Frommer's®

W9-ANF-321

Cruises
& Ports of Call

From U.S. & Canadian Home Ports to the Caribbean, Alaska, Hawaii & More

2006

by Heidi Sarna & Matt Hannafin

Here's what the critics say about Frommer's:

"Amazingly easy to use. Very portable, very complete."

—*Booklist*

"Detailed, accurate, and easy-to-read information for all price ranges."
—*Glamour Magazine*

"A thorough and entertaining look at the cruise world."

—*Chicago Tribune*

"Frommer's Guides have a way of giving you a real feel for a place."
—*Knight Ridder Newspapers*

WILEY

Wiley Publishing, Inc.

Published by:

Wiley Publishing, Inc.
111 River St.
Hoboken, NJ 07030-5774

ISBN-13: 978-0-7645-8846-4
ISBN-10: 0-7645-8846-X

Editor: Naomi P. Kraus
with Jennifer Moore
Production Editor: Heather Wilcox
Cartographer: Elizabeth Puhl
Photo Editor: Richard Fox
Production by Wiley Indianapolis Composition Services

For information on our other products and services or to obtain technical support, please
contact our Customer Care Department within the U.S. at 800/762-2974, outside the
U.S. at 317/572-3993 or fax 317/572-4002.

Wiley also publishes its books in a variety of electronic formats. Some content that
appears in print may not be available in electronic formats.

Manufactured in the United States of America

5   4   3   2   1

Contents

Part 1: Planning, Booking & Preparing for Your Cruise

3 Things to Know Before You Go   65

4 The Cruise Experience   76

Part 2: The Cruise Lines & Their Ships

5 The Ratings & How to Read Them   96

6 The Mainstream Lines   110

7 The Ultraluxury Lines   275

8 Small Ships, Sailing Ships & Adventure Cruises   326

Part 3: The Ports

9 The Ports of Embarkation   426

List of Maps

About the Authors

Heidi Sarna is a freelance writer living in New York City with her husband and toddler twin sons. Coauthor of *Cruising For Dummies* and a contributor to several other guidebooks, she also writes regular travel columns for Frommers.com and *Porthole* cruise magazine. She's written for many magazines and newspapers, including *Gourmet, Condé Nast Traveler, Parenting, Bridal Guide,* and *Travel Weekly.*

Matt Hannafin is a freelance writer, editor, and musician based in Brooklyn, New York. Co-author of the upcoming *1,000 Places in the U.S.A. & Canada to See Before You Die* (a sequel to the 2004 bestseller) and *Cruising For Dummies,* he also writes regular travel columns for Frommers.com, the *Boston Herald,* and *Porthole* cruise magazine. He's contributed to dozens of other books, magazines, and websites, including *Gourmet* and *Travel Weekly.*

Acknowledgments

A select group of travel writers and travel experts contributed to this book. **Mike Driscoll,** editor of the probing industry newsletter *Cruise Week,* provided insights into current booking trends. **Dr. Christina Colon** updated our Miami coverage and accompanied Matt on his rounds of Hawaii. Coconut monkey head, anyone? Our editor, **Naomi Kraus,** provided an up-to-the-minute look at NCL's new Hawaii program and kept our Orlando coverage up-to-date. Cruise expert **Art Sbarsky** kept us up-to-date on Windstar and Silversea. *Travel Weekly* cruise editor **Rebecca Tobin** updated our review of Holland America and its new Signature of Excellence initiative. Merchant Marine officer and travel writer **Ben Lyons** wrote our new, expanded review of Delta Queen Steamboat Company. Ship authority and world traveler **Ted Scull** kept our coverage of river cruise routes fresh, and **Mark Chesnut** helped keep our Caribbean, Hawaii, and Bermuda coverage current. **Darlene Simidian** updated our section on Costa Cruises and helped with the research for Cruise West and several of the Caribbean ports. Travel journalist **Marilyn Green** jumped in at the last minute with a review of the new *Costa Magica.* Thanks! For their work in previous editions of this book, big thanks go to *SeaTrade Cruise Review* U.S. editor **Anne Kalosh;** writer and traveler extraordinaire **Ken Lindley;** *Miami Herald* columnist and Frommer's author **Lesley Abravanel;** and passenger ship expert **Alan Zamchick.** Lastly, Matt would like to thank his fiancee, **Rebecca,** for bearing with him during deadline month. Heidi thanks her twin sons, **Kavi and Tejas,** for being such good sailors at the ripe old age of three (10 cruises and counting), and gives a big hug to hubby **Arun** for putting up with the crazy cruising life all these years.

An Invitation to the Reader

In researching this book, we discovered many wonderful places—hotels, restaurants, shops, and more. We're sure you'll find others. Please tell us about them, so we can share the information with your fellow travelers in upcoming editions. If you were disappointed with a recommendation, we'd love to know that, too. Please write to:

Frommer's Cruises & Ports of Call 2006
Wiley Publishing, Inc. • 111 River St. • Hoboken, NJ 07030-5774

An Additional Note

Please be advised that travel information is subject to change at any time—and this is especially true of prices. We therefore suggest that you write or call ahead for confirmation when making your travel plans. The authors, editors, and publisher cannot be held responsible for the experiences of readers while traveling. Your safety is important to us, however, so we encourage you to stay alert and be aware of your surroundings. Keep a close eye on cameras, purses, and wallets, all favorite targets of thieves and pickpockets.

Other Great Guides for Your Trip:

Frommer's USA

Frommer's Caribbean Ports of Call

Frommer's Alaska Cruises & Ports of Call

Frommer's Caribbean

Frommer's Mexico

Frommer's Canada

Frommer's Hawaii

Frommer's Bermuda

Frommers.com

Now that you have the guidebook to a great trip, visit our website at **www.frommers.com** for travel information on more than 3,000 destinations. With features updated regularly, we give you instant access to the most current trip-planning information available. At Frommers.com, you'll also find the best prices on airfares, accommodations, and car rentals—and you can even book travel online through our travel booking partners. At Frommers.com, you'll also find the following:

- Online updates to our most popular guidebooks
- Vacation sweepstakes and contest giveaways
- Newsletter highlighting the hottest travel trends
- Online travel message boards with featured travel discussions

Cruising 2006: 10 Million Cruise Fans Can't Be Wrong

If you've picked up this book, it's unlikely we have to talk you into a cruise—that idea's probably already in your head. And anyway, it's not our job to try to talk you into anything. We know some people just love traveling by ship and others just hate it. We also know that some people just *assume* they'd hate it, without having the full story.

Because, y'know, it's a pretty big story, and new chapters are being added every year. Time was, the cruise biz was a pretty homogenous cow, attracting mostly older folks plus a smattering of honeymooners and party-makers. They're all still there, of course, but today so is everyone else: young families, young professionals, young couples in Harley shirts, baggy-jeans teens, middle-aged gym rats, multigenerational family reunion groups, red staters, blue staters, and a contingent of Canadians and other foreigners to help us all get along.

In a certain sense, it's an old-fashioned kind of vacation—a hearkening back to the old European Grand Tours, with travelers hitting a region's high points in quick succession—bam, bam, bam—then getting back aboard ship to socialize with people who were strangers until circumstance pushed them together. In another sense, though, cruising is a totally modern kind of vacation, the newest ships packed with every possible widget to win over prospective travelers and turn them into repeat customers. We'll be honest, though. It's not this stuff that grabs us—not the three-story show lounges or sushi bars, not the rock-climbing walls or the hot rock massages or the planetariums, either. It's simply being at sea on a ship. It's the teak decks, white steel railings, thick mooring lines, and proud funnels. It's the feeling that you've untethered yourself from the world, as you stand on deck at night, lean over the rail, and watch the waves break around your ship's bow as it heads to the next port of call. The sea: It's a powerful thing.

CRUISING TODAY: NEW SHIPS, MORE PAX

Check out this statistic: Between 2000 and 2005, the major lines launched 68 new cruise ships, and that's not even counting foreign and small-ship cruise lines. Fortunately for the industry, they've been able to persuade more and more passengers (or "pax" in agent-speak) aboard to fill all those ships: Just over 3.6 million North Americans took a cruise in 1990. By 2000 that number was up to 6.8 million. Among the major travel options, cruising was probably the least affected by the attacks of September 11, 2001, bouncing back quickly after some initial cancellations. As cruise lines began to position their ships to more home ports around the country so nervous travelers wouldn't have to fly (see below), cruising boomed. By 2004, the total number of cruising North Americans was up to 9 million, with U.S. lines carrying a total of 10.6 million counting foreign nationals.

As we head toward 2006, the cruise lines' decade-long building spree is finally slowing down, with only three major newbuilds introduced in 2005 and fewer than half a dozen in the lineup for 2006. With bookings up and the need to fill more new ships decreasing, prices—which were ridiculously low through 2003 and into 2004—have been leveling off. You still won't pay brochure rates (see below), but the days of $400 weeklong cruises are probably over, at least for now.

THE REAL SCOOP ON CRUISE PRICES

Cruise pricing is really . . . well, dumb. Beyond the fuzzy math that often makes the new ships the cheapest to book, you also have the problem of brochure prices. Check out Brochure X, which lists a weeklong sailing at $1,900 per person for a standard outside cabin. Now click over to your favorite travel agency's website and you'll probably see that same cruise going for $575. What gives?

Just like new-car prices, cruise line brochure prices are notoriously inflated—in fact, some lines are talking about dropping them from brochures altogether. In the meantime, you should basically just plain ignore brochure rates. Everything, and we mean everything, is discounted due to stiff competition between cruise lines. Other guidebooks and articles print those inflated brochure prices anyway, leaving it up to you to take a guess at what the real price may be. We don't. Instead, we've partnered with **Just Cruisin' Plus,** a respected agency specializing in cruises, to provide you with the **actual prices** consumers were paying for cruises aboard all the ships reviewed in this book. Each review shows you approximately how much you can expect to pay for an inside cabin (one without windows), an outside cabin (with windows or a balcony), and a small suite. In chapter 2, we've provided a chart that shows how these prices compare with the published brochure rates. How much of a difference could it be? Think about this: The brochure rate for a 6-night western Caribbean cruise aboard Royal Caribbean's beautiful *Jewel of the Seas* is $1,988 for a low-end outside cabin. In reality, however, people who booked during our sampling period (June 2005 cruises, priced in mid-Apr) were able to get that same cabin for $798. Ka-ching.

AND NOW, COMING TO A PORT NEAR YOU . . .

For the past few years, the big trend in the cruise world is putting ships where people can get to them. It seems like an obvious idea, but for decades the cruise lines only nibbled around its edges, homeporting most of their ships in Miami, Fort Lauderdale, Los Angeles, and a few other major ports and forcing people to fly there before their vacation could get underway. Today, ships are sailing regularly from more than two dozen **U.S. and Canadian home ports,** so unless you live in Nebraska, there's a good chance you can drive to your ship—saving yourself both time and money. While you're doing that, you may just want to stick around and see the sights, 'cause some of those port cities are pretty interesting, whether you're sailing to the **Caribbean** from New York, Charleston, Jacksonville, or New Orleans; to **Alaska** from Seattle, San Francisco, or Vancouver; to **Bermuda** from Baltimore, Boston, or Philly; to the **Mexican Riviera** from Los Angeles or San Diego; to **Hawaii** from Ensenada or right from Honolulu; or to **New England** from Norfolk or Quebec City. When you add in small ships sailing from places like Warren, Rhode Island; Astoria, Oregon; Alexandria, Virginia; and Memphis, Tennessee, you realize there's a whole lot of country out there to explore. In chapter 9, "The Ports of Embarkation," we discuss the high points of all the major cruise home ports, giving you the lowdown on what to see if you're only going to be there for a day or two pre- or post-cruise. Chapters 10 through 16 give you the scoop on all the major ports of call in all the so-called "homeland cruising" regions, with info on sights and attractions to see on your own as well as recommendations for the best shore excursions.

FINDING A SHIP IS EASY, BUT WILL YOU CLICK?

Comparing cruise ships and lines is like scanning an online dating site: "Attractive young cruise ship with nice body and good personality seeks friend for dating, possible relationship." The ship looks good, but we all know how photos can lie. And the descriptions, how can you trust them?

Just like in dating, there are ships that you'll get along with and ships that you won't. It's all a matter of personality. Your dream ship is probably out there, somewhere—it's just a matter of figuring out what you want. If those huge Vegas-style floating resorts you see advertised on TV aren't your cup of tea, there are also quiet, refined ships where you're left to do your own thing, with outstanding service staff standing by in case you need anything, anything at all. Other ships are more like intimate B&Bs, where the vibe is casual, the cabins are cozy, and the focus is all on history, culture, and the outdoors. A few are honest-to-god sailing ships, with masts and sails to offer nostalgic adventure.

Chances are there's a ship out there with your name on it, and we're here to help you wade through the different options and experiences. To do this, we've divided the cruise lines into three main categories—**mainstream lines** (chapter 6), **ultraluxury lines** (chapter 7), and **adventure lines** (chapter 8)—and developed a rating system that judges them only against other ships in the same category—megaships against megaships, luxe against luxe, small ship against small ship.

CRUISE TRENDS & TASTES

Every year brings real advances to the cruise biz, as well as some trends that might stick around for a while before fizzling—remember the cigar bars that were all the rage a few years ago? And remember when Internet centers were a novelty? Here's what's new and hot today. As for tomorrow, look into our crystal ball . . .

- **A few lines fold, others raise:** Ten years ago there were at least half a dozen small and midsize cruise lines holding their own, often in the budget end of the market. Not any more. Most of the shakeout happened between 1999 and 2001, but 2004 also saw the demise of **Royal Olympic Cruises'** U.S. division and **Festival Cruises** (aka First European). Royal Olympic's European division was on the ropes too as this book went to press. Meanwhile, **MSC Cruises** made a series of bold moves intended to increase its presence, purchasing two of Festival's almost new ships at auction, hiring former Celebrity president Richard Sasso to head its North America division, launching the new 58,000-ton *Opera* (sister to its year-old *Lirica*), and ordering two new megaships. **Oceania Cruises,** which sprang into being in 2003, continued to rack up good reviews while adding a third ship to its fleet of intimate 684-passenger twins. Like *Regatta* and *Insignia,* the *Nautica* formerly sailed for Renaissance Cruises, which went belly-up in 2001.

- **New ships:** Only three major new vessels launched in 2005 (NCL's *Norwegian Jewel* and *Pride of America* and Carnival's *Carnival Liberty*), and at press time five new megaships were scheduled to launch in 2006. **Costa Cruises** will introduce the new 3,800-passenger, 112,000-ton *Costa Concordia* in summer 2006. The "other" Italian line, **MSC Cruises,** will debut its first megaship, an as-yet-unnamed 3,000-passenger model, in June 2006. Down in Hawaii, **NCL's** 2,400-passenger, 92,100-ton *Pride of Hawai'i* will join sister ship *Pride of America* in April. **Princess** is also planning a sister to the 3,100-passenger, 113,000-ton *Caribbean Princess,* due in May 2006. As usual, **Royal Caribbean** is planning to one-up them all by introducing the 3,600-passenger, 160,000-ton *Freedom of the Seas,* the first of its so-called Ultra-Voyager ships, which will reclaim the "world's biggest" title from Cunard's *QM2.*

- **New terminals in weird places:** In May 2004, Royal Caribbean unveiled its new Cape Liberty cruise port in **Bayonne, NJ,** across the Hudson from Manhattan. It seemed a weird choice, but maybe represented a new phase in the cruise industry's home-porting movement: not only spreading ships around the country, but spreading them around congested population centers, too. Eight months later, New York announced that it would open a secondary cruise terminal to help alleviate congestion at the old west side piers. Located in the old industrial neighborhood of **Red Hook, Brooklyn,** the new terminal is scheduled to open in late 2005.

- **A new lease on life for older ships:** Ships are always being refurbished, but recently cruise lines have upped the ante, giving several old vessels really extreme makeovers. **Royal Caribbean** got the ball rolling back in June 2003, refitting its 1991-vintage *Monarch of the Seas,* and in 2004 and 2005 continued with *Empress* and *Sovereign of the Seas.* In addition to having its decor upgraded, each vessel saw the addition of some au courant attractions, such as a gourmet coffee bar and a Latin nightclub. In mid-2005 the line went a step further in redoing 1997's *Enchantment of the Seas,* reviving the 1990s trend of "stretching" older ships by literally sawing them in half like magicians' assistants, inserting a new midsection full of cabins and entertainment features, then welding them back together again. **Holland America** has also been busy revitalizing its older vessels, starting in October 2004 with 1994's *Ryndam,* the first vessel to be upgraded to the line's full "Signature of Excellence" standards. Other older HAL vessels are slated to be upgraded to one degree or another by early 2006. See ship reviews in chapter 6 for full info.

- **Bigger ships in Bermuda:** It's been an axiom forever that Bermuda cruises are offered on smallish ships, a consequence of strict rules designed to protect the island's hotel industry and prevent overcrowding. But, since cruise lines are no longer building smallish ships, things eventually had to change, and now they have. Beginning in 2005, Bermuda began hosting some of the largest ships in the world, including Royal Caribbean's 3,114-passenger *Voyager of the Seas*, sailing from the line's new port in Bayonne, New Jersey. More megaships are sure to follow.

- **Brand-name entertainment options:** Standing out from the crowd is always among the biggest challenge facing every cruise line. Lately, some have begun making deals with big names from outside the cruise biz to help them spiff up their image. **Celebrity Cruises,** for example, has teamed up with **Cirque du Soleil** to bring its brand of fantasy circus magic to the line's megaships. **Norwegian** followed by announcing a partnership with the famed **Second City** improv comedy group. Over at **Cunard,** the cobranding was with London's **Royal Academy of Dramatic Arts,** whose graduates and students perform short plays and offer readings, workshops, and acting classes on *QM2*'s transatlantic crossings. The ship's Cunard ConneXions learning program also includes talks on music, modern art, literature, marine science, ocean liner history, cooking, and other topics, led by instructors and lecturers from Oxford University and elsewhere, while programs in the ship's planetarium have been created by NASA, the American Museum of Natural History, and others.

- **Active shore excursions & postcruise extensions:** We've been stuck on enough slow-mo tour buses to know that the right excursions can make or break your trip. As the age of the average cruiser continues to come down, lines have begun programming more active tours, such as biking, hiking, horseback riding, river rafting, glacier treks, and dog-sledding. Other excursions focus on history and culture. For those who want even more action, many lines offer multiday pre- and post-cruise tours, some with an adventurous bent. Celebrity Cruises has taken the lead among the mainstream lines with its **Celebrity Xpeditions** program, which lets cruisers tack trips to the Great Pyramids of Egypt, Switzerland's majestic Matterhorn, the Incan city of Machu Picchu, and mysterious Easter Island onto their cruise. Many of the ultraluxury lines offer similar adventurous extensions.

- **Expanded golf offerings:** Onboard golf programs have hit the big time in the past 2 years, with **Carnival, Holland America, Celebrity, Seabourn, Princess,** and **Silversea** all featuring programs created by Florida's Elite Golf Cruises that offer onboard instruction (including use of split-screen computer swing coaching), guided golf excursions, computer simulators that mimic play at three dozen of the world's top courses, and various pro-shop-style extras. **Norwegian Cruise Line** has also gone big into golf on its new Hawaii cruises, offering golf excursions at every port, bookable separately or as a package deal. *Pride of Aloha* and *Pride of America* have onboard pro shops offering club rental and golf accessories.

- **Bigger teen centers:** Teenagers can be a tough crowd to please, but the cruise lines sure are trying—maybe because, as Carnival's design guru Joe Farcus told us, "Teens are our future." We say again, *ka-ching!* **Carnival** itself has huge teen centers on its Conquest-class vessels. **Royal Caribbean**'s *Mariner, Navigator,* and *Sovereign of the Seas* each have three separate areas for teens and also offer teen spa treatments. **Disney Cruise Line** recently upgraded its teen centers, mixing dorm and trendy coffee-shop styling. Other ships with great teen facilities include **NCL**'s *Norwegian Dawn, Star, Spirit, Sun,* and *Pride of America;* **Princess**'s Grand- and Diamond-class vessels; and **Holland America**'s Vista-class ships and the older *Maasdam,* which include a teen-only sun deck in the stern.

- **Onboard cellphone service:** It used to be that the only way to call home from a ship was via satellite phone at a cost of $8 or $9 a minute. Starting in 2004, though, cruise lines began using a technology that allows people to use their cellphones, even while far out at sea. At press time, Royal Caribbean, Celebrity, NCL, Costa, and Crystal's *Crystal Serenity* are hooked up, and Carnival, HAL, and MSC Cruises are looking into it. Our prediction? Every major line will be cellular enabled within a year. Ringers off, please. (See chapter 3, "Things to Know Before You Go," for more details.)

- **Internet Wi-Fi:** Aren't wires just so 20th century? All Carnival, Princess, Holland America, and NCL vessels now have wireless hot zones so passengers who sail with their laptops can connect in a number of lounges. **Seabourn**'s three luxury vessels and Carnival's ***Carnival Valor*** go them all one better, with Wi-Fi access in every part of the ship, bow to stern.

- **Expanded prebooking options:** One of the downsides of ships carrying 3,000 passengers is that there's more competition for prime appointment times at the spa and for some

small-group shore excursions. As a consequence, the first day of some cruises will see long lines to sign up. Cruise lines are finally starting to address this problem through online prebooking. At present, most of the major cruise lines offer some degree of **prebooking for shore excursions.** Only Crystal, Silversea, Princess's *Caribbean Princess* and *Sapphire Princess,* and Cunard's *QM2* (for suite guests and past Canyon Ranch customers) are set up to **prebook spa appointments,** though most lines say they're looking into it.

- **Automatic tipping:** Say goodbye to the days when tipping your waiter meant slipping a little envelope from your tux pocket and pressing it into his hand. Today, Carnival, Costa, Holland America, NCL, Oceania, and Princess all add an automatic gratuity to your onboard account. In most cases it can be adjusted at your discretion. See chapter 3, "Things to Know Before You Go," for more details.

SAFETY AT SEA: MORE SECURITY, FEWER GERMS

For better or worse, we're currently living in a security-obsessed world. People have to show ID to get into office buildings and take off their shoes to go through airport X-rays, so you'd better believe security measures are in place on cruise ships, too.

All the major cruise lines have their own **dedicated onboard security forces** who monitor people coming aboard (passengers, crew, delivery people, and contractors) and keep an eye out during the cruise, and we're not just talking the kind of rent-a-cops you see at your local convenience store. Some lines have even hired ex–Navy SEALs as top-level security consultants and have trained deck officers in how to react to takeover attempts. Other security measures are also in place, but the cruise lines prefer to keep them under their hats.

Immediately following September 11, all cruise ships went to Security Level III, the highest dictated by the Coast Guard, and between then and 2004 a series of new regulations went into effect that mandated a no-visitors policy; X-ray of all hand-carried bags; screening of checked bags; the use of sniffer dogs; a security zone of at least 300 feet around all cruise ships, plus concrete barriers; patrol boats, and sometimes Coast Guard escorts at some ports; and the screening of all ship's stores, mail, and cargo before they're brought aboard. Many of these systems were already in place at most cruise lines and ports, so passengers generally don't notice much difference. Other changes have been made in the back office, including a rule that ships must submit a complete list of passengers and crew to the Coast Guard 96 hours before arriving at a U.S. port. Internationally, new regulations issued by the International Maritime Organization (IMO) require all ports around the world to operate within a consistent framework to address security issues.

On a day-to-day basis, passengers will mostly notice ship security when boarding, both initially and at the ports of call. Most cruise lines photograph passengers digitally at embarkation and then match their pictures to their faces every time they get back aboard thereafter. Digital passcards also allow them to tell instantly who's aboard at any given time. Many lines have also hired additional security personnel—in some cases Gurkhas, the famed Nepalese fighters—to assist officers at the gangway and be on hand as needed.

The other major cruise safety issue that occasionally hits the news is **norovirus** (aka Norwalk-like virus), a stomach bug that causes nausea, vomiting, and diarrhea. An extremely common bug that hits some 23 million Americans a year (mostly on land), it's also extremely contagious. According to the Centers for Disease Control (CDC), people infected with norovirus can pass the bug on from the moment they begin feeling ill to between 3 days and 2 weeks after they recover—meaning the cruise ship outbreaks reported between 2003 and 2005 were probably the result of contagious passengers bringing the infection aboard, rather than of unsanitary practices on the ships themselves. Face it, cruise ships are a lot like kindergarten: When one kid shows up sick, everybody gets sick.

In any case, don't worry too much. It's no fun to have your vacation spoiled by illness, but norovirus causes no long-term health effects for most people. Persons unable to replace liquids quickly enough—generally the very young, the elderly, and people with weakened immune systems—may become dehydrated and require special medical attention, but that's about the worst of it. More good news: Outbreaks have been on the downswing since they first were reported. Cruise lines are keeping a close eye on boarding passengers for signs of illness, and have further stepped up their already vigilant sanitation routines to reduce the chance of transmission.

The Best of Cruising

People are always asking us which are our favorite ships, and we always say, "Well, what do you like to do when you're *not* on a ship?" In this section we've broken out different kinds of cruises, interests, and destinations to help you find one that best matches what you're looking for. You'll find complete information on each pick in part 2, "The Cruise Lines & Their Ships," and part 3, "The Ports."

1 Our Favorite Mainstream Ships

Mainstream ships are the big boys of the industry, carrying the most passengers and providing the most diverse cruise experiences to suit many different tastes, from party-hearty to elegant and refined.

- **Celebrity's Millennium class & Century class:** With their elegant decor, incredible spas, great service, edgy art collections, and the best alternative restaurants at sea, *Millennium, Infinity, Summit,* and *Constellation* are just the best mainstream megaships out there. Class, charm, personality—what's not to like? Celebrity's older Century-class ships (*Century, Galaxy,* and *Mercury*) aren't too far behind, either, and the line's prices are far lower than you'd expect. See p. 142 and 147.

- **Royal Caribbean's Radiance class & Voyager class:** The most elegant vessels Royal Caribbean has produced to date, *Radiance, Brilliance, Serenade,* and *Jewel of the Seas* combine a sleek, seagoing exterior; a nautically themed interior; and acres of windows. The Voyager ships—*Voyager, Explorer, Adventure, Navigator,* and *Mariner*—are the archetypal activities ships, and maybe the first vessels to satisfy the old "city at sea" cliché. See p. 261 and 264.

- **Princess's Diamond class & Coral class:** Princess's huge but cozy *Diamond* and *Sapphire Princess* are its most beautiful ships to date, combining gorgeous exterior lines with wood-heavy, old-world lounges; an innovative dining plan; and a great covered promenade that allows you to stand right in the ship's bow. The smaller *Coral Princess* and *Island Princess* are big winners, too, with similar decor and a smaller size that lets them traverse the Panama Canal. See p. 238 and 242.

2 Best Luxury Cruises

Here's the very best for the cruiser who's used to traveling deluxe and who doesn't mind paying for the privilege. These ships have the best cuisine, accommodations, and service at sea.

- **Silversea *Shadow* and *Whisper:*** The best overall highbrow small-ship line. With its cuisine, roomy suites, and over-the-top service—including complimentary and free-flowing Philipponnat champagne—Silversea is the crème de la crème of high-end cruises. See p. 319.

- **Crystal *Symphony* and *Serenity:*** Carrying 940 to 1,080 passengers, these are the best midsize ships out there, big enough to offer lots of dining, entertainment, and fitness options, and small enough to bathe passengers in luxury. See p. 277.

- **Radisson Seven Seas *Navigator* and *Voyager:*** Not only are cabins aboard these midsize 490- and 700-passenger, all-suite ships roomy, but their huge bathrooms are fabulous. To top it off, food and service on both are among the very best at sea. See p. 296.
- **Cunard *Queen Mary 2:*** QM2 has her very own niche in the luxe market— and in the cruise market as a whole, for that matter. While too enormous to offer the kind of intimate luxury you'll get with *Silversea, Seabourn,* and *Sea-Dream,* she is able to give you a pretty close idea of what life aboard the great old ocean liners was like, and that's pretty luxe all by itself. See p. 288.
- **SeaDream Yacht Club *SeaDream I and II:*** What's not to love? These cool 110-passenger yachts are elegant but casual, and carry along jet skis, mountain bikes, and kayaks for jaunts around ports like St. Barts and Jost Van Dyke. See p. 313.

3 The Most Romantic Cruises

Of course, all cruises are pretty romantic when you consider the props they have to work with: the undulating sea all around, moonlit nights on deck, cozy dining and cocktailing, private cabin balconies. Here are the best lines for getting you in the mood.

- **Star Clippers:** With the wind in your hair and sails fluttering overhead, the top decks of the four- and five-masted *Royal Clipper* and *Star Clipper* provide a most romantic setting. Below decks, the comfy cabins, lounge, and dining room make these ships the most comfortable adventure on the sea. See p. 392.
- **Cunard:** Like real royalty, *Queen Mary 2* was born with certain duties attendant to its station, and one of the biggest of those duties is to embody the romance of transatlantic travel and bring it into the new century. Take a stroll around that promenade deck, dine in that fabulous dining room, and thrill to be out in the middle of the Atlantic on nearly a billion dollars worth of Atlantic thoroughbred. See p. 288.
- **SeaDream Yacht Club *SeaDream I & II:*** With comfy Balinese daybeds lining the teak decks, toys like MP3 players and high-powered binoculars at your fingertips, and free-flowing champagne, these 110-passenger playboy yachts spell romance for the spoiled sailing set. See p. 313.
- **Windstar Cruises:** Pure romance is a day with your loved one in a private cove with *Wind Surf* or *Wind Spirit* anchored offshore, bobbing calmly on the waves, sails furled. Windstar offers a truly unique cruise experience, giving passengers the delicious illusion of adventure and the ever-pleasant reality of great cuisine, service, and itineraries. See p. 415.
- **Celebrity Cruises:** Big, stylish, and glamorous, Celebrity's Millennium- and Century-class ships are romantic like an Art Deco nightclub from the '30s, and the Millennium ship's alternative restaurants will make you feel like you're *in* the '30s, with their great period detailing. See p. 134.
- **Sea Cloud Cruises:** Really, when it comes right down to it, what setting is more movie-star romantic than a zillionaire's sailing yacht? That's what you get with *Sea Cloud,* once owned

by Edward F. Hutton and Marjorie Merriweather Post, with some cabins retaining their original grandeur. See p. 391.

- **Windjammer Barefoot Cruises:** They may not be everybody's idea of

romantic, but if you and your significant other have always dreamed of chucking it all and taking off on a Harley, these are the ships for you: rum-swigging, T-shirt-wearing, ultra-free, and quirky as hell. See p. 402.

4 Best Cruises for First-Timers

Short cruises are a good way to test the waters. Here are our favorites in a variety of styles.

- **Royal Caribbean *Monarch* and *Majesty of the Seas* (3- and 4-night Bahamas and Baja):** Mainstream ships that only offer 3- and 4-night cruises tend to be the oldest and most knocked-around ships in a line's fleet, and while *Monarch* and *Majesty* aren't spring chickens, they are being kept up better than most, with *Monarch* (on the West Coast) having undergone a major refurbishment in spring 2003 and *Majesty* (on the East Coast) scheduled for one as this book goes to press. With high passenger density and flashy interiors, these cruises promote a high-energy atmosphere. See p. 271.
- ***Disney Wonder* (3- and 4-night Bahamas):** *Wonder* sails 3- and 4-night

Bahamas family cruises, which gives passengers the option of booking a 4- or 3-day stays at Walt Disney World for a total weeklong vacation. Cabins were designed with families in mind, as were the ship's activities, and to top it off *Wonder's* even a classy ship with lovely ocean-liner lines. See p. 168.

- **Royal Caribbean *Voyager of the Seas* (5-night New England/Canada):** Besides being one of the biggest passenger ships ever, period, *Voyager* is the biggest ship sailing the New England/Canada circuit from New York in summer and fall. If you're worried about being bored on your first cruise, don't be here: Five days might not even be enough time to see the whole ship, much less the ports. This sucker's big. See p. 264.

5 Best Cruises for Families with Kids

More families are cruising than ever before, and lines are beefing up their kids and teens facilities to keep everybody happy. All the lines included here offer supervised activities for three to five age groups between ages 2 or 3 and 17 and have well-stocked playrooms, wading pools, kids' menus, and cabins that can accommodate three to five people. They also offer group and/or private babysitting. See "Cruises for Families," in chapter 1 and the cruise line reviews in chapters 6 through 8 for more info.

- **Disney Cruise Line:** This family magnet offers the most sophisticated and high-tech seagoing children's program in the world, bar none. Huge play areas, family-friendly cabins (the majority have two bathrooms—a sink and toilet in one and a shower/tub combo and a sink in the other), baby nursery, and the ubiquitous Mickey all spell success. Plus, the 3- and 4-night Bahamas cruises aboard the *Disney Wonder* are marketed in tandem with stays at Walt

Disney World, so you can have your ocean voyage and your Cinderella Castle, too. See p. 162.

- **Royal Caribbean:** The huge Voyager-class ships are truly theme parks at sea, with features such as onboard rock-climbing walls, ice-skating rinks, in-line skate rinks, miniature golf, burger-joint diners, and Disney-esque Main Streets running down their centers, with parades and other entertainment throughout the day. The Radiance-class ships are also a great family choice, offering rock climbing and miniature golf. All this is in addition to bigger-than-normal kids' playrooms, teen centers, wading pools, and video game rooms, plus regulation-size basketball, paddle ball, and volleyball courts. Even the line's older ships have impressively roomy kids' facilities. See p. 254.

- **Carnival Cruise Lines:** Despite a let-the-good-times-roll allure that appeals to adults, Carnival goes out of its way to amuse people of all ages, and does a particularly fine job with kids 2 to 15 years old. A few hundred per cruise is pretty normal, with as many as 700 to 800 on Christmas and New Year's cruises. You'll find the biggest and brightest playrooms in the fleet on the Conquest-class vessels, with computer stations, a climbing maze, a video wall showing movies and cartoons, arts and crafts, and oodles of toys and games, plus great water slides out on the main pool deck. Carnival's **Destiny-** and **Spirit-class** ships are pretty great, too. See p. 112.

- **Princess Cruises:** The Grand-class ships and *Coral* and *Island Princess* each have a spacious children's play-room and a sizable piece of fenced-in outside deck for toddlers and one for older kids, with a wading pool. Teen centers have computers, video games, and a sound system, and the ones on the Grand-class ships even have teen hot tubs and private sunbathing decks. See p. 231.

- **Norwegian Cruise Line:** The kids' facilities on the line's new *Norwegian Dawn* and *Norwegian Star* are fantastic, with a huge, brightly colored crafts/play area, a TV corner full of bean-bag chairs, an enormous ball-jump/play-gym, a teen center, and a large outdoor play/pool area that even has a Jacuzzi just for kids. Parents will appreciate the many restaurant options on board, while kids can dine in tiny chairs at a kid-size buffet of their own. See p. 201.

- **Cunard:** Though you'd hardly expect it from such a seriously prestigious line, the *QM2* has a great program, and facilities, for kids, starting at age 1. Aside from Disney, no other line offers such extensive care for children so young. There's even a special daily children's teatime that's perfect as an early dinner, and the children's pro-gramming is free of charge up until midnight daily. See p. 288.

6 Best Cruises for Pure Relaxation

Sometimes it's all about doing absolutely nothing, but some ships are better at let-ting you do nothing (in style and com-fort) than others.

- **SeaDream Yacht Club:** SeaDream's two intimate, 110-passenger yachts deliver an upscale yet very casual experience without regimentation. Cabin beds are fitted with fine Frette linens, but the best snooze on board is to be had in 1 of the 18 queen-size, Bali-style sun beds that line each ves-sel's top deck. Each features an extra-thick mattress, teak bed tables, sea views, and is ensconced in its own raised, semi-partitioned "bedroom." Reading lights are provided at night, and some guests just end up sleeping out here. See p. 313.

- **Oceania Cruises:** Aboard Oceania's two midsize, classically styled ships, the dress code is "country club casual" at all times; you can show up for dinner in whenever you like; activities and entertainment are small-scale and personal; itineraries visit many quiet, refined ports; and the cabin beds are some of the best at sea (see below). Step aboard, take a deep breath, and *relax*. See p. 225.

- **Celebrity Cruises:** If your idea of relaxation involves regular massages, lolling around in ornate steam rooms, mud baths, and hydrotherapy pools, and then letting your limbs tingle in gorgeous solariums, Celebrity's Millennium-class ships are tops. Afterward, have a long, relaxed dinner at the ships' amazing alternative restaurants (among the best at sea), then decide what kind of pillow you want: The line's "ConciergeClass" suites

feature a whole menu of different kinds, plus tension-absorbing mattresses and comfy duvets. See p. 134.

- **American Safari Cruises:** Every October and November, luxury small-ship line American Safari offers a series of 3- and 4-night California Wine Country cruises aboard its 22-passenger yacht, *Safari Quest*. Days are spent on private tours of various vineyards and estates, with wine tastings, art tours, gourmet lunches, and even a massage by a local therapist included in the rates (which, FYI, are pretty high). In the late afternoon you can take out a kayak and explore the rivers on your own, then come back and soak in the top-deck hot tub. Ahhhh. See p. 337.

- **Star Clippers:** You won't find better ships for the Caribbean, really, than Star Clippers' two tall-masted modern clipper ships, with acres of sail shining in the sun and you down below them in a deck chair, listening to sailors working the winches, heading for the next small yachting port. No megaship bustle here. See p. 392.

7 Cushiest Cabin Amenities

Sometimes it's all about not leaving your cabin, and these selections will help you with that decision. (Note that we've only included features that are available in every cabin on the ship discussed. Top-level suites on nearly every ship also have amenities that you wouldn't believe. It's good to be king.)

- **Best Beds for the Average Joe: Oceania Cruises.** While the ultraluxe lines all offer plush duvets, fine linens, and great mattresses, Oceania has transplanted luxury bedding to the mainstream/premium market with its signature "Tranquility Beds," a confection of 350-thread-count Egyptian

cotton sheets and duvet covers, down duvets, custom-designed extra-thick mattresses, and the best down pillows we've ever used. Every cabin has 'em. Viva democracy! See p. 225.

- **Best Cabin Bathrooms: Radisson Seven Seas** *Navigator* **and** *Voyager,* **Silversea** *Shadow* **and** *Whisper.* Every single bathroom on these ships has a separate shower stall and a full-size bathtub long enough for a normal-size human to actually recline in, as well as a long marble counter flanked by two sets of tall shelves, with high-end bath products to pamper you even more. See p. 296 and 319.

- **Best Bath Products: Silversea, Sea-Dream, and Seabourn.** The luxury lines have the market cornered on luxuriant bath products. On Sea-Dream there is shampoo, conditioner, bath and facial soaps, shower gel, and lotions by Bvlgari. On Silversea, they're from Italy's Aqua di Parma, and on Seabourn passengers enjoy bath products from Molton Brown, plus a selection of soaps from Hermes, Chanel, Bronnley, or Bijan. See p. 319, 313, and 305.

- **Best Stateroom Goodies: Seabourn.** Seabourn's package of complimentary "Signature Delights" includes personalized stationery, Tumi luggage tags and document portfolio, a CD of classic jazz and bottle of champagne in your stateroom, plus a minibar stocked with liquor and soft drinks, a fruit basket that's replenished daily, and aromatherapy bath selections from Molton Brown. See p. 305.

8 Best Cuisine

Here's where you'll find the finest restaurants afloat, with food rivaling what you'd find at the best restaurants in the world's major cities.

- **Celebrity Cruise Line:** It doesn't get any better than the alternative restaurants on the **Millennium-class ships,** all supervised by chef and restaurateur Michel Roux of the Waterside Inn, one of England's few three-star Michelin restaurants. Reservations are required in these intimate, elegantly designed spots. *Millennium's* Olympic restaurant boasts the actual gilded French walnut wood paneling used aboard White Star Line's *Olympic,* sister ship to *Titanic;* while sister ships *Infinity, Summit,* and *Constellation* have restaurants themed around artifacts from the SS *United States, Normandie,* and *Ile de France.* A highly trained staff dotes on diners with tableside cooking, musicians play elegant period pieces, and the entire decadent experience takes about 3 hours. It costs $25 a person, but it's well worth it. See p. 134.

- **Silversea Cruises:** Hit it on a sunset departure from port and the windowed, candlelit Terrace Cafe alternative restaurant on each of this line's four ships becomes a window to the passing scenery and a home for some of the best food at sea. Reservations are required for the fixed theme menu, with the Asian night starting with sushi and sashimi, while a French feast begins with foie gras and is followed by a scallop and ratatouille salad, beef tenderloin, and a warm chocolate tart with raspberries. (Excellent wines and all spirits are included in the cruise rates.) See p. 319.

- **Crystal Cruises:** While all the food you'll get on these ships is first-class, their reservations-only Asian specialty restaurants are the best at sea, especially *Serenity's* Silk Road restaurant, overseen by Master Chef Nobuyuki "Nobu" Matsuhisa. The accouterments help set the tone, too—chopsticks, sake served in tiny sake cups and decanters, and sushi served on thick blocky square glass platters. An Asian-themed buffet lunch, offered at least once per cruise, gives passengers an awesome spread, from jumbo shrimp to chicken and beef satays to stir-fry dishes. See p. 277.

- **Radisson Seven Seas Cruises:** The award-winning chefs aboard all the line's ships produce artful culinary presentations that compare favorably to those of New York's or San Francisco's top restaurants, and the waiters are some of the industry's best. See p. 296.

- **Seabourn Cruise Lines:** There's nothing quite like dining on the outdoor deck of *Legend* and *Pride*'s Veranda Café, where casual dinners are offered most nights. With the ships' wakes shushing just below, it's a rare opportunity to dine with the sea breezes and starry night sky surrounding you. Asian, Mediterranean, and steakhouse-style menus are featured. See p. 305.
- **Oceania Cruises:** Oceania's dining experience is near the top in the mainstream category, with menus created by renowned chef Jacques Pepin and with passengers able to choose between dinner at four different restaurants, all of them excellent.

Service is doting and fine-tuned, even at the casual semi-buffet option, offered on an outdoor terrace that's elegant and totally romantic at sunset. See p. 225.
- **Norwegian Cruise Lines:** NCL gets onto this list by sheer weight of numbers. Get this: The *Norwegian Sun, Star, Dawn,* and *Jewel* each offer 9 or 10 different dining options, including multiple main dining rooms, multiple specialty restaurants, teppanyaki rooms, and casual options. While the fare in the main dining rooms is totally average, it's quite good in some of the alternative venues, including the sushi bar and the elegant French/continental Le Bistro. See p. 201.

9 Best Cruises for the Party Set

Whether you're traveling solo or with your significant other, these ships can keep you in a party mood all day and night.

- **Windjammer Barefoot Cruises:** If you have an informal attitude, these cruises are a great bet, extremely dress-down and very, very, very casual. It's amazing what a little wind, waves, stars, and moonlight can do for your social skills—and the free rum punch, $2 beers, and visits to legendary Caribbean beach bars don't hurt, either! There are a handful of rowdy singles-only cruises annually—erotic tart-eating contest, anyone? See p. 402.
- **Carnival Cruise Lines:** Lots of men and women in their 20s, 30s, and 40s seek out Carnival's "fun ships" for their wild-and-crazy decor and around-the-clock excitement. What else would you expect from ships with names such as *Fantasy, Inspiration,* and *Sensation?* The Pool Deck is always bustling (especially on the

3- and 4-nighters), with music playing so loudly you'll have to go back to your cabin to think, and the discos and nightspots hop until the early morning hours. The ships are big, offering many places to meet and mingle. See p. 112.
- **Royal Caribbean:** This line draws a good cross section of men and women from all walks of life. As with Carnival, a decent number of passengers are singles and in their 20s, 30s, and 40s, especially on the short 3- and 4-night weekend cruises. For an exciting Saturday-night-out-on-the-town barhopping kind of thing, the **Voyager-class ships** feature a truly unique multideck, boulevard-like promenade running down the center of each ship, its ground floor lined with shops, bars, restaurants, and entertainment outlets, and multistory atria at either end. See p. 254.
- **Norwegian Cruise Line:** Between bustling 3- and 4-night itineraries and weeklong cruises on ships with

up to 10 restaurants and tons of bars, NCL is pretty much always hopping. There are tons of activities all day and some of the best entertainment at sea.

An added plus: The ships all have casual dress codes and open-seating dining, creating more mingling opportunities. See p. 201.

10 Best Beaches

All warm-water cruises offer easy access to beaches, either close to the dock or, more likely, via a short taxi ride. These are some of the best in the various regions.

- **In the Eastern & Southern Caribbean:** So many . . . Palm Beach, Aruba; the Gold Coast beaches (Paynes Bay, Brandon's Beach, Paradise Beach, Brighton Beach), Barbados; Cane Garden Bay, Tortola, British Virgin Islands; Dickenson Bay, Antigua; Grand Anse Beach, Grenada; Diamond Beach, Martinique; Pinney's Beach, Nevis; St-Jean Beach and Grand Cul-de-Sac, St. Barts; Cupecoy Beach and Orient Beach, Sint Maarten/St. Martin; Pigeon Point Beach, Tobago; Trunk Bay, St. John; and Paradise Beach, Nassau, Bahamas. All are within a taxi ride of the cruise piers. See chapter 10.

- **In the Western Caribbean:** Grand Cayman's Seven Mile Beach is a stretch of pristine sand easily accessible via a short taxi ride from Georgetown. Meanwhile, Jamaica's own Seven Mile Beach is located in Negril, which is closer to Montego Bay than to Ocho Rios. At Playa Del Carmen, the beaches at Chankanaab National Park and nearby Playa San Francisco and Playa Palancar are also good bets. See chapter 10.

- **On the Mexican Riviera:** For those in search of a back-to-basics beach, the best and most beautiful is Playa La Ropa, close to Zihuatanejo. Next door, the wide beach at Playa Las Gatas is pocked with restaurants and snorkeling sites. At Puerto Vallarta, spectacularly wide Banderas Bay offers 26 miles of beaches, including popular Playa Los Muertos, full of *palapa* restaurants, beach volleyball, and parasailing. Acapulco is all about beaches, of which the best include Caleta, Caletilla, and the beach on Roqueta Island. Ditto for Cabo San Lucas, with its famous Lovers Beach at Land's End, where the Pacific meets the Sea of Cortez. See chapter 12.

- **In Hawaii:** Hawaii *is* beaches, hundreds of 'em. But because you'll be arriving by ship and only have limited time, you have to concentrate on ones that aren't too far off. Among the best that are accessible by taxi are Ala Moana Beach Park and Waikiki Beach on Oahu, the former a lot like L.A.'s casual Venice Beach, the latter a bit like Miami's vibrant South Beach. A bit farther afield, Lanikai Beach is just too gorgeous to be real. On the Big Island, Hapuna Beach regularly wins kudos as the state's most beautiful beach, and it's not too far from where you come ashore in Kailua-Kona. You'll have a longer taxi ride on Maui to visit Kapalua Beach, the island's prize stretch. On Kauai, try Poipu Beach, with stretches of sand as well as a grassy lawn graced by coconut trees. We saw a Hawaiian monk seal here sunning himself on the sand, with police tape around him like he was a crime scene. See chapter 14.

11 Best Small-Ship Adventure Cruises

Among the small-ship lines, some offer great opportunities for real adventure, whether you're talking about getting out into the wilderness, interacting with wind and wildlife, or just sailing to places you never imagined you'd go.

- **Glacier Bay Cruiseline (Alaska):** Glacier Bay Cruiseline's small ships are the best for exploring wild Alaska. *Wilderness Explorer,* carrying only 31 passengers, spends all its time in wilderness areas, with passengers kayaking and hiking almost every day. *Wilderness Adventurer* mixes this experience with visits to a few tiny fishing towns. See p. 367.

- **Cruise West and Clipper Cruise Line (Alaska/Russian Far East):** Want a real expedition? Cruise West's *Spirit of Oceanus* and Clipper's *Clipper Odyssey* offer 2-week cruises that sail from mainland Alaska, through the Aleutian Islands, then across the Bering Sea to the Russia Far East, visiting coastal towns and wilderness areas. See p. 349 and 342.

- **Maine Windjammer Association (Maine coast):** You get a fairly relaxing adventure, but an adventure nonetheless because these are real sailing ships, relying on the coastal winds for propulsion. If you like, you're welcome to learn the ropes of sailing while aboard, as you sail to small islands around Penobscot Bay. See p. 378.

- **Clipper, Cruise West, Lindblad, and American Safari Cruises (Baja/Sea of Cortez):** Gray whales winter along the coast of Mexico's Baja peninsula, and all four of these lines give you a chance to get up close and personal with the big beasties. Other days are spent cruising the uninhabited and sparsely inhabited islands of the Sea of Cortez, with their starkly gorgeous landscape. Optional postcruise tours include a visit to the magnificent Copper Canyon, larger and deeper than the U.S. Grand Canyon. See p. 342, 349, 374, and 337.

12 Best History & Learning Cruises

And then there are ships that are oriented toward learning about the region through which you're sailing, or that are parts of history themselves.

- *Delta Queen* **(Mississippi River):** The wooden, 174-passenger *Delta Queen* was built in 1926 and is one of the great links to the Mississippi's stern-wheeler past. Cruises are a celebration of Americana, with lots of history and river lore, meals that feature Cajun and Southern cooking, and a music program heavy on Dixieland jazz and swing. Special theme cruises focus on the Civil War and antebellum home visits. See p. 359.

- **American Canadian Caribbean (Erie Canal/Finger Lakes):** Designed to be able to sail in puddles, it seems, ACCL's ships can navigate through the narrow, shallow waters of the old northeast canal system, with much time spent in the region's rivers and lakes, plus visits to historic sites such as Fort Ticonderoga, Cooperstown and the Baseball Hall of Fame, West Point, and the old Erie Canal. Some cruises are timed to coordinate with New England's fall foliage season. See p. 329.

- **Clipper Cruise Line (U.S./Canada East Coast):** The beautiful *Clipper*

Adventurer, probably the most beautiful of the small adventure and expedition ships, offers a cruise that sails almost the entire east coast of the U.S., from Halifax, Nova Scotia, to Savannah, Georgia. Stops include historic Revolutionary War towns such as Lexington and Concord, the Gettysburg National Military Park, Washington, D.C., Colonial Williamsburg, Virginia, and Charleston, South Carolina. See p. 342.

- **Imperial Majesty (Bahamas):** This one's a bit of a ringer. The itinerary visits nowhere you'd normally call historic, but *Regal Empress,* the line's one ship, is historic in and of itself. Built in 1953, it's one of the only real old ocean liners still operating in the American market. By 2010, Coast Guard regulations will make it impossible for old vessels like this to sail, so if you want to see what ocean ships were like in the mid–20th century, *Regal Empress* is one of your last options. And it's cheap, too! See p. 190.
- **Maine Windjammer Association (Maine Coast):** The Maine Windjammer Association really is an association, with 14 owner-operator members operating real schooners. Several of them date back to the 19th century and early 20th, including the 22-passenger *Lewis R. French, Stephen Taber,* and *Isaac H. Evans;* the 29-passenger *Grace Bailey;* and the 40-passenger *Victory Chimes,* which appears on the back of Maine's state quarter. Cruises let you become familiar with old-style sailing ships and learn something about handling the sails, all while tooling around the bays and coves of the gorgeous Maine coast. See p. 378.
- **Cruise West, Lindblad, Glacier Bay, and American Safari Cruises (Columbia and Snake rivers):** Follow in the steps of Lewis and Clark through the rivers of the Pacific Northwest, transiting locks and dams, visiting Indian petroglyphs, and experiencing one of the most beautiful river landscapes in the U.S. Some cruises also offer recreational activities such as kayaking, while others visit vineyards in Washington's wine country. See p. 349, 374, 367, and 337.

13 Best Cruises for Sports Nuts & Gym Rats

Many cruise ships today are a far cry from the days when no one did anything more active than shuffleboard and a walk around the deck. In fact, we've heard of people who actually *lost* weight on their cruise by taking advantage of all the active options available. Here are some of the best.

- **Best Cruises for Onboard Sports:** Royal Caribbean's five Voyager-class ships win hands down with their full-size basketball courts, rock-climbing walls, miniature golf courses, in-line skating tracks, and ice-skating rinks. See p. 254.
- **Best Onboard Gyms:** Once relegated to dank little rooms, onboard gyms now hold pride of place, usually occupying spacious digs on one of the top decks and boasting wraparound windows, aerobics rooms, and as many exercise machines, free weights, and spinning bikes as most large dry-land gyms. The best are aboard **Carnival's Destiny-class ships** (p. 112); **Holland America Vista-class ships** and *Rotterdam, Amsterdam, Volendam,* and *Zaandam* (p. 171); and **Royal Caribbean's Voyager-class ships** (p. 254).

- **Best Golf Cruises:** While practically all the major cruise lines offer golf excursions and some level of golf instruction (usually at an outdoor driving net), several lines go the extra mile. **Carnival, Holland America, Celebrity, Princess,** and ultraluxe lines **Seabourn** and **Silversea** all feature programs created by Florida's Elite Golf Cruises that offer comprehensive golf-cruise vacations. In addition to onboard instruction, hi-tech computer simulators allow virtual play that mimics some three dozen of the world's top courses, with software that analyzes your swing to give a perfect real-time simulation. In port, the programs bundle priority tee times, early debarkation, transportation, golf pro escort, cart rental, and greens fees into one excursion cost. See p. 112, 171, 134, 231, 305, and 319.

- **Best Snorkeling and Scuba Cruises:** Virtually any warm-water cruise you take will offer snorkeling on shore excursions, and certified scuba divers can often arrange their own trips. In the Caribbean, islands with particularly good waters for snorkeling

and diving include Bonaire, Grand Cayman, Cozumel (especially at the Chankanaab National Park), Curaçao, and the U.S. Virgin Islands (at Buck Island Reef). In Central America, the waters off Belize (especially it's famous Blue Hole) and Honduras's Roatan Island offer great waters, and Hawaii is known as one of the best dive destinations in the world. See chapters 10 and 14 for more information on these destinations.

- **Best Onboard Sports Bars:** Royal Caribbean's **Voyager-class ships** (p. 254) all have a golf-themed sports bar up at the very highest level of the ship, with TVs for viewing the games and enormous windows for viewing everything else. The first three ships of the series, *Voyager, Explorer,* and *Adventure,* also have a second, more rah-rah sports bar along their indoor Royal Promenade, with free nacho chips and hot pretzels. The sports bars on NCL's older *Norwegian Dream* and *Norwegian Wind* (p. 201) are also pretty great, with a real bar feel, a few comfortable round booths, and a total lack of chichi.

14 Best Ships for Spa-Goers

One company (Steiner Leisure) runs the vast bulk of cruise ship spas, but facilities vary.

- **Celebrity Cruises:** Celebrity's **Millennium-class** and **Century-class ships** are at the top of the spa heap. Their huge and exceedingly attractive AquaSpas manage to combine a huge repertoire of the latest wraps, packs, soaks, and massages with striking aesthetics inspired by Japanese gardens and bathhouses and Moorish and Turkish spas. Facilities include saunas, mud baths, massage rooms, Turkish baths, and thalassotherapy pools (a sort of giant New Age hot tub). See p. 134.

- **Cunard:** *QM2*'s two-story, 20,000-square-foot spa was designed and is operated by Canyon Ranch, one of the most famous spas in North America. Done up in a vaguely Art Deco and nautical motif, the place looks as good as it feels. More than 50 therapists dole out the latest treatments, and you can finish off your spa time with a dip in the ultrarelaxing aquatherapy pool. See p. 288.

- **Windstar Cruises:** The intimate, 308-passenger *Wind Surf* has extensive spa facilities for a ship this size, with prebookable spa packages combining six or more treatments tailored to both men and women. See p. 415.

- **Royal Caribbean:** The two-level spa complexes aboard the line's **Voyager-class ships** are among the largest and best accoutered out there. A peaceful waiting area has New Age tropical bird-song music piped in overhead. Ahhhh, relaxation—until you get your bill. The **Radiance-class ships** have huge exotically themed solariums and 13 treatment rooms, including a special steam-room complex featuring heated, tiled chaise longues and special showers simulating tropical rain and fog. See p. 254.
- **Radisson Seven Seas:** Radisson's spas are among the few not run by the ubiquitous Steiner. Instead, the French spa company Carita imports staffs and hairdressers from Parisian salons, and offers company specialties such as the Rénovateur exfoliating process as well as such cruise spa standards as hydrotherapy, reflexology, aromatherapy, body wraps, facials, manicures/pedicures, and anti-stress, therapeutic, and hot-rock massage. See p. 296.
- **Norwegian Cruise Line:** The *Norwegian Dawn* really ratcheted up the line's commitment to spa culture, with facilities located off a lofty, sunlit entrance atrium done up in greenery and a Mayan design theme. A big thumbs up goes to the spa's indoor pool complex, an elegant space with a large lap pool, hot tub, jet-massage pool, and sunny windowed seating areas. See p. 201.

15 Best Shopping Cruises

Folks who lament our consumer culture should look into the small-ship lines in chapter 8, where shopping hardly ever rears its head. If vacationing means an opportunity to indulge your plastic gland, though, the following ports and ships will give you the fix you crave.

- **In the Caribbean:** Aside from places such as Progresso, Mexico (which is just a dock that allows easier access to the peninsula's Mayan ruins), all the ports in the Caribbean have at least a few stores or souvenir stands. Most have a sprawling market or complexes near the cruise ship docks that blend seamlessly with the shopping streets beyond. If a ship is coming to an island, people there will be ready to sell you stuff. The biggest shopping ports are Charlotte Amalie, St. Thomas; Nassau and Freeport, Bahamas; Christiansted, St. Croix; San Juan, Puerto Rico; Georgetown, Grand Cayman; Philipsburg and Marigot, St. Martin; and Oranjestad, Aruba. Expect jewelry, perfume, cosmetics, clothing, liquor, arts and crafts, and souvenirs, with about an equal mix of chain stores and locally owned shops. At some smaller ports, such as Dominica, you'll still find good indigenous Caribbean arts (that island's Caribe Indian baskets are gorgeous), but on the whole the "island crafts" you'll find are pretty lame and/or made in Hong Kong. The American islands (Puerto Rico and the U.S. Virgins) allow you to bring home more cheap booze duty-free (see chapter 3). See chapter 10.
- **In Alaska:** If you've cruised in the Caribbean, you'll have a bit of déjà vu when you step off your ship in Skagway, Juneau, or Ketchikan and see chain stores such as Little Switzerland. Mixed in among the jewelry and perfume, though, you'll also have the opportunity to see art created by the vibrant Alaska Native cultures of Southeast, the Tlingit, Haida, and Tsimshian. Paintings, sculpture, carved masks, and ornate ceremonial rattles are frequently gorgeous, but also frequently very, very expensive.

Ketchikan and Skagway are a bit too shopping-frantic for our tastes. We prefer Juneau and the much less busy Sitka. See chapter 11.

- **On the Mexican Riviera: Puerto Vallarta** is the best shopping bet among the Mexican Riviera ports, combining typical tourist shopping with opportunities for buying real works of art. Dozens of galleries are dedicated to Mexican modern art, while the city's proximity to the High Sierras means it's also a center for gorgeous Huichol Indian art. Among the other ports usually included on Riviera itineraries, Cabo San Lucas is a veritable shopping mall, though only distinctive if you're in the market for tequila and T-shirts. See chapter 12.

- **In Hawaii:** For those who like to do some serious window-shopping, head to Kalakaua Avenue at Oahu's Waikiki Beach. Here you can find everything from Coach bags to board shorts, all on a bustling strip complete with statues, reflecting pools, street performers, and at dusk, flaming Tiki torches and alfresco dining. It's Beverly Hills meets Greenwich Village. Lahaina, Maui, has a lovely historic district that offers great beachfront shopping on Front Street. By the courthouse, artists congregate under a big banyan tree, creating a sort of open-air gallery. See chapter 14.

- **In New England and Canada:** You won't have time to go New England antiquing in the traditional get-in-the-car-and-drive way, but New England/Canada itineraries offer some good shopping ports. Newport, Rhode Island's downtown is full of cutesy boutiques and shops selling nautically themed merchandise, the latter of which you'll also find a lot of along the hilly streets of New Bedford, Massachusetts. In Boston, head for historic Faneuil Hall and the adjacent Quincy Market, or to Newbury Street if you've got money to burn—it's Boston's version of New York's Fifth Avenue. If you're sailing from New York, you can just *go* to Fifth Avenue, with pricey shops stacked end-to-end from 42nd Street to 57th, or head downtown to SoHo or Chelsea for art. In Portland, Maine, the L.L.Bean outlet is within striking distance at nearby Freeport. See chapter 15.

Part 1

Planning, Booking & Preparing for Your Cruise

With advice on choosing and booking your ideal cruise and tips on getting ready for the cruise experience.

1

Choosing Your Ideal Cruise

Forget the "overfed, newlywed, nearly dead" stereotype of cruising. That's old school. Today, you can sail a floating country club to little yachting islands in the Caribbean, bop around Hawaii in the first new U.S.-flagged cruise ships in generations, take an expedition from Alaska over to the Russian Far East, take the *Queen Mary 2* across the pond to England, sail among the reefs and indigenous cultures of Central America, or explore North America's great rivers on floating B&Bs. There are also trips programmed with your needs and preferences in mind, whether you're a senior, a traveling family, a swinging single, a wheelchair user, or a swinging, wheelchair-using granddad. There are also active adventure cruises, cruises geared to fine food and wine, cruises with a cultural or historic bent, and, of course, the classic fun-in-the-sun relaxation escape. In this chapter, we'll introduce you to the lot of them.

1 Homeland Cruise Regions in Brief

Whether because of convenience or an aversion to flying (that is, the cost of flying or the fear of it), the idea of cruising from a port within driving distance has a lot of appeal for a lot of folks. And anytime a lot of folks want to do something, you can be sure the cruise lines will be right there on the spot, ready to hand them an umbrella drink. Today, you can cruise to the Caribbean from Miami or from New York, New Orleans, Houston, and about 10 other ports. You can visit Bermuda on ships that depart from Boston, New York, Philadelphia, and Baltimore. Alaska, Mexico, and Hawaii are now accessible from half a dozen embarkation ports along the West Coast. With all of these choices, there's a good chance you can drive right up to the gangway. In the chapters that follow, we cover all regions to which you can cruise from 19 U.S. and 3 Canadian home ports. Below is a snapshot of those regions, to get you started.

CARIBBEAN/BAHAMAS/CENTRAL AMERICA

When most of us think of a cruise, we think of the islands. We imagine pulling up in our gleaming white ship to a patch of sand and palm tree paradise, a steel band serenading us as we stroll down the gangway in our shorts and flip-flops and into the warm sun. Well, the good news is that this image is a pretty darn accurate depiction of many ports in the Caribbean, Bahamas, and Central America. Sure, some are crowded with other cruise ships and passengers and many are pretty weak in the palm tree department, but you're guaranteed nearly **constant sunshine** and plenty of beaches. On some you'll find lush **rainforests, volcanic peaks, Mayan ruins,** winding **mountain roads,** and beautiful **tropical flowers.** And all of them have **great beaches** and that laid-back don't-hurry-me island pace.

Most Caribbean cruises are a week long, though you'll also find 5-, 6-, 8-, 9-, 10-, and 11-night sailings. Cruises to The Bahamas are usually 3- and 4-nights, though many Caribbean routes also include a stop in Nassau or one of the cruise lines' private Bahamian islands. Stops at Cozumel, Playa del Carmen, and other spots along Mexico's Yucatán Peninsula are common, as increasingly are visits to Central American ports like Belize City, Belize, and Roatan, Honduras. You'll find itineraries usually stick to one region of the Caribbean, either **eastern** (typically calling on some combination of the U.S. Virgin Islands, Puerto Rico, St. Martin, and The Bahamas), **western** (usually Grand Cayman, Jamaica, Cozumel, and Key West, and sometime Belize or Honduras), or **southern** (less defined, but often departing from San Juan and including Aruba, Curaçao, Barbados, St. Lucia, Antigua, or Grenada). Small-ship cruises frequently visit the less-developed islands, mostly in the eastern and southern Caribbean, including the beautiful British Virgin Islands and ports such as St. Barts, Dominica, Nevis, and the tiny islands of the Grenadines. **Season:** Year-round, with the greatest number of ships cruising here between October and April.

THE PANAMA CANAL

Imagine the particularly 19th-century kind of hubris it took to say, "Let's dig a huge canal all the way across a country, linking two oceans." Imagine, too, the thousands of workers who pulled it off. Both those things are much on the mind of people today as they sail through the Panama Canal, one of the great engineering achievements of all time. There's a lot of history here, as well as a lot of rich Central American culture to explore on port days surrounding your transit. Many ships offer only two Panama Canal cruises annually, when repositioning between their summer season in Alaska and the fall/winter season in the Caribbean, but these days many cruise lines are including **partial Canal crossings** as part of extended western Caribbean itineraries from Florida, sailing through the Canal's locks westbound to Gatun Lake, docking for a day of excursions, and then sailing back out in the evening. The big draw on these itineraries is the pure kick of sailing through the Canal, whose walls pinch today's megaships so tight that there might not be more than a few feet on either side. The Canal's width is so much on shipbuilders' minds that they coined a term—*panamax*—to describe the largest ships that are able to transit. **Season:** Roughly November through April.

ALASKA & BRITISH COLUMBIA

Alaska is America's frontier, a land of mountain, forest, and tundra just remote enough and harsh enough that it remains mythic, even if some of its towns do have Starbucks. The main draws here are all things grand: huge glaciers flowing down from the mountains, enormous humpback whales leaping from the sea, eagles soaring overhead, and forests that seem to go on forever. Alaska Native culture figures in too, with the Tlingit, Haida, and Tsimshian tribes all holding considerable power in everyday life, from the arts to the business world. Most cruises concentrate on the Southeast Alaska panhandle (the ancestral home of those three tribes), which stretches from Ketchikan in the south to Yakutat in the north, with British Columbia to the east and the vast reaches of interior Alaska and Canada's Yukon Territory to the north. Typical cruises sail either round-trip from Seattle or Vancouver, British Columbia, or north- or southbound between Vancouver and one of Anchorage's two major port towns, Seward and Whittier. Both options concentrate on ports and natural areas along the Southeast's **Inside Passage,** the intricate web of waterways that link the region's thousands of forested islands. Highlights of most itineraries include glaciers (famous Glacier Bay or several others), the old prospector town of Skagway, state capital Juneau, and boardwalked Ketchikan in the south. Cruises between Vancouver and Anchorage may also visit natural areas along the **Gulf of Alaska,** such as College Fjord and Hubbard

Glacier. Small-ship cruises frequently visit much smaller towns and wilderness areas on the Inside Passage. Some avoid civilization almost entirely, and a few particularly expeditionary (and expensive) cruises sail far west and north, past the Aleutian Islands, and cross the Bering Sea into the Russian Far East. **Season:** Roughly from mid-May through mid-September, although some smaller ships start up in late April.

THE MEXICAN RIVIERA & BAJA

The so-called Mexican Riviera is the West Coast's version of the Caribbean—a string of sunny ports within proximate sailing distance of San Diego, LA, and San Francisco. The first stop geographically is Cabo San Lucas, a party-oriented town at the southern tip of the Baja Peninsula, with the Pacific Ocean on one side and the Sea of Cortez on the other. Think beaches, beer, and bikinis, with thatched palapa bars providing some character. From there, cruises head southeast to such ports as Puerto Vallarta, Mazatlán, Acapulco, Ixtapa, and Manzanillo, a stretch famed for white-sand beaches, watersports, deep-sea fishing, and golf, with some history thrown in for good measure. Hernando Cortes blew through the region in the 1520s looking for treasure, and in the 1950s and '60s Hollywood did the same, mining the area both for locations and for off-camera relaxation. Small-ship lines also offer **Baja/Sea of Cortez** cruises that concentrate on the peninsula's small towns, natural areas, and remarkable whale-watching. These cruises typically sail from Cabo or the state capital, La Paz. **Season:** The heaviest traffic is October through April, though ships sail year-round—especially short 3- and 4-night cruises that stop in Cabo or Ensenada, just south of the U.S./Mexico border. Small ships typically cruise Baja in the winter months.

BERMUDA

Perhaps the one place in the world where you'll have a chance to see hundreds of British men's knees, Bermuda is a beautiful island chain known for its powdery pink sand beaches, created by pulverized shells and coral over the eons; golf courses; and sane and friendly manner. The locals really do wear brightly colored Bermuda shorts with jackets, ties, and knee-highs, but don't feel obligated to join them. **Hamilton** and **St. George's** are Bermuda's two main port towns, though the largest ships will dock on the west end at the **Royal Naval Dockyard.** Ships pull alongside piers at all three places and it barely takes 2 minutes to walk into town. There's plenty to do, too, from shopping in Hamilton for English wool and Irish linens, to checking out the many historical sites, which range from the 300-year-old St. Peter's Church to the impressive nautical exhibits at the Dockyard's Maritime Museum. Most people, though, are headed for Bermuda's many dreamy beaches, which are easily accessible by taxi or motor scooter. To keep things from getting too chaotic, Bermuda limits the number of ships allowed to call there, so there are generally just six doing 7-night cruises from New York, Boston, Philadelphia, Baltimore, and occasionally Norfolk, Virginia. **Season:** Late April through early October.

HAWAII

If a place can simultaneously be the number-one honeymoon destination in America *and* one of the few places to which the Brady Bunch schlepped Alice and the kids, it must have something going for it, right? It does: Hawaii is gorgeous, with an almost embarrassing richness of stunning beaches, hula girls, and hunky Polynesian men, and the weather really is perfect all the time, putting both locals and visitors in a friendly and mellow mood. Learn to surf, go to a luau, snooze on the sand, enjoy the local coffee, or check out the native Hawaiian culture, which the locals are fiercely proud of. The past survives alongside the modern world in a vibrant arts scene, which includes traditional Polynesian dance and music, as well as painting, sculpture, and crafts. And the diverse landscape of the islands ranges from fuming volcanoes to crashing surf, serene beaches, lush jungles, and abundant orchids and other tropical flowers. Pearl Harbor is another important attraction.

For the foreseeable future, Norwegian Cruise Line rules the roost in Hawaii, with three ships (and a fourth on the way) doing year-round cruises round-trip from Honolulu. Other lines typically visit the islands in April, May, September, and October, on their way between seasons in Alaska and the Caribbean. The four main calls are to **Oahu,** with the famous Waikiki beach; **Maui,** home of the historical town of Lahaina; **Kauai,** the most natural and undeveloped of the four; and the **Big Island,** where the state's famous volcanoes reside, including Mauna Kea and the still-active Kilauea. **Season:** Year-round; the islands are about the same latitude as Jamaica.

EASTERN CANADA/NEW ENGLAND

Humpback, finback, and minke whales, lobster pots, Victorian mansions, and lighthouses on windswept bluffs are just a taste of what a journey along the coast of New England and Canada has in store for cruise passengers. America and Canada were born in these parts, so you'll be in for lots of **historical sites** along the way, from Boston's Paul Revere House to Halifax, where *Titanic* victims were brought (and many buried) after the ship's tragic sinking nearly 100 years ago. Itineraries may include passing through **Nantucket Sound,** around **Cape Cod,** and into the **Bay of Fundy** or **Gulf of St. Lawrence.** Some ships traverse the St. Lawrence Seaway or the smaller Saguenay River. The classic time to cruise here is in autumn, when a brilliant sea of **fall foliage** blankets the region, but as the route becomes more and more popular, cruise lines are scheduling 4- to 12-night trips in spring and summer, too. Big 2,000-passenger-plus ships cruise here as well as much smaller vessels carrying a tenth of that load. Most sail to or from New York, Boston, Montréal, and Québec City. **Season:** Most ships cruise here in September and October, with a few lines also offering late spring and summer sailings.

U.S. RIVER CRUISES

So who needs the ocean? If your interests run toward history, culture, and nature, a river cruise is a fantastic option. Small ships sail throughout the year, navigating the historic **Mississippi River** system to cities and towns of the South; sailing through the **California Wine Country** for tastings, tours, and meals at noted vineyards; following Lewis and Clark down the Pacific Northwest's **Columbia and Snake rivers;** and even offering cruises on the **Erie Canal** and the rivers of New England, timed to take in the fall foliage. Some of these ships (like the American Canadian Caribbean Line vessels) are tiny and basic, carrying fewer than 100 passengers and designed to sail in very shallow, narrow waterways. Others (like the *Delta Queen* and American West ships) are vintage or re-created stern-wheelers that evoke classic 19th-century river travel. **Season:** Throughout the year in different regions. (See small ship reviews in chapter 8 for itineraries.)

2 Itineraries: The Long & the Short of It

Decided where you want to go? So now you have to hone in on the itineraries that are available. Do you just want to get away for a few days, or are a few weeks more your style? Do you want an itinerary that visits somewhere different every day, or are you looking forward to some relaxing sea days, too? And, if you're flying or driving a long way to the cruise's home port, do you want to spend a few days seeing that part of the country as well, before or after your cruise? Options are what you have; choices are what you need to make.

LONG CRUISE OR SHORT?

The vast majority of cruises are **7 nights** long and depart on a Saturday or Sunday, whether we're talking Caribbean, Alaska, Hawaii, or Mexico. Many of us like the weeklong vacation concept, but if you're looking to spend less money or you're a first-time cruiser interested in testing the waters, you can pick from a slew of 2-, 3-, 4-, and 5-night cruises, and even a few 6-nighters. Many of the **3- and 4-night cruises** sail from Florida to The Bahamas or from California to Baja, Mexico. You can also find a lot of **4- and 5-night cruises** to the Caribbean and Bahamas, as well as 4- and 5-night New England/Canada cruises in the summer and fall. Naturally, these depart on different days of the week, with some timed to sail over the weekend.

On the one hand, shorter cruises make sense if you're not sure you'll like the cruise experience, but they probably won't show you cruising in its best light. Why? Because mini-sailings are geared to people who can only get away for a few days and want to pack as much party into a short time as possible. (This is especially true of the 3-night weekend cruises offered by Carnival and Royal Caribbean.) Longer cruises are generally mellower. There's also the fact that cruise lines tend to put their oldest, most beaten-up ships on short-cruise schedules, saving their new ships for their bread-and-butter weeklong itineraries.

Longer cruises, ranging from **9, 10, and 12 nights** to multiweek voyages, allow you to really feel like you've gotten away, and settle into the community on board your ship. Longer cruises tend to be relaxed and steady, and are popular with older folks who have the time and money to travel. You'll find a few longer sailings in Alaska, the Caribbean, and New England/Canada, and also many long **repositioning cruises,** offered when ships leave one cruise region and sail to another (for instance, heading from Alaska to the Caribbean in stages). These are often deeply discounted and sometimes visit unusual ports, but they often also spend several days at sea between ports.

DAYS AT SEA VS. DAYS IN PORT

When evaluating an itinerary, take a look at its day-by-day schedule. A few ships will visit a different port every day, but it's much more typical for them to have at least 1 or 2 days at sea—either because they have to sail a long way between ports, or just to give passengers a chance to rest (and spend some money on board, while they're at it). Many cruises these days—especially ones that sail from more northerly home ports to Caribbean destinations—are spending up to 3 days at sea on a 7-night itinerary and 4 on an 8-night itinerary. That's not a bad thing if your main vacation goal is to decompress, but if your goal is to see a lot of different ports, this is not an ideal situation. Ditto if you think you'll get "are we there yet?" antsy between ports.

CRUISETOURS & ADD-ONS

Cruise lines offer a variety of options for extending your vacation on land, either before or after your cruise. These range from simple 1- and 2-night add-on **hotel packages** to longer resort stays and full-blown land tours of a week or longer. The latter, known as **cruisetours,** are offered mostly in Alaska, where Holland America, Princess, Royal Caribbean, and Celebrity have elaborate hotel and transportation infrastructure. Many parts of inland Alaska can be accessed this way—Denali National Park, Fairbanks, Wrangell–St. Elias National Park, Nome, and Kotzebue included. If you've a mind to, you can even go all the way to the oil fields of the North Slope of Prudhoe Bay, hundreds of miles north of the Arctic Circle. Many tours also head east into Canada, spending time in the starkly beautiful Yukon Territory or heading to Banff, Lake Louise, and Jasper National Park in the Canadian Rockies.

Caribbean-bound ships originating in Florida often offer extensions to Orlando's theme parks. Disney, naturally, is tops in this regard, offering seamless 1-week land/sea vacations, with 3 days in the park and 4 aboard *Disney Wonder,* or vice versa. Other regions offer their own specialties: Small-ship cruises in Baja, for example, typically offer an extension to the amazing Copper Canyon, larger than the U.S. Grand Canyon.

3 Different Boats for Different Folks

Different cruise lines offer different kinds of experiences, but judging physical factors such as the size and age of the ship are also part of choosing your ideal cruise. What kind of boat floats your boat?

MEGASHIPS (1,800–3,600 PASSENGERS)

For the past dozen years, the so-called "megaships" have dominated the market, carrying upwards of 1,800 passengers and offering an onboard experience any city-dweller will recognize: food and drink available at any hour, entertainment districts filled with neon and twinkling lights, monumental architecture, big crowds, and a definite buzz. You often won't see the same faces twice from day to day, and, in fact, if you don't plan specific times and places to meet up with your spouse, lover, or friend, you may roam the decks for hours looking for them. (Some passengers even bring a set of walkie-talkies to stay in touch—annoying to the rest of us, maybe, but it keeps them happy.) The megas have as many as 12 or 14 passenger decks full of shops, restaurants, bars, and lounges, plus cabins of all shapes and sizes. Most have a grand multistory atrium lobby, three or four swimming pools and hot tubs, theaters, a pizzeria, a specialty coffee shop, and one or more reservations-only restaurants. Mammoth spas and gyms boast dozens of exercise machines and treatment rooms, and vast children's areas include splash pools, playrooms, and video arcades. Countless activities are offered all day long, including dance lessons, wine tastings, fashion shows, art auctions, aerobics classes, bingo, bridge, cooking demonstrations, pool games, computer classes, and trivia contests. And at night you have a choice of piano bars, discos, martini and champagne bars, sports bars, casinos, theaters, and show lounges.

But even the megas aren't all alike. **Carnival** and **Costa**'s ships are the most theme-park-like, with their over-the-top decor and ambience. **Royal Caribbean**'s and **NCL**'s megas (especially their newer ships) are more like Times Square hotels, blending a lot of flash with some elegant areas. **Princess** goes for a sort of Pottery Barn design sense and fun but not-too-daring activities and shows, and **Holland America**'s and **Disney**'s megas blend tradition with some bright, modern spaces. **Celebrity** is king in terms of sleek modern decor and a near-upscale ambience.

As a general rule, these ships are so large that they're limited as to where they can go. Ships in the 100,000-ton range are too big to fit through the Panama Canal, and so operate from the same coast year-round—West Coast ships doing Mexico itineraries in winter and Alaska in summer, say; East Coast ships either staying in the Caribbean year-round or spending the summers sailing in Europe or New England/Canada. Some ports also lack docking facilities to accommodate these huge ships, meaning you either won't visit them at all or you'll have to be tendered ashore in shuttle boats.

SHIP SIZE COMPARISONS

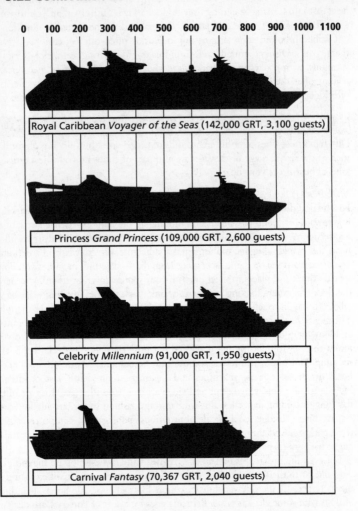

0   100   200   300   400   500   600   700   800   900   1000   1100

Royal Caribbean *Voyager of the Seas* (142,000 GRT, 3,100 guests)

Princess *Grand Princess* (109,000 GRT, 2,600 guests)

Celebrity *Millennium* (91,000 GRT, 1,950 guests)

Carnival *Fantasy* (70,367 GRT, 2,040 guests)

Ships in this chart represent the range of sizes sailing in the Caribbean in 2005. See reviews in chapters 6–9 for sizes of ships not shown here, then compare. Note that GRT=gross register tons, a measure of the interior space used to produce revenue on a vessel. One GRT=100 cubic feet of enclosed, revenue-generating space.

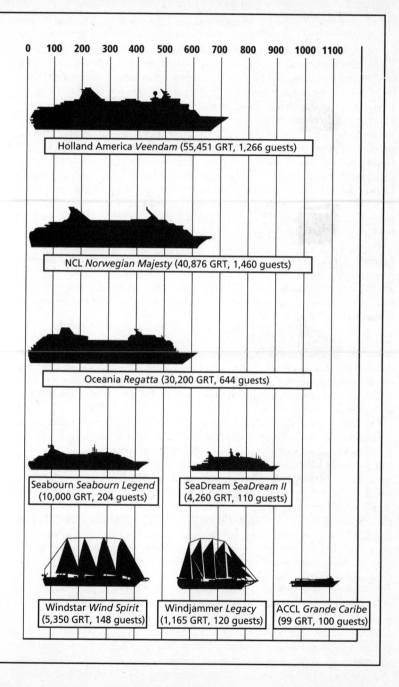

0   100   200   300   400   500   600   700   800   900   1000   1100

Holland America *Veendam* (55,451 GRT, 1,266 guests)

NCL *Norwegian Majesty* (40,876 GRT, 1,460 guests)

Oceania *Regatta* (30,200 GRT, 644 guests)

Seabourn *Seabourn Legend* (10,000 GRT, 204 guests)

SeaDream *SeaDream II* (4,260 GRT, 110 guests)

Windstar *Wind Spirit* (5,350 GRT, 148 guests)

Windjammer *Legacy* (1,165 GRT, 120 guests)

ACCL *Grande Caribe* (99 GRT, 100 guests)

MIDSIZE SHIPS (600–1,800 PASSENGERS)

For a while it looked as if midsize vessels were going the way of the dodo, but the past couple years has seen a small resurgence in their fortunes, and a number of older but still not *old*-old midsize ships continue soldiering on.

The term *midsize* is, of course, relative. Measuring in at between 20,000 and 60,000 gross tons, most of these ships are still larger than some of the great old ocean liners. *Titanic,* for instance, was only 46,000 tons. They're plenty big and spacious enough to provide a diverse cruise experience, though you won't find the range of activities you do on the megaships. Consider that a good thing: For some people, a more toned-down, lower-key cruise is just what the doctor ordered. Most of **Holland America**'s fleet fits that description, aside from its mega-size Vista-class ships. **MSC Cruises** operates two 58,600-ton, 1,590-passengers vessels in the Caribbean, and is really embracing the midsize zeitgeist in their onboard programming. **Oceania Cruises** operates three even smaller vessels, carrying only 684 passengers apiece in a country-club type setting. **NCL** also still offers several midsizers, though they're the older ships in their fleet and are already on the chopping block. (All will have left the fleet by 2009.)

Among the true ultraluxury lines, midsize is about as big as it gets excluding Cunard's megaliners. **Crystal** and **Radisson** both operate ships in the 50,000-ton range, carrying 700 to 940 passengers—a telling figure when you consider that MSC and NCL's similarly sized ships pack in twice as many passengers. Along with high-toned service, cuisine, and amenities, personal space is a major difference between the mainstream and luxe lines.

SMALL SHIPS (12–450 PASSENGERS)

If the thought of sailing with thousands of other people makes you want to jump overboard, a smaller ship may be more up your alley. Small ships are ideal for those who crave a calm, intimate experience where conversation is king. As in a small town, you'll quickly get to know your neighbors, since you'll see the same faces at meals and on deck throughout the week.

The small ships in this book can be broken down into four groups: sailing ships, coastal and river cruisers, expedition ships, and small luxury ships.

Sailing ships have sails. How obvious is that? But what's not necessarily obvious is how much—or how little—those sails are used to actually propel the ship. On Maine's coast, the 14 independently owned ships of the **Maine Windjammer Association** are honest-to-god sail-powered vessels, most without engines of any kind. If the wind stops blowing, their only option is to let down their motorized yawl boat and try to push the ship into wind. The ships of **Windjammer Barefoot Cruises, Star Clippers,** and **Windstar,** on the other hand, usually operate under wind power for a part of each cruise, but they have engines to do most of the pushing. All these vessels tend to attract as many passengers in their 30s as in their 70s, all of them looking for something a little different than a regular cruise.

Most of the other small ships in this book are coastal and river cruisers—small vessels designed to sail in protected coastal waters and rivers. Very casual (and for the most part relatively plain), these ships offer a cruise oriented heavily toward nature, wildlife watching, culture, and history, with onboard naturalists to help interpret what you see. In addition to coastal cruisers, **Cruise West** and **Clipper Cruises** also operate tougher expedition ships able to sail in the open ocean. Rounding out the small-ship options are the nostalgic Mark Twain–style stern-wheelers of **Delta Queen** and

American West, which turn the clock back on trips along the Mississippi, the Pacific Northwest's Columbia and Snake rivers, and Alaska's Inside Passage.

See "Active Travel & Adventure Cruises," below, and chapter 8, "Small Ships, Sailing Ships & Adventure Cruises," for more details on all these options.

The small luxury ships of high-end lines such as **Seabourn, Silversea,** and **SeaDream** offer a refined, ultraelegant ambience. Cabins are spacious, gracious waiters serve gourmet meals on fine china, and guests dress to impress. These ships also offer few activities besides watersports, putting more emphasis on quiet relaxation and quiet, more high-end ports, such as St. Barts. **American Safari Cruises** operates truly tiny yachts carrying only 12 and 22 passengers. Service-oriented like the luxe ships, they also offer an adventure-travel vibe, with lots of built-in active excursions.

OLD SHIP OR NEW?

The age of a ship used to be a bigger topic than it is now. The 2000 edition of this book included no fewer than 12 really old vessels, 10 of which have either been sold off, laid up, or scrapped. Aside from Cunard's classic *QE2* (now sailing primarily from England), the small luxury yacht *Sea Cloud,* and most of the Maine Windjammer Association fleet, the only truly antique ship in this book is Imperial Majesty's old and endearing *Regal Empress,* a liner built in 1955 and still going strong, if a little worn around the edges. She's probably the last chance you'll have to sail on a mid-century liner.

The majority of ships in this book, by contrast, have been built in the past 16 years, though a few date to the late 1980s. Those older ships are generally a bit dated, though some cruise lines are doing a lot of work to bring them up-to-date. Royal Caribbean, for instance, is updating the interiors of their older ships to look more like their new ones, and offer some of the same options.

4 Cruises for Families

There's a reason so many families with kids go on cruises—it's easy! Okay, as the mother of young twin boys, traveling is never "easy" with kids, but a cruise is sure convenient, not to mention safe and relaxing for mom and dad. Cruise lines have been going to great lengths to please parents and kids alike, as families become an ever larger and more influential segment of the cruising public. In fact, since 2000, Royal Caribbean, among the most family-friendly lines, has seen more than a 50% increase in the number of kids under 3 cruising with their parents. Same story with Carnival, which now carries 300% more children under 18 than in 1995. The latest trends? Catering to toddlers and teens. Royal Caribbean introduced daily playgroups for parents and toddlers (6 months–3 years), while elaborate teen facilities are all the rage across the industry. Lines know teens are their future business, and they do their best to keep teenagers entertained and out of mischief.

It's the megaships that cater most to families and attract the largest numbers of them, with playrooms, video arcades, and complimentary **supervised activities** generally provided for children ages 2 or 3 to 17 (generally young children must be potty-trained to participate), and programs broken down into several age categories. Some lines set a minimum age for children to sail aboard (usually 6–12 months), but Disney offers a supervised nursery for ages 3 months and up, and it wouldn't surprise us if this became a trend. See the individual cruise line reviews for details.

Disney offers the most family-friendly ships at sea today, followed by **Royal Caribbean,** whose ships (especially the Voyager- and Radiance-class ships) have huge play areas. The post-1990 **Carnival** ships do a pretty good job, too (and kids as young as 4 months are included in the group babysitting program), as do the new **Norwegian** ships (especially the new *Norwegian Dawn* and *Norwegian Star,* with their awesome kids' center) and all **Princess** and **Celebrity** ships built after 1993, when family cruising was becoming more mainstream. Even lines traditionally geared to older folks are getting in on the kid craze. Holland America is just finishing up a renovation of all of its ships' kids' facilities, and the *QM2*'s kids' facilities and programs are the best-kept secrets at sea.

See the section "Best Cruises for Families with Kids," on p. 10, for more info.

BABYSITTING   To ensure that parents have a good time, too, there are adults-only discos and lounges, and babysitting in the evenings until about 1 to 3am on many ships (though not all). After the complimentary daylong roster of supervised activities wraps up somewhere between about 7 and 10pm, most mainstream lines offer **group babysitting** slumber-party style in the playroom starting at about 10pm, usually for ages 3 to 12, at a cost of about $4 to $6 per hour per child. Some lines, though, accommodate younger kids. Disney's nurseries take children as young as 3 months and Carnival includes kids as young as 4 months; they have toys, cribs, and nap areas geared to infants and toddlers. The counselors will even change diapers! **Private in-cabin babysitting** by a crewmember is also offered by several lines (Celebrity, Royal Caribbean, and most high-end lines) at a steeper $8 to $10 per hour for the first child and/or second (sometimes it's a few bucks more for a sibling). Using a private babysitter every night isn't cheap, but Heidi's gone this route when cruising with her twin toddlers and swears by it—how else to dine and have a cocktail or two in peace after a long baby-centric day? (Of course it's key that your kids are good sleepers, so they can be tucked in and asleep before the sitter arrives to avoid meeting a new face at bedtime.)

FAMILY-FRIENDLY CABINS   Worried about spending a whole week with the family in some cramped little box? Depending on your budget, you may not have to.

Of course, a family of four can share a cabin that has bunk-style third and fourth berths, which pull out of the walls just above the pair of regular beds, and a few lines, such as Carnival and NCL ships, will even accommodate a fifth person on a rollaway bed on certain ships if space permits. If you've got a baby, a crib can be brought in if requested in advance. But there's no other way to slice it: A standard cabin with four people in it will be cramped, and with one bathroom . . . well, you can imagine. However, when you consider how little time you'll spend in the cabin, it's doable, and many families take this option. The incentive to share one cabin is price—whether children or adults, the rates for third and fourth persons sharing a cabin with two full-fare (or even heavily discounted) passengers are usually about half of the lowest regular rates. Norwegian Cruise Line allows children under 2 to sail free with two full-fare passengers (though you must pay port charges and government taxes for the kids, which will run about $100–$200 per person). Disney offers a reduced rate of $99 per 3- and 4-night cruise and $139 per 7-night cruise for children under 3, and Crystal has offered free passage for all children under 12 for summer sailings in Alaska. *Note:* Because prices are based on double adult occupancy of cabins, single parents sailing with children usually have to pay adult prices for their kids, though deals for single parents are offered every once in a while.

If you can afford it, and equate space with sanity, **consider booking a suite or junior suite.** Many have a pullout couch in the living room (or, better yet, two separate bedrooms) and can accommodate up to three or four children. *Disney Magic* and *Wonder* boast the family-friendliest cabins at sea: The majority of the ships' 875 cabins are equipped with two bathrooms and a sitting area with a sofa bed, plus there's a tub and minifridge. (While minifridges or minibars are fairly standard these days, tubs are a

Family Cruising Tips

Here are some suggestions for better sailing and smoother seas on your family cruise.

- **Reserve a crib.** If you'd like a crib brought into your cabin, request one when booking your cruise.
- **Minifridges/minibars are standard on most new ships.** Ships more than 5 or 10 years old may only offer them in suites. And if yours is a minibar stocked with beer and peanuts, you can ask your steward to clear it out so you have space for milk and snacks.
- **Bring baby food.** If your infant is still on jar food, you'll have to bring your own; ships don't supply it, with the exception of Crystal Cruises (with prior notice). And don't forget diapers either.
- **Keep a tote with you on embarkation day.** Fill it with diapers, baby food, bathing suits, or anything you'll need for the afternoon. After boarding a big ship, it may take a few hours for your luggage to be delivered to your cabin.
- **Pack some basic first-aid supplies, and even a thermometer.** Cruise lines have limited supplies of these items, and charge for them, too. If an accident should happen on board, virtually every ship (except the smallest ones) has its own infirmary staffed by doctors or nurses. Keep in mind that first aid can usually be summoned more readily aboard ship than in port.
- **Warn younger children about the danger of falling overboard,** and make sure they know not to play on the railings.
- **Make sure your kids know their cabin number** and what deck it's on. The endless corridors and doors on the megaships often look exactly alike, though some are color-coded.
- **Prepare kids for TV letdown.** Though many ships today receive satellite TV programming, you won't get the range of options you have at home.

rarity unless you're splurging on a suite.) They're like minisuites and comfortably sleep families of three or four—but, of course, you pay more for all of this. The ships' bona fide suites accommodate families of five to seven. Royal Caribbean's and Princess's newest ships have family suites as well—the minisuites on the Grand class are great for families—but remember, they're no bargain: You pay for the larger size and beefed-up amenities.

If you have older kids, it may just be cheaper to book **connecting cabins**—two separate standard cabins with interconnecting doors, which allows you to be close to each other, but separate. Almost every ship reviewed in this book offers connecting cabins, with the exception of most small ships and a small handful of midsize and megaships.

TAKING THE KIDS ON SMALL SHIPS   If your children are at least 10 or 12, some of the casual, off-beat cruises (for example, aboard Windjammer's *Legacy* and *Polynesia* and Star Clippers' *Royal Clipper*) can be loads of fun for some kids and educational to boot. You won't find a kids' playroom stuffed with toys, TVs, video games, or many other kids on board for that matter, but these cruises are more about exploring the ports anyway, so you'll only be aboard ship in the evenings. If your child is

Getting Married on Board or in Port

If you'd like to have your marriage and honeymoon all in one, you can legally get hitched on many cruises, either aboard ship or at one of your ports of call.

Practically all the mainstream lines offer wedding packages, with Carnival, Princess, and Royal Caribbean being the romance leaders, followed by NCL, Celebrity, Disney, Holland America, and Costa. In almost all cases a local justice of the peace, notary, or minister must officiate; so even if you choose to hold your ceremony aboard ship, it will have to take place while the ship is in port, not at sea. Eight of Princess's ships (the Diamond-, Coral-, and Grand-class ships) have **wedding chapels** on board, as do Royal Caribbean's Voyager-class ships, Carnival's Spirit-class ships, and NCL's *Norwegian Sun, Star, Dawn,* and *Pride of America.* Other ships hold ceremonies in lounges that are decorated for the occasion.

If you want non-sailing family and friends to attend, you can hold the ceremony and reception at your port of embarkation, before the ship leaves. Guests will be on a special list with port security, though they'll have to bring the requisite ID to board. Ceremonies can also be arranged at various ports of call, including Aruba, Barbados, Grand Cayman, St. Thomas, Sint Maarten, San Juan (Puerto Rico), Ocho Rios and Montego Bay (Jamaica), and Cozumel (Mexico) in the Caribbean; Nassau in The Bahamas; Key West, Florida; Bermuda; and Juneau and Ketchikan, Alaska. If you've always wanted to be married on a beach or by a tropical waterfall, this is the way to go. In Alaska, you can even arrange to be married on the ice of Juneau's Mendenhall Glacier courtesy of **Temsco** (© **877/789-9501;** www.temscoair.com), which also handles glacier helicopter tours for the cruise lines. If contemplating marriage in a port of call, remember that your cruise itinerary limits how far afield you can go, since ships generally stay in port for only 3 to 10 hours.

Wedding packages generally start around $750 for shipboard ceremonies; that price usually includes the services of an officiant (though you can bring your own if you prefer), a bouquet and boutonniere, champagne and keepsake glasses, a wedding cake, and the services of a photographer but not the photos themselves—those will cost extra, should you choose to buy them. The $750 package offered by Carnival—one of the big leaders in shipboard weddings—accommodates eight people including the bride and groom. Prices go up from there based on the complexity and size of any reception you want to have (from a simple open bar and hors d'oeuvres to

inquisitive and somewhat extroverted (not to mention well behaved), he or she may be able to talk with the crew and learn how a sailing ship operates.

5 Cruises for Honeymooners & Anniversary Couples

You want romance? You're in luck. Practically all cruises have what it takes to make your honeymoon or anniversary cuddly and cozy: moonlit nights, the undulating sea all around, dimly lit restaurants, and maybe a private balcony or whirlpool tub in your a formal meal in the ship's restaurant) and by port, with the top price being $2,145. Additional guests can be accommodated at a rate of $24 per person. Ceremonies can also be performed off-ship in port, at higher prices.

THE LEGAL DETAILS   No matter where you choose to wed, you must arrange for a marriage license from the U.S. or foreign port far in advance of the cruise itself. Policies vary from country to country, so you'll save a lot of headaches by having the cruise line help you with the details. When you're arranging your cruise, the line or your travel agent can fill you in on the rules and regulations of your marriage port and assist you with the application form and any other paperwork. Carnival and Princess have actual wedding departments to help you with these matters; other lines handle wedding planning through their guest-relations office or refer you to a wedding consultant with whom they work. Be sure to check with these departments before booking your cruise to be sure wedding space is available on the date you have in mind.

HAVING THE CAPTAIN OFFICIATE   Have your heart set on the big boss performing your marriage rites at sea? If so, you've got only one choice: Princess Cruises. Their Diamond-, Coral-, and Grand-class ships are currently the only ones where the captain himself does the honors, performing six or seven civil ceremonies a week. Adorned with fresh flower arrangements, stained glass, and warm caramel-wood furniture, the ships' charming wedding chapels seat about three dozen. Assistant pursers, decked out in their handsome dress blues, are available to escort a bride down the mini-aisle. Three different ceremony packages are offered, starting at $1,800 per couple (plus $400 for licensing fees). Depending on which you choose, they include photography, video, music, and salon treatments for the bride. You can also arrange onboard receptions that can be custom-tailored with a variety of options—hors d'oeuvres, champagne, wedding cake, and so on. Friends and relatives who aren't sailing can even monitor the wedding courtesy of the ships' chapel web-cams, which broadcast an updated photo every minute or so. (Look at the very bottom of the Princess website homepage for "Bridge Cams." Pick a ship, then click on "wedding chapel" from the drop-down menu.) Don't wait till the last minute if you're considering Princess for your wedding, as there's often a waiting list.

cabin. Of course, different ships are romantic to different kinds of people. The megaships offer a big, flashy kind of romance, like a trip to Vegas without the dry heat. The ultraluxury lines are more like a trip to Paris, with gourmet cuisine, fine wine, perfect service, and the finest bed linens. And some of the small-ship lines are like staying at a Vermont B&B—though others are more like a Motel 6, but with a better view. Beyond the ships themselves are the ports of call, offering experiences that are variously exotic, charming, exciting, and sybaritic.

HONEYMOON & ANNIVERSARY PACKAGES

Besides their inherent romantic qualities, cruises are a good honeymoon choice for lots of reasons—Sunday departures, so couples who marry on Saturday can leave the next day. Some lines offer honeymooner freebies such as a special cake in the dining room one night, or an invitation to a private cocktail party. Couples celebrating anniversaries are often invited as well. To get your share of freebies, be sure to tell your travel agent or the cruise line reservation agent that you'll be celebrating on the cruise. Beyond the freebies, the cruise lines aren't shy about selling a variety of **honeymoon/anniversary packages.** You'll get a pamphlet describing the available packages when you receive your cruise tickets in the mail. NCL's $79 Honeymoon Package is about average for its price range, and includes champagne and strawberries at embarkation, a dinner for two with complimentary wine at the ship's specialty restaurant, an invitation to a cocktail party, a keepsake photo, and canapés in your cabin one evening. Their $229 Deluxe Package adds breakfast in bed one day and two 25-minute massages at the spa. All the mainstream lines offer similar deals, with packages in the $300 to $500 range generally piling on more spa treatments, champagne, shore excursions, canapés, chocolate-covered strawberries, and the like. These packages must be ordered before the cruise.

Ultraluxe lines such as Silversea, Seabourn, Radisson, SeaDream, and Crystal are less involved in these kinds of promotions, but that's because free champagne and canapés, terry bathrobes, whirlpool bathtubs, and five-course dinners served in your cabin are all a matter of course.

VOW-RENEWAL & "ROMANCE" PACKAGES

Some lines offer vow-renewal packages for couples who'd like to celebrate their marriage all over again, or packages that simply add romance to a vacation. On Holland America, for example, couples can renew their vows at a special group ceremony at sea, catered with drinks and cold hors d'oeuvres; the $129 package includes a floral arrangement in your cabin, a photo and photo album, a certificate presented by the captain, and dinner for two at the Pinnacle alternative restaurant. Princess offers souped-up vow-renewal packages for $205 and $485 per couple. The former includes the ceremony, an orchid bouquet and boutonniere, a bottle of champagne and souvenir champagne glasses, a framed formal portrait of the ceremony, a commemorative certificate signed by the captain, and a framed photo of the ceremony; the latter adds a champagne breakfast in bed, two terry-cloth robes, a visit to the spa for half-hour massages or facials, canapés or petit fours in your stateroom every evening, and a personalized invitation from the captain to visit the bridge while in port. These are fairly representative of what's offered by the other mainstream lines.

6 Cruises for Gay Men & Lesbians

A number of specialized travel agencies offer cruises for gay men and/or lesbians, either chartering a full ship outright or reserving blocks of cabins with cruise lines that are known to be particularly gay-friendly. Full-charters typically bring aboard their own entertainers (as well as the ship's usual entertainment staff) and program many of their own activities. Hosted group trips typically have cocktail parties for group members and specially programmed activities on board and in port.

- **Atlantis Events Inc.,** 9200 Sunset Blvd., Suite 500, West Hollywood, CA 90069 (© 800/628-5268 or 310/859-8800; www.atlantisevents.com), offers all-gay charters with lines such as Celebrity, Royal Caribbean, and NCL. In addition to the lines' own entertainment, Atlantis brings aboard its own featured performers. Past guests have included Patti LuPone, Cybill Shepherd, and Chaka Khan.

- **Friends of Dorothy Travel,** 1177 California St. Suite B, San Francisco, CA 94108-2231 (© 800/640-4918 or 415/864-1600; www.fodtravel.com), offers many full-gay charters with lines such as Celebrity, NCL, and the ultraluxe SeaDream Yachts, as well as hosted tours on *Queen Mary 2* and other ships.
- **Olivia Cruises and Resorts,** 4400 Market St., Oakland, CA 94608 (© 800/631-6277 or 415/962-5700; www.olivia.com), offers full-ship charters targeted specifically to the lesbian community, mostly aboard Holland America's ships. Guest performers for 2004 and 2005 included k. d. lang, the Indigo Girls, Wynonna Judd, Shawn Colvin, and Melissa Etheridge, plus the cast of Showtime's *The L Word.*
- **Pied Piper Travel,** 330 W. 42nd St., Suite 1804, New York, NY 10036 (© 800/874-7312 or 212/239-2412; www.piedpipertravel.com), offers hosted gay cruises that include various onboard parties and activities and arranged visits with the gay community at the various ports of call.
- **R Family Vacations,** 2 Washington Ave., Nyack, NY 10960 (© 866/732-6822; www.rfamilyvacations.com), was founded by Rosie O'Donnell's partner Kelli O'Donnell, along with gay travel veteran Gregg Kaminsky. Trips are targeted to the gay and lesbian family market.
- **RSVP Vacations** (© 800/328-7787; www.rsvpvacations.com) offers full ship charters on lines like Holland America and Star Clippers. All sailings are targeted to both gay men and lesbians, and bring aboard their own guest performers. RSVP works through more than 10,000 different travel agencies, which can be located by calling the 800 number or checking the website above.

7 Active Travel & Adventure Cruises

It's true: Cruises *can* be active and adventurous, whether you want to really get off the beaten track on an expeditionary small ship or just keep your heart-rate elevated a few hours a day on a megaship.

ADVENTURE & EXPEDITIONARY CRUISES

A few years ago we met this great Australian couple in Alaska. They'd wanted to see the state for years, and wanted to really get into its forests and see its wildlife, but they didn't have time to do a 3-week wilderness trek. Their solution? They booked aboard one of Glacier Bay Cruiseline's ships, where every day was spent hiking, kayaking, or visiting tiny fishing towns. It was a perfect choice for them. Glacier Bay is one of the most physically active cruise lines in this book, but almost all the small-ship lines offer the ability to go "off-road," far from the usual ports of call.

Vessels that offer nature-oriented cruises basically break down into three types. **Coastal and river cruisers** are built to take people into narrow, shallow waters where you'd never find a big ship. Small (generally carrying fewer than 150 people) and usually pretty plain, these ships offer a casual cruise oriented heavily toward nature, wildlife watching, culture, and history, with onboard naturalists to help interpret what you see. **Expedition ships** are similar in size and character to the coastal cruisers, but they're built tougher and have stabilizers, allowing them to sail in open ocean—often as far as Asia, Europe, Antarctica, South America, and the Russian Far East. **Sailing ships** put a classic twist on the cruise experience. Some are classic or re-created rigged vessels that rely on wind for all or most of their propulsion. Others are rigged for show only, and have engines to do the real work.

Aboard all these ships there are few of the usual activity options, but that's by design: Their focus is on what's outside the vessel, not inside. Most offer itineraries that mix visits to large and small ports with days spent steering through natural areas in search of wildlife, but some are more active than others. Lindblad Expeditions, Glacier Bay, and American Safari Cruises, for instance, build activities such as hiking, kayaking, and exploring by inflatable launch into their adventure itineraries. Ditto for some of the more expeditionary trips offered by Cruise West and Clipper. On Star Clippers' sailing ships, those inflatable launches might be used to take passengers water-skiing or on banana-boat rides.

KEEPING ACTIVE ON THE MAINSTREAM & LUXE SHIPS

Ships started becoming more active around the dawn of the 1990s, and today it's unheard of for a new megaship to launch without a huge gym (the biggest exceeding 10,000 sq. ft., with dozens of exercise machines), jogging tracks, and sports decks that may have basketball courts, golf nets, and rock-climbing walls (the latter a hallmark of Royal Caribbean). A handful of smaller and mostly high-end ships concentrate on watersports, with retractable or floating watersports platforms to allow easy swimming, water-skiing, and windsurfing right from the ship. See "Keeping Fit: Gyms, Spas & Sports," in chapter 4, for an overview, and the "Pool, Fitness, Spa & Sports Facilities" section of each ship review in part 2 for a rundown on which ship has what.

ACTIVE SHORE EXCURSIONS

On shore, the cruise lines are offering more and more active excursions. No need to sit on a bus for 3 hours sweating if you'd rather be feeling the burn. Along with snorkeling and diving, options such as biking, hiking, kayaking, horseback riding, and river rafting are offered in many ports from the Caribbean to Alaska and beyond. For more details, see the port reviews in part 3.

8 Cruises for Young People

"So which are the ships for young people?" We get this question all the time, and the answer is, there aren't any. That is, there aren't any that attract *only* young people, just like there aren't many hotels or resorts that do. Most ships are a mixed bag of ages, with couples in their 40s, 50s, and 60-plus making up the majority, along with a growing percentage of younger couples, often with kids. Destination plays into the balance, with the Caribbean and Mexican Riviera attracting a sizable young crowd as well as lots of retirees. Alaska, Europe, New England/Canada, and Asia itineraries, on the other hand, draw mostly an older, 50-plus crowd (though you will see families with young kids in Alaska and Europe during the summer). That said, here are some general guidelines about ships and the ages of the people you'll find on them.

The **youngest crowds,** in the 20s-to-40s range, are typically found on 2-, 3-, and 4-night warm-weather cruises (and next on the 7-night cruises) on mainstream lines such as Carnival, Royal Caribbean, and NCL. Young-at-heart types, who may be 54 or 67 or 72 but who wear bikinis and short-shorts and drink piña coladas for lunch, will also be attracted to those lines, as well as to smaller fun-loving lines such as Windjammer and Star Clippers.

The **oldest folks,** upward of 60, will be the vast majority on luxury lines such as Seabourn, Silversea, Cunard, and Radisson. Holland America, a mainstream line, has also traditionally attracted a mature crowd, though they're trying hard to broaden their demographic, particularly on their newer megaships. Among the small-ship lines, you'll find a generally older crowd aboard American Canadian Caribbean, American Cruise Lines, American West, Delta Queen, and RiverBarge Excursions, as well as on port-to-port itineraries offered by Cruise West and Clipper.

9 Cruises for People with Disabilities & Health Issues

Though most of the cruise industry's ships are foreign-flagged and are not required to comply with the **Americans with Disabilities Act,** the newest ships have all been built with accessibility in mind, and some older ships have been retrofitted to offer access. Most ships that can accommodate wheelchair-bound passengers require that they be accompanied by a fully mobile companion. The ship reviews in chapters 6 through 8 include information about access and facilities in the "Cabins" sections, but be sure to discuss your needs fully with your travel agent prior to booking.

See the "Onboard Medical Care" box below for information on medical facilities aboard ship.

ACCESSIBLE CABINS & PUBLIC ROOMS   Most ships have a handful of cabins specifically designed for travelers with disabilities, with extra-wide doorways, large bathrooms with grab bars and roll-in showers, closets with pull-down racks, and furniture built to a lower height. The "Ships at a Glance" chart on p. 98 identifies ships with accessible cabins, and the "Cabins" section in each of the ship reviews in chapters 6 through 8 indicates how many. The vast majority of the ships reviewed in the **mainstream** and **luxury** categories (chapters 6 and 7) have accessible cabins, but of the **adventure ships** in chapter 8, only Delta Queen's *American* and *Mississippi Queen,* Cruise West's *Spirit of '98* and *Spirit of Oceanus,* and Clipper's *Clipper Odyssey* are even moderately wheelchair-friendly.

Most public rooms on newer vessels have ramps, and some also have lifts to help passengers with disabilities into the pools. A few older ships still have small sills or lips in cabin and bathroom doorways, originally created to contain water, which may rise as high as 6 to 8 inches. Those that do may be able to install temporary ramps to accommodate wheelchair users. This must be arranged in advance.

ELEVATORS   Most elevators aboard today's megaships are wide enough to accommodate wheelchairs, but make sure before booking. Sailing ships and most small vessels do not have elevators. Due to the size of the megaships (where it can sometimes be a long way from place to place), cabins designed for wheelchair users are intentionally located near elevators. If you don't use a wheelchair but have trouble walking, you'll want to choose a cabin close to an elevator to avoid a long hike.

TENDERING INTO PORT   If your ship is too large to dock or if a port's docks are already taken by other vessels, your ship may anchor offshore and shuttle passengers to land via small boats known as *tenders.* Some tenders are large and stable and others are not, but the choppiness of the water can be a factor when boarding either way, so if you use a wheelchair or have trouble walking, it may be difficult or impossible to get aboard. For liability reasons, many lines forbid wheelchairs to be carried onto tenders, meaning you may have to forgo a trip ashore and stay on board when in these ports. An exception to this is Holland America, which has a wheelchair-to-tender transport system aboard all of their ships except *Prinsendam.* The system works by locking a wheelchair on a lift, which transports it safely between the gangway and the tender.

Check with your travel agent to find out if itineraries you're interested in allow your ship to dock at a pier. Note that weather conditions and heavy traffic may occasionally affect the way your ship reaches a port.

Onboard Medical Care

The vast majority of ships have a nurse and sometimes a doctor aboard to provide medical services for a fee. Most of their cases involve seasickness, sunburn, and the like, but they may also be required to stabilize a patient with a more serious ailment until he or she can be brought to a hospital at the next port of call (or, in extreme cases, be evacuated by helicopter). If they're very unlucky, the medical staff may also have to deal with an outbreak of **norovirus,** the flulike gastrointestinal bug that's hit a few ships in the past 3 years. More common than the common cold, the virus causes vomiting, stomach cramps, diarrhea, and general nausea for a few days, and is caused by simple contagion: One infected passenger comes aboard, leaves his germs on a handrail, and all of a sudden everyone's sick—just like kindergarten. Though outbreaks are rare, cruise lines have stepped up their already vigilant sanitation routines to further reduce the chance of transmission.

All large ships have **staffed infirmaries,** but if you have special needs, check with the line to see exactly what medical services are provided. The quality of ships' staffs and facilities can definitely vary. Generally, big ships have the best-equipped facilities and largest staff since they're dealing with such a huge number of passengers and crew. In 2003, the author of an extensive *New York Times* article concluded that **Holland America** and **Princess** had the best onboard medical facilities, as well as the most generous pay packages for their doctors. Princess's Grand- and Coral-class ships, for instance, carry at least one and sometimes two doctors as well as two to five nurses, and are linked via a live video and camera system with U.S.-based medical centers. All Holland America ships can consult 24 hours a day (via phone or e-mail) with the University of Texas Medical Branch at Galveston, and their Vista-class ships have a teleradiology system that allows X-rays to be transmitted to a shoreside medical facility. (Princess's *Sea Princess* and Carnival's Spirit- and Conquest-class ships also have this system.) HAL's *Amsterdam* has the capability to do live television telemedicine conferencing and transmit X-rays to shoreside medical facilities. Note that shipboard doctors are not necessarily certified in the United States, and aren't always experts in important areas such as cardiology.

Small ships (those discussed in chapter 8) generally don't carry onboard medical staff since they sail close to shore and can evacuate sick passengers quickly. Usually, some crewmembers have nursing or first-aid experience. Small ships always carry doctors when sailing more far-flung international itineraries.

TRAVEL-AGENT SPECIALISTS   A handful of experienced travel agencies specialize in booking cruises and tours for travelers with disabilities. **Accessible Journeys,** 35 W. Sellers Ave., Ridley Park, PA 19078 (© **800/846-4537** or 610/521-0339; www.disabilitytravel.com), organizes both group and individual cruises on accessible ships, with accessible airport transfers and shore excursions, as well as an escort on group tours. **Flying Wheels Travel,** 143 W. Bridge St., Owatonna, MN 55060 (© **507/451-5005;** www.flyingwheelstravel.com), is another option.

2

Booking Your Cruise & Getting the Best Price

We're sorry to break it to you, but there's no magic secret to getting the best price on your cruise. Just when you think you have a foolproof strategy for saving big, conditions within the industry and the travel agent community shift and your grand plan is exactly the wrong way to go. In this chapter we've laid out the best booking strategies for 2006, along with other money-saving suggestions and booking tips.

1 Cruising 2006: Early Bird Gets Worm

The old tenet of supply-and-demand determines cruise rates: When the lines have more ships than they can fill, prices are low. Over the past decade, the cruise lines built so many new ships at such a frenetic pace that that's exactly what happened. Brochure prices—already unrealistic and inflated—became totally meaningless in the face of rampant discounting, which only got more frenzied as sailing dates approached and berths remained empty. If you waited till the last minute to book your cruise, chances were that the cruise lines would almost be giving 'em away. After all, it's better to get $400 for a berth than to sail with it empty and get nothing at all.

Well, those days are over. The great flurry of shipbuilding that raged from the late '90s through 2004 has finally slowed, demand has caught up with supply, and prices are back up to where they were in the late '90s, especially during the most popular cruising seasons. Cruises are still affordable, but industry sources say rates are about 8% higher in the Caribbean than they've been in the past year or two, and are about 10% higher in Alaska. Mike Driscoll, editor of industry bible *Cruise Week*, says you can expect to pay roughly $100 more, probably several hundred more, for a cruise this year versus 2 or 3 years ago. "Barring some geopolitical catastrophe, I see prices heading up and stabilizing," he says. "Last-minute shoppers will not be rewarded with bargains like they have been for the past 5 years."

So what does this mean? After preaching in previous years that booking at the last minute would land you the best deal, the sermon is over. There are always exceptions—slow periods such as September and October and non-holiday weeks in November and December—but today **your best strategy is booking early,** say about 4 to 6 months out.

As for the actual booking process, cruise lines still tend to do what they've been doing for years, relying on traditional **travel agents** and **websites** to sell their product, rather than retaining huge in-house reservations departments. For tips on using both online and brick-and-mortar agencies to the best advantage, see "Agents & the Web: Finding the Best Deals," later in this chapter.

2 The Prices in This Guide

Just like the airbrushed models dancing and lounging all over the cruise lines' brochures, the prices printed in those brochures aren't real, varying from just a little more than people really pay to wildly inflated. Apparently, even the cruise lines are ignoring them these days: We've heard from a reliable industry insider that many lines are planning to phase them out altogether. In any case, remember that **you'll always pay less,** except aboard some of the specialized small-ship lines.

Many cruise guides and magazines print these brochure rates despite knowing how useless they are in the real world, but we've come up with a new approach, working with Nashville, Tennessee–based Just Cruisin' Plus (© **800/888-0922;** www.just cruisinplus.com) to present a sample of the **actual prices** people are paying for cruises aboard all the ships in this book. You can see the difference for yourself. The brochure rate for a 7-night western Caribbean cruise aboard Princess Cruises' beautiful *Caribbean Princess* is $1,239 for a low-end outside cabin. In reality, however, during our sampling period (June 2005 cruises, priced in mid-Apr) customers were able to get that same cabin for $649. Can we say huge difference? In the ship-review chapters, we've listed these realistic prices for every ship, and in the "Price Comparisons: Discounted Rates vs. Brochure Rates" table in this chapter, we've shown how the brochure prices for every ship stack up against what consumers actually pay. The table gives prices for the lowest-priced **inside cabins** (ones without windows) and lowest-priced **outside cabins** (with windows) aboard each ship, and the ship reviews in chapters 6 through 8 also provide sample discount prices for the cheapest **suites.** Remember that cruise ships generally have many different categories of cabins within the basic divisions of inside, outside, and suite, all priced differently. The rates we've listed represent the *lowest-priced* (which usually equates to smallest) in each division. If you're interested in booking a roomier, fancier cabin or suite, the price will be higher, with rates for high-end inside cabins being close to those for low-end outsides, and rates for high-end outsides being close to those for low-end suites.

Remember that rates are always subject to the basic principles of supply-and-demand, so those listed here are meant as a guide only and are in no way etched in stone—the price you pay may be higher or lower, depending on when you book, when you choose to travel, whether any special discounts are being offered by the lines, and a slew of other factors. All rates are cruise-only, per person, based on double occupancy, and, unless otherwise noted, include **port charges** (the per-passenger fee each island charges the cruise line for entry). Government fees and taxes are additional.

3 The Cost: What's Included & What's Not

Overall, a cruise adds up to great value and convenience when you consider that your main vacation ingredients—accommodations; meals and most snacks; stops at ports of call; a packed schedule of activities; use of gyms, pools, and other facilities; and shows, cabaret, jazz performances, and more—are covered in the cruise price. Just don't think it's all free. To beef up their bottom lines as much as possible, cruise lines are pushing a slew of **added-cost onboard extras.** Of course you can always just say "no." But if you're like most of us, you'll have an "oh, what the heck" attitude once you step across that gangway. So, when figuring out your budget, be sure to figure in the additional costs you'll incur for shore excursions (which can run from $25 up to $500), bar drinks and specialty coffees, spa treatments ($25–$500 plus tip), souvenirs, and even fresh

Price Comparisons: Discounted Rates vs. Brochure Rates

Cruise Line	Ship	Itinerary (region / number of nights)	Lowest-Priced Inside Cabin (discounted / brochure)	Lowest-Priced Outside Cabin (discounted / brochure)	Lowest-Priced Suite (discounted / brochure)
American Canadian Caribbean Line	Grande Caribe	Intracoastal Waterway / 14	$2,925 / $2,925	$3,335 / $3,335	N/A
	Grande Mariner	Erie Canal / 12	$2,455 / $2,455	$2,795 / $2,795	N/A
	Niagara Prince	Hudson & Lake Champlain / 12	$2,455 / $2,455	$2,795 / $2,795	N/A
American Safari Cruises	Safari Escape	Pacific Northwest / 7	$2,795 / $2,795	$4,795 / $4795	N/A
	Safari Quest	California Wine Country / 4	$2,295 / $2,295	$2,495 / $2,495	N/A
	Safari Spirit	Pacific Northwest / 7	$2,995 / $2,995	$4,795 / $4,795	N/A
Carnival	Carnival Conquest	W. Caribbean / 7	$529 / $1,649	$679 / $1,899	$1,329 / $2,599
	Carnival Destiny	S. Caribbean / 7	$529 / $1,649	$679 / $1,849	$1,279 / $2,599
	Carnival Glory	E. Caribbean / 7	$529 / $1,749	$679 / $1,899	$1,399 / $2,599
	Carnival Legend	E. Caribbean / 8	$599 / $1,899	$749 / $2,099	$1,449 / $2,799
	Carnival Liberty	W. Caribbean / 8	$649 / $1,799	$799 / $1,999	$1,499 / $2,799
	Carnival Miracle	W. Caribbean / 7	$499 / $1,749	$649 / $1,949	$1,379 / $2,599
	Carnival Pride	Mexican Riviera / 7	$579 / $1,649	$729 / $1,949	$1,399 / $2,599
	Carnival Spirit	Mexican Riviera / 8	$619 / $1,899	$769 / $2,099	$1,669 / $2,949
	Carnival Triumph	Canada/NE / 7	$599 / $1,649	$749 / $1,899	$1,499 / $2,599
	Carnival Valor	E. Caribbean / 7	$519 / $1,749	$669 / $1,899	$1,349 / $2,599
	Carnival Victory	E. Caribbean / 7	$499 / $1,649	$649 / $1,849	$1,299 / $2,599
	Celebration	Bahamas / 5	$319 / $849	$3,79 / $1,089	$979 / $1,749
	Ecstasy	W. Caribbean / 5	$339 / $999	$419 / $1,089	$949 / $1,549
	Elation	W. Caribbean / 7	$449 / $1,349	$539 / $1,489	$1,279 / $2,179
	Fantasy	Bahamas / 4	$269 / $849	$329 / $929	$619 / $1,279
	Fascination	W. Caribbean / 4	$249 / $849	$299 / $979	$619 / $1,279
	Holiday	W. Caribbean / 5	$359 / $999	$459 / $1,149	$1,059 / $1,749
	Imagination	W. Caribbean / 5	$359 / $999	$469 / $1,149	$1,069 / $1,749
	Inspiration	W. Caribbean / 5	$379 / $999	$469 / $1,149	$1,089 / $1,749
	Paradise	Baja/Mexico / 4	$309 / $849	$389 / $979	$779 / $1,379
	Sensation	W. Caribbean / 5	$359 / $999	$459 / $1,149	$1,049 / $1,749
Celebrity	Century	Panama Canal / 10	$999 / $2,779	$1,180 / $3,259	$3,000 / $5,439
	Constellation	E Caribbean / 12	$1,500 / $2,379	$1,700 / $2,679	$6,000 / $11,479
	Galaxy	Panama Canal / 12	$1,710 / $2,179	$1,880 / $2,719	$3,850 / $6,359

Price Comparisons: Discounted Rates vs. Brochure Rates

Cruise Line	Ship	Itinerary (region / number of nights)	Lowest-Priced Inside Cabin (discounted / brochure)	Lowest-Priced Outside Cabin (discounted / brochure)	Lowest-Priced Suite (discounted / brochure)
	Infinity	Panama Canal / 14	$1,400 / $2,519	$1,950 / $3,419	$3,850 / $7,219
	Mercury	Mexican Riviera / 10	$1,030 / $2,479	$1,150 / $3,199	$3,300 / $8,599
	Millennium	E. Caribbean / 7	$950 / $1,759	$1,100 / $2,159	$3,850 / $9,859
	Summit	Alaska / 7	$930 / $1,900	$1,205 / $2,500	$4,250 / $8,800
	Zenith	Bermuda / 7	$1,200 / $1,785	$1,250 / $2,015	$3,050 / $5,985
Clipper	Clipper Odyssey	Alaska / Bering Sea / 15	N/A	$7,750 / $7,750	$11,120 / $11,120
	Nantucket Clipper	Charleston / Savannah / 7	N/A	$1,953 / $2,170	N/A
	Yorktown Clipper	Costa Rica / Panama Canal / 7	N/A	$$2,549 / $2,830	N/A
Costa	Costa Magica	W. Caribbean / 7	$899 / $1,499	$1,099 / $1,600	$2,599 / $3,199
	Costa Mediterranea	W. Caribbean / 7	$599 / $999	$699 / $1,249	$1,500 / $2,349
Cruise West	Pacific Explorer	Costa Rica / Panama / 7	N/A	$1,720 / $2,199	N/A
	Spirit of Alaska	Columbia / Snake Rivers / 7	$1,182 / $1,549	$1,722 / $2,149	N/A
	Spirit of Columbia	Pacific Northwest / 7	$1,500 / $1,849	$2,040 / $2,449	N/A
	Spirit of Discovery	Pacific Northwest / 7	N/A	$2,272 / $2,649	N/A
	Spirit of Endeavour	Napa Valley / 4	N/A	$1,448 / $1,599	N/A
	Spirit of '98	Alaska / 8	N/A	$3,999 / $3,999	$6,749 / $6,749
	Spirit of Oceanus	Alaska / 11	N/A	$5,061 / $5,599	$7,041 / $7,799
Crystal	Crystal Serenity	Panama Canal / 10	N/A	$2,995 / $5,695	$6,620 / $9,505
	Crystal Symphony	Panama Canal / 10	N/A	$2,095 / $5,070	$6,495 / $9,000
Cunard	Queen Mary 2	Canada / New England / 12	$2,749 / $3,439	$3,549 / $4,439	$8,999 / $11,249
Delta Queen	American Queen	New Orleans / Natchez / 4	$833 / $1,110	$1,339 / $1,785	$2,010 / $2,680
	Delta Queen	Nashville / Chattanooga / 6	N/A	$1,670 / $1,670	$4,020 / $4,020
	Mississippi Queen	St. Louis / St. Paul / 7	$1,895 / $1,895	$2,925 / $2,925	$4,685 / $4,685
Disney	Disney Magic	W. Caribbean / 7	$799 / $1,699	$1,059 / $2,099	$1,379 / $2,499
	Disney Wonder	Bahamas / 4	$519 / $899	$719 / $1,249	$839 / $1,499

Price Comparisons: Discounted Rates vs. Brochure Rates

Cruise Line	Ship	Itinerary (region / number of nights)	Lowest-Priced Inside Cabin (discounted / brochure)	Lowest-Priced Outside Cabin (discounted / brochure)	Lowest-Priced Suite (discounted / brochure)
Glacier Bay Cruiseline	Executive Explorer	Alaska / 10	N/A	$3,295 / $3,295	$4,095 / $4,095
	Wilderness Adventurer	Alaska / 8	$2,999 / $2,999	$3,469 / $3,469	N/A
	Wilderness Discoverer	Columbia River / 7	$1,200 / $1,200	$1,599 / $1,599	N/A
	Wilderness Explorer	Alaska / 6	N/A	$1,465 / $1,465	N/A
Holland America	Amsterdam	Hawaii / 15	$1,602 / $4,185	$1,999 / $4,910	$6,879 / $11,710
	Maasdam	S. Caribbean / 11	$1,299 / $2,154	$1,299 / $2,604	$3,379 / $6,574
	Noordam	E. Caribbean / 10	$1,449 / $1,929	$1,659 / $2,319	$5,079 / $6,669
	Oosterdam	Mexican Riviera / 7	$799 / $1,340	$799 / $1,680	$2,222 / $3,850
	Ryndam	Mexican Riviera / 10	$1,099 / $1,886	$1,099 / $2,335	$6,540 / $11,760
	Statendam	Alaska / 7	$949 / $1,265	$1,305 / $1,773	$2,799 / $3,909
	Veendam	Alaska / 7	$849 / $1,266	$1,149 / $1,750	$2,521 / $3,765
	Volendam	Alaska / 7	$949 / $1,265	$1,165 / $1,666	$2,400 / $3,579
	Westerdam	E. Caribbean / 7	$799 / $1,319	$799 / $1,659	$2,375 / $3,829
	Zaandam	Alaska / 7	$999 / $1,337	$1,364 / $1,858	$2,949 / $4,122
	Zuiderdam	E. Caribbean / 7	$599 / $1,319	$699 / $1,659	$1,313 / $3,829
Imperial Majesty	Regal Empress	Bahamas / 2	$189 / $229	$269 / $289	$499 / $499
Lindblad Expeditions	Sea Bird	Columbia River / 7	$2,490 / $2,490	$3,940 / $3,940	N/A
	Sea Lion	Alaska / 7	$3,980 / $3,980	$5,850 / $5,850	N/A
MSC Cruises	Lirica	E. Caribbean / 7	$545 / $1,400	$745 / $1,750	$1,595 / $2,650
	Opera	E. Caribbean / 7	$545 / $1,400	$745 / $1,750	$1,795 / $2,650
Norwegian	Norwegian Crown	Bermuda / 7	$979 / $1,399	$1,009 / $1,579	$2,609 / $3,799
	Norwegian Dawn	Bahamas/ Florida / 7	$809 / $1,579	$879 / $1,679	$3,799 / $5,099
	Norwegian Dream	Alaska / 11	$1,479 / $1,779	$1,549 / $2,099	$ 4,469 / $4,699
	Norwegian Jewel	E. Caribbean / 7	$1,135 / $1,579	$1,175 / $1,779	$3,625 / $4,799
	Norwegian Majesty	Bermuda / 7	$773 / $1,349	$853 / $1,449	$2,683 / $4,599
	Norwegian Spirit	Alaska / 7	$953 / $1,149	$1,003 / $1,399	$3,203 / $4,099
	Norwegian Star	Mexican Riviera / 8	$901 / $1,399	$986 / $1,679	$3,371 / $4,099
	Norwegian Sun	Alaska / 7	$1,043 / $1,229	$1,293 / $1,349	$3,473/ $4,299
	Norwegian Wind	Hawaii / 11	$1,167 / $1,649	$1,167 / $1,799	$3,644 / $3,799

Price Comparisons: Discounted Rates vs. Brochure Rates

Cruise Line	Ship	Itinerary (region / number of nights)	Lowest-Priced Inside Cabin (discounted / brochure)	Lowest-Priced Outside Cabin (discounted / brochure)	Lowest-Priced Suite (discounted / brochure)
	Pride of Aloha	Hawaii / 7	$749 / $3,799	$899 / $4,499	$2,779 / $7,899
	Pride of America	Hawaii / 7	$849 / $3,299	$999 / $2,999	$2,479 / $6,499
	Pride of Hawai'i	Hawaii	not yet available	not yet available	not yet available
Oceania	Insignia	South America / 10	N/A	$1,499 / $4,798	$2,999 / $7,798
	Regatta	S. Caribbean / 10	$999 / $2,598	$1,199 / $2,998	$2,499 / $5,598
Princess	Caribbean Princess	W. Caribbean / 7	$559 / $1,149	$649 / $1,239	$2,099 / $2,749
	Coral Princess	Panama Canal / 10	$1,249 / $1,449	$1,449 / $1,674	$3,324 / $3,524
	Dawn Princess	Mexican Riviera / 10	$899 / $1,119	$1,099 / $1,349	$2,449 / $2,699
	Diamond Princess	Alaska / 7	$899 / $1,309	$899 / $1,549	$3,209 / $3,609
	Golden Princess	S. Caribbean / 7	$649 / $1,049	$759 / $1,259	$2,149 / $2,549
	Grand Princess	W. Caribbean / 7	$549 / $889	$649 / $1,039	$2,099 / $2,549
	Island Princess	Alaska / 7	$1,049 / $1,549	$1,249 / $1,749	$3,449 / $3,949
	Regal Princess	Mexican Riviera / 10	$999 / $1,699	$1,099 / $1,799	$2,549 / $2,549
	Sapphire Princess	Mexican Riviera / 7	$649 / $1,149	$799 / $1,379	$2,099 / $2,399
	Sea Princess	S. Caribbean / 14	$1,399 / $1,499	$1,599 / $1,799	$3,699 / $3,999
	Star Princess	W. Caribbean / 7	$549 / $1,039	$649 / $1,239	$2,099 / $2,549
	Sun Princess	Alaska / 7	$799 / $1,299	$1,199 / $1,699	$3,189 / $3,539
Radisson Seven Seas	Seven Seas Mariner	Alaska / 7	N/A	$2,967 / $4,805	$2,967 / $4,805
	Seven Seas Navigator	Canada/ New England / 7	N/A	$2,606 / $6195	$3,281 / $7,495
	Seven Seas Voyager	W. Caribbean / 7	N/A	$2,458 / $4,705	$2,458 / $4,705
Royal Caribbean	Adventure of the Seas	S. Caribbean / 7	$849 / $1,609	$999 / $1,919	$2,579 / $5,299
	Brilliance of the Seas	Panama Canal / 10	$1,299 / $2,199	$1,449 / $2,449	$3,849 / $5,779
	Empress of the Seas	S. Caribbean / 11	$1,019 / $1,789	$1,199 / $2,109	$3,859 / $5,259
	Enchantment of the Seas	Canada/ New England / 7	$869 / $1,499	$1,099 / $1,729	$3,829 / $5,049
	Explorer of the Seas	E. Caribbean / 7	$859 / $1,609	$898 / $1,879	$2,349 / $5,329
	Grandeur of the Seas	W. Caribbean / 9	$799 / $1,968	$899 / $2,418	$2,699 / $5,418
	Jewel of the Seas	W. Caribbean / 6	$699 / $1,688	$798 / $1,988	$2,099 / $5,438

Price Comparisons: Discounted Rates vs. Brochure Rates

Cruise Line	Ship	Itinerary (region / number of nights)	Lowest-Priced Inside Cabin (discounted / brochure)	Lowest-Priced Outside Cabin (discounted / brochure)	Lowest-Priced Suite (discounted / brochure)
	Legend of the Seas	W. Caribbean / 7	$649 / $1,349	$798 / $1,579	$3,379 / $4,129
	Majesty of the Seas	Bahamas / 4	$269 / $629	$2,99 / $679	$1,239 / $2,279
	Mariner of the Seas	W. Caribbean / 7	$809 / $1,579	$948 / $1,849	$2,349 / $5,299
	Monarch of the Seas	Baja/Mexico / 4	$319 / $679	$3,49 / $799	$1,379 / $2,409
	Navigator of the Seas	E. Caribbean / 7	$869 / $1,639	$1,049 / $2,029	$2,349 / $5,329
	Radiance of the Seas	Alaska / 7	$969 / $1,590	$1,139 / $2,070	$2,099 / $4,110
	Rhapsody of the Seas	W. Caribbean / 7	$559 / $1,379	$659 / $1,579	$1,899 / $4,129
	Serenade of the Seas	S. Caribbean / 7	$759 / $1,748	$859 / $2,048	$2,399 / $5,488
	Sovereign of the Seas	Bahamas / 4	$269 / $629	$2,99 / $649	$1,199 / $2,279
	Splendour of the Seas	W. Caribbean / 5	$359 / $909	$429 / $1,049	$1,399 / $3,179
	Vision of the Seas	Mexican Riviera / 7	$549 / $1,049	$649 / $1,279	$1,899 / $3,379
	Voyager of the Seas	W. Caribbean / 7	$759 / $1,888	$898 / $2,088	$2,349 / $5,538
Seabourn	Seabourn Legend	Panama Canal / 14	N/A	$4,995 / $8,325	$8,271 / $13,785
	Seabourn Pride	E. Caribbean / 7	N/A	$2,987 / $4,595	$7,461 / $7,325
SeaDream	SeaDream I	S. Caribbean / 7	N/A	$2,637 / $5,138	$7,917 / $12,488
	SeaDream II	S. Caribbean / 7	N/A	$2,637 / $5,138	$7,917 / $12,488
Silversea	Silver Cloud	S. Caribbean/ South America / 12	N/A	$5,411 / $7,570	$6,671 / $9,370
	Silver Shadow	Alaska / 12	N/A	$5,496 / $7,245	$6,771 / $8,945
	Silver Whisper	S. Caribbean / 9	N/A	$2,347 / $4,545	$2,897 / $5,645
Star Clippers	Royal Clipper	S. Caribbean / 7	$1,780 / $1,780	$2,100 / $2,100	$3,800 / $3,800
	Star Clipper	S. Caribbean / 8	$1,970 / $1,970	$2,200 / $2,200	$4,165 / $4,165
Windjammer	Amazing Grace	Panama/ Costa Rica / 7	N/A	$639 / $990	$1,890 / $1,890
	Legacy	S. Caribbean / 6	N/A	$1,045 / $1,045	$1,345 / $1,345
	Mandalay	S. Caribbean / 13	$2,105 / $2,105	$2,405 / $2,405	$2,805 / $2,805
	Polynesia	S. Caribbean / 6	N/A	$1,320 / $1,320	$1,420 / $1,420
	Yankee Clipper	S. Caribbean / 6	$900 / $1,000	$1,100 / $1,200	$1,300 / $1,400
Windstar	Wind Spirit	S. Caribbean / 7	N/A	$2,036 / $2,660	$2,995 / $3,938
	Wind Star	W. Mediterranean / 7	N/A	$2,656 / $3,480	$5,078 / $5,078
	Wind Surf	S. Caribbean / 7	N/A	$1,961 / $2,560	$3,085 / $4,058

flowers and custom-tailored suits if your self-restraint is really low. **Gratuities** are also not included on most lines, which pay their service staff minimal salaries on the assumption that they'll make most of their pay in tips. Generally, you can expect to tip about $70 per person during a weeklong cruise. (For more on tipping, see chapter 3, "Things to Know Before You Go.") If you're the gambling type, you're a prime candidate for increasing your ship's revenue stream, whether your game is craps or bingo, scratch-off cards or Caribbean stud poker. Sources tell us that many onboard slot machines have even been rigged to work faster, so passengers spend more money.

Some of the most luxurious and expensive lines—Silversea, Seabourn, and SeaDream Yacht Club—come closest to being truly all-inclusive by including all alcoholic beverages and gratuities in their cruise rates. Radisson Seven Seas includes gratuities as well, but offers free wine only at dinner. Aside from these aberrations, though, you can expect to shell out at least another $250 to $500 per person for an average 7-night cruise, and easily double that if, for instance, you have a bottle of wine with dinner every night, a couple of cocktails after, go on three $75 shore excursions, hit the ships' $25-per-person alternative restaurants a few times, try your luck at bingo, and buy some trinkets in the onboard shops or at the ports of call. Of course, just as at a hotel, you'll also pay extra for items such as ship-to-shore phone calls and e-mails, massages, manicures, facials, haircuts, fancy coffees, and medical treatments in the ship's infirmary. If you're not cruising from a port you can drive to, then you'll have to figure in **airfare to the ship,** which is rarely included in cruise prices.

4 Money-Saving Strategies

From early-booking discounts to last-minute deals, from sharing cabins to senior and frequent-cruiser discounts, there are a lot of ways to save money on your cruise. Read on to find out how.

As they have for years, cruise lines continue to offer substantial **early-booking discounts.** Since last-minute bookings no longer guarantee the great savings they did just a few years back, chances are you'll get a better price by booking about 4 to 6 months before your cruise departs. Price aside, when booking early you naturally have much more assurance of getting exactly what you want in terms of cruise line, ship, and everything else.

If you're in the habit of traveling at the last minute, you may still be able to snag some deals this way, especially during slow periods like September, October, and non-holiday weeks in November and December. The main thing you may sacrifice when booking late is a measure of choice: You'll have to take the ship, itinerary, and cabin category that's available, whether it's the one that you wanted or not. Getting airfare at the last minute may be tough, too. Plus, most last-minute deals are completely non-refundable; if you book a week before the cruise, for example, the full fare is due upfront and you get zip back if you change your mind a few days later.

You'll find **last-minute deals** advertised online and in the travel section of many Sunday newspapers, especially the *Miami Herald, LA Times,* and *New York Times.* You should also check with a travel agent that specializes in cruises. See "Agents & the Web: Finding the Best Deals," later in this chapter.

From time to time some cruise lines offers discounts to **seniors** (usually defined as anyone 55 years or older), so don't keep your age a secret, and always ask your travel agent about these discounts when you're booking. For discounts in general, the best

Average Cost of Onboard Extras

Just so you're not shocked when your shipboard account is settled at the end of your trip, here are some average prices for onboard extras.

Laundry	$1–$6 per item
Self-service laundry	$1–$2 per load
Pressing	$1–$4 per item
5×7-inch photo from ship photographer	$7–$10
Scotch and soda at an onboard bar	$3.95–$6
Bottle of beer (domestic/imported)	$3.50/$6
Bottle of wine to accompany dinner	$10–$300
Glass of wine	$5–$10
Bottle of Evian water (.5 liters/1.5 liters)	$1.95/$3.25
Can of Coca-Cola	$1.50–$2
Ship-to-shore phone call or fax	$4–$15 per minute
Cell phone calls at sea	$1.70 per minute
Sending e-mails	50¢–$1 per minute
50-minute massage	$109–$139
Sunscreen, 6-ounce bottle	$10
Disposable camera	$15–$20

organization to belong to is **AARP,** 601 E St. NW, Washington, DC 20049 (© **888/ 687-2277;** www.aarp.org), the biggest outfit in the United States for people 50 and over.

If you've cruised with a particular cruise line before, you're considered a valued **repeat passenger** and will usually be rewarded with 5% to 10% discounts on future cruises. Depending on how many times you've sailed, you may also get cabin upgrades, invitations to private cocktail parties, priority check-in at the terminal, casino vouchers, logo souvenirs, special mailings and newsletters, and maybe even a free cruise if you've racked up enough sailings. The catch to all of this is that repeat-passenger discounts often cannot be combined with other pricing deals, particularly in the case of the mainstream lines.

If you're really a serious repeater, though, the generous booty you get on the small upscale ships can add up. After you sail a total of 140 days with Seabourn, for instance, you're entitled to a free 14-day cruise, while Silversea passengers get a free 7-night cruise after sailing 350 days and a free 14-night cruise after 500 days. After your 20th Crystal cruise, you get your choice of a business-class air upgrade, a $1,500 shipboard credit, or a $1,200 discount on the cruise, among other perks. Some of the small adventure-oriented lines offer similar deals. ACCL, for instance, gives passengers an 11th cruise free after their 10th paid cruise of at least 12 nights.

Some cruise lines offer reduced **group rates** to folks booking at least eight or more cabins, but this is really based on supply-and-demand. If a ship is selling well, group deals may not be available, but if it isn't, lines have a lot more incentive to wheel and deal. Carnival even guarantees that if individual fares fall below what a group has already paid, group members get the difference back in the form of a shipboard credit. Groups may be family reunions and the like, but travel agents also may create their own "groups" whose members don't even know they're part of one. Quick explanation: The travel agent reserves a block of cabins on a given ship and the cruise line in turn gives them a discounted group rate that agents can pass on to their clients. The cruise line benefits because they're potentially selling a lot of cabins through agency X, and the agent benefits because they can offer their clients a good price. So, always ask your travel agent if you can be piggyback onto some group space.

Very small groups—three or four people max in most cases—can share one cabin if it's equipped with **third or fourth berths** (sofa beds or bunk-style berths that pull down from the ceiling or wall). Disney, Carnival, and NCL go one better by offering family cabins that can accommodate five people—Disney's even have 1½ bathrooms. The rates for third, fourth, and fifth passengers in a cabin, whether adults or children, are typically 50% or more off the normal adult fare. You can also look into **sharing a suite.** Many can accommodate five to seven people, and some are almost outlandishly roomy.

Solo passengers generally get socked with something called the **single supplement,** which entails a charge that adds 50% to 100% to the standard per person cruise fare— a consequence of cruise lines basing their revenue expectations on two people sharing every cabin. Some lines are quietly foregoing or reducing this kind of supplemental charge if a ship isn't filling up as a particular departure date approaches, but there's no way to predict this kind of thing. A few lines (HAL and Windjammer barefoot) offer a **cabin-share service** that matches you with a same-gender roommate. If the cruise line can't find a roommate for you, you'll probably get the cabin at the regular double occupancy rate anyway. Very few ships offer cabins specifically designed for solo passengers anymore.

5 Agents & the Web: Finding the Best Deals

Today, practically everybody has a website, and the difference between so-called **Web-based cruise sellers** and more **traditional travel agencies** is that the former rely on their sites for actual bookings, while the latter use theirs as glorified advertising space to promote their offerings, doing all actual business in person or over the phone. With a few exceptions the cruise lines also have **direct-booking engines** on their own sites, but we don't recommend using them. Why? Because agents and Web-based sellers may have negotiated group rates with the lines, be part of a consortium with whom a line is doing an upgrade promotion, or have other deals going that enable them to offer you lower rates. Though it may sound peculiar, the cruise lines actually prefer that you book through third parties because having agents and sites do the grunt work allows the lines to maintain small reservations staffs and, simultaneously, maintain goodwill in a system that works—something they have to consider because the vast majority of cruises are booked through agencies of one type or another. Typically, cruise lines report that about 90% of their bookings come from travel agencies.

WHICH OFFERS BETTER PRICES?

As far as cruise prices go, there's no absolutely quantifiable difference between the real live travel agents (whether your hometown brick-and-mortar mom-and-pop agency or a big anonymous mega-agency) and Internet-based cruise sellers. In 2004 and 2005, the major lines starting doing something they had talked about for years, offering all agencies large or small the same rates—a major coup for small agencies who have been struggling to keep up with the Expedias of the world. At press time, Carnival, Norwegian, Royal Caribbean, Crystal, and Celebrity had declared in one way or another that they would offer all agencies the same rates, and further, that they would have no dealings with any agency who publicly (via print or website advertising) doled out rebates to clients—that is, gave their customers additional discounts by sacrificing some of their own commissions. As quoted in industry bible *Cruise Week,* Crystal Senior Vice resident Bill Smith summed it up: "Whatever the agent and the customer finally decide upon in their private negotiations is one thing, but if agents go out and publicly negotiate pricing below our pricing, it's a problem." The lines believe rebating and cutthroat discounting among agencies cheapens the cruise product; lines want travel agents to emphasize the benefits of cruise vacations, not just the fact that one agent is offering a cheaper price than another. Still, though industry insiders predict all the major lines will level the playing field by 2006, don't think there aren't any loopholes. For example, at press time Royal Caribbean was offering one of its top-producing agencies bottles of wine for any clients booking Royal Caribbean. Other agencies have offered customers gift cards or other incentives in lieu of reduced rates.

WHICH PROVIDES BETTER SERVICE?

Since pricing is closer to being equitable across all types of cruise agencies than ever before, it's really service that distinguishes one agency from another. Most websites give you only a menu of ships and itineraries to select from, plus a basic search capability that takes into account only destination, price, length of trip, and date, without consideration of the type of cruise experience each line offers. That's fine if you know exactly what you want, and are comfortable on the computer. If, on the other hand, you have limited experience with cruising and with booking on the Web, it may be better to see a traditional agent, who can help you wade through the choices and answer your questions. For instance, a good agent can tell you which cabins have their views obstructed by lifeboats; which are near loud areas such as discos and the engine room; which ships and itineraries you should avoid if you're not looking for a party vibe; and, in general, what the major differences are between cabin categories. A lot of this kind of detailed information won't be found on the Web. You need to hear it from a person.

Keep in mind, though, that you need to find an agent who really knows the business— and this applies to every type of agent: those who work out of their home or an agency office, those who work for large conglomerates and deal mostly over the phone, and those who man toll-free numbers associated with Web-based sellers. Some are little more than order-takers: They may not know much more than pricing, and may never even have been on a cruise themselves. This system works okay for selling air travel, where the big question is coach or first-class, case closed; but a lot more variables are associated with booking a cruise. An experienced cruise agent—someone who's sailed on or inspected a variety of ships and booked many customers aboard in the past—will be able to tell you about special promotions (like free bottles of wine) and help out and act as an intermediary should any problems arise with your booking, order special extras such as a bottle of champagne in your cabin when you arrive, and in general make your planning easy.

So, how do you know if an agent is any good? The best way, of course, is to use one who has been referred to you by a reliable friend or acquaintance. This is particularly valuable these days, when agents are being pressed to squeeze more profit from every sale, making them less likely to take the time to discuss options. When searching for a good agent, it can't hurt if an agent is an **Accredited Cruise Counselor (ACC),**

Be Savvy & Beware of Scams

With the number of offers a potential cruise buyer sees, it can be difficult to know if an agency is or isn't reliable, legit, or, for that matter, stable. It pays to be on your guard against fly-by-night operators and agents who may lead you astray.

- **Get a referral.** A recommendation from a trusted friend or colleague (or from this guidebook) is one of the best ways to hook up with a reputable agent.
- **Use the cruise lines' agent lists.** Many cruise line websites include agency locator lists, naming agencies around the country with whom they do business. These are by no means comprehensive lists of all good or bad agencies, but an agent's presence on these lists is usually another good sign of experience.
- **Beware of snap recommendations.** If an agent suggests a cruise line without asking you a single question first about your tastes, beware. Because agents work on commissions from the lines, some may try to shanghai you into cruising with a company that pays them the highest rates, even though that line may not be right for you.
- **Always use a credit card to pay for your cruise.** It gives you more protection in the event the agency or cruise line fails. When your credit card statement arrives, make sure the payment was made to the cruise line, not the travel agency. If you find that payment was actually made to the agency, it's a big red flag that something's wrong. If you insist on paying by check, you'll be making it out to the agency, so it may be wise to ask if the agency has default protection. Many do. (*Note:* The only exception to this is when an agency is running a charter cruise—for example, a music cruise with special entertainment.)
- **Always follow the cruise line's payment schedule.** Never agree to a different schedule the travel agency comes up with. The lines' terms are always clearly printed in their brochures and usually require an initial deposit, with the balance due no later than 75 to 45 days before departure. If you're booking 2 months or less before departure, full payment is usually required at the time of booking.
- **Keep on top of your booking.** If you ever fail to receive a document or ticket on the date it's been promised, inquire about it immediately. If you're told that your cruise reservation was canceled because of overbooking and that you must pay extra for a confirmed and rescheduled sailing, demand a full refund and/or contact your credit card company to stop payment.

Master Cruise Counselor (MCC), or **Elite Cruise Counselor (ECC),** designations doled out by the Cruise Lines International Association (CLIA), an industry trade organization. Many of the cruise lines' websites list **preferred agencies** (generally broken down or searchable by city or state), as does the CLIA site at **www.cruising.org**. Many of the most reliable agencies are also members of **agent groups,** like Virtuoso and Signature Travel Network. In the sections below, we list some of the best agencies and also evaluate the major cruise-selling websites.

6 Recommended Agencies & Websites

Out of some 19,000 U.S. travel agencies, 15% (or about 3,000 agencies) sell 90% of all cruise travel in North America; about 10% to 15% of those are considered cruise-only. Agencies come in all shapes and sizes, from small neighborhood stores to huge chain operations. Like banking, telecommunications, and media, the travel industry has been rife with consolidation over the past decade, so even that mom-and-pop travel agency on Main Street may turn out to be an affiliate of a larger agency.

Even though you'll get similarly low rates from both traditional and Web-based agencies these days, we can't stress enough that service counts for something, too. There's value in using a travel agent you've worked with in the past or one who comes highly recommended by someone you trust. A good agent will be there for you if problems arise.

TRADITIONAL AGENCIES SPECIALIZING IN MAINSTREAM CRUISES

To give you an idea of where to begin, here's a sampling (by no means comprehensive) of both cruise-only and full-service agencies that have solid reputations selling cruises with mainstream lines such as Princess, Carnival, Royal Caribbean, Celebrity, Holland America, and Norwegian. A few are affiliated with the big chains; most are not. While all have websites to promote current deals, the agencies listed primarily operate from a combination of walk-in business and toll-free telephone-based business.

- **The Cruise Company,** 10760 Q St., Omaha, NE 68127 (© **800/289-5505** or 402/339-6800; www.thecruisecompany.com)
- **Cruise Holidays,** 7000 NW Prairie View Rd., Kansas City, MO 64151 (© **800/ 869-6806** or 816/741-7417; www.cruiseholidayskc.com)
- **Cruises By Brennco,** 6600 College Blvd., Suite 130, Overland Park, Kansas City, MO 66211 (© **800/955-1909** or 816/942-1000; www.brennco.com)
- **Cruises Only,** 100 Sylvan Rd., Suite 600, Woburn, MA 01801 (© **800/278-4737;** www.cruisesonly.com), is part of NLG, the largest cruise retailer in the world.
- **Cruise Value Center,** 6 Edgeboro Rd., Suite 400, East Brunswick, NJ 08816 (© **800/231-7447** or 732/257-4545; www.cruisevalue.com)
- **Dynamic Travel & Cruises,** 2325 E. Southlake Blvd., Southlake, TX 76092 (© **800/766-2911** or 817/481-8631; www.dynamictravel.com)
- **Just Cruisin' Plus,** 5640 Nolensville Rd., Nashville, TN 37211 (© **800/888-0922** or 615/833-0922; www.justcruisinplus.com)
- **Mann Travel & Cruises/123Travel,** 4400 Park Rd., Charlotte, NC 28209 (© 800/835-9828, www.123travel.com)

Another way to find a reputable travel agency in your town is by contacting one of a handful of **agency groups** or **consortiums,** which screen their members. The following groups, whose members specialize in mainstream cruises, all maintain websites that allow you to search for local agencies with your zip code or city: **TravelSavers** (© **800/366-9895;** www.travelsavers.com) is a group of about 1,200 agencies; **Cruise Ship Centers** (© **800/707-7327;** www.cruiseshipcenters.com) has about 80 locations in Canada; and **Vacation.com** (© **800/843-0733;** www.vacation.com) is the largest group in the U.S., with some 6,000 members. **Carlson Wagonlit Travel** (www.carlson travel.com) and **Cruise Holidays** (www.cruiseholidays.com) are both large, reputable chains and their websites allow you to find a local branch near you.

TRADITIONAL AGENCIES SPECIALIZING IN LUXURY CRUISES

This sampling of reputable agencies, both cruise-only and full-service, specializes in selling ultraluxury cruises such as Cunard, Seabourn, Silversea, Crystal, Radisson Seven Seas, and SeaDream Yacht Club.

- **Concierge Cruises & Tours,** 13470 N. Sunset Mesa Dr., Marana, AZ 85653 (© **800/940-8385** or 520/572-6377)
- **Cruise Professionals,** 130 Dundas St. E., Suite 103, Mississauga, Ontario L5A 3V8, Canada (© **800/265-3838** or 905/275-3030; www.cruiseprofessionals.com)
- **Cruises of Distinction,** 42557 Woodword Ave., Bloomfield Hills, MI 48304 (© **800/434-5522** or 248/332-2020; www.cruisesofdistinction.com)
- **Golden Bear Travel,** 16 Digital Dr., Novado, CA 94949 (© **800/551-1000** or 415/382-8900; www.goldenbeartravel.com)
- **Largay Travel,** 625 Wolcott St., Waterbury, CT 06705 (© **800/322-9481** or 203/757-9481; www.largaytravel.com)
- **Strictly Vacations,** 108 W. Mission St., Santa Barbara, CA 93101 (© **800/447-2364;** www.strictlyvacations.com; expert on Windstar)

The following agency groups have members who specialize in luxury cruises. All maintain websites that allow you to search for local agencies with your zip code or city. Agency members often get perks to pass on to clients, from cabin upgrades to private cocktail parties. **Virtuoso** (© **800/401-4274;** www.virtuoso.com) is a consortium of more than 310 member agencies nationwide, including some on the list above. To find an agency in your area, call their toll-free number or e-mail **information@virtuoso. com**. Another group is **Signature Travel Network** (© **800/339-0868;** www.signature travel.com), with about 200 member agencies on the West Coast. To find an agency in your area, call or email **info@signaturetravelnetwork.com**.

WEB-BASED AGENCIES SPECIALIZING IN MAINSTREAM CRUISES

The following sites are reputable Web-based cruise specialists. All allow searches by destination, date of travel, length of cruise, and price range, as well as cruise line or ship if you know exactly what you want, and all allow you to book online for at least some if not most lines. In many cases, though, this does not involve a live connection with the cruise line's reservations database, so you'll have to wait up to 24 hours for a confirmation via e-mail, fax, or phone call. Sometimes you can research your cruise online but have to call a toll-free number when you're ready to get down to business. Keep in mind, these websites are constant works in progress, adding new features all the time.

- **Cruise.com** (www.cruise.com; © **800/303-3337** or 888/333-3116)
- **Cruise411.com** (www.cruise411.com; © **800/553-7090**)
- **Expedia** (www.expedia.com; © **800/397-3342**) is the largest Web-based cruise seller in the world.
- **Icruise.com** (www.icruise.com; © **866/942-7847** or 212/929-6046)
- **Travelocity** (www.travelocity.com; © **877/815-5446**) is the second-largest Web-based cruise seller in the world.
- **eCruises.com** (www.ecruises.com; © **800/438-2686**)

7 Choosing Your Cabin

When it comes right down to it, choosing a cabin is really a question of money. From a windowless lower-deck cabin with upper and lower bunks to a 1,400-square-foot suite with a butler and mile-long private veranda, cruise ships can offer a dozen or more stateroom categories that differ by size, location in the ship, amenities, and, of course, price. To see what we mean, go to the Cruises Only website (www.cruisesonly.com) for 360-degree tours and photos of most ships.

It's traditionally been a rule of thumb that the higher up you are and the more light that gets into your cabin, the more you pay; the lower you go into the bowels of the ship, the cheaper the fare. On some of the more modern ships, however, that old rule doesn't always ring true. On ships launched recently by Carnival, for instance, designers have scattered their most desirable suites on midlevel decks as well as top decks, thereby diminishing the prestige of an upper-deck cabin. For the most part, though, and especially on small ships, where most cabins are virtually identical, cabins on higher decks are still generally more expensive, and outside cabins (with windows or balconies) are more expensive than inside cabins (those without). Outside cabins whose windows are obstructed by lifeboats will be cheaper than ones with good views.

EVALUATING CABIN SIZE

Inch for inch, cruise ship cabins are smaller than hotel rooms. Of course, having a private balcony attached to your cabin, as many do, makes your living space that much bigger.

A roomy **standard cabin** is about 170 to 180 square feet, although some of the smallest are about 85 to 100 square feet. Disney has some of the more spacious standard cabins at sea, at 226 square feet. Celebrity's standards are spacious enough at around 170 to 175 square feet, with those on its Millennium-class ships sometimes as big as 191 square feet. Carnival and Holland America's are about 185 square feet or more. By way of comparison, equivalent standard cabins on a good number of ships in the Norwegian and Royal Caribbean lines are quite a bit smaller—try 120 to 160 square feet—and can be cramped. Cabins on the small-ship lines such as Windjammer, Clipper, and ACCL can be very snug—on the order of 70 to 100 square feet.

Smoking at Sea . . . or Not

All ships covered in this book prohibit smoking in all restaurants, theaters, and such places as shops and the library. If you want to light up, most bars and lounges have smoking sections, and you're free to have a cig out on deck. You can also have a butt in your cabin or on your balcony. Now, if you're looking for a nonsmoking cabin because you're concerned about the lingering smells from a previous smoker, with a few exceptions, you're out of luck. The vast majority of cruise lines do not designate cabins smoking or nonsmoking (with the exception of Disney: They designate all of their cabins nonsmoking). Why? It's impossible to control (for example, someone books a nonsmoking cabin and then smokes anyway). Further, it would be a big fat headache for the cruise lines' inventory department—how many cabins should be set aside for smokers? Do they sit empty if not enough smokers book the cruise?

Luckily, cabins are cleaned well between cruises, if necessary by shampooing the rug or using air purifiers. Matt, a fairly smoke-sensitive nonsmoker, can't recall ever walking into a cabin and smelling residual smoke.

All the standard cabins on the high-end lines are roomy—in fact, many of the high-end ships are "suite only." For example, on Silversea's *Silver Shadow* and *Silver Whisper,* cabins are 287 square feet, plus a 58-square-foot balcony. Across the board, from mainstream to luxe, **suites and penthouses** are obviously the most spacious, measuring from about 250 square feet up to over 1,400 square feet, plus private verandas.

Most cruise lines publish schematic drawings in their brochures, with square footage and, in some cases, measurements of length and width, which should give you some idea of what to expect. (We also include square footage ranges for inside cabins, outside cabins, and suites in the cruise ship descriptions in chapters 6–8.) Consider measuring off the dimensions on your bedroom floor and imagining your temporary oceangoing home, being sure to block out part of that space for the bathroom and closet. As a rough guideline, within a cabin of around 100 square feet, about a third of the floor space is gobbled up by those functional necessities.

Now, while you may be thinking, "Gee, that's really not a lot of space," remember that, like a bedroom in a large house, your cabin will, in all likelihood, be a place you use only for sleeping, showering, and changing clothes.

THE SCOOP ON INSIDE CABINS VS. OUTSIDE CABINS

Whether you really plan to spend time in your cabin is a question that should be taken into account when deciding whether to book an inside cabin or an outside cabin (that is, one without windows or one with windows or a balcony). If you plan to get up bright and early, hit the buffet breakfast, and not stop till the cows come home, you can probably get away with booking an inside cabin and save yourself a bundle. Inside cabins are generally neither as bad nor as claustrophobic as they sound. Many, in fact—such as those aboard most of the Carnival and Celebrity fleets—are the same size as the outside cabins, and most cruise lines design and decorate them to provide an illusion of light and space.

If, on the other hand, you want to lounge around and take it easy in your cabin, maybe ordering breakfast from room service and eating while the sun streams in—or, better yet, eating out *in* the sun, on your private veranda—then an outside cabin is definitely a worthwhile investment. Remember, though, that if it's a view of the sea you want, be sure when booking that your window or balcony doesn't just give you a good view of a lifeboat or some other obstruction (and remember, there are likely to be balconies on the deck right above your balcony, so they're more like porches than actual verandas). Some cruise line brochures tell you which cabins are obstructed, and a good travel agent or a cruise line's reservation agent can tell you which cabins on a particular ship might have this problem.

OTHER CABIN MATTERS TO CONSIDER

Unless you're booking at the last minute (like a few weeks or less before sailing), as part of a group, or in a cabin-share or cabin-guarantee program (which means you agree to a price, and find out your exact cabin at the last minute), you can work with your agent to pick an exact cabin. If possible, try to go into your talks with some idea of what kind of cabin category you'd like, or at least with a list of must-haves or must-avoids. Need a **bathtub** rather than just a shower? That narrows your choices on most ships. Want **connecting cabins** so you and your kids, friends, or relatives can share space? Most ships have 'em, but they sometimes book up early, as do cabins with **third or fourth berths** (usually pull-down bunks or a sofa bed). Almost all ships have cabin TVs these days, but a few don't. Want an **elevator** close by, to make it easy to get

MODEL CABIN LAYOUTS

Typical Outside Cabins
- Twin beds (can usually be pushed together)
- Some have sofa bed or bunk for third passenger
- Shower (tubs are rare)
- TV and music
- Window or porthole, or veranda

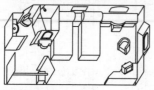

Outside Cabin

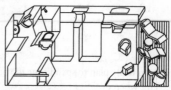

Outside Cabin with Veranda

Typical Suites
- King, queen, or double beds
- Sitting areas (often with sofa beds)
- Large bathrooms, usually with tub, sometimes with Jacuzzi
- Refrigerators, sometimes stocked
- TVs w/VCR and stereo
- Large closets
- Large veranda

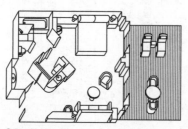

Suite with Veranda

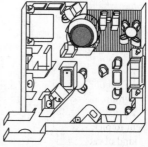

Grand Suite with Veranda

Thanks to Princess Cruises for all photos and diagrams.

READING A SHIP'S DECK PLAN

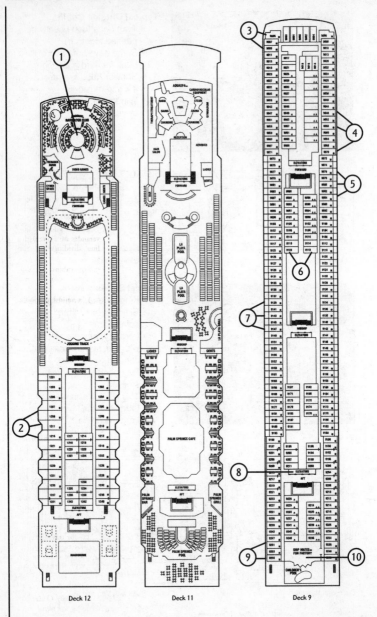

Deck 12   Deck 11   Deck 9

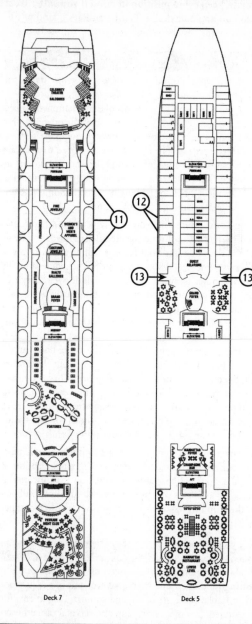

Deck 7   Deck 5

Some cabin choice considerations:

1. **Note the position of the ship's disco** and other loud public areas, and try not to book a cabin that's too close or underneath. This disco is far from any cabins—a big plus.

2. **Cabins on upper decks** can be affected by the motion of the sea. If you're abnormally susceptible to seasickness, keep this in mind.

3. **Ditto for the cabins in the bow.**

4. **Outside cabins without verandas** appear as solid blocks of space.

5. **Outside cabins with verandas** are shown with a line dividing the two spaces.

6. **Inside cabins** (without windows) can be real money-savers.

7. **Cabins amidships** are the least affected by the motion of the sea, especially if they're on a lower deck.

8. **Cabins that adjoin elevator shaftways** might be noisy (though proximity makes it easier to get around the ship).

9. **Cabins in the stern** can be affected by the motion of the sea, and tend to be subject to engine vibration.

10. **Cabins near children's facilities** may not be the quietest places, at least during the day.

11. **Check that lifeboats** don't block the view from your cabin. The lifeboats in this example adjoin public rooms, and so are out of sight.

12. **Cabins for travelers with disabilities** are ideally located near elevators and close to the ship's entrances (#13).

(Thanks to Celebrity Cruises for use of Mercury's *deck plan.)*

between decks? Is the view out the cabin's windows obstructed by lifeboats or other ship equipment? Most importantly, **keep cabin position in mind if you suffer from seasickness.** A midships location on a middle deck is best because it's a kind of fulcrum point, the area least affected by the vessel's rocking and rolling in rough seas.

8 Booking Your Air Travel

Except during special promotions, airfare is rarely included in cruise rates for Caribbean, Alaska, Mexico, and New England/Canada cruises, though it often is on Europe and Asia itineraries. So if you can't drive to your port of embarkation and need to fly to get to Miami, New York, San Juan, New Orleans, or one of the other 20-plus home ports, you'll have to either purchase airfare on your own through an agent or online, or buy it as a package with your cruise. The latter is often referred to as an **air add-on** or **air/sea package.** You can usually find information on these programs in the back of cruise line brochures and on their websites, along with prices on flights from more than 100 U.S. and Canadian cities to the port of embarkation. Here are the pros and cons to booking your airfare through the cruise line.

- **Pros:** When you book through the cruise line, you usually get round-trip transfers between the airport and the ship. A uniformed cruise line employee will be in the airport to direct you to the right bus, and your luggage will be taken from the airport to the ship. The cruise line will know your airline schedule and, in the event of delayed flights and other unavoidable snafus, will do what they can to make sure you get to the ship. For instance, during the abnormally fierce hurricane season in fall 2004, those who had booked the cruise lines' air package were given priority when it came to rebooking. People who book their air transportation and transfers separately are on their own.

- **Cons:** Odds are it will be more expensive to book through the cruise line than on your own. In the past, cruise lines offered more competitive fares, but the airlines aren't giving them the bulk discounts they used to, meaning prices have gone up. Consequently, fewer passengers are now booking the lines' air packages. Also, if you book through the lines, you probably won't be able to use any frequent-flier miles you've accumulated, and the air add-on could require a circuitous routing—with indirect legs and layovers—before you finally arrive at your port of embarkation.

If you choose to arrange your own air transportation, make absolutely sure that airfare is not included as part of your cruise contract. It rarely is with the exception of Europe and Asia cruises, but if it is, you're often granted a deduction (usually around $250 per person) off the cruise fare. Passengers who book their own flight can still buy **transfers from the airport to the ship** through their cruise line, but it's often cheaper to take a taxi, as is the case in Miami and Fort Lauderdale.

9 Prebooking Your Dinner Table & Arranging Special Diets

In addition to choosing your cabin when booking your cruise, on most ships you can also choose an **early or late seating** for dinner, and sometimes even put in a request for the size table you're interested in (tables for 2, 4, 8, 10, and so on). Assignments for breakfast and lunch are rarely required, as almost every ship also serves a casual breakfast in its buffet restaurant throughout the morning. At night, though, early seatings allow you to get first dibs on shipboard nightlife (or, conversely, promptly hit the sack), while late seatings allow you to linger a little longer over your meal. Lately, though, more lines—especially Norwegian and, to a slightly lesser extent, Princess—are junking this traditional early-late paradigm (in at least some of their restaurants) in favor of **open-seating dining** in which you simply show up when hunger pangs strike. For a more detailed discussion, see "Onboard Dining Options," on p. 87.

If you follow a **special diet**—whether vegetarian, low-salt, low-fat, heart-healthy, kosher, halal, or any other, or if you have certain food allergies—make this known to your travel agent when you book, or at least 30 or more days before the cruise, and make sure your diet can be accommodated at all three meals (sometimes special meal plans will cover only breakfast and dinner). The vast majority of ships offer vegetarian meals and health-conscious choices as part of their daily menus these days (Crystal even offers kosher food as part of its daily offerings), but it can't hurt to arrange things ahead of time. A cruise is not the place to go on an involuntary starvation diet.

10 Booking Pre- & Post-Cruise Hotel Stays

Cruise lines often offer hotel stays in the cities of embarkation and debarkation, and because most of these cities are tourist attractions in their own right, you may want to spend some time in New York, Oahu, or Vancouver before you sail, or drive to Disney World from Port Canaveral. The cruise lines' package deals usually include hotel stays and transportation from the hotel to the ship (before the cruise) or from the docks to the hotel (after the cruise). Inquire with your travel agent, and compare what the line is offering with what you may be able to arrange independently. Nowadays especially, you may be able to get a hotel stay much cheaper.

11 Cancellations & Insurance

Given today's unpredictable geopolitical situation, cancellation and insurance are hot topics, and ever-changing cruise line policies and procedures mean that it pays to stay informed.

What should you do if the cruise you've booked is canceled before it departs? A cruise could be canceled because of shipyard delays (if you've booked an inaugural cruise), or because of the outbreak of an infectious disease, mechanical breakdowns (such as nonfunctioning air-conditioning or an engine fire), the cruise line going out of business, act of war, or an impending hurricane.

"Though not as important as just after 9/11, insurance was sure a big help to those who bought it for cruises during the 2004 hurricane season," says *Cruise Week* editor Mike Driscoll.

That said, in today's competitive market, cruise lines have been making extraordinary efforts to appease disappointed passengers, whether they bought insurance or not. Typically, a line will reschedule the canceled cruise and offer passengers big discounts on future cruises—after all, they don't want the bad press they'd get if they cheated hundreds or thousands of people. There are, however, no set rules on how a line will compensate you in the event of a cancellation.

Now, if the shoe's on the other foot and you need to cancel your own cruise, you'll generally get a refund—most lines give you every cent back if you cancel at least 2 to 3 months before your departure date, although details vary from line to line. If you cancel closer to departure, you'll usually get a partial refund up until anywhere about 15 days before the cruise. After that, you won't get any refund at all, even if you cancel for medical reasons. Exceptions? In early 2003, in response to the impending war with Iraq and the general uneasiness in the Middle East, many lines liberalized their cancellation and insurance policies for their European cruises, and, in some cases, all their itineraries, including the Caribbean, in order to encourage bookings. They covered cancellations for any reason whatsoever up to a day before sailing, issuing full (or 90%) credits for a future cruise. For example, SeaDream Yacht Club's generous policy, which still remains in effect, allows you to cancel your cruise for any reason up to the day of departure and get a credit for a future cruise, redeemable within the next 2 years. Since policies can change frequently in response to world events, before booking find out the line's cancellation policy.

For all of these reasons—worries about travel, worries about cruise lines canceling or going belly up, sudden illness or other emergencies, missed flights that cause you to miss the ship, or even if you just change your mind—you may want to think about purchasing **travel insurance.**

If you're just worried about missing the ship, go a day early and spend your money on a hotel and nice dinner instead. If you're worried about medical problems occurring during your trip, on the other hand, travel insurance may be more vital. Except for the small coastal cruisers described in chapter 8, most cruise ships have an infirmary staffed by a doctor and a nurse or two; but in the event of a dire illness, the ship's medical staff can only do so much. Therefore, you may want a policy that covers **emergency medical evacuation** and, if your regular insurance doesn't cover it, the potential cost of major medical treatment while away from home.

There are policies sold through the cruise lines (with details varying from line to line) and others sold independently. Both have pros and cons.

CRUISE LINE POLICIES VS. THIRD-PARTY INSURERS

A good travel agent can tell you about policies sold through the cruise lines and ones sold independently of the lines. No matter which you choose, it's absolutely crucial to read the fine print because terms vary from policy to policy.

Both kinds typically reimburse you in some way when your trip is affected by unexpected events (such as canceled flights, plane crashes, dockworkers' strikes, or the illness or death of a loved one, as late as the day before or day of departure) but not by "acts of God," such as hurricanes and earthquakes (the exception being if your home is made uninhabitable, putting you in no mood to continue with your cruise plans). Both also typically cover **cancellation of the cruise** for medical reasons (yours or a family member's); **medical emergencies** during the cruise, including evacuation from the ship; lost or damaged luggage; and a cruise missed due to airline delays (though some only cover delays over 3 hr.). Neither kind of policy will reimburse you if your travel agent goes bankrupt, so using a travel agent you're very familiar with or who has been recommended to you is the safest precaution you can take. (And, of course, *always use a credit card,* never a check. If a corrupt travel agent cashes it, or a decent one just goes out of business, then you could get screwed.) Most cancellation policies also do not cover cancellations due to work requirements.

THIRD-PARTY COVERAGE   Even though agents get a commission for selling both cruise line policies and independent policies, most agents and industry insiders believe that non–cruise line policies are the best bet because some, such as Access America (see below), will issue insurance to those with **preexisting medical conditions** if the condition is stable when purchasing the insurance (a doctor would have to verify this if you ever made a claim) and if you purchase the policy within 14 days of your initial deposit on the cruise. They also offer **supplier-default coverage** that kicks in if a cruise line goes bankrupt, which a handful did between 2000 and 2003.

Still, you shouldn't be afraid to book a cruise. A well-connected travel agent should see the writing on the wall months before a cruise line fails—commissions will slow or stop being paid, phone calls won't be returned, and industry trade publications will report on any problems. The less customer-service-driven cruise sellers may not stop pushing a troubled cruise line, however, and may continue selling these lines up to the very last minute.

According to the Fair Credit Billing Act, if you paid by credit card (and again, you should), you'll generally get your money back if you dispute the charge within 60 days of the date the charge first appears. If you paid in full 4 months before the cruise, you'll likely be out of luck going the credit-reimbursement route and may have to resort to litigation. Also, while many lines post a multimillion-dollar bond with the Federal Maritime Commission, creating a fund from which they can reimburse creditors should they fail financially, it's no guarantee you'll get all or any of your money back. Technically, the bond covers cruise payments for all passengers embarking from U.S. ports, but since the line would have banks or other vendors to pay off first, you'd likely get only pennies on the dollar, if that. Still, it's better that a cruise line have a bond than not—and if you learn that a line is having trouble making bond payments, it may be a sign of serious financial woes.

Policies are available from reputable insurers such as **Access America,** Box 71533, Richmond, VA 23286 (© **866/807-3982;** www.accessamerica.com), and **Travel Guard International,** 1145 Clark St., Stevens Point, WI 54481 (© **800/826-4919;** www. travelguard.com), whose websites maintain lists of the lines they cover (or no longer cover); these are helpful in figuring out which lines may be considered financially shaky.

CRUISE LINE COVERAGE   Cruise lines offer their own policies, many of them administered by New York–based **BerkelyCare** (© **800/453-4069**). If you opt for this type of policy out of sheer convenience (the cost is added right onto your cruise fare), keep in mind they do not cover you in the event of a cruise line bankruptcy (though using a credit card can save you here; see above) or for cancellation of your cruise due to preexisting medical conditions, which is usually defined as an unstable condition existing within 60 days of your buying the insurance. Some lines' policies, including Carnival, Costa, Silversea, and Crystal, will issue a cruise credit for the penalty amount if a medical claim is deemed preexisting, and issue you cash if you cancel for a covered reason. Generally, the cancellation penalty imposed by the cruise line would be 100% of the cruise fare, for example, if you cancel a few days before the cruise (assuming you've paid in full), or it could be just $300 if you cancel right after making the initial cruise deposit.

Sounds like the third-party policies win hands down, right? Well, to make it just a little more complicated, a handful of cruise line policies are actually better in some areas than outside policies. For example, since 1995, **Princess Cruises** has had an insurance policy that allows you to cancel for all the reasons that an outside policy would (illness, injury) and get cash reimbursement or they will let you cancel for any reason whatsoever (from fear of flying to a bad hair day) up until the day of departure and have 75% to 90% of the normal penalty for canceling your cruise applied toward a future trip. **Norwegian** introduced a similar policy in 2001, the same year **Celebrity** and **Royal Caribbean** started offering their "any reason" policy, which provides a cruise credit for 75%. For an extra $100 above their standard insurance fee (or $250 if purchased alone), high-end **Silversea** allows you to cancel cruises for any reason 1 to 14 days before sailing and get a credit for 100% of the penalty amount (including airfare if booked through Silversea), applicable toward any cruise within the following 12 months. Many other lines offer similar cancellation plans. The cruise lines using the BerkelyCare policies (see above) also reimburse passengers for days missed on a cruise—say, if you missed your flight and had to join up with the cruise 2 days later— covering hotel costs during the missed days and transportation to the ship (though typically only to a max of $500). Keep in mind, cruise line policies do change, so before purchasing insurance be sure you understand exactly what you're getting.

12 Putting Down a Deposit & Reviewing Tickets

In this age of last-minute booking, you typically need to pay in full when making your reservation. If you're booking several months or more ahead of time, then you have to leave a deposit to secure the booking. Depending on the policy of the line you selected, the amount will either be fixed at a predetermined amount or represent a percentage of the ticket's total cost. The length of time cruise lines will hold a cabin without a deposit is getting shorter by the minute. It seems pretty clear, in this age of near-obsessive "shopping around," that the cruise lines are doing their part to discourage it. It used to be a cruise could be held for a week before you had to plunk down cash; most lines have now shortened this window to 1 to 3 days (exceptions include exotic itineraries that aren't ultracompetitive). Carnival, for instance, now requires a deposit within 24 hours.

The balance of the cruise price is due anywhere from about 60 to 90 days before you depart; holiday cruises may require final payments earlier, perhaps 90 days before departure. The payment schedule for groups is more liberal. Booking at the last minute usually requires payment in full at the time of booking.

Credit card payments are made directly to the cruise line, but payments by check are made out to the agency, which then passes payment on to the cruise line. As we've said repeatedly, it's preferable by far to pay by credit card, for the added protection it offers.

"Except in certain circumstances, if the travel agency asks, prefers, or insists on running your credit card through the agency processing terminal, it is a *major* red flag that most often should send you running from the building," says Charlie Funk, co-owner of Just Cruisin' Plus in Nashville. The only exception to this is when an agency is doing a charter with special entertainment and the cruise is only offered through the agency.

Carefully review your ticket, invoice, itinerary, and/or vouchers to confirm that they accurately reflect the departure date, ship, and cabin category you booked. The printout usually lists a specific cabin number; if it doesn't, it designates a cabin category. Your exact cabin location will then be assigned to you when you board ship.

If you need to cancel your cruise after putting down a deposit, you'll get all or most of your money back, depending on how close you are to departure. With Royal Caribbean, for instance, customers get a 100% refund if they cancel more than 70 days ahead. Less than 30 days from the cruise, the refund drops to 50%, and within the last week it's your loss.

3

Things to Know Before You Go

You've bought your ticket and you're getting ready to cruise. Here are a few details you need to consider before you go.

1 Passports & Visas

For decades, U.S.-based cruise ships have operated under rules that permit U.S. citizens to travel to Canada, Mexico, and the Caribbean without need of a passport, but that all seems to be changing. As of mid-2005, new rules proposed by the U.S. departments of State and Homeland Security may soon do away with that loophole, meaning even passengers taking weekend jaunts to the Bahamas will soon need a passport—no ifs, ands, or buts.

Called the **Western Hemisphere Travel Initiative,** the rule changes are part of the Intelligence Reform and Terrorism Prevention Act of 2004, and at press time were in a review period. The final ruling was due to be issued in late 2005 and will likely recommend implementation of the plan. If so, the first phase is coming up fast. If implemented according to the proposed schedule (which is the main bone of contention with the cruise industry), all U.S. citizens traveling to the Caribbean, Bermuda, and Central and South America will be required to carry passports as of **December 31, 2005.** One year later, the rules would affect travelers to Mexico and Canada (thus affecting Mexican Riviera cruises and Canada/New England cruises, as well as any Alaska cruises beginning or ending in Vancouver), and on December 31, 2007, passports would be required for all air, sea, and land border crossings.

The bottom line? "Generally," says Carnival spokeswoman Jennifer De La Cruz, "our advice to guests is that if they're traveling on a cruise in 2006 or beyond, they should plan to get a passport. These rules are likely to be finalized in the not-too-distant future and it's difficult to predict whether or not there will be any modification to the implementation timeline."

Time to go passport shopping. Don't dillydally either, because U.S. passport services are likely to be deluged when and if the new rules take effect. Passport applications generally take 6 to 8 weeks to process, though expedited service is also available (see below).

If you don't currently have a passport or need to replace an expired one, the **U.S. State Department website** (http://travel.state.gov) provides information. You can also inquire at your local passport acceptance facility or call the **National Passport Information Center** (© 877/487-2778). Fees for new passports are $85 adult, $70 children under 16. Renewals cost $55. If you're leaving within a few weeks, you can pay an additional $60 fee to have your passport expedited for delivery within 2 weeks.

As you would before any trip abroad, make two photocopies of your documents and ID before leaving home. Take one set with you as a backup (keeping it in a different piece of luggage from the one holding your originals) and keep one at home.

Vaccinations Required?

Travel to the Caribbean does not generally warrant inoculations against tropical diseases. Ditto for the Mexican ports you might be visiting. The Centers for Disease Control (CDC) recommends prescription anti-malarial drugs for travelers in certain parts of Central America, including Panama's San Blas Islands and Honduras's Roatan Island—both of them cruise destinations. CDC recommendations and warnings can be viewed at **www.cdc.gov/travel/destinat.htm**.

After using your passport or proof of citizenship to board ship at the beginning of your cruise, the cruise line might hang onto your documents for the duration of your cruise, thus allowing them to facilitate clearance procedures quickly at each port. Your documents are returned to you after departing the last foreign port of call, en route back to your home port.

Non-U.S./Canadian citizens departing from and/or returning to the U.S./Canada should check with their travel agent or cruise line to determine required paperwork. Generally, you'll need a valid passport, alien-registration card as applicable, and any visas required by the ports of call.

2 Money Matters

Know how they say cruises are all-inclusive vacations? They're lying. True, the bulk of your vacation expenses are covered in your fare, but there are plenty of extras. We've detailed the specifics in "The Cost: What's Included & What's Not," in chapter 2. In this section, we'll examine the way monetary transactions are handled on board and in port.

ONBOARD CHARGE CARDS

Cruise ships operate on a cashless basis. Basically, this means you have a running tab and simply sign for what you buy on board during your cruise—bar drinks, meals at specialty restaurants, spa treatments, shore excursions, gift-shop purchases, and so on—then pay up at the end. Very convenient, yes—and also very, very easy to forget your limits and spend more than you intended to.

Shortly before or after embarkation, a purser or check-in clerk will take an imprint of your credit card and issue you an **onboard charge card,** which, on most ships, also serves as your room key and as your cruise ID, which you swipe through a scanner every time you leave or return to the ship. Some ships issue separate cards for these functions, or a card and an old-fashioned room key. Some adventure lines that carry 100 or fewer passengers just ask for your cabin number for onboard purchases.

On the last night of your cruise, an **itemized account** of all you've charged will be slipped beneath your cabin door. If you agree with the charges, they'll automatically be billed to your credit card. If you'd rather pay in cash or if you dispute any charge, you'll need to stop by the office of the ship's cashier or purser. There may be a long line, so don't go if you don't have to.

BRINGING CASH ASHORE

The cashless system works just fine on board, but remember, you'll need cash in port. Many people get so used to not carrying their wallets aboard ship that they get off in port and find themselves without any money in their pockets—a minor annoyance if your ship is docked and it just means trudging back aboard for cash, but a major annoyance if it's anchored offshore and you have to spend an hour ferrying back and forth by tender.

Credit cards are accepted at most port shops, but we recommend having some real cash, ideally in small denominations, to cover the cost of taxi rides, tips to tour leaders, or purchases you make from craft markets and street vendors. Information on local currency is included in chapters 9 through 16, but for the most part you don't have to worry about exchanging money at all. In the Caribbean, the U.S. dollar is the legal currency of the U.S. Virgin Islands, Puerto Rico, and (oddly enough) the British Virgin Islands, but vendors on islands that have their own currency will also usually accept dollars. Even on islands such as Guadeloupe and Les Saintes, where they may prefer euros (they're both French possessions), we've never had our U.S. dough turned away. Mexican, Central American, and Canadian ports are similarly dollar-friendly, and Alaska and Hawaii are, of course, states. Americans have it so easy . . . .

If you're running low on cash, **ATMs** are easy to find in nearly every cruise port covered in this guide, often right at the cruise terminal. Remember that you'll get local currency from machines where the dollar isn't the legal tender, so don't withdraw more than you need. Many megaships also have ATMs (surprise, surprise: usually near the casino), but you can expect to be charged a hefty fee for using them—up to $5 in addition to what your bank charges you.

Many lines, such as Carnival and Royal Caribbean, will cash **traveler's checks** at the purser's desk, and sometimes **personal checks** of up to about $200 to $250 (but sometimes only when accompanied by an American Express card, for guarantee). You can also often get a **cash advance** through your Visa, MasterCard, or Discover card.

Except aboard some of the ultraluxury lines, **gratuities for the crew** are not normally included in the cruise rates, though many lines these days are either automatically adding a suggested gratuity to your end-of-cruise bill or offering passengers the option of charging gratuities. Where this is not the case, you should reserve some cash so that you won't feel like Scrooge at the end of your cruise. See "Tipping, Customs & Other End-of-Cruise Concerns," later in this chapter, for more on this subject. Information on how each line deals with gratuities is included in the "Service" section of each line review in chapters 6 through 8.

3 Keeping in Touch While at Sea

Some people take a cruise to get away from it all, but others are communication addicts. For them, today's megaships offer a spectrum of ways to keep in touch.

CELLPHONES & SAT-PHONES

Look out, here they come. Over the past couple of years, technology has become available that allows cellphone users to make and receive calls while aboard ship, even when far out at sea. **Costa Cruises** was the first to introduce it, aboard the new *Costa Fortuna* in late 2003, but fall 2004 was when things really took off, with **Norwegian Cruise Line, Royal Caribbean,** and **Celebrity** all announcing plans to go cellular fleetwide by the end of 2005. Costa has also expanded cell service beyond *Fortuna* to its vessels *Atlantica, Europa, Romantica,* and *Tropicale.* At press time, industry big-gun Carnival hasn't made a firm decision on the cellular issue, though its sister line Holland America is investigating the possibilities. Among the luxury lines, **Crystal Cruises'** *Crystal Serenity* is the only vessel wired for service at press time, though. Silversea is also looking into the possibility.

Get ready: Your boss will be calling you in the hot tub any minute now.

Wireless Maritime's service is available to most passengers with GSM phones that operate at 900 MHz and 1900 MHz, which are common in the United States. In addition to regular voice and text messaging, the service—which kicks in once a ship sails beyond range of shoreside towers—lets passengers with data-capable GSM/GPRS devices access data services such as e-mail and picture messaging. Passengers are billed by the carrier to which they subscribe at roaming rates set by that carrier, just as if they were roaming on land instead of at sea.

Though each user's carrier sets its own rates, expect charges of roughly $1.70 per minute. That ain't cheap, but it's nowhere near the average $8 or $9 per minute (and sometimes up to $15 a minute) cruise lines typically charge for **in-cabin satellite-phone service.**

In addition to cabin sat-phones and cell service, each ship has a central phone number, fax number, and e-mail address, which you'll sometimes find in the cruise line's brochure and usually in the documents you'll get with your tickets. Distribute these to family members or friends in case they have to contact you in an emergency. It also can't hurt to leave behind the numbers of the cruise line's headquarters and/or reservations department, both of whom will be able to put people in touch with you.

INTERNET & E-MAIL AT SEA

Aside from some of the small, adventure-oriented ships in chapter 8, pretty much every cruise ship has computers from which passengers can send and receive e-mail and browse the Internet. In many cases, their computer centers are decked out with state-of-the-art flat-screen monitors, plush chairs, coffee bars, and Web-cams so users can send their vacation pictures to family and friends. They're often open around the clock, and many offer classes for computer novices.

E-mail access is usually available through the Web via your Earthlink, AOL, Hotmail, Yahoo, or other personal account, with charges calculated on a per-minute basis (usually between 50¢ and $1) or in pre-purchased blocks (say, $40 for a 3- or 4-night cruise or $90 for a 7-night cruise). A few ships still offer e-mail through temporary accounts you set up once aboard ship, with rates averaging roughly $1 to $4 per message.

Many ships built over the past several years (including the newest Celebrity, Crystal, Costa, HAL, NCL, Oceania, Royal Caribbean, Cunard, Radisson, SeaDream, and Silversea ships) have been wired with **dataports** in all, most, or some cabins and suites, allowing passengers who travel with laptops to log on in privacy. The cost for these services tends to be higher than access in the Internet centers. **Wireless Internet**

The *Frommer's Cruises* Onboard Cellphone Etiquette Pledge

We hate to hear them ringing on city buses, commuter trains, restaurants, theaters, museums, public restrooms, and even on the street, so how much more will we hate it now that cellphones are invading cruise ships, too? That's why we're asking you all to take the *Frommer's Cruises* Onboard Cellphone Etiquette Pledge: *I, _____, do solemnly swear that I will have mercy on my fellow passengers. I will turn off my ringer. I will speak in soft tones. I will keep my conversations short and conduct them whenever possible in the privacy of my own cabin. And I will never, ever carry my phone into the dining room, the theater, or the library. I swear.*

Plugging in Your Gadgets

All ships reviewed in this book run on 110 AC current (both 110 and 220 on many), so you won't need an adapter.

(Wi-Fi) is another new trend, offered aboard all the Carnival, Holland America, NCL, and Princess vessels, usually in designated areas such as the atrium and some public rooms. A few ships—the small luxury ships of Seabourn and the huge new *Carnival Valor*—offer wireless access everywhere on board. To take advantage of this service you must have a wireless card for your laptop, rent a card, or rent a laptop, then purchase minutes either on an as-used basis or in packages of 33 to 500 minutes.

KEEPING ON TOP OF THE NEWS

News junkies take note: Most ships have CNN and sometimes other news stations as part of their regular TV lineup. Many ships also maintain the tradition of reprinting headline news stories pulled off the wire and slipping them under passengers' doors each morning.

4 Packing for the Different Cruise Climates

One of the great things about cruising is that even though you'll be visiting several countries (or at least several ports) on a typical weeklong itinerary, you won't be living out of your suitcase: You just check into your cabin on day 1, put your clothes in the closet, and settle in. The destinations come to you. But what exactly do you need to pack? Eveningwear aboard ship is pretty much the same wherever you go, but your destination definitely affects what you'll need during the day.

SHIPBOARD DRESS CODES (OR LACK THEREOF)

Ever since Norwegian Cruise Line started the casual trend back at the turn of the 20th century, cruise lines have been toning down or turning off their dress codes. During the day, no matter what the itinerary, you'll find T-shirts, polo shirts, and shorts or khakis predominating, plus casual dresses for women and sweat shirts or light sweaters to compensate for the air-conditioning. The vibe is about the same on the luxury lines, though those polos and khakis probably sport better labels. On the megaships, retractable glass roofs mean the pool scene keeps going strong whether you're in the sunny Caribbean or icy Alaska. So, pack that **bathing suit,** as well as a cover-up and sandals if you want to go right from your deck chair to one of the restaurants or public rooms. If you plan on hitting the gym, don't forget sneakers and your **workout clothes.**

Evenings aboard ship used to be a lot more complicated, requiring passengers to pack for more situations than today's cruises demand. On most lines these days, **formal nights** have either melted away entirely or slid closer to what used to be considered semi-formal. When Oceania Cruises started up in 2003, its dress code was set as "country club casual" every single night, on every voyage. NCL has also pretty much ditched formal nights completely, though its "optional formal" captain's cocktail night accommodates those who choose to dress up. Disney Cruise Line has toned formality down to the point where a sport jacket is considered dressy enough. Most other mainstream lines still have 2 traditional formal nights during any 7-night itinerary—usually the second and second-to-last nights of the cruise, the former for the captain's cocktail party. For these, imagine what you'd wear to a nice wedding: Men are encouraged to

Tuxedo Rentals

Despite the casual trend, there's usually a contingent of folks on board who like to get all decked out—and why not? After all, how many chances do you get these days to dress like you're in a Fred Astaire/Ginger Rogers movie? If you don't own a tux or don't want to bother lugging one along, you can often arrange a rental through the cruise line or your travel agent for about $75 to $120 (the higher prices for packages with shirts and shoes). In some cases, a rental offer arrives with your cruise tickets; if not, a call to your travel agent or the cruise line can facilitate a rental. If you choose this option, your suit will be waiting in your cabin when you arrive.

---

wear tuxedos or dark suits; women dress in cocktail dresses, sequined jackets, gowns, or other fancy attire. If you just hate dressing up, women can get away with a blouse and skirt or pants—and, of course, jewelry, scarves, and other accessories can dress up an otherwise nondescript outfit. (Most cabins have personal safes where you can keep your good jewelry when you're not wearing it.) Men can get away with a blue blazer and tie if they choose to. **Casual nights** (sometimes called "smart casual" or something similar) make up the rest of the week, though some lines still cling to an old distinction between full casual (decent pants and collared shirts for men, and maybe a sport jacket; dresses, skirts, or pantsuits for women) and informal or semi-formal (suits or sport jackets; stylish dresses or pantsuits). Suggested dress for the evening is usually printed in the ship's daily schedule. Cruise lines also usually describe their dress codes in their brochures and on their websites.

Most of the **ultraluxury lines** maintain the same ratio of formal, semi-formal, and casual nights, with passengers tending to dress on the high end of all those categories. Tuxedos are very common. That said, even the luxe lines are relaxing their dress standards. Seabourn doesn't even request ties for men except on formal nights anymore, and Windstar and SeaDream have a casual "no jackets required" policy every single day, though dinners usually see some men in sport jackets and women in nice dresses.

Aboard all the **small-ship lines** covered in this book, it's very rare to see anything dressier than a sports jacket at any time, and those usually appear only for the captain's dinner. Most of these lines are 100% casual 100% of the time, with passengers sometimes changing into clean shirts, trousers, and dresses at dinner.

DRESSING FOR YOUR DESTINATION

The cruise destinations covered in this book divide fairly easily into warm-weather regions (Caribbean, Central America, Mexican Riviera, Hawaii, and Bermuda) and the cooler northern regions of Alaska and its milder neighbor on the other side of the continent, New England/Canada.

WARM-WEATHER ITINERARIES

In the **Caribbean,** the temperature stays within a fairly narrow range year-round, averaging between 75°F and 85°F (24°C–29°C), though in summer the combination of sun and humidity can get very intense, especially at midafternoon. Trade winds help cool things off on many of the islands, as may rainfall, which differs island to island— Aruba, for instance, is very dry, while it seems to rain briefly every other time we're in Nassau. Winter is generally the driest season throughout the region, but even then it can be wet in mountainous areas, and afternoon showers often give the shores a good

Average Temperatures in the Cruise Regions*

Destination	Jan	Feb	Mar	Apr	May	June	July	Aug	Sept	Oct	Nov	Dec
Eastern Caribbean	70/83	70/84	71/85	73/86	74/87	76/87	76/88	76/89	76/89	75/88	74/86	72/84
Western Caribbean	65/82	66/84	72/86	73/90	75/90	75/90	75/90	75/91	75/90	73/86	72/84	70/82
Southern Caribbean	73/82	73/82	73/84	75/88	76/88	76/88	77/88	77/88	77/88	76/87	77/84	74/83
Panama Canal/ Central America	76/84	76/84	76/85	77/86	76/87	75/86	75/85	75/85	75/87	74/86	74/84	75/84
Southeast Alaska	19/29	23/34	27/39	32/47	39/55	45/61	48/64	47/63	43/56	37/47	27/37	23/32
Mexican Riviera	72/87	72/87	72/87	72/87	76/89	77/89	77/89	77/89	77/88	77/88	75/88	73/88
Bermuda	61/69	60/68	60/69	63/71	68/75	73/81	77/85	78/86	76/84	72/80	67/75	63/70
Hawaii	65/78	65/78	66/78	68/79	70/81	72/83	73/84	74/85	73/85	72/83	70/81	67/79
Canada/New England*	19/30	19/30	25/40	34/48	41/57	50/66	57/73	57/73	54/68	45/57	36/48	25/37

*Temperatures are in degrees Fahrenheit, representing average lows and highs. Canada/New England temperatures represent Halifax, Nova Scotia. Temperatures farther south along the coast will be on the high side of the temperature range. **Note:** Humidity can make summer temperatures in warm-weather destinations seem hotter, while Alaska's damp climate can make its summer temperatures seem colder.*

soaking, sometimes just for a few minutes, sometimes for hours. Temperatures on Mexico's Yucatán Peninsula and in **Central America** can feel much hotter, especially on shore excursions to the humid interior. Hurricane season lasts officially from June 1 to November 30, traditionally the low cruise season.

The **Mexican Riviera** is traditionally sunny, with average daytime temperatures in the mid-80s. Showers are brief and usually occur at night, when the temperature drops by about 10 degrees. Humidity is moderate during the November to April dry season and higher from May to October.

Hawaii is, of course, paradise. Along the coast, daytime temperatures are usually between the mid-70s and mid-80s, while the mountains can be quite a bit cooler, with summer daytime temperatures in the 60s. On the leeward side of the islands, away from the wind, temperatures occasionally get into the low 90s, while the high slopes of Mauna Kea, the state's highest volcanic peak, are regularly covered with snow in the winter.

Bermuda, too, enjoys a wonderfully temperate climate due to the proximity of the Gulf Stream, which flows between the island and North America. There's no rainy season and no typical month of excess rain. Showers may be heavy at times, but the skies clear quickly. During the April-to-October cruise season temperatures stay in the mid-70s to mid-80s, and even in summer the temperature rarely rises above 85°F (29°C), with a breeze cooling things down at night.

WHAT TO PACK No matter which warm-weather region you'll be visiting, casual daytime wear aboard ship means shorts, T-shirts or polos, sundresses, and bathing suits. The same dress code works in port too, but in many places it's best to cover the skimpy bikini top if straying from the beach area. Bring a good pair of **walking shoes** or sandals if you intend to do more than lie on the beach, and **aqua-socks** might also be a good idea if you plan to snorkel, take inflatable launches to shore, or participate in watersports. They're also very good for shore excursions that traverse wet, rocky terrain, such as Jamaica's Dunn's River Falls trip. They're cheap to buy, but if you forget, many cruise lines rent them for excursions for about $5 a pair. A folding umbrella or lightweight raincoat or poncho is a good idea for destinations that experience regular tropical showers.

Lastly, remember to pack sunglasses, a hat, and **sunscreen.** All are available aboard ship and in the ports, but sunscreen in particular will be a lot cheaper at your local market than in a gift shop. You might also consider bringing a **plastic water bottle** that you can refill aboard ship, rather than buying overpriced bottled water in port.

ALASKA ITINERARIES

While Southeast Alaska, where most cruises sail, has more temperate year-round weather than the rest of the state, summers here are still unpredictable. In May, when the cruise season gets going, we've experienced icy rain at the waterline and hiked in new snow at the top of Juneau's Mount Roberts—but we've also seen a lot of beautiful, crisp, sunny days. June is the driest of the 3 true summer months, July the warmest (and also the busiest), and August the month where you'll usually experience the most rain. Rainy weather usually continues into September, though we've sailed here as the season wrapped up and had sunny days all week long. Some towns are rainier than others no matter what time you sail—Ketchikan, for instance, gets about 150 inches of precipitation annually, more than three times Juneau's total. In general, daytime summer temperatures are usually in the 50s and 60s, though the damp climate can make it seem colder (as can wind, proximity to glaciers, and excursions to higher elevations). Some days can also be nicely warm, getting up into the 70s or occasionally into the 80s. The all-time high temperature in Juneau was 90°F (32°C) in July 1975—a real rarity.

This far south you won't experience the famed midnight sun, though days still seem to go on forever. In June, Juneau gets about 18 hours of sunlight—sometimes at 10pm there's still enough to read by. Farther north, in Anchorage, Denali, and Fairbanks, the sun dips below the horizon for only a little over 4 hours on some June days. Summer temperatures here are roughly comparable to those in Southeast.

WHAT TO PACK   The rule for Alaska is layering. In addition to some lightweight clothing to wear aboard ship (including a bathing suit, as most megaships have covered pool areas), you'll want to bring some variation of the following items for daytime use:

- A lightweight, waterproof coat or jacket
- Two sweaters or fleece pullovers, or substitute a warm vest for one
- Two to four pairs of pants or jeans
- Two pairs of walking shoes (preferably waterproof)
- A warm hat and gloves
- Long underwear if you're on a May/September shoulder-season cruise
- A folding umbrella

Despite the cool temperatures and sometimes overcast conditions, you'll still want to pack **sunglasses and sunscreen,** especially if you'll be doing a lot of active shore excursions or spending a lot of time on deck, whale-watching. That's also the reason you'll want to bring **binoculars** and/or a good **camera,** preferably with a telephoto or zoom lens and with lots of digital memory or film. Regarding binoculars, many of the small-ship adventure lines have enough aboard for all passengers, but it can't hurt to bring your own if you have them. Because whales, eagles, and bears aren't the only wildlife in Alaska, you'll also do well to pack some **mosquito repellant.** Bugs aren't as big a problem in Southeast as in the more central parts of the state, but if you get into the forest on shore excursions, they can still get annoying.

EASTERN CANADA/NEW ENGLAND ITINERARIES

Temperatures on summer Canada/New England cruises are usually very pleasant, averaging in the 60s and 70s. Temperatures in Nova Scotia will be on the low end of that scale, often dipping into the 50s at night, while you can expect hot temperatures if you're sailing from New York, where summer days are often in the 80s or 90s.

Temperatures in Boston are usually in the 70s in summer. On September/October fall foliage cruises, expect temperatures in Canada to range from the low 40s to the low 60s. Rain-wise, the situation is unpredictable. We've experienced bright, crisply sunny days followed by a full 24-hour socker of a storm. Fog is also common, especially on New Brunswick's Fundy Coast and the Atlantic Coast of Nova Scotia.

WHAT TO PACK   A lighter version of layering is called for here, with a long-sleeve shirt or light sweater over your T-shirts, polos, and dresses. Pack a combination of shorts and long casual pants as well, plus good walking shoes and a light jacket for use in the evenings. Fall cruises call for a bit heavier clothing, but you'll rarely experience really bone-chilling cold on these cruises. As always, remember your sunblock, sunglasses, hat, and folding umbrella.

SUNDRIES

Except on the small ships, most vessels have a **laundry service** on board and some dry cleaning, too, with generally about a 24-hour turnaround time; a price list will be in your cabin. Cleaning services tend not to be cheap—$1 or $1.50 per pair of socks, $2.50 to $3 for a T-shirt, and $9 to dry-clean a suit—so if you plan to pack light and wear the same outfit several times, consider the self-service laundry rooms aboard some ships (Carnival, Crystal, Princess, and Holland America, among others). The small-ship lines often provide no laundry service at all.

Like hotel rooms, most cabins (especially those aboard the newest and the most high-end ships) come with **toiletries** such as soap, shampoo, conditioner, and lotion, although you still may want to bring your own products—the ones provided often seem watered down. If you forget something, all but a few of the smallest ships in this book have at least one shop on board, selling razor blades, toothbrushes, sunscreen, film, and other sundries, usually at inflated prices.

Most cabins also have **hair dryers** (the "Cabins & Rates" charts in chapters 6–8 tell you which have them and which don't), but they tend to be weak, so don't expect miracles—if you have a lot of hair, bring your own. All ships reviewed in this book run on 110 AC current (both 110 and 220 on many), so you won't need an adapter.

You don't need to pack a **beach towel,** as they're almost always supplied on board (again, except aboard some small-ship lines). If you insist on big and fluffy, however, you might want to pack your own. Bird-watchers and whale-watchers will want their **binoculars** and manuals, golfers their clubs unless they intend to rent, and snorkelers their gear (which can also be rented, usually through the cruise lines).

If you like to read but don't want to lug hefty novels on board, most ships of all sizes have libraries stocked with books and magazines. Some are more extensive than others. Most ships also stock paperback bestsellers in their shops.

5 Tipping, Customs & Other End-of-Cruise Concerns

We know you don't want to hear about the end of your cruise before you've even gone, but it's best to be prepared. Here's a discussion of a few matters you'll have to take care of before heading home.

TIPPING

Most cruise lines pay their service staff low base wages with the understanding that the bulk of their income will come from tips. Each line has clear guidelines for gratuities, which are usually printed in their brochures and on their website, on your cruise documents, and in the daily schedule toward the end of your trip. The traditional way of tipping was to simply hand your waiter, assistant waiter, and cabin steward cash in a little envelope, but these days more and more lines—Carnival, Costa, Oceania, Holland America, and Princess, to be exact—are automatically adding tips to passengers' onboard account (generally between $8.50 and $11.50 per person, per day total), with the amount adjustable if you request it at the purser's desk before the end of the cruise. Norwegian Cruise Line goes a step further, with a $10-per-person, per day nonrefundable service charge. Some lines, such as Royal Caribbean and Disney, give you the option of paying cash directly to staff or adding the gratuities onto your account. Some small-ship lines pool the tips and divide them equitably among all crew. Ultra-luxury lines Silversea, Seabourn, SeaDream, and Radisson include tips in the cruise rates. Windstar promotes its "tipping not required" policy, but "required" is the operative word: Tipping really is expected.

Suggested tipping amounts vary slightly with the line and its degree of luxury, from about $9 to $13 total per passenger, per day, and half that for children. As a rule of thumb, each passenger (not each couple) should expect to tip at least $3.50 per day for their cabin steward, $3.50 for their dining room waiter, and about $2 for their assistant waiter, and sometimes 75¢ for their headwaiter. Some lines suggest you tip the maitre d' about $5 per person for the week and slip another couple bucks to the chief housekeeper, but it's your choice. If you've never even met these people, don't bother. Guests staying in suites with butler service should also send $3.50 per day his way. A 15% gratuity is usually included on every **bar bill** to cover gratuities to bartenders and wine stewards. The captain and other professional officers definitely do not get tips. It'd be like tipping your doctor.

On lines that follow traditional person-to-person gratuity policies, tip your waiter and assistant waiter during the cruise's final dinner, and leave your cabin steward his or her tip on the final night or morning, just before you disembark. Tip spa personnel immediately after they work on you, but note that on some lines, Steiner's spa personnel automatically add a tip to your account unless you indicate otherwise, so inquire first before adding one yourself.

DISEMBARKING

It's a good idea to begin packing before dinner on your final night aboard. Be sure to fill out the luggage tags given to you and attach them securely to each piece. You'll be asked to leave your luggage outside your cabin door by midnight or so, after which service staff will pick it up and spirit it away. Two points here: (1) First-time cruisers always worry about leaving their bags out in public, but we've never heard an instance of anything being stolen; (2) because ship's personnel have to get thousands of pieces of luggage into bins and off the ship, don't expect your luggage will be treated gently. Rather than packing bottles of duty-free liquor and other breakables, carry them off the ship yourself.

Once you debark, you'll find your bags waiting for you in the terminal, organized by the colored or numbered tags you attached. Attendants are standing by to help you should your bag not be where it's supposed to be.

Ships normally arrive in port on the final day between 6 and 8am, and need at least 90 minutes to unload baggage and complete docking formalities. So no one disembarks much before 9am, and sometimes it may be 10am before you're allowed to leave the ship, usually via debarkation numbers assigned based on flight times. (Not surprisingly, suite passengers get expedited debarkation.) Have breakfast. Have coffee. Have patience.

In the cruise ship terminal, claim your luggage and then pass through Customs before exiting. This normally entails handing the officer your filled-out declaration form as you breeze past, without even coming to a full stop. There are generally porters available in the terminals (to whom it's traditional to pay $1–$2 per bag carried), but you may have to haul your luggage through Customs before you can get to them.

U.S. CUSTOMS

Except for some small-ship itineraries in Alaska and U.S. rivers, and NCL's cruises in Hawaii, all the other ships in this book will visit at least one foreign port on their itinerary, meaning you'll have to go through Customs and be subject to duty-free purchase allowances when you return. We've found clearing Customs at U.S. cruise ports usually painless and speedy, with officials rarely asking for anything more than your filled-out declaration form as they nod you through. Better safe than sorry, though. Keep receipts for all purchases you make abroad. And, if you're carrying a particularly new-looking camera or expensive jewelry (and are a particularly nervous type), you may want to consider carrying proof that you purchased them before your trip. Similarly, if you use any medication containing controlled substances or requiring injection, carry an original prescription or note from your doctor.

Depending on which countries you visited, your **personal exemption** will be $800 or $1,600. There are also limits on the amount of alcoholic beverages (usually 1 liter), cigarettes (1 carton), cigars (100 total, and no Cubans!), and other tobacco products you may include in your personal duty-free exemption.

The standard personal duty-free allowance for U.S. citizens is $800, an amount that applies to **Mexico, Canada,** and most of the **Caribbean** islands. If returning directly from the **U.S. Virgin Islands,** you may bring in $1,600 worth of merchandise duty-free, including 5 liters of alcohol, of which at least 1 liter should be a product of those islands. If you visit only Puerto Rico, an American commonwealth, you don't have to go through Customs at all.

As you may be visiting both foreign and U.S.-territory ports, things get more complicated: If, for instance, your cruise stops in the U.S. Virgin Islands and The Bahamas, your total limit is $1,600, of which no more than $800 can be from The Bahamas. Note that you must declare on your Customs form all gifts received during your cruise.

Joint Customs declarations are possible for family members traveling together. For instance, for a husband and wife with two children, the total duty-free exemption on goods from the U.S. Virgin Islands is $5,400.

Note that most meat or meat products, fruit, plants, vegetables, or plant-derived products will be seized by U.S. Customs agents unless they're accompanied by an import license from a U.S. government agency. The same import rules apply even if you are returning from Puerto Rico, Hawaii, and the U.S. Virgin Islands.

For more specifics, visit the **U.S. Customs Service** website at **www.customs.gov**. Canadian citizens should look at the **Canada Border Services Agency** site (www.cbsa.gc.ca), and citizens of the U.K. should visit the **U.K. Customs and Excise** site (www.hmce.gov.uk).

The Cruise Experience

Cruise ships evolved from ocean liners, which were once the only way of crossing from point A to point B if there was an ocean in between. This was often no easy matter, entailing a real journey of several weeks, often in harsh winter weather. Competition quickly came down to two elements over which the shipping lines had some control: speed (get me off this damn ship as fast as possible) and comfort (don't rush on my account, I'm having a great time). While the former was great for businessmen in a rush, the latter had more intriguing possibilities, and it wasn't long before ship owners began offering pleasure cruises around scenic parts of the world, lavishing their passengers with shipboard comforts between ports of call. And thus the cruise industry was born.

Today, while the cruise experience varies from ship to ship, the common denominator is choice, with nonstop entertainment and activities, multiple dining options, and opportunities to be as sociable or private as you want to be. On most of the big ships, you can run from an aerobics class to ballroom dancing, then to a computer class or informal lecture, then to a wine tasting session or goofy poolside contest—all before lunch. On warm-weather itineraries you can choose to do nothing more than sunbathe in a quiet corner of the deck all day, and in Alaska you can camp out on deck with your binoculars, scanning for whales. It's your choice. In the pages that follow, we'll give you a taste of cruise life, starting from the beginning.

1 Checking In, Boarding & Settling into Your Cabin

It's cruise day. If you've flown to your city of embarkation, uniformed attendants will be standing at the ready at baggage claim, holding signs bearing your cruise line's or ship's name and waiting to direct you to buses bound for the terminal. You've probably already paid for these **transfers** when you bought your ticket. If not, you can arrange them now, or take a taxi to the ship. If you've driven to the port, it's just a matter of parking and trundling your luggage into the terminal. If it's still morning or early afternoon, don't feel rushed. Remember, another shipload of passengers is just getting off, and cabins still need to be cleaned, supplies loaded, and paperwork and Customs documents completed properly before you can board. Even if your ship has been berthed since 6am, new passengers are often not allowed on board until about 1pm, though lines are increasingly offering preboarding—which means you can get on at 11am or noon, have lunch, and start checking out the ship, though your cabin probably won't be ready till early afternoon. See chapter 9, "The Ports of Embarkation," for more information on flying, driving, and parking.

When you arrive at the port, you'll find an army of **porters** to help transport your luggage into the terminal—for a price (usually $2 per bag)—and another army of smiling cruise line employees waiting to direct you to the check-in desks. Once inside, your tagged luggage will be taken from you, scanned, and delivered to your cabin, sometimes arriving not long after you check in but more often showing up a few hours later. For this reason, it's a good idea to pack a small **essentials bag** you can carry on board with you, containing a change of clothes and maybe a swimsuit, plus a pair of sunglasses and any toiletries, medications, or other essentials you may need immediately.

Once in the terminal, you'll hand over your cruise tickets, show **ID** (two forms generally; see "Passports & Visas," in chapter 3, for information on acceptable ID), and give an imprint of your credit card to establish your **onboard account** (see "Money Matters," in chapter 3, for more on this). Depending upon when you arrive and the crowd situation, you may find yourself waiting in line for an hour or more, but usually it's less.

For security reasons, cruise lines do not allow unofficial **visitors** on board ship, so if friends or relatives brought you to the pier, you'll have to say your goodbyes on land.

Once on board, you may be guided to your **cabin** (you don't need to tip the person who leads you, though we usually give $1 or $2, especially if he's carried our bags), but in many cases you'll have to find it on your own. Soon after you do, your **cabin steward** will probably stop by to introduce him- or herself, inquire if the configuration of beds is appropriate (that is, whether you want separate twin beds or a pushed-together double), and give you his or her extension so that you can call if you need anything. If your steward doesn't put in an appearance, feel free to call housekeeping to request anything you need. The brochures and **daily programs** in your cabin will answer many questions you may have about the day's activities, the recommended dress for dinner that night, and what the ship's safety procedures are. There may also be a **deck plan** that will help you find your way around. If not, you can pick one up at the guest services desk—signs near the staircases and elevators should be able to guide you there.

With a few notable exceptions, cruise ships have **direct-dial telephones** in cabins, along with instructions on how to use them, and a directory of phone numbers for the departments or services on board. You can call anywhere in the world from most cabins' phones via satellite, but you'll break the bank to do it, with charges ranging from around $3 to about $15 a minute, with $8 or $9 being about average. It's cheaper to call home from your **cellphone** (if your ship is appropriately wired) or from a public telephone in port, or to send e-mail from the Internet center. (See "Keeping in Touch While at Sea," in chapter 3, for more info.)

Most ships sailing the Caribbean have North American–style **electrical outlets** (twin flat prongs, 110 AC current), and some have outlets for both European current (220 AC) and North American. Keep in mind, there's often only one outlet for your curling iron or hair dryer, and it's usually above the desk or dresser, rather than in the bathroom.

Most ships also have **in-cabin safes** for storing your valuables, usually operated via a self-set combination. On ships that don't offer them, you can usually check valuable items at the purser's desk.

A **lifeboat safety drill** will be held either just before or after sailing. It's required by the Coast Guard, and attendance is mandatory. Check to make sure your cabin has enough life preservers for everyone in your party, since you'll have to wear them to the drill. (Hope you look good in orange.) If you need extra—or for that matter, if you need additional blankets or pillows—let your steward know ASAP.

A History of Cruising

It wasn't until the late 19th century that British shipping companies realized they could make money not just by transporting travelers, cargo, mail, and immigrants from point A to point B, but also by selling a luxurious experience at sea. Most historians agree that the first cruise ship was Peninsular & Oriental Steam Navigation Company's *Ceylon*, which in 1881 was converted to a lavish cruising yacht for carrying wealthy, adventurous guests on world cruises. A few years later, in 1887, North of Scotland, Orkney & Shetland Steam Navigation's *St. Sunniva* was launched as the first steamer built expressly for cruising.

The Germans joined the cruise trade in 1891 when the Hamburg-America Line sent its *Augusta Victoria* on a Mediterranean cruise, and during the early 1900s, more and more players entered the picture, spending warmer seasons crossing the Atlantic and Pacific and offering pleasure cruises the rest of the year. During these boom years, competition became fierce between famous shipping lines such as **Cunard,** White Star, Hamburg-America, French Line, North German Lloyd, **Holland America,** Red Star Line, and others, which all sought to attract customers by building the largest, fastest, or most luxurious new vessels, with extravagant appointments you'd never find on a modern cruise ship—stained-glass ceilings, frescoes, ornate wooden stairways, and even plaster walls. (Oddly, onboard activities and entertainment were relatively sparse amid all the grandeur. Besides lavish social dinners, about the only pastimes were reading, walking around the deck, and sitting for musical recitals.) These same ships, with their first-class ballrooms, smoking lounges, and suites decorated with the finest chandeliers, oriental rugs, and artwork, also carried immigrants in inexpensive, bare-bones steerage accommodations, with second-class cabins available between these two polar extremes. This multiclass system survived until the late 1960s, and even today you can see vestiges of it in the *QM2*'s dining rooms, which are assigned to passengers depending on the level of cabin they book.

Soon after Cunard launched its popular 2,165-passenger *Mauretania* and *Lusitania* in 1906, the White Star Line's J. Bruce Ismay envisioned a trio of the largest and most luxurious passenger vessels ever built, designed to appeal to rich American industrialists. The first of these sisters, the 2,584-passenger, 46,000-ton *Olympic,* was in service by 1911, introduced with such fanfare that the 1912 launch of the second sister, *Titanic,* was not nearly as anticipated. Still, that ship soon became the most famous of all time, through the most tragic of circumstances. Vestiges of Ismay's dream ships survive today on Celebrity Cruise's *Millennium,* whose alternative restaurant is decorated with original carved wall panels from the *Olympic,* salvaged before the ship was scrapped in 1935.

The Brits and Germans continued building bigger and bigger ships up until **World War I,** when almost all vessels were requisitioned to carry soldiers, supplies, and weaponry. Many grand ships were lost in the conflict, including Cunard's *Lusitania* and the third of Ismay's trio, launched in 1914 as the *Britannic* and sunk by a mine in 1916.

After World War I, the popularity of cruising increased tremendously, and more ships were routed to the Caribbean and Mediterranean for long, expensive cruises—Cunard's *Mauretania* and its new running mate *Aquitania* were both yanked off the Atlantic for a millionaire's romp through the Med, carrying as few as 200 pampered passengers in the lap of luxury. As they headed to warmer climes, many ships' traditional black hulls were painted white to help them stay cool in those pre-air-conditioning days. This became a tradition itself, to the point where in the 1960s and 1970s nearly all ships sailing in the Caribbean and western Mexico were painted a dazzling white.

By the 1930s, shipboard activities and amenities were becoming much more sophisticated, with morning concerts, quoits, shuffleboard, bridge, Ping-Pong, motion pictures, and the first "swimming baths" (that is, pools) appearing on board, though these were often no more than burlap or canvas slung over wooden supports and filled with water. The first permanent outdoor pools appeared in the 1920s, and in the 1930s, the large outdoor pool on the *Rex* actually included a patch of sand to evoke Venice's Lido beach. When the great French liner *Normandie* made its maiden voyage in 1935, its first-class dining room boasted the cruising world's first air-conditioning system.

World War II saw the great liners again called into service. Cunard's *Queen Elizabeth* and *Queen Mary* and Holland America's *Nieuw Amsterdam* completed distinguished wartime service and sailed on into the postwar years, but many great liners never made it back to civilian life. *Normandie,* probably the greatest and most beautiful liner of all time, burned and capsized in New York while being converted into a troopship.

Shipboard travel boomed in the 1950s, and for the first time, pleasure cruising became accessible to the growing middle class, with onboard life enhanced by pool games, bingo, art classes, dance lessons, singles' parties, and midnight buffets—all of which you'll still find on ships today. By the 1960s, however, jet planes had replaced ships as the public's transportation of choice, and the boom was over. Increasingly expensive to maintain, many of the great 1950s liners were sent to the scrap yards.

The industry seemed doomed; but in the early 1960s, two Norwegian cargo and tanker ship operators, Christian and Knut Kloster, began offering Caribbean cruises aboard the 11,000-ton *Sunward* from a home port in Miami, and soon the Caribbean cruise trade exploded. **Royal Caribbean Cruise Line** was formed in January 1969, and in the late '60s and early '70s, Royal Viking, **Carnival, Princess, Costa,** and **Holland America** joined the lucrative circuit. It was in 1968, on board Costa's *Carla C.* (at the time chartered to Princess Cruises and sailing Mexican Riviera and Panama Canal cruises from Los Angeles) that American writer Jeraldine Saunders was inspired to write the novel *The Love Boat,* later made into a popular television series that introduced millions to cruising.

2 Exploring the Ports of Call: Shore Excursions vs. Going It on Your Own

How you spend your time in port can make the difference between a great cruise experience and a total, howling disappointment. The ports covered in this guide vary greatly, from quiet **undeveloped islands** such as Jost Van Dyke in the Caribbean, where yours will likely be the only ship in sight, to **bustling towns** such as Charlotte Amalie on St. Thomas and Ketchikan in Alaska, both of them jam-packed with ships and souvenir shops. Due to factors such as accessibility of local transportation, condition of roads, terrain, and the amount of time your ship is in port (which can range from 4 or 5 hr. to 10 or more), some ports are easy to **explore independently,** others less so. In the port chapters that come later in this guide, we'll advise you which ports of call are good bets for solo explorations (and whether you should go it on foot or by taxi, motor scooter, ferry, or otherwise) and where you should sign up for an **organized shore excursion.**

When it comes to going on your own, one downside is that you'll be forgoing the kind of narrative you get from a guide, and may miss out on some of the historical and cultural nuances of a particular attraction. On the other hand, you may find your own little nuances, things that an organized tour skips over as being too minor to bother with. Touring alone allows you to avoid groups and crowds, and hopefully connect with the destination in a more personal way. When going the solo route, though, be sure you know exactly when your ship departs for the next port—the captain won't wait forever if you're late, leaving you on your own to get to the next port of call.

Sometimes a port's real attractions may be miles (sometimes a lot of miles) from where your ship is docked—a common enough occurrence in Hawaii, Alaska, and Mexico's Yucatán Peninsula, among other places. In such cases, touring on your own could be an inefficient use of your time, entailing lots of hassles and planning, and possibly costing more. Here, the shore excursions offered by the cruise lines are a good way to go. Under each port review we'll run through a sampling of both the best excursions and the best sights and activities you can see and do on your own.

Shore excursions run the gamut, from snoresville bus tours and catamaran booze cruises to more stimulating options like snorkeling, jungle walks, whale-watching, and glacier helicopter treks. For those who like a little sweat in their port visit, there are more **physically challenging options** than ever, such as kayaking, horseback riding, mountain biking, dog-sledding, and river rafting. There's a decent selection of tours in all of the regions covered in this guide (generally at least 10–20 per port), with the greatest number offered in Alaska, Hawaii, and the Caribbean. Keep in mind that **shore-excursion prices** vary from line to line, even for the exact same tour. Also note that some cruise lines may not offer all these tours, while others may offer even more. Note also that the excursions can often fill up fast, especially on the megaships, so don't dawdle in signing up. When you receive your cruise documents and/or confirmation numbers, or at the latest when you board the ship, you'll get a listing of the excursions offered for your itinerary. To get a jump on things, most lines list their shore excursions on their website, and Carnival, Celebrity, Costa, Crystal, Disney, Holland America, NCL, Princess, Radisson Seven Seas, Royal Caribbean, and Silversea all allow you to **prebook or pre-reserve them,** either online or through some other system. It's a good option if you have your heart set on a particular site. If you change your mind once on board, cruise line policies vary, with some allowing you to switch to another tour or get an onboard credit for the amount, as long as you cancel out at least 24 hours in advance. Read the fine print before signing up.

If a tour offered by your ship is booked up, you can try to book it independently once you get to port. The popular Atlantis submarine tour, for example—offered at Grand Cayman, Nassau, St. Thomas, among others—usually has an office/agent in the cruise terminals or nearby. In Juneau, it's easy to walk over to the Mt. Roberts Tramway and buy a ticket yourself for the hull up the mountainside.

Other options include contacting an outside company, such as **Port Promotions** (www.portpromotions.com), at least a few weeks before your cruise. This tour company will arrange many of the same tours the lines do, often for a few bucks less, and also put together custom tours tailored to your group's needs. Port Promotions currently offers tours in the Caribbean, Alaska, Hawaii, and Europe.

3 A Typical Day at Sea: Onboard Activities

Most of the mainstream lines and the larger luxury ships offer an extensive schedule of activities throughout each day, especially during days at sea, when the ship isn't visiting a port. To keep track of the games, contests, lessons, and classes, ships print a **daily program,** which is placed in your cabin the previous evening, usually while you're at dinner. A cruise director and his or her staff are in charge of the festivities and do their best to ensure that a good time is had by all. As a general rule, the smaller the ship, the fewer the activities: Midsize ships like Oceania's *Regatta* and *Insignia* are intentionally low-key (as are most of the ultraluxury ships), while most of the small adventure lines shun organized activities unless they involve the nature, culture, and history of their destinations.

ONBOARD LEARNING OPPORTUNITIES

For years, lists of shipboard classes read as if they'd been lifted straight out of the Eisenhower-era home-entertainment playbook: napkin-folding, vegetable-carving, scarf-tying, mixology, and the like. Old habits die hard, so you'll still find these kinds of things aboard many ships, but in the past few years it seems that the cruise lines have finally started to catch up to the modern world. Today, most mega- and midsize ships also offer **informal lectures** on subjects such as personal investing, health and nutrition, the arts (and crafts), handwriting analysis, and computers (word processing, digital photography, website design, and so on). Don't expect to gain valuable life-skills or credits toward your college degree—these are mostly hourlong sessions, and tend to be pretty basic—but they make a nice addition to the day.

Many lines also feature **cooking demonstrations** and **wine-tasting seminars,** the former often resembling the kind you see on TV, complete with model kitchen and video monitors for an up-close view of the preparations. Wine tastings are usually conducted by the ship's sommeliers, though some lines bring aboard guest experts. There's usually a $5 to $15 charge for wine tastings. Royal Caribbean's *Navigator of the Seas* and *Mariner of the Seas* both have wine bars created in association with Mondavi and several other California vineyards. Classes in wine appreciation are held here throughout the week, and passengers can stage their own tastings by ordering special "wine flight" tasting menus.

Dance classes (most frequently salsa, country, and ballroom) are usually held several times a week, taught by one of the onboard entertainers. Staff from the gym, spa, and beauty salon offer frequent seminars on **health, beauty, and fitness,** with topics including skin and hair care, detox for weight loss, and wrinkle reductions. These seminars are free, but they have an ulterior motive: getting you to sign up for not-so-cheap spa treatments or buy expensive beauty products. Just remember: *You don't have to.*

Some of the mainstream lines are heading more in the enrichment direction than others. **Holland America,** for instance, is broadening its lecture series as part of its big "Signature of Excellence" push, and adding a special theater aboard each ship as a home for its culinary arts program. **Princess** launched its ScholarShip@Sea program in early 2003, offering courses in computers, photography, floral arranging, cooking, ceramics, arts and crafts, and specialized lectures (varying by voyage) that might include personal finance, nutrition, geography, natural history, wellness, the performing arts, marine biology, and maritime history, among others. **Celebrity Cruises** offers a similar program, with between two and five lecturers on each cruise.

In general, the ultraluxury lines have more refined and interesting enrichment programs. **Crystal**'s Creative Learning Institute (CLI), for example, offers classes targeted toward enhancing quality of life, and was developed in association with organizations and schools such as the Society of Wine Educators, Pepperdine University, Sotheby's, and Barnes&Noble.com, all of which provide lecturers. Offered year-round on every cruise, the program is divided into five "centers," including wine and food, arts and entertainment, business and technology, "lifestyle" (including floral design, interior design, book clubs, and language instruction by Berlitz), and "wellness." The wine and food seminars offered include Cocktail Making, Wine Appreciation, Chocolate, Spa Cuisine, and Beer Essentials. Aboard *Queen Mary 2*'s transatlantic crossings, **Cunard** is offering a similar program developed in association with Oxford University and featuring talks on history, global politics and cultural trends, theater, science, music, literature, and more.

ONBOARD GAMES

Sometimes you just have to let your hair down, and believe us, most cruises give you every opportunity. Almost all the mainstream lines continue a tradition of staging **wacky poolside contests** on days at sea, with passengers competing to see who can do the best belly-flop, who has the hairiest back, and who can stuff the most Ping-Pong balls into their bathing suits. Sometimes passengers are teamed up for relay races that require members to pass bagels to one another with their teeth. **Costa** is particularly big on this kind of thing, with their ridiculously good-looking "animation staffs" abetting passengers in games such as "Election of the Ideal Couple," which is less election than trial by ordeal. It's laugh-out-loud funny, staged at a frantic, circuslike pace.

And it's not just the classic party ships that let their hair down. At its weekly deck parties, Holland America sometimes features a team **water-bottle relay** in which one person chugs a bottle of water, and, as the line's description says, "puts it in their swim suit." The other team members each get a sponge, which they use to fill that bottle with ice water from a bucket on the other side of the deck. Other cruises might have a **ship-building contest,** with groups of passengers constructing vessels from junk they find around the ship, then sending them for sea trials in one of the hot tubs. Small-ship lines such as Cruise West even get in on this kind of action, with passengers using tabletop items to construct sculptures at one dinner a week. The winner gets a bottle of wine.

Game shows, such as the **Newlywed/Not-So-Newlywed Game,** are ever popular. Volunteer yourself or just listen to fellow passengers blurt out the truth about their personal lives—just like on *Oprah!* **Disney** and **Carnival** often stage very realistic game-show-type games, with buzzers, contestant podiums, and digital scorekeeping. On **Disney's** *Disney Magic,* the *Who Wants to Be a Mouseketeer* show rewards people who solve all 10 Disney trivia questions with a free 7-night cruise.

If you're a performer at heart, volunteer for the weekly **passenger talent show** held aboard many ships. Among the more bizarre displays we've seen: an elderly lady aboard *Norwegian Sun,* wearing red hot pants and heels and lip-synching Shirley Temple's "On the Good Ship Lollipop." Or, head to the nightclub and wiggle your way into the **hula-hoop or twist competitions.** Gaming fans can sign up for **trivia quizzes,** do puzzles, or join **chess, checkers, bridge, and backgammon tournaments.**

SHIPBOARD CASINOS & GAMES OF CHANCE

Almost every cruise ship has a **casino** (save for the small, adventure-oriented ships, the Disney ships, and NCL's *Pride of America* and *Pride of Aloha*). The biggest and flashiest are aboard the Carnival, Royal Caribbean, Costa, Celebrity, and Princess megaships, with literally hundreds of slot machines, and dozens of roulette, blackjack, poker, and craps tables. Smaller luxury lines such as Radisson and Seabourn have scaled-down versions, while the small adventure- and learning-oriented ships (those reviewed in chapter 8) have none at all. Stakes aboard most ships are relatively low, with maximum bets rarely exceeding $200. Average minimum bets at blackjack and poker tables are generally $5 or $10; the minimum at roulette is typically 50¢ or $1.

Ships are free to offer gambling in international waters, but local laws almost always require onboard casinos to close down whenever a ship is in port. Big gamblers should keep this in mind when cruising to Bermuda, where ships stay in port for 3 whole days, with no gambling whatsoever during that period. Also, Hawaii law prohibits casino gambling on ships sailing round-trip from the state, so there are no casinos on NCL's *Pride of America* and *Pride of Aloha.* In Alaska, where ships sail mostly in the protected waters of the Inside Passage, a dispensation allows shipboard casinos to stay open except when ships are within 3 miles of a port.

Children are not permitted to enter onboard casinos; the minimum age is generally 21.

Most ships also have a **card room,** which is usually filled with serious bridge or poker players and is occasionally supervised by a full-time instructor. Most ships furnish cards for free, although some charge $1 or so per deck. Another time-honored shipboard tradition is **horse racing,** a very goofy activity in which toy horses mounted on poles are moved around a track by hand, based on rolls of the dice. Passengers bet on the outcome, and the end of the cruise features an "owners cup" race and best-dressed-horse show.

ART AUCTIONS

You'll find shipboard art auctions either a fun way to buy pictures for your living room or an incredibly annoying and blatantly tacky way for the cruise lines to make more money by selling a lot of marginally interesting or just plain awful originals and some good but fantastically overpriced lithographs and animation cels to unsuspecting passengers—not that we're taking sides, of course. They're big business on mainstream and ultraluxury lines, held three or four times a week for an hour or 2 at a time. From a stage or in one of the ship's lounges, the auctioneer (a salesman for an outside company that arranges the shows) briefly discusses a selection of the hundreds of works displayed around the auction space, sometimes paintings by well-knowns such as Peter Max and Erté; lithographs by greats such as Dalí, Picasso, and Miró; animation cels, often by Disney; and many pieces by artists you've never heard of. The art, framed or unframed, is duty-free to U.S. citizens and is packed and mailed home to the winner. The one big plus about these auctions? **Free champagne,** and they'll keep bringing it to you whether you bid or not. Just look interested.

4 Keeping Fit: Gyms, Spas & Sports

Since the early 1990s, cruise lines have been making their spa and fitness areas bigger and more high-tech, moving them out of windowless corners of bottom decks and into prime top-deck positions with great views from floor-to-ceiling windows. The best of them—aboard the Celebrity, Royal Caribbean, Princess, Carnival, Norwegian, and Holland America ships—probably beat out your gym at home, with dozens of state-of-the-art workout machines, large aerobics rooms, spinning and yoga classes, and spa treatments that run from the basic to the bizarre. Sports areas are also getting super-sized on some ships, and options you'd never have imagined possible on a ship just a few years ago are becoming almost commonplace.

GYMS: AN ANTIDOTE TO THE MIDNIGHT BUFFET

The well-equipped **fitness centers** on the megaships may feature a dozen or more treadmills and just as many stationary bikes (some with virtual-reality screens!), step machines, upper- and lower-body machines, free weights, and aerobics rooms. Expect great gym facilities on Carnival's Conquest, Spirit, and Destiny classes; Princess's Grand and Coral classes; NCL's *Dawn, Spirit, Star, Jewel, Sun,* and *Pride of Aloha;* Royal Caribbean's Radiance- and Voyager-class ships; Holland America's Vista-class ships; and Celebrity's Millennium-class. Working out on your own is of course free, as are many basic aerobics and stretching classes, but if you want to take a trendier class such as boxing, spinning, Pilates, yoga, or tai chi, it'll usually cost you $10 a class. **Personal training sessions** are usually also available for around $75 a pop.

Older ships, usually those built before 1990, often do not devote nearly as much space and resources to fitness areas. Gyms on such ships are generally smaller and more spartan, but you'll find at least a couple of treadmills, a stationary bike or step machine, and some free weights on all but the smallest, most adventure-oriented cruise lines. On ships with limited or no gym facilities, aerobics and stretching classes will often be held out on deck or in a lounge.

ONBOARD SPORTS OPTIONS

If you're into sports, the megaships pack the most punch, with jogging tracks; outdoor volleyball, basketball, and paddle-tennis courts; plus several pools for water polo, volleyball, aqua aerobics, and swimming. The most mega of the megas—Royal Caribbean's enormous Voyager-class ships—go entirely off the deep end, packing a bona fide ice-skating rink, an outdoor rock-climbing wall, an in-line skating track, a full-size basketball court, miniature golf, and lots more. The rock-climbing walls have now been added to the entire RCI fleet, some of which have other cool sports options of their own. The Radiance-class ships, for instance, have gyro-balanced pool tables, and during her recent refurbishment *Enchantment of the Seas* was outfitted with bungee trampolines.

GOLF

In old movies, you always see the stars whacking golf balls off the backs of ships. Well, you can't do that anymore—the environment, you know—but today's ships are catering to golfers in other ways, and more than ever before. While practically all the major cruise lines offer some level of golf instruction or excursions, several go the extra mile.

For instance, **Carnival** (www.carnivalgolf.com), **Holland America** (www.holland americagolf.com), **Celebrity** (www.celebritycruisesgolf.com), **Seabourn** (www. seabourngolf.com), **Princess** (www.princessgolf.com), and **Silversea** (www.silversea golf.com) all feature programs created by Florida's Elite Golf Cruises (www.elitegolf cruises.com) that offer comprehensive onboard golf academies with various combinations of instruction, guided golf excursions in almost every port of call, and pro-shop-style extras. On board, **computer simulators** allow virtual play that mimics some three dozen of the world's top courses, including Scotland's St. Andrews, North Carolina's Pinehurst, and California's Pebble Beach. Using Microsoft Links software, the system analyzes every nuance of a golfer's swing to give a perfect real-time simulation of the shot on a 10-by-12-foot screen. The hitting mat even simulates different fairway conditions, from light rough to sand. Mini-competitions are held on most sea days for all levels of players, from beginners to serious competitors. Prices for the simulators range from $25 to $50 per person, per session. Elite Golf's relationship with Nike Golf offers guests **professional club fitting** on board, with options to rent or buy. Other Nike Golf products and apparel are also available on board.

The full Elite Golf program is currently available aboard Carnival's *Victory, Triumph, Destiny,* and *Inspiration;* Holland America's *Oosterdam, Zuiderdam, Westerdam,* and *Prinsendam;* Celebrity's *Century, Constellation, Galaxy, Infinity, Mercury, Millennium,* and *Summit;* and Princess's *Golden, Caribbean, Diamond,* and *Sapphire Princess* (with plans to go fleetwide this year). Though these lines' other ships aren't equipped for simulated play, almost all offer a full-time onboard golf professional who schedules private, couple, or group **lessons.** You can also have your stroke analyzed via V1 digital video coaching, which uses a split-screen to compare your stroke side-by-side with that of various golf legends—which could either be totally demoralizing or totally inspiring, depending on your frame of mind. In port, **golf excursions** bundle early debarkation, transportation, priority tee times, golf pro escort, cart rental, and greens fees into one excursion cost, with clubs and golf shoes available for demo, rental, or purchase if you don't want to lug your own. Days at sea may include clinics, demonstrations, and onboard putting contests. Professional tournaments and group golf events can also be arranged with Elite Golf Cruises on any of their golf academy vessels.

Elsewhere in cruise world, **SeaDream Yacht Club**'s 110-passenger vessels are equipped with golf simulators and Orlimar titanium drivers and irons. **Royal Caribbean** also offers golf simulators and miniature golf courses on their Radiance- and Voyager-class ships (with mini-golf also available on *Splendour* and *Legend of the Seas*), and arranges golf excursions in select ports.

Norwegian Cruise Line has gone big into golfing on its new Hawaii cruises, offering excursion packages at several courses each day, including Puakea, Poipu Bay, Princeville, and Kauai Lagoons (Kauai); Volcano Golf & Country Club, Mauna Lani Resort, Hapuna, and Big Island Country Club (Hawaii); and Makena, Elleair Maui, Wailea, and The Dunes at Maui Lani (Maui). Excursions run from $95 to $245 per person, or you can opt for an $850 package that includes play at Poipu Bay, Kauai Lagoons, Hapuna, Wailea, and The Dunes At Maui Lani. A wide variety of Callaway clubs are available for rent on board (as are golf shoes), and the onboard pro shop offers balls, hats, visors, gloves, shirts, and more.

SPORTS FOR COUCH POTATOES

No need for all you sports-loving couch potatoes to be deprived. Most megaships have **dedicated sports bars** with large-screen televisions broadcasting ESPN and whatever live games are available that day. Even those that don't have sports bars might outfit a public area or bar with televisions for viewing during popular sporting events such as the Super Bowl. If you want to watch the game from the comfort of your cabin, no problem: **ESPN** is available on cabin TVs on most of the mainstream and ultraluxe lines.

ONBOARD SPAS: TAKING RELAXATION ONE STEP FURTHER

If your idea of a heavenly vacation is stripping down to a towel and having someone rub mystery oil over your whole body, choose a cruise ship with a well-stocked spa. It won't be hard. For the past 15 years, spas have been big business on cruise ships, and have gotten progressively more amazing as the years have gone on. The largest, newest, and best are perched on top decks and boast great views from 8 or 10 treatment rooms, where you can choose from dozens of massages, mud packs, facials, and even teeth whitening, as well as some much more esoteric treatments, many of allegedly Asian origin, many offered as part of high-priced packages.

If you've taken a few cruises and noticed that the spas on different lines look suspiciously alike, that's because almost all of them (as well as the ships' hair salons) are staffed and operated by the London-based firm **Steiner Leisure.** NCL, Oceania, and Silversea's spas are operated by a company called **Mandara,** but (surprise!) they're owned by Steiner, too. Companies bucking the Steiner hegemony include Radisson Seven Seas (whose spas are run by **Carita**), Cunard (whose *QM2* spa is run by **Canyon Ranch**), and Star Clipper's *Royal Clipper,* which is an entirely in-house operation.

The young, mostly British women (and occasionally men) Steiner employs are professional and charming in their little green outfits, but we've found the quality of the treatments to be inconsistent. As at any spa, on land or sea, your enjoyment is literally in the hands of the individual therapist, and their level of experience and finesse. Overall, we've found that **massages** are a pretty safe bet, whether you choose a standard neck massage, a full-body shiatsu massage, or a deep-tissue sports massage (which can verge on painful but gives you the most bang, wallop, and burn for your buck). The highest profile massage today is the **hot lava stone massage,** in which the therapist rubs you down with heated river rocks and oil—think soothing rather than invigorating.

We've found other treatments to often be disappointing and not worth the money—unless you live in a place where access to unusual spa and beauty treatments is limited. For the same fifty bucks you spend on a pedicure aboard ship you could get two much better ones in New York, but if you live in, say, rural North Dakota? Well, it's your vacation. Live it up.

A word about some of the more exotic and expensive treatments, such as electrode facials and **Ionithermie** slimming/detox, which allegedly stimulates cells, releases toxins, and contributes directly to weight loss: Whenever we've asked for details, it's clear most spa staffers don't have much of a clue about them beyond the descriptions they've memorized. We suspect—and this is just our opinion, mind you—that that's because they're a load of hooey.

Here's a sampling of treatments and their standard Steiner rates:

- 25-minute Swedish massage: $60 to $72
- 50-minute full-body massage: $89 to $128
- 75-minute hot stone massage: $142 to $190
- 50-minute facial: $89 to $109
- Manicure: $25 to $44
- Pedicure: $40 to $61

Note that rates for identical treatments can vary by as much as $20 from ship to ship. Treatments are charged to your onboard account. Usually they do not include a **gratuity,** but on a few lines Steiner does add them directly to your bill. Before you sign, ask your therapist or the desk attendant whether a tip is included, and write one in if not. Of course, if you were unhappy with your treatment, you're not required to tip at all.

It's almost guaranteed that at the end of your session, just as you're coming out of semiconscious trance, your Steiner or Mandara therapist will give you an itemized list of expensive **creams, exfoliants, moisturizers, toners,** and **masks** that will help you get the spa effect at home—all for just a couple hundred bucks. In fact, on a recent *Norwegian Dawn* cruise, Heidi's massage therapist spent a whopping 15 minutes telling her how Gwyneth Paltrow and the other stars swore by the $124 Elemis face cream she was pushing. Enough already. The products are often very good, but the sales pitch is just a little too shameless. So, remember our mantra: *You can say no*— unless, of course, you're in a spending mood. See "Best Ships for Spa-Goers" in the "Best of Cruising" chapter to see which ships have the best facilities.

Tip: Make your spa appointments on the 1st day out to snag the best times.

5 Programs for Kids & Teens

With the cruise lines in overdrive to please the little people these days, kids amenities and services rival those offered for adults. Dedicated playrooms, camplike counselors, computers, state-of-the-art video arcades, pools, and new teen centers have most kids so gaga for cruising, you'll have to drag them away kicking and screaming at the end of the week. Even if your kids are too young to join the programming (which typically starts at age 2 or 3), there are more options than ever. In this age of play dates, it's no surprise that a line, Royal Caribbean, recently introduced daily 45-minute **playgroups** for infants, toddlers, and parents.

The youngest kids frolic in toy- and game-stocked **playrooms,** listen to stories, and go on treasure hunts; older kids keep busy with arts and crafts, **computer games,** lip-sync competitions, pool games, volleyball, and now many more educational activities focused on art, science, music, and exercise. There's usually a TV showing movies throughout the day, and, for the younger ones, there are ball bins and plastic jungle gyms to crawl around in. Many megaships have shallow kiddie pools for diaper-trained young'ins, sometimes sequestered on an isolated patch of deck.

The newest ships of the mainstream lines invite hard-to-please **teens** to hang out in their very own space, complete with a dance floor, bar (nonalcoholic of course), video wall for movie watching, video arcade, and sometimes private Internet area. The best facilities are on the *Carnival Valor, Glory,* and *Conquest; Disney Wonder* and *Magic;* Royal Caribbean's Voyager and Radiance classes; *Norwegian Dawn* and *Star;* and the *Grand, Golden, Star,* and *Caribbean Princess.*

See "Cruises for Families" in chapter 1 for more details, including information on **babysitting.**

6 Onboard Dining Options

In no other area is cruising experiencing as much change as in its dining rituals. In just the past 5 or 6 years, traditional five-course, assigned-seating meals in formal dining rooms have been overshadowed on many vessels by the numerous **casual dining options** that allow passengers not only to dress down but also to dine with complete flexibility, choosing when, with whom, and where they want to eat, with several different restaurant options. In mid-2000, **Norwegian Cruise Line** got the ball rolling with its Freestyle Cruising arrangement, which boils down to passengers being able to dine anytime between 5:30pm and midnight in any of several venues, with the last seating at 10pm. **Oceania Cruises**' much smaller ships operate on essentially the same system, and **Princess**'s "Personal Choice" dining scheme offers passengers the option of choosing flexible or traditional dining.

Formal or casual aside, the bottom line is that cruise lines are willing to feed you till you pop, and these days are offering more and more cuisine options, too. On the megaships, you can get elegant **multicourse meals** served in grand two- and three-story dining rooms; make reservations at an intimate specialty restaurant for Asian, Italian, French, Tex-Mex, Pacific Northwest, or Creole cuisine; drop in at the ship's buffet restaurant or cafe for an ultracasual meal; hit the **midnight buffet** or take in some **24-hour** pizza, ice cream, pastries, and specialty coffees, with some sushi to top it all off. Carnival offers pizza, Caesar salad, and garlic rolls 24 hours a day, and many lines now deliver pizza to your cabin! Disney has a burger and hot dog counter by the pool, and Royal Caribbean's Voyager-class ships have entire 1950s-style diners out on deck. The midsize ships generally have fewer choices, though Oceania's vessels, which carry only 684 passengers apiece, have four different venues at dinner, including Italian and steakhouse specialty restaurants and an alfresco restaurant serving Spanish dishes. The ultraluxe lines are offering alternatives, too.

All but the most cost-conscious cruise lines will attempt to satisfy reasonable culinary requests, so if you follow a **special diet,** inform your line as early as possible, preferably when booking your cruise, and make sure they'll be able to satisfy your request at all three meals. **Vegetarian dishes** and a selection of **healthier, lighter meals** (usually called "spa cuisine" or "light and healthy options") are available as a matter of course on just about every ship at breakfast, lunch, and dinner, and several lines, including Carnival, Crystal, and Royal Caribbean, also offer **low-carb** meals. Most lines offer kosher options at meals, but you'll get better choices at **Chosen Voyage,** 5812 Hobart St., Pittsburgh, PA 15217 (© **877/462-4673;** www.chosenvoyage. com), a company that charters small and midsize ships and adapts all the kitchens and dining rooms on board for kosher cooking.

Some of the small-ship lines need advance notice for any special requests. Most large ships will provide kosher and halal meals if requested in advance, but expect them to be prepackaged.

TRADITIONAL DINING

Though casual and specialty dining are all the rage, most ships still continue to offer formal, **traditional dinners** in at least one restaurant, generally from about 6:30 to 10pm. Ships carrying fewer than 400 passengers generally have one **open-seating dinner,** where guests can stroll in when they want and sit with whomever they choose. Those carrying more than 400 passengers typically have two **assigned seatings** in one or more main dining rooms. Under Princess's flexible dining plan, its ships offer a combination of both, with one or more restaurants on each ship offering open restaurant-style seating and another offering traditional early and late seating. Disney, which gained a reputation early on for being more Disney than cruise line, puts a unique twist on things by offering two seatings in three main themed dining rooms that passengers and their servers rotate through over the course of the cruise.

Most ships still require you to reserve either the early or late seating (sometimes called 1st and 2nd seating) when booking your cruise. **Early seating** (served at around 6:30pm) is for those who prefer dining early and are ready to leave the table once the dishes are cleared. Elderly passengers and families with children tend to choose this seating. If you choose **late seating** (served at around 8:30pm), you won't have to rush through pre-dinner showering and dressing after an active day in port, and the meal tends to be more leisurely, allowing you to linger over coffee and after-dinner drinks.

If you get assigned to the first seating and you want the second, or vice versa (or you get no assignment at all), see the maitre d' staff, who will probably have a table set up in the dining room during your initial embarkation for this purpose. Most can accommodate your wishes, if not on the first night of sailing, then on the second. Ditto if you find that you don't get along with your assigned tablemates. Most of the time you'll be seated at a table for between 4 and 10 people. If you want privacy, you can request a table for two, but unless you're sailing aboard one of the smaller, more upscale ships, don't get your hopes up, as couples' tables are usually few and far between.

Seven-night cruises offering traditional dining generally have 2 **formal nights** per week, when the dress code in the main dining room calls for dark suits or tuxedos for men and cocktail dresses or fancy pantsuits for women (but remember, on most ships you can dine casually in the buffet restaurant any evening and skip the formal stuff). Other nights in the main dining rooms are designated informal and/or casual. Ten- to 14-night cruises have 3 formal nights. (See "Packing for the Different Cruise Climates," in chapter 3, for more information.)

Though some ships still offer early and late seatings for breakfast and lunch (served around 7 and 8:30am and noon and 1:30pm, respectively), most ships are now offering open-seating setups within certain hours.

Smoking is prohibited in virtually all ships' dining rooms.

SPECIALTY DINING

Variety + intimacy = specialty dining. Over the past several years, all the mainstream lines and most of the luxe lines have retooled their ships' interiors to make room for a greater number of small, alternative dining venues, where 100 guests or so can sample various international cuisines with sometimes elaborate presentations. Following the trend of socking passengers with extra charges to make up for lower fares, the cost for dining at most of these restaurants ranges from $10 up to the more typical $20 to $25 per person. Frankly, sometimes the food isn't any better than in the main dining rooms (especially in Holland America's, Carnival's, and Costa's specialty restaurants), but the venues are at least quieter and more intimate. The best, without a doubt, are on the Celebrity, Crystal, Silversea, and Radisson ships. NCL also gets special mention for having so damn many of them—six, on the line's newest ships, plus casual choices. Here's what's available on each of the lines.

Specialty Dining: Who's Got What

Cruise Line & Ships	Type of Specialty Restaurants	Extra Charge
Carnival		
Spirit and Conquest classes	Steakhouse/Seafood	$25 per person
Celebrity		
Millennium class	Continental	$30 per person
Costa		
Costa Atlantica, Costa Mediterranea	Italian	$23 per person
Crystal		
Crystal Serenity	Asian, Sushi, Italian	"suggested" $6 tip
Cunard		
Queen Mary 2	Mediterranean	$30 per person
	Chef's Galley	$30 per person
	Italian, Asian, Carvery	No extra charge
Disney		
Disney Magic, Disney Wonder	Italian	$10 per person
Holland America		
Fleetwide	Pacific Northwest	$20
Norwegian		
Dawn, Star, Spirit	Steakhouse	$20 per person
	French/Continental	$15
	Pan-Asian	$12.50
	Sushi	a la carte pricing, $10–$15
	Teppanyaki	a la carte pricing, $10–$15
	Tapas, Italian	no extra charge
Majesty, Dream, Wind, Crown	French/Continental	$15 per person
Pride of Aloha	Pan-Asian, Italian	$12.50 per person
	French/Continental,	$15 per person
Pride of America	Pan-Asian, Italian	$12.50 per person
	French/Continental,	$15 per person
	Steakhouse	$20 per person
Sun	Italian	$12.50 per person
	French/Continental,	$15 per person
	Pan-Asian,	$15 per person
	Sushi, Teppanyaki	a la carte pricing, $10–$15
	Tapas	no extra charge
Oceania		
Regatta, Insignia	Italian, Steakhouse	no extra charge

Cruise Line & Ships	Type of Specialty Restaurants	Extra Charge
Princess		
Caribbean Princess	Italian trattoria	$20
	Steakhouse	$15
	Caribbean	no extra charge
Diamond, Sapphire	Italian, Steakhouse, Southwestern, Asian	no extra charge
	Italian trattoria	$20 per person
Golden, Grand, Star	Italian trattoria	$20 per person
	Steakhouse	$15 per person
Coral, Island Princess	Italian trattoria	$20 per person
	Steakhouse	$15 per person
Sun class	Steakhouse	$15 per person
	Sit-down pizzeria	no extra charge
Radisson		
Seven Seas Mariner	French, International	no extra charge
Seven Seas Voyager	French, American	no extra charge
Navigator	Italian	no extra charge
Royal Caribbean		
Radiance class	Italian, Steakhouse	$20 per person
Voyager class, Empress of the Seas	Italian	$20 per person
Seabourn		
Legend, Pride	Asian, Mediterranean, Steakhouse*	no extra charge
Silversea		
Shadow, Whisper	Italian and Mediterranean	no extra charge

* Seabourn hosts varying theme nights in one restaurant aboard each ship.

CASUAL DINING

If you'd rather skip the formality and hubbub of the main dining room, all but the tiniest ships serve breakfast, lunch, and dinner in a **casual, buffet-style cafe restaurant,** so you never have to put on a tie if you don't want to. Usually located on the Lido Deck, with indoor and outdoor poolside seating, these restaurants serve a spread of both hot and cold items. On the megas, a grill may be nearby where, at lunchtime, you can get burgers, hot dogs, and often chicken and veggie-burgers; sometimes you can find specialty stations offering taco fixings, deli sandwiches, or Chinese food, too. On most ships, breakfast and lunch buffets are generally served for a 3- to 4-hour period, so guests can stroll in and out whenever they desire, but many of the mainstream lines also keep portions of their Lido cafes open almost round the clock. Most lines serve dinner buffet-style nightly as well in the Lido restaurants, but some offer a combination of sit-down service and buffet.

BETWEEN-MEAL SNACKING

If hunger pangs get the best of you between lunch and dinner, almost all the mega- and midsize ships have complimentary **pizzerias** (24 hr. daily on Carnival's ships) and **self-serve frozen yogurt and ice-cream machines** (usually free, with a few exceptions like Princess), as well as cafes or coffee shops where you can grab a snack, sandwich, or specialty coffee (the latter, plus ultrarich cakes and pastries, at an extra charge). The upscale lines and some of the mainstreamers (such as Celebrity, Princess, Oceania, and Holland America) offer **afternoon tea service,** serving finger sandwiches, pastries, and cookies along with tea and coffee. Carnival and several others do their own, less fancy versions. Most of the small-ship lines serve **pre-dinner snacks and hors d'oeuvres** on deck or in the main lounge or bar area.

The **midnight buffet,** a staple of cruising back in the '80s and '90s, has been scaled back in recent years, in part because so many casual dining options are available for late-night snacking. Today, you'll usually find it offered in all its overwhelming extravagance only once or twice a week on most lines, with heaps of elaborately decorated fruits, vegetables, pastries, cold cuts, pasta, and sometimes shrimp and other treats, with an ice sculpture to top off the festive mood. Sometimes the nighttime feast will be focused on a culinary theme, such as Tex-Mex, Caribbean, or chocolate. On nights when there's no buffet, smaller **snack stations** will be set up instead, or servers will cruise the ships with trays of hors d'oeuvres—which keeps drinkers where the cruise lines want them: at the bar, running up their tabs.

If you'd rather not leave your cabin, most ships offer **24-hour room service** from a limited menu. Suite guests can often order the same meals being served in the dining room delivered to their rooms course by course.

7 Onboard Entertainment

Entertainment is a big part of the cruise experience on almost all ships, but especially on the megaships of Carnival, Royal Caribbean, Celebrity, Costa, Princess, NCL, and Holland America, which all offer an extensive variety throughout the day. Afternoons, you can dance on deck with the **live dance band,** which we'll lay 10-to-1 will be jamming calypso music or tunes by Bob Marley and Jimmy Buffett. Or put on your waltzing shoes and head inside to one of the lounges for some **swing dancing.** Lines such as Holland America, Crystal, NCL, Oceania, and Royal Caribbean often feature a 1940s-style big band playing dance tunes. One of the most pleasant concerts we've seen aboard a ship was in the atrium's Aquarium Bar on RCI's *Voyager of the Seas,* where a trio played big band and classical stuff that so inspired two passengers, that they got up and joined the musicians, belting out Italian opera songs like real pros. A huge crowd gathered to watch; it was really good.

Pre-dinner entertainment starts to heat up around 5pm, and continues all night to accommodate passengers dining early and late. Head to the **piano bar** for a cocktail or do some pre-dinner dancing to some small-group jazz.

Usually twice in any weeklong cruise, there's apt to be **Vegas-style musical revues** performed early and late in the main show lounge, with a flamboyant troupe of anywhere from 4 to 16 feather-boa-and-sequin-clad male and female dancers sliding, kicking, and lip-synching as a soloist or two belts out show tunes and pop faves. Expect a lot of Andrew Lloyd Webber, "YMCA," at least one tune each from *Grease, Footloose,* and *A Chorus Line,* and maybe a few Rodgers and Hammerstein classics thrown in for class. A live orchestra accompanies most of these productions, though unfortunately not all (recorded music is used on Holland America's Vista-class ships, for example). While the quality of these shows industry-wide is inconsistent, opinion here at Casa Frommer's is divided on the whole revue format, with Heidi enjoying the medleys "if the singing's good—which, granted, it isn't always" and Matt thinking most of them are "all flash and no substance." Two lines we can agree on, though, are Disney and NCL. Disney offers absolutely the best shows at sea, with characters and stories based on its parent company's classic films. Recent shows on NCL are also standouts, with strong soloists and really original staging, choreography, and choice of material.

Nights when the shows aren't scheduled may feature a **magic show** complete with sawing in half a scantily clad assistant and pulling rabbits from a hat; **acrobatic acts** and **aerialists** (always a big hit); **headline soloists,** some of them quite good (such as singer Jane L. Powell, a perennial NCL favorite whose amazing range takes her from Louis Armstrong to Bette Midler); or **guest comedians or specialty acts,** such as Costa's regular operatic recitals, Oceania's pianists, and Royal Caribbean's a cappella singing groups. **Comedians** frequently perform in the main theater or a second performance space, sometimes doing PG- and R-rated material at an early show and then running the X up the mast at an adults-only midnight performance. Raising the humor bar, Norwegian Cruise Line recently announced a partnership with the famed Second City improv comedy group.

The **disco** gets going on most ships around 9 or 10pm and works it until 2 or 3am or sometimes later. Sometimes a live band plays until about midnight, when a DJ takes over until the wee hours, spinning tunes from the '70s through to today; sometimes there's only a DJ. A **karaoke session** may also be thrown in for an hour or 2 in the afternoon or evening.

An alternative to the disco or the main show may be a pianist or jazz trio in one of the ship's romantic nightspots, or a **themed party** such as NCL's Miami salsa bash or the '50s sock hops put on by many lines. For a quiet evening, lines such as Holland America, Celebrity, Crystal, and Disney have cinemas showing **recent-release movies.**

To prove not all innovative entertainment has to be big, Celebrity features **strolling vocal quartets** that roam around the ships in the evening, performing wherever people are gathered. Celebrity has also introduced an intriguing, difficult-to-put-into-words performance inspired by fantasy circus troupe **Cirque du Soleil,** a partner in the new entertainment offering. Taking place nightly in the observation lounges on the *Constellation* and *Summit,* which are appropriately decorated for the occasion, outrageously costumed dancers perform and interact with guests. On Royal Caribbean's Voyager-class ships, a troupe of **clowns** performs impromptu juggling, acrobatic, and comedy routines in various public areas. At different points of the cruise they also give juggling lessons and provide a little talk on clown history and technique. Big thumbs up! Along similar lines, on a recent Carnival *Valor* cruise, a couple of entertainers high up on stilts danced and waved around windsocklike flags on the pool deck. Ships carrying 100 to 400 passengers have fewer entertainment options and a more mellow evening ambience overall. The high-end lines may feature a quartet or pianist performing before dinner and maybe a small-scale song-and-dance revue afterward, plus dancing in a quiet lounge. The small adventure-oriented ships may at most have a solo performer before and after dinner, or **local musicians and/or dancers** aboard for an afternoon or evening.

8 Shopping Opportunities on Ship & Shore

Even the smallest ships have at least a small shop on board selling T-shirts, sweatshirts, and baseball caps bearing the cruise line logo. The big new megaships, though, are like minimalls, offering as many as 10 different stores selling items such as toiletries and sundries (film, toothpaste, candy, paperback books, even condoms), as well as totes, **T-shirts,** mugs, toys, key chains, and other cruise line logo souvenirs. You'll find **formal wear** such as sequined dresses and jackets, silk dresses and scarves, purses, satin shoes, cummerbunds, ties, and tuxedo shirts, as well as perfume, cosmetics, jewelry (costume and the real stuff), and porcelain figurines.

A few ships have **name-brand stores.** Many of Carnival's ships, for instance, have Fossil boutiques on board, selling mostly watches. The Disney ships, of course, have shops selling Disney souvenirs, clothing, and toys. And appropriately, Cunard's new *QM2* has a Harrods shop offering lots of those cute stuffed bears, green totes, and biscuits. The high-end lines, such as Silversea, Crystal, and Radisson, have boutiques selling fine jewelry, bags, and accessories (many cuts, and dollars, above the standard stuff sold on mainstream lines).

All merchandise sold on board while a ship is at sea is **tax-free** (though you must declare them at Customs when returning to the U.S.); to maintain that tax-free status, the shops are closed whenever a ship is in port. Prices can vary, though; and just like a resort, items such as disposable cameras, sunscreen, candy, and snack foods will cost substantially more than you'd pay at home. On the other hand, by midcruise there are often decent sales on things like T-shirts, tote bags, jewelry, and booze.

See "Best Shopping Cruises" in "The Best of Cruising" chapter for the best shopping islands.

Before each port of call, the cruise director or shore-excursion manager gives a **port talk** about that place's attractions and shopping. Now, it's no secret that many cruise lines have mutually beneficial deals with certain shops in every port (generally of the touristy chain variety), so on the big, mass-market ships especially, the vast majority of the port info disseminated will be about shopping. Better bring along your own guidebook (this one!) if you want information on history or culture. The lines often recommend a list of shops in town where they say the merchandise is guaranteed, and if the stone falls out of the new ring you bought at one of them once you get home, the cruise lines say they'll try to help you get a replacement. Don't hold your breath, though; the whole thing is a bit ambiguous. If you're not an expert on jewelry or whatever else it is you want to buy, it may be safer to shop at these stores; however, you won't get much of a taste for the local culture in one of them. Browsing at outdoor markets and in smaller craft shops is a better way to get an idea of the port's local flavor.

Part 2

The Cruise Lines & Their Ships

Detailed, in-depth reviews of all the cruise lines sailing from U.S. and Canadian home ports and a few Caribbean islands, with discussions of the type of experience they offer and the lowdown on all their ships.

5

The Ratings & How to Read Them

The following three chapters are the heart and soul of this book, our expert reviews and ratings of the cruise lines operating in the American market. This chapter is your instruction manual, with hints on how to use the reviews to compare the lines and find the one that's right for you.

1 Cruise Line Categories

To make your selection easier (and to make sure you're not comparing apples and oranges), we've divided the cruise lines into three distinct categories, given each category a chapter of its own, and rated each line only in comparison with the other lines in its category (see more about this in "How to Read the Ratings," below). The categories are as follows:

THE MAINSTREAM LINES (chapter 6) This category includes the most prominent players in the industry, the jack-of-all-trades lines with the biggest ships, carrying the most passengers and providing the most diverse cruise experiences to suit many different tastes, from party-hearty to elegant and refined. With all the competition in the industry today, these lines tend to offer good prices, too. Mixed in among these lines you'll find a few oddballs, including budget lines and midsize European lines.

THE ULTRALUXURY LINES (chapter 7) These are the Dom Perignon of cruises, offering elegant, refined, and doting service, extraordinary dining, spacious cabins, and high-toned entertainment aboard intimate, finely appointed small and midsize vessels—and at a high price.

SOFT-ADVENTURE LINES & SAILING SHIPS (chapter 8) If you don't like crowds; want an experience that revolves around nature, history, or culture; want to visit out-of-the-way ports; or prefer quiet conversation to a large ship's roster of activities, these small, casual ships may be your cup of tea.

2 Reading the Reviews & Ratings

Each cruise line's review begins with **The Line in a Nutshell** (a quick word about the line in general) and **The Experience,** which is just what it says: a short summation of the kind of cruise experience you can expect to have aboard that line, followed by a few major **pros and cons.** The **Ratings Table** judges the individual elements of the line's cruise experience compared with the other lines in the same category (see below for ratings details). The text that follows fleshes out these summations, providing all the details you need to get a feel for what kind of vacation the cruise line will give you.

The individual **ship reviews** give you details on each vessel's accommodations, facilities, amenities, comfort level, upkeep, and vital statistics—size, passenger capacity, year launched and most recently refurbished, number of cabins, number of crew, and so on—to help you compare. Size is described in terms of **gross register tonnage (GRT),** which is a measure not of actual weight but of the interior space (or volume) used to produce revenue on a ship: 1 GRT equals 100 cubic feet of enclosed, revenue-generating space. By dividing the GRTs by the number of passengers aboard, we arrive at the **passenger/space ratio,** which gives you some idea of how much elbowroom you'll have on each ship. To compare the amount of personalized service you can expect, we have the **passenger/crew ratio,** which tells you approximately how many passengers each crewmember is expected to serve—though this doesn't literally mean a waiter for every two or three passengers, since "crew" includes everyone from officers to deckhands to shop clerks.

Note that when several vessels are members of a class—built on the same design, with usually only minor variations in decor and attractions—we've grouped the ships together into one **class review.**

HOW TO READ THE RATINGS

To make things easier on everyone, we've developed a simple ratings system based on the classic customer-satisfaction survey, rating both the cruise line as a whole and the individual ships as poor, fair, good, excellent, or outstanding on a number of important qualities. The **cruise line ratings** cover all the elements that are usually consistent from ship to ship within the line (overall enjoyability of the experience, dining, activities, children's program, entertainment, service, and value), while the **individual ship ratings** cover those things that vary from vessel to vessel—quality and size of the cabins and public spaces, comfort, cleanliness and maintenance, decor, number and quality of dining options, gyms/spas (or, for the small-adventure lines that don't have gyms and spas, "Adventure & Fitness Options"), and children's facilities—plus a rating for the overall enjoyment of the onboard experience. To provide an **overall score,** we've given each ship an overall star rating (for example, ★★★½) based on the combined total of our poor-to-outstanding ratings, translated into a 1-to-5 scale:

1	=	Poor	4	=	Excellent
2	=	Fair	5	=	Outstanding
3	=	Good			

In instances where the category doesn't apply to a particular ship (for example, none of the adventure ships has children's facilities), we've simply noted "not applicable" (N/A) and absented the category from the total combined score, as these unavailable amenities would be considered a deficiency only if you plan to travel with kids.

Now for a bit of philosophy: The cruise biz today offers a profusion of experiences so different that comparing all lines and ships by the same set of criteria would be like comparing a Park Avenue apartment to an A-frame in Aspen. That's why, to rate the cruise lines and their ships, we've used a **sliding scale,** rating lines and ships on a curve that compares them only with others in their category—mainstream with mainstream, luxe with luxe, adventure with adventure. Once you've determined what kind of experience is right for you, you can look for the best ships in that category based on your particular needs. For example, if you see in the "Small Ships, Sailing Ships & Adventure Cruises" chapter that Windstar achieves an "outstanding" rating for dining, that

continues

Ships at a Glance

Cruise Line	Ship	Frommer's Star Rating	Year Built
ACCL (soft adventure): A family-owned New England line operating tiny, no-frills ships that travel to offbeat places, carrying casual, down-to-earth older passengers.	**Grande Caribe**	★★★	1997
	Grande Mariner	★★★	1998
	Niagara Prince	★★★	1994
American Safari Cruises (soft adventure): The most luxurious of the small-ship soft-adventure lines.	**Safari Escape**	★★★★	1983
	Safari Quest	★★★★	1992
	Safari Spirit	★★★★	1981
Carnival (mainstream): The Wal-Mart of cruising, Carnival specializes in colorful, jumbo-size resort ships that deliver plenty of bang for the buck. If you like the flash of Vegas and the party-hearty atmosphere of New Orleans, you'll love Carnival's brand of flamboyant fun.	**Carnival Conquest**	★★★★½	2002
	Carnival Destiny	★★★★½	1996
	Carnival Glory	★★★★½	2003
	Carnival Legend	★★★★	2002
	Carnival Liberty	★★★★½	2005
	Carnival Miracle	★★★★	2004
	Carnival Pride	★★★★	2001
	Carnival Spirit	★★★★	2001
	Carnival Triumph	★★★★½	1999
	Carnival Valor	★★★★½	2004
	Carnival Victory	★★★★½	2000
	Celebration	★★★	1987
	Ecstasy	★★★½	1991
	Elation	★★★½	1998
	Fantasy	★★★½	1990
	Fascination	★★★½	1994
	Holiday	★★★	1985
	Imagination	★★★½	1995
	Inspiration	★★★½	1996
	Paradise	★★★½	1998
	Sensation	★★★½	1993

* *Tonnage calculations for small ships are often calculated differently than those of larger ships, making passenger/space figures difficult to gauge.*

Gross Tonnage	Passenger Capacity (Double Occupancy)	Passenger/Space Ratio	Passenger/Crew Ratio	Wheelchair Access	Sailing Regions	Full Review on Page
99	100	N/A*	5.5 to 1	no	Intracoastal Waterway, Caribbean, Chesapeake Bay, Erie Canal/Hudson River, New England Islands	334
99	100	N/A*	5.5 to 1	no	Intracoastal Waterway, Panama Canal, Erie Canal/Great Lakes, New England Islands	334
99	60	N/A*	5 to 1	no	Mississippi River, Erie Canal/ Great Lakes, Maine Coast, Hudson River/Lake Champlain, Intracoastal Waterway	334
N/A*	12	N/A*	2 to 1	no	Pacific Northwest/ British Columbia, Alaska	340
99	22	N/A*	2 to 1	no	Mexico/Sea of Cortez, Alaska, Pacific Northwest, California Wine Country	340
N/A*	12	N/A*	1.7 to 1	no	Pacific Northwest, Alaska	340
110,000	2,974	37	2.5 to 1	yes	Caribbean	121
101,353	2,642	38.5	2.6 to 1	yes	Caribbean	127
110,000	2,974	37	2.5 to 1	yes	Caribbean	121
88,500	2,124	41.5	2.3 to 1	yes	Caribbean	124
110,000	2,974	37	2.5 to 1	yes	Caribbean	121
88,500	2,124	41.5	2.3 to 1	yes	Caribbean	124
88,500	2,124	41.5	2.3 to 1	yes	Mexican Riviera	124
88,500	2,124	41.5	2.3 to 1	yes	Mexican Riviera, Hawaii, Alaska	124
102,000	2,758	37	2.6 to 1	yes	Caribbean	127
110,000	2,974	37	2.5 to 1	yes	Caribbean	121
102,000	2,758	37	2.6 to 1	yes	Caribbean	127
47,262	1,486	32	2.2 to 1	yes	Bahamas/Key West	133
70,367	2,040	34.5	2.2 to 1	yes	Caribbean	130
70,367	2,040	34.5	2.2 to 1	yes	Caribbean	130
70,367	2,040	34.5	2.2 to 1	yes	Bahamas	130
70,367	2,040	34.5	2.2 to 1	yes	Bahamas, Caribbean	130
46,052	1,452	31.5	2.2 to 1	yes	Caribbean	133
70,367	2,040	34.5	2.2 to 1	yes	Caribbean	130
70,367	2,040	34.5	2.2 to 1	yes	Caribbean	130
70,367	2,040	34.5	2.2 to 1	yes	Ensenada/Catalina Island	130
70,367	2,040	34.5	2.2 to 1	yes	Caribbean	130

Ships at a Glance

Cruise Line	Ship	Frommer's Star Rating	Year Built
Celebrity (mainstream): Celebrity offers the best of two worlds: If you like elegance without stuffiness, fun without bad taste, and pampering without a high price, Celebrity is king.	**Century**	★★★★½	1995
	Constellation	★★★★★	2002
	Galaxy	★★★★½	1996
	Infinity	★★★★★	2001
	Mercury	★★★★½	1997
	Millennium	★★★★★	2000
	Summit	★★★★★	2001
	Zenith	★★★★	1992
Clipper (soft adventure): Clipper's comfortable small ships focus on offbeat ports of call, learning, and mingling with your fellow passengers. It's the ideal small-ship cruise for people who've tried Holland America or one of the other mainstream lines but want a more intimate cruise experience.	**Clipper Odyssey**	★★★★	1989
	Nantucket Clipper	★★★	1984
	Yorktown Clipper	★★★	1988
Costa (mainstream): Imagine a Carnival-style megaship hijacked by an Italian circus troupe: That's Costa. The words of the day are fun, festive, and international.	**Costa Magica**	★★★★	2004
	Costa Mediterranea	★★★½	2003
Cruise West (soft adventure): Family-owned Cruise West is the preeminent small-ship line in Alaska, and over the past decade it's branched out to include trips in warmer destinations, too. Most of its itineraries are port-to-port and geared to older, well-traveled, intellectually curious passengers.	**Pacific Explorer**	★★★½	1995
	Spirit of Alaska	★★★½	1980
	Spirit of Columbia	★★★½	1979
	Spirit of Discovery	★★★½	1976
	Spirit of Endeavour	★★★½	1983
	Spirit of Glacier Bay	★★★½	1971
	Spirit of '98	★★★★	1984
	Spirit of Oceanus	★★★★★	1991
Crystal (luxury): Fine-tuned and fashionable, Crystal gives passengers pampering service and scrumptious cuisine aboard ships large enough to offer generous fitness, dining, and entertainment facilities.	**Crystal Serenity**	★★★★½	2003
	Crystal Symphony	★★★★½	1995

Gross Tonnage	Passenger Capacity (Double Occupancy)	Passenger/Space Ratio	Passenger/Crew Ratio	Wheelchair Access	Sailing Regions	Full Review on Page
70,606	1,750	41	2 to 1	yes	Caribbean	147
91,000	1,950	46	2 to 1	yes	Caribbean, Bermuda	142
77,713	1,896	41	2 to 1	yes	Panama Canal, Caribbean	147
91,000	1,950	46	2 to 1	yes	Mexican Riviera, Alaska, Hawaii	142
77,713	1,896	41	2 to 1	yes	Mexican Riviera, Alaska, Pacific Northwest	147
91,000	1,950	46	2 to 1	yes	Caribbean	142
91,000	1,950	46	2 to 1	yes	Hawaii, Panama Canal, Alaska	142
47,225	1,374	34.5	2.1 to 1	yes	Caribbean, Bermuda	150
5,218	128	41	1.8 to 1	partial	Northwest Alaska/Russia	346
1,471	100	14.7	3.2 to 1	no	Caribbean, Central America, Intracoastal Waterway, Chesapeake Bay/Hudson River, Coastal Maine, French Canada, Great Lakes	347
2,354	138	17	3.5 to 1	no	Caribbean, Central America/ Panama Canal, Mexico/ Sea of Cortez, California Wine Country, Alaska	347
105,000	2,720	38.6	2.5 to 1	yes	Caribbean	157
85,000	2,112	40	2.3 to 1	yes	Caribbean	160
1,716	100	17	3 to 1	no	Central America	356
97*	78	N/A	3.7 to 1	no	Alaska, Pacific Northwest	358
97*	78	N/A	3.7 to 1	no	Alaska, British Columbia	358
94*	84	N/A	4 to 1	no	Alaska, Pacific Northwest	358
99*	102	N/A	3.6 to 1	no	Alaska, Mexico/Sea of Cortez, British Columbia, California Wine Country	356
95*	46	N/A	2.9 to 1	no	Alaska	358
96*	96	N/A	4.2 to 1	partial	Alaska, Pacific Northwest	355
4,500	114	39.5	2 to 1	no	Alaska, Bering Sea/Russia	353
68,000	1,080	63	1.7 to 1	yes	Caribbean, Mexican Riviera	283
51,044	940	52.5	1.7 to 1	yes	Canada/New England, Panama Canal, Caribbean	285

Ships at a Glance

Cruise Line	Ship	Frommer's Star Rating	Year Built
Cunard (luxury): A legendary line with a nearly legendary new vessel—the largest ocean liner in the world.	Queen Mary 2	★★★★★	2004
Delta Queen (soft adventure): Real live stern-wheel steamboats plying the Mississippi River system and beyond.	American Queen	★★★★	1995
	Delta Queen	★★★★	1927
	Mississippi Queen	★★★★	1976
Disney (mainstream): Family ships where both kids and adults are catered to equally, and with style.	Disney Magic	★★★★½	1998
	Disney Wonder	★★★★½	1999
Glacier Bay Cruiseline (soft adventure): The top choice in Alaska for hardcore adventure cruises, with most itineraries focused on kayaking, hiking, and wildlife watching. On some cruises you can go a full week and hardly see another human besides the people on your ship.	Executive Explorer	★★★½	1986
	Wilderness Adventurer	★★★½	1984
	Wilderness Discoverer	★★★½	1992
	Wilderness Explorer	★★★½	1969
Holland America (mainstream): Holland America has been in business since 1873, and has managed to hang on to more of its seafaring history and tradition than any line today except Cunard. It offers a moderately priced, classic, and casual yet refined cruise experience.	Amsterdam	★★★★	2000
	Maasdam	★★★★	1993
	Noordam	★★★★	2006
	Oosterdam	★★★★	2003
	Rotterdam	★★★★½	1997
	Ryndam	★★★★	1994
	Statendam	★★★★	1993
	Veendam	★★★★	1996
	Volendam	★★★★½	1999
	Westerdam	★★★★	2004
	Zaandam	★★★★½	2000
	Zuiderdam	★★★★	2002
Imperial Majesty (mainstream): One of the few real vintage ships left.	Regal Empress	★★	1953
Lindblad Expeditions (soft adventure): One of the most adventure-oriented small-ship lines, concentrating on wilderness and wildlife.	Sea Bird	★★★½	1982
	Sea Lion	★★★½	1981

Gross Tonnage	Passenger Capacity (Double Occupancy)	Passenger/Space Ratio	Passenger/Crew Ratio	Wheelchair Access	Sailing Regions	Full Review on Page
150,000	2,620	57	2.1 to 1	yes	Transatlantic, Caribbean, Ensenada, Mexico/Central & South America, Canada/ New England	293
3,707	436	8.5	2.6 to 1	yes	U.S. River Cruises	365
3,360	174	19.3	2.1 to 1	no	U.S. River Cruises	363
3,364	414	8	2.6 to 1	yes	U.S. River Cruises	365
83,000	1,754	47.5	1.8 to 1	yes	Caribbean	168
83,000	1,754	47.5	1.8 to 1	yes	Bahamas	168
98*	49	N/A	2.4 to 1	no	Alaska	372
89*	63	N/A	3.4 to 1	no	Alaska	370
95*	82	N/A	3.9 to 1	no	Alaska, Pacific Northwest	370
98*	31	N/A	2.4 to 1	no	Alaska	373
61,000	1,380	44	2.1 to 1	yes	Hawaii, Caribbean, Canada/ New England	182
55,451	1,266	44	2.1 to 1	yes	Caribbean, Canada/ New England	187
85,000	1,848	46	2.3 to 1	yes	Caribbean	178
85,000	1,848	46	2.3 to 1	yes	Mexican Riviera, Alaska	178
56,652	1,316	43	2.2 to 1	yes	No U.S. ports for 2006	182
55,451	1,266	44	2.1 to 1	yes	Caribbean, Alaska, Mexican Riviera	187
55,451	1,266	44	2.1 to 1	yes	Alaska	187
55,451	1,266	44	2.1 to 1	yes	Caribbean, Alaska	187
63,000	1,440	44	2.2 to 1	yes	Caribbean, Alaska	184
85,000	1,848	46	2.3 to 1	yes	Caribbean, Alaska	178
63,000	1,440	44	2.2 to 1	yes	Panama Canal, Alaska, Mexican Riviera, Hawaii	184
85,000	1,848	46	2.3 to 1	yes	Caribbean, Alaska	178
21,909	875	24	2.4 to 1	partial	Bahamas	193
100	70	N/A	3.2 to 1	no	Pacific Northwest, Mexico/ Sea of Cortez, Alaska	377
100	70	N/A	3.2 to 1	no	Pacific Northwest, Mexico/ Sea of Cortez, Alaska	377

Ships at a Glance

Cruise Line	Ship	Frommer's Star Rating	Year Built
MSC Cruises: Italian line offers midsize ships and gadget-free fun.	**Lirica**	★★★½	2003
	Opera	★★★½	2004
Norwegian (mainstream): NCL makes its mark with its always-casual, open-seating dining, and while its older ships aren't perfect, its newer ones are much better, with *Sun, Star, Dawn,* and *Pride of Aloha* giving the newest Royal Caribbean and Princess ships a run for their money. The line's new U.S.-flagged ships also give it dominance in Hawaii, where it's the only cruise line able to offer cruises entirely in Hawaiian waters.	**Norwegian Crown**	★★★½	1988
	Norwegian Dawn	★★★★½	2002
	Norwegian Dream	★★★	1992
	Norwegian Jewel	★★★★½	2005
	Norwegian Majesty	★★★	1992
	Norwegian Spirit	★★★★½	1999
	Norwegian Star	★★★★½	2002
	Norwegian Sun	★★★★	2001
	Norwegian Wind	★★★	1993
	Pride of Aloha	★★★★	1999
	Pride of America	not yet in service	2005
	Pride of Hawai'i	not yet in service	2006
Oceania (mainstream): New casual premium line operating two smallish, intimate ships with great service and cuisine.	**Insignia**	★★★★	1998
	Regatta	★★★★	1998
Princess (mainstream): With a fleet of mostly large and extra-large megaships, including some of the biggest at sea, L.A.-based Princess offers a quality mainstream cruise experience with a nice balance of tradition and innovation, relaxation and excitement, casualness and glamour.	**Caribbean Princess**	★★★★½	2004
	Coral Princess	★★★★½	2003
	Dawn Princess	★★★★	1995
	Diamond Princess	★★★★★	2004
	Golden Princess	★★★★½	2001
	Grand Princess	★★★★½	1998
	Island Princess	★★★★½	2003
	Regal Princess	★★★½	1991
	Sapphire Princess	★★★★★	2004
	Sea Princess	★★★★	1998
	Star Princess	★★★★½	2002
	Sun Princess	★★★★	1997

Gross Tonnage	Passenger Capacity (Double Occupancy)	Passenger/Space Ratio	Passenger/Crew Ratio	Wheelchair Access	Sailing Regions	Full Review on Page
58,600	1,586	37	2.1 to 1	yes	Caribbean	199
58,600	1,756	33.5	2.1 to 1	yes	Caribbean	199
34,250	1,050	32.5	2 to 1	yes	Caribbean, Bermuda	223
92,250	2,224	41.5	2 to 1	yes	Caribbean, Bahamas, Canada/ New England	212
50,760	1,748	29	2.8 to 1	yes	Caribbean	221
92,100	2,376	38.8	2 to 1	yes	Caribbean	212
40,876	1,460	30	2.7 to 1	yes	Caribbean, Bermuda	219
76,800	1,960	38.4	2 to 1	yes	Caribbean, Bahamas	212
92,250	2,224	41.5	2 to 1	yes	Mexican Riviera, Alaska	212
78,309	1,960	40	2 to 1	yes	Caribbean, Alaska	216
50,760	1,748	29	2.8 to 1	yes	Hawaii, Alaska	221
77,104	2,002	38.5	2 to 1	yes	Hawaii	207
81,000	2,146	37.7	2.1 to 1	yes	Hawaii	207
92,100	2,400	38.7	2.3 to 1	yes	Hawaii	207
30,200	684	44	1.8 to 1	yes	Amazon/Caribbean	229
30,200	684	44	1.8 to 1	yes	Caribbean/Amazon, Mexico/ Panama Canal	229
116,000	2,600	37.4	2.4 to 1	yes	Caribbean	246
91,627	1,970	46.5	2 to 1	yes	Panama Canal, Alaska	242
77,000	1,950	39.5	2.2 to 1	yes	Mexican Riviera, Alaska	250
113,000	2,670	42.5	2.4 to 1	yes	Alaska	238
109,000	2,600	42	2.4 to 1	yes	Canada/New England, Caribbean	246
109,000	2,600	42	2.4 to 1	yes	Caribbean	246
91,627	1,970	46.5	2 to 1	yes	Hawaii, Alaska	242
70,000	1,590	44	2.3 to 1	yes	Mexican Riviera, Panama Canal/Mexican Riviera/Central America, Caribbean/Amazon	252
113,000	2,670	42.5	2.4 to 1	yes	Mexican Riviera, Alaska	238
77,000	1,950	39.5	2.2 to 1	yes	Caribbean	250
109,000	2,600	42	2.4 to 1	yes	Caribbean	246
77,000	1,950	39.5	2.2 to 1	yes	Caribbean	250

Ships at a Glance

Cruise Line	Ship	Frommer's Star Rating	Year Built
Radisson Seven Seas (luxury): Radisson carries passengers in style and extreme comfort. Its brand of cruising is casually elegant and subtle, and its cuisine is near the top.	Seven Seas Mariner	★★★★½	2001
	Seven Seas Navigator	★★★★	1999
	Seven Seas Voyager	★★★★½	2003
Royal Caribbean (mainstream): Royal Caribbean offers some of the most activity-packed, best-looking, best-designed, and just plain fun megaships in the biz. Along with NCL, they're also out in the forefront of innovation, always challenging the status quo regarding what can and can't be done aboard ships.	Adventure of the Seas	★★★★½	2001
	Brilliance of the Seas	★★★★½	2002
	Empress of the Seas	★★★½	1990
	Enchantment of the Seas	★★★½	1997
	Explorer of the Seas	★★★★½	2000
	Grandeur of the Seas	★★★½	1996
	Jewel of the Seas	★★★★½	2004
	Legend of the Seas	★★★½	1995
	Majesty of the Seas	★★★	1992
	Mariner of the Seas	★★★★½	2003
	Monarch of the Seas	★★★	1991
	Navigator of the Seas	★★★★½	2003
	Radiance of the Seas	★★★★½	2001
	Rhapsody of the Seas	★★★½	1997
	Serenade of the Seas	★★★★½	2003
	Sovereign of the Seas	★★★	1988
	Splendour of the Seas	★★★½	1996
	Vision of the Seas	★★★½	1998
	Voyager of the Seas	★★★★½	1999
Seabourn (luxury): Seabourn's ships are floating pleasure palaces, giving passengers doting service and nearly the finest (if not the finest) cuisine at sea.	Seabourn Legend	★★★★	1992
	Seabourn Pride	★★★★	1988
SeaDream (luxury): An upscale yet casual line without the traditional regimentation.	SeaDream I	★★★★½	1984
	SeaDream II	★★★★½	1985
Silversea (luxury): Silversea caters to guests who won't settle for anything but the best, with free-flowing champagne and exceptional service.	Silver Shadow	★★★★★	2000
	Silver Whisper	★★★★★	2001

Gross Tonnage	Passenger Capacity (Double Occupancy)	Passenger/Space Ratio	Passenger/Crew Ratio	Wheelchair Access	Sailing Regions	Full Review on Page
50,000	700	71.4	1.6 to 1	yes	Mexican Riviera, Caribbean, Alaska	300
33,000	490	67.3	1.5 to 1	yes	Canada/New England, Panama Canal, Tahiti/Hawaii, Caribbean	302
46,000	700	65.7	1.6 to 1	yes	Caribbean	300
142,000	3,114	45.5	2.7 to 1	yes	Caribbean	264
90,090	2,100	43	2.5 to 1	yes	Panama Canal	261
48,563	1,602	30.5	2.4 to 1	yes	Caribbean	273
80,700	2,252	36	2.7 to 1	yes	Caribbean	268
142,000	3,114	45.5	2.7 to 1	yes	Caribbean	264
74,137	1,950	38	2.5 to 1	yes	Caribbean, Bermuda	268
90,090	2,100	43	2.5 to 1	yes	Caribbean	261
74,137	1,804	38.5	2.5 to 1	yes	Caribbean	268
73,941	2,390	31	2.9 to 1	yes	Bahamas	271
142,000	3,114	45.5	2.7 to 1	yes	Caribbean	264
73,941	2,390	31	2.9 to 1	yes	Ensenada/Catalina/San Diego	271
142,000	3,114	45.5	2.7 to 1	yes	Caribbean	264
90,090	2,100	43	2.5 to 1	yes	Caribbean, Alaska	261
78,491	2,000	39	2.5 to 1	yes	Caribbean	268
90,090	2,100	43	2.5 to 1	yes	Caribbean, Alaska	261
73,192	2,292	32	2.7 to 1	yes	Bahamas	271
69,130	1,804	38.5	2.5 to 1	yes	Caribbean	268
69,130	2,000	39	2.5 to 1	yes	Mexican Riviera, Alaska	268
142,000	3,114	45.5	2.7 to 1	yes	Bermuda. Caribbean	264
10,000	208	48	1.5 to 1	yes	Panama Canal, Caribbean	310
10,000	208	48	1.5 to 1	yes	Caribbean, Canada/New England, U.S. East Coast	310
4,260	110	39	1.2 to 1	no	Caribbean	317
4,260	110	39	1.2 to 1	no	Caribbean	317
28,258	388	73	1.3 to 1	yes	Caribbean, Central America, Alaska	323
28,258	388	73	1.3 to 1	yes	Caribbean, Panama Canal, Canada/New England	323

Ships at a Glance

Cruise Line	Ship	Frommer's Star Rating	Year Built
Star Clippers (sailing ships): Classic clipper ships with all the amenities.	**Royal Clipper**	★★★★	2000
	Star Clipper	★★★½	1992
Windjammer (sailing ships): Ultracasual and delightfully carefree, this eclectic fleet of cozy, rebuilt sailing ships (powered by both sails and engines) lures passengers into a fantasy world of pirates-and-rum-punch adventure.	**Amazing Grace**	★★½	1955
	Legacy	★★★½	1959
	Mandalay	★★	1923
	Polynesia	★★	1938
	Yankee Clipper	★★	1927
Windstar (sailing ships): The no-jackets-required policy aboard Windstar sums up the line's casually elegant attitude. The ships feel like private yachts—they're down-to-earth, yet service and cuisine are first-class.	**Wind Spirit**	★★★½	1988
	Wind Star	★★★½	1986
	Wind Surf	★★★★	1990

means that among the lines in that category/chapter, Windstar has the best cuisine. It may not be up to the level of, say, the ultraluxurious Seabourn (it's not), but if you're looking for a sailing-ship cruise that also has great food, this line would be a great bet.

3 Evaluating & Comparing the Listed Cruise Prices

As we explain in detail in chapter 2, the cruise lines' brochure prices are almost always wildly inflated—they're the "sticker prices" cruise line execs would love to get in an ideal world. In reality, passengers typically pay anywhere from 10% to 50% less. Instead of publishing these inflated brochure rates, then, we've worked with Nashville's **Just Cruisin' Plus** (© 800/888-0922; www.justcruisinplus.com) to provide you with samples of the **actual prices** customers were paying at press time. Other travel agencies and online sites will generally offer similar rates. Each ship review includes per diem prices (the total cruise price divided by the number of days) for the following three basic types of accommodations:

- Lowest-priced inside (without windows) cabin
- Lowest-priced outside (with windows) cabin
- Lowest-priced suite

Remember that cruise ships generally have several categories of cabins within each of these three basic divisions, all priced differently, and that the prices we've listed

Gross Tonnage	Passenger Capacity (Double Occupancy)	Passenger/Space Ratio	Passenger/Crew Ratio	Wheelchair Access	Sailing Regions	Full Review on Page
5,000	227	22	2.2 to 1	no	Caribbean	398
2,298	170	13.5	2.5 to 1	no	Caribbean	400
1,525	94	16.5	2.4 to 1	no	Caribbean, Central America	411
1,165	120	9.5	2.8 to 1	no	Caribbean, Bahamas	409
420	72	6	2.6 to 1	no	Caribbean	413
430	126	4	2.8 to 1	no	Caribbean	413
327	64	5	2.2 to 1	no	Caribbean	413
5,350	148	36	1.6 to 1	no	Caribbean	423
5,350	148	36	1.6 to 1	no	Caribbean	423
14,745	308	48	1.9 to 1	no	Caribbean	420

represent the *lowest* categories for inside and outside cabins and suites. Remember, too, that since this book covers cruises in several different regions, the prices we've listed are not applicable to all sailings—cruises in Alaska and Hawaii, for instance, are almost always more expensive than comparable cruises in the Caribbean. These prices are meant as a guide only and are in no way etched in stone—the price you pay may be higher or even lower, depending on when you choose to travel, when you book, what specials the lines are offering, and a slew of other factors. Prices listed include **port charges** (the per-passenger fee ports charge for ships to dock) but do not include taxes.

See chapter 2, "Booking Your Cruise & Getting the Best Price," for more details on pricing and to compare our discount prices with the cruise lines' published brochure rates (in the "Price Comparisons: Discounted Rates vs. Brochure Rates" table). Seeing how much you'll probably save can be a real eye-opener.

A NOTE ON ITINERARIES

Our fleet itinerary tables give you an idea of which ships sail which regions, and when. See the cruise lines' websites or a travel agent for full details on each itinerary. Note that we have not listed repositioning cruises—those trips offered only when a ship moves from one region to another (for instance, sailing from the Caribbean to Alaska).

6

The Mainstream Lines

These are the shopping malls of cruise ships, with lots to do, lots to eat, lots to buy on board, and lots of other people sharing the experience with you—sometimes as many as 3,000 of them, plus a thousand or more crew. Want action? Just walk out your cabin door. Want quiet? Hide out on your private balcony or burrow into a quiet lounge while everybody else is at the pool (or, if you want *real* quiet, consider booking one of the luxury or small-ship cruises described in chapters 7 and 8).

Since the mainstream category is, well, mainstream (meaning the most popular), it's the one that's seen the most growth, innovation, and investment in recent years, so the ships, as a general rule, are remarkably new—and also remarkably big. This is the category where the **megaships** reside, those hulking 1,200- to 3,200-passenger floating resorts that offer the widest variety of activities and entertainment. Most of the lines in this chapter (but particularly the "Big Four"—Carnival, Royal Caribbean, Princess, and Norwegian) have been pumping billions into building newer, bigger, and fancier ships, offering a wide variety of cabin sizes and layouts, a mix of formal and informal dining options, a wide array of entertainment (heavy on the Vegas style), sports facilities, bars, Internet cafes, giant spas, and more activities than you can possibly squeeze into a day.

The intense competition between cruise lines means they're constantly trying to outdo each other with cool stuff you'd never expect to find on a cruise ship, from rock-climbing walls and ice-skating rinks to pottery studios, planetariums, and multi-million-dollar art collections. You can choose from a dizzying number of things to do, from dancing lessons, bingo, and game-show contests to lectures on finance and nutrition, classes on photography and website design, and wine tastings. Mixers encourage singles to mingle and grandmothers to pull out the grandkid pictures, while nutty contests by the pool encourage passengers to toss away all restraint as they try and stuff the most Ping-Pong balls down their bathing suits or swim across the pool with a bagel in their mouths. Overall the atmosphere is very social, especially on warm-weather cruises in the Caribbean, Bahamas, Bermuda, and Mexico, where passengers are sunning, strutting, and sipping their favorite drink out on deck. Steer clear, of course, if you suffer from agoraphobia.

Now granted, the term "mainstream" covers a lot of ground, and that's the point. These ships are generalists, attempting to offer a little something for almost everyone—all ages, backgrounds, and interests, from tattooed, blue-collar beer-drinkers to sake-sipping PhDs with subscriptions to *Smithsonian*. As a rule, though, big-ship cruises to sunny spots tend to attract the youngest mix of fun-loving, like-to-party passengers (lots of 20s, 30s, and 40s), while itineraries in Alaska and New England tend to appeal more to a mellower crowd mostly in their 40s, 50s, and on up.

Frommer's Ratings at a Glance: The Mainstream Lines

1 = poor   **2** = fair   **3** = good   **4** = excellent   **5** = outstanding

Cruise Line	Enjoyment Factor	Dining	Activities	Children's Program	Entertainment	Service	Worth the Money
Carnival	4	3	3	4	3	3	4
Celebrity	5	4	5	3	3	5	5
Costa	3	2	4	2	3	2	3
Disney	4	3	3	5	5	3	4
Holland America	4	4	3	2	4	5	5
Imperial Majesty	3	3	2	1	2	3	3
MSC Cruises	3	3	4	3	3	3	4
Norwegian	4	4	4	4	4	4	5
Oceania	4	4	2	N/A	3	4	4
Princess	4	4	4	4	4	4	4
Royal Caribbean	5	4	5	4	4	4	5

Note: Cruise lines have been graded on a curve that compares them only with the other mainstream lines. See "How to Read the Ratings," in chapter 5, for a detailed explanation of the ratings methodology.

The more elegant and refined of the lines are commonly referred to as **premium,** a notch up in the sophistication department from others that are described as **mass-market.** Quality-wise, for the most part they're all on equal footing and, overall, are more alike than they are different, especially in regards to dining and entertainment. Ditto for lines like Oceania and MSC, whose fleets of midsize ships are almost throwbacks to the days before supersizing. For even more of a throwback there's Imperial Majesty, with its one midsize antique ocean liner. Though these lines have little in common with the Carnivals and Royal Caribbeans of the world, they're in this chapter because they offer well-rounded cruises for a fairly diverse mix of passengers.

DRESS CODES   The sad truth for you old-fashioned types is that no one dresses up these days. Not in the office, not to a Broadway show, and not on a mainstream cruise—at least not very often. Maybe there will be a backlash, but for now black ties and pearls have given way to cargo shorts and sandals, and nobody bats an eye when passengers stroll into the formal dining room wearing jeans. Norwegian Cruise Line was the first to completely do away with "mandatory" formal nights, though formal-wear is optional for the captain's cocktail party. Aside from Oceania and Imperial Majesty, the rest of the lines in this chapter still have 2 formal (or "formal optional") nights a week that call for dark suits or tuxedos for men and cocktail dresses, sequined numbers, or fancy pantsuits for women—and there still are some people who like to get all gussied up. The other 5 nights are some combination of semiformal and casual, though the trend is increasingly going all-casual, with slacks and polo shirts common for men and dresses, pantsuits, or skirts and tops for women. Guests are asked not to wear shorts and T-shirts in the formal dining rooms, but you'll see that some people do anyway. Daytime is casual.

1 Carnival Cruise Lines

3655 NW 87th Ave., Miami, FL 33178-2428. ℂ **800/227-6482** or 305/599-2200. Fax 305/405-4855. www.carnival. com.

THE LINE IN A NUTSHELL The Wal-Mart of cruising, Carnival specializes in colorful, jumbo-size resort ships that deliver plenty of bang for the buck. If you like the flash of Vegas and the party-hearty of New Orleans, you'll love Carnival's brand of flamboyant fun. **Sails to:** Caribbean, Mexican Riviera, Alaska, Canada/New England, Hawaii (plus Europe, transatlantic).

THE EXPERIENCE Nobody does it better in the party department. The line with the most recognized name in the biz serves up a very casual, down-to-earth, middle-American Caribbean vacation. While food and service are pretty average—not surprising considering the large numbers served—that doesn't stop the line from trying to offer a higher-quality vacation. Recent enhancements include switching from plastic to china in the buffet restaurants, and equipping cabins with thicker towels, duvet blankets, and more TV channels. The fleet has even gone wireless, offering "Wi-Fi" Internet access throughout each ship.

"The Carnival of today is very different than 10 or 20 years ago," Carnival president and CEO Bob Dickinson said recently.

Indeed, on many ships in the fleet you'll find a sushi bar, supper club, wine bar, coffee bar, and great amenities for children. Like the frat boy who graduated to a button-down shirt and an office job, Carnival has definitely moved up and on. But like that reformed frat boy who stills like to meet his old pals for happy hour every week, Carnival hasn't lost touch with its past. Sure, the line's decor, like its clientele, has mellowed since its riotous, party-hearty beginnings, but each ship is still an exciting, bordering-on-nutty collage of textures, shapes, and images. Where else but on these floating play lands would you find life-size mannequins of Hollywood stars such as Marilyn Monroe and Humphrey Bogart, bar stools designed to look like baseballs and bats, or real oyster-shell wallpaper? The outrageousness of the decor is part of the fun. Evolved yes, dull no.

"We are who we are; we're still the fun ships," Dickinson reminds us.

Pros

- **Fun, theme-park ambience:** The fanciful decor on these vessels is unmatched.
- **Large standard cabins:** At 185 square feet or larger, Carnival's standard inside and outside cabins are among the roomiest in the mainstream category.
- **Melting pot at sea:** You name 'em, they'll be on a Carnival cruise, from frisky 20-something singles and honeymooners to *Leave It to Beaver* families with young kids to grandparents along for the show.
- **An insomniac's delight:** When passengers on most ships are calling it a night, Carnival's guests are just getting busy with diversions such as midnight adult comedy shows, raging discos, and 24-hour pizza parlors.

Cons

- **You're never alone:** Not in the hot tubs, on shore excursions, in the pool, while sunbathing, at the gym, at the frozen-yogurt machine . . .
- **No enrichment stuff:** Activities are pretty much confined to fun and games on the pool deck; no guest speakers and classes like most other mainstream lines offer.

Compared with other mainstream lines, here's how Carnival rates:

	Poor	Fair	Good	Excellent	Outstanding
Enjoyment Factor				✓	
Dining			✓		
Activities			✓		
Children's Program				✓	
Entertainment		✓			
Service		✓			
Worth the Money				✓	

CARNIVAL: BIG LINE, BIG FUN

Carnival has enjoyed an extended run as Big Cheese of the cruise world. The assets of its parent company, Carnival Corporation, are enormous and growing: In addition to its own fleet of 21 ships, Carnival Corp. holds full ownership of Cunard, Seabourn, Costa, Windstar, and Holland America Line—all told, the company has a stake in 12 cruise brands in North America, Europe, and Australia. And, in April 2003, Carnival beat out Royal Caribbean to acquire P&O Princess, adding yet another major cruise brand to its cruise dynasty. When all is said and done, Carnival Corp. will operate a combined fleet of 77 ships, with another 13 scheduled for delivery over the next few years.

The origins of the Miami-based company were as precarious as they were accidental. Company patriarch Ted Arison, a somewhat reclusive billionaire who passed away in 1999, had sold an airfreight business in New York in 1966 and intended to retire to his native Israel to enjoy the fruits of his labor—after a few more little ventures. After he negotiated terms for chartering a ship, he assembled a group of paying passengers, then discovered that the ship's owner could no longer guarantee the vessel's availability. According to latter-day legend, a deal was hastily struck whereby Arison's passengers would be carried aboard a laid-up ship owned by Knut Kloster, a prominent Norwegian shipping magnate. The ship was brought to Miami from Europe, and the combination of Arison's marketing skill and Kloster's hardware created an all-new entity that, in 1966, became the corporate forerunner of Norwegian Cruise Line.

After a bitter parting of ways with Kloster, Carnival got its start in 1972 when Arison bought *Empress of Canada,* known for its formal and somewhat stuffy administration, and reconfigured it into Carnival's first ship, the anything-but-stuffy *Mardi Gras.* After a shaky start—the brightly painted ship, carrying hundreds of travel agents, ran aground just off the coast of Miami on its first cruise—Arison managed to pick up the pieces and create a company that, under the guidance of astute and tough-as-nails company president Bob Dickinson and chairman Micky Arison (Ted's son), eventually evolved into the most influential trendsetter in the cruise ship industry. The rest is history, as they say.

Today, Carnival's fleet includes 21 ships, most of which cruise the Caribbean and Bahamas year-round. The 110,000-ton 2,974-passenger *Carnival Liberty,* sister to *Valor, Conquest,* and *Glory,* is slated to debut in July 2005.

PASSENGER PROFILE

In the old days, Carnival was as party-oriented as a college frat house, with about the same vibe: Heidi sailed in 1996 when more than 500 graduating high-school seniors practically took over (and ruined) a cruise on *Celebration*. She still gets nightmares. Guidelines implemented in early 1997 put a stop to all of that, mandating that no one under 21 can sail unless sharing a cabin with an adult over 25, with exceptions made for married couples and young people traveling with their parents in separate cabins. So, while you'll still find teen groups on board (especially Mar–June), things are not what they were.

A Carnival cruise is a huge melting pot—couples, singles, and families; young, old, and lots in between. I've met doctors on Carnival cruises as well as truck drivers. And no matter what their profession, you'll see people wearing everything from Ralph Lauren shirts and Gucci glasses to Harley-Davidson T-shirts and tattoos. Carnival estimates about 30% of passengers are under age 35, another 40% are between 35 and 55, and 30% are over age 55. At least half of all passengers are first-time cruisers. While it's one of the best lines to choose if you're single, Carnival's ships certainly aren't overrun by singles—families and couples are definitely in the majority. The line's 3-, 4-, and 5-night cruises tend to attract the most families with kids and the highest number of 20- and 30-something single friends traveling together in groups.

Regardless of their age, passengers tend to be young at heart, ready to party, and keyed up for nonstop, round-the-clock activities. Many have visited the casinos of Las Vegas and Atlantic City and the resorts of Cancún and Jamaica, and are no strangers to soaking in sardine-can hot tubs, sunbathing, hitting the piña coladas and beer before lunch, and dancing late into the night.

The typical Carnival passenger likes to dress casual, even at dinner, with jogging suits, jeans, and T-shirts just as prevalent as Dockers, sundresses, and Hush Puppies on all but formal nights—and even on formal nights, it's not uncommon for some passengers to run back to their cabins to change out of their dressier duds and put on shorts or jeans before heading out to the discos and bars. Tuxedos are in the minority here. As a cruise director on the *Carnival Legend* recently told Heidi, "the cut-off is shorts." Otherwise, just about anything else goes.

DINING

Like most lines these days, Carnival offers a raft of dining options. Though not to the degree of flexibility that NCL, and to a lesser extent Princess, offers, Carnival's newest Spirit- and Conquest-class ships offer about as many dining venues as you'll really need.

TRADITIONAL   In its two-story "formal" dining rooms (and take formal with a grain of salt—some Carnival passengers don't seem to know anything but T-shirts and jeans), Carnival's food quality and presentation, while much improved from its early

---

Carnival's Vacation Guarantee

Unhappy with your Carnival cruise? Dissatisfied guests may disembark at their first non-U.S. port of call and, subject to some restrictions, get a refund for the unused portion of their cruise and reimbursement for coach-class airfare back to their ship's home port. To qualify, passengers must inform the ship's purser before their first port of call.

days, is still pretty average, and for the most part on par with Royal Caribbean, Princess, and NCL. Carnival's fare is fine if you've got humble-enough tastes. You'll find interesting dishes, such as honey-basted filet of salmon, roasted quail, and West Indian pumpkin soup, on the dinner menus, in addition to such all-American favorites as lobster and prime rib, plus pasta dishes, grilled salmon, broiled halibut, and Thanksgiving-style turkey served with all the trimmings. Unfortunately, the preparation is uneven (as is true on many of the mainstream lines), one night your entree is great, the other it's blah. At lunch, you'll find appetizers such as sushi and fried calamari, and entrees such as focaccia filled with arugula, roasted peppers, and fresh mozzarella, and a linguini dish in a light tomato sauce with julienne of tomatoes and hickory smoked ham. Healthier **"Spa Carnival," vegetarian,** and **low-carb choices** are also on each menu.

Despite the hectic pace and ambience, dining service is usually friendly and some-what classier than in earlier years, if not always the most efficient. The staff still pre-sents dessert-time song-and-dance routines, although the parades of flaming Cherries Jubilee and Baked Alaska have, for safety reasons, been curtailed. Sophistication goes only so far, however: The line still has its waiters handle all wine service, rather than employing sommeliers.

In a nod to a more flexible system in its formal restaurants, Carnival offers **four dif-ferent seatings** on most ships rather than the traditional two. However, because you can choose only to dine early (5:45 and 6:15pm) or late (8 or 8:30pm), with the line selecting your exact time, it's hardly more flexible (though it's better for the galley staff, who have a more spaced window to prepare meals). The Spirit-class ships retain the traditional two seatings.

SPECIALTY   *Carnival Spirit,* which debuted in spring 2001, was the line's first to have a reservations-only restaurant, a two-level venue serving steaks and other dishes for a $25-per-person cover charge (plus tip and not including wine). Subsequent Spirit-class and Conquest-class ships—and all future Carnival ships—have this inti-mate alternative venue. Here, service is more gracious, and dedicated sommeliers are on hand to take your wine order. Menus are leather-bound, and elegant table settings feature beautiful Versace show plates and Rosenthal, Fortessa, and Revol china. Tables for two and four are available, and a musician or two serenades diners with soft bal-lads. There's even a dance floor. The menu includes steaks, from New York strip to porterhouse and filet mignon, as well as dishes such as grilled lamb chops, a fish dish, and king crab claws. The experience is intentionally designed to be slow and linger-ing, so don't go if you're looking for a fast meal. The food and service are the most doting you'll find on Carnival (in fact, on a recent *Legend* cruise, almost too attentive, with a server at our table nearly every few minutes).

CASUAL   At the opposite end of the alternative-dining spectrum, guests aboard all Carnival ships can opt to have any meal in the buffet-style Lido restaurants at no extra charge. For an unstructured and casual dinner, walk in any time between about 6 and 9:30pm for serve-yourself entrees such as chicken, pasta, stir-fry, and a carving station. At lunch, buffets in the Lido feature the usual suspects—salads, meats, cheeses, pastas, grilled burgers, and chicken filets, and several hot choices such as fish and chips, roast turkey, or stir-fry. The lunchtime buffets also feature specialty stations, serving up things such as pasta or Chinese food or a Cajun fish dish. The new ships have deli stations for sandwiches, and at press time the older ships in the fleet were being retrofitted with them. At times, the buffet line gets backed up as passengers wait for bins to be restocked and servers scramble to fill them. Though the food is unmemorable, recent upgrades to tableware are not: Kudos to Carnival for bringing in colorful ceramic sugar bowls, salt and pepper shakers, and dinnerware and tossing out the generic white plastic stuff.

SNACKS & EXTRAS But wait, there's more: Carnival ships give you 24-hour pizza (anywhere from 500–800 pies are flipped a day!), calzones that are surprisingly tasty, Caesar salad with or without chicken, and self-serve soft ice cream and frozen yogurt, as well as a complimentary **sushi bar** in the promenade on the newest ships (on older ships, sushi is served in the Lido buffet restaurants at lunch and/or dinner), and a deli on some vessels. There are nightly **midnight buffets** in the Lido restaurants, with a gala, pull-out-all-the-stops buffet once per cruise. The newest ships also have specialty (read: not free) coffee and pastry bars, some with milkshakes and banana splits, too.

All ships offer **24-hour room service,** with a new limited menu including items like a focaccia sandwich with grilled zucchini, fresh mozzarella, and portobello mushrooms, plus the standard tuna salad, cookies, fruit, and so on. Kids can select from **children's menus.** For kids under age 21, there are convenient **Fountain Fun Cards** that can be purchased for unlimited soft-drink purchases (from $8 for 2-night cruises, up to $32 for 8-day voyages). There's an adult version too, charging between $11 for 2-night cruises and $44 for 8-nighters.

ACTIVITIES

Carnival doesn't skimp in the keeping-busy department, so there's never a dull moment—you can run from one activity to the next all day long if you want to, though there's not as much variety as aboard lines such as Norwegian and Celebrity (read: no enrichment lectures, though with the introduction of the line's new Presidential Wine Club, with its subscription-based home wine delivery and annual Presidential Wine Club cruises, maybe that'll change). By day, the main pool decks are the heart of the action, and between the blaring bands (and I mean loud—don't expect to have a conversation without shouting) and microphone-wielding social hosts whipping up interest in pillow-fighting competitions, belly-flop contests, or Austin Powers dancing lessons, you'll barely be able to hear yourself think. Lest things get too out of hand, uniformed security guards watch over the pool deck and bars. On all but the line's oldest ships, it's a little quieter up on the second tier of the Sun Deck, and each ship has a quieter pool and sunbathing area at the stern, sans loudspeakers. Spirit-class vessels have a second midships pool separated from the main action by a bar and solid dividers that keep most of the noise out and provide a more serene lounging space; one of the four pools on the Conquest-class ships is quieter and covered by a retractable glass roof.

Slot machines begin clanging by 8 or 9 in the morning in the **casinos** when the ships are at sea (tables open at 11am), and waiters and waitresses start tempting passengers with trays of fruity theme cocktails long before the lunch hour. Expect to hear the ubiquitous art auctioneer shouting into a microphone about some Peter Max masterpiece (all mainstream lines hold **art auctions** several times a week, but on a recent *Valor* cruise, the über-amplified screaming match was held smack dab in the middle of the atrium lobby—Heidi found the whole thing obnoxious). There are **line-dancing and ballroom classes,** trivia contests, facial and hairdo demonstrations, singles

---

Handy Hot Line

Carnival offers a 24-hour hot line for help with unexpected snafus or emergencies. Call ☎ **877/885-4856** toll-free, or 305/406-4779.

---

and newlywed parties, game shows, shuffleboard, bingo, art auctions, and movies. You can spend some time in the roomy gyms on the Fantasy-, Destiny-, Spirit-, and Conquest-class ships (and take the handful of **free aerobics classes** or the ones they charge $10 for, such as Pilates, yoga, and spinning) or playing volleyball on the top deck, or treat yourself to one of dozens of relaxing (and expensive) treatments in the Steiner-managed **spas.** All ships have covered and lighted golf driving nets, with **golf pros** sailing on board to give lessons, with video analysis starting at $25 for a 15-minute session and $80 for an hour. Pros also accompany guests on golf excursions on shore, and clubs, golf shoes, balls, gloves, and other paraphernalia are available for rent.

Not surprisingly, with this pace, you won't find any focus on quiet times except in the subdued, handsome-looking library/game rooms and 24-hour **Internet centers** on each ship; you'll also find wireless "Wi-Fi" service fleetwide as well. There are no educational lectures on art, history, or other cerebral topics, such as you'll find aboard Celebrity, Norwegian, HAL, and other lines, though recently the line started offering **arts and crafts lessons** on sea days, to the tune of activities such as decorating your own sun visor with glitter and paint.

CHILDREN'S PROGRAM

Carnival is right up there with the best ships for families—the line estimates that about 500,000 kids will have sailed aboard its ships in 2005. In fact, the line claims it carries a whopping 400% more children under 18 today than in 1995. Some 600 to 800 children per cruise is pretty normal, and there can be as many as 1,000 on Christmas and New Year's cruises. There are a lot of children around in summer too, when it'll be difficult to find a kid-free hot tub. On Carnival's post-1990 ships, the **child facilities** are fairly extensive, with the Conquest-class, Spirit-class, and Destiny-class ships, as well as *Elation* and *Paradise,* offering the biggest and brightest playrooms in the fleet, featuring a climbing maze, arts and crafts, oodles of toys and games, a 16-monitor video wall showing movies and cartoons, and computer stations loaded with the latest educational and entertainment software. The facilities on the line's older ships—including the oldest, *Celebration* and *Holiday*—are no competition.

The **Camp Carnival program** offers supervised kids' activities on sea days from 9am to 10pm (and 2–10pm on port days) for ages 2 through 14 in four age groups: toddlers 2 to 5, juniors 6 to 8, intermediates 9 to 11, and teens 12 to 14. Ten to 16 counselors (all of whom are trained in CPR and first aid) organize the fun and games on each ship, which include face painting, computer games, puzzles, fun with Play-Doh, picture bingo, pirate hat–making, and pizza parties for toddlers. For juniors, there's PlayStation 2, computer games, ice-cream parties, story time and library visits, T-shirt coloring, and swimming. For intermediates, there are scavenger hunts, trivia and bingo, Ping-Pong, video-game competitions, arts and crafts, computer games, dance classes, and talent shows. There are even **"homework help" sessions** available for kids who need to keep up while on vacation as well as new educational activities, that include art projects with papier-mâché, oil paintings, and watercolors; music appreciation, which gets kids acquainted with different musical instruments; science projects where kids can make their own ice cream and create minihelicopters; and a fitness program that encourages today's couch-potato computer-head kids to actually get up and run around. Teen clubs are geared to 12 to 14 year olds (the cruise director's department schedules activities for the 16–18 set), and are quite elaborate on the newest ships. Besides karaoke parties, computer games, scavenger hunts, talent shows, card and trivia games, and Ping-Pong, teens can watch movies there and go to dance parties. Most ships are also equipped with iMacs, but there is no Internet center for teens only like some ships offer. Of course, teens can also hang out in the video arcades—the newest ships have virtual-reality games and air-hockey tables. For something more refined, Carnival now offers a collection of spa treatments geared to teens.

As if that's not enough, the entire fleet has children's wading pools, and for bigger kids there's that great signature snaking slide at the main pool of each ship.

Parents wanting a kid-free evening can make use of the supervised children's activities, offered from 7 to 10pm nightly, after which time group **slumber-party-style babysitting** for ages 4 months through age 11 is available till 3am in the playroom. No private babysitting is available. In addition to these hours, Carnival also now offers group babysitting between 8am and noon on port days for the under 2 set, for $6 per hour for the first child, $4 per hour for each additional child. On sea days between noon and 2pm, you can also drop off children under two at the rate above, or parents may use the playroom with their babies for these 2 hours at no charge. And yes, counselors will change diapers (though parents are asked to provide them along with wipes)! Parents with kids age 8 and under checked into the children's program get free use of beepers on most ships, in case their kids need to contact them. A handful of strollers are available for rent fleetwide for $25 for 7- and 8-night cruises (less for shorter cruises) as well as a limited number of bouncy seats, travel swings, and Game Boys for rent.

Mom and Dad can get an earlier start on their kid-free evening, when the counselors supervise **kids' mealtime** in the Lido restaurant between about 6 and 7pm in a special section reserved for kids; it's offered nightly except the first night of the cruise, and, on cruises 5 nights or longer, it's also not offered on the last night. The children's dining room menu, printed on the back of a fun coloring/activity book (crayons are provided), features the usual favorites—hot dogs, hamburgers, french fries, chicken nuggets, pepperoni pizza, peanut-butter-and-jelly sandwiches, banana splits, Jell-O, and a daily special.

A turndown service for kids includes complimentary chocolate-chip cookies on their pillows at bedtime on formal nights. Cribs are available if requested when making your reservations. Children must be at least 4 months old to sail on board.

ENTERTAINMENT

Aboard its newer megaships, Carnival has spent millions on stage sets, choreography, and sound equipment. The theaters on the Destiny-class, Spirit-class, and Conquest-class ships are spectacular three-deck extravaganzas, and the casinos are so large you'll think you've died and gone to Vegas; but even aboard its smaller, older ships, Carnival consistently offers some of the most lavish entertainment extravaganzas afloat.

My, what an inefficient way to fish.

Ring toss, good. Horseshoes, bad.

Faster! Faster! Faster!

We take care of the fiddly bits, from providing over 43,000 customer reviews of hotels, to helping you find our best fares, to giving you 24/7 customer service. So you can focus on the only thing that matters. Goofing off.

travelocity
You'll never roam alone.

Carnival Fleet Itineraries

Ship	Itineraries
Carnival Conquest	**7-night W. Carib:** Round-trip from New Orleans, LA, year-round.
Carnival Destiny	**7-night S. Carib:** Round-trip from San Juan, PR, year-round.
Carnival Glory	**7-night E. & W. Carib:** Round-trip from Port Canaveral, FL, year-round (itineraries alternate weekly).
Carnival Legend	**8-night S. & W. Carib:** Round-trip from Ft. Lauderdale, FL, Oct–Apr (itineraries alternate weekly). **8-night Carib:** Round-trip from New York, NY, Apr–Oct.
Carnival Liberty	**6-night W. Carib:** Round-trip from Ft. Lauderdale, FL, year-round. **8-night W. Carib/Central America:** Round-trip from Ft. Lauderdale, FL, year-round.
Carnival Miracle	**7-night W. Carib:** Round-trip from Tampa, FL, year-round.
Carnival Pride	**7-night Mexican Riviera:** Round-trip from Long Beach, CA, year-round.
Carnival Spirit	**8-night Mexican Riviera:** Round-trip from San Diego, CA, Oct 2005–Apr 2006. **12-night Hawaii:** Ensenada to Honolulu and Honolulu to Vancouver, Apr 2006. **7 night Gulf of Alaska:** North- or southbound between Vancouver, BC, and Whittier/Anchorage, AK, May–Aug 2006. **7-night Alaska Inside Passage:** Round-trip from Vancouver, BC, May–Aug 2006.
Carnival Triumph	**7-night E. & W. Carib:** Round-trip from Miami, FL, year-round (itineraries alternate weekly).
Carnival Valor	**7-night E. & W. Carib:** Round-trip from Miami, FL, year-round (itineraries alternate weekly).
Carnival Victory	**7-night E. & W. Carib:** Round-trip from Miami, FL, year-round (itineraries alternate weekly).
Celebration	**4- & 5-night Bahamas/Key West:** Round-trip from Jacksonville, FL, year-round.
Ecstasy	**4- & 5-night W. Carib:** Round-trip from Galveston, TX, year-round.
Elation	**7-night W. Carib:** Round-trip from Galveston, TX, year-round.
Fantasy	**3- & 4-night Bahamas:** Round-trip from Port Canaveral, FL, year-round.
Fascination	**3-night Bahamas & 4-night W. Carib:** Round-trip from Miami, FL, year-round (itineraries alternate).
Holiday	**4- & 5-night W. Carib:** Round-trip from Mobile, AL, year-round.
Imagination	**4- & 5-night W. Carib:** Round-trip from Miami, FL, year-round.
Inspiration	**4- & 5-night W. Carib:** Round-trip from Tampa, FL, year-round.
Paradise	**3-night Ensenada & 4-night Ensenada/Catalina Island:** Round-trip from Long Beach, CA, year-round (itineraries alternate).
Sensation	**4- & 5-night W. Carib:** Round-trip from New Orleans, LA, year-round.

Carnival megaships each carry about 8 to 16 flamboyantly costumed dancers (fewer on *Celebration* and *Holiday*) for twice-weekly **Vegas-style musicals.** One or two live soloists carry the musical part of the show, while dancers lip-sync the chorus. A 6- to 10-piece orchestra of traditional and digital instruments deftly accompanies the acts each night, sometimes enhanced by synchronized recorded music. You'll also find comedians, jugglers, acrobats, rock 'n' roll bands, country-and-western bands, classical string trios, pianists, and Dorsey- or Glenn Miller–style big bands, all performing, if not simultaneously, at least during the same cruise, and sometimes on the same night. Special entertainment may include a local mariachi band when a ship's in port late in Cozumel.

Besides the main theater, most entertainment happens somewhere along the indoor Main Street–like promenade (except on the Spirit-class ships, which are more spread out). Many are called the "Something-or-other Boulevard" or "Something-or-other Way," it stretches along one entire side of each ship and is lined with just about the entire repertoire of the ships' nightclubs, bars, lounges, patisseries, and disco and casino. One bar on all the Fantasy-, Destiny-, Spirit-, and Conquest-class ships welcomes cigar smoking, and fleetwide, cigars are sold at the pool bar and during midnight buffets.

By day, entertainment includes an ultraloud Caribbean-style calypso or steel-drum band performing Bob Marley tunes and other pop songs on a deck poolside (though usually decent, on a recent *Valor* cruise the singer was tone-deaf—painful at those decibels—but then again, who would notice after a few piña coladas?), and a pianist, guitarist, or string trio playing in the atria of the line's newest ships.

SERVICE

All in all, a Carnival ship is a well-oiled machine, and you'll certainly get what you need—but not much more. When you board, for instance, you're welcomed by polite and well-meaning staff at the gangway, given a diagram of the ship's layout, and then pointed in the right direction to find your cabin on your own, carry-on luggage in tow. Chalk it all up to the size of the line's ships. It's a fact of life that service aboard all megaliners is simply not as attentive as that aboard smaller vessels—with thousands of guests to help, your dining-room waiter and cabin steward have a lot of work ahead of them and have little time for chitchat. Lines can get long at the breakfast and lunch buffets and, at certain times, at the pizza counter, though there always seem to be plenty of drink waiters and waitresses roaming the pool decks, looking to score drink orders. And these days, they're hawking drinks in classier uniforms, which have, for the most part, been upgraded over the past few years to a more subdued style (bye-bye fuchsia and bright blue).

Service certainly doesn't benefit from Carnival's **automatic tipping policy.** Like most of the major lines these days, gratuities for the crew are automatically added to your account at the end of your cruise to the tune of $10 per person per day fleetwide, and they're divvied up among the staff automatically. You can adjust the amount—or eliminate it completely and hand out cash in envelopes—by visiting the purser's desk. On Carnival and the other lines with automatic tipping policies, we've found waiters and cabin stewards don't seem as eager to please as they did when the tip carrot was hanging directly over them.

There is a **laundry service** aboard each ship for washing and pressing only (with per-piece charges), as well as a handful of **self-service laundry rooms** with irons and coin-operated washers and dryers. There's a liquid soap and shampoo dispenser in cabin bathrooms fleetwide, plus a small basket of trial-size toiletries (only refilled upon request).

The Conquest Class:
Carnival Conquest •
Carnival Glory • Valor •
Liberty (preview)

The Verdict

Like a stretch model of the slightly shorter Destiny-class vessels and souped up with a supper-club concept from the Spirit series, the Conquest class also brings the fleet's largest children's and teen's facilities—all packaged in a pastiche of both pleasing and jarring colors and design themes.

Carnival Conquest *(photo: Carnival Cruise Lines)*

Specifications

Size (in tons)	110,000	Year Launched	
Passengers (double occ.)	2,974	*Conquest*	2002
Passenger/Space Ratio	37	*Glory*	2003
Total Cabins/Veranda Cabins	1,487/556	*Valor*	2004
Crew	1,160	*Liberty*	2005
Passenger/Crew Ratio	2.5 to 1	Last Major Refurbishment	N/A

Frommer's Ratings (Scale of 1–5)   ★★★★½

Cabin Comfort & Amenities	4.5	Dining Options	4
Ship Cleanliness & Maintenance	5	Gym, Spa & Sports Facilities	5
Public Comfort/Space	4.5	Children's Facilities	4.5
Decor	4	Enjoyment Factor	4

These 110,000-ton 2,974-passenger sisters are the largest Carnival vessels to date, with the fourth and final sister, *Carnival Liberty,* following in July 2005. The $500-million Conquest-class ships closely resemble the Destiny series, though they stretch about 60 feet longer and add Spirit-class features such as supper clubs. If all berths are occupied, each Conquest liner can carry an eyebrow-raising 3,700-plus passengers (that's not counting more than 1,000 crew). These mondo megas boast more than 20 bars and lounges, Carnival's largest children's facilities, and an entire, separate zone dedicated to teens. Each has a state-of-the-art "teleradiology" system that enables the ship's doctors to digitally transmit X-rays and other patient information to medical facilities on shore for consultation on a broad range of medical situations.

Cabins & Rates

Cabins	Per Diems from	Sq. Ft.	Fridge	Hair Dryer	Sitting Area	TV
Inside	$76	185	yes	yes	no	yes
Outside	$97	185–220	yes	yes	yes	yes
Suite	$192	275–345	yes	yes	yes	yes

CABINS Standard outside cabins measure a roomy 220 square feet. These categories (6A and 6B) take up most of the Riviera and Main decks. Of the ship's outside cabins, 60% (556 of 917) offer balconies. The standard balcony cabins (categories 8A–8E) measure a still ample 185 square feet plus a 35-square-foot balcony. For those who simply must have a bigger balcony, a little extra dough buys an "extended balcony" (60 sq. ft.) or "wraparound large balcony." There's only a handful of these category-9A accommodations, and they're tucked all the way aft on the Upper, Empress, and Verandah decks. The 42 suites are a full 275 square feet plus a 65-square-foot balcony, and bigger still are the 10 Penthouse Suites at 345 square feet plus an 85-square-foot balcony. Most of the suites are sandwiched in the middle of the ship on Deck 7 and between two other accommodations decks, eliminating the danger of noisy public rooms above or below. Specially designed family staterooms, at a comfortable but not roomy 230 square feet, are located one deck below the children's facilities, and a couple of them can be connected to the room next door. In lieu of a private veranda, these family staterooms feature floor-to-ceiling windows for ocean views.

All categories of cabins come with a TV, safe, hand-held hair dryer (not the wall-mounted, wimpy variety), stocked minifridge (items consumed are charged to your onboard account), desk/dresser, chair and stool, and bathroom with shower. A handy new amenity in standard bathrooms is the makeup/shaving mirror. Curiously, telephones do not have voice mail.

There are 28 cabins for passengers with disabilities.

PUBLIC AREAS The Conquest ships are bright and playful—a sort of Mardi Gras feel instead of the dark and glittery Las Vegas look some of the older ships in the fleet sport. Architect Joe Farcus was inspired by the great Impressionist and post-Impressionist artists—not only their paintings but also their color palette—so *Conquest* bursts with sunny yellows and oranges and vivid blues and greens. Maybe Farcus is running a little low on inspiration these days, as the *Glory*'s theme revolves around "color," with public rooms bearing names such as the White Heat Dance Club, the Amber Palace (show lounge), and On The Green (golf-themed sports bar). On the *Valor,* a liberally applied "heroism" theme connects everything from the Bronx Bar Yankee-themed sports bar with white leather barstools and banquettes designed to look like baseballs, to the One Small Step disco, a tribute to Neil Armstrong's walk on the moon a la weird minivolcano-like craters that stand several feet tall and glow with LED lighting.

The general arrangement of public areas on these ships closely resembles that of the Destiny class with a pair of two-story main dining rooms (one midships, one aft), a three-deck-high showroom in the bow, and a secondary lounge in the stern.

As on the Destiny ships, here, too, passengers step across the gangway and into the base of a soaring, nine-deck-high atrium, dressed to the nines in each ship's respective theme. On the *Conquest,* for example, it's a mural collage of works by masters such as Claude Monet, Paul Gauguin, and Edgar Degas, with backlit flowers of Murano glass popping up from the granite-topped atrium bar. Each vessel sports 22 bars and lounges, many of these rooms clustered on the Atlantic and Promenade decks.

The 1,400-seat Show Lounge stages Carnival's big production shows. On the *Valor,* it's called Ivanhoe and it's complete with knights in shining armor a la Sir Walter Scott's classic tale. There's also a secondary entertainment venue for dance bands and late-night comedians, as well as a piano bar, wine bar (the best place for people-watching, as its open to the main promenade), and another live music venue where combos belt out oldies, country, and requests.

Nobody does disco better than Carnival. You can groove on an enormous floor (on the *Conquest,* it's a jungle ambience straight from the exotic paintings of Henri Rousseau; on the *Valor,* it's all about the moon), or just perch with a drink on funky barstools (lotus-shaped on the *Conquest,* for example). One deck down is the ships' most elegant lounge, done in wood paneling and dark, rich colors. The Internet Café is oddly tucked away off a back corner of the room.

The casinos sprawl across 8,500 square feet, packing in almost 300 slot machines and about two dozen gaming tables. Tucked off to one side is the sports bar.

The ships boast by far the biggest children's facilities in the fleet: At 4,200 square feet, Children's World and the separate teen center combined are more than triple the space for kids and teens on Destiny-class ships. Children's World sits atop the spa (instead of sharing the same deck as on the Destiny vessels) and holds an arts-and-crafts station, video wall, computer lab, PlayStation 2 game units, and lots of fun toys for younger children, from play kitchens to push toys, mini–sliding boards, farm sets, and more. The enclosed adjacent deck offers a dipping pool. The ships' nod to teenagers is a big nod. Teen facilities on earlier ships were, at most, a room, but here's a space so large it forms its own secondary promenade branching off the main one. The teen area has a soda bar and separate dance floor flowing into a huge video games area with air hockey tables, which is open to all passengers.

DINING OPTIONS   Each ship has a pair of two-story main restaurants, styled in keeping with each ships' theme. On the *Conquest,* a monumental sunflower marking the entrance to Monet is by the Murano glass artist Luciano Vistosi, while the artwork in the Renoir Restaurant is inspired by the cafe scene in the painting *Lunch at the Restaurant Fournaise.* On the *Valor,* the Washington and Lincoln dining rooms won't win any design awards; described by the line as "contemporary colonial," what oddly dominates the decor are bright peach colored walls . . . hmmm. As Heidi's husband is fond of saying, "You can't eat ambience." Well, then bring out the lobster. You'll see broiled tail on the menu once a cruise, and there are six desserts nightly. Low-fat, low-carb, low-salt Spa Carnival Fare, vegetarian dishes, and children's selections are available.

The Conquest-class ships borrow the by-reservation supper club from the Spirit-class ships. The venue serves USDA prime-aged steaks, king crab claws, and other deluxe items for a $25-per-person cover charge. On the Spirit ships, the club sits under a glass portion of the ship's funnel for a more dramatic setting, but the Conquest ships' room has low ceilings and a more intimate feel. The best food and most refined service on board are here, where dinner is meant to stretch over several hours and several bottles of wine (for which there's an extra charge).

Breakfast, lunch, and dinner are served in the two-story restaurant on the Lido Deck, where you'll also find a 24-hour pizza counter (the mushroom and goat cheese pies are scrumptious). Separate buffet lines (more than on the Destiny ships, to alleviate crowding) are devoted to Asian and American dishes, deli sandwiches, salads, and desserts. A new concept (on the upper level) is Sur Mer: Carnival modestly describes this as a fish-and-chips shop, but the choices include such goodies as calamari, lobster salad, and bouillabaisse. There's no charge here or for the stand-up sushi bar down on the main promenade, but the pastries, cakes, and specialty coffees at the patisserie cost a couple of bucks each.

There's also 24-hour room service with new menus including items such as a chicken fajita with greens and guacamole in a jalapeno and tomato wrap, plus the standard tuna salad, cookies, fruit, and so on.

POOL, FITNESS, SPA & SPORTS FACILITIES   The ships' four swimming pools include the main pool with its two huge hot tubs and a stage for live (and realllly loud) music. If you don't love reggae and calypso, don't go here. This space is where all the action (and noise) of pool games plus the occasional outbreak of line dancing occurs. (Anyone for the Electric Slide?) Carnival's trademark twisty slide shoots into a pool one deck up. The aft pool, covered by a retractable glass dome, usually provides a more restful setting, although the pizzeria and burger grill are here (along with two more oversize hot tubs). The fourth pool is the one for kiddies outside the playroom.

The ships' 12,000-square-foot health club and salon with neat his and hers ocean-view steam and sauna rooms perches high on Deck 11. Though the decor is a real yawner—it's as though Farcus simply forgot about the waiting area and locker room—you'll find today's latest treatments available, from hot (well, warmed) rock massages to hair and scalp massages. The spa is run by Steiner, the company that controls most cruise ship spas. On the fitness side, you'll find the non-trendy aerobics classes offered for free (like stretching and step), and the cool stuff everyone wants to do, like Pilates and spinning, going for $10 a class. There's a hot tub that sits in a glass-enclosed space jutting into the fitness room.

The jogging track loops above an open deck so that no cabins underneath get pounded.

The Spirit Class: Carnival Spirit • Pride • Legend • Miracle

The Verdict

Bright and fun like the larger Destiny-class vessels, with the same multistory dining and entertainment venues, the Spirit class also boasts some more cool stuff such as a reservations-only restaurant and wedding chapel.

Carnival Spirit *(photo: Gero Mylius, Indav Ltd.)*

Specifications

Size (in tons)	88,500	Year Launched	
Passengers (double occ.)	2,124	*Spirit*	2001
Passenger/Space Ratio	41.7	*Pride*	2001
Total Cabins/Veranda Cabins	1,062/682	*Legend*	2002
Crew	930	*Miracle*	2004
Passenger/Crew Ratio	2.3 to 1	Last Major Refurbishment	N/A

Frommer's Ratings (Scale of 1–5)   ★★★★

Cabin Comfort & Amenities	5	Dining Options	4
Ship Cleanliness & Maintenance	4	Gym, Spa & Sports Facilities	4
Public Comfort/Space	4	Children's Facilities	4
Decor	4	Enjoyment Factor	4

When the $375-million Carnival *Spirit* debuted in April 2001, she ushered in a new class for the fun-ship line. Bigger than Carnival's eight Fantasy-class ships and smaller than its three Destiny-class vessels, the 2,124-passenger, 88,500-ton, 960-foot *Spirit, Pride, Legend,* and *Miracle* update Carnival's rubber-stamp style with a handful of innovations and more elegance, placing them closer to the newest Royal Caribbean and Princess vessels than to Carnival's earlier fun ships. The Spirit ships eliminate the cluster of nightclubs in favor of stretching the music venues from bow to stern on Decks 2 and 3, and there's an appealing supper club, which the subsequent Conquest-class has also adopted. A state-of-the-art "teleradiology" system enables the ship's doctors to digitally transmit X-rays and other patient information to medical facilities on shore for consultation on a broad range of medical situations.

Interestingly, the Spirit-class ships bear more than a little resemblance to Costa's 6-year-old *Costa Atlantica* and newer sister *Mediterranea:* Their hull and superstructure were built from identical plans, and Carnival design guru Joe Farcus did the decor for them all.

Cabins & Rates

Cabins	Per Diems from	Sq. Ft.	Fridge	Hair Dryer	Sitting Area	TV
Inside	$76	185	yes	yes	some	yes
Outside	$97	185	yes	yes	yes	yes
Suite	$197	275–300	yes	yes	yes	yes

CABINS   The Spirit-class ships have verandas on more than 60% of their cabins, though most are pretty small, with a wood-tone plastic chair, a small table, and a deck chair. (Cabins with larger balconies are amidships and aft on Decks 6, 7, and 8.) Their 213 inside cabins and outsides without balconies are a roomy 185 square feet (standard outsides with balconies are the same size plus a 40-sq.-ft. balcony). Of the 44 category-11 suites, most measure 275 square feet, plus an 85-square-foot balcony, while 10 located at the stern of Decks 4 through 8 measure 245 square feet, plus a jumbo wraparound 220-square-foot balcony. The six category-12 suites measure 300 square feet, plus a 115-square-foot balcony. On Deck 4, all category-5A cabins have lifeboats obstructing the view, though they do have sliding-glass doors that allow you to lean out into the fresh air.

In a subtle departure from the minimalist, somewhat cold cabin decor of the rest of Carnival's older ships, the *Spirit*'s cabins are warmer and more sophisticated, with toasted-caramel wood-tone furniture and mango- and coral-hued upholstery, drapes, and bedspreads. The pointy lighting fixtures are more stylish but don't throw a lot of light on the desk mirror. Also, there are none of those great little reading lights over the beds like the rest of the fleet offers, just lamps on the night tables.

All cabins, even the least expensive inside ones, have a decent amount of storage space in both closets and drawers (with small leather handles that some people find difficult to grab hold of), plus a safe, TV, desk and stool, chair, well-designed bathroom with a shower stall that is a tad larger than that on other ships, and glass shelves on either side of the large mirror to stash your toiletries. Just about all cabins have a small sitting area with a sofa and coffee table (some insides have only a chair and table), and all have a real hair dryer (stored in the desk/vanity drawer).

There are 16 cabins for passengers with disabilities.

PUBLIC AREAS   Carnival designer Joe Farcus works his whimsy once again aboard the Spirit-class ships, blending marble, wood-veneer walls, tile mosaic work, buttery leathers, rich fabrics, copper and bronze, Art Nouveau and Art Deco themes, and all manner of glass lighting fixtures. Though a somewhat subdued bronzy color-scheme defines many public areas, these ships still are glitzy and blinding in the same fun Vegas way as the rest of the Carnival fleet.

A string trio or pianist performs throughout the day at the lower-level lobby bar that anchors each ship's spectacular, jaw-dropping, nine-deck atrium, even more of a central hub than aboard earlier Carnival ships owing to its placement amidships. Just about all the indoor action is on Decks 2 and 3, where you'll find the piano bar (on *Spirit*, it's a neat Oriental-style spot with carved rosewood detailing, paper-lantern lighting fixtures, a red lacquer piano, and rich Chinese silk walls; on *Legend*, it's an understated tribute to Billie Holiday in stainless steel), large sports bar, disco, jazz nightclub (where karaoke and other contests are held), cafe (where you can purchase specialty coffees and pastries), combination library and Internet center (with a ridiculously spare book collection), elegant string of shops, modern-style wedding chapel, and sprawling photo gallery, where pictures can be digitally enhanced with borders. The low-ceilinged lounge tucked into the bow on Deck 1, at the end of a corridor of cabins, is so well hidden it's often empty.

The three-level showrooms are something to see; on *Spirit*, Farcus had Verdi's Egypt-themed opera *Aida* in mind when he covered it head to toe in brightly painted gold-and-blue King Tut–style sarcophagi and hieroglyphics (on the *Legend*, it's a flashy Mediterranean-style movie palace). Sightlines are severely limited from parts of the Deck 2 and Deck 3 level, so arrive early if you want a decent view. The disco is a two-story barrel-shaped place with a giant video wall; on *Spirit*, the funky spot has a Jackson Pollock–inspired splatter-painted design. On the *Miracle*, the disco was made to look like a gothic castle in ruins with faux stonewalls.

The ships' broad outdoor promenade is wonderfully nostalgic (almost), but unfortunately does not wrap around the entire ship; near the bow you are channeled through a door and the promenade suddenly (and oddly) becomes enclosed and narrower, turning into a cute but kind of odd jungle-themed area lined with comfy chairs and small tables with views through jumbo-size portholes. The kids' playroom and a video arcade are tucked away in the far forward reaches of the bow on Decks 4 and 5. Playrooms are divided into three sections connected via tunnels and offer sand-art, a candy-making machine, a computer lab with a handful of iMacs and PlayStations, and other diversions. They're of decent size, but nowhere near the size and scope of what you'll find on the Conquest-class fleetmates or on Royal Caribbean's Radiance- and Voyager-class ships and Disney's *Magic* and *Wonder*. The video arcade is huge, with 30-plus machines, including air hockey and foosball.

DINING OPTIONS   Unlike most of the fleet, the Spirit ships have one sprawling, two-story, 1,300-seat formal dining room (offering the traditional early and late seating). They're pleasant places to dine, especially if you can snag an intimate booth or a table along the glass railing on the second level, with views of the scene below. The Spirit ships were the first in the Carnival fleet to also offer an alternative reservations-only restaurant for more intimate and elegant dining, for a cover charge of $25 per person. The newer Conquest class also has them. Main drawback on the Spirit class: Rowdy crowd noise sometimes filters up from the atrium bar below. In the huge, well-laid-out indoor/outdoor casual buffet restaurant, menu items range from standard

American to French, Italian, and Asian; sushi is offered in the buffet restaurant at lunch. Don't expect to be bowled over by the preparation and service unless Denny's is your idea of gourmet. On a recent cruise, desserts looked better than they tasted.

As aboard the rest of the fleet, there's delicious 24-hour pizza and Caesar salad offered from a counter in the buffet restaurant. You can get a tasty deli sandwich from the New York Deli all day long, and self-serve frozen yogurt and soft ice cream are also on hand. Caviar and champagne combos are available in certain bars on each ship.

POOL, FITNESS, SPA & SPORTS FACILITIES The Spirit-class spas are the only ones in the fleet to have any decor to speak of; the rest have had a bland, institutional look, as though Farcus forgot to design them. The *Spirit*, for instance, sports a Greek-inspired motif of white fluted columns and images of Greek gods on the walls. The multilevel gyms are based loosely on a Greek amphitheater, and though they're more than adequate, with dozens of machines, they're a bit more cramped than the huge spaces on the Conquest- and Destiny-class ships.

In general, there are lots of places for sunbathing across the three topmost decks, including the area around the two main pools amidships on the Lido Deck, as well as around a third pool on the aft end of this deck. All told, there are four hot tubs (including one in the gym), plus a jogging track, combination volleyball/basketball court, and shuffleboard. A fun, snaking water slide for kids and adults is sequestered high up and aft on a top deck, and adjacent is a small, sort of forlorn, fenced-in kids' wading pool. With no shade up on this part of the ship, don't forget to put sunscreen on your kiddie's delicate skin—or your own, for that matter.

The Destiny Class: Carnival Destiny • Triumph • Victory

The Verdict

These three behemoths capture the classic Carnival whimsy with mind-boggling design features, yet have a somewhat mellower color scheme than the line's older ships—but let's not split hairs, they're still bright.

Carnival Destiny *(photo: Carnival Cruise Lines)*

Specifications

Size (in tons)		Total Cabins/Veranda Cabins	
Destiny	101,353	*Destiny*	1,321/480
Triumph/Victory	102,000	*Triumph/Victory*	1,379/508
Passengers (double occ.)		Crew	1,000
Destiny	2,642	Passenger/Crew Ratio	2.6 to 1
Triumph/Victory	2,758	Year Launched	
Passenger/Space Ratio		*Destiny*	1996
Destiny	38.5	*Triumph*	1999
Triumph/Victory	37	*Victory*	2000
Last Major Refurbishment	N/A		

Frommer's Ratings (Scale of 1–5)   ★★★★½

Cabin Comfort & Amenities	5	Dining Options	3.5
Ship Cleanliness & Maintenance	4	Gym, Spa & Sports Facilities	5
Public Comfort/Space	4.5	Children's Facilities	4
Decor	4	Enjoyment Factor	4.5

Taller than the Statue of Liberty, these 13-deck ships cost $400 to $440 million apiece and carry 2,642 passengers based on double occupancy and 3,400-and-change with every additional berth filled (and some cruises do indeed carry a full load). All three are nearly identical, though *Triumph* and *Victory* are a tad larger than *Destiny* (having an additional deck at top) and are reconfigured in a few minor ways. *Destiny* was the first cruise ship ever built to exceed 100,000 tons, and her sheer size and spaciousness inspired the cruise industry to build more in this league: After her debut, Princess launched the 109,000-ton Grand class, Royal Caribbean introduced the massive 142,000-ton Voyager class, Cunard rolled out the 150,000-ton *Queen Mary 2*, Carnival's 110,000-ton Conquest ships debuted, and Royal Caribbean's 160,000-ton Ultra Voyager ships are in the works . . . what's next?

Cabins & Rates

Cabins	Per Diems from	Sq. Ft.	Fridge	Hair Dryer	Sitting Area	TV
Inside	$78	185	no	yes	no	yes
Outside	$99	185–220	no	yes	yes	yes
Suite	$195	275–345	yes	yes	yes	yes

CABINS   The Destiny-class sisters, along with the new Conquest-class ships, have the line's biggest standard outside cabins, with the category-6A and -6B cabins (which take up most of the Riviera and Main decks) measuring 220 square feet (and that's not including the balcony); the rest of the fleet's standard outsides measure 185 square feet—still very roomy. If that's not enough, more than 60% of the *Destiny* sisters' outside cabins (480–508 of them) have sitting areas and private balconies. That's compared to a paltry 54 private verandas out of 618 outside cabins on Carnival's Fantasy-class ships.

There are two categories of suites: Veranda Suites measuring 275 square feet, plus a 65-square-foot balcony; and Penthouse Suites where you can live like a king with 345 square feet, plus an 85-square-foot balcony. Both are located on Deck 7, smack dab in the middle of the ship. Specially designed family staterooms, at a comfortable but not roomy 230 square feet, are located convenient to children's facilities, and many of them can be connected to the stateroom next door. In lieu of a private veranda, these family-friendly staterooms feature floor-to-ceiling windows for ocean views. All standard cabins have a TV, safe, hair dryer, desk, dresser, chair and stool, and bathroom with shower.

A total of 25 cabins on *Destiny,* 27 on *Triumph,* and 30 on *Victory* are wheelchair accessible.

PUBLIC AREAS   At the time these ships were designed, Carnival interior designer Joe Farcus never had so much public space to play with, and he took full advantage.

The ships are dominated by staggering nine-deck atria with casual bars on the ground level, and the three-deck-high showrooms are a sight—*Destiny's* was the first of this magnitude on any cruise ship, and subsequent models tread a fine line between outrageous and relatively tasteful: for example, *Triumph's* wacko chandelier, which looks like DNA strands made from crystal golf balls, topped with little Alice-in-Wonderland candleholders. The ships' mondo casinos span some 9,000 square feet and feature more than 300 slot machines and about two dozen gaming tables.

Many of the ships' 12-plus bars and entertainment venues are located along the bustling main drag of the Promenade Deck. The Sports Bar on each ship boasts multiple TV monitors projecting different sporting events. Each ship has a wine bar, a cappuccino cafe, and a piano bar, which aboard *Triumph* is a bizarre New Orleans–themed place called the Big Easy, sporting thousands of real oyster shells covering its walls (collected from New Orleans' famous Acme Oyster House—only on Carnival!). Each also has a sprawling disco with a wild decor: On *Victory,* an Arctic motif features black faux-fur bar stools, while *Triumph's* decor is a little more reserved, with goofy little Barney-purple chairs and glass panels and tubes filled with bubbling water throughout. One deck below is an elegant lounge for a drink or a cigar: On *Triumph,* it's a clubby place called the Oxford Bar, with dark wood paneling, leather furniture, and gilded picture frames (too bad you can hear the disco music pounding above late at night). The ships' Internet centers are adjacent to this lounge.

Each ship has several shopping boutiques, a spacious beauty salon, a library, a card room, and a fairly large children's playroom and video arcade.

Note: As part of *Victory's* oceans-of-the-world theme, sculpted seahorses support the staircase railings throughout the ship. All fine and dandy, but their protruding snouts are hazardous if you don't watch where you're going. Heidi got a wicked black-and-blue mark on her leg to prove it.

DINING OPTIONS   Each ship has a pair of two-level dining rooms with ocean views from both the main floor and the mezzanine level, as well as a two-story indoor/outdoor casual buffet restaurant that includes two specialty food stations that make Asian stir-fry and deli-style sandwiches to order; sushi is also served in the buffet restaurant at lunch. There's also a grill section for burgers, fries, and kielbasa-size hot dogs, a salad bar, and a dessert island. Specialty coffee bars and patisseries sell gourmet goodies for a few bucks a pop, and caviar and champagne combos are available in certain bars on each ship.

POOL, FITNESS, SPA & SPORTS FACILITIES   Along with the Conquest-class ships, the Destiny-class facilities are the most generous among the Carnival vessels, with four pools (including a kids' wading pool); seven hot tubs; and a 214-foot, two-deck-high, corkscrew-shaped water slide.

The tiered, arena-style decks of the sprawling midships Lido pool area provide optimal viewing of the band and stage, pool games, and all the hubbub that happens in this frenetically busy part of the ship. Along with two hot tubs, *Destiny* has swim-up bars at two of its main pools; *Triumph* and *Victory* eliminated the swim-up bars in exchange for more deck space, larger pools, and the addition of a wading area a few inches deep surrounding the pools. Unfortunately, this area can be very difficult to get across, due to a lack of obvious "corridors" through all the deck chairs. The aft pool area on all three ships features two hot tubs and a retractable roof that covers it all, enabling deck activities and entertainment to continue even in rainy weather. On *Triumph* and *Victory,* the big stage adjacent to the Main Continent pool is even bigger than the one on *Destiny,* and it has been reconfigured to allow more space for guests at deck parties, and to make the pool deck more open and visually appealing. Another modification is the placement of a small performance stage aft on the Lido Deck near the New World pool.

Even though the ships' huge gyms aren't as large as those on Royal Caribbean's Voyager class, Carnival's are much roomier and actually feel bigger. The two-deck-high spa and fitness centers feature more than 30 state-of-the-art exercise machines, including virtual-reality stationary bikes. There are men's and women's saunas and steam rooms, and a pair of hot tubs. Spas offer all the latest treatments (at the latest high prices), but as on all Carnival ships (except for the newer Spirit class), they're surprisingly drab, and the only place to wait for your masseuse is on a cold, high-school-locker-room bench, wrapped in a towel—no robes are provided (unless, supposedly, you ask for one). So much for ambience. There are separate aerobics rooms (though they're smaller than they used to be, as half the space was snapped up to create a teen room a few years back).

The well-stocked 1,300-square-foot indoor/outdoor children's play center has its own pool and is nicely sequestered on a top deck, out of the fray of the main pool deck areas. The ships also have virtual-reality video arcades that promise hours of fun.

The Fantasy Class: Fantasy • Ecstasy • Sensation • Fascination • Imagination • Inspiration • Elation • Paradise

Fantasy *(photo: Carnival Cruise Lines)*

The Verdict

These time-tested favorites are the line's original megas, and their whimsical decor and endless entertainment and activities spell excitement from the get-go, though they feel a tad outdated compared to Carnival's newer classes.

Specifications

Size (in tons)	70,367	*Sensation*	1993
Passengers (double occ.)	2,040	*Fascination*	1994
Passenger/Space Ratio	34.5	*Imagination*	1995
Total Cabins/Veranda Cabins	1,020/54	*Inspiration*	1996
Crew	920	*Paradise*	1998
Passenger/Crew Ratio	2.2 to 1	*Elation*	1998
Year Launched		Last Major Refurbishment	
Fantasy	1990	*Fantasy*	2003
Ecstasy	1991		

Frommer's Ratings (Scale of 1–5)

Cabin Comfort & Amenities	4	Dining Options	3
Ship Cleanliness & Maintenance	4	Gym, Spa & Sports Facilities	3.5
Public Comfort/Space	4	Children's Facilities	4
Decor	3.5	Enjoyment Factor	4

These Fun Ships and their risqué names offer a successful combination of hands-on fun and a glamorous, fantasyland decor, with acres of teak decking plus all the diversions, distractions, and entertainment options for which Carnival is famous. They really are fun! (Or are they cheesy? It's such a fine line.) Each was built on the same cookie-cutter design at Finland's Kvaerner Masa shipyard (at a cost of $225 to $300 million each . . . a bargain compared to the $500-million price tag of a new ship today), and they are nearly identical in size, profile, and onboard amenities, with different decorative themes. These ships have been run hard and they look a bit worn out compared to their newer fleetmates, but you won't notice a thing after a couple of Carnival Funship drink specials!

From the first ship of the series *(Fantasy)* to the last *(Paradise)*, the ships' decor evolved toward a relatively mellow state (note, *relatively*). *Fantasy* features a Roman-themed entertainment promenade inspired (loosely, of course) by the ancient city of Pompeii, with a faux-stone floor, terra-cotta urns, Doric columns, and electric torches—but where's the flowing lava? In late 2003, the ship underwent a major refurbishment, which included a brand new atrium bar (like the *Elation* and all newer ships), completely overhauled cabins, redesigned promenade, and new carpeting and wall coverings throughout much of the other areas.

Ecstasy follows a city-at-sea theme, with no shortage of neon-metallic skyscraper imagery. *Fascination* is big on flashy fantasy, with a retina-shattering chrome atrium and a heavy Broadway and Hollywood movie-star theme, with life-size (though worn-looking) mannequins of legends such as John Wayne and Marilyn Monroe; while *Sensation* avoids obvious razzle-dazzle in favor of artwork enhanced with ultraviolet lighting, sound, and color. Aboard *Imagination,* miles of fiber-optic cable make the mythical and classical artwork glow in ways the Greek, Roman, and Assyrian designers of the originals never would have imagined. *Inspiration* was reportedly inspired by artists such as Toulouse-Lautrec and Fabergé, and architects such as Frank Lloyd Wright—though in a . . . brighter style. You'll find a Greek mythology theme on the *Elation* that's all about Carnival-style "classic" columns, flutes, and harps, while the *Paradise* pays tribute to classic ocean liners. The newest of the Fantasy-class ships—the *Paradise* and the *Elation*—sport a few improvements over their sisters, including an expanded kids' playroom and the hublike atrium bar. The *Sensation* has also recently added an atrium bar (the rest of this class will likely get the atrium bars added at some point). By the way, the *Paradise,* touted as the line's only completely nonsmoking ship when she debuted in 1998, changed its policies in late 2004; you can now light up in designated areas, like on the rest of the fleet.

Cabins & Rates

Cabins	Per Diems from	Sq. Ft.	Fridge	Hair Dryer	Sitting Area	TV
Inside	$70	185	no	no	no	yes
Outside	$87	185	no	no	no	yes
Suite	$190	330	yes	no	yes	yes

CABINS   Accommodations range from lower-deck inside cabins with upper and lower berths to large suites with verandas, king-size beds, sitting areas, and balconies. As with the entire fleet, standard cabins here are roomy (at least 185 sq. ft.) and minimalist in design, with stained-oak trim accents and conventional, monochromatic colors such as salmon red—subdued compared to the flamboyance of the public areas. The cabins are not big on personality but are functional and well laid out. There are 26 demi-suites and 28 suites, all with private verandas. The 28 330-square-foot suites each have a whirlpool tub and shower, an L-shaped sofa that converts into a foldaway bed, a safe, a minibar, a walk-in closet, and sliding-glass doors leading to a 70-square-foot private balcony, and are positioned midway between stern and bow, on a middle deck subject to the least tossing and rocking during rough weather.

All cabins, even the least expensive inside ones, have enough storage space to accommodate a reasonably diverse wardrobe, and feature safes, TVs, desk and stool, chair, reading lights for each bed, and bathrooms with roomy showers and generous-size mirrored cabinets to store your toiletries.

About 20 cabins on each ship are suitable for passengers with disabilities.

DINING OPTIONS   In addition to a pair of big one-story dining rooms with windows, there's a large indoor/outdoor casual buffet restaurant. You'll also find specialty coffee bars and patisseries on *Elation, Ecstasy,* and *Paradise* selling gourmet goodies for a couple of bucks a pop. There's a complimentary sushi bar serving fresh, tasty sushi in late afternoons on all but the *Sensation,* with sake available for an extra charge. Caviar and champagne combos are available in certain bars on each ship.

PUBLIC AREAS   Each ship boasts the same configuration of decks, public lounges, and entertainment venues, including a six-story atrium flanked by glass-sided elevators, casinos, new Internet centers, and at least eight bars, plus several (usually packed) hot tubs. The cluster of disappointing shops on each ship is surprisingly cramped and won't be winning any design awards; it's much better on the newer ships.

POOL, FITNESS, SPA & SPORTS FACILITIES   Although totally blah in the decor department, the 12,000-square-foot spas and fitness areas are well-enough equipped. Each has a roomy, mirrored aerobics room and a large, windowed, Pepto Bismol–colored gym with (last time we counted) seven treadmills, five stationary bikes, two rowing machines, two step machines, and dozens of free weights. Each has men's and women's locker rooms and massage rooms (both areas surprisingly drab and institutional feeling), as well as a sauna and steam room, whirlpools, and three swimming pools, one of which has a spiraling water slide. The Sun Deck of each ship offers an unobstructed ⅛-mile jogging track covered with a rubberized surface.

Holiday • Celebration

The Verdict

Fun ships, yes, but these older Carnival vessels are outdated and frumpy compared to their slick, glamorous newer sisters. To compensate, Carnival has been basing them at offbeat home ports, like Mobile (AL) and Jacksonville (FL).

Celebration *(photo: Carnival Cruise Lines)*

Specifications

Size (in tons)		*Holiday*	726/10
Celebration	47,262	Crew	
Holiday	46,052	*Celebration*	670
Passengers (double occ.)		*Holiday*	660
Celebration	1,486	Passenger/Crew Ratio	2.2 to 1
Holiday	1,452	Year Launched	
Passenger/Space Ratio		*Holiday*	1985
Celebration	32	*Celebration*	1987
Holiday	31.5	Last Major Refurbishment	
Total Cabins/Veranda Cabins		*Holiday*	1998
Celebration	743/10	*Celebration*	1999

Frommer's Ratings (Scale of 1–5)   ★★★

Cabin Comfort & Amenities	3	Dining Options	3
Ship Cleanliness & Maintenance	3	Gym, Spa & Sports Facilities	2
Public Comfort/Space	3	Children's Facilities	3
Decor	3	Enjoyment Factor	4

Take them for what they are: near relics. Museum pieces, really. Refreshing if today's new mega ships are too big for your liking and nostalgic if you can appreciate the design ideals of the disco era. The decor encompasses all the colors of the rainbow, with healthy doses of chrome, brass, and mirrors a la the late 1970s, early 1980s—Tony Manero would go gaga. These medium-size, nearly identical ships were built some 20 years ago for about $100 million to $170 million apiece. Sure, they can't compare with their new post-1990 sisters in the style and amenities departments, but they're often priced less and you can enjoy that wild-and-crazy brand of Carnival fun if your expectations are reasonably low.

There's no atrium, and the pool deck of each ship can get crowded and cramped at high noon. Refurbishments over the past few years on *Celebration* included replacing hot tubs with new models; installing new carpeting, tile, counters, and equipment for the buffet restaurants; and adding a new video-game arcade and a photo gallery. The cramped Lido buffet restaurants on both have been remodeled, creating a more open area; teak flooring was replaced with tile and carpeting; and a new pizzeria was also installed. *Holiday*'s 1998 enhancements were similar, and also included refurbishment of the spa, gym, and several entertainment areas.

Cabins & Rates

Cabins	Per Diems from	Sq. Ft.	Fridge	Hair Dryer	Sitting Area	TV
Inside	$67	186	no	no	no	yes
Outside	$84	186	no	no	no	yes
Suite	$204	374	yes	no	yes	yes

CABINS   Like the standard cabins in the entire Carnival fleet, they're big. Done in blond-wood tones with pinky-red accenting, they're clean and uncluttered, though nothing to write home about, and are all virtually identical. Beds can be configured as twins or doubles, and each cabin has piped-in stereo music as well as a wall-mounted TV. The medium-size bathrooms have showers.

At 374 square feet, the 10 suites on the Verandah Deck of each ship are as large and comfortable as those offered aboard vessels charging a lot more. Each has a whirlpool tub and shower, an L-shaped sofa that converts into a foldaway bed, a safe, a minibar, a walk-in closet, and sliding-glass doors leading to an 87-square-foot private balcony.

Just over a dozen cabins are wheelchair accessible. There are no connecting cabins.

PUBLIC AREAS   You may need to keep your sunglasses on even when you're inside: Public areas explode with color in that original outrageous (even scary) Carnival way. We're talking healthy doses of fuchsia, black, red, chrome, brass, glass, and neon. On *Celebration,* there's a bar designed like the inside of a trolley car, and the Red Hot Piano Bar is just that—all red. On *Holiday* one bar features an authentic British bus from 1934. In all, each ship has seven bars, six entertainment lounges, a casino, a disco, a library, and a video arcade. There's also a children's playroom, a beauty salon, and shops. Elevators interconnect all eight decks.

DINING OPTIONS   Two main one-story dining rooms and one casual indoor/outdoor buffet restaurant serve breakfast, lunch, and dinner. On *Celebration,* you'll find a complimentary sushi bar open in late afternoons, with sake available for an extra charge.

POOL, FITNESS, SPA & SPORTS FACILITIES   Even though the gyms and spas were remodeled and expanded in 1998 and 1999, you can tell fitness just wasn't a big priority when these ships were built—they're tiny and drab, with a sauna for men and women and a small hair salon. Each ship has two hot tubs and three pools, including a small wading pool for children and a pool with a snaking water slide.

2 Celebrity Cruises

1050 Caribbean Way, Miami, FL 33132. ☎ **800/437-3111** or 305/539-6000. Fax 800/722-5329. www.celebrity.com.

THE LINE IN A NUTSHELL   Celebrity offers the best of two worlds: If you like elegance without stuffiness, fun without bad taste, and pampering without a high price, Celebrity is king. **Sails to:** Caribbean, Panama Canal, Alaska, Mexican Riviera,

Bermuda, Hawaii, Canada/New England (plus Europe, transatlantic, South America, Asia, South Pacific).

THE EXPERIENCE   With the most elegant big ships in the industry, Celebrity offers a refined cruise experience, yet one that is fun and active. Each ship is spacious, glamorous, and comfortable, mixing sleekly modern and Art Deco styles and throwing in cutting-edge art collections to boot.

An exceedingly polite and professional staff contributes greatly to the elegant mood. Dining-wise, Celebrity shines with its dashing alternative restaurants on the Millennium-class ships. Featuring the signature cuisine of celebrity chef Michel Roux, they're the best at sea for both quality of food and their gorgeous decor.

Like all the big-ship lines, Celebrity offers lots for its passengers to do, but its focus on mellower pursuits and innovative programming sets it apart. Niceties such as roving a cappella groups lend a warmly personal touch, while expert-led seminars on topics like astronomy, photography, personal investing, and history offer a little more cerebral meat than the usual.

Celebrity gets the "best of" nod in a lot of categories: The AquaSpas on the line's megaships are up there with the most attractive at sea, the art collections the most compelling fleetwide, the decor the most original, and the onboard activities and entertainment among the most varied. Celebrity pampers suite guests with butler service, and treats all guests to in-cabin pizza delivery.

Pros

- **Spectacular spas:** Beautiful and well equipped, the spas on the Millennium- and Century-class ships are the best at sea today.
- **Best alternative restaurants at sea:** Service, food, and wine are simply excellent; and the Millennium-class restaurants' elegant decor incorporates artifacts from cherished old liners, such as *Olympic, Normandie,* and SS *United States.*
- **Innovative everything:** Entertainment, spas, and cuisine are some of the most innovative in the industry. The latest: acupuncture and holistic healing theme cruises and Cirque du Soleil–inspired shows.

Cons

- **Too much to do:** Okay, while this might not actually be a legitimate negative, there really are just so many cool things to do, you may not be able to squeeze them all in.

Compared with other mainstream lines, here's how Celebrity rates:

	Poor	Fair	Good	Excellent	Outstanding
Enjoyment Factor					✓
Dining				✓	
Activities					✓
Children's Program			✓		
Entertainment			✓		
Service					✓
Worth the Money					✓

CELEBRITY: THE BEST OF TWO WORLDS

What's not to love? Celebrity offers moderately priced cruises that feel like they should cost a lot more.

The line's roots go back to the powerful Greek shipping family Chandris, whose patriarch John D. Chandris founded a cargo shipping company in 1915. The family expanded into the cruise business in the late 1960s and by 1976 had the largest passenger-cruise fleet in the world. In the late 1970s, they introduced the down-market Chandris-Fantasy Cruises, which served a mostly European clientele. In 1989, the Chandris family dissolved Fantasy and created Celebrity Cruises, building great ships that got better each time. The company's rise to prominence was so rapid and so successful that in 1997 it was courted and acquired by the larger and wealthier Royal Caribbean Cruises, Ltd., which now operates Celebrity as a sister line to Royal Caribbean International, retaining their crisp navy-blue-and-white hulls and rakishly angled funnels decorated with a giant X (actually the Greek letter *chi,* for Chandris). With their distinctive profiles and striking art collections (featuring works by Robert Rauschenberg, Damien Hirst, Jasper Johns, David Hockney, and others), they're some of the most distinctive and stylish ships out there, but even so Celebrity's had some trouble distinguishing itself in the marketplace. Some new efforts, though—including the **Celebrity Xpeditions** adventure program (with trips to the Galapagos, Arctic, and Antarctic, and adventure excursions on many other sailings), an entertainment partnership with **Cirque du Soleil,** and the line's first cruise in Southeast Asia—are bound to attract attention.

PASSENGER PROFILE

Celebrity tries to focus on middle- to upper-middle-income cruisers, and even wealthy patrons who want the best megaship experience out there (while happily nestled in one of the line's amazing Penthouse Suites); but with Celebrity's rates more or less comparable to those of Carnival and Royal Caribbean, you'll find a very wide range of folks aboard, those who appreciate the elegance of its ships, and those who could care less. Clients who choose their cruise based on more than just price like Celebrity because it's not Carnival and because it offers a well-balanced cruise, with lots of activities and a glamorous, exciting atmosphere that's both refined and fun.

Most passengers are couples in their 40s, though you'll see passengers of all ages, with a decent number of honeymooners and couples celebrating anniversaries, as well as families with children in summer and during the holidays.

DINING

TRADITIONAL   While Celebrity loves touting executive chef Michel Roux and his food, and while the dining service is tops in the mainstream category, the cuisine in the main dining rooms isn't really that much better than what's being served these days on the newest Royal Caribbean, Princess, and Disney ships. When you're serving dinner to 800 people at once, it can only be so good (it's the specialty restaurants, below, that really excel). In the main dining rooms, a dinner menu is likely to feature something along the lines of escargot a la bourguignon, chilled melon soup, filet of halibut on a bed of zucchini spaghetti enhanced with an apple cider beurre blanc; duckling a l'orange; or a prime rib. To balance such heartiness, at every meal Celebrity offers lighter "spa" fare, such as a broiled king salmon or roast pork loin stuffed with sun-dried tomatoes (calorie, fat, cholesterol, and sodium breakdowns are listed on the back of the menu); and a vegetarian menu is available upon request. Wine-wise, Chef Roux's choices are offered in a wide price range to suit every budget, with many French choices. Plus, Celebrity recently introduced a line of proprietary wines called Celebrity Cruises Cellarmaster Selection. The wines can also be purchased online at www.celebrityvineyards.com. The first two varieties released were a 2002 Russian River Valley Chardonnay and a 2001 Sonoma County Cabernet Sauvignon. Seems like every cruise line in town is hopping *on* the wagon, even Carnival started a wine club recently.

SPECIALTY Celebrity really shines with the cuisine, service, and ambience offered in the intimate alternative restaurants on the Millennium-class ships. Here, Michel Roux and his impressively high service and food standards make the experience well worth the $30 cover charge (the highest cover charge on a ship that we know of). There seem to be more waitstaff than diners in the restaurants, which seat just over 100 passengers; Caesar salads and zabaglione are prepared tableside, and an excellent cheese trolley is presented at the end of the meal (the fine selection, from blues to sharps and mild goat cheeses, is flown in from Paris). At a dinner in *Infinity*'s elegant SS United States restaurant, the charming maitre d' carved our crispy roasted Long Island duckling with the finesse of a concert pianist. All the maitre d's are highly trained, often by a member of Michel Roux's shoreside restaurant staff, and keep standards way up on the four Millennium-class ships.

Menus are similar throughout the four specialty restaurants, though there's at least one thing on each restaurant's menu that was inspired by a dish served on the venue's namesake, such as Waldorf Pudding in the Olympic restaurant, which is prepared as it was on the original liner. Otherwise, expect very similar dishes, for example, appetizers such as a creamy lobster broth, tartare of salmon garnished with quail eggs, and goat cheese soufflé with tomato coulis, followed by entrees such as sea bass brushed with tapenade, shrimp scampi flambéed in Armagnac, Steak Diane, and rack of lamb coated with mushroom duxelles and wrapped in a puff pastry. For dessert, you can't go wrong with chocolate soufflé or a plate of Michel Roux's favorite bite-size desserts. Wines by the glass and bottle are suggested with each dish, and while many are pricey, some are affordable, and Mr. Roux knows how to pick an exquisite wine.

CASUAL As with most lines today, alternative casual dining is available in the Lido restaurant on most nights (though on a recent *Zenith* cruise, the lighting was awfully bright and the taped music too loud). Waiters serve entrees such as salmon, pasta, gourmet pizzas, and chicken between about 6 and 9:30pm by reservation only (although if there's space, walk-ins are accepted, too), unlike Carnival and Royal Caribbean, which offer buffet-style alternative restaurants. During dinnertime, Celebrity also offers a **sushi bar** in one section of the Lido restaurant serving both appetizer-size portions and full meals. Celebrity's breakfast and lunch buffets in the Lido restaurant are on par with lines such as Royal Caribbean and Princess, with features like a made-to-order pasta bar and a **pizza** section.

Light breakfast eaters or those looking for a pre- or post-breakfast snack, will want to grab an incredibly good croissant from **Café Cova** (the croissants are free, but you have to pony up a few bucks for an accompanying latte or cappuccino). The ships also have outdoor grills offering burgers and such. Each Millennium-class ship has a **Spa Cafe** in a corner of the thalassotherapy pool area where you can get low-cal treats for lunch or dinner from noon to 8pm, including raw veggie platters, poached salmon with asparagus tips, vegetarian sushi, and pretty salads with tuna or chicken, or enjoy a quick spa breakfast of items such as bagels and lox, fresh fruit, cereal, and boiled eggs.

SNACKS & EXTRAS A nice touch that appears on all formal nights, plus one other night, is a late-night culinary soiree known as **Gourmet Bites,** in which a series of upscale canapés and hors d'oeuvres, such as fish tempura and roasted garlic lemon chicken, are served by roving waiters in the ship's public lounges between midnight and 1am. There's a traditional midnight buffet on the final formal night; otherwise, themed buffets, such as Oriental, Italian, Tex-Mex, or tropical smorgasbords, are offered at lunch in the Lido restaurant.

At least once per cruise fleetwide, the line offers what it calls **Elegant Tea,** an impressive little event in which white-gloved waiters serve tea, finger sandwiches, scones, and desserts from rolling trolleys. You sure won't find this on Carnival. The line's 24-hour room service allows passengers to order off the lunch and dinner menus during those hours. And not only is Celebrity's pizza tasty and available throughout the afternoon fleetwide, but you can also get it delivered to your cabin (in a box and pouch like your local pizzeria uses) between 3 and 7pm and 10pm and 1am daily.

ACTIVITIES

Celebrity's ships offer lots of options for those who want to stay active, but they also cater to those who want to veg—on a recent *Zenith* cruise to Bermuda, **"quiet time by the pool"** was actually listed on the daily activities schedule from noon to 1:30pm (the pool band only started up at 3:30). Don't get us wrong, these ships aren't sleepy; they're just not rowdy in any way. If you'd rather chug beers by the pool while listening to loud music and watching (or joining) a men's hairy legs contest, then your better bet is a Carnival or Royal Caribbean cruise bound for the Caribbean or Bahamas. In the past few years, Celebrity has made a concerted effort to bring its onboard experience as close to a luxury line as possible.

If you like to stay busy, Celebrity's innovative repertoire of activities includes **complimentary enrichment lectures.** Up to four featured speakers/performers on every cruise may include caricature artists (on weeklong Caribbean and Bermuda sailings), naturalists (on Alaska, Hawaii, and South America sailings), chefs from well-regarded shoreside restaurants, and wine experts who offer onboard seminars and pre-dinner tastings. From time to time actors, politicians, and journalists also sail aboard and hold talks. For 2005, the lineup included Irving R. Levine, former NBC News Chief Economics Correspondent, former Clinton advisor and now FOX news political analyst Dick Morris, and actors Ernest Borgnine and Larry Hagman (okay, they're no Brad Pitt or George Clooney, but they probably have some good stories to tell from the old days!). In 2005, a neat new partnership with *National Geographic Traveler* magazine debuted, featuring writers and photographers from the magazine on several sailings.

The line also offers its Acupuncture at Sea program fleetwide now, after first being introduced in 2003. Now stop rolling your eyes, it's no odder than the rock-climbing walls or pottery-making studios other lines offer! (Just hope the seas don't get choppy during your session—ouch!) On all cruises, two to four doctors specializing in Oriental medicine are on hand to give free talks on acupuncture and other holistic health treatments as well as offer acupuncture and medicinal herbal treatments (for a fee) for pain management, smoking cessation, weight loss, stress management, and other ailments. The program is conducted out of a dedicated space on the Millennium ships, in the second level of the former Notes music rooms, and on the others, in modified meeting rooms.

If you're not the "try something new type," Celebrity also has the tried-and-true stuff to do too, from wine tastings (at $8 per person) to horse racing, bingo, bridge, art auctions, trivia games, arts and crafts, cooking demos, computer classes (from Web page design to the basics of Excel), and ballroom and line-dancing lessons. Celebrity isn't big on rowdy pool games, so the liveliest might be a gals versus guys volleyball match. During the day, a live pop band plays on the pool deck for a couple of hours.

If you prefer curling up with a good book in some quiet nook, you'll have no problem finding one. On *Galaxy* and *Mercury,* you can find some peace in the far corners of the Sky Deck and on the aft Penthouse Deck. On the Millennium sisters, the uppermost deck aft, near the jogging track, harbors a cluster of deck chairs away from the main-pool fray. Inside there are many hideaways, including **Michael's Club,** the edges of Rendez-Vous Square, and lounge chairs at the spa's thalassotherapy pool (on all but *Zenith*). The ships have impressive spas and gyms, especially the bigger ships, and offer various aerobic-type classes throughout the day; basic ones are free, and the cool ones, such as **Pilates and yoga,** are now $10 a person. All the ships have about 18 workstations for e-mail and Internet access, but only on the Millennium-class ships are they in one, great, oceanview computer center location. On the *Century, Galaxy, Mercury,* and *Zenith,* clusters of computers are in several different locations (these ships, after all, were not built with Internet cafes in mind). The Millennium-class ships also offer **Internet access in every cabin and suite** for guests who bring their laptops. You'll also enjoy the interactive system wired to all cabin TVs fleetwide, which is a great way for Celebrity to get you to spend more money! Besides ordering room service from on-screen menus, you can select the evening's wine in advance of dinner, play casino-style games, or browse in "virtual" shops for a wide selection of merchandise for delivery directly to your home at the end of your cruise. You can also order pay-per-view movies, including some adult titles (free movies are shown on the TV, too).

If you'd like to spend some time calling your friends and family back home (and tell them what a great time you're having), you can do that, too. At press-time, Celebrity announced its fleet would be wired for cellphone access by the end of 2005.

CHILDREN'S PROGRAM

Although it did not originate that way, Celebrity has evolved into a cruise line that pampers kids as well as adults, especially during the summer months and holidays, when 400+ children on a Caribbean or Bermuda cruise is typical. If there are more than 12 kids aboard, the line's Club X program kicks in. Each ship has a playroom (called the Ship Mates Fun Factory on the Millennium-class and the Century-class ships, and the Children's Playroom on *Zenith*), supervised activities practically all day long, and private and group babysitting evenings. *Galaxy, Mercury,* and Millennium-class ships also have wading pools, and the Millennium-class's indoor/outdoor facilities are by far the best in the fleet, with features like ball bins, slides, and jungle gyms.

During kid-intensive seasons, namely summers, activities are geared toward four age groups between the ages of 3 and 17. Kids ages 3 to 6, dubbed "Ship Mates," can enjoy treasure hunts, clown parties, T-shirt painting, dancing, movies, ship tours, and ice-cream-sundae-making parties. "Cadets," ages 7 to 9, have T-shirt painting, scavenger hunts, board games, arts and crafts, ship tours, and computer games. Your 10- to 12-year-old may want to join the "Ensign" activities, such as karaoke, computer games, board games, trivia contests, arts and crafts, movies, and pizza parties. For teens ages 13 to 17 (and divided into two groups, 13–15 and 16–17) who don't think themselves too cool to participate, the "Admiral T's" group offers talent shows, karaoke, pool games, and trivia contests. For the 3 to 12 set, Celebrity recently introduced **"Celebrity Science Journeys,"** which expose kids to fun and educational activities, from learning about insects and thunderstorms, to listening to dolphins and whales communicate under water. The Century-class and Millennium-class ships have attractive teen discos/hangout rooms (on the *Zenith,* bars and lounges are used for teen activities before they're opened for adults). Special activities offered in the summer include summer-stock theater presentations, which involve three age groups: The Ship Mates and Cadets sing, dance, and act, and the Ensigns direct and produce the plays. The Young Mariners Club offers kids the chance to get a behind-the-scenes look at the cruise ship, with activities and tours related to the entertainment, food and beverage, and hotel departments. Junior Olympics are held poolside and the whole family is encouraged to cheer on the kids who compete in relay races, diving, and basketball free throws. There are also masquerade parties, where Ship Mates and Cadets make their own masks and then parade around the ship. For toddlers under age 3, parents can borrow a "treasure box" from the playroom, which includes toys and books.

On formal nights during summers and holidays (and other times of the year if there are enough kids on board), a complimentary **parents' night out program** allows Mom and Dad to enjoy dinner alone while the kids are invited to a pizza party with the counselors. Group babysitting in the playroom is available for ages 3 to 12 between noon and 2pm on port days, and every evening from 10pm to 1am for children ages 3 to 12, for $6 per child per hour. Private in-cabin babysitting in the evening by a female crewmember is available on a limited basis for $8 per hour for up to two children (kids must be at least 6 months old); make your request 24 hours in advance. There is no minimum age for sailing.

ENTERTAINMENT

In the spirit of offering something a little different and a little more interesting than their peers, in 2004, Celebrity announced a partnership with fantasy circus troupe **Cirque du Soleil.** The observation lounges on *Constellation* and *Summit,* the two ships that at press time were offering the show, are transformed for 2 hours every evening into "The Bar at the Edge of the Earth," where guests engage in interactive performances (as opposed to a straight stage show) with surreal Cirque characters. Typically one or two performers are from the company's actual traveling circus, while the rest are from the ship's entertainment staff. Once per cruise, there is also a Cirque du Soleil Masquerade Ball when guests are invited to don masks (currently, there's no charge for this gala). Otherwise, Celebrity continues to offer some nice, understated entertainment touches such as strolling **a cappella groups, harpists,** and **classical trios** performing in various parts of each ship.

Celebrity also offers the popular favorites, such as **Broadway-style musicals** led by a sock-it-to-'em soloist or two and a team of lip-syncing dancers in full Vegas-esque regalia. On the Millennium-class and the Century-class ships, these shows are performed on some of the best-equipped, highest-tech stages at sea, with hydraulic orchestra pits, trap doors, turntables, sets that move along tracks in the stage floor, lasers, and a video wall showing images that coincide with the performance. Showrooms aboard all Celebrity ships have excellent acoustics and sightlines that are among the most panoramic and unobstructed at sea.

Other nights in the showroom you'll find magicians, comedians, cabaret acts, and passenger talent shows.

When you tire of Broadway-style entertainment, you'll find that all the ships have cozy lounges and piano bars where you can retreat for a romantic nightcap. In these more intimate lounges, the music is often laid-back jazz or music from the big-band

Celebrity Fleet Itineraries

Ship	Itineraries
Century	**7-night E. Carib:** Round-trip from Ft. Lauderdale, FL, Jan–Feb 2006. Alternates with **9- & 10-night W. Carib:** Round-trip from Miami, FL, Jan–Apr and Dec 2006. **4- & 5-night W. Carib:** Round-trip from Miami, FL, Nov–Dec 2006.
Constellation	**7-night S. Carib:** Round-trip from San Juan, PR, Jan–Mar and Dec 2006. **9- & 12-night Bermuda/Carib:** Round-trip from Bayonne, NJ, Mar–Apr 2006. **10- & 11-night E./S. Carib:** Round-trip from Ft. Lauderdale, FL, Nov–Dec 2006.
Galaxy	**11- & 12-night Panama Canal:** Round-trip from Galveston, TX, Jan–Apr 2006. **7- & 11-night S. Carib:** Round-trip from San Juan, PR, Dec 2006.
Infinity	**10- & 11-night Mexican Riviera:** Round-trip from San Francisco, CA, Apr 2006. **7-night Alaska Inside Passage:** Round-trip from Vancouver, BC, June–Aug. **14-night Hawaii:** Round-trip from San Diego, CA, Oct 2006.
Mercury	**8-, 10- & 11-night Mexican Riviera:** Round-trip from San Diego, CA, Jan–Apr and Oct–Dec 2006. **7-night Alaska Inside Passage:** Round-trip from Seattle, WA, May–Sept 2006. **3- & 4-night Pacific Northwest:** Round-trip from Seattle, WA, Sept–Oct 2006.
Millennium	**7-night E. Carib:** Round-trip from Ft. Lauderdale, Jan–Apr and Dec 2006.
Summit	**13- & 14-night Hawaii:** Round-trip from Los Angeles, CA, Jan and Mar–Apr 2006. **14-night Panama Canal:** East- or westbound between Ft. Lauderdale, FL, and Los Angeles, CA, Feb 2006. **7-night Gulf of Alaska:** North- or southbound between Vancouver, BC, and Seward/Anchorage, AK, May–Sept 2006.
Zenith	**4- & 5-night W. Carib:** Round-trip Miami, FL, Jan–Apr 2006. **7-night Bermuda:** Round-trip from Bayonne, NJ, Apr–Oct 2006. **10-night W. Carib:** Round-trip from Tampa, FL, Nov–Dec 2006.

era, spiced with interpretations of contemporary Celine Dion– or Whitney Houston–type hits. There's also the elegant and plush **Michael's Club** piano lounges, for a cordial and some quiet conversation. Each ship has late-night disco dancing, usually until about 3am. You'll also find karaoke and recent-release movies in the theater on the Millennium-class and Century-class ships.

Each ship has a rather spacious **casino,** and while they may not be as Vegasy as the ones on Carnival, they're bustling enough to put gamblers in the mood.

SERVICE

Overall, service is polite, attentive, cheerful, and especially professional. Staff wear white gloves at embarkation as they escort passengers to their cabins. Waiters have a poised, upscale-hotel air about them, and their manner contributes to the elegant mood. There are very professional sommeliers in the dining room, and waiters are on hand in the Lido breakfast and lunch buffet restaurants to carry passengers' trays from the buffet line to a table of their choice. Poolside, attendants are on hand to periodically pass out refreshing chilled towels along with sorbet. When it comes to tipping, Celebrity, like Royal Caribbean, invites passengers to give crew cash at the end of the cruise in the traditional method, or upon request, have them added to passengers' onboard charge accounts. We've found that across many lines cash tipping is more personal and definitely seems to keep the waiters and cabin stewards more motivated to please.

If you occupy a suite on any of the ships, you'll get a **tuxedo-clad personal butler** who serves afternoon tea, complimentary cappuccino and espresso, and complimentary pre-dinner hors d'oeuvres, bringing them right to your cabin. If you ask, he'll handle your laundry, shine your shoes, make sewing repairs, and deliver messages. For instance, on one sailing with Heidi's mother, the butler brought her a glass of juice each night after learning that she needed it to take her medication. Your butler will serve you a full five-course dinner if you'd rather dine in your cabin one night, and will even help you organize a cocktail party for your cruising friends, in either your suite or a suitable public area. (You foot the bill for food and drinks, of course.)

Other hedonistic treats bestowed upon suite guests include a bottle of champagne on arrival, personalized stationery, terry robes, a Celebrity tote bag, oversize bath towels, priority check-in and debarkation, express luggage delivery at embarkation, and complimentary use of the soothing indoor thalassotherapy pools on the Century-class ships, whose use otherwise carries a charge. Suite guests can even book an in-cabin massage daily between the hours of 7am and 8pm.

If you want the sweet life without actually booking a suite, Celebrity offers a suite-like class of cabins fleetwide called the **ConciergeClass** state rooms; though the size of the cabins is smaller than the suites and you don't get butler service, you do get perks from fresh flowers and fruit to personalized stationery, a choice of pillow, over-size towels, fancy bathrobes, a bottle of champagne, and first dibs on everything from dining to shore excursions. You'll pay more for these cabins (currently about 228 on each of the Millennium-class ships, about twice as many as on the other ships in the fleet) than a standard stateroom, but less than a bona fide suite.

Celebrity is the only mainstream line that provides cotton robes in all cabins fleetwide, and, in all cabins on the Millennium- and Century-class ships, you'll find minifridges stocked with drinks and snacks (if consumed, each item is billed on passengers' onboard accounts).

Laundry and dry-cleaning services are available fleetwide for a nominal fee, but there are no self-service laundry facilities.

The Millennium Class: Millennium • Infinity • Summit • Constellation

The Verdict

Total knockouts, Celebrity's newest and biggest offer all the leisure, sports, and entertainment options of a megaship and an atmosphere that combines old-world elegance and modern casual style. Without a doubt, they're the classiest megas at sea.

Millennium *(photo: Celebrity Cruises)*

Specifications

Size (in tons)	91,000	Year Launched	
Passengers (double occ.)	1,950	*Millennium*	2000
Passenger/Space Ratio	46	*Infinity*	2001
Total Cabins/Veranda Cabins	975/590	*Summit*	2001
Crew	999	*Constellation*	2002
Passenger/Crew Ratio	2 to 1	Last Major Refurbishment	N/A

Frommer's Ratings (Scale of 1–5)   ★★★★★

Cabin Comfort & Amenities	5	Dining Options	5
Ship Cleanliness & Maintenance	5	Gym, Spa & Sports Facilities	5
Public Comfort/Space	5	Children's Facilities	4
Decor	5	Enjoyment Factor	5

The Golden Age of sea travel may have ended about the same time top hats went out of style, but who's saying we can't have a new, more casual golden age of our own? Celebrity's Millennium-class ships may just be the vessels to ring it in.

In creating its newest ships, Celebrity took the best ideas from the wonderful *Century, Galaxy,* and *Mercury* and ratcheted them up, in terms of both scale and number: bigger ships, bigger spas and theaters, more veranda cabins, more dining options, more shopping, more lounges, and more sports and exercise facilities, plus more of the same great service, cuisine, and high-style onboard art for which the company is already known. In addition, they have state-of-the-art gas-turbine propulsion systems that produce less pollution and offer a smoother, quieter ride for passengers.

Cabins & Rates

Cabins	Per Diems from	Sq. Ft.	Fridge	Hair Dryer	Sitting Area	TV
Inside	$123	170	yes	yes	yes	yes
Outside	$152	170–191	yes	yes	yes	yes
Suite	$483	251–1,432	yes	yes	yes	yes

CABINS   Improving upon Celebrity's already-respectable cabins, the Millennium-class ships push the bar up yet another notch, with their elegant striped, floral, or patterned fabrics in shades such as butterscotch and pinkish terra cotta, along with Deco-style lighting fixtures and marble desktops. As with the rest of the fleet, standard inside and outside cabins are a roomy 170 square feet, and come with a small sitting area, stocked minifridge, TV, safe, ample storage space, cotton robes, and shampoo and soap dispensers built right into the shower. Only thing missing? Individual reading lights above the beds (though there are table lamps on nightstands).

Premium and Deluxe staterooms have slightly larger sitting areas and approximately 40-square-foot verandas. The 12 simply titled "Large" oceanview staterooms in the stern measure in at a very large 271 square feet and have two entertainment centers with TVs/VCRs, a partitioned sitting area with two convertible sofa beds, and very, very, very large 242-square-foot verandas facing the ships' wake.

New perks were rolled out in mid-2003 for a majority of the cabins on the Sky Deck of each Millennium-class vessel; most are 191 square feet or larger, and all have balconies. Passengers booking these cabins—called ConciergeClass staterooms—get a bunch of cushy extras, from a bottle of champagne to a choice of pillow, oversize towels, double-thick Frette bathrobes, priority for just about everything (dining, shore excursions, luggage delivery, embarkation, and disembarkation), and cushioned chairs and high-powered binoculars on the 41-square-foot balconies. Whew! Expect to pay more for these cabins than a regular standard, but they're still generally priced lower than suites (the main difference is that the suites also get butler service; the Concierge-Class staterooms don't). But (there's always a but!), unfortunately many of the

ConciergeClass and the Deluxe Oceanview cabins on the Sky Deck are somewhat in the shadows of the overhanging deck above (where the buffet restaurant, pool deck, and spa are located), which juts out farther than the three decks below it. Also, the balconies of the cabins at the aft and forward end of the Sky Deck are not completely private, since they jut out farther than the deck above (keep your clothes on).

In the suite category, Celebrity has gone all out, offering not only 24-hour butler service, but four levels of accommodations, from the 251-square-foot Sky Suites with balconies to the eight 467-square-foot Celebrity Suites (with dining area, separate bedroom, two TV/VCR combos, and whirlpool bathtub, but no verandas) and the 538-square-foot Royal Suites (also with a separate living/dining room, two TV/VCR combos, a standing shower and whirlpool bathtub, and a huge 195-sq.-ft. veranda with whirlpool tub). At the top of the food chain are the massive Penthouse Suites, which measure 1,432 square feet. They're as good at it gets, with herringbone wood floors, a marble foyer, a computer station, a Yamaha piano, and a simply amazing bathroom with ocean views and a full-size hot tub. Did we mention a 1,098-square-foot veranda that wraps around the stern of the ship and features a whirlpool tub and full bar? (The only downside is you sometimes feel the vibrations of the engines a few decks below.) If these suites have a Park Avenue feel, it's no wonder. The designer, Birch Coffey, also does apartments for New York's elite.

Passengers requiring use of a wheelchair have a choice of 26 cabins, from Sky Suites to balcony cabins and inside staterooms.

PUBLIC AREAS   There's simply nothing else at sea like the Grand Foyer atrium. The stunning hub of all four ships, each rectangular, three-deck area features a translucent, inner-illuminated onyx staircase that glows beneath your feet. All around are giant silk flower arrangements and topiaries. Off on the port side, guests can ride between decks on oceanview elevators (on a recent Panama Canal cruise, one passenger decided the elevators provided the best views on the ship and spent the day riding up and down). Overlooking the Foyer and the ocean, an attractive Internet center has 18 computer stations. These ships are masterpieces of rich velveteen and suedes, golden brocades, burled woods, and ornate topiaries.

In each ship's bow is the elegant three-deck theater, partially illuminated by what look like torches all around the room, an amazingly realistic trick produced by projecting blue and orange lights on a strip of thin cloth that's blown by a fan from below. The effect gives the rooms a warm, flickering, elegant glow (we've since seen these cool torches on other new ships, too). Seating on all three levels is unobstructed, except in the far reaches of the balconies.

For specialty coffees and freshly baked pastries (for an extra charge), the appealing Cova Café is a bustling, Italian-style cafe you could almost imagine being in Venice, with rich fabrics, cozy banquettes, and wood-frame chairs. You'll also find elegant martini, champagne, and caviar bars, as well as brighter, busier lounges for live music. For the real dancing, though, head up to the 100% stunning observation lounge/disco. Three circular levels break up the windowed room, which, without the use of any barriers, make the huge space seem more intimate.

Other rooms include the two-deck library, staffed by a full-time librarian; an oceanview florist/conservatory (created with the help of Paris-based floral designer Emilio Robba and filled mostly with silk flowers and trees, some of which are for sale); and the huge, high-tech conference center and cinema. Celebrity's signature Michael's

Club is a quiet, dignified piano bar, replete with fake fireplace and comfy leather club chairs (not much used during the day, it's a great place to snuggle up with a good book), and excellent for an after-dinner drink. The casinos are extensive; *Millennium*'s is decorated in an opulent Beaux Arts design, with faux-marble columns and mythological Greco-Roman sculptures, rich damask curtains, mosaic floor tiling, and wall frescoes.

The ships' Emporium Shops keep shopaholics in heaven, with names such as Escada Sport, Tommy Hilfiger, Swarovski (crystal), and Fendi (purses). There's also plenty of less expensive souvenir stuff.

For kids, the Shipmates Fun Factory has both indoor and outdoor soft-surface jungle gyms, a wading pool, a ball-bin, a computer room, a movie room, an arts-and-crafts area, a video arcade, a teen center, and more. The kids' facilities on the Millennium ships are the line's best.

DINING OPTIONS   The main dining rooms are beautiful two-level spaces that are very much in the style of Celebrity's earlier Century-class ships. A huge window in the stern and oversize round windows along both sides admit natural light, and a central double staircase provides a dramatic entrance (though the only downside to these lovely rooms is the vibrations felt from the engines a few decks below). The *Summit*'s dining room boasts a 7-foot bronze *La Normandie,* an Art Deco sculpture that originally overlooked the grand staircase on the SS *Normandie* ocean liner, in the center of its lower level. The piece, which is supposed to depict the goddess Athena, but looks an awful lot like George Washington in drag, was residing near the pool at the Fountainebleau Hotel in Miami before the line purchased it.

The pièce de résistance on these ships, however, is their alternative, reservations-only restaurants, which offer dining experiences unmatched on any other ship today. *Millennium*'s is the Edwardian-style Olympic restaurant, whose main attraction is several dozen hand-carved and gilded French walnut wall panels that were made by Palestinian craftsmen for the A La Carte restaurant aboard White Star Line's *Olympic,* sister ship to the *Titanic,* which sailed from 1911 to 1935. *Infinity*'s SS United States restaurant features etched-glass panels from the 1950s liner of the same name, which claimed fame for its speed crossing the Atlantic from New York—a record that has never been broken. (The ship is still around, though it sits disused and moldering at a pier in Philadelphia.) The *Summit*'s Normandie restaurant features original gold-lacquered panels from the smoking room of the legendary *Normandie,* while the *Constellation*'s Ocean Liners restaurant has artifacts from a variety of luxury liners, including sets of original red-and-black lacquered panels from the 1920s *Ile de France,* which add a whimsical Parisian air. The dining experience Celebrity has created to match these gorgeous rooms is nothing short of amazing: 130 guests (but never seated all at once, and 75 per night is typical) are served by a staff of about 23, including 8 dedicated chefs, 6 waiters, 5 maitre d's, and 4 sommeliers, all trained personally by executive chef Michel Roux and his senior staff. Dining here is a 2- to 3-hour commitment. Gracious service includes domed silver covers dramatically lifted off entrees by several waiters in unison when meals are delivered. Cuisine is a combination of Roux specialties with original recipes from the ships the restaurants are named after (such as the Long Island duckling featured on the original SS *United States*), and includes the first use of tableside flambé cooking at sea. A great cheese selection is offered from a marble-topped trolley, and in the menu, Roux suggests wines for each course (and they're not cheap). For atmosphere, a pianist or a piano/violin duo performs early-20th-century salon music. It's $30 a person to dine there, but, in this case, it's well worth it—you'd pay a fortune for this experience if you had it on land. No children under age 12 are allowed and reservations are required.

The huge but well-laid-out indoor-outdoor buffet restaurant on all four ships is open for breakfast, lunch, and dinner, offering regular buffet selections plus pizza, pasta, and ice-cream specialty stations. Waiters often carry passengers' trays to their tables and fetch coffee, a service level few other megaships match.

POOL, FITNESS, SPA & SPORTS FACILITIES   The spas on the Millennium-class ships are gorgeous and simply sprawling, with 25,000 square feet taken up with hydrotherapy treatment rooms, New Agey steam rooms and saunas (some chamomile-scented, some mint-scented, some with a shower that simulates a tropical rainforest, some with heated tiled couches and eucalyptus scents). A large bubbling thalassotherapy pool, with soothing pressure jets, in a solarium-like setting, is under a glass roof that also shelters a seating area where guests can grab a casual breakfast or lunch from the AquaSpa Cafe. The pool is free to all adult guests (unlike the one on the Century-class ships, which is $10 per day). Lots of pricey spa packages, from about $200 to $400, combine a complement of Eastern- or Western-influenced treatments using things such as coconut and frangipani scented oil and heated massage rocks to pamper guests. Although they sound heavenly, Heidi has never been totally satisfied with any of these fancy treatments she's tried; considering how expensive they are, the treatments have often been rushed and some therapists have seemed inexperienced or tired (you would be, too, after a 10- to 12-hr. day), and less than enthusiastic. (This is often true with Steiner spas on other lines, too, but it's more disappointing on Celebrity, which promotes its spas so heavily.) We're not telling you to avoid the spa, just stick with the basic massages when you go there; you can't go wrong with a classic shiatsu.

Next door to the spa there's a very large gym with dozens of the latest machines and free weights, and a large aerobics floor.

Up top, the Sports Deck has facilities for basketball, volleyball, quoits, and paddle tennis. Just below, on the Sunrise Deck, are a jogging track and a golf simulator. Below that is the well-laid-out pool deck, where you'll find two pools, four hot tubs, a couple of bars, and a multistoried sunning area. Head up to the balcony level above the pool, at the stern or bow of the ship, for quieter sunbathing spots.

The Century Class: Century • Galaxy • Mercury

The Verdict

Three of the most attractive and all-around appealing megaships at sea. Down-to-earth and casual, this trio also manages to be elegant and exciting.

Mercury *(photo: Matt Hannafin)*

Specifications

Size (in tons)		Crew	
Century	70,606	*Century*	843
Galaxy/Mercury	77,713	*Galaxy/Mercury*	900
Passengers (double occ.)		Passenger/Crew Ratio	2 to 1
Century	1,750	Year Launched	
Galaxy/Mercury	1,896	*Century*	2006
Passenger/Space Ratio	41	*Galaxy*	1996
Total Cabins/Veranda Cabins		*Mercury*	1997
Century	875/61	Last Major Refurbishment	N/A
Galaxy/Mercury	948/220		

Frommer's Ratings (Scale of 1-5)   ★★★★½

Cabin Comfort & Amenities	5	Dining Options	4
Ship Cleanliness & Maintenance	4	Gym, Spa & Sports Facilities	5
Public Comfort/Space	5	Children's Facilities	4
Decor	5	Enjoyment Factor	5

With these three sisters, beginning with the *Century* in 1995, Celebrity ushered in some of the most beautiful ships to be built in modern times, though at about 10 years old apiece, they're no longer spring chickens in the new-ship-obsessed cruise world. Known collectively as the Century class, they're more or less equivalent in size and amenities. Of the three ships, the one that's the most dissimilar to its mates is the first, *Century.* It's lighter by 7,000 tons and has a capacity for 120 fewer guests, a smaller children's playroom (and no wading pool), and a brighter, glitzier feel—though at press time, *Century* was to receive a major $55-million face-lift in spring 2006. *Galaxy* and *Mercury* are warmer and more reminiscent of classic ocean liners, but with a modern feel. The decor casts a chic and sophisticated mood, with lots of warm wood tones as well as rich, tactile textures and deep-toned fabrics, from faux zebra skin and chrome to buttery soft leathers, velvets, and futuristic-looking applications of glass and marble.

It's difficult to say what's most striking on these three ships. The elegant spas and their 15,000-gallon thalassotherapy pools? The distinguished Michael's Club piano lounges with their leather wingbacks and velvet couches? The two-story old-world dining rooms set back in the stern, with grand floor-to-ceiling windows allowing diners to spy the ship's wake glowing under moonlight? An absolutely intriguing modern-art collection unmatched in the industry?

Take your pick—you won't go wrong.

Cabins & Rates

Cabins	Per Diems from	Sq. Ft.	Fridge	Hair Dryer	Sitting Area	TV
Inside	$115	170–175	yes	yes	no	yes
Outside	$130	170–175	yes	yes	some	yes
Suite	$317	246–1,433	yes	yes	yes	yes

CABINS   Simple yet pleasing decor is cheerful and based on light-colored furniture and monochromatic themes of muted purple-blue, green, or pinky red. Standard inside and outside cabins are larger than the norm (although not as large as Carnival's 185-footers), and suites, which come in four categories, are particularly spacious, with marble vanity/desk tops, Art Deco–style sconces, and rich inlaid wood floors. Some, such as the Penthouse Suite, offer more living space (1,219 sq. ft., expandable to 1,433 sq. ft. on special request) than you find in many private homes, plus such wonderful touches as a private whirlpool bath on the veranda. Royal Suites run about half that size (plus 100-ft. balconies) but offer touches such as French doors between the bedroom and seating area, both bathtub and shower in the bathroom, and TVs in each room. *Galaxy* and *Mercury's* 246-square-foot Sky Suites offer verandas that, at 179 square feet, are among the biggest aboard any ship—bigger, in fact, than those in the more expensive Penthouse and Royal suites on these ships (you may want to keep your robe on, though, as people on the deck above can see down onto part of the Sky Suite verandas). All suite bathrooms have bathtubs with whirlpools and magnified makeup mirrors. Like the Millennium-class, the Century-class ships also now offer Concierge-Class staterooms, which are located mostly on the Sky and Penthouse decks. Though a tad less cushy than the regular suite amenities (cabins are smaller and you're not entitled to the services of a butler), if you book a ConciergeClass cabin you get many of the same perks, including a bottle of champagne, choice of pillow, oversize towels, double-thick Frette bathrobes, and priority for just about everything (dining, shore excursions, luggage delivery, embarkation, and disembarkation).

All cabins are outfitted with built-in vanities/desks, stocked minifridges (accounts are billed for any snacks or drinks consumed), hair dryers, cotton robes, radios, and safes. Closets and drawer space are roomy and well designed, as are the bathrooms, and all standard cabins have twin beds convertible to doubles. Cabin TVs are wired with an interactive system that allows guests to order room service from on-screen menus, select wine for dinner, play casino-style games, or go shopping.

Note that the sternmost cabins on Vista Deck are right next to the children's center—a consideration if you want to spend lots of quiet time inside.

Eight of the cabins aboard each ship (one inside and seven outside) were specifically designed for passengers with disabilities.

PUBLIC AREAS   All three ships are designed so well that it's never hard to find a quiet retreat when you want to feel secluded but don't want to be confined in your cabin.

Each vessel boasts a cozy Michael's Club piano bar, decorated like the parlor of a London men's club. They're great spots for a fine cognac or a good single-malt Scotch while enjoying soft background music. On *Century* and *Galaxy,* Michael's Club piano bar maintains its wood-paneled clubbiness somewhat better than aboard the *Mercury,* where it wraps around the main atrium and lets onto a very uncozy view of the shopping below. Still, you can't beat the high-backed, buttery-leather chairs.

For those who don't find that clubby ambience appealing, Tastings Coffee Bar offers an alternative, with specialized upscale java (at an extra cost). There's also the popular Rendez-Vous Square, arranged so that even large groups can achieve a level of privacy and couples can find a nook of their own. Champagne bars appear aboard *Galaxy* and *Mercury,* and the latter also sports a nice, modern Deco-looking martini bar set in the ship's aft atrium—our only complaint is the audible clanging of the casino's slot machines, which seems to get trapped and amplified by the atrium's drum shape. Various other bars, both indoor and outdoor, are tucked into nooks and crannies throughout all three ships.

The multistoried, glass-walled nightclubs/discos are spacious, sprawling, and elegant in a clean, modern way, yet designed with lots of cozy nooks for romantic conversation over champagne. Each of the three ships has double-decker theaters with unobstructed views from almost every seat (though avoid those at the cocktail tables at the back of the rear balcony boxes, unless you have a really long neck) and state-of-the-art equipment such as cantilevered orchestra pits and walls of video screens to augment the action on the stage.

Libraries aboard the ships are comfortable, but not as big or well stocked as they could be.

DINING OPTIONS   The two-story formal dining rooms on all three ships are truly stunning spaces reminiscent of the grand liners of yesteryear, with wide, dramatic staircases joining the two levels and floor-to-ceiling walls of glass facing astern to a view of the ship's wake. If you lean toward the dramatic, don a gown or tux and slink down the stairs nice and slow like a 1940s Hollywood starlet—there aren't many places you can do that these days.

Each ship also has an indoor/outdoor buffet restaurant open for breakfast, lunch, and dinner, as well as pizza and ice-cream stations.

POOL, FITNESS, SPA & SPORTS FACILITIES   Pool decks aboard these vessels feature a pair of good-size swimming areas rimmed with teak benches for sunning and relaxation. Even when the ships are full, these areas don't seem particularly crowded. Aboard *Galaxy* and *Mercury,* retractable domes cover one of the swimming pools during inclement weather.

The ships' spacious, windowed, 10,000-square-foot AquaSpa and fitness facilities are some of the best at sea today. The gym wraps around the starboard side of an upper forward deck like a hook, the large spa straddles the middle, and a very modern and elegant beauty salon faces the ocean on the port side. The focal point of these spas is a 115,000-gallon thalassotherapy pool, a bubbling cauldron of warm, soothing seawater. After a relaxing 15- or 20-minute dip, choose a massage or facial, or, if you're a gambler (because the fancy stuff is hit or miss in the quality department), something more exotic, such as a Rasul treatment (a mud pack and steam bath for couples), herbal steam bath, or a variety of water-based treatments involving baths, jet massages, and soft whirling showers. A dip in the thalassotherapy pool is $10; it's free if you've signed up for a massage or other treatment. There are also saunas and steam rooms (including *Mercury*'s impressive Turkish hammam, with its uniformly heated surfaces and beautiful tile work). As aesthetically pleasing to the eye as they are functional, each of the AquaSpas employs a design theme—a Japanese bathhouse on *Century* and *Galaxy*, and a Moroccan motif on the *Mercury*.

The gyms are generously sized and there are also aerobics classes in a separate room (trendy classes like Pilates and spinning are $10 a pop; the farty ones are free . . . figures) and an outdoor jogging track on an upper deck, a golf simulator, and one deck that's specifically designed for sports.

Zenith

The Verdict

Combining the gentility of classic cruising with the fun and glamour of today's exciting megaships, this midsize, casually elegant ship is a very pleasing package.

Zenith *(photo: Celebrity Cruises)*

Specifications

Size (in tons)	47,225	Crew	628
Passengers (double occ.)	1,374	Passenger/Crew Ratio	2.1 to 1
Passenger/Space Ratio	34.5	Year Launched	1992
Total Cabins/Veranda Cabins	687/0	Last Major Refurbishment	1999

Frommer's Ratings (Scale of 1–5)   ★★★★

Cabin Comfort & Amenities	4	Dining Options	3
Ship Cleanliness & Maintenance	4	Gym, Spa & Sports Facilities	3
Public Comfort/Space	4	Children's Facilities	3
Decor	4	Enjoyment Factor	4

In this day of mondo ships carrying 2,000 to 3,000 passengers, this midsize ship carrying about 1,400 guests is wonderfully more intimate. An exceptionally wide indoor promenade gives passengers the feeling of strolling along a boulevard within the ship's hull. Like its megaship sisters, this smaller ship boasts a distinctive art collection with pieces by the likes of Warhol and Hockney, and after a multi-million-dollar refurbishment back in 1999, it also offers such signature Celebrity elements as a Michael's Club lounge, patisserie, martini bar, and enlarged spa facilities. Still, next to the stylish new decor you'll find chrome and other shiny remnants of the original early-1990s scheme rearing their ugly heads in places such as the main dining room, giving the ship two distinct personalities.

Sister ship *Horizon* left the fleet in fall of 2005 and was turned over to Island Cruises, the brand name of Sunshine Cruises Limited, a joint venture between Royal Caribbean Cruises L.d. and First Choice Holidays PLC, one of the United Kingdom's largest integrated tour operators. Are the days numbered for *Zenith*, too?

Cabins & Rates

Cabins	Per Diems from	Sq. Ft.	Fridge	Hair Dryer	Sitting Area	TV
Inside	$171	172	no	yes	no	yes
Outside	$179	172	no	yes	some	yes
Suite	$436	270–500	yes	yes	yes	yes

CABINS As on the Century-class ships, accommodations offer a decent amount of space, with all inside and standard outside cabins measuring 172 square feet, with the exception of some oddly shaped smaller insides amidships on the Caribbean Deck. The muted blue, green, or burnt orange fabrics and accouterments are tasteful, subdued, and relatively well maintained. All cabins have roomy bathrooms with showers, spacious closets and drawers, hair dryers, cotton robes, safes, TVs, glass-topped coffee tables, desks, and marble-topped vanities. The solitary lamp on the nightstand by the bed(s) is pretty inadequate for nighttime reading. Some cabins have stocked minifridges (accounts are billed for any snacks or drinks consumed).

Six cabins are positioned all the way aft, with windows facing a classically romantic view of the ship's wake, though bear in mind the children's playroom is right in the midst of these cabins. So, if you're planning on quiet daytimes in your cabin and will sail during school holidays, you may not want to book one of them.

The 20 roomy suites are about 25 square feet bigger than most of the suites on the Century-class ships (the only difference being that the *Zenith* doesn't have any private verandas). Each suite has a marble bathroom with whirlpool tub, a sitting area, a minibar, and butler service. There are two Royal Suites at 500 square feet, each with large sitting rooms, dining table and chairs, marble bathrooms, walk-in closets, VCR, CD player, minibar, and butler service.

Be careful when booking if views are important to you: Most of the category-7 outside cabins on the Bahamas Deck have views blocked by lifeboats. Cabins on the Florida Deck have portholes. Also, note that the sternmost cabins on Europa Deck are right next to the children's center—a consideration if you want to spend lots of quiet time inside.

Four cabins are wheelchair accessible.

PUBLIC AREAS Late-1990s refurbishments improved on the original interior design; but there are still remnants of the latter remaining, so you'll see a schizophrenic mix of a nautical, clubby, plush, and warm ambience and an '80s modern, metallic feel. There is not a multideck atrium, nor excessive flashiness (a big plus for some people).

Without a doubt, the most attractive space on the ship is the elegant Michael's Club lounge, with wingback chairs, leather couches, brocade fabrics, and even a faux fireplace. Opening off the same short hallway is a library and a card room. Another appealing place is the spacious, nautical-themed bar/observation lounge on the Marina Deck, called Fleet Bar. It has floor-to-ceiling windows, navy-blue furniture, and honey-brown wood accents.

Amidships is the Rendezvous Lounge and Rendezvous Bar, where, especially on formal nights, guests can show off their finery and relax with cocktails before heading to the adjacent dining room. There's a really elegant martini bar in the same area (though, unfortunately, it's sort of in the middle of the main drag to the dining room and bustling photo gallery) plus an art gallery offering the same kind of works you'll see at onboard art auctions. The Zodiac Club is a lounge by day and disco by night. The attractive Cova Café offers specialty coffees and chocolates as well as champagne, wine, and liquors in a lovely setting; it's a dark and cozy place for a pre-dinner drink. The modern, minimalist, two-level Celebrity Show Lounge aboard each ship has good sightlines from all seats except those on the edges of the balcony level.

The playroom is small, though it has windows. There's also a video arcade.

DINING OPTIONS   The dining room is the most chrome-intensive place on board (ceiling, railing, chair frames, and pillars), smacking of that sort of 1980s-era wedding-hall look, yet it's still comfortable and pleasing enough, with banquette seating for tables along the sides of the rooms. The indoor/outdoor buffet restaurant, serving breakfast, lunch, and dinner, was refurbished a few years back and now features separate islands for drinks and food, keeping lines to a minimum; it also now features darker wood detailing and fabrics for a more elegant look.

POOL, FITNESS, SPA & SPORTS FACILITIES   Ample space is dedicated to recreation, including two good-size swimming pools that never seem to be overcrowded, even when the ships are full. The newly renovated top-deck spa and fitness area has floor-to-ceiling windows and resembles the spas aboard Celebrity's larger ships, and although it doesn't offer as many of the more exotic treatments or have the thalassotherapy pool featured on the larger ships, it has several spa-treatment rooms and a Seraglio steam/mud room (like the Rasul on the larger ships). The gym is on the small side—too small, for instance, to hold fitness classes (they're held instead in one of the nightclubs).

The ship's beautiful tiered decks at the stern offer many quiet places for lounging in view of the ships' hypnotic wake when underway. Each has a cluster of three hot tubs aft on an upper deck.

Other recreation facilities and options include a golf driving net used for lessons with the pro, shuffleboard, Ping-Pong table, and a small jogging track.

3 Costa Cruises

200 S. Park Rd., Suite 200, Hollywood, FL 33021-8541. ℂ **800/462-6782** or 954/266-5600. Fax 954/266-2100. www.costacruises.com.

THE LINE IN A NUTSHELL   Imagine a Carnival megaship hijacked by an Italian circus troupe: That's Costa. The words of the day are fun, festive, and international, with two Italian-American megaships providing the venue. Expect a really good time, but don't set your sights too high for cuisine. **Sails to:** Caribbean.

THE EXPERIENCE   For years, Costa has played up its Italian heritage as the main factor that distinguishes it from Carnival, Royal Caribbean, and the rest, and today, even though the line employs fewer Italian crewmembers than in the past, that's still true. You'll find more pasta dishes on the menu than other lines offer; more classical music among the entertainment offerings; Italian-flavored activities facilitated by a young, mostly Italian, and ridiculously attractive "animation staff"; and a huge number of Italian-Americans among the passengers. Physically, the line's new ships are a hybrid: modern mainstream megaships that bear more than a passing resemblance to Carnival's newest vessels, with interiors designed by Carnival's designer-in-chief Joe Farcus, who took inspiration from Italy's traditions of painting and architecture but still stuck close to his signature "more is more" style—think Venice a la Vegas.

Over the past year, the line has implemented a new crew training program that's improved overall service—one of our bugaboos with Costa in the past.

Pros

- **Italian flavor:** Entertainment, activities, and cuisine are presented with an Italian carnival flair.
- **Very active, very fun:** There are a lot of activities, and Costa passengers love to participate, creating a festive and social environment morning to night.

Cons

- **Average dining:** While the pizza is excellent and some of the pasta dishes work well, overall the cuisine only gets a "C" compared with the other big mainstream lines.

COSTA: CONTINENTAL FLAVOR IN THE CARIBBEAN

Costa's origins are as Italian as could be. In 1860, Giacomo Costa established an olive-oil refinery and packaging plant in Genoa. After his death, his sons bought a ship called *Ravenna* to transport raw materials and finished products from Sardinia through Genoa to the rest of Europe, thereby marking the founding of Costa Line in 1924. Between 1997 and 2000, Carnival Corporation bought up shares in Costa until it became whole owner. Today Costa's Italianness is as much a marketing tool as anything else, but it must be working: The line's presence in Europe is huge, and in the past 3 years it's introduced three new megaships (*Costa Mediterranea* in June 2003, *Costa Fortuna* in Nov 2003, and *Costa Magica* in Nov 2004), with the 3,800-passenger, 112,000-ton *Costa Concordia,* the largest passenger ship in Italian history, due in summer 2006 and an as-yet-unnamed sister ship due in 2007.

PASSENGER PROFILE

Most of Costa's ships sail in Europe, where they sail with 80% to 85% Europeans. In contrast, the 2,112-passenger **Costa Mediterranea** and 2,720-passenger **Costa Magica** are marketed to Americans for winter Caribbean sailings, attracting passengers of all ages who want lots of fun and action, and like the idea of "Cruising Italian Style," as the line's ad slogan goes. Italian-Americans are heavily represented aboard every Caribbean cruise, and in general Costa passengers are big on participation, the goofier the better: Witness, for instance, the number of passengers wearing togas on Roman Bacchanal Toga Night. And we've never seen as many guests crowding the dance floor, participating in contests, or having a go at bocce ball or mask-painting as aboard this line's ships.

Compared with the other mainstream lines, here's how Costa rates:

	Poor	Fair	Good	Excellent	Outstanding
Enjoyment Factor			✓		
Dining		✓			
Activities				✓	
Children's Program		✓			
Entertainment			✓		
Service		✓			
Worth the Money			✓		

In the Caribbean, Costa appeals to retirees and young couples alike, although there are more passengers over 50 than under. Typically you won't see more than 40 or 50 kids on any one cruise except during holidays such as Christmas and spring break, when there may be as many as 500 children on board. About 90% to 95% of passengers are from North America, with the remainder mostly from Europe and South America. Because of the international mix, public announcements, lifeboat drills, and some entertainment are given in both English and Italian. The cruise director is often American or British during Caribbean sailings, but much of the activities staff is comprised of multilingual Italians.

DINING

In general, file Costa's cuisine under "average," though there are exceptions. Pastas are totally authentic and are often very good, the pizza is fantastic, and on a recent cruise the roast turkey with trimmings and the Caribbean lobster tail in tarragon sauce went over big. Most guests at our table ordered two each of the latter.

TRADITIONAL   Each dinner menu features five courses from a different region of Italy—Liguria one night, Sicily the next, etc.—plus several alternatives for each course, including the traditional pasta course. Much of the pasta is made on the ship (lasagna and cannelloni, for instance), while the fettuccini, spaghetti, and raviolis are shipped in from Italy. Many of these dishes are heavy on the cream and so are richer than some Americans are used to, but they're definitely the highlight of the food aboard. If you feel like a change from the pasta course, try one of the interesting risottos—a crabmeat-and-champagne selection on our last cruise was divine. Otherwise, expect cruise staples such as poached salmon, lobster tail, grilled lamb chops, roast duck, and beef tenderloin, plus always-available classic selections such as Caesar salad, baked or grilled fish or chicken, and spaghetti with tomato sauce. Soups sounded interesting on the menu, but tended to be bland. Vegetarian options such as polenta with greens and bell peppers stuffed with rice are available at each meal, though they tend to be uninspired—sometimes the vegetables your tablemate got with his steak look much more appetizing. Health and Wellness menu selections are listed with their calorie, fat, and carbohydrate breakdown. On the second formal night, flaming baked Alaska is paraded through the dining room and complimentary champagne is poured. Other desserts include tiramisu, gelato, zabaglione (meringue pie), and chocolate soufflé, which was the best dessert we had while aboard.

SPECIALTY   Each ship features a reservations-only alternative restaurant ($23 per person) offering Mediterranean dishes such as rigatoni served with lobster and tomatoes, or grilled lamb chops. A Tuscan steakhouse menu is also available. The ambience is considerably quieter and more romantic than in the main dining room, with pleasant piano music and a small dance floor if you feel like a waltz between courses. *Magica's* Vincenza Club Restaurant is outstanding, with an adventurous menu by restaurateurs Zefferino and a romantic ambience, all Versace china, dark woods, and Italy-inspired art. If you order wine, you're in for a show, with a steward decanting your bottle using a steady hand and a candle.

CASUAL   Each ship offers a large buffet restaurant with six serving stations. Breakfast is a standard mix of eggs, meats, fruits, cereals, and cheeses. At lunch, several of the stations will serve standard dishes while others will be given over to a different national or regional cuisine (Spanish, Greek, Asian, and so forth). Casual dining is also available nightly till 9:30pm. **Pizza,** offered in one section of the buffet from noon to 2am, is made in ovens right behind the counter and served fresh. It looks a little weird, but trust us, it's fantastic—one of the highlights of the food on board. On our last *Mediterranea* cruise, someone from the line quipped that because it was real Italian pizza (very thin, without excess cheese and sauce), you can eat as much as you like and not get fat. We *believe* him. Out on deck there's a **grill** serving burgers and hot dogs, as well as a **taco bar** at lunch. If you're looking for another afternoon snack, head over to the ice-cream station in the buffet area, which offers daily specials like fresh banana or coconut, along with traditional flavors.

SNACKS & EXTRAS   Most cruise lines seem to have scrapped their **midnight buffets,** but Costa still offers them nightly, often focusing on a theme taken from that evening's activity. On Mediterranean Night, the buffet offers pastry, fruits, desserts, pastas, and savories from Spain, Greece, France, and Turkey. On another night, the guests head below to the ship's massive galley for the buffet. Look for the polenta with mushroom sauce there—on our last cruise it was superb. **Room service** is available 24 hours a day. Suite guests can order full meals delivered; all others can choose from various sandwiches, appetizers, and a full bar menu.

ACTIVITIES

More than anything else, Costa is known for its lineup of exuberant and often Italian-inspired activities, and passengers on these ships love to participate. Three nights per 7-night cruise are given over to Italian and Mediterranean themes. **Festa Italiana** turns the ship into an Italian street festival where guests are encouraged to wear the colors of the Italian flag and participate in bocce ball, tarantella dance lessons, pizza-dough tossing, Venetian-mask making, and Italian karaoke. **Serata Tropical** is a deck party with a Mediterranean twist, where guests can enjoy ethnic dancing and ice-carving demonstrations amid the typical Caribbean deck party trimmings. **Mediterranean Night** transforms various parts of the ship to represent France, Turkey, Greece, and Spain, with appropriate skits, activities, singing, and games. The highlight of many cruises is **Roman Bacchanal Toga Night,** when at least some of the guests don bed sheets, with many repeat passengers bringing their own custom models and toga accouterments (though the line provides bedsheets and tying instructions for those who don't). The evening ends with the hysterical Roman Bacchanal show, which is half slapstick vaudeville and half passenger talent show. After each act, Julius Caesar (and the audience) decides whether to send the performers to the buffet or throw them to the lions. It's a hoot.

During the day, activities include **Italian language and cooking classes,** as well as traditional cruise staples such as jackpot bingo, bridge, arts and crafts, dance classes, shuffleboard, art auctions, horse racing, Ping-Pong, and fun poolside competitions in which teams have to put on Roman-style costumes or don silly hats. Each ship also has a combo library and Internet center, as well as a large card room. **Enrichment lectures** focus on topics such as personal finance, romance, and the benefits of a good night's sleep. **Aerobics and stretch classes** are usually held on the covered pool area's dance floor, and because its stage is designed with a high, vaulted ceiling, the music and the instructor's calls can be very, very loud and boomy—don't pick this time and place for a quiet read. Live steel-drum music is featured throughout the day in the same area. Luckily, there's lots of deck space across several levels for sunbathing, so you

Costa Fleet Itineraries

Ship	Itineraries
Costa Magica	**7-night E. & W. Carib:** Round-trip from Ft. Lauderdale, FL, Dec 2005–Apr 2006 and Nov–Dec 2006 (itineraries alternate weekly).
Costa Mediterranea	**7-night E. & W. Carib:** Round-trip from Ft. Lauderdale, FL, Nov 2005–Apr 2006 and Dec 2006 (itineraries alternate weekly).

can escape the noise if you want to. In the stern, a fun all-ages water slide operates a couple of hours a day.

For avid duffers there's a golf-driving net, as well as **private onboard golf lessons** with a golf professional (30-min. lessons are $35; hourlong lessons are $60). The pro will also accompany guests who sign up for golfing shore excursions to some of the best courses in the Caribbean.

A **Catholic Mass** is held almost every day in each ship's small chapel.

CHILDREN'S PROGRAM

Costa's kids' programs are not nearly as extensive as those available on other lines such as Disney and Royal Caribbean, but then, there are usually far fewer children on board in the first place. At least two full-time youth counselors sail aboard each ship, with additional staff whenever more than a dozen kids are on the passenger list. Both ships offer **supervised activities** for kids 3 to 18, divided into two age groups unless enough children are aboard to divide them into three (3–6, 7–12, and 13–18 years) or four (3–6, 7–10, 11–14, and 15–18). The **Costa Kids Club,** for ages 3 to 12, includes such activities as Nintendo, galley tours, arts and crafts, scavenger hunts, Italian-language lessons, bingo, board games, face painting, movies, kids' karaoke, and pizza and ice-cream-sundae parties. The ships each have a pleasant children's playroom and a teen disco. If there are enough teens on board, the **Costa Teens Club** for ages 13 to 18 offers foosball and darts competitions, karaoke, and other stuff.

When ships are at sea in the Caribbean, supervised Kids Club hours are from 9am to noon, 3 to 6pm, and 9 to 11:30pm. The program also operates during port days, but on a more limited basis.

Two nights a week there's a great complimentary **Parents' Night Out program** from 6 to 11:30pm during which kids 3 and older (they must be out of diapers) are entertained and given a special buffet or pizza party while Mom and Dad get a night out alone. All other times, **group babysitting** for ages 3 and up is available every night from 9 to 11:30pm at no cost, and from 11:30pm to 1:30am for $10 per child per hour. No private, in-cabin babysitting is available.

Children must be at least 3 months old to sail with Costa; under two's sail free.

ENTERTAINMENT

Although the passengers are mostly American and the location is the Caribbean, the main entertainment focus aboard Costa is Italian, with concerts, operatic soloists, puppet or marionette shows, mimes, acrobats, and cabaret, all produced with an Italian bent but with no language skills required. On a recent cruise, one of the shows had a unicycle-riding, ball-balancing, flame-juggling, plate-spinning entertainer—the kind you used to see on *The Ed Sullivan Show*. Other featured performers included an operatic tenor singing a program of high-note crowd pleasers and a classical pianist performing Beethoven and Gershwin. The line's production shows mostly follow the typical song-and-dance revue formula, with both good elements (the "Out of This World" show framed the numbers with a vague time-travel storyline, and a few of its sections showed real creativity) and bad (the male soloist on *Mediterranea* was the worst we've ever seen on a ship). Participatory shows are much more fun overall, and more in tune with what Costa passengers seem to want. The "Election of the Ideal Couple," and a *Newlywed Game* takeoff for instance, both clip along at an a frantic pace, with the cruise staff helping and hindering as appropriate to get the most laughs. Who knew the criterion for being an ideal couple was the ability to burst a balloon with your butt?

Both ships have glitzy casinos as well as hopping discos, which often get going only after 1am.

SERVICE

In past years our main complaint about Costa was its service, which on particularly bad nights resembled a Three Stooges skit. While it's still not the Four Seasons, our last cruises showed marked improvement, with waiters seeming better trained and more polished, cabin stewards more attentive and helpful, and everyone more accommodating and friendly. Kudos to whatever new training programs have been put in place. They're working.

There are no self-service laundry facilities on any of the Costa ships.

Costa Magica

The Verdict

The largest Italian cruise ship ever, *Magica* continues Costa's trend toward heavily decorated, Carnival-like interiors, but with a lighter, almost feminine feel and a "journey through Italy" theme.

Costa Magica *(photo: Costa Cruises)*

Specifications

Size (in tons)	105,000	Crew	1,068
Passengers (double occ.)	2,720	Passenger/Crew Ratio	2.5 to 1
Passenger/Space Ratio	38.6	Year Launched	2004
Total Cabins/Veranda Cabins	1,358/522	Last Major Refurbishment	N/A

Frommer's Ratings (Scale of 1–5)

★★★★

Cabin Comfort & Amenities	4	Dining Options	4
Ship Cleanliness & Maintenance	4	Gym, Spa & Sports Facilities	5
Public Comfort/Space	4	Children's Facilities	3
Decor	4	Enjoyment Factor	4

Costa Magica, along with sister ship *Costa Fortuna* (which sticks to the Mediterranean), is Costa's and Italy's largest ship—at least until the larger *Costa Concordia* debuts in June 2006. Elegant and rather feminine in decor compared to the drama of the earlier *Atlantica,* which it replaces in the Caribbean this year, *Magica* is still crowded with rich detail everywhere, but in a manner more like a medieval manuscript, with interwoven images themed as a journey through Italy's magical places. Walk through and you'll see evocations of the Costa Smeralda, Poitano, Portofino, Trentino, and Sicily, from the Renaissance to today. The ship's largest, most dramatic sculpture, a 16-foot set of terra-cotta forms titled "Between Memory and Vision," located near the Costa Smeralda dining room, seems to be a symbol for the rather dreamy mood of the ship. There's nothing dreamy about the nightlife, however: As on most Costa ships, *Magica*'s disco is very lively, and many public rooms stay crowded long after the last show has finished.

Cabins & Rates

Cabins	Per Diems from	Sq. Ft.	Fridge	Hair Dryer	Sitting Area	TV
Inside	$128	160	yes	yes	no	yes
Outside	$157	160	yes	yes	yes	yes
Suite	$371	275–345	yes	yes	yes	yes

CABINS   Standard cabins tend toward elegant, with soft, warm colors and magic-themed prints by Augusto Vignali. Of the 1,358 cabins, 465 have balconies, as do the 58 suites. Inside cabins are very well designed, with two closet areas, a fairly generous amount of drawer space, twin or queen bed configuration, and showers. Outside staterooms with verandas are the same size with an additional 65 square feet of private balcony, including lounge chairs and a small table. Suites range from 275 square feet with 65-square-foot balconies to 345 square feet with 85 square feet of private veranda. All staterooms have minibars, hair dryers, and safes, and suites have whirlpool baths. Some of the furnishings, especially lamps, are unusual and charming, and at passenger request it may soon be possible to order them.

Twenty-seven staterooms are wheelchair accessible.

PUBLIC AREAS   Because *Magica*'s public areas reflect different parts of Italy, the mood varies strongly. Dance and theater imagery dominates the Spoleto ballroom, reflecting the Spoleto "Two Worlds" art festival, while the Sicily Casino has an uncanny atmosphere taken from the region's folklore and traditional puppetry. Sixty-five large puppets of medieval knights, court jesters, and musicians are dotted among the tables and slot machines. From the casino you can keep an eye out for the beginning of the action in the disco, which seems to suddenly fill in response to an invisible summons. The bi-level, glass wrapped space has a polished brass sun, sand effects on the floor, and wall mosaics invoking the waves of the Italian beach resort Grado. In sharp contrast, the Bressanome Library has an ecclesiastical theme, befitting a place (the namesake, not the library) that was a Bishop's see for centuries. Adults and children wait in turn to retreat into the tall, blue, phone-booth sized enclosed chairs, which are modeled on ecclesiastical thrones. They make a great place for a private read. The striking three-level Urbino Theater has a gold dome with an extremely impressive Murano glass chandelier and inlaid wood paneling forming the shape of musical instruments. One of the most enchanting areas on board is the huge, 3,600-square-foot Grand Bar Salento, with fat gold columns and a ceiling above the dance floor that's covered with images from the Baroque churches of Lecce. The space is almost constantly in use. *Magica's* nine-deck atrium is lined with a photographic collage of Italy's most loved regions—a sort of summary of the ship—and the bronze sculpture there has one of several haunting titles found among the ship's art: "There were four of us and now there are three of you."

DINING OPTIONS Although Costa's food has been uneven, the choices aboard the *Magica* show great improvement, and the Vincenza Club Restaurant is outstanding. The menu by restaurateurs Zefferino has items that may be too exotic for some, but more conservative tastes have plenty of steaks, seafood, fowl, and vegetables to choose from, along with outrageously good desserts and wines. The ambience is romantic, with Versace china and gold napkins standing out against rich, dark woods and shining goldware, with friezes from Palladio's villas reproduced around a giant skylight. The two main restaurants, Costa Smeralda and Portofino, have lighting concealed in pods in the walls to create magical effects. The Bellagio restaurant is unusually elegant for an informal buffet, with domes and columns, plus light fixtures shaped like arms and heads emerging from the walls—shades of Cocteau's *Beauty and the Beast*? In addition to more consistently high food quality, Costa now offers more choices for vegetarians and passengers looking for sugar-free and other diet choices. Pizza and pastas are very good indeed, and the soft-serve ice-cream machine gets so much use we expect it'll just melt down someday.

POOL, FITNESS, SPA & SPORTS FACILITIES The 4,600-square-foot Saturnia Spa is proof that not all Steiner-run spas are alike. The Saturnia is exceptionally spacious—most land-based salons don't have the expanse and decor this one has—and a huge wall of glass extends the space even more. One very unusual feature: a pair of dedicated leather pedicure thrones with massage action. The multi-level gym is similarly beautiful and well equipped with Pilates balls, free weights, and yoga mats. The Technogym equipment can be programmed to parameters set for you by one of the ship's personal trainers, with a digital key that will repeat the program every time you use it. Spinning bikes, treadmills, yoga classes, and health seminars supplement the range of skincare treatments, facials, wraps, and massages. A Turkish bath and sauna are also available.

The main pool area is built like an amphitheater and is clearly a place to see and be seen. The Positano Lido pool, aft under a removable glass roof, is overlooked by an impressive bronze sculpture of Poseidon, and on our cruise the pool and Jacuzzis were in use in the evenings as well as daytime. A third pool area is dedicated to children and their attendant families.

Costa Mediterranea

The Verdict

Is it a carnival or is it Carnival? Decorated in a Europe-meets-Vegas style, with spacious public rooms and an almost futuristic-looking atrium-top specialty restaurant, *Mediterranea* is eye-candy for the ADD set.

Costa Mediterranea *(photo: Costa Cruises)*

Specifications

Size (in tons)	85,000	Crew	920
Passengers (double occ.)	2,112	Passenger/Crew Ratio	2.3 to 1
Passenger/Space Ratio	40	Year Launched	2003
Total Cabins/Veranda Cabins	1,056/678	Last Major Refurbishment	N/A

Frommer's Ratings (Scale of 1–5) ★★★½

Cabin Comfort & Amenities	4	Dining Options	3
Ship Cleanliness & Maintenance	4	Gym, Spa & Sports Facilities	4
Public Comfort/Space	4	Children's Facilities	3
Decor	4	Enjoyment Factor	4

Along with European-based sister ship *Costa Atlantica, Mediterranea* ushered in the future for Costa, being a kind of European version of the "Fun Ships" operated by sister company Carnival. In fact, they're almost identical, built along the same lines as Carnival's Spirit-class ships and with interiors designed by Carnival's designer-in-chief, Joe Farcus. Build megaship, add tomato sauce, and stir. At nearly 1,000 feet long, *Mediterranea* cuts a sleek profile, and her bright yellow, barrel-like smokestack, emblazoned with a big blue Costa C, distinguishes her from her Carnival cousins.

Despite the obvious success of the Spirit-class design (six Carnival and Costa ships are based on it, and Holland America has adapted it for their Vista-class vessels), we're not completely in love with it. The main public decks have a zigzagging layout that lacks the easy flow of some competitors, and some areas in the bow are downright bizarre: For instance, the wide outdoor promenade on Deck 3 ducks indoors as it goes forward, becoming a long, strange, marble-floored lounge. Is it a place to sit? Is it a place to walk? No one seems to know, so it gets hardly any use. But maybe that's a plus, making its little marble tables, wicker chairs, and small couches decent places to escape the crowds.

Cabins & Rates

Cabins	Per Diems from	Sq. Ft.	Fridge	Hair Dryer	Sitting Area	TV
Inside	$86	160	yes	yes	no	yes
Outside	$100	210	yes	yes	yes	yes
Suite	$214	360-650	yes	yes	yes	yes

CABINS   All cabins feature caramel-color wood tones and warm autumn-hued fabrics that create a pleasant environment, and well over half of the cabins have private balconies. Each has a stocked, pay-as-you-go minifridge, hair dryer, personal safe, and more than adequate storage space, and all outside cabins have sitting areas with couches. The views from all category-4 cabins on Deck 4 are completely obstructed by lifeboats, and the category-6 balcony cabins directly above, on Deck 5, are partially obstructed as well. Bathrooms have good storage space.

The 32 Panorama suites on Deck 5 and 6 measure 272 square feet, plus a 90-square-foot balcony with attractive granite coffee tables, wooden chairs, and desks. Suites have large couches that can double as a bed, two separate floor-to-ceiling closets, lots of drawer space, and large bathrooms with bathtubs, marble counters, and double sinks. Adjacent is a dressing room with a vanity table, drawers, and a closet. The Grand Suites are the largest accommodations aboard. Six are located amidships on Deck 7 and measure 372 square feet, plus 118-square-foot balconies; the other eight are aft on Decks 4, 6, 7, and 8 and measure 367 square feet, plus 282-square-foot balconies.

Eight cabins are wheelchair accessible.

PUBLIC AREAS   Interiors on the *Mediterranea* are inspired by noble 17th- and 18th-century Italian *palazzi,* and are heavy on dance and theater imagery—in fact, they're heavy on just about everything. From her carpets to her decorated ceilings, hardly any surface aboard *isn't* decorated somehow. When you first lay eyes on her Alice in Wonderland–like fantasyland atrium, for instance, it's a bit jarring, all bright colors, glowing light panels, textured and sculpted metal surfaces, Roman-style ceiling murals, and fiber-optic squid swarming up eight decks. Soon, though, you'll grow attached to the buttery-soft red leather chairs (including several pairs of pleasantly absurd ones with towering tall backs) and huge framed black-and-white photographs of dancers that fill the space, with its dramatic central bar and more intimate wings spreading out port and starboard. Just astern, another bar/lounge leads to the two-story dining room.

The ship's disco is a darkish, two-story, cavelike space with video-screen walls, fog machines, and translucent dance floors. The three-level theater has velvety high-backed seating and very high-tech and elaborate stages. Downstairs, on the lowest passenger deck, a smaller show lounge used for late-night comedy acts, karaoke, and cocktail parties is decorated with an underwater motif, but don't worry, you're still above the waterline. There's also a big glitzy casino with a festive Vegas-style mood, several large lounges that feature musical entertainment in the evenings, a smallish but pleasant library/Internet center, and a roomy, elegant card room. A kids' playroom, teen center, large video arcade, and Catholic chapel (one of these things is not like the others . . .) are all squirreled away in the bow on Decks 4 and 5.

Biggest complaint? Inadequate signage in stairwells and elevator banks to tell passengers where they are and where the various public rooms are located.

DINING OPTIONS   Aside from an elegant two-story dining room, there's a two-story alternative, reservations-only restaurant high up on Deck 10, charging guests $23 per person for the privilege of dining (suite guests can go free of charge once per cruise). Its atmosphere is its best feature, with dim lights, candlelight, fresh flowers, soft live music, and lots of space between tables. On our last cruise the *Corzetti al pesto* (pasta with basil sauce) was very good, while the sea bass and flounder entrees were not great. The roasted rack of lamb was presented with a bit more care than in the main restaurant, and the chocolate parfait sabayon was a decadent and elegant finish. For a quieter and more romantic mood, the alternative restaurant is a nice change of pace, but don't linger past 10pm if you don't want cigar smoke to spoil your elegant dinner: That's when the restaurant's second story becomes a cigar lounge.

For casual breakfast, lunch, and (6 nights a week) dinner, head to the sprawling indoor/outdoor buffet restaurant. Soft ice cream and pizza made with herbs and fresh mozzarella are served from stations here. Look up when you get to the very end of the restaurant, before heading out to the stern pool area: There's a huge, amazing Murano glass chandelier up there that you'd never notice unless you craned your head on purpose.

POOL, FITNESS, SPA & SPORTS FACILITIES *Mediterranea*'s gym is a pleasant tiered affair with machines on many different levels and a large hot tub in the center. The spa offers your typical menu of treatments, including 50-minute massages, facials, and reflexology treatments. There are three pools on Deck 9, two of them in the loud, active main pool area and another in the stern. Above the latter is a neat water slide for all ages. Other sports and relaxation amenities include four hot tubs, a golf driving net, and a combo volleyball, basketball, and tennis court. If you explore, you'll find lots of deck space for sunbathing and hiding away with a deck chair and a page-turner.

4 Disney Cruise Line

P.O. Box 10210, Lake Buena Vista, FL 32830. ℂ **800/951-3532** or 888/325-2500. Fax 407/566-3541. www.disney cruise.com.

THE LINE IN A NUTSHELL Disney's the big cheese when it comes to family fun. Though Royal Caribbean, Carnival, Celebrity, and Princess all devote significant attention to kids, it took Disney to create vessels where both kids and adults are really catered to equally, and with style. If you love Disney, you'll love these two floating theme parks. **Sails to:** Caribbean, Bahamas.

THE EXPERIENCE Both classic and ultramodern, the line's two ships are like no others in the industry, designed to evoke the grand transatlantic liners but also boasting a handful of truly innovative features, including extra-large cabins for families, several restaurants through which passengers rotate on every cruise, fantastic Disney-inspired entertainment, separate adult pools and lounges, and the biggest kids' facilities at sea. In many ways, the experience is more Disney than it is cruise (for instance, there's no casino); but, on the other hand, the ships are surprisingly elegant and well laid out, with the Disneyisms sprinkled around subtly, like fairy dust, amid the Art Deco and Art Nouveau design motifs. Head to toe, inside and out, they're a class act.

Disney's is nothing if not organized, so its 3- and 4-night cruises aboard *Disney Wonder* are designed to be combined with a Disney theme park and hotel package to create a weeklong land/sea vacation. You can also book these shorter cruises (as well as *Disney Magic*'s weeklong cruises) separately.

Pros

- **Kids' program:** In both the size of the facilities and the range of activities, it's the most extensive at sea.
- **Entertainment:** The line's family-oriented musicals are some of the best onboard entertainment today.

- **Family-style cabins:** All have sofa beds to sleep families of at least three, and the majority have 1½ bathrooms.
- **Innovative dining:** No other ships have diners rotating among three different but equally appealing sit-down restaurants.

Cons

- **Limited adult entertainment:** There's no casino or library, and adult nightclubs tend to be quiet after busy family days.
- **Small gyms:** Considering the ships' large size, their gyms are tiny.
- **Packed pools:** Though there are three pools, they get pretty sardine-can-like on sunny days, especially the kids' pools.
- **Expensive:** Compared to peers Royal Caribbean, Celebrity, Carnival, and Princess, Disney cruises tend to run a few hundred dollars more. Why? There are only two ships and lots of Disney-lovers to fill them.

DISNEY: THE OLD MOUSE & THE SEA

For at least half a century now, Disney has been in the business of merging modern-day expectations and cutting-edge technology with a nostalgic sense of American culture: for childhood innocence, for the frontier, for an idealized turn-of-the-century past, for our mythic heroes. And whether you're a fan or a critic, it's indisputable that at this point the company itself has become a part of our culture. There are probably few people alive—and certainly few Americans—who could fail to recognize Disney's more high-profile creations: Mickey, Donald Duck, Sleeping Beauty, "When You Wish Upon a Star." They've become part of our national identity. And that's why *Disney Magic* and *Disney Wonder* work so well. In nearly every aspect of the onboard experience, they have what most other ships lack: a cultural frame of reference that's recognized by almost everyone.

Many Disney passengers purchase their cruises as part of 7-night seamless land/sea packages that combine 3- or 4-night cruises with 4- or 3-night pre-cruise park stays. Disney buses shuttle passengers between Orlando and the ship—about an hour's drive, during which an orientation video imparts some info about the cruise experience. At Disney's swank cruise terminal at Port Canaveral, check-in is usually made easier and faster because guests who have come from the resorts already have their all-purpose, computerized Key to the World cards, which identify them at boarding, get them into their cabins, and serve as their onboard charge cards. (If you're just doing the cruise, you get your Key to the World card when you arrive at the terminal.) You

Compared with other mainstream lines, here's how Disney rates:

	Poor	Fair	Good	Excellent	Outstanding
Enjoyment Factor				✓	
Dining			✓		
Activities			✓		
Children's Program					✓
Entertainment					✓
Service			✓		
Worth the Money				✓	

don't have to worry about your luggage, either: It's picked up at the resort and delivered to your cabin soon after you board.

PASSENGER PROFILE

Disney's ships attract a wide mix of passengers, from honeymooners to seniors, but naturally a large percentage is made up of young American families with children (with a smallish number of foreign passengers as well). Because of this, the overall age demographic tends to be younger than that aboard many of the other mainstream ships, with many passengers in their 30s and early-to-mid 40s. The bulk of the line's passengers are first-time cruisers, and since the line attracts so many families (sometimes large ones), more than half of its bookings are for multiple cabins.

DINING

While Disney's food is average cruise fare, its dining concept sets it apart from the big-ship crowd.

TRADITIONAL   The neat catch with Disney's version of set dining is that there are three restaurants that passengers (and their servers) rotate among for dinner over the course of the cruise. On one night, passengers dine on dishes such as roasted duck, garlic-roasted beef tenderloin in a green peppercorn sauce, or herb-crusted Atlantic cod in *Magic*'s elegant 1930s-era **Lumiere's** restaurant or *Wonder*'s equally elegant nautical-themed **Triton's.** On another night, they enjoy the likes of potato-crusted grouper, baby back pork ribs, or mixed grill in the tropical **Parrot Cay** restaurant. And on the third, they nosh on maple-glazed salmon, pan-fried veal chop, or roasted chicken breast with smashed potatoes at **Animator's Palate,** a bustling eatery with a gimmick: It's a sort of living animation cel, its walls decorated with black-and-white sketches of Disney characters that over the course of the meal gradually become filled in with color. Video screens add to the illusion, and the waiters even disappear at some point to change from black-and-white to full-color vests. It's kinda corny, but fun.

Each restaurant has an early and a late seating, and similar groups are scheduled to rotate together as much as possible (for example, families with young children, adults alone, and families with teens). **Vegetarian options** are offered at all meals, and kosher, halal, low-salt, low-fat, and other **special diets** can be accommodated if you request them when you book your cruise, or soon thereafter; once you're aboard, a chef and head server will meet with you to determine your exact needs. Kids' menus start with appetizers such as fruit cocktail and chicken soup before heading on to such familiar entree items as meatloaf, ravioli, pizza, hot dogs, hamburger, Jell-O and mac-and-cheese. The wine list is fair, and includes bottles by Silverado Vineyards, owned by members of the Disney family.

Magic's 7-night itineraries have 1 formal night and 1 semiformal night. The rest of the evenings are casual (no jackets or ties necessary). *Wonder* is casual throughout the cruise, though (on both ships) sports jackets are recommended for men dining in Palo and Lumiere's/Triton's. Overall, on Heidi's recent 3-night *Wonder* cruise, many went ultra caz: You could always count on a number of people in shorts and flip-flops at dinner (except for Palo's).

SPECIALTY   Both ships also have a romantic adults-only restaurant called **Palo,** serving Italian specialties such as tortellini stuffed with crab meat, grilled salmon with risotto, and excellent gourmet pizzas, like one topped with barbecued chicken, black olives, and spinach. A decent selection of Italian wines is available, and the dessert menu includes a fine chocolate soufflé and a weird-but-tasty dessert pizza. The restaurant itself is horseshoe-shaped and perched way up on Deck 10 to offer a 270-degree view. Service is attentive but not overly formal, and you don't have to dress up, though a jacket for men may be nice. Reservations are essential, and should be made immediately after you board, as the docket fills up fast ($10 per person cover charge).

CASUAL   Breakfast and lunch are served in several restaurants, both sit-down and buffet. Casual dinners are served on nights 2 though 6 in Topsiders *(Magic)* and Beach Blanket *(Wonder)*, the indoor/outdoor buffet. This poorly designed and cramped buffet venue is the one dining outlet on the ships that just doesn't work—Heidi found trying to squeeze through the throngs with kids and trays in tow during busy breakfast and lunch times practically qualified as a circus trick.

SNACKS & EXTRAS   A boon for families with fussy kids, Pluto's Dog House, on the main pool deck, is always bustling because of its complimentary chicken tenders, fries, burgers, nachos, bratwurst and other quick snacks served from lunch through the dinner hour. Stations for pizza and ice cream (with lots of toppings) are nearby and equally as popular. More highbrow options include champagne brunch (for $10 per person) on 4- and 7-night cruises and an afternoon tea on the *Magic*'s 7-night itineraries ($5 per person). On 7-night cruises, themed dining ops include breakfast with the Disney characters (for picture taking and posting), afternoon iced tea and cookies with Peter Pan's pal Wendy, and the new Pirates in the Caribbean dinner and deck party. It starts as a themed dinner in the restaurants, with waiters and passengers in pirate garb, and entree choices like Black Beard's jumbo crab cakes, then moves up on deck for a party with music and lots of special effects, from black lighting to pirates repelling from the funnel.

If you, or your kids, are soda junkies, Disney is the only mainstream line that dispenses the stuff for free! Since mid-2004, you can pour yourself a fountain soda (and then another and another) from a poolside station 24-7 on both ships, which can add up to a substantial savings for you by the end of the cruise. There's also the new Cove Café, in the space formerly occupied by the Common Grounds teen center, serving gourmet coffees and light fare for adults (at an extra cost).

The **24-hour room service** menu includes kid favorites such as pizza and cookies. (Though Heidi was on hold for a looooonggggg time when she tried to order lunch for her kids. Seems many others had the same idea.)

ACTIVITIES

Unlike on pretty much every other cruise ship, there's no casino of any kind on board, not even a card room. These are family ships. Activities on both vessels include basketball, Ping-Pong, and shuffleboard tournaments; sports trivia contests; weight-loss, health, and beauty seminars; bingo, Pictionary, and other games; wine tastings; and singles mixers (though these family-focused ships aren't great choices for singles). Each ship also has a spa and a surprisingly small gym (given the entire ship's size). During sea days aboard *Magic*, there are also galley tours, informal lectures on nautical themes and Disney history, Q & As with the captain, and home entertaining and cooking demos. Film buffs and Disney aficionados will appreciate backstage theater tours, drawing and animation sessions, and talks from people involved with Disney's Broadway, film, and television productions. All these activities are complimentary except wine tasting, which costs a hefty $12 per person. There are also dance classes, movies, and that cruise stalwart the Not-So-Newlywed Game, which Disney calls "Match Your Mate." All 7-night itineraries offer a captain's cocktail party with complimentary drinks once per cruise, and all 3- and 4-night cruises host nonalcoholic welcome receptions starring Disney characters. Sports fanatics can watch "the game" in the Diversions sports pub.

CHILDREN'S PROGRAM

Not surprisingly, with potentially hundreds of kids on any given sailing (1,000 is typical), Disney's kids' facilities are the most extensive at sea, with at least 50 counselors supervising the fun for five age groups between 9am and midnight daily. Nearly half a deck (comprising two huge play spaces and a nursery) is dedicated to kids. The **Oceaneer Club,** for ages 3 to 7 (with separate activities for ages 3–4 and 5–7), is a kid-proportioned playroom themed on Captain Hook. Kids can climb and crawl on the bridge, ropes, and rails of a giant pirate ship, as well as on jumbo-size animals, barrels, and a sliding board; get dressed up from a trunk full of costumes; dance with Snow White and listen to stories by other Disney characters; or play in the kiddie computer room. The interactive **Oceaneer Lab** offers kids ages 8 to 12 a chance to work on computers, learn fun science with microscopes, build from an enormous vat of Legos, do arts and crafts, hear how animation works, and construct their own radio show. Activities are arranged for two groups, ages 8 to 9 and 10 to 12, and both rooms are open till at least midnight, and till 1am on certain days. To keep things fresh, new activities are being introduced all the time (some 24 in 2004, for example) for the 3 to 12 set. There's also a video arcade, though it's really cramped compared to most on Royal Caribbean and Princess ships. Kids can eat lunch and dinner with counselors in the Topsider and Beach Blanket buffet restaurants all but the first evening of the cruise.

For teens (13–17), there's a new teen hangout called **The Stack** on the *Magic* and **Aloft** on the *Wonder*, where the ESPN Skybox sports bar used to be. Three times the size of the old Common Grounds teen room and more isolated from mom and dad, the teen centers, each with a different design motif, have two separate rooms, one with video screens for movies and the other a teen disco with a teens-only Internet center. Dance parties, karaoke, trivia games, improv comedy lessons, and workshops on photography are offered for teens on all cruises. There are even more options on 7-night sailings, including learning how to DJ!

Neither ship offers private babysitting services. Instead, the **Flounder's Reef Nursery** for kids ages 3 months to 3 years operates from 6pm to midnight daily, and also for a few hours during the morning and afternoon (hours vary according to the day's port schedule). No other line offers such extensive care for babies. Stocked with toys and decorated with *Little Mermaid*–themed bubble murals and lighting that gives an "under the sea" look, the area also has one-way portholes that allow parents to check on their kids without the little ones seeing them. The space has cribs and counselors do change diapers (though you must supply them). The price is $6 per child per hour, and $5 for each additional child in a family (with a 2-hr. minimum). Parents get a tuned beeper when they first check in to the nursery, or the kids' program, so that counselors can contact them anywhere on the ship if their child needs them.

When the ship calls on **Castaway Cay,** Disney's private island in the Bahamas, kids can head for Scuttle's Cove, a veritable paradise for the 12 and under set. There are barrels to crawl through, a giant whale-dig site to explore, and more; kids' counselors

Disney Fleet Itineraries

Ship	Itineraries
Disney Magic	**7-night E. & W. Carib:** Round-trip from Port Canaveral, FL, year-round (itineraries alternate weekly).
Disney Wonder	**3- & 4-night Bahamas:** Round-trip from Port Canaveral, FL, year-round.

are on hand to supervise the fun if mom and dad want to head to Serenity Bay, the adults-only beach. For families who want to play together, there are bike rentals and lots more. For details, see section 1, "The Cruise Lines' Private Islands," in chapter 9.

ENTERTAINMENT

Disney's fresh, family-oriented entertainment is some of the very best at sea today. On both ships, after-dinner performances by Broadway-caliber entertainers in the nostalgic Walt Disney Theatre include Disney Dreams, a sweet musical medley of Disney classics, taking the audience from *Peter Pan* to *The Lion King; Hercules, A Muse-ical Comedy*, a salute to the popular Disney film that's part story, part song, and part stand-up comedy (with lots of pop-culture references and enough slyness to keep adults entertained as well; the brilliant Hades character is a Robin-Williams-meets-Harvey-Fierstein hoot); and the *Golden Mickeys*, a tribute to Disney films through the years that combines song and dance, animated film, and special effects. On both ships, the stage design allows for lots of magic, with actors flying above the boards and disappearing in and out of trap doors, but the most refreshing thing about these shows is that they have story lines—rare almost to the point of extinction in the cruise world, which mostly presents musical revues.

Who Wants to Be a Mouseketeer? is a fun **audience-participation show** based on the millionaire quiz show and featured on 7-night itineraries. On Disney's version, the questions are all Disney trivia and the prizes are shipboard credits and a 7-night cruise for the big winner. Family game shows (including a trivia contest called "Mickey Mania" and another "Sound Waves," in the spirit of *Name That Tune*) and karaoke take place nightly in the **Studio Sea family nightclub.** Adults (18 and older) can take advantage of the **adults-only entertainment area** in the forward part of Deck 3, with its three themed nightclubs: one quiet, with piano music or soft jazz (with the kids safely tucked away in the Flounder's Reef nursery, Heidi and her husband enjoyed a great evening listening to Daryl Lockhart tickle the ivories in the romantic Cadillac Lounge on the *Wonder*); one dance club; and the third, Diversions, a combination sports pub and karaoke bar. Another nightspot is the **Promenade Lounge,** where live classic pop music is featured daily. The **Buena Vista Theater** shows movies day and evening.

SERVICE

Just as at the parks, Disney staff hails from some 60 countries, including the United States. Service in the dining rooms is efficient and precise, but leans toward friendly rather than formal. Maintenance workers and stewards keep public areas and cabins exceptionally clean and well maintained, and inconspicuous security guards are on duty 24 hours a day to make sure nothing gets out of hand (you know how Mickey can get after one too many martinis . . .). Overall, things run very smoothly.

Though the ships typically sail full and are bustling, the crew seems to remain perpetually good natured and smiley. On Heidi's recent *Wonder* sailing, everyone from the young crewmember doling out non-stop trays of chicken tenders at Pluto's Dog House to the gals working at the nursery and the ultrasmooth maitre d's at the restaurants, seemed to really like their jobs. The "happy to serve" mentality trickles right on up to the officer level too: The captain personally autographs guests' scrapbooks, photographs, and mementos in a public area at least once per cruise, while top officers participate in the beloved Disney "pin-trading" sessions. So, what makes everyone work so dang hard? Hotel Director Mike Mahendran told Heidi that performance expectations are high, but that it certainly doesn't hurt that crew members earn 10% to 30% more than the industry standard, and enjoy other perks that foster productivity.

It's no great surprise that travel agents tell us many guests rate service among the top features of a Disney Cruise.

Services include **laundry** and **dry cleaning** (the ships also have self-service laundry rooms) and 1-hour photo processing. Tips can be charged to your onboard account, which most passengers opt for, or you can give them out in the traditional method: cash.

Disney Magic •
Disney Wonder

The Verdict

The only ships on the planet that successfully re-create the grandeur of the classic transatlantic liners, albeit in a modern, Disneyfied way.

Disney Magic *(photo: Disney Cruise Line)*

Specifications

Size (in tons)	83,000	Passenger/Crew Ratio	1.8 to 1
Passengers (double occ.)	1,754*	Year Launched	
Passenger/Space Ratio	47.5	*Magic*	1998
Total Cabins/Veranda Cabins	877/378	*Wonder*	1999
Crew	950	Last Major Refurbishment	2003/2004

** **Note:** With children's berths filled, capacity can go as high as 3,325.*

Frommer's Ratings (Scale of 1–5)   ★★★★½

Cabin Comfort & Amenities	5	Dining Options	4.5
Ship Cleanliness & Maintenance	5	Gym, Spa & Sports Facilities	3
Public Comfort/Space	4	Children's Facilities	5
Decor	5	Enjoyment Factor	5

These long, proud-looking ships carry 1,754 passengers at the rate of two per cabin, but since Disney is a family company and its ships were built expressly to carry three, four, and five people in virtually every cabin, the ship could theoretically carry a whopping 3,325 passengers. Although numbers rarely reach that high, Hotel Director Mike Mahendran told Heidi they rarely carry fewer than 2,500 passengers.

Though service is a high point of a Disney cruise and the ships are well laid out, these high numbers mean certain areas of the ship will feel crowded at times, namely the kids' pool area, the buffet restaurants, and the photo gallery and shops after dinner.

Cabins & Rates

Cabins	Per Diems from	Sq. Ft.	Fridge	Hair Dryer	Sitting Area	TV
Inside	$124	184–214	yes	yes	yes	yes
Outside	$165	226–268	yes	yes	yes	yes
Suite	$203	259–1,029	yes	yes	yes	yes

CABINS   The Disney ships offer the family-friendliest cabins at sea, with standard accommodations equivalent to the suites or demi-suites on most ships—they're about 25% larger than the industry standard. All of the 877 cabins have at least a sitting area with a sofa bed to sleep families of three (or four if you put two small children on the sofa bed, as Heidi did when her boys were just under 2 years old). Some cabins also have one or two pull-down bunks to sleep families of four or five. Nearly half have private verandas. One-bedroom suites have private verandas and sleep four or five comfortably; two-bedroom suites sleep seven. Outside cabins that don't have verandas have jumbo-size porthole windows.

The decor is virtually identical from cabin to cabin, combining modern design with nostalgic ocean-liner elements such as a steamer-trunk armoire for kids, globe- and telescope-shaped lamps, map designs on the bedspreads, and a framed black-and-white 1930s shot of Mr. and Mrs. Walt Disney aboard the fabled ocean liner *Rex*. Warm wood tones predominate, with Deco touches in the metal and glass fittings and light fixtures. The majority of cabins have two bathrooms—a sink and toilet in one and a shower/tub combo and a sink in the other (both of them compact, though with ample shelf space). This is something you won't find in any other standard cabin industry-wide, and it's a great boon for families. All cabins have a minifridge (empty), hair dryer, safe, TV, shower-tub combo, sitting area, and lots of storage space.

One-bedroom suites are done up with wood veneer in a definite Deco mood. Sliding frosted-glass French doors divide the living room from the bedroom, which has a large-screen TV, queen-size bed (which can be split to make two twins), chair and ottoman, dressing room, makeup table, and whirlpool tub in the bathroom. A second guest bathroom is located off the living room, which also has a bar and a queen-size sofa bed. The veranda extends the length of both rooms. Two-bedroom and Royal suites are also available.

Sixteen cabins are fitted for wheelchair users.

PUBLIC AREAS   Both ships have several theaters and lounges, including an adults-only area with three separate venues: a piano/jazz lounge, disco, and sports-pub-cum-karaoke bar. There's also a family-oriented entertainment lounge called Studio Sea for game shows, karaoke, and dancing; the Promenade Lounge for classic pop music in the evenings; and a 24-hour Internet cafe with eight flat-screen stations. The new Cove Café (where Common Grounds teen center used to reside) is a comfy place for gourmet coffees or cocktails in a relaxed setting with books, magazines, Internet stations, and TVs. A 270-seat cinema shows recent-release and classic Disney movies.

The children's facilities, as you'd expect, are the largest of any ship at sea (see "Children's Program," above, for details).

Throughout, both ships have some of the best artwork at sea, owing to Disney's vast archive of animation cels, production sketches, costume studies, and inspirational artwork, featuring characters we've all grown up with. Other art—notably the "Disney Cruise Line Seaworthy Facts" near the photo shop and A-to-Z of seagoing terms near the theater—was created specifically for the ships and gets a big, big thumbs up. Canned music pumped into the public areas and corridors tends toward big-band music and crooner tunes or surf-type pop.

DINING OPTIONS   Disney's unique rotation dining setup has guests sampling three different restaurants at dinner over the course of their cruise, with an adults-only specialty restaurant also available, by reservation only (see "Dining," above). At breakfast and lunch, the buffet-style spread in *Magic*'s Topsider and *Wonder*'s Beach Blanket restaurants offers deli meats, cheeses, and rice and vegetable dishes, as well as a carving station, salad bar, and a dessert table with yummy chocolate-chip cookies. Though the culinary offerings are fine, the layout and tiny size of the place are not. During the morning rush, for example, it's tough to squeeze through the place, let alone with kids and a tray full of breakfast. Be prepared to dine elsewhere if the place is packed.

Options for afternoon noshing poolside include Pinocchio's Pizzeria; Pluto's Dog House for hot dogs, hamburgers, chicken tenders, fries and more; and Scoops ice-cream bar (which also includes a generous selection of toppings). There's 24-hour room service from a limited menu, but no midnight buffet unless you count the spread offered at the evening deck party held once per cruise. Instead, hors d'oeuvres are served to passengers in and around the bars at about midnight.

POOL, FITNESS, SPA & SPORTS FACILITIES   The pool deck of each ship has three pools: Mickey's Kids' Pool, shaped like the mouse's big-eared head, with a great big white-gloved Mickey hand holding up a snaking yellow slide (this pool can get crooooww-ded!); Goofy's Family Pool, where adults and children can mingle; and the Quiet Cove Adult Pool, with whirlpools, poolside Signals Bar, and a new coffee spot called Cove Café. On sunny days, the kids' pool will feel like a sardine can—watch those canon balls! A consolation prize for families with young children, adjacent is a splash pool with circulating water for diaper-wearing babies and toddlers. It's the only one at sea as the lines' official party line is no diaper-wearing children (and that includes pull ups and swim diapers) are allowed in any pool, wading or adult, for hygiene reasons.

Just beyond the adult pool area is a spa and the tiny, surprisingly drab fitness center (tiny compared to those aboard Carnival, Holland America, and most of the other mainstream lines), with a small aerobics room, seven treadmills, dumbbells, and a handful of cycle, elliptical, and Cybex machines. The gyms are so much of an afterthought that it's even difficult to find them, via a circuitous route through the spa. Nice view once you get there, though: The gyms' forward windows look down onto the bridge, where you can watch the officers at work. The 8,500-square-foot, Steiner-managed Vista Spa & Salon is much more impressive, with attractive tiled treatment rooms and a thermal suite with a sauna, steam room, misting shower, and heated contoured tile chaise longues. Among the many treatments are a selection geared to teens.

Both ships have an outdoor Sports Deck with basketball and paddle tennis. There's also shuffleboard and Ping-Pong, and joggers and walkers can circuit the Promenade Deck, which is generally unobstructed (though the forward, enclosed section may be closed off when the ship is arriving and departing port because it's adjacent to the anchor mechanisms).

5 Holland America Line

300 Elliott Ave. W., Seattle, WA 98119. ℭ **877/724-5425** or 206/281-3535. Fax 800/628-4855. www.holland america.com.

THE LINE IN A NUTSHELL   Holland America has been in business since 1873, and has managed to hang on to more of its seafaring history and tradition than any line today except Cunard. It offers a moderately priced, classic, and casual yet refined cruise experience. **Sails to:** Caribbean, Panama Canal, Alaska, Mexico, Hawaii, Canada/New England.

THE EXPERIENCE   Holland America consistently delivers a solid product with old-world elegance. Though the line has been retooling itself to attract younger passengers and families, it still caters mostly to older folks, and so generally offers a more sedate and stately experience than other mainstream lines, plus excellent service for the money. Its fleet, which until a few years ago consisted of midsize, classically styled ships, is in the process of being supersized, and the new Vista-class megaships are a mite bolder in their color palate, that's for sure. New or old, the vessels are all well maintained and have excellent (and remarkably similar) layouts that ease passenger movement. More so on the pre-Vista-class ships, throughout the public areas of the fleet you'll see flowers that testify to Holland's place in the floral trade, Indonesian fabrics and woodcarvings that evoke the country's relationship with its former colony, and seafaring memorabilia that often harks back to Holland America's own history.

Pros

- **Great service:** HAL's primarily Indonesian and Filipino staff is exceptionally gracious and friendly.
- **Traditional classic ambience:** The Vista-class ships are pushing the HAL envelope, but overall the line's ships are classy, with impressive art collections and a touch of traditional ocean-liner ambience.
- **Chocolate!** The once-per-cruise dessert extravaganzas and the occasional spreads of sweets guarantee you'll gain a few pounds.
- **Great gyms:** HAL's gyms are some of the largest, most attractive, roomiest, and best stocked at sea today.

Cons

- **Sleepy nightlife:** While there are always a few stalwarts and a couple of busyish nights, these aren't party ships. If you're big on late-night dancing and barhopping, you may find yourself partying mostly with the entertainment staff.
- **Fairly homogenous passenger profile:** Although younger faces are starting to pepper the mix (especially on 7-night cruises to warm weather destinations), most HAL passengers still tend to be low-key, fairly sedentary 55-plus North American couples.

Compared with the other mainstream lines, here's how HAL rates:

	Poor	Fair	Good	Excellent	Outstanding
Enjoyment Factor				✓	
Dining				✓	
Activities			✓		
Children's Program		✓			
Entertainment				✓	
Service					✓
Worth the Money					✓

HOLLAND AMERICA: GOING DUTCH

One of the most famous shipping companies in the world, Holland America Line was founded in 1873 as the Nederlandsch-Amerikaansche StoomvAart Maatschappij (Netherlands-American Steamship Company). Its first ocean liner, the original *Rotterdam,* took her maiden, 15-day voyage from the Netherlands to New York City in 1872. By the early 1900s, the company had been renamed Holland America and was one of the major lines transporting immigrants from Europe to the United States, as well as providing passenger/cargo service between Holland and the Dutch East Indies via the Suez Canal. During World War II, the company's headquarters moved from Nazi-occupied Holland to Dutch-owned Curaçao, then the site of a strategic oil refinery, and after the war the company forged strong links with North American interests. The line continued regular transatlantic crossings up until 1971, and then turned to offering cruises full-time. In 1989, it was acquired by Carnival Corporation, which improved the line's entertainment and cuisine while maintaining its overall character and sense of history. Today, most of HAL's vessels are named for other classic vessels in the line's history—*Rotterdam,* for example, is the sixth HAL ship to bear that name—and striking paintings of classic HAL ships by maritime artist Stephen Card appear in the stairways on every ship.

In addition to introducing its first three megaships in the past few years, HAL is also in the midst of a fleetwide upgrade program it calls "Signature of Excellence," a $225-million initiative that will upgrade dining, accommodations, service, and activities by November 2006 (most ships will be refitted by the time this book goes to press in late 2005). All staterooms are to be outfitted with flat-panel plasma TVs and DVD players, extra-fluffy towels and terry-cloth bathrobes, plus new massage showerheads, lighted magnifying makeup mirrors, and salon-quality hair dryers. Already in place fleetwide by the time this guide hits the bookstores, are plush triple-sheeted mattresses and 100% Egyptian cotton bed linens in all cabins. Suites will get new duvets, fully stocked minibars, and personalized stationery, and all suite guests will have access to a new one-touch 24-hour concierge service and exclusive concierge lounge. In addition to an expanded lecture series, each ship will get a special demonstration kitchen where a Culinary Arts program will offer interactive programs about food and wine. More changes are in store for HAL's pre-Vista-class vessels, including a combination lounge, library, coffee shop, and Internet cafe called the "Explorations Café, Powered by the New York Times" (featuring NYT crossword puzzles and online news); and dramatically upgraded facilities for kids—see the review of the Statendam-class ships later in this section for more details. Spa facilities will be enhanced to match the Greenhouse Spas introduced on the line's Vista-class megaships, with new treatments, expanded fitness and treatment facilities, a thermal suite (a kind of New Age steam room), and a hydrotherapy pool. In terms of who has what, the *Amsterdam, Volendam,* and *Zuiderdam* are slated to get their Signature upgrades during dry docks just after this guide is published (fall 2005), while the *Veendam, Maasdam,* and *Oosterdam* are scheduled for 2006. The rest of the fleet was already up to snuff at press time.

Though Holland America offers cruises in every major region covered in this book, it's particularly strong in Alaska. In 1971, it acquired Westours, a pioneering tourism company founded by Chuck West (who also created small-ship line Cruise West), and over the years it's acquired more and more Alaska properties, including trains, river cruisers, and hotels. The line operates one of the most extensive land-tour operations in the state, so many passengers opt to combine their cruise with a visit to Denali and Kenai Fjords national parks, Fairbanks, and/or Canada's Yukon Territory and Kluane National Park.

PASSENGER PROFILE

For years, HAL was known for catering to an almost exclusively older crowd, with most passengers in their 70s on up. Today, following intense efforts to attract younger passengers, about 40% of the line's guests are under age 55 (with the average age being 57), with a few young families peppering the mix, especially in summers and during holiday weeks. While the average age skews a bit lower on the newer Vista-class ships, HAL just isn't Carnival or Disney, and their older ships especially were designed with older folks in mind—a few even have fold-down seats in the elevators.

Passengers tend to be amiable, low-key, better educated than their equivalents aboard sister line Carnival, and much more amenable to dressing up—you'll see lots of tuxedos and evening gowns on formal nights. Though you'll see some people walking laps on the Promenade Deck, others taking advantage of the ships' large gyms, and some taking athletic or semi-adventurous shore excursions, these aren't terribly active cruises, and passengers overall tend to be sedentary. HAL has a very high repeat-passenger rate, so many of the people you'll see aboard will have sailed with the line before.

Parties for solo travelers (only 30–40 of whom tend to be on any particular cruise) encourage mixing, and you can ask to be seated with other solo passengers at dinner. On cruises of 10 nights or longer, gentlemen hosts sail aboard to provide company for single women, joining them at dinner as well as serving as dance partners.

DINING

Much improved over the years, Holland America's cuisine skirts close to the top of the mainstream heap, though it's not up to the gold standard of Celebrity's specialty restaurants.

TRADITIONAL   In the line's lovely formal restaurants, appetizers include sevruga caviar, prawns in spicy wasabi cocktail sauce, deep-fried hazelnut brie, and duck and black-bean quesadillas; the soup-and-salad course always includes several options, from a plain house salad and minestrone to Bahamian conch chowder and chilled watermelon soup; and main courses are heavy on **traditional favorites** such as broiled lobster tail, grilled salmon, beef tenderloin, roast turkey, seared tuna steak, grilled pork chop, and filet mignon. Those wanting something less substantial can try **light and**

healthy dishes such as seared duck breast, pan-seared grouper, and fresh fruit medley. Some vegetarian entrees are available on the main menu, but you can also ask for a **full vegetarian menu,** with half a dozen entrees and an equal number of appetizers, soups, and salads. (Don't miss the tofu stroganoff and celery-and-stilton soup if they're offered—yum.) Children can enjoy tried-and-true staples such as pizza, hot dogs, burgers with fries, chicken fingers, and tacos, plus chef's specials such as pasta and fish and chips. The **wine list** comprises about 70% U.S. vintages, with the rest from Europe, Chile, and Australia. **Dessert** features some wonderful chocolate creations, plus delicate items such as a tropical trifle with salmonberries, raspberries, pineapple, kiwi, and coconut cream. HAL recently expanded its dinner times to four seatings, so guests can request 5:45, 6:15, 8, or 8:30pm.

SPECIALTY   Aboard every vessel, the Pinnacle Grill offers **Pacific-Northwest cuisine,** including dishes like Dungeness crab cakes, pan-seared rosemary chicken with cranberry chutney, wild mushroom ravioli with pesto cream sauce, or lamb rack chops with drizzled mint sauce, plus premium beef cuts, all complemented with regional wines from Chateau Ste. Michelle, Canoe Ridge, Willamette Valley Vineyards, and others. The cover charge here is $20 per person. On a recent *Westerdam* cruise, the service was top rate and the food exceeded our expectations—don't miss the opportunity to dine here at least once per cruise. Make reservations as early as possible when you come aboard. In addition to dinners, alternative restaurants are also open for lunch on sea days.

CASUAL   As has become industry standard, **casual dining** is available each night in the ships' buffet-style Lido restaurants, which also serve breakfast and lunch. They're some of the best-laid-out buffets at sea, with separate stations for salads, desserts, drinks, and so on, keeping lines and crowding to a minimum. Diners here are offered open-seating from about 6 to 8pm. Tables are set with linens and a pianist provides background music, but service is buffet-style, with waiters on hand to serve beverages. The set menu features the basics: Caesar salad, shrimp cocktail, or fresh-fruit-cup appetizer; French onion soup; freshly baked dinner rolls; and four entree choices, which may include salmon, sirloin steak, roast chicken, and lasagna, served with a vegetable of the day and a baked potato or rice pilaf. At lunch, the buffet restaurants offer deli sandwiches, pasta, salads, stir-fry, burgers, and, sometimes, Mexican dishes. Pizza and ice-cream stations are open till late afternoon. Out on the Lido Deck, by the pool, a **grill** serves hamburgers, hot dogs, veggie and turkey burgers, and a special of the day, such as knockwurst or spicy Italian sausage, between about 11:30am and 5pm. A **taco bar** nearby offers all the fixings for tacos or nachos, but it's open only till 2:30pm (so much for nachos and beer after your shore excursion). Once a week, the Lido also hosts a **barbecue buffet dinner.**

SNACKS & EXTRAS   Once per cruise, a special Royal Dutch High Tea features teatime snacks and music provided by the ships' string trio, making it one of the most truly "high" among the generally disappointing high teas offered on mainstream lines. On other days, a more standard **afternoon tea** has waiters passing around teeny sandwiches and cookies in one of the main lounges. Pizza, soft ice cream, and frozen yogurt round out the afternoon offerings.

Free hot canapés are served in some of the bars/lounges during the cocktail hour, and free iced tea and lemonade are served on deck, one of many thoughtful touches provided at frequent intervals by the well-trained staff. Each of the Vista-class ships also has a sailing-ship-themed **Windstar Café** serving specialty coffees, pastries, and snacks for an extra charge. On the other ships the newly added **Explorations Café** has a coffee bar that serves a premium Starbucks blend, for a charge.

Each evening around midnight, a spread of snacks is available in the Lido restaurant, and at least once during each cruise the dessert chefs get to go wild in a midnight **Dessert Extravaganza.** Cakes are decorated with humorous themes, marzipan animals guard towering chocolate castles, and trays are heavy with chocolate-covered strawberries, truffles, cream puffs, and other sinful things.

Room service is available 24 hours a day and is typically efficient and gracious (though on a recent *Westerdam* cruise, Heidi was on hold for 10 or 15 min. before she could place her order on several occasions).

ACTIVITIES

Though varied and fun, HAL's onboard activities tend to be low-key. You can take ballroom dance lessons; take an informal class in photography; play bingo or bridge; sit in on a trivia game or Pictionary tournament; participate in Ping-Pong, golf-putting, basketball free-throw, or volleyball tournaments; take a gaming lesson in the casino or an aerobics class at the gym; take a guided tour of the ship's art collection or a backstage theater tour; go high-toned at a wine tasting; or go low-toned at the goofy pool games, which may be as innocuous as a relay race or as totally goofy as a water-ballet contest or another that the line describes this way: "Two teams battle to see who can stuff the most spoons down the swimsuit." Sodom and Gomorrah. . . . Some cruises also feature model shipbuilding contests in which you can only use junk you can find around the ship, with seaworthiness tested in one of the ship's hot tubs. Each ship's **Internet center** is open 24 hours a day. The Vista-class ships also have an extensive **golf instruction** program with onboard pros, equipment rental, and computer-aided coaching. The newest offering is the **Culinary Arts** program, which includes free cooking demos, usually twice per 7-day cruise (go early to get a front-row seat, or sit in the back and watch the food preparation on the flat-panel TVs around the room), and more intimate, hands-on cooking classes (available for a charge).

Activities pick up a bit at night, with pre-dinner cocktails and dancing. After dinner, you may attend a Fabulous Fifties party or a country-and-western night, take part in a slot-machine tournament or Night-Owl Pajama Bingo, or take in a show or movie (see "Entertainment," below).

On 7-night Alaska cruises, Native artists demonstrate traditional arts such as ivory and soapstone carving, basket weaving, and mask making as part of the line's **Artists in Residence Program,** created under the auspices of Anchorage's Alaska Native Heritage Center. Another program offered during visits to Glacier Bay brings a member of the Huna tribe aboard to talk about the land, which the Huna have called home for centuries. In Hawaii and Mexico, cultural dancers perform for passengers.

CHILDREN'S PROGRAM

Holland America isn't Disney—and they don't claim to be—but they're trying harder to cater to families with children. The biggest change to the Club HAL program is the lowering of the age minimum from 5 down to 3. Activities are programmed for three age brackets (3–8, 9–12, and 13–17), with one supervisor for every 30 kids. You'll find the most children on cruises during summers and holiday weeks. At these times, there may be as many as 300 to 400 kids aboard the Vista-class ships, especially in the Caribbean, though around 100 to 200 is typical overall. Each evening, kids receive a program detailing the next day's activities, which may include arts and crafts, youth sports tournaments, movies and videos, scavenger hunts, PlayStations, disco for teens, storytelling for younger kids, miniature golf, charades, "candy bar bingo," Ping-Pong, and pizza, ice-cream, and pajama parties. Activities are not scheduled while a ship is in port, though in the Caribbean the line does offer kids' activities on its private beach, Half Moon Cay (see section 1, "The Cruise Lines' Private Islands," in chapter 9). *Maasdam* and the newer Vista-class ships have dedicated "KidZone" playrooms and separate teen centers, and the other vessels are having them installed. Until then, they continue HAL's old practice of using multipurpose rooms for kids' activities when necessary. While the dedicated centers are an improvement (with computers, a large-screen TV for movies, an audio system, video games, and a dance floor) they lack a real "kid" feel, not to mention the ball-jumps, padded climbing and crawling areas, and fanciful decor that make kids' facilities aboard Disney, Royal Caribbean, Carnival, Celebrity, Princess, and NCL so compelling—although the new teen-only areas being added under HAL's Signature of Excellence, designed to look like an artist's loft indoors and a funky beach outdoors, are pretty cool. All the ships have small video-game rooms.

Group babysitting in the playroom is offered between 10pm and midnight for $5 per hour for ages 3 to 12. In-cabin babysitting is also offered assuming a crewmember is available. The cost is $8 an hour for the first child (minimum age 12 weeks), and $5 per hour for additional kids. Inquire at the guest services desk.

There is no age minimum for children to sail aboard.

ENTERTAINMENT

Don't expect HAL's shows to knock your socks off, but hey, at least they're trying. Each ship features small-scale **Vegas-style shows,** with live music (except on the Vista-class ships, where, we're told, there isn't enough space for a live orchestra in the main show lounges—ain't that the pits?), laser lights, and lots of glimmer and shimmer, and some sailings of *Volendam* feature a show based on the Barry Manilow song "Copacabana." Overall, though, you'll find better quality entertainment from the soloists, trios, and quartets playing jazz, pop, and light-classical standards.

Recent-release movies are shown an average of twice a day in an onboard cinema, with free popcorn available for the full movie effect. There's also a **crew talent show** once a week, in which crewmembers (Indonesians one week, Filipinos the next) present songs and dances from their home countries. On one 2002 cruise, a performance of "My Way" by 14 crewmembers wielding tuned bamboo angklung rattles was a real highlight of the cruise. It was, in fact, one of the most thoroughly bizarre things we've ever seen, and lots of fun. **Passenger-participation shows** are a different animal, with passengers lip-syncing tunes from the '50s and '60s as part of the Rockin' Rolldies show, then joining twist and hula-hoop contests in the sock hop that follows.

Aboard each ship, one of the lounges becomes a disco in the evening, with a small live band generally playing before dinner and a DJ taking over for after-dinner dancing. The new Vista-class ships have the line's first dedicated discos, and on the other ships, the Crow's Nest lounges have been redecorated for a more disco-y feel.

SERVICE

Holland America is one of the few cruise lines that maintains a training school (a land-based facility in Indonesia known within HAL circles as "ms Nieuw Jakarta") for the

Holland America Fleet Itineraries

Ship	Itineraries
Amsterdam	**15-night Hawaii:** Round-trip from San Diego or between San Diego and Ensenada, Dec 2005 and Feb–Apr 2006. **30-night Hawaii, Tahiti & Marquesas Islands:** Round-trip from San Diego, Jan 2006. **10-night Canada/New England:** North- or southbound between New York, NY, and Montreal, QB, Sept–Oct 2006. **10-night S. Carib/Panama Canal:** Round-trip from Ft. Lauderdale, FL, Oct–Dec 2006.
Maasdam	**7-night Canada/New England:** North- or southbound between Boston, MA, and Montreal, QB, Oct 2005 and May, June, Aug, and Sept 2006. **10- & 11-night E./S. Carib:** Round-trip from Norfolk, VA, Oct–Dec 2005, Jan–Mar 2006, and Nov–Dec 2006.
Noordam	**10- & 11-night E. Carib:** Round-trip from New York, NY, Feb–Apr and Oct–Dec 2006.
Oosterdam	**7-night Mexican Riviera:** Round-trip from San Diego, CA, Oct 2005–Apr 2006 and Oct–Dec 2006. **7-night Alaska Inside Passage:** Round-trip from Seattle, WA, May–Sept 2006.
Ryndam	**7-night Alaska Inside Passage:** North- or southbound between Vancouver, BC, and Anchorage/Seward, May–Sept 2006. **10-night Mexican Riviera:** Round-trip from San Diego, CA, Oct–Nov 2005 and Oct–Dec 2006.
Statendam	**15-night Hawaii:** Round-trip from San Diego, CA, Oct–Nov 2005. **7-night Alaska Inside Passage:** North- or southbound between Vancouver, BC, and Anchorage/Seward, May–Sept 2006.
Veendam	**7-night Alaska Inside Passage:** North- or southbound between Vancouver, BC, and Anchorage/Seward, May–Sept 2006. **7-night W. Carib:** Round-trip from Tampa, FL, Nov–Dec 2005, Jan–Apr 2006, and Oct–Dec 2006.
Volendam	**7-night Alaska Inside Passage:** Round-trip from Vancouver, BC, May–Sept 2006. **10-night S. Carib:** Round-trip from Ft. Lauderdale, FL, Jan–Mar and Oct–Dec 2006.
Westerdam	**7-night Alaska Inside Passage:** Round-trip from Seattle, WA, May–Sept 2006. **7-night E. & W. Carib:** Round-trip from Ft. Lauderdale, Nov–Dec 2005, Jan–Apr 2006, and Oct–Dec 2006 (itineraries alternate).
Zaandam	**7-night Alaska Inside Passage:** Round-trip from Seattle, WA, May–Sept 2006. **10-night Panama Canal:** Round-trip from Ft. Lauderdale, FL, Oct 2005–April 2006. **10-night Mexican Riviera:** Round-trip from San Diego, CA, Oct–Dec 2005 and Oct–Dec 2006. **15-night Hawaii:** Round-trip from San Diego, CA, Oct–Dec 2006.
Zuiderdam	**7-night E. Carib:** Round-trip from Ft. Lauderdale, FL, Oct 2005–Mar 2006 and Oct–Dec 2006. **7-night Alaska Inside Passage:** Round-trip from Vancouver, BC, May–Sept 2006.

selection and training of staffers, resulting in service that's efficient, attentive, and genteel. The soft-spoken, primarily Indonesian and Filipino staffers smile more often than not and will frequently remember your name after only one introduction, though they struggle occasionally with their English. (Be cool about it: Remember, you probably can't speak even a word of Bahasa Indonesia or Tagalog.) During lunch, a uniformed employee may hold open the door of a buffet, and at dinnertime, stewards who look like vintage hotel pages walk through the public rooms ringing a chime to formally announce the dinner seatings.

Like many other lines these days, HAL automatically adds **gratuities** to passengers' shipboard accounts, at the rate of $10 per day, adjustable up or down at your discretion.

Prinsendam Drops By

In addition to the ships reviewed in this chapter, Holland America's small, boutique-size *Prinsendam* will also sail a series of cruises to the eastern and southern Caribbean and Central America in December 2005 and December 2006. Launched in 1988, with a tonnage of 38,000 tons and a passenger capacity of only 793, the vessel sailed as *Royal Viking Sun* for Royal Viking line and Cunard and as *Seabourn Sun* for Seabourn before being transferred to Holland America in 2002.

This is a change from the line's old "No Tipping Required" policy, which always should have had a parenthetical after it that read "but it's expected anyway." A 15% service charge is automatically added to bar bills and dining room wine accounts.

Only the Vista-class ships come with minifridges standard in cabins. On the other vessels, they can be rented for $2 a day (inquire before your cruise if you're interested). All cabins have complimentary fruit baskets on embarkation day. A new early-boarding program allows guests to get aboard in the port of embarkation as early as 11:30am, when some lounges and facilities will be open for their use, although cabins generally won't be ready until 1pm.

Onboard services on every ship in the fleet include **laundry** and **dry cleaning.** Each ship—except the new Vista-class ships, oddly enough—also maintains several **self-service laundry rooms** with irons.

The Vista Class: Zuiderdam • Oosterdam • Westerdam • Noordam (preview)

Zuiderdam *(photo: Holland America Line)*

The Verdict

Holland America's first foray into mega-size ships marry traditional HAL style with a partying Caribbean feel; by the time the Westerdam was launched, and the kinks were worked out, the relationship was working.

Specifications

Size (in tons)	85,000	Year Launched	
Passengers (double occ.)	1,848	*Zuiderdam*	2002
Passenger/Space Ratio	46	*Oosterdam*	2003
Total Cabins/Veranda Cabins	924/623	*Westerdam*	2004
Crew	800	*Noordam*	2006
Passenger/Crew Ratio	2.3 to 1	Last Major Refurbishment	2005/2006

Frommer's Ratings (Scale of 1–5)   ★★★★

Cabin Comfort & Amenities	4.5	Dining Options	4
Ship Cleanliness & Maintenance	4	Gym, Spa & Sports Facilities	4.5
Public Comfort/Space	4	Children's Facilities	3
Decor	3.5	Enjoyment Factor	4

Built on a similar design as Carnival's Spirit-class ships, *Zuiderdam* (named for the southern point of the Dutch compass, and with a first syllable that rhymes with "eye"), *Oosterdam* (eastern, and with a first syllable like the letter "O"), and *Westerdam* are Holland America's biggest ships to date, though their 85,000-ton, 1,848-passenger size doesn't put them anywhere in the running among today's true behemoths. Still, the line hopes they'll help it finally shed its image as your grandmother's cruise line and compete better for the all-important baby-boomer and family cruise dollars. Can't fault them for that, but let's just say hipness isn't something you can grow overnight. *Zuiderdam,* the first of the series, came off totally unnatural, like a 60-something banker trading in his Mercedes and suits for a red Corvette and tight black jeans. Its peculiar style—mixing ultrabright Carnival-esque colors, stark W Hotel modernism, and the traditional style for which HAL was previously known—was toned down some for sister ship *Oosterdam,* introduced in 2003. A little bit brighter than the old HAL but not embarrassingly so, this ship was a great improvement. By the time the *Westerdam* came on the scene, the new look was refined; though there still are ultra bright pockets, like the lemon yellow and grape leather furniture in the piano bar. Overall, the ship's a winner. In the spirit of learning from their mistakes, HAL has gone back and tweaked parts of the *Zuiderdam,* replacing some of the loudest carpeting with darker shades, for example, and even removing some of the more jarring "art" pieces. The giant red lips are gone and so is the ice block sculpture in the disco, which was replaced with a more benign wall of video screens. All three sisters are extraordinarily spacious, with large standard cabins, stylish two-level dining rooms, and distinctive specialty restaurants.

All descriptions in this review refer to *Zuiderdam, Oosterdam,* and *Westerdam.* A fourth sister, *Noordam,* is scheduled to debut in February 2006. It replaces the old 1984 *Noordam,* which left the HAL fleet in November 2004.

Cabins & Rates

Cabins	Per Diems from	Sq. Ft.	Fridge	Hair Dryer	Sitting Area	TV
Inside	$115	185	yes	yes	no	yes
Outside	$123	194–200	yes	yes	yes	yes
Suite	$338	298–1,000	yes	yes	yes	yes

CABINS   Cabins in all categories are comfortable and, as aboard every HAL ship, are among the industry's largest, with a simple decor of light woods, clean lines, and subtly floral bedding. Overall, more than two-thirds of them have verandas, with the deluxe veranda suites and staterooms in the stern notable for their deep balconies, nearly twice the size of those to port and starboard. You get a romantic view of the ship's wake, too, but since the decks are tiered back here, residents of the cabins above you can see right down. Keep your clothes on.

Standard outside and veranda cabins all have a small sitting area and a tub in the bathroom—a relatively rare thing in standard cabins these days. Closet space in all categories is more than adequate for 7-night cruises, with nicely designed fold-down shelves and tie rack. Dataports allow passengers to access e-mail and the Internet from every cabin, using their own laptops.

Suites run from the comfortably spacious Superior Veranda Suites (with wide verandas, large sofa bed, walk-in closet, separate shower and bath, and extra windows) to the Penthouse Veranda Suites, extremely large multi-room apartments with a flowing layout, pantry, palatial bathrooms with oversize whirlpool baths, and ridiculously large private verandas with a second, outdoor whirlpool. Their decor is reminiscent of 1930s moderne style. Guests in every suite category have use of a concierge lounge whose staff will take care of shore excursion reservations and any matters about which you'd normally have to wait in line at the front desk. The lounge is stocked with reading material, coffee, and juice, and a continental breakfast is served daily.

Twenty-eight cabins are wheelchair accessible.

PUBLIC AREAS   Public rooms on the Vista-class ships run the gamut from the traditional to the modern, from the lovely to the not-so-lovely. The color schemes are a real stew, from strong eye-opening oranges, red, and purples, to the much more sedate champagnes and deep blues. Among the more traditional spaces is the signature Explorer's Lounge, a venue for quiet musical performances and high tea. *Oosterdam's* and *Westerdam's* stick to the understated, elegant style you see on other HAL ships, while on *Zuiderdam* it's dressed up with slightly brighter colors and more modern furniture. The top-of-the-ship Crow's Nest lounge, an observation lounge during the day and nightclub/disco at night, offers wide-open views, comfortable leather recliners toward the bow (a perfect reading perch during days at sea), and even a few rococo thrones on the starboard side, good for "wish you were here" cruise photos. The rear port corner of the Crow's Nest is the most truly elegant lounge area aboard, with high-style Deco chairs and soft leather sofas.

Lower Promenade Deck is the hub of indoor activity on these ships. In the bow, the three-deck Vista Lounge is the venue for large-scale production shows, while the Queen's Lounge at midships hosts comedians and other cabaret-style acts. Between the two there's a casino, a peculiarly decorated (read: really flashy) piano bar that reminds us of Marvin the Martian from the old Bugs Bunny cartoons. There's also HAL's first-ever dedicated discos, but they're uninspired at best (and, on *Zuiderdam,* just butt-ugly). Our favorite room, the Sports Bar, looks as little like the standard rah-rah sports-hero-and-pennants sports bar as you can imagine, with comfortable free-form leather seating and brushed-metal vase-shaped table lamps. *Très* chic. Only the multiple TVs give away the place's true identity.

One deck up, the traditional Ocean Bar wraps around the understated three-deck atrium—whose focal point on all ships is a Waterford crystal chandelier—with bay windows to port and starboard looking out onto the promenade and the room's namesake. Moving forward, you pass through the drab shopping arcade, whose displays spill right into the central corridor courtesy of retractable walls, forcing you to browse as you walk from stem to stern. A lot of lines are doing this and it's a pretty crass sales pitch; it gets a big thumbs down from us. Once you get through, you come to the traditional-looking library with its ocean-liner-style writing tables and very nontraditional (but very cool) funky blonde-wood swivel chairs with spring-adjusting back support. By the end of 2006, the entire Vista class will have an Explorations Café, a combination specialty coffee shop, Internet center, and library, plus a Culinary Arts demonstration kitchen (see Statendam-class review for more details).

Other public rooms include the Main Deck's Atrium Bar, a very comfortable small-scale nook vaguely reminiscent of a 1930s nightclub; the wicker-furnitured outdoor Lido Bar on the Lido Deck (which unfortunately lacks the charm of similar spaces on the line's older ships); and the KidZone and WaveRunner children/teen centers, which are a bit bare, though roomy and sunny. Art in the public areas includes some nice humorous paintings by Hans Leijerzapf, maritime artwork by Stephen Card, replica 18th-century Dutch engravings and commedia dell'arte statues, and jazz sketches and paintings by Wil van der Laar. *Oosterdam*'s Java Corner has several sketches of landmark Frank Lloyd Wright designs.

Oceanview elevators at port and starboard midships are a little boxy, closing off some of the inspiring views that were intended. Much better views are to be had from outdoor areas forward on Decks 5, 6, and 7, and from an area just forward of the gym, above the bridge. You can even check a ship's compass here.

DINING OPTIONS   The main Vista Dining Room is a two-deck affair, decorated traditionally but with nice touches of modernism, for instance in the *Zuiderdam*'s black, high-backed wooden chairs, which are very sharp. The ship's alternative Pacific Northwest restaurant, the 130-seat Pinnacle Grill, wraps partially around the three-deck atrium in a design that's maybe a bit too open—ask for a table by the windows or in the aft corner for a cozier experience. Aside from this quibble, the design is appealing, with marble floors, bright white linens, gorgeous Bvlgari place settings, and ornate, organically sculpted chairs by Gilbert Libirge, who also created the ships' beautiful, batik-patterned elevator doors.

Diners wanting something more casual can opt for the well-laid-out Lido buffet restaurant; the outdoor Grill for burgers, dogs, and the like; or the Windstar Café, serving specialty coffees (for a cost), snacks, and light meals in a tall-ship atmosphere.

POOL, FITNESS, SPA & SPORTS FACILITIES   As aboard all the HAL ships reviewed in this book, the Vista-class ships boast some of the largest gyms around, with a full complement of cardio equipment and weight machines arranged in tiers around the cardio floor, with a large hot tub in the center. There's also a basketball/volleyball court on the Sports Deck and a computerized golf simulator one deck down, on Observation Deck. The Greenhouse Spa is fully 50% larger than any other in the HAL fleet, and besides offering the usual massage, mud, and exotic treatments, it has a couple of HAL firsts: a thermal suite (a series of saunas and other heat-therapy rooms) and a hydrotherapy pool, which uses heated seawater and high-pressure jets to alleviate muscle tension. Oddly, there's no compelling design motif, like you'd find in other signature spas. Around the pool, extra-heavy wooden lounge chairs are thick-padded and nap-worthy. The pool area doesn't quite work on *Zuiderdam*, where the colors are jarring and the materials cheap looking, but as in many other areas, *Oosterdam*'s and *Westerdam*'s is a vast improvement, very pleasant all around.

Outdoors, the wraparound Promenade Deck is lined with classy wooden deck chairs—a nice touch of classic ocean liner style—and is popular with walkers and joggers. The main pool deck is the hub of outdoor activity on sea days, with hot tubs, music, and pool games, and can be covered with a sliding roof in inclement weather. The hallmarks of the pool area on both ships are giant bronze animal statues—from a polar bear, to penguin and dolphin. Another pool, in the stern on Lido Deck, is a quieter alternative.

Rotterdam • Amsterdam

The Verdict

Modern throwbacks to the glory days of transatlantic travel without the stuffiness or class separation, these attractive sisters offer great features, from classic art to rich mahogany woodwork and elegant yet understated public rooms.

Amsterdam *(photo: Holland America Line)*

Specifications

Size (in tons)		*Amsterdam*	690/172
Rotterdam	56,652	Crew	
Amsterdam	61,000	*Rotterdam*	593
Passengers (double occ.)		*Amsterdam*	647
Rotterdam	1,316	Passenger/Crew Ratio	
Amsterdam	1,380	*Rotterdam*	2.2 to 1
Passenger/Space Ratio		*Amsterdam*	2.1 to 1
Rotterdam	43	Year Launched	
Amsterdam	44	*Rotterdam*	1997
Total Cabins/Veranda Cabins		*Amsterdam*	2000
Rotterdam	658/161	Last Major Refurbishment	2004/2005

Frommer's Ratings (Scale of 1–5)   ★★★★½

Cabin Comfort & Amenities	4.5	Dining Options	4
Ship Cleanliness & Maintenance	4	Gym, Spa & Sports Facilities	4.5
Public Comfort/Space	5	Children's Facilities	3
Decor	5	Enjoyment Factor	4.5

With 3 years separating them, near-twins *Rotterdam* and *Amsterdam* combine classic elegance with contemporary amenities and provide a very comfortable cruise, especially on itineraries of 10 nights and longer. *Rotterdam,* the sixth HAL ship to bear that name, is popular with passengers who previously sailed aboard the legendary *Rotterdam V,* which was sold off in 1997. At press time, it appears that *Rotterdam* will not be sailing from any U.S. ports in 2006.

Cabins & Rates

Cabins	Per Diems from	Sq. Ft.	Fridge	Hair Dryer	Sitting Area	TV
Inside	$107	182	no	yes	yes	yes
Outside	$133	197	no	yes	yes	yes
Suite	$459	225–937	yes	yes	yes	yes

CABINS   Unlike the beige color schemes of the older Statendam-class ships, the decor here is livelier, with corals, mangoes, blues, and whites brightening things up.

The standard cabins are among the most spacious at sea and offer enough hanging and drawer space for 10-night-plus cruises. Bathrooms are generous as well, with bathtubs in all but the standard inside cabins (and, on *Amsterdam,* in a handful of outsides as well). Each cabin has a sitting area, a desk, a safe, two lower beds convertible to a queen, and great reading lights above each bed, in addition to the line's new amenities: flat-panel plasma TVs and DVD players, extra-fluffy towels and terry-cloth bathrobes, new massage shower heads, lighted magnifying makeup mirrors, and salon-quality hair dryers. Beds now have plush triple-sheeted mattresses and 100% Egyptian cotton bed linens.

Veranda Suites are 225 square feet and have a 59-square-foot private veranda; Deluxe Veranda Suites measure 374 square feet and have a 189-square-foot veranda and a dressing room. Both have sitting areas, whirlpool tubs, and stocked minibars, and are kept stocked with fresh fruit. Penthouse Suites measure 937 square feet and have a 189-square-foot veranda, living room, dining room, guest bathroom, and an oversize whirlpool tub. All suite guests have use of a concierge lounge whose staff will take care of shore excursion reservations and any matters about which you'd normally have to wait in line at the front desk. The lounge is stocked with reading material, and a continental breakfast is served daily.

Twenty-one cabins are wheelchair accessible.

PUBLIC AREAS   Both ships have great, easy-to-navigate layouts that allow passengers to move easily among public rooms. Most of the inside public areas are concentrated on two decks; ditto for the pools, sunning areas, spa, sports facilities, and buffet restaurant, which are all on the Lido and Sports decks.

Overall, the ships give you the feeling of an elegant old hotel, with dark red and blue upholstery and leathers, damask fabrics, mahogany tones, and gold accents. Artwork is everywhere, from the stairwells to the walkways on the Promenade and Upper Promenade decks. Aboard *Amsterdam,* the theme is Dutch and nautical; aboard *Rotterdam* it's continental and Asian. In *Amsterdam*'s atrium, a clock tower combines an astrolabe, a world clock, a planetary clock, and an astrological clock. You can't miss it; it's been wedged into the space with barely an inch to spare. *Rotterdam*'s passengers are greeted in the atrium by a large reproduction Flemish clock.

The Ocean Bar serves complimentary hot hors d'oeuvres before dinner nightly, and passengers pack into the bar to listen and dance to a lively trio. More elegant is the Explorer's Lounge, whose string ensemble performs a classical repertoire. Nearby is the open-sided piano bar, featuring a red lacquered baby grand piano.

The Crow's Nest observation lounge/disco gets fairly little use during the day unless there's a special event being held (such as line-dance classes), but it's a popular spot for pre-dinner cocktails and after-dinner dancing. Near the room's entrance on *Amsterdam* you'll see the *Four Seasons* sculptures originally created for the old *Nieuw Amsterdam* in 1938, and purchased back by the line from a private collector. On *Rotterdam,* a highlight of the Crow's Nest is the life-size terra-cotta human and horse figures, copies of ancient statues discovered in Xian, China.

The main showroom, perhaps the brightest of the rooms, is done in red and gold and is more a nightclub than a theater. Sit on the banquettes for the best sightlines, as alternating rows of individual chairs sit lower and don't permit most passengers to see over the heads of those in front of them. The balcony offers decent sightlines.

Other public rooms include a large casino, library, card room, a movie theater, and a computer room with eight flat-screen computers for e-mailing or surfing the Net.

By the end of 2005, just after this guide is published, both ships will have an Explorations Café, a combination specialty coffee shop, Internet center, and library. The kids' facilities will also be enhanced and there will be a new Culinary Arts demonstration kitchen (see Statendam-class review for more details).

DINING OPTIONS   Aboard both ships, the attractive two-level formal dining rooms have floor-to-ceiling windows and an elegant, nostalgic feel, and never seem crowded. The Pinnacle Grill seats fewer than 100 diners and offers romantic, intimate Pacific Northwest cuisine in an elegant setting. The only downside here: no windows. And be careful of those funky chairs; they tip forward if you lean too far toward your soup. Aboard *Amsterdam,* make a point of looking at the paintings, all of which have a joke hidden somewhere on the canvas—look for the RCA "his master's voice" dog on the Italian rooftop, and for Marilyn Monroe by the lily pond.

As in the rest of the fleet, casual buffet-style breakfast, lunch, and dinner are offered in the Lido restaurant, a bright, cheerful place done in corals and blues. It's a well-laid-out space, with separate salad, drink, deli, dessert, and stir-fry stations. There's a taco bar poolside at lunchtime, and pizza is available in the afternoon.

POOL, FITNESS, SPA & SPORTS FACILITIES   *Amsterdam* and *Rotterdam* have spacious, well-equipped gyms with a very large separate aerobics area, floor-to-ceiling ocean views, plenty of elbowroom, and a decent spa, which will be upgraded by late 2005 as part of the line's enhancement program. There's a pair of swimming pools: one amidships on the Lido Deck, with a retractable glass roof and a pair of hot tubs, and another smaller, less trafficked and thus more relaxing one in the stern, letting on to open views of the ships wake. Both ships have great wraparound Promenade decks lined with wooden deck chairs, a quiet and nostalgic spot for reading, snoozing, or—especially on *Amsterdam*'s Alaska itineraries and *Rotterdam*'s Europe cruises—scoping the scenery.

There's a combo volleyball and tennis court on the Sports Deck, and Ping-Pong tables on the Lower Promenade in the sheltered bow.

Volendam • Zaandam

The Verdict

These handsome ships represent a successful marriage of HAL's usual elegance and gentility with a well-done dose of classy modern pizzazz.

Volendam *(photo: Holland America Line)*

Specifications

Size (in tons)	63,000	Passenger/Crew Ratio	2.2 to 1
Passengers (double occ.)	1,440	Year Launched	
Passenger/Space Ratio	44	*Volendam*	1999
Total Cabins/Veranda Cabins	720/197	*Zaandam*	2000
Crew	647	Last Major Refurbishment	2005

Frommer's Ratings (Scale of 1–5)

✦✦✦✦½

Cabin Comfort & Amenities	4.5	Dining Options	4
Ship Cleanliness & Maintenance	4	Gym, Spa & Sports Facilities	4.5
Public Comfort/Space	5	Children's Facilities	3
Decor	5	Enjoyment Factor	4.5

Introduced at the turn of the century, *Volendam* and *Zaandam* marked Holland America's first steps into a more diverse, mainstream future, offering an experience designed to attract the vital 40-something boomers while still keeping the line's core older passengers happy. The ships have alternative restaurants, Internet centers, and huge gyms that many lines attracting younger crowds can't match, but their overall vibe is more traditional than Carnival, Princess, and Royal Caribbean—and, for that matter, than the line's newer and much more glitzy Vista-class vessels. These are classy, classic ships, but with just a touch of funk to keep things from seeming too old-fashioned—note the autographed Bill Clinton saxophone and Iggy Pop guitar in *Zaandam's* elegant Sea View Lounge.

Cabins & Rates

Cabins	Per Diems from	Sq. Ft.	Fridge	Hair Dryer	Sitting Area	TV
Inside	$140	186	no	yes	yes	yes
Outside	$180	196	no	yes	yes	yes
Suite	$382	284–1,126	yes	yes	yes	yes

CABINS   In a word: roomy. These standard cabins are among the largest in the industry, and with a much more modern, daring look than on the line's older ships. Fabrics are done in salmon-red, burgundy, gold, and bronze, and walls in a striped pale-gold fabric, hung with gilt-framed prints. Bathrooms are roomy and well designed, with adequate storage shelves and counter space. All outside cabins have shower/tub combos (short tubs, but tubs nonetheless), while inside cabins have only showers. Cabin drawer space is plentiful, and closets are roomy, with great shelves that fold down if you want to adjust the configuration of space. There's a storage drawer under each bed.

All cabins have sitting areas, plus Holland America's new Signature of Excellence enhancements, from flat-panel plasma TVs and DVD players, to extra-fluffy towels and terry-cloth bathrobes, new massage shower heads, lighted magnifying makeup mirrors, and salon-quality hair dryers. Beds now have plush triple-sheeted mattresses and 100% Egyptian cotton bed linens.

On the Verandah and Navigation decks, 197 suites and minisuites have balconies, including the single gorgeous Penthouse Suite, which measures 1,126 square feet, including veranda, and is adorned with one-of-a-kind pieces such as 19th-century Portuguese porcelain vases and Louis XVI marble table lamps.

Twenty-one cabins are wheelchair accessible.

PUBLIC AREAS   *Volendam's* public areas are floral-themed; *Zaandam's* sport musical motifs. Aboard *Volendam,* each aft staircase landing has a still-life painting of flowers, and a spot outside the library has a collection of elaborate delft tulip vases (ironically, with fake silk tulips). You could even call the gorgeous graduated colors in the show lounge seating florally themed, with colors from magenta to marigold creating a virtual garden in bloom. *Zaandam*'s theme is exemplified by one of the more bizarre and inspired atrium decorations we know of—a huge, mostly ornamental baroque pipe organ decorated with figures of musicians and dancers—as well as by numerous musical instruments scattered around the ship in display cases, from a classic Ornette Coleman–style plastic Grafton sax in the Sea View Lounge to the elaborate Mozart harpsichord display (with busts and a candelabra) outside the card room. The display of electric guitars in the atrium stair tower, signed by Queen, Eric Clapton, the Rolling Stones, and others, might represent a little too much wishful thinking on HAL's part about attracting younger passengers. Or does it represent the aging of the '60s generation?

In general, as aboard almost the entire HAL fleet, public areas are very easy to navigate. Corridors are broad, and there's little chance of getting lost or disoriented. Surfaces and fabrics overall are an attractive medley of subtle textures and materials, from tapestry walls and ceilings to velveteen chairs, marble tabletops, and smoky glass. *Volendam* even has a red-lacquer piano and suede walls woven to resemble rattan. *Zaandam*'s pianos are all funky: The one in the piano bar is painted to look as though it's made of scrap lumber and rusty nails; the one in the Lido restaurant is downright psychedelic.

The warm and almost glowingly cozy Explorer's Lounge is a favorite area, along with the nearby Sea View Lounge and the adjacent piano bar, with its round, pill-like leather bar stools and plush sofas. On busy nights, the Ocean Bar can get crowded by the bar, but there's usually plenty of space across the room or near the dance floor, where a live jazz band plays danceable music before and after dinner.

The ever-popular Crow's Nest nightclub has been redesigned as part of the Signature enhancements and now has features like banquettes in bright, modern colors and translucent white floor-to-ceiling curtains that function both as decor and moveable enclosures for private events. Cocktail mixology classes and other events are offered here during the day; after dinner, it becomes the ships' disco and nightclub. As on the other HAL vessels, the ships' main showrooms are two-story affairs with movable clusters of single seats and banquettes on the ground level in front of the stage so passengers can get comfortable.

Both vessels have impressive art and antiques sprinkled throughout their public areas. The booty on *Volendam* includes an authentic Renaissance fountain outside the casino (the ship's most pricey piece), an inlaid marble table in the library, and a small earthenware mask dating back to 1200 B.C. that's kept in a display case near the Explorer's Lounge. On *Zaandam*, an area outside the library features reproductions of Egyptian jewelry and a huge repro Egyptian statue fragment.

By the end of 2005, just after this guide is published, both ships will have an Explorations Café, a combination specialty coffee shop, Internet center, and library. The kids' facilities will also be enhanced, and there will be a Culinary Arts demonstration kitchen (see Statendam-class review for more details).

DINING OPTIONS The two-story main dining rooms are glamorous, framed with floor-to-ceiling windows and punctuated by dramatic staircases. A classical trio serenades guests from a perch on the top level. Just outside the second level of the dining room is a place you ladies won't want to miss: a wonderful powder room with ocean views and lots of elbowroom for primping, with vanity tables and stools in one room and the toilets and sinks adjacent. Both ships also feature HAL's fleetwide Pacific Northwest specialty restaurant, the Pinnacle Grill (see "Dining," on p. 173).

The Lido buffet restaurants are efficiently constructed, with separate stations for salads, desserts, and beverages, cutting down on the chance of monstrously long lines. A sandwich station serves its creations on delicious fresh-baked breads.

POOL, FITNESS, SPA & SPORTS FACILITIES   The gyms on these ships are downright palatial and among the best at sea, with floor-to-ceiling windows surrounding dozens of state-of-the-art machines, and so much elbowroom that you might wonder if some equipment is out getting serviced. Hey, no complaints here. The adjacent aerobics areas are huge too—nearly as big as the ones at our gyms back home. By late 2005, the spa and hair salons will be upgraded.

Three pools are on the Lido Deck: a small and quiet aft pool (behind the Lido buffet restaurant) and the main pool and wading pool, located under a retractable glass roof in a sprawling area that includes the pleasant, cafelike Dolphin Bar, with rattan chairs and shade umbrellas. There are more isolated areas for sunbathing above the aft pool on a patch of the Sports Deck and in little slivers of open space aft on most of the cabin decks. The Sports Deck also has a pair of practice tennis courts, as well as shuffleboard. Joggers can use the uninterrupted Lower Promenade Deck to get their workout.

The Statendam Class: Statendam • Maasdam • Ryndam • Veendam

Veendam *(photo: Holland America Line)*

The Verdict

These attractive midsize vessels are an increasing oddity in an industry where each new ship is bigger than the last. Public areas are functional and appealing, with just a dash of glitz and collections of European and Indonesian art.

Specifications

Size (in tons)	55,451	Year Launched	
Passengers (double occ.)	1,266	*Statendam*	1993
Passenger/Space Ratio	44	*Maasdam*	1993
Total Cabins/Veranda Cabins	633/149	*Ryndam*	1994
Crew	602	*Veendam*	1996
Passenger/Crew Ratio	2.1 to 1	Last Major Refurbishment	2004–2006

Frommer's Ratings (Scale of 1–5)   ★★★★

Cabin Comfort & Amenities	4	Dining Options	4
Ship Cleanliness & Maintenance	4	Gym, Spa & Sports Facilities	4
Public Comfort/Space	5	Children's Facilities	3*
Decor	4	Enjoyment Factor	4.5

* *Children's facilities are in the process of being upgraded.*

These four vessels are, like all the HAL ships, extremely well laid out and easy to navigate. Touches of marble, teak, polished brass, and multi-million-dollar collections of art and maritime artifacts lend a classic ambience, and many decorative themes emphasize the Netherlands' seafaring traditions. The onboard mood is low-key (though things get dressy at night), the cabins are large and comfortable, and there are dozens of comfortable nooks all over the ships in which you can curl up and relax. *Ryndam* was the first HAL ship to roll out of the dry dock with all its Signature of Excellence enhancements in place, and our descriptions refer to that vessel; the upgrades to *Statendam, Veendam,* and *Maasdam* will be completed by spring 2006.

Cabins & Rates

Cabins	Per Diems from	Sq. Ft.	Fridge	Hair Dryer	Sitting Area	TV
Inside	$121	186	no	yes	yes	yes
Outside	$144	197	no	yes	yes	yes
Suite	$356	284–1,126	yes	yes	yes	yes

CABINS   Cabins are roomy, unfussy, and comfortable, with light-grained furniture and floral or Indonesian batik-patterned curtains separating the sleeping area from the sitting area. White-gloved stewards add a hospitable touch. All cabins have twin beds that can be converted to a queen and, in some cases, a king, all with plush triple-sheeted mattresses and 100% Egyptian cotton bed linens. About 200 cabins can accommodate a third and fourth passenger on a foldaway sofa bed and/or an upper berth. Closets and storage space are larger than the norm, and bathrooms are well designed and well lit, with bathtubs in all but the lowest category. All cabins have personal safes and music channels, plus new enhancements that include flat-panel plasma TVs and DVD players, extra-fluffy towels and terry-cloth bathrobes, new massage shower heads, lighted magnifying makeup mirrors, and salon-quality hair dryers.

Outside cabins have picture windows and views of the sea, though those on the Lower Promenade Deck have pedestrian walkways (and, occasionally, pedestrians) between you and the ocean. Special reflective glass prevents outsiders from spying in during daylight hours. To guarantee privacy at nighttime, you have to close the curtains. No cabin views are blocked by dangling lifeboats or other equipment.

Minisuites are larger than those aboard some of the most expensive lines, such as SeaDream. Full suites are 563 square feet, and the Penthouse Suite sprawls across a full 1,126 square feet. Six cabins are outfitted for passengers with disabilities, and public areas are also wheelchair friendly, with spacious corridors, wide elevators, and wheelchair-accessible public toilets.

PUBLIC AREAS   For the most part, public areas are subdued, consciously tasteful, and soothing. The Sky Deck offers an almost 360-degree panorama where the only drawback is the roaring wind. One deck below, almost equivalent views are available from the ever-popular Crow's Nest nightclub, which has been redesigned in a fresh, new way. Highlights include a glowing bar, banquettes in bright, modern colors, and translucent white floor-to-ceiling curtains that function both as decor and moveable enclosures for private events. Cocktail mixology classes and other events are offered here during the day; after dinner, it becomes the ships' disco and nightclub. The ships' small, three-story atria are pleasant enough and refreshingly unglitzy, housing the passenger-services and shore-excursions desks as well as officers' offices.

The ships' two-story showrooms are modern and stylish, and unlike aboard most ships, which have rows of theater-like seats or couches, their lower levels are configured with cozy groupings of cushy banquettes and chairs that can be moved. The balcony, however, has very uncomfortable bench seating, with low backs that make it impossible to lean back without slouching.

The new Explorations Café replaces the ships' libraries and game rooms, and we bet the new space will be popular: Set right in the thick of things, you can while away hours here. Lounge chairs face the big picture windows and come equipped with music stations and headphones. Shelves of books, DVDs, and games line the walls, and a magazine stand holds current issues of popular magazines plus the latest edition of the *New York Times,* when the ship can get it (and no, they're not flying in copies during sea days). If you're a crossword buff you can tackle the *Times'* puzzles embedded on computer screens under glass in the room's cafe tables (wax pencils are provided). Explorations also functions as the Internet Cafe, but passengers toting their Wi-Fi enabled laptops can take advantage of wireless hotspots throughout the ship. Until *Veendam* and *Maasdam* get an Explorations Café in 2006, they'll still have a large, tranquil library with floor-to-ceiling windows. A small selection of books and board games can be signed out, and writing tables with HAL-logo stationery is available; next door, there's a spacious card room and an Internet center with eight flat-screen stations.

A cozy piano bar is nestled in a quiet nook next to the elegant Explorer's Lounge, a popular venue for high tea in the afternoon and for elegant light classical and parlor music after dinner. A live band plays for dancers before dinner in the very popular Ocean Bar, and the nice-size casinos are spacious though not as pleasingly designed as aboard the line's newer ships. A small movie theater shows films three times a day, and this space also houses the new Culinary Arts demonstration kitchen—the movie screen descends in front of the kitchen during showtimes. Across the hall from the theater is an attractive new wine bar and shop where guests can take part in tastings, one white wine and one red each day, and buy wine for that night's dinner at a discount.

Maasdam has a small children's and teen's area on the top deck, but HAL is making big changes to the kids' areas. The youngest kids play in a room decorated like a giant paint box, and pre-teens have a karaoke machine and video games. Lucky teens, however, get the Oasis, a top-deck sun deck with a wading pool with waterfall, teak deck chairs, hammocks, colorful Astroturf, and lamps designed as metal palm trees, all enclosed by a bamboo fence. This would be a great space for group events on sailings with few kids aboard.

DINING OPTIONS   These ships have elegant, two-story main dining rooms at the stern, with dual staircases swooping down to the lower level for grand entrances and a music balcony at the top where a duo or trio serenades diners. Ceilings are glamorous with their lotus-flower glass fixtures, and two smaller attached dining rooms are available for groups. HAL's Pacific Northwest specialty restaurant, the Pinnacle Grill (see "Dining," on p. 173), has a classy modern feel to it.

The casual indoor/outdoor buffet restaurant is well laid out, with separate stations for salads, desserts, and drinks, which helps keep lines to a minimum. The restaurant serves breakfast, lunch, and dinner daily, and its pizza and ice-cream stations are open until just before dinner. An outdoor grill on the Lido Deck serves burgers and other sandwich items throughout the afternoon, and a nearby station allows you to make your own tacos or nachos at lunch.

POOL, FITNESS, SPA & SPORTS FACILITIES   Each ship has a sprawling expanse of teak-covered aft deck surrounding a swimming pool. One deck above and centrally located is a second swimming pool plus a wading pool, hot tubs, and a spacious deck, all under a sliding glass roof to allow use in Alaska, or in inclement weather elsewhere. Imaginative, colorful tile designs and a dolphin sculpture add spice, and the attractive Dolphin Bar, with umbrellas and wicker chairs, is one of our favorite spaces on board, the perfect spot for a drink and snack in the late afternoon after a shore excursion.

The Sports Deck of each ship has combo basketball/tennis/volleyball courts, and the Lower Promenade Deck offers an unobstructed circuit of the ship for walking, jogging, or just lounging in the snazzy, traditional-looking wooden deck chairs. The ships' roomy, windowed Ocean Spa gyms are some of the most attractive and functional at sea, with a couple of dozen exercise machines, a large aerobics area, steam rooms, and saunas. The redesigned Greenhouse Spas are an improvement, each including new thermal suites with a hydrotherapy whirlpool and heated tile loungers.

The Forward Observation Deck is accessible only via two stairways hidden away in the forward (covered) portion of the Promenade Deck, and so gets little use. There's no deck furniture here, but standing in the very bow as the ship plows through the ocean is a wonderful experience.

6 Imperial Majesty Cruise Line

2950 Gateway Dr., Pompano Beach, FL 33069. © **954/956-9505.** Fax 954/971-6678. www.imperialmajesty.com.

THE LINE IN A NUTSHELL   Imperial Majesty operates nothing but 2-night round-trips between Fort Lauderdale and Nassau, year-round. The one big reason to sail? The line's ship, the 1953-vintage *Regal Empress*, is probably the last chance you'll ever get to sail on a real, old-fashioned ocean liner. They don't make 'em like this anymore. **Sails to:** Nassau, Bahamas.

THE EXPERIENCE   If you want to get a glimpse of what ocean travel was like in the 1950s, plunk down a couple hundred bucks and take a quick ride aboard *Regal Empress*. Today, the 53-year-old vessel is more over-the-hill vaudeville trouper than glamorous star, but she's one of the very few ships left where you can see the kind of woody interiors and chunky steelwork that characterized the great old liners. She's a real ship-ship, totally unlike today's hotel-like megaships. Former owners Regal Cruises (see below) kept her in good shape, initiating several well-planned refurbishments that ripped out bad, glitzy '80s additions and reemphasized the classic elements of her decor. Let's not be dishonest, though: The *Empress* shows her age, and for every classic element there's a worn one to balance it, like scuffed cabin walls, stained or sagging ceiling tiles, and a "been at sea too long" smell in some areas. Quirks and all, though, the *Regal Empress* is an absolute classic—and with international maritime regulations mandating retirement for vessels like this by 2010, time is running out.

Pros

- **She's a time machine:** Lots of old wooden wall paneling survives, providing a window back to the old *An Affair to Remember* days.
- **Classic nautical lines:** The ship's long, bowed hull and tiered aft decks cut a snazzy, classic profile in this age of boxy look-alike megaships.
- **It's cheap:** Cruises in high season start at $179 per person, and rates can get as low as $129. The best suite on the ship goes for $499 per person.

Cons

- **Wear and tear:** On a vessel like this, "ship-shape" means keeping her running and safe, not shiny and new. The crew does a great job keeping her clean, but 53 years of hard use show through in innumerable scrapes, scratches, scuffs, and bruises.
- **Feels crowded:** For her size, this ship carries a lot of passengers, and because there aren't too many public rooms, things can get crowded. That said, maybe crowds are good on a 40-hour good-time cruise.

REGAL EMPRESS: OLD, CHEAP & CHARMING

Here's something you don't hear about every day: On April 18, 2003, U.S. marshals swooped in and literally arrested *Regal Empress* in Florida, clapping her in irons and forcing cancellation of an Easter weekend cruise after more than 800 passengers had already boarded. The action came after an engine-repair company secured a lien on the vessel to cover a $729,000 bill owed by the ship's then-owner, Regal Cruises. Only 10 days later, Regal announced it was ceasing operations.

The incident was a blow to ship lovers, who assumed the old *Regal Empress*—built as the Greek ocean liner *Olympia*—would be sold for scrap. An initial government auction on May 16 netted no takers, but on May 23 the ship was finally won by Fort Lauderdale–based Imperial Majesty for a cool $1.75 mil.

Saved? For now. By 2010, though, *Empress*'s kind of woody interiors and mazelike layout will be prohibited by international safety regulations. After that you'll only be able to see this kind of ship in the movies. There's still some hope for *Empress,* though: In late 2004 Rhode Island state senator Leonidas Raptakis began working with representatives of the Greek government to purchase and preserve the ship as a museum of Greek maritime history, either in Greece or New England. See **www.ssmaritime.com/olympiacampaign.htm** for information.

PASSENGER PROFILE

At any given time, about 50% of passengers book the ship as part of land-sea package deals, often sold via telemarketers. The other 50% are generally South Florida locals and vacationers looking to add a quick Bahamas hop to their Florida vacation. A fair number are first-timers sampling the cruise experience before committing to a longer voyage.

DINING

The dining experience on *Regal Empress* is surprisingly pleasant, with most meals served both inside at the formal restaurant and at the indoor-outdoor buffet, which is also the venue for a daily midnight buffet themed on Italian, Latin, and other dishes.

Compared with other mainstream lines, here's how Imperial Majesty rates:

	Poor	Fair	Good	Excellent	Outstanding
Enjoyment Factor			✓		
Dining			✓		
Activities		✓			
Children's Program	✓				
Entertainment		✓			
Service			✓		
Worth the Money			✓		

Imperial Majesty Fleet Itineraries

Ship	Itineraries
Regal Empress	**2-night Bahamas:** Round-trip from Fort Lauderdale to Nassau, year-round.

TRADITIONAL   There are two seatings for each meal in the *Empress*'s attractive, wood-paneled Caribbean dining room, which retains much of its original ocean-liner charm with etched glass, ornate wall sconces, oil paintings, and an original mural of New York. The cuisine, while not gourmet in any way, is decent and served professionally by a fleet of waiters and their assistants. Main courses tend to be classic cruise fare: prime rib, catch of the day, chicken cordon bleu, and veal scaloppine, with appetizers such as shrimp cocktail, prosciutto with melon, and spinach and feta strudel. Soups and salads (including good gazpacho and Greek salad) round out the courses, and there's always one **vegetarian option** such as spinach quiche or linguini Toscana. Desserts include a perfectly acceptable napoleon, cheesecake, and mousse, plus an assortment of ice creams and (predictably, but still charming) a baked Alaska paraded around the room with some flair by the waitstaff.

CASUAL   The buffet adjoins the stern pool area and serves lunch on embarkation day and breakfast on day 2 and disembarkation day. Breakfast offers a good selection of fruits, meats, eggs, omelets, and pastries. Lunches include the usual salads, cheese, fruit, cold cuts, and meats, plus good pasta. On the opposite side of the stern bar, an open-air grill serves burgers, hot dogs, and pizzas.

ACTIVITIES

As you're only aboard for 2 nights, the range of activities is limited to bingo, gambling, dancing, drinking, and karaoke, and on night 2 all guests are invited to a complimentary champagne reception with the captain. At port in Nassau, the line offers several extra-cost shore excursions to Blue Lagoon Island, including simple beach runs, parasailing, snorkeling, glass-bottom boat tours, and stingray swims.

CHILDREN'S PROGRAM

Just behind the pool deck there's a small, very drab **children's room** where a youth counselor supervises activities for kids 3 and up for a few hours each evening. Expect coloring contests, movies, arts and crafts, and pizza parties, plus a Kids Disco Party in the ship's regular adult disco on night 2. There are also seven video game machines bunched together in the rear section of the enclosed promenade, aft. No babysitting is available.

ENTERTAINMENT

Let's start by saying we're suckers for this kind of budget entertainment. Limited facilities, no sets, a punishing schedule—how can you not root for them? In the not-very-grand **Grand Lounge,** a seven-member song-and-dance troupe and three-piece "orchestra" (all from Romania when we were aboard) gives its all on the small, low-ceilinged stage, with rapid costume changes and big smiles to keep things lively. Elsewhere, the completely charming **Commodore Lounge** has a pianist from 8:30pm till after midnight, and the **Mermaid Lounge** next door has live dance music and karaoke throughout the evening. Down one of the ship's many mysterious stairways, the drab **Mirage disco** thumps until late night, while a trio performs on the pool deck.

SERVICE

Service is better than you might expect from such an inexpensive line. The dining staff is professional and experienced, cabin stewards and ship maintenance staff are top-notch (they have to be, as the old ship requires constant care), and the friendly bartenders at the Pool Bar have their job down pat. As booze sales are a big part of the line's revenue, stewards are constantly roving the public areas asking if you need a drink, but it never gets to the point of annoyance. Room service is not available; nor is laundry service.

Regal Empress

The Verdict

However worn around the edges, this indomitable old war horse retains some charming vestiges of old ocean-liner days.

Regal Empress *(photo: Matt Hannafin)*

Specifications

Size (in tons)	21,909	Crew	365
Passengers (double occ.)	875	Passenger/Crew Ratio	2.4 to 1
Passenger/Space Ratio	18.5	Year Launched	1953
Total Cabins/Veranda Cabins	457/10	Last Major Refurbishment	1997

Frommer's Ratings (Scale of 1–5)   ★★

Cabin Comfort & Amenities	2	Dining Options	2.5
Ship Cleanliness & Maintenance	3	Gym, Spa & Sports Facilities	1
Public Comfort/Space	2	Children's Facilities	1
Decor	2.5	Enjoyment Factor	3

Now 53 years young, *Regal Empress* is the oldest cruise ship in the U.S. market. Built in Scotland in 1953 as a two-class Greek Line ocean liner called the *Olympia,* the ship made her debut sailing from Glasgow and Liverpool to New York. In 1970, long after air travel killed the transatlantic trade, she switched to cruising, but by 1974 ended up mothballed at a pier in Piraeus, Greece, where she languished until 1983. In 1984, after a major refitting, she sailed as the *Caribe I* ("The Happy Ship") for now-defunct Commodore Cruise Lines. She was sold to Regal in 1993, then to Imperial Majesty 10 years later. Today, the *Empress* is a hodgepodge of old and new, with some of her original ocean-liner decor existing side by side with cheap lounge furnishings. On one sailing after her last major renovation, we heard a passenger say of the interior, "It's not dull, but it could use a little more glitter." We disagree. In fact, for us it's the lack of glitter that really makes the *Empress* worthwhile—the rich wood paneling that covers the main stair landings, the dining room, and the purser's lobby; the sunken seating clusters port and starboard in the cozy Commodore Lounge (our favorite spot for cocktails and conversation); and the little-used but delightful old-fashioned enclosed promenade.

The ship's layout is also peculiarly charming, owing to years of alterations and also to the fact that she was originally built as a two-class ocean liner, carrying 138 first-class passengers and 1,169 tourist-class, with her layout configured to keep the two mostly separate. Today, with the areas merged for use by everyone, the *Regal Empress* is full of odd little stairways leading from deck to deck, doors that go where you wouldn't think they would, and corridors that twist and turn like an English hedge maze. It's like an old house: quirky and unique, and as different as can be from the open design of most modern ships.

Cabins & Rates

Cabins	Per Diems from	Sq. Ft.	Fridge	Hair Dryer	Sitting Area	TV
Inside	$95	80–106	no	no	no	yes
Outside	$135	116–120	no	no	no	yes
Suite	$250	216–408	yes	yes	yes	yes

CABINS   Because cruises are only 40 hours long it doesn't really matter what cabin you book, but you sure do have a lot of choices: As with most old ships, the *Empress*'s 457 cabins vary widely in size, location, and configuration, with the smallest measuring a cramped 80 square feet and the largest suites a spacious 410 square feet. The majority are about 100 to 120 square feet, including many inside cabins without views. Cabins look their age for the most part, with drab walls and sparse furnishings, though bright matching drapes and bedspreads cheer things up a bit. Ceilings are low in the cabins as well as in the corridors outside. Closet space is more than adequate since all you need is an overnight bag for these trips. All cabins have televisions and telephones. Bathrooms are generally small and cramped.

Suites E and F and minisuites U90 and U91 on the Upper Deck are the most distinctive cabins aboard, with their woody interiors and odd-though-appealing shapes. In late 1997, 10 suites were reconfigured to include large private verandas. A few also have very bizarre, unattractive enclosed balconies (actually forward sections of the enclosed promenade, now partitioned off) with hot tubs. Unless you just can't live without a Jacuzzi, we'd give 'em a pass.

Sixty-seven cabins can be configured for four through bunk-bed arrangements. Others are configured for single passengers. Two cabins are accessible to wheelchairs, but overall this ship is not a good option for people with mobility problems.

PUBLIC AREAS   The Pool Bar is the hub of outdoor action and is a total classic, with a chunky, caramel-colored wood bar. Inside, the Grand Lounge is used for stage performances and bingo. One deck down, the smoky casino is either cheesy looking or retro-cool, depending on your perspective. The disco, however, is just plain drab. Up on Sun Deck, the Mermaid Lounge nightclub is a pleasant space with a large dance floor and glass-brick, brass-railed bar. A bit of trivia: This lounge used to be the first-class swimming pool, back in the old days. You can still see the mechanism that was used to retract its glass ceiling.

For us, the best room on the ship (and one of our favorite rooms on any ship, period) is the Commodore Lounge, a clubby, intimate bar with sunken seating areas to port and starboard. A pianist performs here in the evenings. For quiet lounging, we also recommend the enclosed promenade decks to port and starboard. Essential in the old days for north Atlantic crossings (where winter cold and winds made outdoor promenades uncomfortable), indoor promenades are now a thing of the past—even the new *Queen Mary 2,* the first ocean liner built in decades, doesn't have one. *Empress* sports rich teak decking, potted trees and plants, and a smattering of couches and small tables for two. This is probably the only chance you'll ever get to experience this aspect of old ship life.

A small card room, kids' playroom, and three-screen Internet center are located behind the Pool Bar.

DINING OPTIONS   See "Dining," above.

POOL, FITNESS, SPA & SPORTS FACILITIES   The ship's tiered aft decks are very attractive in that classic liner kind of way, with one small pool and two hot tubs surrounded by deck chairs and tables. For a private moment alone with the sea, take the stairs down from here (or exit the rear starboard-side doors of the Grand Lounge) and walk to the very stern. It's a spot many passengers never explore. Ditto for the forward observation deck just below the bridge, accessible via a stairway on the enclosed promenade. There's no gym, but a tiny massage room and beauty salon are located on the Upper Deck, near the passenger services desk.

7 MSC Cruises

6750 N. Andrews Ave., Fort Lauderdale, FL 33309. © **800/666-9333.** www.msccruises.com.

THE LINE IN A NUTSHELL   What a difference a year makes. Once a catch-as-catch-can line offering cheap cruises on a fleet of older ships, MSC is busily retooling itself into a player in the American market. Its sugar-daddy European owner and high-profile U.S. management team plan to turn it into a premium line on par with Holland America and Celebrity—and who knows, maybe they can. **Sails to:** Caribbean (plus Europe, South America).

THE EXPERIENCE   Based in Italy, where it was born as an adjunct of Mediterranean Shipping Company, the world's second-largest container-shipping operation, MSC's all about "Italian style." You're probably thinking, "What, another Costa?" Not exactly. Where Costa goes for a flashy megaship vibe, MSC is deliberately low-key in the decor and whoopee department. Its two U.S.-based ships, the identical, midsize *Lirica* and *Opera,* were launched in 2003 and 2004 and are almost a throwback to an earlier era of cruising, carrying "only" 1,590 passengers and with almost none of the pop-culture themes and flashiness of most modern ships. Ditto for the onboard ambience, which is in the process of being retuned by the new U.S. management team. New head-man Rick Sasso, formerly president of Celebrity Cruises, has his eye on re-creating what he sees as cruising's glory days. "The seventies were my favorite era in cruising," he told us. "It was all about the experience then: the personality of the brand and the way passengers interacted with each other." The idea is a line that doesn't rely on gadgets and gimmicks, but where the staff helps the passengers have a great time simply interacting with each other. Though the long list of improvements Sasso and team intend to make at MSC weren't fully implemented at press time, we can see the direction they're going, and we like it.

Pros

- **Human-size ships:** Small enough to be homey and big enough that they don't get boring, *Lirica* and *Opera* are surprisingly spacious despite being pipsqueaks compared to the competition's megaships.
- **Fun activities:** As at Costa, the European staff knows how to get people in the mood for fun.
- **Unusual entertainment touches:** While production shows can lapse into the usual Vegas-style song-and-dance, circus-style contortionists, acrobats, and stilt performers add a nice touch.

Cons

- **Small cabins:** Standard inside and outside cabins are only 140 square feet, and 247-square-foot suites would pass for junior suites aboard most vessels.
- **Tiny shower stalls:** Showers in cabin bathrooms are among the smallest in the cruise business.
- **No alternative dining:** In the evening, the only alternative to the two dining rooms is the buffet or pizza.

MSC: ITALIAN LINE GOES INTERNATIONAL

The cruise wing of Mediterranean Shipping Company, one of the world's largest container-shipping operations, MSC came into being in 1990, concentrating on the European market. In 1998 it bought the Big Red Boat *Atlantic* from defunct Premier Cruises and began offering 11-night Caribbean cruises for both Europeans and Americans. And that, essentially, was the line's story until last year, when things started to change fast. In April 2004 MSC purchased Festival Cruises' ship *European Vision* after that company's financial meltdown; in May it hired former Celebrity president Richard Sasso to head its North America division; in June it launched the new 58,000-ton *Opera;* and in August it bought *European Vision's* sister ship, *European Stars. Vision* and *Stars* (renamed *Armonia* and *Sinfonia*) are almost identical to MSC's *Lirica* and *Opera,* all of them having been built by France's Alstom Marine, which was also responsible for *Queen Mary 2.* Two new MSC megaships are currently on order with Alstom, one for delivery in June 2006 and another for 2007. In December 2004 MSC launched its first two-ship Caribbean season ever, deploying *Lirica* and *Opera* on 7- and 11-night cruises while simultaneously launching a major retooling of their product, aiming to transform it from a low-priced European niche line into a more high-toned premium line catering to an international audience. The transformation is ongoing, but the combination of the new U.S. management team and the parent company's deep pockets gives us confidence in MSC's future.

Compared with other mainstream lines, here's how MSC rates:

	Poor	Fair	Good	Excellent	Outstanding
Enjoyment Factor			✓		
Dining			✓		
Activities				✓	
Children's Program			✓		
Entertainment			✓		
Service			✓		
Worth the Money				✓	

PASSENGER PROFILE

The typical age range is mid-40s and up, and while MSC's Mediterranean itineraries tend to carry 85% European and 15% "other" (including North Americans), Caribbean itineraries are exactly reversed, with Americans dominating. Also, while European itineraries tend to carry a lot of kids, those in the Caribbean don't except at holidays. Announcements in the Caribbean are made in two languages, English and Italian, in that order.

DINING

Dining service is traditional, with a very European sensibility. While that sounds dandy, it also presented some annoyances to Americans on our late-2004 cruise—no after-dinner coffee, no Sweet'n'Low type artificial sweeteners, breakfast buffet selections skewed more toward European tastes, and slow service. Management is aware that this probably won't do for many American passengers. "We're going to offer the best of both worlds," said new pres Rick Sasso. "We'll give them their corn flakes"— as well as bagels, sweeteners, late-night coffee, and other American favorites—"but we'll do it with a European flair." Training is in progress to speed up the service, and they've even added several Jamaican chefs to the kitchen staff because, according to another exec, "Europeans don't know how to cook bacon."

TRADITIONAL   Two formal dining rooms serve traditional breakfast, lunch, and dinner in two fixed seatings, with an emphasis on Italian cuisine. Six-course lunches include appetizers like smoked salmon tartare, tomatoes stuffed with tuna mousse, and barbecued chicken wings; a soup of the day; choice of salads; pasta selections like ravioli, risotto with pears and Bel Paese cheese, and traditional spaghetti; and main courses that might include pan-roasted chicken breast in a Riesling wine sauce, sliced sirloin, Caribbean red snapper fillet, frittata with zucchini and Swiss cheese, or a plain old turkey sandwich. A selection of vegetables, cheeses, and desserts rounds out the offerings, along with a special **vegetarian menu,** burgers and dogs from the grill, and **healthy-choice options.**

Expect about the same for dinner, with appetizers like lamb-and-mushroom quiche, avocado boat with seafood salad, and crispy fried spring rolls; a salad of the day; three soup selections, such as Trieste-style red beans soup, oxtail broth with sherry, and chilled orange and tomato cream soup; pasta selections such as risotto with artichokes and fresh mint leaves and pappardelle pasta with white veal ragout; and main courses like rock Cornish hen with mushrooms and crispy bacon, prime rib, grilled mahi-mahi fillet, and vegetable couscous with raisins and cashews. As at lunch, there's also a vegetarian menu, healthy menu, and a selection of cheeses and desserts (including sugar-free desserts), plus a **bread of the day** and an **Italian regional specialty.** An "always available" list includes steak, chicken, salmon fillets, Caesar salad, baked potato, and corn on the cob.

SPECIALTY   None.

CASUAL   The Le Bistrot Cafeteria serves all three meals buffet-style, with dinner available from 6 to 8pm.

SNACKS & EXTRAS   Pizza, burgers, and other items are available from the pool-deck grill during the day. From late afternoon to late night, the grill serves pizza and **Italian specialty snacks.** Inside, the ship offers one of the few daily **midnight buffets** left in the industry.

MSC Fleet Itineraries

Ship	Itineraries
Lirica	**7-, 10- & 11-night Carib:** Round-trip from Fort Lauderdale, FL, Dec 2005–Apr 2006.
Opera	**7-night E. Carib:** Round-trip from Fort Lauderdale, FL, Jan–Apr 2006.

ACTIVITIES

Activities on MSC tend toward cruise traditions, many of them with a European sense of fun. Outside, expect a round of **goofy pool games,** including water polo, treasure hunts, and various team games, plus foosball, darts, and **golf tournaments,** the latter on a putting green that wraps around the top deck. Goofiness continues in the evenings, with the kind of participatory games for which Italian ships are known. Leave your self-consciousness at home. Flamenco and tango **dance lessons** might be held in one of the lounges, while guests such as former U.S. ambassadors offer **informal lecturers.** Other classes include Italian language, basic computer use, and cooking, and the spa and salon staffs put on the usual raft of **beauty demonstrations.** Next door, the gyms offer stretching and standard aerobics classes, plus Pilates and yoga at an added charge ($14 per class, or five for $55). Other activities include cards and bingo, gambling in the **casinos,** arts and crafts, and various meet-and-greet events such as singles and honeymooners cocktail parties.

CHILDREN'S PROGRAM

Each ship has a smallish (if cute) children's center, while other kid-centric activities around the ship might include "baby disco" and balloon-tying shows. Private babysitting can be arranged through the main desk.

ENTERTAINMENT

Evening entertainment is centered around the extra-wide stage of each ship's main theater, where shows on a recent voyage were a mixed bag. The usual Vegas song-and-dance routines drew yawns, but several shows drew on European circus traditions, featuring contortionists, acrobats, and stilt performers. It's that European influence—also evident at audience-participation shows and in the lively disco—that distinguishes MSC's entertainment from the American cruise lines. New shows were added to the theater's lineup for *Lirica* and *Opera's* Caribbean season, including a Spanish show with flamenco and modern dancers, an Italian-style show featuring tenor Enrico Scotto, a classic concert, and a magic show. Quieter options around the ship include daytime films in the main theater and music in the jazz bar and piano bar, right around the corner from an Internet center that looks peculiarly like a reception desk. Sit at one of the terminals on embarkation day and odds are good someone will ask you how to get to the buffet.

SERVICE

On our late-2004 *Opera* cruise, the main complaint we heard was about slow and indifferent service. Although several members of the international bar and cabin-service staff were extremely personal, friendly, and attentive, service overall was marked by inconsistency, and MSC's much-vaunted Italian waiters just didn't live up to the hype.

To their credit, MSC's new management team was acutely aware of these problems and began an immediate program to improve them. By the time the ships' Caribbean season began there was a definite improvement in overall attentiveness and friendliness, and we were pleased to note that the friendliest and most efficient crewman we'd met in October had already been promoted from the bar to be a waiter in the main restaurant. That bodes well.

Room service is available 24 hours a day from a limited menu. **Laundry service** is also available, though there are no self-serve laundries.

Lirica • Opera

The Verdict

Straightforward midsize vessels. Rather than hitting guests over the head with self-consciously "fun" decor, they just present a venue in which passengers and staff can create their own good times.

Opera *(photo: MSC)*

Specifications

Size (in tons)		Crew	
Lirica	58,600	*Lirica*	760
Opera	58,600	*Opera*	800
Passengers (double occ.)		Passenger/Crew Ratio	
Lirica	1,586	*Lirica*	2.1 to 1
Opera	1,756	*Opera*	2.2 to 1
Passenger/Space Ratio		Year Launched	
Lirica	37	*Lirica*	2003
Opera	33.5	*Opera*	2004
Total Cabins/Veranda Cabins		Last Major Refurbishment	
Lirica	795/132	*Lirica*	N/A
Opera	878/200	*Opera*	N/A

Frommer's Ratings (Scale of 1–5)   ★★★½

Cabin Comfort & Amenities	3.5	Dining Options	3
Ship Cleanliness & Maintenance	4	Gym, Spa & Sports Facilities	3.5
Public Comfort/Space	4	Children's Facilities	3
Decor	3	Enjoyment Factor	4

Opera and *Lirica* almost seem like a different species from today's brand of enormomegaships, lacking any kind of overt gimmicks—no planetariums, no rock-climbing walls, no "decorate-every-surface" design schemes. What they are are ships on which people can get together to talk, loll in the pool, throw away their inhibitions, and relax, without having their senses overwhelmed. Whether that's a good thing or not depends on your point of view. It's what management says they're going for, but will vacationers get it? We'll see.

Another aspect of *Lirica* and *Opera*'s old-fashionedness? Their moderate size, which is on par with Holland America's well-loved Statendam-class ships. Long and low, both vessels seem a lot larger than they really are, with a surprising amount of space both in their public rooms and out on the pool deck. For this, credit their small cabins.

Cabins & Rates

Cabins	Per Diems from	Sq. Ft.	Fridge	Hair Dryer	Sitting Area	TV
Inside	$78	140	yes	yes	no	yes
Outside	$106	140	yes	yes	no	yes
Suite	$242	236–247	yes	yes	yes	yes

CABINS   Cabins come in only four varieties: standard 140-square-foot inside cabins, 140-square-foot oceanview and balcony cabins, and suites that would pass for junior suites aboard most vessels. Though not palatial, staterooms are pleasantly and unfussily decorated, with simple light-wood trim and upholstery patterns, good lighting and storage, and niceties such as a writing/makeup desk and minibar. Balcony cabins seem roomier than they are thanks to strategically placed mirrors and extremely wide balcony doors. Bathrooms, on the other hand, are stuck with some of the smallest shower stalls in the industry—the only serious design flaw noted on board, and one they probably can't do much about. Suites have larger tub/shower combos.

Four cabins on *Lirica* and five on *Opera* are wheelchair accessible.

PUBLIC AREAS   Decor on MSC is as far a cry from Carnival's over-the-top themed decor as it is from the more reserved, stylish decor of Celebrity. Somewhere between plain and restrained, *Opera* and *Lirica*'s public areas are done up in blonde woods, floral and geometric carpets, functional solid-colored chairs and banquettes, and a smattering of marble, brass, and mirrors.

Most public rooms are on two adjoining decks, starting with the main forward theater with its extra-wide stage. Avoid seats in the back corners, which offer lousy sightlines even when other passengers don't stand at the rail in front of them, completely blocking off the view. Heading aft there's a coffee bar wrapped around the small, comfortable atrium; a lounge for music, karaoke, and other entertainment; several shops; a casino; an intimate piano bar; and several nook lounges and seating areas. One deck down, just below the theater, is a bar/lounge that's your best bet for a quiet evening drink, as it's off the main evening traffic routes. A library and card room adjoins. Atop the ship is a disco/observation lounge with several dance floors and a generally hopping vibe.

Kids get a playroom tucked weirdly into the same complex as the spa, gym, and beauty salon, in the bow on the pool deck. On *Opera,* the room has a Buffalo Bill wild west theme, with a puffy, cushioned cacti, western wall paintings, and signs pointing to Monument Valley, the Colorado River (a wide blue line meandering across the floor), and Fort Laramie, a large play structure. Counselors are on hand to organize activities, but remember (as a memorable sign said when we were aboard), "It's not possible entry in the mini-club if is not present one animator!"

DINING OPTIONS   Each ship's two restaurants are downright old-fashioned, eschewing the multiple levels, grand staircases, columns, and chandeliers common aboard most megaships in favor of a simple one-story approach. Decor is restrained to the point of being irrelevant—just warmly colored walls and carpets, a smattering of ceiling and fixture lights, and lots of people dining at tables that are maybe just a little too close together.

A standard buffet restaurant occupies the stern of the pool deck, with an outdoor seating area separated off from the main pool. An outdoor grill serves pizza, burgers, and the like. Pizza and Italian specialty snacks are also served indoors from late afternoon till late night.

POOL, FITNESS, SPA & SPORTS FACILITIES   The main recreation deck has two pools and two hot tubs. Like many other spaces on board, it's almost a throwback to early 1990s ship design, a plain old pool deck without unnecessary frills. A jogging track wraps around the deck above.

Gyms are only adequate for the number of people on board, with about a dozen aerobics machines, another dozen weight machines, free weights, and a small aerobics floor. Spa treatment rooms encircle the space, with a pre- or post-treatment "relaxation room" off to one side. Up on the top deck, a golf putting green encircles the stern.

8 Norwegian Cruise Line

7665 Corporate Center Dr., Miami, FL 33126. ℂ **800/327-7030** or 305/436-4000. Fax 305/436-4126. www.ncl.com.

THE LINE IN A NUTSHELL   NCL makes its mark with its always casual, open-seating dining and a nearly constant stream of innovations, which include three ships now sailing year-round among the Hawaiian islands. Its newest ships are standouts, giving Royal Caribbean and Princess a run for their money. **Sails to:** Caribbean, Panama Canal, Alaska, Mexican Riviera, Bermuda, Hawaii, Canada/New England (plus South America, Europe).

THE EXPERIENCE   Back in the mid- to late '90s, NCL operated a mixed-bag fleet of older ships whose onboard vibe was only a couple steps above budget. What a difference a few years makes. Today NCL is one of the top players in the industry, with innovative itineraries, a fleet of mostly new megaships, a casual onboard atmosphere, quality entertainment, and a staggering number of dining choices. As of last year, it also has a lock on the Hawaiian market, with the only two ships legally able to sail entirely within the 50th state, without having to hit a foreign port to comply with U.S. cabotage laws. (See long, convoluted, legalistic explanation below.)

Pros

- **Hawaii, Hawaii, Hawaii:** If you want to sail the islands, NCL is your #1 pick, offering the only cruises that never leave state waters.
- **Flexible dining:** NCL's "freestyle cruising" dining policy lets you dine when and where you want, dressed however.
- **Restaurants galore:** With between 6 and 10 places to have dinner, you won't know where to turn.
- **Above-average entertainment:** In addition to above-average Vegas-style shows and musical groups, NCL also has a new deal with the Second City comedy troupe, providing extra ha-ha on *Norwegian Dawn*.

Cons

- **Small cabins:** Though with each new ship they seem to get a little bigger, at about 110 to 165 square feet, standard inside and outside cabins are a tighter squeeze than most of the competition, including Carnival's 185-square-foot standards.
- **Several below-average older ships:** At least for the next few years, NCL is still saddled with a few remnants of its past. They've got NCL's casual esthetic and some of its dining options, but they feel tinny and have few if any balcony cabins.

NCL: SAY ALOHA TO INNOVATION

Talk about pulling yourself up by your bootstraps. Norwegian was one of the pioneers of the North American cruise market, beginning in 1966 as an alliance between Norwegian ship owner Knut Knutson and Israeli marketing genius Ted Arison, who later started Carnival Cruises. After these auspicious beginnings, the line spent many years relegated to the industry's back seat behind biggies Carnival and Royal Caribbean, but beginning in 1997 it began a sequence of moves that transformed it into a true leader and innovator.

The biggest change came in 2000, when NCL introduced its groundbreaking **Freestyle Cruising** concept, a move that, it's safe to say, changed the face of cruising forever. The new program did away with fixed dining times, seating assignments, and formal dress codes, leaving passengers free to choose when and where they want to dine among a variety of venues. Traditional tipping also went away, replaced by a system where gratuities are added directly to passenger accounts. In an industry long ruled by traditions it was a bold experiment, and its success inspired an industrywide trend.

Over the next couple years, NCL pressed ahead with another new project: **Taking over the Hawaii cruise market.** U.S. laws designed to protect American shipping prevent foreign-flagged vessels from sailing itineraries solely between American ports, requiring them to make sometimes-long detours to foreign ports. This is particularly difficult in isolated Hawaii, forcing many ships to sail from foreign mainland ports such as Ensenada, Mexico, or visit really out-of-the-way stops such as Fanning Island in the Kiribati Republic. In late 2002, NCL acquired the unfinished hulls of two "Project America" ships that had been begun in the U.S. by now-bankrupt American Classic Voyages. Intense lobbying in Congress led to a deal in which NCL was able to have these vessels completed at a German shipyard yet still sail under the U.S. flag. As part of the fine print, NCL was also able to reflag the foreign-built *Norwegian Sky*, renaming it *Pride of Aloha* and operating it under the company's new U.S.-flag brand **NCL America** with U.S. officers and crew, sailing round-trip from Honolulu and concentrating exclusively on the islands. This is something no competing line is currently able to offer.

Compared with other mainstream lines, here's how NCL rates:

	Poor	Fair	Good	Excellent	Outstanding
Enjoyment Factor				✓	
Dining				✓	
Activities				✓	
Children's Program				✓	
Entertainment				✓	
Service				✓	
Worth the Money					✓

NCL is also on a major modernization kick, having made arrangements for its Asian parent company, Star Cruises, to take over all the older Norwegian vessels over the next 3 years. This will leave NCL with a totally up-to-date fleet, including five new ships launched between 1999 and late 2002 (*Spirit, Star, Sun, Dawn,* and *Pride of Aloha*), two launched just as this book went to press (*Pride of America* and *Norwegian Jewel*), the second Project America ship set to debut in April 2006 *(Pride of Hawai'i)*, and two 2,400-passenger megaships on order for 2007. And out there, somewhere in fantasyland, is also a tantalizing possibility: In April 2003, NCL announced that it had purchased the **SS *United States,*** built in 1952 to be the fastest, safest ship at sea. Though laid up since 1969 (at present in Philadelphia), the ship still holds the record for transatlantic passage by an ocean liner. NCL's plans are vague at best. Some speculate that the line purchased *United States* (as well as the old, 1951-built SS *Independence,* which spent years sailing for defunct American Hawaii Cruises) to prevent competitors from purchasing and refurbishing them as competition to NCL's Hawaii operation. Or maybe they really *do* intend to relaunch them. Stay tuned.

PASSENGER PROFILE

NCL as a rule attracts a diverse lot, and passengers in general are younger, more price-conscious, and more active than those aboard lines such as HAL, Celebrity, and Princess. Typical NCL passengers are couples ages 25 to 60, and include a fair number of honeymooners and families with kids during summers and holidays. Kids under age 2 travel free. The atmosphere aboard all NCL vessels is informal and well suited to casual types, party-makers, and first-time cruisers.

DINING

All the restaurants on all NCL ships follow an open-seating policy each and every evening, allowing you to dine whenever you like within the 5:30 to 10pm window, sitting with whomever you want (rather than having a table preassigned), and dressed however you like (management says anything goes except jeans, shorts, and tank tops, but we've seen those in the restaurants, too). This flexible setup really works for families, groups, and anyone else who doesn't want to be tied down to fixed timings and tables, and who dreads the idea of being seated with a bunch of strangers with whom you'll have to chitchat for a week. On the other hand, if you end up sitting with people you like, you can always make plans to dine with them again.

The night of the captain's cocktail party is officially an "optional formal" night, meaning you don't have to wear a suit, tie, or fancy dress, but for those who would like to, this is the night to do so. On a recent cruise, we were surprised how many people chose to dress up.

TRADITIONAL   The main dining rooms, like the rest of the ships' eating venues, operate with open seating and casual dress codes, so the only really "traditional" thing about them is their ambience: large, elegant, and similar to dining rooms on Royal Caribbean, Carnival, Princess, and Celebrity. The food is similar, too. You can usually count on such choices as grilled swordfish with lemon-caper sauce, salmon or poached sea bass, beef Wellington, broiled lobster tail, chicken Parmesan, fettuccine Alfredo, or perhaps a Jamaican jerk pork roast, Wiener schnitzel, or roast prime rib. The wine lists appeal to standard mid-American tastes, and prices aren't offensively high. Once a week, the main dining rooms serve an intriguing and amusing **President's Menu.** Created by former White House chef Henry Haller, it features some former presidents' and first ladies' favorite dishes, such as Betty Ford's Garden Salad with Olive Oil Dressing and Richard Nixon's North Atlantic Crab Soup.

A **light choice** (prepared with recipes from NCL partner *Cooking Light* magazine) and a **vegetarian entree** are available at lunch and dinner. **Children's menus** feature the popular standards: burgers, hot dogs, grilled cheese sandwiches and french fries, spaghetti and meatballs, ice-cream sundaes, and even something you may not expect: vegetable crudités and cheese dip.

SPECIALTY   In addition to one or two main dining rooms, each ship has between two and eight smaller alternative specialty restaurants serving food that's up there with the best of the mainstream competition (though nowhere near the alternative restaurants on Celebrity's Millennium-class vessels).

Each ship has a French/Continental restaurant called **Le Bistro,** and the line's newest ships also offer choices such as pan-Asian, Italian, Japanese, Pacific Rim, and Spanish/tapas. The food in Le Bistro (where you'll pay a $12.50 per-person cover charge) is better than that in the main dining rooms, and includes items such as a yummy Caesar salad made right at your table, a delicious salmon filet in sorrel cream sauce, a juicy beef tenderloin, and a marvelously decadent chocolate fondue served with fresh fruit. Often, tables are available for walk-ins, but make your reservations— available only a day in advance—as soon as possible to be on the safe side. Reservations aren't always necessary for lunch.

CASUAL   In addition to the numerous sit-down venues highlighted above (all of them casual in their own way), all NCL ships also have a standard informal buffet with indoor/outdoor seating, open 24 hours a day. The newer the ship, the better designed this outlet is, serving stir-fries and theme offerings like an all-vegetarian Indian buffet in addition to popular standards like burgers. See ship reviews for more details.

SNACKS & EXTRAS   Snacking ops include pizza and ice cream offered throughout the day from the Lido buffet restaurant, a coffee bar serving specialty java and other beverages, and 24-hour room service for pizza, sandwiches, and other munchies. One port day per week on most of the fleet, you can drool over the popular **Chocoholic Extravaganza** buffet, offering everything from tortes to brownies.

ACTIVITIES

You'll find the most action aboard the larger, newer ships, but all offer decent rosters. You can take cha-cha lessons; watch a cooking demo; play bingo, shuffleboard, or basketball; attend an art auction or spa or beauty demonstration; and on some cruises, sit in on enrichment lectures about classic ocean liners, nutrition, personal investing, or other topics. There are snorkeling demonstrations in the pool, makeovers, talent shows, wine tastings (for $10 per person), and trivia contests, plus silly poolside competitions to keep you laughing all afternoon long. In Hawaii, *Pride of Aloha* and *Pride of America* offer many activities themed on Hawaiian arts and culture. See ship review for details.

Internet cafes offer e-mail and Internet access fleetwide. For those wanting flexibility in their Web-surfing, a Wi-Fi wireless system lets you log on from various places on all the line's ships using your own or a rented laptop and an NCL network card. You can also use your **cellphone,** even far out at sea: NCL was the first major line to embrace the new technology that makes it possible, and now everybody seems to be getting in on the act. (See "Keeping in Touch," in chapter 3.)

Gyms fleetwide are open 24-hours. The newer ships feature classes like cardio kickboxing and spinning, the latter of which carries a $5 charge (cheaper than most lines,

NCL Fleet Itineraries

Ship	Itineraries
Norwegian Crown	**13- & 14-night E./S. Carib:** Round-trip from Philadelphia, PA, Mar–Apr 2006. **5-, 6- & 7-night Bermuda:** Round-trip from Philadelphia, PA, Apr–June 2006. **7-night Bermuda:** Round-trip from New York, NY, June–Oct 2006.
Norwegian Dawn	**7-night Florida/Bahamas:** Round-trip from New York, NY, May–Aug 2006. **7-night Canada/New England:** Round-trip from New York, NY, Sept–Oct 2006. **10-night E. Carib:** Round-trip from New York, NY, Jan–Apr and Oct–Dec 2006. **11-night W. Carib:** Round-trip from New York, NY, Jan–Mar and Oct–Dec 2006.
Norwegian Dream	**7-night W. Carib:** Round-trip from Houston, TX, Jan–Apr 2006.
Norwegian Jewel	**7-night E. & W. Carib:** Round-trip from Miami, FL, Jan–Apr 2006.
Norwegian Majesty	**7-night W. Carib:** Round-trip from Charleston, SC, Jan–Apr 2006. **7-night Bermuda:** Round-trip from Boston, MA, May–Oct 2006. **7-night Bermuda:** Round-trip from Charleston, SC, Oct–Nov 2006.
Norwegian Spirit	**10- & 11-night E./S. Carib:** Round-trip from New York, NY, Jan–Feb and Oct–Dec 2006. **7-night Florida/Bahamas:** Round-trip from New York, NY, Feb–May 2006. **6-night Florida/Bahamas:** Round-trip from New York, NY, May–Sept 2006. Alternates with **8-night E. Carib:** Round-trip from New York, NY, May–Sept 2006.
Norwegian Star	**8-night Mexican Riviera:** Round-trip from Los Angeles, CA, Jan–Apr 2006. **7-night Alaska Inside Passage:** Round-trip from Seattle, WA, May–Sept 2006.
Norwegian Sun	**7-night W. Carib:** Round-trip from New Orleans, LA, Jan–Apr 2006. **7-night Alaska Inside Passage:** Round-trip from Seattle, WA, May–Sept 2006.
Norwegian Wind	**10-night Hawaii/Kiribati:** Round-trip from Honolulu, HI, Jan–Mar 2006. **7-night Alaska Inside Passage:** Round-trip from Vancouver, BC, May–Sept 2006.
Pride of Aloha	**7-night Hawaii:** Round-trip from Honolulu, HI, year-round.
Pride of America	**7-night Hawaii:** Round-trip from Honolulu, HI, year-round.
Pride of Hawai'i	Not yet announced, but probably 7-night Hawaii, round-trip from Honolulu, year-round.

which typically charge $10). All ships except *Norwegian Majesty* have golf driving cages where guests can practice their putting and swinging at their leisure. In port, NCL's Dive-In program offers at least one snorkeling and one scuba excursion at almost every Caribbean port, escorted by the ship's certified instructors. In Hawaii, the line offers a comprehensive program of **golf excursions** to some of the islands' best courses, including Ko'olau on Oahu, Poipu Bay and the Prince Course on Kauai, Mauna Lani Resort and Hapuna Golf Course on the Big Island, and Kapalua and Wailea on Maui. The Hawaii ships also have an onboard pro shop.

CHILDREN'S PROGRAM

NCL's Kids Crew program offers year-round supervised activities for children ages 2 to 17, divided into four age groups: Junior Sailors, ages 2 to 5; First Mates, ages 6 to 8; Navigators, ages 9 to 12; and teens, ages 13 to 17. Activities include sports competitions, dances, face painting, treasure hunts, magic shows, arts and crafts, cooking classes, T-shirt painting, and even a Circus at Sea. Children get their own Cruise News detailing the day's events. Unlimited soda packages are $16 for kids under age 17 on 7-night cruises, and a "Teen Passport" coupon book is available for teens—for $30 they get up to 20 nonalcoholic drinks such as Virgin Daiquiris.

Each ship has a playroom, and with each new ship the line introduces, the kids' facilities get better. The facilities on the newer ships *Dawn, Star, Spirit, Sun,* and *Pride of America* are the best by far, huge spaces that include a separate teen center and a wading pool, as well as a large, well-stocked playroom. The *Dawn, Star,* and *Jewel* have wonderful spaces with a huge combo climbing maze and ball bin indoors and a kids' pool and hot tub area outside with a fun, wacky theme (dinosaurs on *Dawn,* rockets on *Star,* tropical sea creatures on *Jewel,* and pirates on *Spirit*). On sea days, the play-rooms are open between 9am and noon, 2 to 4:30pm, and then 7:30 to 10pm; on port days the hours are 3 to 5pm and 7:30 to 10pm. At the discretion of the coun-selors, play areas are open to babies/toddlers if accompanied by a parent (usually dur-ing slow off-season periods).

Once per 7-night cruise the ships offer a **Mom and Dad's Night Out,** when kids dine with counselors. Otherwise, **group babysitting** for kids aged 2 to 12 is offered nightly between 10pm and 1am (and 9am–5pm on port days) for $5 per child per hour, plus $3 an hour for each additional child. Counselors do not do diapers; par-ents are given beepers so they can be alerted when it's time for the dirty work. Private babysitting is not available.

ENTERTAINMENT

NCL offers some of the best entertainment of all the mainstream lines. A recent cruise on *Norwegian Sun* offered the best entertainment we've seen at sea in years, from the always-awesome NCL singer Jane L. Powell and her excellent accompanying band to a talented piano-playing singer covering Billy Joel and Cat Stevens, a Bill Cosby–style comedian who kept everyone in stitches, and production shows with an impressive cast (including pairs of ballroom dancers and acrobats), choreography, costumes, and set design. Performances of Bollywood- and South Beach–inspired shows on *Norwe-gian Dawn* are also standouts, as are the ship's new revues featuring sketch comedy, songs, and improvisation by members of the famed **Second City comedy troupe,** many of whose alumni (including Bill Murray, Mike Myers, John Belushi, and Gilda Radner) went on to join the pantheon of comedy greats. On the Hawaii ships, 1 night a week is devoted to Polynesian music and dance, with uniformly good production shows and house bands rounding out the schedule.

For closet entertainers, the line puts on **Star Seeker,** its version of the *American Idol* talent-show program, giving adults and kids the chance to prove themselves in one of the show lounges. Videos of the winners are sent to NCL's shoreside entertainment department for consideration as a one-time entertainer aboard a future free NCL cruise.

Serious gamblers should consider only *Star, Dawn,* and *Sun* because these three ships boast the fleet's biggest and splashiest **casinos.** Note that because of Hawaiian law, *Pride of Aloha* and *Pride of America* do not have casinos aboard, nor any kind of gambling.

All the ships have bars where you can slip away for a quiet rendezvous, and small tucked-away corners for more intimate entertainment, including pianists and cabaret acts. Music for dancing is popular aboard all the ships and takes place before or after shows, and each ship has a late-night disco.

SERVICE

Fleetwide, cabin service, room service, and bar service tend to be speedy and efficient. Dining service is a mixed bag: On a recent cruise service in the main dining room was accommodating but less than stellar, while service in the Le Bistro and Il Adagio alterna-tive restaurants was very sharp and attentive. Service in the well-laid-out buffet restaurants on *Star, Dawn, Spirit,* and *Sun* is efficient; lines move quickly and bins are continually filled. On NCL's older ships, conditions are more cramped and lines often back up.

NCL got a lot of flack about poor service when *Pride of Aloha* debuted in July 2004, owing to its all-American crew's complete lack of shipboard experience. Intensive training over the succeeding months improved the situation, but at press time it was still uneven. On the plus side, crewmembers were almost uniformly friendly and helpful, and passengers love the fact there are no English-as-a-second-language problems to deal with. On the downside, staff can at times get a little too blasé. A hotel director with whom we spoke stressed that their goal is to match the standards of an international crew, but they still have a bit more work to do.

Fleetwide, tipping is done automatically, with a $10 per day **service charge** added to each passenger's onboard account ($5 for kids 3–12). Though officially nonrefundable, the charge can be adjusted if you've experienced serious problems that the customer-service staff was unable to remedy.

NCL ships offer **laundry** and **dry-cleaning service,** but *Norwegian Dawn* is the only ship in the fleet that offers self-service launderettes and ironing facilities (on Decks 5, 7, 9, 10, and 11).

NCL America: Pride of Aloha • Pride of America • Pride of Hawai'i (preview)

The Verdict

Sailing from Honolulu, concentrating solely on the islands, and with Hawaii themes playing a major part in the onboard atmosphere, these vessels are literally in a class by themselves.

Pride of Aloha *(photo: NCL)*

Specifications

Size (in tons)		Crew	
Pride of Aloha	77,104	*Pride of Aloha*	1,000
Pride of America	81,000	*Pride of America*	1,000
Pride of Hawai'i	92,100	*Pride of Hawai'i*	1,000
Passengers (double occ.)		Passenger/Crew Ratio	
Pride of Aloha	2,002	*Pride of Aloha*	2 to 1
Pride of America	2,146	*Pride of America*	2.1 to 1
Pride of Hawai'i	2,400	*Pride of Hawai'i*	2.3 to 1
Passenger/Space Ratio		Year Launched	
Pride of Aloha	38.5	*Pride of Aloha*	1999
Pride of America	37.7	*Pride of America*	2005
Pride of Hawai'i	38.7	*Pride of Hawai'i*	2006
Total Cabins/Veranda Cabins		Last Major Refurbishment	
Pride of Aloha	1001/257	*Pride of Aloha*	2004
Pride of America	1,073/665	*Pride of America*	N/A
Pride of Hawai'i	1,188/540	*Pride of Hawai'i*	N/A

Frommer's Ratings (Scale of 1-5)   ⭐⭐⭐⭐*

Cabin Comfort & Amenities	3	Dining Options	4
Ship Cleanliness & Maintenance	4	Gym, Spa & Sports Facilities	4
Public Comfort/Space	4	Children's Facilities	3.5
Decor	4	Enjoyment Factor	4

* *Since* Pride of Hawai'i *had not yet launched at press time, these ratings refer to* Aloha *and* America *only.*

If you take a cruise in Hawaii, chances are you'll be taking it with NCL. Why? Because if you don't, it means you'll have to sail from or to a foreign port (such as Ensenada, Mexico) and spend days at sea either before or after you see the islands. For the foreseeable future, NCL has a lock on interisland Hawaii cruises, which it gained by having the only large U.S.-flagged cruise ships in the business. (See legal explanation earlier in this review.) After some start-up problems associated with training its U.S. staff, the operation is humming along just fine, and though NCL's kind of mass-market cruise isn't for everybody, it definitely has its points, such as . . .

- **All Hawaii, all the time:** Because *Aloha* and *America* are U.S.-flagged and U.S.-crewed, they're in compliance with U.S. cabotage laws, which forbid foreign-flagged vessels from sailing itineraries composed only of U.S. ports. And since Hawaii's islands are all relatively close together, the *Pride* itineraries can visit a port every single day.
- **All-American crew:** American crews are as rare as dodo birds on today's ships, but on the *Prides* practically everybody's American, save a handful of foreign passengers.
- **Overnights in port:** Most cruise itineraries have passengers reboarding by 6pm so the ship can sail to its next port, but NCL's itineraries include overnight stays in Kauai and Maui, giving you an opportunity to sample nightlife ashore and get a better feel for both of these beautiful islands.
- **Enough shore excursions to choke a horse:** NCL offers nearly 150 excursion options in port, allowing you to create a Hawaii itinerary to suit your preferences, from easy bus tours to adventurous excursions to golf outings at some of the islands' best courses. For more information on shore excursions in Hawaii, consult chapter 14.

On the downside, these are busy, noisy ships—especially in summer and during holidays, when many families with kids sail. Things can get tight out on deck and in lines for buffets, early dinners at the restaurants, and sometimes to get on and off ship in port. Second, because these cruises put so much emphasis on the port experience, with many excursions starting in early morning and taking up most of the day, passengers tend to come back to the ship, eat an early dinner, and crash. The cruise director with whom we spoke said the ship's passengers tend to be of the "early to bed, early to rise" variety, so if you want a cruise with lots of onboard activities and a heavy nightlife, this isn't the one for you. Lastly, although prices for the cruises themselves are relatively low, expect lots of **extra costs,** from the $10-a-day automatic gratuity to expensive drinks, pricey Internet access, and the bundle you're bound to spend on shore excursions or renting cars in port. Because most of the islands' real attractions aren't near the port facilities, you have to take an excursion or rent a car if you're going to see anything worth seeing.

As *Pride of Hawai'i* is not scheduled to launch until April 2006, this review deals entirely with *Pride of Aloha* and *Pride of America*.

Cabins & Rates

Cabins	Per Diems from	Sq. Ft.	Fridge	Hair Dryer	Sitting Area	TV
Inside	$151	121–147	yes	yes	yes	yes
Outside	$203	149–154	yes	yes	yes	yes
Suite	$435	321–512	yes	yes	yes	yes

CABINS   Yes, cabins on both *Pride* vessels are pretty, with wood-grain walls and carpets, upholstery, and bedspreads done in vibrant, Hawaiian-accented pinks, blues, oranges, purples, and greens, but spacious they're not. Continuing a longstanding NCL tradition, the vast majority of standard outsides and insides measure about 40 square feet smaller than Carnival's standards. Storage space is limited to a single hanging closet and several drawers in the main cabin. Be prepared to use your suitcase to store whatever else doesn't fit. All have a small sitting area or desk, a minifridge (not stocked), a hair dryer, TVs, and coffee- and tea-making equipment. On *Pride of America,* all cabins have a dataport to accommodate laptop users. Bathrooms are adequately sized. Balcony cabins come in particularly handy on the run between Kona and Hilo, letting you watch the lava flowing from Kilauea Volcano without changing out of your pajamas. The captain turns the ship 360 degrees at the optimum viewing point, so cabins on both sides get a view. The majority of *Pride of America*'s outsides have balconies, including cabins located almost all the way forward toward the ship's bull-headed bow— some to port and starboard, some facing front with recessed, forward-facing balconies.

Six cabins on *Aloha* and 23 on *America* are equipped for wheelchairs. The ships offer laundry and dry-cleaning service but do not have self-serve launderettes.

PUBLIC AREAS   *Pride of Aloha*'s decor draws from the beauty of Hawaii's tropical landscape, full of pinks, blues, oranges, purples, and greens—a welcome change from the cruise world's ubiquitous Caribbean imagery. You'll find references to Hawaiian culture and history throughout the ship, from orchids to outrigger canoes, beaches, fish, waterfalls, and colonial plantations. The ship has nearly a dozen bars, including a surfing-themed sports bar, two large poolside bars, a coffee bar, an Internet cafe, a library, and the dark and cozy Captain Cook's Bar and Churchill's Cigar Club, the latter a dimly lit nook with oversize soft leather furniture and an out-of-the-way location. It's the most appealing place on the ship for a quiet drink, though tolerance for smoke is required. Up on Deck 12, the Plantation Club lounge is a pleasant getaway, with quiet piano or guitar music, cozy tables, and a decor of palms and black-and-white photos of old Hawaii. One deck down in the bow, the Outrigger Lounge is a very woody observation lounge/disco, with rattan chairs, tropical foliage, outrigger canoes, and carpeting that suggests the ocean. Hawaiian dance and crafts classes are held here throughout the week. Most other recreation venues are on Decks 5, 6, and 7, including the centerpiece Kumu Cultural Center, a museum of Hawaiian culture with displays on Hawaiian woodworking, boatbuilding and navigation, music, history, and classic Hawaii travel kitsch. A large video screen shows movies on culture, marine life, and other topics throughout the day. On the same deck, a pro shop serves as a focal point for NCL America's extensive golf program. On Deck 6, the Blue Hawaii show lounge hosts karaoke, dancing, and other small-scale entertainments amid pop-culture Hawaiian decor. In the stern, the two-story Stardust Lounge theater is the venue for large-scale revues. For kids, a huge children's area includes a sprawling playroom with cathedral-high ceilings, a teen center with a large movie screen and a pair of foosball games, and a video arcade. A children's wading pool is located outdoors on Deck 12.

Pride of America's decor matches her name, with public rooms throughout decorated to celebrate aspects of American culture and geography. Giant photographs of the Grand Canyon, Monument Valley, Mt. Rainier, the Golden Gate Bridge, the Chicago Skyline, and other sites adorn her stairtowers, and U.S. themes dominate the decor of many of the restaurants (see below). *America,* the ship—that is, the old United States Line's vessel SS *America*—is the motif of the SS *America* Library, which holds memorabilia and artifacts of the vessel as well as a scale model built specifically for the room. Despite her intended year-round Hawaiian itineraries, *America* actually employs relatively little Hawaiian imagery beyond some art, some carpeting and upholstery, and the small Hawaiian cultural display in the atrium. A hint that NCL might have non-Hawaii plans for the ship in future? Stay tuned. For now at least you can enjoy Hawaii's own Kona Beer on tap in the (hmmm . . .) Gold Rush Saloon, with its prospector decor. For a more elegant drinking experience, head to the Napa Wine Bar, which, with its stone-pattern walls, box-shaped light fixtures, and light woods and upholsteries, straddles the line between Napa Valley casual and hip 1950s lounge. In a nice touch, a door opens to outdoor seating on the Promenade Deck. Nearby, Pink's Champagne and Cigar Bar spans the width of the ship, with bright Hawaii-patterned carpeting and a contrastingly 19th-century casino-looking chandelier hovering above its piano-bar piano. Way up on Deck 13, the small, intimate, and beautifully designed Lanai Bar & Lounge is located next to one of the largest dedicated meeting spaces at sea, with auditoriums and meeting facilities for up to 550 participants. For kids, the Rascal's Kids Club offers an elaborate indoor jungle gym, a movie room full of beanbag chairs, computer terminals, a large play space, and a protected outdoor splash pool with tube-slide. Next door, the teen center is designed like an adult lounge, with a "bar," dance floor, and games.

Because of Hawaiian law, there's no casino or any other gambling on any of the *Pride* ships. If you've got a jones, head to the card room, where you might find a secret game of Texas Hold 'Em in progress. The password is "swordfish."

DINING OPTIONS   Above all else, NCL excels in the restaurant department. For breakfast, lunch, and dinner, each *Pride* ship has two main dining rooms whose almost-elegant decor belies their often casually dressed customers. For dinner, you can also choose from several extra-charge alternative restaurants, which offer superior service, presentation, and cuisine.

Aboard *Pride of Aloha,* the Royal Palm Bistro, high atop the ship opposite the Plantation nightclub, serves French/Mediterranean cuisine in a pseudo-colonial Hawaiian decor. On Deck 11, Pacific Heights serves Pan-Pacific cuisine, including local fish, steak, Asian dishes, and (hmmm . . .) pizza, which you can get free late into the night. Most interesting of the three is the Kahili Restaurant, a long, narrow space stretched along the starboard side of Deck 5. Serving Italian cuisine in a setting of elegant burlwood paneling, cozy booths, and windowside tables for two, the restaurant is a little hard to find, located at the bottom of a stairway from Deck 6. The per-person charge is $15 for Kahili and the Royal Palm Bistro, $12.50 for Pacific Heights. Reservations are required for dinner in all of the specialty restaurants, though you can sometimes get a table as a walk-in. For casual dining there's a large but poorly organized indoor/outdoor casual buffet restaurant on the pool deck serving all three meals plus snacks in between. If you arrive and find a huge line, slip outside to the covered Lanai Deck in the stern, where there are additional lines that get much less use.

Pride of America's two main restaurants are the Skyline Restaurant, with its Art Deco decor and skyscraper motifs, and the mucho Americano Liberty Restaurant, with its greeting statues of George Washington and Abe Lincoln, its stars-and-ribbons carpeting, its soaring-eagle-motif glass ceiling, its glass Mount Rushmore, and its bunting-style curtains that give it the look of an old-time political rally. Passengers can also choose from several intimate, extra-cost options: the Lazy J Texas Steakhouse, where waiters serve in cowboy hats; Jefferson's Bistro, an elegant venue modeled after the president's home, Monticello, and serving French cuisine; the Little Italy Italian restaurant; and East Meets West, a Pan-Asian restaurant with attached sushi/sashimi bar and teppanyaki room. Alternative, reservations-only restaurants carry a charge of $12.50 to $20 per person. For late-night cravings, the Cadillac Diner serves burgers, shakes, and other diner fare 24 hours, with additional seating outside on the promenade deck. On Deck 11, the Aloha Cafe buffet is designed with multiple serving islands both inside and out, rather than a few long central lines.

Because of these ships' emphasis on port calls, restaurants tend to be busiest early, with long lines often forming right at 5:30. The later you dine, the less the wait and the better the service, since the staff won't be as rushed. *Tip:* It's easier to get reservations at alternative restaurants for the first couple of nights and on luau night in Maui, when most passengers stay ashore.

POOL, FITNESS, SPA & SPORTS FACILITIES   The well-stocked oceanview gyms on these ships are open 24 hours a day, and the adjacent aerobics room has floor-to-ceiling windows and a great selection of stretching, step, and other traditional classes at no extra charge, and spinning, kickboxing, and other trendy choices for which they'll squeeze an extra $10 a pop out of ya. Nearby, the spa and beauty salon offer ocean views as well, plus (on *Pride of America* only) a small outdoor "Oasis Pool." Out on deck, *Pride of Aloha* has a pair of pools with a cluster of four hot tubs between them; one deck up is a combo basketball/volleyball court, a pair of golf driving nets, and shuffleboard. There's also a kids' wading pool and some cute mini-chaise-longues located far forward on the Sports Deck, where there's also a fifth hot tub. *Pride of America*'s pool deck, her central outdoor space, is a bit underwhelming, perhaps an admission that whatever the line came up with, it couldn't compete with Hawaii's beaches. Look to the deck above, however, for a couple of fun toys: a trampoline with bungee harness to keep you from flying over the side, and a "spaceball challenger" gyroscope in which passengers, suitably strapped in, can revolve 360 degrees in any direction, like astronauts in outer space. Wraparound promenade decks on both ships offer a great stroll.

Norwegian Spirit • Star • Dawn • Jewel

The Verdict

Really original megaships don't come along too often these days, but these babies are it, with a mix of classy and fun spaces, a lively Miami-esque atmosphere, awesome kids' facilities, and more restaurant options than you'll likely have time to sample.

Norwegian Dawn *(photo: NCL)*

Specifications

Size (in tons)		Dawn	1,112/509
Spirit	75,338	Jewel	1,188/510
Star	91,000	Crew	
Dawn	92,250	Spirit	985
Jewel	92,100	Star	1,126
Passengers (double occ.)		Dawn	1,126
Spirit	1,966	Jewel	1,200
Star	2,240	Passenger/Crew Ratio	2 to 1
Dawn	2,224	Year Launched	
Jewel	2,376	Spirit	1999
Passenger/Space Ratio		Star	2001
Spirit	38.3	Dawn	2002
Star	40.5	Jewel	2005
Dawn	41.5	Last Major Refurbishment	
Jewel	38.8	Spirit	2004
Total Cabins/Veranda Cabins		Star	2001
Spirit	980/390	Dawn	N/A
Star	1,120/515	Jewel	N/A

Frommer's Ratings (Scale of 1–5)   ★★★★½

Cabin Comfort & Amenities	4	Dining Options	5
Ship Cleanliness & Maintenance	5	Gym, Spa & Sports Facilities	4
Public Comfort/Space	5	Children's Facilities	5
Decor	4.5	Enjoyment Factor	4.5

Talk about innovation: These ships get straight A's. Want dining choice? These ships have between 8 and 10 different restaurants apiece, from fancy steakhouses and teppanyaki restaurants to casual Tex-Mex and burger joints. Want something other than the generic Caribbean theme so prevalent on many ships? The ships instead have a healthy dose of Latin Miami in their music and decor, especially appropriate for *Dawn* and *Spirit*'s innovative New York–Caribbean itineraries, which visit Miami as a port of call. Want the biggest suites aboard any ship, anywhere? The ships' Garden Villas spread out over a mind-blowing 5,350 square feet and feature private gardens, multiple bedrooms with extravagant baths, separate living rooms, full kitchens, and private butler service. Zowie! Zowie, too, on their price: $26,000 a week for 6 guests. Normal cabins, on the other hand, come at normal prices.

Onboard programs are innovative too, featuring fewer of the ho-hum napkin-folding classes that once defined ship life and more computer- and health/nutrition-oriented workshops. The production shows in the striking theaters have a fresh feel too, incorporating hip-hop, India-inspired Bollywood themes, lots of Latin music, and even the occasional hint of storyline into honest-to-God exciting musical revues. Childrens' centers are such a knockout—so huge and completely kid-centric—that we wished we were 5 again. Ditto for our reaction to the buffet restaurant's Kids' Café, a miniaturized version of the adult cafe, accurate down to tiny chairs and a miniature buffet counter. It's the cutest thing going.

Don't get us wrong, this isn't paradise: Though many spaces aboard the ships approach high style (*Dawn* and *Star*'s elegant Gatsby's Champagne Bar, for instance), hints of NCL's recent near-budget past still hide in the wings, including the individually wrapped butter pats used even in the fancy restaurants, fast-food-style napkin dispensers in the buffet, and spindly metal-frame chairs and end tables in most cabins. But those are minor quibbles. Overall, these ships are winners. They're nearly identical in layout, though each succeeding ship in the series improved on the one before in size and amenities.

Norwegian Jewel, the newest of the series, is scheduled to launch just after this book goes to press, so is not reviewed here. *Norwegian Spirit,* which came to NCL from the Star Cruises fleet, is slightly smaller than her sisters and has a slightly different layout.

Cabins & Rates

Cabins	Per Diems from	Sq. Ft.	Fridge	Hair Dryer	Sitting Area	TV
Inside	$132	142	yes	yes	yes	yes
Outside	$140	158–166	yes	yes	yes	yes
Suite	$421	229–5,350	yes	yes	yes	yes

CABINS Though not overly large compared to some in the industry (particularly those of Carnival and Holland America's ships), standard cabins on these ships are larger than elsewhere in the NCL fleet. Decor is a mix, with stylish elements, such as cherrywood wall paneling and snazzy rounded lights; kitschy elements, such as bright island-colored carpeting; and cheap touches, such as spindly chairs and end tables, and wall-mounted soap dispensers in the bathrooms. Each comes with a small TV and minifridge, a tea/coffeemaker (an amenity rarely offered), private safe, and cool, retro-looking Aliseo hair dryers hanging in a coiled silver wall mount. Closet and drawer space provide more than enough space for weeklong sailings, and bathrooms in all categories are well designed, with large sinks whose faucets swing out of the way, a magnifying mirror inset in the regular mirror, adequate though not exceptional counter/shelf space, and (in all but inside cabins) shower, toilet, and washstand compartments (shower and toilet are behind their own little doors). Balconies in standard cabins accommodate two metal pool chairs and a small table, but aren't terribly roomy.

Spirit cabins have a similar decor to *Star* and *Dawn,* including the cherrywood wall paneling, but having originally been marketed in Asia, they also boast much larger cabin bathroom units. The *Spirit*'s great loos have separate toilet, shower, and washstand compartments divided by sliding doors. Plus, to accommodate families of all sizes, a good number of cabins can be combined to create two-, three-, and four-bedroom suites; and most cabins also have a sofa bed, pop-up trundle bed, and a pull-down berth to accommodate families.

Minisuites on the *Dawn* and *Star* provide about 60 more feet of floor space than standard cabins, with a large fold-out couch, a curtain between the bed and the sitting area, and a bathtub, while the four so-called "Romance Suites" (in the stern on Deck 10) really are, with 288 square feet of space, stereo with CD/DVD library, bathroom with separate shower and tub, nice wooden deck chairs on the balcony, and a romantic view over the ship's wake. Penthouse Suites offer the same, plus gorgeous bathrooms with a whirlpool tub and tiled, seaview shower stall; a larger balcony; and a walk-in closet. Those on Deck 11 offer a separate kids' room and bathroom. Those facing the bow on Decks 9 and 10 have large windows and deep balconies, but safety requirements mandate that instead of a nice glass door, the balconies are accessed via an honest-to-God steel bulkhead that's marked, "For your own safety, open only when the vessel is in port." The ship's four Owner's Suites are huge, with two balconies (one facing forward, as just described, and another, more accessible one on the side), living and dining areas, powder room, guest bath, and 750 square feet of space; compared to the two Garden Villas up on Deck 14, however, these suites are peasant's quarters. The Garden Villas are, in a word, HUGE, the biggest at sea today, with three bedrooms, enormous living rooms, private Italian gardens with hot tub, panoramic views all around, private butler service, grand pianos, and totally extravagant seaview bathrooms with whirlpool tubs. They're priced beyond the range of . . . well, pretty much everybody.

Twenty cabins are wheelchair accessible.

PUBLIC AREAS   From the moment you step aboard into the ships' large, broad, skylit atrium lobby, with a coffee bar at ground level and a band performing on its large stage, you'll be in a party mood. Public areas throughout are fanciful and extremely spacious, done in a mix of bright, Caribbean- and Miami-themed decor and high style Art Deco, with lots of nooks and some downright wonderful lounges and bars mixed in among all the restaurant choices. On *Dawn,* art throughout mixes primitivist folk paintings, modern art depicting famous world buildings such as the Petronas Towers and the Great Pyramids, Andy Warhol silk-screens, and classic works from the great masters Matisse, Renoir, van Gogh, and Monet. There's even art outdoors, with landscapes, Matisse dancers, and other themes painted along the length of the Promenade Deck and a burst of colorful stars and streamers running back from the bow, intended as an homage to the old steamship tradition of passengers throwing streamers from the deck as their ship pulls away from the dock.

On Deck 7, the main entertainment deck, a multi-deck theater has a thousand seats sloping down to a large stage flanked with opera boxes where musicians sometimes perform. There's also a nightclub for smaller-scale cabaret entertainment and dancing and a British-themed pub with piano entertainment, a big-screen TV for sports, and tasty fish and chips. It's pleasant enough (if often smoky), but this bar's big flaw is that it serves as a de facto corridor, so it gets more traffic than a cozy space should. Behind the bar, all by itself in the stern and taking up the full width of the ship, the Galleria Shops are a veritable department store at sea.

Deck 12 features a complex of "sit-down" rooms, including a comfortable cinema with traditional theater seats, a library, a card room, a reading room, a "lifestyles" room (used for classes, private functions, and so on), several meeting rooms, and a small wedding chapel. Forward of these is an observation lounge/disco; on the *Dawn* it's got bright, amoeba-shaped chairs and couches in the starboard rear corner—totally *Alice in Wonderland,* totally fun. Up top, on Deck 13, *Dawn* and *Star* feature a bar/lounge with a 1930s and '40s theme, a marble-topped bar, brown leather seating around small cocktail tables, and artwork depicting the Rat Pack, Bogart, James Cagney, Groucho Marx, and other Hollywood legends. A piano player entertains in the evening. *Spirit* and *Star* also feature a covered outdoor Bier Garten stocked with German pilsner, hefeweizen, and wheat beers, it also offers beer amenities like weisswurst and pretzels.

For kids, these ships have some of the better facilities at sea, with a huge, brightly colored crafts/play area, a big-screen TV room stuffed full of beanbag chairs, a huge ball-jump/crawling maze play-gym, a computer room, and a nursery with tiny little beds. Outside, the pool area is fantastic. On the *Dawn,* it's right out of *The Flintstones,* with giant polka-dotted dinosaurs hovering around faux rock walls, slides, a paddling pool, and even a kids' Jacuzzi. The *Star*'s has a space-age rocket theme. There are video arcades and teen centers on all three ships, with computers, a dance floor equipped with a sound/video system, and a soda bar.

Other rooms include a spacious casino; a very high-style, cathedral-ceiling champagne bar with a sweeping staircase and piano entertainment; and an Internet center. On *Dawn* and *Star,* the Havana Club, with seating for only 12, is an almost private room for cigars, port, cognacs, and whiskey.

DINING OPTIONS   These ships are all about their restaurants: *Dawn* and *Star* each have 10 and *Spirit* has 8, including a steakhouse, Asian venue, and Italian cafe. Main dining rooms include the elegant, chandelier-lit Venetian *(Dawn)* and ornate French-style Versailles *(Star)* offering a traditional European-style dining experience; the Aqua, a lighter, more modern space serving contemporary dishes (some designed by former White House executive chef Henry Haller); and a third smaller venue on the *Dawn* called Impressions, which is decorated in the style of a 19th-century French dining room.

Dawn and *Star* each have three alternative restaurants that carry a $12.50 to $17.50 per person cover charge. Pan-Asian restaurants have a very open feel (think high-end food court), a separate conveyor-belt sushi and sake bar, and an intimate Japanese teppanyaki room, where meals are prepared from the center of the table as guests look on. (Cover charge is $12.50; a la carte pricing in teppanyaki room is $10–$15.) Le Bistro serves classic and nouvelle French cuisine in an atmosphere of floral tapestry upholstery and fine place settings. *Dawn*'s is adorned with original Impressionist paintings by van Gogh, Matisse, Renoir, and Monet, lent from the private collection of Tan Sri Lim Kok Thay, chairman and CEO of Star Cruises, NCL's parent company. Cover charge here is $12.50 per person. There's also a steakhouse ($17.50 per-person cover) and, on *Star,* a modern outlet serving Pacific Rim–style fare ($12.50 cover or a la carte pricing).

For more casual fare, there's the Blue Lagoon, a 24-hour spot for burgers, fish and chips, stir-fry, and other snacks, and typical buffet fare is served at the top-of-the-ship buffets. Out on deck, each ship has a casual grill serving up burgers, dogs, and fries during the day. Other casual dining venues on *Dawn* and *Star* include a Tex-Mex/tapas restaurant for goodies like sangria, tamales, black bean soup with chorizo, enchiladas, quesadillas, and Mexican chocolate mascarpone cheesecake. We can't spare 50 pages to go on and on about the ships' extensive food offerings, so we'll just say . . . and there's more!

POOL, FITNESS, SPA & SPORTS FACILITIES   Main pool areas have the feel of a resort, ringed by flower-shaped "streetlamps" and terraces of deck chairs leading down to the central pool and hot tubs. A huge bar running almost the width of the ship serves ice cream on one side, drinks on the other. Nice space, but the real plaudits go to the spa, especially on *Dawn*, where you'll find a large lap pool, hot tub, jet-massage pool, and sunny windowed seating areas furnished with wooden deck chairs, the latter harking back to the classic indoor pools on the transatlantic liners. The rest of the spa is similarly stylish, with a sunlit entranceway that rises three decks high and is decorated with plants and Mayan reliefs, a juice bar, and 21 rooms offering the standard massages and beauty/relaxation treatments. The gym, by way of contrast, is blah: large, with a room for cycling classes, an aerobics studio, a very large free-weights area, and dozens of aerobics and weight machines, but it won't win any awards in the design department.

Outside there's an extra-long jogging track, a sports court for basketball and volleyball, two golf-driving nets, and facilities for shuffleboard and deck chess, plus acres of open deck space for sunning both aft on Deck 14 and forward on the tiered Sun Deck, where a lone hot tub looks out over the bow.

Norwegian Sun

The Verdict

If you like your ships big but intimate, *Sun* has a cozier feel than the newer *Dawn* and *Star,* yet still features multiple restaurants and lots of cabins with balconies.

Norwegian Sun (photo: Matt Hannafin)

Specifications

Size (in tons)	78,309	Crew	968
Passengers (double occ.)	1,960	Passenger/Crew Ratio	2 to 1
Passenger/Space Ratio	40	Year Launched	2001
Total Cabins/Veranda Cabins	1,001/432	Last Major Refurbishment	N/A

Frommer's Ratings (Scale of 1–5)   ✪✪✪✪

Cabin Comfort & Amenities	4	Dining Options	4.5
Ship Cleanliness & Maintenance	4	Gym, Spa & Sports Facilities	4
Public Comfort/Space	4	Children's Facilities	3.5
Decor	4	Enjoyment Factor	4

Norwegian Sun was the second megaship built for NCL's modern era (after *Norwegian Sky,* since renamed *Pride of Aloha*), and blazed the trail that all the later ships followed, with 9 restaurants, 12 bars, and everything else designed with casual cruising in mind.

Cabins & Rates

Cabins	Per Diems from	Sq. Ft.	Fridge	Hair Dryer	Sitting Area	TV
Inside	$149	118–191	yes	yes	yes	yes
Outside	$185	154–173	yes	yes	yes	yes
Suite	$496	264–570	yes	yes	yes	yes

CABINS   *Sun* is heavy on suites and minisuites, the latter of which measure a roomy 264 to 301 square feet (plus 68- to 86-sq.-ft. balconies) and have walk-in closets, sitting areas, and bathtubs. Twenty 355- to 570-square-foot Penthouse and Owner's suites (with 119- to 258-sq.-ft. balconies) include the services of a butler and concierge who will get you on the first tender in ports, make dinner reservations, and generally try to please your every whim. The pair of penthouses also has a separate living room and dining area.

Among the regular balcony cabins, categories BA, BB, and BC (which take up most of Decks 8–10) are laid out awkwardly, with the twin beds and the closet-dresser unit positioned too close together. A person dragging a suitcase or pushing a stroller has to twist up like a pretzel to squeeze by. Other than that, the decor is pleasant with caramel wood veneers, attractive gilt-framed artwork, and navy, gold, and Kelly green fabrics and carpeting. Storage space is plentiful, so much so that on a recent cruise we couldn't even manage to fill up all the shelves. The bathrooms have a pair of shelves above the counter and a really useful one in the shower, though otherwise the skinny shower stalls are a tight squeeze for all but Kate Moss–types. Cabins at the forward end of Deck 6 have large portholes that look out on the ship's wraparound Promenade Deck, popular with walkers and runners, so you'll probably want to have your curtains closed most of the time unless you like being peeped on.

Every cabin has a small sitting area, a minifridge (not stocked), a hair dryer, TV, desk and chair, and a coffee-/tea-maker. Bathrooms are equipped with shampoo and liquid-soap dispensers attached right to the wall (and the shampoo is halfway decent, too), as more and more ships are doing these days. Suites are stocked with robes for use during the cruise.

Twenty cabins are equipped for wheelchairs.

PUBLIC AREAS   The ships are bright and sun-filled due to an abundance of floor-to-ceiling windows. Surrounding the understated three-level atrium on several levels are a bar, clusters of chairs creating relaxing pockets, and an area where a pianist performs. The color scheme is a pleasing, unjarring pastiche of mostly cool blues, sages, deep reds, and soft golds blended with marble, burled-wood veneers, and brass and chrome detailing. There are nearly a dozen bars, including a sports bar, a wine bar, a nightclub/disco centrally located amidships, two large poolside bars, a coffee bar, an Internet cafe, and a dark and cozy cigar club. As on *Pride of Aloha,* the latter is one of the nicest nooks on the ship, with soft ballads coming from the adjacent piano bar and oversize soft leather furniture to sink into—just as long as you're not coughing from the smoke.

In addition to the so-so main theater there's also an attractive observation lounge wrapped in windows high atop the ship, with live music at night. The casino is large and flashy enough, though not over the top. The layout of the shops (where you can spend your casino winnings—ha!) is attractive, with a wide streetlike corridor cutting between the main boutiques and a long jewelry counter. As the passage is the only way to get between the casino and show lounge, you're forced to browse whether you want to or not.

For kids, the ship's huge children's area includes a sprawling playroom with cathedral-high ceilings, a teen center with a large movie screen and a pair of foosball games, a video arcade, and a wading pool.

DINING OPTIONS   Breakfast, lunch, and dinner are served in two main dining rooms with many tables for two and four. At dinner you can also choose from six alternative restaurants, including Le Bistro, an elegant space with lots of windows and several comfy round booths with cushy pillows as well as regular tables ($12.50 cover charge). There's also the Il Adagio Italian restaurant, a long, skinny space between the two main restaurants, where the lighting is low and the views are good from both the raised round booths along the wall and the tables for two at the windows ($12.50 cover charge). The shrimp scampi and veal chop with wild mushroom ragout are tasty, and so is the homemade mushroom ravioli and Mediterranean seafood cocktail. Caesar salads are prepared from scratch tableside, and the warm chocolate hazelnut cake is to die for.

Sun's sushi bar serves expertly prepared, fresh-tasting maki and California rolls (at about $2 per roll) along with nigiri sushi and sashimi (most are $2 or $3 for two pieces) with authentic Japanese place settings; you can get a delicious and filling combo platter for $8. The adjacent teppanyaki venue does lunch and dinner just like Benihana, with the theatrical cutting and flinging of shrimp, chicken, beef, and whatever else you order from the a la carte menu. Nearby is a tapas restaurant, an attractive room decorated with tile mosaic and terra-cotta pottery, and serving an odd and mediocre-tasting assortment of finger food, from fried seafood balls to ribs, olives, seafood salad, and falafel, along with sangria and a selection of Mexican (not Spanish) beer. At dinnertime, live Spanish music is featured; at lunch the mood is more casual. Pacific Heights is a health-oriented dinner venue featuring light Pacific Rim and Asian Fusion cuisine, where calories, fat, protein, and other similar stats are listed on the menu. Entrees include macadamia-crusted monkfish, and grilled pork chops with applesauce and roasted cabbage rolls. Reservations are required for dinner in all of the specialty restaurants, though you can sometimes get a table as a walk-in.

The casual buffet restaurant is large but poorly organized, and is often backed up at mealtimes. Open 24 hours, the buffet serves snacks (including pizza and jumbo really yummy homemade cookies) between meals. Pizza is also available from room service 24 hours a day.

POOL, FITNESS, SPA & SPORTS FACILITIES   *Sun's* well-stocked oceanview gym is open 24 hours a day, and the adjacent aerobics room has floor-to-ceiling windows and a great selection of no-charge traditional classes (including stretch classes and step classes) as well as spinning, kickboxing, and other trendy choices that carry a $5 charge. At the nearby spa, you can wait for your treatment in a serene sitting area that has a wall of glass facing the hypnotic sea. Heidi got the best shiatsu massage of her life here, so good she signed up for a second.

Out on deck is a pair of pools with a cluster of four hot tubs between them. One deck up are the combo basketball/volleyball court, a pair of golf driving nets, and shuffleboard. The kids' wading pool and some cute mini-chaise-longues are conveniently tucked along the starboard side of the Sports Deck.

Norwegian Majesty

The Verdict

Though *Majesty* really doesn't excel in any one area, it's still an understated, informal midsize ship, with good food and enough entertainment and activity options to keep everyone occupied.

Norwegian Majesty *(photo: NCL)*

Specifications

Size (in tons)	40,876	Crew	620
Passengers (double occ.)	1,460	Passenger/Crew Ratio	2.7 to 1
Passenger/Space Ratio	28	Year Launched	1992
Total Cabins/Veranda Cabins	730/0	Last Major Refurbishment	1999

Frommer's Ratings (Scale of 1–5)   ★★★

Cabin Comfort & Amenities	3	Dining Options	2
Ship Cleanliness & Maintenance	4	Gym, Spa & Sports Facilities	3
Public Comfort/Space	4	Children's Facilities	3
Decor	4	Enjoyment Factor	3

Most things that are only 14 years old are considered fairly new, but that rule doesn't apply to cruise ships, and so today the 1992 vintage *Norwegian Majesty* is a veritable antique. An extensive 1999 refurbishment and reconstruction spruced up the outside decking, carpets, and cabin decor, and added many new rooms by literally sawing the ship in half like a magician's assistant and putting her back together with a new pre-constructed midsection. While hardly dazzling, the humble *Majesty* is an appealing midsize next to modern megaships that are two or three times her size.

Cabins & Rates

Cabins	Per Diems from	Sq. Ft.	Fridge	Hair Dryer	Sitting Area	TV
Inside	$110	108	no	yes	no	yes
Outside	$122	108–145	some	yes	no	yes
Suite	$383	235	yes	yes	yes	yes

CABINS   Originally built to be a Baltic ferry, *Norwegian Majesty* was retooled into a cruise ship before she ever left the shipyard. Unfortunately, her cabins were designed with short 3- and 4-night cruises in mind; today, with the vessel sailing mostly 7-night

Bermuda and Caribbean itineraries, those small cabins can seem particularly small. The suites (18 of them) are more than adequate, with bathtubs and tile bathrooms, sitting areas, and enough room to move. Most Superior Oceanview Staterooms are barely adequate at 145 square feet, but in lower inside and outside categories (which make up a good portion of the total cabins) it gets even tighter at a ridiculous 108 square feet. All cabins have hair dryers, safes, and televisions, and cabins far forward and far aft have minifridges.

Some cabins on the Norway and Viking decks have views that are obstructed by lifeboats. On the Promenade Deck, cabin windows look out onto the promenade, meaning you may open your curtain in the morning and see a jogger's head bob by. The best non-suite accommodations are the category C rooms on the Majesty Deck, especially the ones in the bow that have windows offering sweeping vistas of the sea ahead.

Seven cabins are equipped for passengers with disabilities.

PUBLIC AREAS   Public areas favor a nice mix of blues, lavenders, ivories, teak, and brass over overt glitz. The Royal Observatory Lounge, tucked away in the bow and offering great views, is the scene of live entertainment nightly, including karaoke. Aside from Deck 7's Frame 52 Disco, the rest of the ship's nightlife is on Decks 5 and 6, including the Rendezvous Lounge piano bar and Royal Fireworks dance lounge for adult contemporary sounds. The Palace Theater could be described as intimate; it could also be described as claustrophobic. Either way, the sightlines are not good, with support columns all around the room, and the low ceiling prevents dancers from getting too energetic. The Polo Club, just outside the theater, usually features a pianist/vocalist. On the opposite end of the long, narrow room is the dark, moody Monte Carlo Casino, a decent place for you and your money to have a parting of ways.

A coffee bar sits next door to the Le Bistro alternative restaurant. Shops are forward from the lobby, and there's also a card room, a small video arcade, a library, a children's playroom, and a meeting room.

DINING OPTIONS   Both the Seven Seas and the Four Seasons dining rooms get quite crowded. Le Bistro, the line's signature alternative restaurant, is a small, intimate room off the corridor that links the two main dining rooms. It charges a $12.50 cover per person.

Although many ships put their buffet restaurant in the stern, this ship's indoor/outdoor Cafe Royale is in the bow, with panoramic windows that allow passengers to see what's ahead. The room is smallish and can be crowded at mealtimes, with long lines. There are outdoor tables on the Sun Deck by the pool, but if you want to stay inside and the Cafe Royale tables are taken, slip down the stairs into the Royal Observatory, another bow-facing room with great views; at dinnertime, it's used as another reservations-only alternative restaurant, this one serving Italian cuisine. In the stern, Piazza San Marco serves pizza, hot dogs, and burgers.

POOL, FITNESS, SPA & SPORTS FACILITIES   Joggers and walkers can circle the ship on the wraparound Promenade Deck 7, which is also home to the Bodywave spa and fitness center. These facilities are not extensive by any means: The workout room is basic and has several weight stations and cardiovascular stations, and there's a separate aerobics room across the hall. On deck, there are two pools and a splash pool for kids, nicely sequestered on the aft end of the Norway Deck.

Norwegian Dream • Norwegian Wind

The Verdict

These two ships are pleasant enough ways to sail if the price is low enough, but their lack of wide-open spaces and the way public rooms lead into one another make them feel either cozy or cramped—take your pick.

Norwegian Wind *(photo: NCL)*

Specifications

Size (in tons)	50,760	Passenger/Crew Ratio	2.8 to 1
Passengers (double occ.)	1,748	Year Launched	
Passenger/Space Ratio	29	*Norwegian Dream*	1992
Total Cabins/Veranda Cabins	874/0	*Norwegian Wind*	1993
Crew	614	Last Major Refurbishment	2001

Frommer's Ratings (Scale of 1–5)   ★★★

Cabin Comfort & Amenities	3	Dining Options	3
Ship Cleanliness & Maintenance	4	Gym, Spa & Sports Facilities	3
Public Comfort/Space	3	Children's Facilities	3
Decor	4	Enjoyment Factor	3

Cruise ship years are a lot like dog years, which means these 13- and 14-year-old ships are ooooold. Originally built as much smaller vessels, they were "stretched" in 1998 at Germany's Lloyd Werft shipyard, with a new 130-foot midsection inserted into each, raising their tonnage from 41,000 to 50,760 and increasing their capacity from around 1,200 passengers to over 1,700. At the time, that was a nifty technological feat, but cutting edge these ships are not. On the plus side, they provide more of an "at sea" feeling than aboard many of today's supersize megaships, with many open decks and a lot of glass letting on to ocean views. Renovations in 2001 added restaurants that allow them to offer the choices promised by NCL's Freestyle dining program.

Cabins & Rates

Cabins	Per Diems from	Sq. Ft.	Fridge	Hair Dryer	Sitting Area	TV
Inside	$120	130–150	no	no	no	yes
Outside	$141	160–176	no	no	some	yes
Suite	$368	270–385	yes	yes	yes	yes

CABINS   Over 80% of cabins aboard these ships are outside, most with sitting areas and picture windows. In general, cabin decor is pleasant and breezy, with wood accents and pastels evocative of the West Indies. Unfortunately, storage space is minimal: Two people can just barely manage, and when a third or fourth person shares a cabin, it can get truly cramped. Bathrooms are also small. At 160 to 176 square feet, the outside deluxe staterooms are smaller than the outside cabins of competitors such as Holland America and Carnival, but among the fleet's largest standard cabins. The top-of-the-line Owner's Suites are 271 square feet, plus a 65-square-foot balcony—large enough, but small compared with what the competition offers. Clustered on the Sun Deck, each of these suites has a living room with convertible double-bed sofa, separate bedroom, minifridge, stereo with CD library, DVD player, and bathroom with tub and shower. The six 384-square-foot Superior Deluxe Penthouse Suites amidships on the Norway Deck have partially obstructed views because of the over-hang from the restaurant above. Avoid them. Lifeboats block the views of the category F and G cabins at midships on the Norway Deck.

Thirteen cabins are wheelchair accessible, and 35 are equipped for passengers with hearing impairments.

PUBLIC AREAS   Both ships are filled with light owing to tiered upper decks fore and aft and walls of windows to port and starboard. Nice, but it also illuminates the chintzy materials used in passageways and stairways, creating a tinny feel. Both also have layout idiosyncrasies owing to their late-'90s stretching, forcing you to walk through some public rooms and up and down stairs in order to get from one end of the ship to another. Most lounges and other public areas are concentrated on the Star Deck, with a few one flight down on the International Deck. The dark, Vegas-style casinos are glitzy, but are on the small side. Lucky's Bar and Dazzles disco see the most late-night action, with many folks also spending lots of time at the Sports Bar & Grill, a real bar-bar for real guy-guys decorated with sports memorabilia and giant-screen TVs. On the International Deck, the library is small and feels like an afterthought. The Observatory Lounge on the Sports Deck, a sequestered oceanview spot behind the gym and spa, has dancing in the evenings. A basketball/volleyball court is just overhead, creating its own kind of thump-thump. A small children's playroom is located on Deck 11.

DINING OPTIONS   *Dream* and *Wind* each have three main dining rooms, of which the most appealing is Terraces, a cozy, three-level restaurant with a 1930s sup-per-club feel and floor-to-ceiling windows facing the stern. The Four Seasons restau-rant is also an attractive spot, with tiered seating and curved walls of windows. Couples who want a romantic dinner should try and reserve one of the oceanview tables for two. The Sun Terrace restaurant is a trattoria serving traditional Italian fare, while Le Bistro is an intimate reservations-only French/Continental restaurant serving just 72 guests. The entrances to three of these restaurants are located on the Interna-tional Deck, and congestion here is common at dinnertime.

Unlike most ships, neither *Wind* nor *Dream* has a traditional casual buffet. Instead, the Four Seasons offers a buffet at breakfast, while sit-down breakfasts and lunches are served in the Sun Terrace and Terraces dining rooms. The small, indoor/outdoor Sports Bar & Grill also serves casual meals: continental-style breakfast; burgers, hot dogs, and salad at lunch; dishes like chili con carne and stir-fry spicy chicken for din-ner; and snacks throughout the day. The outdoor Pizzeria adjacent to the main swim-ming pool offers a limited breakfast buffet, plus pizza, pasta, and a salad bar at lunch.

POOL, FITNESS, SPA & SPORTS FACILITIES   With their attractive dark wooden decking and crisp blue-and-white striped canvas umbrellas, the pool decks have a sort of European beach-resort feel. Each ship has two pools, the larger of which, on the Sun Deck, has a swim-up bar and two hot tubs. The main problem here is that high walls added when the ships were stretched cut off sea views for those lounging poolside, and create a closed-in, claustrophobic feeling. For panoramic views of sea and sky, you have to walk up to the Sports Deck or to the small pool aft on the International Deck, where rows of deck chairs surround an almost purely decorative keyhole-shaped pool.

Gyms on both ships are cramped and inadequately equipped considering the vessels carry some 1,700 passengers. On a recent cruise, people sometimes had to wait to use the four treadmills, four stairsteppers, and four stationery bikes. The small spa offers the typical range of treatments as well as his and hers saunas. Both the gym and spa are located right underneath the Sky Deck's basketball/volleyball court, so expect some intense banging when a game is in progress.

The Sports Deck has Ping-Pong tables and a golf driving range. Joggers can work out on the wraparound Promenade Deck.

Norwegian Crown

The Verdict

Remember the 1980s TV show *Dynasty*? *Norwegian Crown* had its heyday in that same era of glitz and glitter, and with the right lighting (and a little nip and tuck during her 2003 dry dock), she still looks pretty good. Her small size is a real plus for folks who don't like their ships supersize.

Norwegian Crown *(photo: NCL)*

Specifications

Size (in tons)	34,242	Crew	525
Passengers (double occ.)	1,078	Passenger/Crew Ratio	2 to 1
Passenger/Space Ratio	31.7	Year Launched	1988
Total Cabins/Veranda Cabins	539/16	Last Major Refurbishment	2003

Frommer's Ratings (Scale of 1–5)   ★★★½

Cabin Comfort & Amenities	4	Dining Options	4
Ship Cleanliness & Maintenance	4	Gym, Spa & Sports Facilities	4
Public Comfort/Space	3	Children's Facilities	3
Decor	3	Enjoyment Factor	4

Norwegian Crown is like an old Hollywood star on her fourth or fifth marriage. Built originally as the *Crown Odyssey* for Royal Cruise Line in 1988, she became the *Norwegian Crown* after NCL acquired Royal. In 2000, NCL moved the ship to another subsidiary, Orient Lines, switching her name back to *Crown Odyssey.* Then, NCL moved the ship back to its own fleet once again, changing her name back to *Norwegian Crown.* No word on what she'll be called when she eventually transfers to Star Cruises. A major refurbishment in 2003 brought the *Crown* more closely in line with the newer ships of the NCL fleet, which offer the line's flexible multiple dining options as well as the full-service Mandara Spa.

Cabins & Rates

Cabins	Per Diems from	Sq. Ft.	Fridge	Hair Dryer	Sitting Area	TV
Inside	$140	160	no	yes	yes	yes
Outside	$144	165	some	yes	yes	yes
Suite	$373	290–615	yes	yes	yes	yes

CABINS   Although the *Crown* was built before balcony fever overtook the ship design industry, her cabins compensate for the paucity of balconies with other amenities, such as large picture windows and whirlpool tubs. Room size ranges from a roomy 160-square-foot minimum for inside cabins, to the 615-square-foot Owner's Suites that have large balconies, king-size beds, and walk-in closets. Even inside cabins have a huge amount of closet space, one of the design elements of a bygone era, when ships were built for long journeys. All cabins have TVs, coffeemakers, safes, hair dryers, and, impressively, Internet connections. Some 50 cabins (numbers 8009–8055) have views partially obstructed by lifeboats. Four new suites on the Penthouse deck were added in the last renovation, along with nine new inside passenger cabins. Four cabins are configured for passengers with disabilities.

PUBLIC AREAS   *Crown* has a design scheme Linda Evans would approve of, full of glass, polished brass, and color schemes heavy on maroons, mauves, and gold. The popular Top of the Crown lounge has a bar topped with blue-pearl granite and cocktail tables mounted on a railing that encircles the room. The Lido Bar includes large windows with high-tech stainless steel support systems that create an airy, modern space. Like the hot teen spaces on the new megaships, the teen and children's center is awash in metallic purples, greens, and oranges, and features a dance floor, state-of-the-art sound and light system, juice bar, and large, multicolored banquettes. A video arcade separates the teen center from the children's center, which is decorated in vibrant, primary colors, and stocked with diversions such as a plasma-screen TV, beanbags for comfortable viewing, and a computer corner.

DINING OPTIONS   Perhaps the most dramatic change to the ship during her February 2003 dry dock was the addition of three new restaurants, bringing the total number to six—quite a choice for a ship of this size. The signature 70-seat alternative restaurant, Le Bistro, is decorated in coral, green, and gold, with large, comfortable wood banquettes. Gold sconces along the walls provide soft, glowy lighting and a romantic atmosphere. At the 40-seat Pasta Café, guests can watch the chef prepare traditional Italian fare from a blue-granite-topped bar. There's also an Asian-themed restaurant called Chopsticks. The three new venues complement the main dining room, the Seven Continents Restaurant, along with the Yacht Club buffet restaurant and Cafe Italia for al fresco pizza and pasta.

POOL, FITNESS, SPA & SPORTS FACILITIES   NCL completely rebuilt the ship's Mandara Spa and gym, and it's now an expanded space done up in light woods and aqua, mint green, and creamy white mosaic tiles. There are now nine treatment rooms, while the beauty salon has four stations facing an expanse of floor-to-ceiling windows. The gym has a separate aerobics room, plus you'll find an indoor pool, hot tubs, and saunas. There's an outdoor pool on the ship's aft deck, and much of the teak decking throughout has been restored.

9 Oceania Cruises

8300 NW 33rd St., Suite 308, Miami, FL 33122. ℂ 800/531-5658 or 305/514-2300. www.oceaniacruises.com.

THE LINE IN A NUTSHELL Oceania is the phoenix that rose from the ashes of Renaissance Cruises, which went belly-up in September 2001. Headed by former Renaissance and Crystal Cruises executives, the new line operates three of Renaissance's ships and mimics some attributes of much pricier lines, with excellent service and cuisine and a quiet, refined onboard feel. **Sails to:** Caribbean (plus Europe, South America, Asia).

THE EXPERIENCE Oceania is positioned as an "upper premium" line intended to fill the gap between big-ship premium lines such as Celebrity and real luxe lines such as Radisson, both in terms of ship size and level of luxury. It's going for a kind of floating country club feel, with a low-key ambience; few organized activities; low-key entertainment; a casual, sporty dress code; an emphasis on cabin comfort; and 10- to 25-night itineraries that favor smaller, less-visited ports such as St. Kitts and St. Barts. Despite such luxe-travel touches, the line's prices are competitive with—and often even lower than—those of the other premium lines.

Pros

- **Excellent cuisine:** In both the main dining room and specialty restaurants, Oceania is near the top among mainstream lines.
- **Excellent, personal service:** The ships' European crews are extremely friendly and eager to please.
- **Intimate size:** Oceania's ships only carry 684 passengers apiece, making for a much more human-scale feel than you get aboard a megaship.
- **Nonsmoking policy:** On these ships, smoking is permitted only in two small areas of the pool deck and nightclub. (Of course, this is a "con" for smokers.)

Cons

- **Few outside decks:** There's only a pool deck, a sun deck, and the deserted promenade/boat deck, which is never used since it has no deck chairs or other furniture. Aside from the many private cabin balconies, you'd have a hard time finding a quiet little outdoor nook.
- **Few activities:** By design, Oceania offers few onboard activities, leaving passengers to their own devices. This is only a "con" if you need constant stimulation.
- **So-so entertainment:** While music aboard is uniformly excellent, show-lounge entertainment could stand some improvement.

OCEANIA: CLASS ACT, COZY SHIPS

Remember Renaissance Cruises? Founded in 1988, it made news in the '90s by building a fleet of identical medium-size ships and going direct to consumers rather than working with travel agents. Both of these were fairly revolutionary moves back then, and, as often happens with revolutions, this one didn't work out too well. Already in bad financial shape when 9/11 hit, the line was forced into bankruptcy when the resultant travel downturn came. Left high and dry, its ships were put up for auction to the highest bidder. Princess scooped up a couple of them (which it now operates as *Pacific Princess* and *Tahitian Princess*), the British line Swan Hellenic got another (which it rechristened *Minerva II*), and Oceania, a new line founded by former Renaissance CEO Frank Del Rio and former Crystal president Joseph Watters, started up with two others, the former *R1* and *R2*. Renamed *Regatta* and *Insignia,* the ships spend half the year in Europe and the other in the Western Hemisphere. A third sister ship, *Nautica,* joined the fleet in late 2005, sailing itineraries to Africa, India, Southeast Asia, and China.

PASSENGER PROFILE

Due partially to the length of these cruises (mostly 12 and 14 days) and partially to the low-key onboard atmosphere, Oceania tends to attract older passengers who prefer to entertain themselves, reading in the library and enjoying the destination-heavy itineraries. Most are Americans, with many from the West Coast and many "returning," having sailed previously with Renaissance. A sprinkling of younger couples usually find themselves on board as well, though children are rare enough to be surprising. Whatever their age, passengers tend to be drawn by the line's all-casual, all-the-time dress code and ambience.

Because of Oceania's stringent no-smoking rules, most passengers are nonsmokers. Aside from one corner of the pool deck and one corner of the Horizons nightclub, smoking is not permitted anywhere on board—even in your cabin or its balcony.

DINING

Oceania's dining experience is one of its strongest suits, with menus created by renowned chef Jacques Pepin (onetime personal chef to Charles de Gaulle and, more recently, one of America's best-known chefs and food writers) and passengers able to choose among four different restaurants for dinner: the main Grand Dining Room, the Mediterranean-style Toscana restaurant, the Polo Grill steakhouse, and the "Tapas on the Terrace" casual outdoor option. All four venues work on an open-seating basis (dine when you want, with whom you want), with meals usually served in a 3-hour window from 6:30 to 9:30pm.

TRADITIONAL The **Grand Dining Room,** the main restaurant aboard each ship, features French-inspired continental cuisine in five courses, with a string quartet providing music at dinner. Appetizers might include grilled marinated prawns, frog leg mousse, and crushed new potatoes with chives and Malossol caviar, and soups might

Compared with other mainstream lines, here's how Oceania rates:					
	Poor	**Fair**	**Good**	**Excellent**	**Outstanding**
Enjoyment Factor				✓	
Dining				✓	
Activities		✓			
Children's Program	N/A*				
Entertainment			✓		
Service				✓	
Worth the Money				✓	

* Oceania offers no children's program.

Oceania Fleet Itineraries*

Ship	Itineraries
Insignia	**12-night Amazon/S. Carib:** Manus (Brazil) to Barbados, Mar 2006.
Regatta	**25-night Caribbean/Amazon:** Round-trip from Miami, FL, Nov–Dec 2005. **12-night S. Carib:** Round-trip from Miami, FL, Dec 2005 and Feb 2006. **10-night S. Carib:** Round-trip from Miami, FL, Jan–Feb 2006. **14-night W. Carib:** Round-trip from Miami, FL, Mar 2006. **16-night Mexico/Panama Canal:** East- or westbound between Miami, FL, and Los Angeles, CA, Jan–Feb 2006.

At press time, itineraries were not available for Oceania's fall 2006 U.S. sailings.

be as traditional as beef oxtail consommé or as unusual as Moroccan harira chicken soup. There are always several salads and a pasta of the day, and entrees are elaborate, well-presented versions of the big faves (lobster tail butterfly, beef Wellington, steamed Alaskan king crab legs), plus some uncommon dishes: sautéed sea bream filet and pheasant breast ballotine stuffed with morel mushrooms. There's always a tasty **vegetarian option,** plus an alternative selection of basics: grilled sirloin, broiled chicken, salmon filet, etc.

SPECIALTY   As an alternative, passengers can make a reservation at the ship's specialty restaurants, the Italian **Toscana** or the **Polo Grill** steakhouse. Tostana is sinfully overwhelming, serving half a dozen antipasti and an equal number of pasta dishes, soups, salads, and *secondi piatti* such as medallions of filet mignon topped with sautéed artichoke and smoked mozzarella; swordfish steak sautéed in garlic, parsley, Tuscan olives, capers, and orvieto wine; and braised double-cut lamb chops in a sun-dried tomato, olive, and roasted garlic sauce. Desserts include the remarkable if weird-sounding chocolate lasagna. Polo Grill serves chops, seafood, and cuts of slow-aged beef, with all the substantial trimmings: seafood appetizers, soups such as New England clam chowder and lobster bisque, straight-up salads such as Caesar and iceberg wedge with bleu cheese and crumbled bacon, and side dishes such as a baked potato, wild mushroom ragout, and creamed spinach. Passengers can make reservations for either restaurant during breakfast or lunch hours at the Terrace Cafe. There's no extra charge, but there's an initial two-reservation limit to ensure that all guests get a chance. If you'd like to dine here more than twice, add your name to the waiting list and you'll be contacted if there's space (which there usually is).

CASUAL   On the casual side, the **Terrace Cafe** is a standard cruise ship buffet serving a range of sides, salads, and main courses. An attached pizzeria serves very tasty thin-crust pies. At lunch the pool deck's grill is also fired up, serving burgers, hot dogs, and specialty sandwiches. In the evening, the outdoor portion of the Terrace is transformed into **Tapas on the Terrace,** a romantic option with regional Spanish and Mediterranean specialties, other ethnic dishes, and home-style favorites served from a buffet. Waiters are on hand to serve drinks and generally be charming.

SNACKS & EXTRAS   **High tea** is served daily at 4pm in the Horizons Lounge, with a good spread of pastries, tea sandwiches, and scones. **Room service** is available 24 hours. Guests in Owners, Vista, and Penthouse suites can have full meals served course by course in their rooms.

ACTIVITIES

By design, activities are not a high priority for Oceania. Expect enrichment lectures themed around the region being visited, fitness and computer classes, informal health and beauty seminars by the spa and salon staff, and a handful of old cruise standards: bingo, shuffleboard, and the like. For people who are self-motivated and/or prefer to spend their time aboard reading on deck or in one of the library's overstuffed leather armchairs, this is ideal. If you like a lot of organized activities, though, this is not the line for you.

Both ships have smallish, 19th-century-style casinos that see a fair amount of action. Internet access is available in Deck 9's Oceania@Sea Internet center and at two terminals in the library. The ships' full-service spas are run by Mandara, a subsidiary of Steiner Leisure, which operates almost every spa at sea.

CHILDREN'S PROGRAM

There are no special facilities on these ships, and the line typically carries very few children.

ENTERTAINMENT

The good news: You won't be assailed by steel-drum bands doing bad Bob Marley covers. Instead, you'll get a 12-piece jazz band on deck in the afternoon and in the club at night; pianists performing Cole Porter, Hoagy Carmichael, and other American standards at the martini bar before dinner; and an occasional string quartet.

The bad news: That's the high point of the onboard entertainment. Each night, the main show lounge presents a headliner, but at least in the line's first season the acts were hit-or-miss, with a Victor Borge–style classical pianist scoring big one night, a card-trick specialist going down in flames the second, and a folk-dance troupe from one of the ports providing a pleasant but essentially amateur program the third. According to Oceania chairman Joseph Watters, the line has no plans to start offering typical song-and-dance revues—for which we whisper a prayer of thanks.

Other entertainment options include the occasional karaoke session or a movie presented out on deck.

SERVICE

The staff in the restaurants are crack troops, delivering each course promptly but without any sense that they're hurrying passengers through their meals. Service balances precision with friendliness, skewing close to the kind of understated professionalism you see on the real luxury lines. The relatively small number of passengers aboard also means service is more personal than you find aboard the megaships. In the bars, staff tend to remember your drink order by the second day, and cabin stewardesses greet their passengers by name in the corridors. Like many other lines, Oceania automatically adds a **gratuity** to your shipboard account ($11.50 per person, per day, which may be adjusted up or down at your discretion). For guests occupying Owner's, Vista, and Penthouse suites, there's an additional $3 per day gratuity added for butler service.

There's a **self-service laundry** and ironing room on Deck 7, in addition to standard laundry, dry cleaning, and pressing service offered by the ship's laundry.

Regatta • Insignia

The Verdict

With their smallish size, understated decor, and serene atmosphere, these mostly non-smoking ships are more like quiet boutique hotels than cruise vessels, and provide a comfortable, laid-back, yet stylish way to see the Caribbean.

Regatta *(photo: Oceania)*

Specifications

Size (in tons)	30,200	Crew	373
Passengers (double occ.)	684	Passenger/Crew Ratio	1.8 to 1
Passenger/Space Ratio	44	Year Launched	1998
Total Cabins/Veranda Cabins	343/232	Last Major Refurbishment	2002–03

Frommer's Ratings (Scale of 1–5)

⭐⭐⭐⭐

Cabin Comfort & Amenities	4	Dining Options	4
Ship Cleanliness & Maintenance	4	Gym, Spa & Sports Facilities	4
Public Comfort/Space	4.5	Children's Facilities	N/A
Decor	4	Enjoyment Factor	4

Imagine an old-style Ritz-Carlton hotel in the shape of a cruise ship and you've pretty much got the idea here. Like all of the former Renaissance vessels, the former *R1* and *R2* are comfortable and spacious ships decorated mostly in warm, dark woods and rich fabrics. They're traditional and sedate, with an emphasis on intimate spaces rather than the kind of grand, splashy ones you'll find on most megaships. Of course, the ships' small size means there'd be no *room* for grand spaces, even if they'd wanted them: Each carries only 684 passengers, making them pipsqueaks in this era of 3,000-passenger giants. But then, their intimacy is one of the main reasons passengers choose them. The atmosphere is relaxed and clubby, with no formal nights that demand tuxedos and gowns.

Cabins & Rates

Cabins	Per Diems from	Sq, Ft.	Fridge	Hair Dryer	Sitting Area	TV
Inside	$100	160	no	yes	yes	yes
Outside	$135	160–216*	no	yes	yes	yes
Suite	$275	322–962*	yes	yes	yes	yes

* *Including veranda.*

CABINS   Staterooms aboard *Regatta* and *Insignia* are straightforward, no-nonsense spaces with a hint of modern European city hotel: plain off-white walls, dark wood trim and furniture, and rich carpeting. The highlight of each, though, is its "Tranquility Bed," an oasis of 350-thread-count Egyptian cotton sheets and duvet covers, down duvets and pillows, custom-designed extra-thick mattresses, and a mound of throw-pillows to prop you up during the late-late show. Spacious balconies have teak decking for a classic nautical look, though the white plastic deck furniture is a bit suburban patio. All cabins have televisions, safes, vanities with mirrors, hair dryers, phones, full-length mirrors, and French-milled toiletries. Closet space is a little skimpy considering the lengthy itineraries these ships sail, but drawer space scattered around the cabin, and space under the beds, make up for this a bit. Overall cabin size is in the 165-square-foot range—not tiny, but not exceptionally large, either. There are also some bizarre little quirks. Light switches, for instance, can be mystifying: There doesn't seem to be any way to turn off the bedside lights until you discover the tiny, almost hidden buttons up near their shades. There are also switches for the overheads right in the headboard, which are very easy to switch on accidentally in your sleep.

Suites include minibars, bathtubs, and a small area with a cocktail table for intimate in-room dining. Ten Owner's Suites measure 786 to 982 square feet and are located at the ship's bow and stern, featuring wraparound balconies, queen-size beds, whirlpool bathtubs, minibars, living rooms, and guest bathrooms. Owners Suites, Vista Suites, and Penthouse Suites feature butler service. Concierge-class staterooms (in between regular cabins and suites) add some warm-and-fuzzy to the amenities: a welcome bottle of champagne, a refrigerated minibar, DVD player, personalized stationary, cashmere throw blanket, complimentary tote bag, priority embarkation, a dedicated check-in desk and priority luggage delivery, priority restaurant reservations, complimentary shoeshine service, and additional bathroom amenities like massaging shower heads, luxury toiletries, and a hand-held hairdryer.

Three cabins on each ship are wheelchair accessible.

PUBLIC AREAS   Overall, these are elegant yet homey ships, with dark-wood paneling, fluted columns, ornate faux-iron railings, gilt-framed classical paintings, Oriental-style carpets, frilly moldings, marble and brass accents, and deep-hued upholstery, all contributing to a kind of "English inn at sea" look. In the bow, the spacious, woody Horizons lounge has floor-to-ceiling windows and brass telescopes on three sides and is used for dancing in the evenings and for various activities during the day. The 345-seat show lounge offers cabaret and variety acts, musical recitals, magic shows, and comedy; and the smallish but comfortable casino offers blackjack, poker tables, roulette, and slots. The attached Martini Bar has a ridiculously long martini list (29 recipes, and 30 kinds of vodka to choose from!) and is a very relaxing space in the pre-dinner hours, when a pianist plays standards. A jazz band performs here in the evenings.

Another notable space is the comfortable library, decorated in a traditional English style with warm red upholstery, mahogany paneling, and faux garden skylight and marble fireplace.

DINING OPTIONS   The main dining room is an elegant single-level space surrounded on three sides by windows. It's spacious and understated, with simple wood-veneer wall panels, wall sconces, and teal carpeting. Tables seating between two and eight are available, though the smaller arrangements go fast. Just outside the maitre d' station is a cozy bar area where you can have a pre-dinner cocktail while waiting for your dinner companions. The ships' two specialty restaurants, the Polo Grill and Toscana, are both located in the stern on Deck 10, and are decorated to match their cuisine: woody, old-Hollywood decor in Polo and a bright white Mediterranean feel and Roman urns and relief in Toscana. The restaurants serve 96 and 90 guests respectively. On Deck 9, the Terrace serves buffet breakfast, lunch, and dinner, the latter out under the stars, with drink service, Spanish cuisine, and candles flickering in lovely hurricane lamps. It's a very romantic spot if you can time your meal to the sunset.

POOL, FITNESS, SPA & SPORTS FACILITIES   The attractive teak pool deck, dotted with canvas umbrellas, offers a pair of hot tubs and plenty of deck chairs for sunbathing. A small jogging track wraps around the pool one deck above, and the Deck 11 Sun Deck has shuffleboard, more lounging space, and a golf driving cage with a full set of clubs for both right- and left-handed passengers. The fully equipped spa on Deck 9 offers a variety of treatments, including aromatherapy massages, hot-stone treatments, and various wraps and facials. Just forward of the spa there's an outdoor hydrotherapy whirlpool overlooking the bow. A decent-size oceanview gym and beauty salon are attached.

10 Princess Cruises

24305 Town Center Dr., Santa Clarita, CA 91355. © 800/PRINCESS or 661/753-0000. Fax 661/259-3108. www.princess.com.

THE LINE IN A NUTSHELL   With a fleet of mostly large and extra-large megaships, including some of the biggest at sea, L.A.-based Princess offers a quality mainstream cruise experience with a nice balance of tradition and innovation, relaxation and excitement, casualness and glamour. **Sails to:** Caribbean, Panama Canal, Alaska, Mexican Riviera, Hawaii, Canada/New England (plus Europe, South America, Asia, South Pacific, Africa and Transatlantic).

THE EXPERIENCE   If you were to put Royal Caribbean, NCL, and Holland America in a big bowl and mix them together, then add a pinch of both British maritime tradition and California style, you'd come up with Princess. Dining, entertainment, and activities are geared to a wide cross section of cruisers: The more traditional-minded can spend some time in the library, join a bridge tournament, enjoy a traditional dinner in a grand dining room, and then take in a show. Those seeking something different can spin a pottery wheel or work toward their PADI scuba certification, and then dine in an intimate Italian or steakhouse restaurant and take in a set of small-group jazz after. The line's largest vessels are large indeed, exceeded in size only by Royal Caribbean's Voyager-class ships and Cunard's *Queen Mary 2*. Still, they manage to offer intimate spaces for quiet time, as well as lots to do.

Pros

- **Lots of dining choices and flexibility:** Each ship offers two or three main dining rooms plus an intimate alternative restaurant or two and a 24-hour buffet. The line's "Personal Choice" program allows you to dine at a fixed time and place or wing it as you go along.
- **Excellent lounge entertainment:** Princess books top-quality entertainers for its piano lounges and smaller showrooms.
- **On top of trends:** From a wide range of enrichment classes to wireless Internet access fleetwide and online spa reservations for a few ships, Princess doesn't rest on its laurels.

Cons

- **Pottery Barn decor:** More of a qualifier than a con: The line's ships are very pleasant, yes, but the sea of beiges and blues is so safe that it can be a bit of a yawn. Artwork in public areas and cabins tends toward bland.
- **Small gyms:** For such large vessels, the gyms are surprisingly small and can even feel cramped.
- **Pricey ice cream:** Unlike other lines, Princess's parlors have no free ice cream during the day—instead the line sells its house brand that's mixed with a variety of toppings.

PRINCESS: SMART CASUAL

The Princess story goes back to 1962, when company founder Stanley McDonald chartered a vessel called the *Yarmouth* for use as a floating hotel at the Seattle World's Fair. In 1965, he officially started Princess Cruises, naming the company after another chartered vessel, the *Princess Patricia,* which offered cruises between Los Angeles, Alaska, and Mexico's Pacific coast. In 1974, Princess was snapped up by British shipping giant P&O, and later in that decade it got a big boost by having its ships featured in the TV series *The Love Boat.* To this day, Gavin "Captain Stubing" MacLeod acts as occasional pitchman for the line, though the original *Pacific Princess* and *Island Princess,* the twin 640-passenger vessels used in the series, finally left the fleet in 1999 and 2002. (Their names have since been assigned to new vessels.) In April 2003, Princess became the latest in a long string of lines scooped up by Carnival Corporation, the 500-pound gorilla of the cruise world. Will the mergers never end?

Although its ships sail to nearly every destination covered in this book, Princess is particularly strong in **Alaska,** where it's been locked in competition with Holland America for decades. Through its affiliate, Princess Tours, it offers more than 40 different cruisetour itineraries in conjunction with its Gulf of Alaska and Inside Passage voyages, visiting Denali National Park, Fairbanks, the Kenai Peninsula, Wrangell–St. Elias National Park, Canada's Yukon Territory, and distant Prudhoe Bay on Alaska's north coast. Guests on these land tours stay in five Princess-owned wilderness lodges and travel via motor coach and the line's domed Midnight Express train cars.

Since 2004, Princess has also had an increased presence in the **Caribbean.**

PASSENGER PROFILE

The majority of Princess's passengers are in their 50s, 60s, and older, though more and more 30- and 40-somethings (and their families) are sailing these days, particularly during summer school holidays. Overall, Princess passengers are less rowdy and boisterous than those aboard Carnival and not quite as staid as those aboard Holland America. Its ships all have extensive kids' facilities and activities, making them suitable for families, while their balance of formal and informal makes them a good bet for a romantic vacation too, with opportunities for doing your own thing mixed in among more traditional cruise experiences. For serious romance—the movie kind, with the uniformed captain performing the ceremony—look to *Coral, Island, Diamond,* and *Sapphire Princess* and the four Grand-class ships, all of which have wedding chapels on board. *Grand* was the first cruise ship to have one, and now a string of other ships have followed suit, including Royal Caribbean's Voyager class, Carnival's Spirit class, NCL's *Sun* and *Dawn,* and others. Princess's ships, though, remain the only ones where the captain conducts ceremonies.

Compared with other mainstream lines, here's how Princess rates:

	Poor	Fair	Good	Excellent	Outstanding
Enjoyment Factor				✓	
Dining				✓	
Activities				✓	
Children's Program				✓	
Entertainment				✓	
Service				✓	
Worth the Money				✓	

DINING

All Princess ships sailing from the U.S. and Canada offer a wide variety of dining options. In general, though, their cuisine doesn't quite live up to the number and attractiveness of their restaurants. Some dishes exceed expectations and others fall flat, but most sit squarely in the "average to tasty" range, approximately on par with what's served aboard Royal Caribbean and Norwegian.

TRADITIONAL   One place where the line shines is in the flexibility of its Personal Choice Dining program, which allows passengers two options: dining at a set time, with set dining companions, in one of the ship's two or three main restaurants, or just wandering in anytime during a 4½-hour window to be seated by the maitre d'. If you're not sure which option you'll prefer once you're on board, sign up for traditional, since it's easier to switch to anytime dining than it is to go the other way 'round. Anytime dining isn't offered aboard the older *Regal Princess,* which has only one dining room.

Whether you choose traditional or flexible dining, your menu in the main dining room will be the same, with several appetizers, soup and salad, and a choice of five to eight dinner entrees that may include prime rib, lobster, king crab legs, turkey and trimmings, mahimahi filet with dill butter sauce, rack of lamb with Dijon sauce, Cornish hen, sautéed frogs' legs, or duck a l'orange. There are always **healthy choices** and **vegetarian options,** too, plus staples such as broiled Atlantic salmon, grilled chicken, and grilled sirloin steak.

The *Diamond Princess* and *Sapphire Princess,* which debuted in March and June 2004, introduced a new dining concept: one main 500-seat dining room for traditional-seating guests and four smaller, 230-seat restaurants for anytime dining. The twist: Each of those four smaller restaurants serves a different **themed cuisine** (Italian, steakhouse, Southwestern, and Asian) in addition to a standard menu that's served in all five venues. You want steak but the husband's got a taste for five-spice Mandarin duckling? This system caters to you both.

Because passengers are unlikely to have the same waitstaff every night of their cruise, all waiter and assistant-server gratuities are automatically added to passengers' onboard accounts as part of a $10 per-person, per-day total (which also covers your cabin steward). Though this may seem to remove the incentive for staff to go the extra mile, we didn't experience any drop in the quality of dining service on our most recent cruises. All tip amounts can be adjusted up or down by visiting the purser's desk at any time during your cruise. Passengers choosing the flexible option but wishing to be served by the same waiter nightly in the main restaurant can usually be seated in his or her section if they make a special request.

Unlike the no-dress-code dress code that's part of NCL's "Freestyle" dining plan, Princess maintains the tradition of holding 2 formal nights per week, with the other nights designated smart casual, which is defined as "an open-neck shirt and slacks for gentlemen and a dress, skirt and blouse, or trouser suit outfit for ladies." Men, however, should take our advice and pack at least a jacket. Otherwise, you may be down in the gift shop buying one after you realize everyone on the ship except you decided to dress for dinner. Trust us on this: We speak from experience.

All of the restaurants offers a **kids' menu,** which offers goodies such as burgers, hot dogs, fish sticks, chicken fingers, and, of course, PB&J sandwiches; this menu is also offered in the Horizon Court during its sit-down Bistro hours 11pm to 4am nightly (though, shame on you if you're kiddies are up that late!!).

SPECIALTY   Except for *Regal,* all Princess ships that sail from the U.S. feature alternative restaurants: an Italian trattoria and steakhouse restaurant on the Grand-class ships, trattoria and New Orleans–style restaurants on *Coral* and *Island Princess,* and a steakhouse and free sit-down pizzeria on the Sun-class ships. *Diamond* and *Sapphire Princess* also feature the Italian trattoria, with its eight-course meals, in addition to their Italian-themed dining rooms. *Regal* offers a sit-down pizzeria only. Prices are $20 per person at the trattoria and $15 at the steakhouse. See the individual ship reviews later in this section for more details. Reservations are recommended for all the alternative restaurants as seating is limited.

CASUAL   Fleetwide, passengers can choose casual dining at breakfast, lunch, and dinner in the 24-hour, buffet-style Horizon Court restaurant. At breakfast, you'll find the usual: fresh fruit, cold cuts, cereal, steam-table scrambled eggs, cooked-to-order fried eggs, meats, and fish. At lunch, you'll find several salads, fruits, hot and cold dishes, roasts, vegetarian choices, and sometimes sushi. Evenings (until 10pm), the space serves a casual buffet dinner that usually has the same dishes as in the main dining room. From 11pm to 4am it serves a late-night menu of pastas, seafood, poultry, and red meats every night, along with a chef's special of the day. The food here is as good as you'll find in the main dining rooms, and the atmosphere is strictly casual.

Real romantics can have dinner served by a dedicated waiter on their private balcony, at a table set with a tablecloth, hurricane candle lamp, and champagne. While the waiter is setting everything up, you and your significant other can have a complimentary cocktail in one of the ship's bars. The whole thing costs $50 per person (and is currently only offered on the Grand-class ships), but what's money against romance? On all the ships, you can order breakfast served on the balcony for $25 per couple.

SNACKS & EXTRAS   Most of the ships also have a poolside grill or two serving burgers, hot dogs, and pizza; a patisserie offering coffee and pastries; an ice-cream bar serving Häagen-Dazs and Princess's house brand for a charge; and 24-hour room service. (The older *Regal* lacks the pizza and ice cream.)

ACTIVITIES

Like the other big mainstream lines, Princess offers onboard activities designed to appeal to a wide range of ages and tastes. For active types, the Grand-class ships and the *Coral, Island, Diamond,* and *Sapphire Princess* all offer basketball/volleyball courts, 9-hole miniature-golf courses, and virtual-reality golf simulators. The latter are also available on the Sun-class ships. Those who prefer to do everything virtually will like the Grand-class's huge virtual/video game rooms, 24-hour Internet centers, and wireless

Internet access fleetwide in the atria for laptop users (wireless cards are available if you don't have one). The line's enrichment program features quality **computer classes** explaining the basics of Web design, Photoshop, and other topics. There are large, well-stocked libraries on every ship for the less digitally inclined, as well as sedate activities such as bingo, cards, and trivia games; traditional shipboard sports such as Ping-Pong and shuffleboard; and more athletic activities, including aerobics classes and water volleyball. There are also recent-release big-screen movies (shown on giant LCD screens on a top outside deck on the *Caribbean* and *Grand Princess,* with plans for the movie screens to be added to all new ships and probably retro-fitted on the older ones at some point, too), dance lessons, activities designed to part you from your cash (such as art auctions and beauty and spa demonstrations), and others designed to part you from your dignity, such as belly-flop contests and the perennial Newlywed/Not-so-Newlywed game. New family-friendly passenger participation activities fleetwide include an American-Idol-style "Princess Idol" competition. In the Caribbean, guests can earn PADI scuba-diving certification while on board (contact the **PADI New Waves Dive Line** at 🕿 **888/919-9819** or check out **www.newwaves.com**). In Alaska, rangers, naturalists, and guest lecturers present talks and slide shows on such topics as the Iditarod sled-dog race, the wildlife and ecology of Glacier Bay and the Tongass National Forest, oceanography and marine life, glaciers, Native Alaskan cultures, and Alaskan history.

In 2003, the line introduced a fleetwide enrichment program it calls **Scholar-Ship@Sea,** offering classes in cooking, computer skills (such as basic Photoshop and Excel), finance, photography, and (an industry first) a pottery workshop. Large-group seminars are free, while small-group and individual classes carry a charge of around $20 to $25 per person. Charges for paint-your-own ceramics are calculated based on the piece you create.

Princess made waves when it announced in 2004 that it was taking the spa operations on the new *Caribbean Princess* in-house (instead of using London-based Steiner, as most lines do). Princess planned to do some things differently in the ship's Asian-themed Lotus Spa: like not putting the hard sell on clients to buy spa products after a treatment (which Steiner is so famous for) and not using electrical equipment in any treatments (namely Steiner's ultrapopular, but circumspect if you ask us, ionothermie treatments that allegedly reduce cellulite). But alas, after just 1 year running the spa in-house, Princess announced in early 2005 they would be going back to Steiner—turns out they were offered a deal they just couldn't refuse. Oh well, so much for bucking the system. The good news is that the spa still looks great, and innovations such as special treatments targeted at teens (facials, manicures, pedicures, and a special body polish and tanning session) and the online reservations system Princess introduced on the *Caribbean Princess* will remain. Online booking is a real boon considering the long lines that often form at the reservations desk on embarkation day. The reservation system, accessed through the Princess website, is also available for spa treatments on the *Sapphire Princess.*

CHILDREN'S PROGRAM

Princess's "Princess Kids" program offers activities year-round for three age groups: **Princess Pelicans** (ages 3–7), **Princess Pirateers** (ages 8–12), and **teens** (ages 13–17), supervised by a staff of counselors, the size of which varies depending upon the number of children aboard. Each ship has a spacious indoor/outdoor children's playroom with a splash pool, an arts-and-crafts corner, game tables, and computers or games consoles, plus a teen center with computers, video games, a dance floor, and a music system. The two-story playrooms on *Golden* and *Grand* have a large fenced-in outside deck dedicated to kids only, including a teen section with a hot tub and private sunbathing area; the new *Caribbean Princess,* as well as the rest of the Grand-class ships, have a great fenced-in outdoor play space for toddlers; and the new *Coral, Island, Diamond,* and *Sapphire Princess* have a small swimming pool for adults adjacent to the outdoor kids deck, allowing parents to relax while their kids play.

Traditional kids' activities include arts and crafts, scavenger hunts, game tournaments, movies and videos, coloring contests, pizza and ice-cream parties, karaoke, dancing, tours of the galley or behind the scenes at the theater, hula parties complete with grass skirts, and teenage versions of *The Dating Game.*

Learning activities on your cruise may include environmental education programs developed by the California Science Center, National Wildlife Federation, the California Coastal Commission, and the Center for Marine Conservation, which teach about oceans and marine life through printed materials and specially created films. The California Science Center program has activities led by youth counselors who have completed special training. The kids' equivalent of an onboard guest lecturers program is also offered occasionally, allowing children to go stargazing with an astronomer, work on their drawing with an animator, and so on.

Children must be at least 6 months of age to sail. When kids are registered in the youth program, their parents are given pagers so that they can be contacted if their children need them. Parents may also rent walkie-talkies through the purser's desk if they want two-way communication with their kids. Two parent "date nights" let adults have a calm evening while kids dine with counselors in a separate restaurant. Teens have their own group night in one of the main dining rooms, complete with photographs and an after-dinner show. Younger kids can then be taken straight to group babysitting in the children's center (available nightly 10pm–1am for kids 3–12; $5 per hour, per child). Princess does not offer private in-cabin babysitting.

On days in port, Princess offers children's center activities straight through from 8am to 5pm (on sea days the center closes for lunch), allowing parents to explore the port while their kids do their own thing. On Princess's private Bahamas beach, Princess Cays, kids can be checked in at a play area supervised by the shipboard youth staff (for details on Princess Cay see section 1, "The Cruise Lines' Private Islands," in chapter 9). In Alaska, kids ages 6 to 12 and teens ages 13 to 17 can participate in the **Junior Ranger and Teen Explorer program,** a joint effort between Princess and the National Parks Service that uses interactive projects to teach kids about Glacier Bay's natural and cultural history.

While Princess really does offer great facilities and amenities for parents and children, it's not a line that's completely gung ho about only catering to families. Therein lies a big advantage—Princess ships aren't overrun with children. In fact, a Princess reservations agent recently told us that they cap the total number of kids under 18 at about 14% to 15% of a ship's capacity. On a recent cruise Heidi took with her young sons on the 3,100-passenger *Caribbean Princess* (3,782 maximum occupancy), that maxed out at about 600 children, which is a far cry from the 800 to 1,200 kids under 17 that lines like Carnival, Disney, and Royal Caribbean routinely see. Sure, she has kids of her own, but she still doesn't want to cruise on a ship with hordes of other kids. Princess offers a great middle ground.

Princess Fleet Itineraries

Ship	Itineraries
Caribbean Princess	**7-night E. Carib:** Round-trip from Ft. Lauderdale, FL, year-round. **7-night W. Carib:** Round-trip from Ft. Lauderdale, FL, May–Oct 2006.
Coral Princess	**10-night Panama Canal:** Round-trip from Ft. Lauderdale, FL, Oct 2005–Apr 2006. **7-night Gulf of Alaska:** North- or southbound between Vancouver and Whittier/Anchorage, May–Sept 2006.
Dawn Princess	**10-night Mexican Riviera:** Round-trip from San Francisco, CA, Oct 2005–May 2006. **7-night Alaska Inside Passage:** Round-trip from Seattle, WA, May–Sept 2006.
Diamond Princess	**7-night Gulf of Alaska:** North- or southbound between Vancouver and Whittier/Anchorage, May–Sept 2006.
Golden Princess	**7-night Canada/New England:** Round-trip from New York, NY, Oct 2005. **7-night S. Carib:** Round-trip from San Juan, PR, Oct 2005–Apr 2006.
Grand Princess	**7-night W. Carib:** Round-trip from Galveston, TX, Nov 2005–Apr 2006.
Island Princess	**15-night Hawaii:** Round-trip from Los Angeles, CA, Oct 2005–Apr 2006. **7-night Gulf of Alaska:** North- or southbound between Vancouver and Whittier/Anchorage, May–Sept 2006.
Regal Princess	**10-night Mexican Riviera:** Round-trip from San Diego, CA, Oct–Nov 2005. **21-night Panama Canal/Mexican Riviera/Central America:** Round-trip from San Diego, CA, Nov 2005. **12-night Caribbean/Amazon:** Ft. Lauderdale, FL, to Manaus, Brazil, Apr 2006. **10-night Alaska Inside Passage:** Round-trip from San Francisco, CA, May–Sept 2006.
Sapphire Princess	**7-night Mexican Riviera:** Round-trip from Los Angeles, CA, Oct 2005–Apr 2006. **7-night Gulf of Alaska:** North- or southbound between Vancouver and Whittier/Anchorage, May–Sept 2006.
Sea Princess	**14-night Carib:** Round-trip from Ft. Lauderdale, FL, and Barbados, Nov 2005–Apr 2006.
Star Princess	**7-night W. Carib:** Round-trip from Ft. Lauderdale, Oct 2005–Apr 2006.
Sun Princess	**10-night E. & S. Carib:** Round-trip from Ft. Lauderdale, Oct 2005–Apr 2006 (itineraries alternate). **7-night Alaska Inside Passage:** Round-trip from Seattle, WA, May–Sept 2006.

* At press time, details on some fall 2006 itineraries were not yet available.

ENTERTAINMENT

Princess has some of the best entertainment at sea, with variety acts on the ships' main stages ranging from Vegas-style song-and-dance revues and cabaret singers to ventriloquists, acrobats and aerialists, stand-up comics, and New Agey violinists. The Sun-class ships offer entertainment in two showrooms, while the newer vessels offer three shows nightly in their main theater and two smaller venues, plus quieter music in a few lounges, including the popular piano bars. At several other venues, including the Wheelhouse Lounge and the atrium, you'll find other pianists, guitarists, or string quartets providing live background music, and out by the pool a deck band plays at various times during the day. For those who would rather participate, there are regular karaoke nights and a passenger talent show. The ships' **casinos** are among the most comfortable at sea, very large and well laid out.

A raft of new family-friendly passenger participation activities, include an *American Idol*-style "Princess Idol" competition and a reality-TV style make-over show, called "If They Could Sea Me Now."

SERVICE

Overall, service is efficient and passengers rarely have to wait in lines, even in the busy Horizon Court buffet restaurants. As is true generally of staff aboard all the mainstream lines, you can expect them to be friendly, efficient, and happy to help, but not of the level you'll find aboard the luxe lines or at fine hotels. Cabin steward service is the most consistent, with dining service only slightly behind. Bar service can occasionally be on the dodgy side, with language barriers sometimes standing between you and your just-right drink. On the plus side, if you become a regular at a certain spot, staff members are apt to remember what you want after a couple of days.

For suite guests, the line recently announced upgrades to its suite amenities fleetwide, including complimentary Internet access, dry cleaning, laundry, and shoe polishing; complimentary corsage and boutonniere on formal nights; expedited embarkation and debarkation; and other perks, including free portrait sessions with the ship's photographer or en suite afternoon tea. It's good to be king . . . or queen . . . or princess.

Through the line's **Captain's Circle loyalty program,** cruisers who have sailed with Princess before are issued specially colored onboard keycards and cabin-door nameplates (gold after taking one to five cruises, platinum after five, and elite after 15) so that staffers will know to be extra helpful. Platinum Captain's Circle members also get expedited embarkation and free Internet access throughout their cruise, while Elite members receive free laundry and dry-cleaning services, a complimentary wine-tasting class, 10% off in the onboard gift shops and more.

Gratuities for all service personnel are automatically added to passengers' shipboard accounts at the rate of $10 per person per day, as they are now on most lines. Adjustments (up or down) can be made by visiting or calling the purser's desk at any time. Passengers who wish to tip more traditionally—dispensing cash in person—can also make arrangements for this through the desk.

All of the Princess vessels offer laundry and dry-cleaning services, and also have **self-service laundromats.**

The Diamond Class: Diamond Princess • Sapphire Princess

The Verdict

Princess's best ships ever—clubby, intimate public areas plus airy outdoor spaces plus A+ dining options add up to five big stars. These are some of the best megaships out there.

Diamond Princess *(photo: Princess Cruises)*

Specifications

Size (in tons)	116,000	Crew	1,100
Passengers (double occ.)	2,670	Passenger/Crew Ratio	2.4 to 1
Passenger/Space Ratio	43.4	Year Launched	2004
Total Cabins/Veranda Cabins	1,337/748	Last Major Refurbishment	N/A

Frommer's Ratings (Scale of 1–5)

★★★★★

Cabin Comfort & Amenities	4.5	Dining Options	5
Ship Cleanliness & Maintenance	5	Gym, Spa & Sports Facilities	4.5
Public Comfort/Space	5	Children's Facilities	5
Decor	4.5	Enjoyment Factor	5

Princess is on a roll. Just 1 year after it scored big with the beautiful *Coral* and *Island Princess,* the Love Boat line has topped itself by building two of the best new mega-ships to come along in years. Built by Mitsubishi Heavy Industries in Nagasaki, Japan, these two vessels are Princess's biggest ever (and third in the world behind *Queen Mary 2* and Royal Caribbean's Voyager-class ships), but they're also poster children for Princess's philosophy of offering "big ship choice with small ship feel." Outside, they're an appealing update of the Grand class's groundbreaking design, but more sleek, graceful, and streamlined, doing away with the Grand's "shopping cart" look by moving the elevated disco down to deck level. The Disco is now perched just behind the funnel, with its pair of purely decorative "jet turbine" pods, which were introduced on *Coral* and *Island* and have become something of a trademark.

The biggest innovation aboard these ships is in their dining program. Extending Princess's "Personal Choice" program (in which passengers choose either traditional, fixed-seating dining or more unstructured "Anytime" dining), *Diamond* and *Sapphire* offer one traditional restaurant and four themed "Anytime" restaurants, for which passengers on the less structured plan can make reservations each evening (see "Dining," below, for more details).

Among the innovations, expect some of the same features that make the Coral- and Grand-class ships such winners: comfortable cabins (tons of 'em with balconies), woody lounges with hints of seagoing history, understated central atrium lobbies, relaxing indoor/outdoor "Conservatory" pool areas, large Asian-themed spas, and—a personal favorite of ours—covered Promenade decks that wrap around the bow, just below the open top deck. When we sailed, we walked up to this perch late one moon-less night and made a discovery: Standing right in the bow, with the whistling wind drowning out the ship's hum and no light coming from above, behind, or to the sides, the starry sky and dark sea merge and you feel as if you're all alone, flying into outer space. Second star to the right, and straight on till morning . . .

Cabins & Rates

Cabins	Per Diems from	Sq. Ft.	Fridge	Hair Dryer	Sitting Area	TV
Inside	$111	168	yes	yes	no	yes
Outside	$121	183–275	yes	yes	no	yes
Suite	$379	354–1,329*	yes	yes	yes	yes

Includes veranda.

CABINS   Though cabins on *Diamond* and *Sapphire* are a bit bigger than those on the Coral- and Grand-class ships, they still stick close to the Princess family look, with upholstery and walls done in easy-on-the-eyes earth tones and off-whites, all trimmed in butterscotch wood. All have safes, hair dryers, minifridges, and TVs broadcasting one of the widest selections of channels at sea. Standard inside and outside cabins are smaller than those aboard the newer Holland America and Carnival ships, but are still comfortable and stylish, and more than 70% of outside cabins have verandas. Like the Coral ships, balconies on these vessels are tiered, avoiding the slab-sided "hotel at sea" look of so many megaships and assuring direct sunlight for those on Decks 8 and 9 (where most of the popular minisuites are located), but, unfortunately, also assuring there's no privacy on those lower balconies—folks standing on the ones above can look right down on you. Standard cabin bathrooms have smallish shower stalls and adequate counter space.

Minisuites provide substantially more space without jumping into the cost stratosphere; have those big, less-than-private balconies; and offer sizable sitting areas with sofa beds and two televisions, one TV facing the sitting area and the other the bed (cheaper and less bothersome, the line told us, than installing a lazy Susan to let one TV swivel). They're ideal for families with children. Bathrooms have bathtubs and more counter space than in standard cabins. Storage space in both standard outsides and minisuites is more than adequate, with a large shelved closet and open-sided clothes rack facing a small dressing alcove by the bathroom door. Sixteen full suites have curtained-off sitting and sleeping areas, very large balconies, complimentary stocked minibar, robes, whirlpool tubs and separate showers in the bathroom, and a walk-in closet. Suite guests are also on the receiving end of the new slew of perks highlighted in the "Service" section above.

Twenty-seven cabins on each ship are wheelchair accessible.

PUBLIC AREAS These ships are huge—a fact you'll learn the first time you have to walk from one end to the other to retrieve something you forgot in your cabin. On the other hand, when you're sitting in one of their cozy lounges or bars, you might well think you're on a 40,000-ton ship, rather than one three times that size. It's an appealing combination, giving passengers a large ship's range of options but packaging it all in a more personal, human-scaled package. You don't feel like you're lost in the crowd.

Most public rooms on these ships are set on Decks 6 and 7. Toward the bow, the two-deck Princess Theater is the main show space, with tiers of upholstered theater seats (with little cocktail tables that fold out of their armrests, airline style) and a pair of opera boxes to either side of the large stage. It's a very minimalist room, and a very appealing one, putting the emphasis on the stage rather than distracting with fanciful decor. Just outside the entrance is the clubby Churchill's, a classically decorated cigar bar with TVs for sports. You'll also find a multipurpose entertainment lounge called Club Fusion, used principally for games (think bingo and "Princess Idol" talent shows) and evening music. Down a spiral staircase in the back of the room, you'll find one of our favorite spaces, the very small, cozy Wake View Bar, a classy nook full of dark wood, leather chairs, and paintings depicting turn-of-the-19th-century tobacconists. TVs are tuned to sports (though the sound is often off), and six portholes overlook the namesake wake. Few people seem to venture down here, so let's keep it to ourselves, okay?

At midships are two of Princess's signature lounge spaces: the English-adventurer-themed Explorer's Lounge and the ocean-liner-themed Wheelhouse Bar, the former a secondary show lounge for comedians, impressionists, and other small-scale entertainment; the latter the prime space aboard for elegant music, with a jazz combo playing in the evenings. Decor matches the name for both rooms, with Egyptian art, jungle-pattern carpeting, clubby furniture, and faux Moorish screens in Explorer's, and leather couches, dark wood, brass candlestick sconces, and paintings of old P&O liners in Wheelhouse. There's dancing here, but the "I love the nightlife, I like to boogie" crowd is more likely to be up in the top-deck disco, the highest point of the ship, with a balcony looking back over the stern if you want to head out for air or romance. (Or a smoke.)

Explorer's jungle theme carries over into the ships' casinos, with their tree-trunk pillars and leafy ceilings. Next door, the three-story atrium is admirably restrained, with lots of creamy marble and wood, understated grillwork art fronting the atrium elevators, and musicians performing throughout the day. Opening off the space are the relaxing library, the charming writing room (how old-fashioned!), several shops, a coffee bar, and Crooners, a Rat Pack–themed bar serving 56 different martini recipes in two sizes: the standard "Sinatra" and the supersize "Deano" *[sic]*. Clusters of low-slung wicker-frame chairs along the windows give a '50s rumpus room effect. Very slinky.

On Deck 7, the ships' Internet Cafes are notable not only for being large and exceedingly stylish (probably the nicest Internet centers we can name on a ship), but for also being cafes in more than just name: A bar toward the back of the room dispenses gourmet coffee for a few bucks, along with free croissants and sweet rolls. Passengers who bring their laptops can connect wirelessly here, as well as in the atrium. Four computer terminals are also located in the atrium's library, and computer classes are generally held in the ship's wedding chapel, just across from the Wheelhouse Bar.

For kids, *Diamond*'s and *Sapphire*'s Fun Zone centers are divided into four separate and sizable rooms, segregating kids by age. Younger tots get a climbing maze, flower-backed chairs, toys, computers, and a great, cushiony amphitheater for watching movies. Teens get a sort of Austin Powers–looking room, brightly colored and looking much like a normal adult bar on many less restrained ships. ("That was on purpose," one Princess exec told us. "What teen wants to be treated like a kid?")

DINING OPTIONS   Passengers opting for traditional dining take their meals in the 518-seat International Dining Room, with its simple but elegant wood-panel walls and classical paintings. "Anytime" diners get four restaurants, each with music and decor to match its theme: Japanese paintings and gorgeous framed kimonos in Pacific Moon (Asian); Anasazi themes and grayed wood floors in Santa Fe (Southwestern); 18th-century European style in Vivaldi (Italian); and totally classic dark wood, sturdy chairs, and subdued lighting gleaming off stainless architectural fixtures in Sterling (steakhouse). Don't miss the onion rings with cayenne sauce in Sterling. Yum.

In addition to the Asian, Southwestern, Italian, and steakhouse menus in these four restaurants, each also lets guests order from the same shipwide menu of the day, which is the same as is served in the main traditional restaurant. Want more? Anyone dining in any restaurant can request a special item from any of the others. And more? Guests in the traditional restaurant are offered the menus of the specialty restaurants throughout the week. Goodbye arguments about where to dine, hello choice.

Guests wanting to gorge long and hard should make a reservation at Sabatini's, the extra-cost ($20) Italian trattoria, which serves eight-course, 2½-hour meals. For ultra-casual dining, head to the Horizon Court buffet.

POOL, FITNESS, SPA & SPORTS FACILITIES   Like most megaships, *Diamond* and *Sapphire* have two pools at midships, a partying main pool out in the sun and a secondary "Conservatory" space with a retractable roof for bad weather. On these vessels, the latter has a large pool, two hot tubs, and a balcony that does double duty as sunning space and venue for the line's pottery-making classes. Our favorite outdoor spaces on board, though, are in the stern, where four decks descend in curved, horseshoelike tiers, creating a multilevel resort with two pools, two hot tubs, two bars, and a magnificent view of the ship's wake.

Another pool, this one an adults-only resistance pool for swimming laps in place, is set in a cleft just outside the large, well-appointed spa, totally minimal in its elegant Asian theme, with a great suite of steam rooms and stone lounging chairs for guests to use before or after their treatment. Next door, the gym is one of the few sour notes on board—well-stocked (and with little TVs on all the aerobics machines), but still inadequately small considering the number of people aboard. Same deal on most Princess ships. When we sailed, it got crowded often. A large aerobics studio is attached, offering spinning, yoga, and other aerobics and fitness classes ($10 for most of them).

Out on Deck 16, at the top of a very quietly marked stairway and almost completely shielded from wind and view, is a small miniature-golf course. More serious golfers can play illusory courses at a virtual-reality center farther forward, near a nicely designed covered and netted sports court suitable for basketball and volleyball.

The Coral Class: Coral Princess • Island Princess

The Verdict

Beautiful, spacious, and at the same time surprisingly intimate, *Coral* and *Island* offer great onboard learning experiences, a nice range of entertainment options and venues, and interesting itineraries.

Coral Princess *(photo: Matt Hannafin)*

Specifications

Size (in tons)	91,627	Crew	981
Passengers (double occ.)	1,970	Passenger/Crew Ratio	2 to 1
Passenger/Space Ratio	46.5	Year Launched	2003
Total Cabins/Veranda Cabins	987/727	Last Major Refurbishment	N/A

Frommer's Ratings (Scale of 1–5)   ★★★★½

Cabin Comfort & Amenities	5	Dining Options	4
Ship Cleanliness & Maintenance	5	Gym, Spa & Sports Facilities	4
Public Comfort/Space	5	Children's Facilities	4
Decor	4	Enjoyment Factor	4.5

Further refining Princess's vision of mega-size ships with an intimate feel, *Coral Princess* and *Island Princess* are some of the loveliest vessels to debut in the past few years. Outside, there are balconies on some 83% of their outside cabins, but their tiered design is a vast improvement over the typical megaship "wall of balconies" look, contributing to clean and flowing profiles. Up top, their futuristic-looking jet-engine-style decorative funnels give you the impression the ships are going to fly right out of the water and into orbit.

Built to juuuuussst be able to squeeze through the Panama Canal (with approximately 2 ft. of space on each side), these ships are extremely spacious and well laid out, and never feel crowded even when full—though they're a fifth larger than the line's Sun-class ships, they carry only 20 more passengers apiece based on double occupancy, meaning more room for you. Understated interiors are both classic and modern, with Internet centers and Times Square–style news tickers right around the corner from woody, almost Edwardian lounges. Our favorite spaces: the clubby Wheelhouse Bar for a before-dinner drink; the bar at the New Orleans–themed Bayou Restaurant for jazz till 'round midnight; the Lotus Pool, a peaceful solarium done up in Balinese style, where your book will have to be damn good to keep you from dozing off; the Princess Theater in mid- or late afternoon on sea days, for recent-release big-screen movies; and the remarkable Universe Lounge, a truly innovative performance space.

Cabins & Rates

Cabins	Per Diems from	Sq. Ft.	Fridge	Hair Dryer	Sitting Area	TV
Inside	$137	160	yes	yes	no	yes
Outside	$130	168–232	yes	yes	no	yes
Suite	$332	323–591*	yes	yes	yes	yes

* Includes veranda.

CABINS   Decor sticks to Princess's fleetwide standard, with upholstery and walls done in easy-on-the-eyes earth tones and off-whites, all trimmed in butterscotch wood. All have safes, hair dryers, minifridges, and TVs broadcasting one of the widest selections of channels at sea. Inside and standard outside cabins are serviceable, but don't expect much room to stretch out—at 160 and 168 square feet respectively, they're on the low end of average in the mainstream category, much larger than on Princess's Sun-class ships and some ships in the Costa and NCL fleets but nowhere near the 185 to 195 square feet you get with the newer Carnival, Holland America, and Disney ships. Private balconies are, to large measure, not *exactly* private: They're set up in descending tiers—a positive in terms of soaking up the sun, a negative if your idea of fun is sitting out there in your birthday suit. Cabins E311 to E623 on Emerald Deck have views obstructed by dangling lifeboats, a fact that's clearly stated in the line's brochures. Standard cabin bathrooms have smallish shower stalls and adequate counter space.

Minisuites provide substantially more space without jumping into the cost stratosphere, and have larger balconies and sizable sitting areas with sofa beds and two televisions, one facing the sitting area and the other the bed—an odd touch since there's no partition, creating total cacophony if you have both on simultaneously. Bathrooms have bathtubs and more counter space than in standard cabins. Storage space in both standard outsides and minisuites is more than adequate, with a large shelved closet and open-sided clothes rack facing a small dressing alcove by the bathroom door. Sixteen full suites have curtained-off sitting and sleeping areas, very large balconies, complimentary stocked minibars, robes, whirlpool tubs and separate showers in the bathroom, and a walk-in closet. Suite guests are also on the receiving end of the new slew of perks highlighted in the "Service" section above.

Twenty cabins on each ship are wheelchair accessible.

PUBLIC AREAS Layout is one of the areas in which these vessels really shine, with decks and public areas arranged so it's always easy to find your way around. Most indoor public spaces are on Decks 6 and 7, starting with the large Princess Theater in the bow. Unlike the ornately decorated two- and three-deck theaters on many new ships, this is a classic sloping one-level space, decorated with no theme whatsoever. You get a good view from every one of the comfortable theater seats, which have little flip-up tables in their arms to hold drinks or, when the room is used for lectures or other enrichment activities, your notebook. Farther aft, the Explorer's Lounge is a smaller-scale show lounge for comedians, karaoke, game shows, and dancing, decorated to evoke the romantic European explorers of the 19th century, with vaguely Islamic tile motifs, African and Asian art pieces, primitivist exotic paintings on the walls, and a dark, woody atmosphere. Important sports events are broadcast here on multiple large screens. In the very stern, the new Universe Lounge is a truly innovative multipurpose space, hosting TV-style cooking demonstrations (with a full kitchen onstage), computer classes (with hookups for 50 computers around the room), lectures, and full-blown production performances on three low interconnected stages, which revolve and rise and segment and contort and do more things than you think a stage could—it's a regular three-ring circus. Shows are tailored to utilize all these options, with much of the action taking place at ground level for a true floor-show feel.

Some standout bars and lounges include the maritime-themed Wheelhouse Bar, an intimate spot decorated in classic dark woods, with heavy leather and corduroy armchairs and love seats, faux marble pillars, domed ceiling lights, and small end-table lamps. In the evening, a small band performs smooth jazz and pop numbers for dancing, and some afternoons the ships' string quartets perform classical repertoire. At one entrance to the lounge, a small museum displays memorabilia from P&O history, including (on *Coral*) an original brass bell from the SS *Oronsay,* children's dolls from the SS *Orsova* and SS *Strathnaver,* postcards sent from the legendary SS *Canberra,* and so on. Nearby, the low-key four-deck atrium is surrounded by the ships shops; the Internet center with its news ticker; Churchill's cigar lounge, a cozy room with big windows, armchairs and sofas seating just 10 people, and a humidor under a portrait of the room's namesake; and Crooner's, a Rat Pack–themed piano bar with a Vegas/martini vibe. A real live crooner performs at the piano each evening.

One level down, the ship's library and card room are both exceptionally large and comfortable, though the layout—with entrances both from the atrium and from the midships elevators/stair tower—means that people often use the rooms as a passageway, adding more bustle than we'd like in a library. Themed casinos (London on *Coral,* Paris on *Island*) and a wedding chapel round out the adult public room offerings, while at the stern on Deck 12, there's the bright and very kid-scaled Fun Zone and Pelican's Playhouse children's center and smallish Off Limits teen center, with computers and a dance floor. Outside are a children's play area and the small Pelican Pool. The ship's bright pottery studio is hidden away back here as well, giving it the feel of a playroom for grown-ups.

DINING OPTIONS To accommodate Princess's Personal Choice concept, two similar dining rooms—the Provence and the Bordeaux—are dedicated to traditional fixed-seating dining and to Anytime Personal Choice dining, respectively. Both single-level rooms are understated and spacious, with lots of elbowroom (except, that is, in the unusually narrow arm chairs at some tables).

There are two specialty restaurants aboard. Sabatini's Trattoria ($20 per person) is a traditional Italian restaurant with an airy decor, open kitchen, cushioned wicker balloon-back chairs, and Italian scenes in faux tilework on some walls. Dinners here are eight-course extravaganzas, with all dishes brought automatically—you just select your main course. Brunches here are similarly over-the-top, with a seafood buffet and a large selection of egg dishes. Next door, the Bayou Cafe and Steakhouse ($15 per person) is a New Orleans–themed restaurant with a subdued, woody ambience, faux brick walls, lantern lighting, and primitivist New Orleans murals on the walls. Dinners here include barbecued alligator ribs appetizers and main courses like seafood gumbo, fried catfish, grilled jumbo prawns, and chicken-and-chorizo jambalaya. Steak lovers can also be sated with varieties from New York Strip to porterhouse. A jazz trio plays during dinner, then continues on till midnight for patrons of the attached bar. Tables are sprinkled with Mardi Gras beads for extra atmosphere.

The ships' 24-hour Horizon Court buffet restaurants are comfortable enough, though the circular layout of the food stations—and no clear path through them—often leads to light chaos. Overlooking the main pool, the Grill serves burgers, dogs, and the like in the afternoon, with very good pizza available one deck down (just forward of the pool) and extra-cost Häagen-Dazs and fresh juices available aftward at the Lotus Pool's ice-cream bar and juice bar. Inside, at the bottom of the atrium, La Patisserie is a pleasant lounge/cafe serving regular coffee free and specialty coffees at extra cost, with cookies and sweets free for the taking. As the room is almost at sea level, it's a great spot from which to watch the waves go by, and it's worth spending at least a minute here as your ship goes through the Panama Canal: The Canal walls are literally only a couple feet away. It's a startling picture.

POOL, FITNESS, SPA & SPORTS FACILITIES   The ships' main pool areas are spacious but surprisingly plain, with a main pool and three large hot tubs surrounded by sunning areas. A steel-drum duo performs on a tiny, low-key stage at one end during the day. Moving toward the stern, the Lotus Pool is a much more interesting area, decorated with a Balinese motif that gives a sense of tranquillity (though if there are lots of kids aboard, that tranquillity probably won't last). Stylish wooden deck chairs here (and more traditional "Royal Teak" ones on the wraparound Promenade Deck) are much more classy than the white plastic loungers around the main pool. A sliding-glass roof protects the Lotus Pool during inclement weather. Up on the Sports Deck there's a wading pool for adults.

Fitness facilities include a surprisingly small gym, though reasonably equipped, plus a relatively large separate aerobics room. Up on the top decks there is a basketball/volleyball court and a computerized golf simulator. There's also a 9-hole miniature-golf course up there, and though it's in the open air you have to enter through a windowless wooden door that makes it look permanently closed. It's not; just go on in.

In the stern on Deck 14, the Balinese-themed Lotus Spa offers the usual massage, mud, and beauty treatments, and features a thermal suite (a unisex room offering various heat treatments) and a lovely seaview salon. For what it's worth—because the spa is run by Steiner (the company that runs almost all cruise ship spas) and since personnel change regularly—we had one of our best cruise ship massages on *Coral Princess,* an almost painful deep-tissue sports massage that left us feeling completely loose and refreshed. On the downside, spa staff repeatedly suggested we sign up for a hot-stone massage or "Asian Lotus Ritual" instead, even though we showed up at the reservation desk having already decided what we wanted. Ostensibly, this was because the sports massage can be very painful (which it can), but could it be just a coincidence that the two therapies they suggested were $50 and $100 more expensive? Hmmm . . .

The Grand Class: Grand Princess • Golden Princess • Star Princess • Caribbean Princess

Grand Princess *(photo: Princess Cruises)*

The Verdict

These huge, well-accoutered vessels are very easy to navigate, never feel as crowded as you'd expect, and are amazingly intimate for their size.

Specifications

Size (in tons)		Crew	
Grand/Golden/Star	109,000	*Grand/Golden/Star*	1,100
Caribbean	116,000	*Caribbean*	1,200
Passengers (double occ.)		Passenger/Crew Ratio	
Grand/Golden/Star	2,600	*Grand/Golden/Star*	2.4 to 1
Caribbean	3,100	*Caribbean*	2.6 to 1
Passenger/Space Ratio		Year Launched	
Grand/Golden/Star	42	*Grand Princess*	1998
Caribbean	37.5	*Golden Princess*	2001
Total Cabins/Veranda Cabins		*Star Princess*	2002
Grand/Golden/Star	1,300/710	*Caribbean Princess*	2004
Caribbean	1,557/881	Last Major Refurbishment	N/A

Frommer's Ratings (Scale of 1–5)   ★★★★½

Cabin Comfort & Amenities	5	Dining Options	4
Ship Cleanliness & Maintenance	4	Gym, Spa & Sports Facilities	5
Public Comfort/Space	5	Children's Facilities	4
Decor	4	Enjoyment Factor	4.5

When she was launched, the 109,000-ton, 2,600-passenger *Grand Princess* was the world's biggest and most expensive cruise ship, costing $450 million, but things change fast: Today, even if you stacked the line's smallest ship, the *Pacific Princess,* on top of her, she still wouldn't be as big as Royal Caribbean's Voyager-class ships, and even they've now been superceded by Cunard's *Queen Mary 2.* Still, *Grand, Golden,* and *Star Princess,* and their slightly larger sister *Caribbean Princess* are massive ships, with 18 decks soaring up to their space-age discos, which hover in the air at their very stern, stretching from port to starboard and resembling the handle on a giant shopping cart. The ships look like nothing else at sea, and though they give an impression of immensity from the outside, inside they're extremely well laid out, very easy to navigate, and surprisingly cozy. In fact, their public areas never feel as crowded as you'd think they would with almost 4,000 people aboard, including passengers and crew. The ultramodern ships even manage to offer a few areas with traditional accents that recall a grander era of sea travel, including the clubby and dimly lit Explorer's and Wheelhouse lounges and the elegant three-story atrium, where classical string quartets perform on formal nights and during embarkation.

Caribbean Princess, which launched in spring 2004, is a slightly larger version of the Grand-class concept (similar layout, but with an extra deck), and sports some new features, including a cafe serving Caribbean dishes. A 113,000-ton sister to *Caribbean Princess* (though not an identical sister) will be delivered in May 2006 and named *Crown Princess* after a vessel that debuted in 1990 and left the Princess fleet in 2002. Like *Caribbean Princess,* she'll sail full-time in the Caribbean, offer feature films on a giant outdoor screen, and serve Caribbean snacks from the Café Caribe buffet. New attractions include more dining venues (an international cafe, a wine and seafood bar, pub fare in the Wheelhouse Bar, and a steak and seafood house) and a "piazza-style" atrium that the line describes as having a street cafe environment. Another sister (again, not identical) to the *Caribbean Princess* is on order at Fincantieri's Monfalcone yard for a spring 2007 delivery; the $525-million ship will be 116,000 tons.

All the Grand-class ships are too big to squeeze through the Panama Canal, so they tend to remain in the Caribbean, sometimes heading to Europe for the summer.

Cabins & Rates

Cabins	Per Diems from	Sq. Ft.	Fridge	Hair Dryer	Sitting Area	TV
Inside	$82	160	yes	yes	no	yes
Outside	$97	165–232	yes	yes	no	yes
Suite	$302	323–1,314*	yes	yes	yes	yes

* *Includes veranda.*

CABINS Though cabins on these vessels are divided into some 35 categories, there are actually fewer than 10 configurations. For the most part, the category differences reflect location—such as amidships versus aft. Cabins are richly decorated in light hues and earth tones, and all have safes, hair dryers, minifridges, and TVs. Storage is adequate and features more closet shelves than drawer space. Cabin balconies are tiered so they get more sunlight, but this also means your neighbors above can look down at you. Be discreet.

A standard outside cabin without a balcony, such as categories F and FF, ranges from 165 to 210 square feet, while insides, such as category JJ, measure 160 square feet. Balcony cabins range from 165 to 257 square feet, including the balcony. At 324 square feet, including the balcony, the 180 minisuites on each vessel are smaller than the 32 minisuites on the Sun-class ships, but are ultra comfortable and offer a roomy sitting area with a full-size pull-out couch, two televisions, minifridge, large bathroom with full tub and shower, generous closet and drawer space, terry robes, and private balconies. When Heidi sailed with her young sons on the *Caribbean Princess* recently, she had two cribs set up in the living area, and there was still plenty of space for playing; storage was so plentiful that, even with the copious gear toddlers require, much of it was left unused.

Two Grand Suites measure 782 square feet and feature all the above amenities plus a hot tub and two bathrooms, one for the toilet, the other for a shower and separate whirlpool tub. There are two 607-square foot family suites that can sleep up to eight, with two bathrooms. Minibars in the suites are stocked once on a complimentary basis with soda, bottled water, beer, and liquor. Suite guests are also on the receiving end of the new slew of perks highlighted in the "Service" section above.

Lifeboats partially or completely obstruct the views from most cabins on Emerald Deck. More than 600 cabins can accommodate a third passenger in an upper berth. Each ship has 28 wheelchair-accessible cabins.

PUBLIC AREAS Even sailing with a full load of passengers (as many as 3,100 on *Grand, Golden,* and *Star* if all additional berths in every cabin are filled, and a whopping 3,782 on *Caribbean Princess*), you'll wonder where everyone is. These are huge ships with a not-so-huge feeling. Because of their smart layout, six dining venues, expansive outdoor deck space divided into four main sections, multiple sports facilities, four pools, and nine hot tubs, passengers are dispersed rather than concentrated into one or two main areas.

Coupled with this smart layout is Princess's pleasing (if not a bit too plain), contemporary decor. Public areas are done up in caramel-colored wood tones and pleasing color schemes of warm blue, teal, and rust, with some brassy details and touches of marble.

While the decor is soothing, the entertainment is pretty hot. Gamblers will love each ship's sprawling and dazzling casino, among the largest at sea at 13,500 square feet. Three main entertainment venues include a well-equipped two-story theater for big Vegas-style musical revues, a second one-level show lounge for smaller-scale entertainment such as hypnotists and singers (this room has major sightline problems caused by structural columns and a shallow pitch in the seating), and the travel-themed Explorer's Club, with murals of Egyptian and African scenes and a band, variety performer, or karaoke nightly. There's also the clubby, old-world Wheelhouse Lounge, offering laid-back pre- and post-dinner dancing in an elegant setting, as well as a woody sports bar and a wine bar selling caviar by the ounce and vintage wine, champagne, and iced vodka by the glass.

Skywalkers multilevel disco/observation lounge, sequestered 150 feet above the ship's stern like a high-tech tree house, is a unique spot offering floor-to-ceiling windows with two impressive views: forward for a look over the ship itself, or back toward the sea and the giant vessel's very impressive wake. It's well positioned away from any cabins (so the noise won't keep anyone up), and there's a funky moving sidewalk that gets you there—it's our favorite disco at sea. Check out the view at sunset.

For kids, the indoor/outdoor Fun Zone kids' play area has tons of games, toys, and computers—the jewel for Heidi, a mother of toddlers, is the outdoor, fenced-in play area. Nearly always deserted (we're told there are rarely more than 10 children under 3 on board any given cruise), with its fleet of three wheelers and minibasketball setup, it's an awesome place to let your little ones run free while you sit on the sidelines and relax. There's a kiddie pool in the vicinity. A separate teen center has several computers, plus video games, a dance floor, and a sound system. On the *Grand* and *Golden,* there's also a neat teens-only sunbathing area with deck chairs and a hot tub, as well as a cavernous and truly amazing arcade, with hang gliding, downhill skiing, fly-fishing, motorcycle-riding machines, virtual-reality rides, and dozens more.

Each ship also has a library, a small writing room, a card room, and a large Internet center. There's an attractive wedding chapel where the captain himself performs about six or seven bona fide, legal marriages every cruise.

DINING OPTIONS   The ships each have three pleasant, one-story main dining rooms, laid out on slightly tiered levels. By way of some strategically placed waist-high dividers, they feel cozy, although the ceilings are a tad on the low side. The 24-hour Horizon Court casual restaurant offers buffet-style breakfasts and lunches, and is designed to feel much cozier than it actually is. With clusters of buffet stations serving stir-fry, beef, turkey, pork, and lots of fruit, salads, cheeses, and more, lines are kept to a minimum and you're hardly aware of the space's enormity. This restaurant turns into a sit-down bistro from 10pm to 4am, with the same dinner menu each night. If you like the idea of New York strip sirloin at midnight, this is the place to go.

For a more intimate yet still casual meal, there are two alternative, reservations-required restaurants. Sabatini's specializes in Italian cuisine, featuring an eight-course menu emphasizing seafood—you better be hungry. Service is first-rate and the food is decent ($20 per person). The second venue is the Sterling Steakhouse ($15 per person), where you can choose your favorite cut of beef from the "Sterling Steakhouse" brand and have it cooked to order. Another alternative is the Café Caribe, a themed buffet carved out of the Horizon Court, serving Caribbean specialties such as jerk chicken, grilled Caribbean rock lobster, whole roast suckling pig, Guiana pepper pots and curries, and paella-style prawns (no cover charge). Musicians play Caribbean music, and passengers can order their meal cooked to taste at the cafe's open kitchen.

POOL, FITNESS, SPA & SPORTS FACILITIES   The Grand-class ships have around 1.7 acres of open deck space, so it's not hard to find a quiet place to soak in the sun. Our favorite spot on a hot, humid day is portside aft on the deck overlooking the swimming pool, where the tail fin vent blows cool air. It's like having an outdoor air-conditioner.

The ships have four great swimming pools, with all except *Caribbean Princess* including one with a retractable glass roof for inclement weather. Another aft, under the disco, feels miles from the rest of the ship, while outside the spa a resistance pool allows you to swim steadily against the current. The fourth pool is for kids. Other recreational offerings include a Sports Deck with a jogging track and paddle tennis, a fun 9-hole putting green, and computerized simulated golf. A new feature—introduced aboard *Caribbean Princess* and later retrofitted to *Grand Princess* and *Star Princess*—is a 300-square-foot outdoor LED movie screen for watching movies under the stars. You can reserve deck chairs for evening feature films, and, yes, there's popcorn (free) and Raisinettes (for a price). It's really great fun.

Spa, gym, and beauty-parlor facilities are located in a large, almost separate part of each ship, surrounding the lap pool and its tiered, amphitheater-style wooden benches. As is the case fleetwide with Princess, the oceanview gym is surprisingly small for a ship of this size, although there's an unusually large aerobics floor. For a short while, the Lotus spas on the *Caribbean* and *Sapphire Princess* were operated in-house, though before this book went to press, Princess turned them back to Steiner (oh well . . . economies of scale always win). A company spokeswoman tells us some of the innovations of the Lotus spa will remain, including online spa reservations (make your booking weeks or months before your cruise and never have to wait in line!) and the Asian decor, featuring black lacquer countertops and Oriental-style furniture. Another thing that will remain, as it does on all of the Grand-class ships, is the spas' unfortunate location: underneath the Sports Deck. Hope there's no basketball game going on during your shiatsu appointment.

The Sun Class: Sun Princess •
Dawn Princess •
Sea Princess

The Verdict

These relaxed, pretty ships are pleasant and comfortable, great for families and for grown-ups who like to enjoy the good life without too much flash.

Sun Princess *(photo: Princess Cruises)*

Specifications

Size (in tons)	77,000	Year Launched	
Passengers (double occ.)	1,950	*Sun Princess*	1995
Passenger/Space Ratio	39.5	*Dawn Princess*	1997
Total Cabins/Veranda Cabins	975/410	*Sea Princess*	1998
Crew	900	Last Major Refurbishment	N/A
Passenger/Crew Ratio	2.2 to 1		

Frommer's Ratings (Scale of 1–5)   ★★★★

Cabin Comfort & Amenities	4	Dining Options	4
Ship Cleanliness & Maintenance	4	Gym, Spa & Sports Facilities	4
Public Comfort/Space	5	Children's Facilities	4
Decor	5	Enjoyment Factor	4

Here's the scoop on *Sea Princess, Dawn Princess,* and *Sun Princess:* They're just like all the other Princess ships, only less so—being among the line's oldest vessels (though still only 8, 9, and 11 years old), they're the ones that led the way toward the design Princess has used ever since. They're pretty ships, with a decor that mixes classic and modern, using materials such as varnished hardwoods, marble, etched glass, granite, and textured fabrics. The look doesn't sock you between the eyes with its daring; in fact, it's a bit plain-Jane—comfortable and quiet, and (so far) aging gracefully. Light color schemes predominate, with lots of beiges, and their layout is very easy to navigate. By the end of the first day you'll know where everything is.

Cabins & Rates

Cabins	Per Diems from	Sq. Ft.	Fridge	Hair Dryer	Sitting Area	TV
Inside	$101	135–148	yes	yes	no	yes
Outside	$114	147–160	yes	yes	no	yes
Suite	$322	365–678*	yes	yes	yes	yes

* Includes veranda.

CABINS   Though cabins on these vessels are divided into some 28 categories, there are actually fewer than 10 configurations—for the most part, the category differences reflect location (amidships versus aft, and so on), and thus price. More than 400 cabins on each vessel boast private balconies, though at about 3×8½ feet, they're small.

And that leads to our main point: The staterooms on these ships are cramped. Standard outside cabins, such as categories BC and BD, are 178 square feet including their balconies, while Carnival's standards, by comparison, are nearly 186 square feet without balconies—on these ships, what little balcony space you gain is deducted from your room.

Guests in each ship's six suites enjoy as much as a sprawling 678 square feet of space, as well as robes to use while aboard (regular cabin passengers can request them, too) and minibars stocked once on a complimentary basis with soda, bottled water, beer, and liquor. Suite guests are also on the receiving end of the new slew of perks highlighted in the "Service" section above. The 32 minisuites on each ship are really nice, with a separate bedroom area divided from the sitting area by a curtain. Each has a pullout sofa, a chair and desk, a minifridge, two TVs, a walk-in closet, and a whirlpool tub and shower in a separate room from the toilet and sink.

All cabins have minifridges, safes, TVs, and hair dryers, and 300 will accommodate third passengers in upper berths. Nineteen cabins on each vessel are wheelchair accessible.

PUBLIC AREAS   These ships have a decidedly unglitzy decor that relies on lavish amounts of wood, glass, marble, and collections of original paintings, statues, and lithographs. The one-story showrooms offer unobstructed views from every seat, and several spaces in the back are reserved for wheelchair-users. The sound systems are good, and lighting is state-of-the-art. The smaller Vista Lounge also presents entertainment, with good sightlines and comfortable cabaret-style seating. The elegant, nautical-motif Wheelhouse Bar is done in warm, dark-wood tones and features small bands, sometimes with a vocalist; it's the perfect spot for pre- or post-dinner drinks.

There's a dark and sensuous disco; a bright, spacious casino; a wine bar selling caviar by the ounce and vintage wine, champagne, and iced vodka by the glass; and lots of little lounges for an intimate rendezvous, such as the Atrium Lounge and a second lounge located on the same deck, immediately aft.

DINING OPTIONS   In these ships' two dining rooms there are no dramatic, sweeping staircases for making an entrance; instead, the rooms feel intimate, broken up by dividers topped with frosted glass. Each ship also has two alternative dining venues. The sit-down pizzeria on Dolphin Deck is open approximately 11am to 2:30pm and 7pm to 1am for casual and quiet dining, with tables seating two, four, and six. Sorry, no takeout or delivery. The Sterling Steakhouse is set out of the wind just outside the Horizon Court, overlooking the main pool. Passengers can choose from four cuts of beef—rib-eye, New York strip, porterhouse, and filet mignon—with starters such as chili, blooming onion, jalapeño poppers, and fresh Caesar salad, plus the usual sides of baked potato or fries, sautéed mushrooms, creamed spinach, and corn on the cob. It's open from 6 to 10pm, reservations are recommended, and the cover charge is $15 per person. On Alaska sailings, the steakhouse option is moved inside to one side of the 24-hour Horizon Court buffet restaurant, which also offers an ultracasual option for all meals, including sit-down bistro-style dinners from 11pm to 4am.

POOL, FITNESS, SPA & SPORTS FACILITIES   The pool decks on these ships are well laid out, with three adult pools (one of them in the stern), one kids' wading pool, and hot tubs scattered around the Riviera Deck. Three spacious decks are open for sunbathing. The ships' gyms are appealing, and though they're on the small side for vessels of this size, they're actually roomier than the ones on the much larger Grand-class ships. Aerobics, stretching, and meditation classes are available in the conversely very roomy aerobics room, and the nearby spas offer the usual massages, mud treatments, and facials. The teak Promenade Deck provides space for joggers, walkers, and shuffleboard players, and a computerized golf center called Princess Links simulates the trickiest holes at some of the world's best golf courses.

Regal Princess

The Verdict

In cruise ship terms, it may be middle-aged and suffering from a lack of outdoor deck space, but Princess's second-oldest ship is still appealing, with one of the industry's sleekest profiles and a huge domed casino/lounge on the very top deck.

Regal Princess (photo: Princess Cruises0

Specifications

Size (in tons)	70,000	Crew	696
Passengers (double occ.)	1,590	Passenger/Crew Ratio	2.3 to 1
Passenger/Space Ratio	44	Year Launched	1991
Total Cabins/Veranda Cabins	795/184	Last Major Refurbishment	2000

Frommer's Ratings (Scale of 1–5)   ★★★½

Cabin Comfort & Amenities	4	Dining Options	3
Ship Cleanliness & Maintenance	4	Gym, Spa & Sports Facilities	3
Public Comfort/Space	3	Children's Facilities	3
Decor	4	Enjoyment Factor	4

Regal Princess was designed by Renzo Piano, the man responsible for the wacko Centre Pompidou in Paris, as well as the reconstruction plans for the reunited Berlin. Between 1991 and 1995 the ship was Princess's most modern, most dramatic, and most frequently photographed vessel, but times change, and today she's already the line's oldest ship. She ain't no dinosaur, though. In early 2000, *Regal's* interior received a major face-lift that updated, upgraded, and generally brought her into the 21st century. Chrome columns and shiny surfaces were replaced by warm earth tones, cherry wood, and marble, giving the ship a much more open feel and bringing it more in line with what you'll find on the Sun- and Grand-class ships.

You'll either adore or dislike the ship's exterior, which its designer has compared to the silhouette of a porpoise moving through the water. All that sleekness comes at a price, though: The vessel's outdoor deck space is insufficient, leading to congestion at deck buffets and around swimming pools whenever the ship is full. There's no uninterrupted Promenade Deck around the periphery of the ship, either. All in all, the emphasis here is on what's inside, not outside.

Cabins & Rates

Cabins	Per Diems from	Sq. Ft.	Fridge	Hair Dryer	Sitting Area	TV
Inside	$100	190	yes	yes	no	yes
Outside	$110	190–210	yes	yes	no	yes
Suite	$255	578*	yes	yes	yes	yes

* Includes veranda.

CABINS   Of 795 cabins total, 624 are outside cabins, but of those only 184—those on Aloha and Baja decks—have private verandas. Spacious standard cabins are done in light-grained wood and warm beiges and peaches, with comfortably upholstered chairs and sofas, safes, and TVs. Bathrooms are compact but comfortable. The 14 suites and 18 minisuites have balconies, sitting areas, bathtubs, and minifridges. Robes are provided for guests in suites, and minibars are stocked once on a complimentary basis. Suite guests are also on the receiving end of the new slew of perks highlighted in the "Service" section above.

Views from category F cabins on the Dolphin Deck are partially obstructed by lifeboats, and the category H outside cabins have only portholes. Ten cabins are wheelchair accessible.

PUBLIC AREAS   *Regal*'s 2000 makeover gave her a stylish look, with soft lighting, more natural-looking materials, and more classic-looking murals and artwork. At the ship's core is the three-story Plaza Atrium, with a grand staircase. The lower level houses the lobby and reception area and a patisserie and wine bar. The ship's signature space, though, is its massive, 13,000-square-foot domed casino-cum-bar-cum-observation-deck. Situated several decks above the other bars, restaurants, and public areas, it feels a million miles from everything else on the ship, and is strikingly dramatic, framed by polished, rounded, bone-white "ribs" arching from ceiling to floor and glassed in by 270 degrees of panoramic curved glass windows. In its casino area, tables and slot machines lie close to a stage, where a piano player or a band keeps you entertained between hands. There's also a two-level show lounge offering Vegas-style entertainment, a champagne and wine bar, a piano bar, a library, a card room, a cinema, and a 2,000-square-foot children and teen center, the latter on the top deck, with ocean views. Like the rest of the fleet, the atrium is wired for Wi-Fi Internet access for anyone toting along their laptop.

DINING OPTIONS   The design of the Palm Court dining room is miles from the kind of consciously grand, romantic rooms on today's crop of ships. It's not unpleasant, mind you, just uninspiring. Up on the Lido Deck, Bravo's serves fresh-baked pizza with a wide-open ocean view, and the Cafe Del Sol buffet restaurant is open 24 hours for meals and snacks.

POOL, FITNESS, SPA & SPORTS FACILITIES   Two pools on the Lido Deck can become crowded when the ship is completely booked. Two hot tubs are adjacent, and there's a small running track one deck up. The *Regal Princess*'s health club/spa is another area that tells you this ain't a new ship. Unlike today's giant gym/spas, which typically perch way at the top of the ship to give inspiring views, *Regal*'s smallish one lies way down deep in the ship, along with steam rooms, saunas, and a tiny beauty salon.

11 Royal Caribbean International

1050 Caribbean Way, Miami, FL 33132. ℭ **800/327-6700** or 305/539-6000. Fax 800/722-5329. www.royal caribbean.com.

THE LINE IN A NUTSHELL   Royal Caribbean offers some of the best-looking, best-designed, most activity-packed, and just plain fun megaships in the biz. Along with NCL, they're also out in the forefront of innovation, always challenging the status quo regarding what can and can't be done aboard ships. **Sails to:** Caribbean, Panama Canal, Alaska, Mexican Riviera, Bermuda, Hawaii, Canada/New England (plus Europe, transatlantic).

THE EXPERIENCE   Though still trailing industry-leader Carnival in terms of size and profit, Royal Caribbean has definitely taken the lead in the excitement and cool-appeal department. You've seen the ads: healthy 30- and 40-somethings hiking across a glacier or kayaking through crystal water as Iggy Pop's "Lust for Life" plays on the soundtrack, then sipping wine on deck as the sun goes down. That's obviously the Madison Avenue take (these are cruise ships after all, not treks to Nepal), but it isn't all just hype: This really is a more youthful product that delivers fun, humor, a touch of class, and a bit of "feel the burn" active excitement, all without charging an arm and a leg. Cruises on these fun, active, and glamorous (but not too over-the-top-glitzy) megaships offer a great experience for a wide range of people, whether your idea of a good time is getting super-active or relaxing in the Solarium pool. There are huge children's centers for the kids, and entertainment for adults is varied and sometimes even novel. Out favorite: the Voyager ships' resident troupe of clowns, who teach juggling, clown history, and makeup application when not doing their act. Decor-wise, these ships are a shade or two toned down from the Carnival brood: Rather than trying to overwhelm the senses, many of their public areas are understated and classy. The Radiance-class vessels are the line's most elegant to date, with a sophistication that's up near the level of Royal Caribbean's sister line, Celebrity Cruises.

Pros

- **Activity central:** With rock-climbing walls, basketball courts, miniature golf, ice skating, and bungee trampolines among the many diversions, these ships are tops in the adrenaline department.
- **Beautiful public areas:** Lounges, restaurants, and outdoor pool decks are well designed, spacious, glamorous, and just plain inviting.
- **Great solariums:** Solariums on the Vision-, Voyager- and especially the Radiance-class ships are oh-so-relaxing oases designed around a theme (Venice, Africa, and so forth), a pool, and a pair of enormous whirlpool tubs.

Cons

- **Small cabins on the older ships:** At just about 120 to 160 square feet, most cabins aboard the line's pre-1999 vessels are downright tiny.

ROYAL CARIBBEAN: HIP SHIPS FOR THE BABY-BOOMER SET

Royal Caribbean was the first company to launch a fleet specializing exclusively in Caribbean ports of call—hence the company name. In the late 1980s it expanded its horizons beyond the Caribbean and now offers cruises in every major cruising region. It's the line that launched the megaship trend (with 1988's 73,192-ton *Sovereign of the Seas*), as well as the mega-megaship trend (with 1999's 3,114-passenger *Voyager of the Seas*), but beyond sheer size its ships have been innovative, challenging the idea of

Compared with other mainstream lines, here's how RCI rates:

	Poor	Fair	Good	Excellent	Outstanding
Enjoyment Factor					✓
Dining			✓		
Activities					✓
Children's Program				✓	
Entertainment				✓	
Service				✓	
Worth the Money					✓

what can fly (float?) on ships. When *Voyager* was launched, industry people pooh-poohed the idea of ice-skating rinks, interior boulevards, and rock-climbing walls on cruise ships. But with five Voyager-class vessels in the water and an even larger model on the way (see the preview later in this section), who's laughing now?

In 1997, Royal Caribbean acquired the smaller and more high-end Celebrity Cruises, which it continues to operate as a separate brand. For the past few years the two lines have been making incursions into Princess and Holland America's dominance of the **Alaska cruisetour** market. They now offer more than 25 options, including some to Whistler and the Canadian Rockies. They're also the only lines offering train service between Anchorage and its distant cruise port in Seward, with 360-degree views available from glass-domed viewing cars. On the other side of North America, the line upped its commitment to the northeast by repositioning the huge *Voyager of the Seas* to a new port in Bayonne, New Jersey (across the Hudson from New York) for Bermuda and Caribbean cruises, and building a new cruise port on the New Jersey side of the Hudson River. In other news, RCI is in the midst of major upgrades to its older vessels, retrofitting them with some of the line's signature features. Details can be found in the individual ship reviews later in this chapter.

PASSENGER PROFILE

You'll find all walks of life on a Royal Caribbean cruise: passengers in their 20s through 60s and older, mostly couples (including a good number of honeymooners), some singles traveling with friends, and also lots of families—nearly 300,000 kids sail with Royal Caribbean annually. While the majority of passengers come from somewhere in North America, the huge Voyager-class ships in particular attract a lot of foreigners, including many Asians and Latin Americans. There are books in the library in French, Spanish, and Dutch; and in-cabin documents (such as room-service menus) are in five languages, including Italian and Portuguese.

Over the past several years the line has been making a push for younger, hipper, more active passengers with their "Get Out There" ad campaign, which portrays the ships as a combination of hyperactive urban health club, chic restaurant district, and adventure-travel magic potion—which of course is a bit of a stretch. They're active, yes, but don't expect the Shackleton expedition. Overall, passengers are energetic, social, and looking for a good time, no matter what their age. And, they want a less glitzy, theme-parkish, and party-on experience than they'll get with RCI's main competitor, Carnival. RCI's shorter 3- and 4-night cruises do tend to attract more of the partying crowd, however, as is the case with most short cruises.

DINING

Royal Caribbean's cuisine falls in the "pretty tasty" to "impressively good" range. Unlike NCL, Oceania, and Princess, which have adopted looser, "walk-in" dining programs, Royal Caribbean sticks to offering early- and late-seating dinners in traditional main dining rooms, with guests assigned a set dinner table. As with all the other mainstream lines, there are also many casual and specialty dining options.

TRADITIONAL   Dinners are offered in two seatings in the main dining rooms, with typical entrees including poached Alaskan salmon, oven-roasted crispy duck served with a rhubarb sauce, sirloin steak marinated with Italian herbs and served over a chunky tomato stew, and shrimp scampi. At lunch and dinner, there's always a **light and healthy option** such as herb-crusted baked cod with steamed red-skinned potatoes and vegetables; or a pasta tossed with smoked turkey, portobello mushrooms, and red-pepper pesto; as well as a **vegetarian option** such as vegetable strudel served in a puff pastry with black-bean salsa. **Low-carb options** were also introduced in mid-2004.

SPECIALTY   Royal Caribbean hasn't gone whole-hog into alternative, extra-charge specialty restaurants the way NCL has. Instead, it's integrated some new dining options into the casual and snacking categories. The Voyager-class ships and *Empress of the Seas* each have one intimate, reservations-only Italian restaurant, Portofino, while the Radiance-class and *Mariner* and *Navigator of the Seas* have Portofino and the Chops Grill steakhouse. They're all attractive and intimate getaways, and food and service are the best on board, justifying the $20-per-person cover charge. Specialty restaurants are being installed on the line's older ships as they're renovated.

CASUAL   Fleetwide, an open-seating casual dinner option is offered every night from 6:30 to 9:30pm in the buffet-style Windjammer Cafe. Meals follow the general theme of dinners in the main restaurants (Italian, Caribbean, and so on) and the room is made a bit more inviting through dimmed lighting and the addition of tablecloths. Long open hours mean this option rarely gets crowded. You can also eat breakfast and lunch in the Windjammer if you don't want the formality of the main dining room. Aboard *Mariner, Navigator,* and *Monarch of the Seas,* the buffet area has an Asian specialty buffet called Jade, serving sushi and a variety of traditional and modern dishes. Aboard *Sovereign of the Seas,* an expanded buffet called the Windjammer Marketplace has a variety of themed islands for different regional cuisine, including Asian, Mediterranean, and Latin, plus a carving station, pasta station, and soup and salad bar.

RCI's Voyager ships and the older *Sovereign of the Seas* have one of the most distinctive casual-dining options at sea: an honest-to-god **Johnny Rockets diner** with red vinyl booths and chrome accents, serving burgers, milkshakes, and other diner staples. There's a $3.95 per-person service charge and sodas and shakes are a la carte (shakes will cost you $3.60 a pop), but that doesn't stop lines from forming during prime lunch and dinner times.

SNACKS & EXTRAS   Voyager-class ships have an extensive coffee shop on the indoor promenade, serving a variety of pastries, sandwiches, and pizza, plus several self-serve soft ice-cream stations, nacho and hot dog type snacks in the sports bars, and a multi-station buffet restaurant. The line's other ships have similar options, with decent pizza served afternoons and late night for those suffering from post-partying munchies, and ice cream and toppings available throughout the day from a station in the Windjammer. The Radiance-class ships and the recently refurbished *Empress* and *Sovereign* all have Latte'tudes coffee shops serving gourmet java, cookies, and other baked goods, and **Ben & Jerry's** ice cream. There are also three pull-out-all-the-stops midnight buffets per week, with "Midnight Treats" hors d'oeuvres served late on the other days.

A fairly extensive **kids' menu** (which is fun in and of itself, with word and picture games and pictures to color in, crayons included) features the usual options: burgers, hot dogs, fries, fish sticks, burritos, oven-fried lemon chicken, spaghetti and meatballs, and pizza, plus lots of desserts.

Room service is available 24 hours a day from a fairly routine, limited menu. During normal lunch and dinner hours, however, a cabin steward can bring many items served in the restaurant to your cabin.

ACTIVITIES

The TV ads don't lie: Royal Caribbean's ships really are activity-packed, though if you want to remain glued to a deck chair and do nothing, that's no problem either.

These ships are known for their sports facilities. Fleetwide, you'll find rock-climbing walls (with multiple climbing tracks and training available) plus lots of typical cruise fare: spa and beauty demonstrations, art auctions, wine tastings, salsa and ballroom dance lessons, bingo, oddball crafts/hospitality classes like napkin folding, "horse race" gambling, and outrageous poolside games like the men's sexy legs contest, designed to draw big laughs. Sports facilities vary by ship: There are ice-skating rinks and in-line skating tracks on the Voyager-class ships; the Radiance-, Voyager-, and Vision-class ships all have combo basketball/volleyball courts; and several ships (the Radiance and Voyager classes as well as *Splendour* and *Legend of the Seas*) feature miniature-golf courses. If shopping can be considered an activity, Royal Caribbean beats out Carnival with its impressive selection of boutiques clustered around the ships' atria.

For those whose goal is to not gain 5 pounds at the buffet, gyms are well equipped fleetwide, with specialized fitness classes such as yoga and cardio-kickboxing available for $10 per person. **Onboard spas** offer the usual range of massages, facials, and other beauty treatments, but here's a piece of advice: If you want a treatment, sign up immediately after boarding, since these are big ships and a lot of people will be competing with you for desirable time slots. If you're flexible, you can often find more openings and special discounts on port days and off times. During a recent rainy stay in Halifax, Heidi signed up for a combo 25-minute back massage and 25-minute mini-facial that was discounted to $89 from $120, not including the tip).

CHILDREN'S PROGRAM

Year-round and fleetwide, Royal Caribbean offers its **"Adventure Ocean"** supervised kids' programs for children **ages 3 to 17** (divided into Aquanauts, ages 3–5; Explorers, ages 6–8; Voyagers, ages 9–11; Navigators, ages 12–14; and older teens ages 15–17). Male and female youth staff all have college degrees in education, recreation, or a related field. Each ship has a children's playroom and facilities for teens, but in general the scope of the kids' facilities on the Voyager- and Radiance-class ships far exceeds that of the rest of the fleet, covering up to 22,000 square feet and including large playrooms, and a large, sequestered outdoor deck with ship-shaped play equipment. Radiance-class ships and *Voyager, Adventure,* and *Explorer* also have a water slide and a kids' pool. Kids' areas on the other vessels are impressive in their own regard, on par with or better than Carnival's Fantasy- and Destiny-class ships. Activities fleetwide include movies, talent shows, karaoke, pizza and ice-cream parties, bingo, scavenger hunts, game shows, volleyball, face painting, and beach parties, and **Internet access** is available to Adventure Ocean kids at half price (25¢ vs. 50¢ for adults).

Three programs mix learning with play. The **"Adventure Science"** program teaches and entertains kids with fun yet educational scientific experiments, while **"Adventure Art,"** offered in partnership with Crayola, focuses on art projects made with the company's crayons, modeling clay, glitter, glue, markers, and paint. The new **"Sail into Story Time"** program uses popular children's books such as *Where the Wild Things Are* and *The Very Hungry Caterpillar* (for ages 3–5) and *The Stinky Cheese Man* and *Do Pirates Take Baths?* (for ages 5–8) as a basis for creative activities, arts and crafts, and dramatic projects designed to spark kids' imaginations. For instance, after reading *Where the Wild Things Are,* they're turned loose for a supervised "wild rumpus." Hey, better here than at home . . .

For younger kids (ages 6 months–3 years), RCI has partnered with **Fisher-Price** on a program of supervised **"play dates"** in which babies and toddlers are invited to daily 45-minute play sessions with their parents. Offered on all but embarkation day, the interactive dates incorporate music, storytelling, and a variety of Fisher-Price toys to advance their lessons—promoting physical development, problem-solving skills, exploring cause and effect or rhythm and movement, and exploring the world around them. Sessions are divided into two groups: Aqua Babies (6–18 months) and Aqua Tots (18 months–3 years). Parents who participate receive a special newsletter that highlights the theme and objectives of each session and offers play tips to implement once you're back home. In your cabin, Fisher-Price TV offers age-appropriate programming for kids.

For teens, each ship has a **teen center,** disco, and a video arcade. *Sovereign of the Seas* has three new teen-only areas, including a dedicated teen sundeck (which is also available on *Mariner, Navigator,* and *Monarch*).

Preview: *Freedom of the Seas*

We're just guessing, of course, but it seems there's a bit of corporate one-upmanship going on between Carnival Corporation and Royal Caribbean. In June 2003, with Carnival subsidiary Cunard about to launch *QM2* and steal the "world's biggest passenger ship" crown, RCI announced plans to build the "Ultra-Voyager," a 158,000-ton, 3,600-passenger vessel that one-ups both the 150,000-ton *QM2* and its own 142,000-ton Voyager ships, the previous heavy-weight champs. A sort of Voyager-class-plus, the Ultra vessels will feature an on-deck water park with jets, sprays, and water cannon, plus two cantilevered hot tubs extending out 12 feet beyond the side of the ship. Anticipating that the ship will appeal to families, RCI has created six different categories of family cabins, able to sleep six to eight passengers. The first of the Ultras, *Freedom of the Seas,* is scheduled to enter service in May 2006, sailing year-round 7-night eastern and western Caribbean itineraries from Miami.

Royal Caribbean Fleet Itineraries

Ship	Inside
Adventure	**7-night Southern Carib:** Round-trip from San Juan, PR, year-round.
Brilliance	**10- & 11-night Panama Canal:** Round-trip from Miami, FL, Jan–Apr and Nov–Dec 2006.
Empress	**11-night E. & Southern Carib:** Round-trip from San Juan, PR, Oct 2005–Apr 2006 and Nov–Dec 2006. **3- & 4-night E. Carib:** Round-trip from San Juan, PR, Oct 2005–Apr 2006.
Enchantment	**4- & 5-night W. Carib:** Round-trip from Ft. Lauderdale, FL, year-round.
Explorer	**7-night E. & W. Carib:** Round-trip from Miami, FL, year-round (itineraries alternate weekly).
Freedom	**7-night W. Carib:** Round-trip from Miami, FL, year-round.
Grandeur	**9-night W. Carib:** Round-trip from Baltimore, MD, Oct–Nov 2005 and May–Nov 2006. **7-night W. Carib:** Round-trip from New Orleans, LA, Dec 2005–Apr 2006 and Dec 2006. **5-night Bermuda:** Round-trip from Baltimore, MD, May–Nov 2006.
Jewel	**8-night E. Carib:** Round-trip from Ft. Lauderdale, FL, Nov 2005–Apr 2006 and Nov–Dec 2006. Alternates with **6-night W. Carib:** Round-trip from Ft. Lauderdale, FL, Nov 2005–Apr 2006 and Nov–Dec 2006. **10-night Bermuda/Carib:** Round-trip from Boston, MA, Sept–Oct 2006.
Legend	**7-night W. Carib:** Round-trip from Tampa, FL, Nov 2005–Apr 2006 and Nov–Dec 2006.
Majesty	**3- & 4-night Bahamas:** Round-trip from Miami, FL, year-round.
Mariner	**7-night E. & W. Carib:** Round-trip from Port Canaveral, FL, year-round (itineraries alternate weekly).
Monarch	**3-night Ensenada & 4-night Ensenada/Catalina/San Diego:** Round-trip from Los Angeles, CA, year-round (itineraries alternate).
Navigator	**7-night E. & W. Carib:** Round-trip from Miami, FL, year-round (itineraries alternate weekly).
Radiance	**7-night E. & W. Carib:** Round-trip from Miami, FL, Nov 2005–Apr 2006 (alternates weekly). **7-night Gulf of Alaska:** North- or southbound between Seward/Anchorage, AK, and Vancouver, BC, May–Sept 2006. **14-night Hawaii:** Round-trip from San Diego, CA, May and Sept 2006. **6-night W. Carib:** Round-trip from Ft. Lauderdale, FL, Oct–Dec 2006. Alternates with **8-night E. Carib:** Round-trip from Ft. Lauderdale, FL, Oct–Dec 2006.
Rhapsody	**7-night W. Carib:** Round-trip from Galveston, TX, year-round.
Serenade	**7-night Southern Carib:** Round-trip from San Juan, PR, Oct 2005–Apr 2006 and Oct–Dec 2006. **7-night Alaska Inside Passage:** Round-trip from Vancouver, BC, May–Sept 2006. **11-night Hawaii:** Honolulu, HI, to Ensenada, Mexico, Oct 2006.
Sovereign	**3- & 4-night Bahamas:** Round-trip from Port Canaveral, FL, year-round.
Splendour	**4- & 5-night W. Carib:** Round-trip from Galveston, TX, Nov 2005–Apr 2006.
Vision	**3-night Baja:** Round-trip from Los Angeles, CA, Jan 2006. **7-night Mexican Riviera:** Round-trip from Los Angeles, CA, Oct 2005–Apr 2006 and Sept–Dec 2006. **7-night Alaska Inside Passage:** Round-trip from Seattle, WA, May–Sept 2006.
Voyager	**5-night Bermuda:** Round-trip from Bayonne, NJ, Oct–Nov 2005. **9-night W. Carib:** Round-trip from Bayonne, NJ, Oct–Nov 2005. **7-night E. & W. Carib:** Round-trip from Miami, FL, Dec 2005–Apr 2006 and Nov–Dec 2006 (itineraries alternate weekly).

Slumber-party-style **group babysitting** for children 3 and up is available in the kids' playroom nightly between 10pm and 1am, and from noon until sailing on days the ship is in port. The hourly charge is $5 per child (kids must be at least 3 years old and potty-trained). Private, in-cabin babysitting for kids 6 months and up is available from off-duty crewmembers 8am to 2am, and must be booked at least 24 hours in advance through the purser's desk. On a recent *Voyager* cruise, Heidi had the services of a sweet Lithuanian cabin stewardess who came to mind her twins each evening at 8:30. The cost: $8 per hour for up to two siblings; $10 per hour for a maximum of three. The 4 hours of adult time to enjoy dinner, drinks, and entertainment: priceless.

Alternatively, the **Adventure Ocean dinner program** is a kind of "get out of parenting free" card for adults, inviting kids to dine with youth staff in the Windjammer Cafe, the Solarium, or Johnny Rockets diner (depending on the ship) from 6 to 7pm, then take part in an activities session till 10pm. This is offered on 3 nights of a 7-night cruise and once or twice on shorter cruises. A complete child's menu is offered.

Children must be at least 6 months old to sail with Royal Caribbean.

ENTERTAINMENT

RCI doesn't scrimp in the entertainment department, with music and comedy acts, some of the best Vegas-style shows at sea, passenger talent shows, karaoke, sock hops, and occasional **"name" groups and soloists,** such as the Platters, the Drifters, the Coasters, John Davidson, and Marty Allen. Other names may not be as familiar, but can be pretty amazing, such as the Knudsen Brothers (www.knudsenbros.com), a five-member family a cappella group that mixes great harmonies, human-beat-box rhythms, and a lot of comedy about their male-pattern baldness. The newer the ship, the larger and more sophisticated the stage, sound, and lighting equipment, with some boasting a wall of video monitors to augment live performances.

Aside from its showrooms and huge glitzy casinos, Royal Caribbean is big on signature spaces, with each ship offering the nautical, woodsy **Schooner Bar** as well as the **Viking Crown Lounge,** an observation-cum-nightclub set high on a top deck and boasting panoramic views of the sea and ship in all directions. The new Latin-themed **Bolero's bars** (aboard *Navigator, Mariner, Monarch, Sovereign,* and *Empress*) serve a mean mojito and have Latin music into the night. Atrium bars also feature live music, often classical trios. One evening on our most recent cruise, two very talented passengers spontaneously began singing as the atrium trio played, attracting a huge crowd. Suddenly the 3,000-passenger ship felt like an intimate cabaret lounge. It was a great moment passengers talked about for the rest of the trip.

SERVICE

In general, dining, bar, and cabin service is surprisingly good considering the sheer volume of passengers with which crewmembers must deal. At meals on a recent cruise we found that even when staff was rushed our water glasses were always filled, wine orders were delivered promptly, and our servers always found time for a little friendly chit-chat as they skated around their tables. Other times we found ourselves greeted with a smile by a crewman polishing the brass, and had busboys in the buffet restaurant going out of their way to bring coffee and water, even though the room is officially self-service. These folks work long, hard days, though, and on ships this size (and especially on those operating quick-turnaround 3- and 4-night cruises) you'll probably run into some crewmembers who look like they need a vacation.

Laundry and **dry-cleaning services** are available on all the ships, but none have self-service laundromats.

The Radiance Class:
Radiance • Brilliance •
Serenade • Jewel of the Seas

The Verdict

Megaship masterpieces! Royal Caribbean's most elegant vessels to date combine shippy lines and nautical decor with a lot of the fun and games of RCI's Voyager class, including rock climbing and miniature golf.

Radiance of the Seas *(photo: RCCL)*

Specifications

Size (in tons)	90,090	Year Launched	
Passengers (double occ.)	2,100	*Radiance*	2001
Passenger/Space Ratio	43	*Brilliance*	2002
Total Cabins/Veranda Cabins	1,050/577	*Serenade*	2003
Crew	857	*Jewel*	2004
Passenger/Crew Ratio	2.5 to 1	Last Major Refurbishment	N/A

Frommer's Ratings (Scale of 1–5)   ★★★★½

Cabin Comfort & Amenities	4	Dining Options	4.5
Ship Cleanliness & Maintenance	5	Gym, Spa & Sports Facilities	5
Public Comfort/Space	5	Children's Facilities	4
Decor	5	Enjoyment Factor	5

These ships are just plain stunning, with some of the adventure features of their larger Voyager-class siblings but a sleeker seagoing profile outside, a more nautical look and feel inside, and acres of windows to bring the two together. When you first board, you'll see one of Royal Caribbean's typical wiry modern art sculptures filling the bright, nine-story atrium, but venture a little farther and you'll see that the ships have a much more traditional interior, with dark wood paneling, caramel-brown leathers, and deep-sea-blue fabrics and carpeting. Outside, some 110,000 square feet of glass cover about half of their sleek exteriors. From Decks 5 through 10 portside, the atrium is an uninterrupted wall of glass facing the sea, with four banks of glass elevators. The Viking Crown Lounge, Singapore Sling's piano bar, Crown & Anchor Lounge, Sky Bar, Windjammer Cafe, and Champagne Bar are wrapped in glass, too, all of which comes in handy in scenic destinations like Alaska, letting passengers view the passing scenery even while still enjoying the ships' indoor offerings.

Just as the decor and design of these ships are new, so are their mechanics. Like the Voyager-class ships, they have an Azipod propulsion system—two submarine-shaped propeller pods anchored to the ship's bottom and able to move like rudders, twirling almost 360 degrees to offer incredible maneuverability. The ships' environmentally friendly GE gas turbine engines are cleaner than the standard diesels and virtually vibration-free. A bit of trivia: That's the meaning of the giant "GTV" (gas turbine vessel) painted on either side of their stern—a new appellation to go with the old SS (steamship) and the more recent MV (motor vessel, for example diesel).

Cabins & Rates

Cabins	Per Diems from	Sq. Ft.	Fridge	Hair Dryer	Sitting Area	TV
Inside	$123	165	yes	yes	yes	yes
Outside	$141	170	yes	yes	yes	yes
Suite	$344	293–1,001	yes	yes	yes	yes

CABINS   Beginning in 1999, RCI began increasing the size of their cabins, one of the major drawbacks on their older ships. Now, with the Radiance class, cabins have gotten even better, with even the smallest insides measuring a roomy and inviting 165 square feet. Some 75% of outside staterooms measure at least 180 square feet and boast 40-square-foot verandas, while the rest have jumbo-size portholes. Nearly as impressive as the cabins' size is their appealing decor of attractive navy blues and copper tones—a nice change from earlier vessels' *Miami Vice* pinks, mints, and baby blues.

All but a handful of suites are located on Deck 10. The best, the Royal Suite, measures 1,001 square feet and offers a separate bedroom, living room with baby grand piano, dining table, bar, entertainment center, and 215-square-foot balcony. Six Owner's Suites are about half that size, with 57-square-foot balconies, a separate living room, a bar, and walk-in closet; and the 35 Grand Suites one step below 358 to 384 square feet, with sitting areas and 106-square-foot balconies. Three 586-square-foot Royal Family Suites have 140-square-foot balconies and two bathrooms and can accommodate six people in two separate bedrooms (one with third and fourth berths) and another two on a pullout couch in the living room. Suite guests are treated to complimentary in-cabin butler service in addition to cabin stewards, and there's also a Concierge Club on Deck 10 where suite guests can request services and grab a newspaper.

All cabins have minifridges, hair dryers, interactive televisions (for buying shore excursions, checking your onboard account, and looking up stock quotes), small sitting areas with mini-couches, lots of drawer space, roomy closets, bedside reading lights, and TVs. Vanity/desks have pullout trays to accommodate laptops, plus modem jacks to connect them to the Internet. Bathrooms are small, with Royal Caribbean's typical hold-your-breath-and-step-in shower stalls, but they do have lots of storage space.

One snag on the balcony front: On each ship, Cabin Decks 7 through 10 are narrower than the rest of the ship, resulting in cabin balconies on Deck 10 (many of them suites) being shaded by the overhang of the deck above. Meanwhile, cabin balconies on the aft and forward ends of Deck 7, being indented, look out onto the top of Deck 6 instead of directly out onto the sea. Balconies on cabins 7652 to 7670 and 7152 to 7170, also aft on Deck 7, are not completely private since the dividers between them don't go all the way to the edge of the space. Keep your clothes on; your neighbors can look right over at you.

Fifteen cabins can accommodate wheelchair users.

PUBLIC AREAS   Overall, these ships are stunners. Our favorite space is the cluster of five intimate, wood-and-leather lounges on Deck 6, which recall the decor of classic yachts, university clubs, and cigar lounges. Expect low lighting, inlaid wood flooring, cozy couches, and Oriental-style area rugs. The best of these rooms is the romantic piano bar and lounge that stretches across each ship's stern, with a bank of floor-to-ceiling windows. For amazing views, don't miss having a cocktail here on a moonlit night. Adjacent is a lovely Colonial-style Billiard Club boasting herringbone wood floors, redwood veneer paneling, and a pair of ultra-high-tech gyroscopic pool tables. No excuse for missing shots: The tables compensate for the ship's movements, staying remarkably level.

The main theaters are refreshingly different from most in the cruise biz, with a cool ambience, warm wood tones, and seating in deep sea-blues and greens. Artful hand-made curtains, indirect lighting, and fiber optics all come together to create a quiet, ethereal look. But guys, watch those protruding armrests: It's very easy to snag your pants pockets on them.

Other public areas include the attractive Casino Royale, with more than 200 slot machines and dozens of gaming tables; a baseball-themed sports bar with interactive games on the bar top; the nautically themed Schooner Bar; a 12-station, 24-hour Internet center; a specialty-coffee bar with several Internet stations; a small library; a conference-center complex with a small movie theater; and, high up on Deck 13, Royal Caribbean's signature Viking Crown Lounge, which is divided between a quiet lounge and a large disco with a rotating bar. Even the ships' high-style public bathrooms are impressive, with their marble floors and counters and funky portholelike mirrors.

The huge kids' area on Deck 12 includes a sprawling playroom divided into several areas, with a video arcade and an outdoor pool with water slide. Teens have their own nightclub, with a DJ booth, music videos, and a soda bar.

DINING OPTIONS   The two-story main dining rooms on all four ships are glamorous and elegant, like something out of a 1930s movie set. Four willowy silk-covered columns dominate the vaulted main floor, and a wide double staircase connects the two decks dramatically—all that's missing are Cary Grant and Katharine Hepburn. On *Serenade,* painter Frank Troia's huge, impressionist *Gala Suite* amplifies the mood, depicting formally dressed couples dancing amid floating globes of light.

The nautically decorated Windjammer Cafe takes self-serve buffet dining to new levels, with 11 food stations (9 inside and 2 outside) set up as islands to keep the lines down and the crowds diffused. It really works. If you prefer taking your meals while reclining, there's a small strip of cozy tables with oversize rattan chairs and big squishy cushions between the indoor and outdoor seating areas.

The cozy 90-seat Chops Grille is an oceanview venue with dark woods, rich upholsteries, and high-backed booths that bring home the meat-and-potatoes mood. You can watch your steak being cooked in the open kitchen. Adjacent is the 130-seat Portofino, an Italian restaurant that also has ocean views. Expect more refined and gracious service than in the main dining room, plus a more leisurely pace (and of course a $20 cover charge). Up on the Sport Deck, the Seaview Cafe is a casual lunch and dinner venue with checkered floors, rattan chairs, and lots of light, serving quick meals such as fish and chips, popcorn shrimp, and burgers.

A counter in the Solarium serves freshly made pizza by the slice, and a coffee shop offers cappuccino and pastries.

POOL, FITNESS, SPA & SPORTS FACILITIES   The Radiance vessels offer tons of recreation outlets and acres of space to flop on a deck chair and sunbathe. At the main pool, passengers pack in like sardines on sunny days at sea, and deck chairs can be scarce during the prime hours before and after lunch—par for the cruise ship course. On *Radiance,* the pool deck is presided over by a 12-foot-high cedar totem pole carved for the ship by Alaska Native artist Nathan Jackson of Ketchikan. How many ships have you seen with their own totem pole?

Much more relaxing are the ships' large, lush Solariums, with their exotic eastern motifs. Tropical foliage and waterfalls impart an Asian-spa mood, and stone reliefs, regional woodcarvings, and statues drive home the mood. The area's adjacent (and popular) pizza counter adds a little pandemonium to the otherwise serene scene (as can kids, if they happen to find the place), but overall this is a great spot to settle in for a lazy afternoon at sea. The padded wooden chaise longues are heavenly. The adjacent spa has 13 treatment rooms and a special steam-room complex with heated tiled lounges and showers that simulate tropical rain and fog.

The Sports Deck has a 9-hole miniature-golf course and golf simulators, a jogging track, a rock-climbing wall attached to the funnel, and a combo basketball, volleyball, and paddle-tennis court. The sprawling oceanview gym has a huge aerobics floor and dozens of exercise machines, including sea-facing treadmills and elliptical stair-steppers.

The Voyager Class: Voyager • Explorer • Adventure • Navigator • Mariner of the Seas

Explorer of the Seas *(photo: Matt Hannafin)*

The Verdict

Sports club meets Vegas meets theme park meets cruise ship, these enormous vessels are real winners if you like your vacations larger than life. As we overheard one little boy say to his father, "This doesn't look like a ship, Daddy. It looks like a city!"

Specifications

Size (in tons)	142,000	Year Launched	
Passengers (double occ.)	3,114	*Voyager*	1999
Passenger/Space Ratio	45.5	*Explorer*	2000
Total Cabins/Veranda Cabins	1,557/757	*Adventure*	2001
Crew	1,176	*Navigator*	2002
Passenger/Crew Ratio	2.7 to 1	*Mariner*	2003
Last Major Refurbishment	N/A		

Frommer's Ratings (Scale of 1–5) ★★★★½

Cabin Comfort & Amenities	4	Dining Options	4.5
Ship Cleanliness & Maintenance	4	Gym, Spa & Sports Facilities	5
Public Comfort/Space	5	Children's Facilities	5
Decor	4	Enjoyment Factor	5

The 3,114-passenger, 142,000-ton Voyager-class ships are the benchmark against which all subsequent megaships have been measured. When they were introduced, they were almost a third larger than the next largest passenger ship (though they've since been bested by Cunard's *QM2*), with features you still won't find anywhere else: a full-size ice-skating rink that puts on great ice-shows twice a week (and skating for passengers at other times), an outdoor in-line skating track (skates can be rented or you can bring your own), and a 1950s-style diner sitting right out on deck. As if that's not enough for you, there's also 9-hole miniature-golf courses and golf simulators; regulation-size basketball, paddleball, and volleyball courts; huge two-level gyms and spas; and the rock-climbing walls that have become one of Royal Caribbean's most distinguishing features. And did we mention they also have monumentally gorgeous three-story dining rooms, florist shops, and a "peek-a-boo" bridge on Deck 11 that allows guests to watch the crew steering the ship?

What really sets these ships apart from any other passenger ship, though, are the four-story, boulevard-like promenades that run more than a football field's length down their center, lined with bars, shops, and entertainment lounges and anchored at each end by huge atria. Called the Royal Promenade, they provide a great place to people-watch, and weirdly enough, you can watch from your cabin if you want to: Three decks of inside cabins have views from bay windows of the "street scene" below.

The strollable feel of these promenades leads to our major conclusion: These vessels are a perfect compromise for couples who can't decide between a tropical cruise and a city vacation. They may, in fact, be the first ships to really live up to the old "city at sea" cliché. And certainly enough people are aboard to warrant the comparison too: Each ship carries 3,114 guests at double occupancy, but since many staterooms have third and fourth berths, total capacity for each vessel can reach as high as 3,838. Remarkably, though, the ships never feel crowded. On our last three sailings we found many public rooms nearly empty during the day and didn't have to wait in line for anything all week, even though more than 3,200 passengers were aboard. As we heard one woman comment to her companion, "I know there are 3,000 people on this ship, but where are they all?" Kudos go to the crew for efficiency, and also to Royal Caribbean for a design that features enough appealing public areas to diffuse crowds comfortably, plus a layout that encourages traffic to flow in several different directions. This keeps crowding down and also means you don't tend to find yourself in the same spots day after day—it's entirely possible to be aboard for 6 days, turn a corner, and find yourself in a room you've never seen before.

Cabins & Rates

Cabins	Per Diems from	Sq. Ft.	Fridge	Hair Dryer	Sitting Area	TV
Inside	$118	160	yes	yes	no	yes
Outside	$137	161–328	yes	yes	some	yes
Suite	$336	277–1,325	yes	yes	yes	yes

CABINS   With the Voyager-class ships, Royal Caribbean finally did something about the major fault of their older vessels, increasing standard cabin size from a tiny 120 to 153 square feet up to a livable 173 square feet for a standard oceanview cabin (including balcony), and 160 square feet for an inside cabin. Bathrooms are still on the cramped side, with little storage space, few amenities (soap and shampoo only), and only a thin sliver of counter, though there's more space out in the cabin on shelves above the desk. The cylindrical shower stalls, though tight for large-size people, have neat sliding doors that keep the water and warmth in. All cabins also have Internet dataports, minifridges, safes, TVs, pleasant pastel color schemes, and hair dryers hidden in a drawer of the vanity—and they're actually powerful enough to do their job.

Of the 1,557 cabins, 939 have ocean views and 757 have verandas. There's a single huge Penthouse Suite; 10 Owner's Suites; and 4 Royal Family Suites that accommodate a total of eight people with two bedrooms plus a living room with sofa bed and a pair of bathrooms. There are also smaller and cheaper family cabins with sofa beds that enable them to sleep six. For voyeurs, the 138 atrium cabins on the second, third, and fourth levels of the four-story Royal Promenade have windows facing the action below, with curtains and soundproofing to keep most of the light and noise out, when you want downtime.

Twenty-six cabins are wheelchair accessible.

PUBLIC AREAS   Each ship has about 3 miles of public corridors, and it can feel like a real hike if your cabin's on one end of the ship and you have to get to the other. Running down the center of each like Main Street is the bustling, four-story Royal Promenade, designed to resemble Memphis's Beale Street or New Orleans's Bourbon Street. Like them, it's lined with shops, bars, and cafes, and features evening musical performances by the ships' various musical groups, including their big bands. Other promenade attractions include an elegant champagne bar, a comfy English/Irish bar with "sidewalk" seating, a self-serve soft ice-cream station with lots of toppings, shops, and a bright cafe that serves pizza, cookies, pastries, and coffee 24 hours a day. *Voyager, Explorer,* and *Adventure* also have a large sports bar here that gets big, raucous crowds when games are broadcast (and puts out free hot dogs and nachos to keep them there), and an arcade stocked with classic 1980s video games. On *Navigator* and *Mariner,* those were scrapped in favor of Vintages Wine Bar, created in collaboration with the Mondavi, Beringer Blass, and Niebaum-Coppola wineries. Full of wood and leather, with terra-cotta floors, attractive vineyard-themed lithographs, and a 600-bottle "cellar," the bars showcase more than 60 vintages. Prices are reasonable and guests can taste any variety before ordering. Classes in wine appreciation are held here throughout the week, and passengers can also stage their own tastings by ordering any of 13 special "wine flight" tasting menus, with selections grouped by taste profile, varietal, or region—for example, Merlots, Australian wines, etc.

A roving quartet of "Krooze Komic" clowns performs elaborate acrobatics shows, teaches juggling classes, and offers impromptu physical comedy throughout the cruise. Twice per cruise, one or more of the clowns present an informal discussion on clown history, archetypes, makeup application, and tricks of the trade. These talks are presented once for adults and later for kids in the ships' large children's centers.

In total, there are some 30 places aboard each ship to grab a drink, including the Viking Crown complex on the top deck, with its elegant jazz club and golf-themed 19th Hole bar; the dark, romantic, nautically themed Schooner Bar; and the clubby cigar bar, tucked away behind a dark door and hosting blackjack games on formal evenings. Aboard each ship, the futuristic or gothic-dungeon-themed disco is entered though a theme-parky "secret passage," while the huge three-story showrooms occupy the opposite end of the kitsch spectrum: beautifully designed, with simple, elegant color schemes and truly lovely stage curtains—the one on *Adventure* decorated with peacock designs, the one on *Explorer* depicting a chorus of women standing under golden boughs amid a rain of leaves. Excellent ice shows as well as game shows and fashion shows are held throughout each cruise at the "Studio B" ice rink, which has a sliding floor to cover the ice during non-skate events.

Each ship has a two-story library-cum-computer-room with about 18 computer stations and Web-cams that allow you to send your picture as an electronic postcard.

There are also sprawling kids' areas with huge oceanview playrooms, teen discos, and jumbo arcades. Families with science-minded kids will appreciate *Explorer's* pair of working $1.5-million laboratories, where scientists from the University of Miami's Rosenstiel School of Marine & Atmospheric Science conduct research on wind patterns, water chemistry, UV and solar radiation, and air pollution via sensors attached to the ship's mast and hull. Over the course of each cruise, these scientists present talks on their research and show off their labs to passengers on free organized tours. Amusingly, cabin TVs have a channel that shows images from various cameras mounted around the ship. In the oceanography lab, the camera is mounted at a spot to which passengers' eyes are drawn during their tour. It took us a minute to realize what we were seeing when we turned on our cabin TV one day and were confronted with a group of people staring right at us, completely immobile.

The best spots for chilling out with a book during days at sea include the seaview Seven of Hearts card room and Cloud Nine Lounge on Deck 14. Those really wanting to get away from people can retreat up the curving stairway to Deck 15's Skylight Chapel, which gets almost no traffic and is even free of piped-in music. (Though it also lacks windows.)

DINING OPTIONS   The three-level main dining rooms on these ships are among the most stunning and classy aboard any of today's megaships, with designs that follow a general European theme. Each level—linked by a large open area and grand staircase at its center—is considered a separate restaurant, though service and menus are consistent throughout. A pianist or piano trio entertains from a platform in the aft end of the room and a huge crystal chandelier hangs overhead, both setting an elegant mood.

For a dining alternative, the oceanview Portofino restaurant serves Italian meals in a cozy setting (and at an additional $20 per person charge), but be sure to reserve a table as soon as you get aboard, as they book up fast.

The pleasant, spacious Island Grill and Windjammer casual buffet restaurants are joined into one large space but have separate lines and stations to keep things moving. On *Navigator* and *Mariner,* this area also incorporates the Asian-themed Jade buffet. There's no outdoor seating per se, but the ship's main pool area is on the same deck, just outside the restaurants' entrances.

Another casual option for lunch, dinner, and late-night snacks is the popular Johnny Rockets, a 1950s-style diner set out on deck and offering burgers, shakes, fries, and the like, with veggie burgers to satisfy non-meateaters. The international waitstaff is cute enough in their '50s-style soda-jerk clothes, but we could do without the cutesy lip-sync-and-dance routines to songs such as "YMCA" and "Respect." There's a $3.95 per-person service charge and sodas and shakes are a la carte (shakes will cost you $3.60 a pop).

POOL, FITNESS, SPA & SPORTS FACILITIES   Each ship has a well-equipped oceanview gym, though the arrangement of machines and the many pillars throughout can make them feel tight when full. Each has a large indoor whirlpool and a huge aerobics studio (among the biggest on any ship), and their two-level spa complexes are among the largest and best accoutered at sea, with peaceful waiting areas where New Agey tropical-birdsong music induces total relaxation—until you get your bill. (Steiner, the company that manages spas aboard most cruise ships, keeps rates steep in 'em all.)

While crowds tend to disperse around the ships' public areas, on sunny days things can get tight out on the main pool decks, creating a kind of tenement-style sunbathing scene. As aboard Carnival's Destiny-class ships, deck chairs are squeezed into every level of the multistoried, amphitheater-like decks, and the vibe can be electric (or at least loud) when the pool band starts playing. Guests seeking something more peaceful can usually find it in the adjacent Solarium, with a second swimming pool and two enormous whirlpool tubs under a sliding roof. Behind the Johnny Rockets diner, *Voyager*, *Adventure*, and *Explorer* have a kids' pool area with a water slide, wading pool, hot tub for adults, and dozens of adorable half-size deck chairs for the kids. On *Navigator* and *Mariner* the area is reserved for teens, with deck chairs for sunbathing, food service several times a week, and an outdoor dance floor with sound and light systems. Deck 13 is the hub of sports action, with the much-touted rock-climbing wall, skating track, miniature-golf course, and basketball court. Appointments must be made to use the more popular options (especially the wall), but this is a good thing as it cuts down on lines.

The Vision Class: Legend • Enchantment • Grandeur • Rhapsody • Splendour • Vision of the Seas

The Verdict

These ships are glitzy and exciting without going overboard, though they're on the frumpy side compared to the newer, snazzier Radiance and Voyager ships.

Rhapsody of the Seas *(photo: RCCL)*

Specifications

Size (in tons)		*Grandeur*	975/212
Legend/Splendour	69,130	*Enchantment*	1,126/248
Grandeur	74,140	*Rhapsody/Vision*	1,000/229
Enchantment	80,700	Crew	
Rhapsody/Vision	78,491	*Legend/Splendour*	720
Passengers (double occ.)		*Grandeur*	760
Legend/Splendour	1,804	*Enchantment*	840
Grandeur	1,950	*Rhapsody/Vision*	765
Enchantment	2,252	Passenger/Crew Ratio	2.5 to 1
Rhapsody/Vision	2,000	*Enchantment*	2.7 to 1
Passenger/Space Ratio		Year Launched	
Legend/Splendour	38.5	*Legend*	1995
Grandeur	38	*Splendour/Grandeur*	1996
Enchantment	36	*Enchantment/Rhapsody*	1997
Rhapsody/Vision	39	*Vision*	1998
Total Cabins/Veranda Cabins		Last Major Refurbishment	N/A
Legend/Splendour	902/231	*Enchantment*	2005

Frommer's Ratings (Scale of 1–5)

★★★½

Cabin Comfort & Amenities	3	Dining Options	3
Ship Cleanliness & Maintenance	4	Gym, Spa & Sports Facilities	4
Public Comfort/Space	4	Children's Facilities	4
Decor	3.5	Enjoyment Factor	4

It's a funny thing with cruise ships. One year they're the newest, hottest, biggest thing on water, and just a few cycles around the sun later you look at them and think, "How quaint. How '90s." They may be just fine, and still offer a great, exciting cruise experience, but things have changed so fast in the cruise biz that even the best ships from the late 20th century can seem dated. That's sort of the story with RCI's Vision-class vessels, but listen, we're not knocking them. These are pretty fine ships, with an open, light-filled feel and many of the same amenities offered by the line's newer, larger ships, including great Solarium pools, hoppin' multilevel discos, well-equipped Internet centers, and sprawling outdoor decks where it's not difficult to find a quiet corner. They've even been retrofitted with rock-climbing walls.

As part of the major "revitalization" program Royal Caribbean began in 2003, *Enchantment of the Seas* is scheduled to go under the knife just as this book goes to press. And we aren't kidding about the knife. Renewing a trend common in the mid-90s, *Enchantment* will literally be sawn in half like a magician's assistant, have a new 73-foot midsection inserted, then be welded back together. Up on the pool deck, which will grow by 50%, two suspension bridges will stretch more than 75 feet, crossing over two new deck areas that jut past lower decks to overhang the water. On one side will be a new island bar, on the other a stage for poolside musical entertainment. Down below, a new "interactive splash deck" will have 64 water jets on the floor, along the perimeter, and in a central dome. Forty of these will be connected to a touchpad system, letting kids spray each other or create their own water ballet. Additions to the nearby Sports Deck will include four bungee trampolines where guests strap into a harness connected to bungee cords, to keep them from flying over the side. The top-side, quarter-mile jogging track will also be augmented with four fitness stops where runners can jump rope; use sit-up/press-up bars to work their arms, back, and stomach; work the calves at a step-up station; and cool down with a series of suggested stretches. Disabled passengers won't be left out, with new accessibility features including pool and Jacuzzi lifts, access to the Splash Deck, a lift to the bungee trampoline area, and improved thresholds and ramps throughout the vessel. Below-deck changes will include the addition of a Latin-themed bar, an expanded casino, a larger shopping area, and a new coffee bar serving Seattle's Best coffee and Ben & Jerry's ice cream—features currently available aboard RCI's newer vessels. No word yet on whether *Enchantment*'s sister ships will get a similar refurbishment anytime soon.

Cabins & Rates

Cabins	Per Diems from	Sq. Ft.	Fridge	Hair Dryer	Sitting Area	TV
Inside	$89	138–174	no	no	yes	yes
Outside	$129	154–237	some	no	yes	yes
Suite	$326	241–1,140	yes	no	yes	yes

CABINS To be polite, cabins are "compact"—larger than on the line's Sovereign-class ships and *Empress of the Seas,* but smaller than those on the Voyager- and Radiance-class ships and on many competitors' vessels (37–52 sq. ft. smaller than Carnival's standard cabins, for example). For big, check out the 1,140-square-foot Royal Suites, which feature a huge marble bathroom with double sinks, a big whirlpool bathtub, and a glass-enclosed shower for two. And what suite would be complete without a baby-grand piano? For something in between, check the roomy 190-square-foot category-D1 cabins, with private verandas, minifridges, small sitting areas with pullout couches, and tons of storage space. All told, about a quarter of each ship's cabins have private verandas, about a third can accommodate third and fourth passengers, and all have an impressive amount of storage space, safes, and TVs. Bathrooms are not the largest you'll ever see, with shower stalls that are a tight squeeze for anyone thicker than a supermodel. Expect a decor of pastel and beige with varnished hardwood trim—not adventurous, but not hideous either.

Each vessel has between 14 and 17 staterooms equipped for wheelchair users.

PUBLIC AREAS Introduced over a period of 3 years, the six Vision-class vessels evolved slightly between the first and last, but for the most part they have a similar look. Promenade and Mariner decks, home to most public rooms, are bright, wide open, and easy to navigate, with corridors converging at a seven-story atrium known as "The Centrum." There, glass elevators take passengers from Deck 4 all the way up to the stunning, glass-walled Viking Crown Lounge on Deck 11, which is a great viewing spot during transits of Alaska's Inside Passage or the Panama Canal. Down below, the Boutiques of the Centrum shopping arcade is much more extensively stocked (and appealing to look at) than those aboard Carnival's Fantasy-class ships, their arch competitors when both were the newest ships at sea.

Throughout each vessel, warm woods and brass, gurgling fountains and green foliage, glass, crystal, and buttery leathers highlight the public areas. Some evoke a private Roman villa; others are deliberately glitzier and flashier. Comfortable spots include the Schooner piano bar, a Royal Caribbean signature with its nautical wood-and-rope decor. It's a great place for a pre-dinner drink or late-night unwinding. Ditto the Champagne Terrace at the foot of the atrium, where you can sip a glass of fine wine or bubbly while swaying to the dance trio.

In contrast to its showcase spaces, each ship also contains many hideaway refuges, including an array of cocktail bars, a library, and card rooms. Hundreds of potted plants and more than 3,000 original artworks aboard each ship add humanity and warmth, though some of that art is, as we said above, "so '90s."

Full musical revues are staged in glittery, two-story showrooms, where columns obstruct views from some balcony seats. The ship's casinos are Vegas-style flashy, with hundreds of gambling stations so densely packed that it's sometimes difficult to move and always difficult to hear. For kids there's a playroom stocked with toys, books, and games, while the nearby teen center goes the video-game route.

DINING OPTIONS The large dining rooms aboard these vessels span two decks connected with a very grand staircase and flanked with 20-foot walls of glass. The rooms are of their era, with lots of stainless steel, mirrors, dramatic chandeliers, and a bit of banquet-hall feel. There's also a large indoor/outdoor buffet restaurant serving breakfast, lunch, and dinner.

POOL, FITNESS, SPA & SPORTS FACILITIES The Steiner-managed spas on these ships offer a wide selection of treatments as well as the standard steam rooms and saunas. Adjacent to the spas are spacious Solariums, each with a pool, lounge chairs, floor-to-ceiling windows, and a retractable glass ceiling. These bright, comfortable spots, designed after Roman, Egyptian, or Moorish models, are a peaceful place to lounge before or after a spa treatment, or any time at all. The gyms are surprisingly small and cramped considering the ships' size, and don't compare to those on Carnival's, Holland America's, and Celebrity's megaships.

Each ship has a higher-than-expected amount of open deck space. The outdoor pool on the Sun Deck has the usual blaring rah-rah music during the day, along with silly contests of the belly-flop variety. A rock-climbing wall, jogging track, shuffleboard, and Ping-Pong round out the on-deck options.

The Sovereign Class: Sovereign • Monarch • Majesty of the Seas

The Verdict

These three ships started Royal Caribbean's trip into megaship land. They aren't spring chickens, but they are a bargain, sailing inexpensive 3- and 4-night cruises on the East and West coasts.

Sovereign of the Seas *(photo: RCCL)*

Specifications

Size (in tons)			
		Sovereign	840
Sovereign	73,192	*Monarch/Majesty*	825
Monarch/Majesty	73,941	Passenger/Crew Ratio	
Passengers (double occ.)		*Sovereign*	2.7 to 1
Sovereign	2,292	*Monarch/Majesty*	2.9 to 1
Monarch/Majesty	2,390	Year Launched	
Passenger/Space Ratio		*Sovereign*	1988
Sovereign	32	*Monarch*	1991
Monarch/Majesty	31	*Majesty*	1992
Total Cabins/Veranda Cabins		Last Major Refurbishment	
Sovereign	1,138/62	*Sovereign*	2004
Monarch/Majesty	1,177/62	*Monarch*	2003
Crew		*Majesty*	N/A

Frommer's Ratings (Scale of 1–5)   ★★★*

Cabin Comfort & Amenities	3	Dining Options	3
Ship Cleanliness & Maintenance	4	Gym, Spa & Sports Facilities	3
Public Comfort/Space	3	Children's Facilities	4
Decor	3.5	Enjoyment Factor	3.5

* *Ratings based on* Monarch *and* Sovereign.

When she was launched in 1988, *Sovereign of the Seas* was the largest passenger vessel built in half a century, and caused such a sensation that Royal Caribbean quickly followed her up with the slightly larger *Monarch* and *Majesty of the Seas*. Times change, though, and today these once-giant ships are literally half the size of their largest fleetmates. A decade and a half of hard use gave them their share of bumps and bruises, but in 2003 Royal Caribbean began a major makeover program designed to hammer out the dents and bring them into the 21st century. *Monarch of the Seas* went under the knife first, with *Sovereign* following in November 2004. Currently, RCI has not scheduled any upgrades for *Majesty*.

Cabins & Rates

Cabins	Per Diems from	Sq. Ft.	Fridge	Hair Dryer	Sitting Area	TV
Inside	$71	120	no	no	no	yes
Outside	$99	120–157	some	no	some	yes
Suite	$318	264–670	yes	no	yes	yes

CABINS   The worst feature of the early RCI ships is their tiny cabins, with standard staterooms averaging a way-too-snug 120 square feet and bathrooms similarly cramped. More than 100 cabins have upper and lower berths to accommodate four, albeit quite tightly. Overall, cabin decor is spartan and uninspired, with pastel fabrics and blond woods, and like other ships of their generation, relatively few have balconies. Closet space is limited, but that isn't a problem on these ships' short itineraries. All cabins have TVs, plus personal safes on *Majesty* and *Monarch* (on *Sovereign*, they're only in cabin categories R, A, B, C, and D; for everyone else, there are lockboxes at the purser's desk). Soundproofing in these cabins isn't the greatest; in some you can hear every word your neighbors say.

Four to six cabins on each ship can accommodate wheelchair users.

PUBLIC AREAS   A dramatic five-story atrium is the focal point of each ship, separating the public areas (which are mostly clustered in the stern) from the cabins forward, an arrangement that minimizes bleed-through noise and also gives the impression that these ships are smaller than they are. Shops, the ship's salon, the Internet center, the library, several information desks, and a champagne bar are all clustered around the atrium at various levels. Elsewhere, you'll find a sprawling casino, a cinema, the popular Schooner piano bar, and (as on all pre-*Voyager* RCI ships) the Viking Crown Lounge, perched on the topmost deck some 150 feet above sea level and letting on to amazing panoramic views. It's a great place for a pre-dinner drink and after-dinner dancing. Down on Decks 5 and 7, the two-story main show lounge is roomy and well planned, with lots of cocktail-table-and-chair clusters for two and a huge stage.

As part of their recent makeovers, *Monarch* and *Sovereign* were fitted with a Boleros Latin Lounge, featuring Latin music, a dueling-piano-players act, and drinks from Brazil, Cuba, and Central America. The ships' children's centers were also expanded and three teen-only hangouts added: the Living Room coffee bar, a disco called "Fuel," and a private outdoor sun deck with dance floor.

DINING OPTIONS   Each ship offers a pair of one-story dining rooms (extensively refurbished on *Sovereign* and *Monarch*), plus a large indoor/outdoor buffet restaurant on Deck 11 serving breakfast, lunch, and dinner. *Monarch*'s buffet also offers an Asian option, and *Sovereign*'s features multiple self-service islands offering regional dishes from Asia, Latin America, the Mediterranean, the U.S., and elsewhere, plus a cooked-to-order pasta station, a carving station, deli, and a soup-and-salad bar. On *Monarch* and *Sovereign* you can also nosh at a new dedicated pizzeria or grab a specialty coffee or Ben & Jerry's ice cream from the Latte'tudes coffee shop. *Sovereign* also features a '50s-style Johnny Rockets diner serving burgers and shakes.

POOL, FITNESS, SPA & SPORTS FACILITIES The deck layout and two good-size swimming pools seem plenty large when they're empty, but the number of passengers who typically sail these short itineraries almost guarantees that they'll fill up, becoming a wall-to-wall carpet of people. That said, there are many patches of more isolated deck space all over each ship, from the quiet slices on the tiered aft decks to two levels of far-forward deck space.

The Sports Deck, up high in the stern, has Ping-Pong tables and a basketball court. The half-moon-shaped gym on Deck 10 is fairly spacious, with a wall of windows facing aft. Treadmills, stationary bikes, step machines, and free weights line the perimeter of the room, facing the sea, and the inner part of the room serves as the aerobics space. A smallish spa is adjacent.

All three ships sport rock-climbing walls, a feature that's become one of Royal Caribbean's signature offerings.

Empress of the Seas

The Verdict

Once known as *Nordic Empress,* this midsize ship received a substantial makeover in spring 2004, bringing her amenities more in line with what's offered on her much larger fleetmates.

Empress of the Seas *(photo: RCCL)*

Specifications

Size (in tons)	48,563	Crew	668
Passengers (double occ.)	1,602	Passenger/Crew Ratio	2.4 to 1
Passenger/Space Ratio	30.5	Year Launched	1990
Total Cabins/Veranda Cabins	800/69	Last Major Refurbishment	2004

Frommer's Ratings (Scale of 1–5)   ★★★½

Cabin Comfort & Amenities	3	Dining Options	3.5
Ship Cleanliness & Maintenance	4	Gym, Spa & Sports Facilities	3
Public Comfort/Space	3	Children's Facilities	4
Decor	4	Enjoyment Factor	4

This once-hefty 48,000-ton vessel is an absolute shrimp compared to her more modern megaship cousins, and in recent years her late-'80s decor was looking pretty dated. In 2004, though, RCI gave her a face-lift that updated the decor of her lobbies, elevators, corridors, and other public areas and transformed some of her lounge spaces into additional dining, entertainment, and fitness areas. The result? She don't look bad, particularly for short cruises.

Cabins & Rates

Cabins	Per Diems from	Sq. Ft.	Fridge	Hair Dryer	Sitting Area	TV
Inside	$93	117	no	no	no	yes
Outside	$109	139	no	no	some	yes
Suite	$351	194–596	yes	no	yes	yes

CABINS At no more than 139 square feet, standard cabins are small, almost half of them are insides, and (despite renovations done in 2004) most bear some of the scuffs and scrapes of 14 years at sea—a combination that practically guarantees passengers will spend more time in the public areas or out in the sun. All cabins have safes and TVs. Drawer and closet space is limited, though cabins accommodating third and fourth guests were fitted with modified wardrobes during the ship's refit, which should address the problem somewhat. Bathrooms are cramped and showers coffin-like, though there's a surprisingly good amount of storage space in them. Upper-end cabins and suites have verandas; outside cabins without them offer rectangular picture windows. Four cabins are wheelchair accessible.

PUBLIC AREAS Considering the relatively small size of this vessel, her six-deck atrium was a pretty astonishing design choice, with light flooding in from above, big windows flanking five decks on either side, and a fountain splashing at its base. Up on the top two decks, *Empress*'s Viking Crown Lounge and disco is a barrel-like two-story space wrapped in windows, with tiny pencil-point lights in the ceiling creating a neat starscape at night, when the place is dark and the music is rocking. As part of her refit, the ship's gym now occupies the disco's balcony—a very weird decision, if you ask us. On Deck 6, the Latin-themed Boleros Bar serves specialty tequilas, excellent mojitos, and live Latin music in the evenings, while the nautical-themed Schooner Bar has sing-along piano entertainment. Other entertainment choices include the casino and the Strike Up the Band Showroom, with its very pink, slick, Atlantic City showroom feel. For kids, the children's center includes a fun climbing maze with tubes and slides.

DINING OPTIONS The ship's two-level dining room has a "futuristic a la 1980s" feel, with floor-to-ceiling windows in the stern and a balcony with circular seating areas protruding from its rim, suggesting flying saucers. Decor here was refurbished in spring 2004, washing away some of its banquet-hall feel. The ship's buffet restaurant, the Windjammer, also got a face-lift, and two new dining options were added: the line's Portofino Italian specialty restaurant and a coffee bar, Latte'Tudes, serving Seattle's Best specialty coffees plus Ben & Jerry's ice cream—for an extra charge, of course.

POOL, FITNESS, SPA & SPORTS FACILITIES On the Sun Deck there are three hot tubs, a generous swimming pool fed by a fountain, a wading pool for children, and enough shady spots to get a break from the sun. When the sun goes down, the deck transforms from sunbathing space into a starlit dance floor, with its fountain, gazebo, and sail-like canopies creating a cozy, almost clubby ambience.

The ship's spa was thoroughly redone in '04 and is now totally modern and welcoming. For workouts, head to that wacky gym, the jogging track, or the rock-climbing wall, then take a good steam after.

7

The Ultraluxury Lines

On these top-shelf cruises, guests don't line up for a look at an ice sculpture or a slice of pepperoni pizza en route to St. Thomas or Nassau; they sip a '98 Bordeaux with their filet de boeuf in truffle sauce while sailing to St. Barts. They order jumbo shrimp from the room-service menu, and take indulgent baths in ritzy marble-covered bathrooms. There are no midnight buffets, dancing waiters, belly-flop contests by the pool, assigned dinner seating (except on the Crystal and Cunard ships), or many of the other typi-cal cruise ship trappings, but instead, doting service, the best food and wine you'll find at sea, and a calm, elegant retreat to call home for a week or two.

These cruise lines' ships are the closest thing you'll find to five-star. Mostly small and intimate, these are the sports cars of cruise ships, and they cater to discerning travelers who don't blink at paying top dollar to be pampered with fine gourmet cuisine and spacious suites with walk-in closets. Formal nights see the vast majority of guests dressed in tuxedos and sparkling dresses and gowns dining in el-egant rooms with the finest linens, stemware, and china. The only exceptions here are the yachts of SeaDream, which take a much more casual approach that suits their more laid-back decor. Aboard all the lines, delicious French, Italian, and Asian cuisine often rivals that of respected shoreside restaurants and is served in high style by large staffs of doting, gracious waiters who know how to please. A full dinner can even be served to you in your cabin, if you like. Still, you shouldn't expect the kind of five-star experience you'd get on land; none of these ultraluxe ships offers the level of service and cuisine you'd find at a Four Seasons or Ritz-Carlton hotel. But while it won't quite be a three-star Michelin experience, the ultraluxe lines are as good as it gets at sea. And they're pretty darn good.

Entertainment and organized activities are more dignified than on other ships—you won't see any raunchy comedy routines or bordering-on-obscene pool games here—and are more limited as guests tend to amuse themselves, enjoying cocktails and conversation in a piano bar, or watching small-scale Broadway-inspired song-and-dance reviews.

With the exception of the large Crystal ships and Cunard's QE2 and QM2, these high-end vessels tend to be small and intimate, carrying just a few hundred passengers. You're not likely to feel lost in the crowd, and staff will get to know your likes and dislikes early on. The onboard atmosphere is much like a private club, with guests trading traveling tales and meeting for drinks or dinner.

While the high-end lines discount at times, they'll still cost two or three times as much as your typical mainstream cruise. Expect to pay at least $2,000 per person for a week in the Caribbean, and easily more if you opt for a large suite or choose to cruise during the busiest times of the year. Many extras are often included in the cruise rates. For instance, Silversea's, Seabourn's, and SeaDream's rates include unlimited wine, liquor, and beverages, along with tips, a stocked minibar, and one complimentary

Frommer's Ratings at a Glance: The Ultraluxury Lines

1 = poor   2 = fair   3 = good   4 = excellent   5 = outstanding

Cruise Line	Enjoyment Factor	Dining	Activities	Children's Program	Entertainment	Service	Worth the Money
Crystal	5	5	5	3	4	4	5
Cunard	5	4	5	5	4	4	5
Radisson Seven Seas	5	4	3	2	3	5	5
Seabourn	5	5	2	N/A*	2	4	4
SeaDream	5	4	3	N/A*	3	5	5
Silversea	5	5	3	N/A*	2	5	4

Note: Cruise lines have been graded on a curve that compares them only with the other lines in the ultraluxury category. See "How to Read the Ratings," in chapter 5, for a detailed explanation of the ratings methodology.

* Lines with N/A rating for children's programs have no program whatsoever.

shore excursion per cruise. Radisson's rates include tips, wine with dinner, one-time stocked minibar, and unlimited soda and bottled water, and Crystal now includes all soft drinks in its rates. Many of these lines also include other free perks the mainstream lines don't, from Godiva chocolates on pillows at night (Silversea), to cotton logo pj's (SeaDream), a CD of classic jazz (Seabourn), luggage tags and document portfolio (Seabourn offers Tumi versions), personalized stationery (Silversea, Seabourn, and Radisson), and high-end bathroom amenities from names such as Bronnely, Molton Brown, and Acqua di Parma.

Most people attracted to these types of cruises are sophisticated, wealthy, relatively social, and used to the finer things in life. Most are well traveled, though not necessarily adventurous, and tend to stick to five-star experiences. These ships are not geared to children, although you'll see more than ever before (especially on holiday sailings and summertime cruises to places such as the Caribbean and Alaska). In this event, babysitting can often be arranged privately with an off-duty crewmember. The larger Crystal ships do have playrooms, and as many as 100 children are not uncommon during holiday cruises.

DRESS CODES   With the exception of SeaDream, these are the most formal cruises out there: For the main dining rooms, you need to bring the tux and the sequined gown—guests dress for dinner on the 2 or 3 formal nights on these cruises. Informal nights call for suits and usually ties for men (though Seabourn, for instance, now officially doesn't require ties except on formal nights) and smart dresses, skirts, or pantsuits for ladies; sports jackets or nice shirts for men and casual dresses or pantsuits for women are the norm on casual nights. That said, like the rest of the industry, even the high-end lines are relaxing their dress codes, heading closer to lines such as Windstar and SeaDream, which espouse a casual "no jackets required" policy during the entire cruise. All the ultraluxe lines now have casual dining venues, so if you just want to throw on a sundress, or polo shirt and chinos, and be done with it, you'll be fine. Even in the formal dining room (albeit on a casual night) on a recent *Seven Seas Navigator* cruise, several 60-plus passengers wore jeans, sneakers, and T-shirts (even if they were the $100 kind).

1 Crystal Cruises

2049 Century Park E., Suite 1400, Los Angeles, CA 90067. © **800/446-6620** or 310/785-9300. Fax 310/785-0011. www.crystalcruises.com.

THE LINE IN A NUTSHELL   Fine-tuned and fashionable, Crystal offers top-shelf service and cuisine on ships large enough to offer lots of outdoor deck space, generous fitness facilities, tons of activities, multiple restaurants, and more than half a dozen bars and entertainment venues. **Sails to:** Caribbean, Panama Canal, Alaska, Mexican Riviera, Hawaii, Canada/New England.

THE EXPERIENCE   Aside from Cunard's *Queen Mary 2,* Crystal has the only truly upscale large ships in the industry. Carrying 940 to 1,080 passengers, they aren't huge, but they're big enough to offer much more than their high-end peers. You won't feel hemmed in and you likely won't be twiddling your thumbs from lack of stimulation. Service is excellent and the line's Asian cuisine is tops. Unlike Seabourn's small ships, which tend to be more calm and staid, Crystal's sociable California ethic and large passenger capacity tend to keep things mingly, chatty, and more active.

Pros

- **Four or five restaurants:** In addition to the formal dining room, there are two or three alternative restaurants (including, on *Serenity,* two with cuisine by famed chef Nobu Matsuhisa), plus a poolside grille, an indoor cafe, and a casual restaurant that puts on great theme luncheon buffets.
- **Best Asian food at sea:** The ships' reservations-only Asian restaurants serve up utterly delicious, authentic, fresh Japanese food, including sushi. At least once per cruise, an Asian-theme buffet lunch offers an awesome spread.
- **Fitness choices:** There's a nice-size gym, paddle-tennis courts, shuffleboard, Ping-Pong, a jogging circuit, golf-driving nets, and a putting green.
- **Enrichment Programs:** No other line has as much, with complimentary computer training classes on every cruise, plus dozens of theme sailings focused on food and wine, art, film, jazz music, wellness, and other subjects.

Cons

- **Least all-inclusive of the luxe lines:** Only nonalcoholic drinks are included in the rates, not tips, booze, and so on.
- **Cabin size:** Accommodations (especially on *Symphony*) are smaller than those aboard Silversea, Seabourn, and Radisson.

Compared with the other ultraluxury lines, here's how Crystal rates:

	Poor	Fair	Good	Excellent	Outstanding
Enjoyment Factor					✓
Dining					✓
Activities					✓
Children's Program			✓		
Entertainment				✓	
Service				✓	
Worth the Money					✓

CRYSTAL: SPARKLING & SPACIOUS

Established in 1990, Crystal Cruises has held its own and even established its own unique place in the high-stakes, super-upscale cruise market. Its ships are the largest true luxury vessels aside from Cunard's venerable *QE2* and new *QM2,* and while not quite as generous in the stateroom department (cabins are smaller than those on Radisson, Silversea, Seabourn, and SeaDream) and the freebies department (Crystal doesn't include complimentary champagne, liquor, and wine in the rates), they provide a truly refined cruise for discerning guests who appreciate really good service and top-notch cuisine. No doubt about it, Crystal is one of our favorite lines.

The line is the North American spinoff of Japan's largest container shipping enterprise, Nippon Yusen Kaisha (NYK). Despite these origins, a passenger aboard Crystal could conceivably spend an entire week at sea and not even be aware that the ship is Japanese-owned and -funded. More than anything else, Crystal is international, with a strong emphasis on European service. The Japanese exposure is subtler, and you'll feel it in the excellent Asian cuisine and tasty sake served in the alternative restaurants and at the Asian-theme buffets. A Japanese activities director is on board to attend to the handful of Japanese passengers you'll see on many cruises.

In late 2005, the line's oldest ship, the 1990-built *Harmony,* left the Crystal fleet to take up service with parent company NYK's Asian cruise division. In announcing the move, Crystal also hinted at future construction of a replacement vessel, though no details are yet available.

PASSENGER PROFILE

Like other high-end lines, Crystal draws a lot of repeat passengers. On many cruises more than 50% hail from affluent regions of California and most step aboard for their second, third, or fourth Crystal cruise. There's commonly a small contingent of passengers (about 15% of the mix) from the United Kingdom, Australia, Japan, Hong Kong, Mexico, Europe, and South America and others. Most passengers are well-heeled couples over 55. A good number of passengers step up to Crystal from lines such as Princess and Holland America.

Many Crystal passengers place great emphasis on the social scene before, during, and after mealtimes, and many enjoy dressing up (sometimes way up) for dinner and adorning themselves with the biggest and best diamonds they own. You'll see no shortage of big rocks and gold Rolexes. The onboard jewelry and clothing boutiques do a brisk business, and it's obvious that women on board have devoted much care and attention to their wardrobes and accessories. On formal nights—2 or 3 of which occur during every 10- or 11-day cruise—the majority of men wear tuxes and many women wear floor-length gowns, although your classic black cocktail dress is just fine. As on most ships, dress codes are much more relaxed during the day.

Though not a kid-centric line compared to the mainstream lines, in the high-end, Crystal is the most accommodating for families with kids. Each ship has a dedicated playroom and supervised activities for ages 3+ are offered when demand warrants it. During the holidays, the summer months of July and August, and on Alaska cruises, 100 or so kids on board is not that unusual.

DINING

Service by the team of ultraprofessional, gracious, European male waiters is excellent. In the main dining room—and to a somewhat lesser degree in the alternative restaurants—table settings are lavish and include fine, heavy crystal and porcelain. Even in the Lido restaurant, waiters are at hand to serve you your salad from the buffet line, prepare your coffee, and then carry your tray to wherever it is you want to sit.

TRADITIONAL   Dinner is served in two seatings in the main dining rooms; lunches and breakfasts are open seating. Cuisine selections include dishes such as coq au vin (braised chicken in burgundy red-wine sauce with glazed onions and mushrooms over a bed of linguine), Black Angus beef tenderloin with burgundy wine gravy, oven-baked quail with porcini mushroom and bread stuffing, or seared sea scallops served with a light lobster beurre blanc over a bed of risotto. At lunch and dinner, there's a light selection—lower in cholesterol, fat, and sodium—such as grilled fresh halibut served with steamed vegetables and herbed potatoes, as well as an entree salad—for example, a mixed salad with grilled herb-marinated chicken breast, lamb, or filet mignon. Vegetarian selections are also featured, such as spinach and ricotta cannelloni or a brochette of Mediterranean vegetables. **Kosher foods** and **low-carb choices** are also available, and sugar-free, gluten-free, and low-fat options are now part of all menus, even at buffets. Virtually any special diet can be accommodated.

In a kind of homage to the California wine industry, Crystal offers one of the most sophisticated inventories of California wines on the high sea, as well as a reserve list of two dozen or so rare wines and an extensive selection of French wines. The line also recently created its own proprietary label called *C Wines,* which features three reserve selections and three premium *C Wines* selections, which are offered by the glass or by the bottle.

SPECIALTY   The line's Asian venues are among the best at sea. *Symphony*'s Jade Garden showcases the Asian cuisine of Wolfgang Puck's acclaimed Santa Monica restaurant, Chinois on Main. Even better, master chef **Nobuyuki "Nobu" Matsuhisa,** known for his restaurants in New York, Miami, L.A., London, Paris, and other cities, partnered with Crystal to create menus for *Serenity*'s Sushi Bar and its Pan-Asian restaurant Silk Road. Dishes feature Nobu's eclectic blends of Japanese cuisine with Peruvian and European influences. In the Sushi Bar, sample the salmon tartare with sevruga caviar or the yellowtail sashimi with jalapeño; in Silk Road, choices include lobster with truffle yuzu sauce and chicken with teriyaki balsamic. While Nobu himself makes occasional appearances on *Serenity,* chef Toshiaki Tamba, personally trained by Nobu, oversees the restaurants.

Aboard both ships, famed restaurateur Piero Selvaggio showcases the cuisine of his award-winning Santa Monica and Las Vegas Valentino restaurants at the Italian "Valentino at Prego." Reservations are required, and there's a suggested $6 gratuity in each of the specialty restaurants.

CASUAL   Excellent themed luncheon buffets—Asian, Mediterranean, Western barbecue, or South American/Cuban, for instance—are generously spread out at lunchtime by the pool, and an extraspecial gala buffet is put on once per cruise in the lobby/atrium. No expense or effort is spared to produce elaborate food fests, with heaps of jumbo shrimp, homemade sushi, Greek salads, shish kabobs, beef satay, stir-fry dishes, and more.

While you can have breakfast in the Lido restaurant, the Bistro serves a late continental breakfast from 9:30 to 11:30am and is open between 11:30am and 6pm for complimentary grazing at the buffet-style spread of cheeses, cold cuts, fruit, cookies, and pastries. Nonalcoholic specialty drinks, such as hazelnut latte and fruit shakes, are complimentary here.

For something casual poolside, the Trident Grill serves casual lunches daily between 11:30am and 6pm for those who'd like something simple and easy poolside (beef, chicken, and salmon burgers; wraps and tuna melts; pizza, hot dogs, and fries; fruit; and a special of the day). You can place your order at the counter and either have a seat at the adjacent tables or head back to your deck chair and let a waiter bring you your lunch. You don't even have to change out of your bathing suit. It also operates several evenings per cruise between 6 and 9pm, offering an open-air ambience and serving dishes such as grilled shrimp, Cobb salad, and gourmet pizza.

SNACKS & EXTRAS   For afternoon tea, it's the ultrachic Palm Court on one of the uppermost decks. A sprawling space with floor-to-ceiling windows and pale-blue and white furniture in leather and rattan, the area gives off an overall light, soft, and ethereal ambience. Pre-dinner and midnight canapés in the lounges include the delicious likes of foie gras, caviar, and marinated salmon.

There is, of course, 24-hour room service, as well as complimentary unlimited non-alcoholic drinks everywhere aboard, from cappuccino to soda and bottled water.

ACTIVITIES

Crystal offers an interesting selection of activities that can fill your day if you care to be so busy. You can count on several **enrichment lectures** throughout a cruise, such as a historian presenting a slide show and speaking about the Panama Canal and how it was built, a former Ambassador speaking about regional politics, or a movie critic talking to guests about Hollywood films. Most speakers are not celebrities, but well-known personalities do occasionally show up. Recent guests have included broadcast icon Barbara Walters; television personality Regis Philbin; actress Doris Roberts; TV journalist Garrick Utley, who appears regularly on CNN; award-winning CBS news correspondent Ike Pappas; Broadway star Joel Grey; singer Maureen McGovern; entertainer Lucie Arnaz (daughter of Lucille Ball and Desi Arnaz); comedian Jonathan Winters; and Olympic gold medalists Nadia Comaneci and Bart Conner.

In addition to each cruises' guest lecturers, some of Crystal's sailings feature **theme programs** with activities built around them, including more than a dozen Wine & Food Festival cruises. These feature a respected wine expert such as Dan Berger who conducts at least two complimentary tastings, and guest chefs such as Nancy Silverton and Anton Mosimann conducting cooking demonstrations for guests and then presenting the results of those lessons at dinner. There are also music-theme cruises from time to time, featuring Big Bands and jazz singers, such as the up-and-coming Liza Lee. Other theme cruises have experts conducting seminars on finance issues, language instruction, and art appreciation, where speakers from the famous auction house Sotheby's are spotlighted.

Guest teachers teach swing, rumba, and merengue dance lessons on some cruises. Group lessons are complimentary, and private lessons can sometimes be arranged with the instructors for about $50 per hour per couple. Crystal is also big on organizing bridge and paddle-tennis competitions, game-show-style contests, and trivia games, as well as providing midafternoon dance music with the resident dance trio or quartet; serving tea to the accompaniment of a harpist; offering interesting arts and crafts such as glass-etching; and even presenting guest fashion shows. Commonly, a golf expert sails on board, too, conducting complimentary group golf lessons by the driving nets several times per cruise (again, private lessons can be arranged; prices start at $50 per hour). A variety of free aerobics classes is also offered in the fitness center, including Pilates and yoga (private personal trainers are available for a fee).

Kudos to the line's **Computer University;** no other line offers anything as extensive. Each ship has a well-stocked 24-hour two-room computer lab with some 30 computer workstations. Passengers can send and receive e-mail via their personal accounts (AOL, Hotmail, and so on) or through a special personal shipboard address they're given with their cruise documents. Computer use is free of charge, while there's a fee for e-mailing and Internet access. You can even rent a laptop computer for use in the comfort of your stateroom ($5 per day), which are all wired for Internet access.

A complimentary 30-course computer curriculum is offered on all cruises, with topics such as a basic introduction to using the computer, understanding the Internet, and creating spreadsheets using Excel. There are also private lessons available for $50 an hour.

CHILDREN'S PROGRAM

Crystal is a sophisticated cruise line that focuses its attention on adults, but more than any other line in the luxury end of the market, it also does its part to cater to the little people. Each ship has a bright children's playroom, primarily used during holiday and summer cruises (mostly in Alaska and Europe), when some 100 kids may be aboard. Both ships have PlayStation video games, computers, and video arcade/teen centers. During busy times, counselors are on hand to supervise activities such as scavenger hunts, arts and crafts, karaoke, and games to take place during several hours in the morning and in the afternoon, for three age groups between 3 and 17. There are kiddy books and videos in the library for guests to take back to their staterooms, and a children's menu in the main dining room as well as favorites at the poolside Trident Grill like hot dogs, hamburgers, and pizza.

For children as young as 6 months, in-cabin babysitting can be arranged privately through the concierge at an hourly rate of $7.50 for one child, $10 for two kids, and $12.50 for three kids. Cribs, highchairs, and booster seats are available, and as for food, if you notify the line ahead of time, they'll special order jars of baby food, at no charge. Or, the chef will puree organic food for your baby. Note that children 11 and under pay 50% of the minimum fare when accompanied by two full-fare guests.

The minimum age for sailing is 6 months.

ENTERTAINMENT

Onboard entertainment is good (and plentiful), but it's certainly not the high point of the cruise. Shows in the horseshoe-shaped, rather plain Galaxy Lounge encompass everything from classical concertos by accomplished pianists to comedy. A troupe of spangle-covered, lip-syncing dancers and a pair of lead singers perform Vegas-style shows with themes such as Cole Porter or a certain Broadway show. From time to time, celebrity entertainers such as Carol Channing, Tommy Tune, Robert Klein, and Marvin Hamlisch, are featured.

Crystal Fleet Itineraries

Ship	Itineraries
Serenity	**10-night E. Carib:** Round-trip from Ft. Lauderdale, FL, Nov 2005. **7- & 14-night Mexican Riviera:** Round-trip from Los Angeles, CA, Dec 2005–Jan 2006. **7- & 10-night Caribbean:** Round-trip from Miami, FL, Nov–Dec 2006.
Symphony	**10- & 11-night Canada/New England:** North- or southbound between New York, NY, and Montreal, Oct–Nov 2005 and Sept–Oct 2006. **10- & 11-night Panama Canal:** North- and southbound between Miami, FL, and Caldera, Costa Rica, Nov 2005–Feb 2006. **8-, 10- & 14-night E./S. Carib:** Round-trip from Ft. Lauderdale, FL, Dec 2005. **7-night Canada/New England:** Round-trip from New York, NY, Sept 2006.

After dinner each night, a second large, attractive lounge is the venue for ballroom-style dancing to a live band, with a coterie of gentleman hosts aboard each sailing to provide dance (and dinner) partners for single ladies. *Serenity* also has a dedicated disco, while on *Symphony* the disco is part of the Starlight lounge. A pianist in the dark, paneled, and romantic Avenue Saloon—our favorite room on board—plays popular show tunes and pop hits before and after dinner, from "New York, New York" to "My Funny Valentine." On both ships you can also enjoy cigars in the Connoisseurs Club, a movie theater showing recent-release movies several times a day (as well as serving as a venue for lectures and religious services), and cabin TVs that feature a wonderfully varied and full menu of movies.

Gamblers will have no problem feeling at home in the roomy **casinos,** which are supervised directly by Caesars Palace Casinos at Sea.

SERVICE

The hallmark of a high-end cruise such as Crystal is its service, so the line's staff is better trained and more attentive than that aboard most other cruise lines, and is typically an international cast: The dining room and restaurant staffs hail from Italy, Portugal, and other European countries, and have trained in the grand restaurants of Europe and North America; and the cabin stewardess who tidies your stateroom is likely to be from Scandinavia, Hungary, or some other European country. Overall, the dining/bar staff is best, outshining the cabin stewardesses, though everyone, even the staff manning the information and concierge desks in the lobby, is endlessly good natured and very helpful—a rare find, indeed. Guests in Penthouse Suites are treated to the services of male butlers. (We might note that the Crystal ships are among the few that have a small pool for their crewmembers, located at the bow of the ship on Deck 5. It pays to keep the crew happy!) As far as tipping goes, most passengers charge gratuities to their onboard accounts, though you can pay in cash if you wish.

All guests are welcomed to complimentary unlimited nonalcoholic drinks everywhere aboard, from cappuccino to soda and bottled water.

In addition to laundry and dry-cleaning services, self-serve laundry rooms are available.

Crystal Serenity

The Verdict

Just when you thought Crystal couldn't get any better, the new *Crystal Serenity* comes on the scene and does just that, offering an ultraelegant cruise with a huge array of onboard choices, from dining to activities and public spaces.

Crystal Serenity *(photo: Crystal Cruises)*

Specifications

Size (in tons)	68,000	Crew	655
Passengers (double occ.)	1080	Passenger/Crew Ratio	1.6 to 1
Passenger/Space Ratio	63	Year Launched	2003
Total Cabins/Veranda Cabins	540/460	Last Major Refurbishment	N/A

Frommer's Ratings (Scale of 1–5)   ★★★★½

Cabin Comfort & Amenities	4.5	Dining Options	5
Ship Cleanliness & Maintenance	5	Gym, Spa & Sports Facilities	5
Public Comfort/Space	4.5	Children's Facilities	3.5
Decor	4	Enjoyment Factor	5

The largest ultraluxury vessel afloat, *Serenity* is 38% bigger than the older *Symphony* but only carries 15% more guests. It's one of the most spacious ships out there, from the beautifully designed public rooms to an expansive pool deck. There's simply no crowding at any time. Former guests will be very pleased that there are no radical changes in style, service, or layout from the *Symphony* and the departed *Harmony,* only subtle improvements, including a sushi bar and rooms built specifically for Crystal's University at Sea. Most recently, the ship was wired for cellphone use, too. In every way, this ship's a star.

Cabins & Rates

Cabins	Per Diems from	Sq. Ft.	Fridge	Hair Dryer	Sitting Area	TV
Outside	$300	202–226	yes	yes	yes	yes
Suite	$620	403–1345*	yes	yes	yes	yes

* Including veranda.

CABINS   Standard staterooms on this ship are about the same size as those on *Symphony,* though the bathrooms and balconies are larger. The majority of standard cabins (categories A and B) are 202 square feet, not including balconies; cabin size is not Crystal's strong suit when compared to the line's luxury peers. There are 100 suites in three different categories, with the largest running 1,345 square feet.

Most of the standard cabins, called "Deluxe Staterooms," have a veranda, while 80 rooms have a large picture window. All feature a seating area, complimentary soft drinks and water, remote TV and DVD (the easy to operate controls are a nice touch), small refrigerator, private safe, computer dataport, bath/shower combo, Egyptian cotton sheets and feather bed toppers, and a pillow menu. Choose from "regular" king and standard-size pillows or four specialty options: hypo-allergenic king- or standard-size pillows, filled with downlike polyfiber; round neck pillows, sotonic elastic foam-filled, for neck or lumbar support; firm standard-size pillows, with 95% feather and 5% down filling; or therapeutic sleep-sensitive standard-size pillows, 100% polyester fiber with head and neck indent. Besides all of this, the Penthouse Stateroom adds in butler service and complimentary beer, while the Penthouse Suites also throw in complimentary liquor and wine setup upon embarkation, a flat screen TV, a separate bedroom area with a vanity, a Jacuzzi tub, a bidet, and a walk-in closet. If you're going straight to the top, the ship's Crystal Penthouses are incredibly spacious abodes, with a separate living room, a dining area, a CD player, three TVs (one in the bathroom if that floats your boat!), a cordless phone, a library, a pantry, and, believe it or not, a small gym.

Decor-wise, wood accents and furniture in the staterooms are on the medium to dark side, creating an elegant atmosphere offsetting the more colorful curtains, wall coverings, upholstery, and bedcovers. The feel is soothing. As aboard *Symphony,* the bathrooms are nicely laid out but still on the small side for a ship of such a high quality. You'll find plenty of drawer and closet space for a cruise of up to about 2 weeks.

Only a handful of cabins either connect or have a third berth available, and none offers four berths. There are eight rooms designated as wheelchair accessible.

PUBLIC AREAS It's difficult to pick a favorite; the public rooms on the *Serenity* are all very appealing. The ship has a quiet, elegant atmosphere, and you certainly won't find glitz; even the casino, Caesars Palace at Sea (which offers Vegas odds, even on craps), is understated. A wonderful feature that harkens back to the glory days of oceangoing travel includes a wide wraparound teak promenade (Deck 7). There are no deck chairs to get in the way of strollers, and lifeboats are a deck below, so the views are free and clear.

Color schemes throughout the ship are muted and very calming, with lots of blues, greens, reds, golds, and grays. Among the most popular lounges on this ship (and aboard *Symphony*) is dark and cozy Avenue Saloon. On the *Serenity,* it has a wonderful round bar and plenty of table seating. The two show lounges, Galaxy Lounge and Stardust Club, offer great sightlines and comfy seating, both theater- and table-style.

Two of the new rooms on *Serenity* are for the **Computer University@Sea,** which has 36 computer stations with Internet access, and for the lines' learning program, which offers classes in partnership with well-known institutions, such as piano instruction by Yamaha, language immersion by Berlitz, art classes conducted by the Parsons School of Design, and wellness programs run by the Cleveland Clinic and the Tai Chi Cultural Center.

The ship has a good library that's well stocked with books, DVDs, and CDs that can be checked out only when the librarian is on duty.

DINING OPTIONS Dining has been a trademark of Crystal's since the line began sailing in 1990, and the *Serenity* carries on the tradition with its two impressive alternative open-seating restaurants, both of which require reservations and a suggested $6 cover charge. In Prego, the surroundings really make you feel you're in a fine Italian restaurant ashore. Menu items range from meats to pastas, fish, and more, and there's also a tasting menu offering items selected by Piero Selvaggio, proprietor of the famous Santa Monica and Las Vegas restaurants, Valentino. On the Oriental side of things, famed chef Nobu Matsuhisa oversees the menus in Silk Road, an ultrastylish space designed in a sea of ethereal mints and whites—there's both a main restaurant and a sushi bar. In the ship's formal restaurant, the Crystal Dining Room, there are two seatings each evening at assigned tables. The lovely decor is a rich blend of dark woods with blue and mauve chairs, all of which have armrests!

The ship's other outlets include the Bistro Café, open for a variety of snacks and beverages all day long, plus the poolside Trident Grill and the Lido Café, which serves buffet-style breakfast and lunch, with some made-to-the-minute specialties such as omelets or pastas. A new addition to this ship is Tastes, a casual venue serving breakfast, lunch, and dinner under the retractable roof near the Neptune Pool. It has a completely separate menu from the other dining areas and is a great dinner alternative when you don't feel like dressing up.

The 24-hour room service menu is quite extensive; at scheduled meal times, guests can order from the Crystal Dining Room menus.

POOL, FITNESS, SPA & SPORTS FACILITIES   There are two reasonably sized pools, one of which features a sliding glass roof. Indoors, the stunning Crystal Spa was designed according to soothing Feng Shui principles, putting you right into relaxation mode. The complex includes a quiet room with very comfortable seating and great aft-facing views for those relaxing moments before or after a spa treatment. The changing rooms have luxurious amenities such as lotions, shampoos, hair dryers, clocks, and bottles of water, while the steam rooms boast large picture windows for great views while you roast! There's also a spacious beauty salon with six complete workstations. There's a gym plus a separate weight room, an aerobics studio, two full-size paddle tennis courts, table tennis, golf driving nets, and a putting green.

Crystal Symphony

The Verdict

A gracious, floating pleasure palace, small enough to feel intimate and personal, yet large enough for a whole range of entertainment, dining, and fitness diversions.

Crystal Symphony *(photo: Crystal Cruises)*

Specifications

Size (in tons)	51,044	Crew	545
Passengers (double occ.)	940	Passenger/Crew Ratio	1.7 to 1
Passenger/Space Ratio	54.3	Year Launched	1995
Total Cabins/Veranda Cabins	480/276	Last Major Refurbishment	2004

Frommer's Ratings (Scale of 1–5)   ★★★★½

Cabin Comfort & Amenities	4	Dining Options	5
Ship Cleanliness & Maintenance	4	Gym, Spa & Sports Facilities	5
Public Comfort/Space	4.5	Children's Facilities	3
Decor	4	Enjoyment Factor	5

Plush, streamlined, extravagantly comfortable, and not as overwhelmingly large as the megaships being launched by less glamorous lines, *Symphony* competes with the high-end Silversea, Radisson, and Seabourn vessels, although she's almost five times as large as Seabourn's, with a broader choice of onboard diversions and distractions. In spring 2004 she underwent a thorough $12-million sprucing up during a 3-week dry dock, resulting in a completely new and expanded spa, an expanded area for her Computer University@Sea program, a new ultra-intimate dining area seating groups of 12, and a spruced up main dining room, library, photo shop, public restrooms, and staterooms.

Cabins & Rates

Cabins	Per Diems from	Sq. Ft.	Fridge	Hair Dryer	Sitting Area	TV
Outside	$210	198–215	yes	yes	yes	yes
Suite	$650	287–782	yes	yes	yes	yes

CABINS   Despite their high price tag, the majority of *Symphony*'s cabins are smaller than the smallest aboard any of the Silversea, Radisson, or Seabourn vessels. They're still quite comfortable though, and cabins with balconies start at 198 square feet, plus 48-square-foot verandas. All staterooms were given an overhaul in early 2004, and a pillow menu was introduced shortly after that (see description in *Serenity* review, above). The pillow collection joins other bedroom amenities introduced recently, including Egyptian cotton sheets and feather bed toppers.

Deck 10 holds the ship's spectacular, attractively styled penthouses; the best measure more than 750 square feet, plus nearly 200-square-foot balconies, and have full-fledged Jacuzzis in their living rooms (with ocean views to boot!), dark-wood furniture, sofas upholstered in silk and satin, plus Oriental rugs and entertainment centers with 35-inch flat-screen TVs, and DVD and CD players. They also enjoy the services of a doting butler in addition to two stewardesses. The other two categories are about 287 and 396 square feet, plus 72- to 98-square-foot balconies.

Overall, color schemes in most staterooms mix pastel pinks, mints, blues, and beiges with pale-wood tones, and are cheerful, breezy, and light. Each cabin has a sitting area, TV with one of the largest selections of programming you'll find at sea, VCR, stocked minibar (snacks and alcoholic beverages consumed are charged to your onboard account except in the Penthouse Suites on Deck 10, where they're complimentary), hair dryer, and safe. While drawer space is adequate in all cabins, the hanging closets are smaller and tighter than you'd expect on ships of this caliber. Bathrooms have both shower and bathtub (a short little one in the lower category cabins), and are mostly tiled. We found the cabins to be not entirely soundproof; we could hear our neighbors talking and hear their television quite easily.

Cabins without verandas have large rectangular windows. The category E cabins located amidships on Decks 7 and 8 have views obstructed by lifeboats. There are no inside cabins.

Seven cabins are wheelchair accessible.

PUBLIC AREAS   Throughout the ship you'll find marble, glass, and hardwood paneling mingling with flowers and potted plants (especially palms). In that classic California style, the color schemes for the most part are light and airy, with plenty of champagnes, grays, whites, and blues. You'll find classy wood tones and dark leather furniture in recently refurbished rooms such as the library and Connoisseur's Club cigar lounge. Passenger throughways are wide and easy to navigate, and the atrium/lobby areas are quite spacious, though hardly cutting edge stylewise with no shortage of shiny surfaces, chrome, and brassy railings.

For drinkin', there are several bar/entertainment lounges, as well as a roaming staff that wanders the public areas throughout the day and much of the night, offering to bring drinks to wherever you happen to be sitting. The dark Avenue Saloon, where polished mahogany, well-maintained leather upholstery, and a live pianist draw passengers in, is one of the prime before- and after-dinner cocktail spots (and our personal favorite, by far). There are also two large entertainment lounges, one for Vegas-style material and another for ballroom dancing to a live band.

There's a large theater for movies and slide lectures, and a hushed library that's outfitted with comfortably upholstered chairs and a worthy collection of books, periodicals, and videos. *Symphony*'s Computer University@Sea areas were expanded during her spring '04 face-lift and now include a 25-seat classroom and an adjacent Internet center. For young kids, *Symphony* has a cute playroom with a tiered movie-viewing nook; for teens there's a teen center/video arcade.

DINING OPTIONS   Designed with curved walls and low, vaulted ceilings, the ship's main dining room is elegant and spacious, with dark wall paneling. Tables are not too close together, and there are well over 20 tables for two, mostly along the side or near the oceanview windows.

The ship's two themed, reservations-only alternative restaurants—the Italian Prego and the pan-Asian restaurant Jade Garden—are right up there with the best at sea. The Vintage Room, an intimate boardroom-style wine cellar, was added during the ship's 2004 refit to host special wine and champagne theme dinners and other events.

A casual indoor/outdoor buffet restaurant is open for breakfast and lunch, and the poolside Trident Grill serves ultracasual dinners several evenings per cruise. The Bistro is open from 9:30am to 6pm for continental breakfast, snacks, specialty coffees, and more.

POOL, FITNESS, SPA & SPORTS FACILITIES   *Symphony* offers a lot of outdoor activities and spacious areas in which to do them. There are two outdoor swimming pools separated by a bar, ice-cream counter, and sandwich grill, as well as two hot tubs. One of the pools is refreshingly oversize, stretching almost 40 feet across one of the sun decks; the other can be covered with a retractable glass roof. The gym and separate aerobics area are positioned for a view over the sea, with plenty of space for the line's complimentary yoga, Pilates, and aerobics (and personal training classes, for a fee). The Steiner-managed spa and beauty salon is accessorized with Feng Shui features including gurgling fountains, incense, wind chimes, crystals, mirrors, and a private canopied teak sun deck to create an atmosphere of peace and relaxation. On deck, there's a pair of golf driving nets, a putting green, a large paddle-tennis court, Ping-Pong tables, and a broad, uninterrupted teak Promenade Deck for walkers and joggers.

The ship's gorgeous and generous tiered afterdecks provide quiet places for an afternoon spent dozing in a deck chair or for quiet repose while leaning against the railing and allowing yourself to become entranced by the ship's wake.

2 Cunard

24303 Town Center Dr., Ste. 200, Valencia, CA 91355-0908. © **800/7CUNARD**. www.cunard.com.

THE LINE IN A NUTSHELL   The most venerable line in the cruise industry, Cunard is a classic, offering a link to the golden age of passenger ships. **Sails to:** Caribbean, New England/Canada, transatlantic (plus Europe, Africa, South America, World Cruise).

THE EXPERIENCE   The Cunard of today is not the Cunard of yesterday, but then again, it is. Formed in 1840 by Sir Samuel Cunard, the line provided the first regular steamship service between Europe and North America, and was one of the dominant players during the great years of steamship travel, which lasted roughly from 1905 to the mid-1960s. In 1969, long after it was clear that jet travel had replaced the liners, the company made what some considered a foolhardy move, launching *Queen Elizabeth 2* and setting her on a mixed schedule, half crossing, half cruising. Through sheer persistence, the ship proved the critics wrong, and by the late 1990s she was still going strong, even if the company went through some rough times.

Today *QE2* is doing cruise duty from Britain, relinquishing her transatlantic routes to the massive *Queen Mary 2,* the first true ocean liner built in more than 30 years. *QM2* is as modern as passenger ships get, and bigger than them all—at least until Royal Caribbean launches the 158,000-ton *Freedom of the Seas* this April. But, she's also an homage to all that went before, designed with oversized grandeur, old-world formality, and even a dose of blatant class structure: Some restaurants and outdoor decks are set aside specifically for suite guests only, if you please. As she's the only Cunarder currently serving the North American market, all details in this review refer to her alone.

Pros

- **Classic ambience:** Despite a few chintzy touches, the ship really does live up to its billing as the grandest afloat, with some rooms that could have come right out of a 1940s liner.
- **S-p-a-c-e:** This ship is absolutely enormous, from her hangar-size ballroom to the massive expanse of her top deck.
- **Comfortable amenities:** Even interior cabins are comfortable (though not gigantic), with extra-large shower stalls and quality toiletries.
- **Pure prestige:** There used to be ships that everyone in the world knew—"Oh, you're sailing on the *Queen Mary,*" they'd say. "That's the ship Marlene Dietrich took on her last crossing." *QM2* is the only ship launched in more than a quarter-century with that kind of broad public cachet.

Cons

- **Not *quite* luxe:** Despite her grandeur, *QM2* carries too many passengers to provide the kind of intimacy and personal feel you get on the other luxe lines—especially those operating small ships (Silversea, SeaDream, and Seabourn), but also on relatively large vessels such as *Crystal Serenity.*
- **Occasional off notes:** If you're going to design a huge corridor of showy Art Deco wall panels, don't make those panels out of plastic. Yuck.

Compared with the other ultraluxury lines, here's how Cunard rates:

	Poor	Fair	Good	Excellent	Outstanding
Enjoyment Factor					✓
Dining			✓		
Activities					✓
Children's Program					✓
Entertainment				✓	
Service				✓	
Worth the Money					✓

CUNARD: GETTING THERE IS HALF THE FUN

Once upon a time, Cunard ruled the waves. Its ships—first *Mauretania* and *Lusitania,* later *Queen Mary* and *Queen Elizabeth*—were the fastest and most reliable at sea. Then somebody invented the jet airliner and the whole passenger-shipping business went to hell. Numbers dropped. Ships went cruising for their bread. Cunard stuck to its guns, though, keeping *QE2* on the Atlantic until sheer doggedness gave it a certain cachet as the last of the old breed. Fleetmates came and went, including the little *Sea Goddess* yachts (now with SeaDream) and a number of midsize ships acquired from other lines, but *QE2* soldiered on.

Back in the head office, things weren't so great. In 1971, Cunard was acquired by the Trafalgar House holding company and began a period of corporate troubles and shuffling ownership. As Commodore Ronald Warwick, master of the *QM2,* told us last year, "Each of the previous owning companies was successful in its own right; however, they were all conglomerates with virtually no focus on passenger shipping. From my perspective, this . . . frequently appeared to put the future of Cunard in doubt."

In April 1998, Carnival Corporation acquired Cunard from the Norwegian company Kvaerner Group. To some it seemed a comedown for the venerable line, but Warwick and other Cunard employees saw it as an unqualified boon. "To my mind," he says, "Carnival Corporation were the white knights that saved us from demise, and when the planning of the *Queen Mary 2* was announced, I experienced a feeling of pleasure and relief. They'd delivered a message to the world and to those of us on the 'shop floor' that they were determined to build on the maritime heritage for which our company has been famous."

Today Cunard is again very famous indeed after all the media attention that accompanied *QM2*'s launch, but it's hardly the old British brand that its advertising might lead you to believe. In late 2004, for instance, the company was swallowed whole by Carnival Corp. subsidiary Princess Cruises. Its operations and sales staffs were merged with Princess's at the latter's suburban Los Angeles headquarters, but a more surprising decision was the removal of several longtime and well-loved Cunard officers (including *QM2*'s Captain Wright and *QE2*'s Captain McNaught) for reassignment to the Princess fleet. It remains to be seen whether Cunard will maintain an independent identity under the Princess umbrella or, like Celebrity Cruises when it was swallowed by Royal Caribbean in 1997, enter a period of identity crisis and uncertain market image.

Though *QE2* is still in service (sailing mostly from the U.K.) and Cunard has a new liner named *Queen Victoria* set to debut in 2007, *QM2* is currently the only Cunard ship operating in North American waters.

PASSENGER PROFILE

In general, Cunard attracts a well-traveled crowd of passengers in their 50s and up, many of them repeaters who appreciate the line's old-timey virtues and are more the 4 o'clock tea crowd than the hot-tub-and-umbrella-drink set. That said, the hoopla surrounding the launch of *QM2* is attracting a much wider demographic, especially on summer Atlantic crossings when families travel together and approximately 60% of passengers are from the U.S. British passengers make up the next largest percentage, and usually several hundred passengers hail from various other nations, making Cunard one of the few truly international cruises.

DINING

TRADITIONAL   Cunard is the last bastion of the old steamship tradition of segregating passengers according to class, though for the most part the practice is limited to dining hours. What this means is that passengers are assigned to one of the three reserved-seating restaurants according to the level of cabin accommodation they've booked: Suite passengers dine in the 206-seat **Queen's Grill;** junior-suite passengers dine in the 180-seat **Princess Grill;** and everyone else dines in the three-deck, 1,351-passenger **Brittania Restaurant**—decor-wise, the most beautiful of the three and a fitting heir to the grand restaurants of the past. The two grill restaurants serve dinner in a single seating, while Brittania has early and late seatings. All three also serve breakfast and lunch in open seatings.

QM2's cuisine sticks close to tradition, with entrees that might include pheasant with southern haggis and port wine sauce, roasted prime rib, grilled lobster with garden pea risotto, and scallion wild-rice crepes with mushroom filling and red pepper sauce. The Grill restaurants also offer the option of requesting whatever dish comes into your head—if they have the ingredients aboard, someone in the galley will whip it up for you. At all three restaurants, **special diets** can be accommodated, and vegetarian and health-conscious Canyon Ranch Spa dishes are available as a matter of course.

SPECIALTY   In the stern on Deck 8, *QM2*'s **Todd English restaurant** is a small 156-seat Mediterranean venue that echoes the original *Queen Mary*'s Verandah Grill, one of that ship's most legendary spaces. Created by celebrity chef Todd English, the restaurant serves elaborate and often very rich lunches ($20 per person) and dinners ($30 per person), with some amazing desserts.

One deck down, the contemporary **Chef's Galley** ($30 per person) serves only a few dozen guests, who get to watch the chef prepare their meal via an open galley and several large monitor screens.

CASUAL   Almost a third of Deck 7 is given over to the **King's Court,** a large buffet with numerous stations designed to minimize lines. Seating is laid out in many small, cozy areas, as opposed to the cavernous layout of most big-ship buffets. At night, the space is partitioned off into three separate casual restaurants: **The Carvery,** serving carved beef, pork, lamb, and poultry along with gourmet English favorites; **La Piazza,** serving pizza, pasta, and other Italian specialties 24-hours; and **Lotus,** a pan-Asian restaurant blending Chinese, Japanese, Thai, and Indian influences. All are free, but reservations are recommended at dinner.

SNACKS & EXTRAS   On Deck 2, the oversized Golden Lion Pub serves English pub grub, while waaaaay up on Deck 12 you can get standard burgers and dogs at the outdoor Boardwalk Café. Traditional **afternoon tea** accompanied by a string quartet is served either in the Winter Garden, a lounge designed after the conservatory at London's Kew Gardens, or the Queen's Room, the ship's most classic, traditional space. **Room service** is available 24 hours a day.

ACTIVITIES

Though Cunard is owned by Carnival Corporation, *QM2*'s onboard vibe couldn't be any more different than her "Fun Ship" cousins. Rather than woo-hoo good times, Cunard concentrates on learning experiences and the arts, with a healthy dollop of pampering to keep things light.

Central to the onboard experience is the 20,000-square-foot **Cunard ConneXions** complex, seven classrooms where instructors and lecturers from Oxford University, *Architectural Digest, Gourmet* magazine, and others present seminars on literature, marine science, ocean-liner history, music and culture of the 1960s, modern art, Shakespeare on film, architectural history, cooking, computer applications, languages, and other topics. Course listings for the Oxford University lecture program (presented on the Transatlantic crossings) are available 90 days ahead on the Cunard website.

Passengers who prefer book learning can take advantage of the largest **library** at sea, a huge, beautifully designed space that actually looks like a library, unlike the typical rooms-with-a-few-bookshelves on most megaships. Next door, a **bookshop** sells volumes on passenger ship history, as well as Cunard memorabilia. Other shops, clustered around *QM2*'s atrium, sell logo-wear, jewelry, fashion, and duty-free items. Continuing the marine-history topic, the ship's **Maritime Quest** (MQ—get it?) history trail offers a museum-quality timeline set up in various places throughout the ship, with an audio tour available to tie it all together.

QM2's impressive, mint-and-bamboo **Canyon Ranch Spa** combines nautical undertones with a modern minimalist motif to create a most relaxing space, with a co-ed thalassotherapy pool and hot tub; thermal suite; a beauty salon with wonderful ocean views; and a staff of more than 50 doling out hot-stone and Thai massage, reflexology, facials, and other acts of expensive kindness in 25 treatment rooms. The ship's gym, which wraps around the bow on Deck 7, is surprisingly small and uninspired for a ship this large and well conceived, but does offer treadmills and stationery bikes with flatscreen TV monitors.

CHILDREN'S PROGRAM

Though you might not expect it from a grand liner that (one imagines) is filled with sophisticated seniors, *QM2* offers great digs for kids. The kids' complex, called **The Zone,** is open to kids ages 1 and up—an extraordinarily young minimum age shared only by Disney's ships. (Most ships with kids' programming welcome kids 3 and up, a few ages 2 and up.) Facilities are divided by age. The 1-to-6 set occupies half of a roomy area with lots of toys, arts and crafts, a play gym and ball bin, and big-screen TVs. There's also a separate **nursery** with 10 crib/toddler-bed combos for napping tots. Just outside the oceanview space is a play gym out aft on Deck 6, with a small pool. Officially it's called the "family deck," though anyone who doesn't mind screeching

Cunard Fleet Itineraries

Ship	Itineraries
Queen Mary 2	**6-night transatlantic:** East- or westbound between Southampton, UK, and New York, NY, Oct–Nov 2005 and Apr–Nov 2006. **12- & 14-night S. Carib:** Round-trip from New York, NY, Nov–Dec 2005. **12-night Carib/S. America:** New York, NY, to Rio de Janeiro, Brazil, Jan 2006. **3-night Ensenada:** Round-trip from Los Angeles, Feb 2006. **14-night Mexico/Costa Rica/South America:** Los Angeles, CA, to Valparaiso, Chile, Mar 2006 (also bookable at 38-night Los Angeles to New York odyssey). **4- & 5-night Canada/New England:** Round-trip from New York, NY, July and Sept 2006. **12-night Canada/New England:** Round-trip from New York, NY, Sept–Oct 2006. **7-night E. & W. Carib:** Round-trip from Ft. Lauderdale, FL, Nov–Dec 2006.

children can lounge there. The other half of the play area is reserved for kids 7 to 17, with the 7-to-12 crowd usually occupying a play area with beanbag chairs, lots of board games, TVs, and a number of Xbox video-game systems. **Activities for teens**— including ship tours, movies and production shows in the theaters, and pizza parties— are usually held elsewhere.

The whole kids' program is staffed by two to three British nannies, who have completed a 2-year program in the discipline back in England, plus two to three activities counselors, many of whom have backgrounds as school teachers. The best part? Aside from 2 hours at lunchtime and an hour or two in the afternoon, The Zone offers complimentary supervised activities and care from 9am to midnight, so you can dine with the adults and know your offspring are being well cared for. You can take your kids to eat earlier in the King's Court buffet restaurant, or there's a special **children's tea** daily from 5 to 6pm in the Chef's Galley.

ENTERTAINMENT

Entertainment aboard *QM2* runs the gamut from plays featuring graduates of Britain's **Royal Academy of Dramatic Arts** to some pretty run-of-the-mill song-and-dance revues. The former perform most of the year as part of a partnership between Cunard and the school, with RADA graduates and students also offering a variety of readings and workshops, including acting classes. Besides theater, *QM2*'s lounges feature a wide variety of **music,** from string quartets in the Winter Garden conservatory to jazz in the Chart Room to high-toned dance music in the gorgeous Queen's Ballroom and low-toned in the **G32 disco.** On Deck 2, the large, beautifully appointed **Empire Casino** is more Monte Carlo than Vegas, with refined art and furnishings rather than the usual clangorous arcade vibe.

Illuminations, a secondary theater on Deck 3, started life as an adjunct to the Cunard ConneXions classrooms and ended up as the world's first oceangoing **planetarium,** presenting a rotating series of 3D films, some of them created in conjunction with noted institutions such as New York's Museum of Natural History and the Smithsonian's National Air and Space Museum.

Up on Deck 12, the Boardwalk Café doubles at night as a venue for **outdoor movie screenings** when weather permits. See the ship review below for a discussion of *QM2*'s other theaters and lounges.

SERVICE

With their classy uniforms and cordial, gracious efficiency, *QM2*'s crew exhibits a polished sort of British demeanor—even when they're actually from the Philippines. That said, the sheer size of the vessels and large number of passengers mean they must do their share of rushing around and keeping up, as aboard all the other huge cruise ships today. The staff have a lot on their plates, which explains why the ship carries more staff now than when she was launched.

Queen Mary 2

The Verdict

Faster than a speeding bullet, more powerful than a locomotive, *QM2* is literally in a class by herself: a modern reinterpretation of the Golden Age luxury liner, bigger than anything that's gone before and built to sail hard seas well into the 21st century.

Queen Mary 2 *(photo: Cunard)*

Specifications

Size (in tons)	151,400	Crew	1,270
Passengers (double occ.)	2,620	Passenger/Crew Ratio	2.1 to 1
Passenger/Space Ratio	57.8	Year Launched	2004
Total Cabins/Veranda Cabins	1,310/879	Last Major Refurbishment	N/A

Frommer's Ratings (Scale of 1–5)   ★★★★★

Cabin Comfort & Amenities	5	Dining Options	4.5
Ship Cleanliness & Maintenance	5	Gym, Spa & Sports Facilities	4.5
Public Comfort/Space	5	Children's Facilities	5
Decor	4.5	Enjoyment Factor	5

Before her launch, we often heard *QM2* referred to by industry types as "Micky's White Elephant"—Micky being Micky Arison, chairman of Carnival Corporation, the criticism referring to the fact that *QM2*'s design and construction sucked up about a billion dollars and 5 years of labor, a record expenditure to match her record-breaking size.

But that was before her launch. That was before the Queen of England did the honors at her naming ceremony. That was before the fireworks and traffic jams that attended her first arrival into every port. And it was definitely before the media glommed onto her as the first really newsworthy ship to be launched since . . . well, since *QE2*, probably. And when you control about half the cruise industry, as Carnival Corp. does, that kind of publicity is priceless.

When all is said and done, *QM2* deserves all the hype. She's a really remarkable ship: classic yet contemporary, refined yet fun, huge yet homey, and grand, grand, grand. The largest passenger ship at sea (at least till April, when *Freedom of the Seas* snatches the title back for Royal Caribbean), she's also the only real ocean liner built since her older sister hit the water in 1969—and that, perhaps, needs some explanation. What is it exactly that makes an ocean liner different?

In a word, "more"—of everything. "We had a working definition that built on the idea of 'enhancement,'" said Stephen Payne, *QM2*'s designer, with whom we spoke in summer 2003. "The ship had to have enhanced strength and sea-keeping characteristics to withstand continuous exposure to North Atlantic conditions; enhanced speed to maintain her schedule [because unlike a cruise ship, a transatlantic liner has no ports that can be skipped to make up time lost to harsh seas]; enhanced passenger facilities to keep her passengers happy for 5 days at sea; and enhanced endurance to allow her great range between refueling." All of these mandates created the ship you see today. The need for speed meant her hull had to be more knife-prowed than a normal cruise ship's. The need for strength meant her steel plating had to be uncommonly thick and her skeleton unusually dense and super-reinforced. The need to battle high waves meant her superstructure had to be set much farther back on her hull than is common on today's cruise ships. The list goes on and on. In a sense, you could almost say that it was the sea itself that designed *QM2*. They were made for each other.

Inside, *QM2* was laid out in such a way that even after a weeklong crossing you might still be finding new places to explore on board. Our favorites? The Queen's Room ballroom on formal night; the classic Chart Room for drinks before dinner; the forward facing Commodore Club with its clubby atmosphere; and the forward observation deck on Deck 11, just below the bridge—probably the best spot aboard when sailing out of New York Harbor. Throughout, artwork functions both as decoration and as mood-enhancement, with iconography that recalls the ocean liner's Golden Age. The most evocative art of all, though, may be a sound: Way up on *QM2*'s funnel, on the starboard side, is one of the original Tyfon steam whistles from the first *Queen Mary*—the same whistle that sounded when the *Mary* made her first crossing in 1936, now on permanent loan from the city of Long Beach, California. Mounted beside an identical replica, it has a low bass "A" note that literally shakes the rafters, and if that doesn't put a smile on your face, nothing will.

Cabins & Rates

Cabins	Per Diems from	Sq. Ft.	Fridge	Hair Dryer	Sitting Area	TV
Inside	$229	194	yes	yes	no	yes
Outside	750	381–2,249*	yes	yes	yes	yes

* *Including veranda.*

CABINS   All of *QM2*'s cabins, from the smallest inside to the largest outside, are decorated in a smooth, contemporary style, with light-blond woods, simple lines, and a clean, uncluttered look. Even standard inside and outside cabins, though by no means huge, have a simple elegance and a nice helping of amenities, including terry robes and slippers, fridge, safe, dataport, interactive TV with e-mail capability, and extra-large showers. The vast majority of cabins are outsides with balconies, most of them recessed back into the superstructure to assure that they stay dry even in the roughest seas. Junior suites are appealingly spacious, each with a wide balcony, sitting area, roomy bathroom with tub, and a large walk-in closet. It only goes up from there, culminating in the enormous duplex suites that perch in the stern on Decks 9 and 10 and are so stratospherically expensive that it's not worth giving details on them here. All suites and junior suites feature Frette linens, flatscreen TVs with Xbox game systems, personalized stationery, pre-dinner canapés, concierge service, a bottle of champagne on embarkation, and use of the Queens Grill Lounge. Queens Grill Suites get fully stocked bars and other niceties, such as use of a large private deck overlooking the stern.

There are 30 wheelchair-accessible cabins total in various cabin grades.

PUBLIC AREAS   Because *QM2* was designed for comfortable sailing in rough seas, most of her public areas are clustered unusually low, down on Decks 2 and 3. At midships, the relatively restrained (and a bit too white) Grand Lobby atrium lets onto two central promenades, decorated with huge Art Deco wall panels. Some are stunning and recall decorated glass panels from the opulent liner *Normandie,* while others are a bit chintzy and miss the mark.

Getting beyond that one flaw, Deck 2's promenade leads down to the elegant Empire Casino and the too-big-to-be-cozy Golden Lion pub. Up one deck, the Veuve Clicquot Champagne Bar (serving a variety of champagne, as well as caviar and foie gras) is decorated with slightly abstracted images of mid-20th-century movie stars and leads into one of the most beautiful rooms on board, The Chart Room, a high-ceilinged space with green-glass Deco maps on one wall, 1940s-style furnishings, and the feel of a great ocean liner. You expect David Niven to come strolling through. Across on the ship's port side, Sir Samuel's Wine Bar is almost a continuation of the Chart Room, offering more lounge space. Forward, the Royal Court Theater is a two-deck grand showroom and the principle theatrical venue on board, seconded by the Illuminations planetarium farther forward, which doubles as a full-size movie theater and lecture hall (see "Entertainment," above).

In the stern on Deck 3, the Queen's Room ballroom perfectly captures the essence of Cunard style, running the full width of the ship and boasting a high, arched ceiling, the largest ballroom dance floor at sea, crystal chandeliers, and a truly royal quality. The G32 nightclub, almost hidden behind silver doors at the head of the Queen's Room, is decorated in industrial style to match its name—"G32" was the number by which *QM2*'s hull was known at the shipyard, before Cunard decided what she'd be called.

Other notable spaces include the Winter Garden on Deck 7, a light, airy space designed to provide an outdoor garden feel on long transatlantic crossings, and the Commodore Club bar/observation lounge on Deck 9, with its wonderful white-leather chairs, dramatic bow views, and attached Churchill's cigar room. There's also a card room hidden away on Deck 11, just behind the observation deck, and the remarkable library and bookshop forward on Deck 8 (see "Activities").

DINING OPTIONS   Decor-wise, the Queens Grill and Princess Grill restaurants, serving suite passengers exclusively, are the very models of restrained good taste, with a series of elegant blown-glass vases their one bold touch. The Britannia Restaurant, on the other hand, is fairly overwhelming, intended to recall *Queen Mary*'s magnificent first-class restaurant and featuring a vaulted, Tiffany-style glass ceiling, a curved balcony that echoes the shape of the *Mary*'s famous bridge, candlelit tables, soaring pillars, and the largest art tapestry at sea, depicting a liner against the New York skyline.

See "Dining," above for more details on the ship's dining experience.

POOL, FITNESS, SPA & SPORTS FACILITIES   The Canyon Ranch Spa is a two-story complex occupying some 20,000 square feet. At the center of its treatment rooms is a co-ed 15×30-foot aqua-therapy pool whose relaxation gizmos include airbed recliner lounges, neck fountains, a deluge waterfall, an air tub, and body-massage jet benches. There's a hot tub adjacent, and nearby is a thermal suite comprised of aromatic steam rooms and an herbal sauna. A beauty salon occupies the top level of the complex, offering tremendous views from its lofty perch. The gym, one deck down, is sort of drab and chopped up, but is perfectly well equipped to make people sweat, with free weights and the latest digitally enhanced climbers, steppers, runners, and rowers.

A more classic exercise is a walk or jog around the wide outdoor Promenade Deck, which encircles the looooooonggg ship on Deck 7 and offers beautiful sea views; three times around equals 1 mile. For some shoulder work, there's a pair of golf simulators adjacent to the covered pool solarium on Deck 12. Other dips include a splash pool and hot tubs way up on Deck 13 and several in the tiered stern. Rounding out the sports options are Ping-Pong, basketball, quoits, a paddle-tennis court, and, of course, shuffleboard—this is a transatlantic liner, after all.

3 Radisson Seven Seas Cruises

600 Corporate Dr., Suite 410, Fort Lauderdale, FL 33334. © **800/285-1835.** Fax 402/501-5599. www.rssc.com.

THE LINE IN A NUTSHELL   Operating a fleet of stylish and extremely comfortable midsize vessels, Radisson offers a casually elegant and subtle luxury cruise experience. Its service is as good as it gets, and its cuisine is near the top. **Sails to:** Caribbean, Alaska, Bermuda, New England/Canada (plus Europe, South America, Antarctica, South Pacific, Australia/New Zealand, World Cruise).

THE EXPERIENCE   If you insist on luxury but like to keep it subtle, Radisson might be your cruise line of choice. Its ships are spacious and understated, with a relaxed onboard vibe that tends to be less stuffy than Seabourn and Silversea. As aboard all the luxury ships (with the exception of the huge *QM2*), entertainment and activities are low-key, with passengers left to enjoy their vacations at their own pace. Dress tends toward casual, though tuxedos and gowns aren't uncommon on formal evenings. Service is friendly and absolutely spot-on, and cuisine is some of the best at sea, both in the formal dining rooms and alternative restaurants. Even if what tickles your fancy isn't on the menu, the chef will prepare it for you. Passengers tend to be unpretentiously wealthy. When last we sailed, our social circle at dinner and in the piano bar included an Atlantic City nightclub owner, a retired recycling executive, a graphic artist, a theatrical casting director, and a woman who owned a string of Taco Bell franchises—all of them aboard to enjoy a quiet, relaxed vacation.

Pros
- **Great dining:** Cuisine is superb, and the main dining room and alternative restaurants operate on an open-seating basis, the latter by reservation.
- **Frequent sales:** Radisson frequently runs great two-for-one and free-air deals, making its rates attractive to mainstream cruisers looking to move up to the luxe world.
- **Lots of private verandas:** The all-suite *Seven Seas Navigator* has them in 90% of hers, and the all-suite *Mariner* and *Voyager* have them in every single stateroom. There are no windowless cabins on any of the line's ships.
- **Amazing bathrooms on *Navigator* and *Voyager*:** Bigger and better than those on Seabourn and Crystal, cabin bathrooms all have separate shower stalls and full-size bathtubs long enough for normal-size humans.

Cons
- **Less all-inclusive than some other luxe lines:** While the line does include gratuities, wine with dinner, and unlimited soda and bottled water, it doesn't throw in any

complimentary shore excursions, and the only free liquor is a one-time loading up of your cabin minibar. Silversea, Seabourn, and SeaDream offer more freebies.

RADISSON: LOW-KEY ELEGANCE

Radisson Seven Seas Cruises got its start in a 1994 merger between Seven Seas Cruises and Carlson (Radisson) -owned Diamond Cruises, and today operates a small fleet of luxurious, globe-trotting ships, including three that sail regularly from U.S. ports (*Seven Seas Navigator, Seven Seas Mariner,* and *Seven Seas Voyager*); the 320-passenger *Paul Gauguin,* which spends the year doing 7- to 14-night cruises in French Polynesia; and the chartered expedition ship *Explorer II,* on which Radisson offers Antarctic cruises each January and February. While many luxury ships hopscotch from cruise region to cruise region, never staying long in any one place, Radisson's ships are often the most frequently seen luxury ships in some ports. *Seven Seas Navigator* offers Caribbean cruises during the winter season and then relocates to New York for the summer and fall, where it's the most luxurious ship in residence (sailing to Bermuda, New England/Canada, and on a "Top of the World" cruise to Greenland, Iceland, and the Baltic). *Seven Seas Mariner* is one of the best ships in Alaska each summer.

In early 2005 Radisson announced that its original ship, the endearing little 350-passenger catamaran **Radisson Diamond,** would be leaving the fleet to take up a new life as a gambling ship in Hong Kong. *Joi Gin, Diamond.* Don't forget to write. On the plus side, her departure leaves Radisson with a much more uniform, modern fleet.

PASSENGER PROFILE

This line appeals primarily to well-traveled and well-heeled passengers in their 50s and 60s, but younger passengers and honeymooners pepper the mix. Many passengers are frequent cruisers who have also sailed on Silversea, Seabourn, and Crystal, or are taking a step up from Holland America, Celebrity, or one of the other mainstream lines. Though they have sophisticated tastes (and can do without inane activities such as napkin-folding classes), they also appreciate the line's less formal ambience. On our recent cruises, casual nights in the formal dining room saw some passengers dressed in polo shirts and jackets and others in nice T-shirts with khakis and sneakers. You're also likely to find some women in full makeup, coiffed 'do, and coordinated jewelry, shoes, and handbags strolling the pool deck, and many men sporting gold Rolexes the size of Texas. A kids' program on summer Alaska and Bermuda sailings and some holiday sailings attract some **families,** but the limited number of third berths in cabins tends to keep the numbers down.

Compared with the other ultraluxury lines, here's how Radisson rates:

	Poor	Fair	Good	Excellent	Outstanding
Enjoyment Factor					✓
Dining				✓	
Activities			✓		
Children's Program		✓			
Entertainment			✓		
Service					✓
Worth the Money					✓

DINING

Superb menus are designed for a sophisticated palate, and the overall cuisine is some of the best in the cruise industry. Nice red and white house wines are complimentary at dinner, and each ship has an extensive menu of vintages from Germany, Italy, and Chile.

TRADITIONAL   In the main restaurants, elaborate and elegant meals are served in open seatings by a staff of mostly Europeans. Caesar salads are tossed to order; appetizers may include oven-roasted pheasant salad or avocado fritters in a spicy sauce; and main entrees include enticing dishes such as zucchini-wrapped chicken breast stuffed with olives and tomatoes, herb-crusted roast leg of lamb, and fresh fish. Each dinner menu offers a **vegetarian option** such as a vegetable curry (plus vegetarian appetizers), and a **light and healthy choice** such as grilled tuna steak in a leek-and-tomato vinaigrette. When you've had enough of fancy, several standards called **simplicity dishes** are also available daily: spaghetti with tomato sauce, filet mignon, and grilled chicken breast or salmon. **Special diets** (kosher, halal, low-fat, low-salt, and so on) can be accommodated at all meals, but for very stringent regimes such as glatt kosher you must make arrangements before your cruise.

Breakfasts include made-to-order omelets, as well as a typical selection of hot and cold breakfast foods. Lunch entrees include a spicy paella as well as rich homemade soups.

SPECIALTY   *Seven Seas Navigator* has only one alternative choice: Portofino, an indoor/outdoor Italian restaurant serving antipasti choices such as marinated salmon rings or Bresaola carpaccio with Parmesan cheese and mushrooms, pasta courses that may include jumbo-prawn risotto, and main courses such as a grilled lobster or *osso buco*. *Mariner* and *Voyager* each have three alternate choices. The 110-seat Signatures restaurants are directed by chefs from Paris's famed Le Cordon Bleu cooking school, while their Latitudes restaurants serve Indochine cuisine, with dishes like Cambodian wafu salad; steamed fresh halibut in a Matsutake mushroom broth with gingered vegetables; and a spiced rack of lamb accompanied by aromatic Jasmine rice, wok-seared snow peas, and fresh sprouts in peanut jus. La Veranda serves Mediterranean and North African dishes in a casual setting. All alternative venues are intimate spaces with tables for two or four. Make reservations early in the cruise, to guarantee yourself a table.

CASUAL   All three vessels have casual buffet restaurants, plus a poolside sandwich grill staffed by waiters.

SNACKS & EXTRAS   Hot hors d'oeuvres are served in the lounges before dinner, and if you take advantage of the 24-hour room service, a steward will come in and lay out a white tablecloth along with silverware and china, whether you've ordered a full-course dinner, a personal pizza, or just a plate of fruit. Plus, you can always get virtually anything by request. Specialty coffees, soft drinks, and mineral water are complimentary at all times, and high tea is served each afternoon.

ACTIVITIES

Days not spent exploring the ports are basically unstructured, with a few activities thrown in for those who aren't pursuing their own relaxation. During the day, there may be ballroom dance classes, wine tastings, art auctions, bingo, and bridge (with instructors sailing on all cruises). *Mariner* and *Voyager* also offer computer classes. Aboard all three ships, each cruise also features a **guest lecturer** drawn from the ranks of former diplomats, writers, anthropologists, and naturalists, often speaking on a topic relevant to the region you're sailing—for example, Colonial America on New England/Canada cruises. Recent speakers have included TV news personalities Hugh

Radisson Fleet Itineraries

Ship	Itineraries
Seven Seas Mariner	**8- & 10-night Mexican Riviera:** Round-trip from Los Angeles, CA, Dec 2005 and Dec 2006. **7-night E. Carib:** Round-trip from Ft. Lauderdale, FL, Mar 2006. **9-night W. Carib:** Round-trip from Ft. Lauderdale, FL, Mar 2006. **7-night Gulf of Alaska:** North- or southbound between Vancouver, BC, and Whittier/Anchorage, AK, May–Sept 2006.
Seven Seas Navigator	**7-night Canada/New England:** North- or southbound between New York, NY, and Montreal, QB, Oct 2005. **17-night Panama Canal:** New York, NY, to Los Angeles, CA, Oct 2005. **26-night Tahiti/Hawaii:** Round-trip from Los Angeles, Nov 2005. **7-, 8-, 10- & 11-night E. Carib:** Round-trip from Ft. Lauderdale, FL, Jan, Mar, and Nov–Dec 2006. **4-, 5- & 7-night E. Carib:** Round-trip from San Juan, PR, Jan–Mar 2006.
Seven Seas Voyager	**5- & 7-night E. & W. Carib:** Round-trip from Ft. Lauderdale, FL, Nov–Dec 2005 and Nov–Dec 2006.

Downs and Garrick Utley, soprano Dame Kiri Te Kanawa, former CIA and FBI director William H. Webster, former national security adviser Robert McFarlane, and top business journalist Marshall Loeb. On some cruises, chefs trained in the Le Cordon Bleu cooking method offer **Le Cordon Bleu Class Culinaire,** an extra-cost ($395) series of cooking workshops. The line also offers a slate of interesting **theme cruises** built around topics like food, wine, film, and chocolate.

More active passengers can work out in the ships' gyms, run on the tracks, or whack some balls into a golf net, then take a massage at the ships' spas, run by the French company **Carita of Paris.** Staffed by Carita-trained therapists and hairdressers imported from Parisian salons, the spas offer company specialties such as their Rénovateur exfoliating process as well as cruise spa standards such as hydrotherapy, reflexology, aromatherapy, body wraps, facials, manicure/pedicures, and anti-stress, therapeutic, and hot-rock massage.

CHILDREN'S PROGRAM

These ships are geared to adults, and mature ones at that, but summer Alaska and Bermuda sailings and select holiday cruises offer a **Club Mariner** kids program in which counselors supervise activities like games, craft projects, and movies for two age groups (6–11 and 12–17). Teens help the counselor select the activities they prefer. On other cruises, an ad-hoc kids program will be put together if enough kids are aboard to warrant it. Minimum age for children to sail aboard is 1 year, and the line reserves the right to limit the number of children under age 3 on any one sailing. **Babysitting** may be available for $25 an hour if a female crewmember is willing to perform the service outside of her regular duty hours.

ENTERTAINMENT

As on most other luxe ships, entertainment is low-key and modest, with most passengers content to spend their evenings exploring the cocktail circuit, singing along in the piano bar, visiting the casino, or dancing to the ships' elegant musical groups. All three ships offer musical revues in their show lounges, and though they're certainly not a high point of the cruises, they add a nice option to the evenings. A recent show on *Navigator* featured hits from the 1930s and 1940s up through the 1980s, including a Village People segment that most people seemed to enjoy—even a 70-plus woman in a wheelchair and oxygen tank, who bobbed her head happily to the song "Feel My Body." *Seven Seas Voyager* has a show called "On a Classical Note," with operatic works by Mozart, Verdi, Rossini, and Puccini and subtitles in English so audiences can follow the action. Occasional sailings offer **themed entertainment**—a doo-wop cruise featuring The Platters, for instance, and a "Spotlight on Classical Music" cruise featuring Anna Maria Alberghetti. Check with the line or your travel agent for a schedule of upcoming theme cruises.

SERVICE

Service is a major plus with Radisson, with a mostly European and Filipino staff striving to fulfill every passenger request with a smile. You rarely, if ever, hear the word "no," and since the passenger-to-crew ratio is quite high, you rarely have to wait for someone else to get served first. Stewardesses care for your cabin ably and unobtrusively, **room service** is speedy and efficient, and restaurant waitstaffs are supremely gracious and professional, with an intimate knowledge of the menu. Bar staff will often remember your drink order after the first day.

Voyager, Navigator, and *Mariner* all have complimentary **self-serve laundries** in addition to standard laundry and dry-cleaning services.

Gratuities are included in the cruise rates, but many passengers end up leaving more anyway at the end of their trip.

Seven Seas Mariner •
Seven Seas Voyager

The Verdict

The 700-passenger, all-suite *Mariner* and *Voyager* are Radisson's largest ships, boasting balconies on every single stateroom, plus extra helpings of Radisson's great pampering treatment.

Seven Seas Mariner *(photo: Radisson)*

Specifications

Size (in tons)		Total Cabins/Veranda Cabins	350/350
Mariner	50,000	Crew	447
Voyager	46,000	Passenger/Crew Ratio	1.6 to 1
Passengers (double occ.)	700	Year Launched	
Passenger/Space Ratio		*Mariner*	2001
Mariner	71.4	*Voyager*	2003
Voyager	65.7	Last Major Refurbishment	N/A

Frommer's Ratings (Scale of 1–5) ★★★★½

Cabin Comfort & Amenities	5	Dining Options	4
Ship Cleanliness & Maintenance	5	Gym, Spa & Sports Facilities	3
Public Comfort/Space	5	Children's Facilities	N/A
Decor	4.5	Enjoyment Factor	4

Introduced in 2001, the all-suite *Seven Seas Mariner* was the first vessel built by any line to offer a private balcony on every single stateroom, and was designed to be exceedingly spacious. Sister ship *Seven Seas Voyager,* which entered service 2 years later, continues this theme and offers improvements in some areas where we found *Mariner* lacking, particularly public room warmth and bathroom layout. In addition, *Voyager* was designed with an efficient one-corridor approach, making for extremely smooth traffic flow in the public areas.

Cabins & Rates

Cabins	Per Diems from	Sq. Ft.	Fridge	Hair Dryer	Sitting Area	TV
Suite	$387	252–1,204*	yes	yes	yes	yes

* These measurements for Seven Seas Mariner *only.* Suites on Voyager *are slightly larger at 306–1,216 square feet.*

CABINS   *Mariner* and *Voyager* are the only all-suite, all-balcony ships at sea, with Deluxe Suites representing the vast majority of the available accommodations. On *Mariner,* they measure 252 square feet, plus a 49-square-foot balcony; on *Voyager,* they've been enlarged to 306 square feet, with a 50-square-foot balcony. Even beyond size, *Voyager's* standard accommodations are superior, with a warmer feel and more over-the-top marble bathrooms, each one with separate shower/bathtub facilities. Conversely, *Mariner's* top-end suites are somewhat larger than *Voyager's,* from the forward-facing, 1,204-square-foot Master Suites (with two balconies, including one enormous 721-sq.-ft. expanse) down to the 359-square-foot Horizon Suites, located in the stern and opening onto expansive views of the ship's wake from their oversized balconies. (*Voyager's* Master Suites have only one balcony, measuring a comparatively tiny 183 sq. ft.)

All staterooms are designed with blond woods and rich fabrics and feature king-size beds convertible to twins, cotton bathrobes, hair dryer, TV/DVD (with movies available from the ships' DVD libraries), stocked refrigerator, safe, and large walk-in closet. Additionally, those on *Voyager* offer e-mail connection. Balconies overall are a little less than private—walls separating them do not extend to the edge of the ship's rail, making it possible to lean out and see what your neighbor is up to. Butler service comes standard in *Mariner's* Master, Mariner, and Grand suites and *Voyager's* Master, Grand, Voyager, Seven Seas, and Penthouse suites. The top three categories of suites on each vessel also offer Bose Wave music systems.

Six suites on *Mariner* and four on *Voyager* are wheelchair friendly.

PUBLIC AREAS   While virtually every room aboard *Mariner* has a clean, fresh appearance, combining smooth blond woods with rich leathers and fabrics and an abundance of glass, marble, and stainless steel, the ship's extremely high space-per-guest ratio can, at times, create a feeling of perhaps too much room. The one-corridor design on *Voyager* helps alleviate this problem while continuing similar design motifs.

Both ships have beautifully laid out two-deck theaters with terrific sightlines from virtually every seat, plus an Observation Lounge sitting high up on the top deck and featuring a semicircular bar, plush chairs and sofas, and a 180-degree view of the sea. It's a particularly attractive room at night. Lower down, each ship also boasts a well-stocked library, a cigar lounge, a card and conference room (popular with bridge players), and a computer center. A very nice feature here is that guests are charged only for transmission time, meaning you can compose a document in Word or another program free of charge, then open your e-mail and paste it in, and only incur a cost while you're in active e-mail mode. *Mariner* also has a dedicated disco, but who needs a disco on a luxe ship? On *Voyager,* the Voyager Lounge serves as the disco at night and (as aboard *Mariner*) as a piano lounge before dinner.

DINING OPTIONS   *Mariner* and *Voyager* each have four restaurants, with the main dining room, the Compass Rose, serving all three meals in single open seatings. Casual breakfasts and lunches are available in the indoor/outdoor La Veranda Restaurant, up near the top of the ship on Deck 11.

Two reservations-only (but no-charge!) restaurants are open for dinner only. Signatures features world-ranging cuisine prepared in classic French style by chefs trained at Paris's famous Le Cordon Bleu School. Latitudes offers a new Indochine menu (see "Dining," above). On *Voyager,* Latitudes has an open galley, allowing guests to watch as items are prepared.

In the evening, half of La Veranda is turned into an excellent candlelit, white-tablecloth Mediterranean Bistro with a combination of waiter and self-service dining. Grilled food is available poolside, and room service runs 24 hours—guests can even have the Compass Rose dinner menu served course by course in their suites during dinner hours.

POOL, FITNESS, SPA & SPORTS FACILITIES   Each ship's one pool and three hot tubs are located on Deck 11. Deck chairs are set up around the roomy pool area, as well as on the forward half of the deck above, where you'll also find a paddle-tennis court, golf driving nets, shuffleboard courts, and an uninterrupted jogging track. Sunbathing doesn't seem to be the biggest priority for Radisson guests, so deck chairs are usually readily available, even on sea days in warm cruising areas.

Each ship's Carita spa is located in an attractive but rather small space. A similarly smallish oceanview gym and separate aerobics area are located in the same area, as well as a beauty salon.

Seven Seas Navigator

The Verdict

Warm and appealing, the 490-passenger *Navigator* is an ideal size for an ultraluxe cruise: small enough to be intimate and large enough to offer plenty of elbowroom, more than a few entertainment outlets, and some of the best cabin bathrooms at sea.

Seven Seas Navigator *(photo: Radisson)*

Specifications

Size (in tons)	33,000	Crew	324
Passengers (double occ.)	490	Passenger/Crew Ratio	1.5 to 1
Passenger/Space Ratio	67.3	Year Launched	1999
Total Cabins/Veranda Cabins	245/215	Last Major Refurbishment	N/A

Frommer's Ratings (Scale of 1–5)   ★★★★

Cabin Comfort & Amenities	5	Dining Options	4
Ship Cleanliness & Maintenance	4	Gym, Spa & Sports Facilities	4
Public Comfort/Space	4	Children's Facilities	N/A
Decor	4	Enjoyment Factor	4.5

Navigator has well-laid-out cabins and public rooms, and if you've been on the Silversea ships, you'll notice a similar layout (especially in the Star Lounge and Galileo Lounge), as the ships were all designed by the same architects and built in the same yard, Italy's Mariotti. While *Navigator*'s interior is very attractive, outside she looks a little bit top-heavy, a consequence of her odd provenance: Her hull was originally built to be a Russian spy ship. When Radisson purchased the uncompleted vessel, they redesigned her superstructure with additional decks. *Trivia:* In 2004, *Navigator* was one of the primary settings for the Pierce Brosnan and Salma Hayek film *After the Sunset.*

Cabins & Rates

Cabins	Per Diems from	Sq. Ft.	Fridge	Hair Dryer	Sitting Area	TV
Suite	$372	301–1,067	yes	yes	yes	yes

CABINS   *Navigator* is an all-suite, all-outside ship, so there's not a bad room in the house. Each elegant suite is done up in shades of deep gold, beige, and burnt orange, with caramel-toned wood furniture and a swath of butterscotch suede just above the beds. Nearly 90% of them have private balconies, with only suites on the two lowest passenger decks having bay windows instead. Of these, the only ones with obstructed views are those on the port side of Deck 6 looking out onto the promenade. The standard suites are a roomy 301 square feet; the 18 top suites range from 448 to 1,067 square feet, plus 47- to 200-square-foot balconies. Passengers in the Master, Grand, and Penthouse A & B suites are treated to butler service in addition to regular service by the staff of all-female room stewardesses. Each suite has a huge marble bathroom with a separate shower stall, a long tub, lots of counter space, and wonderful Aveda bath products. Along with those on *Seven Seas Voyager* and Silversea's *Silver Whisper,* they're the best bathrooms at sea today.

Every suite has a sitting area with couch, terry robes, a pair of chairs, desk, vanity table and stool (with an outlet above for a hair dryer or curling iron), TV/DVD (with movies available from an onboard library), minibar stocked with two complimentary bottles of wine or spirits, private safe, and a wide walk-in closet with a tall built-in dresser. The safe is on top of the dresser, so don't do what Heidi did: leave the safe door open, bend over to rummage through a drawer, and then Bam!, smack your head on the way back up. She gave herself quite a lump. The top three categories of suites on each vessel also offer Bose Wave music systems.

Four suites are wheelchair accessible.

PUBLIC AREAS   Full of autumn hues and deep blues, *Navigator*'s attractive decor is a marriage of classic and modern design, with contemporary wooden furniture, chairs upholstered in buttery leather, walls covered in suede, and touches of stainless steel, along with silk brocade draperies, dark-wood paneling, burled veneer, and marble. The ship has lots of intimate spaces, so you'll never feel overwhelmed the way you sometimes do on larger ships.

Most of the public rooms are on Decks 6 and 7, just aft of the three-story atrium and main elevator bank (whose exposed wiring and mechanics could have been better disguised). The well-stocked library has 10 computers with e-mail and Internet access. A card room is adjacent. Across the way, the cozy Navigator Lounge, paneled in mahogany and cherry wood, is a popular place for pre-dinner cocktails—which means it can get tight in there during rush hours. Next door is the Connoisseur Club cigar lounge, a somewhat cold and often underutilized wood-paneled room with umber leather chairs. Down the hall is the roomier Stars Lounge, with a long, curved, black-granite bar and clusters of oversize ocean-blue armchairs around a small dance floor. A live music duo croons pop numbers here nightly. The attractive dark-paneled casino with its striking mural is bound to attract your eye, even if you don't gamble.

Galileo's Lounge, surrounded by windows on three sides, is our favorite spot on board in the evening, when a pianist is on hand and the golden room glows magically under soft light. When the doors to the deck just outside are open on a balmy, star-soaked night, dancers spill out from the small dance floor, creating a truly romantic, dreamy scene. By day, Galileo's is a quiet venue for continental breakfast, high tea, seminars, and meetings, and is also a perfect perch from which to view the seascape.

The stage of the twinkling two-story Seven Seas Lounge is large enough for the kind of sizable, Vegas-style, song-and-dance revues typical of much larger ships—a rarity in the luxe market. While sightlines are good from the tiered rows of banquettes on the first level, views from the sides of the balcony are severely obstructed.

The cheerful windowed Vista observation lounge is used for meetings and is another great scenery-viewing spot. It opens directly out to a huge patch of forward deck space just over the bridge.

DINING OPTIONS   There are two restaurants, the formal Compass Rose dining room and the more casual Portofino Grill, which serves buffet-style breakfast and lunch and is transformed every evening into a very cozy, dimly lit, reservations-only restaurant specializing in Tuscan cuisine with southern Italian accents, with many tables for two. Its menus are inspired by Chef Angelo Elia of Fort Lauderdale's Casa D'Angelo Ristorante. The Compass Rose, a pleasant, wide-open room done in warm caramel-colored woods, offers a single, open seating at all meals. There's also a casual grill on the pool deck for burgers, grilled-chicken sandwiches, fries, and salads at lunchtime, and a **Coffee Corner** on Deck 6, with complimentary deluxe coffees available (from a machine) 24 hours a day.

POOL, FITNESS, SPA & SPORTS FACILITIES   The oceanview gym is bright and roomy for a ship of this size, and a separate aerobics room offers impressively grueling classes, such as circuit training and step. A pair of golf nets and two Ping-Pong tables are available for guest use, but they're situated high on Deck 12 in an ash-plagued nook just behind the smokestacks, and are accessible only by a hard-to-find set of interior crew stairs. The whole area looks like an afterthought. At the pool area, a wide set of stairs joins a balcony of deck chairs to a large pool and pair of hot tubs on the deck below. Adjacent to the gym is *Navigator*'s six-room Carita spa.

4 Seabourn Cruise Line

6100 Blue Lagoon Dr., Suite 400, Miami, FL 33126. ☎ **800/929-9391** or 305/463-3070. www.seabourn.com.

THE LINE IN A NUTSHELL Small and intimate, these quiet, comfortable megayachts lavish all guests with personal attention and very fine cuisine.

THE EXPERIENCE Strictly upper-crust Seabourn caters to guests who are well mannered and prefer their fellow vacationers to be the same. Generally, they aren't into pool games and deck parties, preferring a good book and cocktail chatter, or a taste of the line's special complimentary goodies, such as free mini-massages on deck and soothing Eucalyptus oil baths drawn in suites upon request.

Due to the ships' small size, guests mingle easily and enjoy mellow pursuits such as trivia games and presentations by guest lecturers. With 157 crewmembers to just 208 guests (a higher ratio than on almost any other line), service is very personal; staff members greet you by name from the moment you check in, and your wish is their command.

Pros

- **Top-shelf service:** Staff seems to know what you need before you ask.
- **Totally all-inclusive:** Unlimited wines and spirits are included, as are gratuities.
- **Excellent dining:** Even the breakfast buffets are exceptional, and having dinner on the outside decks of the Veranda Café, with the churning wake shushing just below you, is divine.
- **Remote ports of call:** These small ships are able to visit less-touristed Caribbean ports that larger ships can't.

Cons

- **Limited activities and nightlife:** There's not a whole lot going on, but most guests like it that way.
- **Shallow drafts mean rocky seas:** Rough seas in the Caribbean are relatively rare, but not unheard of. Because the ships are small, they can get tossed around a lot more (and in less-rough waters) than larger vessels.
- **Aging vessels:** When compared to the newer ships of its competitors, Seabourn's 14- to 18-year-old *Legend* and *Pride* lack luster and suffer from some unfortunate design decisions, namely the configuration of the pool deck.
- **No balconies:** The sliding-glass doors that have been added to many of the suites are an improvement, but no substitute for the real thing.

Compared with the other ultraluxury lines, here's how Seabourn rates:

	Poor	Fair	Good	Excellent	Outstanding
Enjoyment Factor					✓
Dining					✓
Activities		✓			
Children's Program	N/A*				
Entertainment		✓			
Service				✓	
Worth the Money				✓	

* *Seabourn has no children's program.*

SEABOURN: THE CAVIAR OF CRUISE SHIPS

Seabourn was established in 1987, when luxury-cruise patriarch Warren Titus and Norwegian shipping mogul Atle Brynestad commissioned a trio of ultra-upscale 10,000-ton vessels from a north German shipyard. They sold out to industry giant Carnival Corporation in 1991 and eventually transferred the ships' registries from Oslo to The Bahamas, somewhat diluting the link to the line's Norwegian roots. That said, you may find your suite minibar stocked with bottles of Norwegian Ringnes Pilsener, captains are Norwegian, and there's no denying the ships' décor is very Scandinavian, with its cool, almost icy sea of pastels. In the spirit of streamlining, in 2001, Carnival Corporation sold the line's *Sea Goddess* vessels to Seabourn's original owner, Brynestad, and, in 2002, transferred the line's 758-passenger *Seabourn Sun* to sister line Holland America. The *Goddess* ships now sail for SeaDream Yacht Club—see the review on p. 313—and *Seabourn Sun* now sails as HAL's *Prinsendam*.

Today, Seabourn finds itself at the top the ultraluxury market, though elbow to elbow with Radisson, Silversea, and Crystal—lines that have newer, bigger ships with more contemporary design and more in the way of entertainment and onboard activities. Though competitors for sure, each of these ultraluxe lines has its own unique draw: Seabourn has by far the smallest and most intimate ships of the four (though larger than SeaDream's yachts, which are more casual and sportier), and the line is playing that up more and more, focusing on its strengths: doting, personalized service, and special little extras; fine food and wine; and a laid-back atmosphere on ships small enough to venture into exotic harbors where megaships can't go. In fact, the line now officially calls itself "The Yachts of Seabourn." French balconies (sliding-glass doors) were added to 36 of the ships' suites in 2000 to better compete with the competition's balcony cabins, and in early 2002 and again in early 2004, even more enhancements were introduced, from complimentary mini-massages on deck to Molton Brown toiletries in suite bathrooms. In mid-2004, Seabourn became one of the first lines to offer wireless, "Wi-Fi," Internet access throughout their ships (not just in certain "hot spots"), for guests with laptops. At least one special shore excursion is complimentary on each cruise.

PASSENGER PROFILE

Seabourn's guests are well-traveled mature adults mostly in their 50s, 60s, and 70s, with an average age, according to a company spokesman, of 53, and are used to the five-star treatment. Many have net worths in the millions. You are likely to encounter former CEOs, lawyers, investment bankers, real-estate tycoons, and entrepreneurs. The majority of passengers are couples, and there is always a handful of singles as well, usually widows or widowers. A number of European and Australian guests frequently spice up the mix (but not more than about 5% in the Caribbean), but no matter what their nationality, these are experienced globe-trotting travelers. While you'll occasionally see families with children during the holidays and summers, it's the exception rather than the rule. These ships do not cater to kids in any way, and passengers prefer it that way.

DINING

Seabourn's cuisine is very, very good and remains one of the line's strong points, as it does with peers Silversea, Crystal, and Radisson.

TRADITIONAL   Fleetwide, dining is offered in a single open seating in the main dining rooms, The Restaurant, allowing guests to dine whenever they choose and with whomever they want, between about 7 and 10pm. Dinner service is high-style, with waiters dramatically lifting silver lids off dishes in unison and almost running at a trot through the elaborate, six-course European service. Typically service is attentive and unobtrusive, and the waitstaff is programmed to please.

Celebrity restaurateur Charlie Palmer, of New York's Aureole fame, is behind the ships' menus, with the ships' chefs training in Palmer's shoreside restaurants. Five entrees change nightly, including one vegetarian. One night may feature dishes such as seared scallops on corn and scallion risotto with roasted sweet pepper puree, pan-roasted halibut with asparagus risotto, grilled venison chops, and a duo of aged sirloin and braised beef short ribs with honey-glazed turnips, mustard greens, and red-wine sauce. There's also a **vegetarian selection** such as soy-glazed shiitakes, a **lighter choice,** with entrees such as crab lasagna with tomato basil coulis, and a standing **a la carte menu** with such staples as Caesar salad, angel-hair pasta, baked salmon, chicken breast, New York strip steak, grilled beef filet, and broiled lamb chops. If nothing on the menu appeals to you, just ask for something you'd prefer: If the chef has the ingredients aboard, he'll prepare whatever you'd like. Want to dine alone as a couple? Not a problem. The maitre d' will be aware of preferences, and will also be aware of solo travelers who may like company.

Formal nights (two per weeklong cruise) are very formal, in spite of the casual world we live in, with virtually every male present in a tuxedo and ladies in sequins and gowns. On other nights, things have relaxed somewhat as Seabourn stays focused on attracting a younger crowd (younger, as in 40- and 50-somethings), and ties are not required. Regardless, passengers always look very pulled together. On formal nights in the Restaurant, the Veranda Café is jackets-only (no tie).

Complimentary wines (about 18 on any given cruise) and champagne are served at lunch and dinner, as well as at any time and place on the ships (ditto for spirits and soft drinks); an extensive list of other vintages is also available. Desserts are varied and scrumptious, including a trio of crème brûlées in flavors such as vanilla, cappuccino, and jasmine.

CASUAL   As a **casual alternative** for breakfast and lunch, the Veranda Café, with indoor and outdoor seating, offers a combination buffet and table-service menu. At breakfast, omelets are made to your specifications and an impressive fresh-fruit selection includes papaya, mango, raspberries, and blackberries; at lunch, you'll find salads, sandwich makings, fresh pasta, and maybe jumbo shrimp, smoked salmon, and smoked oysters, plus hot sliced roast beef, duck, and ham on the carving board. Every evening per cruise, including on formal nights, the Veranda Café also serves a more intimate and casual dinner for about 35 to 40 guests (reservations are required). The outdoor seating offers a rare opportunity to dine with the sea breezes and night sky surrounding you—it's a beautiful thing. Menus here are simpler than in The Restaurant, and focus on themes such as Asian, Mediterranean, French, and steakhouse-style cuisine. Dine here for the atmosphere (it's wonderful), not the food—it's often better in the main dining room. At press time, the Veranda Café was scheduled for a facelift and enhanced menus in late 2005.

One night on each warm-weather itinerary includes a **festive buffet dinner** served out on deck by the pool (jumbo shrimp and caviar can also be ordered poolside, or anywhere else, at no charge—aren't you salivating just reading this?), and **silver-service beach barbecues**—complete with china and linen, and, of course, champagne and **caviar** in the surf—are also a big hit in remote ports such as Virgin Gorda, Jost Van Dyke, or tiny Mayreau in the Grenadines.

Seabourn Fleet Itineraries

Ship	Itineraries
Seabourn Legend	**14-night Panama Canal:** North- or southbound between Ft. Lauderdale, FL, and Caldera, Costa Rica, Nov 2005–Mar 2006 and Nov–Dec 2006. **16-night S. Carib:** Round-trip from Ft. Lauderdale, FL, Dec 2005. **7-night S. Carib:** Round-trip from St. Thomas, USVI, Mar–Apr 2006. **5- & 7-night E. Carib:** East- or westbound between Ft. Lauderdale, FL, and St. Thomas, USVI, Mar and Apr 2006.
Seabourn Pride	**7-night S. Carib:** Round-trip from Barbados, Nov 2005 and Nov–Dec 2006. **7-night E. Carib:** Barbados to Ft. Lauderdale, FL, Dec 2005 and Nov–Dec 2006. **7-night S. Carib/Amazon:** Round-trip from Barbados, Nov–Dec 2005. **16-night E./S. Carib:** Round-trip from Ft. Lauderdale, FL, Dec 2005. **8-night Canada/New England:** North- or southbound between Gloucester, MA, and Quebec City, QB, Oct 2006. **12-night U.S. East Coast:** Gloucester, MA, to Nassau, Bahamas, Oct 2006.

SNACKS & EXTRAS **Room service** is available 24 hours a day on all ships. During normal lunch or dinner hours, your private multi-course meal can mirror the dining room service, right down to the silver, crystal, and porcelain. Don't expect the same level of service dining this way (courses may arrive together) as you would in the ships' restaurants, but do expect a very cushy, lazy way of "ordering in" one night. Outside of mealtimes, the room-service menu is more limited, though you can order treats such as jumbo shrimp and caviar along with the more humdrum burgers, salads, sandwiches, and pastas. In-cabin breakfasts are popular, and you can have your eggs prepared any way you like them.

ACTIVITIES

The Seabourn ships are sociable because of their small size, but don't offer too much in the way of organized activities; typically they offer trivia contests, galley tours, computer classes, **wine tastings,** bridge tournaments, and the ever popular Liar's Club. The lack of in-your-face, rah-rah activities is what most passengers like about Seabourn, though each ship does have a cruise director to organize things. Public announcements are few, and, for the most part, passengers are left alone to enjoy conversation and pursue their own personal peace.

Each of the ships has a retractable **watersports marina** that unfolds from its stern, weather and sea conditions permitting, allowing passengers direct access to the sea for water-skiing, windsurfing, sailing, snorkeling, banana-boat riding, kayaking, and swimming. Each cruise features at least one and often two **guest lecturers** discussing upcoming ports as well as other random topics. Noted chefs, scientists, historians, authors, or statesmen may be aboard, or maybe a wine connoisseur, composer, anthropologist, TV director, or professor, presenting lectures and mingling with guests. From time to time, the line manages to bring aboard celebrities; past guests have included actor Alan Arkin, journalist Bernard Kalb, *Jeopardy!* host Alex Trebek, singer/actress Michelle Phillips, author Paul Theroux, and actress Jill Eikenberry.

The ships each have four computers offering e-mail and Internet access in a small business center. Movies are available for viewing in cabins, and movies are sometimes shown out on deck as well, under the stars (and with popcorn, too!). Suites also have a Bose Wave CD player, and each ship has a library of music and unabridged best-selling books on disc.

CHILDREN'S PROGRAM

These ships are not geared to children, but there are no restrictions against them (as long as they're at least 1 year old), so you may occasionally see a young child. He or she will probably be a very bored child, however, as the line provides no special programs, no special menus, and no special kids' concessions. In a pinch, you may be able to arrange to have an available crewmember provide babysitting service.

ENTERTAINMENT

There are two roomy entertainment lounges, and both have small stages where a cabaret singer or two, solo instrumentalist (harpist, pianist, violinist), quartet, or maybe a comedian or puppeteer performs. As Seabourn continues to try to loosen up a bit, though, lighter, more fun and participatory entertainment is replacing the more traditional fare, especially in the Caribbean. On a recent cruise, we were delighted to watch three cruise staff members doing a lively 1950s/1960s rock 'n' roll show, one playing the goofy, gum-chewing, bobby-socks-wearing coed who exhorted the audience to come up on the dance floor (several couples did). Another night, a hilarious Steve Allen–style comedian/pianist delighted the audience with his wisecracking wit and musical talents.

Before dinner, a pianist plays and sings for cocktailers in The Club; adjacent is the small, rather drab casino with a handful of card tables and slots. You'll also find a pianist playing in the observation lounge on Deck 8, where passengers enjoy cocktails, a little dancing, and quiet conversation.

Due to the ships' small size, there are obviously no big production shows with sets and elaborate costume changes like those you'd find on the larger ships of Silversea, Radisson, and Crystal. This seems to please most guests, who choose a Seabourn cruise exactly because it isn't large enough to offer splashier shows.

SERVICE

With the minor exception of some uneven dining service and the occasional forgetful cabin stewardess, the service staff is outstanding: friendly, courteous, eager to please, discreet, and highly competent. Most are European and most have gained experience at the grand hotels of Europe; the cabin staff is all female. They're among Seabourn's most valuable assets. All gratuities are included in the rates.

If you don't want to deal with lugging your luggage to the airport (or your car), Seabourn offers a service where you can ship your bags directly to the ship and back.

Laundry and **dry cleaning** are available. There are also complimentary self-service laundry rooms.

Seabourn Pride •
Seabourn Legend

The Verdict

These smallish megayachts remain among the top in the market, though they're in a class by themselves—they just don't offer the same experience as the larger and newer (and less intimate) ships of ultraluxury lines such as Radisson, Silversea, and Crystal, which have more entertainment options and brighter decor.

Seabourn Legend *(photo: Seabourn Cruise Line)*

Specifications

Size (in tons)	10,000	Passenger/Crew Ratio	1.5 to 1
Passengers (double occ.)	208	Year Launched	
Passenger/Space Ratio	48.1	*Pride*	1988
Total Cabins/Veranda Cabins	100/6	*Legend*	1992
Crew	157	Last Major Refurbishment	2000

Frommer's Ratings (Scale of 1–5)   ★★★★

Cabin Comfort & Amenities	4	Dining Options	3.5
Ship Cleanliness & Maintenance	4	Gym, Spa & Sports Facilities	3
Public Comfort/Space	5	Children's Facilities	N/A
Decor	3	Enjoyment Factor	4

Got the time? Got the money? Come aboard these sleek, attractive ships for a cruise to just about any Caribbean port you'd want to visit, plus fall foliage cruises that hug the East Coast and call on the top spots. Even with just 208 passengers, you can be as social or as private as you wish, with no rowdiness or loud music and no one exhorting you to get involved. While you're aboard, your ship is your floating boutique hotel or your private yacht. You make the call.

Cabins & Rates

Cabins	Per Diems from	Sq. Ft.	Fridge	Hair Dryer	Sitting Area	TV
Suite	$392	277–575	yes	yes	yes	yes

CABINS   Just about everything on a Seabourn cabin has the feel of an upscale Scandinavian hotel. All cabins are outside, offer ocean views, and measure 277 square feet. Almost all are identical. Color schemes, a bit on the dull side, are either ice blue or champagne-colored, with lots of bleached oak or birch-wood trim, as well as mirrors and spotlight lighting. While only the top six Owner's Suites have proper balconies, 36 regular suites on Decks 5 and 6 have French balconies with sliding doors and a few inches of balcony for your feet (the rest of the suites have picture windows). While you can't fit a chair on one, they do allow sunlight to pour into the cabin, as well as offer a great view up and down the length of the ship. You can sit on the sofa or in a chair and read while sunning yourself out of the wind and out of view. You can also sleep with the doors wide open, going to sleep with the sounds and smells of the ocean—unless, of course, the officers on the bridge decide to lock the doors. If seas get even a little choppy or the wind picks up a hair, a flick of a switch locks your door automatically and there's not a darn thing you can do about it. (Remember, these ships are small, so you're not that far above the water line. They like to avoid waves and sea spray getting into those lovely suites.)

The two Classic Suites measure 400 square feet, and two pairs of Owner's Suites are 530 and 575 square feet and have verandas, dining areas, and guest powder rooms. Their dark-wood furnishings make the overall feeling more like a hotel room than a ship's suite, but, as is true of any cabins positioned near the bow of relatively small ships, they can be somewhat uncomfortable during rough seas. Owner's Suites 05 and 06 have obstructed views.

The best features of the suites are their bathrooms and walk-in closets, with plenty of hanging space for Seabourn's extended cruises. Drawer space, on the other hand, is minimal. White marble bathrooms include a tub and shower (depending on the ship, 10–14 suites have only showers), and lots of shelf, counter, and cabinet space. Those on *Seabourn Pride* have twin sinks; those on *Legend* have single sinks. Molton Brown bath products plus designer soaps by Chanel, Bijan, Hermès, and Bronnley are provided for guests along with the use of terry bathrobes, slippers, world atlas, and umbrellas. In the line's continuing quest to pamper guests with complimentary perks (to make up for the aging hardware of the ship itself), in their staterooms at embarkation, guests will find a complimentary CD of romantic jazz favorites and document portfolios and luggage tags by Tumi, a high-end luggage company.

The coffee table in the sitting area can be pulled up to become a dining table, and the complimentary minibar is stocked upon arrival with two bottles of liquor or wine of your choice (a request form comes with your cruise documents) and a chilled bottle of champagne. Unlimited bottled water, beer, and soft drinks are restocked throughout the cruise. Ice is replenished twice daily (more often on request), and bar setups are in each room. There's a desk, hair dryer, safe, radio/CD player (music and book CDs are available for borrowing), and at press time, new flat-screen TVs and DVD players were to be added to all suites by early 2006. Fresh fruit and a flower complete the suite scene.

Connecting cabins are available. Some are marketed as 554-square-foot Double Suites, and that's exactly what they are: two 277-square-foot suites, with one converted to a lounge. There are four wheelchair-accessible suites.

PUBLIC AREAS   A double, open-spiral, brass-railed staircase links the public areas, which are, overall, duller than you'd expect on ships of this caliber. Step onto most ships today and you'll "oooh" and "ahhh" at the decor. Not so here, where the minimalist Scandinavian design ethic is in play. For the most part, public rooms are spare and almost ordinary looking. Art and ornamentation are conspicuous by their absence, with the exception of the small lobby area in front of the purser's desk on Deck 5, where attractive murals of ship scenes liven up the curved walls.

The forward-facing observation lounge on Sky Deck is the most attractive public room, a quiet venue all day long for reading or cards, the spot for afternoon tea (during which a pianist provides background music), and a good place for a drink before meals. A chart and compass on the wall outside will help you pinpoint the ship's current position, and a computerized wall map lets you track future cruises.

The Club piano bar in the stern offers great views during daylight hours, is packed before dinner, and sometimes offers after-dinner entertainment such as a *Name That Tune* game or a cabaret show for those who stay up past 10pm. Hors d'oeuvres are served here both before and after dinner. A tiny, cramped casino is adjacent, with a couple of blackjack tables, a roulette wheel, and about 10 slots. The downstairs show lounge is a dark, tiered, all-purpose space for lectures, the captain's cocktail party, and featured entertainers such as singers, comedians, and pianists.

One of the best places for a romantic, moonlit moment is the isolated patch of deck far forward in the bow on Deck 5, where a lone hot tub also resides.

DINING OPTIONS   The formal Restaurant, located on the lowest deck, is a large low-ceilinged room with elegant candlelit tables. (With the lights low, you can hardly notice the old bright peach and gray paint job on the columns and moldings.) It's open for breakfast, lunch, and dinner; officers, cruise staff, and sometimes guest lecturers host tables at dinnertime. If you're not in the mood for the formal dining room, the recently spruced-up Veranda Café (which now features new German-made Rosenthal porcelain tableware in a contemporary style), serves a combination buffet and full-service breakfast and lunch; the fresh-fruit selection at breakfast is very impressive. On most nights (including formal nights), it's open for dinner, too, on a reservations-only basis, with restaurateur Charlie Palmer consulting on the creation of the menus, as he does in the main restaurant. Dishes are prepared around themes such as "Steak House Traditions," including steaks, fish, and chicken grilled with creamed spinach and potatoes; and "Citrus & Ginger Asian," a combination of Japanese, Thai, and Chinese flavors. In good weather, it's a real treat and very romantic to dine at one of the arc of awning-covered tables located aft, overlooking the wake, with the wind and surf serenading you.

A special of the day—pizza with pineapple topping or fresh ingredients for tacos— is also available at the pleasant Sky Bar, overlooking the Lido Deck, for those who don't want to change out of their swimsuits. You'll also find burgers, chicken, hot dogs and grilled items at the Sky Bar. On sunny days, themed lunches also are often set up here.

POOL, FITNESS, SPA & SPORTS FACILITIES   The outdoor pool, which gets little use, is awkwardly situated in a shadowy location aft of the open Deck 7, between the twin engine uptakes and flanked by lifeboats that hang from both sides of the ship. A pair of whirlpools is better located just forward of the pool. A third hot tub is perched far forward on Deck 5; it's wonderfully isolated and a perfect spot (as is the whole patch of deck here) from which to watch a port come into sight or fade away.

A retractable, wood-planked watersports marina opens out from the stern of each ship so that passengers can hop into sea kayaks or go windsurfing, water-skiing, or snorkeling right from the vessel. An attached steel mesh net creates a protected saltwater pool when the marina is in use.

The gym and Steiner-managed spa are roomy and well equipped for ships this small, and are located forward of the Lido Deck. Yoga and Pilates as well as more traditional aerobics classes are offered in a lounge or on deck, and you'll find two saunas, massage rooms, and a beauty salon.

5 SeaDream Yacht Club

2601 S. Bayshore Dr., Penthouse 1B, Coconut Grove, FL 33133. (C) **800/707-4911** or 305/631-6100 Fax 305/631-6110. www.seadreamyachtclub.com.

THE LINE IN A NUTSHELL   Intimate cruise-ships-turned-yachting-vessels, SeaDream's two small ships deliver an upscale yet casual experience without the regimentation of traditional cruise itineraries and activities.

THE EXPERIENCE   SeaDream—a line created a few years ago by Seabourn founder Atle Brynestad with that line's two *Sea Goddess* ships—will entice those who value impeccable service, a mellow atmosphere, and a good batch of sevruga Malossol caviar. But the line seeks another kind of traveler as well: one who straddles a WaveRunner, barhops in Monte Carlo, and enjoys a spontaneous mountain-bike trek. But this isn't just the wealthy man's *Survivor* episode. Pampering is still a major focus—in fact, tickets for a SeaDream cruise were included in the decadent gift baskets given out at the Sundance Film Festival in 2005—and the line's flexible itineraries and fluid daily schedules should appeal to landlubbers used to resort vacations.

Pros

- **Flexible itineraries:** Captains have the authority to duck inclement weather by visiting a different port or to extend a stay off an island because of perfect snorkeling conditions.
- **Truly all-inclusive:** Unlimited wines and spirits as well as tips are included in the rates.
- **Late-night departures from key ports:** Instead of leaving port around cocktail hour—just when things begin to get interesting—the ships will stay late or even overnight in places such as St. Barts to allow passengers a night of carousing on terra firma.
- **Cool tech stuff:** These ships were built in the mid-1980s, but they've been outfitted for the 21st century. Every cabin is equipped with a flat-screen TV, Internet access, and CD and DVD players; and jet skis, MP3 players, and Segway Human Transporters are available for passenger use.

Cons

- **Rough seas:** While the intimacy of these ships can be a selling point, their size can be a detriment: They bob like buoys in even mildly rough waters, and the diesel engines sometimes produce a shimmying sensation.
- **Limited entertainment:** When you're not sipping a late-evening drink in Virgin Gorda or St. Barts, you're probably watching the lounge act, but don't expect Broadway-style pyrotechnics and scantily clad chorus girls. A piano player and a sidekick are the sum total of the ship's entertainment.

SEADREAM: YOUR YACHT AWAITS

In fall 2001, Norwegian entrepreneur Atle Brynestad, who founded Seabourn in 1987 and chaired the company for a decade, bought out Carnival Corporation's stake in Seabourn's *Sea Goddess I* and *Sea Goddess II,* then worked with former Seabourn and Cunard president and CEO Larry Pimentel to form the SeaDream Yacht Club, reintroducing the ships as twin yachts. *SeaDream II* was redesigned and refitted at a Bremerhaven, Germany, shipyard and was unveiled in Miami in February 2002. Her sister ship debuted 2 months later, following her own refurbishment.

The mantra from management is that these vessels are not cruise ships. They are yachts and have been painstakingly renovated to invoke the ambience of your best friend's private vessel, on the theory (as president and CEO Pimentel told us recently) that "cruising is about what happens inside the vessel; yachting is about what happens outside." Toward this end, deck space has been expanded and refurbished with such touches as queen-size Sun Beds. The Main Salon is cozy, with fabrics and art hand-picked by Linn Brynestad, the owner's spouse. The dress code steers clear of the traditional tux and sequins dress-up night by favoring "yacht casual" wear. Some men wear jackets, but never ties. Itineraries are designed so that ships stay overnight in three-quarters of the ports they visit because, as Pimentel explained, "There's no sense in leaving a port at 5 if it doesn't start really happening till 11."

With many crewmembers having migrated to SeaDream from the *Goddess* days, meticulous attention to detail and personalized service are still the ships' greatest assets.

PASSENGER PROFILE

Most passengers are in their 40s to 60s, are 70% American (with Brits and other Europeans making up most of the remainder), and are not veteran cruisers. In theory, they have refined tastes but balk at the rigid structure of cruise itineraries. They're happy to strike up a game of backgammon beside the pool, or venture into town with the chef in search of the evening's special fish. They want top-notch service and gourmet food, but are secure enough to dispense with a stuffy atmosphere. At least that's the plan.

More than 50% of the line's business comes from full charters of the ships, often by large (rich) families. Smaller groups can take advantage of a deal that gives one free cabin for every four booked, up to a maximum of 25 cabins. Still, groups of 50 are a significant presence on ships this size, so when booking, inquire whether there will be any large groups aboard, to avoid the "in crowd/out crowd" vibe.

DINING

TRADITIONAL   Dining is a high point of the SeaDream experience. Daily five-course dinners in the Dining Salon include five entrees that change nightly, with a healthy selection among them. Dishes such as the sautéed foie gras with cassis glaze and candied apples and a coconut soufflé with vanilla sauce won raves on a recent cruise. You'll find a vegetarian option and a la carte items such as linguini with pesto and rosemary marinated lamb chops. The kitchen will prepare **special requests** provided the ingredients are on board. **Local specialties,** such as fresh fish from markets in various ports, are likely to be incorporated into the menu. Open-seating dining is offered from 7:30 to 10pm, and table arrangements include everything from the nine-seat captain's table to cozier places for two (though during the evening rush, it's not easy to snag one). Unlike the practice on the former *Sea Goddesses,* there are no formal evenings. Jackets are not required; some men wear them, but many just stick to collared shirts.

Guests can venture "out" for dinner by requesting a spot in advance at one of several private alcoves on Deck 6, or even on the bridge. These special dining ops may not be advertised heavily on board—you'll have to ask for them.

CASUAL   The partially covered, open-sided Topside Restaurant on Deck 5 serves breakfast and lunch daily, with guests choosing from a buffet or menu.

SNACKS & EXTRAS   Room service is available 24 hours a day for those who don't want to pause their DVD player. You'll also find sandwiches, wraps, pastries, and other snacks throughout the day in the Topside Restaurant's buffet area or at the pool.

Dining highlights from the old *Sea Goddess* cruises are carried over here, including lavish **beach barbecues,** called the Caviar and Champagne Splash, on Jost Van Dyke and Virgin Gorda. As you lounge on a quiet beach gazing out toward the anchored ship, you'll see the captain standing at the bow of a Zodiac boat zooming toward the beach, looking like George Washington crossing the Delaware, but in decidedly better weather and absolutely bluer water. The captain's soldiers, 20-something European stewards in Hawaiian shirts, hop into the surf carrying a life preserver that doubles as a floating serving tray for an open tin of sevruga Malossol caviar, encircled by little dishes of sour cream, chopped egg, and minced onion. Two stewards perform ceremonial running front flips into the surf with champagne bottles in hand, then pop off the corks in unison. Meanwhile, other crewmembers are tending the barbecues, preparing grilled lobster tails, barbecued spare ribs, carved roast beef, baked potatoes, salads, and fresh fruit. Passengers feast under umbrellas at tables set with proper china and hotel silver brought ashore by the staff. It doesn't get much better than this.

The line's **open-bar policy** means that unlimited alcoholic beverages are served throughout the vessels, though cabin minifridges are stocked only with complimentary beer and soft drinks. If you want wine and spirits for your minifridge, you'll have to pay. Advance requests for favorite libations are encouraged. Each ship's wine cellar includes some 3,500 bottles, of which an excellent selection is complimentary.

ACTIVITIES

Considering the small size of these ships, they have a surprising array of indoor and outdoor activities. The best part is that few of them are organized and none of them require an announcement over the ship's intercom (read: peace and quiet). Cabins offer DVD and CD players, flat-screen TVs, and Internet accessibility. Internet access is also available in the library. Guests have access to portable MP3 players that (talk about a homey touch) were programmed by CEO Pimentel's 18-year-old son, who loaded them with 170 hours of music from all genres, from pop to jazz to classical. There are about 25 on each ship; pick them up at the reception desk.

Outdoor enthusiasts are encouraged to take advantage of the toys at each ship's **Watersports Marina,** which is outfitted with sea kayaks, Sunfish, and WaveRunners (keep in mind, if seas are at all choppy, the marina isn't lowered). **Mountain bikes** are carried aboard ship for guest use onshore. Golf lovers can head toward the bow on Deck 6 to practice their swing on a **golf simulator.** The newest toy: a **Segway Human Transporter,** an upright two-wheel *Jetsons*-like scooter. Five are available on each yacht, and you can take a spin at $49 an hour, either on your own or on special Segway shore excursions, which instantly make you the center of attention at every port where they're offered.

One to two shore excursions are offered per port (at additional cost), with possibilities including a regatta on St. Martin and visits to The Baths on Virgin Gorda. Guests can also join the captain on a kayaking or snorkeling jaunt he may be leading to a quiet Virgin Gorda cove, meet up with the chef to scout for local produce, or follow the bartender for a night out to a local watering hole such as Foxy's on Jost Van Dyke.

SeaDream Fleet Itineraries

Ship	Itineraries
SeaDream I	**4-, 6-, 7- & 9-night E. & S. Carib (several routes):** Round-trip from San Juan, PR, and between San Juan and St. Thomas, St. Thomas and St. Martin, and St. Martin and San Juan, Oct 2005–Apr 2006. **3-, 6- & 7-night E./S. Carib:** Round-trip from St. Thomas, USVI, Nov–Dec 2006.
SeaDream II	**4-, 6-, 7- & 9-night E./S. Carib (several routes):** Round-trip from St. Thomas, Barbados, and Antigua, and between West Palm Beach and St. Thomas, St. Thomas and Barbados, St. Thomas and St. Martin, and Antigua and Barbados, Nov 2005–Apr 2006. **6-, 7- & 8-night E./S. Carib (several routes):** Round-trip from San Juan, Barbados, or St. Thomas, or between San Juan and Barbados or Barbados and St. Thomas, Nov–Dec 2006.

CHILDREN'S ACTIVITIES

Though the only actual restriction is that children under age 1 are prohibited, these ships are by no means kid-friendly. There are no babysitting services or child-related activities. Teens, though, may enjoy these cruises' emphasis on watersports and unstructured activities. Keep in mind, the standard Yacht Club staterooms can accommodate only three people; the third person/child sleeps on the couch (which doesn't pull out). If you've got a larger family, you'll have to spring for two staterooms. The rate for a child up to age 12 is $100 per day and $200 per day for children over 12; in both cases it is assumed that they'll be sharing a stateroom with two adults.

ENTERTAINMENT

Tunes are served up nightly on a white glass-topped Yamaha in the Piano Bar. Three nights a week in the Main Salon, guests can catch a spirited **cabaret vocalist** with digitized accompaniment followed by dancing. On a few cruises in the Caribbean, **local bands** are brought on for the night. A **casino** on Deck 4 has two poker tables, four slot machines, and two electronic poker machines.

On 1 evening during each cruise, a screen is set up on deck for a **movie** under the stars, which passengers can view poolside (or even from the pool).

SERVICE

Given the small number of guests and large number of crew, everyone is quick to satisfy whims and commit your name to memory, though make sure that your first drink is your favorite; you may find fresh ones reappearing automatically throughout the evening. The dining room waitstaff is courteous and knowledgeable, though a bit harried as most passengers, even though seating is open, tend to dine about the same time each evening. As aboard the Silversea ships, cabin bathrooms are stocked with Bvlgari amenities and guests all get a complimentary set of SeaDream pj's. **Laundry, dry cleaning,** and **pressing** are available, but there is no self-service laundry.

SeaDream I • SeaDream II

The Verdict

The service, cuisine, and intimacy of the old *Sea Goddess* ships in an even better package, with flexible itineraries and laid-back atmosphere designed to pry landlubbers from their resorts and out to sea.

SeaDream II *(photo: SeaDream Yacht Club)*

Specifications

Size (in tons)	4,260	Passenger/Crew Ratio	1.2 to 1
Passengers (double occ.)	110	Year Launched	
Passenger/Space Ratio	39	*SeaDream I*	1984
Total Cabins/Veranda Cabins	55/55	*SeaDream II*	1985
Crew	89	Last Major Refurbishment	2002

Frommer's Ratings (Scale of 1–5)   ★★★★½

Cabin Comfort & Amenities	5	Dining Options	3.5
Ship Cleanliness & Maintenance	4	Gym, Spa & Sports Facilities	4
Public Comfort/Space	4.5	Children's Facilities	N/A
Decor	4	Enjoyment Factor	5

Care for a chronology? The year is 1984, and Sea Goddess Cruises begins offering luxury small-ship cruises for very affluent travelers. Unfortunately, not enough affluent travelers are interested, and within 2 years the line sells out to Cunard, which takes over operation of its two vessels and retains a similar approach, featuring impeccable service and cuisine. In 1998, Carnival Corporation purchases Cunard and transfers the *Sea Goddess* ships to its Seabourn division, which operates similar-size luxury vessels. Then, in August 2001, Carnival sells the ships to Atle Brynestad, founder of Seabourn Cruises. Brynestad then brings aboard former Seabourn and Cunard president and CEO Larry Pimentel as co-owner, chairman, and CEO of the new line, and hires a raft of other ex-Cunard executives to fill the company's top spots.

Man, the business world is complicated. But because this line is geared to affluent travelers, we thought you might be interested. Now let's get to the details.

Cabins & Rates

Cabins	Per Diems from	Sq. Ft.	Fridge	Hair Dryer	Sitting Area	TV
Suite	$377	195–450	yes	yes	yes	yes

CABINS All of the 54 one-room, 195-square-foot, oceanview suites are virtually identical, with the bedroom area positioned alongside the cabin's large window (or portholes in the case of Deck 2 suites) and the sitting area inside, the exact opposite of most ship cabin layouts. Soundproofing between cabins is good and engine noise minimal, as all cabins are located forward and amidships.

Each cabin has twin beds that are convertible to queens, a couch (which can accommodate a child or third person), plenty of mirrors, a minibar and minifridge stocked with complimentary beer and soft drinks (if you want wine and spirits for your minifridge, you'll have to pay), a telephone, fresh flowers, terry robes, plush towels branded with the SeaDream logo, multiple jet massage showers, and a hair dryer. The light-colored wood cabinetry, furniture, and softgoods are all brand new. Beds are outfitted with luxurious Belgian linen, made of Egyptian cotton. Tech items include CD and DVD players, portable MP3 players (25 are available from the reception desk), and a flat-screen TV with Internet capability. Passengers can also use the TVs to browse and buy from the SeaDream Collection, which includes the usual logo items but also lets you bring part of your SeaDream experience home—for instance, the Hadeland crystal glasses and Porsgrund china used aboard ship (produced in workshops owned by SeaDream's founder) or the brand of mountain bikes, WaveRunners, jet skis, and so on that are carried aboard the vessels.

There are 16 staterooms that are connectable to form eight 390-square-foot Commodore Club Staterooms. The gorgeous 450-square-foot Owner's Suite has a bedroom, living room, dining area, main bathroom with bathtub and separate oceanview shower, and guest bathroom.

These ships are not recommended for passengers requiring the use of a wheelchair: Doorways leading to staterooms are not wide enough, many thresholds in public areas are several inches tall, and tenders that shuttle passengers from ship to shore in many ports cannot accommodate wheelchairs. Though there are elevators, they don't reach all decks.

PUBLIC AREAS   The SeaDream yachts retain much of *Sea Goddess's* former sophisticated decor. Stained wood floors, Oriental carpets, and striking exotic floral arrangements delight the eye. The Main Salon and its small but popular alcove bar remain the focus of the cocktail hour. One deck above in the Piano Bar, a singing pianist taps out his favorites along with any that you may request. Next door are the ship's small casino, a gift shop, and a library furnished with comfy chairs and area carpets and stocked with everything from military history to Oprah Book Club favorites.

The favorite place to socialize has to be the Top of the Yacht Bar amidships on Deck 6, which has been designed with teak decking, rattan furniture, and contrasting blue-striped cushions. The bar area is partially covered and offers alcove seating. On this deck you'll also find a flotilla of queen-size Sun Beds for reading, sunbathing, or napping; they're slightly elevated at the stern of the ship to allow for uninterrupted ocean viewing. For those who might want to sleep on deck one night, management will allow it and outfit beds with blankets. There's a large collection of original artwork by exclusively Scandinavian artists, located throughout the ship and commissioned or otherwise chosen by Linn Brynestad.

DINING OPTIONS   Dinners are served in the main dining room. On 1 or 2 nights during the trip, a festive dinner is served in the open-sided, teak-floored Topside Restaurant, and some special meals are served on the beach during port calls. (See "Dining," above, for details.)

POOL, FITNESS, SPA & SPORTS FACILITIES   Much of the redesign of these ships was informed by the experience one would have on a yacht. As yachting is about being outdoors, the open spaces on the SeaDream ships have been vastly improved. Stake an early claim to a Sun Bed because they're prime real estate. Eight of them are aftward on Deck 6, and more are forward, near the golf simulator. Aft on Deck 3 is the pool area, with comfortable lounge chairs and umbrellas, tables, a bar, and, not too far away, a hot tub. A covered deck above has more chairs.

Toward the bow on Deck 4 are the beauty salon, spa, and gym, the latter of which has four treadmills with flat-screen TVs, an elliptical machine, two stationary bikes, and free weights (and lowish ceilings if you're on the tall side). Classes include aerobics, yoga, and tai chi. The uninterrupted ocean views add a calming diversion while you're burning calories. The teak-lined spa, the Asian Spa and Wellness Center, has three treatment rooms and features the usual decadent (and pricey) suspects, including wraps, facials, and massages, plus more exotic options such as hot lava rock massages, a spice and yogurt scrub, and a cucumber and aloe wrap. A full-day treatment package is offered, which you can enjoy in the spa or in the privacy of your own stateroom for $500 a person.

6 Silversea Cruises

110 E. Broward Blvd., Fort Lauderdale, FL 33301. ℂ **800/722-9955.** Fax 954/522-4499. www.silversea.com.

THE LINE IN A NUTSHELL   It doesn't get better than free-flowing Philipponnat Royale Reserve champagne and marble bathrooms stocked with Italian Acqua di Parma bath products. These gorgeous ships offer the best of everything.

THE EXPERIENCE   Fine-tuned and genteel, a Silversea cruise caters to guests who won't settle for anything but the best. The food and service are the best at sea, and the ships' Italian-style decor is warm and inviting. Nothing seems to have been forgotten in the creation of the plush Silversea fleet. Tables are set with Christofle silver and Schott-Zwiesel crystal. These are dignified vessels for a dignified crowd that likes to dress for dinner. If you want the VIP treatment 24–7, this is your cruise line.

Pros
- **Doting service:** Gracious and ultraprofessional, the Silversea crew knows how to please well-traveled guests with high expectations.
- **Truly all-inclusive:** Unlimited wines and spirits, including the house champagne (Philipponnat Royale Reserve), as well as tips, are included in the rates.
- **Excellent cuisine:** Rivaling the best restaurants ashore, cuisine is as exquisite as it gets at sea. Each ship has two alternative venues for dinner, buffets are bountiful, and the room-service menu includes such extravagant snacks as jumbo shrimp.
- **Large staterooms and great bathrooms:** At 287 square feet, plus 58-square-foot balconies, *Silver Whisper*'s and *Shadow*'s staterooms are bigger than Seabourn's and Crystal's, and the huge marble bathrooms are the best at sea (along with those on *Seven Seas Navigator* and *Voyager*).

Cons
- **Stuffy crowd:** Of course, not every guest fits that bill, but expect a good portion of the crowd on any cruise to be, shall we say, reserved.

SILVERSEA: THE CROWN JEWELS

Silversea Cruises was conceived in the early 1990s by the Lefebvre family of Italy, former owners of Sitmar Cruises, an Italian shipping company dating back to 1938 that was sold to P&O Cruises in the late '80s. Created to cater to discerning travelers looking for an ultraluxurious cruise experience, the line's four ships were built and outfitted at shipyards in Italy and no expense was spared in their design.

Compared with the other ultraluxury lines, here's how Silversea rates:

	Poor	Fair	Good	Excellent	Outstanding
Enjoyment Factor					✓
Dining					✓
Activities			✓		
Children's Program	N/A*				
Entertainment		✓			
Service					✓
Worth the Money				✓	

* Silversea has no children's program.

When the line introduced 296-passenger *Silver Cloud* and *Silver Wind* in 1994, the new line joined Seabourn right at the top of the heap, with features such as stateroom balconies and a two-level show lounge giving them the edge and raising the bar for ultraluxury cruising. With the introduction of the larger, even more impressive *Silver Shadow* and *Silver Whisper* in 2000 and 2001, that bar was raised even higher, with larger staterooms and huge marble bathrooms, dimly lit and romantic cigar lounges, and more entertainment lounges—all in all, the absolute height of style, paired with itineraries that spanned the globe. Recent enhancements include several new alliances with Italian companies. You'll now find bath amenities from Acqua di Parma, a renowned Italian fragrance house; the ships all have Loro Piana boutiques, which sell high-end Italian clothes and accessories; and each has an Italian art collection (for show and for sale), from a company called Italian Factory, which represents new Italian artists. The ships also sport a new Italian alternative-dining venue, La Terrazza (still called Terrace Cafe for breakfast and lunch).

PASSENGER PROFILE

While Silversea's typical passenger mix is 48-plus, shorter cruises and Caribbean sailings often skew the mix a tad younger, adding at least a handful of 30- and 40-something couples to the pot. Typically, about 70% of passengers are American and they're well traveled, well heeled, well dressed, and well accessorized: five-carat diamonds and gold Rolexes the size of Texas are de rigueur. Most guests are couples, though singles and small groups of friends traveling together are usually part of the scene too. Many have cruised with Silversea before, and they expect the best of everything. 'Hup hup!

DINING

Gourmet foodies should consider a Silversea cruise for the food alone. The cuisine is well prepared and presented, and creative chefs continually come up with a wide variety of dishes in the ships' three restaurants. Each has a formal open-seating venue and two more casual options. There are plenty of tables for two in all restaurants, though in the main dining room, you may have to wait for one.

TRADITIONAL The Restaurant is the elegant main dining room. While the cuisine is not as impressive as that of the more intimate and casual La Terrazza, The Restaurant offers delicious meals and a lot more choice, and entrees such as a pan-fried filet of lemon sole, roast lamb saddle with artichoke-garlic stuffing, and marinated crab and leek salad and star anise are very good. The wine list in both restaurants is excellent, and several complimentary wines are suggested at each meal from more than 40 choices. You can also choose one of the wines not included in the complimentary list—a $745 1990 Château Margaux, anyone? The sky's the limit on a Silversea cruise.

SPECIALTY   Each ship now has two **casual alternatives** serving for dinner; both require reservations. Open most evenings for dinner, La Terrazza, formerly called the Terrace Cafe, is a lovely windowed venue now offering Italian cuisine under the watchful eye of chef Marco Betti, owner of the award-winning Antica Posta restaurants in Atlanta, Georgia, and Florence, Italy.

The second alternative venue, called Le Champagne aboard the *Shadow* and *Whisper,* offers nightly fixed menus created by renowned European chef Joachim Koerper. The German native earned the coveted Michelin two stars for his Girasol restaurant in Moraira, Spain. These very intimate and elegant dining spaces may also be reserved for private dinner parties. The typical fixed menu may start off with the likes of an *amuse bouche* (mini starter course such as a lobster medallion served on lentils), followed by a marble foie gras terrine with fresh fig chutney, gazpacho soup, roast veal loin with Mediterranean couscous and basil sauce, and all topped off by a dessert course featuring rosemary crème brûlée with olive oil ice cream. Most evenings, both venues will be open for dinner.

CASUAL   Burgers, sandwiches, and salads are served poolside at lunchtime, in addition to service in The Restaurant and the buffet-style Terrace Cafe (which is transformed into La Terrazza evenings), and once per cruise, passengers are invited into the galley for the traditional galley brunch. It features more than 100 delectable dishes, from stone crab claws to pickled herring, Hungarian goulash, rabbit a la Provençal, and German bratwurst. A red carpet is rolled out, literally, through the galley, and it's a most festive affair, with the chef on hand to chat with guests about the feast.

SNACKING & EXTRAS   The line's **24-hour room-service menu** includes such decadent choices as caviar and jumbo shrimp cocktail, and you can order it as many times as you like. Plus, if you'd rather dine in one evening, you can order off The Restaurant's menu (during its dinnertime operating hours) and have your meal served, course-by-course, on a table in your suite, which is set with linens and china. There's an elegant white-gloved tea service in one of the lounges on most days.

ACTIVITIES

Aside from trivia games, card tournaments, stretch and aerobics classes, and bridge tours, Silversea excels in its more cerebral pursuits. **Wine-tasting seminars** are excellent, and the line's enrichment lectures are varied and interesting; at least one guest speaker is featured on every sailing. They include guest lecturers such as Fred McLaren, a retired Navy captain and professor, who does a slide show and talk on his adventures diving 12,500 feet down in a Russian MIR submersible to explore the remains of the *Titanic*. Other lecturers include Lynn Sherr, award-winning ABC News correspondent and author, and Brian Jones, who together with his Swiss colleague Bertrand Piccard, pulled off one of the most daring feats in aviation history—the first circumnavigation of the earth in a hot air balloon. The lines culinary theme cruises, in partnership with Relais & Châteaux, are hosted by Relais Gourmands chefs and

Silversea Fleet Itineraries

Ship	Itineraries
Silver Shadow	**7- & 9-night E. & S. Carib (several routes):** Round-trip from Barbados and San Juan or between Miami and Barbados, Barbados and San Juan, San Juan and Ft. Lauderdale, or Ft. Lauderdale and Barbados, Oct–Dec 2005. **12-night Central America:** Round-trip from Ft. Lauderdale, Nov 2005. **14-night Carib:** Round-trip from Ft. Lauderdale, Dec 2005. **10-night Gulf of Alaska:** Anchorage, AK, to Vancouver, BC, June 2006. **9-, 10- & 12-night Alaska Inside Passage (several routes):** Round-trip from Seattle or San Francisco or north-/southbound between either Vancouver and Seattle or Vancouver and San Francisco, June–Aug 2006.
Silver Whisper	**4-, 7-, 9-, 10- & 14-night Carib (several routes):** Round-trip from Ft. Lauderdale, Barbados, Antigua, or San Juan or between Ft. Lauderdale and either Barbados, Antigua, or Curaçao, Nov 2005–Apr 2006. **15-night Panama Canal:** Ft. Lauderdale, FL, to San Diego, CA, Feb 2006. **10-night Panama Canal:** San Diego to Caldera, Costa Rica, and Caldera to San Juan, PR, Mar 2006. **9-, 10-, 11- & 12-night Canada/New England (several routes):** Round-trip from New York, Boston to Montreal, Montreal to New York, or New York to Montreal, Sept–Oct 2006.

feature demos and tastings in the ships' new Viking Cooking Schools, which include Viking cooking stations so that guests can cook along with the guest chefs.

Other pursuits include language classes and golf and computer-learning lessons. Plus, on the *Shadow* and *Whisper,* there are special golf cruises that feature PGA golf pros, golfing excursions, and the latest video-teaching technology.

Lighter activities include a dip in the pool or two hot tubs, or a visit to the golf driving net, the Internet center, or boutiques, which include "The Fine Jewelry Room." Here you'll find high-end gold, diamond and gemstone pieces from top designers.

And the ships' Balinese-inspired Mandara spa beckons with its flower-strewn copper foot bowls, warm massage rocks, and other Asian-inspired treatments. To avoid waiting in an invariably long line on the first day of the cruise to make your appointments, you can now book your treatments online before your cruise (at www.silver sea.com).

CHILDREN'S PROGRAM

These ships are not geared to children, though every so often one or two are aboard. Babysitting may be arranged with an available crewmember (no guarantee); otherwise, no activities or services are offered specifically for children. The minimum age for sailing is 12 months.

ENTERTAINMENT

For evening entertainment, the ships each have a small casino, a combo entertaining each evening in the nightclub adjacent to the show lounge, a pianist in another lounge, and dozens of in-cabin movies, including oldies and current films. The small-scale song-and-dance revues in the two-level show lounges are a pleasant after-dinner diversion, but don't expect the talent to knock anyone's Gucci socks off; low-brow Carnival and Royal Caribbean do a better job at Vegas-style entertainment. It's the nonstandard stuff that Silversea excels at. Popular **theme cruises** from time to time feature classical musicians and guest chefs and renowned wine experts conducting demonstrations and talks. The pace is calm, and that's the way most Silversea guests like it; most are perfectly content to spend their after-dinner hours with cocktails and conversation.

SERVICE

The gracious staff knows how to please discerning guests. Staff members are friendly and remember your name, but are never obtrusive or pushy. Waiters and stewardesses are as discreet as the guests are, and chances are you'll never hear the word "no." The room-service menu includes choices such as caviar and jumbo shrimp cocktail; at dinnertime you can also order from The Restaurant's menu and have it served to you in your suite course by course. Unlimited wines, Philipponnat Royale Reserve champagne, spirits, and soft drinks are included in the rates, as are gratuities. Hot and cold canapés are served in the lounges before dinner, and Godiva chocolates are left on suite pillows each evening.

Other perks a small high-end line such as Silversea offers is flexible embarkation and disembarkation. For a charge of $100 to $150 a person, you can board the ship and get into your suite as early as 10:30am (normal embarkation is 3pm); likewise, you can disembark as late as 5pm (and have lunch on the ship). Normally, guests disembark in the morning an hour or 2 after the ship arrives in port.

You can also avoid waiting in lines on board by pre-booking spa appointments online up to 48 hours before sailing. On can also pre-book shore excursions (up until 7 nights before sailing) on Silversea's website as well.

Laundry and **dry cleaning** are available. There are also **self-service laundry** rooms.

Silver Shadow • Silver Whisper

The Verdict

The most beautiful, well-run ships you can find in the ultraluxe market, they're as good as it gets if you're on a quest for mighty fine cuisine, service, and suites.

Silver Shadow *(photo: Silversea Cruises)*

Specifications

Size (in tons)	28,258	Passenger/Crew Ratio	1.3 to 1
Passengers (double occ.)	388	Year Launched	
Passenger/Space Ratio	73	*Silver Shadow*	2000
Total Cabins/Veranda Cabins	194/157	*Silver Whisper*	2001
Crew	295	Last Major Refurbishment	N/A

Frommer's Ratings (Scale of 1–5)   ★★★★★

Cabin Comfort & Amenities	5	Dining Options	5
Ship Cleanliness & Maintenance	5	Gym, Spa & Sports Facilities	4
Public Comfort/Space	5	Children's Facilities	N/A
Decor	5	Enjoyment Factor	5

With these ships, Silversea sets the bar very high for the rest of the ultraluxe ships. Not only is Silversea ultra-all-inclusive, with unlimited wines and spirits covered in the rates along with gratuities, but on *Shadow* and *Whisper,* all the right chords are struck. The ships are small enough to be intimate, but large enough to offer a classy two-story show lounge, dark and romantic cigar lounge, three dining venues, impressive spa and gym, and some really great suites.

Cabins & Rates

Cabins	Per Diems from	Sq. Ft.	Fridge	Hair Dryer	Sitting Area	TV
Suite	$261	287–1,435*	yes	yes	yes	yes

* Includes balconies.

CABINS The suites on these all-suite ships don't leave anything to be desired—the setting is simply sublime. With a chilled bottle of Philipponnat Royale Reserve at your side, settle down in the comfy sitting area and bask in the ambient luxury. Private balconies are attached to three-quarters of the plush staterooms, which measure a roomy 287 square feet or more. They're done up in an ultrapleasant color scheme focused on rich blues and soft golds, along with coppery-brown wood tones—a welcome contrast to the bland champagne-colored Seabourn suites. Each Silversea suite has a walk-in closet, minibar, DVD player, sitting area, lighted dressing table with hair dryer, writing desk, and wonderful marble-covered bathrooms stocked with Acqua di Palma toiletries. The separate shower stall and extra-long bathtub, along with double sinks, make these among the best loos at sea; only Radisson's *Seven Seas Navigator* and *Voyager* have bathrooms this good. All beds have feather-down pillows and duvets, and Turkish cotton linens. The largest of the four two-bedroom Grand Suites are really something else, measuring 1,435 square feet and come with three bathrooms, a pair of walk-in closets, an entertainment center, two verandas, and a living room and dining area. The Grand, Royal, and Owner's suites have flat-screen televisions as well.

PUBLIC AREAS The corridors and stair landings of these classy ships are bathed in lots of deep Wedgwood blue and golden peach fabrics and carpeting, along with warm caramel wood tones, while the color scheme throughout the public rooms is a rich medley of blood-red velveteens and golden brocades, as well as strong blues and teals. The low-key main lobby area, where the purser's desk resides, branches out into a pair of attractive four-deck-high staircases with shiplike railings. The ships have a quite impressive two-story show lounge with tiered seating and lots of cozy clusters of chairs; The Bar, just outside of the show lounge's first level, is a social hub, with a long bar, dance floor, and plenty of seating. The Observation Lounge, high on Deck 10 overlooking the bow, is a great place for some quiet time, to relax, read, and watch the scenery outside unfold through the floor-to-ceiling windows. You'll find a radar screen, astronomical maps, binoculars, and reference books, and during the day, a self-service water and juice bar. On Deck 8 at the stern, the windowed Panorama Lounge also affords great sea views and lots of comfortable seating. By day, enjoy a continental breakfast or high tea here, while by night, a pianist serenades dancers on the small dance floor when the venue becomes an intimate nightspot. The Humidor cigar lounge has a walk-in humidor and is a dark, cozy, and plush spot for cocktails—even nonsmokers can't help but be drawn to the ambience. There's also a small casino and attached bar, card room with felt-topped tables, boutique, and pool bar.

DINING OPTIONS   In The Restaurant, the main dining room, a live trio plays romantic oldies, and guests are invited to take a spin around the small dance floor. There are plenty of tables for two, though during popular times you may have a short wait for one. Breakfast, lunch, and dinner are served here in high style, while a more casual buffet-style breakfast and lunch are offered in the indoor/outdoor Terrace Cafe. Even in the casual venue, service is doting, and waiters rush to carry plates to tables and are on hand to serve drinks and clear plates moments after you finish eating. A special pasta dish is prepared made-to-order by a chef for guests who do lunch in the Terrace Cafe. Come evenings, the venue becomes La Terrazza, which serves an Italian menu; reservations are required.

A third venue for dinner, called Le Champagne, opened on both ships in early 2004. The very intimate 24-seat restaurant is on Deck 7 next to the Terrace Cafe, where the Le Champagne wine-tasting room was located, and reservations are required.

POOL, FITNESS, SPA & SPORTS FACILITIES   Old-style wooden chaise longues padded with royal blue cushions line the open decks (though like many new ships, some decks are covered with a jolting grass-green AstroTurf in lieu of beautiful teak). There are plenty of places to retire with a good book or an afternoon snooze, either near the pool on Deck 8, or at the stern on that deck. You'll also find a nice sized pool, pair of hot tubs, and a golf cage.

The spa, gym and hair salon occupy much of Deck 10, and are spacious for ships of this size. There's a separate workout room with the latest exercise machines as well as separate aerobics room; the spa features a pleasant subtle Asian decor, but you'll hardly notice once you're getting some fabulous treatment from one of the expert masseuses.

Small Ships, Sailing Ships & Adventure Cruises

Small ships operate in most of the regions covered in this book, providing a more intimate, casual, and up-close experience than you'll get with the typical mid- or mega-size ship. Whereas big ships allow you to see a region while immersed in a vibrant, resortlike atmosphere, small ships allow you to see it from the waterline, without distraction from anything that's not an inherent part of the locale—no glitzy interiors, no big shows or loud music, no casinos, no spas, and no crowds, as the majority of these ships carry fewer than 100 passengers. Whether sailing through Alaska's coastal wilderness, along the Erie Canal or the Mississippi River, between tiny islands in the Caribbean, or from vineyard to vineyard in California's Wine Country, you're immersed in your destination from the minute you wake up to the minute you fall asleep, and for the most part you're left alone to form your own opinions.

Of the lines reviewed in this chapter, most operate small, motorized **coastal and river cruisers** that are like floating B&Bs, with a main public lounge, a dining room, and little else besides cabins and open decks. A few of these lines also operate slightly larger ships with deep drafts that are suitable for longer open-sea cruises. Four of the lines we review—Star Clippers, Windstar, Windjammer Barefoot Cruises, and the independently owned schooners of the Maine Windjammer Association—operate honest-to-god **sailing ships,** the former two with a yachtlike vibe, the latter two more like summer camps for adults (though for different reasons). Beyond these physical distinctions, the experience provided by these lines breaks down into two main subcategories.

Soft-adventure cruises are more or less the anti-cruise, dispensing with the whole "spend a few hours in port, see the sights, do some shopping" zeitgeist. Instead, these ships often stick to wilderness areas entirely, only occasionally making a port call, usually at tiny, out-of-the-way towns. The primary focus is on outdoor activities such as hiking, kayaking, tide-pooling, and snorkeling, with inflatable landing craft bringing passengers from ship to shore. Resident naturalists are usually on hand to explain what you're seeing. Lines that provide this kind of experience include Glacier Bay Cruiseline, Lindblad Expeditions, the Maine Windjammer Association, and (in some cases) Cruise West and Clipper.

Port-to-port cruises tend to follow the cruise model a little more closely, visiting ports most days as well as visiting great natural sites. Because of their shallow draft (the amount of ship below the waterline), though, these vessels can visit small, out-of-the-way ports as well as the popular ones frequented by the megaships. On board, the vibe is a less intense version of what you'll find on the soft-adventure lines, with passengers who are interested in bird-watching, botany, marine life, and history, and want to see it all from a more casual, human-scale vessel. Lines providing this kind of trip include American Canadian Caribbean, American West Steamboat Company, Clipper, Delta Queen, and Star Clippers. American Safari Cruises straddles the adventure/port divide pretty evenly, offering a luxe trip that also includes a lot of time out in the wild.

Windjammer Barefoot Cruises, a line that operates a fleet of clunky, charming old sailing ships and one diesel ship, primarily in the Caribbean and Central America, is in a category all by itself. While its ships sail the same kind of itineraries as the other port-to-port lines, there's not as much focus on outdoor or enrichment-type activities—just the occasional casual hike, snorkeling session, or beach volleyball game. The line's passengers are mostly out to have a good time—and what's wrong with that? Windstar is more like a standard premium or pseudo-luxe cruise experience, visiting a mix of large and small ports most days.

There are also a handful of ships that sail what might be called **expedition cruises,** though for the most part these operate in Antarctica and other regions not covered in this book. Both Cruise West and Clipper, though, have vessels that sail from Alaska across the Bering Sea into the Russian Far East, taking in the Aleutian Islands and some little-visited parts of coastal Alaska in the process. Even Windjammer has gotten in on this act, and theirs might be the greatest expedition of all: a 2-month cruise on the diesel cargo/passenger ship *Amazing Grace* between Trinidad and Tahiti—fully halfway around the world.

A few caveats on the small-ship experience:

- **For the most part, don't expect luxury:** Except for the American Safari yachts, the Star Clippers and Windstar vessels, and a few other standouts, most of these ships are pretty basic. Food is usually good but not gourmet. Cabins are generally very small and most lack amenities such as TVs or telephones. You also won't find room service or overly doting stewards, but in their place you do tend to get very personal attention, as crew and passengers get friendly fast. See individual reviews for details.

- **If you're not a self-starter, stay away:** With the possible exception of Windjammer Barefoot and Windstar, these ships aren't for people who need constant stimulation. On board, you're on your own to entertain yourself. Rather than the usual cruise song-and-dance, entertainment usually takes the form of informal lectures; occasional video presentations on wildlife, history, and culture; and maybe a crew talent show. And that's it.

- **Weak stomach? Think before you book:** As there are no stabilizers on most of these smaller ships, the ride can be bumpy in rough seas. This is only a potential problem, however, for weak-stomached folks sailing in the Caribbean, Baja, and some New England/Canada itineraries, which sometimes cross open water. You won't have to worry about rough seas (or any seas at all) on river cruises, or when sailing Alaska's Inside Passage or the East Coast's Intracoastal Waterway, which comprise mostly protected waters.

- **Check your bank balance, too:** You might think that because small ships lack the amenities of the megaships, their cruises would be cheaper—but you'd be dead wrong. Check this fact: Often, you can literally get a full 7-night cruise with some of the mainstream lines for the same price as *2 days* with American Safari Cruises or Lindblad, among the priciest small-ship operators. Cruises with the other small-ship lines tend to be cheaper, though you'll rarely find a weeklong trip starting at less than $1,200 to $1,500 (Windjammer Barefoot Cruises and the Maine Windjammers being the exceptions).

What accounts for this? Demand, for one thing. When you only have a couple hundred beds to fill and are offering a great product, people will pay. The other reason is that many of these ships, particularly in Alaska, sail only part of the year, so they only have 4 months to make their annual nut.

Before you choke on your donut and call Carnival, though, let's do a little **cost-benefit analysis.** Megaship cruises are touted as all-inclusive vacations, but they almost never are: After you pay your base fare, you're still apt to spend hundreds or even thousands more on shore excursions, spa treatments, and all the extra options offered on ship and shore. On a small ship, though, that balance between up-front and hidden costs can be quite a bit different. Aside from alcohol, there's almost nothing aboard on which to spend money, but more importantly, some lines include **shore excursions** in the base fare. On the more adventure-oriented ships, *all* off-ship activities may be included, so if you refrain from running up a bar tab, you could get through the week without ever dipping into your wallet, at least 'til it's time to tip the crew.

- **Most of these ships do not carry a doctor or nurse:** Since they mostly sail close to land, it's easy to get sick passengers to medical care ashore. Ships that do sail more far-flung itineraries will carry medical staff.
- **Most aren't good for kids:** Of the ships in this chapter, only two (Windjammer Barefoot's *Legacy* and *Polynesia*) ever have children's programs. American Safari, Clipper, Cruise West, Delta Queen, Glacier Bay, Lindblad, and Star Clippers schedule some family-oriented sailings in high season, and families also show up occasionally on some Windstar and Maine Windjammer vessels, but most of these ships are so adult-oriented that kids would be as out of place as Martians.
- **Small ships are not appropriate for people with serious mobility problems:** Of the ships reviewed here, only Cruise West's *Spirit of '98* and *Spirit of Oceanus,* Clipper's *Clipper Odyssey,* and Delta Queen's *American* and *Mississippi Queen* are even moderately wheelchair-friendly.

A NOTE ON LINE/SHIP RATINGS   Because the small ship experience is so completely different from the megaship experience, we've had to adjust our ratings. For instance, because all but a tiny fraction of these ships have just one dining room for all meals, we can't judge them by the same standard we use for ships with 5 or 10 different restaurants. So, we've set the default **Dining Options** rating for these ships at

---

The Scoop on Small-Ship Tonnage

When reading the reviews in this chapter, bear in mind that small-ship lines often measure their ships' gross register tonnage or GRTs (a measure of internal space, not actual weight) differently than the large lines. There's not even a definite standard within the small-ship market, so to compare ship sizes its best to just look at the number of passengers aboard. Also note that where GRTs measures are nonstandard, passenger/space measurements are impossible or meaningless.

Frommer's Ratings at a Glance: The Small-Ship Lines

1 = poor   2 = fair   3 = good   4 = excellent   5 = outstanding

Cruise Line	Enjoyment Factor	Dining	Activities	Children's Program	Entertainment	Service	Worth the Money
American Canadian Caribbean	4	3	4	N/A	3	3	3
American Safari Cruises	4	4	5	N/A	2	4	4
Clipper	4	4	4	N/A	3	4	4
Cruise West	4	3	4	N/A	2	4	4
Glacier Bay	5	3	5	N/A	2	4	4
Lindblad Expeditions	5	4	5	N/A	2	4	4
Maine Windjammer Assoc.*	5	3	3	N/A	3	3	5
Star Clippers	5	4	4	N/A	3	4	5
Windjammer Barefoot Cruises	4	3	3	3	3	3	5
Windstar	5	4	2	N/A	2	4	4

Note: Cruise lines have been graded on a curve that compares them only with the other lines in the Soft-Adventure and Sailing Ships category. See chapter 5 for the ratings methodology. With the exception of Windjammer Barefoot's *Legacy* and *Polynesia,* none of the lines and vessels in this chapter offers a children's program. Lines we've covered in mini-reviews have not been rated.

* Because the Maine schooners are all owner-operated, programs vary significantly. These ratings should be taken only as a general indication of fleetwide quality.

3, or "good," with points deducted if a restaurant is particularly uncomfortable and points added for any options above and beyond. Similarly, we've changed the "Gym & Spa Facilities" rating to **Adventure & Fitness Options** to reflect the fact that on small ships the focus is what's outside, not inside. Options covered in this category might include kayaks, trips by inflatable launch, bow-landing capability, an A-1 ice rating (allowing Arctic and Antarctic sailing), and frequent hiking, tide-pooling, and/or snorkeling trips.

DRESS CODES   The word is *casual.* Depending on the region sailed, polo shirts, khakis or shorts, and a fleece pullover and Gore-Tex shell will pretty much take care of you all week. On Windjammer you could show up to dinner in your bathing suit and not feel out of place. On warm-weather cruises, consider bringing a pair of aqua-socks or rubber sandals, as you may be going ashore in rubber landing crafts and have to step out into the surf.

1 American Canadian Caribbean Line

461 Water St., Warren, RI 02885. ✆ **800/556-7450** or 401/247-0955. Fax 401/247-2350. www.accl-smallships.com.

THE LINE IN A NUTSHELL   A family-owned New England line, ACCL operates tiny, no-frills ships that travel to offbeat places and attract a well-traveled, extremely casual, and down-to-earth older crowd. **Sails to:** U.S./Canada river/coastal cruises, Caribbean, Central America.

THE EXPERIENCE   ACCL began in 1966 when Rhode Island shipbuilder Luther Blount realized there was a demand for small-ship sailing on the rivers, canals, and coast of New England and Canada. Over the years, his vessels have gone well beyond their regional home, and now offer cruises down the Intracoastal Waterway and in the Caribbean and Central America. With an innovative, exploratory design, Blount's extremely informal small ships won't win any awards for decor (they are, in fact, about the most bare-bones vessels you'll find in terms of amenities, service, and meals), but that's not what they're all about. Instead, this is a line that gets passengers close to the real life of the regions it visits, whether you want to explore historic American towns and check out fall foliage along the Erie Canal, visit tiny islands such as Bequia in the Caribbean, or play connect the dots among New England's islands. Many of ACCL's generally friendly and almost universally older passengers have sailed with the line before, and appreciate its lack of glitz and gimmicks, as well as "just us folks" features such as a BYOB policy.

Pros

- **Casual and unpretentious:** If you're looking for a relatively cost-effective, do-it-yourself, and slow-paced adventure, these tiny yet innovative vessels are tops.
- **Innovative itineraries and ships:** Itineraries are one of a kind and imaginative, and the ships' technical innovations allow an up-close experience.
- **BYOB policy:** ACCL's BYOB policy provides substantial savings on bar bills. The bus or van that transports passengers from the airport or hotel to the ship stops at a reasonably priced liquor store en route so those interested can stock up on their beverage of choice.

Cons

- **No frills:** Cabins are tiny, decor is bland, bathrooms are minuscule, and there are no beach towels, so bring your own. Meals are served family-style.
- **No place to hide:** When the ships are at or near full capacity, they're very, very full. Your cabin is your only sanctuary, and thin cabin walls will make you feel closer to your neighbors than you may prefer.
- **Minimal port information:** For a line that's so destination-oriented, ACCL's ships have a surprising lack of books and naturalists/historians to provide background on history, culture, and nature.

AMERICAN CANADIAN CARIBBEAN: SLOW & EASY

Master shipbuilder and ACCL founder/builder/captain Luther Blount began his career in 1949, and has designed and built more than 300 vessels since in his Warren, Rhode Island, shipyard. Blount built his first cruise ship, the 20-passenger *Canyon Flyer,* in 1966, and over the years has gradually increased both size and capacity while remaining faithful to his original concept that small is the only way to cruise. His company now operates a fleet of three vessels, the newest two of which, *Grande Caribe* and *Grande Mariner,* are, he told us, "about as perfect as I can build for what I'm doing." Each vessel's unusually shallow 6½-foot draft combines with more than 20 patented Blount innovations to allow it to sail in narrow, shallow waterways and nudge directly up onto pristine, dockless shores, disembarking passengers via a ramp that extends from the bow. Who needs a pier? Some 85% to 90% of the company's cruises sail in domestic waters, with the rest visiting the Caribbean and Central America.

All told, American Canadian Caribbean is a delightfully rare find. It's one of the few family-owned cruise lines (with 89-year-old Luther still living at the shipyard and

Compared with the other small-ship lines, here's how ACCL rates:

	Poor	Fair	Good	Excellent	Outstanding
Enjoyment Factor				✓	
Dining			✓		
Activities				✓	
Children's Program	N/A				
Entertainment			✓		
Service			✓		
Worth the Money			✓		

keeping a hand in, though daughter Nancy runs the company on a day-to-day basis) and one of the few that designs, builds, maintains, and markets its own ships. If you sail this line, you're guaranteed an unusual, "what you see is what you get" experience: friendly, homespun, and visiting some places few other ships go. Just be sure you know what you're getting into. Read on . . .

PASSENGER PROFILE

This ultracasual line appeals to a sensible, early-to-bed crowd of mostly senior couples in their 60s through 80s, with the average age being 72. While some are physically fit, there are usually a few walking with canes and using hearing aids. Besides senior couples, there may be a few mother-daughter teams. All are attracted by the line's casual atmosphere (windbreakers and wash-and-wear sportswear is about as fancy as these folks get on vacation) and want to visit some unusual, interesting ports while simultaneously avoiding overcrowded ones. That said, ACCL's passengers tend to be less adventurous than those on other small-ship lines, so ACCL doesn't offer hard-core activities such as water-skiing or excursions in inflatable Zodiac boats.

ACCL has one of the most loyal followings of any line, so it's not unusual to have 65% to 70% repeaters on the average cruise. Many have sailed with the other small-ship lines, as well as some of the bigger, more luxurious lines. Travel programs for seniors, such as Elderhostel, are also popular with the typical ACCL passenger.

These ships won't appeal to the vast majority of young couples, singles, honeymooners, and families. Children under age 14 are prohibited, and the line offers no children's facilities or activities. Passengers sailing solo can take advantage of a **"Willing to Share" program,** in which the line will pair you with another solo passenger, thus avoiding the 175% rate you'd pay if booking a cabin just for yourself. If there turns out not to be another solo aboard, you get the cabin for the cheaper rate anyway. On the other side of the spectrum, when three passengers share a cabin each gets a 15% discount.

Warning: Ceilings on all ACCL ships are set at not much more than 6 feet, 4 inches—something to take into consideration if you're very tall.

DINING

Wholesome, all-American food is well prepared, but overall is nothing special. The daily menu, with selections for all three meals, is posted every morning on the blackboard in the dining room. Meals are served promptly at 8am, noon, and 6pm every day and are announced by one of the crew clanging a bell as he or she passes through the corridors and lounge. Rather than wandering in gradually, everyone typically arrives within a few minutes. Mixing with your fellow passengers at meals is mandatory since dining is open seating, communal-style for all meals, at tables primarily seating eight. There are no tables for two and just one or two set for four.

Early risers will find "eye-opener" coffee and fruit juices available beginning at 6:30am in the lounge. At breakfast, waiters deliver melon slices and a different hot dish every morning, such as scrambled eggs with bacon, Belgian waffles, pancakes, French toast, and cheese omelets. Passengers can also choose from a buffet of hot or cold cereal, yogurt, and fruit. Lunch is the lightest meal of the day and consists of homemade soup (such as tomato basil, vegetable, or beef orzo) along with turkey, ham and cheese, and tuna sandwiches on freshly baked bread, plus a salad, chips, fruit, and dessert. Dinners begin with a salad and fresh bread followed by a main entree such as roast beef or chicken, along with vegetables and rice or potatoes, plus dessert. Fresh fish is common on Caribbean and Central America itineraries, especially those that include Belize. One cook told us about a fisherman in St. Lucia who paddled up to the ship and asked if they'd like to buy some fresh tuna. When the cook asked how he'd know it was fresh, the man said, "Give me 10 minutes," then went off and caught one. The same fisherman now supplies the line whenever its ships are in port. Occasional **theme nights** spotlight dishes from Italy, the Caribbean, the American West, and so forth, and there's usually a barbecue on the top deck at least once per cruise, weather permitting.

With only one entree per meal, anyone wanting an alternative meal (such as fish instead of beef) can be accommodated only if he or she notifies the kitchen before 10am. In general, owing to the average passenger age, ACCL cooks try to keep things low in salt and fat. Passengers following other **special diets,** such as vegetarian, can be accommodated with advance notice.

SNACKS & EXTRAS   A variety of teas, as well as coffee and hot chocolate, is available round the clock, as are fresh fruit, pretzels, and other snacks at the bar, and biscotti at the coffee station. Fresh-baked cookies and muffins are served between meals, and any baked goods left over from breakfast, lunch, and dinner are also left out for passenger noshing.

The line's **BYOB policy** is a real money-saving system for passengers—a bottle of rum we bought in Panama City, for example, cost less than $5—about the cost of one drink on most ships. Passengers' beer and wine are stored in a cooler near the bar, and there are separate shelves there for liquor bottles. To avoid drinking someone else's booze, all bottles and cans are labeled with the passengers' cabin number. Soft drinks, along with tonic and soda water, are provided free of charge at the bar. On the first and last night of each cruise, hourlong welcome and goodbye parties offer an open stocked bar (for all drinks but beer), as well as jumbo-shrimp cocktails, smoked salmon, or something similar.

The line has no room service.

ACTIVITIES

With the exception of occasional informal lectures, a few printed quizzes, cooking demonstrations, and bridge and galley tours, daytime activities are oriented toward recreational pursuits off the ship during calls at river/coastal towns and remote islands and beaches. River, canal, and coastal cruises concentrate on visits to historically rich Colonial ports, plus exploration of the region's flora and fauna, with area guides and naturalists leading visits to wildlife sanctuaries and parks. In the Caribbean and Central America, a platform at the stern of the ship lets passengers step right into the

ACCL Fleet Itineraries

Ship	Itineraries
Grande Caribe	**14-night Intracoastal Waterway:** North- or southbound between Warren, RI, and Stuart, FL, Nov 2005 and Apr 2006. **11-night Virgin Islands & E./S. Carib:** Round-trip from St. Thomas or between St. Martin and Antigua, Dec 2005–Feb 2006. **11-night Bahamas:** Round-trip from Nassau, Mar–Apr 2006. **7-night Chesapeake Bay:** Between Baltimore, MD, and Alexandria, VA, May 2006. **12-night Erie Canal:** Round-trip from Warren, RI, June–July and Sept–Oct 2006. **5-night New England Islands:** Round-trip from Warren, RI, July–Aug 2006.
Grande Mariner	**14-night Intracoastal Waterway:** North- or southbound between Warren, RI, and Stuart, FL, Nov 2005 and May and Nov 2006. **11-night Panama Canal:** Round-trip from Panama City, Dec 2005–Jan 2006. **7- & 11-night Belize:** Round-trip from Belize City, Feb–Mar 2006. **7-night Colonial Intracoastal:** North- or southbound between Jacksonville, FL, and Charleston, SC, Apr 2006. **15-night Erie Canal/Great Lakes:** West- or eastbound between Warren, RI, and Chicago, IL, June and Aug 2006. **6-night Lake Michigan:** Round-trip from Chicago, IL, June–Aug 2006. **5-night New England Islands:** Round-trip from Warren, RI, Sept 2006. **12-night Erie Canal:** Round-trip from Warren, RI, June–July and Sept–Oct 2006.
Niagara Prince	**14-night Mississippi:** New Orleans, LA, to Chicago, IL, May 2006. **6-night Lake Michigan:** Round-trip from Chicago, IL, June–July 2006. **15-night Erie Canal/Great Lakes:** West- or eastbound between Warren, RI, and Chicago, IL, June 2006. **7-night Maine Coast:** Round-trip from Portland, ME, July–Sept 2006. **10-night Hudson River/Lake Champlain:** Round-trip from Warren, RI, Sept–Oct 2006. **14-night Intracoastal Waterway:** Warren, RI, to Stuart, FL, Nov 2006.

water for snorkeling, swimming, kayaking, or taking a ride in a Blount-designed 24-passenger glass-bottom boat, used to view coral formations and tropical fish.

The amount of time spent at each port varies from a few hours to an entire morning or afternoon, and the ship usually remains anchored or docked at night, allowing passengers to explore restaurants and/or nightspots ashore. The typically short distance between stops is covered during daylight, which is particularly nice on fall foliage cruises in New England. The cruise director (who also doubles as the purser and supervises housekeeping) is in charge of all passenger activities. Select cruises, including those to Belize, typically carry full-time naturalists aboard, but the line does not consistently have the variety or quality of onboard experts you'll find on more outdoors- and learning-oriented lines such as Glacier Bay, Lindblad, and Clipper. If this is important to you, ask the line's reservations agents which cruises will have experts aboard; they always know well in advance. Because no list of recommended background reading is supplied before the cruise (and because there's only a small library aboard, in the lounge), passengers should do their own research ahead of time and bring appropriate guidebooks.

Instead of a daily printed schedule, the agenda of activities and ports of call is posted every morning on a bulletin board, and the cruise director runs through the day's schedule after breakfast.

Aside from the destination-oriented activities, the main evening events are card playing and a movie from the ship's video collection, shown after dinner on the large-screen TV in the lounge. Of course chatting with new friends under the stars on the top deck is a popular pastime, as this set tends to be a well-traveled interesting bunch.

CHILDREN'S PROGRAM

The minimum age for children on board is 14 years old, and there are no special facilities even for those who clear that mark. This is not a line for young people.

ENTERTAINMENT

Amusement is mostly of the do-it-yourself variety, such as board games, puzzles, and reading. The BYOB cocktail hour is a time for songs (accompanied on the lounge piano, assuming there's a passenger aboard who plays), announcements, and an occasional informal talk about an upcoming sight or experience. Sometimes, **local entertainers,** such as Dixieland bands on Mississippi River itineraries, living history performers on the Intracoastal Waterway, and Garifuna dancers in Belize, will be invited aboard for an evening or will perform for passengers in port.

SERVICE

The ship's staff is mostly made up of Americans, many of whom hail from the Northeast, including Rhode Island, ACCL's home state. For many, serving aboard the vessel is like a summer job, and they probably won't be doing this type of thing as a career. What they lack in experience, though, they make up for in enthusiasm and friendliness. As on most small ships, all of them double on many jobs that bigger ships have segregated into separate departments. You may see your cabin attendant waiting tables at dinner, for instance.

Service is adequate in the dining room—about what you'd find at a friendly local restaurant. Cabins are made up once a day after breakfast, and towels are changed every other day. There's no laundry service or room service.

Grande Caribe • Grande Mariner • Niagara Prince

The Verdict

Functional and no-frills, these three near-sisters are well-thought-out vehicles for transporting passengers to remote ports—no more, no less.

Grande Mariner *(photo: ACCL)*

Specifications

Size (in tons)	99*	Passenger/Crew Ratio	
Passengers (double occ.)		*Niagara Prince*	4.9 to 1
Niagara Prince	84	*Caribe/Mariner*	5.5 to 1
Caribe/Mariner	100	Year Launched	
Passenger/Space Ratio	N/A*	*Niagara Prince*	1994
Total Cabins/Veranda Cabins		*Grande Caribe*	1997
Niagara Prince	42/0	*Grande Mariner*	1998
Caribe/Mariner	50/0	Last Major Refurbishment	
Crew		*Niagara Prince*	1999
Niagara Prince	17	*Caribe/Mariner*	N/A
Caribe/Mariner	18		

* See note on p. 328 regarding small-ship tonnage and passenger/space measurements.

Frommer's Ratings (Scale of 1–5)

★★★

Cabin Comfort & Amenities	2	Dining Options	3
Ship Cleanliness & Maintenance	4	Adventure & Fitness Options	3.5
Public Comfort/Space	3	Children's Facilities	N/A
Decor	2	Enjoyment Factor	3

Sisters *Grande Mariner* and *Grande Caribe* are the culmination of 30 years of ACCL's "small ship equals good ship" corporate philosophy, and though they're definitely the most comfortable and appealing vessels the line has ever built, they're still as basic as cruise ships come, with tiny, spartan cabins and no-fuss decor. Ditto and then some for the smaller, older *Niagara Prince,* which has an even tighter layout. No one books these ships expecting luxury, though. Seaworthy and practical, they all have the innovative exploratory features for which ACCL is known: a shallow draft and retractable wheelhouse that allow them to sail through shallow canals and under low bridges, bow ramps that allow them to pull right up to pristine beaches, and a platform in the stern for swimming and launching the ships' glass-bottom boats and sailboats.

Cabins & Rates

Cabins	Per Diems from	Sq. Ft.	Fridge	Hair Dryer	Sitting Area	TV
Inside	$205	80–120	no	no	no	no
Outside	$233	80–120	no	no	no	no

* Expect to pay between $50 and $200 per person on top of advertised fares, as port charges are not bundled into ACCL's rates. (Per diems above include port charges.) Cabin footage measurements for the smaller Niagara Prince are 78 to 96 square feet.

CABINS   Imagine a box with four light-colored walls, single beds (only some of which can be arranged into a double), a small closet, a few drawers, and some wall hooks—and that's it. Fancy they're not. There are no TVs or radios, little room for couples to maneuver, and the head-style bathrooms are tiny beyond belief, with toilet and sink actually *in* the shower stall, to save room. Passengers around 6 feet or taller, be aware of the low bridge over the toilet, and anyone with privacy issues should be sure to inquire before booking, as most bathrooms have only a curtain between them and the cabin, while a few on *Mariner* have doors. Bathrooms have soap and towels only.

Cabins have either a sliding glass window or a small porthole, and some have bunk beds, just like summer camp. All cabin doors lock from the inside only—there are no keys, which is common with these kinds of small, friendly ships. Cabins in the rear of the ships may experience some engine vibration. None of the cabins are wheelchair accessible and the ship has no elevators, but a stair lift connects the top three decks for those who have difficulty walking.

PUBLIC AREAS   The smallest of these ships, the two-deck *Niagara Prince,* has a single lounge connected to its dining room, while the larger *Mariner* and *Caribe* have much better and more spacious-feeling arrangements, with their lounges on the top deck and dining rooms below. All the lounges are furnished with couches and chairs, a large-screen TV, a bar, board games and puzzles, and a random selection of books and magazines (bring your own books if you like to read). They serve as the venue for all onboard activities and socializing. During the day, many passengers view the scenery from the open top deck, which is furnished with deck chairs and partially covered by a large awning to provide shade in sunny weather. Open decks along the port and starboard sides, a small area in the bow, and a quiet open area in the stern are great spots for up-close wildlife watching.

DINING OPTIONS   All meals are served in a single small dining room that resembles a church cafeteria.

ADVENTURE & FITNESS OPTIONS   None of the ACCL ships has any exercise facilities, swimming pools, or spas. Passengers can walk around the Sun Deck's narrow but passable perimeter, but otherwise any exercise you get will be in port, or on the occasional swim from the ship's stern platform.

2 Mini-Review: American Cruise Lines

741 Boston Post Rd., Suite 200, Guilford, CT 06437. ℂ **800/814-6880**; www.americancruiselines.com.

THE LINE IN A NUTSHELL   Concentrating on the U.S. East Coast, Connecticut-based American Cruise Lines operates three new U.S.-flagged vessels with unusually large cabins, a casual onboard vibe, and an emphasis on American history and culture. Like other small-ship lines, the prices aren't cheap, but they're far from the priciest, with weeklong sailings starting around $2,400 per person. **Sails to:** U.S. river cruises.

THE EXPERIENCE   Its all about the destinations. Taking off from ports up and down the eastern seaboard, American Cruise Lines' three small ships—the 49-passenger *American Eagle* (2000) and *American Glory* (2002) and the much larger, 92-passenger *American Spirit* (2005)—keep the focus on the country's historic towns and cities, usually docking within a few blocks of museums, shops, and historic districts. For those who don't want to explore on their own, shore excursions are offered at a nominal price ($10–$20 per person on average), and usually include tours of local museums, tours detailing a port's architecture and history, and visits to historic homes. Guest lecturers (including historians, wildlife experts, local experts, etc.) join the ships at each port to provide additional context via informal lectures.

All three of the line's vessels were built at its own shipyard in Salisbury, Maryland, and while they're a bit boxy and uninspired on the outside, they're refreshingly large and bright within. Cabins average more than 200 square feet—nearly twice the size offered by main regional competitor American Canadian Caribbean. All cabins are outside, with large picture windows, a writing desk, TVs, adequate storage, and roomy bathrooms. At least 14 on each ship have private balconies. Three public lounges (one large enough for everyone aboard, the other two smaller reading rooms) and multiple outdoor decks provide passengers plenty of elbow room. Each evening sees a complimentary cocktail and hors d'oeuvres party followed by dinner in the single dining room, which seats all passengers comfortably. A young American crew serve menus tailored to the cruising region—for instance, Maryland crab cakes on Chesapeake Bay cruises, lobster on cruises in coastal Maine, and Key lime pie on the Great Rivers of Florida cruise.

American Cruise Lines Fleet Itineraries

Ship	Itineraries
Entire fleet	**6- to 14-night River Cruises:** Cruises to the Maine coast; the coastal islands of Massachusetts, Connecticut, and Rhode Island; Chesapeake Bay; the mid-Atlantic Intracoastal Waterway; the historic antebellum South; Florida's inland waterways and Lake Okeechobee; and the Hudson River for fall foliage. Sails from New London, CT; Providence, RI; Baltimore, MD; Bangor, ME; Charleston, SC; Jacksonville, FL; and Fort Myers, FL.

3 American Safari Cruises

19221 36th Ave. W., Suite 208, Lynnwood, WA 98036. © 888/862-8881. Fax 425/776-8889. www.amsafari.com.

THE LINE IN A NUTSHELL American Safari Cruises offers one of the most luxurious and yet adventurous experiences in the small-ship market—and also one of the most expensive. **Sails to:** Alaska and British Columbia, Sea of Cortez/Baja, U.S./Canada coastal/river cruises.

THE EXPERIENCE Unlike the competition's mostly basic vessels, American Safari's ships are honest-to-god yachts, carrying only 12 and 22 passengers apiece in plush comfort, with homey lounges, hot tubs, and large cabins. Everything except gratuities is included in the base price, including alcoholic beverages and shore excursions. But then, they'd better be: Eight-night cruises typically run upwards of $5,000 per person.

Despite the yacht feel, American Safari's cruises are actually pretty adventurous, with some days spent kayaking in the wilderness and others visiting small ports of call, sometimes overnighting there for a taste of the local nightlife. A passenger-crew ratio of about two to one ensures that a cold drink, a clever meal, or a sharp eagle-spotting eye is never more than a request away, and during the day passengers have a lot of flexibility: If some want to kayak and others want to go wildlife-watching in an inflatable, no problem. It's good to be king.

Pros

- **Almost private experience:** With only one or two dozen fellow passengers, it's like having a yacht to yourself.
- **Built-in shore excursions:** All off-ship excursions are included in the cruise fare.
- **Onboard amenities:** Not many ships in the small-ship market can boast such large cabins, public lounges so homey and comfortable, or an oceanview hot tub. These yachts can.
- **Night anchorages:** The route taken allows time for the vessels to overnight at anchor, which means you get a quieter night's sleep and get to see all the scenery you're passing through, without missing anything at night.

Cons

- **The price:** Even when taking the included excursions, drinks, and transfers into account, the price is still high. You pay for all that luxury.

Compared with the other small-ship lines, here's how ASC rates:

	Poor	Fair	Good	Excellent	Outstanding
Enjoyment Factor				✓	
Dining				✓	
Activities					✓
Children's Program	N/A				
Entertainment		✓			
Service				✓	
Worth the Money				✓	

AMERICAN SAFARI CRUISES: LUXE ADVENTURE

American Safari Cruises (once upon a time known as American Yacht Safaris) was formed in 1996, operating a single yacht (the 21-passenger *Safari Quest*) on itineraries in Alaska's Inside Passage. Today, the line has three vessels, with a whopping total of 45 beds. That's less than half what most of the other lines in this chapter can offer on any one of their ships. The *Safari Spirit* was re-christened in May of 2005 (after a total overhaul and refurb following an encounter with an uncharted rock in 2003), as the line's most luxurious ship.

The company offers cruises in Alaska and British Columbia, Mexico's Sea of Cortez/Baja, the Columbia and Snake rivers, and the California Wine Country, traveling by day and anchoring in a secluded bay or outside a small town at night. Professional naturalists sail on all Alaska, Pacific Northwest, and Baja itineraries, leading off-vessel exploration and answering questions on board. Wine Country trips include private tours and wine tastings. On board, the vibe is upscale, the adventure quotient high, and the bragging rights for passengers extreme. This is one classy operation.

PASSENGER PROFILE

Passengers—almost always couples—tend to be more than comfortably wealthy, with guests on Alaska cruises tending to fall in the 44 to 75 age range and those on other itineraries skewing younger, from the young 40s to the upper 60s. Most hope to get close to nature without sacrificing luxury. They've paid handsomely for food, drink, and service, all of which are close to overwhelming. Dress is always casual, with comfort being the prime goal. An advantage of the ships' small size is that if you can round up enough friends, you can rent the ships as full charters, for which good discounts are available.

DINING

ASC's shipboard chefs are always on the lookout for quality goods, bartering with fishing boats for the catch of the day, raiding local markets for the freshest fruits and vegetables, and packing in ingredients for any special requests they've gotten from passengers. All meals are served family-style, and multi-course dinners may feature thyme-infused king salmon, cracked crab, rack of lamb with herb crust, fresh seafood file gumbo, beef Wellington, or roasted duck with orange blackberry sauce. Dress is always casual, and the tone of the table service varies by meal: Expect paper napkins at lunch and cloth serviettes at dinner. **Special dietary requests** (vegetarian, and so forth) can be accommodated with advance notice. On Wine Country cruises, the chef

American Safari Cruises Fleet Itineraries

Ship	Itineraries
Safari Escape	**7-night Pacific Northwest/British Columbia:** Round-trip from San Juan Island, WA, Oct 2005 and Sept–Oct 2006. **8-night Alaska Inside Passage:** North- or south-bound between Juneau, AK, and Prince Rupert, BC, May–Sept 2006.
Safari Quest	**8-night Mexico Sea of Cortez:** Round-trip from La Paz, Baja California Sur, with guests transferring overland from Los Cabos at beginning and end of cruise, Dec 2005–Apr 2006. **7-night Alaska Inside Passage:** North- or southbound between Juneau and Sitka, AK, May–Sept 2006 (includes 2 full consecutive days in Glacier Bay National Park). **11-night Pacific Northwest (Columbia/Snake Rivers):** East- or westbound between Astoria, OR, and Lewiston, ID, Sept–Oct 2006. **3- & 4-night California Wine Country:** Round-trip from San Francisco, CA, Oct–Nov 2006.
Safari Spirit	**7-night Pacific Northwest:** Round-trip from San Juan Island, WA, Oct 2005 and Sept–Oct 2006. **7-night Alaska Inside Passage:** Round-trip from Juneau, AK, May–Aug 2006.

will discuss with guests why he picked certain wines to accompany the meals, and in Alaska the chef will stock up on local seafood and offer an **all-you-can-eat salmon bake,** crab feed, or halibut feast.

SNACKS & EXTRAS   Between meals, snacks such as Gorgonzola and brie with pears, walnuts, and table crackers are set out. There's also a 24-hour coffee/tea facility, an early-risers' breakfast, and a fully stocked bar from which passengers may serve themselves at will.

ACTIVITIES

For such a luxurious operation, ASC is surprisingly outdoorsy, with expedition leaders accompanying passengers on off-vessels exploration. In Alaska, you might take out a Zodiac boat or kayak to investigate shoreline black bears or river otters, or to navigate fjords packed with ice floes and lolling seals. Expeditions include trips to boardwalked cannery towns, Tlingit villages, and tiny villages such as Meyer's Chuck, population about 50, give or take. Activities throughout the day are well spaced, and there are many opportunities to see wildlife. In the Sea of Cortez, expect a warm-weather version of same, with a pack-mule ride from the beach into the hills, snorkeling with juvenile sea lions, and a gourmet picnic served on a deserted beach.

CHILDREN'S PROGRAM

Most sailings have no programs or facilities whatsoever for kids, but occasional sailings in Alaska and the Sea of Cortez are targeted to families (and called "Kids in Nature," or KIN, cruises), with naturalists giving kids lessons in the region's flora and fauna. At the end of the trip, they each get a few "graduation gifts," including a video documenting their week on board and a "University of Whales" diploma.

ENTERTAINMENT

The main lounge is the social center of each ship, a place for guests to relax, listen to an informal lecture by the ship's naturalist, play a game of cards or Scrabble, or watch a movie from the ship's library on the big-screen TV. From time to time, the ship docks at a town with a measure of nightlife—at the least, you'll get to shoot a game of pool; at best, the passengers will all head out together for a pub-crawl.

SERVICE

Crewmembers are cheerful and discreet, fussing over such details as the level of cilantro in lunchtime dishes or making elaborate cocktails from the bar. They've even been known to call ahead to upcoming ports to arrange for a passenger's favorite brand of beer to be brought aboard. Surprisingly for such an all-inclusive line, gratuities are not included in the rates, and the company recommends a gratuity of 5% to 10%, to be divided up among the whole crew. And when you're paying $4,000 to $7,500 for a cruise, that ain't chicken feed.

Laundry service is not available except in "emergency situations."

Safari Spirit • Safari Escape • Safari Quest

The Verdict

Sleek and stylish, these three ships are the closest thing to private yachts you'll ever find, with an experience that mixes luxury and adventure.

Safari Quest *(photo: American Safari Cruises)*

Specifications

Size (in tons)		*Escape*	6
Spirit	N/A*	*Quest*	9
Escape	N/A*	Passenger/Crew Ratio	
Quest	100*	*Spirit*	1.7 to 1
Passengers (double occ.)		*Escape*	2 to 1
Spirit	12	*Quest*	2 to 1
Escape	12	Year Launched	
Quest	22	*Spirit*	1981
Passenger/Space Ratio	N/A*	*Escape*	1983
Total Cabins/Veranda Cabins		*Quest*	1992
Spirit	6/0	Last Major Refurbishment	
Escape	6/0	*Spirit*	2005
Quest	11/0	*Escape*	2002
Crew		*Quest*	2001
Spirit	7		

* See note on p. 328 regarding small-ship tonnage and passenger/space measurements.

Frommer's Ratings (Scale of 1–5) ★★★★

Cabin Comfort & Amenities	5	Dining Options	3
Ship Cleanliness & Maintenance	4	Adventure & Fitness Options	4
Public Comfort/Space	4	Children's Facilities	N/A
Decor	4	Enjoyment Factor	5

More private yachts than cruise ships, American Safari Cruises' vessels are an oddity in the cruise community: One old fella we met called them "Tupperware ships," a pretty accurate description for their exceedingly sleek, contoured, Ferrari-looking exteriors. Inside, you're welcomed to poke around almost everywhere, adding to the feeling that you're vacationing with friends, not sailing on a commercial ship.

Cabins & Rates

Cabins	Per Diems from	Sq. Ft.	Fridge	Hair Dryer	Sitting Area	TV
Outside	$399	112–164	no	yes	some	yes

CABINS Staterooms are comfortable, with large, firm beds; good or at least adequate light; and TV/VCRs, with guests welcome to take movies from the ship's library. The *Spirit* has the largest cabins, and after its overhaul in 2005, is considered the most luxurious of the fleet. Bathrooms are roomy and have showers (a shower-tub combo on the *Spirit*). Best accommodations are the Admiral's Cabins, which have large picture windows, a small sitting area, plus other features like a cedar-lined sauna or small balcony (varies by cabin). There are no special facilities for travelers with disabilities and with the exception of one cabin for solo travelers on the *Safari Quest*, there are no cabins designed specifically for single occupancy.

PUBLIC AREAS Sitting rooms are intimate and luxurious, and look as if they'd been transported whole from a spacious suburban home. Four or five prime vantages for spotting wildlife (including a hot tub) ensure as little or as much privacy as you desire. All public rooms have generous panoramic views for cold or inclement weather.

DINING OPTIONS All three meals are served on a burnished mahogany table in a casual room on the *Spirit* and *Escape,* and at a cluster of round tables on the *Quest,* usually when the ship is at anchor.

ADVENTURE & FITNESS OPTIONS All three ships carry sea kayaks for passenger use and inflatable launches for off-vessel exploration, and there's a hot tub for relaxing when you get back aboard. Each of the yachts has two fitness machines on board.

4 Mini-Review: American West Steamboat Company

2101 4th Ave., Suite 1150, Seattle, WA 98121. © 800/434-1232. Fax 206/340-0975. www.americanweststeam boat.com.

THE LINE IN A NUTSHELL Southern charm in northern climes. Inside and out, American West Steamboat's two vessels are modeled after paddlewheel riverboats from the 1800s, and offer an experience heavy on history and charm. You don't feel like you're on a cruise ship, but rather, staying at a charming hotel in New Orleans' French Quarter. **Sails to:** Southeast Alaska, Pacific Northwest river cruises.

THE EXPERIENCE Want to sail on a vessel where the livin' is easy, the fish (or at least the whales) are jumping, and . . . you get the idea. Carrying 235 and 146 passengers, respectively, *Empress of the North* and *Queen of the West* are all about nostalgia, offering cruises that mix port calls with time spent cruising wild areas. Guests attracted to the ships for their historic feel are equally interested in the history of the ports, so cruises feature **expert lecturers** on the sailing regions, giving lectures in the ship's main showroom and providing narration on each port of call prior to arrival. One shore excursion per port is included in the cost of the cruise. *Empress of the North* is the first stern-wheeler to sail Alaska's Inside Passage in more than a century.

American West Fleet Itineraries

Ship	Itineraries
Empress of the North	**7-night Pacific Northwest (Columbia/Snake Rivers):** Round-trip from Portland, OR, Feb–Apr and Oct–Dec 2006. **7-night Alaska Inside Passage:** Round-trip from Juneau, AK, May–Sept 2006. **7-night Pacific Puget Sound/Canada:** Round-trip from Seattle, WA, Sept 2006.
Queen of the West	**7-night Pacific Northwest (Columbia/Snake Rivers):** Round-trip from Portland, OR, Mar–Nov 2006.

The vessels themselves are homey yet elegant, with rocking chairs, cushy couches, and a mixture of Alaska Native and Americana-style art. Due to their relatively large size—at least as compared to most other small ships—the *Empress* and *Queen* pack a lot of punch. Like most of their competition, one main restaurant serves all three very filling meals, but you can also get continental breakfast and burgers, hot dogs, sandwiches, and homemade chili and soup at lunch in the Calliope Bar & Grill. You can also hear the calliope, on which the cruise director on our recent sailing would sometimes perform. In the evening, the show lounge offers small-scale entertainment, including jazz soloists and small song-and-dance revues. At the stern, the Paddle Wheel Lounge is the spot for cocktails, card games, scenery gazing, and watching the bright red paddlewheel churning away. Staterooms and suites are quite lovely, and decorated much like cozy bedrooms, with dark-wood tones, flowery bedspreads, lace curtains, and semi-ornate lighting fixtures. The majority of suites and staterooms have verandas, with the rest offering large picture windows. There is no room service, except breakfast in the suites and also dinner in the two-room suites.

Most guests average between 65 and 70 years old, are retired and fairly well traveled, and have sailed on a range of traditional premium and upscale lines. Most seem to be "day" people. In an effort to appeal to a broader age group, entertainment now includes music from the '50s, '60s and '70s (as opposed to the '30s and '40s). The line is seeing more extended families cruising together, including grandparents, parents, and kids. Rates start around $3,300 per person for weeklong Alaska cruises, and $2,300 (and sometimes as low as $1,700, depending on season) for Columbia/Snake River cruises.

5 Clipper Cruise Line

11969 Westline Industrial Dr., St. Louis, Missouri 63146-3220. ℂ **800/325-0010** or 314/655-6700. Fax 314/655-6670. www.clippercruise.com.

THE LINE IN A NUTSHELL   Clipper's comfortable small ships focus on offbeat ports of call, learning, and mingling with your fellow passengers. It's the ideal small-ship cruise for people who've tried Holland America or one of the other mainstream lines but want to try a more intimate cruise experience. **Sails to:** Caribbean/Central America, Alaska, U.S./Canada river and coastal cruises (plus Europe, South America, South Pacific, Antarctica, Asia, Australia/New Zealand).

THE EXPERIENCE   Clipper caters to mature, seasoned, easygoing, relatively affluent, and well-traveled older passengers seeking a casual and educational vacation experience heavy on the nature, history, and culture of the ports visited. Naturalists and historians sail on all itineraries to provide context, and a cruise director helps organize the days, answers questions, and assists passengers. The line falls mostly on the "port-to-port" side of small-ship cruising, offering a less active, more learning-focused experience than more adventure-driven lines like Glacier Bay. Rather than kayaking around an iceberg, Clipper's passengers are more likely to try and identify the seabird sitting on top of it. Like most of the other small-ship lines, Clipper isn't cheap, though it's by no means the most expensive of the bunch.

Pros

- **Great learning opportunities:** Historians, naturalists, and guest lecturers sail aboard, offering lectures and accompanying guests on shore excursions.
- **Informal atmosphere:** No need to dress up here—everything's casual.
- **Interesting itineraries:** Clipper covers a huge range of destinations, offering many U.S. river cruises as well as great Alaska, Russian Far East, and Central America trips.
- **Young, enthusiastic crews:** While they may not be the most experienced, they're sweet and hardworking, and add a homey feel to the trip.

Cons

- **Noisy engines on _Yorktown_ and _Nantucket_:** If you can help it, don't book a cabin on the lowest deck (Main Deck), where noise from the engines can get quite loud.

CLIPPER: CASUAL SHIPS, ENLIGHTENING TRIPS

Based in St. Louis of all places, Clipper was founded in 1982 and is a subsidiary of deluxe-tour operator INTRAV. Like Lindblad Expeditions, the line rarely schedules its ships to do the same itineraries for more than a few weeks at a time, instead moving from region to region, with no one place serving as a real home port. Effectively, the ships are on a constant trip around the world, boarding passengers to sail different segments of one very long itinerary. Longer seasons in the Caribbean and Alaska are the exceptions to this rule.

The line operates both small coastal cruisers and larger, more substantial vessels for expeditional ocean voyages. The sleek, yachtlike, 128-passenger _Clipper Odyssey_ sails primarily in Asia, Australia, New Zealand, and the South Pacific, but also offers several Alaska voyages, including one that crosses into the Russian Far East and visits some of Alaska's most remote islands. Two coastal ships, the 102-passenger _Nantucket Clipper_ and 138-passenger _Yorktown Clipper,_ are cozy and relatively plain, but offer a nice mix of itineraries that cover Alaska, the Caribbean, the Great Lakes, and coastal

Compared with the other small-ship lines, here's how Clipper rates:

	Poor	Fair	Good	Excellent	Outstanding
Enjoyment Factor				✓	
Dining				✓	
Activities				✓	
Children's Program	N/A				
Entertainment			✓		
Service				✓	
Worth the Money				✓	

and river waters of the U.S./Canada coasts. The 122-passenger *Clipper Adventurer,* one of our very favorite ships, is not sailing from any U.S. ports this year except as part of fully chartered trips. Farther afield, she offers cruises from Antarctica to Europe to South America.

PASSENGER PROFILE

The majority of Clipper passengers are well-traveled 45- to 75-year-old couples (and occasionally singles) who are attracted by the casual intimacy of small ships and by the opportunity to actually learn something about the places they visit. Most are well educated though not academic, casual, and adventurous in the sense that they're up for a day of snorkeling and hiking but are happy to get back to their comfortable ship afterward. As a company spokesman noted a few years back, "Our aim is to offer an experience that adds something special to one's understanding of the world while providing a sense of enjoyment."

Clipper attracts a remarkably high number of repeat passengers: On any given cruise, 40% or more of the passengers will have sailed with the line before. Many have also sailed with other small-ship lines, such as Lindblad Expeditions, Cruise West, and ACCL.

DINING

The fare is all-American, prepared by attendees of the Culinary Institute of America, and incorporates local ingredients whenever practical. While relatively simple in ingredients and presentation, it's the equal or better of most cuisine served on the big mainstream lines.

Full breakfast is served in the dining room, with cereals and lighter fare also available in one lounge. Similarly, at lunch you can get a full meal in the dining room or create your own sandwich from an assortment of cold cuts in the lounge. Dinner is served in a single open seating in the dining room and offers four courses with five main entree options: seafood (perhaps herb-marinated halibut or stuffed lobster tail), a meat entree (such as roast duck, veal Marsala, or prime rib), a pasta entree, a **"starch and vegetables" entree** (such as steamed vegetables over saffron rice), and a **vegetarian option** (such as marinated grilled portobello mushroom, vegetarian lasagna, or 10-vegetable couscous). Clipper can accommodate special diets or restrictions (lactose intolerance, food allergies, low-fat, and so forth) if you give them 3 weeks' warning before your cruise, but their galleys are not equipped to provide kosher meals.

Weather and time permitting, there's a barbecue on deck at least once during each weeklong cruise.

Though the onboard dress code is casual at all times, many passengers will put on sports jackets and dresses for dinner, and some men wear ties for the captain's welcome-aboard and farewell parties.

SNACKS & EXTRAS Snacks are available throughout each day in the lounge, including mighty fine "Clipper Chipper" chocolate-chip cookies (whose recipe is posted on the line's website, in case you're interested). Like almost all small ships, the Clipper ships don't offer room service unless you're too ill to attend meals.

ACTIVITIES

As aboard the other small-ship lines, Clipper's activities are designed to focus your attention on the environment, history, and culture of the region you're visiting, giving you the opportunity to return home from your vacation not only relaxed but also enriched. Like the other primarily port-to-port lines, its ships spend most days in port,

Clipper Fleet Itineraries

Ship	Itineraries
Clipper Odyssey	**14-night Northwest Alaska & Russia's Kamchatka Peninsula:** Round-trip from Anchorage, AK, June 2006.
Nantucket Clipper	**7-night E./S. Carib:** Round-trip from St. Thomas, USVI, Dec 2005–Jan 2006 and Dec 2006. **7-night Central America:** Belize City to Puerto Cortes, Honduras, Feb 2006. **7-night Intracoastal Waterway:** North- or southbound between Jacksonville, FL, and Charleston, SC, Mar–Apr and Nov 2006. **11-night "Colonial & Civil War"** **U.S. East Coast:** North- or southbound between Alexandria, VA, and Charleston, SC, May and Nov 2006. **10-night Chesapeake Bay/Hudson River:** North- or southbound between Alexandria, VA, and New York, NY, Oct 2005 and May and Nov 2006. **7-night Coastal Maine:** North- or southbound between Boston, MA, and Bangor, ME, May–June and Oct 2006. **8-night St. Lawrence Seaway/Thousand Islands:** North- or southbound between Quebec City, QB, and Buffalo, NY, June–July 2006. **14-night French Canada/Great Lakes:** Between Quebec City, QB, and Chicago, IL, July and Sept 2006. **7-night Lake Michigan:** Round-trip from Chicago, IL, Aug–Sept 2006. **7-night Hudson River Fall Foliage:** Round-trip from New York, NY, Oct 2006.
Yorktown Clipper	**7-night E./S. Carib:** Round-trip from St. Thomas, USVI, Dec 2005–Jan 2006 and Dec 2006. **7-night Central America/Panama Canal:** Between San Jose, Costa Rica, and Panama City, Panama, Feb, Nov, and Dec 2006. **7-night Mexico Sea of Cortez:** Round-trip from La Paz, Baja California Sur, Feb and Mar 2006. **5-night California Wine Country:** Round-trip from Redwood City, CA, Oct 2005. **7-night California Wine Country:** Round-trip from Redwood City, CA, Apr–May and Oct–Nov 2006. **7-night Alaska Inside Passage:** Round-trip from Juneau, AK, May–Sept 2006. **7-night Pacific Northwest:** North- or southbound between Seattle, WA, and Vancouver, BC, Oct 2005 and Sept–Oct 2006.

where passengers can go off on their own or choose from a range of extra-cost shore excursions.

At least one naturalist always sails with each ship, and occasionally a historian as well. These experts will often offer casual, complimentary walks in port and will also accompany passengers on many extra-cost shore excursions, to provide added-value info. Throughout the cruise, these same staff members also offer a series of informal lectures, which on our last trip included talks on reef fish identification, the nature and geology of the Caribbean islands, American Revolution history, and plant life. In warm-weather destinations, towels and snorkeling gear are provided free.

CHILDREN'S PROGRAM

Though Clipper offers no babysitting or any children's facilities or programs of any kind, several sailings per year are designated as "family departures," while others— including their popular Virgin Islands cruises and Baja whale-watching cruises—are targeted to multi-generational families (grandparents, parents, children). Aside from these cruises, children are very rare birds indeed on these ships.

ENTERTAINMENT

As is typical, these ships offer minimal entertainment, though in some ports local musicians may be brought aboard for an evening. A weeklong Caribbean cruise a few years ago saw passengers entertained by a steel-drum band, an acoustic island-music trio, and a full modern island band, as well as a tropical fashion show in which one of the models was none other than a recent Miss St. Kitts. Recent-release movies may also be shown in a lounge (or, on *Clipper Odyssey*, on cabin TVs). *Clipper Odyssey* and *Yorktown Clipper* also have pianos in one lounge, in case a passenger feels like entertaining; and a small library on each ship is stocked with books on the regions the ship visits, plus a smattering of bestsellers.

SERVICE

Service staff aboard *Nantucket Clipper* and *Yorktown Clipper* is basically collegiate or post-collegiate Americans having an adventure before getting on with whatever it is they're getting on with. Aboard *Clipper Odyssey*, the staff is international. Whatever the mix, these folks tend to be pleasantly competent amateurs: friendly, willing to work, and happy to help. But don't be surprised by the occasional slip-up; remember, these are casual ships, not Silversea.

There is laundry service aboard *Clipper Odyssey*, but not on *Nantucket Clipper* or *Yorktown Clipper*.

Clipper Odyssey

The Verdict

Clipper's sleekest and most spacious vessel, with some of the largest staterooms in the small-ship market and some of its most wide-ranging itineraries, including a trek from Alaska to the Russian Far East.

Clipper Odyssey *(photo: Clipper Cruise Line)*

Specifications

Size (in tons)	5,218	Crew	72
Passengers (double occ.)	128	Passenger/Crew Ratio	1.8 to 1
Passenger/Space Ratio	41	Year Launched	1989
Total Cabins/Veranda Cabins	64/9	Last Major Refurbishment	1999

Frommer's Ratings (Scale of 1–5) ★★★★

Cabin Comfort & Amenities	4	Dining Options	3
Ship Cleanliness & Maintenance	4	Adventure & Fitness Options	5
Public Comfort/Space	5	Children's Facilities	N/A
Decor	3.5	Enjoyment Factor	4

Clipper Odyssey was built in Tsu, Japan, in 1989 based on a design by Dutch yacht architects Studio Acht. Acquired by Clipper in 1999, she's the line's Pacific Ocean ship, offering itineraries that range from Australia/New Zealand through Japan to the Russian Far East, the latter reached via expeditionary cruises from Alaska. In 2004, while en route through Alaska's Aleutian Islands, the ship hit a rock and sustained hull damage that forced cancellation of several cruises while repairs were made. She was sailing again by mid-September.

This vessel is one of only a handful of small ships with an elevator, making it a better bet than most for people with mobility problems. All public rooms and one cabin are wheelchair accessible, but the gangway is not.

Cabins & Rates

Cabins	Per Diems from	Sq. Ft.	Fridge	Hair Dryer	Sitting Area	TV
Outside	$517	175–230	yes	yes	yes	yes
Suite	$741	310	yes	yes	yes	yes

CABINS Cabins average 186 square feet, making them among the largest in the usually cozy small-ship market. All are outside, with two lower beds or one queen bed, plus a sitting area with sofa, piped-in music channels, safes, minifridges, and TVs. Bathrooms all have bathtubs (a real rarity on small ships), and the eight deluxe cabins and the single suite all have small private verandas (ditto). With the exception of the category-1 cabins on A Deck, which have portholes, all other cabin categories have picture windows.

PUBLIC AREAS The *Odyssey* boasts more extensive public rooms than your average small ship, with the usual lounge/bar augmented by a second lounge and a library. There's also an outdoor bar on the Lido Deck, and even a small beauty salon. Two open outdoor decks provide plenty of sunning and viewing space.

DINING OPTIONS A single dining room serves all meals in a single open seating. Light breakfast and lunch items are also available in the lounge.

ADVENTURE & FITNESS OPTIONS *Odyssey* is one of only four small ships in this book to offer a heated outdoor pool, a small gym, and a dedicated jogging track. Inflatable launches allow off-vessel exploration, and a glass-bottom boat allows passengers to view undersea life without getting wet.

Nantucket Clipper • Yorktown Clipper

The Verdict

Like a pair of your favorite walking shoes, these low-frills yet comfortable small ships carry passengers along America's rivers and coasts, then head to Baja and Central America for the winter.

Yorktown Clipper *(photo: Clipper Cruise Line)*

Specifications

Size (in tons)			
		Yorktown	69/0
Nantucket	1,471	Crew	
Yorktown	2,354	*Nantucket*	32
Passengers (double occ.)		*Yorktown*	40
Nantucket	102	Passenger/Crew Ratio	
Yorktown	138	*Nantucket*	3.2 to 1
Passenger/Space Ratio		*Yorktown*	3.5 to 1
Nantucket	14.7	Year Launched	
Yorktown	17	*Nantucket*	1984
Total Cabins/Veranda Cabins		*Yorktown*	1988
Nantucket	51/0	Last Major Refurbishment	N/A

Frommer's Ratings (Scale of 1–5)

★★★

Cabin Comfort & Amenities	3	Dining Options	3
Ship Cleanliness & Maintenance	4	Adventure & Fitness Options	2
Public Comfort/Space	3	Children's Facilities	N/A
Decor	3	Enjoyment Factor	4

The impression we kept coming back to when discussing the cozy cabins and lounges of these ships was that someone had taken one of the Holland America or Princess ships and shrunk it to one-fiftieth its normal size. Though not boasting the many bright public rooms of those large vessels, the four-deck *Yorktown* and *Nantucket Clipper* offer similar clean styling redone in more casual and easy-to-live-with colors, while also offering a small ship's ability to take passengers into shallow-water ports and other out-of-the-way locations far from the megaship crowd.

Cabins & Rates

Cabins	Per Diems from	Sq. Ft.	Fridge	Hair Dryer	Sitting Area	TV
Outside	$279	93–204	no	yes	no	no

CABINS   Although small (an average cabin on *Nantucket Clipper* is 93–123 sq. ft.; the average on the *Yorktown* is 110–140 sq. ft.), cabins are very pleasantly styled, with blond-wood writing desks, chairs, and bed frames; "better than a bare wall"–style paintings; and a goodly amount of closet space, plus additional storage under the beds. There are no phones or TVs, but each cabin does have piped-in music channels. Cabins have no safes as such, but two drawers in the closet can be locked, and passengers can lock valuables in each ship's safe, located on the bridge.

Cabins come in six categories, differentiated mostly by their location rather than their size. Beds are either permanently fixed into an "L" position (better for tall people) or set parallel to one another and abutted by wall and headboard. Some cabins have twin beds that can be pushed together to make a double, and some contain upper berths to accommodate a third person. Each ship has three or four extra-large cabins measuring 163 to 204 square feet.

All cabins have picture windows except for a few category-1 cabins on the Main Deck, which have portholes. All cabins on each ship's Promenade Deck and a handful at the stern on the Lounge Deck open onto the outdoors rather than onto an interior corridor, and whereas we normally prefer this simply because it makes us feel closer to nature, here it doesn't matter because the doors open out—meaning you can't leave the door open to breezes without blocking the deck walkway. It's worth noting that passengers in the Promenade Deck cabins should also be careful when opening their doors from the inside, lest they inadvertently brain some fellow passenger out taking a walk around the deck.

Cabin bathrooms are compact, though not nearly as tiny as aboard rivals American Canadian Caribbean and Glacier Bay. Toilets are wedged between the shower and sink area and may prove tight for heavier people. Bathrooms have showers but no tubs.

There are no cabins suitable for travelers with disabilities, and no elevators between decks.

PUBLIC AREAS   Each ship has four decks and only two indoor public areas: the dining room and the Observation Lounge. The pleasant lounge has big windows, a bar, a small but informative library, a piano, and enough space to comfortably seat everyone on board for lectures and meetings. It's the main hub of onboard activity. Other than that, there are no cozy hideaways other than your cabin. There is, though, plenty of outdoor deck space for those who like to linger over a sunset or under the stars.

DINING OPTIONS   All meals are served in the one dining room, which is spacious and comfortable. Snacks are also offered in the lounge throughout the day, along with coffee, tea, and other drinks.

ADVENTURE & FITNESS OPTIONS   The only onboard fitness options are walking or jogging around the deck (18 laps = 1 mile). When anchored in calm waters, you can sometimes go swimming and snorkeling right from the ship, courtesy of a small platform that's lowered into the water. Inflatable launches allow off-vessel exploration.

6 Cruise West

2301 5th Ave., Suite 401, Seattle, WA 98121. ℂ **800/426-7702** or 206/441-8687. Fax 206/441-4757. www.cruisewest.com.

THE LINE IN A NUTSHELL   Family-owned Cruise West is the preeminent small-ship line in Alaska, and over the past decade it's branched out to include trips in warmer destinations too. Most of its itineraries are port-to-port and geared to older, well-traveled, intellectually curious passengers. There are also a handful of more expeditionary sailings on the deep-water *Spirit of Oceanus*. **Sails to:** Alaska, Central America, Sea of Cortez/Baja, U.S./Canada river/coastal cruises (plus South Pacific, Asia).

THE EXPERIENCE   Like all small ships, Cruise West's eight vessels can navigate tight waterways, visit tiny ports, and scoot up close to shore for wildlife watching, but for the most part these are not adventure cruises. Much like competitor Clipper Cruise Line, Cruise West tends more toward casual, relaxed ships with an emphasis on watching nature from the deck than on trekking out into it: On most cruises, a quick excursion by inflatable launch is as active as it gets. At sea, the lack of organized activities leaves you free to scan for wildlife, peruse the natural sights, talk to the other guests, or read. In port—whether one of the large, popular ports or a less visited one—the line offers a good slate of shore excursions oriented mostly to nature and history. *Spirit of Oceanus,* the only one of the line's vessels built for sailing open seas, offers incredible sailings to the Russian Far East (aka Siberia), as well as winter trips to the South Pacific and Japan.

Pros

- **The staff:** The line's friendly, enthusiastic staffs are a big plus, making guests feel right at home.
- **Great shore excursions:** Cruise West's list includes some real gems.
- **Comfort and old-fashioned style:** Two of the line's ships—the oceangoing *Spirit of Oceanus* and the *Spirit of '98,* a re-creation of a late-19th-century coastal steamer—offer snazzier surroundings than most of their small-ship competitors.

Cons

- **Wacky bathrooms on some ships:** *Spirit of Alaska* has uncomfortable head-style bathrooms, while *Columbia* and *Discovery* have their sinks out in the cabin.

Compared with the other small-ship lines, here's how Cruise West rates:

	Poor	Fair	Good	Excellent	Outstanding
Enjoyment Factor				✓	
Dining			✓		
Activities				✓	
Children's Program	N/A				
Entertainment		✓			
Service				✓	
Worth the Money				✓	

CRUISE WEST: ALASKA'S SMALL-SHIP LEADER & THEN SOME

Cruise West is the legacy of Chuck West, a man who arrived in Alaska after serving as a pilot in World War II, liked what he saw, and decided to share it with others. After offering the first flightseeing tours above the Arctic Circle, he went on to found Alaska's first hotel chain and first motorcoach sightseeing line, then in the mid-1980s he started experimenting with multi-night, daylight-only yacht cruises on the Inside Passage. Overnight cruises followed, and the rest is history. Today, Cruise West, run by West's son Dick, is the largest small-ship line in America, offering cruises in Alaska, British Columbia, the Columbia and Snake rivers, the California Wine Country, the Baja Peninsula/Sea of Cortez, and Central America.

Though primarily oriented to port-to-port cruising, Cruise West also offers some more outdoors-oriented and exploratory cruises. Its flagship, the 114-passenger *Spirit of Oceanus*, sails 13- and 24-night Bering Sea/Russian Far East expedition cruises that are among the most far-ranging in the small-ship category, taking in Siberian native communities and incredibly remote islands off the Alaskan coast. Closer to home, the spartan *Spirit of Alaska* sails a number of adventure cruises that concentrate on Alaska's outdoors, while the *Pacific Explorer* does the same in Panama and Costa Rica. The little day-cruiser *Sheltered Seas* still offers the original Cruise West experience from back in the '80s: 4-, 5-, and 8-night excursions visiting wild areas by day and stopping each night in small port towns, where guests stay in local hotels and get to experience the place like locals.

PASSENGER PROFILE

Passengers with Cruise West tend to be in the 50–75 demographic (often at the high end of that range), financially stable, well educated, and intellectually curious. Many have sailed with the mainstream lines but came to Cruise West in search of something more intimate and less frenetic. When we sailed last summer, our fellow passengers included two State Department employees, several teachers, a retired bank president, and a magazine art director. On another cruise, the passenger list included a group of 30-odd Yale alumni, including one 80-something lady from New Haven who was set on doing every active shore excursion she could—hiking, kayaking, the lot. Ditto for a 40-ish couple from Pennsylvania we met in 2003, who, in between activities, had a list of local experiences they were bent on sampling, including a delicacy known as halibut cheeks. All these people wanted to visit Alaska's ports and see its natural wonders in a relaxed, dressed-down atmosphere—which is what Cruise West is all about.

Like a Road Trip, but by Boat

In addition to the ships profiled here, Cruise West's 70-passenger day cruiser *Sheltered Seas* offers what it calls **Daylight Yacht Tours,** a series of 4-, 5-, and 8-night trips that cruise Alaska's waterways by day and bring you ashore in port each evening, where passengers can take a prearranged tour of the town and/or dinner before heading to their hotel for the night. Many of these towns are too small to attract the larger cruise ships, but by the time you arrive even the other small ships will have departed, meaning you get to experience the town the way the locals do. If you can't decide between cruising Alaska and seeing it by land, this is an option worth exploring. As with Cruise West's other itineraries, additional travel by rail or motor coach allows visits to Fairbanks and Denali National Park. **Rates:** 4-night trips from $1,753, 5-night from $2,371, 8-night from $3,275. Prices include all shore accommodations, port charges, luggage handling, onboard services, and onboard meals.

DINING

Breakfast, lunch, and dinner are served at set times at one unassigned seating. An early riser's buffet is set out in the lounge before the set breakfast time, but if you're a late riser you'll miss breakfast entirely, as no room service is available. At all meals the fare is fairly average home-style American—not overly fancy, but varied enough. Chefs make a point of stocking up on fresh seafood while in port. **Vegetarian options** aren't particularly notable, but are offered at every meal, as are **heart-healthy entrees** and staple favorites like steak, chicken, and fish. With advance notice, the galley can accommodate other special diets (vegetarian, kosher, low-salt, low-fat). *Spirit of Oceanus* has a buffet option at breakfast and lunch. Aboard all ships, a buffet-style lunch and/or dinner may be served on the top deck in good weather.

SNACKS & EXTRAS   A late-afternoon snack is provided every day to tide passengers over until dinner, and the chef will occasionally whip up a batch of cookies. Pretzels, nuts, and other crunchy snack foods are usually left out in the lounge/bar, where there's also a 24-hour coffee/tea/cocoa station.

ACTIVITIES

As with other small ships, Cruise West vessels don't offer much in the way of onboard diversions. What activities there are may include post-dinner discussions of the port or region to be visited the next day, afternoon talks by expert guests while at sea, and perhaps a tour of the bridge or galley. Onboard fitness options are limited to walking around the open decks. A complimentary excursion is offered at each port, as well as a full slate of extra-cost excursions. Sometimes these complimentary excursions are very worthwhile—as at the Alaska Native town of Metlakatla, where passengers are treated to a wonderful performance by a Native music and dance troupe, or on the California Wine Country cruises, which include luncheons and tours at various wineries. Other times, though, the included excursions are just short bus tours and don't compare with the more exciting extra-cost excursions. Occasionally, expedition

Cruise West Fleet Itineraries

Ship	Itineraries
Pacific Explorer	**7-night Costa Rica & Panama:** Round-trip from San José, Costa Rica, Nov–Dec 2005, June–July 2006, and Nov–Dec 2006. **9-night Costa Rica & Panama:** Between Panama City, Panama, and San José, Costa Rica, Dec 2005 and Jan–Apr and Dec 2006.
Sheltered Seas	**4- & 5-night Alaska Daylight Cruise:** North- or southbound between Ketchikan and Juneau, AK, May–Aug 2006.
Spirit of '98	**8-night Alaska Inside Passage:** North- or southbound between Juneau and Ketchikan, AK, May–August 2006. **7-night Pacific Northwest (Columbia/Snake Rivers):** Round-trip from Portland, OR, Apr and Sept–Oct 2006.
Spirit of Alaska	**3- & 4-night Glacier Bay:** Round-trip from Juneau, AK, May–Aug 2006. **8-night Alaska Inside Passage:** Round-trip from Juneau, AK, May–Aug 2006. **7-night Pacific Northwest (Columbia/Snake Rivers):** Round-trip from Portland, OR, Sept–Oct 2006.
Spirit of Columbia	**3- & 4-night Prince William Sound:** Round-trip from Anchorage, AK, May–Aug 2006. **7-night British Columbia:** Round-trip from Seattle, WA, Apr and Sept–Oct 2006.
Spirit of Discovery	**8-night Alaska Inside Passage:** Round-trip from Juneau, AK, May–Aug 2006. **7-night Pacific Northwest (Columbia/Snake Rivers):** Round-trip from Portland, OR, Apr and Sept–Oct 2006.
Spirit of Endeavor	**8-night Alaska Inside Passage:** North- or southbound between Juneau and Ketchikan, AK, May–Aug 2006. **7-night Mexico Sea of Cortez:** Round-trip from Cabo San Lucas, Baja California Sur, Dec 2005–Mar 2006. **7-night British Columbia:** Round-trip from Seattle, WA, Apr and Sept–Oct 2006. **3- & 4-night California Wine Country:** Round-trip from San Francisco, CA, Oct–Nov 2005 and Oct–Nov 2006.
Spirit of Glacier Bay	**3- & 4-night Glacier Bay:** Round-trip from Juneau, AK, May–Aug 2006.
Spirit of Oceanus	**11-night Alaska Inside Passage:** North- or southbound between Vancouver, BC, and Anchorage, AK, May–Aug 2006. **13-night Bering Sea:** Round-trip from Anchorage, June–Aug 2006.

leaders will take passengers for a spin in the ships' inflatable Zodiac boats, getting close in to shore. Kayaking is also available on some itineraries.

At least one and sometimes two cheerful and knowledgeable "expedition leader" naturalists accompanies each trip to answer passengers' questions about flora, fauna, geology, and history, and other experts are brought aboard at various ports to add to the experience. On Columbia and Snake river itineraries, for instance, a Nez Perce poet and storyteller comes aboard to talk about the region's native peoples. *Spirit of Oceanus*'s longer itineraries sail with several historians, naturalists, and cultural experts, who provide numerous in-depth lectures throughout the cruise.

CHILDREN'S PROGRAM
No children's program is available.

ENTERTAINMENT

As is standard with small-ship lines, entertainment is almost nonexistent, and what you do get will be catch-as-catch-can. One evening the crew might put on a talent show featuring skits, music, magic, and whatever else they can drum up. Passengers sometimes get involved. Another evening, during dinner, passengers might be set the task of creating art from whatever's on their tables, with the winning table getting a bottle of wine for their effort. Some cruises also bring local musicians and dancers aboard to perform. *Pacific Explorer, Spirit of Endeavor, Spirit of '98,* and *Spirit of Oceanus* have TV/VCRs in their cabins and a shelf of videos in the lounge for passengers to take at will. *Spirit of Oceanus* and *Spirit of '98* both have pianos in their lounges, though it's primarily passengers playing them.

SERVICE

The line strives for a family feeling, employing young, energetic crews comprised mostly of American college students. Crewmembers do double- and triple-duty, waiting tables at breakfast, making beds and cleaning cabins, polishing the handrails, and unloading baggage at the end of the trip. They may not be consummate pros, but they do go out of their way to learn your name and offer personal service. Passengers tend to find them adorable. Crews aboard *Spirit of Oceanus* and *Pacific Explorer* are international. Laundry service is available only on *Spirit of Oceanus* and *Pacific Explorer.*

Spirit of Oceanus

The Verdict

Spirit of Oceanus is one of the most luxurious small-ships in the market, an ocean cruiser able to sail far-flung itineraries in style and comfort. Her cabins are downright huge.

Spirit of Oceanus *(photo: Cruise West)*

Specifications

Size (in tons)	4,500	Crew	59
Passengers (double occ.)	114	Passenger/Crew Ratio	2 to 1
Passenger/Space Ratio	39.5	Year Launched	1991
Total Cabins/Veranda Cabins	57/12	Last Major Refurbishment	2001

Frommer's Ratings (Scale of 1–5)   ★★★★★

Cabin Comfort & Amenities	5	Dining Options	5
Ship Cleanliness & Maintenance	4	Adventure & Fitness Options	5
Public Comfort/Space	5	Children's Facilities	N/A
Decor	5	Enjoyment Factor	5

The name says it all. Unlike all the other Cruise West ships, *Spirit of Oceanus* was built for sailing in open (rather than coastal) waters, allowing the line to offer more wide-ranging itineraries. The ship was built in 1991 as *Renaissance V,* one of the original vessels of now-defunct Renaissance Cruises. She sailed briefly for Star Cruises before Cruise West bought and refurbished her in 2001. Today, she's the line's largest and most luxurious ship, with more public rooms, a small gym, an elevator, and even a hot tub on the top deck. Her decor is more private yacht than cruise ship, with corridors and cabins paneled in glossy wood-look paneling studded with gleaming brasswork, and her cabins are absolutely massive. Her incredible 12- & 13-night Alaska Bering Sea/Russian Far East cruises (among the very best cruises we've ever taken) make the average Inside Passage cruise seem like a trip on the Circle Line. At the opposite pole of those Siberian outings, winters see the vessel sailing to the South Pacific and Japan.

Cabins & Rates

Cabins	Per Diems from	Sq. Ft.	Fridge	Hair Dryer	Sitting Area	TV
Outside	$460	215–250	yes	yes	yes	yes
Suite	$640	277–353	yes	yes	yes	yes

CABINS All 57 staterooms aboard are outsides with picture windows or (in a few cases) large portholes, and range in size from 215 to 353 square feet, which ranks them among the largest in the small-ship world. Each has a couch, TV/VCR, minifridge, marble-topped vanity, a walk-in closet or wardrobe, and a comfortably sized bathroom. Decor is a far cry from the usual off-white walls and modular furnishings of most small ships. Instead, their walls are paneled in dark, polished wood-tones, with rich carpeting giving a yachtlike (or boutique hotel) look. Twelve staterooms on Sun and Sports decks have private teak balconies, but the cabins themselves are actually smaller than those without balconies—what you gain in outside, you lose in inside.

Spirit of Oceanus is one of the few small ships with an elevator—a boon to folks with mobility problems—though no cabins are designed specifically for passengers with wheelchairs.

PUBLIC AREAS Public rooms include the main Oceanus Lounge—the venue for frequent lectures and slide presentations by the ship's large staff of naturalists and historians—and the smaller Oceanus Club, a combo bar and reading room with a baby grand that gets infrequent use. Nooks opening off from the Club are stocked with games and a small book and video library (where the ship's one computer is also located, for e-mailing only). On Alaska/Bering Sea trips, passengers go off-vessel most days via inflatable Zodiac landing boats, with rubber boots provided by the line. (Bring rain gear, though, as trips ashore are often wet.) South Pacific and Japan itineraries also include destination-specific activities built into the trip price.

DINING All meals are served in single open seatings in the pleasantly decorated Pacifica Restaurant on the Main Deck. For breakfast and lunch, passengers also have the option of going to the partially covered outdoor buffet on Sun Deck—a very pleasant perch in most weather, offering great views of the surrounding scenery.

ADVENTURE & FITNESS OPTIONS There's a small gym on the Sports Deck, with free weights, a step machine, and exercise bike, and two treadmills. A hot tub is located outside, just behind the Bistro buffet. Several inflatable launches allow frequent off-vessel exploration.

Spirit of '98

Spirit of '98 *(photo: Cruise West)*

The Verdict

Built as a replica of a 19th-century coastal steamer, *Spirit of '98* is one of the most distinctive small ships you'll ever see.

Specifications

Size (in tons)	96*	Crew	23
Passengers (double occ.)	96	Passenger/Crew Ratio	4.2 to 1
Passenger/Space Ratio	N/A*	Year Launched	1984
Total Cabins/Veranda Cabins	49/0	Last Major Refurbishment	1995

* See note on p. 328 regarding small-ship tonnage and passenger/space measurements.

Frommer's Ratings (Scale of 1–5) ★★★★

Cabin Comfort & Amenities	4	Dining Options	4
Ship Cleanliness & Maintenance	4	Adventure & Fitness Options	2
Public Comfort/Space	4	Children's Facilities	N/A
Decor	4	Enjoyment Factor	5

The *Spirit of '98* is a time machine. Built in 1984 as a replica of a 19th-century steamship and extensively refurbished in 1995, it carries its Victorian flavor so well that some of the people we've met on board think the ship really is a hundred years old. If you want to get a look at her, rent Kevin Costner's movie *Wyatt Earp,* whose ending was filmed on board. Also, Sue Henry's 1997 mystery novel *Death Takes Passage* is set entirely aboard the *'98* and provides detailed descriptions of the ship.

Cabins & Rates

Cabins	Per Diems from	Sq. Ft.	Fridge	Hair Dryer	Sitting Area	TV
Outside	$500	81–228	some	no	some	yes
Suite	$843	550	yes	no	yes	yes

CABINS   Cabins are comfortable and of decent size, continue the Victorian motif (except in their bathrooms), and feature TV/VCR combos and either twin, convertible twin, or double beds with firm, comfortable mattresses. Deluxe cabins have a minifridge, a seating area, and a trundle bed to accommodate a third passenger. One Owner's Suite provides a spacious living room with meeting area, large bathroom with whirlpool tub, king-size bed, stocked bar with refrigerator, TV/VCR, stereo, and enough windows to take in all of Alaska at one sitting.

Cabin 309, located on the upper deck, is fully wheelchair accessible, and there's an elevator connecting most passenger decks, though it doesn't get up to the Sun Deck. Two cabins are for solo passengers.

PUBLIC AREAS   The Grand Salon is the ship's bar/lounge, with a suitably plinky-sounding player piano, a 24-hour tea/coffee station, and a small library and video shelf. The room continues the ship's 19th-century design theme with pressed-tin ceilings (aluminum actually, but why be picky?), balloon-back chairs, ruffled draperies, and plenty of polished woodwork and brass. Another lounge space, a small bar called Soapy's Parlour after Skagway's legendary con man, sits just aft of the dining room. There's only a bartender at mealtimes, though, and it otherwise gets little use—meaning it's a good spot to sneak off and read. Out in the air, passengers congregate in the large bow area, on the open top deck (where staff will sometimes set up a bar on nice days), or at the railing in front of the bridge, which is open except when the ship is passing through rough water.

DINING OPTIONS The Klondike Dining Room is beautifully decorated and large enough to seat all guests in booths and round center tables. The booths seem to suffer less ambient noise than the round tables in the middle, so try to snag one of those if you can.

ADVENTURE & FITNESS OPTIONS The Upper Deck circles the ship, allowing walking for exercise. Inflatable launches allow off-vessel exploration.

Spirit of Endeavour • Pacific Explorer

The Verdict

Neither of these ships will knock your socks off with their style, but they will get you out to some beautiful spots in comfort.

Spirit of Endeavour *(photo: Matt Hannafin)*

Specifications

Size (in tons)		Crew	
Endeavour	99*	*Endeavour*	28
Explorer	1,716	*Explorer*	33
Passengers (double occ.)		Passenger/Crew Ratio	
Endeavour	102	*Endeavor*	3.6 to 1
Explorer	100	*Explorer*	3 to 1
Passenger/Space Ratio		Year Launched	
Endeavour	N/A*	*Endeavor*	1983
Explorer	17	*Explorer*	1995
Total Cabins/Veranda Cabins		Last Major Refurbishment	
Endeavour	51/0	*Endeavour*	1999
Explorer	50/0	*Explorer*	1998

* See note on p. 328 regarding small-ship tonnage and passenger/space measurements.

Frommer's Ratings (Scale of 1–5)

★★★½

Cabin Comfort & Amenities	3	Dining Options	3
Ship Cleanliness & Maintenance	4	Adventure & Fitness Options	2/3*
Public Comfort/Space	3	Children's Facilities	N/A
Decor	3	Enjoyment Factor	5

* Endeavor/Explorer

Spirit of Endeavour formerly sailed as the *Newport Clipper* of Clipper Cruise Line and has a nearly identical design as that line's *Yorktown Clipper,* with the same kind of low-key, comfortable feel. The boxier but similar-size *Pacific Explorer* was launched in 1995 as the *Temptress Explorer* of Costa Rica's Temptress Adventures, and was taken over by Cruise West in 1998.

Cabins & Rates

Cabins	Per Diems from	Sq. Ft.	Fridge	Hair Dryer	Sitting Area	TV
Outside	$362*	108–155	some	no	no	yes

* Prices cheaper for Central America itineraries.

CABINS   Comfortable and decently furnished, cabins aboard *Endeavour* and *Explorer* have firm, comfortable twin beds or a double bed, TV/VCR, adequate closet space, and decent-size bathrooms. All cabins have large view windows except a handful of forward Main Deck cabins on *Endeavour,* which have portholes. *Endeavour* does boast a writing desk in each of her cabins, plus minifridges in her Deluxe cabins. Two of those Deluxe cabins can accommodate a third person in a pull-down Pullman berth. There are no special facilities aboard for travelers with disabilities.

PUBLIC AREAS   Aboard *Endeavour,* the plush lounge/bar is the only public lounge on the ship, with a bar, book and video library, and 24-hour tea/coffee station. *Pacific Explorer* has two sizable lounges, one of which functions as the ship's library/reading room. On the top deck, *Explorer's* Tortuga Bar is the main social area aboard, with seating in the open or under an overhang. The bar keeps Costa Rica's Imperial Beer on tap.

DINING OPTIONS   Each ship has a single large dining room down by the waterline, with windows on both sides. This was the spot from which we sighted our first bear on our last trip, midway through our main course, and the captain obligingly made a U-turn, cut his engines, and let the ship drift within easy view for almost 30 minutes. Dessert was served after.

ADVENTURE & FITNESS OPTIONS   Cruises aboard *Pacific Explorer* tend to concentrate more on the outdoors than most other Cruise West itineraries, and most excursions are built into her rates, including guided hikes, kayaking, and snorkeling. Aboard *Endeavour* you can walk a circuit around the Upper Deck for exercise. Inflatable boats, launched from a deck at the back of the ship, allow off-vessel exploration.

Spirit of Glacier Bay • Spirit of Discovery • Spirit of Columbia • Spirit of Alaska

The Verdict

Utilitarian small ships that have been in service since the '70s, these three offer Cruise West's same intimate cruise experience, but the word of the day is "spartan."

Spirit of Alaska *(photo: Cruise West)*

Specifications

Size (in tons)		*Discovery*	21
Glacier Bay	95*	*Columbia/Alaska*	21
Discovery	94*	Passenger/Crew Ratio	
Columbia/Alaska	97*	*Glacier Bay*	2.9 to 1
Passengers (double occ.)		*Discovery*	4 to 1
Glacier Bay	46	*Columbia/Alaska*	3.7 to 1
Discovery	84	Year Launched	
Columbia/Alaska	78	*Glacier Bay*	1971
Passenger/Space Ratio	N/A*	*Discovery*	1976
Total Cabins/Veranda Cabins		*Columbia*	1979
Glacier Bay	25/0	*Alaska*	1980
Discovery	43/0	Last Major Refurbishment	
Columbia/Alaska	39/0	*Glacier Bay*	2000
Crew		*Discovery*	1992
Glacier Bay	16	*Columbia/Alaska*	1995

* *See note on p. 328 regarding small-ship tonnage and passenger/space measurements.*

Frommer's Ratings (Scale of 1–5)

★★★½

Cabin Comfort & Amenities	3	Dining Options	3
Ship Cleanliness & Maintenance	4	Adventure & Fitness Options	2
Public Comfort/Space	3	Children's Facilities	N/A
Decor	3	Enjoyment Factor	5

Though of slightly dissimilar sizes and passenger capacities, these four vessels are extremely similar, all offering the friendly Cruise West experience, though in a somewhat plainer package than with their fleetmates. Though they're older ships, all have been kept in good condition. Interestingly, the *Glacier Bay, Alaska,* and *Columbia* (as well as Glacier Bay Cruiseline's *Wilderness Adventurer* and *Wilderness Discoverer*) were originally built by Captain Luther Blount for his American Canadian Caribbean Line, and therefore share a problem common to all Blount vessels: They're not good choices for very tall people, as ceilings throughout are set at little more than 6 feet, 4 inches; many beds are also too short for those 6 feet, 2 inches or taller. On the other hand, the *Alaska* and *Columbia* have ACCL's patented bow ramp, which, in combination with their shallow draft, allows the ships to basically beach themselves, disembarking passengers right onto shore in wild areas without ports.

Cabins & Rates

Cabins	Per Diems from	Sq. Ft.	Fridge	Hair Dryer	Sitting Area	TV
Inside*	$169	80	no	no	no	no
Outside	$246	95–128	some	no	some	some

* Inside cabins on Spirit of Alaska *and* Spirit of Columbia *only.*

CABINS   Cabins aboard all four ships are very snug (smaller than those aboard their fleetmates) but comfortable, with light, B&B-ish decor and lower twin or double beds. (Aboard the *Discovery,* one category has upper and lower bunks, and deluxe cabins have queen-size beds.) Storage space is ample, and most Bridge and Lounge Deck cabins feature picture windows. Bathrooms aboard the *Discovery* and *Columbia* are slightly better than those aboard the *Alaska,* which has tight, head-style arrangements (sink and toilet in the shower stall). None of the cabins on any of these ships accommodate wheelchairs.

PUBLIC AREAS   All four ships have a lounge with a bar, 24-hour tea/coffee station, and a book and video library. Lounges are a little too small to accommodate all passengers when the ships are full.

DINING OPTIONS   A single dining room serves all meals.

ADVENTURE & FITNESS OPTIONS   Inflatable launches allow off-vessel exploration.

7 Delta Queen Steamboat Company

Robin Street Wharf, 1380 Port of New Orleans Pl., New Orleans, LA 70130. (✆) 800/543-1949. Fax 504/585-0630. www.deltaqueen.com.

THE LINE IN A NUTSHELL   Delta Queen offers one of the best cruising experiences you'll find anywhere. Plying the Mississippi River system from New Orleans to as far north as St. Paul and as far east as Pittsburgh, the line offers a good old-fashioned cruise that's more Mark Twain than Las Vegas, full of history and river lore, Cajun and Southern cooking, and a music program heavy on Dixieland jazz and swing. The vessels themselves are virtual museum pieces, whether an actual antique like the 1927-built *Delta Queen,* or a re-created one like 1995's *American Queen.* **Sails to:** U.S. river cruises.

THE EXPERIENCE   Life on the Mississippi is definitely different, with the riverboats often tying their lines to trees rather than piers, and the stage (aka gangway) let down right onto muddy riverbanks. On board, the main activity is watching the river go by—its traffic, its commerce, its scenery and towns—while a resident historian (or "Riverlorian") spins tales and offers lessons about river life, culture, and history. Sit yourself down in a rocking chair or porch swing and just watch open land and forests go by, mile after mile. Unlike the ocean with its distant horizon, you can measure your progress by watching the riverbank go by only a few hundreds yards away, always looking expectantly around the next bend to see what's there. Maybe it'll be some small town, or maybe a group of kids running down to the bank to wave and hear the boat's mighty whistle. The boat, and by extension you, are an integral part of it all, fitting in perfectly in a way the Caribbean megaships don't.

All around, DQ offers more lavishing surroundings and better food and service than you'll find on the no-frills small ships, and its boats have an intimacy and personality that bigger cruise ships lack. Throw in a healthy dose of the Mighty Mississippi and you have a totally unique and memorable cruise.

Pros

- **Old-fashioned fun:** From flying kites on the stern to playing the boisterous steam calliope, life onboard is surprisingly fun and certainly carefree.
- **America, America . . . :** These all-American ships are awash in American nostalgia, with an authentic flavor you won't find on other cruises. Visits to small, charming ports like Henderson, KY, and Madison, IN, drive home the point.
- **History:** The *Delta Queen* is a National Historic Landmark, and just being on the river is enough to make Mark Twain come alive. Between the Riverlorian talks and historical ports, you'll never have as much fun learning about the past again.

Cons

- **Limited Activities:** While the historical program is great and the live music is first rate, don't expect cruise ship activities like gambling, yoga, or late-night partying.

DELTA QUEEN: BIG WHEEL KEEPS ON TURNIN'

It used to be that stern-wheelers were a main source of transportation in the interior of the country, with lavish boats outdoing each other in speed and comfort. Supposedly, service was common enough that a flashing lantern on shore was enough to signal a passing boat to stop and pick up passengers. Cruising with Delta Queen, which has ties going back to 1890, it sometimes seems that nothing has changed. On our first night on board the *Delta Queen,* we found ourselves unexpectedly coming alongside the riverbank at 10pm to stop where a car, not a lantern, was flashing its lights at us. Soon we were nestled against the bank to embark a flight-delayed passenger, and within minutes we were underway again, caught somewhere between the early 20th century and the early 21st.

Delta Queen's three steamboats have significantly different characteristics: The wooden, 174-passenger **Delta Queen** is small and genuinely old-fashioned: Built in 1927, she's a time machine and a National Landmark. The 414-passenger **Mississippi Queen** (1976) and the 436-passenger **American Queen** (1995) are sort of

Compared with the other small-ship lines, here's how Delta Queen rates:

	Poor	Fair	Good	Excellent	Outstanding
Enjoyment Factor					✓
Dining			✓		
Activities			✓		
Children's Program		✓			
Entertainment					✓
Service				✓	
Worth the Money				✓	

purpose-built, nostalgic, and ersatz elegant, with a few cruise ship amenities. Itineraries are as varied as the boats themselves, sailing the Mississippi, Ohio, Cumberland, Tennessee, Illinois, and Kanawha rivers, plus the Gulf Coast Intracoastal Waterway. Trips from New Orleans visit Antebellum homes and plantations, while trips farther north scrape through the Rust Belt. From bustling cities such as Cincinnati and Pittsburg to small towns where the biggest attraction is the National Quilt Museum (Paducah, KY), you'll see a varied picture of America.

PASSENGER PROFILE

Delta Queen passengers have historically been almost exclusively American, in their sixties and up and fiercely loyal. The company has made great efforts in the last few years, however, to lower the average age by bulking-up their children's program and offering short 3- and 4-night cruises out of New Orleans. Expect to see some families on the *Mississippi* and *American Queen* from May to August and during the holidays, including kids traveling with their grandparents. The old *Delta Queen* does not offer any "riverbonding" cruises and will continue to attract an older crowd.

Passengers should note that no doctors are carried aboard. In an emergency, the boats simply pull up along the riverbank to await medical help.

DINING

Compared to some of the smaller, more adventurous lines, the food on board Delta Queen is decidedly more varied and complex and compares favorably with mainstream cruise ships. On all three boats, food runs toward Middle American, Southern, and Cajun, with consistently satisfying prime rib, roast duck, fried oysters, catfish stuffed with crab and wild rice, ravioli stuffed with shrimp, seafood gumbo, garlic and leek soup, Mississippi Mud Pie, and praline and pecan cheesecake. Local specialties are a favorite, and **fried alligator** might even show up one night at a New Orleans Moonlight Buffet! Meals are served in traditional style, with passengers assigned to a set table for lunch and dinner.

SNACKS & EXTRAS   It doesn't sound like much, but freshly popped **popcorn** is a Delta Queen staple. Grab a bag, sit out on the rocking chairs on deck, and watch the river go by. It doesn't get any better than this—unless, perhaps, you dig into the bottomless basket of **fresh chocolate-chip and peanut butter cookies.**

ACTIVITIES

You know how you sometimes feel you need a vacation to recover from your vacation? Not so on Delta Queen, where the boat's pace averages 6 mph—and yours does too. Learning about the river is the focus of most days, with an onboard historian/Riverlorian describing passing areas, showing you where you are on a chart, or weaving facts and stories about the river into daily talks. Some are given during breakfast and discuss the river's history and culture, while ones at night might explain the river's navigation lights. (*Note:* The Riverlorian program is not offered on *American Queen*'s 3- and 4-night itineraries.) Other activities include films (both historical and current), a lecture from a Mark Twain impersonator, and **calliope concerts** on deck, in which everyone gets to play a few notes. But the most popular sport on board is definitely **kite flying.** After putting together your own kite from a kit, head to the top deck and try to get your bird in the air without getting it tangled with other lines, caught under a passing bridge, or landing in the Mississippi.

Delta Queen Fleet Itineraries

Ship	Itinerary
American Queen	**3- & 4-night Mississippi River:** Round-trip from New Orleans, LA, Oct 2005–June 2006. **6- & 7-night Mississippi River:** Round-trip from New Orleans or between New Orleans and Memphis, TN, June–Aug 2006.
Delta Queen	**4-, 5-, 6-, 7-, 11- & 12-night river cruises (multiple routes):** Sailing between Cincinnati and Pittsburgh, Cincinnati and Nashville, Nashville and Chattanooga, Chattanooga and Cincinnati, Pittsburgh and New Orleans, New Orleans and Galveston, New Orleans and Mobile, New Orleans and Pensacola, New Orleans and St. Louis, round-trip from New Orleans, and round-trip from Galveston, year-round.
Mississippi Queen	**5-, 6-, 7- & 11-night river cruises (multiple routes):** Sailing between St. Louis and St. Paul, St. Louis and New Orleans, New Orleans and Memphis, New Orleans and St. Louis, Memphis and Nashville, and round-trip from New Orleans, year-round.

CHILDREN'S PROGRAM

While seniors will always outnumber toddlers on Delta Queen, an improved children's program has been drawing increased numbers of families over the past few years. On *Mississippi Queen* and *American Queen*'s summer and holiday **"riverbonding" cruises,** a family activity coordinator encourages kids to unplug from video games and TV and keeps them occupied instead with knot tying, mini-golf tournaments, and the like. While typical children's programs entertain kids separately from their parents, Delta Queen encourages activities in which the whole family can participate, including a new collection of family-oriented shore excursions in which everyone tours a plantation house through the eyes of the children who once lived there, whitewashes a fence like Tom Sawyer, or tours a Cajun swamp. *Note:* The *Delta Queen* does not offer this program and does not have any facilities for children.

ENTERTAINMENT

Delta Queen is based in New Orleans, so expect high-quality live music and evening entertainment. **Riverboat-style shows** feature vaudeville singers and a heavy emphasis on Dixieland jazz. Dancers appreciate the nightly **big band concerts.** Theme nights are popular, especially on the 3- and 4-night cruises, which might feature Cajun Night, Blues Night, or a Mardi Gras Ball. *American Queen* and *Mississippi Queen* have more elaborate evening shows, mostly because they have an actual stage for performers. Lastly, despite their being riverboats, none of the DQ vessels have **casinos** on board.

SERVICE

Service on Delta Queen isn't polished in a luxe-cruise way, but it sure is more fun, with the crew managing to be friendly and entertaining as well as thoroughly efficient. Everyone on board is a character, and many have been with the company a decade or more. Case in point, our waiter Choo-Choo, who teased busboy Maurice one night for not being at the table the moment we sat down—"Just remember what it says in the Bible," he intoned to us in his best drawl, "He may not be there when you want him, but he'll be there on time."

Room service is only available from a very limited breakfast menu.

Delta Queen

The Verdict

Like your favorite B&B, the 1927-built *Delta Queen* oozes charm, personality, and a welcoming friendliness. It's a classic in a league of its own.

Delta Queen *(photo: Delta Queen)*

Specifications

Size (in tons)	3,360	Crew	80
Passengers (double occ.)	174	Passenger/Crew Ratio	2.1 to 1
Passenger/Space Ratio	19.3	Year Launched	1927
Total Cabins/Veranda Cabins	80/0	Last Major Refurbishment	1998

Frommer's Ratings (Scale of 1–5)   ★★★★

Cabin Comfort & Amenities	3.5	Dining Options	3
Ship Cleanliness & Maintenance	4	Adventure & Fitness Options	2
Public Comfort/Space	4	Children's Facilities	N/A
Decor	5	Enjoyment Factor	5

When we first caught sight of *Delta Queen* nudged against a riverbank, dripping muddy water from her slowly turning paddlewheel, she looked both perfectly in sync with her surroundings and perfectly out of place. Was she a lonely relic from a long-gone time, or were we intruders on her world, where she'd been carrying on commerce as usual for a hundred years? It seemed amazing that such a boat still existed, much less still carried passengers.

Built in 1927, *Delta Queen* is the real deal: Nothing seems contrived or fake (because it isn't) and antiques *are* the decor, not just elements dropped in to add authenticity and hominess. While not originally built for the Mississippi river, the boat has a long and proud history, with her hull originally fabricated in Scotland, then shipped to California for final assembly. Costing the then exorbitant price of $1 million, she was known for her fine interiors as she carried overnight passengers between San Francisco and Sacramento. (Her sister, the *Delta King*, still survives as a restaurant in Sacramento.) During WWII, the government took her over, painted her gray, and used her to ferry troops around San Francisco Bay. In 1949 Capt. Tom Greene bought her, literally packed her in a big box, and towed her to New Orleans, making her the first steamboat to transit the Panama Canal. Because her superstructure is built almost entirely of wood, her career has been threatened numerous times by newer fire regulations, but her legions of loyal fans have secured her future with exemptions from the U.S. Congress.

Cabins & Rates

Cabins	Per Diems from	Sq. Ft.	Fridge	Hair Dryer	Sitting Area	TV
Outside	$278	55–229	no	no	some	no

CABINS   With their stained-glass windows and acres of wood paneling, the cabins aboard *Delta Queen* couldn't be further from the cookie-cutters on today's modern ships. Size ranges from tight upper-and-lower-berth cabins with pipe racks for storage to plush if not overly spacious cabins with queen-size beds. Every cabin is outside (though a few have obstructed views) and many feature windows or doors that can be opened to allow the fresh air in. Charmingly, almost all open up directly onto the Promenade decks, which creates a neighborly feel with chairs and rockers situated just outside. Just as charmingly, there are no telephones or TVs in any of the cabins.

Every cabin has its own personality and history: One cabin on Sun Deck is where President Jimmy Carter (one of three presidents to sail aboard) stayed for a week in 1979. Another cabin is said to be haunted by the ghost of the late owner of the company, Ma Greene. Don't laugh, either: Crewmembers take Ma Greene's ghost very seriously, and many swear up and down that they've interacted with her as she keeps an eye on her beloved boat.

Delta Queen has no wheelchair-accessible cabins, nor is there an elevator on board.

PUBLIC AREAS   Wood, wood, and more wood! Beautifully maintained and very comfortable, *Delta Queen* seems more like an upscale Southern home or warm B&B than a normal cruise ship, with her rich wood interiors, overstuffed couches, and numerous antiques. The Cabin Lounge is the lower of two forward lounges, graced with fluted columns and potted plants, and is suitable for reading, cards, and tea. The wooden grand staircase with shiny brass steps rises to the Victorian-style Texas Lounge, with its bar, daytime games, singer-pianist, and popcorn machine. The Betty Blake Lounge is an interior room between the cabins on Cabin Deck and is full of exhibits about the company's history. It's named after the woman who lobbied Congress for years to secure *Delta Queen*'s continued career. The Orleans Room, serving meals in two seatings, doubles as an old-fashioned music hall featuring ragtime, Dixieland, jazz, and blues. Passengers can even visit the engine room, where you'll see spotless brass fittings and gauges. Watching the slow, heaving Pitman arms turning the thrashing red wooden paddlewheel is hypnotic, and a very far cry indeed from the strictly "off limits" culture of most modern ships.

DINING OPTIONS   Forget Freestyle Dining or 10 different restaurants. On *Delta Queen,* the one dining room on board used to be a freight deck and features tin ceilings and an ironwood floor. One day, the room might be transformed with checker cloth tablecloths into a "picnic" area, complete with denim-clad waiters bringing drinks in wagons; serving corn, chicken, and catfish; and scattering plastic ants across the table while crooning, "It's just like a real picnic, isn't it?" Food on the *Delta Queen* can often be a bit better than the *Mississippi Queen* and *American Queen,* as the smaller number of passengers makes for more individual preparation. A light breakfast snack is served in the Cabin Lounge for those not wishing to take a full meal in the Orleans Room.

ADVENTURE & FITNESS OPTIONS   *Delta Queen* passengers tend to be older and the ship has basically non-existent exercise facilities, save for an exercise bike and elliptical trainer positioned on the stern by the paddlewheel. Shore excursions tend to be fairly low-key, activity wise.

Mississippi Queen •
American Queen

The Verdict

Match the charm and history of the *Delta Queen* with some of the comforts and amenities of a newer ship, and you'll get the *Mississippi* and *American Queens*. While not as cozy, these boats still deliver authentic and spirited America's river travel.

American Queen *(photo: Delta Queen)*

Specifications

Size (in tons)		American Queen	222/31
Mississippi Queen	3,364	Crew	
American Queen	3,707	*Mississippi Queen*	157
Passengers (double occ.)		*American Queen*	167
Mississippi Queen	414	Passenger/Crew Ratio	2.6 to 1
American Queen	436	Year Launched	
Passenger/Space Ratio		*Mississippi Queen*	1976
Mississippi Queen	8	*American Queen*	1995
American Queen	8.5	Last Major Refurbishment	
Total Cabins/Veranda Cabins		*Mississippi Queen*	1996
Mississippi Queen	206/100	*American Queen*	1991

Frommer's Ratings (Scale of 1–5)

★★★★

Cabin Comfort & Amenities	4	Dining Options	4
Ship Cleanliness & Maintenance	4	Adventure & Fitness Options	3
Public Comfort/Space	4	Children's Facilities	2
Decor	5	Enjoyment Factor	5

Treading the line between modern and old-fashioned, these grand riverboats feel authentic while offering modern amenities like plunge pools, a gym, and private balconies. Don't expect a regular cruise ship, though. The largest stern-wheeler in history, the *American Queen* is grand and magnificent, a tiered wedding cake of filigree and curlicues crowned with two huge fluted smokestacks. Ornamentation and decoration are everywhere, framing an assortment of vintage period pieces and antiques. Even her engine is a vintage steam plant, rescued and restored from a 1930 U.S. Army Corps dredge (though unlike *Delta* and *Mississippi Queen,* her steam plant and paddlewheel are assisted by a modern propulsion system). She looks so beautiful and authentic that it's hard to imagine she was built in the 1990s—and even harder to imagine how much effort and expense Delta Queen put into her, when most other companies would have cut corners.

The *American Queen* is now mostly based year-round in New Orleans on 3- and 4-night cruises, offering spiced up activities (Beatles music, deck parties, seafood boils, more interactive shore excursions) in an effort to lower Delta Queen's notoriously older clientele. Coupled with attractively priced hotel stays in New Orleans, this is a great way to see if the steamboating experience is right for you.

You wouldn't think the *Mississippi Queen* and the *QE2* have much in common, right? Well, James Gardner, who designed the *QE2* in the 1960s, designed the *Mississippi Queen* in the 1970s. Unfortunately, he didn't get the *MQ* quite as right as he did the *QE2*, and for many years, she seemed more like a floating Holiday Inn than a true steamboat, and became many people's least favorite of the trio. Delta Queen got wise, however, and in 1996 gave her a top-to-bottom refurbishment and a new Victorian interior. Today she spends her year wandering the river system, with itineraries ranging from 3 to 14 nights. Some of her more popular trips include fall foliage sailings along the Upper Mississippi and the Great Steamboat Race, during which she sails alongside *Delta Queen* for 2 weeks in a spirited competition that also includes games between each boat's passengers. Several theme cruises, including Civil War, Gardens, and the Great Steamboat Era, are very popular.

Cabins & Rates

Cabins	Per Diems from	Sq. Ft.	Fridge	Hair Dryer	Sitting Area	TV
Inside	$208	68–140	No	No	No	No
Outside	$335	87–353	No	No	Some	No

CABINS Cabins on the *American Queen*, like almost every other part of the ship, are elaborately decorated, complete with Tiffany-style lamps and plenty of storage space. Decorative moldings and trim surround each cabin door and ceiling, and most cabins feature a large bathroom and tub, as well as a huge sink and a tiled floor. As aboard *Delta Queen*, many cabins open up to the common decks via French doors, creating a neighborly feel. Other cabins have a large bay window or private balconies, and some suites feature extra-spacious balconies with views that rival that from the pilothouse. Cabins that open to the deck have a small stained-glass transom window to let fresh air in.

Mississippi Queen's cabins are a bit more standard and are small when compared to modern cruise ships, though approximately half offer private balconies. (Given that the *MQ* was built in 1976, this design was way ahead of its time.) The privacy is a trade-off, however, meaning a loss of some of the friendly community feel found on the other boats. It also means the only common Promenade Deck is located at the very top of the ship near the pool area. While it seems a small detail to some, it does create a different feel on board.

American Queen has a number of cabins designed for solo passengers. *American Queen* has nine wheelchair-accessible cabins; *Mississippi Queen* has one.

PUBLIC AREAS *American Queen*'s decor is one of the most impressive afloat, with details so numerous you could spend a week just exploring the public rooms. The Ladies' Parlor welcomes anyone to lounge on the swooning couch, facing a fireplace whose wooden mantle is cluttered with black-and-white "ancestral" photographs and flanking vases. Floor lamps with linen shades, silver tea sets, a rosewood pump organ, and floral wallpaper all add to the lovely room—a cozy spot to read or simply gaze out at the river through the rooms French doors and pretty curtained bay window. Across the passageway is the Gentlemen's Card Room, a masculine, clubby lounge complete with a Boar's Head on the wall (which covers a TV, of all things). Just aft, the Mark

Twain Gallery is a museum space and lounge full of antique furniture, a model of the *Delta Queen,* and views down onto the J. M. White Dining Room below. Further aft on Cabin Deck, the Grand Saloon is an impressive showroom, modeled after grand opera houses of the 1800s and featuring cozy private boxes perfect for watching the shows. The liveliest spot is all the way aft at the Engine Room Bar, where banjo playing, ragtime, and jazz go on late into the night while moody, rhythmic light flickers off the spinning paddlewheel outside the windows. At the Observation Deck's Chart Room, passengers can peruse books about the river, or pretend to drive via the large mounted steering wheel, or enlist the Riverlorian's help in charting the boat's progress. For such a relatively small vessel, *American Queen* has an astonishing variety of spaces.

Most of the *Mississippi Queen*'s public rooms are located on the Observation Deck, with cabins both above and below. The abundance of private balconies detracts somewhat from the ship, as there are not the numerous Promenade decks that are found on the *Delta* and *Mississippi Queen.* Linking the boat's seven decks is a Grand Staircase, crowed by a *trompe l'oeil* ceiling. At the very front of Observation Deck is the Wheel House, which (like the *AQ*'s Chart Room) acts as home to the Riverlorian, with charts by which passengers can track their progress on the river. Aft is the Grand Saloon, used for most activities during the day and as a showroom at night. Overlooking the boat's 36-foot wide paddlewheel is the appropriately named Paddlewheel Lounge, offering commanding views of the river from the two-story windows that line three of its sides. Other public areas include the Golden Antlers Bar, the Forward Lounge, the open-air Calliope Bar, a movie theater, library, and even a beauty salon. The Engine Room is open to passengers on both boats.

DINING OPTIONS   Breakfast, lunch, and dinner are all served in the ship's dining rooms, but there's also a buffet breakfast and lunch served in the Front Porch of America. The *American Queen*'s J. M. White Dining Room is spectacular and memorable. Recalling the main cabin lounge aboard its late-19th-century namesake steamboat, it has a pair of soaring two-deck sections decorated with white filigree woodwork, colorful tapestries, and two huge, gilded antique mirrors. The Front Porch of America, a feature on all three steamboats, is aptly named for its sweeping views over the bow and furnishings of white wicker chairs and painted rockers. Light and casual, the room offers a constant stream of soft ice cream, lemonade, and baskets of freshly baked cookies. Grab some and head out to the porch swings and rocking chairs. Hot dogs and hamburgers are available on the open decks by the Calliope Bar, high above the spinning paddlewheel, and a late-night snack is usually served in one of the lounges.

ADVENTURE & FITNESS OPTIONS   Each ship has a small gym and pool, and a fitness instructor sails with *American Queen*'s shorter jaunts from New Orleans. Oh, and there's a Ping-Pong table on the top deck.

8 Glacier Bay Cruiseline

2101 4th Ave., Suite 2200, Seattle, WA 98121. (C) **800/451-5952** or 206/623-7110. Fax 206/623-7809. www.glacier baycruiseline.com.

THE LINE IN A NUTSHELL   Glacier Bay Cruiseline is the top choice in Alaska for hardcore adventure cruises, with most itineraries focused on kayaking, hiking, and wildlife-watching. On *Wilderness Adventurer* and *Wilderness Explorer*'s itineraries, you can go a full week and hardly see another human besides the people on your ship. Trips aboard *Wilderness Discoverer* and *Executive Explorer* merge the outdoors with a more standard port-to-port itinerary. **Sails to:** Alaska, Pacific Northwest river cruises.

THE EXPERIENCE Glacier Bay offers an ultracasual, outdoors-oriented cruise experience for passengers who couldn't give two hoots about luxury. Good thing, because the line's fleet includes three of the most spartan ships in the market, 31- to 86-passenger coastal cruisers with bare-bones cabins and public areas. The onboard atmosphere is casual and friendly, with naturalists on hand to help passengers get out there and experience Alaska at ground level. Our favorite Glacier Bay moment occurred one morning in 1998, when we launched our kayak into an icy early-season rain, paddled out of sight of the ship, and came upon two black bears ambling along the shore, maybe 15 yards away, still groggy from their winter hibernation. We put up our oars and drifted, watching until they disappeared into the bush a few minutes later, then continued kayaking for another hour before heading back for lunch. Now that's Alaska.

Wilderness Adventurer, Explorer, and *Discoverer* all carry a fleet of professional, two-person sea kayaks, and naturalists sail with all cruises to provide insight. Outdoors excursions are included in the cruise price, and *Wilderness Discoverer* and *Executive Explorer*'s port-to-port itineraries also offer extra-cost excursions in towns such as Skagway and Haines.

Pros

- **Kayaking!** Launched from a platform at the ship's stern, the kayaks provide a great way to get out there and see Alaska close-up.
- **Informality:** It's casual all the way, and you and the crew will bond in no time.
- **Focus on environment and Alaska's culture:** By avoiding the big towns on most cruises, Glacier Bay is able to show you the real Alaska.

Cons

- **Bare-bones ships:** Aside from *Executive Explorer,* Glacier Bay's ships are as basic as they come, with tiny cabins and public areas that aren't much fancier than a church cafeteria.

GLACIER BAY: ALASKA'S BEST WILDERNESS SHIPS

Glacier Bay Cruiseline (formerly Alaska's Glacier Bay Tours & Cruises) has been around for almost 4 decades under several owners, including the Alaska Native corporation Goldbelt. New owners took the helm in 2004 and pledged to maintain the line's active-adventure orientation.

Compared with the other small-ship lines, here's how Glacier Bay rates:

	Poor	Fair	Good	Excellent	Outstanding
Enjoyment Factor					✓
Dining			✓		
Activities					✓
Children's Program	N/A				
Entertainment		✓			
Service				✓	
Worth the Money				✓	

Glacier Bay Fleet Itineraries

Ship	Itineraries
Executive Explorer	**7-night Alaska Inside Passage:** North- or southbound between Juneau and Ketchikan, AK, May–Aug 2006.
Wilderness Adventurer	**7-night Alaska Inside Passage:** Round-trip from Juneau, AK, May and Aug–Sept 2006. **8-night Prince William Sound:** Round-trip from Anchorage, AK, June–Aug 2006.
Wilderness Discoverer	**7-night Alaska Inside Passage:** North- or southbound between Juneau and Sitka, AK, June–Aug 2006. **7-night Pacific Northwest (Columbia/Snake Rivers):** East- or westbound between Portland, OR, and Richland, WA, Sept–Oct 2006.
Wilderness Explorer	**6-night Alaska Glacier Bay/Icy Strait:** Round-trip from Juneau, AK, May–Aug 2006.

PASSENGER PROFILE

Glacier Bay's typical passengers are active individualists, overwhelmingly interested in nature and wildlife and completely uninterested in the usual sightseeing-and-shopping cruise experience. All want a casual, dress-down, no-pretense vacation, and enjoy the fact that captains on Glacier Bay's adventure itineraries have the freedom to sail wherever passengers will get the best Alaska experience that day, taking into account factors such as weather and wildlife sightings. Passengers tend to be on the youngish side, with as many couples in their 40s and 50s as in their 60s and 70s, and a scattering of 30-, 80-, and 90-somethings filling out the list. If you're particularly tall—say, 6 feet 4 inches or over—note that ceilings on *Wilderness Adventurer, Discoverer,* and *Explorer* are quite low.

DINING

Meals are pretty standard middle-American fare (plus the requisite Alaskan salmon) and are served in single open seatings in the main dining room. Dinners include a choice of two entrees, typically a fresh fish such as halibut or salmon and a chicken or beef dish. **Special diets** (vegetarian, low-fat, low-salt) can be accommodated if the line is given advance warning, but they're not set up to do kosher meals. Depending on the weather, the chef's team will sometimes prepare and serve barbecued seafood (prawns, crabs, and so forth) out on the top deck. One dinner per cruise is designated the captain's dinner, and here the cuisine is ratcheted up a notch, perhaps to lobster and free champagne.

SNACKS & EXTRAS Pre-dinner snacks of the chicken-wing and nacho variety are served daily in each ship's lounge/bar. Other than that, coffee, tea, the occasional bowl of chips, and the fresh cookies baked at midafternoon are the only snacks available between scheduled mealtimes.

ACTIVITIES

Activities offered by the adventure vessels are the integral elements of the trip: kayaking, hiking, and wildlife-watching. Two full-time onboard naturalists keep an eye on activities, wildlife and sea life viewing, and give informal presentations highlighting the natural and historical aspects of the region. Guest lecturers sometimes sail as well, or come aboard to give readings of Alaskan stories or presentations on glaciers, marine life, whales, and other natural topics. Days on the line's port-to-port vessels (*Wilderness Discoverer* and *Executive Explorer*) are similar to those offered by Cruise West and Clipper, with visits to both large and small port towns and other days spent sailing in wild areas such as Glacier Bay, Tracy Arm, and Misty Fjords.

CHILDREN'S PROGRAM

None on most sailings. However, the line does offer several cruises every summer designated for families, with supervised children's activities and special 50%-off rates for kids 18 and under.

ENTERTAINMENT

The usual for small ships: board games (passenger vs. crew Pictionary on one of our trips!) and a TV/VCR in the lounge of each ship, on which passengers can view tapes on wildlife, Alaska history, and Native culture, plus a few feature films. *Wilderness Explorer* also has a piano for passenger use.

SERVICE

One of the line's greatest strengths is the extreme informality of the passenger/crew dynamic—the two groups tend to become so friendly so fast that after a couple of days you'll find off-duty deckhands watching nature videos with passengers in the lounge and naturalists sitting with passengers on the top deck at night, watching the stars. As with most small-ship lines, members of the staff do double- and triple-duty, cleaning the cabins, serving meals, and loading and unloading your luggage. There are no laundry facilities, and no room service.

Wilderness Adventurer • Wilderness Discoverer

Wilderness Discoverer *(photo: Glacier Bay)*

The Verdict

These ships are pretty much the jeeps of the cruise world: rough and ready vehicles for getting you out to the real Alaska.

Specifications

Size (in tons)		Crew	22
Adventurer	89*	Passenger/Crew Ratio	
Discoverer	95*	*Adventurer*	3.4 to 1
Passengers (double occ.)		*Discoverer*	3.9 to 1
Adventurer	63	Year Launched	
Discoverer	82	*Adventurer*	1984
Passenger/Space Ratio	N/A*	*Discoverer*	1992
Total Cabins/Veranda Cabins		Last Major Refurbishment	
Adventurer	32/0	*Adventurer*	2000
Discoverer	41/0	*Discoverer*	2001

* See note on p. 328 regarding small-ship tonnage and passenger/space measurements.

Frommer's Ratings (Scale of 1–5)   ★★★½

Cabin Comfort & Amenities	3	Dining Options	3
Ship Cleanliness & Maintenance	4	Adventure & Fitness Options	5
Public Comfort/Space	3	Children's Facilities	N/A
Decor	3	Enjoyment Factor	5

Wilderness Adventurer and *Wilderness Discoverer* were purchased from American Canadian Caribbean Line, where they sailed as the *Caribbean Prince* and *Mayan Prince,* respectively. Like all ACCL ships, they were built with an incredibly shallow draft that allows them to sail places other ships can't go. In addition, Glacier Bay has outfitted both vessels with a fleet of stable two-person sea kayaks and a dry-launch platform in the stern that allows passengers to take off right from the ship. Some other small-ship operators offer kayaking, but in every other instance they're launched from shore, and are not as high quality as the craft Glacier Bay uses. The downside to the ships' ACCL legacy is that that line has always made very spartan vessels, with bare-boned cabins and public areas. However, that doesn't matter to Glacier Bay passengers, who are looking for adventure, not cushy comfort. Tall passengers should note that ceilings are very low on these ships. If you're 6 feet 4 inches or more, you'll bump your head.

Cabins & Rates

Cabins	Per Diems from	Sq. Ft.	Fridge	Hair Dryer	Sitting Area	TV
Inside	$171	70	no	no	no	no
Outside	$228	77–196	no	no	some	some

CABINS *Basic* is the word. Though decor is pleasant enough, most of the cabins on these ships are just big enough for two to maneuver in simultaneously, and closet space is minimal (though there's more space under the beds). All AA- and A-class cabins (plus Deluxe cabins on the *Discoverer*) have picture windows, while cabins on the lower deck are smaller than the rest and have no closet, nightstand, or windows. Some AA cabins can accommodate a third person, albeit tightly. Bathrooms are referred to as "marine heads," meaning one little space with a toilet, a sink, and a shower head sticking out of the wall. In effect, the whole bathroom is the shower. Four "suites" on the *Wilderness Discoverer* offer a little more legroom, plus queen beds, TV/VCRs, and doors that open onto the Observation Deck. No cabins are wheelchair accessible.

PUBLIC AREAS The public rooms on both ships—the forward lounge and adjacent dining room—are similarly bare-boned but are lined with windows, so even at mealtimes you can keep watch for natural wonders. The lounges have TV/VCR setups and a selection of tapes, plus a small library, board games, and a 24-hour tea/coffee station. On both ships, prime outdoor viewing areas are in the bow and stern of the main deck and on the top deck (a portion of which is covered with a plastic tarp for viewing in rainy weather). These three spots are where passengers spend most of their time on board, making any deficiencies in the interior decor pretty much a moot point.

DINING OPTIONS Each ship has a single simple dining room able to serve all passengers comfortably.

ADVENTURE & FITNESS OPTIONS Each ship carries a fleet of sea kayaks and inflatable launches, and excursions using both are built into their itineraries, as are hikes in the rainforest. You can also walk laps around each ship's Sun Deck.

Executive Explorer

The Verdict

Glacier Bay's most comfortable ship, a speedy catamaran sailing to Alaska's large and small ports.

Executive Explorer *(photo: Glacier Bay)*

Specifications

Size (in tons)	98*	Crew	18
Passengers (double occ.)	49	Passenger/Crew Ratio	2.7 to 1
Passenger/Space Ratio	N/A*	Year Launched	1986
Total Cabins/Veranda Cabins	24	Last Major Refurbishment	2005

* See note on p. 328 regarding small-ship tonnage and passenger/space measurements.

Frommer's Ratings (Scale of 1–5)   ★★★½

Cabin Comfort & Amenities	3	Dining Options	3
Ship Cleanliness & Maintenance	4	Adventure & Fitness Options	2
Public Comfort/Space	3	Children's Facilities	N/A
Decor	3	Enjoyment Factor	4

Though she looks like a wedge of cheese as she steams through the Inside Passage, *Executive Explorer* is actually Glacier Bay's fastest and most comfortable vessel, a three-deck catamaran with comfortable cabins and spacious public rooms. A few years back we arrived in Ketchikan on another vessel just as *Executive Explorer* was getting ready to depart. Her passengers got on board, the captain started the engines, and zoom! she took off like a sports car and zipped out of sight. This is one speedy little boat.

Cabins & Rates

Cabins	Per Diems from	Sq. Ft.	Fridge	Hair Dryer	Sitting Area	TV
Outside	$330	120	no	no	no	no
Suite	$410	140	yes	no	yes	yes

CABINS The most comfortable cabins in the Glacier Bay fleet, though most are still pretty basic. All have large viewing windows, twin beds that can be converted to a double, and considerable closet space. Bathrooms are the same kind of head-style arrangements found on the line's other vessels (with the toilet essentially in the shower stall), with sinks out in the main part of the cabin. On the Upper Deck, two President's Staterooms face forward over the bow, just below the bridge, providing exceptional views, with two full walls of windows. Much larger than the other cabins on board, they're furnished with TV/DVD, a minifridge, queen-size bed, and larger closets. No cabins are wheelchair accessible.

PUBLIC AREAS   Like most small ships, *Executive Explorer* has only two public rooms, one comfortable main lounge right in the bow, with large windows all around, and one dining room. The lounge has a bar, a small library, board games, and a TV. An open top deck and a covered area on the middle deck are the best spots for wildlife viewing.

DINING OPTIONS   The single, simple dining room is able to serve all passengers comfortably.

ADVENTURE & FITNESS OPTIONS   *Executive Explorer* carries no fitness equipment and no kayaks, and due to her shape there are no wraparound outdoor decks on which to do laps.

Wilderness Explorer

The Verdict

Probably the most basic ship in this book, *Wilderness Explorer* also lives up to its name, offering itineraries that take passengers away from the things of man.

Wilderness Explorer *(photo: Glacier Bay)*

Specifications

Size (in tons)	98*	Crew	13
Passengers (double occ.)	31	Passenger/Crew Ratio	2.4 to 1
Passenger/Space Ratio	N/A*	Year Launched	1969
Total Cabins/Veranda Cabins	18/0	Last Major Refurbishment	N/A

* See note on p. 328 regarding small-ship tonnage and passenger/space measurements.

Frommer's Ratings (Scale of 1–5)   ★★★½

Cabin Comfort & Amenities	2	Dining Options	3
Ship Cleanliness & Maintenance	4	Adventure & Fitness Options	5
Public Comfort/Space	2	Children's Facilities	N/A
Decor	3	Enjoyment Factor	5

The tiny, 31-passenger *Wilderness Explorer,* which the line refers to as its "cruising base camp," offers the most active cruise experience available in Alaska, basically diving right into wilderness and staying there till it's time to go home. Cruises are structured so passengers are out hiking and sea kayaking most of each day, with the ship used only as a place to eat, sleep, and get from place to place. Only 1 day in the middle of each cruise is spent mostly aboard ship, with a brief stop at Glacier Bay Lodge. Like Glacier Bay's other ships, the *WEX* was built by Luther Blount's American Canadian Caribbean Line, way back in 1969—which makes it not only one of the smallest and most basic ships in this book, but one of the oldest. Blount sure does build tough boats.

Cabins & Rates

Cabins	Per Diems from	Sq. Ft.	Fridge	Hair Dryer	Sitting Area	TV
Outside	$244	48–216	no	no	no	no

CABINS   Tiny, tiny, tiny. All cabins feature upper and lower bunks, the same kind of head-style bathrooms as aboard the *Wilderness Adventurer* and *Discoverer,* and minimal storage space. Tiny windows in A-class cabins let in light but aren't much good for seeing the sights. AA-class cabins are one deck up and have more space and actual windows, while one 216-square-foot Deluxe cabin is located right behind the wheelhouse and has more space and windows at both port and starboard. One cabin is designated for solo passengers. No cabins are wheelchair accessible.

PUBLIC AREAS   The *WEX* has one lounge with a bar, 24-hour tea/coffee station, a shelf of books, and a TV/VCR. Though very small, it's pleasantly decorated, with a leather couch and a spinet piano for passenger use. While aboard, the topside Observation Deck gets a lot of use, and is partially covered for inclement weather.

DINING OPTIONS   One dining room and snacks in the lounge. What more do you want?

ADVENTURE & FITNESS OPTIONS   These cruises are based entirely around active adventure via sea kayaks and hiking. Inflatable launches are also carried on board.

9 Lindblad Expeditions

96 Morton St., New York, NY 10014. ℂ **800/397-3348** or 212/765-7740. Fax 212/265-3770. www.expeditions.com.

THE LINE IN A NUTSHELL   Lindblad Expeditions is one of the most adventure- and learning-oriented small-ship lines, offering itineraries that stay far away from the big ports, concentrating instead on wilderness and wildlife. **Sails to:** Alaska, Columbia and Snake rivers, Sea of Cortez/Baja, Central America (plus Europe, Arctic Norway, Antarctica, South America, Galapagos).

THE EXPERIENCE   Operating cruises worldwide for 25 years, Lindblad has a more international, professional feel than Glacier Bay Cruiseline, its main adventure competitor in Alaska, whose vibe is totally laid-back local. It's a similarly casual, jeans- and-fleece experience, though, and designed to appeal to the intellectually curious traveler seeking a vacation that's educational as well as relaxing. Your time is spent learning about the outdoors from high-caliber expedition leaders and guest scientists, many of them aboard as part of Lindblad's alliance with the National Geographic Society. Days are spent observing the world around you, either from the ship or on kayaking, motor-launch, and hiking excursions, which are included in the cruise price. Flexibility and spontaneity are key, with the captain able to alter his route at any time to follow a pod of whales or school of dolphins. Depending on weather and sea conditions, there are usually two or three excursions every day.

Pros

- **Great expedition feeling:** Lindblad's programs offer innovative, flexible itineraries, outstanding lecturers/guides, and a friendly, accommodating staff.
- **Alliance with National Geographic:** Beyond providing top-notch lecturers aboard ship, Lindblad's new relationship with the Geographic Society means its ships are actively engaged in scientific research, with passengers right in the thick of things.
- **Built-in shore excursions:** Lindblad programs its shore excursions as an integral part of its cruises, with all excursion costs included in the cruise fare. And they better be, because these trips are . . .

Cons

- **Very expensive:** Lindblad's cruise fares are among the highest in the small-ship market.

LINDBLAD: LEARNING CRUISES FOR THE WELL-HEELED

In 1984, Sven-Olof Lindblad, son of adventure-travel pioneer Lars-Eric Lindblad, followed in his father's footsteps by forming Lindblad Expeditions. From the beginning, the line has specialized in providing environmentally sensitive adventure/educational cruises to remote places in the world, with visits to a few large ports thrown in for good measure. In 2004, though, the company's commitment to true exploration went to a new level when it formed an alliance with the **National Geographic Society.** Beginning this year, NGS scientists, photographers, and film crews will sail aboard Lindblad's ships to both provide guests with an enhanced experience and to conduct actual research on sea and land. The line's most adventure-oriented vessel, the *Endeavour,* will be rechristened *National Geographic Endeavour* and be fitted with advanced research equipment, while an NGS advisory group that includes NGS explorer-in-residence Sylvia Earle will help develop research, conservation, and educational initiatives for the fleet.

The line's two Alaska ships, the identical, 70-passenger *Sea Bird* and *Sea Lion,* are like Glacier Bay's ships: more jeeps than sports cars, with small cabins and basic public areas. In addition to Alaska, these ships also sail Washington and Oregon's Columbia and Snake rivers and Mexico's Baja Peninsula. Another vessel, the 64-passenger *Sea Voyager,* is based in Central America and Baja year-round, while *National Geographic Explorer* sails many of the line's most exploratory sailings, occasionally sailing a single voyage through the Caribbean. In the Galapagos, Lindblad operates two vessels year-round, the 48-passenger *Islander* and the 80-passenger *Polaris.*

Compared with the other small-ship lines, here's how Lindblad rates:

	Poor	Fair	Good	Excellent	Outstanding
Enjoyment Factor					✓
Dining			✓		
Activities					✓
Children's Program	N/A				
Entertainment		✓			
Service				✓	
Worth the Money				✓	

Lindblad Expeditions Fleet Itineraries

Ship	Itineraries
Sea Bird/ Sea Lion	**Pacific Northwest (Columbia/Snake rivers):** Round-trip from Portland, OR, Oct 2005 and May and Sept–Nov 2006. **6-night 7-night Mexico Sea of Cortez:** Round-trip from La Paz, Baja California Sur, Jan–July 2006. **7-night Alaska Inside Passage:** North- or southbound between Juneau and Sitka, AK, May–Aug 2006.
Sea Voyager	**7-night Central America (several routes):** Round-trip from San Jose, Costa Rica, and north or southbound between San Jose and Panama City, Panama, Oct 2005– Apr 2006, July–Aug 2006, and Nov–Dec 2006.

PASSENGER PROFILE

Lindblad tends to attract well-traveled and well-educated professionals—usually age 55+ but often including a few younger couples and occasionally families—who are looking for an active, casual, up-close experience with their destinations. Most tend to be interested in wildlife (particularly whale- and bird-watching) and in the culture and history of the region they're visiting.

DINING

Hearty buffet breakfasts and lunches and sit-down dinners feature a good choice of hot and cold dishes, with the chef buying many of his fresh ingredients from ports along the way and many meals reflecting regional culture and tastes. Although far from haute cuisine, dinners are well prepared and presented and are served at single open seatings that allow passengers to get to know each other by moving around to different tables. Dinners may include entrees such as filet mignon, glazed shallots with red-wine sauce and giant scallops, and pasta primavera with spinach fettuccine. Lecturers and other staff members dine with passengers. **Vegetarian options** are available at every meal, and other special diets (low-fat, low-salt, kosher, and so forth) can be accommodated with advance notice. Weather permitting, *Sea Bird* and *Sea Lion* offer **deck barbecues** and sometimes **beach barbecues,** where permitted.

SNACKS & EXTRAS   Appetizers served in the late afternoon include items such as fruit and cheese platters, and baked brie with pecans and brown sugar.

ACTIVITIES

During the day, most activity takes place off the ship, aboard Zodiac boats and/or on land excursions. While on board, passengers entertain themselves with the usual small-ship activities: wildlife watching, reading, and engaging in conversation. Four to five **naturalists,** one historian, and an undersea specialist sail with each cruise (the most carried by any of the small-ship lines), presenting lectures and slide shows throughout each cruise and also leading guest exploration on shore. Many voyages also feature guest scientists, photographers, and lecturers from the **National Geographic Society.**

CHILDREN'S PROGRAM

There are no organized programs on regular cruises, but Lindblad does offer several family-oriented cruises every year in Alaska, Baja, and Central America, with a "Family Coordinator" providing learning activities for kids. Passengers under age 21 get 25% off the regular rates.

Lindblad Central America Cruises

In addition to the ships profiled here, Lindblad also operates the 64-passenger *Sea Voyager,* which sailed as the Temptress Adventures vessel *Temptress Voyager* before being acquired and refurbished by Lindblad in 2001. The vessels sail from Central American homeports most of the year, visiting Costa Rica and Panama and putting the emphasis on the region's jungle and marine life. Panama cruises also incorporate the history of the Canal. In spring the vessel sails in Mexico's Baja peninsula.

ENTERTAINMENT

Each evening the onboard naturalists lead discussions recapping the day's events, and, after dinner, documentary and feature films are occasionally screened in the main lounge. In some regions, local musicians come aboard from time to time to entertain. Books on nature and wildlife are available from each ship's small library.

SERVICE

Dining-room staff and room stewards are affable and efficient and seem to enjoy their work. As with other small ships, there's no room service unless you're ill and unable to make it to the dining room, and no laundry service.

Sea Lion • Sea Bird

The Verdict

Fairly utilitarian expedition vessels, *Sea Bird* and *Sea Lion* are designed to get you out into the wilderness, with naturalists aboard to teach you something about it too.

Sea Bird *(photo: Lindblad Expeditions)*

Specifications

Size (in tons)	100*	Passenger/Crew Ratio	3.2 to 1
Passengers (double occ.)	70	Year Launched	
Passenger/Space Ratio	N/A*	*Sea Lion*	1981
Total Cabins/Veranda Cabins	36/0	*Sea Bird*	1982
Crew	22	Last Major Refurbishment	N/A

* See note on p. 328 regarding small-ship tonnage and passenger/space measurements.

Frommer's Ratings (Scale of 1–5)   ★★★½

Cabin Comfort & Amenities	3	Dining Options	3
Ship Cleanliness & Maintenance	4	Adventure & Fitness Options	4
Public Comfort/Space	3	Children's Facilities	N/A
Decor	3	Enjoyment Factor	5

The shallow-draft *Sea Lion* and *Sea Bird* are identical twins, right down to their decor schemes and furniture. Unfancy, with just two public rooms and utilitarian cabins, they're very similar to several other small ships in this chapter, including the ACCL ships, Glacier Bay's *Wilderness Adventurer* and *Discoverer,* and Cruise West's *Spirit of Alaska.* As a matter of fact, *Spirit of Alaska* and the two Lindblad ships all sailed at one time for the now-defunct Exploration Cruise Lines.

Cabins & Rates

Cabins	Per Diems from	Sq. Ft.	Fridge	Hair Dryer	Sitting Area	TV
Outside	$356	95–110	no	no	some	no

CABINS   Postage-stamp cabins are tight and functional rather than fancy. No cabins are large enough to accommodate more than two, and each features twin or double beds, an adequate closet and drawers under the bed for extra storage, and a sink and mirror in the main room. Behind a folding door lies a Lilliputian bathroom with a head-style shower (toilet opposite the shower nozzle). All cabins have picture windows that open except the lowest-price cabins, which have small "portlights" that provide light but no view. Top-level cabins have a seating area. No cabins are wheelchair accessible.

PUBLIC AREAS   Public space is limited to an observation lounge that serves as the nerve center for activities, plus the open areas on the Sun Deck and in the bow. In the lounge, you'll find a bar and a library of atlases and books on Alaska's culture, geology, history, plants, and wildlife.

DINING OPTIONS   A single dining room serves all meals.

ADVENTURE & FITNESS OPTIONS   Each cruise involves frequent hikes in wilderness areas, accessed via Zodiac landing craft. You can also walk around the Upper Deck for exercise.

10 Maine Windjammer Association

P.O. Box 317, Augusta, ME 04332-0317. ✆ 800/807-WIND. www.sailmainecoast.com.

THE LINE IN A NUTSHELL   Actually, it's not a line. Unlike every other company in this book, the Maine Windjammer Association is instead a loose consortium of 14 privately owned classic schooners—some built as far back as 1871, some fairly new—that offer sail-powered summer trips along the gorgeous mid-Maine coast. It's the most natural cruise you'll ever take. **Sails to:** Mid-Maine coast.

THE EXPERIENCE   Let's take a poll: How many of you harried, cell-phone-toting, e-mail obsessed, 21st-century go-go types dream of going quietly off-line for a while, back to some kind of ideal summertime memory—you in a sailboat on the open water, cozy bunks and kerosene lamps at night, stars in the sky, and quiet all around? Aboard Maine's fleet of old-time schooners, that's exactly what you get, on mostly 3- to 6-night cruises that run from $395 to $875. With no engines (on most vessels), little electricity, and only the most basic accommodations, these ships offer their passengers the chance to get away for a few days of pure magic and a reminder that days don't all have to be rushed and multitasked. Days are filled with sailing and walks around quaint Maine towns, and evenings are pure serenity.

Pros

- **Off-the-grid experience:** You can hardly get away more than this, and with the ships relying almost exclusively on sail power (and policing what goes over the side pretty rigidly), it's an environmentally friendly way to cruise, too.
- **Relaxation in the pure sense of the word:** Passengers on these ships have no obligations and nothing to distract them from just sitting back and enjoying. The experience is casual all the way, and you and the crew will bond in no time.
- **Classic ships:** Some of the association's member vessels date from as far back as 1871, and fully half the fleet has been named to the National Register.
- **Gorgeous scenery:** The Penobscot Bay region is one of the most picturesque sailing grounds anywhere, made all the more gorgeous by other schooners off in the distance. It's a perfect match of vessel and venue, picking up where New England's great 19th-century whaling ships and cargo schooners left off.

Cons

- **Rustic accommodations:** Cabins are almost universally tiny, most with only rudimentary furniture and lighting. This is actually a plus for many passengers, who come seeking just that kind of experience.
- **Few private facilities:** Only nine cabins in the whole fleet have private toilets (known as "heads" in the windjammer world). Otherwise, ships have two or more shared toilets and showers.
- **Few activities:** Again, it's why a lot of people sign up, but if you need a lot of organized stimulation, look elsewhere.

MAINE WINDJAMMIN': A CURE FOR THE 50-HOUR WORKWEEK

It all began in the 1930s, decades after steamships had supplanted the schooners and other sail craft that had been the mainstay of commerce and transportation for centuries. In Maine, formerly one of the top boatbuilding regions of the country, the

Compared with the other small-ship lines, here's how the MWA rates:

	Poor	Fair	Good	Excellent	Outstanding
Enjoyment Factor					✓
Dining			✓*		
Activities			✓*		
Children's Program	N/A*				
Entertainment		✓*			
Service			✓*		
Worth the Money					✓*

* Since the Maine schooners are all owner-operated, programs vary significantly. These ratings should be taken as only a general indication of fleetwide quality. Ratings for "activities" and "entertainment" should be read in the spirit of these cruises, which are entirely outdoors-oriented, with few organized activities. There's also very little of what you'd traditionally call "service." If you want a drink, you bring it aboard yourself, and there's no cabin service unless something goes drastically wrong. Meals are often prepared by the same people who trim the sails. There are no real children's programs aboard any of these ships.

boats that had escaped the scrap yard were in danger of simply rotting away from despair and disuse. In 1936, though, Maine artist Frank Swift began offering pleasure cruises on one of the old vessels, confident that people would be glad to escape the bustle of modern life for a few days of relaxation and simple pleasures. As Swift later recalled of his first trip, "We had only three lady passengers from Boston. The next time, I believe, we took off without any passengers." But Swift didn't give up, and soon his trips were in such demand that over the next 3 decades he not only grew his fleet but also lured other captains into the business. By 1977, there were so many schooners operating in coastal Maine that it only made sense for them to pool their advertising and marketing dollars. And thus the Maine Windjammer Association was born. You can request information for all ships from the address and phone number above and get basic info on the individual schooners (and links to their Web pages) through the association website. Bookings must be made directly with the captain of each schooner. Full contact information for each is listed below.

PASSENGER PROFILE
The Maine Windjammers attract passengers of all ages, though most tend to fall between ages 30 and 80. Many are returning passengers who sail a particular schooner every year, often coordinating with other passengers they've met on previous trips. Many others are sailors themselves who enjoy helping out or taking a turn at the wheel. Most folks know the kind of experience they're signing on for, but first-timers often aren't quite prepared for just how rustic it can be. Bob Tassi, owner/captain of the schooner *Timberwind,* told us that, "initially, a lot of passengers experience some sense of shock, especially if they're not sailors and don't understand what a boat is. They have a romantic vision, and I think despite your best efforts to be honest with them—to say look, these are really small cabins—unless you've been on a boat you can't picture that. Something happens to you, though. You can see it in the eyes of people who get on the boat Sunday night and they're very anxious about the accommodations, and claustrophobia, and only two toilets, but then suddenly by Wednesday they almost transform. Where they were checking their messages and looking at cellphones, all of a sudden that stuff gets put away, and something gets inside of them, and they become windjammer people. Very few go away unhappy."

DINING
Meals on all the schooners are prepared on wood stoves in rustic galleys and served out on deck, picnic style. Expect traditional New England staples such as fresh seafood, chowder, roasts, Irish soda bread, and homemade ice cream. The cooks can accommodate vegetarian and some other special diets, but be sure to mention your needs when you book. At night, after dropping anchor, dinner is served by lantern light. Chances are, other schooners will be anchored not far away. You'll hear them off across the water, singing folk songs or saluting you with blasts from their tiny brass signal cannons. A few passengers or crew may even brave the frigid Maine water and swim over for a visit.

All the ships are BYOB, with coolers and ice provided if you've got beer to keep chilled. During the day, snacks are usually available in the galley. Once per cruise, most of the ships debark passengers onto a quiet, rocky beach for a traditional **lobster bake**—sometimes with champagne.

Maine Windjammer Association Fleet Itineraries

Ship	Itineraries
Entire fleet	**2- to 6-night Maine coastal cruises:** The whole fleet sails from Rockland, Rockport, and Camden, ME, late May through mid-Oct.

ACTIVITIES

An exact opposite of the typical cruise experience, the Maine schooners sail during the day and anchor in protected coves every night. In the evenings or mornings they'll often run a small boat to shore to allow passengers to explore small fishing towns and uninhabited islands. You can also see the sights at your port of embarkation, since all the schooners encourage guests to arrive a day before sailing and spend the night on board.

Many guests are either actual or wannabe sailors and enjoy the effort that goes into setting these rare seabirds to flight—hauling the sails, raising the centerboard, or hand-cranking the anchor from the bay's floor (the latter much harder than it looks—trust us). Otherwise, days aboard are totally unstructured, leaving guests free to talk ship with the captain, take a turn at the wheel, climb the rigging for a watchman's view, or simply read or stare out over the water, looking for seals, porpoises, puffins, and every once in a while a minke whale. An easy intimacy develops fast, and since the mid-Maine coast is a cruising paradise, passengers can expect to encounter any number of other schooners, sloops, and other sailcraft. Often, two or more ships will take each other on in an informal race.

CHILDREN'S PROGRAM

Many of the Maine Windjammers have restrictions on young children sailing aboard (see individual reviews below). Others accept children as young as 5, but there are no formal programs to keep them entertained. When we last sailed, a Texas couple was aboard with their 6-year-old daughter, who spent the week playing with the captain's young son. The schooner became a whole world to explore, the week an opportunity to use the imagination most kids cede to TV and video games.

ENTERTAINMENT

None to speak of, though many of the schooner captains and crew are musicians who may break out their instruments in the evening. Guests who play are encouraged to bring acoustic instruments.

SERVICE

Don't expect much. Crew aboard these ships are *really* crew—the folks who haul the sails and swab the decks. In their spare time they do the dishes, clean the shared restrooms, and mend what needs mending. The first mate might also be the cook (and, often enough, the spouse of the captain). For the most part, you're on your own.

American Eagle

American Eagle *(photo: Maine Windjammer Assoc.)*

Launched in 1930, *American Eagle* was a fishing schooner for 53 years before being refurbished for passenger sailing. She was named a National Historic Landmark in 1991 and is the only schooner in the area certified to sail internationally, enabling her to make annual cruises to Canada.

- **Ambience:** Quiet. There's often a cribbage game in the galley, and in the evening Capt. John Foss holds storytime, with pieces appropriate to the day's sights. Guests spend an hour a day on shore, minimum.
- **Cabins:** Cabins are fitted with hot and cold running water, reading lights, natural lighting, and some heat in the spring and fall.
- **Bathrooms/Showers:** Two shared heads below deck, each with a wash sink. One shower in the midships compartment.
- **Size:** 92 ft.
- **Passengers:** 26 (min. age 12).
- **Homeport:** Rockland.
- **Contact:** Captain John Foss, P.O. Box 482, Rockland, ME 04841. ✆ 207/594-8007; www.schooneramericaneagle.com.

Angelique

Angelique *(photo: Maine Windjammer Assoc.)*

Launched in 1980 for passenger sailing, she's the only non-schooner in the fleet, rigged instead as a gaff topsail ketch with distinctive dark-red sails.

- **Ambience:** Quiet, with no organized activities. There's music if someone brings aboard an instrument and isn't shy. (There's also a piano in the deckhouse salon.) Guests can go ashore both morning and evening if time allows.
- **Cabins:** Cabins have upper and lower bunks or double beds. All have running water and reading lights.
- **Bathrooms/Showers:** Three shared heads below deck, and three showers.
- **Size:** 95 ft.
- **Passengers:** 29 (min. age 12).

- **Homeport:** Camden.
- **Contact:** Yankee Packet Company, P.O. Box 736, Camden, ME 04843. © **800/282-9989;** www.sailangelique.com.

Grace Bailey

Grace Bailey *(photo: Maine Windjammer Assoc.)*

Launched in 1882, *Grace Bailey* came to Maine for cargo work in 1910. Designated a National Historic Landmark in 1990, she's won and placed multiple times in the Windjammer Association's annual Great Schooner Race.

- **Ambience:** Quiet, with no predetermined activities. There's music if any musicians are aboard (there's a piano in the after-cabin lounge). Guests can often go ashore in the mornings, with hiking time also available during the lobster bake on longer sailings.
- **Cabins:** Rustic cabins with upper and lower bunks, a water basin, and battery-powered lights.
- **Bathrooms/Showers:** Three shared heads below deck. One hot/cold freshwater shower.
- **Size:** 80 ft.
- **Passengers:** 29 (min. age 16, but younger teens can be accommodated with supervision).
- **Homeport:** Camden.
- **Contact:** Maine Windjammer Cruises, P.O. Box 617, Camden, ME 04843. © **800/736-7981;** www.mainewindjammercruises.com.

Heritage

Heritage *(photo: Maine Windjammer Assoc.)*

Built by her captains on a 19th-century model, *Heritage* was launched in 1983 for the Windjammer trade.

- **Ambience:** Flexible to whatever the group on board is interested in: singing, storytelling, games, piracy, and/or quiet. Guests are able to go ashore several times a week, as time permits.

- **Cabins:** Cabins have hot and cold running water and 12-volt cellphone charging outlets. Two cabins have private heads—talk about luxury!
- **Bathrooms/Showers:** Three shared heads. One hot/cold freshwater shower.
- **Size:** 95 ft.
- **Passengers:** 30 (min. age 12, but past guests may bring younger children).
- **Homeport:** Rockland.
- **Contact:** Schooner Heritage, P.O. Box 482, Rockland, ME 04841. ℘ **800/648-4544;** www.schoonerheritage.com.

Isaac H. Evans

Isaac H. Evans *(photo: Maine Windjammer Assoc.)*

Launched in 1886, the *Evans* spent 85 years working Delaware Bay as an oyster schooner before switching to passenger sailing in Maine. Named to the National Register, she's currently the only Maine schooner exclusively owned and operated by a woman.

- **Ambience:** Varies, with games, music, and activities programmed if passengers want them. Guests are able to go ashore at least once per day, sometimes twice. Some sailings are themed: on photography, hiking, knitting, etc.
- **Cabins:** Cabins have hot and cold running water, electric reading lights, windows for light and ventilation, and more than the average number of extras (soap, lotion, shampoo, and so on). Six cabins have double beds; the rest have upper and lower berths.
- **Bathrooms/Showers:** Two shared heads. One enclosed shower whose water is heated by the galley's wood stove.
- **Size:** 65 ft.
- **Passengers:** 22 (min. age 6, though younger children are sometimes considered).
- **Homeport:** Rockland.
- **Contact:** Capt. Brenda Walker, P.O. Box 791, Rockland, ME 04841. ℘ **877/238-1325;** www.midcoast.com/~evans.

J & E Riggin

J & E Riggin *(photo: Maine Windjammer Assoc.)*

Launched in 1927, *Riggin* worked as an oyster dredger before being rebuilt for passenger sailing in 1977. Known for her speed, she won the first and only oyster schooner race ever held on Delaware Bay, and has won the Great Schooner Race several times. She was named a National Historic Landmark in 1991.

- **Ambience:** Days are quiet, while nights usually see music, games, and storytelling. Guests can usually go ashore in the mornings for an hour or two. Co-captain Anne Mahle is known for her cooking, and has published a cookbook of the dishes served on board.
- **Cabins:** All cabins have quilts, reading lights, a porthole, and a sink with cold running water and handmade soap.
- **Bathrooms/Showers:** Two shared heads and one hot/cold shower, all on deck. **Size:** 89 ft.
- **Passengers:** 24 (min. age 12, but summer family cruises take kids as young as 6).
- **Homeport:** Rockland.
- **Contact:** Capt. Jon Finger and Anne Mahle, 136 Holmes St., Rockland ME 04841. ℂ **800/869-0604;** www.riggin.com.

Lewis R. French

Lewis R. French *(photo: Maine Windjammer Assoc.)*

Built in Maine in 1871, the *French* is the oldest schooner in the fleet (along with *Stephen Taber*) and the only Maine-built 19th-century schooner still in existence. She operated as a cargo schooner until 1971, after which she was converted for passengers and named to the National Register.

- **Ambience:** There are no planned events, leaving guests to make their own atmosphere. Guests can go ashore almost every day for 1 or 2 hours. Smoking is not allowed on board. Nor are cellphones, TVs, or loud radios.
- **Cabins:** Cabins have cold running water and a window for ventilation.
- **Bathrooms/Showers:** Two shared heads and one hot/cold freshwater shower, all on deck.
- **Size:** 64 ft.
- **Passengers:** 22 (min. age 16).
- **Homeport:** Camden.
- **Contact:** Capt. Garth Wells, P.O. Box 992, Camden, ME 04843. ℂ **800/469-4635;** www.schoonerfrench.com.

Mary Day

Mary Day *(photo: Maine Windjammer Assoc.)*

Launched in 1962, *Mary Day* was the first schooner built specifically as a windjammer and the first coastal schooner built in Maine since 1930.

- **Ambience:** Games and music are encouraged aboard *Mary Day*, with Captain Barry King often playing guitar. Guests are able to go ashore every day for an hour or more, and the weekly lobster bake allows for 3 hours ashore on a remote beach.
- **Cabins:** Cabins have cold running water, reading lights, skylights and windows, and unusually high headroom (9 ft. in most).
- **Bathrooms/Showers:** Two heads and two hot/cold showers, all on deck.
- **Size:** 90 ft.
- **Passengers:** 30 (min. age 15).
- **Homeport:** Camden.
- **Contact:** Schooner Mary Day, P.O. Box 798, Camden, ME 04843. ✆ **800/992-2218;** www.schoonermaryday.com.

Mercantile

Mercantile *(photo: Maine Windjammer Assoc.)*

Launched in 1916, *Mercantile* hauled cargo before Windjammer founder Frank Swift converted her for passengers in 1942. She was named a National Historic Landmark in 1990.

- **Ambience:** Onboard experience is tailored to the passengers aboard, with music and games offered if anyone's interested. When possible, guests can go ashore in the mornings, with hiking time available during the lobster bake (on longer sailings).
- **Cabins:** Rustic cabins with bunks, a water basin, and battery-powered lights.
- **Bathrooms/Showers:** Two heads below deck and a third in the galley/dining area. One hot/cold freshwater shower.
- **Size:** 78 ft.
- **Passengers:** 29 (min. age 16, but younger teens can be accommodated).
- **Homeport:** Camden.

- **Contact:** Maine Windjammer Cruises, P.O. Box 617, Camden, ME 04843. © 800/736-7981; www.mainewindjammercruises.com.

Mistress

Mistress *(photo: Maine Windjammer Assoc.)*

The smallest ship in the windjammer fleet, *Mistress* was launched in 1960 as a blend of traditional schooner and private yacht. A local blacksmith did all her ironwork, and much of her hardware was secured from an old-time ship's chandlery in Nova Scotia.

- **Ambience:** Onboard experience is tailored to the passengers, with music, games, and time ashore offered based on interest. Lobster bakes are included on 4- and 5-day cruises, with time for hiking.
- **Cabins:** Each of her 3 private cabins has its own head, sink, and private companionway from the deck. Two have double beds, the other upper and lower bunks.
- **Bathrooms/Showers:** Three private heads. One sun shower for impromptu washups during warm weather, plus stops at friendly B&Bs and inns, where passengers may use the showers.
- **Size:** 46 ft.
- **Passengers:** 6 (min. age 16 unless booking whole boat).
- **Homeport:** Camden.
- **Contact:** Maine Windjammer Cruises, P.O. Box 617, Camden, ME 04843. © 800/736-7981; www.mainewindjammercruises.com.

Nathaniel Bowditch

Nathaniel Bowditch *(photo: Maine Windjammer Assoc.)*

Built in East Boothbay, Maine, and launched in 1922 as a private racing yacht, *Bowditch* won class honors in the Bermuda Cup in the 1920s and during WWII was used by the Coast Guard for submarine surveillance. She fished the North Atlantic in the postwar years and was rebuilt for the passenger trade in the early 1970s.

- **Ambience:** Music is encouraged, and games and puzzles are kept in the galley for passenger use. Guests are able to go ashore most days. Quiet time is encouraged after 8pm.
- **Cabins:** Rustic cabins with either double or single beds, barrel water, and reading lights. Some cabins have skylights.
- **Bathrooms/Showers:** Three shared heads below deck. One hot/cold shower on deck, with a privacy curtain set up while the ship is at anchor.
- **Size:** 82 ft.
- **Passengers:** 24 (min. age 14, but designated family sailings accept kids as young as 5).
- **Homeport:** Rockland.
- **Contact:** Capt. Owen & Cathie Dorr, 4 Gay Pl., Rockland, ME 04841. ✆ **800/ 288-4098;** www.windjammervacation.com.

Stephen Taber

Stephen Taber *(photo: Maine Windjammer Assoc.)*

Like the *Lewis R. French, Stephen Taber* was built way back in 1871, and is the oldest sailing vessel in continuous service in the U.S. She hauled lumber, stone, and produce up and down the eastern seaboard for a full century, and is now listed on the National Register.

- **Ambience:** The *Taber* is known as a fun vessel, and a day's sail often ends with music and stories. Guests are able to go ashore once or twice daily, weather permitting. Operated by the same family for over a quarter century, the *Taber* is known for her food (former captain Ellen Barnes, mother of the current captain, has published many of their recipes in the cookbook *A Taste of the Taber*) and draws a huge number of repeat passengers—upwards of 70% on most sailings.
- **Cabins:** Cabins have running water, lights, windows, and enough head-room to stand and dress.
- **Bathrooms/Showers:** Two shared heads and one hot-water shower, all on deck.
- **Size:** 68 ft.
- **Passengers:** 22 (min. age 14).
- **Homeport:** Rockland.
- **Contact:** Capt. Noah Barnes, Windjammer Wharf, P.O. Box 1050, Rockland, Maine 04841. ✆ **800/999-7352;** www.mainewindjammers.com.

Timberwind

Timberwind *(photo: Maine Windjammer Assoc.)*

Built in Portland, Maine, in 1931, *Timberwind* spent the first 38 years of her life stationed 18 miles off Portland Head, taking pilots to meet large ships and navigate them in. She was converted for passenger sailing in 1969 and designated a National Historic Landmark in 1992. She's one of the most rustic vessels in the fleet.

- **Ambience:** Quiet, with days spent sailing and guests able to go ashore most days for 1 to 3 hours. Music-lovers might be particularly interested in this vessel since her owner, Capt. Bob Tassi, was a Nashville studio engineer before chucking it all to become a schoonerman. Evenings frequently find him on guitar, and a framed portrait of Frank Sinatra graces the rustic galley.
- **Cabins:** Tiny varnished-wood cabins have small electric lights but do without running water (instead, there's an enamel basin, a stack of towels, and a small oak water barrel). Beds are either bunks or doubles.
- **Bathrooms/Showers:** Two shared heads below deck. One on-deck shower with privacy curtain.
- **Length:** 70 ft.
- **Passengers:** 20 (min. age 5).
- **Homeport:** Rockport.
- **Contact:** Schooner Timberwind, PO. Box 247, Rockport, ME 04856. © **800/ 759-9250;** www.schoonertimberwind.com.

Victory Chimes

Victory Chimes *(photo: Maine Windjammer Assoc.)*

Launched in 1900, *Victory Chimes* is the largest U.S.-flagged commercial sailing vessel and the only classic three-masted schooner still operating. Her image adorns the back of the Maine State Quarter, minted in 2003.

- **Ambience:** There are no scheduled activities, though music and games often break out. Guests can go ashore in the morning and evening every day for 1 to 2 hours.

- **Cabins:** Cabins have bunk beds, portholes, 110-volt outlets, reading lights, and sinks with hot and cold running water. Most have upper and lower berths. There are also 3 single cabins, 1 cabin with twin beds, 1 that sleeps 4, and 4 cabins with double beds and private toilets.
- **Bathrooms/Showers:** Three shared heads (two on deck, one below). Two showers.
- **Size:** 132 ft.
- **Passengers:** 40 (min. age 10).
- **Homeport:** Rockland.
- **Contact:** Victory Chimes, P.O. Box 1401, Rockland, ME 07841. 𝒞 **800/745-5651;** www.victorychimes.com.

11 Mini-Review: RiverBarge Excursions

201 Opelousas Ave., New Orleans, LA 70114. 𝒞 **888/282-1945.** Fax 504/365-0000. www.riverbarge.com.

THE LINE IN A NUTSHELL   Barging vacations have grown in popularity over the last 3 decades, especially in England and Continental Europe, and now the concept is available in the U.S. through RiverBarge Excursions, a company created by New Orleans towboat and barge owner Eddie Conrad. Sailing year-round, the company's 198-passenger *River Explorer* navigates the waterways of the Midwest and the South, visiting riverfront cities such as Memphis, St. Louis, Cincinnati, and New Orleans. Itineraries are both cheaper and more inclusive than those of their main competitor, the Delta Queen Steamboat Company. **Sails to:** U.S. river cruises.

THE EXPERIENCE   Built in 1998, the *River Explorer* is actually three different vessels lashed together like train cars. A towboat (the *Miss Nari*) is the rig's engine, with two three-deck hotel barges behind: the *DeSoto* for the cabin accommodations and the *LaSalle* housing the public spaces. The complete vessel has a length of 730 feet and a width of 54 feet, sized to fit into the locks of the Intracoastal Waterway. The interior design is spacious, modern in decor, and features huge windows for viewing the passing riverscape. The favorite perch is the Guest Pilot House, a forward-facing observation lounge with charts to study and communications between river pilots to listen to. The *River Explorer*'s actual navigating pilot is one deck above, and visitors are welcome to drop in, but only when the barge is tied up. The Lobby, aft of the Guest Pilot House, provides lounge and banquette seating. Etched glass panels decorate the seatbacks, depicting river bridges. A midships lounge known as the Governor Galvez Room has books and videos for passenger use and board games and cards to enjoy at three octagonal tables. The Sprague, the two-level show lounge, is the setting for storytelling, local entertainment, and bingo.

The Galley, a huge light-filled space on the lowest passenger deck, serves all meals. Breakfast is a buffet, with omelets to order, and the buffet lunch (called "dinner" here) offers hot and cold selections, with dishes such as catfish and shrimp reflecting the cruising region. Dinner ("supper") has traditional table service and includes an appetizer, soup, salad, choice of two or three entrees, and freshly baked cakes and pies. Preparation is consistently good, and regular menu items are typical Middle American.

Cabins are named after states and arranged in order of their entry into the Union. The square footage is generous, and while all have the same layout, the upper deck rooms have narrow balconies. Large picture windows slide open, and amenities include twin or queen-size beds, TV/VCR, fridge, desk, two chairs, and decent hanging and drawer space. All bathrooms have full tubs and showers.

RiverBarge Excursions Fleet Itineraries

Ship	Itineraries
River Explorer	**3- to 9-night River Cruises:** Sailings available year-round on the Mississippi, Atchafalaya, Illinois, Ohio, Cumberland, and Tennessee rivers and the Intracoastal Waterway paralleling the Gulf of Mexico, sailing from Cincinnati, OH; Galveston and Port Isabel, TX; St. Louis, MO; Louisville, KY; Memphis and Nashville, TN; and New Orleans, LA.

Covered and open outdoor deck space stretches nearly the complete length of the top deck. There's bar service up here, and hot and cold hors d'oeuvres are served before dinner.

Weeklong itineraries tend to start around $2,200 per person, give or take $100 to $300, depending on season.

12 Mini-Review: Sea Cloud Cruises

32–40 N. Dean St., Englewood, NJ 07631. ℂ **888/732-2568** or 201/227-9404. Fax 201/227-9424. www.sea cloud.com.

THE LINE IN A NUTSHELL   Germany-based Sea Cloud Cruises caters to a well-traveled clientele looking for a deliciously exotic five-star sailing adventure, and an international one too: Typical Caribbean cruises draw about 30% American passengers, 30% German, 20% British, and the rest from elsewhere in Europe. A trip aboard one of the line's sailing ships—the antique *Sea Cloud* or the modern replica *Sea Cloud II*—will spoil small-ship lovers forever. **Sails to:** Caribbean (plus Europe).

THE EXPERIENCE   In 1931, Wall Street tycoon E. F. Hutton commissioned construction of the four-masted sailing ship *Hussar* from the Krupp family shipyard in Kiel, Germany. Outfitting of her interior was left to Hutton's wife, heiress and businesswoman Marjorie Merriweather Post, who spent 2 years on the task, eventually drafting a full-scale diagram showing every detail of her design, down to the placement of antiques. After the couple's divorce, Post renamed the vessel *Sea Cloud* and sailed her to Leningrad, where second husband Joseph E. Davies was serving as U.S. ambassador. WWII saw the vessel commissioned to the U.S. Navy, which removed her masts and used her as a floating weather station. After the war the vessel went though numerous hands: first back to Post, then to Dominican dictator Rafael Leonidas Trujillo Montinas, then to a number of American owners before she was finally purchased by German economist and seaman Hartmut Paschberg. A lover of great ships, Paschberg and a group of Hamburg investors put up the money for an 8-month overhaul that restored *Sea Cloud*'s original grandeur, full of marble, gold, and mahogany detailing. Today the ship offers cabins for 64 passengers, the luckiest (and richest) of whom can stay in Post's own museum-like suite, with its Louis XIV–style bed and nightstands, marble fireplace and bathroom, chandeliers, and intricate moldings. The other original suites are similarly if less sumptuously furnished. Standard cabins are comfortable but lack the suites' time-machine quality. Still, everyone aboard gets to enjoy a taste of the past in the main restaurant, with its dark-wood paneling, brass trimmings, and nautical paintings.

Sea Cloud Fleet Itineraries

Ship	Itineraries
Sea Cloud & Sea Cloud II	**6- to 13-night E. & S. Carib:** Several different itineraries from island home ports, Dec 2005–Apr 2006 and Nov 2006–Apr 2007.

On the larger *Sea Cloud II,* an elegant lounge is designed with rich mahogany woodwork, ornate ceiling moldings, leather club couches, and overstuffed bucket chairs. *Cloud II* has several opulent suites, one with burled wood paneling and a canopy bed. Otherwise, on both ships, the standard cabins are very comfortable, but ordinary in comparison. Those on *II* have small sitting areas, and all cabins have marble bathrooms with showers, TV/VCRs, telephones, safes, hair dryers, and bathrobes.

The dining room on each ship accommodates all guests in a single, open seating, and fine wines and beer are complimentary at lunch and dinner. Breakfast and some lunches are offered buffet style, while the more formal dinners are served on elegant candlelit tables set with white linens, china, and silver. Most men wear jackets nightly, though the 2 formal nights on each cruise are not black-tie affairs—jackets and ties work just fine. Most cruises also feature a barbecue night out on deck.

These being small sailing ships, organized activities are few; it's the ships themselves that entertain, and watching the crew work the riggings, plus visits to less-touristed ports such as Les Saintes, Dominica, Bequia, Mayreau, Tobago, and St. Barts. Only 1 day of each cruise is spent at sea. Outside decks of both ships are covered with lines, winches, cleats, brass compasses, wooden deck chairs, and other shippy accouterments, providing a wonderfully nostalgic and nautical setting, and a **sailing class** is offered on every cruise. *Cloud II* also has a library, a small gym, and a swimming platform. Evenings may include piano music and mingling over cocktails. Other occasional activities may include talks by resident guest lecturers; local musicians who come aboard for a few hours; and **"open houses,"** where guests enjoy champagne and caviar on the Main Deck before touring each other's cabins (with the residents' permission, of course).

Weeklong *Sea Cloud* cruises in the Caribbean run from $3,720 to $7,559. Sailings aboard *Sea Cloud II* run from $3,786 to $6,812.

THE FLEET The two *Clouds* are closest in look and style to Star Clippers' tall ships, though smaller and more upscale. The 64-passenger, 2,532-ton, four-masted *Sea Cloud* (1931) is in a class by itself, while its newer incarnation, 94-passenger, 3,849-ton, three-masted schooner *Sea Cloud II* (2001), is a wonderful copy.

The company's other vessels, 90-passenger *River Cloud I* (1996) and 88-passenger *River Cloud II* (2001), traverse the rivers of Europe.

13 Star Clippers

4101 Salzedo Ave., Coral Gables, FL 33146. ✆ **800/442-0551** or 305/442-0550. Fax 305/442-1611. www.star clippers.com.

THE LINE IN A NUTSHELL It doesn't get much better than this if you appreciate tall ships. With the sails and rigging of classic clipper ships and some of the cushy amenities of modern megas, a cruise on this line's 170- to 228-passenger beauties spells adventure and comfort. **Sails to:** Caribbean (plus Asia and Europe).

THE EXPERIENCE The more ships we've sailed on, the more Star Clippers stock goes up. Few other lines offer the best of two worlds in such an appealing package. On the one hand, the ships offer comfortable, almost cushy public rooms and cabins. On the other, they espouse an unstructured, let-your-hair-down, hands-on ethic— you can climb the masts (with a harness, of course), help raise the sails, crawl into the bow netting, or chat with the captain on the open-air bridge.

On board, ducking under booms, stepping over coils of rope, leaning against railings just feet above the sea, and watching sailors work the winches are constant reminders that you're on a real working ship. Furthermore, listening to the captain's daily talk about the next port of call, the history of sailing, or some other nautical subject, you'll feel like you're exploring some of the Caribbean's more remote stretches in a ship that really belongs there—an exotic ship for an exotic locale. In a sea of look-alike megaships, *Star Clipper* and newer *Royal Clipper* stand out, recalling a romantic, swashbuckling era of ship travel.

Pros

- **Hands-on experience:** You never have to lift a finger if you don't want to, but if you do, you're free to help out.
- **Comfortable amenities:** Pools, a piano bar and deck bar, a bright and pleasant dining room serving tasty food, and a clubby, wood-paneled library balance out the swashbuckling spirit. *Royal Clipper* also boasts a gym, a small spa, and marble bathrooms.
- **Rich in atmosphere:** On these ships, the ambience is a real treat.
- **Offbeat itineraries:** Itineraries take passengers to remote places such as the Grenadines and French West Indies.

Cons

- **No fitness equipment on *Star Clipper*:** The newer *Royal Clipper* has a fitness center, but on *Star Clipper* you're out of luck for anything but a massage.

STAR CLIPPERS: COMFY ADVENTURE

Clipper ships—full-sailed, built for speed, and undeniably romantic—reigned for only a brief time on the high seas before being driven out by steam engines and iron (and then steel) hulls. During their heyday, however, these vessels, including famous names such as *Cutty Sark, Ariel,* and *Flying Cloud,* engendered more romantic myths than any before or since, and helped open the Pacific Coast of California during the gold rush of 1849, carrying much-needed supplies around the tip of South America from Boston and New York.

Compared with the other small-ship lines, here's how Star Clippers rates:

	Poor	Fair	Good	Excellent	Outstanding
Enjoyment Factor					✓
Dining				✓	
Activities				✓	
Children's Program	N/A				
Entertainment			✓		
Service				✓	
Worth the Money					✓

By the early 1990s, despite the nostalgia and sense of reverence that had surrounded every aspect of the clippers' maritime history, nothing that could be technically classified as a clipper ship had been built since *Cutty Sark* in 1869. Enter Mikael Krafft, a Swedish-born industrialist and real-estate developer with a passion for ship design and deep, deep pockets, who invested vast amounts of personal energy and more than $80 million to build *Star Flyer* and *Star Clipper* at a Belgian shipyard in 1991 and 1992.

To construct these 170-passenger twins, Krafft procured the original drawings and specifications of Scottish-born Donald McKay, a leading naval architect of 19th-century clipper-ship technology, and employed his own team of naval architects to solve such engineering problems as adapting the square-rigged, four-masted clipper design to modern materials and construction. In mid-2000, Krafft went a step further, launching the 228-passenger *Royal Clipper*, a five-masted, fully rigged sailing ship inspired by the famed *Preussen*, a German clipper built in 1902. The *Royal Clipper* now claims the title of the largest clipper ship in the world, and she's a stunning sight.

When compared with Windjammer Barefoot Cruises, which operates original (if modernized) sailing ships, and Windstar Cruises, which operates less authentic electronically controlled sailing ships, Star Clippers is smack dab in the middle—more luxurious and a bit more expensive than the bare-boned, no-frills Windjammer and less formal and expensive than Windstar (though the posh *Royal Clipper* gets pretty close to Windstar level). Overall, the experience is quite casual, and salty enough to make you feel like a fisherman keeling off the coast of Maine, without the physical hardship of actually being one. As Krafft put it on one sailing, "If you want a typical cruise, you're in the wrong place."

All the Star Clippers vessels are at once traditional and radical. They're the tallest and among the fastest clipper ships ever built, and are so beautiful that even at full stop they seem to soar. As opposed to ships such as Windstar's *Wind Surf*, a bulkier cruise vessel that just happens to have sails, Star Clippers' ships do generally rely on sails alone for about 25% to 35% of the time; the rest of the time, the sails are used with the engines. Each ship performs superlatively—during *Star Clipper*'s maiden sail in 1992 off the coast of Corsica, she sustained speeds of 19.4 knots, thrilling her owner and designers, who had predicted maximum speeds of 17 knots. The *Royal Clipper* was designed to make up to 20 knots under sail (14 max under engine alone), and on a recent cruise, she easily hit 15 knots one afternoon. During most cruises, however, the crew tries to keep passengers comfortable and decks relatively horizontal, so the vessels are kept to speeds of 9 to 14 knots with a combination of sail and engine power.

PASSENGER PROFILE

With no more than 228 passengers aboard the largest ship in the fleet, each Star Clippers cruise seems like a triumph of individuality and intimacy. The line's unusual niche appeals to passengers who might recoil at the lethargy and/or sometimes forced enthusiasm of cruises aboard larger, more typical vessels. Overall, the company reports that a whopping 60% of passengers on average are repeaters back for another Star Clippers cruise.

While you're likely to find a handful of late-20-something honeymoon-type couples and an extended-family group or two, the majority of passengers are well-traveled couples in their 40s to 60s, all active and intellectually curious professionals (such as executives, lawyers, and doctors) who appreciate a casual yet sophisticated ambience and enjoy mixing with fellow passengers. During the day, polo shirts, shorts, and topsiders are standard issue; and for dinner, many passengers simply change into cleaner and better-pressed versions of the same, with perhaps a switch from shorts to slacks for most men. However, men in jackets and women in snazzy dresses aren't uncommon on the night of the captain's cocktail party.

With a nearly even mix of North Americans and Europeans (most often from Germany, Austria, Switzerland, France, and the U.K.) on a typical Caribbean cruise, the international onboard flavor is as intriguing as the ship itself. Announcements are made in English, German, and French.

DINING

Although the quality can still be inconsistent, Star Clippers' cuisine has evolved and improved over the years as the line has poured more time and effort into it, with an enhanced menu that includes four well-presented entree choices at each evening meal. All meals are open seating, with tables for four, six, and eight in the restaurant; the dress code is always casual (though some guests don jackets on the night of the captain's cocktail party). Breakfast and lunch are served buffet style and are the best meals of the day. The continental cuisine reflects the line's large European clientele and is dominated at breakfast and lunch by cheeses (such as brie, French goat cheese, and smoked Gouda), as well as marinated fish and meats. Breakfasts also include a hot-and-cold buffet spread and an omelet station, where a staff member will make your eggs the way you like them. Late-afternoon snacks served at the Tropical Bar include such munchies as crudités, cheeses, and chicken wings.

Dinners consist of appetizers, soup, salad, dessert, and a choice of five main entree choices: seafood (such as lobster and shrimp with rice pilaf), meat (beef curry, for example), vegetarian, a chef's special, and a light dish. Dinner choices such as fusilli in a tomato sauce, grilled Norwegian salmon, and herb-crusted rack of lamb are tasty, but tend toward the bland side. Most dinners are sit-down (as opposed to the occasional buffet spread up on deck), and service can feel a bit rushed and frenetic during the dinner rush. Breakfast and lunch don't get as crowded because passengers tend to eat at staggered times. Waiters and bartenders are efficient and friendly, and depending on the cruise director, often dress in costume for several theme nights each week.

A worthwhile selection of wines is available on board, with a heavy emphasis on medium-priced French, German, and California selections.

SNACKS & EXTRAS   Coffee and tea are available from a 24-hour coffee station in the piano bar. On *Star Clipper,* room service is available only for guests who are sick and can't make it to the dining room; on *Royal Clipper,* passengers staying in the 14 suites and Owner's Suites get 24-hour room service.

Built for Speed

Every other week, when *Royal Clipper* and *Star Clipper* itineraries overlap off the coast of Dominica and the wind is favorable, the ships engage in a race under sail alone. It's great fun (and a great photo op) to watch the captain running energetically around the bridge, barking orders to the staff. A small but really loud minicannon is fired to start the race, and then each ship blasts her horn three times, whipping passengers into a competitive frenzy. Not to handicap the race too much, but the larger and more powerful *Royal Clipper* usually ends up the winner—on a recent cruise, she hit 14.5 knots while doing so.

ACTIVITIES

If you want action, shopping, and dozens of organized tours, you won't find much of what you're looking for on these ships and itineraries—in fact, their absence is a big part of the line's allure. For the most part, enjoying the experience of being on a sailing ship and socializing with fellow passengers and crewmembers is the main activity, as it is on most any ship this size. Plus, the ships are in port every single day, so boredom is not an issue.

The friendliness starts at the get-go, with smiling waitstaff offering guests complimentary fruit drinks as they board. Throughout the cruise, the captain gives **informal talks** on maritime themes, and, at least once a day, the cruise director speaks about the upcoming ports and shipboard events (though port info may not be as in-depth as you'd expect; on a recent *Royal Clipper* cruise, the cruise director provided only very scant information). Within reason, passengers can lend a hand with deck duties, observe the mechanics of navigation, **climb the masts** (at designated times and with a safety harness), and have a token try at handling the wheel when circumstances and calm weather permit. Each ship maintains an **open-bridge policy,** allowing passengers to wander up to the humble-looking navigation center at any hour of the day or night (you may have to ask to actually go into the chart room, though).

Other activities may include a brief engine-room tour, morning exercise classes on deck, excursions via tender to photograph the ship under sail, in-cabin movies, and hanging out by the pools (three on *Royal Clipper,* two on *Star Clipper*). Of course, sunbathing is a sport in and of itself. Best spot for it? In the bowsprit netting, hanging out over the water. It's sunny, it's a thrill in itself, and it's the perfect place from which to spot dolphins in the sea just feet below you, dancing in the bow's wake. Massages are available on both ships, too, at a reasonable $65 an hour: On *Star Clipper,* they're doled out in a spare cabin or a small cabana on deck; Royal has a dedicated massage room, divided into two areas by a curtain. The *Royal Clipper* also has a small gym.

Port activities are a big part of these cruises. Sailing from one island to another and often arriving at the day's port of call sometime after 9am (but usually before 11am, and usually after a brisk early-morning sail), the ships either dock alongside the shore right in town or anchor offshore and shuttle passengers back and forth by tender. On many landings, you'll have to walk a few feet in shallow water between the tender and the beach.

Activities in port revolve around beaches and watersports, and all are complimentary. That's partly because owner Mikael Krafft is an avid scuba diver and partly because itineraries focus on waters that teem with marine life; each ship offers (for an extra charge) the option of PADI-approved **scuba diving.** Certified divers will find all the equipment they'll need on board. Even uncertified/inexperienced divers can pay a fee for scuba lessons that will grant them resort certification and allow them to make a number of relatively simple dives (on every sailing there's a certified diver on the watersports staff). There's also snorkeling (complimentary equipment is distributed at the start of the cruise), water-skiing, windsurfing, sailing, and banana-boat rides offered by the ship's watersports team in all ports. The ships carry along Zodiac motorboats for this purpose, and *Royal Clipper* has a retractable marina at its stern for easy access to the water. Because there are few passengers on board and everything is so laid back, no sign-up sheets are needed for these activities; guests merely hang out by the gangway or on the beach until it's their turn.

Star Clippers Fleet Itineraries

Ship	Itineraries
Royal Clipper	**7-night S. Carib:** Round-trip from Barbados, Nov 2005–Apr 2006 and Nov–Dec 2006.
Star Clipper	**7-night E. Carib:** Round-trip from St. Martin, Nov 2005–Apr 2006 and Nov–Dec 2006.

Ships tend to depart from their ports early so that they can be under full sail during sunset. Trust us on this one: Position yourself at the ship's rail or dawdle over a drink at the deck bar to watch the sun melt into the horizon behind the silhouetted ships' masts and ropes. It's something you won't forget.

CHILDREN'S PROGRAM

An experience aboard a sailing ship can be a wonderfully educational and adventurous experience, especially for self-reliant children who are at least 10 years old. That said, this is not generally a line for young kids (though the line has no age restrictions, with no supervised activities and no babysitting unless a well-intentioned crewmember agrees to volunteer his or her off-duty hours). The exception is during holiday seasons such as Christmas, when families are accommodated and some children's activities are organized by the watersports staff, including treasure hunts, beach games, and arts and crafts.

ENTERTAINMENT

Some sort of featured entertainment takes place each night after dinner by the Tropical Bar, which is the main hub of activity on both ships. There's a crew talent show one night that's always a big hit with passengers; other nights may offer a trivia contest, dance games, or a performance by local entertainers (such as a steel-drum band) who come on board for the evening. A keyboard player is on hand to sing pop songs before and after dinner, but the twangy renditions of tunes such as "Chattanooga Choo Choo" and "Day-O" don't really fit in with the ships' otherwise rustic ambience. Most nights, disco music is put on the sound system and a section of the deck serves as an impromptu dance floor, with the action usually quieting down by about 1am.

You can borrow DVDs from the library or watch the movies that are shown each day on cabin TVs in English, German, and French if you feel like vegging. Besides that, it's just you, the sea, and conversation with your fellow passengers.

SERVICE

Service is congenial, low-key, unpretentious, cheerful, and reasonably attentive. During busy times, expect efficient but sometimes distracted service in the dining rooms; and during your time on deck, realize that you'll have to fetch your own bar drinks and whatever else you may need. *Royal Clipper* has a second bar on the top deck adjacent to the pools, but even on *Star Clipper,* you're never more than a 30-second walk from a cool drink.

The crew is international, hailing from Poland, Switzerland, Russia, Germany, Romania, Indonesia, the Philippines, and elsewhere, and their presence creates a wonderful international flavor on board. Crewmembers are friendly and usually good-natured about passengers who want to help with the sails, tie knots, and keep the deck shipshape. Because English is not the mother language of some crewmembers, though, certain details may get lost in the translation.

Officers, the cruise director, and the watersports team may dine with passengers during the week, and if you'd like to have dinner with the captain, just go up to the bridge one day and ask; he may oblige you (it depends on the captain). Unlike a lot of other small-ship lines, Star Clippers has a nurse aboard all sailings. **Laundry service** is available on both ships; *Royal Clipper* also offers dry cleaning.

Royal Clipper

The Verdict

This stunning, fully rigged, five-masted, square-sail clipper is a sight to behold; and the interior amenities, from marble bathrooms to an Edwardian-style three-level dining room, are the company's most plush.

Royal Clipper *(photo: Star Clippers)*

Specifications

Size (in tons)	5,000	Crew	105
Passengers (double occ.)	228	Passenger/Crew Ratio	2.2 to 1
Passenger/Space Ratio	22	Year Launched	2000
Total Cabins/Veranda Cabins	114/14	Last Major Refurbishment	N/A

Frommer's Ratings (Scale of 1–5)   ★★★★

Cabin Comfort & Amenities	4	Dining Options	4.5
Ship Cleanliness & Maintenance	5	Adventure & Fitness Options	4
Public Comfort/Space	4	Children's Facilities	N/A
Decor	3	Enjoyment Factor	5

Clipper's biggest and poshest ship to date—and at 439 feet in length, one of the largest sailing ships ever built—the 5,000-ton, 228-passenger *Royal Clipper* boasts more luxurious amenities than the line's older ships, including marble bathrooms, roomier cabins, a small gym and spa, and three pools. In fact, the ship even gives the somewhat tired-looking 15+-year-old Windstar ships a run for their money in the amenities department, while still offering a more rustic ambience. With five masts flying 42 sails that together stretch to 56,000 square feet, *Royal Clipper* is powerful too, able to achieve 20 knots under sail power only, and 14 knots under engine power. (Still, as on *Star Clipper*, the sails are more for show, and typically the engines are also in use 60%–80% of the time, especially at night.) Engines or not, for true sailors and wannabes, the web of ropes and cables stretched between *Royal Clipper's* sails, masts, and deck—along with the winches, *Titanic*-style ventilators, brass bells, wooden barrels, and chunky anchor chains cluttering the deck—are constant and beautiful reminders that you're on a real ship. So are the creaking, rolling, and pitching.

The bottom line: This ship is a big winner for those who like the good life, but in a gloriously different way than any mainstream megaship could ever offer.

Cabins & Rates

Cabins	Per Diems from	Sq. Ft.	Fridge	Hair Dryer	Sitting Area	TV
Inside	$254	113	no	yes	no	yes
Outside	$300	148	no	yes	no	yes
Suite	$543	255–320	yes	yes	no	yes

CABINS   The ship's 114 cabins are gorgeous and roomy, done up in a nautical motif with navy-blue and gold fabrics and dark-wood paneling. All but six are outsides with portholes and measure some 20 to 30 feet larger than cabins aboard *Star Clipper;* they're equivalent in size to the standard cabins on many Royal Caribbean and Norwegian Cruise Line ships, though they're about 40 square feet smaller than Windstar cabins. (On the other hand, they're about 50 sq. ft. larger than the typical cabins on Windjammer's ships.) Bathrooms are marble in all but the six inside cabins, and all have brass and chrome fittings and plenty of elbowroom, as well as brass lighting fixtures, a vanity/desk, hair dryer, safes, telephones, and TVs with DVD players. One problem: There are no full-length closets in the cabins—but then again, who's bringing an evening gown?

Some 22 cabins on the Main and Clipper decks have a pull-down third berth, but unfortunately it's only about 2 feet above the beds, so even when folded up, it juts out enough so that you can't sit up in bed without bumping your head.

Six tight 113-square-foot inside cabins on the Clipper Deck (category 6) and four outside cabins in the narrow forward section of the bow on the Commodore Deck (category 5) tend to be the best cabin bargains, if you're looking to save a buck. (See chapter 2, "Booking Your Cruise & Getting the Best Price," for more information about cabin categories.)

The 14 Deluxe Suites located forward on the Main Deck are exquisite, with private balconies, sitting areas, minibars, and whirlpool tubs. The Main Deck also has two Owner's Suites measuring 355 square feet; they're connectable, so you could conceivably book them together to create a 710-square-foot suite. Each boasts a pair of double beds, a sitting area, a minibar, and—count 'em—two marble bathrooms. Neither suite has a balcony. Suite guests get 24-hour butler service.

There are no connecting cabins, nor any wheelchair-accessible cabins.

PUBLIC AREAS   *Royal Clipper* is like no other small sailing ship we've ever set foot on, with a three-level atrium and frilly multilevel dining room that are more like what you'd find on a much larger ship. Like the cabins, the decor of the ship's main lounge, library, and corridors follows a strong nautical thread, with navy-blue and gold upholstery and carpeting complementing dark-wood paneling.

The open-air Tropical Bar, with its long marble and wood bar, is the hub of evening entertainment and pre-dinner hors d'oeuvres and drinks, while the more elegant piano lounge just inside hosts the weekly captain's cocktail party. (As on *Star Clipper,* the ceiling of the piano bar is the glass bottom of the main swimming pool, so shave those legs, girls!) A clubby library is adjacent to the Tropical Bar aft on the Main Deck, and far forward on this deck is an observation lounge, where you'll find two computers with e-mail and Internet capabilities. On a recent cruise, we didn't see one person set foot in this room.

On the lowest deck, under the waterline and adjacent to the gym, is a little lounge called Captain Nemos, where an underwater spotlight allows you to see fishy creatures swim past the portholes while at anchor (though we never saw anyone using it when we were recently on the ship).

DINING OPTIONS Compared to the dining room on *Star Clipper*, the one on *Royal Clipper* is much plusher in its deep-red velveteen upholstery and dark paneling, and is spread out over three levels. With its brilliant blue sea-scene murals, white moldings and fluted columns, frilly ironwork railings and staircase, and dark-red upholstery, it's vaguely reminiscent of a room on an early-20th-century ocean liner— and somewhat out of place on an otherwise rustic ship. The buffet table is in the center on the lowest level, with seating fanning out and up. Breakfast and lunch are buffet style and dinner is sit-down. You may notice that the low overhang from the staircase makes maneuvering around the buffet table in the dining room a bit tricky.

ADVENTURE & FITNESS OPTIONS Considering her size, *Royal Clipper* offers amazing recreation facilities, with three pools, a gym, and a small spa. (By contrast, *Star Clipper* has two pools and no gym or spa.) The spa boils down to one massage room divided by only a curtain into two treatment areas. Leave your American inhibitions behind because not only do you get no modesty towel with these European-style rubs, but the room is so small that you can hear the muffled whispers and massage strokes of the masseuse on the other side of the curtain. Still, the treatments are expertly doled out at a reasonable $65 an hour.

The ship also has a retractable watersports marina at its stern for easy access to kayaking, sailing, and swimming.

Star Clipper

The Verdict

With the sails and rigging of a classic clipper ship and the creature comforts of a modern mega, the 170-passenger *Star Clipper* offers a wonderfully rustic and cozy way to do the Caribbean.

Star Clipper *(photo: Star Clippers)*

Specifications

Size (in tons)	2,298	Crew	72
Passengers (double occ.)	170	Passenger/Crew Ratio	2.5 to 1
Passenger/Space Ratio	13.5	Year Launched	1992
Total Cabins/Veranda Cabins	85/0	Last Major Refurbishment	N/A

Frommer's Ratings (Scale of 1–5)   ★★★½

Cabin Comfort & Amenities	3	Dining Options	3.5
Ship Cleanliness & Maintenance	4	Adventure & Fitness Options	3
Public Comfort/Space	3	Children's Facilities	N/A
Decor	3	Enjoyment Factor	5

Life aboard *Star Clipper* means hanging out up on deck, and that's where most passengers spend their days. It's a beautiful sight to take in the sea and next port of call through the ship's rigging, a throwback to a simpler age. There's plenty of passenger space, including the many little nooks between the winches, ropes, and other equipment that appealingly clutter the decks of these good-looking working ships. Even with a full load, the ship rarely feels too crowded, except at dinner. Much of the sail-trimming activity occurs amidships and near the bow, so if you're looking to avoid all bustle, take yourself off to the stern.

Cabins & Rates

Cabins	Per Diems from	Sq. Ft.	Fridge	Hair Dryer	Sitting Area	TV
Inside	$246	97	no	yes	no	no
Outside	$275	118–129	no	yes	no	yes

CABINS Cabins are compact, but feel roomy for ships of this size and were designed with a pleasant nautical motif—blue fabrics and carpeting, portholes, brass-toned lighting fixtures, and a dark-wood trim framing the off-white furniture and walls. The majority of cabins have portholes, two twin beds that can be converted into a double, a small desk/vanity with stool, and an upholstered seat in the corner. Storage space is more than adequate for a 7-night casual cruise in a warm climate, with both a slim floor-to-ceiling closet and a double-width closet of shelves; there's also storage space below the beds, desk, nightstand, and chair. Each cabin has a telephone, hair dryer, and safe, and all but the six smallest windowless inside cabins have a color television (though no DVD players).

Standard bathrooms are very small but functional, with marble walls, a nice mirrored storage cabinet that actually stays closed, and a narrow shower divided from the rest of the bathroom by only a curtain; surprisingly, the rest of the bathroom stays dry when the shower's being used. The sink is fitted with water-saving (but annoying) push valves that release water only when they're pressed.

The eight Deluxe Cabins measure about 150 square feet, open right out onto the main deck, and have minibars and whirlpool bathtubs. Because of their location near the Tropical Bar, though, noise can be a problem, especially if there are late-night revelers at the bar. Take note: The ship's generator tends to drone on through the night; cabins near the stern on lower decks get the most of this noise, though it sometimes filters throughout the lowest deck. Note that four cabins shares walls with the dining room, and cabins 311 and 310 actually open right into the dining room itself (so be sure and be dressed before peeking outside to see what's on the menu).

Note that the only difference between the cabins in categories 2 and 3 is a quieter location and a few square feet of space.

None of the units is a suite except for one carefully guarded (and oddly configured) Owner's Suite in the aft of the Clipper Deck that's available to the public only when it's not being set aside for special purposes or occupied by the owner himself (which happens quite often). There are also no connecting cabins, and no cabins designed for wheelchair accessibility. Lacking an elevator, these ships are not recommended for passengers with mobility problems.

PUBLIC AREAS The handful of public rooms include the dining room; a comfy piano bar; the outside Tropical Bar (sheltered from the sun and rain by a canopy); and a cozy, paneled library with a decorative, nonfunctioning fireplace, a good stock of titles, and a computer with e-mail and Internet access. Receiving messages is free, and debit cards for sending messages can be purchased from the purser.

The roomy yet cozy piano bar has comfy banquette seating and is a romantic place for a drink. That area and the outdoor Tropical Bar are the ship's hubs of activity.

Throughout, the interior decor is pleasant but unmemorable, mostly white with touches of brass and mahogany or teak trim—not as upscale-looking as *Royal Clipper* (or vessels operated by Windstar), but cozy, appealing, well designed, and shipshape.

DINING OPTIONS All meals are served in the single dining room, which has mahogany trim and a series of thin steel columns that pierce the center of many of the dining tables—mildly annoying, but necessary from an engineering standpoint. The booths along the sides, seating six, are awkward when couples who don't know each other are forever getting up and down to let their tablemates in and out. With tables only for six and eight, and no assigned seating, each evening you can dine with a different set of friends, or maybe make some new ones. The *Royal Clipper*'s roomier dining-room layout avoids this problem.

ADVENTURE & FITNESS OPTIONS The ship's two small pools are meant more for dipping than swimming. Both have glass portholes, the one amidships peering from its depths into the piano bar. The pool near the stern tends to be more languid and is thus the favorite of sunbathers, whereas the one amidships is more active, with more noise and splashing and central to the action. At both, the ship's billowing and moving sails occasionally block the sun's rays, although this happens amidships much more frequently than it does at the stern.

While there's no gym of any sort, aerobics and stretch classes are frequently held on deck between the library and the Tropical Bar. You can sign up for a massage (at $65 an hour) that's doled out in an empty cabin or in a semi-private area of the top deck.

14 Windjammer Barefoot Cruises

1759 Bay Rd., Miami Beach, FL 33139 (P.O. Box 190-120, Miami Beach, FL 33119). © **800/327-2601** or 305/672-6453. Fax 305/674-1219. www.windjammer.com.

THE LINE IN A NUTSHELL Ultracasual and delightfully carefree, this eclectic fleet of cozy, rebuilt sailing ships (powered by both sails and engines) lures passengers into a fantasy world of pirates-and-rum-punch adventure.

THE EXPERIENCE When you see that the captain is wearing shorts and shades and is barefoot like the rest of the laid-back crew, you'll realize Windjammer's vessels aren't your typical cruise ships. Their yards of sails, pointy bowsprits, chunky portholes, and generous use of wood create a swashbuckling, storybook look; and while passengers don't have to fish for dinner or swab the decks, they are invited to help haul the sails, take a turn at the wheel, sleep out on deck whenever they please, and (with the captain's permission) crawl into the bow net. With few rules and lots of freedom, this is the closest thing you'll get to a real old-fashioned Caribbean adventure, visiting off-the-beaten-track Caribbean ports of call. The ships are ultra-informal, and hokey yet endearing rituals make the trip feel like summer camp for adults. Add in the line's tremendous number of repeat passengers (and a few of its signature rum swizzle drinks) and you have an experience that's ultracasual, ultrafun, and downright chummy.

Pros

- **Informal and carefree:** You can wear shorts and T-shirts (and go barefoot) all day—even to dinner and to the bar.
- **Friendly and down-to-earth:** Crew and passengers mix and mingle, and in no time the ships feel like one big happy family at sea.
- **Adventurous:** With the sails flapping and wooden decks surrounding you, it's no great leap of faith to feel like a pirate on the bounding main.
- **Cheap:** Windjammer's rates are lower than those of Star Clippers and significantly lower than those of Windstar Cruises, and bar drinks are a steal.

Cons

- **Tiny cabins:** No polite way to say it: Cabins are cramped.
- **Loose port schedule:** Sailings usually follow the routes described in the brochures, but one destination may be substituted for another if a particularly adverse wind is blowing, or if there's a storm.

WINDJAMMER: LETTING IT ALL HANG OUT

In a class by itself, Windjammer promises a wind-in-your-hair barefoot adventure with zero pretense. These classic tall ships ooze with character and are almost as real and rustic as they come—except maybe for those sound-alike folks up north, the Maine Windjammer Association.

With five sailing ships and one diesel-driven, passenger-carrying supply vessel, Windjammer has the largest fleet of its kind at sea today (the runner-up is reportedly the Norwegian government). In this age of homogenous, cookie-cutter megaships that barrel their way through the Caribbean headed to crowded ports, the line's tiny, eclectic, and appealingly imperfect vessels are a breath of fresh, rustic air. Sure, Windjammer's ships use their engines as much or more than their sails, because it's just not practical to rely on the wind if you hope to maintain any kind of schedule, but whenever possible, the captain will navigate under sail alone for at least a short while. Except for sailing purists who might be disappointed with the use of engines, the Windjammer experience is hard to beat.

From an inspired if unintentional beginning, Windjammer has grown into one of the major lines for people who want a down-to-earth cruise alternative. The famous and now semiretired Captain Mike Burke—Cap'n Mike, as he's been known for the past half century—founded the company in 1947 with one ship, and for years ran down-and-dirty party cruises popular with singles, purchasing sailing ships rich in

Compared with the other small-ship lines, here's how Windjammer rates:

	Poor	Fair	Good	Excellent	Outstanding
Enjoyment Factor				✓	
Dining			✓		
Activities			✓		
Children's Program			✓*		
Entertainment			✓		
Service			✓		
Worth the Money					✓

Children's program is available on Legacy and Polynesia only.

history but otherwise destined for the scrap yard and transforming them into one-of-a-kind vessels.

Legend has it that Burke, released from navy submarine duty in 1947, headed for Miami with $600 in back pay, intending to paint the town red. He succeeded. The next morning, he awoke with a blinding headache and no money, on the deck of a 19-foot sloop moored somewhere in The Bahamas. Mike Burke had apparently bought himself a boat. Using a mostly empty bottle of Scotch, he christened the boat *Hangover*, and the rest is history. He lived aboard to save money, and then started ferrying friends out for weekends of sailing and fishing. Demand escalated, and Burke quit his full-time job to become a one-man cruise line. In later years, his six children (including company president Susan) have assisted him in his ventures, renovating the vessels at the line's shipyard in Trinidad.

Though the wild-and-crazy Windjammer that used to advertise in *Hustler* and promised its passengers they'd get a "bang" out of their vacation, has mellowed through the years, the line still offers just about the most adventurous laid-back way to island hop in the Caribbean. No cruise can be all bad when it includes complimentary bloody marys in the morning, rum swizzles at sunset, and wine (albeit really cheap wine) with dinner. There are no keys for the cabins, rum punch is served in paper cups, daily announcements are written in magic marker on a bulletin board, chances are the purser doubles as the nurse and gift-shop manager, and itineraries are only partially finalized before a ship's departure and may vary based on wind and tides.

Who needs swimming pools and shuffleboard? That stuff's for those other cruise ships; Windjammer offers the basic ingredients for a let-your-hair-down T-shirts and shorts adventure with some of the Caribbean's more offbeat islands as the incredible backdrop. That isn't to say Windjammer hasn't rolled with the times like any other cruise line. Through the years, since Mike Burke's children have taken over control of the company, a few more "mainstream" features have been added, such as an activities mate (aka cruise director) to organize more activities for passengers, improved food quality, and a summertime kids' program on *Legacy, Amazing Grace,* and *Polynesia.*

Though you can't climb the masts anymore—the line dislikes being sued by passengers who've had one too many rum swizzles and fallen off—many captains will allow you to sit out in the bow rigging, as a bunch of us did one memorable night a few years back, after much, much champagne. Despite any changes, though, the rum still flows freely and the wind still blows through the rigging, and what more could a wannabe pirate really want? Yo-ho-ho, y'all.

PASSENGER PROFILE

Can we say nutty, quirky, nonconformist? That's why Windjammer is so appealing: It's different—a rare concept in today's mostly homogenous megaship cruise world. Unlike some "all things to all people" lines, Windjammer is for a particular kind of informal, fun-loving, down-to-earth passenger, and though some compare the experience to a continuous frat party, we wouldn't go that far. In fact, the passenger and age mix gives lie to that description. From honeymooning couples in their 20s to grandparents in their 70s, the line attracts a broad range of adventurers who like to have fun and don't want anything resembling a highly regimented vacation. Passengers are pretty evenly divided between men and women, and 15% to 20% overall are single. Due to her long itineraries and less romantic appearance, passengers aboard the *Amazing Grace* commissary ship tend to be older than those aboard the sailing ships, mostly

60-plus; exceptions include summers, when the *Grace* attracts more families with its 7-night itineraries and kids' programs.

Many passengers love the Windjammer experience so much that they return again and again. The record is still held by the late "Pappy" Gomez of Cleveland, Ohio, who sailed with Windjammer more than 160 times, but many, many others have sailed with the line 30 to 50 times. The line's supply officer told us he never steps aboard one of the ships without seeing passengers he's sailed with before. There's even a reunion of sorts called the Jammerfest that has Windjammer die-hards flocking to Miami for a weekend blitz: Windjammer throws one of the parties and the groupies pick up their hotel, airfare, and everything else. Shows you just how far a Windjammer fan will go to keep the party alive.

Young children should probably not go (in fact, the line doesn't accept passengers under 6), nor should anyone prone to seasickness (there's quite a bit of that the first days out) or anyone wanting to be pampered (there's none of that during any day out). These ships are not for people with disabilities, either.

DINING

When it comes to dining, "slide over and pass me the breadbasket" about sums it up. Family-style and informal, there's nothing gourmet about the food, which ranges from mediocre to quite tasty. All breads and pastries are homemade, and at dinner, after soup and salad are served, passengers can choose from two main entrees, such as curried shrimp and roast pork with garlic sauce. Don't be surprised if the waiters ask for a show of hands to see who wants what. Unlimited carafes of cheap red and white wine are complimentary. Tasty breakfasts include all the usual, plus items such as eggs Benedict, and lunches include items such as lobster pizza and apple salad. Both of these meals are served buffet style. At certain islands, the crew lugs ashore a picnic lunch for an afternoon beach party, and each sailing usually includes an on-deck barbecue one evening. There are two open seatings for dinner, marked by the clang of a loud barnyard-style bell, usually around 6:30 and 8pm. Many dishes overall are rooted in Caribbean tradition. The chef will accommodate **special diets,** including vegetarian and low-salt. And don't be shy if it's your birthday: The chef will make you a free cake and serve it at dinner.

SNACKS & EXTRAS   Bloody marys are free at breakfast, and each evening at about 5pm, gallons of complimentary **rum swizzles** are dispensed along with hors d'oeuvres that may include homemade plantain chips and salsa, spicy meatballs, chicken fingers, and cheese and crackers. Guests gather on deck, often still in their sarongs and shorts, mingling in the fresh sea air as island music plays in the background. On one of our trips, a woman sang a silly song she wrote about the cruise and the people she had met, as the line's supply officer accompanied her on his flute.

ACTIVITIES

Windjammer deliberately de-emphasizes the activities that dominate life aboard larger vessels, although it may occasionally host an on-deck crab race, knot-tying demonstration, or talk on astronomy or some aspect of sailing. Otherwise, your entertainment is up to you. If the weather's fine and you want to help trim the sails, you may be allowed to lend a hand. If conditions are right and the captain amenable, passengers can jump overboard, literally, and go for a swim when the ships are anchored offshore.

Just about every day is spent in port somewhere. Generally at least once per cruise, on one of the ships' beach visits—to Jost Van Dyke, perhaps—the activities mate organizes **team games** reminiscent of mid-1960s cocktail-party movies (think Cary Grant and Audrey Hepburn in the nightclub scene in *Charade*). It's the usual embarrassing stuff: Passengers twirl hula-hoops while dressed in snorkel gear; pass cucumbers to each other, clasping them only with their thighs; or flop onto slippery foam mats and try to swim to and around a landmark. Silliness, in other words—but it does make for instant camaraderie. After all, after someone's seen you act this dumb, they've seen it all. In other ports, there may also be **organized hikes.**

Snorkeling gear (mask, fins, snorkel, and carrying bag) rents for $25 per week, and you can pay $75 to earn your PADI scuba certification on the *Legacy* and *Polynesia*. Certified PADI dive instructors now sail aboard both ships year-round and teach passengers of all skill levels, including beginners and kids. Certified divers can jump right in and do daily one- and two-tank dives ($55 and $85), night dives, and cave dives, in certain ports, plus dolphin dives ($169) and shark dives ($89).

For the other ships in the fleet, **one-tank scuba dives** from outside agencies cost around $50 at the ports of call. (Novice divers pay $85 for a "resort course.")

There are a handful of **theme cruises** every year, including about six for singles only, plus typically a photography theme sailing and a few focusing on astronomy and even pirates (the later being Windjammer's wacky pirate's week cruises, described by a company source like this: "We get a bunch of insane Windjammer types together to enjoy a lot of pirate theme crap," from costume parties to pirate trivia, boat building, treasure hunts, and lots of rum swigging). Sounds fun to us!

CHILDREN'S PROGRAM

Though this is not a children-oriented line in any traditional sense of the word—there are no video arcades, movies, and teen discos—two of Windjammer's ships do offer kids' programs during the summer for families looking for a little adventure. The *Legacy, Polynesia,* and *Grace* have a "Junior Jammers" kids' program for ages 6 to 17 that

---

The Stowaway Gimmick, Some Deals & Some Charges

Stowaways: Rather than fork over a bundle for a hotel the night before your cruise, you can stay aboard your docked Windjammer ship for a relatively modest $55 per person, double occupancy. That's fine, and a good deal, but it's actually a gimmick: The cruises are 5 nights long, and most passengers opt for the 6th night as a stowaway, so what it comes down to is Windjammer getting dozens of people to pay extra for a night that other cruise lines just bundle into their cruise prices.

Children's rates: Children 6 to 12 sharing a cabin with two adults pay 50% of the adult fare. In June, July, and August on *Legacy, Polynesia,* and *Grace,* children 6 to 12 are free and teens pay 50% of the adult fare.

Port charges: Five-night cruises generally run $65 per person. Port charges for 13-day outings cost $150 per person.

can draw as many as 40 kids a cruise in the summer—a full third of the passenger total (pretty much guaranteed to cramp an old salt's party). Both ships offer counselors for two main age groups (6–11 and 12–17) who supervise a roster of summer-camp-style activities between 9am and 9pm daily (they do many activities in empty cabins on the *Poly* and in unused public rooms on the *Legacy* and *Grace*). Programs for younger kids focus on activities such as arts and crafts, face painting, hair braiding, building sand castles, knot tying, hoisting the sails, and visits to the bridge, while teens can do stuff such as sailing, snorkeling, navigating, and kayaking. There are also introductory scuba classes for 8- to 10-year-olds and 11- to 16-year-olds. Do keep in mind, cabins are small and slippery decks aren't sympathetic to running children.

We would not recommend bringing young kids aboard the line's other ships, which don't have any programs or babysitting. For teens, if they can go a week without e-mail and Game Boys, and can divert themselves the same way adults do, with conversation, shore excursions, reading, and watching the wide blue sea, then a week on a tall ship would be a memorable experience for them.

No children under 6 are allowed aboard any ship in the Windjammer fleet. Unlike most megaship lines, which require passengers to be at least 21 years old unless accompanied by parents, Windjammer's minimum unaccompanied age is 17.

ENTERTAINMENT

Part entertainment, part education, the **Captain's "Story Time"** held each morning out on deck is the first event of the average day on a Windjammer ship. It's a short talk that's 20% ship business; 40% information about the day's port call, activities, or sailing route; and 40% pure humor (on one trip we took, a joke about a cat and a certain part of a woman's anatomy was par for the course). At these morning meetings, the captain will come out and shout "Good morning, everybody!" and the passengers—many of whom have taken these trips before and know the drill—bark back in chorus, "Good morning, Captain SIR!"

The Windjammer crowd loves every minute of it. In fact, the line's accessible and down-to-earth captains are often a part of the entertainment themselves—passengers love them and are like groupies at a rock concert, whether fawning over quiet, charming, and Marlboro-Man-handsome Captain Matt, who is often at the helm of *Mandalay*, or chatting with the more fatherly Captain Casey, who, as a senior captain, rotates among all the ships of the fleet.

In general, social interaction is centered on the bars and top Sun Deck. There's typically a passenger talent show one night; a local pop band is brought on board for a few hours of dancing once or twice a week; and there's a weekly **barbecue buffet dinner and costume party**—a Windjammer tradition that has passengers (and crew) decked out as cross-dressers, pirates, and other characters (Captain Matt looked mighty dashing as Captain Hook on a cruise a few years ago). Bring your own get-up or rummage through the pile of shabby costumes the crew hauls out before the party. Either way, it's a ball! Otherwise, there's almost no organized nightlife.

After dinner, head up to the on-deck bar (drinks are cheap: $2 for a Red Stripe or Heineken and $3.50 for the most expensive cocktail) or grab a chair or mat and hit the deck. Generally, the ships stay late in one or two ports so that passengers can head ashore to an island watering hole.

Windjammer Fleet Itineraries*

Ship	Itineraries
Amazing Grace	**7-night E./S. Carib (several routes):** Between Trinidad and Antigua, Antigua and Tortola, and Antigua and Trinidad, Oct 2005–Jan 2006 and Oct 2006–Jan 2007. **13-night E./S. Carib:** North- or southbound between Freeport, Bahamas, and Trinidad, Jan–Apr 2006. **7-night Central America:** Between Balboa, Panama, and Playa Herradura, Costa Rica, June–Aug 2006.
Legacy	**6-night E./S. Carib:** Round-trip from St. Thomas, USVI, Dec 2004–May 2006. **4-, 5- & 8-night Bahamas:** Between Miami, FL, and Nassau, Bahamas, summer.
Mandalay	**13-night E./S. Carib:** Between Grenada and Antigua, Nov 2005–May 2006. **6-night British Virgin Islands:** Round-trip from Tortola, Apr–Sept 2006.
Polynesia	**6-night E./S. Carib:** Round-trip from Sint Maarten, Dec 2005–May 2006 and Dec 2006. **6-night ABC Islands (Aruba, Bonaire, Curaçao):** Round-trip from Aruba, May–Oct 2006.
Yankee Clipper	**6-night E./S. Carib:** Round-trip from Grenada, year-round.

* The fact is, nobody—not even Windjammer's staff—seems to know exactly where the line's ships go, at least not very far ahead of time. But really, it doesn't matter: The islands are always small and beautiful, and the ambience is always wacky. We were aboard for a week once and couldn't remember where we'd been when we got home. We still aren't sure, but we do know we had a great time. A company spokeswoman told us this is fairly common.

SERVICE

Windjammer tends to attract a staff that shares founder Mike Burke's appreciation for the wide-open sea and barely concealed scorn for corporate agendas and workaday priorities. Many are from the same Caribbean islands the line's ships visit. Service is friendly and efficient but not doting, matter-of-fact and straightforward rather than obsequious. Unlike more upscale cruise lines, with Windjammer there's no master/servant relationship between passengers and staff—the crewmembers just happen to steer the ship or serve dinner or drinks, and will chat like regular folks when they're not. They're a good bunch.

Windjammer's wacky tall ships offer a quaint version of the computerized account system the big lines use to keep track of passengers' onboard purchases. The bar operates on a **doubloon system,** which is a kind of debit card for drinks that amounts to a round paper card passengers purchase and the bartender punches holes in.

Windjammer also offers wedding packages these days, just like the big-ship guys do. Could be pretty neat to tie the knot under the riggings of one of the line's tall ships. Do it on deck or on a beach shoreside in Antigua, Aruba, Grenada, Tortola, Nevis, St. Thomas, and other places. You can get married Saturday or Sunday before the cruise, or on Monday morning before the ship's departure; ceremonies officiated by Windjammer captains (not legally binding though, so get the license first) can take place on Monday or Tuesday during your cruise. The line has a wedding consultant to help with the details, including all the legal stuff. Packages range from $500 to $1,600 per couple, with the top-end option including the services of a local wedding coordinator and a non-denominational local officiant, photographer, topical bouquet, boutonniere, wedding cake, champagne toast, dinner with the captain, and more. The line also offers vow renewal ceremonies officiated by the captain and complimentary honeymoon gift baskets that include a bottle of bubbly and special T-shirts.

Legacy

The Verdict

The brightest, newest, and most spacious of Windjammer's ships, *Legacy* is a real winner in our book, with comfortable cabins, good-size private bathrooms, a cheerful dining saloon with large round booths, and a sprawling expanse of outdoor deck space. Even when full, the ship doesn't feel crowded.

Legacy *(photo: Windjammer)*

Specifications

Size (in tons)	1,165	Crew	43
Passengers (double occ.)	122	Passenger/Crew Ratio	2.8 to 1
Passenger/Space Ratio	9.5	Year Launched	1959
Total Cabins/Veranda Cabins	61/0	Last Major Refurbishment	1997

Frommer's Ratings (Scale of 1–5)

★★★½

Cabin Comfort & Amenities	2	Dining Options	3
Ship Cleanliness & Maintenance	4	Adventure & Fitness Options	N/A
Public Comfort/Space	4	Children's Facilities	N/A*
Decor	3	Enjoyment Factor	5

*Legacy *has a children's program but no dedicated facilities.*

Rebuilt and relaunched in 1997 as the line's largest and most modern ship, *Legacy* was originally built in 1959 as a motored research vessel for the French government, designed with a deep keel that gave her additional balance during North Atlantic and North Sea storms. At the time, she was one of several government-owned ships sending weather reports to a central agency in Paris, which used them to predict storm patterns on the French mainland. The advent of global satellites made the vessel obsolete, and she was bought in 1988 by Windjammer, which over the course of a decade poured over $10 million into a massive reconfiguration at the family-managed Windjammer shipyard in Trinidad. Four steel masts and 11 sails were added, plus accouterments the vessel needed for 7-day barefoot jaunts through the Caribbean. Although still tiny compared to a megaship, at 1,165 tons she's larger than any other vessel in the Windjammer fleet, and is the only one that offers some itineraries from the mainland U.S.

Some hard-core Windjammer veterans consider *Legacy* a wimpy addition to the venerated rough-and-tumble fleet, feeling that it's just not a real yo-ho-ho pirate adventure without their cramped, bare-bones lifestyle. When the vessel was launched, stalwart Windjammer fans wondered whether her comfort level and (gasp!) children's program meant the old days were gone forever. It was like seeing a group of 30- or 40-somethings returning to their favorite college-era dive bar and finding it newly sheathed in wood paneling, with brass lamps in place of the neon lights, and light jazz on the jukebox instead of "Born to Run."

Well, here's the scoop: Though she is indeed the most comfortable of the Windjammer lot, she still embraces that irreverent Windjammer spirit. It takes only a glance at the carved wooden figurehead on the ship's prow—an image of line founder Cap'n Mike Burke in a tropical-print shirt, beer in one hand and a ship's wheel in the other—to see that this is still very much a laid-back, partying vessel. She's just a slightly cushier one.

Cabins & Rates

Cabins	Per Diems from	Sq. Ft.	Fridge	Hair Dryer	Sitting Area	TV
Outside	$184	85	no	no	no	no
Suite	$234	160	no	no	yes	yes

CABINS Cabins aboard *Legacy* are a little larger and more comfortable than those aboard the line's older ships, but if you're used to sailing aboard typical large cruise ships, they'll probably seem cramped. Berths are either doubles or bunk beds, and if you're in the upper portion of the latter, watch your head: More than one passenger has woken up and knocked himself silly on the metal porthole cover, which projects from the wall when open. You'd do well to sleep with your feet toward it.

Suites—both the Admiral Suites and Burke's Berth, which is the best in the house—offer windows instead of portholes, plus space for a third occupant. There are a handful of single cabins, plus triple- and quad-berth options in the Commodore-class cabins, though this affords a minimum of personal space. Burke's Berth is the only cabin aboard that has an entertainment center, a bar, and a vanity.

Storage in all cabins is perfectly adequate for this type of T-shirt-and-shorts cruise, with each containing a small closet/drawer unit and having additional space under the bed. Bathrooms offer enough maneuvering space, but it's a crapshoot on the small, curtained showers—some have a raised lip that contains the runoff and some don't, making for a perpetually wet bathroom floor. Lip or no, small and spartan or not (compared to those offered on larger and glitzier ships), these facilities are still far better than the head-style facilities aboard the other Windjammer sailing ships.

There are no connecting cabins, and as with all the Windjammer ships, *Legacy* has no wheelchair-accessible cabins, and is not a good option for people with disabilities.

PUBLIC AREAS The top deck, with a large canopied area at its center, is the social focus of the cruise, the space where the rum swizzles are dispensed at sunset, where visiting bands perform at night, and where the captain conducts his daily morning "Story Time" session. The ship's bar is also located on this deck, as is the requisite barrel of rum—a real barrel, from which the bartender siphons off what he needs every day.

The Poop Deck offers the best sunbathing space, although shade from the raised sails could force you to move often. Passengers lounge on patio-style white plastic recliners or on the blue cushions strewn about, which many passengers also use to sleep out on deck under the stars, something the line fully encourages.

Navigation of the ship is often from a ship's wheel mounted out in open air near the bow. When seas are calm and sailing is easy, the crew offers passengers a chance to steer. Unlike the practice on most larger cruise ships, *Legacy*'s bow is generally open to passengers, allowing you (if the captain approves) to do your Leonardo DiCaprio "King of the World" bit, or, even better, to climb out on the netting that projects to the tip of the bowsprit and lounge there while the blue Caribbean Sea splashes and sprays below you. Don't miss this opportunity if it's offered—trust us.

The only other interior public room is a small and not terribly appealing lounge that offers a TV/video arrangement and a smattering of books and board games. In an entire week aboard, the only person we saw using this room was a 10-year-old boy watching movies. Everyone else was outside, playing.

DINING OPTIONS All meals are served in the comfortable aft dining room, fitted with large circular tables (a bummer if you're stuck in the middle, three or four people from freedom) and decorated with faux tropical plants. Evening hors d'oeuvres are served out on deck.

ADVENTURE & FITNESS OPTIONS As aboard the rest of the line's ships, there are none. No pool, spa, no gym, no jogging track. Aboard ship, the most exercise you're likely to get is if you volunteer to help hoist the sails. In port, however, you'll have such options as snorkeling, scuba diving, sea kayaking (the ship carries its own kayaks aboard), and hiking to help you work off dessert.

Amazing Grace

The Verdict

If you're looking for a slow, easy, and cheap tour of the Caribbean and like the novelty of being on a supply ship as it does its rounds, a trip on this semi-charming tub is bound to create lasting memories.

Amazing Grace *(photo: Windjammer)*

Specifications

Size (in tons)	1,525	Crew	40
Passengers (double occ.)	92	Passenger/Crew Ratio	2.4 to 1
Passenger/Space Ratio	16.5	Year Launched	1955
Total Cabins/Veranda Cabins	46/0	Last Major Refurbishment	1995

Frommer's Ratings (Scale of 1–5)   ★★½

Cabin Comfort & Amenities	2	Dining Options	2.5
Ship Cleanliness & Maintenance	2.5	Adventure & Fitness Options	N/A
Public Comfort/Space	3	Children's Facilities	N/A
Decor	3	Enjoyment Factor	3

Amazing Grace, the only engine-only Windjammer vessel, is the closest thing to a banana boat in the cruise industry, moving doggedly and regularly through most of the Caribbean, meeting up with the line's sailing ships in various ports to drop off provisions.

Built as the *Pharos* in Dundee, Scotland, in 1955, the *Grace* mostly carried supplies to isolated lighthouses and North Sea oil rigs, but once or twice it was pressed into service as a weekend cruiser for the queen of England. The vessel was acquired by Windjammer in 1988 and still retains some vestiges of her British past despite many modernizations. If you come aboard expecting to be treated like royalty, however, you'll be sorely disappointed. This is not a fancy vessel, and the lack of organized activities on her long 13-night trips forces you to create your own mischief. Because of her large hold and deep draft, she's the most stable vessel in the fleet.

Guests are noticeably more sedentary, definitely older, and less party-oriented than those aboard the line's more raffish sail-powered vessels. Most tend to turn in by 10pm. As one bartender on the ship told us a while back, "If we have a young person aboard, they probably made a mistake."

Cabins & Rates

Cabins	Per Diems from	Sq. Ft.	Fridge	Hair Dryer	Sitting Area	TV
Outside	$101	45	yes	no	yes	no
Suite	$280	375	yes	no	yes	yes

CABINS Cabins are utterly without frills and very small, but they're still a tad roomier than others in Windjammer's fleet. About half contain the varnished paneling from the ship's original construction; the others are more modern, with almost no nostalgic value. Although there's a sink in each cabin, some do not contain toilets and showers, requiring you to use the shared facilities, which can only be so tidy at any given time considering you're not the only one using them. Don't reject these bathroomless cabins out of hand, though, since they're also the ones with the original varnished paneling. Non-honeymooners often rent the Honeymoon Suite near the stern because of its slightly larger size. There's also the funky, wood-paneled Burke's Berth, *Grace's* version of a Penthouse Suite. Its two rooms feel a lot like a rustic hunting lodge (minus the taxidermy), with such neat features as a marble-and-teak bathroom with a sunken tub, skylights above the double bed, entertainment center, and a private porch area at the stern.

There are no connecting cabins and no wheelchair-accessible cabins.

PUBLIC AREAS Though a trip on this ship can be a cool experience (for the right person), there's no avoiding the fact that it is indeed a glorified freighter. A bar/lounge faces forward across the bow, another sits in open air on the stern, and there's a TV room for between drinks. Some of the greatest authenticity preserved from the ship's early days is a piano room and a smoking room/library, which sports etched-glass doors and mahogany walls. Because large sections of this vessel (the storage areas) are off-limits to passengers, many people tend to gravitate to the deck areas (including the lovely Promenade Deck) for reading, napping, or whatever.

DINING OPTIONS The ship's single dining room has booth-type tables that seat up to eight passengers.

ADVENTURE & FITNESS OPTIONS   There's no swimming pool, gym, or fitness facility. Instead, you'll get your exercise during snorkeling and scuba sessions at the ports of call.

Mandalay • Yankee Clipper • Polynesia

The Verdict

Bound by wood and sails, these oddball little ships have led fascinating and long lives, and today promise adventure, good times, and offbeat ports for a bargain price.

Yankee Clipper *(photo: Windjammer)*

Specifications

Size (in tons)		Crew	
Mandalay	420	*Mandalay*	28
Yankee Clipper	327	*Yankee Clipper*	29
Polynesia	430	*Polynesia*	45
Passengers (double occ.)		Passenger/Crew Ratio	
Mandalay	72	*Mandalay*	2.6 to 1
Yankee Clipper	64	*Yankee Clipper*	2.2 to 1
Polynesia	112	*Polynesia*	2.5 to 1
Passenger/Space Ratio		Year Launched	
Mandalay	5.8	*Mandalay*	1923
Yankee Clipper	5.1	*Yankee Clipper*	1927
Polynesia	3.8	*Polynesia*	1938
Total Cabins/Veranda Cabins		Last Major Refurbishment	
Mandalay	36/0	*Mandalay*	1982
Yankee Clipper	32/0	*Yankee Clipper*	1984
Polynesia	50/0	*Polynesia*	2002

Frommer's Ratings (Scale of 1–5)   ★★★

Cabin Comfort & Amenities	2	Dining Options	3
Ship Cleanliness & Maintenance	3	Adventure & Fitness Options	N/A
Public Comfort/Space	3	Children's Facilities	N/A*
Decor	3	Enjoyment Factor	5

* Polynesia *has a children's program but no dedicated facilities.*

Despite different origins and subtle differences in the way they react to the wind and weather, all of these sailing ships share many traits, so we've opted to cluster them into one all-encompassing review. All are roughly equivalent in amenities, activities, and onboard atmosphere; and because each has been extensively refurbished, they have more or less equivalent interior decors. As for their capabilities as sailing ships, Captain Stuart Larcombe, who has served aboard them all, told us that the award goes to *Mandalay* (now that *Flying Cloud*, once a spy ship for the Allied navy in World War II, was retired in 2002). For adventure and interesting ports of call, though, they're all absolutely top-notch, and we advise selecting your ship based on itinerary rather than the ships' minor physical differences.

What make the ships most unique are their histories. *Mandalay* was once the *Hussar IV*, the fourth in a line of same-name yachts built for financier E. F. Hutton, and was, by some accounts, the most sumptuous private yacht in the world. Later, she was commissioned as a research vessel by Columbia University, which sailed her for 1.25 million miles trying to develop theories about continental drift, which have since been proven correct. It's estimated that by the early 1980s, half the knowledge of the world's ocean floor was gathered by instruments aboard this ship.

Yankee Clipper, once the only armor-plated sailing yacht in the world, was built in 1927 by German industrial and munitions giant Krupp-Werft. Allegedly, Hitler once stepped aboard to award the Iron Cross to one of his U-boat commanders. Seized by the United States as booty after World War II, the ship eventually became George Vanderbilt's private yacht and the fastest two-masted vessel sailing off the California coast, once managing 22 knots under full sail. Burke bought the ship just before it was due to be broken down for scrap, then gutted, redesigned, and rebuilt it, stripping off the armor in the process. Renovations in 1984 added a third mast, additional deck space, and cabin modifications. Although not as streamlined as she was originally, she's still a fast and very exciting ship.

Polynesia, built in Holland in 1938, was originally known as *Argus*, and served as a fishing schooner in the Portuguese Grand Banks fleet. Windjammer bought her in 1975, gave her a good scrubbing to wash out the fish smell, and performed a complete reconfiguration of the cabins and interior spaces, adding lots of varnished wood. Less stylish-looking than many of her thoroughbred siblings, she nonetheless remains one of Windjammer's most consistently popular ships, on the one hand due to her handful of annual singles cruises, on the other because she's one of only two Windjammer ships (along with *Legacy*) that offers a children's program.

Cabins & Rates

Cabins	Per Diems from	Sq. Ft.	Fridge	Hair Dryer	Sitting Area	TV
Inside	$160	40–70	no	no	no	no
Outside	$195	40–70	no	no	no	no
Suite	$230	95	some	no	yes	some

CABINS There's no getting around it: Cabins are cramped, just as they would have been on a true 19th-century clipper ship. Few retain any glamorous vestiges of their original owners, and most are about as functional as they come, though wood paneling in *Mandalay* and *Yankee Clipper*'s cabins gives a pleasantly rustic feel. They're all adequate enough, however, and it's the adventurous thrill of sailing on one of these ships that you come for, not luxurious accommodations.

Each cabin has a minuscule bathroom with a shower, many of which function with a push-button—for every push you get about 10 seconds' worth of water—that you'll wind up keeping your finger on the whole time while trying to wash with the other hand. On many vessels, hot water is available only during certain hours of the day, whenever the ships' galleys and laundries aren't using it. Be prepared for toilets that don't always function properly, and retain your sense of humor as they're repaired.

Storage space is limited, but this isn't a serious problem because few passengers bring much with them. Many cabins have upper and lower berths, some have lower-level twins, and a few have doubles (so much for romance). Some standard cabins on *Polynesia* and *Grace* don't have portholes; the rest all do. On *Mandalay* aft deck cabins share a bathroom but are kind of nifty because they have a skylight and a little balcony. They're good for families, couples sailing together, and people who are willing to balance lack of private bathroom against double beds and some extra amenities, such as a minifridge. *Polynesia* offers three windowless cabins that sleep four people.

Some vessels have a limited number of suites with minifridges that, although not spacious by the standards of larger ships, seem to be of generous proportions when contrasted with the standard cabins. *Polynesia*'s recent refit included the creation of 10 windowed suites on Deck A (the highest cabin deck), with twin beds that can be converted to doubles; before her renovation, the ship had only 2 suites.

Other than a pair of cabins connecting on *Mandalay*, there are no connecting cabins on these ships. There are no wheelchair-accessible cabins on any of these ships.

PUBLIC AREAS   What glamour may have been associated with these ships in the past is long gone, lost to the years or in the gutting and refitting they required before entering Windjammer service. There's still a lot of rosewood, mahogany, and other woods left; but today it mixes with more practical steel rather than gilt, and makes an appropriate backdrop for passengers so laid-back that few bother to ever change out of their bathing suits and T-shirts. The ships' teak decks are the most popular areas on these ships, and many passengers adopt some preferred corner as a place to hang out.

DINING OPTIONS   Dining rooms are cozy, and paneled to a greater or lesser extent in wood, though overall they've been designed for efficiency. All are air-conditioned except aboard *Mandalay*, whose dining room is open-air, kept cool by evening breezes. *Polynesia*'s recent and extensive refit redecorated her dining saloon and bar with an appropriately Polynesian look, incorporating bamboo and Tiki masks.

ADVENTURE & FITNESS OPTIONS   These ships are too small to offer health clubs, saunas, or the fitness regimens so heavily promoted aboard larger ships, and none has a swimming pool. You'll get an adequate amount of exercise, however, during hikes, snorkeling, diving and swimming off the side of the ships, and scuba sessions conducted at the ports of call.

15 Windstar Cruises

300 Elliott Ave. W., Seattle, WA 98119. © 800/258-7245 or 206/281-3535. Fax 206/281-0627. www.windstar cruises.com.

THE LINE IN A NUTSHELL   Windstar walks a tightrope between luxury line and sailing-ship line, with an always-casual onboard vibe, beyond-the-norm itineraries, and first-class service and cuisine.

THE EXPERIENCE You say you want a cruise that visits interesting ports; offers super-friendly yet efficient, on-the-nose service; serves excellent cuisine; offers active options like watersports from a retractable platform in the stern; has sails for a romantic vibe; and still doesn't cost an arm and a leg? You pretty much only have one option: Windstar.

This is no barefoot, rigging-pulling, paper-plates-in-lap, sleep-on-the-deck kind of cruise, but a refined yet down-to-earth, yachtlike experience for a sophisticated, well-traveled crowd who wouldn't be comfortable on a big ship with throngs of tourists. On board, stained teak, brass details, and lots of navy-blue fabrics and carpeting lend a traditional nautical ambience, and while the ships' proud masts and white sails cut a traditional profile, they're also ultra-state-of-the-art, controlled by a computer so that they can be furled or unfurled at the touch of a button. Despite the ships' relatively large size (*Wind Surf* is one of the world's largest sailing ships, if not the largest), they're able to travel at upwards of 12 knots under sail power alone, though more usually the sails are up as a fuel-saving aid to the diesel engines.

Pros

- **Sails:** While you won't get a full-on sailing experience here like you do with the Maine Windjammer ships (which rely solely on wind power, and are hoisted and controlled by hand), you do get the ambience, plus the karmic fillip of knowing the sails help save fuel. Plus, the towering masts make it really easy to find your ship in port—just look up.
- **Service:** Like parent company Holland America, Windstar employs mostly Indonesian and Filipino staff, many of whom stay aboard for years. They're extremely professional and friendly as all-get-out. How do they remember everyone's names so quickly?
- **Cuisine:** Few small ships can match Windstar for the quality and ambience of their dining experience, with cuisine by renowned Los Angeles chef Joachim Splichal served in open-seating restaurants where guests can usually get a table for two.
- **Informal and unregimented days:** Beyond "don't wear shorts in the dining rooms," there's no real dress code here, and most men don't even bother with sport jackets at dinner. Similarly, there are zero rah-rah activities, keeping days loose and languid: Explore ashore (the itineraries visit a port almost every day) or kick back and relax aboard ship without a lot of distraction.

Cons

- **Limited activities and entertainment:** This is intentional, but if you need lots of organized hoopla to keep you happy, you won't find much here.
- **No verandas:** If they're important to you, you're out of luck.
- **The theme song:** Some folks like it, but the song they play in the stern bar every time the ships leave port (Vangelis's "Conquest of Paradise," from the film *1492*) gets stuck in our head and gnaws away for days.

WINDSTAR: CASUAL ELEGANCE UNDER SAIL

We're happy there's a company like Windstar in the frequently homogenous cruise industry. It's an individual. It's got personality. It's part of a huuuuuuuuuuuuge corporate empire (Carnival Corporation, via immediate parent company Holland America), but that only manifests in the back office. Out front, it's a friendly, almost old-fashioned operation, small-scale and full of employees who've been with the line

Compared with the other adventure lines, here's how Windstar rates:

	Poor	Fair	Good	Excellent	Outstanding
Enjoyment Factor					✓
Dining				✓	
Activities		✓			
Children's Program	N/A*				
Entertainment		✓			
Service					✓
Worth the Money				✓	

* Windstar has no children's program.

for years. Reportedly, many repeat passengers check to make sure their favorite cabin steward, waiter, captain, or host/hostess will be aboard before they'll book a particular sailing.

The line got its start in 1984, founded by a consortium of two ship-owners and Jean Claude Potier, a former U.S. head of the legendary French Line. From the start, it was all about the sails—and specifically about a new cruise ship design by the Finnish ship-building company Wartsila. Dubbed the "Windcruiser," the concept combined 19th-century sailing ship technology with modern engineering to create a kind of vessel never seen before in the cruise ship world: huge by sailing-ship standards, with at least 21,489 square feet of computer-controlled staysails that furl and unfurl at the touch of a button and can work on their own or in concert with a diesel-electric engine. The concept worked then, and it works now: As you see a Windstar ship approaching port, with its long, graceful hull and masts the height of 20-story buildings, you'll forget all about the giant megaships moored nearby and think, "Now that's a ship."

At press time, Windstar was gearing up to announce a fleetwide refurbishment program called "Degrees of Difference." Similar to parent company HAL's recent "Signature of Excellence" initiative, it will address all aspects of the passenger experience.

PASSENGER PROFILE

People who expect high-caliber service and very high-quality cuisine but dislike the formality of the other high-end ships (as well as the mass-mentality of the megaships) are thrilled with Windstar. Most passengers are couples in their late 30s to early 60s, with the average around 51. Overall, an amazing 60% to 70% of passengers are repeaters, back for their annual or semi-annual dose of Windstar. There are also usually a handful of honeymoon couples on board any given sailing—a good choice on their part, as Windstar ranks high on our list of most romantic cruise lines. The line gets very few families with young kids—rarely more than 6 or 7 on any sailing, and those usually in the 10+ age range, and only during school holiday periods.

Overall, Windstar's sophisticated and well-traveled passengers are more down-to-earth than guests on the luxury lines, but not as focused on nature and learning than guests on most of the small-ship adventure lines. Most want something different from the regular cruise experience, eschew the "bigger is better" philosophy of conventional cruising, and want their vacation to focus more on the ports than on onboard activities. These cruises are for those seeking a romantic escape and who like to visit islands and ports not often touched by regular cruise ships.

Windstar caters to corporate groups, too, with about 25% of its annual cruises booked as full charters or hosting affinity groups.

DINING

Windstar's cuisine is tops in the small-ship category and is a high point of the cruise, served in two or three always casual restaurants.

TRADITIONAL   Dinner is served primarily in each ship's spacious, nautically appointed main restaurant, though the vibe here is less formal and regimented than aboard most larger ships. At dinner, the line's **no-jackets-required** policy means guests do the "casual elegance" thing—pants or casual dresses for women and trousers and nice collared shirts for men—and its open-seating policy means you can show up when you want (within a 2-hr. window) and dine with whomever you want. Restaurants aboard all three ships are set up with an unusual number of tables for two (proving that Windstar is serious about its romantic image), and there's rarely a wait.

The cuisine here was created by chef/restaurateur **Joachim Splichal,** 1991 winner of the James Beard Foundation's "Best California Chef" award and *Bon Appetit's* "Restaurateur of the Year" for 2002. Think straightforward dishes incorporating regional touches and surprising twists. Appetizers may include golden fried Brie served with cranberry sauce and crispy parsley, or a sweet shrimp and crab salad. Among the main courses, you may see a grilled local fish served with a roast corn salsa and sweet plantains, sautéed jumbo prawns served with garlic spinach and spaghetti, or an herb-and-peppercorn-coated prime rib of beef. Desserts such as an apple tart with raspberry coulis and chocolate crème brûlée are beyond tempting. An impressive **wine list** includes California, Australian, New Zealand, Spanish, French, and South African vintages. At press time, Windstar had just announced that it had commissioned 100 new recipes from Mr. Splichal, 70 of which will be introduced in the main restaurants and 30 of which will be served in *Wind Surf's* alternative restaurant, the Bistro (see below). Splichal and his culinary team were scheduled to spend 3 weeks aboard the line's ships, perfecting the new menus and recipes alongside Windstar's executive chefs. Windstar's culinary team will also refresh their Splichal training at the chef's signature restaurant Patina, in Los Angeles.

Vegetarian dishes and **healthy "Sail Light" choices** designed by light-cooking expert Jeanne Jones are available for breakfast, lunch, and dinner; fat and calorie content is listed on the menu. The light choices may feature Atlantic salmon with couscous and fresh vegetables, or a Thai country-style chicken with veggies and oriental rice. The vegetarian options may feature a fresh garden stew or a savory polenta with Italian salsa.

ALTERNATIVE   Windstar's largest ship, the *Wind Surf,* offers alternative dining at the casual, 128-seat Bistro, an intimate space with an understated fantasy garden motif and slightly more eclectic menu choices. Reservations are required, but there's no additional fee.

CASUAL   Breakfast and lunch are available at the buffet-style Veranda Cafe, which offers a generous spread as well as a specialty omelet station at breakfast and a grill option at lunch. Waiters will bring the latter to your table, so there's no waiting. You can also opt for a simple continental breakfast at the sternside Compass Rose bar.

The once-a-week evening **barbecues** on the pool decks of the *Star* and *Spirit* are wonderful parties under the stars, with an ample and beautifully designed buffet spread, tables set with linens, and (often) a Caribbean-style band adding ambience. On

Windstar Fleet Itineraries

Ship	Itineraries
Wind Spirit	**10- & 11-night E. Carib:** Round-trip from St. Thomas, USVI, Dec 2005. **7-night E. Carib:** Round-trip from St. Thomas, USVI, Dec 2005–Mar 2006 and Dec 2006.
Wind Star	**10- & 11-night Costa Rica:** Sailing between Puerto Limon and Caldera, Dec 2005. **7-night Costa Rica:** Round-trip from Caldera, Costa Rica, Dec 2005–Mar 2006 and Dec 2006.
Wind Surf	**10- & 11-night E./S. Carib:** Round-trip from Barbados, Dec 2005. **7-night E. Carib:** Round-trip from Barbados, Dec 2005–Apr 2006 and Dec 2006.

the *Wind Surf,* there's a gala buffet dinner once per cruise in the main lounge, which is transformed into a third dining room for the evening, with a culinary theme matching your cruise region. All three ships also offer weekly barbeque lunches on deck.

SNACKS & EXTRAS   Snacks, including pizza and hot dogs, are available from the pool bar in the afternoons. Speedy **room service** offers continental breakfast; a menu of a about a dozen sandwiches, salads, seafood, and steaks from 11am to 10pm; and a dozen more snack items (from popcorn and chips-and-salsa to a cheese platter or beef consommé) 24 hours a day. During restaurant hours you can have anything from the restaurant's menu served in your cabin, speedy and hot.

ACTIVITIES

Since Windstar's itineraries emphasize days in port over days at sea (in the Caribbean, most cruises either hit a port every day or spend 1 day at sea per week), its ships offer few organized activities, leaving days relaxed and unregimented—the way guests prefer it. The handful of scheduled diversions that are available usually include casino gaming lessons, walk-a-mile and stretch classes on deck, and an occasional vegetable-carving or food-decorating demonstration. At ports where the ships anchor offshore (which is most of them, in the Caribbean), passengers can enjoy kayaking, sailing, water-skiing, snorkeling, windsurfing, and banana-boat rides from a **watersports platform** that's lowered from the stern, weather and sea conditions permitting. You can also swim off of the platform on *Wind Spirit* and *Star,* though not on the larger *Wind Surf* for safety reasons. Up top, the pool deck offers a small pool and hot tub, deck chairs, and an open-air bar, and is conducive to sunbathing and conversation. Other open areas, especially on the larger *Wind Surf,* offer quiet spots for reading.

In port, the company's shore excursions tend to be more creative than usual, and the onboard hosts or hostesses (aka cruise directors, who sometimes double as shore excursions managers and jacks-of-all-trades) are usually very knowledgeable about the ports and are able to point passengers toward good spots for bird-watching, snorkeling, or a nice meal. Brief orientation talks are held before port visits.

The ships each maintain an open-bridge policy, so at most times you're free to walk right in to chat with the captain and officers on duty. There's an extensive DVD and CD collection from which passengers can borrow for use in their cabins, and all three ships have some level of Internet connectivity—*Wind Surf* at its dedicated Internet/business center (with eight computers), and *Star* and *Spirit* via two computers in their libraries, which offer e-mail access only (no surfing). At press time, a spokeswoman for the line said Wi-Fi access would be available on all three ships in the near future (see chapter 3 for more on this trend).

CHILDREN'S PROGRAM

Because children sail infrequently with Windstar, no activities are planned for them. What kids do appear on board are generally ages 10 and up, but there are rarely more than six or seven on any sailing, and those only during school breaks. The ships' DVD libraries stock some children's films. The minimum age for children to sail is 2 years.

ENTERTAINMENT

For the most part, passengers entertain themselves, though each ship does carry a cadre of musicians who provide tunes for evening dancing and background. Most evenings, passengers either retire to their cabins; head for the modest **casino** with its slots, blackjack, roulette, and Caribbean stud poker; or go up to the pool bar for a nightcap under the stars. Sometimes after 10 or 11pm, disco/pop music is played in the lounge if guests are in a dancing mood, and once per cruise a Holland America–style **crew show** allows the ship's Indonesian and Filipino crewmembers to strut their stuff in traditional and contemporary music and dance. It's always a crowd-pleaser.

SERVICE

Windstar is a class operation, as reflected in its thoughtful service personnel. The staff smiles hello and often learns passengers' names within the first hours of sailing. Dining staff is efficient and first-rate as well, but not in that ultraprofessional, military-esque, five-star-hotel, Seabourn kind of way. That's not what Windstar is all about. The line operates under a **tipping-not-required policy,** although generally guests do tip staff as much as on other ships; on Windstar, as on Holland America, there's just less pressure to do so.

Wind Surf

The Verdict

The big boy. An enlarged version of Windstar's 148-passenger ships, the 308-passenger *Wind Surf* is a sleek, sexy, super-smooth sailing ship offering an extensive spa and lots of suites along with an intimate yacht-like ambience.

Wind Surf *(photo: Windstar Cruises)*

Specifications

Size (in tons)	14,745	Crew	190
Passengers (double occ.)	308	Passenger/Crew Ratio	1.6 to 1
Passenger/Space Ratio	48	Year Launched	1990
Total Cabins/Veranda Cabins	154/0	Last Major Refurbishment	2005

Frommer's Ratings (Scale of 1–5)   ★★★★

Cabin Comfort & Amenities	4	Dining Options	3.5
Ship Cleanliness & Maintenance	3.5	Gym, Spa & Sports Facilities	5
Public Comfort/Space	4	Children's Facilities	N/A
Decor	4	Enjoyment Factor	4.5

Wind Surf is the pumped-up big sister of Windstar's smaller original vessels, the *Wind Star* and *Wind Spirit*. Built on the same "Windcruiser" concept as her smaller sisters at French shipyard Societe Nouvelle des Ateliers et Chantiers du Havre, she originally sailed for Club Med Cruises (as *Club Med I*), until purchased by Windstar in 1997.

Despite a passenger capacity more than double that of her sister ships (308 vs. 148), *Wind Surf* maintains the feel of a private yacht, but also something more: Unlike almost any ship today, she mimics the size and flavor of some older, more intimate ocean liners, with a real seagoing feel that's rare among today's breed of cruise ships. It's this ambience, too, that sets her off from all the other "small" ships in this chapter, with amenities and an onboard vibe closer to a very high-end mainstream ship or a casual luxe vessel. In essence, *Wind Surf* is in a class by herself, offering one of the few cruise experiences that really bridges the gap between casual-luxe and adventure, at prices often as low as $1,500 per week.

In late 2005 (after this book goes to press), *Wind Surf* is scheduled for a multi-million-dollar face-lift that will replace all her sails as well as sprucing up her interiors and other aspects of the Windstar experience.

Cabins & Rates

Cabins	Per Diems from	Sq. Ft.	Fridge	Hair Dryer	Sitting Area	TV
Outside	$280	188	yes	yes	no	yes
Suite	$441	376	yes	yes	yes	yes

CABINS   Cabins come in only two flavors: regular 188-square-foot staterooms, and suites that are exactly double that size—because they were created after Windstar's purchase of the ship by combining two regular cabins. Decor is nearly identical in all cabins and suites, with shippy white walls, varnished wood detailing, patterned upholstery and bedding, and understated carpets. Amenities include flat-screen TVs, DVD/CD players, minibar, terry-cloth bathrobes, and large desk/makeup tables. Cabins are roomy (matching some of the largest standard cabins on mainstream ships) and storage space is adequate, though not overly generous. Largish, teak-trimmed bathrooms are artfully designed and more appealing than those aboard many other luxury ships, and contain a hair dryer, plenty of towels, and more-than-adequate storage space. Another hair dryer (one with enough power to actually dry hair) is stowed out in the main cabin.

Thirty suites on Deck 3 have a single large space divided into a comfortable sitting area and a bedroom (with a thick curtain to separate them as needed), plus his-and-hers bathrooms, each with shower and toilet. No cabins or suites have balconies or even picture windows. Instead, chunky portholes add to the ship's nautical ambience. Go with it. We loved 'em.

Wind Surf has two elevators (unlike the other Windstar ships, which have none), but no cabins tailored for wheelchairs. The vessel is not recommended for people with serious mobility problems.

PUBLIC AREAS   All around, *Wind Surf* is the roomiest of the three Windstar ships, with an airy layout and a passenger-space ratio that matches that of the luxe Seabourn ships.

The vessel's main public room is its nautically decorated main lounge, a bright and airy space with well-spaced tables for four spread around a decent size dance floor and bandstand. Passengers gather here in the evening for cocktails, music, and port talks, as well as gambling in the adjoining casino. Aft, the Compass Rose bar may be the most popular spot aboard, with indoor/outdoor seating, a view over the wake, and music in the evenings. A second small stern lounge, the tiny, adorable Terrace Bar, is the venue for evening "Cigars Under the Stars" sessions, with classic wood paneling, thick leather couches and barstools, and more seating and tables just outside, on deck.

Midships on Main Deck, just aft of the Lounge, a large library has comfortable couches, large tables, a small selection of books, and a contrastingly large and varied selection of DVDs that passengers can check out at the front desk for viewing in their cabins. Binders also hold a selection of music CDs, though most are collections—better for people who want background than for real music connoisseurs. Four card tables are set up just outside the library, along the deck's port-side corridor, and the ship's one shop is located just astern, next to the main reception desk. The library has two computers set up for passenger use, but they're not connected to the Web. For that, you'll have to find the Internet center, whose eight computers offer standard Internet and e-mail access. It's hidden down a transverse passageway forward on the Bridge Deck, next to the ship's 60-seat conference facility.

DINING OPTIONS *Wind Surf* offers three dining venues: the main restaurant on Main Deck, the casual alternative Bistro on Star Deck, and the buffet-style Veranda restaurant, also on Star Deck. The Restaurant has 34 tables for two, making it easy for couples to get a romantic dinner alone. Dinners are open-seating, served in a 2-hour window between 7:30 and 9:30pm. Dinner in the cozy Bistro is by reservation only, with a different menu than that served in the restaurant.

As on the other Windstar ships, a combo buffet and a la carte breakfast and lunch are served in the glass-enclosed Veranda, which also has outdoor seating. Guests can also get grilled lobster, shrimp, ribs, hamburgers, hot dogs, sausages, veggie burgers, and vegetables from the Grill, right outside the Veranda's doors.

POOL, FITNESS, SPA & SPORT FACILITIES *Wind Surf* has the most elaborate fitness and spa facilities in the Windstar fleet, outclassing most facilities on other similar-size ships. At the spa, therapists dole out a variety of massages and other treatments in rooms that may look suspiciously familiar: They were created out of regular cabins when Windstar expanded the spa. Spa packages geared to both men and women can be purchased in advance through your travel agent, with appointment times made once you're on board, or you can simply book individual treatments.

The ship's totally glass-walled gym is located on the top deck and is surprisingly well stocked for this size vessel, with four treadmills, several step machines and elliptical trainers, four bikes, a full Cybex weight circuit, dumbbells, a ballet bar, and a rowing machine with water resistance. A separate aerobics room one deck below offers a full schedule of yoga, Pilates, "Body Blitz," and self-defense classes for $11 a pop (or $68 for an unlimited pass), plus free aerobics, stretching, fitball, and abs classes.

There are two pools on board: one on the top deck, beneath the sails, and another in the stern, alongside two hot tubs. For joggers, a full-circuit teak promenade wraps around the Bridge Deck.

Wind Spirit • Wind Star

The Verdict

Two of the most romantic, cozy-yet-roomy small ships out there, these vessels look chic and offer just the right combination of creature comforts and first-class cuisine, along with a casual, laid-back, unstructured ethic.

Wind Spirit *(photo: Windstar Cruises)*

Specifications

Size (in tons)	5,350	Passenger/Crew Ratio	1.6 to 1
Passengers (double occ.)	148	Year Launched	
Passenger/Space Ratio	36	*Wind Spirit*	1988
Total Cabins/Veranda Cabins	74/0	*Wind Star*	1986
Crew	90	Last Major Refurbishment	2003

Frommer's Ratings (Scale of 1–5)   ★★★½

Cabin Comfort & Amenities	4	Dining Options	3.5
Ship Cleanliness & Maintenance	3.5	Gym, Spa & Sports Facilities	2
Public Comfort/Space	4	Children's Facilities	N/A
Decor	4	Enjoyment Factor	4.5

Despite these ships' high-tech design and a size significantly larger than that of virtually any private yacht afloat, they nonetheless retain the grace and lines of classic clipper ships—from the soaring masts to the needle-shaped bowsprit—with practically none of the associated discomforts. They're the kind of lived-in, well-sailed vessels that a certain kind of passenger latches onto forever, and keeps coming back to year after year. To keep things fresh, both received a face-lift in late 2003, and they're expecting another as this book goes to press.

Cabins & Rates

Cabins	Per Diems from	Sq. Ft.	Fridge	Hair Dryer	Sitting Area	TV
Outside	$291	188	yes	yes	no	yes
Suite	$428	220	yes	yes	yes	yes

CABINS   All cabins are nearly identical, with a burgundy and navy color scheme, flatscreen TV, DVD/CD player, minibar, a pair of large round portholes with brass fittings, a compact closet, bathrobes, and fresh fruit. Like the ships' main public rooms, cabins have wood accents and trim, and are attractive and well constructed, with a square footage exceeding most small ships and matching the size of the largest standard cabins on the mainstream ships. Teak-decked bathrooms, largish for ships this size, are better laid out than those aboard many luxury vessels, and contain a hair dryer, plenty of towels, and compact but adequate storage space. Another hair dryer (one with enough power to actually dry hair) is stowed out in the main cabin. Both ships have one Owner's Cabin that gives a little more breathing room, at 220 square feet.

Although all the cabins are comfortable, cabins amidships are more stable in rough seas—a rule of thumb aboard all ships. Note that the ships' engines, when running at full speed, can be a bit noisy.

This line is not recommended for passengers with serious disabilities or those who are wheelchair bound. There are no elevators on board, access to port is often by tender, and there are many raised doorsills.

PUBLIC AREAS   There aren't a lot of public areas on these small ships, but they're more than adequate as passengers spend most of their time in port. The four main rooms include two restaurants, a library, and a vaguely nautical-looking bar/lounge with cozy, partitioned-off nooks and clusters of comfy caramel-colored leather chairs surrounding a wooden dance floor. This is where passengers congregate for port talks, pre- and post-dinner drinks, dancing, and performances by local musicians and dancers. A second bar is out on the pool deck, and also attracts passengers before and after dinner for drinks and sometimes cigar-smoking under the stars.

The small wood-paneled library manages to be both nautical and collegiate at the same time. Guests can read, play cards, or check out one of the hundreds of DVDs and CDs. You can send and receive e-mail via two library computers in the library, though there's no actual Internet access.

DINING OPTIONS   The yachtishly elegant, dimly lit main restaurant is styled with teak trim and paneling, rope-wrapped pillars, navy-blue carpeting and fabrics, and other nautical touches. It's the sole dinner venue, and also serves lunch occasionally. The Veranda breakfast and lunch restaurant is a sunny, window-lined room whose tables extend from inside onto a covered deck. Unfortunately, you have to go outside on deck to enter the restaurant, so if it's raining, you'll get wet.

POOL, FITNESS, SPA & SPORTS FACILITIES   Each ship has a tiny swimming pool and an adjacent hot tub in the stern. Deck chairs around the pool can get filled during sunny days, but there's always space available on the crescent-shaped slice of deck above, outside the Veranda restaurant, and in a nice patch of deck forward of the bridge. Deck 4 offers an unobstructed wraparound deck for walkers.

The ships' small gyms offer elliptical trainers, recumbent bikes, ballet bar, free weights, and a flat-screen TV. Not bad for ships this size. Massages and a few other types of treatments are available out of a single massage room next to the hair salon on Deck 1. Don't fault it just on size, though: One of the best massages we've ever had at sea was on the *Wind Spirit*.

Part 3

The Ports

With guides to the 21 big U.S. and Canadian ports of embarkation, overviews of the major river cruise routes, and advice on things to see and do—on your own and via organized shore excursions—in 58 ports of call.

9

The Ports of Embarkation

Time was, cruises only left from the corners of the U.S.—from Florida to the Caribbean, from New York and Boston to Canada's Maritimes and Bermuda, to Alaska from Vancouver (not in the U.S., but damn close), and to the Mexican Riviera from L.A. and San Diego. That's already a lot of options, but the question remained: Why stop there? Both coasts are full of cities with excellent port facilities, and cruise ships are, after all, ships, not trains on rails. They can sail from anywhere, as long as the water's deep enough.

That realization began dawning on the cruise industry around the turn of the millennium, then grew into a full-blown self-preservation policy after 9/11, when the public's avoidance of air travel threatened to leave ships empty. Once the worst of the jitters wore off, the efficacy of the alternative-home-porting trend had been proven, and there was no going back to business as usual.

So, let's offer a cordial welcome to such cities as Baltimore; Philadelphia; Galveston; Houston; Seattle; Norfolk, Virginia; and even Bayonne, New Jersey. The big ships are on their way, and so are you. In this chapter, we'll provide some information on what there is to see and do in each of the 20 major U.S. and Canadian embarkation ports. Cruise lines generally offer pre- and post-cruise hotel packages for passengers wanting to extend their vacation or add in some decompression time between boat and home, but in case you want to make your own arrangements, we've also included some distinctive hotel and restaurant choices. Hotel prices listed here are standard rack rates for double rooms unless stated otherwise, and may be lower in off seasons. For more extensive information on any of these cities, check the relevant Frommer's city, state, or regional guide.

PORTS NOT COVERED IN THIS CHAPTER While **San Juan (Puerto Rico),** and **Honolulu (Hawaii)** are both major ports of embarkation, they're also major ports of call for ships sailing through, and therefore appear in chapters 10 and 14, respectively. Two other ports, **Jacksonville, Florida,** and **Mobile, Alabama,** are currently only hosting one ship apiece (Carnival's *Celebration* in Jacksonville and Carnival's *Holiday* from Mobile), so are not covered in this book.

FLYING TO THE PORT Whether you purchase air travel on your own or through the cruise line, you have two main options for getting to the port: taking a **taxi** or purchasing **transfers** from the cruise line. We've included taxi prices in all these reviews, so compare them against your cruise line's transfer prices to see which you prefer. While cruise line transfers allow you to fall into the warm, let-'em-take-care-of-everything embrace of the cruise line (and meet some of your fellow passengers before you even board),

Choosing a Chain

In addition to the hotels listed in this chapter, the big motel and hotel chains are represented in most of the port cities.

- **Best Western,** ℂ 800/780-7234; www.bestwestern.com
- **Clarion,** ℂ 877/424-6423; www.clarioninn.com
- **Comfort Inn,** ℂ 800/424-6423; www.comfortinn.com
- **Comfort Suites,** ℂ 800/424-6423; www.comfortsuites.com
- **Courtyard by Marriott,** ℂ 800/321-2211; www.courtyard.com
- **Days Inn,** ℂ 800/329-7466; www.daysinn.com
- **Doubletree,** ℂ 800/222-8733; www.doubletree.com
- **Econo Lodge,** ℂ 800/424-6423; www.econolodge.com
- **Holiday Inn,** ℂ 800/465-4329; www.holiday-inn.com
- **Howard Johnson,** ℂ 800/466-4656; www.hojo.com
- **Motel 6,** ℂ 800/466-8356; www.motel6.com
- **Quality Inn,** ℂ 800/424-6423; www.qualityinn.com
- **Red Roof Inns,** ℂ 800/733-7663; www.redroof.com

you'll often have to wait a while for the bus to load up and go. A taxi is, of course, speedier.

DRIVING TO THE PORT All the ports of embarkation in this chapter offer secure parking for passengers who drive to the ship. We've included basic driving directions and parking prices in all the reviews. Your cruise line and/or travel agent will also provide info.

1 Anchorage, Alaska

Anchorage, which started as a tent camp for workers building the Alaska Railroad in 1914, stands between the Chugach Mountains and the waters of upper Cook Inlet. It was a sleepy railroad town until World War II, when the opening of a couple military bases livened things up a bit. Even with that, though, the city did not start becoming a city in earnest until the 1950s, when the Cold War (and Alaska's proximity to the ol' Evil Empire) spurred a huge investment in infrastructure. Today, Anchorage enjoys the unlikely distinction of being incorrectly perceived as the state capital by pretty much everybody in the Lower 48, simply because it seems so obvious that it should be. (Trivial Pursuit answer: Juneau is the real capital; see chapter 11.) It also boasts good restaurants, good museums, and a nice little zoo. Outside town, the world-class **Alaska Native Heritage Center** is a 26-acre celebration of Alaska's five major Native groups, while a little farther out Mount Alyeska ski resort is one of Alaska's best. And always, of course, there is wilderness, so close that moose regularly annoy gardeners, and bears sometimes amble though town.

Anchorage's downtown area is a manageable 8-by-20 blocks, though its wide streets aren't the kind you feel compelled to walk around. Still, there's quite a few shops (mostly touristy, but with some gems sprinkled through), plus the museum, a few smaller historic attractions, and the must-do **Coastal Trail** along Knik Arm, so plan to spend at least a half or full day. If you have time, plan another half-day at the Native Heritage Center or a day trip about 50 miles south along the incredibly scenic inlet known as **Turnagain Arm.**

GETTING TO ANCHORAGE & THE PORT

From the south, cruising around the Kenai Peninsula to get to Anchorage would add another day to itineraries, so the vast majority of ships dock instead in southerly **Seward** (about 125 miles from Anchorage, on the southeast coast of the Kenai) or **Whittier** (in the northwestern waters of Prince William Sound) then shuttle passengers into the city by bus or train. Most offer excursions in the port area that include transportation into town or to the international airport afterward. If you're arriving by plane before your cruise, you'll land at the **Anchorage International Airport,** located within the city limits, a 10- to 15-minute drive from downtown. Taxis run about $25 for the trip downtown. By car, there is only one road into Anchorage from the rest of the world: the Glenn Highway. The other road out of town, the Seward Highway, leads to the Kenai Peninsula.

GETTING AROUND   Most **car-rental** companies operate at the airport. A midsize car costs about $70 a day, with unlimited mileage. Advanced bookings are recommended. **Taxis** are available in town at a rate of $2 per mile plus a $2 initial fee. Anchorage's $1.50-per-ride People Mover **bus system** is an effective way of moving to and from the top attractions and activities.

BEST CRUISE LINE SHORE EXCURSIONS

Shore excursions in Anchorage often carry restrictions based on whether (and when) you're sailing from Seward or Whittier and whether you're staying over in Anchorage proper.

Exit Glacier & Seward ($45; 3 hr.): At the head of Resurrection Bay in Kenai Fjords National Park, Exit Glacier is one Alaska's most approachable, with viewing just a half-mile walk from the parking lot through an alder forest. Additional nature paths are available.

Seward Sportfishing ($210; 6 hr.): A half-day excursion on Resurrection Bay, targeting whatever fish are in season during your visit. Alaska law requires a fishing license, purchasable aboard your fishing boat for $10 cash. You'll need a credit card to have your catch processed and sent home.

Prince William Sound Kayaking ($99, 3 hr.): Offered on cruises from Whittier, this tour takes you to one of Prince William Sound's deepwater fjords for a guided paddle around gorgeous waterfalls and rock formations.

EXPLORING ANCHORAGE ON YOUR OWN

Anchorage's downtown area is pleasant, but don't expect an old-fashioned Alaskan town: Most of its buildings were leveled in the 1964 earthquake, which at a magnitude of 9.2 was more powerful than the one that hit Southeast Asia in December 2004, generating the deadly tsunami. At Fourth Avenue and E Street, the 1936 **Old City Hall** offers an interesting display of city history in its lobby, including dioramas of the early streetscape. Today, downtown Anchorage is thoroughly modern, albeit in an Alaskan way, with stretches of touristy shops interspersed with government buildings, shops for locals, a few seedy stretches, and occasional dashes of homespun

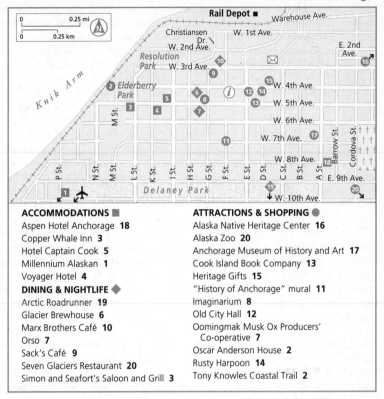

Downtown Anchorage

Rail Depot ■ Warehouse Ave.

Christiansen Dr.   W. 1st Ave.
W. 2nd Ave.   E. 2nd Ave.
Resolution Park   W. 3rd Ave. **10** **16**
9
2 Elderberry Park   **15** W. 4th Ave.
6 *i* **12** **14**
5 **8** **13** W. 5th Ave.
3 **7** W. 6th Ave.
4
11 W. 7th Ave.   **17**
W. 8th Ave.   **18**
Knik Arm
M St.
P St.   N St.   M St.   L St.   K St.   I St.   H St.   G St.   F St.   E St.   D St.   C St.   B St.   A St.   Barrow St.   Cordova St.
E. 9th Ave.
Delaney Park
1 **19** W. 10th Ave.   **20**

0   0.25 mi
0   0.25 km

ACCOMMODATIONS ■
Aspen Hotel Anchorage **18**
Copper Whale Inn **3**
Hotel Captain Cook **5**
Millennium Alaskan **1**
Voyager Hotel **4**
DINING & NIGHTLIFE ◆
Arctic Roadrunner **19**
Glacier Brewhouse **6**
Marx Brothers Café **10**
Orso **7**
Sack's Café **9**
Seven Glaciers Restaurant **20**
Simon and Seafort's Saloon and Grill **3**

ATTRACTIONS & SHOPPING ●
Alaska Native Heritage Center **16**
Alaska Zoo **20**
Anchorage Museum of History and Art **17**
Cook Island Book Company **13**
Heritage Gifts **15**
"History of Anchorage" mural **11**
Imaginarium **8**
Old City Hall **12**
Oomingmak Musk Ox Producers' Co-operative **7**
Oscar Anderson House **2**
Rusty Harpoon **14**
Tony Knowles Coastal Trail **2**

public art: Check out Bob Patterson's **"History of Anchorage" mural** at 7th Avenue and F St., which depicts exactly that.

Our pick of the number-one downtown activity is taking a walk along the **Tony Knowles Coastal Trail,** which offers gorgeous views out over the water. The trail runs through downtown and along the waters of Knik Arm for about 12 miles, from the western end of Second Avenue to Kincaid Park. You can hop on at several points, including via **Elderberry Park,** at the western end of Fifth Avenue, where you'll also find the **Oscar Anderson House** museum (© **907/274-2336;** www.anchorage historic.org). Built in 1915 for Swedish butcher Anderson and his family, it's a quaint dwelling surrounded by a lovely little garden, with a tour that provides a glimpse into the city's short history. Furnishings include a working 1909 player piano. Admission is $3.

The **Anchorage Museum of History and Art,** 121 W. Seventh Ave., between A and C streets (© **907/343-4326;** www.anchoragemuseum.org), is the state's largest museum. Most visitors tour the large Alaska Gallery, an informative and enjoyable walk through the history and some of the anthropology of the state and its Native peoples. The art galleries present Alaskan works from yesterday and today, along with photos of pre-quake Anchorage and Alaskan pop-culture artifacts. The museum gets Alaska's best touring and temporary exhibits, and its restaurant, operated by the excellent Marx Brothers Cafe, serves some of the best lunches to be had downtown. Admission costs $6.50. A $21 combo ticket will also get you admission and a free shuttle to . . .

. . . The 26-acre **Alaska Native Heritage Center,** 8800 Heritage Center Dr. (© **800/315-6608;** www.alaskanative.net), located about 15 minutes from downtown Anchorage. Opened in 1999, the center introduces visitors to the lives and cultures of the state's five major Alaska Native groupings: Southeast's Tlingit, Eyak, Haida, and Tsimshian tribes; the Athabascans of the Interior; the Inupiat and St. Lawrence Island Yupik Natives of the far north; the Aleuts and Alutiiqs of the Aleutian Islands; and the Yup'ik and Cup'ik tribes of the extreme west. A central "Welcome House" holds a small museum displaying some remarkable Native carvings and masks; a workshop where Native craftspeople demonstrate their techniques; a theater presenting a rotating series of films on Native culture; and a rotunda where storytelling, dance, and music performances are presented throughout the day. Outside, spaced along a walking trail around a small lake, are five traditional dwellings representing the five regions. Native staffers are on hand at each to provide information about the dwellings. Though the center is offered as a shore excursion by most ships, it's worth going on your own if you're interested in Native culture, since the tours don't give you enough time to experience all the place has to offer. Admission is $21. A free shuttle leaves regularly from the Anchorage Museum, the Anchorage Visitors Center at 4th Avenue and F Street, the center's downtown gift shop on 4th Avenue (see "Shopping," below), and several other sites. Times are posted at all pickup points, or call © 907/330-8000.

If you're traveling with kids, Anchorage offers a few kid-centric options, including **The Imaginarium,** 727 W. Fifth Ave., between G and H streets, Suite 140 (© **907/ 276-3179;** www.imaginarium.org), a science museum with a strong Alaska theme to many of the displays, including a saltwater touch tank. Admission is $5.50 adults, $5 kids. The **Alaska Zoo,** 4731 O'Malley Rd., about 8 miles from downtown (© **907/ 346-3242;** www.alaskazoo.org), is another option, with gravel paths meandering through the woods past natural flora and local wildlife like bears, seals and otters, musk oxen, Dall sheep, moose, caribou, and waterfowl—all of which you may see on your cruise, but not this close-up. There are also elephants, Siberian tigers, yaks, and Bactrian camels, which you won't see from the ship unless you're having flashbacks. Admission is $9 adults, $5 kids. To get there, take either the old or new Seward Highway south to O'Malley Road, turn left, and travel for about 1½ miles.

ATTRACTIONS IN SEWARD & WHITTIER

Most people pass through Seward and Whittier without a second glance on their way to Anchorage, but if you have time, there are a few interesting sights to see in these two port towns. In Seward, the spectacular **Alaska SeaLife Center,** right on the waterfront at Mile 0 of the Seward Highway (© **800/224-2525;** www.alaskasealife.org), allows scientists and visitors (the latter through windows) to study the sea lions, porpoises, sea otters, harbor seals, fish, and other forms of marine life that abound in the area, as well as the umpteen species of local seabirds. Admission costs $14.

As for Whittier, the most amazing thing about the town is that almost the entire population lives in a single 14-story concrete building known as the **Begich Towers.** It was built during the 1940s, when Whittier's strategic location on the Alaska Railroad and at the head of a deep Prince William Sound fjord made it a key port in the defense of Alaska, and after a while everybody just migrated here to make things easier. Kids don't even have to go outside to get to school in winter—a tunnel leads right from the tower to the school building.

SHOPPING

The **Cook Island Book Company,** 415 W. Fifth Ave. (© **907/258-4544;** www. cookinlet.com), sits amid a block of gift shops and seems unpromising from the outside, but inside is a huge stock of Alaska-oriented books organized by subject: Native culture, history, art, fishing, out-of-print, etc. The shop also stocks fiction and other general topics. Definitely worth a stop.

Many stores in Anchorage carry Native-looking arts and crafts, but most are just touristy knock-offs. Give 'em your back and head for the good stuff instead. The **Oomingmak Musk Ox Producers' Co-operative,** 604 H St. at 6th Avenue (© **888/ 360-9665;** www.qiviut.com), is a co-op owned by 250 Alaska Native women in villages across the state. All of their products are knitted from *qiviut* (*kiv*-ee-oot), the light, warm, silky underhair of the musk ox, which is collected from shedding animals. Each village has its own knitting pattern. They're expensive—adult caps start at $155, scarves at $245—but considering the rarity and beauty of the work, they're a bargain. Their website has a "letters" page with notes sent by the knitters, discussing their work. **The Rusty Harpoon,** at 411 W. 4th Ave. (© **907/278-9011;** www.rustyharpoon gifts.com), also has authentic Native items, less expensive crafts, and reliable, longtime proprietors. Both buy only direct from Native artists they know. The Alaska Native Heritage Center's **Heritage Gifts,** 333 W. 4th Ave. (© **907/272-5048**), also has a good selection of art, books, and music.

WHERE TO STAY

Rooms can be hard to come by in Anchorage in the summer, so be sure to arrange lodging as far in advance of your trip as possible, whether through your cruise line or on your own. Here are some good options:

The **Hotel Captain Cook,** 4th Avenue and K Street (© **800/843-1950;** www. captaincook.com), is Alaska's great, grand hotel, where royalty and rock stars stay. Rates: from $260. Right across the street from the Anchorage Museum, the fairly stylish **Aspen Hotel Anchorage,** 108 E. 8th Ave. (© **866/GUEST4U;** www.aspenhotels ak.com), offers rooms appointed with just about everything, including microwaves, refrigerators, DVD players, and high-speed Internet dataports. Rates: from $169. The small, unpretentious, and centrally located **Voyager Hotel,** 501 K St. (© **800/247- 9070;** www.voyagerhotel.com), has large, light rooms with kitchens, and gets consistent raves from travelers. Rates: from $169. The casual **Copper Whale Inn,** 440 L St. (© **907/258-7999;** www.copperwhale.com), takes up a pair of clapboard houses overlooking Elderberry Park right on the coastal trail downtown, with charming rooms of every shape and size. Rates: from $165 (rooms with shared bath from $145).

If you want a place near the airport, try the **Millennium Alaskan,** 4800 Spenard Rd. (© **800/544-0553;** www.millenniumhotels.com), which advertises itself as having "the feel of a world-class lodge"—a claim that's pretty accurate. Rates: from $270.

DINING & NIGHTLIFE

Though hardly a culinary or nightlife capital, Anchorage does have a few good restaurants if you want an evening out before or after your cruise. For an active, hardy experience, the **Glacier Brewhouse,** 737 W. 5th Ave. (© **907/274-BREW;** www.glacier brewhouse.com), offers a tasty, eclectic, and ever-changing menu served in a large dining room with lodge decor, where the pleasant scent of the wood-fired grill hangs in the air. They brew five hearty beers behind a glass wall. If it's crowded (and it often is), head for the large bar area, where you can just hover like a vulture till a table opens up. Main courses: $10 to $28. The **Marx Brothers Café,** 627 W. 3rd Ave. (*©* **907/ 278-2133;** www.marxcafe.com), began as a hobby among three friends and has become a standard of excellence in the state. The cuisine is varied and creative, ranging from Asian to Italian, but everyone orders the Caesar salad made at the table. The decor and style are studied casual elegance. Main courses: $28 to $50. **Sack's Café,** 328 G St. (*©* **907/274-4022;** www.sackscafe.com), is the most fashionable restaurant in Anchorage, and one of the best, with an ever-changing menu that mixes Alaskan seafood with Italian influences and eclectic touches. Main courses: $16 to $31. **Orso,** 737 W. 5th Ave. (*©* **907/222-3232**), offers superb wood-grilled steaks and locally caught seafood as well as excellent pastas, all in an ornate dining room. Main courses: $16 to $26. **Simon and Seafort's Saloon and Grill,** 420 L St. (*©* **907/274-3502**), is one of Anchorage's great dinner houses with a turn-of-the-century decor, a cheerful atmosphere, and fabulous sunset views of Cook Inlet. Prime rib and seafood are the specialties. Main courses: $16 to $40. Lighter meals are served at the bar. For the best, most original takeout burgers in town, head for **Arctic Roadrunner,** with locations at 2477 Arctic Blvd. at Fireweed Lane (*©* **907/279-7311**), and 5300 Old Seward Hwy. at International Airport Road (*©* **907/561-1246**). Try the Kodiak Islander, which has peppers, ham, onion rings, and God knows what else on top.

For a memorable dining experience out of town, the Mount Alyeska Resort's **Seven Glaciers Restaurant** (*©* **800/880-3880;** www.alyeskaresort.com) offers views that match its name. Located 2,300 feet up a tramway on the mountainside, the restaurant serves trendy and beautifully presented dinners in a sumptuous dining room floating above the clouds. Notable menu selections include the cold smoked and grilled Alaskan salmon and the Alaskan king crab. Main courses: $28 to $52. It's at 1000 Arlberg Ave. in Girdwood, a funky little town 37 miles south of Anchorage along Turnagain Arm.

2 Baltimore, Maryland

"Charm City" has welcomed visitors since 1729. Founded as a shipping and shipbuilding town and later transformed into a manufacturing center (General Motors and Bethlehem Steel have been a part of the east Baltimore landscape for decades, and a Domino Sugar sign dominates the Inner Harbor), the city rode the new-economy wave of the '90s with more service industries and nonprofits. Tourism plays an ever-increasing role in the local economy, with a combination of historical sites, museums, a revitalized harbor area, and friendly people drawing visitors, and now cruise lines, too.

GETTING TO BALTIMORE & THE PORT

All cruise vessels depart from the Port of Baltimore's Seagirt Marine Terminal, on the Broening Highway, about 7 miles from the Inner Harbor, where many of the best attractions and hotels are located. If you're arriving by plane, you'll likely fly into **Baltimore/Washington International Airport** (*©* **800/I-FLY-BWI**), located 10 miles south of downtown Baltimore, off I-295 (the Baltimore-Washington Pkwy.). To get to Baltimore, take I-195 west to Route 295 north, which will take you into downtown. **Taxis** to the port or downtown hotels run about $20. **SuperShuttle** (*©* **800/258-3826;** www.supershuttle.com) also operates vans every half-hour between the airport and all major downtown hotels for $11 per person one-way, $18 round-trip.

Baltimore

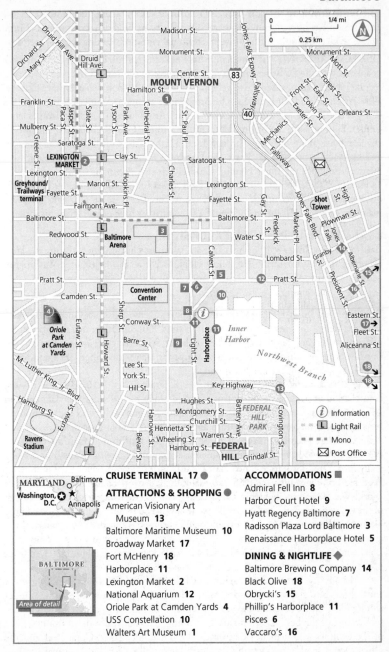

CRUISE TERMINAL 17 ●

ATTRACTIONS & SHOPPING ●

American Visionary Art
  Museum **13**
Baltimore Maritime Museum **10**
Broadway Market **17**
Fort McHenry **18**
Harborplace **11**
Lexington Market **2**
National Aquarium **12**
Oriole Park at Camden Yards **4**
USS Constellation **10**
Walters Art Museum **1**

ACCOMMODATIONS ■

Admiral Fell Inn **8**
Harbor Court Hotel **9**
Hyatt Regency Baltimore **7**
Radisson Plaza Lord Baltimore **3**
Renaissance Harborplace Hotel **5**

DINING & NIGHTLIFE ◆

Baltimore Brewing Company **14**
Black Olive **18**
Obrycki's **15**
Phillip's Harborplace **11**
Pisces **6**
Vaccaro's **16**

If you're driving to the port from I-95 north or south, take Keith Avenue/Exit 56. Turn left on Keith Avenue until it merges into Broening Highway, and take this 1 mile to the Seagirt Marine Terminal. Use the terminal entrance. Parking costs $7 per day.

GETTING AROUND   If you plan to stay near the harbor, it's much easier to walk or take one of the $6 water taxi services that traverse the Inner Harbor. There's also regular metered car-taxi service to get you to the port. On foot, you only have to know a few streets to get your bearings. The **promenade** around the Inner Harbor will take you to Federal Hill and the American Visionary Arts Museum, the Maryland Science Center, Harborplace, the National Aquarium, and the USS *Constellation*. The promenade extends along the water through Inner Harbor East to Fells Point and Canton, and makes for a pretty walk. **Pratt** and **Lombard streets** are the two major east-west arteries just above the Inner Harbor. **Charles Street** is Baltimore's main route north and home to some good restaurants. **St. Paul Street** is the major route south. If you're driving around, expect things to be fairly easy. The streets are on a straight grid, and many are one-way. All the major **rental-car** companies have offices at the airport.

BEST CRUISE LINE SHORE EXCURSIONS

Baltimore City Tour ($39, 2½ hr.): Take in Baltimore's historic sites, visiting the Harborplace, Babe Ruth's birthplace, Johns Hopkins University, Baltimore's Washington Monument, Fort McHenry, and the historic ships berthed at the Seaport.

EXPLORING BALTIMORE ON YOUR OWN

Baltimore's old **Inner Harbor** is the starting point for most visitors. Once a major seaport, the freight business ground to a halt in the 1960s, but it's been a destination for pleasure boaters and tall ships since the city began revitalizing the area in the late '70s. In addition to **restaurants** and extensive **shopping** (see below), there are a number of historic attractions in the neighborhood.

The **USS** *Constellation,* moored at 301 E. Pratt St. (© **410/539-1797;** www. constellation.org), is a stunning triple-masted sloop-of-war originally launched in 1854. It's the last Civil War–era vessel afloat. Tour her gun decks, visit the wardrooms, see a cannon demonstration, and learn about the life of an old-time sailor. Admission is $6.50. More seagoing history is to be had at the **Baltimore Maritime Museum** (© **410/396-3453;** www.baltomaritimemuseum.org). Located at Piers 3 and 5, it's really four museums in one. The Coast Guard Cutter *Taney* survived the bombing of Pearl Harbor, the submarine USS *Torsk* sank the last two Japanese merchant ships of World War II, and the lightship *Chesapeake* spent 40 years anchored near the mouth of the Chesapeake Bay. The "screwpile"-style Seven-Foot Knoll Lighthouse looks more like a New England UFO than a traditional lighthouse. Built in 1856, it marked the entrance to Baltimore's harbor for 133 years before being moved to its current location. Admission to all four is $7 adults, $4 kids. Tickets are available at Pier 3, in front of the National Aquarium, and at the USS *Constellation* Building on Pier 1.

At the nearby **National Aquarium,** 501 E. Pratt St. (© **410/576-3800;** www. aqua.org), visitors can walk into a room surrounded by patrolling sharks, wander among the coral reefs, follow the yearly migration of fish, and visit a rainforest on the roof at one of the best aquariums in the country. Though you walk in front of most of the exhibits, you actually walk inside the doughnut-shaped Coral Reef and the Open Ocean shark tanks, getting up close. There's also a Marine Mammal Pavilion that's home to a family of dolphins and a new exhibit re-creating the canyons of Australia. Admission costs $17.50 adults, $9.50 kids.

Oh, say, can you see by the dawn's early light? Apparently Francis Scott Key could back in 1814, when the British attacked star-shaped **Fort McHenry,** which sits on a point in the harbor at East Fort Avenue (© 410/962-4290; www.nps.gov/fomc). It was the sight of the fort's enormous 15-star flag that showed the fort's 1,000 defenders had held their ground, halting the British offensive and inspiring the U.S. national anthem. After that day the fort never again came under attack, but it remained an active fort on and off for the next hundred years. Today, it's both a National Park and a National Historic Shrine and still flies its huge flag, which takes about 20 people to manage when it's raised and lowered daily. Stop by at 9:30am or 4:30pm (7:30pm June–Aug) to join in. The fort's buildings display historical and military memorabilia, and you can tour the restored barracks, commander's quarters, guardhouse, and powder magazine. Admission $5; free under 16.

The **Walters Art Museum,** 600 N. Charles St. (© 410/547-9000; www.thewalters.org), with its collections of ancient art, medieval armor, and French 19th-century painting, has always been one of Baltimore's great attractions, telling the story of Western civilization through its permanent collection, which covers some 55 centuries. Admission is $8; closed Monday and Tuesday.

For something different, visit the **American Visionary Art Museum,** 800 Key Hwy., at the base of historic Federal Hill on the south side of the Inner Harbor (© 410/244-1900; www.avam.org). You can't miss it: Just look for the multicolored, 55-foot wind-powered sculpture out front. As defined by the museum, visionary art is "art produced by self-taught individuals, usually without formal training, whose works arise from an innate personal vision that revels foremost in the creative act itself." This can range from narrative embroideries by Holocaust survivors to the 10-foot model of the *Lusitania* that dominates a first-floor gallery—made from 193,000 matchsticks. All in all, it's some of the more interesting art you'll ever see. Admission costs $9; closed Monday.

Baseball fans will want to try and catch a game at Oriole Park at Camden Yards, 333 W. Camden St. (© 410/685-9800; www.theorioles.com). If there's a home game during your visit, do whatever it takes to get a ticket: It's a real Baltimore experience. Games are usually held at 1:35 or 7:35pm, with tickets going for about $9 to $32.

SHOPPING

The Inner Harbor is Baltimore's prime shopping district, with malls and hundreds of shops. **Harborplace** (© 410/332-0060; www.harborplace.com) is actually three separate locations with more than 160 stores. Between them, they sell everything from onion rings to diamond rings. The **Light Street Pavilion** has the most food stalls and restaurants, with some souvenir shops. The **Pratt Street Pavilion** offers specialty stores, clothing and jewelry shops, and more restaurants. **The Gallery,** a mall in the Renaissance Harborplace Hotel, has three floors of shops and a food court on the fourth.

For a more classic taste of the city, head to one of its centuries-old markets. The 200-year-old **Broadway Market,** on South Broadway between Fleet and Lancaster streets, has two large covered buildings staffed by local vendors selling fresh produce, flowers, crafts, and an assortment of ethnic and raw-bar foods, ideal for snacking, a quick lunch, or a picnic. You'll even find an old-fashioned Baltimore tradition: "sweet potatoes," soft white candies powdered with cinnamon. The **Lexington Market,** 400 W. Lexington St. (© **410/685-6169;** www.lexingtonmarket.com), claims to be the oldest continuously operating market in the United States, having opened for business in 1782. This Baltimore landmark houses more than 140 merchants, selling prepared ethnic foods (for eat-in or take-away), fresh seafood, produce, meats, baked goods, sweets, even freshly grated coconut. It's worth a visit for the aromas, flavors, sounds, and sights, as well as good shopping. Bring cash, as credit cards are not accepted. Closed Sunday.

WHERE TO STAY

A number of hotels are located in the Inner Harbor and Fells Point neighborhoods, the latter Baltimore's original seaport and home to the first shipyards. Both are located a maximum of 7 miles from the cruise terminal.

The **Hyatt Regency Baltimore,** 300 Light St. (© **800/233-1234;** www. hyatt.com), was the Inner Harbor's first hotel 20 years ago and still has its best location, just a few steps from everything. Rooms have breathtaking harbor views and the amenities are terrific. Rates: $125 to $300.

The **Harbor Court Hotel,** 550 Light St. (© **800/824-0076;** www.harborcourt. com), strives for quiet dignity, refinement, and graciousness, with exquisitely furnished rooms. Rates: $220 to $250.

The **Renaissance Harborplace Hotel,** 202 E. Pratt St. (© **800/468-3571;** http://renaissancehotels.com), is also located right in the middle of everything, across the street from Harborplace and the Inner Harbor. Rooms are very large, and many have great views. Rates: $129 to $309.

The French Renaissance–style **Radisson Plaza Lord Baltimore,** 20 W. Baltimore St. (© **800/333-3333;** www.radisson.com), opened in 1928, so if you love grand old hotels with modern conveniences, this is the one for you. The entrance features marble columns, hand-carved artwork, brass fixtures, and chandeliers, and the Inner Harbor is only 5 blocks away. Rates: $179 to $279.

In Fells Point (southeast of the Inner Harbor), the **Admiral Fell Inn,** 888 S. Broadway (© **800/292-4667;** www.admiralfell.com), is composed of seven buildings built between 1790 and 1920, and blends Victorian and Federal-style architecture. Originally a boardinghouse for sailors, later a YMCA and then a vinegar bottling plant, the inn now includes an antiques-filled lobby and library and guest rooms individually decorated with Federal period furnishings. Rates: $215 to $265.

DINING & NIGHTLIFE

Baltimore used to be very quiet after dark, but not anymore. We suggest heading to the Inner Harbor or Fells Point for some of the town's legendary seafood and an evening out.

Fells Point, the neighborhood where Baltimore began, is one of the city's best areas for seafood, and the benchmark of all the eateries here is **Obrycki's,** 1727 E. Pratt St. (© **410/732-6399**). This is the quintessential crab house, where you can crack open steamed crabs in their shells and feast on the tender, succulent meat. There's crab soup, crab cocktail, crab balls, crab cakes, crab imperial, and soft-shell crabs, and the rest of the menu is just as tempting. Main courses; $15 to $29. At the **Black Olive,** 814 S. Bond St. (© **410/276-7141;** www.theblackolive.com), a Greek taverna located just beyond the busier streets of Fells Point, the combination of Greek fare and the freshest seafood is magic. Choose the catch of the day and trust the chef to make it wonderful. Main courses: $22 to $32. Reservations required.

In a city where lots of restaurants have good views, the view from **Pisces,** 300 Light St. in the Inner Harbor's Hyatt Regency (© **410/528-1234**), tops them all, overlooking the Inner Harbor, Camden Yards, and the downtown skyline. The interior is sleek and modern and the menu small but intriguing, stressing seafood. Main courses: $15 to $29. Of more than a dozen restaurants and sidewalk cafes in the festive Harborplace development, **Phillip's Harborplace,** on level 1 (© **800/648-7067**), is a standout, and the best place for good, reasonably priced seafood featuring crab in many forms—soft-shell, crab and lobster sauté, crab cakes, crab imperial, and all-you-can-eat portions of steamed crabs. Phillips also offers takeout in the Light Street Pavilion. Main courses: $15 to $30.

To top off a perfect day, drop by **Vaccaro's,** 222 Albemarle St. in Little Italy, near Fells Point (© **410/685-4905**), for Italian desserts, coffee, and cappuccino. There's also a location at the Light Street Pavilion in Harborplace. For something more sudsy, try the **Baltimore Brewing Company,** 104 Albemarle St., between Little Italy and the Inner Harbor (© **410/837-5000**). The home of DeGroen's beer, this microbrewery is part German restaurant, part beer hall, its large drinking area lined with sturdy picnic tables.

3 Boston, Massachusetts

Founded in 1630 along the Charles River, Boston is a port of call on many itineraries that sail from New York and is also an embarkation port for a handful of New England/Canada cruises (many of them terminating in Montréal or Québec City). Of all the New England ports it has perhaps the richest history, beginning from the earliest days of America's settlement through the Revolution and beyond. Wend your way through the city's many important historical sights via the Freedom Trail walking tour, hitting sites from the USS *Constitution* (aka Old Ironsides) to the Paul Revere House. In other neighborhoods, stroll past the beautiful Victorian-era town houses in the stylish Back Bay and Beacon Hill areas, or head across the Charles River to Cambridge for a romp around the classic ivied campus of Harvard, founded nearly 400 years ago. Then again, you can skip the past and focus on pure fun, whether it's shopping, perhaps at Faneuil Hall Marketplace, or pub hopping—the beloved *Cheers* bar (at least the exterior used in the opening credits) is on Beacon Street, while a replica of the interior is in Faneuil Hall.

GETTING TO BOSTON & THE PORT

All ships dock at the **Black Falcon Cruise Terminal,** located in the Boston Marine Industrial Park in the South Boston Waterfront District. There's nothing here but ships and sheds, but the heart of Boston is only a couple miles away, and tour buses and taxis line up to meet cruise passengers. For more information, call **Massport** at © **800/235-6426** or check out www.massport.com. By air, you'll arrive at Boston's **Logan International Airport** (www.massport.com/logan), located in East Boston, 3 miles across the harbor from downtown and about 7 miles from the cruise terminal. A taxi to the port costs about $15 for two passengers and the drive takes about 30 to 45 minutes, depending on traffic. **Back Bay Coach** (© **888/222-5229** or 617/746-9909) runs vans frequently from outside the airport's baggage claim to the port and other points in town. It costs $10 per passenger each way.

If you're coming by car from the Massachusetts Turnpike traveling east, go toward Logan Airport. Pass the I-90/I-93 interchange and enter a tunnel eastbound. In the tunnel, take Exit 25/South Boston. At the traffic lights, you will be at Congress Street. Turn right onto Congress Street. Follow to the end and turn right onto Northern Avenue and proceed into the Marine Industrial Park. Continue to the end and turn right onto Tide Street and an immediate right onto Drydock Avenue. Make a left at the Design Center (Design Center Place), which will be immediately across from the entrance to the EDIC Parking Garage. The Black Falcon Terminal is the adjacent building on the water. Parking costs $12 per day.

GETTING AROUND   The best way to see the historic heart of Boston is on foot. If you don't sign up for one of your ship's organized tours, hop in the shuttle bus some cruise lines provide or grab a taxi at the pier and drop $15 for the 3-plus-mile ride to the Boston Common, a good starting point for walking tours. Once in town, spend the day walking, join a hop-on hop-off trolley tour, or take advantage of Boston's efficient subway system, the "T" (short for MBTA), which has stops all over the city. Subway fares run from $1.25 to $3 for adults; bus fares are 90¢.

BEST CRUISE LINE SHORE EXCURSIONS

Freedom Trail Walking Tour ($32, 3½ hr.): While you can easily do this well-marked walk on your own, if you'd like a guide to explain the highlights, this excursion is a good choice.

Fenway Park Tour ($59, 3½ hr.): America's oldest major league ballpark, Fenway is a major pilgrimage site for baseball fans. Visitors tour the press box and broadcast booths, the Red Sox Hall of Fame Club, the .406 Club, the dugout seats, and sometimes the famous left field wall known as "the Green Monster."

Biking Along the Charles River ($59, 3 hr.): After a short bus ride to Boston Common, hop on your borrowed bike and follow the experienced guide through the Common and along the Public Garden to Arthur Fiedler Footbridge. Here the small group turns onto the paved trail along the Esplanade on the Charles River, with views of MIT and Harvard before crossing the river into Cambridge. While peddling enjoy views of the Back Bay skyline with its high-rises and church steeples, and cross back into Boston to visit the Hatch Memorial Shell, the Boston Pops Orchestra's bandstand.

Beacon Hill Walking Tour ($46, 3 hr.): This walking tour begins in the Back Bay neighborhood. The guide leads the group past Trinity Church and adjacent Hancock Tower, along the boutiques and cafes of Newbury Street, through the lush Public Garden, and for a quick beer at the Cheers Pub, the one that inspired the beloved TV show. Move on to Boston Common, the narrow streets and brick sidewalks of Beacon Hill, and finally to Quincy Market.

The Path of Paul Revere ($49, 4 hr.): This bus ride through Boston follows the route of Paul Revere's famous ride to Lexington. In Concord, drive along "Author's Row" for views of the homes of Nathaniel Hawthorne, Ralph Waldo Emerson, and Louisa May Alcott. Once in Lexington, see where 77 Minutemen faced 700 British soldiers at the very first battle of the American Revolution. Eight Minutemen were killed; the wounded were taken to Buckman Tavern, today restored to its 18th-century state.

Lexington & Concord Tour ($99, 7½ hr.): Outside Boston, the towns of Lexington and Concord witnessed the first battle of the Revolutionary War. Tour includes the

Old North Church, where Paul Revere ordered two lanterns to be hung, warning of the British advance by sea; Lexington Green, where the first skirmish of the war took place; and the Old North Bridge, where the American militia met the British forces. Most tours also stop at Harvard Yard, the USS *Constitution,* and for lunch at the Oyster House, America's oldest continuously operating restaurant.

Mayflower & **Plimoth Plantation Tour** ($99, 7½ hr.): Step aboard a full-scale replica of the *Mayflower,* take a gander at Plymouth Rock, then have a lobster lunch at Plimoth Plantation, a living museum where actors re-create 17th-century life.

EXPLORING BOSTON ON YOUR OWN

Boston's cruise port is located in an industrial section of town. There's nothing of note within easy walking distance, but downtown is a short distance by taxi or public transit. Grab a copy of the free *Where Boston* magazine in the terminal and use its map to walk the city's famed **Freedom Trail,** a 3-mile string of well-marked sites that tells the story of America's Revolution, beginning at **Boston Common,** the country's oldest public park, and ending at the 18th-century battleship **USS *Constitution,*** aka Old Ironsides. Sites along the way include the **Boston Latin School,** the first public school in the Colonies, dating back to 1635; the 1712-built **Old State House,** where the Declaration of Independence was first read publicly; the site of the **Boston Massacre;** the **Paul Revere House,** home of the famous Revolutionary War figure who warned that the British were coming; **Faneuil Hall,** an indoor/outdoor mall restaurant/shopping market that was once an important meeting place where the likes of John Hancock, Susan B. Anthony, and John F. Kennedy spoke to the masses; and **Old North Church,** where the famous lanterns signaled Paul Revere's midnight ride.

If you're not psyched about walking the whole thing, join a trolley tour that loops through the city's historic districts, with 20 stops and more than 100 points of interest. Try Brush Hill Tours' **Beantown Trolley** (© **781/986-6100;** www.beantown trolley.com), which offers 1½-hour tours on vintage-style red trolleys, visiting sites on the Freedom Trail as well as other parts of the city. You can hop on and off all day long for $24 per adult (which includes a harbor cruise May–Oct). Stops include the Shaw Memorial across from the State House, where you can buy tickets.

SHOPPING

One of best features of shopping in Massachusetts is that there's no sales tax on clothing priced below $175. On that bright note, the top shopping area is Boston's **Back Bay.** Dozens of classy galleries, shops, and boutiques make **Newbury Street** a world-famous destination. Nearby, the **Shops at Prudential Center** and **Copley Place** (linked by an enclosed walkway across Huntington Ave.) bookend a giant retail complex that includes the posh department stores **Neiman Marcus** and **Saks Fifth Avenue.** The adjacent **South End,** though less commercially dense, boasts a number of art galleries and quirky shops. Another popular spot is **Faneuil Hall Marketplace,** where you'll find the shops, boutiques, and pushcarts at Boston's busiest attraction sell everything from cosmetics to costume jewelry, sweaters to souvenirs.

If the hubbub at Faneuil Hall and in the Back Bay overwhelms you, stroll over to Beacon Hill. Picturesque **Charles Street,** at the foot of the hill, is a short but commercially dense street noted for its excellent gift shops and antiques dealers. One of Boston's oldest shopping areas is **Downtown Crossing,** a traffic-free pedestrian mall along Washington, Winter, and Summer streets near Boston Common, with big-name stores like **Filene's, Filene's Basement, Macy's, H&M,** and **Barnes & Noble. Harvard Square** in Cambridge, with its bookstores, boutiques, and T-shirt shops, is about 20 minutes from downtown Boston by subway on the red line.

WHERE TO STAY

You've got a lot of choice in Boston's many appealing neighborhoods, from B&Bs to boutique hotels and major chains, but don't expect great bargains. Like New York, rates are generally on the high side during spring and summer. Here's a sampling of hotels in downtown Boston (which includes most of the Freedom Trail and the Waterfront, Faneuil Hall Marketplace, the Financial District, and Downtown Crossing areas) and near the airport, both convenient access points to the cruise terminal.

The **Boston Harbor Hotel,** 70 Rowes Wharf, at the Waterfront and Faneuil Hall Marketplace (© **800/752-7077;** www.bhh.com), is one of the finest choices in town—and certainly the prettiest, whether you approach its landmark arch from land or sea (the Airport Water Shuttle stops here). The 16-story brick building is within walking distance of downtown and the waterfront attractions, and it prides itself on offering top-notch service to travelers pursuing both business and pleasure. Rooms have wonderful harbor and skyline views. Rates: from $295.

The chief appeal of the **Boston Marriott Long Wharf,** 296 State St. (© **800/ 228-9290;** www.marriottlongwharf.com), is its easy access to downtown and waterfront attractions. The terraced brick exterior of the seven-story, 389-room hotel is one of the most recognizable sights on the harbor. Rates: from $249.

Harborside Inn, 185 State St. (© **888/723-7565;** www.harborsideinnboston. com), a renovated 1858 warehouse across the street from Faneuil Hall Marketplace and the harbor, is a short walk from the Financial District. You get a lot for your money here: The nicely appointed guest rooms have queen-size beds, hardwood floors, Oriental rugs, and Victorian-style furniture. The rooms surround a sky-lit atrium; those with city views are more expensive but can be noisier. Rates: from $159.

You can't beat the **Four Seasons,** 200 Boylston St. (© **800/819-5053;** www.four seasons.com), for exquisite service, a beautiful location, elegant guest rooms and public areas, a terrific health club, and wonderful restaurants. If you can afford it, this is unquestionably the place to stay. Each room in the 16-story brick-and-glass building has a great view. Rates: from $425.

The **Hampton Inn Boston Logan Airport,** 2300 Lee Burbank Hwy., Revere (© **800/426-7866;** www.hamptoninn.com), is on an ugly commercial-industrial strip, but it's just 1.5 miles from the airport and 3 miles from downtown Boston. A free 24-hour shuttle bus serves the 227-room hotel transporting guests to and from the airport and nearby restaurants. The hotel also has a pool, and the rates include continental breakfast. Rates: from $135.

DINING & NIGHTLIFE

Downtown, people have poured into **Durgin-Park,** 340 Faneuil Hall Marketplace (© **617/227-2038;** www.durgin-park.com), since 1827 for huge portions of delicious food, famously cranky waitresses, and a rowdy atmosphere where CEOs share tables with students. Feast on prime rib the size of a hubcap, lamb chops, fried seafood, and roast turkey. Fresh seafood arrives twice daily. Main courses: $7 to $30. If you want to check out America's oldest restaurant (which also happens to be Boston's best raw bar), visit **Ye Olde Union Oyster House,** 41 Union St. (© **617/227-2750;** www.union oysterhouse.com). The place opened in 1826 and looks much the same as it did then, with a menu of traditional New England seafood. Daniel Webster and John Kennedy were regulars. Main courses: $17 to $30. For French fare, consider **Les Zygomates,** 129 South St. (© **617/542-5108;** www.winebar.com), a delightful bistro and wine bar in a high-ceilinged, brick-walled space. A popular business-lunch destination, Les Zygomates has a chic, romantic atmosphere at night, when live jazz (in its dining room) helps set the mood. Main courses: $18 to $25.

In Cambridge, **Jasper White's Summer Shack,** 149 Alewife Brook Pkwy., Cambridge (© **617/520-9500;** www.summershackrestaurant.com), is a one-of-a-kind 300-seat place with picnic-table style seating and baby blue leather booths, serving up its signature pan-roasted lobster, plus all kinds of seafood, from clam rolls to steamers. Go for the food and the experience. Main courses: $5 to $28. (Jasper White's also has a location in the Back Bay, at 50 Dalton St.; © 617/867-9955.) For more mainstream, there's **Legal Sea Foods** (www.legalseafoods.com), a local family-run chain known for its top-quality seafood. There are nine locations around Boston and Cambridge, including 255 State St., on the waterfront (© **617/227-3115**); 36 Park Sq., between Columbus Avenue and Stuart Street (© **617/426-4444**); and Copley Place, 2nd level (© **617/266-7775**). Main courses: $8 to $35. For burgers in Harvard Square, go to **Mr. Bartley's Burger Cottage,** 1246 Mass. Ave. (© **617/354-6559**), famous for its burgers, onion rings, and a down-to-earth atmosphere. Most items are under $9.

Boston's Italian-American enclave, the North End, has dozens of restaurants; many are tiny and don't serve dessert or coffee. To satisfy those cravings, hit the *caffès* for coffee and fresh pastry in an atmosphere where lingering is welcome. Try **Caffè dello Sport,** 308 Hanover St. (© **617/523-5063**), and **Caffè Vittoria,** 296 Hanover St. (© **617/227-7606**). There's also table service at **Mike's Pastry,** 300 Hanover St. (© **617/742-3050;** www.mikespastry.com), a bakery that's famous for its bustling takeout business and its cannoli.

Nightlife listings can be found in the city's two main newspapers, the *Boston Globe* and *Boston Herald,* or in free publications, available at newspaper boxes around town, like the weekly *Boston Phoenix, Improper Bostonian,* and *STUFF@Night.* Closing time for clubs is 2am, and, since 2004, a smoking ban covers all bars, clubs, and restaurants in the city.

Boston's bar scene was the inspiration behind the TV show *Cheers.* The Bull & Finch Pub, the original bar that inspired the show, is now known as **Cheers Beacon Hill,** 84 Beacon St. (© **617/227-9605;** www.cheersboston.com). Another Cheers, at Quincy Market in Faneuil Hall (© **617/227-0150;** www.cheersboston.com), has an interior modeled after the show's. Nearby, the jam-packed **Black Rose,** 160 State St. (© **617/742-2286;** www.blackrosepub.com), books live Irish music. For jazz, head to either **Regattabar,** at the Charles Hotel, 1 Bennett St., Cambridge (© **617/661-5000;** www.regattabarjazz.com), or **Scullers,** in the Doubletree hotel, 400 Soldiers Field Rd. (© **617/562-4111;** www.scullersjazz.com). Both regularly book top-name acts. Weirdly, one of the hottest nightlife destinations in town is a bowling alley: **Kings,** 10 Scotia St. (© **617/266-2695;** www.backbaykings.com), a 25,000-foot complex in a former movie theater in the Back Bay neighborhood. It has 20 bowling lanes (four of them private), an eight-table billiards room, and a restaurant and lounge.

4 Cape Canaveral & Cocoa Beach, Florida

Known as the "Space Coast" because of nearby Kennedy Space Center, the Cape Canaveral/Cocoa Beach/Melbourne area boasts 72 miles of beaches, plus fishing, golfing, and surfing. The area is only an about an hour west of Orlando's theme parks, which explains why long-underutilized Port Canaveral is now busier than ever before, offering many 3- and 4-night cruise options (often sold as packages with pre- or post-cruise visits to the Orlando resorts) as well as weeklong itineraries. This year, Port Canaveral has even become a port of call, with NCL's *Norwegian Dawn* visiting on her round-trip Florida/Caribbean itineraries from New York.

Outside the port area, Cape Canaveral is . . . well, it's no Miami. Highways, strip malls, chain stores, and tracts of suburban homes predominate from the port area south into Cocoa Beach, where most of the hotels, restaurants, and beaches discussed here are located. The central areas of Cocoa Beach are mildly more interesting, with some great '50s/'60s condo and hotel architecture, but stylish they're not.

GETTING TO CAPE CANAVERAL & THE PORT

Port Canaveral is located at the eastern end of the Bennett Causeway, just off State Road 528 (the Bee Line Expwy.), the direct route from Orlando. From the port, 528 turns sharply south and becomes State Road A1A, portions of which are known as Astronaut Boulevard and North Atlantic Avenue. For information about the port, contact the Canaveral Port Authority (© **888/767-8226** or 321/783-7831; www.portcanaveral.org). Those flying in will probably land at the **Orlando International Airport** (© **407/825-2001;** www.orlandoairports.net), a 45-mile drive from Port Canaveral via S.R. 528, or **Melbourne International Airport** (www.mlbair. com), a straight drive from I-95 to SR 528. Cruise line representatives will meet you if you've booked air and/or transfers through the line. **Cocoa Beach Shuttle** (© **800/633-0427** or 321/784-3831) offers shuttle service between Orlando's airport and Port Canaveral; the trip costs $27 per person each way. By car, Port Canaveral and Cocoa Beach are accessible from virtually every interstate highway along the East Coast. Most visitors arrive via Route 1, Interstate 95, or S.R. 528. Parking at the port costs $10 a day.

GETTING AROUND   Cars are vital. Most **car-rental** companies operate at the Orlando airport, as do several taxi services. The fare to Port Canaveral is a hefty $85-plus, but taxis charge the same rate for up to 9 passengers, so if you're traveling with a group, this might be a good option.

BEST CRUISE LINE SHORE EXCURSIONS

The cruise lines offer excursions to **Kennedy Space Center** ($60, 6 hr.) and the Orlando theme parks ($88/7 hr. to **Universal Studios** or **Islands of Adventure,** $27/8½ hr. transfer-only to **Walt Disney World,** with guests responsible for their own park tickets), as well as pre- and post-cruise stays in Orlando and at local beach resorts. Disney Cruise Line (of course) is the leader in linking cruisers to Orlando, with *Disney Wonder*'s 3- and 4-night itineraries specifically designed to integrate 3- and 4-night stays at the Disney resorts.

THE ORLANDO THEME PARKS

All it took was a sprinkle of pixie dust in the 1970s to begin the almost-magical transformation of Orlando from a swath of swampland into the most visited tourist destination in the world. Today it's home to three giants—Walt Disney World, Universal Orlando, and SeaWorld—whose local offerings include seven of the eight most popular theme parks in the United States. Many cruises from Port Canaveral are sold as land-sea packages that include park stays, but if you decide to visit Orlando before or after your cruise, it's essential to plan ahead. Otherwise, the number of attractions begging for your time and the hyper-commercial atmosphere can put a serious dent in your psyche, your wallet, and your stamina. Even if you had 2 weeks, it wouldn't be long enough to hit everything, so don't even try. Stay selective, stay sane. That's our motto. Here's some basic info on each of the main parks. If you plan to spend a considerable amount of time here, we suggest picking up a copy of *Frommer's Walt Disney World & Orlando 2006*.

WALT DISNEY WORLD

Walt Disney World is the umbrella above four theme parks: the **Magic Kingdom, Epcot, Disney–MGM Studios,** and **Animal Kingdom,** which drew a combined attendance of over 41 million paying customers in 2004, according to *Amusement Business* magazine. Besides its theme parks, Disney has an assortment of other venues, including three water parks, several entertainment venues, and a number of shopping spots. It's all located southwest of Orlando off Interstate 4, west of the Florida Turnpike. For information, vacation brochures, and videos, contact the Walt Disney World Co. (© 407/ 934-7639; www.disneyworld.com) at least 6 weeks in advance of your trip.

TICKET PRICES & HOURS At press time, 1-day, one-park tickets for any one of the four parks were a whopping $60 for adults, $48 for children 3 to 9 (plus tax). Discounted multiday, multipark tickets are available; many land-sea cruise packages include these passes. Park hours vary, so call ahead or go to **www.disneyworld.com** to check. Generally, expect 9am to 8pm hours, though the parks may open earlier and stay open later depending on special events and the economy. Epcot is usually open 10am to 9pm.

THE MAGIC KINGDOM The most popular theme park on the planet offers some 40 attractions, plus restaurants and shops, in a 107-acre package. Its symbol, **Cinderella Castle,** forms the hub of a wheel whose spokes reach to seven "lands" simulating everything from an Amazonian jungle to Colonial America. If you're traveling with little kids, this is the place to go.

EPCOT This 260-acre park (the acronym stands for Experimental Prototype Community of Tomorrow) has two sections. **Future World** is centered on Epcot's icon, a giant geosphere that looks like a big golf ball. Major corporations sponsor the park's 10 themed areas, and the focus is on discovery, scientific achievements, and tomorrow's technologies in areas running from energy to undersea exploration. The **World Showcase** is a community of 11 miniaturized nations surrounding a 40-acre lagoon. All of these "countries" have indigenous architecture, landscaping, restaurants, and shops; and cultural facets are explored in art exhibits, dance or other live performances, and innovative films. This park definitely appeals more to adults than children, but it has few thrill rides. If that's a requirement, go elsewhere. *Note:* Hiking through this park will often exhaust even the fittest person—some folks say Epcot really stands

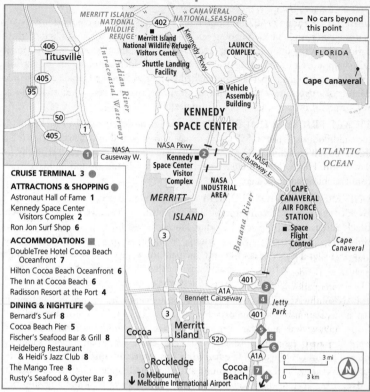

MERRITT ISLAND
NATIONAL
WILDLIFE
REFUGE

CANAVERAL
NATIONAL SEASHORE

■ Merritt Island
National Wildlife Refuge
Visitors Center

■ Shuttle Landing
Facility

LAUNCH
COMPLEX

— No cars beyond
this point

Titusville

FLORIDA

Cape Canaveral

■ Vehicle
Assembly
Building

KENNEDY
SPACE CENTER

ATLANTIC
OCEAN

NASA Pkwy

NASA
Causeway W.

Kennedy ■
Space Center
Visitor
Complex

NASA
Causeway E.

NASA
INDUSTRIAL
AREA

MERRITT

ISLAND

CAPE
CANAVERAL
AIR FORCE
STATION

■ Space
Flight
Control

Cape
Canaveral

CRUISE TERMINAL 3 ●

ATTRACTIONS & SHOPPING ●
Astronaut Hall of Fame **1**
Kennedy Space Center
    Visitors Complex **2**
Ron Jon Surf Shop **6**

ACCOMMODATIONS ■
DoubleTree Hotel Cocoa Beach
    Oceanfront **7**
Hilton Cocoa Beach Oceanfront **6**
The Inn at Cocoa Beach **6**
Radisson Resort at the Port **4**

DINING & NIGHTLIFE ◆
Bernard's Surf **8**
Cocoa Beach Pier **5**
Fischer's Seafood Bar & Grill **8**
Heidelberg Restaurant
    & Heidi's Jazz Club **8**
The Mango Tree **8**
Rusty's Seafood & Oyster Bar **3**

Bennett Causeway

Jetty
Park

Cocoa

Merritt
Island

Cocoa
Beach

Rockledge

To Melbourne/
Melbourne International Airport

0   3 mi
0   3 km

for "Every Person Comes Out Tired"—so we recommend splitting your visit over 2 days if possible.

DISNEY–MGM STUDIOS   You'll probably spy the **Earrfel Tower**—a water tower outfitted with gigantic mouse ears—before you enter this 110-acre park, which Disney bills as "the Hollywood that never was and always will be." You'll find pulse-quickening rides such as the Aerosmith-themed **Rock 'n' Roller Coaster** and the **Twilight Zone of Terror,** and movie- and TV-themed shows such as **Jim Henson's Muppet*Vision 3D,** as well as some wonderful street performers. Adults and kids both love it, and, best of all, it can be done comfortably in 1 day.

ANIMAL KINGDOM   This 500-acre park opened in 1998, combining animals, elaborate landscapes, and a handful of rides. It's a conservation venue as much as an attraction, though, so it's easy for most of the animals to escape your eyes here (unlike at Tampa's Busch Gardens, the state's other major animal park). The thrill rides are better at Busch, but Animal Kingdom has much better shows, such as **Tarzan Rocks!** and **Festival of the Lion King.** The park is good for both adults and children and can be done in a single outing, but if you come on a hot summer day, come early or it's unlikely you'll see many of the primo animals, who are smart enough to seek shade.

UNIVERSAL ORLANDO

Universal Orlando (© 407/363-8000; www.universalorlando.com) is Disney's number-one competitor in the ongoing "anything you can do we can do better" theme-park brawl. Although it's a distant second in terms of attendance, it's unquestionably the champion at entertaining teenagers and the older members of the thrill-ride crowd, with two major parks—the original **Universal Studios Florida** and the newer **Islands of Adventure**—plus an entertainment district and several resorts. It's located at Universal Boulevard, Orlando, off Interstate 4.

TICKET PRICES & HOURS   A 1-day/one-park ticket costs $60 for adults, $48 for children 3 to 9 (plus 6.5% tax); a 2-day, two-park Unlimited-Access Pass is $105 for adults, $95 for children 3 to 9. The parks are open 365 days a year, generally from 9am to 6pm, though often later, especially in summer and around holidays. Call to confirm hours before you go.

UNIVERSAL STUDIOS FLORIDA   Even with fast-paced, grown-up rides such as **Back to the Future, Terminator** (should they change it to Governator?), and **Men in Black Alien Attack,** Universal Studios Florida is fun for kids. And as a plus, it's a working motion-picture and TV studio, so filming is occasionally done at Nickelodeon's sound stages or elsewhere in the park. A talented group of actors portraying a range of characters from Universal films usually roams the park. You can do the park in a day, although you'll be a bit breathless when you get to the finish line.

ISLANDS OF ADVENTURE   This 110-acre theme park opened in 1999 and it is, bar none, *the* Orlando theme park for thrill-ride junkies. With areas themed on Dr. Seuss, Jurassic Park, and Marvel comics, the park successfully combines nostalgia with state-of-the-art technology. Roller coasters roar above pedestrian walkways and water rides slice through the park. **The Amazing Adventures of Spider-Man** is a 3-D track ride that is arguably the best all-around attraction in Orlando; the **Jurassic Park River Adventure**'s 70-foot drop scared creator Steven Spielberg into jumping ship before going over; and **Dueling Dragons** draws more raves from coaster crazies than any other in Orlando. Unless it's the height of high season, the park can be done in a day. It is not, however, a park for families with young kids: 9 of the park's 14 major rides have height restrictions. If, however, you have teens, or are an adrenaline junkie, this is definitely the place for you.

SEAWORLD

A 200-acre marine-life park, **SeaWorld** (© 407/351-3600; www.seaworld.com) explores the deep in a format that combines conservation awareness with entertainment—pretty much what Disney is attempting at Animal Kingdom, but SeaWorld got here first, and its message is subtler and a more integrated part of the experience. The park is fun for everyone from small children to adults (who doesn't like dolphins and whales?) and is easily toured in a single day. The pace is much more laid-back than at Universal or Disney, so it makes for a nice break if you're in the area for several days. SeaWorld has a handful of high-tech roller coasters such as **Journey to Atlantis** and **Kraken,** but, all in all, the park can't compete in this category with Disney and Universal. On the other hand, those parks don't let you discover the crushed-velvet texture of a stingray or the song of a sea lion, not to mention the killer whale **Shamu,** the park's star attraction, and the six other resident orcas. The park entrance is at the intersection of Interstate 4 and State Road 528 (the Bee Line Expwy.), 10 minutes south of downtown Orlando and 15 minutes from Orlando International Airport.

TICKET PRICES & HOURS   A 1-day ticket costs $60 for ages 10 and over, $48 for children 3 to 9 (plus 6.5% tax); age 2 and under, free. The park is usually open 9am to 6pm, later during summer and holidays.

EXPLORING CAPE CANAVERAL & COCOA BEACH ON YOUR OWN

Port Canaveral probably wouldn't be on the cruise industry's radar if it weren't so close to Orlando, and most passengers shuttle directly from theme park to pier rather than spending any significant time here. Nevertheless, anyone interested in the space program and its history should plan to arrive a day early (or stay a day after) to check out Kennedy Space Center and the Astronaut Hall of Fame. There are also a number of attractive beaches.

KENNEDY SPACE CENTER & THE ASTRONAUT HALL OF FAME

Set amid 150,000 acres of marshy wetlands favored by birds, reptiles, and amphibians, the **Kennedy Space Center** (𝕮 **321/449-4444;** www.kennedyspacecenter.com) has been at the center of America's space program since 1969, when astronauts took off from here to the moon. Even if you've never really considered yourself a science or space buff, you can't help but be impressed by the achievements the place represents. The only public access to the center (Hwy. 405) leads directly to the **Kennedy Space Center Visitor Complex,** which has real NASA rockets, the actual Mercury Mission Control Room from the 1960s, and numerous exhibits and films that look at space exploration from the 50s to today. There's a rocket garden displaying now-obsolete Redstone, Atlas, Saturn, and Titan rockets; a daily "Encounter" with a real astronaut; several pricey dining venues; and an obligatory gift shop selling a variety of space memorabilia and souvenirs. Two space-related IMAX movies (one in 3-D) shown on five-and-a-half-story-high screens are informative and entertaining.

While you could spend your entire day at the visitor complex, you must take the included **KSC Tour** or an extra-cost optional tour to see the actual space center, where rockets and shuttles are prepared and launched. Buses for the included tour operate continuously, leaving every 15 minutes and making stops at the **LC-39 Observation Gantry,** with a dramatic 360-degree view over launch pads where space shuttles blast off, and the impressive **Apollo/Saturn V Center,** which includes artifacts, photos, interactive exhibits, and the 363-foot **Saturn V,** the most powerful rocket ever launched by the United States. At each stop you can get off, look around, then take the next bus that comes along. Plan to take the tour early in your visit and be sure to hit the restrooms before boarding—there's only one out on the tour. The optional, guided **NASA Up-Close tour** ($22, 3 hr.) visits KSC's industrial area to see NASA headquarters and get up-close to the Space Shuttle launch pads, KSC's landing facilities, the massive Vehicle Assembly Building, the gigantic Crawler Transporters, and the International Space Station Center, where scientists and engineers prepare additions to the space station now in orbit. The **Cape Canaveral Then and Now tour** ($22, 3 hr.) visits the original launch sites of the Mercury, Gemini, and Apollo programs, including the launch complex where Alan Shepard lifted off on America's first human spaceflight, and Apollo Launch Pad 34, the site of the tragic Apollo 1 fire. Participants relive the launch of America's first satellite at the Air Force Space and Missile

Museum, and also visit the Apollo/Saturn V Center (see above). Optional tours frequently sell out in advance, so call for reservations.

At the Visitors complex, don't miss the **Astronaut Memorial,** a moving black-granite monument that has the names of the U.S. astronauts who have died on missions or while in training. The 60-ton structure rotates on a track that follows the movement of the sun, causing the names to stand out above a brilliant reflection of the sky.

Near the intersection of Routes 1 and 405, across the Indian River to the west of KSC, the **U.S. Astronaut Hall of Fame** features displays, exhibits, and tributes to the heroes of the Mercury, Gemini, and Apollo space programs. Film presentations introduce visitors to the origins of rocketry and to the sheer power of the rockets themselves, and displays of personal memorabilia offer insight into the astronauts' lives. Displays of NASA memorabilia include actual Mission Control terminals (at which you can sit to access interactive information) and, most mind-blowing of all, the actual Apollo 14 command module *Kitty Hawk,* whose plaque bears the inscription "This spacecraft flew to the moon and back January 31 February 9, 1971." Nuff said.

But let's get down to brass tacks. The Astronaut Hall of Fame offers one main thing the rest of the KSC Visitors Complex doesn't: the chance to pretend you're an astronaut through various simulations, including a **G-force simulator** that spins at high speed to simulate four times the force of gravity; a **Mission to Mars** rover simulation that sends you bumping over the surface of the red planet (this one's skippable if you're short on time); and a **Walk on the Moon** weightlessness simulation, using harnesses and counterweights. Now the warnings: Simulators are off-limits to folks under 48 inches, and if you tend to suffer from motion sickness, you'll probably want to avoid everything except the weightlessness simulation. Also, be sure to allow at least a few minutes between simulations, even if you've got a cast-iron constitution. Trust us on this one.

Kennedy Space Center is accessible via State Road 405, just off U.S. 1. The Visitors Complex, including the Astronaut Hall of Fame, is open daily, except Christmas and certain launch days, from 9am to 5:30pm. The last bus tour departs at 2:15pm at the Visitors Complex. Maximum Access Admission (including all exhibits, Astronaut Encounter, IMAX space films, the KSC tour, and the Astronaut Hall of Fame) is $37 adults, $27 kids 3 to 11. Parking at the Visitors Complex and Hall of Fame is free, but there is no shuttle between the two. Be sure to pick up maps as you enter each branch, and expect to spend most of the day here to get the full experience: You'll need at least 2 hours to see the Visitors Complex (plus another couple to see the IMAX films), another 2 to see the highlights of the included tour (plus another 2 or 3 if you linger at the tour stops or take one of the guided tours), and at least another 2 to see the Astronaut Hall of Fame.

BEACHES

Though the Cape Canaveral/Cocoa Beach area doesn't have the spectacular beach culture of Miami, it doesn't lack for pleasant coastline, much of which is famous for surfing. The following beaches (or "parks" in the local lingo) are located within an easy drive of the port area. Closest to the cruise ship port and actually part of the larger port complex, the clean, nicely landscaped 4½-acre **Jetty Park,** 400 E. Jetty Rd. (*C* **321/ 783-7111**), is the most elaborate of the local beaches, perched at a point from which the whole expanse of the Cape Canaveral/Cocoa Beach coastline stretches away to the south. A snack bar, bathrooms, showers, picnic facilities, a children's playground, and fishing are available. Parking costs $5 per car. Follow the signs after entering the port area, near where State Road 528 and the A1A intersect. A series of beaches are accessible (and generally signposted) off the A1A heading south from the port. The **Cocoa Beach Pier** area, off the A1A at Meade Avenue, is a great surfing spot with volleyball, an open-air bar, and a party atmosphere. **Lori Wilson Park,** farther south at 1500 N. Atlantic Ave., is another nicely landscaped area on the order of Jetty Park, with bathrooms and showers; a rustic boardwalk with some shaded picnic areas and benches; a nature center; and The Hammock, a ¼-mile boardwalk nature trail that winds through ferns, twisted trees, and other Jurassic Park–looking foliage, while butterflies flutter by and spiders eye them from their webs. Parking is free.

SHOPPING

Let's be unkind: You could shop here, but why bother? The offerings in Cape Canaveral and Cocoa Beach are mostly the kind of national mall shops that you've probably got at home, so save your energy and dollars for the Caribbean. An exception—as much for the experience as for the goods—is the **Ron Jon Surf Shop,** 4151 N. Atlantic Ave./A1A (© 321/799-8888; www.ronjons.com). Inside the blue and yellow, South Beach–looking Art Deco building is enough au courant beachwear to transform you and a good-size army into surfer dudes. The store also rents beach bikes, body boards, surfboards, kayaks, beach chairs, and other equipment by the hour, day, or week. It's open 24 hours a day, 365 days a year.

WHERE TO STAY

While the area has a wealth of cheap beach hotels, few are really notable, so we'll concentrate on a few that are.

The **Radisson Resort at the Port,** 8701 Astronaut Blvd./A1A (© **800/333-3333;** www.radisson.com/capecanaveralfl), is only a 5-minute drive from the port and offers comfortable rooms and very comfortable two-room suites that are a great option for families, featuring a bedroom with a Jacuzzi and a sofa bed in the living room. Cruise passengers arriving by car can leave their vehicles free in the hotel's lot during their cruise and take the free Radisson shuttle to and from the port. Rates: from $139.

At the other end of the spectrum, **The Inn at Cocoa Beach,** 4300 Ocean Beach Blvd., just off the A1A behind the Ron Jon Surf Shop (© **800/343-5307;** www.theinnatcocoabeach.com), is almost entirely couples-oriented, presenting itself as more of a personalized inn than a traditional hotel. Almost all of its 50 comfortable, romantic B&B-style rooms face the ocean and have rocking chairs on their balconies. Two parrots and two dogs are members of the hotel "staff," and guests are treated to daily breakfast, afternoon tea, and evening wine-and-cheese socials. Rates: from $135.

The **Hilton Cocoa Beach Oceanfront,** 1550 N. Atlantic Ave./A1A (© **800/ 445-8667;** www.cocoabeachhilton.com), is the most upscale of the beachfront mainstream hotels, though it looks more like a downtown business hotel that's been transplanted to the seashore. Rooms are spacious but have smallish picture windows only; none offers a balcony. Rates: from $130. (TV fans take note: The Hilton is near a street called "I Dream of Jeannie Lane.")

The six-story **DoubleTree Hotel Cocoa Beach Oceanfront,** 2080 N. Atlantic Ave. (© **800/552-3224;** www.cocoabeachdoubletree.com), is the pick of the full-service beachside hotels, with oceanview balconies in every room. Rates: from $125.

DINING & NIGHTLIFE

Bernard's Surf, 2 S. Atlantic Ave., Cocoa Beach (© **321/783-2401;** www.bernards surf.com), was opened by Bernard Fischer in 1948, and today photos testify to the many astronauts who've celebrated their safe return to Earth with the restaurant's steak and seafood. The latter is provided by the Fischer family's own boats. At the same address, **Fischer's Seafood Bar & Grill** is a *Cheers*-like lounge popular with the locals, serving fried combo platters, shrimp and crab claw meat, and the like. **Rusty's** is another casual option, with spicy seafood gumbo, raw or steamed oysters, burgers and sandwiches, pasta, and so on. **Rusty's Seafood & Oyster Bar,** 628 Glen Cheek Dr., Port Canaveral (© **321/783-2033;** www.rustysseafood.com), on the south side of Port Canaveral harbor, serves the same menu but with views of the fishing boats and cruise ships heading in and out of the port. Bernard's main courses are $16 to $40; at the others, everything's about $5 to $20.

The Mango Tree, 118 N. Atlantic Ave./A1A, between North 1st and North 2nd streets (© **321/799-0513;** www.themangotreerestaurant.com), is the most beautiful and sophisticated restaurant in Cocoa Beach, serving gourmet seafood, pasta, chicken, and Continental dishes in a plantation-home atmosphere, amid grounds lush with tropical foliage. Main courses: $15 to $39.

In downtown Cocoa Beach, the **Heidelberg Restaurant,** 7 N. Orlando Ave./A1A at the Minuteman Causeway (© **321/783-6806**), serves German and Continental dinner cuisine such as beef filet stroganoff, goulash, roast duck, sauerbraten, and grilled loin pork chops. Main courses: $15 to $23. The adjoining **Heidi's Jazz Club** (© **321/ 783-4559;** www.heidisjazzclub.com) has music nightly except Mondays, with a jam session Sundays from 7 to 11pm. See their website for a schedule of performances.

The **Cocoa Beach Pier,** 401 Meade Ave., off the A1A, and ½ mile north of State Road 520 (© **321/783-7549;** www.cocoabeachpier.com), juts out 800 feet over the Atlantic, offering a casual beer-and-fruity-drinks atmosphere, an open-air bar with live music most nights, an ice-cream shop, sit-down seafood restaurants, and an arcade, plus beach equipment rentals and volleyball right next door on the sand.

5 Charleston, South Carolina

In the closing pages of *Gone With the Wind*, Rhett tells Scarlett that he's going back home to Charleston, where he can find "the calm dignity life can have when it's lived by gentle folks, the genial grace of days that are gone." In spite of all the changes and upheavals over the years, Rhett's endorsement of Charleston still holds true, sans slavery and petticoats. Near fanatical preservationists have assured that architecturally, at least, the Old South lives on here, and they've even managed to hold on to some of its graciousness, too. It's one of the best-preserved cities in the South, boasting 73 pre-Revolutionary buildings and more than 600 built before the 1840s. With its cobblestone streets and horse-drawn carriages, jasmine and wisteria fragrances, and stately old homes, it's a nice little time machine of a place, totally conscious of its historical nature but gratifyingly averse to turning itself into an Old South theme park.

GETTING TO CHARLESTON & THE PORT

The **Port of Charleston's** 18,000-square-foot cruise ship terminal (© **843/958-8298;** www.port-of-charleston.com) is located at 196 Concord St., at the foot of Market Street, smack in the heart of the historic district. You can easily walk anywhere you

Charleston

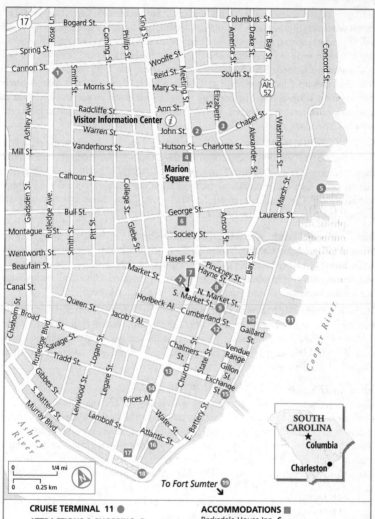

CRUISE TERMINAL 11 ●

ATTRACTIONS & SHOPPING ●
Aiken-Rhett House **3**
Battery/White Point Gardens **18**
Charleston Museum **2**
Edmondston-Alston House **16**
Fort Sumter Visitor Education Center **5**
Fort Sumter **19**
Heyward-Washington House **13**
Nathaniel Russell House **14**
Old City Market **9**
Old Exchange & Provost Dungeon **15**

ACCOMMODATIONS ■
Barksdale House Inn **6**
Embassy Suites Historic Charleston **4**
Market Pavilion **10**
Planters Inn **7**
Two Meeting Street Inn **17**

DINING & NIGHTLIFE ◆
Anson **8**
A. W. Shucks **12**
Club Habana **7**
Hominy Grill **1**

need to go. People arrive by plane at **Charleston International Airport** (© 843/767-7009; www.chs-airport.com), located in North Charleston, 12 miles from the terminal. If you've made arrangements for transfers through your cruise line, a representative will meet your arriving flight and direct you to shuttle buses. **Taxis** are available to downtown for about $20. For those arriving by car, take I-95 north or south, then I-26 (SE) toward Charleston. Exit at East Bay Street, turn left onto Market Street, then right on Washington. The entrance to the terminal will be on your left. **Parking lots** are located near the terminal, with a shuttle service to take you to the pier. Parking is $12 per day.

GETTING AROUND   You can walk around the Historic District easily right from the cruise docks. Narrated horse-drawn **carriage tours** are available at Market Street from several operators. **Palmetto Carriage Tours** (© 843/723-8145; www.charleston carriage.com) uses mule teams and takes off from the red barn behind the Rainbow Market. Tickets are available at 40 N. Market St. From there, exit out back and through the parking lot to the barn. A 1-hour tour costs $19 for adults.

BEST CRUISE LINE SHORE EXCURSIONS

Historic Charleston Carriage Tour ($23, 1 hr.): As hokey as carriage tours may seem, this is actually a nice way to see old Charleston. The leisurely ride just seems to match the pace of the place. You'll pass carefully restored 18th- and 19th-century homes and buildings as your guide gives some historical perspective.

Historic Charleston & Boone Hall ($42–$56, 4 hr.): Tour Charleston's historic district by bus, and also get out of town to see the historic Boone Hall Plantation, with its *Gone With the Wind* ambience. You can tour the lovely Georgian plantation house as well as the slave quarters, built from brick made on the plantation in the 1800s. The tour includes cookies and lemonade on the porch.

EXPLORING CHARLESTON ON YOUR OWN

Charleston's streets are laid out in an easy-to-follow grid. The main north-south thoroughfares are King, Meeting, and East Bay streets. Tradd, Broad, Queen, and Calhoun streets cross the city from east to west. South of Broad Street, East Bay becomes East Battery. The cruise terminal is located in the **Downtown** neighborhood, which extends north from Broad Street to Marion Square at the intersection of Calhoun and Meeting streets. You can't miss the **Old City Market** here (see "Shopping," below), since it shoots straight at the terminal like an arrow. Meeting Street, Church Street, and all the other streets east to the waterfront are full of gorgeous homes and shady gardens, plus many of the historical attractions.

Not far from the City Market, the **Old Exchange & Provost Dungeon,** 122 E. Bay St. (© 843/727-2165; www.oldexchange.com), served as a prison during the American Revolution, then in 1873 became Charleston's City Hall. Its large collection of antique chairs was donated in 1921 by the local Daughters of the American Revolution, and its dungeon (which you can tour led by a costumed docent) displays the only visible chunk of Charleston's original city wall, the Half-Moon Bastion. We could do without its hokey animatronic displays, though. Admission is $7.

The **Nathaniel Russell House,** 51 Meeting St. (© 843/722-3405; www.historic charleston.org/russell.html), is one of the finest examples of Federal architecture you'll ever see. Built in 1808, it's noted for a "free-flying" staircase, spiraling unsupported for three floors. The staircase's elliptical shape is repeated throughout the house. The interiors are ornate with period furnishings, especially the elegant music room with its golden harp and neoclassical-style sofa. Admission runs $8. For a $14 combined ticket you can also visit the **Aiken-Rhett House,** 48 Elizabeth St. (© **843/723-1623;** www. historiccharleston.org/aiken.html), built by merchant John Robinson in 1818 and then expanded by Governor and Mrs. William Aiken in the 1830s and 50s. Like other Charlestonians of their time, the Aikens furnished their home with crystal and bronze chandeliers, classical sculpture, and paintings purchased on trips to Europe. Today, many of those objects are still in the rooms for which the Aikens bought them. Original outbuildings include the kitchens, slave quarters, stables, privies, and cattle sheds.

The **Charleston Museum,** 360 Meeting St. (© **843/722-2996;** www.charleston museum.org), was founded in 1773, making it the first and oldest museum in America. The collections preserve and interpret the social and natural history of Charleston and the South Carolina coastal region, with early crafts, historic relics, and a series of hands-on exhibits for children. Admission is $8 adults, $4 kids. A $14 combined ticket also gets you admission to the museum's **Heyward-Washington House,** 87 Church St. (© **843/722-0354;** www.charlestonmuseum.org/heyward.asp), built in 1772 by Daniel Heyward, "the rice king" of Charleston. It was also the home of Thomas Heyward Jr., a signer of the Declaration of Independence. President George Washington bedded down here in 1791. Many of the fine period pieces in the house are the work of Thomas Elfe, one of America's most famous cabinetmakers. Admission to the house alone is $8.

At the southernmost point of the historic area stands the **Battery** (aka the White Point Gardens), where the Cooper and Ashley rivers converge. It has a landscaped park shaded by palmettos and live oaks, with walkways lined with monuments and other war relics. Virtually every home around here is of historic or architectural interest, including the **Edmondston-Alston House,** 21 E. Battery (© **843/722-7171;** www.middletonplace.org), an 1825 house originally built in Federal style and later modified to a Greek Revival style. Inside are heirloom furnishings, silver, and paintings. Robert E. Lee once found refuge here when his hotel uptown caught fire. Admission costs $7. The house is a property of the Middleton Place Foundation, which also operates the Middleton Place estate, 14 miles northwest of town.

Head back toward the cruise terminal along the seawall on East Battery and Murray Boulevard to absorb Charleston's riverfront ambience and catch the distant view of **Fort Sumter,** where the first shot of the Civil War was fired on April 12, 1861. Confederate forces launched a 34-hour bombardment of the fort, leading Union forces to surrender and the government in Washington to declare war. Amazingly, Confederate troops held onto Sumter for nearly 4 years, by the end of which time continual Northern bombardment had reduced it to a heap of rubble. You can visit the fort with **Fort Sumter Tours/SpiritLine Cruises** (© **800/789-3678;** www.spiritline cruises.com), which runs ferries across Charleston Harbor from town to the fort. You can buy tickets at Liberty Square's Fort Sumter Visitor Education Center, near the foot of Calhoun Street. The 2¼-hour tour consists of approximately 1 hour at Fort Sumter plus a 30-minute harbor cruise in each direction. Park rangers are on hand at the fort to answer your questions, and you can explore gun emplacements and visit a small museum filled with artifacts related to the siege. Ferry tickets cost $12, and tours are offered two or three times a day, usually at 9:30am, noon, and 2:30pm, though there are seasonal variations. Call or check the website to confirm times.

SHOPPING

Located within sight of the cruise ships docks, the **Old City Market** comprises four open-sided buildings that run from East Bay Street up to Meeting Street. The market originally sold foodstuffs, including meat, fish, and local produce, but today it's packed with vendors selling local art, food, books, clothing, and souvenirs. One stand-out item here is **sea-grass baskets** woven by Gullah women, descendents of coastal slaves who maintain a distinct culture on South Carolina's islands.

King Street is known for its shopping, with antiques at the south end of the street, clothes and jewelry along the main stretch, and housewares and interior décor along North King (aka Upper King).

If you fall for the period furniture you see in the historic houses, you can buy reproductions online from the **Historic Charleston Foundation,** which operates the Nathaniel Russell House, the Aiken-Rhett House, and several other historic properties. See their website at www.historiccharleston.org.

WHERE TO STAY

There are quite a few distinctive accommodations in Charleston located within spitting distance of the cruise pier.

The **Embassy Suites Historic Charleston,** 337 Meeting St. (© **843/723-6900;** www.embassysuites.com), is located close to the visitor center, on Marrion Square in the original home of the 19th-century Citadel Military College. It's listed in the National Register of Historic Places and features British West Colonial Plantation decor and two-room suites. Rates: from $169.

Close to the dock, the **Market Pavilion,** 225 E. Bay St. (© **877/440-2250;** www.marketpavilion.com), offers opulent old-Charleston-style guest rooms with old-world decor, heavy plaster crown moldings, mahogany, and four-poster beds. There's also the wonderful rooftop Pavilion Bar and the excellent Grill 225 restaurant. Rates: from $299.

Barksdale House Inn, 27 George St. (© **888/577-4980;** www.barksdalehouse.com), is a neat, tidy, and well-proportioned Italianate building about ¼ mile north of the City Market, constructed as an inn in 1778 and later altered and enlarged. Bedrooms have four-poster beds and many have working fireplaces—as if you need more heat in often-sweltering Charleston. Rates: from $135.

The **Planters Inn,** 112 N. Market St. (© **800/845-7082;** www.plantersinn.com), next to the City Market, is an opulent yet tasteful and cozy enclave of Colonial charm, and one of the finest small luxury hotels in the South. Spacious rooms have hardwood floors, marble baths, and 18th-century decor. Afternoon tea is served in the lobby and the Peninsula Grill's setting has a 19th-century charm unlike any other restaurant in Charleston. The menu changes frequently, with main courses in the $20 to $35 range. Rates: from $170.

Two Meeting Street Inn, 2 Meeting St. (© **843/723-7322;** www.twomeetingstreet.com), has the most enviable location in the city, right across from the Battery, looking over the intersection of the Charles and Ashley rivers. The house was built in 1892 as a wedding gift from a prosperous father to his daughter. Inside, the proportions are as lavish and gracious as the Gilded Age could provide. Rates: from $175.

DINING & NIGHTLIFE

Foodies flock to Charleston for refined Low Country cookery as well as an array of French and international specialties. Among the best is **Anson,** 12 Anson St., in the City Market area (© **843/577-0551;** www.ansonrestaurant.com), which blends the grace notes of a big New York restaurant with Low Country charm and cuisine. The setting is a century-old, brick-sided ice warehouse, and the decor is full of Corinthian pilasters salvaged from demolished colonial houses, with enough Victorian rococo for anyone's taste. Main courses: $15 to $29.

A. W. Shucks, 70 State St. (© **843/723-1151;** www.a-w-shucks.com), is a hearty, casual oyster bar in restored warehouse located next to City Market, around the corner from East Bay Street. The menu highlights oysters and clams on the half-shell, tasty seafood chowders, deviled crab, and a wide beer selection. Main courses: $13 to $20.

Farther from the market area, **Hominy Grill,** 207 Rutledge Ave. (© **843/937-0930;** www.hominygrill.com), features simply and beautifully prepared dishes inspired by the kitchens of the Low Country. It has gained a devoted family following, who come here to feast on such specialties as oven-fried chicken with spicy peach gravy. From the market, head north on Meeting Street, turn left on Calhoun, and walk 7 blocks west to Rutledge. Main courses: $11 to $20.

For a heady after-dinner experience, head to **Club Habana,** 177 Meeting St. (© **843/853-3720;** www.clubhabana.com). With the ambience of a private club, this martini and wine bar located on the second floor of a 200-year-old building lets you relax in any of three Gilded Age salons. The club specializes in exotic cigars and martinis, and serves appetizers, desserts, fruit and cheese plates, and even some miniature beef Wellingtons. It's upstairs from Tinder Box Internationale, selling new and vintage pipes, pipe tobacco, and cigars.

6 Fort Lauderdale, Florida

Broward County's Port Everglades is the second-busiest cruise port in the world, drawing more than 3.5 million cruise passengers a year. It boasts the deepest harbor on the eastern seaboard south of Norfolk, 12 ultramodern cruise ship terminals, and an easy access route to the Fort Lauderdale–Hollywood International Airport, less than a 5-minute drive away.

GETTING TO FORT LAUDERDALE & THE PORT

Port Everglades is located about 23 miles north of Miami within the city boundaries of Fort Lauderdale, Hollywood, and Dania Beach. I-595 will take you right onto the grounds. For information, contact **Port Everglades** (© **954/523-3404;** www.broward.org/port). If you're coming by air, you'll land at the **Fort Lauderdale–Hollywood International Airport** (© **954/359-6100**), located less than 2 miles from Port Everglades (5 min. by bus or taxi), making this the easiest airport-to-cruiseport trip in Florida. If you've booked air or transfers through the cruise line, a representative will show you to your shuttle after you land. If you haven't, taking a taxi to the port costs less than $10. If you're driving, the port has three passenger entrances: Spangler Boulevard, an extension of State Road 84 East; Eisenhower Boulevard, running south from the 17th Street Causeway/A1A; and Eller Drive, connecting directly with Interstate 595. Interstate 595 runs east-west, with connections to the Fort Lauderdale–Hollywood Airport, Interstate 95, State Road 7 (441), Florida's Turnpike, Sawgrass Expressway, and Interstate 75. Parking is available in two large garages for $12 a day.

GETTING AROUND   For a taxi, call **Yellow Cab** (© **954/565-5400**). Rates start at $2.75 for the first mile and $2 for each additional mile. **Broward County Mass Transit** (© **954/357-8400**) runs bus service throughout the county. One-day passes are $2.50. **Water Taxi** (© **954/467-6677;** www.watertaxi.com) offers all-day passes for $5, sailing between Oakland Park Boulevard and Southeast 17th Street along the Intracoastal Waterway, and west along the New River into downtown Fort Lauderdale.

BEST CRUISE LINE SHORE EXCURSIONS

Everglades Airboat Ride ($36, 2½ hr.): The Seminole Indians called it Pahay Okee, the "grassy water," and on this 30-minute airboat ride you'll get to see some of the area's indigenous wildlife, including water birds and American alligators. A longer version of this tour ($48, 4 hr.) also visits the Flamingo Gardens and Wildlife Sanctuary, an old homestead that now houses a free-flight aviary.

Fort Lauderdale Highlights ($39, 4 hr.): Travel by bus along Fort Lauderdale Beach, past the Bahia Mar Yacht Basin, down Las Olas Boulevard ("the Rodeo Drive of Fort Lauderdale"), and among the more than 300 miles of navigable natural waterways and artificial canals that have earned the city its "Venice of the Americas" nickname.

EXPLORING FORT LAUDERDALE ON YOUR OWN

Fort Lauderdale Beach, a 5-mile strip along Florida A1A, gained fame in the 1950s as a spring-break playground, popularized by the movie *Where the Boys Are,* but today the scene is a lot more affluent and family-oriented. In addition to the beaches (see below), there are a few other attractions that might float your boat.

The **Museum of Discovery & Science,** 401 SW Second St. (© 954/467-6637; www.mods.org), is an excellent interactive science museum with an IMAX theater. Check out the 52-foot-tall "Great Gravity Clock" in the museum's atrium. Admission costs $14. The **Museum of Art,** 1 E. Las Olas Blvd. (© 954/763-6464; www.moafl. org), is a truly terrific small museum whose permanent collection of 20th-century European and American art includes works by Picasso, Calder, Warhol, Mapplethorpe, Dalí, Stella, and William Glackens. African, South Pacific, pre-Columbian, Native American, and Cuban art are also on display. Admission is $7; closed Mondays.

Bonnet House, 900 N. Birch Rd. (© 954/563-5393; www.bonnethouse.org), a plantation-style home and 35-acre estate, survives in the middle of an otherwise highly developed beachfront condominium area, offering a glimpse into the lives of Fort Lauderdale's pioneers. Admission costs $10; guided tours offered Wednesday through Sunday approximately 10am to 3pm (call to confirm).

In the walk-through, screened-in aviary at **Butterfly World,** Tradewinds Park South, 3600 W. Sample Rd., Coconut Creek, west of the Florida Turnpike (© 954/977-4400; www.butterflyworld.com), visitors can watch newly hatched butterflies emerge from their cocoons and flutter around as they learn to fly. There are more than 150 species in residence. Admission is $18; open daily 9am to 5pm, Sunday 1 to 5pm.

BEACHES

Backed by an endless row of hotels and popular with visitors and locals alike, the **Fort Lauderdale Beach Promenade** is located along A1A, also known as Fort Lauderdale Beach Boulevard, between SE 17th Street and Sunrise Boulevard. The fabled strip from *Where the Boys Are* is Ocean Boulevard, between Las Olas and Sunrise boulevards. On weekends, parking at the oceanside meters is difficult to find. **Fort Lauderdale Beach** at the Howard Johnson is another perennial local favorite. A jetty

Fort Lauderdale

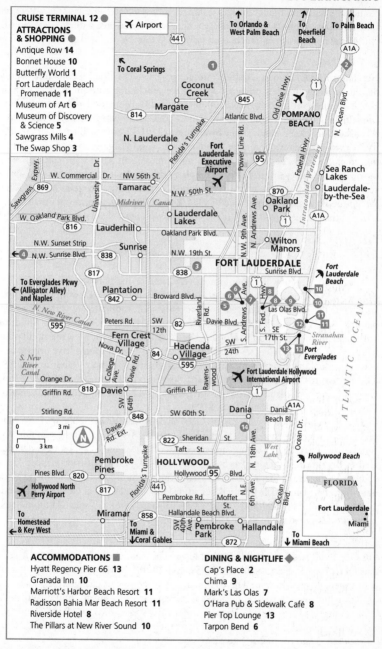

CRUISE TERMINAL 12 ●

ATTRACTIONS & SHOPPING ●

Antique Row **14**
Bonnet House **10**
Butterfly World **1**
Fort Lauderdale Beach Promenade **11**
Museum of Art **6**
Museum of Discovery & Science **5**
Sawgrass Mills **4**
The Swap Shop **3**

✈ Airport

To Orlando & West Palm Beach

To Deerfield Beach

To Palm Beach

↖ To Coral Springs

Coconut Creek

Margate

POMPANO BEACH

Atlantic Blvd.

Old Dixie Hwy.

N. Ocean Blvd.

N. Lauderdale

Fort Lauderdale Executive Airport

Power Line Rd.

Sea Ranch Lakes

Lauderdale-by-the-Sea

Intracoastal Waterway

Federal Hwy.

W. Commercial Dr.   NW 56th St.

Tamarac

N.W. 50th St.

Oakland Park

Sawgrass Expwy.

University Dr.

Midriver Canal

W. Oakland Park Blvd.

Lauderhill

Lauderdale Lakes

Oakland Park Blvd.

Wilton Manors

N.W. Sunset Strip

Sunrise

N.W. 19th St.

N.W. 9th Ave.

N. Andrews Ave.

N.W. Sunrise Blvd.

FORT LAUDERDALE

Sunrise Blvd.

Fort Lauderdale Beach

To Everglades Pkwy. (Alligator Alley) and Naples

Plantation

Broward Blvd.

Las Olas Blvd.

N. New River Canal

Peters Rd.

Davie Blvd.

SE 17th St.

Stranahan River

Port Everglades

Fern Crest Village

Hacienda Village

SW 24th

Nova Dr.

College Ave.

Davie Ave.

S. New River Canal

Orange Dr.

Davie

Fort Lauderdale Hollywood International Airport

Griffin Rd.

Griffin Rd.

Ravenswood

Stirling Rd.

SW 60th St.

Dania

Dania Beach Bl.

Ocean Dr.

A T L A N T I C   O C E A N

Davie Rd. Ext.

Sheridan St.

Taft St.

West Lake

Hollywood Beach

Pembroke Pines

HOLLYWOOD

Hollywood Blvd.

Pines Blvd.

FLORIDA

Hollywood North Perry Airport

Pembroke Rd.

Moffet St.

N.E. 6th Ave.

Ocean Blvd.

Fort Lauderdale

Miami

Miramar

Hallandale Beach Blvd.

To Homestead & Key West

To Miami & Coral Gables

Pembroke Park

Hallandale

To Miami Beach

0   3 mi
0   3 km

ACCOMMODATIONS ■

Hyatt Regency Pier 66 **13**
Granada Inn **10**
Marriott's Harbor Beach Resort **11**
Radisson Bahia Mar Beach Resort **11**
Riverside Hotel **8**
The Pillars at New River Sound **10**

DINING & NIGHTLIFE ◆

Cap's Place **2**
Chima **9**
Mark's Las Olas **7**
O'Hara Pub & Sidewalk Café **8**
Pier Top Lounge **13**
Tarpon Bend **6**

bounds the beach on the south side, making it rather private, although the water gets a little choppy. High school and college students share this area with an older crowd. One of the main beach entrances is at 4660 N. Ocean Dr. in Lauderdale-by-the-Sea.

SHOPPING

Not counting the discount "fashion" stores on Hallandale Beach Boulevard, visitors should know about a few other shopping places, including **Antique Row,** a strip of U.S. 1 around North Dania Beach Boulevard (in Dania, about 1 mile south of Fort Lauderdale–Hollywood International Airport) that holds about 200 antiques shops. Most shops are closed Sunday. **The Swap Shop,** 3291 W. Sunrise Blvd. (© 954/791-SWAP; www.floridaswapshop.com), is one of the world's largest flea markets. In addition to endless acres of vendors, there's a mini-amusement park, a 13-screen drive-in movie theater, and even a free circus, complete with elephants, horse shows, high-wire acts, and clowns. It's open daily. About 10 miles outside town, **Sawgrass Mills,** 12801 W. Sunrise Blvd. at Flamingo Road (© 954/846-2300; www.sawgrassmillsmall.com), is one of the premier outlet malls in the country, with more than 400 big-name stores.

WHERE TO STAY

Fort Lauderdale Beach has a hotel or motel on nearly every block, and the selection ranges from run-down to luxurious.

The **Hyatt Regency Pier 66,** located very close to the port at 2301 SE 17th St. (© 800/233-1234; www.pier66.hyatt.com), is a circular landmark with large rooms. Its famous Piertop Lounge, a revolving bar on its roof, is often filled with cruise ship patrons. Rates: from $199. **Marriott's Harbor Beach Resort,** located just south of Fort Lauderdale's strip at 3030 Holiday Dr. (© 800/222-6543; www.marriottharbor beach.com), is set on 16 acres of beachfront property. Most rooms have private balconies overlooking either the ocean or the Intracoastal Waterway. Rates: from $299. The **Radisson Bahia Mar Beach Resort,** 801 Seabreeze Blvd. (© 800/327-8154; www.radisson.com/ftlauderdalefl), is scattered over 42 acres of seacoast, adjacent to Florida's largest marina. Rates: from $199.

The **Riverside Hotel,** 620 E. Las Olas Blvd. (© 800/325-3280; www.riverside hotel.com), which opened in 1936, is a local favorite. Try for one of the ground-floor rooms, which have higher ceilings and more space. Rates: from $129. **La Casa del Mar Bed & Breakfast,** 3003 Granada St. (© 954/467-2037; www.lacasadelmar.com), is a Spanish Mediterranean–style place with 10 individually furnished rooms. It's only a block away from Fort Lauderdale Beach. Rates: from $110. **The Pillars at New River Sound,** 111 N. Birch Rd. (© 800/800-7666; www.pillarshotel.com), is a small 23-room hotel, the best of its size in the region. Rates: from $169.

DINING & NIGHTLIFE

Las Olas Boulevard is the hub for restaurants in Fort Lauderdale. Look there for **Mark's Las Olas,** 1032 E. Las Olas Blvd. (© 954/463-1000), the showcase of Miami restaurant mogul Mark Militello. The continental gourmet menu changes daily and may include white duck with sweet potato vanilla bean purée or a superb sushi-quality tuna. Main courses: $14 to $46. **Il Tartufo,** 2400 E. Las Olas Blvd. (© 954/767-9190), serves oven-roasted specialties and other Italian standards, plus a selection of fish baked in rock salt. Main courses: $15 to $22.

Cap's Place, 2765 NE 28th Court (© 954/941-0418; www.capsplace.com), is a famous old-time seafood joint, offering good food at reasonable prices. The restaurant is on a peninsula; you get a ferry ride over (see their website for directions). Mahimahi and snapper are popular and, like the other meat and pasta dishes here, can be prepared any way you want. Main courses: $14 to $33. **Tarpon Bend,** 200 SW 2nd St. (© 954/523-3233), is one of the few places where the fishermen still bring the fish to the back door. The oysters from the raw bar are shucked to order, and the steamed clambake (with half a Maine lobster, clams, potatoes, mussels, and corn on the cob) is scrumptious and served in its own pot. Main courses: $12 to $15

The restaurant and patio bar at the **Day's Inn Bahia Cabana Beach Resort,** 3001 Harbor Dr./A1A (© 954/524-1555; www.bahiacabanaresort.com), are charming and laid-back, serving inexpensive American-style dishes on a covered open-air deck overlooking Fort Lauderdale's largest marina; the Fort Lauderdale water taxi makes a stop here. Main courses: $10 to $17.

Strolling the strip of restaurants and bars along **Fort Lauderdale Beach** makes for a nice night out, but if you want something a bit higher-toned, the revolving **Piertop Lounge,** in the Hyatt Regency at Pier 66 (© 954/525-6666), is the area's most famous bar, with a 360-degree panoramic view of Fort Lauderdale. The bar completes a revolution every 66 minutes, and has a dance floor and live music, including blues and jazz. **O'Hara Pub & Sidewalk Café,** 722 E. Las Olas Blvd. (© 954/524-1764), is often packed with a trendy crowd who comes to listen to live R & B, pop, blues, and jazz. Call their jazz hot line (© 954/524-2801) to hear the lineup.

7 Galveston, Texas

Galveston, one of the first big alternative ports developed for Caribbean-bound megaships, is a city and beach resort on a barrier island just off the mainland that averages about 2 miles wide and 30 miles long. Ships departing from Galveston can reach the open sea in about 30 minutes, compared to several hours of lag time from the Port of Houston—which sits inland, some 50 miles to the north, on the edge of the Houston Ship Channel, above Galveston Bay.

The port city's main attractions are the downtown historic district; the Strand, with its Victorian commercial buildings and houses; and the beaches, which draw crowds of Houstonians and other Texans during the summer. And Galveston's very history is a fascinating attraction, too.

At the end of the 19th century, Galveston was a thriving port and a fast-growing city with a bright future. In fact, it was the largest city in Texas and had the third busiest port in the country. Of course, being on the Gulf meant the risk of a hurricane, but the prevailing thought held that the shallow bottom on the western shore of the Gulf of Mexico would prevent the formation of large waves and blunt the force of any approaching storm. This assumption held sway despite the fact that a storm completely wiped out the Texas port town of Indianola in 1886. But more evidence to the contrary came in the form of a massive storm that hit Galveston in September 1900.

It came ashore at night with a 20-foot surge that washed completely over the island. Houses were smashed into matchwood and their dwellers spilled out into the dark waters. By morning more than 6,000 islanders—1 out of every 6—were drowned. It remains the worst natural disaster ever to strike the United States. Those who remained went to work to prevent a reoccurrence of the disaster. Galveston erected a stout seawall that now stretches out along 10 miles of shoreline with several jetties of large granite blocks projecting out into the sea. It also filled in land under the entire city, raising it 17 feet in some places and jacking up all the surviving houses to the new level. Today, Galveston is a vibrant port city and a hub for cruises to the western Caribbean.

GETTING TO GALVESTON & THE PORT

The **Texas Cruise Ship Terminal** at the Port of Galveston is at Harborside Drive and 25th Street, on Galveston Island. It's reached via I-45 south from Houston. For information, call ✆ **409/766-6113** or check out www.portofgalveston.com or www. galvestoncvb.com.

If you're flying in, you'll land at one of two Houston airports: **William P. Hobby Airport** (south of downtown Houston, and about 31 miles, or a 45-min. drive, from the terminal) or **George Bush Intercontinental Airport** (just north of downtown Houston, and about 54 miles, or an 80-min. drive, from the terminal). Information on both is available at the Houston Airport System website, www.houstonairport system.org. Bush is the larger airport and it's international. If you've arranged air transportation and/or transfers through the cruise line (see chapter 2, "Booking Your Cruise & Getting the Best Price"), a cruise line representative will direct you to shuttle buses that take you to the port. Taxis are also available. **United Cab** (✆ **713/699-0000**) charges $80 per carload from Hobby Airport and $125 from George Bush Intercontinental Airport. The following companies provide service from the port to the airports only (not the other way around): **Yellow Cab Company** (✆ **409/763-3333**) for $70 to Hobby and $110 to Bush and **Galveston Limousine Service** (✆ **800/640-4826** or 409/744-5466), which charges $30 per person to/from Hobby and $35 to/from Bush. Round-trip rates are $50 and $60, respectively. All three companies require reservations.

If you're driving to the port, I-45 is the main artery for those arriving from the north. To get to the terminal, follow I-45 South to Exit 1C (at Harborside Dr./Hwy. 275); it's the first exit after the causeway. Turn left (east) onto Harborside Drive and continue for about 5 miles to the cruise terminal. Long-term parking at the port is available. The lots are ½ mile from the cruise ship terminal, and shuttle buses transport passengers between the lots and the terminal, where porters are available to carry luggage.

GETTING AROUND Within walking distance of the port's two terminals is the historic **Strand District,** Galveston's revitalized downtown, with shops, art galleries, museums, and eateries lining its quaint brick streets. If you're looking for a taxi and there aren't any waiting (which is often the case during prime embark- and debarkation times), call one of the companies listed in "Getting to Galveston & the Port," above. Most of Galveston's hotels, motels, and restaurants are located along the seawall from where Broadway meets the shore all the way west past 60th Street. If you're on the seawall around 25th Street (near the visitor center), you can take the **Galveston Island Rail Trolley** to the Strand District. The fare is $1 from the seawall to the Strand, but to ride just around the Strand is free.

BEST CRUISE LINE SHORE EXCURSIONS

City Tour ($47, 3½ hr.): Because Galveston is only a port of embarkation, the cruise lines generally offer only one choice, the basic city tour. For guests with late departing

Galveston

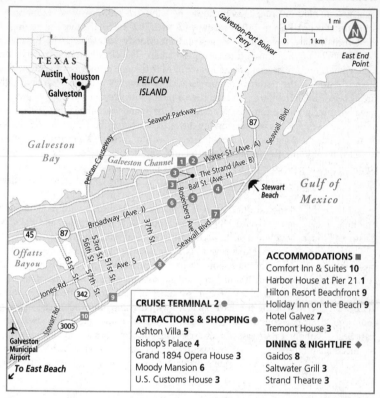

Galveston-Port Bolivar Ferry

East End Point

| 0 | | 1 mi |
| 0 | | 1 km |

TEXAS

Austin ★ Houston

Galveston

PELICAN ISLAND

Seawolf Parkway

87

Seawall Blvd.

Galveston Bay

Galveston Channel Water St. (Ave. A)

Pelican Causeway

The Strand (Ave. B)

Ball St. (Ave. H)

Stewart Beach

Gulf of Mexico

Rosenberg Ave.

Broadway (Ave. J)

37th St.

Seawall Blvd.

45 87

53rd St.

56th St.

51st St.

Ave. S

Offatts Bayou

61st St. 57th St.

Jones Rd.

342

Stewart Rd.

9

3005

10

Galveston Municipal Airport

To East Beach

CRUISE TERMINAL 2 ●

ATTRACTIONS & SHOPPING ●
Ashton Villa **5**
Bishop's Palace **4**
Grand 1894 Opera House **3**
Moody Mansion **6**
U.S. Customs House **3**

ACCOMMODATIONS ■
Comfort Inn & Suites **10**
Harbor House at Pier 21 **1**
Hilton Resort Beachfront **9**
Holiday Inn on the Beach **9**
Hotel Galvez **7**
Tremont House **3**

DINING & NIGHTLIFE ◆
Gaidos **8**
Saltwater Grill **3**
Strand Theatre **3**

flights, this bus tour is an ideal way to spend the day and often ends at the Houston (Bush) Intercontinental Airport. The tour passes through Galveston's scenic and historic Strand district, and then in Houston, through the downtown theater and museum districts and Hermann Park, home to the Houston Zoo. Before heading to the airport, tours pass through River Oaks, Houston's most prestigious residential neighborhood.

EXPLORING GALVESTON ON YOUR OWN

If you've only got a few hours before you have to board your cruise, focus on the **Strand National Historic Landmark District,** the heart of Galveston in the late 1800s and early 1900s, and just steps from the cruise terminals. The **East End Historic District** and the old **Strand District** are north of Broadway, and are both National Historic Landmarks, along with the Tall Ship *Elissa*, a three-masted sailing ship that's the focus of the **Texas Seaport Musuem** (© **409/763-1877;** www.tsm-elissa.org) located at Pier 21, near the cruise dock. The Historic District is the old silk-stocking neighborhood that runs from 9th to 19th streets between Broadway and Church Street. It has many lovely houses that have been completely restored. Three large mansions-turned-museums have regular tours: **Ashton Villa,** 2328 Broadway (© **409/762-3933;** www.galvestonhistory. com); the **Bishop's Palace,** 1402 Broadway (© **409/762-2475**), the most interesting of the bunch because there's more to see; and the **Moody Mansion,** 2618 Broadway (© **409/762-7668**). Admission to each is $6 adults. The city's historical preservation society holds tours of several private houses in May (inquire at the visitor center). The Strand District is the restored commercial district that runs between 19th and 25th streets between Church Street and the harbor piers. When cotton was king, Galveston was a booming port and commercial center, and the Strand was dubbed the "Wall Street of the Southwest." What you see now are three- and four-story buildings along 6 blocks of the Strand and along some of the side streets; many of these are Victorian iron-fronts, so called because the facades included structural and decorative ironwork. This was a common building practice before the turn of the 20th century, and you won't find a better-preserved collection of these buildings anywhere else in the United States. Nowadays the Strand is a shopping and dining area that offers a wide variety of stores.

Be sure and head to Postoffice Street, a restored historic district with more than 25 buildings, including the **Grand 1894 Opera House,** still in operation, and the **U.S. Customs House,** now home of the Galveston Historical Foundation.

The beaches are another of Galveston's most popular attractions. They may not measure up to those of the most popular beach destinations; the sand is a light tan color instead of white but it's all sand and no rocks, and although the water isn't turquoise, it's at a wonderful temperature for much of the year. **East Beach** and **Stewart Beach,** operated by the city, have pavilions with dressing rooms, showers, and restrooms, ideal for day-trippers. Stewart Beach is located at the end of Broadway, and East Beach is about a mile east of Stewart Beach. All of the beaches are free; many of the nicest are on the west side of the island. Another activity popular with visitors and locals alike is to walk, skate, or ride a bike atop the seawall, which extends 10 miles along the shoreline.

SHOPPING

Galveston has more than 20 art galleries on the Strand, Pier 21, and in the Postoffice Street Entertainment District. The **Strand** is also known for its quaint antiques, art, and memorabilia shops.

WHERE TO STAY

The Tremont House: A Wyndham Historic Hotel, 2300 Ship's Mechanic Row (© **409/763-0300** or 800/WYNDHAM; www.wyndham.com), is a 117-room gem located in the heart of the Strand neighborhood. A replica of the original 1839-built hotel, which stood nearby, this Tremont occupies the 1879-built Leon & H. Blum Building, and has been designed to re-create the atmosphere of its 19th-century namesake. Rates: from $119.

The many properties on Seawall Boulevard include the 149-room **Hilton Resort Beachfront,** 5400 Seawall Blvd. (© **409/744-5000** or 800/HILTONS; www.hilton. com), rates: from $129; **Holiday Inn on the Beach,** 5002 Seawall Blvd. (© **409/ 740-3581** or 713/222-2032; www.holidayinnonthebeach.com), rates: from $87; and the 100-room **Comfort Inn & Suites,** 6302 Seawall Blvd. (© **800/221-2222;** www. comfortinn.com), rates: from $99.

Harbor House at Pier 21, No. 28–Pier 21 (© **409/763-3321** or 800/874-3721; www.harborhousepier21.com), is a 42-room very modern-styled hotel built on a pier and overlooking the harbor. It's very close to the Strand District and many restaurants. Rates: from $114.

Hotel Galvez, 2024 Seawall Blvd. (© 409/765-7721 or 800/WYNDHAM; www.wyndham.com), Galveston's historic grand hotel, is located on the shore facing the seawall and one of the municipal beaches. It has 231 rooms and is on the trolley line leading to the Strand district. Rates: from $179.

DINING & NIGHTLIFE

Seafood is what people come to Galveston for, and there's quite a variety. There are local outlets of chain restaurants such as Landry's and Joe's Crab Shack, which do a credible job, but here are a couple of Galveston's best seafood outlets. **Gaidos,** 3800 Seawall Blvd. (© 409/762-9625; www.gaidosofgalveston.com), is a Galveston tradition that has been owned and operated by the Gaido family for four generations, so it's no surprise the seafood is fresh and the service attentive. The soups and side dishes are mostly traditional Southern and Gulf Coast recipes that are comfort food for the longtime customers. The stuffed snapper is the best we've had. Main courses: $14 to $33. **Saltwater Grill,** 2017 Postoffice St. (© 409/762-FISH), located in an old building near the Strand, prints up a menu daily that usually includes some inventive seafood pasta dishes, a fish dish with an Asian bent, gumbo and/or bouillabaisse, and a few non-seafood options. Main courses: $12 to $27.

When it comes to nightlife, it's not exactly New Orleans caliber here, but there are enough bars and restaurants along the seawall, and in the historic Strand and Postoffice Street districts, to pleasantly while away an evening. For concerts, musicals, and plays, check out the 200-seat **Strand Theatre,** 2317 Ships Mechanic Row (© 877/787-2639; www.galveston-thestrand.org), in the heart of the historic district, or the elegant **Grand 1894 Opera House** (© 490/765-1894; www.thegrand.com) for Broadway productions, orchestral performances, and other impressive entertainment.

8 Los Angeles, California

L.A. isn't a city or even a county; it's a whole planet to itself, its nation-states linked by dozens of superhighways that turn into slow-mo performance art at rush hour. The place is just as sunny, smoggy, movie-happy, rich, poor, sybaritic, hard-boiled, New-Agey, and unreal as the movies make it seem, and so obsessively catalogued by those same movies that you'll be having déjà vu every other minute of your visit, spotting places you've seen on the silver screen. We had an argument with a friend once about which U.S. city would be most recognizable to anybody, anywhere in the world. We said New York, she said L.A., and while we still stick with our opinion, we have to admit she had a point.

Now here's the downside to L.A.'s abundance: Unless you stay for several weeks you won't have a hope in hell of getting a real handle on the place. It's just too big, too diverse, and takes a much bigger guidebook to cover—one like *Frommer's Los Angeles,* for instance. Hint, hint.

GETTING TO L.A. & THE PORT

There are two major cruise centers in L.A., the **World Cruise Center,** off Harbor Boulevard in San Pedro (© 310/SEA-PORT; www.portoflosangeles.org), and Carnival Corporation's **Long Beach Cruise Terminal,** 10 miles west at 231 Windsor Way,

Long Beach (www.sanpedro.com/spcom/crusshp2.htm). The World Cruise Center is the busier of the two, hosting Carnival, Celebrity, Crystal, Cunard, HAL, NCL, Princess, Radisson, Royal Caribbean, and Silversea. The Long Beach terminal is pretty much all Carnival, all the time, though Princess also docks here on occasion.

Most visitors fly into **Los Angeles International Airport** (© 310/646-5252; www.lawa.org/lax), better known as LAX. This behemoth is situated ocean side, between Marina del Rey and Manhattan Beach, about 18 miles north of the World Cruise Center. You may also opt to fly into **Long Beach Municipal Airport,** 4100 Donald Douglas Dr. (© 562/570-2600; www.lgb.org), if you're heading right to the port and don't intend to stay on after. (JetBlue offers excellent fares to Long Beach.) To get to the World Cruise Center from LAX, drive south on I-405, then south on I-110. Exit at Harbor Boulevard, go straight through the intersection and right into the World Cruise Center. Parking is $11 per day. To get to the Long Beach Terminal, take I-405 south to the 710 south and continue till you see signs for the *Queen Mary* (that's the old, original *Queen Mary*—see "Exploring L.A. on Your Own," below). At the *Queen Mary* entrance, stay to the far right of the parking ticket taker and follow the signs.

GETTING AROUND   Even though L.A. has been steadily building its public-transportation infrastructure, getting around without a car is still like trying to see Mars without a space suit. All the major rental-car companies are represented at the airports, but if you want to look like a star on the freeways, you can rent a Maserati, Ferrari, Porsche, Bentley, or pretty much anything else (even a Cooper Mini!) at either **Budget Beverly Hills Car Collection,** 9815 Wilshire Blvd. (© 800/227-7117 or 310/881-2335; www.budgetbeverlyhills.com), or **Beverly Hills Rent-A-Car,** 9732 Little Santa Monica Blvd., Beverly Hills (© 800/479-5996 or 310/274-6969; www.bhrentacar.com). Both offer airport pickup service and complimentary delivery to local hotels.

BEST CRUISE LINE SHORE EXCURSIONS

Universal Studios Tour ($80, 7 hr.): A bus ride takes you to huge Universal Studios, where you board the "Glamour Tram" for a backstage look at the movie biz (see description under "Exploring L.A. on Your Own," below).

Disneyland ($93, 8 hr.): Disneyland, the original Disney theme park, lies about an hour's drive from the terminal in Anaheim. Once you get there, you're on your own to explore; but even though it's a small world (after all), 5 or 6 hours may not be enough for the kids. If that's the case, visit on your own, maybe staying nearby (see "Where to Stay," below).

EXPLORING L.A. ON YOUR OWN

Los Angeles is a very confusing city in that its "downtown" isn't considered the center of the city. In fact, there really *is* no center—just a whole bunch of neighborhoods and independently incorporated communities that run into each other and spread out as far as the eye can see. The best way to grasp the geography is to break it into six regions, roughly west to east: **Santa Monica** and the beach communities, **L.A.'s Westside** and **Beverly Hills, Hollywood** and **West Hollywood, Downtown,** the **San Fernando Valley,** and **Pasadena** and environs. You'll probably concentrate your visit in the city's western districts, since that's where the majority of tourist attractions, restaurants, and shops are. Despite the opening of the Disney Concert Hall and the

Los Angeles

Staples Center (a major sports and entertainment arena), most short-stay visitors never make it as far east as Downtown.

There are so many things to see and do in this town that most *residents* never see and do them all, so in this section we'll be concentrating on the quintessential L.A. experience of taking a big swan dive into pop culture and swimming around. Begin your adventure on Hollywood Boulevard at the **Hollywood Walk of Fame,** between Gower and La Brea (and also Vine St. between Yucca and Sunset Blvd.). Currently more than 2,200 past and present celebrities have bronze medallions on the world's most famous sidewalk, each one set in the center of a terrazzo star. You'll need a history book for some of them (who's Blanche Thebom again?), but you'll be surprised by how many will pop your brain buttons. A complete list of stars and their addresses is available online at **www.hollywoodcoc.org.** This part of Hollywood is a funky mix of touristy shops and businesses catering to the local rocker and biker culture. And then, of course, there are the Scientologists, who own a lot of the local real estate.

At the corner of Hollywood Boulevard and Highland Street, the massive 8¾-acre **Hollywood & Highland** entertainment complex (© 323/467-6412; www.hollywood andhighland.com) has all the top-end merchants as well as studio broadcast facilities, restaurants, nightclubs, cinemas, the Lucky Strike Lanes "upscale bowling alley/ lounge," a hotel (see "Where to Stay," below), and the **Kodak Theatre,** home of the Academy Awards. The mall's other centerpiece is the open-air **Babylon Court,** designed after a set from the 1916 film *Intolerance,* with giant elephant-topped pillars and a colossal arch that frames the Hollywood sign in the distance, up on Mt. Lee. (Trivia: The sign started as an advertisement for the "Hollywoodland" housing development. It was only later that it lost the "land" and was adopted as the symbol of the movie industry.)

Between Highland and La Brea Avenue is the famed **Grauman's Chinese Theatre,** 6925 Hollywood Blvd. (© 323/464-8111; www.manntheaters.com), one of the world's great movie palaces, opened in 1927 by impresario Sid Grauman. Visitors by the millions flock to the theater for its famous entry court, where stars such as Gary Cooper, Elizabeth Taylor, Ginger Rogers, and more than 160 others set their signatures and hand-/footprints in concrete.

From Hollywood, you're in an ideal position to set off on a drive along **Sunset Boulevard,** the street, the myth, the legend. This is a must for first-time visitors because you'll see a cross section of everything that is L.A.—legendary clubs, studios, hotels, and zip codes that you'll instantly recognize from movies and TV. The 45-minute drive takes you from Hollywood's seedy/starry streets to flamboyant **West Hollywood,** past glittering **Beverly Hills,** through **Brentwood** (O.J.'s old neighborhood), into the secluded enclave of **Pacific Palisades,** and finally to the sea. From there, you can head north to Malibu's fabled beaches (land of *Baywatch*) or head south along the coast to the funkier beach town of **Santa Monica.** Park at the **Santa Monica Pier** and head south on foot toward **Venice Beach** along the carnival-like **Ocean Front Walk.** You haven't visited L.A. properly until you've toured the area on the right kind of wheels (in-line skates), taken in the human carnival around you, noshed on cheap boardwalk food, watched a few street performers, and bought some cheap sunglasses or ethnic garb—all while enjoying the blue sea, wide beach, and the world's vainest weight lifters, who pump themselves up at an outdoor gym right in the heart of things.

Venice is street theater, but if you want to see some of the big-budget kind, you'll want to tour one of the movie studios. **Warner Brothers Studios,** 4301 W. Olive Ave., at Hollywood Way, Burbank (© **818/972-TOUR;** www.wbstudiotour.com), offers the most comprehensive tour, taking visitors on a 2¼-hour drive-and-walk around the studio's faux streets. After a brief introductory film, you'll pile into glorified golf carts and cruise past parking spaces marked with stars' names, then walk through active film and television sets, where you'll get a glimpse of how the biz really works. Sometimes you can also visit working sets to watch actors filming. Reservations are required, and children under 8 are not admitted. Bring valid photo ID. Tours are $35 per person, departing every 30 minutes on weekdays (9am–4pm May–Sept; 9am–3pm Oct–Apr).

The "other" studio tour is at **Universal Studios Hollywood,** Hollywood Freeway (Universal Center Dr. or Lankershim Blvd. exits), Universal City, in the San Fernando Valley (© **800/UNIVERSAL** or 818/622-3801; www.universalstudioshollywood. com), but this isn't just a working studio; it's also one of the world's largest amusement parks. The main attraction continues to be the Studio Tour, a 45-minute guided tram ride around the company's 420 acres, passing stars' dressing rooms and visiting famous back-lot sets. The rest of the experience is thrill rides themed on blockbusters such as *Back to the Future, Terminator 2* (Look out! The Governator might get you!), and *Shrek.* Admission is $52 adults, $42 for kids under 48 inches tall; free under age 3; open daily, 10am to 6pm on weekdays, 9am to 7pm on weekends.

Just outside the gate is **Universal CityWalk** (© **818/622-4455;** www.citywalk hollywood.com), a 3-block-long pedestrian promenade crammed with flashy name-brand stores, themed nightclubs, theme restaurants (the Hard Rock Cafe and others) a 3-D IMAX theater, an 18-screen cinema, NASCAR virtual racing, and more, More, MORE! Getting in is free, but after that you're on your own. It's open until 9pm weekdays, 11pm Friday and Saturday.

Now, lest we forget, **Disneyland** is also not so far away, at 1313 Harbor Blvd. in Anaheim, an hour south of Downtown L.A. on the I-5 (© **714/781-4565;** www. disneyland.com). The complex is divided into several themed "lands" ranging from the archetypal Main Street U.S.A. to Adventureland, inspired by Asia, Africa, and South America. For our money, no ride in the park (or in its Florida cousin for that matter) has ever topped **It's a Small World,** a slow-moving indoor river ride in which

---

Culture? You Want Culture?

If you have any energy left after being a shameless L.A. tourist, pay a visit to the **Getty Center,** 1200 Getty Center Dr. (© 310/440-7300; www.getty.edu), the Richard Meier–designed cultural cornerstone that displays collector J. Paul Getty's enormous collection of art, ranging from antiquities to impressionist painters, contemporary photography, and graphic arts. Admission is free, but you have to pay and make a reservation to park your car, which is *so* L.A. For more culture, there's also **Museum Row,** a stretch of Wilshire Boulevard just east of Beverly Hills that counts about a dozen different institutions, from the **Los Angeles County Museum of Art,** 5905 Wilshire (© 323/857-6000; www. lacma.org), to the **La Brea Tar Pits** and George C. Page Museum of La Brea Discoveries, 5801 Wilshire (© 323/934-PAGE; www.tarpits.org).

creepy dolls of all the world's children sing their saccharine song through hinged mouths. When it was built in the '50s, could Walt have known that he was envisioning every bad acid trip that happened in the '60s? It's a classic. Admission to the park costs $50 ages 10 and up, $40 ages 3 to 9. Multiday passes are also available, as are resort accommodations.

For cruise travelers with a sense of history, one of the most vital attractions in all L.A. has to be the **RMS *Queen Mary,*** 1126 Queen's Hwy. in Long Beach, at the end of I-710 (© **562/435-3511;** www.queenmary.com). One of the greatest ocean liners ever, she's now moored permanently in Long Beach, in the same complex that holds Carnival's Long Beach terminal. Though many of her original furnishings are long gone, she's still the only surviving example of this particular kind of 20th-century elegance, from her staterooms' tropical hardwood paneling to her incredible Deco artwork and miles of Bakelite handrails. Stroll her teakwood decks and with just a little imagination you're back in 1936. Admission $23, kids $12. *Queen Mary* also functions as a hotel, with rates starting at $109. Several onboard restaurants also offer brunches and dinners, at various rates.

Just across the harbor is the huge **Aquarium of the Pacific,** 100 Aquarium Way, off Shoreline Drive (© **562/590-3100;** www.aquariumofpacific.org), featuring re-creations of three Pacific areas, from the warm tropics to the frigid Bering Sea. More than 12,000 creatures inhabit its the three-story tanks, from sharks and sea lions to delicate sea horses and moon jellies. Admission costs $19 adults, $11 kids 3 to 11.

BEACHES

Los Angeles County's 72-mile coastline sports more than 30 miles of beaches, most of which are operated by the **Department of Beaches & Harbors,** 13837 Fiji Way, Marina del Rey (© **310/305-9503;** www.beaches.co.la.ca.us). Parking costs between $2 and $14. For recorded **surf conditions** and coastal weather forecast, call © **310/ 457-9701** or click on www.surfrider.org/cal5.asp. The following are the best beaches in L.A., listed from north to south.

Jam-packed on warm weekends, **Zuma Beach County Park** is L.A. County's largest beach park, located off the Pacific Coast Highway, a mile past Kanan Dume Road. Although it can't claim to be the most scenic beach in the Southland, Zuma has the most comprehensive facilities: plenty of restrooms, lifeguards, playgrounds, volleyball courts, and snack bars. The southern stretch, toward Point Dume, is **Westward Beach,** separated from the noisy highway by sandstone cliffs.

Not just a pretty white-sand beach but an estuary and wetlands area as well, **Malibu Lagoon State Beach** is the historic home of the Chumash Indians. The entrance is on the Pacific Coast Highway south of Cross Creek Road. Marine life and shorebirds teem where the creek empties into the sea, and the waves are always mild.

Highway noise prevents solitude at short, narrow **Topanga State Park,** located where Topanga Canyon Boulevard emerges from the mountains. Why go? Ask the surfers who wait in line to catch Topanga's excellent right point breaks. There are restrooms and lifeguard services here, and across the street you'll find one of the best fresh fish restaurants around. Three miles along the Pacific Coast Highway, between Sunset Boulevard and the Santa Monica border, the popular **Will Rogers State Beach** has friendly waves, competitive volleyball games, restrooms, lifeguards, and a snack hut in season.

Santa Monica State Beach, on either side of the Santa Monica Pier, is popular for white sands and accessibility. A paved path runs along here, allowing you to walk, bike, or skate to Venice. To the south, wide, friendly **Manhattan Beach** was once a hangout for the Beach Boys. Today it's lined with beautiful oceanview homes and has some of the best surfing around, plus restrooms, lifeguards, and volleyball courts. Not far away are the wide **Hermosa Beach** and **Redondo Beach.**

SHOPPING

Rodeo Drive & the Golden Triangle, between Santa Monica Boulevard, Wilshire Boulevard, and Canon Drive in Beverly Hills, is the city's (and one of the world's) most famous shopping districts, and so chichi and pricey that it's almost like a theme park, with the theme being *money.* Couture shops from high fashion's Old Guard are located along these hallowed blocks, along with plenty of newer high-end labels. Come and gawk. Crossing Wilshire a ways east of Rodeo, the blocks of **La Brea Avenue** north of Wilshire are L.A.'s artiest shopping strip, home to lots of great urban antiques stores dealing in Art Deco, Arts and Crafts, 1950s Moderne, and the like. You'll also find vintage clothiers, furniture galleries, and other warehouse-size stores, as well as some of the city's hippest restaurants.

In Hollywood, scruffy but fun **Melrose Avenue** is the city's funkiest shopping district, with many secondhand and avant-garde clothing shops as well as good restaurants and almost guaranteed celebrity-sightings. The original **Fred Segal** complex—breezy, ultrahip boutiques linked like departments of a single-story fashion maze—is at 8100 Melrose (© **323/655-3734**). Shops include the latest apparel for men, women, and toddlers, plus lingerie, shoes, hats, luggage, cosmetics, workout/lounge wear, and a cafe. Fred Segal also has major star-spotting potential. A few blocks to the north, **Amoeba Music,** 6400 Sunset Blvd. (© **323/245-6400;** www.amoebamusic.com), was described to us by a noted L.A. music critic as "the best record store in the *world,*" and after way too many visits, we have to agree. They carry *everything,* with a huge selection of used CDs and vinyl as well as new disks and videos. A few blocks to the south, **West Third Street** between Fairfax and Robertson is a trendy strip that features some Melrose Avenue émigrés, along with terrific up-and-comers, cafes, and the like. *Fun* is more the catchword here than *funky,* and the shops are a bit more refined than those along Melrose. It's all anchored on the east end by the **Farmers Market,** 6333 W. 3rd St. (© **323/933-9211;** www.farmersmarketla. com), a sprawling marketplace with food and produce stalls, a gourmet market, and a wine bar. The original market was just a bunch of Depression-era farmers setting up stands to sell produce, but eventually permanent buildings grew up, including the trademark shingled 10-story clock tower. **The Grove,** 189 The Grove Dr. (© **888/ 315-8883** or 323/900-8080; www.thegrovela.com), is a huge retail complex at the market's eastern end, with all the usual high-end mall stores and architectural styles ranging from Art Deco to Italian Renaissance.

Santa Monica, location of several of our recommended hotels, is also a great place for shopping. **Main Street,** stretching from Pico Boulevard to Rose Avenue, between 4th Street and Neilson Way, is an excellent street for strolling, crammed with a combination of mall standards and upscale, left-of-center individual boutiques. You can also find plenty of casually hip cafes and restaurants. The primary strip connecting Santa Monica and Venice, Main Street has a relaxed, beach-community vibe that sets it apart from similar strips. The **Third Street Promenade,** a pedestrians-only stretch of 3rd between Broadway and Wilshire Boulevard, is packed with chain stores and boutiques as well as dozens of restaurants and three multi-screen cinemas. It's one of the most popular shopping areas in the city, bustling into the evening.

WHERE TO STAY

If surf and sand comprise the So Cal image in your mind's eye, book a hotel along Santa Monica Bay, on the city's west side, stretching from Redondo Beach in the south to Malibu in the northwest. The more southerly properties are an easy drive to or from the cruise terminals, and all of them are a fairly easy drive to Beverly Hills shopping and the Hollywood attractions.

The Beach House at Hermosa Beach, 1300 The Strand, Hermosa Beach (℃ 888/895-4559; www.beach-house.com), sports a Cape Cod style that suits the on-the-sand location. It's luxurious and romantic, with 96 beautifully designed and outfitted split-level studio suites. Rates: from $224.

Best Western Marina Pacific Hotel & Suites, 1697 Pacific Ave., Venice (℃ 800/421-8151; www.bestwestern.com), is a haven of smart value just off the Venice Boardwalk. Spacious rooms are brightened with beachy colors, the one-bedroom suites are terrific for families (with kitchens and balconies), and many rooms have at least partial ocean views. Rates: from $149.

Shutters on the Beach, 1 Pico Blvd., Santa Monica (℃ 800/334-9000; www.shuttersonthebeach.com), is a Cape Cod–style luxury hotel that sits directly on the beach, a block from Santa Monica Pier. Each room has a beachview balcony. Try to get one of the beach-cottage rooms overlooking the sand, which are more desirable and no more expensive than those in the hotel's towers. Rates: from $445.

The eight-story, Art Deco **Georgian Hotel,** 1415 Ocean Ave. (℃ 800/538-8147; www.georgianhotel.com), boasts luxury, loads of historic charm, and a terrific ocean-view location, just across from Santa Monica's beach and pier. Established in 1933, the place was popular among Hollywood's golden-age elite, who enjoyed its veranda lounge and beautifully designed guest rooms. Rates: from $185.

Casa Malibu, sitting on its own beach at 22752 Pacific Coast Hwy., in Malibu (℃ 800/831-0858), is a leftover jewel from Malibu's golden age that doesn't try to play the sleek resort game. Instead, the modest, low-rise inn sports a traditional California-beach-cottage look that's cozy and timeless, with 21 comfortable, charming rooms. More than half have ocean views, but even those facing the courtyard are quiet and offer easy beach access via wooden stairs to the private beach. Rates: from $95.

If you don't care to stay by the beach, here are some choices for different personality/family types:

Nestled in the Bel-Air Estates, inland toward Beverly Hills, the **Hotel Bel-Air,** 701 Stone Canyon Rd. (℃ 800/648-4097; www.hotelbelair.com), is a stunning Mission-style hotel spread over 12 luxuriant garden acres. All in all, it's one of the most beautiful, romantic, and impressive high-end hotels in all of California. Expect the best of everything. Rates: from $395. For Oscar-winner wannabes, the **Renaissance Hollywood Hotel,** 1755 N. Highland Ave. (℃ 800/HOTELS-1; www.renaissance hollywood.com), is part of the Hollywood & Highland complex (see "Exploring L.A. on Your Own," above). On Oscar night, it's the headquarters for a frenzy of participants and paparazzi, but the rest of the year it's just a centrally located hotel with a nice respect for its location—think guest rooms like swinging '50s bachelor pads, with wood-paneled headboards and Technicolor furniture. Rates: from $239.

While it's east of the prime Sunset Strip action, the **Days Inn Hollywood,** 7023 Sunset Blvd., between Highland and La Brea (© **800/329-7466;** www.daysinn.com), is safe and convenient, and extras such as free underground parking and continental breakfast make it an especially good value for travelers on a budget. Some rooms have microwaves, fridges, and coffeemakers. Rates: from $59.

In Downtown L.A., the historic **Millennium Biltmore Hotel,** 506 S. Grand Ave. (© **800/245-8673;** www.thebiltmore.com), opened in 1923 and has hosted presidents, kings, and Hollywood celebrities, all of them drawn by its old-world charm, its grand lobby, and its warmly elegant rooms. Its Gallery Bar and Cognac Room is one of the best places in town to have a cocktail, and Sai Sai is one of the best Japanese restaurants in downtown L.A. Rates: from $189.

Here are a couple choices if you want to stay near the cruise terminals. Located in quaint seaside San Pedro, adjacent to the World Cruise Center, is the **Sheraton Los Angeles Harbor Hotel,** 601 S. Palos Verdes St. (© **888/890-9888;** www.sheraton laharbor.com). Each room offers an ocean or hillside view, and restaurants, boutiques, art galleries, harbor excursions, and two championship golf courses are practically right outside. Rates: $99 to $169. In downtown Long Beach, the **Hilton Long Beach,** 701 W. Ocean Blvd. (© **800/HILTONS** or 562/983-3400; www.hilton.com), is central to both the Long Beach and San Pedro cruise ship terminals and about a mile from the Aquarium of the Pacific and the restaurants, nightlife, and shopping along Pine Avenue. Rates: $169 to $239.

DINING & NIGHTLIFE

For a dinner that channels the ghost of Old Hollywood, head to **Musso & Frank Grill,** 6667 Hollywood Blvd., Hollywood (© **323/467-7788**). This comfortable, dark-paneled room, virtually unchanged since 1919, begs you to order up one of L.A.'s best martinis and some chops or the legendary chicken pot pie, and listen to the longtime waitstaff wax nostalgic about the days when Orson Welles held court and Faulkner, Fitzgerald, and Hemingway all popped in for a drink between writing screenplays. Main courses: $12 to $35. You'll always find living celebrities, on the other hand, frequenting the Sunset Strip hot spots, the most sizzling of which is the Mondrian hotel and its chic Chino-Latin restaurant, **Asia de Cuba,** 8440 Sunset Blvd., West Hollywood (© **323/848-6000;** www.mondrianhotel.com). Main courses: $23 to $69, served family-style (to be shared). Celebrity dieters can be glimpsed bypassing the eats for the A-list-only **Skybar** on the other side of the pool. The perennial power-spot **The Ivy,** 113 N. Robertson Blvd., West Hollywood (© **310/274-8303**), attracts L.A.'s more conservative celebrities. Main courses: $25 to $50.

Many great restaurants are clustered around the Santa Monica area. For some of the best California cuisine in town, head to chef/owner Michael McCarty's eponymous **Michael's,** 1147 3rd St., Santa Monica (© **310/451-0843;** www.michaelssanta monica.com). Main courses: $28 to $39. The **Border Grill,** 1445 4th St., Santa Monica (© **310/451-1655**), fills the ticket if you're craving a taste from south of that border. Main courses: $13 to $25. From here, you can head for Venice's Ocean Front Walk for some primo people-watching. The **Sidewalk Café,** 1401 Ocean Front Walk, Venice (© **310/399-5547**), offers unobstructed views of parading skaters, bikers, skateboarders, musclemen, break dancers, street performers, sword swallowers, and other participants in the daily carnival. You can also get your dinner here, if you think you won't be distracted. Main courses: $8 to $18. Farther to the north, the **Saddle**

Peak Lodge, 419 Cold Canyon Rd., Calabasas (© **818/222-3888;** www.saddlepeak lodge.com), is a converted hunting lodge in the hills above Malibu. Candlelit tables, a crackling fireplace, and a *Wine Spectator* award-winning wine list make it a romantic favorite. Main courses: $25 to $38.

For seafood, head downtown to the **Water Grill,** 544 S. Grand Ave., Downtown (© **213/891-0900;** www.watergrill.com), a beautiful contemporary fish house that serves imaginative dishes influenced by America's regional cuisines. An absolutely huge raw bar features the best clams, crabs, shrimp, and oysters available, and the fish is so fresh it practically jumps onto the plate. Main courses: $25 to $36.

In Redondo Beach, not far north of the World Cruise Center, the Portofino Hotel & Yacht Club's cozy **Breakwater,** 260 Portofino Way (© **800/468-4292** or 310/379-8481; www.hotelportofino.com/dining.cfm#), specializes in surf, turf, and jazz, with candlelit tables and a glowing fireplace overlooking the Portofino marina. Main courses: $17 to $46.

Bar none, the most classic L.A. thing you can do after the sun goes down is take a picnic dinner to the **Hollywood Bowl,** 2301 N. Highland Ave., Hollywood (© **323/850-2000;** www.hollywoodbowl.org). In addition to being the summer home of the Los Angeles Philharmonic, the Bowl hosts visiting performers ranging from chamber music quartets to jazz greats to folk humorists. The imposing white band shell always elicits appreciative gasps from first-time Bowl-goers. Don't forget your bottle of wine. If you prefer your entertainment with a roof, the new **Walt Disney Concert Hall,** at First Street and Grand Avenue, Downtown (© **213/972-7211;** www.disneyhall.com/wdch), should fit the bill. The strikingly beautiful hall, designed by Frank Gehry, has a dazzling 2,265-seat auditorium, plus a cafe, bookstore, gift shop, and Joachim Splichal's flagship restaurant, **Patina** (© **213/972-3331;** www.patinagroup.com/patina; main courses: $31–$39). The concert hall is open to the public for viewing, but to witness it in its full glory, attend a concert by the world-class philharmonic.

9 Miami, Florida

It's the most Latin city in the U.S., with a hot-hot-hot club scene, sparkling beaches, crystal clear waters, and more palm fronds, glittering hotels, and red sports cars than you'll find anywhere outside Monte Carlo and Rio. On top of all that, Miami is also the undisputed cruise capital of the world, with more than four million passengers passing through yearly, and more supersize ships berthing here than anywhere else.

GETTING TO MIAMI & THE PORT

The **Port of Miami** is at 1015 N. America Way on Dodge Island (© **305/371-7678;** www.miamidade.gov/portofmiami), reached via a four-lane bridge from Miami's downtown district. **Miami International Airport** (© **305/876-7000;** www.miami-airport.com) is about 8 miles west of downtown Miami and the port (about a 15-min. drive). If you've arranged air transportation and/or transfers through the cruise line, a cruise line rep will direct you to shuttle buses to the port. Taxis are also available; the fare is about $21. Blue taxis serve only the immediate area around the airport; yellow taxis serve all other destinations, including the port. **SuperShuttle** (© **305/ 871-2000**) charges $12 per person to the port, with two pieces of luggage.

If you're arriving by car from the north, take I-95 to I-395 and head east on I-395, exiting at Biscayne Boulevard. Make a right and go south to Port Boulevard. Make a

Miami

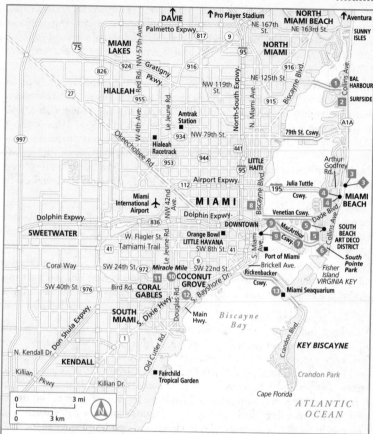

CRUISE TERMINAL 7 ●

ATTRACTIONS & SHOPPING ●
Bal Harbour Shops 1
Bass Museum of Art 4
Bayside Marketplace 9
CocoWalk and the Streets of Mayfair 12
Lincoln Road shopping 5
Miami Seaquarium 13
Miracle Mile 10
South Beach Art Deco district 5

ACCOMMODATIONS ■
The Beach House Bal Harbour 2
Best Western South Beach 5
Biltmore Hotel 11
Biscayne Bay Marriott 8
Crest Hotel Suites 5
Eden Roc Renaissance Resort 3
Fontainebleau Hilton 3

The Hotel 5
Hotel Astor 5
Hotel Inter-Continental Miami 9
Hotel Ocean 5
Indian Creek Hotel 4

DINING & NIGHTLIFE ◆
The Forge 3
Joe's Stone Crab 6
Joia 6
Larios on the Beach 5
Lincoln Road pedestrian mall 5
Nobu 4
Pacific Time 5
Skybar 5
Spris 5
Sushi Samba Dromo 5
Tantra 5
Van Dyke Café 5

left and go over the Port Bridge. Coming in from the northwest, take Interstate 75 to State Road 826 (Palmetto Expwy.) south to State Road 836 east. Exit at Biscayne Boulevard. Make a right and go south to Port Boulevard. Make a left and go over the Port Bridge. Parking lots right at street level face the cruise terminals. Parking runs $12 per day.

GETTING AROUND   Taxis start at $1.70 for first ¼ mile and cost $2.20 for each additional mile. Fares to some frequently traveled routes are standardized. Almost two dozen taxi companies serve Miami-Dade Country, including **Yellow Cab** (© 305/444-4444) and, on Miami Beach, **Central** (© 305/532-5555). There's also the **Metromover** (© 305/770-3131), a 4½-mile elevated line that circles downtown, stopping near important attractions and shopping (including Bayfront Park and Bayside Marketplace). It runs daily from about 5am to midnight, and is fun if you've got time to kill. There are 21 stations spaced about 2 blocks apart each, and service is free.

BEST CRUISE LINE SHORE EXCURSIONS

Parrot Jungle Island ($40, 4 hr.): Parrot Jungle Island is actually a botanical garden, wildlife habitat, and bird sanctuary all rolled into one, featuring parrot shows, ape and monkey experiences, and open aviaries.

Everglades Airboat Ride ($45, 4 hr.): The Seminole Indians called the Everglades Pahay Okee, the "grassy water," and on this 40-minute airboat ride you'll get to see some of the area's indigenous wildlife, including water birds and American alligators.

EXPLORING MIAMI ON YOUR OWN

A sizzling, multicultural mecca, Miami offers the best in cutting-edge restaurants, unusual attractions, entertainment, shopping, beaches, and the whole range of hotels, from luxury to boutique, kitschy to charming. Miami's best attraction is actually a neighborhood, the **South Beach Art Deco district,** located at the southern end of Miami Beach below 20th Street. It's filled with outrageous and fanciful 1920s and 1930s architecture, plus outrageous and fanciful 21st-century people. This treasure-trove, usually just called "the Beach" or "SoBe," features more than 900 pastel-painted buildings in the Art Deco, streamline moderne, and Spanish Mediterranean Revival styles. The district stretches from 6th to 23rd streets, and from the Atlantic Ocean to Lennox Court. Ocean Drive boasts many of the premier Art Deco hotels.

Also in South Beach, the **Bass Museum of Art,** 2121 Park Ave. (© 305/673-7530; www.bassmuseum.org), is Miami's most progressive art museum, with an expanded building designed by Arata Isozakii; a permanent collection of European paintings from the 15th through the early 20th centuries (including Dutch and Flemish Old Masters); and collections of textiles, period furnishings, objects d'art, ecclesiastical artifacts, and sculpture. Rotating exhibits include pop art, fashion, and photography. Admission is $6 for adults, $4 seniors and students.

The adjoining **Coral Gables** and **Coconut Grove** neighborhoods are fun to visit for their architecture and ambience. In Coral Gables, the Old World meets the New as curving boulevards, sidewalks, plazas, fountains, and arched entrances evoke Seville. Today, the area is an Epicurean's Eden, boasting some of Miami's most renowned eateries as well as the University of Miami and the ½-mile-long Miracle Mile, a 5-block retail mecca (see "Shopping," below). Coconut Grove, South Florida's oldest settlement, remains a village surrounded by the urban sprawl of Miami. It dates back to the early 1800s, when Bahamian seamen first sought to salvage treasure from the wrecked vessels stranded along the Florida Reef. Mostly people come here to shop, drink, dine, or simply walk around and explore.

Just minutes from the Port of Miami in Key Biscayne, the **Miami Seaquarium,** 4400 Rickenbacker Causeway (© **305/361-5705;** www.miamiseaquarium.com), is a delight. Performing dolphins such as Flipper, TV's greatest sea mammal, perform along with Lolita the Killer Whale. You can also see endangered manatees, sea lions, tropical-theme aquariums, and the gruesome shark feeding. Admission is $26 adults, $21 kids.

BEACHES

A 300-foot-wide sand beach runs for about 10 miles from south of **Miami Beach** to **Haulover Beach Park** in the north. (For those of you who like to get an all-over tan, Haulover is a nude beach.) Although most of this stretch is lined with a solid wall of hotels, beach access is plentiful, and you are free to frolic along the entire strip. A wooden boardwalk runs along the hotel side from 21st to 46th streets—about 1½ miles. You'll find lots of public beaches here, wide and well maintained, with life-guards, toilet facilities, concession stands, and metered parking (bring lots of quarters). Lifeguard-protected public beaches include 21st Street, at the beginning of the boardwalk; 35th Street, popular with an older crowd; 46th Street, next to the Fontainebleau Hilton; 53rd Street, a narrower, more sedate beach; 64th Street, one of the quietest strips around; and 72nd Street, a local old-timers' spot. On the southern tip of the beach is family-favorite **South Pointe Park,** where you can watch the cruise ships. **Lummus Park,** in the center of the Art Deco district, is the best place for people-watching and model-spotting. The stretch between 11th and 13th streets is a gay beach. The beach from 1st to 15th streets is popular with seniors.

In Key Biscayne, **Crandon Park,** 4000 Crandon Blvd. (© **305/361-5421**), is one of metropolitan Miami's finest white-sand beaches, stretching for some 3½ miles. There are lifeguards, and you can rent a cabana with a shower and chairs for $20 per day. Saturday and Sunday the beach can be especially crowded.

SHOPPING

Most cruise ship passengers shop right near the Port of Miami at **Bayside Market-place,** 401 Biscayne Blvd. (© **305/577-3344;** www.baysidemarketplace.com), a mall with 150 specialty shops, street performers, live music, and some 30 eateries, including a Hard Rock Cafe and others serving everything from Cuban to crepes. Many restaurants have outdoor seating right along the bay for picturesque views of the yachts harbored there. It can be reached via regular shuttle service from the port or by walking over the Port Bridge.

Bal Harbour Shops, 9700 Collins Ave. (© **305/866-0311;** www.balharbourshops. com), is one of the most prestigious fashion meccas in the country, with big-name stores including Chanel, Prada, Armani, Neiman Marcus, Saks Fifth Avenue, and dozens of others.

In South Beach, **Lincoln Road,** an 8-block pedestrian mall, runs between Washington Avenue and Alton Road, near the northern tier of the Art Deco district. It's filled with popular shops such as Victoria's Secret and Banana Republic, interior-design stores, art galleries, and clothing boutiques, as well as coffeehouses, restaurants, and cafes. Despite the recent influx of commercial anchor stores, Lincoln Road still manages to maintain its funky, arty flair, attracting an eclectic, colorful crowd. Or try **Espanola Way,** a small pedestrian road with a European feel that starts at 15th Street and Collins.

Coconut Grove, centered around the confluence of Main Highway and Grand Avenue, is the heart of the city's boutique district and features two open-air shopping and entertainment complexes, **CocoWalk,** 3015 Grand Ave. (© **305/444-0777**), and the less compelling **Streets of Mayfair,** 2911 Grand Ave. (© **305/448-1700**).

In Coral Gables, **Miracle Mile,** actually a ½-mile stretch of SW 22nd Street between Douglas and Le Jeune roads (aka 37th and 42nd aves.), features more than 150 shops.

WHERE TO STAY

Two hotels—the 34-story **Hotel Inter-Continental Miami,** 100 Chopin Plaza (© **800/327-3005;** www.miami.interconti.com; rates: from $139), and the **Biscayne Bay Marriott,** 1633 N. Bayshore (© **800/228-9290;** www.marriott.com; rates: from $149), are located right across the bay from the cruise ship piers, near Bayside Marketplace. Thanks to Miami's good highway network, though, you can stay virtually anywhere in Greater Miami and still be within 10 to 20 minutes of your ship.

SOUTH BEACH Two blocks from the beach, the Art Deco, comfy-chic **Hotel Astor,** 956 Washington Ave. (© **800/270-4981;** www.hotelastor.com), was originally built in 1936, and has made significant renovations to its guest rooms and public areas, and opened a new restaurant, the Metro Kitchen and Bar. Rates: from $125.

The upscale **Hotel Ocean,** 1230 Ocean Dr. (© **800/783-1725;** www.hotelocean. com), is a Mediterranean enclave with 27 beautiful suites appointed with Art Deco furniture, soundproof windows, terraces facing the ocean, and massive bathrooms with French toiletries. Original fireplaces add to the coziness, even if you're not likely to use them. Rates: from $190. **The Hotel,** 801 Collins Ave., at the corner of Collins and 8th Street (© **305/531-2222;** www.thehotelofsouthbeach.com), is a Deco gem with a stylishly whimsical interior designed by haute couturier Todd Oldham. Rates: from $205.

It's hard to find a hotel on South Beach with both good value and excellent service, but the **Crest Hotel Suites,** 1670 James Ave (© **800/531-3880;** www.cresthotel.com), delivers. It's one of Miami's best bargains and coolest hotels, retaining its original 1939 Deco architecture but with a thoroughly modern interior. Rates: from $155. If you're on a budget but want a cozy Deco feel, try the **Best Western South Beach,** 1050 Washington Ave. (© **888/343-1930;** www.bestwestern.com). Rates: from $125.

MIAMI BEACH At the **Indian Creek Hotel,** 2727 Indian Creek Dr., at 28th Street (© **800/491-2772;** www.indiancreekhotelmb.com), each room is an homage to the 1930s Art Deco age. Rates: from $69. **The Beach House Bal Harbour,** 9449 Collins Ave., in Surfside (© **800/327-6644;** www.rubellhotels.com/beach.html), brings a taste of Nantucket to Miami with soothing hues, comfortable furniture, oceanfront views, and a Ralph Lauren–decorated interior. Rates: from $155.

The **Eden Roc Renaissance Resort,** 4525 Collins Ave. (© **800/327-8337;** www.edenrocresort.com; rates: from $179), and the **Fontainebleau Hilton,** next door at 4441 Collins Ave. (© **800/HILTONS;** www.fontainebleau.hilton.com; rates: from $209), are both popular, modernized 1950s resorts evoking the bygone Rat Pack era.

CORAL GABLES   The famous **Biltmore Hotel,** 1200 Anastasia Ave. (© 800/ 448-8355; www.biltmorehotel.com), opened its doors in 1926, and has hosted the likes of Al Capone and the duke and duchess of Windsor. The place is a national landmark, with the largest hotel pool in the continental United States as well as a 300-foot bell tower modeled after the Cathedral of Seville. Rates: from $159. Even if you're not staying here, you can take a free tour on Sundays at 1:30, 2:30, and 3:30pm, conducted by the Dade Heritage Trust.

DINING & NIGHTLIFE

Count on **South Beach** as your dining and nightlife spot, with dozens of first-rate restaurants and cafes. With very few exceptions, the places on **Ocean Drive** are crowded with tourists and priced accordingly. You'll do better to venture a little farther onto the pedestrian-friendly streets just west. The **Lincoln Road** pedestrian-mall area is so packed with places offering great food and atmosphere that it would take a full guidebook to list them all. We recommend strolling and browsing. A couple standout outdoor cafes here are **Spris,** a pizzeria at 731 Lincoln Rd. (© **305/673-2020;** www.spris.cc), and the **Van Dyke Cafe,** 846 Lincoln Rd. (© **305/534-3600**). Prices at Spris range from $5 to $14; main courses at the Van Dyke from $9 to $17. For a culinary trendsetter, try **Pacific Time,** 915 Lincoln Rd. (© **305/534-5979;** www.pacific time.biz), where you can enjoy a taste of the Pacific Rim with a deliciously modern South Beach twist. Main courses: $21 to $30. **Sushi Samba Dromo,** 600 Lincoln Rd. (© **305/673-5337**), features a fusion of Brazilian, Peruvian, and Japanese cuisine (main courses $17–$39; sushi priced by the piece); and **Nobu,** 1901 Collins Ave., at the Shore Club (© **305/695-3232**), is, of course, legendary for its nouvelle Japanese cuisine. Main courses: $10 to $30; Omakase ("chef's choice") menu from $70. Even if Gloria Estefan weren't co-owner of **Larios on the Beach,** 820 Ocean Dr. (© **305/ 532-9577**), the crowds would still flock to this bistro, which serves old-fashioned Cuban dishes such as *masitas de puerco* (fried pork chunks). Main courses: $8 to $27.

At the legendary **Joe's Stone Crab,** 11 Washington Ave., Miami Beach, between South Point Drive and 1st Street (© **305/673-0365**), about a ton of stone-crab claws are served daily during stone-crab season from October to May (usually closed May 15–Oct 15), and since the place doesn't take reservations the wait for a table can be up to 2 hours. Crab prices vary depending on the market rate, but average $63 for a serving of jumbo crab claws, $43 for large claws. If the sky's the limit in the budget, try **Tantra** at 1445 Pennsylvania Ave. (© **305/672-4765;** www.tantrarestaurant.com). Inside, you're greeted by the sound of water cascading down a wall into a small pool, and the feel of real grass underfoot. The dark and exotic interior completes the mood. For a taste as over the top as the setting, try the grilled lobster risotto, and indulge in one of the specialty martinis, all of them served with a real flower floating languidly in your glass. Main courses: $28 to $69. Stay late and watch the serene mood transform into a frenzied party scene.

After dark, look for the klieg lights to direct you to the hot spots of South Beach. While the blocks of Washington Avenue, Collins Avenue, and Ocean Drive are the main nightlife thoroughfares, you're more likely to spot a celebrity in a more off-the-beaten-path eatery such as **Joia,** 150 Ocean Dr. (© **305/674-8871**), a popular, chic Italian spot with an upstairs lounge called Pure Lounge (that's anything but); or **The Forge,** 432 41st St. (© **305/538-8533**), an ornately decorated rococo-style steakhouse with a fine wine selection. Main courses: $22 to $65. Also popular are the hotel bars, such as the Shore Club's hot, hauter-than-thou celeb magnet **Skybar,** 1901 Collins Ave. (② **877/640-9500;** www.shoreclub.com).

For a change of pace from the fast-paced glitz of South Beach or the serene luxury of Coral Gables, head for **Little Havana,** where pre-Castro Cubans commingle with young artists who have begun to set up performance spaces in the area. It's located just west of downtown Miami on SW 8th Street. In addition to authentic Cuban cuisine, the cafe Cubano culture is alive and well.

10 Montréal, Québec

A good number of New England/Canada cruises start or end in the beautiful city of Montréal, an island set deep into the St. Lawrence River southwest of Québec City. Many ships sail between Montréal and Boston or New York, so unless you stay on an extra night or two in a local hotel, you won't have time to do the city justice.

Canada's second largest city, Montréal has a strong French heritage going back to the 16th century, when French explorer Jacques Cartier arrived there in 1535, believing the wide St. Lawrence River was the ocean and the way to the Orient. Oh well. Cartier's settlement was nothing more than an outpost until 1642, when the colony of Ville-Marie was founded by the soldiers of Paul de Chomedey, Sieur de Maisonneuve. Like Québec City, the fur and timber trade put Montréal on the map. When the British captured Québec City in 1759, for a short time Montréal was the capital of New France until, that is, it was also taken by the English. Today, the legacies of both the French and English survive in force. French speakers, known as Francophones, make up about 66% of the city's population, while most of the remaining population speaks English and is known officially as Anglophones. Although both groups are decidedly North American, their vast differences help give Montréal its unique appeal.

History aside, Montréal is also a very cosmopolitan city, with modern skyscrapers and thriving businesses. The city also has its famous parallel subterranean universe to feel pride in. The city's Underground Pedestrian Network, at times a confusing maze, was created to keep Montréalers warm during the frigid winters, and you'll find more than 1,600 shops, 40 banks, 200 restaurants, 10 Métro stations, and about 30 cinemas down there.

GETTING TO THE PORT & MONTREAL

Cruise ships call at the **Iberville Cruise Terminal** at the Port of Montréal on De la Commune Street in Old Montréal (Vieux-Montréal in French). For more information, call the Montréal Port Authority ② **514/283-7011** or check out **www.port-Montreal.com.**

If you're flying in, you'll come through **Montréal-Trudeau Airport** (② **514/ 394-7377** or 800/465-1213; www.admtl.com); a taxi between downtown Montréal and the airport is a flat rate of US$23 (C$31) and takes about 20 minutes.

Driving from NYC, get on Interstate 87 north to link up with Canada's Autoroute 15 at the border, and the entire 400-mile journey is on expressways. Likewise, from Boston, I-93 north joins I-89 just south of Concord, New Hampshire (Boston to Montréal is about 320 miles). At White River Junction there is a choice between continuing on I-89 to Lake Champlain, crossing the lake by roads and bridges to join I-87 and Canada Autoroute 15 north, or picking up I-91 at White River Junction to

Montréal

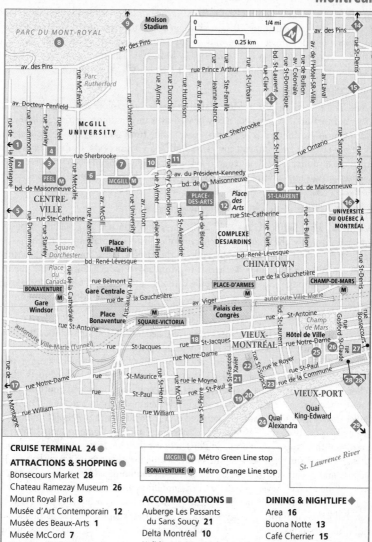

CRUISE TERMINAL 24 ●

ATTRACTIONS & SHOPPING ●

Bonsecours Market **28**

Chateau Ramezay Museum **26**

Mount Royal Park **8**

Musée d'Art Contemporain **12**

Musée des Beaux-Arts **1**

Musée McCord **7**

Notre Dame Basilica **22**

place Jacques-Cartier **25**

Pointe-à-Callière
(Montréal Museum of
Archaeology and History) **19**

rue Notre-Dame
"Antiques Alley" **17**

Sherbrooke Antiques district **1**

MCGILL Ⓜ Métro Green Line stop

BONAVENTURE Ⓜ Métro Orange Line stop

ACCOMMODATIONS ■

Auberge Les Passants
du Sans Soucy **21**

Delta Montréal **10**

Holiday Inn Montréal-
Midtown **11**

Hôtel Le Germain **6**

Hôtel Le St-James **18**

Hôtel Nelligan **23**

La Maison Pierre du Calvet **27**

Ritz-Carlton Montréal **2**

Sofitel **4**

DINING & NIGHTLIFE ◆

Area **16**

Buona Notte **13**

Café Cherrier **15**

Le Bourlingueur **20**

Le Jardin Nelson **28**

Le Taj **3**

Les Halles **5**

Milos **9**

Nuances **29**

Toqué! **14**

go due north toward Sherbrooke, Québec. At the border, I-91 becomes Canada Route 55 and joins Canada Route 10 west through Estrie to Montréal. The Trans-Canada Highway, which connects both ends of the country, runs right through Montréal. Once in Montréal, follow the signs to Old Montréal. The street that runs alongside the Old Port is De la Commune. Parking is US$11 (C$15) per day.

GETTING AROUND

Ships land up right in Vieux-Montréal, so it's easiest to explore this multidimensional city's old treasures on foot. For a city of well over three million, getting to know and getting around Montréal is remarkably easy. Aside from walking, the Métro (subway) system is fast and efficient, and costs US$2.50 (C$3.35) per ride. Plenty of taxis queue up at the terminal if you'd rather go that route for sightseeing, though you should note that drivers do not serve as guides. Rates are metered, with an initial US$2 (C$2.70) charge.

BEST CRUISE LINE SHORE EXCURSIONS

Montréal Highlights (US$49, 2½ hr.): Because Montréal is generally a port of embarkation only, the cruise lines generally offer just a basic city tour on the day passengers disembark, and it typically ends at the airport. This bus tour of Montréal's most famed attractions includes a visit to Mont Royal, which towers above the city, plus a drive through the major shopping districts, and finally to Old Montréal to get a look at the remarkable concentration of 17th-, 18th- and 19th-century buildings.

EXPLORING MONTREAL ON YOUR OWN

If you only have a few hours before your cruise departs, a stroll around the **Old Town,** or Vieux-Montréal, is a must. The city was born here in 1642, down by the river at Pointe-à-Callière; and today, especially in summer, activity centers around **place Jacques-Cartier,** where cafe tables line narrow terraces and sun worshipers, flower sellers, itinerant artists, street performers, and strolling locals and tourists congregate—it's a perfect locale for some good old-fashioned people-watching. The area is larger than it might seem at first, bounded on the north by rue St-Antoine and close to rue St-Jacques, once the "Wall Street" of Montréal and still home to some banks, and on the south by the Vieux-Port (Old Port), a linear park bordering rue de la Commune that gives access to the river and provides welcome breathing room for cyclists, in-line skaters, and picnickers. To the east, Vieux-Montréal is bordered by rue Berri, and to the west by rue McGill. Several small but intriguing museums are housed in historic buildings, and the architectural heritage of the district has been substantially preserved. The restored 18th- and 19th-century buildings have been adapted for use as shops, boutique hotels, studios, galleries, cafes, bars, offices, and apartments. Take a walk through the district in the evening, when many of the finer buildings are illuminated. Among the most worthwhile sites is the Gothic-Revival **Notre-Dame Basilica,** 110 Notre-Dame St. W. (© 514/842-2925; www.basiliquenddm.org), built in 1829, with a stunning interior of sculpted wood, gold leaf, and stained glass. Admission is US$2.50 (C$4) adults. The tin-plated, silver-domed **Bonsecours Market,** 350 Saint-Paul St. E. (© 514/872-7730; www.marchebonsecours.qc.ca), a lively place built in 1847 overlooking the St. Lawrence River, is lined with cafes and small galleries. The 18th-century **Château Ramezay Museum,** 280 Notre-Dame St. E. (© 514/861-3708; www.chateauramezay.qc.ca), is another must. Formerly the governor's home, it's now a history museum with exhibits on Montréal and Québec. Admission is US$5 (C$7) adults, US$2.50 (C$4) kids.

Another worthwhile pursuit to make sure you fit in is a walk to the **Mount Royal Park,** where a small village of Iroquois were living when French explorer Cartier first arrived in the 16th century. Montréal is named for it—the "Royal Mountain"—and it's a soothing urban pleasure to drive, walk, or take a horse-drawn carriage, or *calèche* as they're also known, to the top for a view of the city, the island, and the St. Lawrence River, especially at dusk. The famous American landscape architect Frederick Law Olmsted, who created Manhattan's Central Park, among others, designed Parc du Mont-Royal, which opened in 1876. On its far slope are two cemeteries—one used to be Anglophone and Protestant, the other Francophone and Catholic—reminders of the linguistic and cultural division that persists in the city. With its skating ponds and trails for hiking, running, and cross-country skiing, the park is well used by Montréalers, who refer to it simply and affectionately as "the mountain."

If you're in town for a few days, you may have time to explore Montréal's other neighborhoods. **Chinatown** is just north of Vieux-Montréal, and it's mostly a neighborhood of restaurants. The **Downtown** area is where you'll find the city's office buildings, important museums, and luxury hotels. Other notable 'hoods include **Rue St-Denis,** which stretches from rue Ste-Catherine est to avenue du Mont-Royal. It's the thumping central artery of Francophone Montréal, running from the Latin Quarter downtown and continuing north into the Plateau Mont-Royal district. Thick with cafes, bistros, offbeat shops, and lively nightspots, it is to Montréal what boulevard St-Germain is to Paris; if you want to know what the students and youth of Montréal are all about, spend an evening here.

SHOPPING

Rue Sherbrooke is a major shopping street for international and domestic designers, luxury items such as furs and jewelry, art galleries, and the Holts department store. **Boulevard St-Laurent** covers everything from budget practicalities to off-the-wall handmade fashions. Look along **avenue Laurier** between St-Laurent and de l'Epée for French boutiques, home accessories shops, and young Québecois designers. **Rue St-Paul** in Vieux-Montréal has a growing number of art galleries, a few jewelry shops, souvenir stands, and a shop that sells kites. **Antiques** can be found along rue Sherbrooke near the Musée des Beaux-Arts and on the little side streets near the museum. More antiques and collectibles, in more than 50 tempting shops one after another, can be found along the lengthening "Antiques Alley" of **rue Notre-Dame,** especially concentrated between Guy and Atwater. **Rue St-Denis** north of Sherbrooke has strings of shops filled with fun, funky items.

Some of the best shops in Montréal are found in city museums. Tops among them are shops in **Pointe-è-Callière,** the Montréal Museum of Archaeology and History in Vieux-Montréal; the **Musée des Beaux-Arts** and the **Musée McCord,** both on rue Sherbrooke in the center of the city; and the **Musée d'Art Contemporain** in the Place-des-Arts. **Rue Ste-Catherine** is home to the city's four top department stores and myriad satellite shops, while **rue Peel** is known for its men's fashions. Montréal's long history as a center for the fur trade buttresses the many wholesale and retail furriers, with outlets downtown and in Plateau Mont-Royal, but nowhere more concentrated than on the "fur row" of **rue Mayor,** between rue de Bleury and rue City Councillors.

WHERE TO STAY

Accommodations in Montréal range from soaring glass skyscraper lodgings to grand boulevard hotels to converted row houses. Stylish inns and boutique hotels are appearing in increasing numbers, especially in Vieux-Montréal. Except in bed-and-breakfasts, visitors can almost always count on discounts and package deals, especially on weekends, when the hotels' business clients have packed their bags and gone home. Here's a sampling:

If you're looking for some history, the restored **Ritz-Carlton Montréal,** 1228 rue Sherbrooke Ouest (© **800/363-0366** or 514/842-4212; www.ritzcarlton.com), has been around since 1913, giving it a half-century lead on the closest competition. Rates: from US$182 (C$243). With ancient cut-stone walls, swags of velvet and brocade, and tilting floors that Benjamin Franklin once trod upon, as well as a baronial dining room and a breakfast nook under a peaked glass roof, **La Maison Pierre du Calvet,** 405 rue Bonsecours (© **866/544-1725** or 514/282-1725; www.pierreducalvet. ca), provokes memories of lovers' hotels by the Seine. Rates: from US$179 (C$239). The first Canadian branch of a French chain, the **Sofitel,** 1155 rue Sherbrooke (© **877/285-9001** or 514/285-9000; www.sofitel.com), matches its luxury rivals in every detail. Rates: from US$121 (C$161).

Hôtel Le Germain, 2050 rue Mansfield (© **877/333-2050** or 514/849-2050; www.hotelgermain.com), helped inspire a boom in small, stylish boutique hotels in Vieux-Montréal with its mix of Asian minimalism and Western comforts. Rates: from US$193 (C$257). **Hôtel Le St-James,** 355 rue St-Jacques (© **866/841-3111** or 514/841-3111; www.hotellestjames.com), raised the boutique bar to an almost impossibly high level with a superbly sybaritic spa, high-tech amenities in the rooms, and a gorgeous grand hall. Rates: from US$230 (C$307). The **Hôtel Nelligan,** 106 rue St-Paul Ouest (© **877/788-2040** or 514/788-2040; www.hotelnelligan.com), opened in 2002, counters with a great full-service restaurant, goose-down duvets on the beds, and a rooftop terrace. Rates: from US$161 (C$215).

For families, the **Delta Montréal,** 475 av. du President-Kennedy (© **877/286-1986** or 514/286-1986; www.deltahotels.com), keeps kids blissfully waterlogged with *two* pools—one inside, one outside—and also has a play center. Rates: from US$114 (C$152).

If you're on a tight budget, the **Holiday Inn Montréal-Midtown,** 420 rue Sherbrooke Ouest (© **800/387-3042** or 514/842-6111; www.basshotels.com), is a good choice. Rates: from US$85 (C$113). Set in a 1723 house in Vieux-Montréal, **Auberge Les Passants du Sans Soucy,** 171 rue St-Paul Ouest (© **514/842-2634;** www.lesanssoucy.com), is a more upscale and stylish B&B than most of its peers, and it's located near the top restaurants and clubs in the old town. Rates: from US$89 (C$119).

DINING & NIGHTLIFE

Rue Crescent is one of Montréal's major dining and nightlife districts and it lies in the western shadow of the downtown skyscrapers. Here you'll find hundreds of restaurants, bars, and clubs of all styles between Sherbrooke and René-Lévesque, centering on rue Crescent and spilling over onto neighboring streets. From east to west, the Anglophone origins of the quarter are evident in the surviving street names: Stanley, Drummond, Crescent, Bishop, and MacKay. The party atmosphere that pervades after dark never quite fades, and it builds to crescendos as weekends approach, especially in warm weather.

Any of a dozen cafes along **St-Denis** will fit the bill if you're looking for food and people-watching ops, especially on weekends, when the **Plateau Mont-Royal area** comes alive. **Café Cherrier,** 3635 rue St-Denis, at rue Cherrier (© **514/843-4308**), might be the most fun, if you can find a seat on the wraparound terrace. Main courses: US$10 to US$14 (C$13–C$19). If great French food is your main goal, then head for **Toqué!** in Old Montréal, 900 place Jean-Paul-Riopelle (© **514/499-2084**), which is in a league of its own. Main courses: US$17 to US$27 (C$23–C$36). At the festive **Nuances,** 1 av. du Casino on the Ile St-Helene (© **514/392-2708**), the gracious dining venue on the top floor of a casino, you'll enjoy superb French and Belgian cuisine and spectacular views of the skyline to boot. Main courses: US$23 to US$32 (C$31–C$43). **Les Halles,** 1450 rue Crescent, between rue Ste-Catherine and boulevard de Maisonneuve (© **514/844-2328**), offers some of the city's best traditional French cuisine as well as an excellent wine selection, with more than 400 labels. Main courses: US$21 to US$29 (C$28–C$39). The deft chef at **Area,** 1429 rue Amherst, near rue Ste-Catherine (© **514/890-6691**), impresses with his updated fusion bistro food and *huge* portions. Main courses: US$12 to US$21 (C$16–C$28).

Now if price is as appetizing to you as the trend quotient, try the all-you-can-eat Indian lunch buffet at **Le Taj,** 2077 rue Stanley, near rue Sherbrooke (© **514/ 845-9015**). Main courses: US$6 to US$14 (C$8–C$19). The interior may not be *très* chic, but at dinner, even the *expensive* four-course table d'hôte at **Le Bourlingueur,** 363 St-François-Xavier, near rue St-Paul (© **514/845-3646**), comes in under US$12 (C$16). Main courses: US$7 to US$11 (C$9.35–C$15).

Of course, French isn't your only choice. For Italian, check out super-chic **Buona Notte,** 3518 bd. St-Laurent, near rue Sherbrooke (© **514/848-0644**), where the pastas, focaccias, and risottos rival the occasional celebrity sightings. Main courses: US$17 to US$26 (C$23–C$35). Greek grills are paramount at **Milos,** 5357 av. du Parc (© **514/272-3522**), and the fish is mere hours from the sea. Main courses: US$21 to US$28 (C$28–C$37). Serious food isn't the lure at **Le Jardin Nelson,** 407 place Jacques-Cartier (© **514/861-5731**). Music—classical or jazz—is what draws the crowds, who partake of sweet or savory crepes or very good pizzas under the crabapple tree in the garden. Main courses: US$9 to US$11 (C$12–C$15).

11 New Orleans, Louisiana

New Orleans is one of America's real city-cities, and by that we mean cities in the European sense of the word, with walkable neighborhoods, gorgeous architecture, a lively street scene, and regular patches of green to lighten the urbanity. It's also a world-class party town, home both to giant annual events (Mardi Gras, Jazz Fest) and to a daily round of eating and drinking that would set lesser cities' heads spinning. Maybe it's the influence of the music—New Orleans is the fabled "cradle of jazz," after all—or maybe it's the hot honeyed air, which wraps the city in an Afro-Caribbean embrace with hints of French colonial decadence mixed in for that certain *je ne sais quoi.* You just can't imagine that people work here. When would they find the time? But we know they do because among other things New Orleans is one of the busiest seaports in the nation, with thousands of cargo vessels and hundreds of cruise ships passing through every year. You can watch the parade as you make the long voyage downriver, passing the fabled Mississippi River Delta as you head out to sea, Caribbean-bound.

GETTING TO NEW ORLEANS & THE PORT

The **Julia Street Cruise Ship Terminal** sits at the foot of Julia Street on the Mississippi River, in the convention center district, a short streetcar or taxi ride away from the edge of the French Quarter. For information, call the **Port of New Orleans** at © 504/522-2551 or check out www.portno.com. By air, you'll arrive at the **Louis Armstrong New Orleans International Airport** (© 504/464-0831), about 15 miles northwest of the port. Cruise line representatives meet all passengers who have booked transfers through the line. For those who haven't, a taxi to the port costs about $28 for two passengers and takes about 45 minutes. **Airport Shuttle** (© 866/596-2699 or 504/592-0555) runs vans at 10- to 12-minute intervals from outside the airport's baggage claim to the port and other points in town. It costs $13 per passenger each way. Tickets can be purchased online at www.airportshuttleneworleans.com.

If you're coming by car, take the I-10 downtown. Take the Tchoupitoulas/St. Peters Street exit, the last one before you cross the Mississippi. Stay to the right, and head toward the New Orleans Convention Center. Turn right onto Convention Center Boulevard, then left onto Henderson Street, which will take you to Port of New Orleans Place. Turn left and continue on to the Cruise Ship Terminal. Long-term parking costs $12 per day; inquire through your cruise line.

GETTING AROUND   **Taxis** are plentiful and taxi stands are easy to find, but you can walk all around the **French Quarter,** the spiritual and temporal hub of the city. Its streets are laid out in an almost perfect rectangle, so it's nearly impossible to get lost. It's also so well traveled that it is nearly always safe, particularly in the central parts, though the fringes can get a little dodgy at night. To head out to the **Garden District,** home of beautiful homes, hop the **streetcar** that runs the length of St. Charles Avenue. The nostalgic cars with wooden bench seats operate 24 hours a day and cost $1.25 per ride (you must have exact change). A transfer from streetcar to bus costs 25¢. You board at the corner of Canal and Carondelet streets in the French Quarter, or at intervals along St. Charles. Streetcar service also runs some 5½ miles along Canal Street, from the French Market through the Central Business District to City Park Avenue. A **VisiTour Pass,** which gives you unlimited rides on all streetcar and bus lines, sells for $5 for 1 day, $12 for 3 days. You can buy passes through selected hotel information counters and retail stores; you'll find a list at **www.norta.com**.

BEST CRUISE LINE SHORE EXCURSIONS

Louisiana Swamp Tour ($52, 4½ hr.): Born on the bayou, or just visiting? Whichever, on this trip you'll ride a double-ended flat-bottom boat into Louisiana's swampland. Alligators abound, as well as bald eagles, nutria, mink, deer, black bears, raccoons, otters, beavers, many species of exotic birds, and cypress trees creeping right up from the water.

Airboat & Plantation Tour ($150, 7 hr.): Travel in a small six-passenger boat for an even closer view of the swamps, then visit the Evergreen Plantation, with one of the few remaining Greek Revival plantation homes on the historic River Road, plus well-preserved outbuildings.

EXPLORING NEW ORLEANS ON YOUR OWN

The **French Quarter** is the oldest part of the city and still the most popular for sightseeing, with block after block full of restaurants, bars, jazz clubs, street performers, amazing old architecture, and more wacko characters than you'll find in a thousand other regular towns all put together. Maybe it's the heat that does it. Made up of about 90 square blocks, the Quarter (also known as the *Vieux Carré,* or "Old Square") was

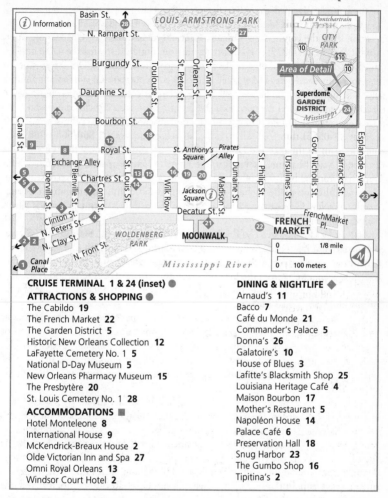

(i) Information

Basin St. ↑

LOUIS ARMSTRONG PARK

N. Rampart St.

Burgundy St.

Dauphine St.

Bourbon St.

Toulouse St.
St. Peter St.
Orleans St.
St. Ann St.

Royal St.

Exchange Alley

St. Louis St.
Conti St.

Chartres St.

Iberville St.
Bienville St.

Clinton St.

N. Peters St.

N. Clay St.

Canal Place

Canal St.

St. Anthony's Square / Pirates Alley

Wilk Row

Jackson Square (i)

Madison St.
Dumaine St.
St. Philip St.
Ursulines St.

Decatur St.

WOLDENBERG PARK

N. Front St.

MOONWALK

FRENCH MARKET

FrenchMarket Pl.

Gov. Nicholls St.
Barracks St.
Esplanade Ave.

Mississippi River

0 — 1/8 mile
0 — 100 meters

Lake Pontchartrain

CITY PARK

Area of Detail

Superdome
GARDEN DISTRICT

Mississippi

CRUISE TERMINAL 1 & 24 (inset) ●

ATTRACTIONS & SHOPPING ●
The Cabildo **19**
The French Market **22**
The Garden District **5**
Historic New Orleans Collection **12**
LaFayette Cemetery No. 1 **5**
National D-Day Museum **5**
New Orleans Pharmacy Museum **15**
The Presbytère **20**
St. Louis Cemetery No. 1 **28**

ACCOMMODATIONS ■
Hotel Monteleone **8**
International House **9**
McKendrick-Breaux House **2**
Olde Victorian Inn and Spa **27**
Omni Royal Orleans **13**
Windsor Court Hotel **2**

DINING & NIGHTLIFE ◆
Arnaud's **11**
Bacco **7**
Café du Monde **21**
Commander's Palace **5**
Donna's **26**
Galatoire's **10**
House of Blues **3**
Lafitte's Blacksmith Shop **25**
Louisiana Heritage Café **4**
Maison Bourbon **17**
Mother's Restaurant **5**
Napoléon House **14**
Palace Café **6**
Preservation Hall **18**
Snug Harbor **23**
The Gumbo Shop **16**
Tipitina's **2**

laid out by the French engineer Adrien de Pauger in 1718, and a strict preservation policy has kept it looking much the way it always has. Its major public area is **Jackson Square** (bounded by Chartres, Decatur, St. Peter, and St. Ann sts.), where musicians, artists, fortunetellers, jugglers, and those peculiar "living statue" guys gather to sell their wares or entertain for change. The main drag, however, is **Bourbon Street,** which is basically Sodom and Gomorrah, though in a good way. Many of the Quarter's best attractions are covered under "Dining & Nightlife," below, but here are some of its more historic highlights.

Incorporating seven historic buildings connected by a brick courtyard, the **Historic New Orleans Collection,** 533 Royal St., between St. Louis and Toulouse (© **504/ 523-4662;** www.hnoc.org), evokes New Orleans of 200 years ago. The oldest building in the complex escaped the tragic fire of 1794. The others hold exhibitions about Louisiana's culture and history. Admission is free; closed Sunday and Monday.

Founded in 1950, the **New Orleans Pharmacy Museum,** 514 Chartres St., at St. Louis (© **504/565-8027;** www.pharmacymuseum.org), is just what the name implies. In 1823, the first licensed pharmacist in the United States, Louis J. Dufilho Jr., opened an apothecary shop here. Today you'll find old apothecary bottles, voodoo potions, pill tile, and suppository molds, as well as the old glass cosmetics counter and a jar of leeches, in case you feel the need to be bled. Admission costs $2; closed Monday.

Constructed in 1795 through 1799 as the Spanish government seat in New Orleans, **The Cabildo,** 701 Chartres St., at Jackson Square (© **800/568-6968**), was the site of the signing of the Louisiana Purchase transfer. It's now the center of the Louisiana State Museum's facilities in the French Quarter, with a multiroom exhibition that traces the history of Louisiana from exploration through Reconstruction, covering all aspects of life, including antebellum music, mourning and burial customs, immigrants, and the changing roles of women in the South. Admission is $5; closed Monday.

Also on Jackson Square, **The Presbytère,** 751 Chartres St. (© **800/568-6968**), was planned as housing for the clergy but is now a Mardi Gras museum that traces the history of the annual event, with everything from elaborate Mardi Gras Indian costumes to Rex Queen jewelry from the turn of the century on display. A re-creation of a float allows you to pretend you are throwing beads to a crowd on a screen in front of you. Admission is $5; closed Monday.

In the Warehouse District, just west of the Quarter, the **National D-Day Museum,** 945 Magazine St. (© **504/527-6012;** www.ddaymuseum.org), was the creation of historian Stephen Ambrose, telling the story of all U.S. amphibious assaults worldwide on that fateful day. Many of the artifacts on display emphasize personal stories, including audio exhibits that tell the experiences of soldiers and civilians alike. Admission is $10.

Aside from the Quarter, the one other neighborhood that absolutely deserves your attention is the **Garden District,** one of the most picturesque areas of the city. It's mostly residential, but what residences. Bounded by St. Charles Avenue and Magazine Street between Jackson and Louisiana avenues, the whole district was originally the site of a plantation, and the land was eventually subdivided and developed as a residential neighborhood for wealthy Americans. Throughout the middle of the 19th century, developers built the Victorian, Italianate, and Greek Revival homes that still line the streets. Take the St. Charles streetcar (see "Getting Around," above) for the full effect.

And then, of course, there are the dead: Because New Orleans is prone to flooding, bodies have been interred aboveground since its earliest days, in sometimes very elaborate tombs that are definitely worth a visit. **St. Louis Cemetery No. 1,** Basin Street between Conti and St. Louis streets, at the top of the French Quarter, is the oldest extant cemetery (1789) and the most iconic. The acid-dropping scene from *Easy Rider* was shot here, prompting the city to declare that no film would ever, ever, ever be shot again in one of its cemeteries. In the Garden District, **Lafayette Cemetery No. 1,** 1427 Sixth St., right across the street from Commander's Palace Restaurant, is another old cemetery that's been beautifully restored. Though both of these cemeteries are usually full of visitors during the day, you should exercise caution when touring, as they've seen some crime over the years.

SHOPPING

Despite what you may think while making your first walk down Bourbon Street, there's more to New Orleans shopping than tourist traps selling cheap T-shirts, alligator snow globes, and other souvenir items—although there are plenty of those too (most of them with an absolutely mind-boggling selection of **hot sauces**).

On Decatur Street across from Jackson Square, **The French Market** has shops selling candy, cookware, fashion, crafts, toys, New Orleans memorabilia, and candles. There is a lot of kitsch, but some good buys are mixed in, and it's always fun to stroll through and grab a few beignets at Café du Monde (see "Dining & Nightlife," below). The French Market is open from 10am to 6pm; Café du Monde is open 24 hours.

From Camp Street down to the river on Julia Street, you'll find many of the city's best **contemporary art galleries.** Of course, some of the works are a bit pricey, but there are good deals to be had if you're collecting, and fine art to be seen if you're not. **Magazine Street** is the Garden District's premier shopping street, with more than 140 shops among the 19th-century brick storefronts and cottages. You'll find antiques, art galleries, boutiques, crafts, and more. The greatest concentration of stores is between Felicity and Washington streets, but if you're so inclined, you could shop your way from here all the way to Audubon Park, hopping over the dry patches on the city bus. Be sure to pick up a copy of *Shopper's Dream,* a free guide and map to most of the stores. It's available all along the street.

WHERE TO STAY

Three streets from Bourbon in the French Quarter, the **Olde Victorian Inn and Spa,** 914 N. Rampart St. (© 800/725-2446; www.oldevictorianinn.com), is a beautifully restored 1840s home, with antiques and reproductions. Some rooms have balconies, and most have fireplaces. The inn can arrange wedding packages that include a service in its courtyard; you can head off for your honeymoon cruise from there! The "spa" in the name refers to the inn's day spa. Rates: from $120.

The **Omni Royal Orleans,** 621 St. Louis St., between Royal and Chartres (© 800/843-6664; www.omniroyalorleans.com), is a most elegant hotel located smack in the center of the Quarter. The lobby is a small sea of marble, and the rooms are sizable and tasteful, full of muted tones and plush furniture, with windows that let you look dreamily out over the Quarter. Rates: from $169.

About 7 blocks from the cruise ship terminal is the atmospheric **Hotel Monteleone,** 214 Royal St., between Iberville and Bienville (© 800/535-9595; www.hotelmonteleone.com), the oldest hotel in the city and also the largest hotel in the French Quarter. Everyone who stays here loves it, probably because its staff is among the most helpful in town. Decor and floor layouts are slightly different in each of the rooms, so ask to see a few different ones. Rates: from $199.

In the Central Business District, just outside the French Quarter and close to the cruise ship terminal, the **Windsor Court Hotel,** 300 Gravier St. (© 888/596-0955; www.windsorcourthotel.com), has been a recipient of the *Condé Nast Traveler's* "Best Hotel in North America" award, so feel free to hold it to a high standard. Accommodations are exceptionally spacious and classy, with large bay windows or a private balcony overlooking the river or the city. Rates: from $215. Also in the CBD, the **International House,** 221 Camp St., just west of Canal (© 800/633-5770; www.ihhotel.com), is a very modern, minimalist hotel that was constructed in an old Beaux Arts bank building. Rooms are simple with high ceilings, ceiling fans, and photos and knickknacks that remind you you're in New Orleans. Rates: from $149.

In the Garden District, the **McKendrick-Breaux House,** 1474 Magazine St. (© **888/570-1700;** www.mckendrick-breaux.com), was built at the end of the Civil War by a wealthy plumber and Scottish immigrant, and today is one of the best guest-houses for value. It's been completely restored to its original charm, with each room furnished with antiques, family collectibles, and fresh flowers. Rates: from $145.

DINING & NIGHTLIFE

Essentially, New Orleans is one giant restaurant and nightlife spot. In 1997, a U.S. survey named it "the fattest city in the country," which makes sense once you've tasted the food at many of the city's best restaurants. Ironically, the city is also home to the authors of *Sugar Busters,* the best-seller about controlling carbohydrates for weight loss, and many of its restaurants are beginning to focus more on health while still maintaining those great N'awlins flavors. After dinner, be sure to head out to the clubs, because this is, after all, the city that gave birth to jazz. Many of the best restaurants and clubs are in the French Quarter.

In business since 1918 and still mighty fine, the legendary **Arnaud's,** 813 Bienville St. (© **504/523-2847;** www.arnauds.com), is set up in three interconnected, once-private houses from the 1700s, and its three Belle Epoque dining rooms are lush with Edwardian embellishments. Menu items include snapper or trout topped with crab-meat, filet mignon, oysters stewed in cream, and classic Bananas Foster. Main courses: $22 to $35. **Bacco,** 310 Chartres St., between Bienville and Conti (© **504/522-2426;** www.bacco.com), a great New Orleans bistro, has an elegant setting with pink faux-marble floors and Venetian chandeliers. You can feast on wood-fired pizzas, regional seafood, and such specialties as black truffle fettuccine and lobster ravioli. Main courses: $19 to $25. **Galatoire's,** 209 Bourbon St., at Iberville (© **504/525-2021**), feels like a bistro in turn-of-the-20th-century Paris, and is one of the city's most legendary places—and one where the locals go for a good meal. Menu items include trout (meunière or amandine), a savory Creole-style bouillabaisse, and a good eggplant stuffed with a purée of seafood. Main courses: $18 to $28.

Louisiana Heritage Cafe, in the Bienville House hotel, 320 Decatur St., at Conti (© **504/299-8800**), serves contemporary Creole cuisine in a formal setting. Entrees include the garlic shrimp and saffron pasta, and a Gulf fish of the day. Main courses: $10 to $20. **The Gumbo Shop,** 630 St. Peter St., at Royal (© **504/525-1486**), is a cheap and convenient place to get solid, classic Creole food. The menu reads like a textbook list of traditional local food: red beans and rice, shrimp Creole, crawfish étouffée. The seafood gumbo with okra is a meal in itself, and do try the jambalaya. Main courses: $7 to $19. **Napoléon House,** 500 Chartres St., at the corner of St. Louis Street (© **504/524-9752**), would have been the home of the lieutenant himself if some locals' wild plan to bring him here to live out his exile had panned out. A landmark 1797 building with an incredible atmosphere, the place is a hangout for drinking and good times, but also serves food. The specialty is Italian muffuletta, with ham, Genoa salami, pastrami, Swiss cheese, and provolone. Main courses: $12 to $24.

Not far outside the Quarter, **Mother's Restaurant,** 401 Poydras St., at Tchoupi-toulas (© **504/523-9656**), has long lines and zero atmosphere, but damn, those po' boys is *goood.* Customers have been flocking here since 1938 for homemade biscuits and red-bean omelets at breakfast, po' boys at lunch, and soft-shell crabs and jamba-laya at dinner. Everything's between $5 and $21. Right on the border of the French Quarter, the open kitchen at **Palace Café,** 605 Canal St., between Royal and Chartres

(© 504/523-1661; www.palacecafe.com), serves contemporary Creole food with a big emphasis on seafood: catfish pecan meunière, andouille-crusted fish of the day, and lots more. Don't miss the white chocolate bread pudding. Main courses: $19 to $28. Outside the Quarter, at the corner of Washington Avenue and Coliseum Street in the Garden District, **Commander's Palace,** 1403 Washington Ave. (© **504/899-8221;** www.commanderspalace.com), still reigns as one of the finest dining choices not only in New Orleans, but in the whole United States—the James Beard Foundation voted it the country's best restaurant in 1996. The cuisine is haute Creole. Try anything with shrimp or crawfish, or the Mississippi quail, or . . . oh hell, just try anything. Main courses: $45.

For a snack any time of the day or night, visit **Café du Monde,** 800 Decatur St., right on the river (© **504/581-2914**). It's basically a 24-hour coffee shop that specializes in beignets, a square, really yummy doughnut-type thing, served hot and covered in powdered sugar. It's a great spot for people-watching, but if you don't want to wait for a table, you can always get a bag of beignets to go. Grab lots of napkins. Moist towelettes would be a good idea too, or maybe just a big wet towel.

Life in "The Big Easy" is conducive to all manner of nighttime entertainment, usually raucous. Do what most people do: Start at one end of **Bourbon Street** (say, around Iberville), walk down to the other end, and then turn around and do it again. Along the way, you'll hear R & B, blues, and jazz pouring out of dozens of bars, be beckoned by touts from the numerous strip clubs, and see one tiny little storefront stall after another sporting hand-lettered signs that say OUR BEER IS CHEAPER THAN NEXT DOOR. It's a scene. Bacchanalian? Yes. Will you spend time in Purgatory for it? Maybe, but it's loads of fun. Grab yourself a big $2 beer or one of the famous rum-based Hurricanes—preferably in a yard-long green plastic cup shaped like a Roswell alien—and join the party.

Most of the places in this section have a cover charge that varies depending on who's performing; some are free. **Preservation Hall,** 726 St. Peter St., just off Bourbon (© **504/ 522-2841** during the day, 504/523-8939 after 8pm; www.preservationhall.com), is a deliberately shabby little hall with very few places to sit and no air-conditioning. Nonetheless, people usually pack the place to see the house band, a bunch of mostly older musicians who have been at this for eons. There's a $5 admission fee. Close by, **Maison Bourbon,** 641 Bourbon St. (© **504/522-8818**), presents authentic and often fantastic Dixieland and traditional jazz. Stepping into the brick-walled room, or even just peering in from the street, takes you away from the mayhem outside. There's a one-drink minimum. **House of Blues,** 225 Decatur St. (© **504/529-2583;** www.hob.com), is one of the city's largest live-music venues. You stand and move among the several bars that pepper the club.

For a classic bar without live music, hit **Lafitte's Blacksmith Shop,** 941 Bourbon St. (© **504/523-0066**), a French Quarter pub housed in an 18th-century Creole blacksmith shop that looks like only faith keeps it standing. Tennessee Williams used to hang out here. If you're looking to get away from the Bourbon scene and hear some real brass-band jazz, head up to **Donna's,** 800 N. Rampart St., at the top of St. Ann Street (© **504/596-6914;** www.donnasbarandgrill.com). There's no better place to hear the authentic sound that made New Orleans famous. The cover varies, but is always reasonable.

One block beyond Esplanade, on the periphery of the French Quarter, **Snug Harbor,** 626 Frenchman St. (© **504/949-0696;** www.snugjazz.com), is a jazz bistro, a classic spot to hear modern jazz in a cozy setting. Sometimes R & B combos and blues are added to the program. There's a full dinner menu in the restaurant, but only appetizers are served in the club. Farther outside the Quarter, jazz, blues, and Dixieland pour out of the nostalgia-laden bar and concert hall **Tipitina's,** way out in the Uptown neighborhood at 501 Napoleon Ave. (© **504/891-8477;** www.tipitinas.com).

12 New York City, New York

Up until the 1950s, New York City was one of the biggest ports in the world for both cargo and passenger vessels, its famous skyline and the Statue of Liberty offering a dramatic approach that no other port could match. So many ships parked their noses against Manhattan's West Side that it was dubbed Luxury Liner Row. All the greats were there, from the *Normandie* to *Queen Mary* and *France,* their horns echoing across midtown. All that ended when the airplane put the liners out of business, allowing people to cross the Atlantic in half a day rather than a week. Never again would the Port of New York see as much traffic, though today it's reclaiming an impressive bit of its former glory as a cruise home port.

Joining a handful of lines that long based ships in NYC for summer and/or fall cruises to Bermuda, New England, and Canada are several Caribbean-bound ships, including NCL's *Norwegian Dawn,* which offers 7-night round-trip cruises year-round to Florida and The Bahamas, as well as longer trips deeper into the Caribbean.

The beauty of New York City is that so many of its motley treasures are within walking distance, its driven citizens as much an attraction as its museums, concert halls, and skyscrapers. Manhattan is a compact place, and most of its streets, north of the Village, follow a simple grid pattern, so it's next to impossible to lose your way.

GETTING TO NEW YORK CITY & THE PORT

The **New York City Passenger Ship Terminal** is at 711 Twelfth Ave., between 46th and 54th streets, on the Hudson River waterfront. It's reached via the Henry Hudson Parkway (aka the West Side Hwy.) via the 54th Street vehicle ramp. Frequently congested on turnaround days, at press time the city had announced a $50 million initiative to significantly improve the port facilities, improving passenger circulation and reducing roadway congestion. For information, call © **212/246-5450** or check out **www.nypst.com**.

At press time, Royal Caribbean was gearing up for its second season offering cruises from its new **Cape Liberty Cruise Port,** across the Hudson from New York, in Bayonne, New Jersey. We know: It doesn't have the same romance. But, it does have the advantage of being less congested, and of offering a great view of the NYC skyline and the Statue of Liberty. The 430-acre man-made peninsula was originally constructed in the late 1930s as a port for international shipping, and was taken over by the U.S. Navy in 1942. It was deeded to the Bayonne Local Redevelopment Authority in December 2002, after the closing of the Navy base. The new port's location—just off the New Jersey Turnpike and I-278, and approximately 15 minutes from the Newark airport—makes it easily accessible to those coming from New Jersey, Long Island, and the New York boroughs of Brooklyn and Staten Island. Passengers coming from Manhattan can connect via a nearby light rail that links with both Amtrak and the PATH subway. To take even more pressure off the busy Manhattan terminals, plans were announced to develop a new cruise terminal by year-end 2005 for gritty **Red Hook, Brooklyn,** right across the harbor from lower Manhattan. By car, the spot is easily accessible to locals as well as to visitors flying into Kennedy, LaGuardia, and Newark airports. While Red Hook itself is heavily industrial, it's just minutes from picturesque Colonial-era Brooklyn Heights (whose riverfront promenade provides one of the best Manhattan views) and the great expanse of the Brooklyn Bridge.

If you're coming in by plane, you'll fly into one of three New York area airports. **John F. Kennedy (JFK) International** is east of Manhattan in the southeastern section of Queens County, 15 miles from midtown Manhattan and a 30- to 60-minute drive from the piers, depending on traffic. **LaGuardia Airport** is east of Manhattan in Queens, 8 miles from midtown Manhattan and a 20- to 40-minute drive from the piers. **Newark International Airport** is west of Manhattan in Essex and Union counties, New Jersey, about 16 miles from midtown Manhattan and a 30- to 60-minute drive from NYC. Information on all three is at the Port Authority of New York & New Jersey website, **www.panynj.gov**. Kennedy and Newark are the larger airports and accommodate both domestic and international flights.

If you've arranged air transportation and/or transfers through the cruise line (see chapter 2, "Booking Your Cruise & Getting the Best Price"), a cruise line representative will direct you to shuttle buses that take you to the port. Taxis are also available. From the airport to the terminal, **yellow New York City Taxis** are usually lined up in great numbers at the airports waiting for fares. From JFK to Manhattan, yellow taxis charge a flat fee of $45 per carload, plus tolls and tip; there is no flat fee from Newark or LaGuardia—you pay the standard metered rate: $2.50 just to get going, then 40¢ for every ⅕ mile (about 4 blocks) thereafter. Newark rides entail an additional $15 surcharge.

Carmel Car Service (© 800/9-CARMEL or 212/666-6666; www.carmelcarservice.com) charges $30 per carload from Manhattan (including the cruise ship piers) to LaGuardia, $44 to JFK, and $43 to Newark; to Manhattan, the rates vary depending on time of day: $28 to $35 from LaGuardia, $40 to $45 from JFK, and $43 to $50 from Newark. Freelance (aka "gypsy") drivers may solicit you in the airport; to avoid being gouged, it's better to stick with a car service or the official NYC yellow taxis. **Super Shuttle** (© 212/258-3826; www.supershuttle.com) vans are another good way to get between the airports and the piers. Fares are $15 to LaGuardia, and $19 to JFK or Newark per person either way (so, it's no bargain if you're a group of three or more). Twenty-four-hour advance reservations are recommended.

If you're coming by car, Manhattan's Henry Hudson Parkway/West Side Highway is the main artery into the port. To get to the terminals at 48th, 50th, and 52nd streets, cars should enter via the vehicle ramp at 54th Street, directly off the highway. Long-term parking at the port, on top of the three terminals, with escalators leading down, is $24 a day if parking for multiple days.

GETTING AROUND   New York's cruise ship piers are close to the heart of town, about 5 long blocks from Times Square. Passengers are a short stroll away from 42nd Street and Times Square and a slightly longer one from Fifth Avenue, Central Park, and many other sites. Much of the Big Apple can be explored on foot (Manhattan is only about 2 miles wide by 13 miles long, with most visitors remaining in its bottom half). If you need a break, hail one of the ubiquitous yellow taxis (meters start at $2.50 and increase 40¢ every ⅕ mile or 40¢ per 90 sec. when stuck in traffic; night and rush-hour surcharges also apply), or hop on the red double-decker **Gray Line** tour buses that crisscross the city (© 800/669-0051 or 212/445-0848; www.graylinenewyork.com); you can join the tour loop at the Circle Line terminal just a few steps south of the cruise ship piers.

New York City

MANHATTAN CRUISE
TERMINAL 4 ●
RED HOOK CRUISE
TERMINAL 40
CAPE LIBERTY CRUISE
TERMINAL 39

ATTRACTIONS & SHOPPING ●
Barneys New York 14
Central Park 2
Chinatown 37
Diamond District 25
Empire State Building 29
"Ladies Mile" stores 32
Macy's/Herald Square 28
Roosevelt Island Tram 16
St. Marks Place 34
Tiffany & Co. 19
Time Warner Center 3
Times Square 9
Zabar's & Fairway 1

ACCOMMODATIONS ■
Doubletree Times Square 8
Hotel Metro 27
Le Parker Meridien 18
Mandarin Oriental 3
Ritz-Carlton 17
Skyline Hotel 6
St. Regis 20
The Kimberly 24
The Muse 26
Waldorf Astoria 23

DINING & NIGHTLIFE ◆
Aix 1
Aquavit 21
Asiate 3
Babbo 33
Corner Bistro 10
Elaine's 12
Eleven Madison Park 31
Gray's Papaya 1
H&H Bagels 5
Home 33
J. G. Melon 13
Joe Allen 7
Joe's Shanghai 38
Katz's Delicatessen 35
La Grenouille 22
Nobu 36
Patsy's Pizzeria 11
Pongal 30
Serendipity 3 15

UPPER WEST SIDE

Lincoln Center

W. 65th St.
W. 64th St.
W. 63rd St.
W. 62nd St.
W. 61st St.
W. 60th St.
W. 59th St.
W. 58th St.
W. 57th St.
W. 56th St.
W. 55th St.
W. 54th St.
W. 53rd St.
W. 52nd St.
W. 51st St.
W. 50th St.
W. 49th St.
W. 48th St.
W. 47th St.
W. 46th St.
W. 45th St.
W. 44th St.
W. 43rd St.
W. 42nd St.
W. 41st St.
W. 40th St.
W. 39th St.
W. 38th St.
W. 37th St.
W. 36th St.
W. 35th St.
W. 34th St.
W. 33rd St.
W. 32nd St.
W. 31st St.
W. 30th St.
W. 29th St.
W. 28th St.
W. 27th St.
W. 26th St.
W. 25th St.
W. 24th St.
W. 23rd St.
W. 22nd St.
W. 21st St.
W. 20th St.
W. 19th St.
W. 18th St.
W. 17th St.
W. 16th St.
W. 15th St.

65th St.

CENTRAL

West Drive

Central Park S.

Columbus Circle

Carnegie Hall

West End Ave.
Amsterdam Ave.
Columbus Ave.
Central Park W.
Tenth Ave.
Ninth Ave.
Broadway
Eighth Ave.
Seventh Ave.

DeWitt Clinton Park

THEATER DISTRICT

MIDTOWN WEST

TIMES SQUARE

Port Authority

GARMENT DISTRICT

Intrepid Sea-Air-Space Museum

Twelfth Ave.
Eleventh Ave.

Lincoln Tunnel
← To New Jersey

Javits Convention Center

Penn Station/ Madison Square Garden

W 32nd St.

W 32nd St.

Tunnel Entrance

Chelsea Park

West Side Hwy.
Eleventh Ave.
Tenth Ave.
Ninth Ave.
Eighth Ave.
Seventh Ave.

Hudson River

Chelsea Piers Sports & Entertainment Complex

Chelsea Piers

CHELSEA

MEAT-PACKING DISTRICT

BEST CRUISE LINE SHORE EXCURSIONS

Manhattan Highlights ($39, 4 hr.): Since New York is only a port of embarkation, the cruise lines generally offer one choice on the day passengers disembark, the basic city tour, that typically ends at one of the local airports. Hop on a bus and see the highlights, from Time's Square to Fifth Avenue's Rockefeller Center and St. Patrick's Cathedral, Lincoln Center, and Central Park, before heading downtown past Macy's to Greenwich Village, Little Italy, Chinatown, and South Street Seaport.

EXPLORING NEW YORK ON YOUR OWN

There's much more to see than we have the space to cover, so here are some easy-to-get-to highlights. In addition to the choices below, don't forget about **Central Park,** the great green swath that is, just by virtue of its existence amidst some of the world's priciest real estate, New York City's greatest marvel.

Lines can be horrible at the concourse-level ticket booth of the **Empire State Building,** so be prepared to wait—or consider purchasing advance tickets online using a credit card at **www.esbnyc.com**. Admission is $14.50 adults; $9.50 to $13.50 kids. For great views, take a ride on the **Roosevelt Island Tram** (© **212/832-4543,** ext. 1). This is the same tram that you have probably seen in countless movies, most recently *Spider-Man.* The Tram originates at 59th Street and Second Avenue, costs $1.50 each way (half price for seniors), and takes 4 minutes to traverse the East River to Roosevelt Island, where there are a series of apartment complexes and parks. During those 4 minutes you will be treated to a gorgeous view down the East River and the eastside skyline with views of the United Nations and four bridges: the Queensboro, Williamsburg, Manhattan, and the Brooklyn Bridge. On a clear day you might even spot **Lady Liberty.** At press time, the statue's observation deck was once again open to the public, and if you get there early enough (no later than noon) to snag a ticket, the views of the city are out of this world. All policies regarding access to the Statue of Liberty and Ellis Island are subject to change at any time; check the official website **(www.nps.gov/stli)** for the latest access information.

There's no doubting that **Times Square** has evolved into something much different from what it was a decade ago when it had a deservedly sleazy reputation. Yet there is much debate whether the old was better than the new. For the real New Yorker, there is not much to offer here; the restaurants aren't very good, the crowds are stifling, and the shops unimaginative major chains. The area has become a sterile Disney-fied celebration of kitsch. Yep, it's a tourist trap, but the neon spectacle is something everyone should witness before returning home. If you are interested in spending more time in the area, here are some of its attractions: ABC's *Good Morning America* has set up a street-facing studio and the **NASDAQ** has an eight-story billboard—the world's largest video screen. The **Virgin Megastore** has a major presence on the square, as do a huge **Toys "R" Us** complete with a 60 ft. Ferris wheel, and **MTV,** which draws busloads of exuberant *Total Request Live* fans to Broadway and 45th Street every weekday afternoon. Forty-second Street between Seventh and Eighth avenues, the former porn peddler's paradise, has been rebuilt from scratch into a family-oriented entertainment mecca. In addition to a spate of beautifully renovated theaters—including the **New Victory,** the **New Amsterdam** (home to *The Lion King*), and the former Selwyn, reinvented as the **American Airlines Theatre** and now the permanent home of the Roundabout Theater Club—the neon-bright block is chock-full with retail and amusements, including **Madame Tussaud's New York,** a six-floor fully interactive new-world version of London's famous wax museum (a steep $31 for adults and $24 for kids 4–12); the multilevel, state-of-the-art **Broadway City** video arcade; and two 20-plus-screen movie complexes.

SHOPPING

Just as there are restaurants on every block, so are there shops. Here's a quick reap: The fish and herbal markets along Canal, Mott, Mulberry, and Elizabeth streets in **China-town** are fun for their bustle and exotica. Dispersed among them (especially along **Canal St.**), you'll find a mind-boggling collection of knock-off sunglasses and watches, cheap backpacks, discount leather goods, and exotic souvenirs. A definite highlight is the **Pearl River** Chinese emporium, a few blocks north of Canal at 477 Broadway. Going north, SoHo, stretching from Broadway east to Sullivan Street, and from Houston down to Broome, is still the epicenter of cutting-edge fashion. Going up even farther, **East 9th Street** between First and Second avenues is lined with an increasingly smart collection of boutiques, including **Jill Anderson** and **Selia Yang,** that sell excellent-quality and affordably priced original fashions for women. If it's strange, illegal, or funky, it's probably available on **St. Marks Place,** which takes over for 8th Street, running east from Third Avenue to Avenue A. You'll also find lots of souveniery things at this permanent street market, from countless T-shirt to boho jew-elry stands. In the West Village, the prime drag for strolling is bustling **Bleecker Street,** where you'll find lots of "discount" leather shops and record stores interspersed with a good number of interesting and artsy boutiques.

On the west side, you'll find major superstores in the elegant, renovated cast-iron buildings of what was once known as the "Ladies' Mile" for its profusion of depart-ment stores. **Filene's Basement, TJ Maxx,** and **Bed Bath & Beyond** are all at 620 Sixth Ave. (at 18th St.), while **Old Navy** is right next door and **Barnes & Noble** is just a few blocks north at 22nd Street. On Broadway, north of Union Square at 19th Street is **ABC Carpet & Home,** a candy store for home decorating buffs. Herald Square—where 34th Street, Sixth Avenue, and Broadway converge—is dominated by **Macy's,** the self-proclaimed world's biggest department store; while in **Times Square,** you can step into Richard Branson's rollicking **Virgin Megastore** and the fabulous **Toys "R" Us** flagship on Broadway and 44th Street. West 47th Street between Fifth and Sixth avenues is the city's famous **Diamond District.** The heart of Manhattan retail is the corner of Fifth Avenue and 57th Street. **Tiffany & Co.,** which has long reigned supreme in the city, sits a stone's throw from **Niketown** and the **NBA Store.** Still, you will find a number of big-name, big-ticket designers radiating from the crossroads, including **Versace, Chanel, Dior,** and **Cartier.** You'll also find big-name jewelers along here, as well as chichi department stores such as **Bergdorf Goodman, Henri Bendel,** and **Saks Fifth Avenue,** all of which help this stretch of Fifth Avenue maintain its classy cachet.

Uptown, Madison Avenue from 57th to 79th streets has usurped Fifth Avenue as *the* tony shopping street in the city; in fact, it boasts the most expensive retail real estate in the world. Bring lots of plastic. This ultradeluxe strip—particularly in the high 60s and 70s—is home to *ultra*-luxurious designer boutiques, with **Barneys New York** as the anchor. Finally, on the Upper West Side, the new kid in town is the massive shopping complex at the foot of the new **Time Warner Center** at Columbus Circle (at the inter-section of Broadway and Eighth Ave., between 58th and 60th sts.), where you'll find big names like Thomas Pink, A/X Armani Exchange, Sephora, and Williams Sonoma to name a few (www.shopsatcolumbuscircle.com). Though you might just want to head uptown a little ways on Broadway for a taste of the real New York in **Zabar's** (at 80th St.) and **Fairway** (at 74th St.), both gourmet-food-store legends.

WHERE TO STAY

There are tons of choices all over town, with rates rarely going below $150 a night, and easily running more than $300, $400, or $500, and we're not even getting into the realm of suites and penthouses. That said, there are often special promotions offered on weekends (when the business travelers have all left town), so rates listed below could be discounted. Here's a sampling of the best hotels at a variety of price points.

If the sky's the limit, you'll pay big bucks for great views at the new **Mandarin Oriental New York**, 80 Columbus Circle (at 60th St.; © **212/805-8800;** www. mandarinoriental.com). Residing in the shiny two-towered Time Warner Center, it occupies floors 34 through 54 of the northwestern tower, and all rooms have great views. They also boast the latest in technology (high-speed Internet access, flatscreen TVs—even in the bathrooms—and the rest of it), plus an elegant decor that marries the Orient with urban New York. Rates: from $655.

Le Parker Meridien, 118 W. 57th St. (© **800/543-4300;** www.parkermeridien.com), the perfect blending of style, service, and amenities, is a hotel that delivers on every front. It's the best choice if you want a little of everything: luxury, high-tech, family-friendly, comfort, and a great central location. Rates: from $295.

New York has many "grand dames," and the **St. Regis,** 2 E. 55th St. (© **212/ 753-4500;** www.stregis.com), is among the best classic elegant hotels that have been around for years. The Beaux Arts beauty on Fifth, who celebrated its 100th anniversary in 2004, offers unrivaled luxury—Louis XVI furniture, crystal chandeliers, and silk wall coverings—and impeccable service. Rates: $400 to $735. Other classics include the **Waldorf Astoria,** 301 Park Ave. (© **800/WALDORF;** www.waldorfastoria.com; rates: from $319).

Ritz-Carlton New York, Central Park, 50 Central Park South (© **212/308-9100;** www.ritzcarlton.com), offers the upscale chain's typically excellent Ritz service, spacious comfortable rooms, understated luxury, and an incredible location overlooking Central Park. Rates: from $550. With artistic interiors and great service, **The Muse,** 130 W. 46th St. (© **877/692-6873** or 212/485-2400; www.themusehotel.com), is the hidden jewel of the Theater District. Rates: from $279.

The **Doubletree Times Square Guest Suites,** 1568 Broadway (© **800/222-TREE;** www.doubletree.com), is great for families, boasting an entire floor of child-proof suites, complete with living rooms and kitchenettes. And your young ones will love the Kids Club (for ages 3–12). Rates: from $289.

The Kimberly, 145 E. 50th St. (© **800/683-0400;** www.kimberlyhotel.com), has great suite deals, with full-fledged one- and two-bedroom apartments—complete with full kitchens—for the same price as most standard Midtown hotels. Free access to a fabulous full-service health club and complimentary sunset cruises in summer add to the incredible value. Rates: from $259. The **Hotel Metro,** 45 W. 35th St. (© **800/ 356-3870;** www.hotelmetronyc.com), is a Midtown gem that gives you a surprisingly good deal, including a marble bath. Rates: from $170. The basic, but newly renovated, **Skyline Hotel,** 725 Tenth Ave. (© **800/586-3400;** www.skylinehotelny.com), is a great option for budget seekers, and it's just a short taxi ride, or walk, if you don't have a lot of bags, from the terminal. Rates: from $179.

DINING & NIGHTLIFE

You can get any type of cuisine imaginable in this foodie city, from Indian to Thai, Ethiopian, Chinese, Japanese, Korean, Portuguese, Argentinean, German, French . . . you get the picture. One of our favorites is **Eleven Madison Park,** 11 Madison Ave. (© 212/889-0905), a magnificent French restaurant on every level. Main courses: $21 to $31. For the best French, however, visit **La Grenouille,** 3 E. 52nd St. (© 212/ 752-1495), which serves the classics with elegant perfection. Main courses: $22 to $34. **Aix,** 2398 Broadway (© 212/874-7400; www.aixnyc.com), is a tri-level restaurant where Chef Didier Virot has put smiles on the faces of West Siders with his novel spin on the cuisine of Provence. Main courses: $20 to $40. In the best views category, **Asiate,** 80 Columbus Circle at 60th Street (© 212/805-8881), in the new Mandarin Oriental hotel, might steal the show at some 34 floors above Central Park. The Japanese/French fare here is divine. Main courses: $69 for three-course prix fixe. Pre-theater diners can't go wrong with **Aquavit,** 65 E. 55th St. (© 212/307-7311; www.aquavit. org), which offers a three-course pre-theater menu for $55 (otherwise, it's $75). Their light Scandinavian cuisine won't weigh you down in your theater seat. After the show, **Joe Allen,** 326 W. 46th St. (© 212/581-6464), is the ultimate Broadway pub—and the meatloaf is marvelous. Main courses: $12 to $27. For great Chinese, hit **Joe's Shanghai,** 9 Pell St. (© 212/233-8888). Main courses: $3 to $22. If it's Italian you're craving, go with **Babbo,** 110 Waverly Place (© 212/777-0303; www.babbonyc.com), where Food Network chef Mario Batali has created the ideal setting for his exciting northern Italian cooking. Main courses: $23 to $29. For top Japanese, hands down it's **Nobu,** 105 Hudson St. (© 212/219-0500), which also happens to have a hand in the menus on Crystal Cruise Lines three ships. Main courses: $8 to $32.

If it's home cooking that gets your goat, go to **Home,** 20 Cornelia St. (© 212/ 243-9579), where the cumin-crusted pork chop sits in a bed of homemade barbecue sauce that's better than Dad used to make, and even Mom would tip her hat to the silky smooth chocolate pudding. Main courses: $16 to $21. **Katz's Delicatessen,** 205 E. Houston St. (© 212/254-2246), is the choice among those who know their kreplach, knishes, and pastrami. The all-beef wieners are the best in a town known for its top-quality dogs. Main courses: $3 to $19. For great pies, as in pizza, visit **Patsy's Pizzeria,** 2287 First Ave. (© 212/534-9783), an East Harlem institution that's been cranking out coal-oven pizza since 1932. It was the favorite of Frank Sinatra, who used to have Patsy's pizzas packed and shipped to him in Vegas. If you got kids, go to **Serendipity 3,** 225 E. 60th St. (© 212/838-3531), a classic ice-cream parlor, but better. Main courses: $5 to $19. Veggies will fall in love with **Pongal,** 110 Lexington Ave. (© 212/696-9458), whose South Indian fare is the yummiest. Main courses: $6 to $11. For cheap, hit **Gray's Papaya,** 2090 Broadway (© 212/799-0243), for a pair of dogs and a fruit drink. If it's bagels you crave, the best are just a few blocks away from the terminal at **H&H Bagels,** Twelfth Avenue and 46th Street (www.handhbagel. com). The competition is fierce in this category but despite arrogantly breaking the $1 barrier for the price of a bagel, H&H still makes the best.

When it comes to nightlife in NYC, where to start? There's **Broadway** for world-class shows; Carnegie Hall and Lincoln Center for symphonies, opera, and ballet; Radio City for concerts and shows; Restaurant Row in midtown for cabaret (like Don't Tell Mama's on W. 46th St.); and the Village for jazz and other live music (like the Blue Note at 131 W. 3rd St.). The list goes on. Assuming you only have a day or two to sample the Big Apple, downtown has the most interesting options, from trendoid **TriBeCa** and **SoHo** lounges where a cosmo goes for the price of a small car, to old-time **Greenwich Village** pubs (such as the **Corner Bistro** on Jane St.) and the handful of live music clubs that have survived since the '50s and '60s in and around Bleecker Street. Still, if Talbots and Brooks Brothers are more your speed, the **Upper East Side,** along Second and Third avenues between about 72nd Street and 96th Street, have no shortage of bars and restaurants, many with outdoor seating during the warm months (from **J.G. Melon** on 74th St. and Third Ave. to **Elaines** on 88th St. and Second Ave.). If you want a classic NYC **disco,** most are on the far reaches of the west side below about 30th Street.

For listings of currents shows, plays, and live music, check out local publications such as *Time Out New York* (www.timeoutny.com), the *Village Voice* (www. villagevoice.com), *New Yorker* (www.newyorker.com), and *New York* magazine (www.nymetro.com).

13 Norfolk, Virginia

Founded in 1682 on two peninsulas formed by the Chesapeake Bay and the Elizabeth and Lafayette rivers, Norfolk is a major seaport and naval base that's replaced its old sailor bars with a modern, spotless downtown of high-rise offices, condos, and all the marinas, shops, and museums that go with them. Interspersed are reminders of the city's past, such as historic houses and the old City Hall, now a museum and memorial to World War II hero General Douglas MacArthur (who was actually born in Little Rock, Arkansas, but always claimed Norfolk). **Downtown** is on the southern side of the city, on the north bank of the Elizabeth River. Bordering downtown to the northwest, **Freemason** is Norfolk's oldest residential neighborhood, with most of its 18th- and 19th-century town houses restored as private homes, businesses, and restaurants. You'll still find a few cobblestone streets here. Northwest of Freemason, across a semicircular inlet known as The Hague, **Ghent** was the city's first subdivision (most houses in "old" Ghent, near The Hague and the Chrysler Museum of Art, were built between 1892 and 1912) and is now its trendiest enclave. Norfolk is one of the newer alternative home ports, with ships sailing to the Caribbean, The Bahamas, and Bermuda.

GETTING TO NORFOLK & THE PORT

Norfolk is located 190 miles southeast of Washington, D.C., and close to the North Carolina border, making it a convenient port for cruisers in the mid-Atlantic states. Ships dock at **Nauticus, the National Maritime Center,** 1 Waterside Dr., at Boush Street (© **800/664-1080;** www.nauticus.org), just steps from the heart of the city. At press time the City of Norfolk had started construction on a new 80,000-square-foot cruise terminal adjacent to the existing facility, which was slated to open in late 2006.

If you happen to be flying, you'll land at **Norfolk International Airport,** on Norview Avenue, 1½ miles north of I-64 (© **757/857-3351;** www.norfolkairport. com). The port is about 7 miles away, and you can get there in 10 minutes via taxi ($20 one-way). There are also shuttle services and car rentals from the airport.

By car, take I-64, exit onto 264 West toward Downtown Norfolk, and take the Waterside Drive exit (Exit 9). Nauticus is four lights down on the left. There are two different parking areas, both close to the dock, serving different ships. Parking is $10 per day. For more information, check **www.cruisenorfolk.org**.

GETTING AROUND   A car is the easiest way to get around this spread-out area, though you can walk the downtown area around the port. For taxis, call **Yellow Cab** (© **757/857-888**).

Norfolk

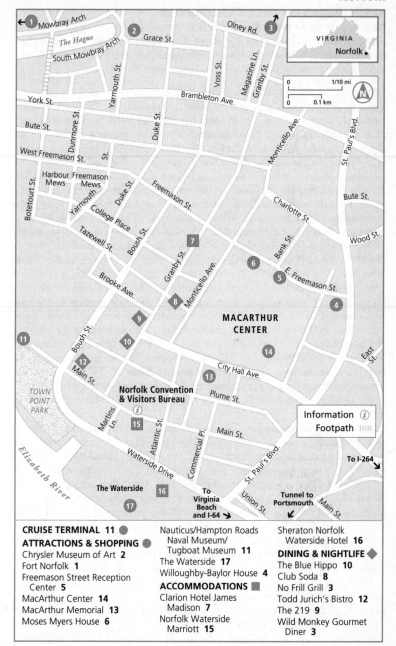

VIRGINIA

Norfolk.

0   1/10 mi
0   0.1 km

Mowbray Arch 1
The Hague
South Mowbray Arch
Grace St. 2
Olney Rd. 3
York St.
Bute St.
West Freemason St.
Yarmouth St.
Dunmore St.
Duke St.
Voss St.
Magazine Ln.
Granby St.
Brambleton Ave.
Monticello Ave.
St. Paul's Blvd.
Harbour Mews
Freemason Mews
Yarmouth
College Place
Duke St.
Freemason St.
Charlotte St.
Bute St.
Wood St.
Botetourt St.
Tazewell St.
Boush St.
Granby St.
7
Monticello Ave.
Bank St.
6
E. Freemason St.
5
Brooke Ave.
8
4
9
MACARTHUR CENTER
10
11
12
Main St.
14
East St.
City Hall Ave.
13
Norfolk Convention & Visitors Bureau
Plume St.
TOWN POINT PARK
Martins Ln.
15
Atlantic St.
Main St.
Commercial Pl.
St. Paul's Blvd.
Information (i)
Footpath |||||
Waterside Drive
Elizabeth River
The Waterside
16
To Virginia Beach and I-64
Union St.
Tunnel to Portsmouth
Main St.
To I-264
17

CRUISE TERMINAL 11 ●
ATTRACTIONS & SHOPPING ●
Chrysler Museum of Art **2**
Fort Norfolk **1**
Freemason Street Reception Center **5**
MacArthur Center **14**
MacArthur Memorial **13**
Moses Myers House **6**

Nauticus/Hampton Roads Naval Museum/ Tugboat Museum **11**
The Waterside **17**
Willoughby-Baylor House **4**
ACCOMMODATIONS ■
Clarion Hotel James Madison **7**
Norfolk Waterside Marriott **15**

Sheraton Norfolk Waterside Hotel **16**
DINING & NIGHTLIFE ◆
The Blue Hippo **10**
Club Soda **8**
No Frill Grill **3**
Todd Jurich's Bistro **12**
The 219 **9**
Wild Monkey Gourmet Diner **3**

499

BEST CRUISE LINE SHORE EXCURSIONS

Norfolk & Virginia Beach Highlights ($39, 3 hr.): There's nothing particularly special about this bus tour, but it's a good bet if you want an overview of the city, visiting the MacArthur Memorial, historic lighthouses, and the First Landing Cross at Cape Henry, where English colonists first came ashore in 1607.

EXPLORING NORFOLK ON YOUR OWN

Right at the port, the large gray building is **Nauticus, the National Maritime Center,** 1 Waterside Dr. at Boush Street (© **800/664-1080;** www.nauticus.org), a museum dedicated to U.S. Naval sea power. The star attraction is the 888-foot USS *Wisconsin,* berthed alongside on the Elizabeth River. A real live battleship, it was built in 1943 and saw duty during World War II, the Korean War, and the Gulf War. It's once again on inactive reserve status, but because it has to be ready to go within 3 months if it's called up, the whole ship is hermetically sealed—meaning you can't go inside. You can, however, walk on board and stare up at the enormous 16-inch guns overhanging its teak main deck. When you leave the *Wisconsin* you'll walk into the **Hampton Roads Naval Museum** (© **757/444-8921;** www.hrnm.navy.mil), with exhibits describing the Civil War battle between the ironclads *Monitor* and *Merrimac* out on Hampton Roads, as well as more info on the Navy's Norfolk history. On the other side of the building, the **Tugboat Museum** (© **757/627-4884**) is actually the *Huntington,* a tug built in 1933 and used by the navy to dock its ships for more than 50 years. The **"Nauticus"** part of the complex is a children's museum on the building's third and fourth floors, with hands-on interactive exhibits and theaters. Admission is free to the naval museum and battleship; Tugboat Museum $2 adults, $1 children; Nauticus $9.95 adults, $7 kids (4–12). Boats also leave from Nauticus and the nearby Waterside center (see "Dining & Nightlife," below) for cruises of the harbor. The most charming of these is the *American Rover* (© **757/627-7245;** www. americanrover.com), a graceful schooner modeled after 19th-century Chesapeake Bay ships. Two-hour cruises cost $15 adults, $10 kids under 12; 3-hour cruises are $22 and $12.

Nearby, **The Waterside** (see "Dining & Nightlife," below) is a general entertainment/shopping/dining area that was one of the first pegs in downtown's revitalization.

A few blocks inland, in Norfolk's old city hall, the **MacArthur Memorial,** MacArthur Square between City Hall Avenue and Plume Street, at Bank Street (© **757/441-2965;** www.macarthurmemorial.org), is the final resting place of the World War II hero and his wife, Jean, their side-by-side marble crypts resting beneath an enormous dome. In a theater next door, a 22-minute film will give you a perspective on Douglas MacArthur's life and help you understand the other exhibits, which include MacArthur's famous corncob pipe, his omnipresent sunglasses, his field cap with its sides rolled down, and a replica of the plaque marking the spot on the USS *Missouri* where MacArthur presided over the surrender of Japan. Admission is free.

Nearby are two historic homes: The **Moses Myers House,** 331 Bank St., is a handsome early-Federal brick town house built by the first Jews to settle in Norfolk, arriving in 1787 and building their home 5 years later. Two Gilbert Stuart portraits of Mr. and Mrs. Myers hang in the drawing room, and some 70% of the overall furniture and decorative arts displayed are original. The fireplace has unusual carvings depicting a sun god—with the features of George Washington. The **Willoughby-Baylor House/Norfolk History Museum,** a block away at 601 E. Freemason St., was built in 1794, and the classic example of Georgian and Federal style architecture is now officially a museum. Both houses are administered by the Chrysler Museum (see below), and tours covering both houses depart on the hour from the **Freemason Street Reception Center,** between the houses at 401 E. Freemason St. (✆ **800/ 368-3097**). Admission is $5; open year-round Wednesday through Saturday 10am to 4pm, with tours offered daily. You can also pick up a map at the reception center that will guide you around the **Cannonball Trail,** a walk-it-yourself heritage trail that connects historic sites downtown.

About a mile to the north, the **Chrysler Museum of Art,** 425 W. Olney Rd., at Mowbray Arch (✆ **757/644-6200;** www.chrysler.org), is Virginia's finest art museum, spanning artistic periods from ancient Egypt to today, with outstanding collections of glass and Art Nouveau furniture, as well as exhibits of ancient Indian, Islamic, Oriental, African, pre-Columbian, French, Italian, and American art and a permanent photo gallery. Admission is $7; closed Monday and Tuesday. While you're in this part of town, drop in to **Fort Norfolk,** Front Street (www.norfolkhistorical.org/fort; make sure you bring proper ID to do a tour). It's the only survivor of 19 harborfront forts authorized by President George Washington in 1794, and helped protect Norfolk during the War of 1812. During the Civil War, Confederate forces seized the fort and used its magazine to supply the ironclad *Merrimac* during its famous battle with the USS *Monitor*.

SHOPPING

Norfolk is one of the better places in Virginia to search for antiques, with more than 30 shops selling a range of furniture, decorative arts, glassware, jewelry, and other items, from both home and overseas. The best place to look is in the old neighborhood of **Ghent** (north of the Chrysler Museum), which over the years has transformed from farmland to wealthy residential enclave to bad neighborhood to bohemian center and now to trendy hipville. A number of shops sit along West 21st Street between Colonial Avenue and Granby Street, which has its own slate of shops.

Downtown Norfolk's centerpiece is the **MacArthur Center,** a $300 million shopping mall built in 1998 and covering the 9 square blocks bordered by Monticello and City Hall avenues, Freemason Street, and St. Paul's Boulevard (✆ **757/627-6000;** www.shop macarthur.com). The main entry is on Monticello Avenue at Market Street. Anchored by Nordstrom and the largest Dillard's department store in existence, it has most of the mall regulars, an 18-screen cinema, a food court, and full-service restaurants.

WHERE TO STAY

The **Sheraton Norfolk Waterside Hotel,** 777 Waterside Dr. (✆ **888/625-5144** or 757/622-6664; www.sheraton.com), sits next door to The Waterside, overlooking busy Norfolk Harbor. A contemporary 10-story hotel, it offers spacious rooms furnished with dark-wood furniture, about a third of them with small balconies facing the river. Rates: from $179.

The **Norfolk Waterside Marriott,** 235 E. Main St. (✆ **800/228-9290;** www. marriott.com), is an elegant 24-story high-rise connected to The Waterside via a covered skywalk. It's got a mahogany-paneled 18th-century-style lobby and sumptuously furnished guest rooms, which recently received $8 million dollars worth of renovations. The indoor pool opens to a sun deck overlooking the river. Rates: from $189.

The **Clarion Hotel James Madison,** 345 Granby St. (✆ **800/CLARION;** www. clarionhotel.com), was built in 1906 and was the first hostelry in Norfolk to provide indoor plumbing. The lobby reflects the hotel's status as Norfolk's grande dame landmark, with polished walnut columns, wing chairs, and a medallion-printed carpet, and the rooms have been renovated and decorated in Colonial style. Rates: from $99.

DINING & NIGHTLIFE

Norfolk's downtown renaissance has turned the 200 block of **Granby Street** into Norfolk's Restaurant Row, with a number of notable restaurants. **The Blue Hippo,** 147 Granby St. (© 757/533-9664), is an urbane bistro operating under the motto "Life is too short to eat boring food." Its kitchen lives up to that standard, blending local produce with flavors from Thailand, Jamaica, and other spice-oriented locales—for example, the crab cakes with Parmesan cheese and black bean crust, served over a wild rice salad. Main courses: $18 to $30. For a more casual evening, try **The 219,** a block north at 219 Granby St. (© 757/627-2896), a storefront cafe that also offers an eclectic mix of cuisines but with more noise and less expense. In addition to seafood, you can also opt for one-person pizzas with such unusual toppings as prosciutto, spinach, and portobello mushrooms. Main courses: $13 to $20, pizzas around $10.

At Boush Street, opposite Nauticus, **Todd Jurich's Bistro,** 150 Main St. (© 757/622-3210; www.toddjurichsbistro.com), offers creative twists on Southern traditions, such as all-lump-meat crab cakes on brioche with lemon mayonnaise. Everything's made with fresh produce, drawn whenever possible from local farms that practice ecologically sound agriculture. Main courses: $18 to $32.

For al fresco dining, try **No Frill Grill** along Colley Avenue in historic Ghent, 806 Spotswood Ave. (© 757/627-4264; www.nofrillgrill.com); its varied menu of southern food and classics includes steaks, seafood, and BBQ. Main courses: $12 to $20. The **Wild Monkey Gourmet Diner,** 1603 Colley Ave. (© 757/627-6462; www.the wildmonkey.com), is an eclectic casual dining experience and a great place for funky diner creations like mac and cheese with lump crab meat and chicken wings in a spicy apricot glaze. Main courses: $10 to $20.

For a little after-dinner nightlife (or dinner, for that matter), try **The Waterside Festival Marketplace** (aka "The Waterside"), between Waterside Drive and the Elizabeth River (© 757/627-3300). This was the catalyst for downtown Norfolk's revitalization, and though the MacArthur Center has eclipsed it as a shopping destination, it's still an after-dark dining and entertainment destination, with bars, comedy clubs, restaurants, and live music. You also may want to check out **Club Soda,** 111 Tazewell St. (© 757/200-SODA), an ultra happening spot along Norfolk's Restaurant Row.

14 Philadelphia, Pennsylvania

Philadelphia today is an inseparable mix of old and new, and one of the new things is the city's resurgence as a cruise port. Several lines, including Celebrity and NCL, use it as an embarkation hub for Bermuda cruises. Scratch the surface of William Penn's "green countrie towne" and you'll find both a wealth of history and plenty of modern distractions. Philadelphia has the largest surviving district of original Colonial homes and shops in the country, with dozens of treasures in and around Independence National Historical Park. It boasts the most historic square mile in America, the place where the United States was conceived, declared, and ratified—and the city and federal governments are investing heavily to show this area off and teach its lessons. Philadelphia offers some of the best dining values and several of the finest restaurants in America. The city is a stroller's paradise of restored Georgian and Federal structures integrated with smart shops and contemporary row house courts to create a working urban environment. It's a center of professional and amateur sports, with more than 9,800 acres of parkland within the city limits. It's a city filled with art, crafts, and music for every taste, with boulevards made for street fairs and parades all year long. From row house boutiques to the Second Continental Congress's favorite tavern, from an Ivy League campus to street artists and musicians, from gleaming skyscrapers to Italian marketplaces, Philadelphia is a city of the unexpected.

There's a tremendous diversity among the 1.5 million residents of this city, spread over 129 square miles—there's the opportunity to sink into the plush seats at the new Kimmel Center and sample gourmet cuisine in the dining room of Zanzibar Blue, and there's also the chance to perch in the bleachers of Citizens Bank Park to watch the Phillies at play. Geographically, Philadelphia sits pretty. Some 60 miles inland, it's the country's busiest freshwater port, controlling the Delaware Valley. Philadelphia occupies a tongue of land at the confluence of the Delaware—one of the largest U.S. rivers feeding into the Atlantic—and the Schuylkill (*school*-kill) rivers. The original settlement, and the heart of Center City today, is the band of solid ground about 5 miles north of the junction's marshland. Since then, of course, the city has drained and used the entire tongue to the south and has exploded into the northeast and northwest.

GETTING TO PHILADELPHIA & THE PORT

Ships dock at Pier 1 of the Philadelphia Cruise Terminal, 5100 S. Broad St. (© 856/968-2052), on the site of the former Philadelphia Naval Base, one of the nation's oldest naval facilities. Though you can't walk to much of anything from the mostly industrial port area, a short taxi ride away are a host of treasures.

If you're flying in, the **Philadelphia International Airport** (www.phl.org) is about 7 miles from downtown Philadelphia and less than 10 minutes from the Philadelphia Cruise Terminal at Pier 1. The airport is easily accessible from Interstates 76, 95, and 476.

Those driving in from points north or south of the city (especially New Jersey), should take I-95 to Exit 17 (Broad St.). If you're arriving from the south, stay to the left and turn left at the first traffic light onto Zinkoff Boulevard. At the next traffic light make a quick left onto Broad Street South and continue straight toward the terminal, where you'll find signs directing you to the parking and drop-off location. From points north, turn left at the second traffic light onto Broad Street and continue to the terminal. Signs will direct you to the parking and drop-off areas. If you're driving in from the west, take I-76 East to Exit 349 (Broad St.). Bear right at the end of the off-ramp onto Broad Street South; it's 1 mile to the terminal. For more extensive driving directions from other locations, see **www.cruisephilly.com**.

Note: The parking facility charges $10 per day, cash or credit, and you must pay your parking fee up front. *All* vehicle passengers must have a photo ID.

GETTING AROUND   Since there may not be any taxis waiting at the terminal, you can call these companies: **Olde City Cab** (© 215/338-0838), **City Cab Company** (© 215/492-6500), or **Quaker City Cab** (© 215/728-8000).

SEPTA (Southeastern Pennsylvania Transportation Authority; © 215/580-7800; www.septa.org) operates an extensive network of trolleys, buses, commuter trains, and subways; if you're having trouble getting a taxi, a SEPTA shuttle bus runs frequently between the terminal area and the Pattison Avenue subway stop, about 2 miles away. In Center City, the Rapid Transit subway cars speed under Broad Street and Market Street, intersecting under City Hall, while the city's buses—purple vans with turquoise

Philadelphia

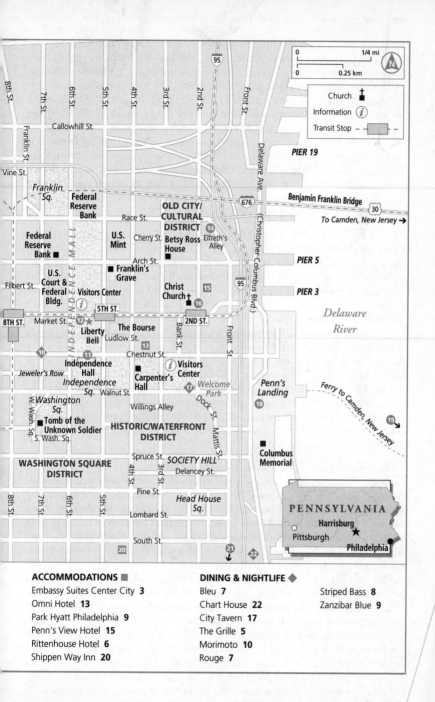

Map Legend

Church	✝
Information	ⓘ
Transit Stop	▭

PIER 19

Benjamin Franklin Bridge

To Camden, New Jersey →

OLD CITY/ CULTURAL DISTRICT

Betsy Ross House 14

Elfreth's Alley

PIER 5

Christ Church 15 16

PIER 3

Delaware River

Franklin Sq.

Federal Reserve Bank

Federal Reserve Bank

U.S. Mint

Race St.

Cherry St.

Arch St.

Franklin's Grave

U.S. Court & Federal Bldg.

Visitors Center

5TH ST.

8TH ST.

Market St. 12

Liberty Bell

The Bourse

Ludlow St. 13

2ND ST.

Bank St.

Front St.

Chestnut St.

Independence Hall

Independence Sq.

Jeweler's Row

10

11

Carpenter's Hall

ⓘ Visitors Center

17

Welcome Park

Penn's Landing 18

Ferry to Camden, New Jersey →

19

Washington Sq.

Tomb of the Unknown Soldier

S. Wash. Sq.

Willings Alley

HISTORIC/WATERFRONT DISTRICT

Dock St.

Mattis St.

Columbus Memorial

WASHINGTON SQUARE DISTRICT

Spruce St.

SOCIETY HILL

Delancey St.

Pine St.

Head House Sq.

Lombard St.

South St.

20

21

22

PENNSYLVANIA

Harrisburg ★

Pittsburgh ○

Philadelphia ●

Vine St.

Callowhill St.

Filbert St.

Franklin St.

8th St. 7th St. 6th St. 5th St. 4th St. 3rd St. 2nd St.

Delaware Ave.

(Christopher Columbus Blvd.)

0   1/4 mi

0   0.25 km

ACCOMMODATIONS ■

Embassy Suites Center City **3**
Omni Hotel **13**
Park Hyatt Philadelphia **9**
Penn's View Hotel **15**
Rittenhouse Hotel **6**
Shippen Way Inn **20**

DINING & NIGHTLIFE ◆

Bleu **7**
Chart House **22**
City Tavern **17**
The Grille **5**
Morimoto **10**
Rouge **7**

Striped Bass **8**
Zanzibar Blue **9**

wings—go pretty much everywhere tourists want to go. Every 12 minutes between 10am and 6pm (Mar 1–Nov 30) the **PHLASH Bus Service** (www.gophila.com/phlash), links Independence Park sites, the Delaware waterfront, the Convention Center, Rittenhouse Square shopping, and Logan Circle. The total loop takes 50 minutes and makes 30 stops. A one-time pass is $1, but get the all-day unlimited ride-pass for $4; $10 for an all-day pass for a family of four. SEPTA also has an all-day $5.50 fare for city buses, but the two systems do *not* accept each other's passes. Children under 6 ride free on both systems. There's also a privately operated **Penn's Landing Trolley** that chugs along Christopher Columbus Boulevard (formerly Delaware Ave.) between the Benjamin Franklin Bridge and Fitzwater Street; you can board at Dock Street or Spruce Street. The fare is $1.50 for adults, 75¢ for children, and the trolley runs Thursday through Sunday from 11am to dusk in the summer. There are also free shuttle-trolleys between the Cruise Terminal and parking facilities.

BEST CRUISE LINE SHORE EXCURSIONS

Philly Highlights ($39, 3 hr.): Because Philadelphia is almost exclusively an embarkation port, most lines only offer the standard city highlights tour for those flying out after about 2 or 3pm. Traveling by bus, you'll pass by Franklin Court, the site of Benjamin Franklin's home; Elfreth's Alley, an oasis of early-18th-century houses believed to be the nations oldest continuously inhabited street; seamstress Betsy Ross's tiny home on Arch Street, with the Stars and Stripes waving outside; as well as the impressive Colonial Christ Church. Your scenic drive will take you past Independence National Historic Park and the famous Liberty Bell, plus Independence Hall where the Declaration of Independence was adopted, and on to Congress Hall, which housed the U.S. Legislature between 1790 and 1800 when Philadelphia was the capital city. A brief stop will be made at the Park Visitors Center before proceeding to the Benjamin Franklin Parkway, a gracious green diagonal modeled after the Champs Elysees in Paris, connecting City Hall, the nation's largest municipal building, to the famous Philadelphia Art Museum resembling a Greek Temple. The tour ends at Philadelphia International Airport.

EXPLORING PHILADELPHIA ON YOUR OWN

Consider Philadelphia's sightseeing possibilities—the most historic square mile in America; more than 90 museums; innumerable colonial churches, row houses, and mansions; an Ivy League campus; and leafy, distinguished parks, including the largest one within city limits in the United States. Philadelphia has come a long way since 1876, when a guidebook recommended seeing the new Public Buildings at Broad and Market streets, the Naval Yards, the old YMCA, and the fortresslike prison (which is still a tourist site as the Eastern State Penitentiary!).

Most of what you'll want to see within the city falls inside a rectangle on a map between the Delaware and Schuylkill rivers in width, and between South and Vine streets in height. It's easy to organize your days into walking tours of various parts of the city. Nothing is that far away. A stroll from City Hall (about 5 miles from the cruise terminal) to the Philadelphia Museum of Art takes about 25 minutes, although the flags and flowers along the Parkway will undoubtedly sidetrack you. A walk down Market or one of the "tree" streets (Chestnut, Spruce, Pine, Locust) to Independence National Historical Park and Society Hill should take a little less time—but it probably won't, as there's so much to entice you on the way. If you'd rather ride, the spiffy PHLASH buses loop past most major attractions about every 12 minutes.

The city is wrapping some of its attractions together in various packages, and the Independence Visitor Center and other locations offer several passes. One is the **RiverPass,** which includes admission to Independence Seaport Museum and its historic ships, Adventure Aquarium, and a round-trip ride on the Freedom Ferry; prices are $30 for adults and $25 for children ages 3 to 12. **Philadelphia Citypass** offers admission to six major attractions, including the Philadelphia Museum of Art, the Franklin Institute, the Zoo, and the Seaport Museum; prices are $36 adults, $22 children 3 to 11, and they may be purchased in advance online at **http://citypass.net/cgi-bin/citypass** (click on "Philadelphia") or at any one of the included attractions. Tickets are good up to 9 days from first use, and they represent about a 50% discount over full admission prices.

If you have just 1 day in Philadelphia, start at the Independence Visitor Center and the adjacent **Liberty Bell** Pavilion in **Independence National Historical Park,** Chestnut Street between 5th and 6th (© **215/597-8974;** admission is free, but you'll need a ticket to join a tour of the park), then move south through Independence Hall and on to residential Society Hill, which is steeped in U.S. history. See what's on at the Academy of Music, the Kimmel Center, the Annenberg Center at the University of Pennsylvania, or the Wachovia Spectrum for sports. If you've got 2 days, spend 1 on this self-guided tour: Starting at **City Hall,** Broad and Market streets (© **215/686-2840**), walk up the Benjamin Franklin Parkway to Logan Circle and spend the afternoon at **Franklin Institute,** at 222 N. 20th St. (© **215/448-1200;** www.fi.edu; admission price varies depending on what you want to see), or the **Philadelphia Museum of Art,** at 26th Street (© **215/763-8100;** www.philamuseum.org). Try to circle back to Rittenhouse Square and the Liberty Place complex before it closes (7pm most nights, 8pm Wed). If you're in town for 3 days, spend the morning of 1 of them in the Old City viewing **Christ Church,** 2nd Street, half a block north of Market (© **215/922-1695**); and **Elfreth's Alley,** 2nd Street between Arch and Race (© **215/574-0560**); then explore the expanding Delaware River waterfront attractions and the **Independence Seaport Museum,** Penn's Landing at 211 S. Columbus Blvd. (© **215/925-5439;** www.phillyseaport.org). Combined admission to the museum and Historic Ship Zone—the USS *Olympia* and USS *Becuna* are both berthed at Penn's Landing—is $9 adults, $6 children. Finally, visit the **Adventure Aquarium,** 1 Aquarium Dr. (© **800/616-JAWS;** www.adventureaquarium.com; admission $14 adults, $11 kids), formerly the New Jersey State Aquarium that was recently renovated to the tune of $40 million, and the newly docked battleship *New Jersey,* both a ferry ride across the Delaware in Camden, New Jersey. The **RiverLink Ferry** (© **215/925-LINK;** www.riverlinkferry.org) runs during business hours every day in summer from Penn's Landing, with departures every 40 minutes. Round-trip fare is $6.

SHOPPING

The best places to look for high fashion and international wares are the specialty shops around **Liberty Place** and **Rittenhouse Square.** You'll find SoHo-style cutting-edge fashion, art, and crafts in the **Old City** area just north of the historic landmarks. For more contemporary items, **Manayunk,** several miles up the Schuylkill River to the northwest of town, is also a hip Philadelphia shopping neighborhood. The new airport retail center carries a surprising number of national names, and the once-funky area on **South Street,** just south of Society Hill, now hosts a clutch of conservative stores that are run more as businesses than as conduits for individual artistic expression. Because restaurants and nightlife now line South Street from

Front to 8th streets, many of the 180 stores here are open well into the evening. Stores in this area offer goods ranging from the genteel to the somewhat grotesque.

It's useful to note that the outskirts (mainly the north) of Philadelphia contain prime examples of the enormous malls now ubiquitous at the interchanges of American superhighways—the 21st-century version of Colonial village squares. You'll find all the luxury chains, and even some branches of downtown Philly's gems, at **King of Prussia Mall** (℃ 610/265-5727; www.kingofprussia.com)—a 450-store behemoth, second only to Minnesota's Mall of America—and at **Franklin Mills** (℃ 610/632-1500; www.franklin-mills-mall.com), an outlet mall that draws four times the traffic of the Liberty Bell.

WHERE TO STAY

For historic accommodations, the top floor of the **Park Hyatt Philadelphia at the Bellevue,** Broad and Walnut streets (℃ 800/223-1234; www.hyatt.com), with its occasionally oddly proportioned rooms, carries traces of a century's worth of history (Thomas Edison designed the fixtures). Rates: from $228. They may not have the history, but rooms at the luxurious **Rittenhouse Hotel,** 210 W. Rittenhouse Sq. (℃ 800/635-1042; www.rittenhousehotel.com), in Center City, offer wonderful views of the Philly landscape, Aveda toiletries in the marble bathrooms, and plush furnishings. Rates: from $235.

Why not wake up to a view of Independence Park through the floral chintz curtains at the **Omni Hotel at Independence Park,** 4th and Chestnut streets (℃ 800/843-6664; www.omnihotels.com)? All of this European-style hotel's guest rooms have views of the Greek Revival Second Bank of the U.S. and a half-dozen of America's Georgian jewels. Rates: from $215. The upper floors of the 52-room **Penn's View Hotel,** Front and Market streets (℃ 800/331-7634; www.pennsviewhotel.com), feel like an exquisite club, with views over the Delaware River. All of the rooms are richly decorated with Chippendale-inspired furnishings. Rates: from $180. Slightly tattered but moderately priced is the **Embassy Suites Center City,** 1776 Benjamin Franklin Pkwy. at Logan Square (℃ 800/362-2779; www.embassy-suites.com), with cute little open-air balconies (yes, the railings are sturdy). And all the rooms are suites with separate bedrooms and living rooms, so parents can have their privacy. Rates: $169.

There are many B&Bs in Philly, but one standout is the **Shippen Way Inn,** 418 Bainbridge St. (℃ 800/245-4873 or 215/627-7266), a tiny row house in Queen Village built around 1750 and lovingly maintained. Rates: from $95.

DINING & NIGHTLIFE

Bars and lounges are everywhere in Philadelphia and they run from neighborhood bars, to after-work blue-collar hangouts, to yuppie social centers, to temples of hipness. Philly's hottest bars occupy, **Rittenhouse Square,** a bastion of propriety that used to roll up its sidewalks at night, but, thanks to some smart entrepreneurs, the stretch along the entire east side (18th St.) now glows with heat lamps and candles, and resounds with murmurs of conversation and the clink of glasses. In 1998, Neil Stein initiated the alfresco movement with his 1920s-style parlor bistro **Rouge,** 205 S. 18th St. (℃ 215/732-6622), which serves a great $15 burger. In 2000, he followed up with **Bleu,** 227 S. 18th St. (℃ 215/545-0342). Main courses: $14 to $28.

For a sense of history and old-style elegance, head for **The Grill,** in the stunning rotunda of the recently renovated bank now housing the Ritz-Carlton Hotel, 10 Ave.

of the Arts (© **215/523-8000**), in the center of town. Surrounded by the soaring dome and windows, the new American cuisine has high expectations to fill but seems to be up to the task. Main courses: $24 to $38.

No place in town is hotter than **Morimoto,** 723 Chestnut St. (© **215/413-9070;** www.morimotorestaurant.com), where the "Iron Chef" of TV fame holds sway amid cool booths and a sea of changing colors. Main courses: $17 to $35.

Crowds make the **Chart House,** 555 S. Columbus Blvd. (formerly Delaware Ave.) at Penn's Landing (© **215/625-8383;** www.chart-house.com), the Convention Center of the Philadelphia restaurant world. The food is amazingly good given the size of this place, and the views of the Delaware River from the restaurant's pier are spectacular. Main courses: $17 to $41.

For $24 to $30, you'll get a tasty, three-course, pre-theater dinner at Philly's hottest jazz spot, **Zanzibar Blue,** 200 S. Broad St. (© **215/732-5200;** www.zanzibarblue.com). Main courses: $18 to $28.

In the historic district, the back garden of **City Tavern,** 138 S. 2nd St., near Walnut Street (© **215/413-1443;** www.citytavern.com), belongs to Independence National Historical Park, and diners are surrounded by century-old trees and Federal-style landmarks while they imbibe their strong ale or punch and dine on an historically faithful 18th-century-recipe potpie. Main courses: $18 to $40.

As you would expect, Philadelphia has a superb reputation for fish houses, and the best in town is **Striped Bass,** 1500 Walnut St. (© **215/732-4444**), located on the most chic dining block in the city. Main courses: $17 to $32.

15 Québec City, Québec

Québec City remains the soul of New France, which throughout the 17th and 18th centuries was an enormous territory that covered the entire area of eastern Canada, eastern United States, the Great Lakes, and Louisiana, and from the Hudson Bay in the North to Florida in the South. In 1608, the French explorer Samuel de Champlain was the first European to claim Québec City, and soon after established a fur trading post. It was the first significant settlement in Canada, and today it is the capital of politically prickly Québec, a province larger than Alaska. The old city, a tumble of colorful metal-roofed houses clustered around the dominating Château Frontenac, is a haunting evocation of a coastal town in the motherland, as romantic as any on that continent. Because of its history, beauty, and unique stature as the only walled city north of Mexico, the historic district of Québec was named a UNESCO World Heritage Site in 1985—one of the only three areas so designated in North America.

Québec City is almost entirely French in feeling, in spirit, and in language; 95% of the population is Francophone. But many of its 508,000 citizens speak some English, especially those who work in hotels, restaurants, and shops where they deal with Anglophones every day. Québec City is also a college town, and thousands of resident young people study English as a second language. So although it is often more difficult in Québec City than in Montréal to understand and be understood, the average Québecois goes out of his or her way to communicate—in halting English, sign language, simplified French, or a combination of all three. Most Québecois are uncommonly gracious, and it is a pleasure to spend time in their company and in their city. Come to Québec and soak up the past.

Few ports are as beautiful as Québec City. Ships large and small call there, a good number starting or ending their itineraries from the port. If yours is one of them, it's a crime not to stay on for an extra night or two at a local hotel for a chance to stroll the historic streets.

Perched on a cliff-top overlooking the St. Lawrence River—the city is split into two sections, the **Lower Town** (or Basse-Ville) and the **Upper Town** (Haute-Ville)—the oldest part of beautiful Québec City, where French civilization in North America was born, dates back nearly 400 years. An old stonewall still embraces the Upper Town.

GETTING TO QUEBEC CITY & THE PORT

The cruise docks at the **Port of Québec,** which includes a bustling commercial shipping operation, are located within walking distance of the historic **Lower Town,** just outside the walled city. The **Upper Town** can be reached via an elevator. For information, call ✆ **418/648-3640** or check out **www.portquebec.ca**.

If you're flying in, you'll land at **Jean-Lesage International Airport** (✆ **418/640-2700;** www.aeroportdequebec.com), a small airport, despite the grand name. A taxi to downtown Québec City is a fixed-rate US$22 (C$27).

If you're driving to the port, from New York City, follow I-87 to Autoroute 15 to Montréal, picking up Autoroute 20 to Québec City. Take 73 nord across the Pont Pierre-Laporte and exit onto boulevard Champlain immediately after crossing the bridge. This skirts the city at river level. Alternatively, take Autoroute 40 from Montréal, which follows the north shore of the St. Lawrence. From Boston, take I-89 to I-93 to I-91 in Montpelier, Vermont, which connects with Autoroute 55 in Québec to link up with Autoroute 20. Or follow I-90 up the Atlantic coast, through Portland, Maine, to Route 201 west of Bangor, then Autoroute 173 to Lévis. A car-ferry there, **Traverse Québec-Lévis** (✆ **418/643-2019;** www.traversiers.gouv.qc.ca), provides a 10-minute ride across the St. Lawrence River; it departs at least every hour and costs about US$8 (C$9.85). Parking at the port costs $15 (C$18) per day.

GETTING AROUND   This port is a walker's paradise. Once you're within or near the walls of the Upper Town, virtually no place of interest is beyond walking distance, and it's definitely the best way to explore the city. Although there are streets and stairs between the Upper and Lower Towns, there is also a **funicular,** which has long operated along an inclined 210-foot track between the Terrasse Dufferin and the Quartier Petit-Champlain. The upper station is near the front of the Château Frontenac and Place d'Armes, while the lower station is actually inside the Maison Louis-Jolliet, on rue du Petit-Champlain. It runs year-round daily and wheelchairs are accommodated. The one-way fare is US$1.25 (C$1.50). If for some reason you aren't up for walking, or if you're going between opposite ends of Lower and Upper Towns, a taxi might be the answer. They're everywhere, and your best bet for getting one is by locating a stand—such as the ones in the Place d'Armes and in front of the Hôtel-de-Ville (City Hall). Restaurant managers and hotel bell captains will also summon them if you ask. Fares are somewhat expensive given the short distances of most rides. The starting rate is US$2.25 (C$2.75), and you should tip an additional 10% to 15%. To call a cab, try **Taxi Coop** (✆ **418/525-5191**) or **Taxi Québec** (✆ **418/525-8123**).

BEST CRUISE LINE SHORE EXCURSIONS

City Walking Tour (US$32, 3 hr.): If you're up for it, the best way to discover Québec's historical side is by walking through the city's narrow cobblestone streets with a knowledgeable guide leading the way. Stroll along the first shopping street in North America,

Québec City

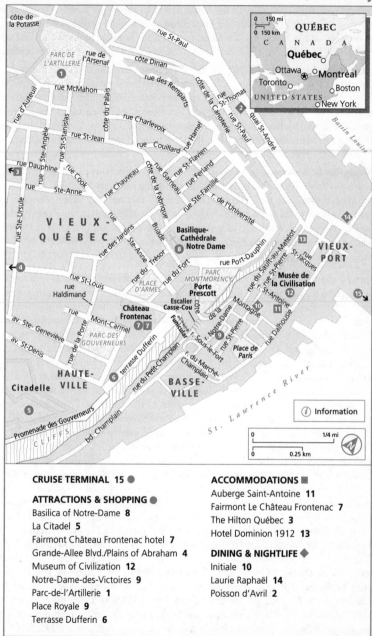

CRUISE TERMINAL 15 ●

ATTRACTIONS & SHOPPING ●
Basilica of Notre-Dame **8**
La Citadel **5**
Fairmont Château Frontenac hotel **7**
Grande-Allee Blvd./Plains of Abraham **4**
Museum of Civilization **12**
Notre-Dame-des-Victoires **9**
Parc-de-l'Artillerie **1**
Place Royale **9**
Terrasse Dufferin **6**

ACCOMMODATIONS ■
Auberge Saint-Antoine **11**
Fairmont Le Château Frontenac **7**
The Hilton Québec **3**
Hotel Dominion 1912 **13**

DINING & NIGHTLIFE ◆
Initiale **10**
Laurie Raphaël **14**
Poisson d'Avril **2**

Le Petit Quartier Champlain, in the Lower Town. In the Upper Town, 3 centuries of history come to life in sites such as la Place d'Armes, la Terrasse Dufferin, Place de l'Hôtel de Ville, and le Musée des Ursulines. Finally, stop for tea at the Fairmont Château Frontenac Hotel, Québec City's best-known landmark, for a plate of delicious pastries.

City Highlights by Bus (US$39, 2½ hr.): Explore the narrow streets and stately residences that have hardly changed in more than 3 centuries. Enjoy panoramic views of the St. Lawrence River from the oldest part of town, drive through the Grande Allée neighborhood for a peak at the Victorian-era homes, and then on to the Château Frontenac landmark hotel, where there's time to explore. Finally, drive on to the Plain of Abraham, where the battle between the French and British armies eventually sealed the fate of the French colony.

Biking the St. Lawrence (US$69, 4½ hr.): If you've maxed out on the history thing, or ate too much on your cruise (or anticipate doing so), start peddling. After being outfitted with a bike and gear, you'll take a 15-minute ferry ride across the St. Lawrence River to the south shore area known as Chaudire-Appalaches, a perfect place for cycling and bird-watching. Ride through quaint villages and past mills and manor homes, before stopping for a light picnic whipped up by the ship's galley.

EXPLORING QUEBEC CITY ON YOUR OWN

Spend a day strolling this beautiful walled city's hilly cobblestone streets—it's a wonderful place for exploring on foot. They're lined with 17th- and 18th-century buildings, cafes, shops, and homes. Québec's Lower Town encompasses the restored Quartier Petit-Champlain, including pedestrian-only **rue du Petit-Champlain; Place Royale** and the small **Notre-Dame-des-Victoires church,** the city's oldest dating back to 1688; and, nearby, the impressive **Museum of Civilization** (www.mcq.org), an excellent interactive museum with rotating exhibits representing historical, current and controversial subjects, is a highlight of any visit. Admission is $11 adults (C$13). Lower is linked to Upper by the funicular on Terrasse Dufferin and by several streets and stairways, including one near the entrance to the funicular. Petit-Champlain is undeniably touristy, but not unpleasantly so: T-shirt vendors have been held in check, though hardly banned. It contains several agreeable cafes and shops. Restored **Place Royale** is perhaps the most attractive of the city's many squares, upper or lower.

When you venture to the Upper Town, an area surrounded by thick ramparts, the highlight is the gorgeous **Fairmont Château Frontenac hotel,** a beauty set high above the St. Lawrence River near the Citadel. Colonial governors used to reside on the site of this turreted castlelike gem with its slanted copper roof. The actual building was erected in 1883 as a prestigious hotel where the likes of Winston Churchill and Queen Elizabeth II have stayed. Linger for a drink or some dinner and savor the magical aura. The other popular attractions in the Upper Town include **Parc-de-l'Artillerie,** 2 rue d'Auteuil (© **418/648-4205;** www.pc.gc.ca/artillerie), admission US$3 (C$4); **Basilica of Notre-Dame,** 20 rue Buade (© **418/694-0665**), free admission; and the **Terrasse Dufferin** pedestrian promenade. At a higher elevation, to the south of the Château, is the **Citadel,** 1 Côte de la Citadelle (© **418/694-2815;** www.lacitadelle. qc.ca), a partially star-shaped fortress begun by the French in the 18th century and augmented often by the English well into the 19th century. Admission is US$6 (C$8). Since most buildings are at least 100 years old, made of granite in similar styles, the Upper Town is visually harmonious. The Terrasse Dufferin promenade attracts crowds in all seasons for its magnificent views of the river and the land to the south, ferries gliding back and forth, and cruise ships and Great Lakes freighters putting in at the harbor below.

Grande-Allée is the western extension of rue St-Louis, from the St-Louis Gate in the fortified walls to avenue Taché. It passes the stately Parliament building, in front of which the Winter Carnival takes place every year (the ice sculptures are installed across the street), as well as the numerous terraced bars and restaurants that line both sides from rue de la Chevrotière to rue de Claire-Fontaine. Later, it skirts the Musée des Beaux-Arts du Québec and the Plains of Abraham, where one of the most important battles in the history of North America took place between the French and the British for control of the city. The city's large modern hotels are also on or near the Grande-Allée.

SHOPPING

Côte de la Montagne, which leads from the Upper Town to the Lower Town as an alternative to the funicular, has a few stores with more tourist-geared items and some crafts and folk art. The Lower Town itself, particularly the **Quartier Petit-Champlain,** just off place Royale and encompassing rue du Petit-Champlain, boulevard Champlain, and rue Sous-le-Fort (opposite the funicular entrance), offers many possibilities—clothing, souvenirs, gifts, household items, collectibles—and is avoiding (so far) the trashiness that often afflicts heavily toured areas. Outside the walls, just beyond the strip of cafes that line Grande-Allée, **avenue Cartier** has shops and restaurants of some variety, from clothing and ceramics to housewares and gourmet foods. The 4 or 5 blocks attract crowds of generally youngish locals, and the hubbub revs up on summer nights and weekends. The area remains outside the tourist orbit.

Dealers in **antiques** have gravitated to rue St-Paul in the Lower Town. To get there, follow rue St-Pierre from the Place Royale, and then head west on rue St-Paul. So far, there are more than 20 shops, with more likely to open, filled with brass beds, knickknacks, Québec country furniture, candlesticks, old clocks, Victoriana, Art Deco and Art Moderne objects, and even the increasingly sought-after kitsch and housewares of the early–World War II period. For unique, the area's **indigenous crafts, handmade sweaters,** and **Inuit art** are among the desirable items not seen everywhere else. An official igloo trademark identifies authentic Inuit (Eskimo) art, which is typically some kind of carvings in stone or bone.

WHERE TO STAY

There are wonderful small hotels and inns within the walls of the Upper Town as well as more than 30 bed-and-breakfasts, and a good number of high-rise hotels within walking distance of the attractions in the old city. Here's a sampling:

The 95-unit **Auberge Saint-Antoine,** 10 rue St-Antoine (© **888/692-2211** or 418/692-2211; www.saint-antoine.com), is an uncommonly attractive boutique hotel set in an 1830 maritime warehouse that boasts its original dark beams and stone floor. Rates: from US$125 (C$149).

If we only had the space to recommend one hotel in the city, **Hotel Dominion 1912,** 126 rue St. Pierre (© **888/833-5253** or 418/692-2224; www.hoteldominion. com), would be it. The owners stripped the inside of the 1912 Dominion Fish & Fruit building down to the studs and pipes and started over. Now there are large rooms and beds covered with feather duvets. Rates: US$130 (C$169).

Fairmont Le Château Frontenac, 1 rue des Carrières (© **800/828-7447** or 418/ 692-3861; www.fairmont.com) is Québec City's magical castle. Dating back to 1883, the hotel has hosted Queen Elizabeth II and Prince Philip, and during World War II, Winston Churchill and Franklin D. Roosevelt had the entire place to themselves for a conference. It was built in phases, following the landline, so the wide halls take crooked paths. Luxurious rooms are outfitted with regal decor and elegant château furnishings. Rates: US$310 (C$349).

The Hilton Québec, 1100 bd. Rene-Levesque est ((℃ **800/447-2411** or 418/ 647-2521; www.hiltonquebec.com), boasts a great location, just across the street from the city walls and near the Parliament. The public rooms are big and brassy, Hilton-style. Rates: US$221 to US$130 (C$279–C$164).

DINING & NIGHTLIFE

This scenic city isn't famous for its food, though its **classic bistros, Italian trattorias,** and other eateries will do just fine. Even the blatantly touristy restaurants along rue St-Louis and around the **Place d'Armes,** many of them with hawkers outside and showy tableside presentations inside, can produce decent meals. As throughout the province, the best dining deals are the table d'hôte—fixed-price—meals. Virtually all full-service restaurants offer them, if only at lunch. As a rule, they include at least soup or salad, a main course, and a dessert. Some places add in an extra appetizer and/or a beverage, all for the approximate a la carte price of the main course alone. Curiously, seafood is not given much attention, considering all that water out there. Game is popular. Remember that for the Québecois, *dîner* (dinner) is lunch, and *souper* (supper) is dinner, though the word *dinner* below is used in the common American sense. Also note that an *entrée* in Québec is an appetizer, while a *plat principal* is a main course.

Initiale, 54 rue St-Pierre (℃ **418/694-1818;** www.restaurantinitiale.com), is an elegant French venue with tall windows, columns, high ceilings and subdued lighting, and delicious fare, such as grilled tuna with lemon marmalade and a tart of white wine and maple syrup. Main courses: US$26 to US$35 (C$30–C$39). **Laurie Raphaël,** 117 rue Dalhousie (℃ **418/692-4555;** www.laurieraphael.com), is a glamorous contemporary French place where main courses run to caribou, quail, rabbit, Arctic char, sea bass, and scallops in unconventional guises, often with Asian touches. Main courses: US$28 to US$41 (C$32–C$45). Located in the historic Old Port area, **Poisson d'Avril,** 115 quai St-Andre (℃ **418/692-1010;** www.poissondavril.net), is one of the city's favorite seafood restaurants. With its classic nautical décor, you'll feel at home ordering the Quebec-style bouillabaisse, or one of the house specialties, from fresh lobster to snow crab and steamed mussels. Main courses: US$10 to US$37 (C$13–C$41)

Although Québec City can't pretend to match the volume of nighttime diversions of exuberant Montréal, there is more than enough after-dark activity to occupy your evenings during an average stay. Apart from theatrical productions, almost always in French, knowledge of the language is rarely necessary to enjoy nighttime entertainment. An after-dinner stroll and a lounge on a bench on **Terrasse Dufferin,** the boardwalk above the Lower Town, may well be your most memorable night on the town. Ferries glide across the river burnished by moonglow, and the stars haven't seemed that close since childhood. Most bars and clubs stay open until 2 or 3am, and there are three principal streets to choose among for nightlife: the **Grande-Allée, rue St-Jean,** and the emerging **avenue Cartier.** Cafes line both sides of the Grande-Allée, and cafe-hopping and people-watching are popular pastimes.

16 San Diego, California

San Diego is best known for its benign climate and fabulous beaches, which combined make the city one big playground on sunny days. With 70 miles of sandy coastline—plus pretty, sheltering Mission Bay—you can choose from a whole slew of watersports, plus biking or skating around splendid Balboa Park, one of the finest urban parks in the country. San Diego was the very first European settlement on the west coast of America, and though it spent a lot of years being looked down on as a conservative, slow-growth Navy town, it's been coming to life over the past decade and a half. Today, the city in the bottom left corner of the U.S. boasts a diverse population and revitalized neighborhoods, and although its population is 1.3 million and rising, you'll find that it hasn't lost its small-town ambience, nor its strong connection with its Hispanic heritage and culture. (Mexico, remember, is just 16 miles to the south.)

San Diego's **downtown** sits at the edge of San Diego Bay, a large natural harbor with flat Coronado on one side and peninsular Point Loma on the other. North from Point Loma is **Mission Bay,** a lagoon that was carved out of tidal estuary in the 1940s, and now a watersports playground. A series of communities are found along the beach-lined coast: Ocean Beach, Mission Beach, Pacific Beach, La Jolla, and, just outside San Diego's city limits, Del Mar. To the south of downtown you'll find **National City,** which is distinguished by shipyards on its bay side, then Chula Vista, and San Ysidro, which ends abruptly at the border (and where the huge city of Tijuana begins, equally abruptly). Inland areas are perhaps best defined by **Mission Valley,** a mile-wide canyon that runs east-west, 2 miles north of downtown, and is perhaps the most congested and least charming part of the city. Along the coast, the city stretches up to **La Jolla,** with its beautiful coastline and filthy rich populace.

GETTING TO SAN DIEGO & THE PORT

San Diego's **B Street Cruise Ship Terminal** is located at 1050 N. Harbor Drive, right in the heart of downtown (© 619/686-6200; www.portofsandiego.org). If you're arriving by air, you'll probably touch down at the **San Diego International Airport** (© 619/400-2400; www.san.org), located just northwest of downtown, along the Bay and close to the piers. Rental cars and metered **taxis** are available, with the latter costing about $7 to the port. If you're coming by car on the I-5 southbound, take the Front Street exit, stay in the right lane for two lights, turn right at Ash Street, and follow until it dead-ends at Harbor Drive. Turn left, and you'll see the pier on your right. Parking is available for $12 per day at the Lane Field facility located on Broadway between Pacific Highway and North Harbor Drive. Additionally, several Park & Ride lots serve both the cruise ship terminal and the airport, with rates ranging from $9 to $24 per day.

GETTING AROUND   Those staying for a short time in the downtown area will be able to cover the close-in attractions (including Balboa Park and Old Town) on foot or using the city buses, or you can also try the narrated **Old Town Trolley Tours** (© 619/298-TOUR; www.historictours.com/sandiego), which provide an easy way to get an overview of the city and tie together visits to several of San Diego's major attractions without driving or resorting to cabs. The trackless trolleys do a 30-mile circular route, and you can hop off at any one of eight stops (including one at the cruise terminal), explore at leisure, and reboard when you please. Trolleys run every half-hour.

Stops include Old Town, the Gaslamp Quarter and downtown area, Coronado, the San Diego Zoo, and Balboa Park. You can begin wherever you want, but you must purchase tickets before boarding (most stops have a ticket kiosk). The tour costs $25 for adults, $15 for kids 4 to 12, for one complete loop; the route by itself takes about 2 hours. The trolleys operate daily 9am to 4pm in winter and 9am to 5pm in summer.

For attractions, accommodations, and beaches in the greater city, having your own wheels is a big advantage. **Taxis** are also available, though other than in the Gaslamp Quarter, after dark, they don't cruise the streets looking for passengers. If you need one, call ahead. Among the local companies are **Orange Cab** (© 619/291-3333), **San Diego Cab** (© 619/226-TAXI), and **Yellow Cab** (© 619/234-6161). The **Coronado Cab Company** (© 935/435-6211) serves Coronado. In La Jolla, use **La Jolla Cab** (© 858/453-4222).

BEST CRUISE LINE SHORE EXCURSIONS

SeaWorld ($59–$67, 7 hr.): San Diego's SeaWorld Adventure Park is one of the largest and best marine life parks in the world. While this tour is about $10 to $20 more than the park's admission price, it's an option if you don't want to worry about arranging your own transportation.

Coronado Cycling Tour ($36, 3½ hr.): From the ship, you'll take a bus and then ferry over to Coronado, where you'll take off on a ride to visit Glorietta Bay, the world-famous Hotel Del Coronado, and Ocean Boulevard with its Victorian mansions and white sandy beaches.

Whale-Watching ($25, 3½ hr.): This fully narrated trip departs right from the pier and heads out in search of California gray whales, which pass San Diego on their 6,000-mile migration from the Arctic to the Baja Coast. This is a seasonal tour that operates from mid-December through the end of March.

EXPLORING SAN DIEGO ON YOUR OWN

Unless you head to the beaches, you'll probably spend most of your time in **downtown** and **Old Town**. The business, shopping, dining, and entertainment heart of the city, the downtown area encompasses the Embarcadero (waterfront), the Gaslamp Quarter, Horton Plaza (see "Shopping," below), and the Convention Center, sprawling over eight individual "neighborhoods." A **Visitor Information Center** is located right across the street from the cruise terminal at the corner of Harbor Drive and West Broadway (© **619/236-1212**).

Right on the waterfront, just a few blocks north of the cruise terminal, are the three classic ships that comprise the **Maritime Museum of San Diego,** 1492 N. Harbor Dr. (© **619/234-9153;** www.sdmaritime.com). The full-rigged merchant vessel *Star of India* dates to 1863, and its impressive masts are an integral part of the San Diego cityscape. The gleaming white steam-powered ferry *Berkeley* (1898) once ran the route between San Francisco and Oakland, and worked round-the-clock to carry people to safety following the 1906 San Francisco earthquake. The sleek *Medea* (1904) is one of the world's few remaining large steam yachts. Other vessels include the HMS *Surprise,* the replica 18th-century Royal Navy frigate used in the film *Master and Commander.* You can board and explore each vessel and check out the collection of maritime artifacts at the museum proper. Admission is $8 adults, $6 kids.

Along the same stretch of the harbor, the **San Diego Aircraft Carrier Museum,** 910 Harbor Dr., at Navy Pier (© **619/544-9600;** www.midway.org), is actually the

San Diego

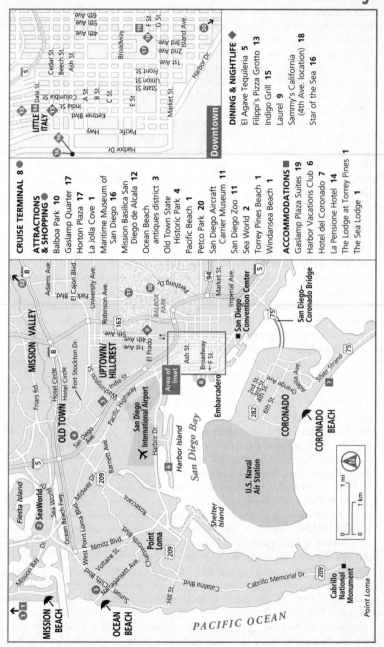

aircraft carrier *Midway,* commissioned in 1945 and a veteran of Vietnam and Gulf War I. In all, more than 200,000 men served aboard the vessel. A self-guided audio tour takes visitors to several levels of the ship, telling the story of life on board. The highlight is climbing up the superstructure to the bridge and gazing down on the 1,001-foot-long flight deck, with various aircraft poised for duty. What really brings the experience to life is the occasional graffiti and other reminders left by the crew. Admission is $13 adults, $10 seniors and veterans, $7 kids 6 to 12. Guided tours are available for an additional cost.

A National Historic District covering 16½ city blocks, San Diego's **Gaslamp Quarter** contains many Victorian-style commercial buildings built between the Civil War and World War I. The center of a massive redevelopment kicked off in the mid-1980s with the opening of the Horton Plaza shopping complex, and the once-seedy area is now packed with trendy boutiques, restaurants, and nightspots. Beautifully restored Victorian commercial buildings will make you think you've stepped back in time. Lit by electric versions of old gas lamps, the Quarter lies between Fourth Avenue to the west, Sixth Avenue to the east, Broadway to the north, and L Street and the waterfront to the south. It makes for good walking and shopping during the day, but the real action here is at night. Immediately southeast of the Gaslamp Quarter is the brand new **PETCO Park,** home of the San Diego Padres.

At the northeast edge of downtown lies **Balboa Park,** one of San Diego's true treasures, sitting on a 1,200-acre square that contains the San Diego Zoo, more than a dozen museums, a classic carousel, wonderful gardens, and splendid architecture. Stop by the **Balboa Park Visitors Center,** located in the House of Hospitality (© **619/ 239-0512;** www.balboapark.org), to learn about free walking and museum tours, or to pick up a brochure about the gardens. Balboa was established in 1868 in the heart of the city, fringed by the early communities of Hillcrest and Golden Hill to the north and east. Tree plantings started in the late 19th century, while the initial buildings were created to host the 1915–16 Panama-California International Exposition; another expo in 1935–36 brought additional developments. The park is divided by Highway 163 into two distinct sections. The narrow western wing is largely grassy open areas that parallel Sixth Avenue. It's a good place for picnics, strolling, and sunning. The main portion of the park, east of 163, contains all of the park's 15 museums (many of them in the beautiful Spanish Colonial Revival buildings that line **El Prado,** the park's east-west thoroughfare), and is bordered by Park Boulevard. This is also where you'll find the world-famous **San Diego Zoo,** 2920 Zoo Dr. (© **619/ 231-1515;** www.sandiegozoo.org), operated by the Zoological Society of San Diego. Founded in 1916 with a handful of animals originally brought here for that same Panama-California Exposition, the zoo now has more than 4,000 creatures in residence, including three giant pandas from the People's Republic of China, wild Przewalski horses from Mongolia, Buerger's tree kangaroos from New Guinea, lowland gorillas from Africa, and giant tortoises from the Galapagos, as well as more than 700,000 plants. The park's Children's Zoo features a nursery with baby animals and a petting area where kids can cuddle up to sheep, goats, and the like. Admission costs $21 adults, $14 kids 3 to 11.

Northwest of the park, heading toward Mission Bay, is San Diego's **Old Town,** where the first settlement of California took place. It's the Williamsburg of the West, allowing you to go back to a time of one-room schoolhouses and village greens, when many of the people who lived, worked, and played here spoke Spanish. Even today, life moves more slowly in this part of the city, where the buildings are old or built to look that way. At the **Old Town State Historic Park,** on San Diego Avenue and Twiggs Street (© **619/220-5422;** www.parks.ca.gov), you don't have to look hard or very far to see yesterday. Dedicated to re-creating the early life of the city from 1821 to 1872, this is where San Diego's Mexican heritage shines brightest. Seven of the park's 20 structures are original, including homes made of adobe; the rest are reconstructed. The park's headquarters is at the Robinson-Rose House, 4002 Wallace St., where you can pick up a map and peruse a model of Old Town as it looked in 1872. Among the park's attractions are La Casa de Estudillo, which depicts the living conditions of a wealthy family in 1872; and Seeley Stables, named after A. L. Seeley, who ran the stagecoach and mail service in these parts from 1867 to 1871. On Wednesday and Saturday, costumed park volunteers re-enact life in the 1800s with cooking and crafts demonstrations, a working blacksmith, and parlor singing. Free 1-hour walking tours are available daily from the Robinson-Rose House. The stillness inside the state park is palpable, especially at night, when you can stroll the unpaved streets and look up at the stars. Admission is free.

Not far from Old Town lies the vast suburban sprawl of Mission Valley. Until I-8 was built in the 1950s, it was little more than cow pastures with a couple of dirt roads, but shopping malls, motels, a golf course, condos, car dealerships, and a massive sports stadium fill the expanse today, following the San Diego River upstream to the **Mission Basilica San Diego de Alcala,** 10818 San Diego Mission Rd. (© **619/281-8449;** www.missionsandiego.com). Established in 1769 above Old Town, this was the first link in a chain of 21 missions founded by Spanish missionary Junípero Serra. It was moved to its present location in 1774 for agricultural reasons, and to separate Native American converts from the fortress that included the original building. The mission was burned by Indians a year after it was built, and when Father Serra rebuilt it he used 5- to 7-foot-thick adobe walls and clay tile roofs—making it less likely to burn again, and in the process inspiring a bevy of 20th-century California architects. It's still an active Catholic parish, and mass is said daily. Admission costs $3.

Head back west toward the water to experience **Mission Bay,** where someone probably took the picture on the postcards you'll send home. Mission Bay is a watery playground perfect for water-skiing, sailing, and windsurfing. The adjacent communities of Ocean Beach, Mission Beach, and Pacific Beach are known for their wide stretches of sand, active nightlife, and casual dining. This is the place to stay if you want to walk barefoot on the sand or are traveling with beach-loving children, and it's also home to **SeaWorld,** 500 Sea World Dr. (© **800/380-3203;** www.seaworld.com), one of the big draws for many visitors coming to San Diego. Owned by Anheuser-Busch, the 189-acre aquatic theme park features performing dolphins, otters, sea lions, walruses, and seals. Several successive 4-ton black-and-white killer whales have held the role of **Shamu,** the park's mascot, performing daily in the **Shamu Adventure,** SeaWorld's most popular show. There's also a slapstick sea lion show "Clyde and Seamore in Deep, Deep Trouble." the fast-paced **Dolphin Show,** and others. Admission costs $51 adults, $41 kids 3 to 9. Discount packages are available that combine SeaWorld with admission to the San Diego Zoo (see above).

BEACHES

San Diego County is blessed with 70 miles of sandy coastline and more than 30 individual beaches that cater equally to surfers, snorkelers, swimmers, sailors, divers, walkers, volleyballers, and sunbathers. Here are some of the best, going south to north. Lovely, wide, and sparkling, **Coronado Beach** is conducive to strolling and lingering, especially in the late afternoon. Waves are gentle here, so the beach draws many Coronado families. South of Mission Bay is **Ocean Beach,** a hot spot for surfers, though the water can be rough for swimming. Above Mission, there's always action at **Pacific Beach,** particularly along Ocean Front Walk, a paved promenade similar to L.A.'s funky Venice Beach promenade. Surfing is popular year-round here, in marked sections, and the beach is well staffed with lifeguards. Just north, **Windansea Beach** is legendary among California's surf elite and remains one of San Diego's prettiest strands. Reached by way of Bonair Street (at Neptune Place), it has no facilities and isn't really ideal for swimming. Come to surf, watch surfers, and soak in the party atmosphere. Up in rich La Jolla, the calm, protected waters of **La Jolla Cove** attract snorkelers and scuba divers, along with a fair share of families to its small beach. The cove's "look but don't touch" policy protects the colorful garibaldi, California's state fish, plus other marine life, including abalone, octopus, and lobster. The unique **San Diego–La Jolla Underwater Park** stretches from here to the northern end of Torrey Pines State Reserve, at the southern end of which you'll find **Torrey Pines Beach,** a fabulous, underused strand, accessed by a pay parking lot ($4) at the entrance to the park. It's rarely crowded, though be aware that at high tide most of the sand gets a soaking. In almost any weather, it's a great beach for walking.

SHOPPING

Downtown, **Horton Plaza,** 324 Horton Plaza (© **619/239-8180;** www.westfield. com/hortonplaza), is the Disneyland of shopping malls and the heart of the revitalized city center, bounded by G Street, Broadway, and First and Fourth avenues. Covering 6½ city blocks, the multilevel shopping center has more than 130 specialty shops, including art galleries, clothing and shoe stores, several fun shops for kids, and bookstores. There's a 14-screen cinema, three major department stores, and a variety of restaurants and short-order eateries. It's almost as much an attraction as SeaWorld or the San Diego Zoo, transcending its genre with a conglomeration of rambling paths, bridges, towers, piazzas, sculptures, fountains, and live greenery. Performers provide background entertainment throughout the year.

North of downtown, compact **Hillcrest** is the hub of San Diego's gay and lesbian community and as such, swank inspiration and chic housewares rule, with scads of places selling trinkets, used books, vintage clothing, and memorabilia, plus some chain stores, bakeries, cafes, and an array of modestly priced globe-hopping dining options. For antiques, head for the **Ocean Beach antiques district** (www.ocean beachsandiego.com) along Newport Avenue, just west of Old Town San Diego and a few blocks from the beach.

WHERE TO STAY

The following picks run the gamut of style as well as location, from Coronado and downtown to up beyond La Jolla.

The **Hotel del Coronado,** 1500 Orange Ave., Coronado (© **800/HOTEL-DEL;** www.hoteldel.com), positively reeks of history. Opened in 1888 and the subject of meticulous restoration, this Victorian masterpiece had some of the first electric lights in existence, and its early days are well chronicled in displays throughout the hotel. Rates: from $285. A more moderate landing is found at La Jolla's **The Sea Lodge,** 8110 Camino del Oro (© **800/640-7702;** www.sealodge.com), where you can walk right onto the wide beach and frolic amid great waves. Lifeguards and the lack of undertow make this a popular choice for families. Though the rooms are plain, the staff is all-pro. Rates: from $169.

The 11-story **Gaslamp Plaza Suites,** 520 E St. (© **619/232-9500;** www.gaslamp plaza.com), is a comfortable landmark (dating from 1913, when it was San Diego's first skyscraper) with superfriendly rates, located smack-dab in the heart of the trendy Gaslamp Quarter. Rates: from $100. In downtown's Little Italy section, **La Pensione Hotel,** 606 W. Date St. (© **800/232-4683;** www.lapensionehotel.com), feels like a small European hotel and offers tidy lodgings at bargain prices. There's an abundance of great dining in the surrounding blocks, and you'll be perfectly situated to explore the rest of town by car. Rates: $80.

You don't need to know much about Craftsman-style architecture to appreciate the taste and keen craftsmanship that went into creating **The Lodge at Torrey Pines,** 11480 N. Torrey Pines Rd., La Jolla (© **858/453-4420;** www.lodgetorreypines.com). The city's only AAA Five Diamond hotel, it sits next to the Torrey Pines Golf Course, San Diego's top links; and you can enjoy a fireplace in your room, sunset ocean views from your balcony, and superb meals at the hotel's A. R. Valentine restaurant. Rates: from $450.

If you haven't gotten enough of sleeping on the water, **Harbor Vacations Club,** 1880 Harbor Island Dr., Marina Cortez, at downtown's G-Dock (© **800/922-4836;** www.harborvacationsclub.com), gives you the opportunity to book a floating hotel room on a power yacht, sailboat, or houseboat. The vessels are docked in a recreational marina on Harbor Island, near the airport and close to downtown. Rates: from $135.

DINING & NIGHTLIFE

You're *sooooo* close to Mexico, might as well have Mexican food, no? The best place in San Diego is, naturally, in Old Town, at **El Agave Tequileria,** 2304 San Diego Ave. (© **619/220-0692;** www.elagave.com). Rather than the "combination plate" fare that's common on this side of the border, this place offers a memorable combination of freshly prepared recipes from Veracruz, Chiapas, Puebla, and Mexico City, along with an impressive selection of boutique and artisan tequilas. Main courses: $16 to $32.

For seafood, try **Star of the Sea,** 1380 N. Harbor Dr., Downtown (© **619/232-7408;** www.starofthesea.com), where you'll find the city's best package of fresh seafood, graceful presentation, and memorable views from the edge of San Diego Bay. Main courses: $26 to $29. Chef Deborah Scott's menu at **Indigo Grill,** 1536 India St., in downtown's Little Italy (© **619/234-6802;** www.cohnrestaurants.com), cleverly fuses the flavors of the Pacific Coast from Mexico to Alaska. The results create the city's most adventurous menu, and one of its most delicious. Main courses: $18 to $29. For gourmet pizza from a wood-fired oven, head for **Sammy's California Wood-fired Pizza,** a local institution with several locations, including 770 Fourth Ave., in the Gaslamp Quarter (© **619/230-8888;** www.sammyspizza.com). Pizza: $8.50 to $9.95. If you want *gigantic* portions (what, that buffet aboard ship wasn't enough for you?), head for **Filippi's Pizza Grotto,** 1747 India St., downtown (© **619/232-5095;** www.realcheesepizza.com), where a salad for one is enough for three, and an order of lasagna must weigh a pound. Filippi's has other locations all over, including Pacific Beach, Mission Gorge, and Escondido. Pizza: $9 to $15.

For more of a class act, the polished service and elegant setting at **Laurel,** 505 Laurel St., next to Balboa Park (© **619/239-2222;** www.laurelrestaurant.com), are urbane and discriminating. The food is prepared with inventive flair and the Rhône-heavy wine list soars, making this a rewarding splurge for a special occasion. Main courses: $19 to $32.

Wherever you choose to dine, finish your evening in the **Gaslamp Quarter,** which always promises a lively evening street scene as well as restaurants, bars, and music venues. Another great option is attending a concert in Balboa Park. Free year-round organ concerts are held on Sundays from 2 to 3pm at the **Spreckels Organ Pavilion,** south of El Prado between Park Boulevard and the Cabrillo Freeway (© **619/ 702-8138;** www.sosorgan.com). The music, enhanced by the organist's commentary, runs the gamut from classical to contemporary. In summer, the free **Twilight in the Park** series (© **619/239-0512;** www.balboapark.org/twilightpark.html) offers a range of music from jazz to classical, world, Latin, gospel, and even oompah, on Tuesday, Wednesday, and Thursday evenings at the Spreckels Pavilion.

17 San Francisco, California

Dot-com bubble? What dot-com bubble?

Things were a little grim in San Francisco after the dot-lifestyle it practically invented turned out to be held together with duct tape. After a couple years of the city shuffling its feet waiting for the good times to come back, though, they apparently have, and the city's stature and future look bright—despite the thick fog bank that blocks out the sun on many days. So what can you expect from the country's most romantic European-style city, which was founded on—and still revels in—the pioneers' boom-or-bust lifestyle? How about the classics, like stunning bay vistas, Victorian architecture, swank boutiques, clanky cable cars, walkable beaches, staunch liberalism, and a hugely influential gay population. Even things that seemed to lose their way in the bad years—the city's storied restaurant scene, for instance—are now back and as happening as ever. San Francisco is open for business.

GETTING TO SAN FRANCISCO & THE PORT

Ships dock at the Port of San Francisco piers along the Embarcadero (© **415/ 274-0400;** www.sfport.com), just a 15-minute walk from Fisherman's Wharf. Parking is $12 per day. Union Square, Powell, and Market streets and the center of downtown can be reached by taxi.

If you're flying in, you'll land at one of the Bay Area's two major airports. **San Francisco International Airport** (© **650/821-8211;** www.flysfo.com) is 14 miles directly south of downtown on U.S. 101. Travel time to downtown during commuter rush hour is about 40 minutes; at other times, it's about 20 to 25 minutes. **BART** (Bay Area Rapid Transit; © **510/464-6000;** www.bart.gov) runs from the airport to downtown, avoiding gnarly traffic and costing a heck of a lot less than taxis and shuttles—about $5 per person to the Embarcadero. Just jump on the airport's free shuttle bus to the International terminal and the BART station. Trains leave approximately every 20 minutes. A **taxi** from the airport to downtown costs $30 to $35, plus tip. **SFO Airporter** buses (© **650/246-8942;** www.sfoairporter.com) depart from outside the lower-level baggage-claim area for downtown San Francisco every 30 minutes from about 5:30am to 10pm. The cost is $14 per person one-way. **SuperShuttle** (© **415/ 558-8500;** www.supershuttle.com) takes you anywhere in the city, charging about $14 depending on your destination, with each additional rider paying $8.

San Francisco

CRUISE TERMINAL 8 ●

ATTRACTIONS & SHOPPING ●
Chinatown temples **13**
City Lights Bookstore **12**
The Exploratorium **2**
Ferries to Alcatraz **7**
Fisherman's Wharf **6**
Golden Gate Bridge **1**
Grace Cathedral **15**
Mission Dolores **25**
Pacific Union Club **15**
The Presidio **2**
San Francisco Museum of Modern Art **21**
SBC Park **23**
Yerba Buena Gardens & Center for the Arts **22**

ACCOMMODATIONS ■
Four Seasons **20**
Marina Inn **5**
Phoenix Hotel **24**
Ritz-Carlton **14**
San Remo Hotel **9**
Savoy Hotel **18**
Union Street Inn **3**
Warwick Regis **19**
Westin St. Francis **17**

DINING & NIGHTLIFE ◆
Caffè Trieste **11**
Delfina **26**
Farallon **17**
Fleur de Lys **16**
Greens Restaurant **4**
Mario's Bohemian
  Cigar Store **10**
Pasta Pomodoro **10**
Tommaso's **12**

Oakland International Airport, about 5 miles south of downtown Oakland (✆ **510/563-3300;** www.flyoakland.com), is a popular alternative to flying directly into San Francisco, and is also accessible on the BART system (see above). Taxis to downtown San Francisco are approximately $45, plus tip. SuperShuttle (see above) costs $25 for the first rider, $15 for each additional person. **Bayporter Express** (✆ **415/467-1800;** www.bayporter.com) is a shuttle service that charges about $26 for the first person and $12 for each additional person to downtown San Francisco.

If you're driving, San Francisco is easily accessible by major highways: **Interstate 5,** from the north, and **U.S. 101,** which cuts south-north through the peninsula from San Jose and across the Golden Gate Bridge to points north. If you drive from Los Angeles, you can take the longer coastal route (437 miles and 11 hr.) or the inland route (389 miles and 8 hr.). From Mendocino, it's 156 miles and 4 hours; from Sacramento, 88 miles and 1½ hours; from Yosemite, 210 miles and 4 hours.

GETTING AROUND You can walk to many attractions from the cruise terminal, including the Embarcadero and sites in the Fisherman's Wharf area, including Ghiradelli Square (once home to the world-famous chocolate factory), the Cannery, the National Maritime Museum, the Museum of the City of San Francisco, and the ferry to Alcatraz. Otherwise, you have lots of transportation options. The San Francisco Municipal Railway, better known as **Muni** (✆ **415/673-6864;** www.sfmuni.com), operates the city's cable cars, buses, and streetcars. Don't miss riding on that classic San Francisco icon, the historic **cable car.** The three lines are concentrated in the downtown area. The most scenic and exciting is the **Powell-Hyde line,** which follows a zigzag route from the corner of Powell and Market streets, over both Nob Hill and Russian Hill, to a turntable at gaslit Victorian Square in front of Aquatic Park (the closet point to the port, near the intersection of Beach and Hyde sts.). The Powell-Mason line starts at the same intersection and climbs Nob Hill before descending to Bay Street, just 3 blocks from Fisherman's Wharf. The third is the California Street line. Rides cost $3.

Buses reach almost every corner of San Francisco and beyond—they even travel over the bridges to Marin County and Oakland. Overhead electric cables power some buses; others use conventional gas engines. All are numbered and display their destinations on the front. Many buses travel along Market Street or pass near Union Square; for safety, avoid taking buses late at night. A bus ride costs $1.25 for adults. If you plan to use public transportation extensively, you might want to invest in a **Muni Street & Transit Map** ($2), sold at the cable car ticket booths at Powell and Market streets and Hyde and Beach streets, as well as in many shops around town.

As comedian Eddie Izzard said, "The fog here is faster than the f*cking **taxis**—of which there are five. Five taxis, all going, 'I got people in.' Then, when you get in, they don't know where they're going." It's a pretty accurate summation. You can often find cabs at the major hotels and downtown during rush hour, but otherwise you'd do better calling ahead to **Veteran's Cab** (✆ **415/552-1300**), **Luxor Cabs** (✆ **415/282-4141**), or **Yellow Cab** (✆ **415/626-2345**). Rates are approximately $2.85 for the first ⅙ mile and $2.25 for each mile thereafter.

BEST CRUISE LINE SHORE EXCURSIONS

Sausalito & Muir Woods ($44, 5 hr.): After a stop in charming Sausalito for bay views and browsing at the town's boutiques, art galleries, and craft shops, your bus heads to 550-acre Muir woods, home to a grove of ancient coastal redwoods. You'll have 1½ hours to hike the area's trails on your own before heading back.

Alcatraz and Sausalito by Bus ($59, 6 hr.): This tour begins with a short drive along the Embarcadero to Fisherman's Wharf where you board the ferry to Alcatraz Island. When you get to Alcatraz Island, a Park Ranger will explain the prison's history before you go inside for a private audio tour. View cells previously inhabited by the Bird Man of Alcatraz and Al Capone. Afterwards, travel back to Fisherman's Wharf by ferry and board your bus for a drive over the Golden Gate Bridge and head for Sausalito, where you're free to walk around town and shop.

EXPLORING SAN FRANCISCO ON YOUR OWN

Just north of the cruise docks, **Fisherman's Wharf** (© 415/956-3493; www.fishermanswharf.org) is almost the definition of "tourist trap," a long coastal shopping mall that stretches from Ghirardelli Square at the west end to Pier 39 at the east. If you like this kind of thing—shops, restaurants, street performers, and the like, few of which have anything intrinsically to do with San Francisco—then linger a bit. If not, stop through for a few minutes to gander at the 600-strong **sea lion colony** that's taken up residence on the west (left) side of Pier 39.

OK, now leave.

From nearby Pier 41, ferries depart throughout the day bound for **Alcatraz Island** (www.nps.gov/alcatraz), the former military post and maximum-security prison that once housed Al Capone, Machine Gun Kelly, and the famous Birdman, Robert Stroud. Now part of the National Park system, "The Rock" offers self-guided tours, ranger-led talks about of its famous "escape-proof" prison, and nature trails that lead onto spectacular San Francisco views and glimpses of the island's abundant wildlife. Ferries are run by the **Blue & Gold Fleet,** Pier 41 (© 415/705-5555; www.blueandgoldfleet.com). Tickets are $16 with headset tour, $12 without. Make your reservation as far in advance as possible, and wear a sweater—it gets cold out there.

Whether traveling to The Rock or not, your next stop should be the intersection of Hyde and Beach, where you can hop the **Powell-Hyde cable car.** Sit or stand near the back, on the left-hand side if possible; that way you get the view down snakelike Lombard Street as well as the spectacular bay view from the top of **Nob Hill.** When the cable cars started running in1873, Nob Hill became the most desirable residential area in the city, chockablock with mansions. Only two survived the earthquake and fire of 1906: the Flood Mansion, which serves today as the **Pacific Union Club,** 1000 California St. at Mason Street, and the **Fairmont Hotel,** 950 Mason St., which was under construction when the earthquake struck and is worth a visit for its spectacular lobby. **Grace Cathedral,** on California Street between Taylor and Jones streets, is notable among other things for its stained-glass windows, depicting Thurgood Marshall, Jane Addams, Robert Frost, John Glenn, and Albert Einstein—representations of divinely inspired human endeavor in law, social work, letters, exploration, and science.

Just northeast of Nob Hill, San Francisco's **Chinatown** gives you a taste of that Asia cruise you couldn't afford this year. The first Chinese immigrants came to San Francisco in the early 1800s to work as servants, and today the city boasts one of the largest Chinese communities in the U.S. Cheesy camera and luggage stores cater to the tourists, but skip those and head for the vegetable and herb markets, restaurants, and shops that cater to Chinese shoppers. The gateway at Grant Avenue and Bush Street marks the entry to Chinatown. On Waverly Place, a street where the Chinese celebratory colors of red, yellow, and green are much in evidence, you'll find three **Chinese temples:** Jeng Sen (Buddhist and Taoist) at no. 146, Tien Hou (Buddhist) at no. 125, and Norras (Buddhist) at no. 109. If you enter, do so quietly so that you do not disturb those in prayer. A block west of Grant Avenue, **Stockton Street,** from 1000 to 1200, is the community's main shopping street, lined with grocers, fishmongers, tea sellers, herbalists, noodle parlors, and restaurants. Here, too, is the Buddhist Kon Chow Temple, at no. 855, above the Chinatown post office.

South of Chinatown and Nob Hill, **Union Square** is the commercial hub of the city, site of most major hotels and department stores. Life is more interesting, though, on the other side of the tracks—or Market Street, as the case may be. There, the neighborhood known as **SoMa** ("South of Market," running between Market, the Embarcadero, and Hwy. 101) was transformed from a district of old warehouses, industrial spaces, and underground clubs into the hub of dot-com-dom in the late '90s, and is now the city's cultural and multimedia center. The **San Francisco Museum of Modern Art,** 151 Third St. (© **415/357-4000;** www.sfmoma.org), holds more than 23,000 works, including paintings and sculptures by Henri Matisse, Jackson Pollock, Willem de Kooning, Richard Serra, Diego Rivera, Georgia O'Keeffe, and Paul Klee. Admission is $10. Closed Wednesdays. The **Center for the Arts at Yerba Buena Gardens,** 701 Mission St. (© **415/978-ARTS;** www.yerbabuenaarts.org), is San Francisco's official cultural facility, presenting music, theater, dance, and visual arts. Cutting-edge computer art, multimedia shows, traditional exhibitions, and performances occupy the center's high-tech galleries. The 5-acre gardens are a great place to relax in the grass on a sunny day, and feature dramatic outdoor sculpture in memory of Martin Luther King, Jr. Between May and October the gardens host a series of free concerts, festivals, and community events. Admission to the galleries is $6. Closed Mondays. At SoMa's waterfront you'll find the stunning **SBC Park,** Third and King streets (© **415/972-2000;** www.sfgiants.com), home of the **San Francisco Giants.** The unobstructed bay vistas take in bobbing boats beyond the outfield. Tickets are hard to come by, but you can try to track them down through www.tickets.com.

Southwest of SoMa, few of San Francisco's neighborhoods are as varied as **Haight-Ashbury,** which gained everlasting fame as a capital of sixties hippy culture. Walk along Haight Street today and you'll encounter a weird mix of aging Deadheads, neo-flower-children, homeless people, throngs of tourists, and the kind of clean-cut yuppies who can afford the steep rents of upper Haight, on the eastern border of Golden Gate Park. Funky-trendy shops, clubs, and cafes still line the commercial district, and if someone offers you a bud they're not talking about beer. To the south, the area of **Castro Street,** between Market and 18th streets is the center of the city's gay community as well as a lovely neighborhood teeming with shops, restaurants, bars, and cafes.

Back up north along San Francisco Bay, the famous **Golden Gate Bridge** connects the City by the Bay with Marin County and the redwoods to the north. Completed in 1937, it's commonly thought of as the world's most beautiful bridge—although the new Millau Bridge in southern France is giving it a run for its money. If at all possible, take a walk across, accessing the walkway from the parking lots on each side of the span.

The bridge is located at the west end of the huge **Presidio** complex; once an army base, it's now an urban national park full of historic buildings, parkland, and a national cemetery. Near the east end of the park, the **Exploratorium,** 3601 Lyon St. (© **415/ 563-7337;** www.exploratorium.edu), is a must for families with kids—though be warned that you'll be there most of the day. Designed for hands-on learning, the museum features more than 650 interactive exhibits exploring all facets of science, letting you touch a tornado, shape an electrical current, and finger-paint on a computer. It's located at the gorgeous **Palace of Fine Arts,** the only remaining building from 1915's Pan-Pacific Exhibition. Admission is $12 adults, $9.50 kids. Closed Mondays.

SHOPPING

San Francisco's most congested and popular shopping mecca is centered on **Union Square** and bordered by Bush, Taylor, Market, and Montgomery streets. Most of the big department stores and many high-end specialty shops are here. Be sure to venture to Grant Avenue, Post and Sutter streets, and Maiden Lane. This area is a hub for public transportation; all Market Street and several other buses run here, as do the Powell-Hyde and Powell-Mason cable car lines. When you pass through the gate to **Chinatown** on Grant Avenue, say good-bye to the world of fashion and hello to a swarm of cheap tourist shops selling everything from linen and jade to plastic toys and $2 slippers. The real gems, however, are tucked away on side streets and in small, one-person shops selling Chinese herbs, art, and jewelry.

Union Street, from Fillmore Street to Van Ness Avenue, caters to the upper-middle-class crowd. It's a great place to stroll, window-shop the plethora of boutiques, try the cafes and restaurants, and watch the beautiful people parade by. Take bus no. 22, 41, or 45. Some of the best shopping in town is packed into the 5 blocks of **Fillmore Street** from Jackson to Sutter in Pacific Heights. It's the perfect place to grab a bite and peruse the high-priced boutiques, crafts shops, and incredible housewares stores. The shopping in the 6 blocks of **upper Haight Street** between Central Avenue and Stanyan Street reflects its clientele, offering everything from incense and European and American street styles to furniture and antique clothes. If your shopping tastes run humble, the tourist-oriented malls along Jefferson Street in the **Fisherman's Wharf** area include hundreds of shops, restaurants, and attractions. If your tastes run more literary, head to **City Lights Bookstore,** 261 Columbus Ave., at Broadway on the east edge of Chinatown (© **415/362-8193;** www.citylights.com). Founded by Beat-poet Lawrence Ferlinghetti in 1953, the three-level shop specializes in world literature, the arts, and progressive politics.

WHERE TO STAY

Looking like a federal building outside and a mansion within, **The Ritz-Carlton,** 600 Stockton St., in Nob Hill (© **800/241-3333** or 415/296-7465; www.ritzcarlton.com), is the best bet for those with more traditional tastes and a hankering for every possible amenity. Rates: from $395. **The Four Seasons San Francisco,** 757 Market St., SoMa (© **800/819-5053** or 415/633-3000; www.fourseasons.com), opened in 2001 and features understated luxury, great service, and oversized rooms with custom-made mattresses. Rates: from $469. The **Westin St. Francis,** 335 Powell St., Union Square (© **800/WESTIN-1** or 415/397-7000; www.westin.com), is a favorite with VIPs for its luxurious rooms and with kids because they get complimentary goodies such as coloring books at check-in. Rates: from $199. Also in Union Square are two great boutique hotels, **The Warwick Regis,** 490 Geary St. (© **800/827-3447** or 415/928-7900; warwicksf.com), and **The Savoy Hotel,** 580 Geary St. (© **800/227-4223** or 415/441-2700; www.thesavoyhotel.com). Rates for both from about $120. Attention to detail, comfortable rooms, and a location along a prime stretch of Union Street make the tiny, six-room **Union Street Inn,** 2229 Union St. (© **415/346-0424;**

www.unionstreetinn.com), an excellent way to experience true San Francisco–style living. Rates: from $179. **The Phoenix Hotel,** 601 Eddy St. (© **800/248-9466** or 415/776-1380), is a favorite with the music and movie set (Sinéad O'Connor, David Bowie, and Keanu Reaves have all laid their heads here) and is one of the only moderate hotels in San Francisco with an outdoor pool. Rates: from $149.

At the small, adorable **San Remo Hotel,** 2237 Mason St. (© **800/352-REMO** or 415/776-8688; www.sanremohotel.com), the rooms may be small and the bathrooms shared, but the North Beach location (walking distance of Fisherman's Wharf), friendly staff, and low prices can't be beat. Rates: from $55. Another top choice for convenient location, room amenities, and budget prices is the **Marina Inn,** 3110 Octavia St., Marina/Pacific Heights (© **800/274-1420** or 415/928-1000; www.marinainn.com). Rates: from $65.

DINING & NIGHTLIFE

Choice dining spots in the city include **Fleur de Lys,** 777 Sutter St., Union Square (© **415/673-7779;** www.fleurdelyssf.com), which offers formal French cuisine in a romantic dining room. A three-course menu costs $68. Whimsical **Farallon,** 450 Post St., Union Square (© **415/956-6969;** www.farallonrestaurant.com), offers high-priced seafood amidst an orgy of oceanic artwork, from jellyfish lamps to sea urchin chandeliers. Main courses: $30 to $37.

Gourmands and everyday diners squeeze into North Beach's **Tommaso's,** 1042 Kearny St., North Beach (© **415/398-9696;** www.tommasosnorthbeach.com), for killer pizza and a no-frills Italian cafe atmosphere. Main courses: $10 to $17. **Pasta Pomodoro,** 655 Union St., North Beach (© **415/399-0300;** www.pastapomodoro.com), serves up heaping plates of fresh pasta at penny-pinching prices. Main courses: $7 to $12. It has several other locations around town. Want a little more atmosphere and more sophisticated Italian cooking? Head to **Delfina,** 3621 18th St., in the Mission District (© **415/552-4055;** www.delfinasf.com). Main courses: $13 to $22.

Greens Restaurant, Building A, Fort Mason Center, Marina/Pacific Heights (© **415/771-6222;** www.greensrestaurant.com), serves inventive vegetarian cuisine in an old waterfront warehouse, with a view of the bay and the Golden Gate Bridge. Main courses: $16 to $20.

North Beach, San Francisco's Italian quarter, stretches from Montgomery and Jackson to Bay Street. It's one of the best places in the city to grab a coffee, pull up a cafe chair, and do some serious people-watching. Nightlife is equally happening; restaurants, bars, and clubs along Columbus and Grant avenues attract folks from all over the Bay Area, who fight for a parking place and romp through the festive neighborhood. Among the area's coffeehouses, we love the authentic atmosphere at **Mario's Bohemian Cigar Store,** 566 Columbus Ave. (© **415/362-0536;** www.mariosbohemiancigarstore.com), and **Caffè Trieste,** 606 Vallejo St. (© **415/392-6739;** www.cafetrieste.com).

At night, dozens of piano bars and top-notch lounges augment San Francisco's lively dance-club culture, and skyscraper lounges offer dazzling city views. The city's arts scene is also extraordinary: The opera is justifiably world renowned, the ballet is on its toes, and theaters are high in both quantity and quality. In short, there's always something going on, so get out there. For up-to-date nightlife information, turn to the *San Francisco Weekly* and the *San Francisco Bay Guardian,* both of which run comprehensive listings. They're available free at bars and restaurants and from street-corner boxes all around the city. *Where,* a free tourist-oriented monthly, also lists programs and performance times; it's available in most of the city's finer hotels. As for bars and lounges, there are hundreds of 'em throughout San Francisco. **Chestnut and Union Street** bars attract a post-collegiate crowd, **Upper Haight** caters to eclectic neighborhood cocktailers, and **Lower Haight** draws snowboarder types. Tourists mix with theatergoers and thirsty businesspeople in **downtown** pubs, while **The Castro** caters to gay locals and tourists.

18 Seattle, Washington

There was a time not too long ago when most Alaska-bound ships sailed from Vancouver, British Columbia, even though Seattle, the home of Starbucks, Microsoft, and grunge, has a fully functioning port right here in the U.S., and not far away. Over the past several years, the cruise lines have recognized and rectified their snubbing of the port, and today a whole slew of ships are sailing from this beautiful and cosmopolitan city, carrying about a half-million passengers. Seattle has shopping, fine restaurants, attractions galore, good air service, culture, and a wide range of accommodations—more, in fact, than you'll be able to take in on just a short pre- or post-cruise visit. It is very much a water-oriented city, set between Puget Sound and Lake Washington, with Lake Union in the center. Practically everywhere you look, the views are of sailboats, cargo ships, ferries, windsurfers, and anglers.

GETTING TO SEATTLE & THE PORT

Cruise ships dock at **Pier 66** (the Bell St. Terminal), right in downtown Seattle, or at the new **Pier 30** terminal, 2431 East Marginal Way S., at the south end of Seattle's downtown waterfront, just a few minutes away by car or taxi. See **www.portseattle. org** for maps and other info. If you're arriving by air, you'll fly into the **Seattle-Tacoma International Airport** (© 800/544-1965), aka **SeaTac,** located about 14 miles south of Seattle and connected to the city by Interstate 5. Generally, allow 30 minutes for the trip between the airport and downtown. A **taxi** downtown will cost you around $30, or you can take the **Seattle Downtown Airporter** (© 800/426-7532; www.graylineofseattle.com) for $10 one-way, $17 round-trip; or **Shuttle Express** (© 425/981-7000), which costs $25 for up to three people to most downtown areas.

If you're arriving by car, you'll likely come in on I-5, which leads right downtown. Alaskan Way, a busy street, runs along the waterfront and past the cruise ship terminal. Parking is $12 per day.

GETTING AROUND   You can walk or take public transportation around downtown Seattle, but if you want a **rental car,** nearly every major company has an outlet at SeaTac. **Seattle Metro** (© 206/553-3000) offers free bus transportation within the downtown area between the hours of 6am and 7pm. The company also operates a waterfront service using old-fashioned streetcars, some of it in the ride-free area, some of it outside. The most it will cost you is $1.50 one-way. Visitors to the Space Needle can use the Seattle Center Monorail from downtown, 1¼ miles away, for $1.50 one-way.

BEST CRUISE LINE SHORE EXCURSUIONS

Seattle Duck Tour ($23 1½ hr.): This WWII-era amphibious tour bus takes you around the Seattle waterfront, historic Pioneer Square, Safeco Field, Pike Place Market, and the downtown shopping district, then drives right into Lake Union to see Gasworks Park, Dale Chihuly's glass studio, and great views of the skyline. For those who don't like to get their wheels wet, there's typically also a regular bus tour that includes the Space Needle and shopping time at Pike Place Market ($45, 3 hr.).

EXPLORING SEATTLE ON YOUR OWN

The **Seattle Waterfront,** along Alaskan Way from Yesler Way North to Bay Street and Myrtle Edwards Park, is the city's single most popular attraction, and much like San Francisco's Fisherman's Wharf area, that's both good and bad. Yes, it's very touristy, with tacky gift shops, saltwater taffy, T-shirts galore, and lots of overpriced restaurants, but it's also home to the Seattle Aquarium, the Pike Place Market and its many vendors, and **Ye Olde Curiosity Shop,** 1001 Alaskan Way (© **206/682-5844;** www.ye oldecuriosityshop.com), a cross between a souvenir store and *Ripley's Believe It or Not.* It's weird! It's tacky! It's always packed! See Siamese-twin calves, a natural mummy, the Lord's Prayer on a grain of rice, a narwhal tusk, shrunken heads, and a 67-pound snail. The collection of oddities was started by oddity-aficionado Joe Standley back in 1899.

At Pier 54, you'll find companies offering sea-kayak tours, sport-fishing trips, jet-boat tours, and bicycle rentals. At Piers 55 and 56, boats leave for 1½-hour harbor cruises as well as trips to **Tillicum Village,** a faux Northwest Native longhouse built for the 1962 Seattle World's Fair, located at Blake Island State Marine Park, across Puget Sound. It's a beautiful spot. **Tillicum Village Tours** (© **206/443-1244;** www.tillicumvillage.com) include a lunch or dinner of alder-smoked salmon and a performance of traditional masked dances. The 4-hour tour costs $69. At Pier 57, you'll find the **Bay Pavilion,** which has a vintage carousel and a video arcade to keep the kids busy.

At Pier 59, you'll find a waterfront park and the **Seattle Aquarium,** 1483 Alaskan Way (© **206/386-4320;** www.seattleaquarium.org), with its well-designed exhibits dealing with the water worlds of the Puget Sound region. One of the aquarium's most popular exhibits is an interactive tide pool and discovery lab that re-creates Washington's wave-swept intertidal zone. From the underwater viewing dome, you get a fish's-eye view of life beneath the waves. Admission is $12 adults, $5 to $8 kids, plus extra for special exhibits.

Inland from the waterfront, between Pike and Pine streets at First Avenue, the historic **Pike Place Market** (© **206/682-7453;** www.pikeplacemarket.org) was originally a farmers market and is now a National Historic District, home to more than 200 local craftspeople and artists who sell their creations here throughout the year, plus excellent restaurants, hundreds of shops, and street performers. Two blocks from the market, behind Jonathon Borofsky's giant *Hammering Man* sculpture, the **Seattle Art Museum,** 100 University St. (© **206/654-3100;** www.seattleartmuseum.org), is a repository for everything from African masks, Old Masters, and Andy Warhol to one of the nation's premier collections of Northwest Coast Indian art. Admission is $7; closed Monday.

Farther west is the **Seattle Center,** which was the epicenter of the 1962 World's Fair and is still home to the fair's futuristic **Space Needle,** 203 Sixth Ave. N. (© **206/443-2111;** www.spaceneedle.com), a 607-foot tower/restaurant thingie that's become the quintessential symbol of Seattle. At 518 feet above ground level, the views from the observation deck are stunning. High-powered telescopes let you zoom in on distant sights, and there's a lounge and two very expensive restaurants inside. Admission is $13 adults, $6 kids. Next door, the newish **Experience Music Project** (© **877/367-5483;** www.emplive.com) is the building that looks like it's in the process of melting. Inside, you'll find displays, interactive music rooms, performance spaces, galleries, and

Seattle

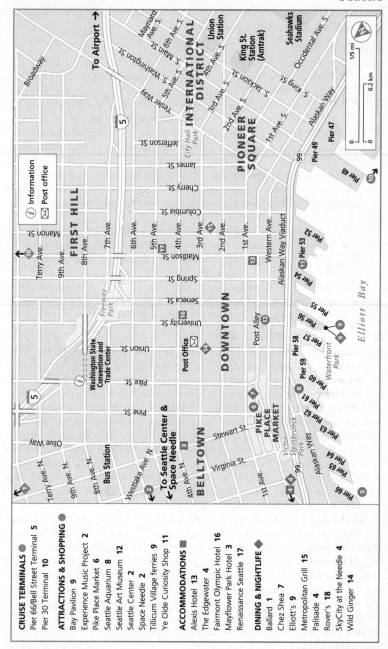

CRUISE TERMINALS ●
Pier 66/Bell Street Terminal **5**
Pier 30 Terminal **10**

ATTRACTIONS & SHOPPING ●
Bay Pavilion **9**
Experience Music Project **2**
Pike Place Market **6**
Seattle Aquarium **8**
Seattle Art Museum **12**
Seattle Center **2**
Space Needle **2**
Tillicum Village ferries **9**
Ye Olde Curiosity Shop **11**

ACCOMMODATIONS ■
Alexis Hotel **13**
The Edgewater **4**
Fairmont Olympic Hotel **16**
Mayflower Park Hotel **3**
Renaissance Seattle **17**

DINING & NIGHTLIFE ◆
Ballard **1**
Chez Shea **7**
Elliott's **9**
Metropolitan Grill **15**
Palisade **4**
Rover's **18**
SkyCity at the Needle **4**
Wild Ginger **14**

research facilities dedicated to all phases of American popular music. Admission is $20 adults, $15 kids, free for kids 6 and under.

WHERE TO STAY

Located in an enviable location halfway between Pike Place Market and Pioneer Square and only 2 blocks from the waterfront, the **Alexis Hotel,** 1007 First Ave. at Madison Street (© **800/426-7033;** www.alexishotel.com), part of the Klimpton group of boutique hotels, is a sparkling gem with a pleasant mix of classic styling and a friendly staff. Rates: from $195. The **Fairmont Olympic Hotel,** 411 University St. (© **888/363-5022;** www.fairmont.com), is one of the bigger, and absolutely one of the most elegant, hotels in Seattle, reminiscent of an Italian Renaissance palace. Rates: from $349.

Built on a pier, **The Edgewater,** 2411 Alaskan Way at Pier 67 (© **800/624-0670;** www.edgewaterhotel.com), is Seattle's only waterfront hotel, even though it looks like a mountain lodge. Rooms feature rustic lodgepole pine furniture and the lobby offers gorgeous sunset views. Rates: from $179.

Renaissance Seattle, 515 Madison St. (© **800/546-9184;** www.renaissancehotels. com), offers larger-than-average rooms, many with views of either Puget Sound or the Cascade Range. Rates: from $189. If shopping or sipping martinis is among your favorite recreational activities, stay at the **Mayflower Park Hotel,** 405 Olive Way (© **800/426-5100;** www.mayflowerpark.com), built in 1927 and connected to the upscale shops of Westlake Center and flanked by Nordstrom and the Bon Marché. In Oliver's Lounge, the hotel also serves up the best martinis in Seattle. Rates: from $150.

DINING & NIGHTLIFE

In a quiet corner of Pike Place Market, **Chez Shea,** 94 Pike St. (© **206/467-9990;** www.chezshea.com), offers candlelit tables, subdued lighting, views of ferries crossing the bay, and superb meals. It all adds up to the perfect combination for a romantic dinner. A three-course dinner (available Tues–Thurs and Sun) is $35; closed Monday. The best waterfront dining in town is at **Palisade,** Elliott Bay Marina, 2601 W. Marina Place (© **206/285-1000;** www.palisaderestaurant.com), which offers a 180-degree view that takes in Elliott Bay, downtown Seattle, and West Seattle. Never mind that it also has great food and some of the most memorable decor of any Seattle restaurant. Main courses: $17 to $65. If you're feeling above it all, pick a restaurant to match. **SkyCity at the Needle,** in the Space Needle at 400 Broad St. (© **800/937-9582**), has the best views in Seattle. Simply prepared steaks and seafood make up the bulk of the menu. Main courses: $20 to $32.

Wild Ginger, 1401 Third Ave. (© **206/623-4450**), is a longtime Seattle favorite, serving Pan-Asian specialties in a stylish and usually very busy setting. Pull up a comfortable stool around the large satay grill and watch the cooks grill little skewers of anything from chicken to scallops to pork to prawns to lamb. Main courses: $9 to $24.

Rover's, 2808 E. Madison St. (© **206/325-7442;** www.rovers-seattle.com), serves the best and most original Northwest cuisine in town, combining local ingredients with classic French cooking. Three prix-fixe menus are available for $80, $90, and $115; a la carte courses are $14 to $20. For the best selection of oysters, head to **Elliott's,** Pier 56, Alaskan Way (© **206/623-4340**), whose oyster bar can have as many as 20 varieties available. Main courses: $16 to $55. For the best steaks, go to

Metropolitan Grill, 820 Second Ave. (© **206/624-3287**), which serves corn-fed, aged beef grilled over mesquite charcoal. Main courses: $18 to $42.

Much of Seattle's evening entertainment scene is clustered in the **Pioneer Square** area. Known for its restored 1890s buildings, it's centered around the corner of First Avenue and Yesler Way. Tree-lined streets and cobblestone plazas make it one of the prettiest downtown neighborhoods, and a plethora of restaurants, bars, and nightclubs make it a happening night scene. Good times are guaranteed, whether you want to hear a live band, hang out in a good old-fashioned bar, or dance. Keep in mind that this neighborhood tends to attract a rowdy crowd, especially late at night. Seattle's other nightlife district is the former Scandinavian neighborhood of **Ballard,** in northwest Seattle, bordering the Lake Washington Ship Canal and Puget Sound, where you'll find more than half a dozen nightlife establishments, including a brew-pub, taverns, bars, and live-music clubs.

19 Tampa, Florida

Tampa was a sleepy port until Cuban immigrants founded Ybor City's cigar industry in the 1880s. A few years later, Henry B. Plant built a railroad to carry tourists into town and constructed his garish Tampa Bay Hotel (now the Henry B. Plant Museum). During the Spanish-American War, Teddy Roosevelt trained his Rough Riders here and walked the Ybor City streets with Cuban revolutionary José Marti. A land boom in the 1920s gave the city its charming, Victorian-style Hyde Park suburb (now a gen-trified area, just across the Hillsborough River from downtown), and the go-go 1980s and 1990s brought skyscrapers, a convention center, a performing-arts center, and lots of shopping and dining options to the downtown area.

On the western shore of Tampa Bay, St. Petersburg is the picturesque and pleasant flip side of Tampa's busy business, industrial, and shipping life. Originally conceived and built primarily for tourists and wintering snowbirds, it's got a nice downtown area, some quality museums, and a few good restaurants.

The Port of Tampa is set amid a complicated network of channels and harbors near historic Ybor City and its deep-water Ybor Channel. Ships sailing from here head primarily to the western Caribbean, the Yucatán, and Central America.

GETTING TO TAMPA & THE PORT

Tampa's cruise terminals are all located along Channelside Drive, close to the heart of things. They're operated by the **Tampa Port Authority** (© **813/905-7678;** www.tampaport.com). If you're coming by air, you'll probably land at **Tampa International Airport** (© **813/870-8700;** www.tampaairport.com), 5 miles west of downtown Tampa, near the junction of Florida 60 and Memorial Highway. If you haven't arranged transfers with the cruise line, the port is an easy 30-minute taxi ride away; the set fare is $20 per car for up to four people. Rental cars are also available from all the major companies.

By car, Tampa lies 188 miles southwest of Jacksonville, 50 miles north of Sarasota, and 245 miles northwest of Miami. From I-75 and I-4 to Terminals 2 and 6, take I-4 West to Exit 1 (Ybor City), go south on 21st Street, then turn right on Adamo Drive (Hwy. 60) and then left on Channelside Drive. For Terminal 7, go south on 21st Street (21st St. merges with 22nd St. after crossing Adamo Dr.), turn right on

Maritime Boulevard, and then go left on Guy N. Verger to Hooker's Point. Parking at the port costs $12 per day.

GETTING AROUND   Taxis in Tampa do not normally cruise the streets for fares; instead, they line up at public loading places, such as the airport, cruise terminal, and major hotels. **Yellow Cab** (© **813/253-0121**) and **United Cab** (© **813/253-2424**) charge about $2 per mile. Should you wish to rent a car, all major rental companies have counters at the airport.

BEST CRUISE LINE SHORE EXCURSIONS

Florida Aquarium ($45, 4 hr.): This state-of-the-art aquarium celebrates the role of water in the development and maintenance of Florida's topography and ecosystems, with more than 10,000 aquatic plants and animals. An overriding theme follows a drop of water as it bubbles through Florida limestone and winds its way to the sea.

BUSCH GARDENS

Admission prices are high, but **Busch Gardens,** 3605 E. Bougainvilla Ave. (© **888/ 800-5447;** www.buschgardens.com), remains Tampa Bay's most popular attraction. The 335-acre family entertainment park features thrill rides, animal habitats, live entertainment, shops, restaurants, and games. The park's zoo ranks among the best in the country, with nearly 3,400 animals.

Montu, the world's tallest and longest inverted roller coaster, is part of **Egypt,** the park's ninth themed area, which also includes a replica of King Tutankhamen's tomb and a sand-dig area for kids. **Timbuktu** is a replica of an ancient desert trading center, complete with African craftspeople at work. It also features a sandstorm ride, a boat-swing ride, a roller coaster, and a video-game arcade. **Morocco,** a walled city with exotic architecture, has Moroccan craft demonstrations and a sultan's tent with snake charmers. The **Congo** features white-water raft rides; Kumba, the largest steel roller coaster in the southeastern United States; and Claw Island, a display of rare white Bengal tigers in a natural setting. **Rhino Rally** is an off-road adventure in 16-passenger "Ralliers," or Land Rovers, which travel a bumpy course that allows views of Asian elephants, buffalo, antelope, and more. Hang on to your hat when a flash flood whisks away the bridge—and your vehicle.

The **Serengeti Plain** is an open area with more than 500 African animals roaming in herds. This 80-acre natural grassy veldt can be viewed from the tram ride, the Trans-Veldt Railway, or the Skyride. **Nairobi** is home to a natural habitat for various species of gorillas and chimpanzees, a baby-animal nursery, a petting zoo, reptile displays, and Curiosity Caverns, where visitors can observe animals active at night. **Bird Gardens,** the original core of Busch Gardens, offers rich foliage, lagoons, and a free-flight aviary holding hundreds of exotic birds, including golden and American bald eagles, hawks, owls, and falcons. This area also features Land of the Dragons, a children's adventure.

For great views while you eat, **Crown Colony** is a multilevel restaurant overlooking the Serengeti Plain. The Anheuser-Busch hospitality center, near the Bird Gardens, is home to a team of Clydesdale horses. Akbar's Adventure Tours, which offers a flight simulator, is located here.

To get to the Gardens, take Interstate 275 northeast of downtown to Busch Boulevard (Exit 33), and go east 2 miles to the entrance on 40th Street (McKinley Ave.). Admission is $56 for adults and $50 for kids 3 to 9 (plus 7% tax). Parking is $7. Park hours are at least 10am to 6pm; hours are usually extended during summer and on holidays. See the website for opening and closing times.

Tampa

Airport

Beach

Lake Carroll

White Trout Lake

University of South Florida

41 275

583 582

301

River

Hillsborough

75

580

Busch Gardens 1

584

587

Temple Terrace

598

580 589

TAMPA

585 574

41 92

2 4

589

Tampa International Airport

Raymond James Stadium

3

3 3

569

YBOR CITY

301

92

See downtown map below

60

75

618

589

5

McKay Bay

4

BUS 41

676

618

685

Old Tampa Bay

Howard Frankland Bridge

4 60

587

Davis Island

Peter O. Knight Airport

676A

To St. Petersburg

Gandy Bridge

92 587 573

Hillsborough Bay

41

East Tampa

0   3 mi
0   3 km

N

Downtown Tampa

275

45

3

MacDill Air Force Base

275

Kay St.

Kay Ave.

Scott St.

Nebraska Ave.

Central Ave.

Orange

India

Governor St.

Scott St.

Nick Nuccio Pkwy.

N. 14th St.

N. 15th St.

3 3

Frank Adamo Dr.

618

Riverfront Park

Doyle Carlton Dr.

N. Boulevard

Laurel St.

N. Tampa Ave.

N. Florida Ave.

Harrison St.

Tyler Street

E. Cass St.

E. Cass St.

Union Station

Twiggs St.

Lee Roy Selmon Crosstown Expwy.

Meridian Ave.

S. 13th St.

Harbor

Banana Docks

Seascape Terminal

Tampa Bay

W. Cass St.

Ashley Dr.

Polk St.

Zack St.

Twiggs St.

Madison St.

Pierce St.

Morgan St.

Marion St.

Jefferson St.

Whiting St.

York

6

7

University of Tampa

E. John F. Kennedy Blvd.

Jackson St.

11

Washington St.

Whiting St.

8

Plant Park

Hillsborough River

North B St.

North A St.

W. John F. Kennedy Blvd.

S. Tampa St.

Florida Ave.

Brorein St.

Whiting St.

13th St.

Whiting St.

Garrison Seaport Terminal/ Port of Tampa

13

14

60

Cleveland St.

Hyde Park

Plant Ave.

9

Brorein St.

10

12

Channelside Drive

Ice Palace

5

Ybor Channel

South Boulevard

618

W. Platt

Platt St.

Tampa Convention Center

S. Ashley Dr.

Garrison Channel

N

CRUISE TERMINAL 5 ●

ATTRACTIONS & SHOPPING ●
Busch Gardens **1**
Florida Aquarium **14**
Henry B. Plant Museum **8**
Tampa Museum of Art **7**
Ybor cigar shops **3**

Ybor City Museum State Park **3**

ACCOMMODATIONS ■
Hilton Garden Inn **3**
Hyatt Regency Tampa **12**
Renaissance Vinoy Resort **6**
Seminole Hard Rock Hotel & Casino **2**
Tampa Marriott Waterside **11**

DINING & NIGHTLIFE ◆
Bern's Steak House **4**
Centro Ybor **3**
Channelside **13**
Columbia Restaurant **3**
Mise en Place **9**

EXPLORING THE REST OF TAMPA ON YOUR OWN

Tampa is best explored by car, as only the commercial district can be covered on foot. If you want to go to the beach, you'll have to head to neighboring St. Petersburg. **Ybor City,** Tampa's historic Latin enclave and one of only three national historic districts in Florida, lies only a mile or so from the cruise ship docks. Once known as the cigar capital of the world, Ybor offers a charming slice of the past with its Spanish architecture, antique street lamps, wrought-iron balconies, ornate grillwork, and renovated cigar factories. Stroll along 7th Avenue, the main artery (closed to traffic at night), where you'll find cigar shops, boutiques, nightclubs, and the famous 100-year-old Columbia Restaurant (see "Dining & Nightlife," below). The **Ybor City Museum State Park,** 1818 9th Ave., between 18th and 19th streets (© **813/247-6323;** www.ybormuseum. org), is primarily devoted to the area's cigar history, with a collection of cigar labels, cigar memorabilia, and works by local artisans. Admission is $3.

Thirteen silver minarets and distinctive Moorish architecture make the stunning **Henry B. Plant Museum,** 401 W. Kennedy Blvd. (© **813/254-1891;** www.plant museum.com), the focal point of the Tampa skyline. This national historic landmark, built in 1891 as the Tampa Bay Hotel, is filled with European and Oriental furnishings and decorative arts from the original hotel collection. Admission is $5; closed Monday. The permanent collection of the **Tampa Museum of Art,** 600 N. Ashley Dr. (© **813/274-8732;** www.tampamuseum.com), is especially strong in ancient Greek, Etruscan, and Roman artifacts, as well as 20th-century art. The museum grounds, fronting the Hillsborough River, contain a sculpture garden and a decorative fountain. Admission is $7 adults; closed Monday.

If you want to see one of the country's largest and busiest ports in action, the **Port Authority of Tampa** (© **813/905-5131**), offers a free 1½-hour tour around Tampa Bay. The 45-passenger *SeePort Adventure* catamaran departs from Terminal 2 Monday through Friday at 9:30am. Reservations are suggested at least 2 weeks in advance.

BEACHES

You have to start at **St. Petersburg,** across the bay, for a north-to-south string of interconnected white sandy shores. Most beaches have restrooms, refreshment stands, and picnic areas. You can either park on the street at meters (usually 25¢ for each half-hour) or at one of the four major parking lots located from north to south at **Sand Key Park** in Clearwater, beside Gulf Boulevard (also known as Rte. 699), just south of the Clearwater Pass Bridge; **Redington Shores Beach Park,** beside Gulf Boulevard at 182nd Street; **Treasure Island Park,** on Gulf Boulevard just north of 108th Avenue; and **St. Pete Beach Park,** beside Gulf Boulevard at 46th Street.

SHOPPING

The most distinctive shopping here is in Ybor City. The place is no longer the major producer of hand-rolled cigars it once was, but you can still watch artisans making stogies at the **Gonzalez y Martinez Cigar Factory/Columbia Cigar Store,** 2103 7th Ave., in the Columbia Restaurant building (© **813/247-2469**). Rollers are on duty Monday through Saturday. You can also stock up on fine domestic and imported cigars at **El Sol,** 1728 E. 7th Ave. (© **813/248-5905**), the city's oldest cigar store; **King Corona Cigar Factory,** 1523 E. 7th Ave. (© **813/241-9109**); and **Metropolitan Cigars & Wine,** 2014 E. 7th Ave. (© **813/248-3304**).

WHERE TO STAY

All of the hotels listed in this section are in downtown Tampa or Ybor City.

The modern, four-story **Hilton Garden Inn,** 1700 E. 9th Ave. (© **800/445-8667;** www.hiltongardeninn.com), is primarily oriented to business travelers, but it's located just 2 blocks north of the heart of Ybor City's dining and entertainment district. Rates: from $89. The **Hyatt Regency Tampa,** Two Tampa City Center at 211 N. Tampa St. (© **800/233-1234;** http://tamparegency.hyatt.com), sits in Tampa's commercial center and also caters mostly to the corporate crowd. Rates: from $149. The **Tampa Marriott Waterside,** 700 S. Florida Ave. (© **800/228-9290;** www. marriotthotels.com), offers a lot of rooms with balconies overlooking the bay or city (the best views are high up on the south side). Rates: from $189.

If the slots on the ship aren't enough for you, the new 500-room **Seminole Hard Rock Hotel & Casino**, 5223 Orient Rd. (© **866/502-7529;** www.hardrockhotel casinotampa.com), has a 130,000-square-foot casino plus several other grand features—stay here if you're looking for lots of excitement. Rates: from $140.

For a special experience farther from the cruise docks, the **Renaissance Vinoy Resort,** 501 Fifth Ave. NE, at Beach Drive in St. Petersburg (© **800/HOTELS1;** www.renaissancehotels.com), is the grande dame of the region's hotels. Built as the grand Vinoy Park in 1925, this elegant Spanish-style establishment reopened in 1992 after a meticulous $93-million restoration. Many of the guest rooms offer lovely views of Tampa Bay. Accommodations in the new wing ("The Tower") are slightly larger than those in the hotel's original core. Rates: from $219.

DINING & NIGHTLIFE

Nightfall transforms Ybor City, Tampa's century-old Latin Quarter, into a hotbed of ethnic food, music, poetry readings, and after-midnight coffee and dessert. The nearly 100-year-old **Columbia Restaurant,** 2117 7th Ave. E. (© **813/248-4961**), occupies an attractive tile-sheathed building that fills an entire city block between 21st and 22nd streets, about a mile from the cruise docks. The aura is pre-Castro Cuba, and the simpler your dish is, the better it's likely to be. Filet mignons; roasted pork; and the black beans, yellow rice, and plantains are flavorful and well prepared. Catch a flamenco show on the dance floor Monday through Saturday. Main courses: $15 to $25. After dinner, all you have to do is stroll along 7th Avenue East between 15th and 20th streets, and you'll hear music blaring out of the clubs that change names and character frequently. Just follow your ears into the one that sounds best to you. With all of the sidewalk seating, it's easy to judge what the clientele is like, too. At **Centro Ybor,** a shopping/entertainment complex between 7th and 8th avenues and 15th and 17th streets (© **813/242-4660;** www.centroybor.com), you'll find a multiscreen cineplex, several restaurants, a comedy club, a large open-air bar, a bunch of typical mall-type stores, and GameWorks, a high-tech entertainment center designed by Steven Spielberg's DreamWorks and Universal Studios. The Ybor City Chamber of Commerce has its Cigar Museum & Visitor Center here (on 8th Ave. next to Centro Espanol).

Although Ybor City is better known, Tampa's trendiest dining scene is actually along South Howard Avenue, between West Kennedy Boulevard and the bay in affluent Hyde Park. That's where you'll find **Mise en Place,** 442 W. Kennedy Blvd., opposite the University of Tampa (© **813/254-5373;** www.miseonline.com), run by chef Marty Blitz and his wife, Maryann, the culinary darlings of Tampa since 1986. They present the freshest of ingredients, with a creative, eclectic menu that changes weekly. Main courses: $15 to $29. Hyde Park is also the home of **Bern's Steak House,** 1208 S. Howard Ave. (© **813/251-2421**), whose steaks are close to perfect. You order according to thickness and weight. Main courses: $27 to $60.

Within steps of the cruise ship piers, the 5-year-old **Channelside,** 615 Channelside Dr., adjacent to the Florida Aquarium (© **813/223-4250;** www.channelsidetampa. com), a shopping, dining, and entertainment complex, continues to grow. Worthwhile eateries include Grill 29, Stumps Supper Club, and Tinatapas.

20 Vancouver, British Columbia

Vancouver is located in the extreme southwestern corner of British Columbia and has the good fortune to be surrounded by both mountains and ocean. Major development over the past decade has ushered in a more international feel, but hasn't diminished the city's quality of life, which includes a rich Northwest Coast Native culture, a thriving Asian community, numerous summertime festivals, and a great arts scene. And those Vancouverites are just so blatantly *nice.* Maybe it's all that fresh air, and proximity to some great Great Outdoors. Who knows, but it makes us want to move here every time we visit.

Though Seattle has usurped some of Vancouver's steam over the past several years, it's still the major southern transit point for Alaska cruises, and is occasionally a port of call as well.

GETTING TO VANCOUVER & THE PORT
Most cruise ships dock at **Canada Place** (© **604/666-7200**) at the end of Burrard Street. The pier terminal is a landmark in the city, noted for its five-sail structure, which reaches into the harbor like a ship setting off. It's located at the edge of the downtown district and is just a quick stroll from the **Gastown** area (see below), with its cafes, art, and souvenir shops; and from Robson Street, where trendy fashions can be found. Right near the pier are hotels, restaurants, and shops. Most visitors arrive by plane, touching down at **Vancouver International Airport,** 8 miles south of downtown. The average taxi fare from the airport to downtown is about US$18 (C$24). **Vancouver Airporter** (© **604/946-8866**) buses also offer service one-way to the city for about US$9 (C$12) per person.

GETTING AROUND You can easily walk the downtown area of Vancouver, but if you want transportation, you've got a few options. Car-rental agencies with local branches include Avis, Budget, Hertz Canada, and Thrifty; and the **Translink system** (© **604 953 3333;** www.translink.bc.ca) includes electric buses, ferries, and the magnetic-rail SkyTrain. **Taxis** are always found around the major hotels and tourist sites.

BEST CRUISE LINE SHORE EXCURSIONS
Coastal Rainforest Adventure (US$73, 3½ hr.): This tour takes you by bus from the skyscrapers of the city to the skyscrapers of Mother Nature, heading through downtown before continuing on to Capilano Canyon, where you'll go on a 2-mile walk through the rainforest. A naturalist guide provides insight on the ecosystem as you go.

Capilano Suspension Bridge & Grouse Mountain Skyride (US$63, 3½ hr.): Visit two highlights of Vancouver, heading from sea level to 4,000 feet. Your tour begins as your bus travels across Lions Gate Bridge that spans Burrard Inlet. Once in North

Vancouver

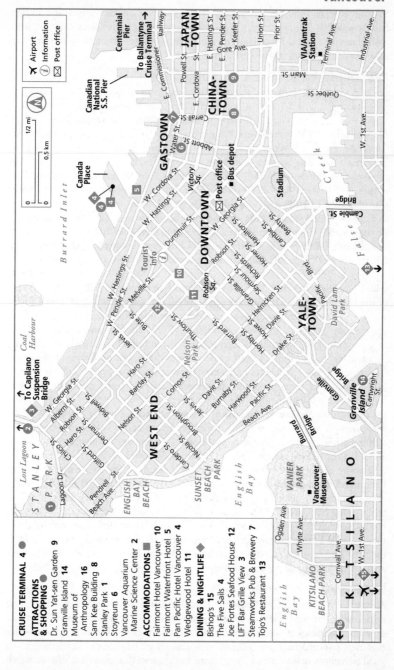

CRUISE TERMINAL 4 ●

ATTRACTIONS & SHOPPING ●
Dr. Sun Yat-sen Garden **9**
Granville Island **14**
Museum of Anthropology **16**
Sam Kee Building **8**
Stanley Park **1**
Stoyreum **6**
Vancouver Aquarium Marine Science Center **2**

ACCOMMODATIONS ■
Fairmont Hotel Vancouver **10**
Fairmont Waterfront Hotel **5**
Pan Pacific Hotel Vancouver **4**
Wedgewood Hotel **11**

DINING & NIGHTLIFE ◆
Bishop's **15**
The Five Sails **4**
Joe Fortes Seafood House **12**
LIFT Bar Grille View **3**
Steamworks Pub & Brewery **7**
Tojo's Restaurant **13**

Airport ✈
Information ⓘ
Post office ✉

0 ⌐ 1/2 mi
0 ⌐ 0.5 km

Burrard Inlet

Centennial Pier
To Ballantyne Cruise Terminal →
Canadian National S.S. Pier
E. Commissioner
Railway

JAPAN TOWN
Powell St.
E. Hastings St.
E. Pender St.
E. Gore Ave.
E. Keefer St.
E. Cordova St.

CHINA-TOWN
Union St.
Prior St.

VIA/Amtrak Station
Terminal Ave.
Industrial Ave.

GASTOWN
Water St.
Carrall St.
Abbott St.
Main St.
Québec St.

Canada Place

W. Cordova St.
W. Hastings St.
Victory Sq.
Post office ✉
Bus depot ■

DOWNTOWN
Dunsmuir St.
W. Georgia St.
Cambie St.
Beatty St.
Hamilton St.
Homer St.
Richards St.
Seymour St.
Granville St.
Howe St.
Hornby St.
Burrard St.
Thurlow St.
Bute St.
Jervis St.
Melville St.
W. Pender St.
W. Hastings St.

Stadium
Cambie St. Bridge
Creek
False Creek
W. 1st Ave.

Tourist info ⓘ
Robson Sq.
Robson St.
Helmcken St.
Davie St.
Drake St.
Pacific
Pacific Blvd.

YALE-TOWN
David Lam Park
Granville Bridge
Granville Island
Cartwright St.

Coal Harbour
To Capilano Suspension Bridge →

Lost Lagoon
STANLEY PARK
Lagoon Dr.
Chilco St.
Gilford St.
Denman St.
Bidwell St.
Cardero St.
Nicola St.
Broughton St.

W. Georgia St.
Alberni St.
Robson St.
Haro St.
Barclay St.
Nelson St.
Comox St.
Pendrell St.
Beach Ave.

WEST END
Nelson Park
Jervis St.
Burnaby St.
Harwood St.
Pacific St.
Beach Ave.

ENGLISH BAY BEACH
English Bay
SUNSET BEACH PARK

VANIER PARK
Vancouver Museum
Ogden Ave.
Whyte Ave.
Cornwall Ave.
W. 1st Ave.

KITSILANO
KITSILANO BEACH PARK
English Bay

Burrard Bridge

539

Vancouver you'll visit the narrow, historic, 450-foot Capilano Suspension Bridge, from whose 230-foot height even the towering evergreens below look tiny. From here, you'll take the Grouse Mountain Skyride to the 4,000-foot summit, where you can hike one of the nature trails or grab lunch.

EXPLORING VANCOUVER ON YOUR OWN

Located within easy walking distance of the pier, **Gastown** is named for "Gassy" Jack Deighton, who in 1867 built a saloon in Maple Tree Square (at the intersection of Water, Alexander, and Carrall sts.) to serve the area's loggers and trappers. The Gastown of today offers cobblestone streets, historic buildings, gaslights, a steam-powered clock (near the corner of Water and Cambie sts.), street musicians, and a touch of Bohemia—as well as boutiques, antiques and art shops, lots of touristy stuff, and lots of restaurants, clubs, and cafes. For something a little educational, check out **Storyeum,** 165A Water St. (© **604/685-8133;** www.storyeum.com), and learn about Canada's West Coast though a multi-media, multi-sensory, storytelling experience set in a unique underground theatre. The neighborhood is bounded by Water and Alexander streets and stretches from Richard Street east to Columbia Street.

Bordering Gastown, Vancouver's historic **Chinatown** is one of the largest in North America (though it doesn't hold a candle to those in New York and San Francisco). In addition to photogenic Chinese gates, bright-red buildings, food, open-air markets selling Chinese wares, and the 6-foot-wide **Sam Kee Building** (8 W. Pender St.), one of the big draws is the **Dr. Sun Yat-sen Garden,** 578 Carrall St. (© **604/689-7133;** www.vancouverchinesegarden.com), a perfectly traditional Chinese garden based on the yin-yang principle. Admission is US$5 (C$6.65). The Chinatown neighborhood is bordered by East Pender and Keefer streets between Carrall Street and Gore Avenue.

Just a few miles from the heart of downtown Vancouver, northwest of the cruise ship terminal, the 1,000 acres of **Stanley Park** contain rose gardens, totem poles, a yacht club, a kids' water park, miles of wooded hiking trails, and great vantage points for views of Lions Gate Bridge. The park is one of Vancouver's gems. On the grounds, the outstanding **Vancouver Aquarium Marine Science Center** (© **604/659-FISH;** www.vanaqua.org) is one of North America's largest and best, housing more than 8,000 marine species, mostly in meticulously re-created environments. Admission is about US$12 (C$16) adults, US$6 to US$10 (C$8–C$13) kids.

If you're up for a 20-minute drive west of downtown, the **University of British Columbia's Museum of Anthropology,** 6393 NW Marine Dr. (© **604/822-3825;** www.moa.ubc.ca), isn't just any old museum. In 1976, architect Arthur Erickson re-created a classic Native post-and-beam structure out of modern concrete and glass to house one of the world's finest collections of West Coast Native art. You enter through doors that resemble a huge, carved, bent-cedar box. Artifacts from potlatch ceremonies flank the ramp leading to the Great Hall's collection of totem poles and a collection of Haida artwork, including masterpieces by sculptor Bill Reid. Admission is US$5 (C$6.65).

SHOPPING

Almost a city within a city, **Granville Island** (a hearty walk southwest of the cruise docks, or an easy taxi ride) is a former industrial site whose warehouses and factories now house galleries, artist studios, restaurants, and theaters. It has so much to offer that even a day may not be enough to experience it all, but you can certainly give it a good shot. Browse for crafts, pick up some fresh seafood, enjoy a great dinner, watch some Shakespeare in the park or attend the latest theater performance, stroll along the waterfront, or simply run through the sprinkler on a hot summer day. Check the website (**www.granvilleisland.com**) for upcoming events and festivals or stop by the information center, behind the Kids Market.

Downtown, not far inland from the cruise docks, **Robson Street** is chockablock with boutiques, souvenir shops, coffeehouses, and bistros. Look for high-end fashions, with a focus on clothes for the younger set. Though a little too heavy on the knick-knack shops, Water Street and Gastown are by no means just a tacky tourist enclave. Look for antique and cutting-edge furniture, galleries of First Nations art, and funky basement retro shops.

WHERE TO STAY

Virtually all of Vancouver's downtown hotels are within walking distance of shops, restaurants, and attractions.

The **Fairmont Hotel Vancouver,** 900 W. Georgia St. (© **800/441-1414;** www.fairmont.com), is the grande dame of Vancouver's hotels. Designed on a generous scale, with a copper roof, marble interiors, and massive proportions, the hotel is all luxury and spaciousness, with marble bathrooms and mahogany furnishings in the guest rooms. Rates: from US$190 (C$253). The **Fairmont Waterfront Hotel,** 900 Canada Place Way (© **800/828-7447;** www.fairmont.com), is an ultramodern, 23-story place right on the harbor, offering spectacular waterfront and mountain views from 70% of the rooms. A concourse links the hotel to the rest of Waterfront Centre, Canada Place, and the Alaska cruise ship terminal. Rates: from US$180 (C$240).

The only boutique hotel in downtown, the **Wedgewood Hotel,** 845 Hornby St. (© **800/663-0666;** www.wedgewoodhotel.com), has racked up numerous honors thanks to its luxurious accommodations (recently renovated), stellar service, and its elegant bar—one of the best in town. The shops of Robson Street are less than a block away. Rates: from US$215 (C$287).

The **Pan Pacific Hotel Vancouver,** 300–999 Canada Place (© **800/937-1515;** www.panpac.com), sits right atop Canada Place, home of the cruise terminal and a convention center. All of the guest rooms are modern, spacious, and comfortably furnished. Try to book a harborside room so you can enjoy the view. Rates: from US$220 (C$293).

DINING & NIGHTLIFE

At **Bishop's,** 2183 W. Fourth Ave. (© **604/738-2025**), owner John Bishop makes every customer feel special, and the candlelight, white linen, and soft jazz don't hurt either. The food is even better, a mix of "contemporary home cooking" like roasted duck breast with sun-dried Okanagan Valley fruits and candied ginger glace. Main courses: US$21 to US$26 (C$28–C$35); reservations required. **The Five Sails,** 999 Canada Place Way, in the Pan Pacific Hotel (© **604/891-2892**), combines truly top-notch food and a killer view of Coal Harbour, the Lions Gate Bridge, and the mountains. Food is an eclectic mix of Thai, Mongolian, Japanese, Vietnamese, and nouvelle influences. Main courses: US$20 to US$26 (C$27–C$35). **Joe Fortes Seafood House,** 777 Thurlow St. (© **604/669-1940**), is a two-story, dark-wood restaurant with an immensely popular bar. The spacious covered and heated roof garden is pure Vancouver, and pan-roasted oysters are a menu staple. Main courses: US$14 to US$17 (C$19–C$23).

For something a little different, **LIFT Bar Grill View,** 333 Menchion Mews (© **604/689-5438;** www.liftbarandgrill.com), has not only awesome views of Coal

Harbour, Stanley Park, and the North Shore mountains, but features dishes, called "whet plates," to be shared. Sample fare such as venison with a chocolate cherry demi-glace, jumbo wild prawns with seared foie gras, and Thai curry duck confit. Main courses: $12 to $18.

For Japanese food, head to **Tojo's Restaurant,** located above an A&W burger joint at 777 W. Broadway (© **604/872-8050**). Hidekazu Tojo's sushi is Vancouver's best, attracting Japanese businessmen, Hollywood celebrities, and anyone else who's willing to pay. Tell Tojo how much you want to spend, and he'll prepare an incredible meal to fit your budget. Reservations required for the sushi bar. Main dishes from US$14 (C$19); complete sushi dinners from US$34 (C$45). Closed Sunday.

After dinner, take a walk through Gastown's cobbled streets (avoiding the panhandlers when you can), dropping in to bars like the **Steamworks Pub & Brewery,** 375 Water St. (© **604/689-2739;** www.steamworks.com), home to a dozen in-house beers and multiple rooms with different moods, from classy old pub to hot London bar to Bavarian beer hall, complete with long benches and enormous copper kettles.

The Caribbean, The Bahamas & the Panama Canal

The Caribbean is the classic cruise destination, tailored to people who want nice white-sand beaches, Tiki bars serving tropical drinks, some hot island music, and sun, sun, sun. Culture and history also have their place. In general, western Caribbean itineraries offer opportunities for visiting the ruins of Mayan cities and temple sites on the mainland, while eastern Caribbean itineraries are more likely to offer reminders of British, French, Spanish, and Dutch colonial history. Panama Canal itineraries mix the lore of that massive construction effort with rich Central American culture. And, of course, there's all that gorgeous scenery, from the lush jungles of Dominica to the arid moonscape of Aruba.

Here's the good news, though: There are hardly any lousy Caribbean islands, though depending on your likes and dislikes, you'll appreciate some more than others. Some—especially St. Thomas and Nassau—are much more touristy and commercial than others, but they'll appeal to shoppers with their large variety of bustling stores. Others—Virgin Gorda, St. John, and Jost Van Dyke, for instance—are quieter and more natural and will appeal to those who'd rather walk along a calm beach or take a drive along a lonely, winding road amid lush tropical foliage. Ports such as St. Barts and Bequia offer a low-key yachting-port atmosphere, while ports such as Key West and Cozumel are all about whooping it up.

HOME PORTS FOR THIS REGION
Though the majority of Caribbean cruises still leave from the traditional Florida ports of **Miami, Fort Lauderdale, Port Canaveral,** and to a lesser extent **Tampa,** you can also sail from Galveston and Houston, Texas; Charleston, South Carolina; Norfolk, Virginia; Jacksonville, Florida; and even New York, Baltimore, and Philadelphia. Some Caribbean islands also commonly serve as home ports, especially Puerto Rico's capital, **San Juan,** but also St. Thomas, Barbados, and others. The upside to these is that you'll start your cruise in the midst of the islands, and probably be able to visit more ports over the course of your trip. The downside is that except for San Juan, it can be more complicated and expensive to fly to these ports than to one of the mainland embarkation points.

LANGUAGE & CURRENCY Both vary by island, though English is spoken widely in all the port towns and the U.S. dollar is commonly accepted everywhere. All prices in this chapter are quoted in U.S. dollars, though we've included information on local currency in the individual reviews.

CALLING FROM THE U.S. & CANADA Most of the islands in this chapter are part of the North American Numbering Plan, meaning you call them just as you would another state or territory on the mainland, adding a "1" before the area code and local number. Where that is not the case (as with Mexico, Belize, the French islands, and so forth), dialing information is included in the port review.

SHOPPING TIPS You'll find it all here, from cheesy tourist souvenirs to jewelry (lots and lots of jewelry), perfume (ditto), and electronics, with some quality indigenous arts available too if you look hard enough. Prices vary by port. Some—such as the U.S. Virgin Islands, St. Barts, St. Martin, and Aruba—are pretty pricey, while ports such as Cozumel, Jamaica, and the Grenadines are cheaper. **Duty-free merchandise** can save you as little as 5% to as much as 50%, so if you have particular goods you're thinking of buying, it pays to check prices at your local discount retailer before you leave home so you'll know whether you're really getting a bargain. Many ports offer particularly good deals on **liquor**, though keep in mind you'll pay tax when coming back into the U.S. if you buy more than your legal limit (see the section on U.S. Customs in chapter 3 for more info).

When shopping, be aware that some items you see offered may not be allowed by U.S. Customs. You may be eyeing that gorgeous piece of **black-coral jewelry,** for instance, but laws prohibiting the trade in endangered species make it illegal to bring many products made from coral and other marine animals back to the United States. (Remember, corals aren't rocks: They're living animals—a single branch of coral contains thousands of tiny coral animals called polyps.) Sea turtles, too, are highly endangered, and sea horses, while not yet protected by laws, are currently threatened with extinction. The shopkeeper selling items made from these creatures probably won't tell you they're questionable from a Customs standpoint, but the Customs agent sure will, and may fine you or, at the very least, confiscate the item if he catches you with it. Better to buy a cheap underwater camera and take pictures of underwater beauties on a snorkeling expedition—you get the memories, the evidence, and a little exercise to boot.

Cuban cigars are also prohibited by U.S. Customs. You'll see them all over the islands, but be aware that, *legally* speaking, you have to smoke 'em before you head for home.

1 The Cruise Lines' Private Islands

Royal Caribbean, Princess, Disney, Holland America, Norwegian, and Costa all have private islands (or parts of islands) that are included as a port of call on many of their Caribbean and Bahamas itineraries. While few offer any kind of true Caribbean culture, they do offer cruisers a guaranteed beach day with all the trimmings and a more private experience than you'll get at most ports' public beaches. Note that aside from Disney's Castaway Cay, none of the islands has a large dock, so passengers are ferried ashore by tender.

CELEBRITY CRUISES See "Royal Caribbean & Celebrity Cruises," below.

COSTA CRUISES Passengers on Costa's eastern Caribbean itineraries spend 1 day at **Catalina Island,** off the coast of the Dominican Republic. This relaxing patch of paradise offers a long beach fringed by palm trees, with activities such as volleyball, beach Olympics, and snorkeling. The area adjacent to the tender dock is the busiest spot, as is to be expected, but if you walk down the beach a bit you'll get a more private, quiet experience (though the coastline gets a little rocky when you get farther out from the dock). Costa provides cruisers with floating beach mats free of charge (most lines charge for them), so you can find your quiet nirvana by paddling out to sea a way. A local island vendor rents jet skis and offers banana-boat rides, the ship's spa staff sets up a cabana to do massages on the beach, and locals often roam around offering them too. (For $25—a fraction of what the ship charges—a local woman gave Heidi a great foot and shoulder massage.) Locals also sell coconuts for $2 apiece, hacking the end off and plunking in a straw or two so you can get at the milk. After you're finished, take it back and they'll whack the thing to pieces with a machete and scrape out the tender coconut meat for you. Music and barbecue round out the day, and there's also a strip of shops hawking jewelry, beachwear, and other souvenirs.

DISNEY CRUISE LINE   A port of call on all *Disney Magic* and *Disney Wonder* cruises, 1,000-acre, 3-×-2-mile **Castaway Cay** is rimmed with idyllically clear Bahamian water and fine sandy beaches. Disney has developed less than 10% of the island, but in that 10% guests can swim and snorkel, rent bikes and boats, get their hair braided ($2 per braid for corn rows), shop, send postcards, have a massage, or just lounge in a hammock or on the beach. Barbecue burgers, ribs, fish, and chicken are available at Cookie's Bar-B-Q, and several bars are scattered around near the beaches.

The island's best quality is its accessibility. Unlike the other private islands, which require ships to anchor offshore and shuttle passengers back and forth on tenders, Castaway Cay's dock allows *Magic* and *Wonder*'s guests to just step right off the ship and walk or take a shuttle tram to the island's attractions. Families can head to their own beach, lined with lounge chairs and pastel-colored umbrellas, where they can swim, explore a 12-acre snorkeling course, climb around on the offshore water-play structures, or rent a kayak, paddle boat, banana boat, sailboat, or other beach equipment. Teens have a beach of their own, where they can play volleyball, soccer, or tetherball; go on a "Wild Side" bike, snorkel, and kayak adventure; or design, build, and race their own boats. Parents who want some quiet time can drop preteens at Scuttle's Cove, a supervised children's activity center for ages 3 to 12 where activities include arts and crafts, music and theater, and scavenger hunts. An excavation site here allows kids to go on their own archaeological dig and make plaster molds of what they find—including a 35-foot reproduction of a whale skeleton. Meanwhile, Mom and Dad can walk, bike, or hop the shuttle to quiet, secluded Serenity Bay, a mile-long stretch of beach in the northwest part of the island, at the end of an old airstrip decorated with vintage prop planes for a 1940s feel. Twenty-five- and 50-minute massages are available here in private cabanas open to a sea view on one side (sign up for your appointment at the onboard spa on the 1st day of your cruise to ensure that you get a spot), and the Castaway Air Bar serves up drinks. Heidi sampled a piña colada and a deep tissue massage at Serenity Bay while her kids were back in the nursery aboard the *Wonder,* and she gives it a giant thumbs up.

Adult- and child-size bicycles can be rented for $6. A 2½-mile out-and-back bike/walking path begins at Serenity Bay, but don't go looking for scenery or wildlife—at best, all you'll see will be the occasional bird or leaping lizard. Parasailing is available for $70 (45 min., airborne 7–9 min.; over age 8 only). All-terrain strollers with canopies and beach wheelchairs are available free of charge.

HOLLAND AMERICA LINE   Located on the Bahamian island of San Salvador, 2,500-acre **Half Moon Cay** is a port of call on most of HAL's Caribbean and Panama Canal cruises (in fact, the line is considering offer two calls to the island on some cruises). The sand here is ultra soft (great for young feet), so go ahead and lay right

The Gulf of Mexico & the Caribbean

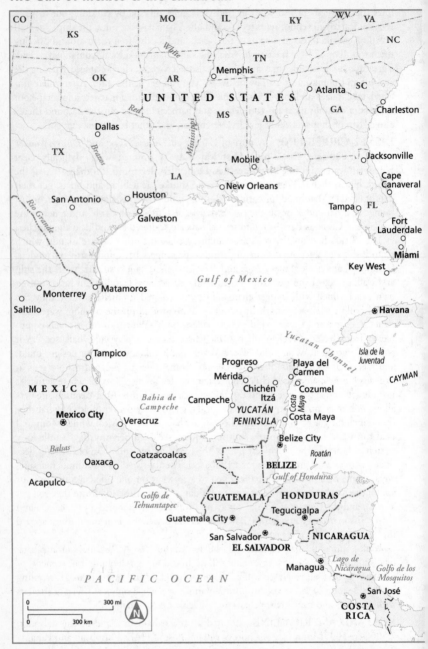

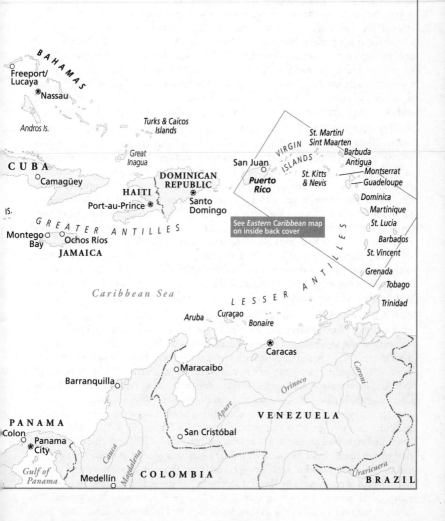

Bermuda

ATLANTIC OCEAN

BAHAMAS

Freeport/
Lucaya

✹Nassau

Andros Is.

Turks & Caicos
Islands

Great
Inagua

CUBA

Camagüey

HAITI

Port-au-Prince ✹

DOMINICAN
REPUBLIC
✹
Santo
Domingo

San Juan

Puerto
Rico

VIRGIN
ISLANDS

St. Martin/
Sint Maarten

Barbuda
Antigua
Montserrat
Guadeloupe

St. Kitts
& Nevis

Dominica

Martinique

St. Lucia

Barbados

St. Vincent

Grenada

Tobago

Trinidad

See *Eastern Caribbean* map
on inside back cover

GREATER   ANTILLES

Montego
Bay

Ochos Ríos

JAMAICA

IS.

LESSER   ANTILLES

Caribbean Sea

Aruba

Curaçao

Bonaire

✹Caracas

Maracaibo

Barranquilla

Orinoco

Caroní

VENEZUELA

Apure

PANAMA

Colon

Panama
City

San Cristóbal

Gulf of
Panama

Cauca

Medellín

Magdalena

COLOMBIA

Uraricuera

BRAZIL

547

down in it or flop on one of the many beach chairs or under a blue canvas sun shade (though you'll have to rent it; they're in limited supply). For something a bit more active, enjoy some of Half Moon's new enhancements. Families will appreciate the new water park at one end of the beach (closest to the tender pier) where there are three water slides on the sand for young children (Heidi's boys loved them!) as well as three more for teens. Just offshore in the shallow turquoise sea, a cluster of floating toy animals—including a crocodile, shark, and octopus—are tethered to the seafloor and perfect for climbing. Other highlights of the beach area include new massage huts as well as air-conditioned, beachfront cabanas available for rent; geared to big spenders, a couple hundred bucks will buy you butler service and an open bar. Away from the main beach area and accessible via a short tram ride, several new shore excursion opportunities include horseback riding ($59 includes a scenic trail ride and a gallop through the surf) and a stingray excursion. Polar opposite from the free-for-all vibe of Grand Cayman's popular Stingray City (see "Grand Cayman," later in this chapter), here just 26 stingrays are corralled in a 150×75-square-foot pen for groups of only 38 guests at a time to pet and feed ($39 per person). You can also sign up for windsurfing, snorkeling, kayaking, scuba diving, deep-sea fishing, parasailing, sailboarding, or aqua-cycling. Half Moon Cay also boasts lunch facilities, several bars, a playground, and even nature trails through a wild bird preserve at a remote part of the island.

NORWEGIAN CRUISE LINE   NCL's private island, **Great Stirrup Cay,** is a stretch of palm-studded beachfront in the southern Bahamas, and was the very first private resort developed by a cruise line in the Caribbean. It's also the most cramped of the cruise line private islands, and part of the shoreline is very rocky. Still, after a piña colada—or two—you probably won't notice its flaws. Rest assured, the bar, lunch, and watersports facilities are hopping, as the sleepy beach turns into an instant party whenever one of the NCL vessels is in port. Music is either broadcast or performed live, barbecues are fired up, hammocks are strung between palms, and there's a definite beach buzz that takes over. Passengers can ride paddle boats, sail Sunfish, go snorkeling or parasailing, hop on a banana boat, join a game of volleyball in the three deep sand courts, get a massage at one of the beachside stations (though they're not very private or quiet), or do nothing more than sunbathe all day long. For kids, organized activities include volleyball tournaments and sandcastle building.

PRINCESS CRUISES   Most of Princess's eastern and western Caribbean itineraries offer a stop at **Princess Cays,** the line's "private island" (a misnomer; as it's really a 40-acre strip off the southwestern coast of Eleuthera in The Bahamas, pretty much cut off from the rest of the island). Along with Holland America's Half Moon Cay, the sand at Princess Cays is among the softest you'll find in the Bahamas. The half-mile of shoreline allows passengers to swim, snorkel, and make use of Princess's fleet of Hobie Cats, Sunfish, banana boats, kayaks, and paddle-wheelers. (If you want to rent watersports equipment, be sure to book it aboard ship or even online, before your cruise, to ensure that you get what you want.) There's also live music, a dance area, and a beach barbecue, and anyone who wants to get away from it all (or sleep off too many rum punches) can head for the several dozen great tree-shaded hammocks at the far end of the beach. For kids, there's a supervised play area with a sandbox and a pirate-ship-themed playground. The Princess shop sells T-shirts and other clothing plus souvenirs of the mug-and-key-chain variety, and local vendors set up stands around the island to sell conch shells, shell anklets, straw bags, and other crafts, and to offer hair braiding.

ROYAL CARIBBEAN & CELEBRITY CRUISES   Many ships of sister lines Royal Caribbean and Celebrity stop for a day at one or another of the line's two private beach resorts, CocoCay and Labadee. At **CocoCay** (aka Little Stirrup Cay), an otherwise uninhabited 140-acre landfall in The Bahamas' Berry Islands, you'll find lots of beach, hammocks, food, drink, and watersports, plus such activities as limbo contests, water-balloon tosses, relay races, and volleyball tournaments. Kids, big and small, will like the aqua park that includes a floating trampoline, water slides, and a sunken airplane and schooner for snorkelers. For something quieter, head for Wanderer's Beach; it's a longer walk from the tender pier than the other beaches, so it tends to be less crowded and quieter. Its calm surf and ultra soft sand make it perfect for families with young children.

Labadee, an isolated, sun-flooded, 270-acre peninsula along Haiti's north coast, is so completely tourist-oriented that you'd never know it was attached to the rest of poverty-stricken Haiti.

Labadee is a rarity among cruise lines' private islands in that it gives you a real glimpse of island culture. At the straightforwardly named "Folkloric Show," a large, colorfully costumed troupe performs Haiti's distinctly African brand of dancing, drumming, and song, while bands at the various bars and restaurants perform the kind of acoustic guitar, banjo, and percussion "mento" music that was a precursor to reggae and other Caribbean styles. It's happy stuff, creating a wonderfully relaxed soundtrack for the whole island. Five beaches are spread around the peninsula, and are progressively less crowded the farther you walk from the dock, where enormous tenders make the short ride to and from the ship. In the Columbus Cove area, a children's aqua-park called Arawak Cay is full of floating trampolines, inflatable iceberg-shaped slides, and water seesaws. Kayaking and parasailing are offered from a dock nearby. At the center of the peninsula, the Haitian Market and Artisan's Market are the port's low points, full of cheesy Africanesque statues and carvings, with touts trying to lure you in with "Sir, let me just show you something over here." Steer clear unless you're desperate for a souvenir. When we were here last, a painter near the dock had much more interesting work for sale.

On both Labadee and CocoCay, organized children's activities include beach parties, volleyball, seashell collecting, and sand-castle building.

2 Antigua

Though it's the largest of the British Leeward Islands, Antigua (pronounced "An-*tee*-gah") is still only 23km (14 miles) long and 18km (11 miles) wide, and offers a much more laid-back experience than you'll get at some of the glitzier Caribbean islands. Nice, relaxing beaches are close to port, and St. John's, the island's capital and main town, is sleepy and undemanding, full of cobblestone sidewalks and weather-beaten wooden houses. Close to port, you can shop lazily in historic, restored warehouses, while away from St. John's, the rolling, rustic island boasts important historic sites. Nelson's Dockyard, for example, was once Britain's main naval station in the Lesser Antilles, and is now a well-maintained national park.

COMING ASHORE   Most cruise ships dock at the **Nevis Street Pier** or **Heritage Quay** (pronounced "Key"), both located in St. John's, the island's only town of any size. From there, you can either walk or take a short taxi ride into town. A handful of smaller vessels drop anchor at English Harbour, on the south coast.

GETTING AROUND   Most of the major attractions here are beyond walking distance. **Taxis** meet every cruise ship. Although meters are nonexistent, rates are fixed by the government, and are posted at the taxi stand at the end of Heritage Quay's pedestrian mall. Drivers often double as tour guides for about $20 per hour for up to four people, with a 2-hour minimum. Tip between 10% and 15% for all rides. Privately operated **buses** are cheaper (little more than $1 to almost anywhere on the island), but service is erratic. Avis, Budget, Hertz, and National all offer **rental cars** on the island, but driving is on the left, signage is inadequate, and you have to buy a $20 temporary driving permit.

LANGUAGE & CURRENCY   The language is **English,** often spoken with a musical West Indian lilt. The Eastern Caribbean dollar (EC$2.72 = US$1; EC$1 = US37¢) is Antigua's official currency, but the U.S. dollar is readily accepted.

BEST CRUISE LINE SHORE EXCURSIONS

Nelson's Dockyard National Park Tour ($46–$59, 3–4½ hr.): After traversing the island's hilly countryside, you'll visit the site of the planet's last surviving, working Georgian dockyard. Many colonial buildings still stand, including forts, residences, and barracks; and several have been converted into restaurants, hotels, shops, and museums. The sea vistas are impressive.

Helicopter to Montserrat Volcano ($240–$261, 2 hr.): In December 1997, the Soufrierre Hills Volcano on the neighboring island of Montserrat blew its top, spewing lava and ash over a huge area and burying large swaths of the island, including the former capital, Plymouth. This trip takes you over both the volcano and the charbroiled highlights of Montserrat's exclusion zone, the area declared off-limits to ground transportation.

Off Road 4x4 Jeep Safari Adventure ($52–$67, 3½–4 hr.): Tour the island's only remaining rainforest via a four-wheel-drive vehicle, and stop at the ruins of forts, sugar mills, and plantation houses. The excursion includes beach time.

Hiking Safari Adventure ($49, 3 hr.): This 4-mile uphill/downhill hike takes you through Antigua's rainforest, offering a panoramic view from one of the island's highest peaks (360m/1,200 ft.).

Jolly Roger Pirate Cruise ($45, 3½ hr.): Aboard this wooden "pirate ship," you can take in some of the island's coastal sights, snorkel, dance on the poop deck, limbo, and walk the plank.

ON YOUR OWN: WITHIN WALKING DISTANCE

St. John's has a few attractions as well as shopping (see below) that can be easily reached on foot. The **Museum of Antigua and Barbuda,** at the intersection of Market Street and Long Street (© **268/462-1469**), traces the history of the nation from its geological birth to the present day. Housed in the neoclassic former courthouse, built in 1750, its exhibits include pre-Columbian tools and artifacts, a replica of an Arawak wattle-and-daub hut, African-Caribbean pottery, and sections dedicated to the island's naval, sugar, and slavery eras. It's open Monday to Friday from 8:30am to 4pm; Saturday from 10am to 2pm. Admission is free, but a donation of $2 is requested. A couple of blocks uphill from the museum, bordered by Church, Long, and Newgate streets, **St. John's Anglican Cathedral** dominates St. John's skyline with its 21m (70-ft.) aluminum-capped twin spires. The original St. John's, a simple wooden structure built in 1681, was replaced in 1720 by a brick building, which was destroyed during an 1843 earthquake. Upon its completion in 1847, the present baroque structure was not universally appreciated: Ecclesiastical architects criticized it as being like "a pagan temple with two dumpy pepper pot towers." The cavernous interior is entirely encased in pitch pine, a construction method intended to secure the building from hurricanes and earthquakes.

ON YOUR OWN: BEYOND THE PORT AREA

One of the major historical attractions of the eastern Caribbean, **Nelson's Dockyard National Park** (© 268/481-5021) lies 18km (11 miles) southeast of St. John's, alongside one of the world's best-protected natural harbors. English ships used the site as a refuge from hurricanes as early as 1671, and the dockyard played a major role during the 18th century, an era of privateers, pirates, and great sea battles. Admiral Nelson's headquarters from 1784 to 1787, the restored dockyard today remains the only Georgian naval base still in use. At its heart, the **Dockyard Museum,** housed in a former Naval Officers' House built in 1855, traces the history of the site from its beginning as a British Navy stronghold to its development as a national park and yachting center. Nautical memorabilia comprise much of the display. Uphill and east of the Dockyard, the **Dow's Hill Interpretation Center** (© 268/481-5045) features an entertaining 15-minute multimedia overview of Antiguan history and an observation platform that affords a 360-degree view of the park. Farther uphill, Palladian arches mark the **Blockhouse,** a military fortification built in 1787 that included officers' quarters and a powder magazine. For an eagle's-eye view of English Harbour, continue to the hill's summit, to the **Shirley Heights Lookout.** Fortified to defend the precious cargo in the harbor below, Fort Shirley's barracks, arched walkways, batteries, and powder magazines are scattered around the hilltop. The Lookout, with its view of the French island of Guadeloupe, was the main signal station used to warn of approaching hostile ships.

The grounds of the national park, which represent 10% of Antigua's total land area, are well worth exploring. Bordered on one side by sandy beaches, the park is blanketed in cactus, tamarind, cinnamon, and turpentine trees, and mangroves that shelter African cattle egrets. An array of **nature trails,** which take anywhere from 30 minutes to 5 hours to walk, meander through the vegetation and offer vistas of the coast. One trail climbs to **Fort Berkeley,** built in 1704 to protect the harbor's entrance. Admission, which is $5 for adults (children under 12 are free), covers the Dockyard, the Dockyard Museum, Dow's Hill Interpretation Center, the Blockhouse, Shirley Heights, and the rest of the park. The complex is open daily from 9am to 5pm, and is within walking distance of cruise ships that dock at English Harbor. Free guided tours of the dockyard last 15 to 20 minutes; tipping is discretionary.

If you've worked up an appetite, the Dockyard's rustic **Admiral's Inn** (© 268/460-1027) offers lunches that usually include pumpkin soup and main courses like local red snapper, grilled steak, and lobster. Built in 1788, the restored brick building originally stored barrels of pitch, turpentine, and lead used to repair ships. Lunch prices run from $12 up.

To see what's billed as the only operational 18th-century sugar mill in the Caribbean, visit **Betty's Hope,** not far from Pares village on the island's east side (© 268/462-1469). On-site are twin mills, the remnants of a boiling house, and a small visitor center, which opens its doors Tuesday through Saturday from 10am till 3pm. Gardeners should be able to spot golden seal bushes, neem trees, and wild tamarinds on the rolling hills. Serene cows saunter lazily on the grounds.

Not far from Betty's Hope, on the extreme eastern tip of the island, **Devil's Bridge** is one of Antigua's most picturesque natural wonders. Over the centuries, powerful Atlantic breakers, gathering strength over the course of their 4,830km (3,000-mile) run from Africa, have carved out a natural arch in the limestone coastline and created blowholes through which the surf spurts skyward at high tide.

Another option for nature lovers, **Wallings Conservation Area** is Antigua's largest remaining tract of tropical rainforest. Located in the southwest, this lush wilderness area features three hiking trails and numerous opportunities to spot wildlife (including many Caribbean birds) and rich vegetation. If you've spent your day at Nelson's Dockyard, pass through the area on the way back to your ship via the circular Fig Tree Drive. Although plagued with potholes, this is the island's most scenic drive. It winds through the tropical forest, passing fishing villages, frisky goats, and old sugar mills along the way.

BEACHES

Antiguans claim that the island is home to 365 beaches, one for each day of the year. True or not, all of them are public, and quite a few are spectacular. Closest to St. John's, **Fort James Beach,** located 5 minutes and a $7 cab fare from the cruise dock, is popular with both locals and tourists. There's volleyball and cricket pretty much daily, and umbrellas and beach chairs are available for rent. For a change of pace, hike up the hill to explore the authentically derelict ruins of Fort James, which once protected St. John's harbor. A bit farther north, a $10 cab ride from the dock, the half-mile beach at **Dickenson Bay** is the island's most bustling, with numerous hotels, restaurants, and watersports vendors. The water is calm, and chairs and umbrellas are available for rent. If you crave complete peace and quiet, head to Antigua's most beautiful beach, at **Half Moon Bay,** isolated at the island's southeast extreme. Waves at the beach's center are great for bodysurfing, while the quieter eastern side is better for children and snorkeling. A restaurant and bar are near the parking lot.

Antigua's **dive sites** include reefs, wall drops, caves, and shipwrecks. To arrange a dive contact **Dive Antigua,** at the north end of Dickenson Bay ((C) **268/462-3483**). A two-tank dive is $79. Reef snorkeling is $30.

SHOPPING

To your right as you leave the docks, **Redcliffe Quay** is Antigua's most interesting shopping complex. Most of the sugar, coffee, and tobacco produced on the island in years past was stored in the warehouses here, and today the restored buildings house an array of boutiques and restaurants. For more local color, turn right (south) once you've reached Market Street and walk 5 blocks to the **Public Market,** which is a good place to sample locally produced fruits and vegetables or to pick up some Antiguan pottery or baskets. Other shopping districts include **Heritage Quay,** right at the dock (home to some 40 duty-free shops) and **St. Mary's Street.**

3 Aruba

Located only 20 miles north of Venezuela, arid Aruba has unwaveringly sunny skies, warm temperatures, and cooling breezes, along with some of the best beaches in the Caribbean, scuba diving, snorkeling, windsurfing, and all the other watersports you'd expect. Away from the beach, Aruba's full of cactus, iguanas, and strange boulder formations. Contrasting sharply with the southern shoreline's beaches, the north coast features craggy limestone cliffs, sand dunes, and crashing breakers. Focused on shopping? The concentration of stores and malls in Oranjestad, the island's capital, is as

impressive as any in the Caribbean. In between purchases, try your luck at one of the island's dozen casinos; two are just steps away from your ship. Aruba's still part of the Netherlands, so there's a Dutch influence, which adds a nice European flavor. Though it has a few small museums, and some centuries-old indigenous rock glyphs and paintings, nobody comes to Aruba for culture or history.

COMING ASHORE Cruise ships arrive at the **Aruba Port Authority,** a modern terminal with a tourist information booth, phones, ATMs, and plenty of shops. From the pier it's a 5-minute walk to the shopping districts of downtown Oranjestad.

GETTING AROUND You'll need transportation to get to most of the beaches. **Taxis** line up at the dock to take you wherever you want to go. Fares are fixed, and every driver has a copy of the official rate schedule (to the beach resorts, it's generally $8–$10). Excellent roads connect major tourist attractions, and all the major **car-rental** companies accept valid U.S. or Canadian driver's licenses. Avis, Budget, Dollar, Hertz, and National all have offices here. There's also good daily **bus service** offering round-trip $2 trips between the beach hotels and Oranjestad. The bus terminal is across the street from the cruise terminal on L. G. Smith Boulevard. Have exact change.

LANGUAGE & CURRENCY   The official language is **Dutch,** but nearly everybody speaks **English.** Spanish and Papiamento are also widely spoken. The **Aruba florin** (AFl) is the official currency (1.77 AFl to US$1; 1 AFl = US56¢), but U.S. dollars are as widely accepted.

CALLING FROM THE U.S.   When calling Aruba from the U.S., dial the international access code **(011)** before the numbers listed in this section.

BEST CRUISE LINE SHORE EXCURSIONS

In addition to the tours described here, cruise lines typically offer about a dozen snorkeling, diving, sailing, and other water-oriented tours.

Off-Road Jeep Adventure ($65–$74; 4½–5 hr.): Take off into Aruba's backcountry in a convoy of four-passenger SUVs, with you behind the wheel and in radio contact with your guide. A stop is made for lunch and swimming.

Island Bike Adventure ($47, 3½ hr.): Explore Aruba's undeveloped northeast coast by mountain bike, pedaling 10 miles and visiting the Natural Bridge (cut by the sea and wind), the Bushiribana Gold Mine, the Alto Vista Chapel, and the California Lighthouse.

Aruba Bar & Pub Crawl ($52, 4 hr.): Travel by antique bus to five different local pubs along the beach, in the countryside, and on Oranjestad's streets, with one free drink included at each. After being dropped off at Carlos 'n Charlie's, you're on your own to get back to the ship. Good luck.

Atlantis Submarine Adventure ($89, 1½ hr.): Cruise 150 feet below the sea in a submarine. During the gentle descent, you'll pass by scuba divers, coral reefs, shipwrecks, and hundreds of curious sergeant majors, damselfish, parrotfish, and angelfish.

ON YOUR OWN: WITHIN WALKING DISTANCE

Aruba's capital has a sunny Caribbean demeanor, with Dutch colonial buildings painted in vivid colors. The main thoroughfare, **L. G. Smith Boulevard,** runs along the waterfront and is crowded with marinas, shopping malls, restaurants, and bars. The harbor is packed with fishing boats and schooners docked next to stalls, where vendors hawk fruits, vegetables, and fish. Two **casinos**—the elegant, 24-hour **Crystal Casino** at the Aruba Renaissance Beach Resort, L. G. Smith Blvd. 82 (© **297/58-36000**), and the less assuming **Seaport Casino,** L. G. Smith Blvd. 9 (© **297/58-36000**)—are located steps from the dock.

For a dash of culture, head to one of the town's small museums, which are open on weekdays only. Squeezed between St. Franciscus Roman Catholic Church and the parish rectory, the small **Archaeological Museum of Aruba,** J. E. Irausquinplein 2A (© **297/58-28979**), highlights the island's Amerindian heritage, with pottery vessels, shell and stone tools, burial urns, and skulls and bones on display; admission is free. There is talk of relocating the museum to a historic building closer to the center of town; call before you plan a visit. To defend the island against pirates, the Dutch erected **Fort Zoutman** in 1796, and added a tower in 1867. Since 1992, the complex has housed the modest **Museo Arubano,** Zoutmanstraat z/n (© **297/58-26099**), which displays prehistoric Amerindian artifacts and remnants from the Dutch-colonial period; admission is $1.75. The small **Numismatic Museum of Aruba,** opposite the cruise ship terminal and next to Royal Plaza (© **297/58-28831**), has meticulous home-made exhibits telling the history of the world through coins, with 35,000 different speci-mens from more than 400 countries; admission is 5 florins and includes a brief tour.

ON YOUR OWN: TOURING BY RENTAL JEEP

The best way to see Aruba's desertlike terrain is to rent a four-wheel-drive vehicle. Car-rental companies have maps highlighting the best routes to reach the attractions. Here's one popular route.

Following the system of roads that traces the perimeter of the island, start clockwise from Oranjestad. Drive past the hotel strip, toward the island's northwesternmost point. Here, the **California Lighthouse** affords sweeping 360-degree views of spec-tacular scenery—gentle sand dunes, rocky coral shoreline, and turbulent waves. The picturesque lighthouse gets its name from the *California,* a passenger ship that sank off the nearby coast in 1916. From here on, your adventure will take you into the island's moonlike terrain, past heaps of giant boulders and barren rocky coastline. The well-maintained road that links the hotel strip with Oranjestad deteriorates abruptly into a band of rubble, and the calm, turquoise sea turns rough and rowdy.

By the time you reach the **Alto Vista Chapel,** about 8km (5 miles) from the light-house, chances are you'll already be coated with red dust that'll contrast nicely with the quaint pale-yellow church, built by native Indians and Spanish settlers in 1750, before the island had its own priest. It was the island's first chapel.

Farther along the northern coast, you'll approach the hulking ruins of the **Bushiribana Gold Smelter.** Built in 1872, its massive stone walls are remnants of Aruba's gold-mining 19th century. Climb the multitiered interior for impressive sea views. Too bad the walls have been marred with artless graffiti. Within view of the smelter, **Natural Bridge** is Aruba's most photographed attraction. Rising 7.5m (25 ft.) above the sea and spanning 30m (100 ft.) of rock-strewn waters, this limestone arch has been carved out over the centuries by the relentless pounding of the surf.

Next, head toward the center of the island and the bizarre **Ayó and Casibari rock formations.** Looking like something out of *The Flintstones,* the gargantuan Ayó rocks served Aruba's early inhabitants as a dwelling or religious site. The reddish-brown pet-roglyphs on the boulders suggest mystical significance.

Farther east, back along the northern coast, **Arikok National Park,** Aruba's show-case ecological preserve, sprawls over roughly 20% of the island. Its premier attrac-tions are a series of caves that punctuate the cliff sides of the area's mesas. The most popular, **Fontein Cave,** has brownish-red drawings left by Amerindians and graffiti etched by early European settlers. Nearby **Quadirikiri Cave** boasts two large cham-bers with roof openings that allow sunlight in, making flashlights unnecessary. Hun-dreds of small bats use the 30m-long (100-ft.) tunnel to reach their nests deeper in the cave. You'll need a flashlight (rentable at the entrance; be sure to ask for spare bat-teries so you're not left in the dark halfway through) to explore the 90m (300-ft.) pas-sageway of **Baranca Sunu,** another cave in the area commonly known as the Tunnel of Love because of its heart-shaped entrance.

Heading southeast toward Aruba's behemoth oil refinery, you'll eventually come to **Baby Beach,** at the island's easternmost point. Like a great big bathtub, this shallow bowl of warm turquoise water is protected by an almost complete circle of rock, and is a great place for a dip after a sweaty day behind the wheel.

BEACHES

All of Aruba's beaches are public, but chairs and shade huts are hotel property. If you use them, expect to be charged. Shade huts located at beaches where there are no hotels are free of charge. **Palm Beach,** home of Aruba's glamorous high-rise hotels, is great for swimming, sunbathing, sailing, people-watching, fishing, and snorkeling. It has two piers and numerous watersports operators, and can get crowded. Separated from Palm Beach by a limestone outcrop, **Eagle Beach** stretches as far as the eye can see. The sugar-white sand and gentle surf are ideal for swimming, and though the nearby hotels offer watersports and beach activities, the ambience is relaxed and quiet. A couple of bars punctuate the expansive strand, and shaded picnic areas are provided for the public. Well-protected **Baby Beach** (see above) is a prime destination for families with young children.

The island's best **snorkeling sites** are around Malmok Beach (also a great **windsurfing** spot) and Boca Catalina, where the water is calm and shallow and marine life is plentiful. **Dive sites** stretch along the entire southern coast, but most divers head for the German freighter *Antilla,* which was scuttled during World War II off the island's northwestern tip, near Palm Beach. The island's largest watersports operators, **Pelican Adventures** (✆ 297/58-63271) and **Red Sail Sports** (✆ 297/58-72302), offer sailing, windsurfing, and water-skiing in addition to one- and two-tank dives ($63 and $89) and snorkeling trips ($38 for 2½ hr., $59 for 4½ hr., champagne brunch sometimes included).

SHOPPING

Caya G. F. Betico Croes (aka Main St.) is the city's major shopping venue, running roughly parallel to the waterfront several blocks inland. **Renaissance Mall** and **Renaissance Marketplace,** right downtown, feature more than 130 stores, 2 casinos, 20 restaurants and cafes, and a movie theater. Just down the road, **Royal Plaza Mall** is chock-full of popular restaurants and generally upscale boutiques. Because the island is part of the Netherlands, **Dutch goods** such as Delft porcelain, chocolate, and cheese are especially good buys. Items from Indonesia, another former Dutch colony, are reasonably priced too. Skin- and hair-care products made from locally produced aloe are also popular and practical. If you're looking for big-ticket items, Aruba offers the usual array of watches, cameras, gold and diamond jewelry, Cuban cigars, premium liquor, English and German china, porcelain, French and American fragrances, and crystal, and its 3.3% duty and lack of sales tax make for some decent prices.

4 Bahamas: Nassau & Freeport

Nassau and Freeport are some of the busiest cruise ports on the Caribbean circuit, even though technically The Bahamas aren't in the Caribbean at all—they're in the Atlantic, north of the Caribbean and less than a hundred miles from Miami. Though holdovers from Great Britain's long colonial occupation linger in some architecture and culture, the vibe here isn't all that much different from parts of Florida, and the ports are totally tourist-oriented, with more shopping than the Mall of America, all surrounded by beaches and casinos.

LANGUAGE & CURRENCY   **English** is the official language of The Bahamas. Its legal tender is the **Bahamian dollar (B$1),** whose value is always the same as that of the U.S. dollar. Both currencies are accepted everywhere on the islands.

Nassau

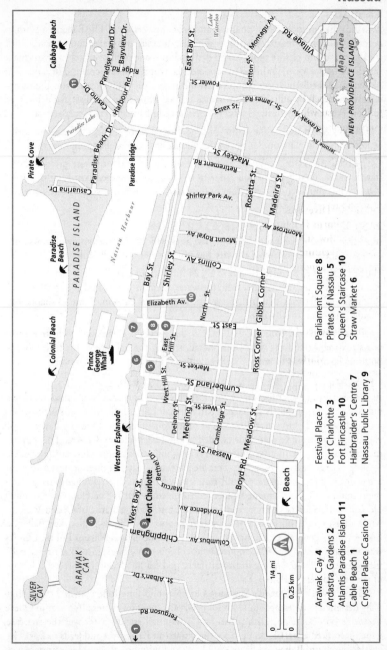

Cabbage Beach

Pirate Cove

Paradise Beach

Colonial Beach

PARADISE ISLAND

Nassau Harbour

Paradise Bridge

Paradise Lake

Casino Dr.
Paradise Island Dr.
Bayview Dr.
Ridge Rd.
Harbour Dr.
Paradise Rd.
Paradise Beach Dr.
Casuarina Dr.

Lake Waterloo

Montagu Av.
Village Rd.
East Bay St.
Fowler St.
Sutton St.
St. James Rd.
Arawak Av.
Jerome Av.
Essex St.
Mackey St.
Retirement Rd.
Shirley Park Av.
Rosetta St.
Madeira St.
Montrose Av.
Mount Royal Av.
Collins Av.
Shirley St.
Bay St.
Elizabeth Av.
North St.
East St.
Gibbs Corner
Ross Corner
East Hill St.
Market St.
Cumberland St.
West Hill St.
West St.
Meeting St.
Delancy St.
Cambridge St.
Meadow St.
Nassau St.
Boyd Rd.
Providence Av.
Marcus
Bethel Dr.
Chippingham
Columbus Av.
St. Alban's Dr.
Ferguson Rd.

Prince George Wharf

Western Esplanade

West Bay St.
Fort Charlotte

ARAWAK CAY

SILVER CAY

NEW PROVIDENCE ISLAND
Map Area

Beach

N

1/4 mi
0.25 km
0

Arawak Cay **4**
Ardastra Gardens **2**
Atlantis Paradise Island **11**
Cable Beach **1**
Crystal Palace Casino **1**

Festival Place **7**
Fort Charlotte **3**
Fort Fincastle **10**
Hairbraider's Centre **7**
Nassau Public Library **9**

Parliament Square **8**
Pirates of Nassau **5**
Queen's Staircase **10**
Straw Market **6**

557

NASSAU

Nassau is the cultural, social, political, and economic center of The Bahamas. With its beaches, shopping, resorts, casinos, historic landmarks, and water and land activities, it's also the island chain's most visited destination—one million travelers a year make their way to the town, and Nassau is one of the world's busiest cruise ship ports. The Nassau/Paradise Island area comprises two separate islands. Nassau is on the northeastern shore of 21-mile New Providence Island, while tiny Paradise Island is linked to New Providence by bridges, and protects Nassau harbor for a 3-mile stretch.

COMING ASHORE   The cruise ship docks at **Prince George Wharf** are in the center of town at Rawson Square, in the middle of Nassau's shopping frenzy.

GETTING AROUND   Walk. The major attractions and stores are pretty concentrated, and if you're really fit you can even trek over to Cable Beach or Paradise Island. (Otherwise, you'll have no problem finding taxis—they'll find you.) There's no good reason to rent a car here.

BEST CRUISE LINE SHORE EXCURSIONS

In addition to the excursions below, cruise lines typically offer a variety of snorkeling, diving, and boat tours. Avoid the city bus tours, which are dull, dull, dull.

Harbor Cruise & Atlantis Resort ($42, 2½ hr.): A tour boat with a local guide shows you the sights (such as they are) from the water, then drops you at the fanciful Atlantis Resort for a brief tour that includes a visit to Predator Lagoon, home to sharks, barracuda, and other toothy fish.

Thriller Powerboat Tour ($50, 1 hr.): A thrill-seeker's excursion, with high-speed boats roaring around the waters off Nassau, scaring the hell out of the fish. Not our personal favorite way to see . . . well, anything, but it sure is fast. Vroom.

ON YOUR OWN: WITHIN WALKING DISTANCE

As you exit from the cruise ship wharf into the main port area, you'll have no choice but to pass through **Festival Place,** a barnlike hall full of little shops and stalls selling arts and crafts, T-shirts, hot sauces, and other touristy items. Outside, hawkers will encourage you to have your hair braided at the **Hairbraider's Centre.** This government-sponsored open-air pavilion attracts braiding experts from all over the island.

Shopping is *the* thing here, but there are a few other sites of interest. Just across Bay Street from Rawson Square (inland from the wharf) are the flamingo-pink government buildings of **Parliament Square,** constructed in 1815. The House of Assembly, old colonial Secretary's Office, and Supreme Court flank a statue of Queen Victoria, while a bust on the north side of the square honors Sir Milo B. Butler, The Bahamas' first governor-general. One block inland, the pink, octagonal **Nassau Public Library** was built as a prison in 1798, and today its collection of books, historical prints, colonial documents, and Arawak Indian artifacts are kept in what were once cells. It's one of the city's oldest buildings.

Slaves carved the **Queen's Staircase** out of a solid limestone cliff in 1793. Originally designed as an escape route for soldiers, each step now represents a year in Queen Victoria's 65-year reign. Lush plants and a waterfall stand guard over the staircase, which is located a few blocks up from the library on East Street and leads to **Fort Fincastle,** Elizabeth Avenue, built in 1793 by Lord Dunmore, the royal governor. An elevator climbs a 38m-high (126-ft.) water tower, where you can look down on the arrowhead-shaped fort. Walk around on your own or hire a guide.

At the corny **Pirates of Nassau museum** at King and George streets (© **242/356-3759;** www.pirates-of-nassau.com), Captain Teach and his fearsome crew guide you through the age of piracy in the lawless Nassau of 1716. Admission is a steep $12 for adults—only worth it if you're with kids, as each adult may bring two children under 12 free; each additional child is $6.

ON YOUR OWN: BEYOND THE PORT AREA

About a mile west of downtown Nassau, just off West Bay Street, **Fort Charlotte** is The Bahamas' largest fort, covering more than 100 hilltop acres and offering impressive views of Paradise Island, Nassau, and the harbor. The complex, constructed in 1788, features a moat, dungeons, underground passageways, and 42 cannons. Nearby, parading pink flamingos are the main attraction at the lush, 5-acre **Ardastra Gardens,** on Chippingham Road (© **242/323-5806;** www.ardastra.com). The graceful birds obey the drillmaster's orders daily at 10:30am, 2:10pm, and 4:10pm. Other exotic wildlife—parrots, boa constrictors, honey bears, macaws, and capuchin monkeys— are less talented but fascinating in their own right, while meandering paths show off the garden's exotic fruit trees, coconut palms, ackee and mango trees, bougainvillea, and hibiscus blossoms. Admission is $12, $6 for children ages 4 to 12.

If you're in the mood for some conch, head for **Arawak Cay,** a small man-made island across West Bay Street from Ardastra Gardens and Fort Charlotte. Join the locals in sampling conch with hot sauce, and wash it down with a cocktail made from coconut water and gin. Farther to the west, the 3,252-sq.-m (35,000-sq.-ft.) **Crystal Palace Casino,** West Bay Street, Cable Beach (© **800/222-7466** or 242/327-6200), is the only casino on New Providence Island.

On Paradise Island, the towering, fancifully designed **Atlantis Paradise Island megaresort** (© **242/363-3000;** www.atlantis.com) is the largest gaming and entertainment complex in the Caribbean, its casino boasting almost 1,000 slot machines and 78 gaming tables, all tied together with a "Lost City of Atlantis" theme. Though only paying hotel guests can use Atlantis' beaches, great slides, and pools, cruise passengers in for the day can visit the casino and restaurants, and sign up for the "Discover Atlantis" tour. The guided excursion, which includes round-trip ferry transport between the ship and property, includes a walk through the resort's sprawling 11-million-gallon lagoon system that boasts more than 200 sea species and 50,000 individual creatures. You'll also tour **The Dig,** a fantastic world of faux Atlantis ruins flooded by the sea. The interconnected passageways, boulevards, and chambers, now inhabited by piranhas, hammerhead sharks, stingrays, and morays, are visible through huge glass windows. It is purported to be the largest man-made marine habitat in the world. To see this part of the resort, you must sign up for the guided "Discovery Tour." Tickets, available at the resort's guest services desks, cost $29 adults, $21 kids 4 to 12, and are free for kids 3 and under. Another tour, available to Disney and Royal Caribbean guests only, gives access to the resort's beaches and restaurants. Atlantis's water slides and pools are for resort guests only.

BEACHES

On New Providence Island, sun worshippers make the 8km (5-mile) pilgrimage to 6.5km (4-mile) **Cable Beach,** which offers various watersports and easy access to shops, a casino, bars, and restaurants. Not on the same level but more convenient for cruise ship passengers, the **Western Esplanade** sweeps westward from the Hilton British Colonial hotel, with changing facilities, restrooms, and a snack bar.

Paradise Beach on Paradise Island is a ferry ride away from Prince George Wharf. The price of admission ($3 for adults, $1 for children) includes use of a shower and locker. An extra $10 deposit is required for towels. Paradise Island has a number of smaller beaches as well, including **Pirate's Cove Beach** and **Cabbage Beach,** the latter of which often fills up with guests of the nearby resorts.

SHOPPING

In 1992, The Bahamas abolished import duties on 11 luxury-good categories, including china, crystal, fine linens, jewelry, leather goods, photographic equipment, watches, and fragrances. Even so, you can end up spending more on an item in The Bahamas than you would at home. True bargains are rare. The principal shopping area is **Bay Street** and the adjacent blocks, which are almost the first things you see when you leave your ship. Here you'll find dozens of duty-free luxury-goods stores, plus hundreds of others selling T-shirts, tourist gimcracks, duty-free booze and cigars, and recordings of Junkanoo music. The crowded aisles of the **Straw Market,** a few blocks west of the docks, display all manner of straw hats, handbags, dolls, place mats, and other items, but be aware that most aren't of the best quality, nor even made locally—much of it has been imported from Asia. Welcome to the global market.

FREEPORT/LUCAYA

Freeport/Lucaya on Grand Bahama Island is visited by far fewer ships than Nassau. Originally intended as two separate developments, Freeport (the landlocked section of town) and Lucaya (which hugs the waterfront) have grown together over the years, offering a mix of sun, surf, golf, tennis, and watersports.

COMING ASHORE   Ships docks at a dreary port in the middle of nowhere, a $15 taxi ride from Freeport and the International Bazaar, center of most of the action.

GETTING AROUND   Once you get to Freeport by **taxi,** you can explore the center of town on foot. Taxis can also take you to farther-flung attractions. The government sets taxi rates, which start at $3 and increase 40¢ for each additional ¼-mile (plus $3 extra per passenger).

BEST CRUISE LINE SHORE EXCURSIONS

Unexso Dolphin Encounter ($80–$89, 3¼ hr.): Pat a dolphin on the nose! On this excursion you can watch, touch, and photograph Flipper, or at least one of his relatives. Organized by Unexso Dolphin Encounter (at Sanctuary Bay).

Kayak Nature Tour ($70–$75, 6 hr.): Visit a protected island creek, kayak through a mangrove forest, explore the island's caves, and take a guided nature walk into Lucayan National Park. The excursion includes lunch and beach time.

ON YOUR OWN: BEYOND THE PORT AREA

Nothing of note is within walking distance of the port. You must take a cab over to Freeport/Lucaya for all attractions.

A couple of miles east of downtown Freeport on East Settlers Way, the 100-acre **Rand Nature Centre** (© **242/352-5438**) serves as the regional headquarters of The Bahamas National Trust. Pineland nature trails meander past native flora and wild birds, including The Bahama parrot. Other highlights include native animal displays (don't miss the boa constrictors), an education center, and a gift shop. Admission is $5. Closed weekends.

Bahamas Golf Excursions

Cruise passengers can arrange to play at the following courses, and some of the cruise lines (Holland America and Carnival, for example) also offer golf packages that include greens fees, transportation, cart rental, and a golf-pro escort.

- **Our Lucaya Beach & Golf Resort,** Royal Palm Way, F-42500, Lucaya (© 242/373-1066; www.ourlucaya.com), offers two 18-hole, par-72 courses. The Lucayan course, designed by Dick Wilson, features well-protected elevated greens, fairways lined with tropical foliage, and doglegs. The links-style Reef course, designed by Robert Trent Jones, Jr., has water traps on 13 of 18 holes. Greens fees are $120 for 18 holes, including cart. Club rentals are $30.
- **South Ocean Golf Course,** Southwest Bay Road, Nassau (© 242/362-4391), is the best course on New Providence Island and one of the best in The Bahamas. Located 30 minutes from Nassau, this 18-hole, par-72 beauty has some first-rate holes with a backdrop of trees, shrubs, ravines, and undulating hills. Greens fees are $90 per person, including cart.

If you'd like a taste of The Bahamas the way they used to be, head for the **Star Club,** on Bayshore Road, on the island's west end (© **242/346-6207**). Built in the 1940s, the Star was Grand Bahama's first hotel, and over the years it's hosted many famous guests. You can order Bahamian chicken in the bag, burgers, fish and chips, or "fresh sexy" ceviche conch salad, or cooked conch prepared as chowder and fritters. But come for the good times and to mix with the locals, not the food. Lunch costs $8. Next door, Austin's Calypso Bar is a colorful old dive if ever there was one.

BEACHES

Xanadu Beach, immediately east of Freeport at the Xanadu Beach Resort, is the premier stretch in the Lucaya area, offering most watersports equipment. It can get crowded at times. **Taíno Beach, Churchill Beach,** and **Fortune Beach** are all conveniently located on the Lucaya oceanfront. A 20-minute ride east of Lucaya, **Gold Rock Beach** may be the island's best. Secluded in Lucayan National Park, it has barbecue pits, picnic tables, and a spectacular low tide. **Barbary Beach,** slightly closer to Lucaya, is great for seashell hunters, and in May and June white spider lilies in the area bloom spectacularly.

SHOPPING

The **International Bazaar,** at East Mall Drive and East Sunrise Highway, next to the Casino at Bahamia, is pure 1960s Bahamian kitsch, and though relentlessly cheerful, it's a little long in the tooth. Each area of the 10-acre, 100-shop complex attempts to capture the ambience of a different region of the globe. Stereotypes abound. Next door, the **Straw Market** features items with a Bahamian touch—baskets, hats, handbags, and place mats. Quality varies, so look around before buying your souvenirs. The **Port Lucaya Marketplace,** on Seahorse Road, is a large shopping-and-dining complex much like the International Bazaar, with steel-drum bands adding some atmosphere. Many of the restaurants and shops overlook a 50-slip marina, and from the boardwalk along the water you can watch the dolphins at the UNEXSO dolphin education and interaction facility.

5 Barbados

No port of call in the southern Caribbean can compete with Barbados when it comes to natural beauty, attractions, and, especially, its seemingly endless stretches of pink and white sandy beaches, among the best in the entire Caribbean Basin. Originally operated on a plantation economy that made its British colonial aristocracy rich, the island is the most easterly in the Caribbean, floating in the mid-Atlantic like a great coral reef. Topography varies from rolling hills and savage waves on the eastern (Atlantic) coast to densely populated flatlands, rows of hotels and apartments, and sheltered beaches in the southwest. The people in Barbados are called Bajans, and you'll see this term used everywhere.

COMING ASHORE   Located about a mile from the capital, Bridgetown, the island's modern and newly expanded cruise ship terminal offers car rentals, taxi services, sight-seeing tours, and a tourist information office, plus shops and scads of vendors.

GETTING AROUND   You'll need transportation to get to the beaches, though you can walk into Bridgetown in about 15 minutes via a new park that's been built along the shoreline between the port and city center. You'll find **taxis** just outside of the cruise terminal. They're not metered, but their rates are fixed by the government. Settle on the rate before getting in.

LANGUAGE & CURRENCY   **English** is spoken with an island lilt. The **Barbados dollar (BD$)** is the official currency (BD$2.08 = US$1; BD$1 = US50¢), but U.S. dollars are commonly accepted.

BEST CRUISE LINE SHORE EXCURSIONS

It's not easy to get around Barbados quickly and conveniently, so a shore excursion is a good idea here.

Kayak & Turtle Encounter ($69, 3½ hr.): A boat ride along the west coast brings you to the beach, where you'll clamber into your kayak for a 45-minute paddle along the shore. Once at the snorkel site, you'll be able to swim with and feed sea turtles.

Mount Gay Rum Distillery & Banks Beer Tour ($42, 3½ hr.): Talk about getting in the spirit. This tour takes you for a tour and tipple at Barbados's number-one rum distillery then heads over to the Banks Brewery for the yeasty side of things.

Rainforest Hike & Cave Adventure ($74, 4 hr.): A guide leads your group through one of Barbados's rainforest gullies, then down into a natural cave.

Harrison's Cave ($49, 2 hr.): Most cruise lines offer a tour to Harrison's Cave in the center of the island (see "On Your Own: Beyond the Port Area," below, for details).

Horseback Riding & Country Drive ($89, 3½ hr.): Horse treks through the heart of the island wind past old plantation houses, sugar cane fields, old sugar factories, small villages, and, if you're lucky, green monkeys scouting for food.

ON YOUR OWN: BEYOND THE PORT AREA

For the purposes of argument, let's consider Bridgetown "beyond walking distance," but, in any case, don't waste too much time here—it's hot, dry, and dusty, and the honking horns of traffic jams only add to its woes. Unless you want to go shopping, you should spend your time exploring all the beauty the island has to offer instead.

All cruise ship excursions visit **Harrison's Cave,** Welchman Hall, St. Thomas (*(C)* **246/438-6640**), Barbados's top tourist attraction. Here you can see a beautiful underground world from aboard an electric tram and trailer. Admission is $16 for adults and $6 for children. If you'd like to go on your own, a taxi ride takes about 30 minutes and costs at least $20 each way. About 1.6km (1 mile) away is the **Flower Forest,** Richmond Plantation, St. Joseph (*(C)* **246/433-8152**), a former sugar plantation that's now a junglelike botanical garden, with paths winding among huge tropical flowers and plants. Admission is $7.50.

Welchman Hall Gully, St. Thomas (Hwy. 2 from Bridgetown; *(C)* **246/438-6671**), is a lush tropical garden owned by the Barbados National Trust. It's 13km (8 miles) from the port (reachable by bus) and features some plants that were here when the English settlers landed in 1627, plus later imports that include cocoa bushes, exotic orchids, and breadfruit trees that are supposedly descendants of the seedlings brought ashore by Captain Bligh, of *Bounty* fame. Many of the plants are labeled and occasionally you'll spot a wild monkey. Admission is $10.

The **Sunbury Plantation House,** 25 minutes from Bridgetown along Highway 5 (*(C)* **246/423-6270**), is the only plantation great house on Barbados whose rooms are all open for viewing. The 300-year-old house is steeped in history, featuring mahogany antiques, old prints, and a collection of horse-drawn carriages. Admission is $10. Signs along the highway will guide you in, right before Six Cross Roads.

BEACHES

Beaches on the island's western "Gold Coast" are far preferable (and closer) than those on the surf-pounded Atlantic side, which are dangerous for swimming. All Barbados beaches are open to the public, even those in front of the big resort hotels and private homes. You'll need to snag a taxi to get to them.

GOLD COAST **Payne's Bay,** with access from the Coach House (*(C)* **246/432-1163**) or Mannie's Suga Suga restaurant (*(C)* **246/419-4511**), is a good beach for watersports, especially snorkeling. There's a parking area here. This beach can get rather crowded, but the beautiful bay makes it worth it. Directly south of Payne's Bay, at Fresh Water Bay, is a trio of fine beaches: **Brighton Beach, Brandon's Beach,** and **Paradise Beach.** Farther north, **Church Point** can get crowded, but it's one of the most scenic bays in Barbados, and the swimming is ideal. Retreat under some shade trees when you've had enough sun. You can also order drinks at the Colony Club Resort's beach terrace.

Snorkelers in particular seek out the glassy blue waters by **Mullins Beach.** There are some shady areas, and you can park on the main road. Just north of here is another good stretch, **Heywoods Beach.**

ON THE SOUTH COAST Just outside Bridgetown, **Carlisle Bay Beach** is popular with locals, and is a great snorkeling spot. Farther south, near Rockley, **Accra Beach** is the biggest on the south coast, and very popular with both locals and visitors. **Sandy Beach,** reached from the parking lot on the Worthing main road, has tranquil waters opening onto a lagoon. This is a family favorite, with lots of screaming and yelling, especially on weekends. Food and drink are sold here. Windsurfers are particularly fond of the trade winds that sweep across wide **Casuarina Beach** even on the hottest summer days. Access is from Maxwell Coast Road, across the property of Casuarina Beach Hotel, where you can get food and drink. **Silver Sands Beach** is to the east of the town of Oistins, near the very southernmost point of Barbados, directly east of South Point Lighthouse and near the Silver Rock Resort. This white sandy beach is a favorite with many Bajans, who probably want to keep it a secret from as many visitors as possible. (Tough luck, Bajans!) Windsurfing is good here, and you can rent boards at **Club Mistral,** at the Silver Sands Resort (© **246/428-6001;** www.club mistralbarbados.com). Open daily 8am to 5pm.

ON THE SOUTHEAST COAST   The southeast coast is known for its big waves, especially at **Crane Beach,** a white sandy stretch backed by cliffs and palms that often appears in travel-magazine articles about Barbados. The beach offers excellent body-surfing, but this is real ocean swimming, not the calm Caribbean, so be careful. This one will cost you about $20 in taxi fare from the cruise pier, each way.

SHOPPING

The shopping-mall-size cruise terminal contains retail stores, duty-free shops, and a plethora of vendors selling arts and crafts, jewelry, liquor, china, crystal, electronics, perfume, leather goods, and great local hot sauce, as well as yummy Punch de Crème (you can get a free sample before buying), a creamy rum drink. Among Barbados handicrafts, you'll find lots of black-coral jewelry, but beware—because black coral is endangered, it's illegal to bring it back to the United States. We suggest looking, but not buying. Local clay potters turn out some really interesting products, some based on designs centuries old.

6 Belize

Located on the northeastern tip of Central America, bordering Mexico on the north, Guatemala to the west and south, and the Caribbean to the east, Belize combines Central American and Caribbean cultures, offering both ancient Mayan ruins and a 298km (185-mile) coral reef that runs the entire length of the country—it's the largest in the Western Hemisphere and the second largest in the world, supporting a tremendous number of patch reefs, shoals, and more than 1,000 islands called cayes (pronounced "keys"), the largest and most populous being Ambergris Caye. (Both Ambergris Caye and Caye Caulker are popular with visitors, but require a flight from Belize City. However, smaller lines like Windstar may just skip Belize City completely and anchor offshore from the cayes and other parts of the mainland, such as southern Dangriga and Placencia.) Unlike many other Caribbean countries, Belize is serious in its dedication to conservation: One-fifth of its total landmass is dedicated as nature reserves, and 7,770 sq. km (3,000 sq. miles) of its waters are protected as well.

Belize City is the economic center of the country. Trying to choose which natural or man-made wonder to explore will be the most stress you'll feel in this very laid-back, diverse, stable, and English-speaking nation, whose population of about 216,000 comprises Creoles, Garifuna (Black Carib Indians), mestizos (a mix of Spanish and Indian), Spanish, Maya, English, Lebanese, Chinese, and Eastern Indians. The country has the highest concentration of Mayan sites among all Central American nations.

COMING ASHORE   A multimillion-dollar pier called **Belize Tourism Village** opened in Belize City in October 2001. While shallow waters mean big ships must still anchor offshore and tender passengers in (a 20- to 30-min. trip), the spiffy pier area now offers a new shopping complex with restaurants, tourist information, and even a tranquil Mayan-themed courtyard.

GETTING AROUND   Taxis are available at the pier, in town, and in resort areas, and are easily recognized by their green license plates. Although the taxis have no meters, the drivers do charge somewhat standard fares, but it's always important to settle what your fare will be prior to hiring a taxi.

LANGUAGE & CURRENCY **English** is the official language of Belize, although Spanish, Creole, Garifuna, and Mayan are spoken throughout the country as well. The Belize Dollar (BZ) has a fixed exchange rate of BZ$1.98 to US$1 (US$1 = BZ51¢). Most establishments, as well as taxis and vendors on the street, take U.S. dollars. In especially touristy areas, just be sure to ask if the price quoted is in U.S. or BZ dollars. Unless otherwise specified, prices in this section are given in U.S. dollars.

CALLING FROM THE U.S. To make a call from the U.S. to Belize, dial the international access code **(011),** the country code **(501),** and then the number of the establishment.

BEST CRUISE LINE SHORE EXCURSIONS

Lamanai ($89, 7½ hr.): Lamanai is one of the largest ceremonial centers in Belize. In the original Mayan language, its name means "submerged crocodile," and you will see various crocodile carvings throughout the site. After a 45-minute drive up the Northern Highway to Tower Hill, you'll board a riverboat and head up the New River. Along the way, through the mangroves, your guide will point out crocodiles basking in the sun, a variety of birds (including jacanas and hawks), delicate water lilies, and other exotic flowers such as black orchids. You'll pass local fisherman and, surprisingly, Mennonite farms—Mennonites from Canada and Mexico began arriving in Belize in 1958 in search of land and a more isolated and simple life, and today their community numbers around 7,000. Landing at the Lamanai grounds, you'll have lunch and then tour the series of temples. There are more than 700 structures, most of them still buried beneath mounds of earth. For a view above the thick jungle, you can climb some of the temples—look in the trees for toucans and spider monkeys playing or napping. You won't mistake the roar of the howler monkey. Your guide may tell you about the red gumbo-limbo tree, whose bark becomes a shade of red and then peels off—it's jokingly referred to as the tourist tree. A small archaeological museum is on the site, as well as a few stands to buy souvenirs.

Altun Ha ($49, 4 hr.): Meaning "water of the rock," Altun Ha is a relatively small site of temples and tombs that was rediscovered in 1957 during expansion of the Northern Highway. This is one of the most extensively excavated sites and was an important trading post during the classical Mayan period. Many treasures were found here, including a carved jade head representing Kinish Ahau, the Mayan sun god. It has become one of the country's national symbols, and is depicted on the nation's currency. The tour includes lunch, and a small gift shop is on-site.

Xunantunich ($88, 7½ hr.): This site, also called Maiden of the Rock, is located near the Guatemalan border overlooking the Mopan River; it was a major ceremonial center during the classic Mayan period. After crossing the river by hand-cranked ferry, you can explore six major plazas surrounded by more than 25 temples and palaces, including *"El Castillo"* (the castle), the largest of the temples. Be sure to climb to the top—it's well worth it for the amazing panoramic view. There's also a new visitor's center with old excavation photos, a scale model, and a few exhibits and souvenir shops. Afterwards, you'll head to San Ignacio for lunch and enjoy a marimba band.

Hol Chan Marine Reserve & Shark Ray Alley ($92, 7½ hr.): You'll head north for an hourlong speedboat ride to **Hol Chan** (Mayan for "little channel"), 6.4km (4 miles) southeast of San Pedro on Ambergris Caye, snorkel the reef for about an hour, and then head off to the Shark Ray Alley dive site, about 5 minutes away, where you'll see and pet dozens of southern stingrays and nurse sharks. Guides bring goodies for them to eat, and they stick around till the food is gone. Remember to bring a disposable underwater camera—if you're going to pet a stingray, you may as well capture it on film! Lunch is on San Pedro, and after eating you can find yourself a rum punch, go shopping, or just hang out at the beach.

Cave Tubing & Jungle Trek ($96, 6¼ hr.): On arriving at Jaguar Paw, you take a 45-minute hike down a jungle trail where your guide will point out various plants and trees used by the ancient Maya for medicinal purposes. When you get to the cave, your guide will hand out flashlights and inner tubes and set you afloat, propelled by the current, through the cave system. On several occasions, you'll emerge into the sunlight before entering another cave. The float lasts about 2 hours, after which you'll have lunch. Bring a change of clothes. Minimum age 12 years.

Belize City Tour ($43, 3 hr.): It's hardly one of the most exciting tours and definitely not a great way to see the natural side of Belize, but if you want to do something quick and easy, this is the tour. It will give you a feel for the city, its colonial architecture, and its culture through a visit to the Belize Maritime Museum and Terminal, the Government House Museum, and St. John's Cathedral, built in 1812, making it the oldest Anglican cathedral in Central America. Around lunchtime, the Mennonite farmers and craftsman are out selling their handmade furniture. Their denim overalls, checked shirts, and straw cowboy hats make them easily recognizable. If you want to combine your city tour with a little nature, the **"City & Sanctuary"** ($52, 4 hr.) tour adds a visit to the **Belize Zoo** (© 220-8004). First created as a haven for animals that were injured and couldn't be returned to the wild, the zoo now houses an impressive array of large cats, primates, reptiles, and birds.

Two-Tank Scuba Dive at Turneffe Atoll ($159, 6 hr.): After a 50-minute boat ride, you arrive at Turneffe Atoll for dives at two different sites with depths of 50 to 70 feet, among reef fish and growths of sponge and coral.

ON YOUR OWN: WITHIN WALKING DISTANCE

Belize City is the hub of the country but doesn't boast the country's major attractions. The historic **harbor district** right around the pier is small and quaint. You'll find a few restaurants, and the **Baron Bliss Park and Lighthouse** is just a short stroll away. After sailing from Portugal, the eponymous baron arrived sick with food poisoning, and remained aboard his yacht for 2 months while local fisherman and administrators treated him kindly and taught him about Belize. He died soon after, but not before changing his will and leaving $2 million to Belize in a trust fund. That money made possible the building of the Bliss Institute Library and Museum and a number of health clinics and markets around the country, as well as helping with the Belize City water system. The baron is considered Belize's greatest benefactor, and Baron Bliss Day, a national holiday, is celebrated on March 9.

Outside the immediate port area, much of the rest of the city is run-down and poor, with narrow, crowded streets and many old colonial structures that are in need of repair. However, since tourism is an important industry in Belize, the country is making an effort to spruce up the city and reduce crime, instituting a squad of Tourism Police to patrol popular tourist areas. Its officers are dressed in brown uniforms.

ON YOUR OWN: BEYOND THE PORT AREA

See "Best Cruise Line Shore Excursions," earlier in this section, for a discussion of the Mayan ruins. Animal enthusiasts might want to visit the **Community Baboon Sanctuary,** located about 48km (30 miles) west of Belize City off the Northern Highway in the Belize District (© 220-2181), which offers a guided tour through forest trails. Through a grassroots effort the villagers and landowners have committed to preserving the habitat necessary to ensure a healthy population of black howler monkeys (known locally as baboons). Those more interested in birding can tour the **Crooked Tree Wildlife Sanctuary,** about 8km (5 miles) farther up the Northern Highway (© 209-7084 or 614-5658). The sanctuary provides a habitat for more than 360 species of birds.

Back in Belize City, if you want to do some gambling, the **Princess Hotel-Casino** is located a couple of kilometers (less than 2 miles) from the cruise pier on Newtown Barricks Road (© 223-2670); it's about 10 minutes and $5 by taxi from the pier.

BEACHES

Compared to many other parts of the Caribbean, the beaches of Belize are neither the biggest nor the widest, but they are relaxing, with very clear water. Areas that offer the best beach sunbathing are in the cayes, including Ambergris Caye, Caye Caulker, Tobacco Caye, and on the mainland to the south in Dangriga and Placencia. There are no beaches near Belize City.

SHOPPING

In general, the best buys in Belize are wooden and slate carvings, Mayan calendars, pottery, ceramics, and furniture made by the Mennonites. At the pier, the new **Tourism Village** offers shops specializing in local souvenirs such as mahogany bowls, jewelry, clothes, assorted carvings, and artwork. A local favorite is **Marie Sharp's hot sauces and jams.** They're served everywhere and can be purchased to take home.

7 British Virgin Islands: Tortola & Virgin Gorda

With small bays and hidden coves that were once havens for pirates (small Norman Island is said to have been the prototype for Robert Louis Stevenson's *Treasure Island*), the BVIs are among the world's loveliest cruising regions. Among its 40-some islands, only Tortola, Virgin Gorda, and Jost Van Dyke (plus Anegada, 16 miles to the north) are of significant size. The English officially annexed the islands in 1672, and today they're a British territory, with their own elected government and a population of about 21,000. Tortola attracts the megaships, while Virgin Gorda and Jost Van Dyke attract the small ships of the Seabourn, SeaDream, Windstar, Star Clippers, and Windjammer Barefoot fleets.

LANGUAGE & CURRENCY   English is spoken here, and the **U.S. dollar** is the legal currency (much to the surprise of arriving Brits).

TORTOLA

Located on the island's south shore, the once-sleepy village and colonial capital of **Road Town** became a bustling center after the 70-acre Wickhams Cay marina brought in a massive yacht-chartering business. The rest of the southern coast is characterized by rugged mountain peaks. On the northern coast are beautiful bays with white sandy beaches, banana trees, mangoes, and clusters of palms.

If your ship isn't scheduled to visit Virgin Gorda but you want to, you can catch a boat, ferry, or launch here and be on the island in no time, since it's only a 12-mile trip.

COMING ASHORE   Visiting cruise ships dock at **Wickhams Cay,** a pleasant 5-minute walk to Main Street in Road Town. You should have no trouble finding your way around.

GETTING AROUND   You can walk around Road Town, and open-air and sedan-style taxis meet every arriving cruise ship to carry passengers to the beaches and other attractions. Fares are set, so ask what you'll be paying before you get in.

BEST CRUISE LINE SHORE EXCURSIONS

Town & Country Excursion ($34, 3½ hr.): Tour the island in an open-air mini-bus, visiting the Botanical Gardens, Cane Garden Bay, Bomba's Full Moon Party Shack at Capoons Bay, and Soper's Hole.

Tortola Snorkeling Adventure ($48, 2½ hr.): Cross the Sir Frances Drake Channel by boat to Normal Island, one of the BVI's prime snorkel sites, full of coral formations, colorful fish, and a group of caves at Treasure Point, where pirate treasure is reputed to have been hidden.

Forest Walk & Beach Tour ($35 3½ hr.): Safari buses take you to Tortola's interior for a 1-mile hike through the Sage Mountain rainforest to the highest point in the Virgin Islands, then head down the Ridge Road for a brief stop at the Botanical Gardens. Minimum age 12 years.

Wreck of the Rhone Two-Tank Certified Dive ($111, 4 hr.): A guided dive to a British ship sunk in an 1867 hurricane, her bow lying almost fully intact in 80 feet of water. All divers must be certified and have dived within the last 2 years.

ON YOUR OWN: WITHIN WALKING DISTANCE

Besides the handful of shops on Main and Upper Main streets in Road Town, there's also a **Botanic Garden** (© 284/494-4557) right in the middle of town, across from the police station. It's open daily from 8am to 6pm and features a wide variety of flowers and plants, including a section on medicinal plants. Admission is free.

ON YOUR OWN: BEYOND THE PORT AREA

You have mainly nature to look at on Tortola. The big attraction is **Sage Mountain National Park,** its peak rising to 1,780 feet, the highest point in the BVIs and USVIs. The park was established in 1964 to protect those remnants of Tortola's original forests not burned or cleared during its plantation era. You'll find a lush forest of mango, papaya, breadfruit, coconut, birch berry, mountain guava, and guava berry trees, many labeled for identification. This is a great place to enjoy a picnic while overlooking neighboring islets and cays. Any taxi driver can take you to the mountain. Before going, stop at the Wickhams Cay tourist office, near the pier, and pick up a brochure with a map and an outline of the park's trails. The two main hikes are the Rain Forest Trail and the Mahogany Forest Trail.

BEACHES

Most of the beaches are a 20-minute taxi ride from the cruise dock. Figure on about $15 per person one-way (some will charge less, about $8–$9 per person if you've got a group), but discuss it with the driver before setting out. You can also ask him to pick you up at a designated time.

A Slice of Paradise: Jost Van Dyke

Covering only 4 square miles, mountainous Jost Van Dyke is an offbeat treat, visited mostly by private yachts and a few small cruise ships such as Windjammer Barefoot Cruises, which often throw afternoon beach parties on the beach at White Bay, with the crew lugging ashore a picnic lunch for a leisurely afternoon of eating, drinking, and swimming. If your ship stays late, don't miss a trip to **Foxy's** (© 284/495-9258), a well-known watering hole at the far end of Great Harbour that's popular with the yachting set as well as locals. It's your classic island beach bar, with music pounding and drinks flowing into the wee hours.

The finest beach is at **Cane Garden Bay** on the island's northwest, across the mountains from Road Town but worth the trip. **Rhymer's** (© 284/495-4639) serves a good if not inexpensive lunch of the conch, whelk, and barbecue sparerib variety (main courses $15 and up). Surfers like **Apple Bay,** also on the northwest side, while next-door Cappoon's Bay is known more for **Bomba's Surfside Shack** (© 284/495-4148), the oldest, most memorable bar on Tortola, covered with Day-Glo graffiti and laced with wire and rejected odds and ends of plywood, driftwood, and abandoned rubber tires. Lunch is $10, and beer and Painkillers, that classic Caribbean rum specialty, are dispensed till the cows come home. At the extreme west end of the island, **Smugglers Cove** is a wide crescent of white sand wrapped around calm, sky-blue water.

SHOPPING
Shopping on Tortola is a minor activity compared to other Caribbean ports. Only British goods are imported without duty, and they are the best buys, especially English china. You'll also find West Indian art, terra-cotta pottery, wicker and rattan home furnishings, Mexican glassware, dhurrie rugs, baskets, and ceramics. Most stores are on **Main Street** in Road Town. The **Pusser's Company Store,** Main Street, Road Town (© 284/494-2467; www.pussers.com), offers a selection of classic travel and adventure clothing, along with Pusser's famous (though not terribly good) rum, which was served aboard British Navy ships for over 300 years. A good, cheap gift item is packets of Pusser's coasters, on which is written the recipe for the Painkiller. Pusser's Road Town Pub is adjacent, serving lunch and, of course, Painkillers.

VIRGIN GORDA
Instead of visiting Tortola, some small cruise ships put in at lovely Virgin Gorda, famous for its boulder-strewn beach known as **The Baths.** The third-largest island in the colony, it got its name ("Fat Virgin") from Christopher Columbus, who thought the mountain framing it looked like a protruding stomach. Megaships that stop at Tortola usually offer a 4½-hour excursion to Virgin Gorda for about $50.

COMING ASHORE   Virgin Gorda doesn't have a pier or landing facilities to suit any of the large ships. Most vessels anchor offshore and tender passengers in to St. Thomas Bay, the port area and yacht harbor for Spanish Town. Ferries from Tortola also berth here.

GETTING AROUND   Taxis are available at the pier and will take visitors to The Baths and area beaches for about $8 per person each way. For a tour of the island, contact Andy Flax of the **Virgin Gorda Tours Association** (c/o the Fischers Cove Beach Hotel; ℰ **284/495-5252**). It'll run you about $40 per couple, and they'll pick you up at the dock if given at least 24-hour notice.

BEST CRUISE LINE SHORE EXCURSIONS

Island Tour & the Baths ($40–$51, 3½ hr.): Most Virgin Gorda tours are variations on this theme, touring the island by open-air bus, stopping at its highest point for a snapshot, taking in the village of Spanish Town, then stopping at Copper Mine National Park, where Amerindian and later European miners once dug for copper. The ruins you see today are what's left of a British operation from 1860. Tours end at the Baths, where you'll have time for swimming, snorkeling, and exploring among the boulders.

ON YOUR OWN: WITHIN WALKING DISTANCE

The Virgin Gorda Yacht Harbour at St. Thomas Bay has several restaurants and shops.

ON YOUR OWN: BEYOND THE PORT AREA

You might also consider cabbing up to glamorous **Little Dix Bay Resort** (ℰ **284/ 495-5555**), established by Laurence Rockefeller in 1965, to enjoy a lunch buffet at an outdoor pavilion that shows off Virgin Gorda's beautiful hills, bays, and sky. Aside from this, most people head for The Baths, which really is spectacular (see "Beaches," below).

BEACHES

The major reason cruise ships come to Virgin Gorda is to visit **The Baths,** where geologists believe ice-age eruptions caused house-size boulders to topple onto one another to form the saltwater grottoes we see today. The pools around The Baths are excellent for swimming and snorkeling (equipment can be rented on the beach), and a crawl between and among the boulders, which in places are very cavelike, is more than a little bit fun. A cafe sits just above the beach for a quick snack or a cool drink. **Devil's Bay,** a great beach just south of The Baths, is usually less crowded. Just north of The Baths is **Spring Bay,** one of the best of the island's beaches, with white sand, clear water, and good snorkeling. Nearby is **The Crawl,** a natural pool formed by rocks that's great for novice snorkelers; a marked path leads there from Spring Bay. **Trunk Bay,** just to the north, is a wide sand beach that can be reached via a rough path from Spring Bay.

  Devil's Bay National Park can be reached by a trail from The Baths. The walk to the secluded coral-sand beach takes about 15 minutes through a natural setting of boulders and dry coastal vegetation.

SHOPPING

The only shopping of note here is right at the Yacht Harbor complex, with a few dive shops, boutiques, and handicraft shops.

8 Cozumel & the Yucatán Peninsula

The island of Cozumel, just off Mexico's Yucatán coast, is one of the busiest cruise ports you'll ever see, with up to 16 ships visiting every day during high season, counting those that anchor offshore and ferry passengers in by tender. All that activity can make the port town of San Miguel seem more like Times Square than the sleepy, refreshingly gritty town it once was, and the pace of transformation doesn't seem to be slowing

The Yucatán's Upper Caribbean Coast

To Progreso

El Cuyo

Holbox

Isla Holbox

Isla Contoy

RÍO LAGARTOS NATURE RESERVE

Chiquilá

Isla Mujeres

Punta Sam

Cancún

Puerto Juárez

Buenaventura

QUINTANA ROO STATE

Isla Cancun

YUCATÁN STATE

180

Croco-Cun

Jardín Botanico

Puerto Morelos

180 D

180 D

Nuevo Xcan

307

To Valladolid & Chichén Itzá

180

Chemax

Punta Bete

Xcaret

Playa del Carmen

Calica

San Gervasio

Pamul

Xpuha

Puerto Aventuras

Yalku Lagoon

San Miguel de Cozumel

Cobá

Akumal

Xelha Lagoon National Park

El Cedral

ISLA DE COZUMEL

Chankanaab Nature Park

Tancah

Tulum

Chunyaxche

Muyil

Boca Paila

Caribbean Sea

Chumpón

Vigia Chico

Punta Allen

0 ⸺ 25 mi

0 ⸺ 25 km

N

Peninsula Vigia Grande

Bahia de la Ascensión

✈ Airport

🚢 Cruise Ship Dock

---- Ferry Route

||||| Reef

◆ Ruins

Felipe Carrillo Puerto

SIAN KA'AN BIOSPHERE RESERVE

To Chetumal & Costa Maya

down: Even if you visited just 5 or 6 years ago, you may not recognize the place. Still, crowds and shiny Miami-wannabe boutiques aside, Cozumel's allure remains its proximity to the ancient Mayan ruins at Tulum and Chichén-Itzá on the mainland. The island's beaches are a big draw, along with diving and shopping for silver jewelry, local handicrafts, and T-shirts from the town's notorious beer pit, Carlos 'n Charlie's.

To see the ruins from here, you must take the 45-minute ferry ride between Cozumel and **Playa del Carmen,** on the mainland, though a few cruise ships call directly at Playa, anchoring offshore. Many ships en route to Cozumel pause in Playa del Carmen to drop off passengers who have signed up for ruins tours. After the tours, passengers take a ferry back to the ship in Cozumel (or, if the tour is by plane, get dropped off at the airport in Cozumel, near downtown). If your ship is not stopping at Playa, bear in mind that the ferry ride back and forth from Cozumel will take almost 2 hours total; if you're more interested in just relaxing, you may want to just hang out on the island.

In recent years, a handful of other Yucatán ports have come onto the scene, including **Calica,** just south of Playa, where there's little more than a pier; **Costa Maya,** about 161km (100 miles) south near the sleepy fishing village of Mahajual; and **Progreso,** on the Gulf coast of the Yucatán, making it the closest to Chichén-Itzá, as well as the city of Merida. At press time, Carnival's long-term plan to develop a new port and pier called the Port of Cancun at Xcaret, just down the road from Playa del Carmen, was still in the negotiation phase.

LANGUAGE & CURRENCY   **Spanish** is the tongue of the land, although **English** is spoken in most places that cater to tourists. The Mexican currency is the **nuevo peso** (new peso). Its symbol is the "$" sign, but it's hardly the equivalent of the U.S. dollar—the exchange rate is about $11 pesos to US$1 ($1 peso = about US9¢). The main tourist stores gladly accept U.S. dollars.

CALLING FROM THE U.S.   You need to dial the international access code **(011)** and **52** before the numbers listed below.

MAYAN RUINS & OTHER MAINLAND ATTRACTIONS

Because all of the sites listed here are quite far from the cruise piers, most cruise passengers visit them as part of **shore excursions.** Admission to the sites is included in the excursion prices, which typically run from $99 (by bus) to $186 (plus $39 airport tax) by plane for Chichén-Itzá and around $87 for a bus to Tulum or Cobá. Chichén-Itzá and Cobá are all-day excursions. Visits to smaller Tulum are often paired with a visit to the Xel-Ha Eco Park, making it a full-day trek ($124). Guests are usually served free and refreshingly coooolllldddd Mexican beer on the bus back after exploring the ruins.

CHICHEN-ITZA   The largest and most fabled of the Yucatán ruins, Chichén-Itzá (meaning "Mouth of the Well of the Itza Family") was founded in A.D. 445 by the Mayans and later inhabited by the Toltecs of central Mexico. At its height, the city had about 50,000 residents, but it was mysteriously abandoned only 2 centuries after its founding. After lying dormant for 2 more centuries, the site was resettled and enjoyed prosperity again until the early 13th century, when it was once more relinquished to the surrounding jungle. The area covers 18 sq. km (7 sq. miles), so you can see only a fraction of it on a day trip. These are some of the highlights.

The best known of Chichén-Itzá's ruins is the magnificent **El Castillo pyramid** (also called the Pyramid of Kukulkán), which was built with the Maya calendar in mind. The four stairways leading up to the central platform each have 91 steps, making a total of 364; when you add the top central platform you get the 365 days of the solar year. On either side of each stairway are nine terraces, for a total of 18 on each face of the pyramid, equaling the number of months in the Maya solar calendar. On the facing of these terraces are 52 panels that represent the 52-year cycle when both the solar and religious calendars would become realigned. The pyramid's alignment is such that on the **spring** or **fall equinox,** light striking the pyramid gives the illusion of a snake slithering down the steps to join its gigantic stone head mounted at the base.

Northwest of El Castillo is Chichén's main **Ball Court (Juego de Pelota),** the largest and best preserved such Mayan ruin anywhere. Carved on both walls of the ball court are scenes showing Mayan figures dressed as ball players and decked out in heavy protective padding. The carved scene also shows a headless player kneeling with blood shooting from his neck; another player holding the head looks on. Here's the way it worked: Players on two teams tried to knock a hard rubber ball through one of the two stone rings placed high on either wall, using only their elbows, knees, and hips. According to legend, the losing players paid for defeat with their lives. Some experts, however, say the victors were the only appropriate sacrifices for the gods. Note the lack of bleacher seating. As the games were played as a ritual, for the entertainment of the gods, only a single judge looked on.

Temples are located at both ends of the ball court. The **North Temple** has sculptured pillars and more sculptures inside, as well as badly ruined murals. The acoustics of the ball court are so good that from the North Temple, a person speaking can be heard clearly at the opposite end, about 136m (450 ft.) away. Near the southeastern corner of the main ball court is the **Temple of the Jaguars,** a small temple with serpent columns and carved panels showing warriors and jaguars. Up the steps and inside the temple, a mural chronicles a battle in a Maya village. To the right of the ball court is the **Temple of the Skulls (Tzompantli),** decorated with rows of skulls carved into the stone platform. When a sacrificial victim's head was cut off, it was impaled on a pole and displayed in a tidy row with others. Also carved into the stone are pictures of eagles tearing hearts from human victims.

Follow the dirt road (actually an ancient *sacbé,* or causeway, made from a white, compacted, claylike soil that made the way visible at night) that heads north from the Platform of Venus. After about 5 minutes you'll come to the **Sacred Cenote,** a great natural well that may have given Chichén-Itzá its name. This well was used for ceremonial purposes, not for drinking water. According to legend, sacrificial victims adorned with gold and other riches were drowned in this pool to honor the rain god Chaac. In the early 20th century, American consul and Harvard professor Edward Thompson bought the ruins of Chichén-Itzá and explored the cenote with dredges and divers, unearthing (and exporting) a fortune in gold and jade.

Due east of El Castillo is one of the most impressive structures at Chichén: the **Temple of the Warriors,** named for the carvings of warriors marching along its walls. It's also called the Group of the Thousand Columns for the rows of broken square pillars that flank it. A figure of Chaac-Mool sits at the top of the temple, surrounded by impressive columns carved in relief to look like enormous feathered serpents. According to scholars, the high priest would tear out a sacrificial victim's heart here and then throw the body down the steps, where another priest would strip off its skin. The high priest would then dress himself in the skin, cross to a nearby platform, and dance.

Lovely, huh? South of the temple is another group of columns (these ones round) that were once an important **market,** controlling the trade in salt on the Yucatán.

South of the market, a cluster of interesting ruins include the **Observatory (El Caracol),** a complex building with a circular tower through whose slits astronomers could observe the cardinal directions and the approach of the all-important spring and autumn equinoxes; the **Edifice of the Nuns (Edificio de las Monjas),** which was named for its resemblance to a European convent; and the **Church (La Iglesia),** one of the oldest buildings at Chichén and was named for its beautiful decorations. Its ceiling, with a Mayan false arch, is a stone replica of the thatched ceiling in a typical Mayan home of the period.

TULUM About 130km (80 miles) south of Cancún and about a 30-minute drive from Playa del Carmen, the small walled city of Tulum is the single most visited Mayan ruin due to its proximity to the ports. It was the only Mayan city built on the coast and the only one inhabited when the Spanish conquistadors arrived in the 1500s. From its dramatic perch atop seaside cliffs, you can see wonderful panoramic views of the Caribbean. Tulum consists of 60 individual structures. Though nowhere near as large and impressive as Chichén-Itzá, the two cities share a similar prominent feature: a ruin topped with a **temple to Kukulkán,** the primary Mayan/Olmec god. Other important structures include the **Temple of the Frescoes,** the **Temple of the Descending God,** the **House of Columns,** and the **House of the Cenote,** which is a well. There's also a sliver of silky beach amidst the site, so bring your bathing suit for a quick refreshing dip. New visitor facilities include a well-stocked bookstore and a soon-to-open museum.

COBA A 35-minute drive northwest of Tulum puts you at Cobá, site of one of the most important city-states in the Mayan empire. Cobá flourished from A.D. 300 to 1000, with its population numbering perhaps as many as 40,000. Excavation work began in 1972, but archaeologists estimate that only 5% of this dead city has yet been uncovered. The site lies on four lakes. Its 81 primitive acres provide excellent exploration opportunities for the hiker. Cobá's pyramid, **Nohoch Mul,** is the tallest in the Yucatán.

XCARET ECOLOGICAL PARK Lying about 6.5km (4 miles) south of Playa del Carmen on the coast, Xcaret (pronounced "Ish-car-*et*") is a 250-acre ecological theme park with small Mayan ruins scattered about the lushly landscaped acres. Visitors can put on life jackets and snorkeling gear and ride the currents through more than a kilometer of well-lit underground caves. You can also swim with dolphins, though this is not included in the cost of excursions. The park has a botanical garden, an aquarium, a sea turtle breeding and release facility, a dive shop, a rotating observation tower, a Mayan village, and two theatres that put on worthwhile cultural shows. Excursions run about $98, and take up a full day from Cozumel.

XEL-HA ECO PARK Farther south of Xcaret, Xel-Ha (pronounced "Shell-*ha*") features a sprawling natural lagoon filled with sparkling blue-green water and surrounded by lush foliage. The use of inner tubes and life vests are included in the admission price, and you can spend a great couple of hours wending your way from one end of the snaking body of calm water to the other, accompanied by schools of tropical fish. Snorkeling gear is available for rental. Xel-Ha has dolphins, too, along with shops, restaurants, and lots of beach chairs. They also offer Snuba and Sea Treking, at an additional cost.

COZUMEL

The ancient Mayans, who lived here for 12 centuries, would be shocked by the million cruise passengers who now visit Cozumel each year, and by the fast-food, raucous-bar, and power-shopping character of San Miguel. Outside town, though, development hasn't squashed the island's natural beauty, and there are still armadillos, brightly colored tropical birds, and lizards scuttling among the dunes. Offshore, the government has set aside 32km (20 miles) of coral reefs as an underwater national park, including the stunning Palancar Reef, the world's second-largest natural coral formation.

COMING ASHORE   It seems like the whole coast of San Miguel is cruise ship berths these days. The newest is **Punta Langosta,** right in the center of town, which puts you just steps from the shops, restaurants, and cafes across the street. (The ferries to Playa del Carmen dock about .4km/¼ mile away.) Other ships pull alongside the well-accoutered **International Pier** (3.2km/2 miles south of San Miguel) or at the **Puerto Maya pier** (another kilometer or so farther south), both about $5 taxi ride from town or a 30- to 45-minute walk from the heart of San Miguel. The beaches are close to the International Pier.

GETTING AROUND

The town of San Miguel is so small you can walk anywhere you want to go. Essentially, there's only one road in Cozumel—it starts at the northern tip of the island, hugs the western shoreline, and then loops around the southern tip and returns to the capital. **Taxis** are available at the piers, and the average fare from San Miguel to most major resorts and beaches is between $10 and $15; between the International terminal and downtown it's about $6. It's customary to overcharge cruise ship passengers, so settle on a fare before getting in. **Motor scooters** and **mopeds** are also a popular means of getting around, and can be rented from (among others) **Auto Rent** (© 987/872-3532) in the Hotel El Cid La Ceiba (right next to the International Pier), and **Rentadora El Dorado** (© 987/872-2383), 181-C Avenida Juarez. The cost is about $30 to $35 per day, including helmet; insurance is an extra $6.

BEST CRUISE LINE SHORE EXCURSIONS

See "Mayan Ruins & Other Mainland Attractions," above, for details on the big mainland excursions. In addition to those below, the cruise lines also offer dozens of different snorkeling, party-boat, and underwater excursions in Cozumel.

Tropical 4x4 Safari Tour ($89, 4½ hr.): Hop in a four-seat Jeep, draw straws to see who gets to drive, and explore the natural side of Cozumel. Much of the roller-coaster-like route is off-road, and the Jeeps travel in a convoy, stopping eventually at a lovely secluded beach for swimming and a picnic lunch.

Mayan Frontier Horseback Riding ($93, 3–4 hr.): Worthwhile horseback-riding tours offer a chance to see Cozumel's landscape, but although they tout visits to Mayan ruins, don't get your hopes up—there's little more than a few refrigerator-size rocks here and there on Cozumel. A bus transports riders to a ranch, where the ride begins.

ON YOUR OWN: WITHIN WALKING DISTANCE

Avenida Rafael Melgar, the principal street along the waterfront, traces the western shore of the island, site of the best resorts and beaches. Most of the shops and restaurants are along this street. The things to do here are basically shop and drink, and boy oh boy are there a lot of choices.

Carlos 'n Charlie's, Av. Rafael Melgar 551 (© **987/869-1446;** www.carlosn-charlies.com), is Mexico's equivalent of the Hard Rock Cafe, but much wilder. Though it moved a few years ago from its old beer-slooped digs into a more sterile Houlihan's-style space right across from the Punta Langosta pier, it's still got deafening music and dancing tourists pounding down yardlong glasses of beer. Many a cruise passenger has stumbled back from this place clutching a souvenir glass as though it were the Holy Grail—dubious proof of a visit to Mexico. Other party spots include the **Hard Rock Cozumel** itself, at Av. Rafael Melgar 2A (© **529/872-5273;** www.hardrock.com), and **Fat Tuesday,** at the end of the International Pier (© **987/872-5130**).

If that's not your scene, you can drop into the small **Museo de la Isla de Cozumel,** on Rafael Melgar between Calles 4 and 6 N (© **987/872-1475**). Once Cozumel's first luxury hotel, it now displays exhibits that take you from pre-Hispanic times and through the colonial era to the present. Admission is $3.

ON YOUR OWN: BEYOND THE PORT AREA

About a $10 taxi ride from the center of San Miguel is the **Chankanaab Nature Park,** Carretera Sur, Kilometer 9 (no phone), where a saltwater lagoon, offshore reefs, and underwater caves have been turned into an archaeological park, botanical garden, and wildlife sanctuary. More than 10 countries have contributed seedlings and cuttings. Some 60 species of marine life occupy the lagoon, including sea turtles and captive dolphins (that you can swim with for $155 for 3 hours, ages 6 and up). Reproductions of Mayan dwellings are scattered throughout the park. There's also a wide white-sand beach with thatch umbrellas and a changing area with lockers and showers. Both scuba divers and snorkelers enjoy examining the sunken ship offshore (there are four dive shops here). Admission is $12.

The few Mayan ruins on Cozumel—**San Gervasio** (north of San Miguel), once a ceremonial center and capital, and **El Cedral** (to the south), site of a Mayan arch and a few small ruins covered in heavy growth—are very, very minor compared to those on the mainland, and only worth visiting if you happen to be in the neighborhood (visiting Playa San Francisco, say, which lies about 3.2km/2 miles from El Cedral).

BEACHES

Cozumel's best powdery white-sand beach, **Playa San Francisco,** stretches for some 4.8km (3 miles) along the southwestern shoreline. You can rent equipment for watersports here, or have lunch at one of the many palapa restaurants and bars on the shoreline. There's no admission to the beach, and it's about a $10 taxi ride south of San Miguel's downtown pier. If you land at the International Pier, you're practically at the beach already.

Playa del Sol, about 1.6km (1 mile) south of Playa del San Francisco, is a decent beach, but expect loud music, lots of booze, and tons of fellow cruisers; many ships offer beach excursions here (with lunch and/or drinks vouchers included). It's not a great spot for families with young children. **Playa Bonita** (sometimes called "Punta Chiqueros") sits in a moon-shaped cove on the island's eastern (windward) side, sheltered from the Caribbean Sea by an offshore reef. It's one of the least crowded beaches, but harder to get to than the others.

SHOPPING

Wall-to-wall shops along the waterfront in San Miguel, starting right across the street from the Punta Langosta pier and stretching in every direction, sell the usual tourist goods, Mexican crafts, and especially **silver jewelry,** which is big business here. The latter is generally sold by weight. Because of the influx of cruise ship passengers, prices are relatively high, but you can and should bargain. If you're docking at the International Pier, a bunch of nice shops in the terminal sell everything from Mexican blankets to jewelry, T-shirts, and handicrafts of all kinds. The pier at Puerta Maya also has a selection of well-stocked gift shops. A fun shop with several locations in the Caribbean is **Del Sol.** Everything they sell changes color in the sunlight, from T-shirts to nail polish and sunglasses.

PLAYA DEL CARMEN

The famed white-sand beach here was relatively untouched by tourists not many years ago, but today the pleasure-seeking hordes have replaced the Indian families who used to gather coconuts for *copra* (dried coconut meat). Shops have sprung up like weeds.

COMING ASHORE   Some cruise ships anchor offshore or at the pier of Cozumel, then send passengers over to Playa del Carmen by tender. Others dock at the **Puerto Calica Cruise Pier** (a former dock for freighters carrying cement), 13km (8 miles) south of Playa del Carmen. Taxis meet each arriving ship here, and drivers transport visitors into the center of Playa del Carmen—which is a good thing since there's nothing to do at Calica save for making a phone call or buying a soda.

GETTING AROUND

BY TAXI   The ferry dock is right in town, near the beach and most major shops. You probably won't need them, but taxis are available to take you anywhere.

BY RENTAL CAR   If you decide to rent a car for the day, Avis, Budget, Hertz, and National all have offices in Playa del Carmen.

SHORE EXCURSIONS

Most visitors head for the Mayan ruins or one of the local water parks the moment they reach shore (see "Best Cruise Line Shore Excursions," in the Cozumel section, above).

ON YOUR OWN: WITHIN WALKING DISTANCE

From where the ferry docks, you can walk to the center of Playa del Carmen, to the beach, and to the small but ever expanding shopping district, which has some pretty trendy boutiques and hip restaurants. **Señor Frog's** (© **984/803-3498**), right at the ferry pier, is another of those "all the beer and shots you can stomach" places, like Carlos 'n Charlie's (p. 576) on the island. For all attractions beyond town, see "Mayan Ruins & Other Mainland Attractions," on p. 572.

SHOPPING

Most shops are along Avenida 5, a stretch of which near the dock is pedestrian-only. The **Rincon del Sol** plaza is a tree-filled courtyard between Calle 4 and Calle 6, built in the colonial Mexican style. It has the best collection of handicraft shops in the area, some of which offer much better quality merchandise than the junky souvenirs peddled elsewhere.

COSTA MAYA

Costa Maya is located near the sleepy fishing village of Mahajual, just over 161km (100 miles) south of Playa del Carmen and not too far from the Mexico/Belize border. Millions of dollars were invested in a pier that opened here not too many years ago, and in a lavish oceanfront shopping and restaurant complex that caters exclusively to the needs of the cruise ship passengers. Princess, Royal Caribbean, Carnival, and Norwegian are among the lines that visit the port. The Mayan ruins of nearby

Kohunlich and Chacchoben are the draw, along with silky white beaches and diving and snorkeling at the Chincorro, Mexico's largest coral atoll.

COMING ASHORE Costa Maya is a self-contained port stop, dropping you right at the purpose-built facilities.

GETTING AROUND **Taxis** line up just outside the pier, and are the only way of getting to sites beyond walking distance. Because of this, prices are steep and non-negotiable. Visiting the Mayan ruins of Kohunlich will set passengers back $65 per person round-trip, while a round-trip ride to Chacchoben comes in around $45 per person. With prices like these, we recommend you book the shore excursions instead (see below).

BEST CRUISE LINE SHORE EXCURSIONS

The Mayan Ruins of Kohunlich ($79, 7 hr.): Located in a secluded jungle setting near the border of Belize, this Mayan city was built between A.D. 200 and 900, spanning the early- through the late-classical periods. The trail to the ruins is marked by a tree that was uprooted and replanted upside down—a means of marking sites used by the apparently brilliant, though obviously eccentric, Mexican archaeologist who first explored the site. Check out the **Plaza of the Acropolis** (where two temples are aligned with the equinox) and the **Temple of the Masks** from the 6th century, where 6-foot stucco masks of the Mayan sun god are remarkably well preserved.

The Mayan Ruins of Chacchoben ($62, 4 hr.): Opened to the public in 1999, this collection of temples dates back to A.D. 360, or the middle of the early-classical period, and played an important role as a trading center for wood, jade, and colorful birds. There are more than two dozen structures, but, to date, less than 5% of the site has been excavated. The first temple encountered is the **Temple of Venus,** a tribute to fertility. The pyramids are in an excellent state of preservation, and their distinctive curved edges and soft lines are particularly beautiful. Climbing to the first plateau affords an impressive view of the surrounding area.

Bike & Kayak Adventure ($48–$54, 3 hr.): Starting off on mountain bikes, you pedal along a dirt road past a small mangrove lagoon with views of the coastline, then through the village of Mahajual (don't blink or you'll miss it), and finally arrive at the beach. After a short refreshment break, trade in your helmet for a paddle and pair up with a partner for a kayak trip out along the nearby reef. The small two-person kayaks are easily launched from the shore and easy to handle. The bike ride back includes another beach stop.

Coral Reef Sail & Snorkel ($54, 3 hr.): A boat takes you to a nearby coral reef, where you can explore with an expert guide.

Dune Buggy Jungle & Beach Safari ($79–$82, 3½ hr.): A drive-yourself convoy excursion in honest-to-god dune buggies (how '60s . . .), leaving from Mahajaul out onto unpaved roads on the way to La Palapa Beach, where you'll have time to swim or use the kayaks and volleyball court.

Jungle Beach Break ($36, no set time): A shuttle operates between the nearby Uvero Beach and the pier every 35 minutes, allowing you to come and go as you please. Not that you'll want to leave the snow-white beaches and crystal-blue water, not to mention the chaise longues and umbrellas; open bar; free snorkel gear; paddle boats; and the sea kayaks, jet skis, and power boats you can rent. Changing rooms with showers and a snack bar are on-site (food not included). Parasailing is also available.

ON YOUR OWN: WITHIN WALKING DISTANCE

If you choose, you could stay right at the one-stop-shop pier complex and still get a taste of the Mayan coast. A 650-seat amphitheatre here offers **cultural shows** daily, from a pre-Hispanic dance drama to a Mexican folkloric performance. There are also activities throughout the day in and around the pier, from guacamole-making classes to aqua-aerobics, games, and contests, plus sprawling restaurants (one with a balcony, the other with outdoor seating and a stage for live music), two saltwater pools, a pool bar, a trampoline, and plenty of shops. Check the daily **entertainment schedule** posted near the restrooms for performance times and activities. Immediately next to the pier is a lovely **private beach club** with umbrellas, chairs, hammock swings, and a small restaurant and bar. There's a small fee for day passes. Enter from the parking lot near the bus departure point.

ON YOUR OWN: BEYOND THE PORT AREA

The only town in the area is the **Mahajaul fishing village,** which until quite recently did not even have electricity. A single main road is lined with a short row of rustic, screened-in restaurants and a miniscule grocery; across the street is a long white beach lined with fishing boats and noticeably devoid of beach umbrellas and sunbathers. Unless you're just curious, there's no real reason to go.

SHOPPING

Because the port at Costa Maya was constructed with the sole purpose of serving American and European cruise ship passengers, you can bet your last enchilada that shopping abounds. There are some 70 shops in a mall-like setting, some of them familiar to the seasoned cruiser, others unique. **Ultra Femme** specializes in fragrances and cosmetics cheaper than you'll find at the duty-free. If it's gold and jewels you're after, head over to **Tanzanite International** for a wide selection and friendly staff, or to **Diamond International** for some great bargains. Next door, you can haggle over "art in silver" at **Taxco Factory.** For something different, head over to the two nearby palapas, where local artisans craft their wares as potential buyers look on.

PROGRESO/MERIDA

Visited by a fraction of the ships that call at Cozumel, Progreso has one major advantage over its rival: proximity to Chichén-Itzá (p. 572), which lies only 2 hours south by motorcoach. This also makes excursions to the ruins considerably cheaper than from Cozumel, averaging about $95 per person. Progreso itself is almost nothing but a port. Ships dock here at the end of a man-made causeway that juts several miles out into the Gulf of Mexico, making it very difficult to visit anything on your own. We recommend taking a tour. Aside from visits to Chichén-Itzá and the smaller Mayan ruins at Uxmal and Dzibilchaltun, cruise passengers can take a tour of **Merida,** the capital of Yucatán state (about 32km/20 miles away), visit the Celestun Estuary Nature Reserve to see pink flamingos in their natural habitat, or take a jeep trek off-road to two local haciendas.

9 Curaçao

As you sail into the harbor of Willemstad, be sure to look for the quaint "floating bridge," the Queen Emma pontoon bridge, which swings aside to open the narrow channel. Welcome to Curaçao (pronounced "Coo-ra-*sow*"), the largest and most populous of the Netherlands Antilles, just 56km (35 miles) north of the Venezuelan coast. Because much of the island's surface is an arid desert, Dutch settlers in the 17th century developed it into a trading post rather than trying to farm, and a huge oil-processing operation located here in the early 20th century resulted in a large population influx and today's curious mixture of bloodlines, including African, Dutch, Venezuelan, and Pakistani. Today the island still retains a Dutch flavor, especially in **Willemstad,** whose harbor is bordered by rows of picture-postcard, pastel-colored, gabled Dutch-colonial houses. While these structures give the town a storybook appearance, the rest of the island looks like the American Southwest, its desertlike landscape dotted with three-pronged cacti, spiny-leafed aloes, and divi-divi trees bent by trade winds.

COMING ASHORE   Cruise ships dock in Willemstad at a megapier just beyond the Queen Emma pontoon bridge, which leads to the duty-free shopping sector and the famous floating market. The adjacent fort houses **Riffort Village,** a shopping/entertainment complex.

GETTING AROUND   From the pier, it's a 5- to 10-minute walk to the center of town, or you can take a **taxi** from the stand. The town itself is easy to navigate on foot. Most of it can be explored in 2 or 3 hours, leaving plenty of time for beaches or watersports. Taxi drivers waiting at the cruise dock will take you to any of the beaches. To be on the safe side, arrange to have your driver pick you up at a certain time and take you back to the cruise dock. Four passengers can share the price of an island tour by taxi, which costs about $18 per person per hour, with a 2-hour minimum. Vans carry up to nine passengers.

LANGUAGE & CURRENCY   Dutch, Spanish, and English are spoken on Curaçao. The official currency is the **Netherlands Antillean florin** (NAf), also called a guilder: US$1 = 1.77 NAf (1 NAf = US56¢). Most places accept U.S. dollars for purchases.

CALLING FROM THE U.S.   When calling Curaçao from the United States, you need to dial the international access code **(011)** before the numbers listed in this section.

BEST CRUISE LINE SHORE EXCURSIONS

Many excursions aren't really worth the price here—you can easily see the town on your own and hop a taxi to the few attractions on the island outside of Willemstad.

Spanish Water Canoe & Snorkeling ($69, 3½ hr.): At Caracas Bay Island, you'll board canoes for a 45-minute paddle alongside mangroves and rock formations, then arrive at Baya Beach where instructors lead snorkeling over a sunken tug boat.

Animal Encounter Scuba Adventure ($89, 4 hr.): Ever want to hand-feed a shark? Here's your chance. Suit up in scuba gear and dive into the shallow (3.6m/12-ft.) water at the Curaçao Seaquarium, where sharks and sea turtles are behind fencing, with holes through which you can hand them their grub while stingrays, parrotfish, and other marine life swim around on your side. Because the water is so shallow, scuba certification isn't required.

ON YOUR OWN: WITHIN WALKING DISTANCE

Willemstad is the major attraction here, and you can see it on foot. After years of restoration, the town's historic center and the island's natural harbor, Schottegat, have been inscribed on UNESCO's World Heritage List. Be sure to watch the **Queen Emma pontoon bridge** in action. It's motorized and a man actually drives it to the side of the harbor every so often so ships and boats can pass through the channel. It's the coolest thing to see. In the **Brionplein** square at the Otrabanda end of the bridge, a statue commemorates Curaçao-born Pedro Luis Brion, who fought for the independence of Venezuela and Colombia as an admiral under Simón Bolívar. **Fort Amsterdam,** site of the Governor's Palace and the 1769 Dutch Reformed church, has the task of guarding the waterfront. The church still has a British cannonball embedded in it. A corner of the fort stands at the intersection of Breedestraat and Handelskade, the starting point for a plunge into the island's major shopping district.

A few minutes' walk from the pontoon bridge, at the north end of Handelskade, is the **Floating Market,** where scores of sailing ships arrive from Venezuela, Colombia, and neighboring West Indian islands, tying up alongside the canal to sell tropical fruits, vegetables, and handicrafts.

Between the I. H. (Sha) Capriles Kade and Fort Amsterdam, at the corner of Columbusstraat and Hanchi di Snoa, is the **Mikve Israel-Emanuel Synagogue.** Dating from 1651, the Jewish congregation here is the oldest in the New World. Next door, the **Jewish Cultural Historical Museum,** Hanchi Snoa 29 (© **599/ 9-461-1633;** www.snoa.com), is housed in two buildings dating from 1728. They were the rabbi's residence and the *mikvah* (bath) for religious purification purposes. Entry is through the synagogue and admission is $2.15.

The **Curaçao Museum,** Van Leeuwenhoekstraat (© **599/9-462-3873**), is housed in a restored 1853 building constructed by the Royal Dutch Army as a military hospital. Today, it displays paintings, objets d'art, and antique furniture, as well as a large collection from the Caiquetio tribes. Admission is $3.25.

ON YOUR OWN: BEYOND THE PORT AREA

Cacti, bromeliads, rare orchids, iguanas, donkeys, wild goats, and many species of birds thrive in the **Christoffel National Park** (© **599/9-864-0363**), located about a 30-minute taxi or car ride from the capital near the northwestern tip of Curaçao. The park rises from flat, arid countryside to 369m (1,230-ft.) **St. Christoffelberg,** the tallest point in the Dutch Leewards. Along the way are ancient Arawak paintings and the **Piedra di Monton,** a rock heap piled by African slaves who cleared this former plantation. Legend says slaves could climb to the top of the rock pile, jump off, and fly back home across the Atlantic to Africa. If they had ever tasted a grain of salt, however, they would crash to their deaths. The park has 32km (20 miles) of one-way trail-like roads. The shortest is about 8km (5 miles) long, but takes about 40 minutes to drive because of its rough terrain. One of several hiking trails goes to the top of St. Christoffelberg. It takes about 1½ hours to walk to the summit (come early in the morning before it gets hot). Admission is $9.

The **Curaçao Sea Aquarium,** off Bhpor Kibra (© **599/9-465-8900;** www. curacao-sea-aquarium.com), displays more than 400 species of fish, crabs, anemones, and other invertebrates, sponges, and coral. This is the site of the "Animal Encounter" excursion described above, and there are also various dolphin swims available, starting at $144. Nonswimmers can see the underwater life from a 14m (46-ft.) semisubmersible observatory. Admission is $15.

Stalactites are mirrored in a mystical underground lake in **Hato Caves,** F. D. Rosseveltweg (© **599/9-868-0379**). Long ago, geological forces uplifted this limestone terrace, which was originally a coral reef. The limestone formations were created over thousands of years by water seeping through the coral. After crossing the lake, you enter two caverns known as "The Cathedral" and La Ventana ("The Window"), where you'll see samples of ancient Indian petroglyphs. Local guides take visitors through every hour. Admission is $6.25.

BEACHES

Curaçao has some 38 beaches, but in general they aren't as good as others in the region. The **Curaçao Seaquarium** has the island's only full-facility, white-sand, palm-shaded beach, but you'll have to pay the full aquarium admission to get in (see "On Your Own: Beyond the Port Area," above). The rest of the beaches are public. Southeast of Willemstad, **Santa Barbara Beach** sits on land owned by a mining company between the open sea and the island's primary watersports and recreational area, known as Spanish Water. It's got pure-white sand and calm water; a buoy line protects swimmers from boats; and there are restrooms, changing rooms, watersports equipment, and a snack bar. The beach has access to the **Curaçao Underwater Park** (© 599/9-462-4242), which stretches from the Breezes Resort to the eastern tip of Curaçao and includes some of the island's finest reefs. **Blauwbaai** (Blue Bay), just north of town, is the largest and most frequented beach on Curaçao, with enough white sand for everybody. Along with showers and changing facilities, there are plenty of shady places to retreat from the noonday sun. At the top of the island, **Westpunt** is known for its gigantic cliffs and the Sunday divers who jump from them into the ocean below. **Knip Bay** and **Playa Abao,** just south of Westpunt, have beautiful turquoise waters.

SHOPPING

Curaçao is a shopper's paradise, with some 200 stores lining Heerenstraat, Breedestraat, and other streets in the 5-block district called the **Punda.** Many shops occupy the town's old Dutch houses. The island is famous for its 5-pound "wheelers" of **Gouda and Edam cheese.** Also look for good buys on wooden shoes, French perfumes, Dutch blue Delft souvenirs, finely woven Italian silks, Japanese and German cameras, jewelry, silver, Swiss watches, linens, leather goods, liquor, and island-made rum and liqueurs, especially Curaçao liqueur, some of which has a distinctive blue color. Some stores also offer good buys on intricate lacework imported from everywhere between Portugal and China. If you're a street shopper and want something colorful, consider a carving or flamboyant painting from Haiti or the Dominican Republic; both are hawked by street vendors at any of the main plazas.

10 Dominica

First things first. It's pronounced "Dome-ee-*nee*-ka," not "Doe-*min*-i-ka." And it has nothing to do with the Dominican Republic. The Commonwealth of Dominica is an independent country, and English, not Spanish, is the official language. The only Spanish commonly understood in Dominica is *mal encaminado a Santo Domingo* ("accidentally sent to the Dominican Republic"), the phrase stamped on the many letters that make it to their proper destination only after an erroneous but common detour.

Dominica is the most lush and mountainous island in the eastern Caribbean, a 29-by 16-mile swatch of crystal-pure rivers, dramatic waterfalls, volcanic lakes, and gargantuan foliage, all accessible via river trips or hikes along undemanding jungle trails. The island's people, primarily descendants of the West African slaves, are another great natural resource. Don't be surprised when you're greeted with a smile and an "okay," the island's equivalent of "hi." Unfortunately, in Roseau, the main city, you may also be greeted by drug dealers offering to sell you some of the local weed—tourism might be a still-developing industry here, but some others are obviously a little further along. The island is also notable for its population of some 3,000 Caribe Indians, the last remaining descendants of the people who dominated the region when Europeans arrived.

COMING ASHORE   Dominica has two cruise ship ports. The most frequented is right in the heart of **Roseau,** the country's capital and largest town. The other is near the northwestern town of **Portsmouth,** with a tourist welcome center and instant access to Fort Shirley and Cabrits National Park.

GETTING AROUND   Fleets of **taxis** and **public minivans** await cruise ship passengers at the Roseau and Portsmouth docks. Drivers are generally knowledgeable about sites and history, and the standard sightseeing rate is from $20 per site per person. The vehicles are unmetered, so negotiate a price in advance and make sure everyone's talking about the same currency.

LANGUAGE & CURRENCY   **English** is Dominica's official language. The **Eastern Caribbean dollar** (EC$2.70 = US$1; EC$1 = US37¢) is its official currency, but U.S. dollars are accepted almost everywhere.

BEST CRUISE LINE SHORE EXCURSIONS

Trafalgar Falls & Emerald Pool Nature Tour ($45, 3½ hr.): Drive to Morne Bruce for a panoramic view of Roseau and learn about local flora and fauna at the Botanical Gardens. Proceed to a lookout point for a majestic view of Trafalgar Falls. Another drive and a 15-minute walk along a relatively easy trail takes you to the Emerald Pool, named for the moss-covered boulders that enclose it. You can splash in the refreshing water if you like, floating on your back to see the thick rainforest canopy, the 50-foot waterfall, and the bright blue sky above you.

Home of the Carib Indians ($54, 5 hr.): Along a rugged portion of Dominica's northeastern coast, the 3,700-acre Carib Territory is home to the world's last surviving Carib Indians. The Caribs today live like most other rural islanders—growing bananas and coconuts, fishing, and operating small shops—but their sturdy baskets of dyed and woven larouma reeds and their wooden canoes (carved from the trunks of massive gommier trees) are evidence of the people's links to the past. The tribe's chief will acquaint you with Carib history, and you'll see a performance by the Karifuna Cultural Group.

Layou Gorge River Tubing ($64, 3 hr.): A 40-minute drive takes you into the Layou Valley, where tubing guides will take you down the river, lined with tall, overhanging cliffs and lush vegetation.

Dominica by Jeep & Swimming at the Titou Gorge ($99, 3½ hr.): A jeep convoy heads up Morne Bruce for a picturesque view, stopping at the Botanical Gardens and the Wotten Waven Sulpher Springs before arriving at the volcanic Titou Gorge, where sheer 20-foot black walls, rock outcrops, caves, and a thundering waterfall provide an exhilarating swimming experience.

Kayak & Snorkel Safari ($59, 3½ hr.): A guided kayaking trip takes you from Soufrière to your snorkeling site at Scotts Head. The bay here is home to an amazing amount of marine life and coral, and its common to see dolphins and frigate birds feeding.

ON YOUR OWN: WITHIN WALKING DISTANCE

IN ROSEAU   As you come ashore, you'll see the **Dominica Museum,** which faces the bay front. Housed in an old market house dating from 1810, the museum's permanent exhibit provides a clear and interesting overview of the island's geology, history, archaeology, economy, and culture. The displays on pre-Columbian peoples, the slave trade, and the Fighting Maroons—slaves who resisted their white slave owners and established their own communities—are particularly informative. Admission is $3. They're usually closed Sundays, but open when a ship is in port.

It took more than 100 years to build the **Roseau Cathedral of Our Lady of Fair Heaven,** on Virgin Lane. Made of cut volcanic stone in the Gothic-Romanesque revival style, it was finally completed in 1916. The original funds to build it were raised from levies on French planters, Caribs erected the first wooden ceiling frame, and convicts on Devil's Island built the pulpit.

On the eastern edge of Roseau, the **Botanical Gardens** lie at the base of Morne Bruce, the mountain overlooking the town. The gardens were established at the end of the 19th century to encourage crop diversification and to provide farmers with correctly propagated seedlings. London's Kew Gardens provided exotic plants collected from every corner of the tropical world, and experiments conducted to see what would grow in Dominica revealed that everything does.

IN PORTSMOUTH   The cruise ship dock at Portsmouth leads directly to 260-acre **Cabrits National Park,** which combines stunning mountain scenery, tropical deciduous forest and swampland, volcanic-sand beaches, coral reefs, and the romance of 18th-century **Fort Shirley,** which, along with more than 50 other major structures, comprises one of the West Indies' most impressive and historic military complexes. Admission is $2.

ON YOUR OWN: BEYOND THE PORT AREAS

Approximately 15 to 20 minutes by car from Roseau, **Trafalgar Falls** is actually two separate falls referred to as the mother and the father falls. The cascading white torrents dazzle in the sunlight before pummeling black lava boulders below. The surrounding foliage comes in innumerable shades of green. To reach the brisk water of the natural pool at the base of the falls, you'll have to step gingerly along slippery rocks, so the nonballetic shouldn't attempt the climb. The constant mist that tingles the entire area beats any spa treatment. The rainbows are perpetual.

Hard-core masochists have an easy choice—the forced march through the **Valley of Desolation** to **Boiling Lake.** Experienced guides say this 6-hour hike is like spending hours on a maximally resistant Stairmaster. So why would any sane person endure this hell? To breathe in the harsh, sulfuric fumes that have killed all but the hardiest vegetation? Because the idea of baking a potato in the steam rising from the earth is irresistible? Maybe to feel the thrill that comes with the risk that you might break through the thin crust that separates you from hot lava? Or could it be the final destination, the wide cauldron of bubbling, slate-blue water of unknown depth? Don't even think of taking a dip in this flooded fumarole: The water temperature is about 190°F (88°C). Can we sign you up?

BEACHES

If your sole focus is beaches, you'll likely find Dominica disappointing. Much of the seacoast is rocky, and many sandy beaches have dark, volcanic sand. There are golden sand beaches as well, but all are located on the northern coast, quite far from Roseau.

SHOPPING

In addition to the usual duty-free items, Dominica offers handicrafts and art not obtainable anywhere else, most notably **Carib Indian baskets** made of dyed larouma reeds and balizier (heliconia) leaves. Designs for these items originated in Venezuela's Orinoco River valley and have been handed down from generation to generation since long before the time of Columbus. Dominican designs and materials are similar to those made today in the Orinoco valley—amazing considering that there's been no interaction between the two peoples for more than 500 years. The Carib basket you buy, therefore, is more than a souvenir; it's a link to the pre-Columbian Caribbean. You can buy Carib crafts directly from the craftspeople in the Carib Territory or at various outlets in Roseau. Prices are ridiculously reasonable.

In Roseau, the cobbled **Old Market Square** is a bustling market located directly behind the Dominica Museum, offering mostly handicrafts and souvenirs. At **Tropicrafts,** at the corner of Queen Mary Street and Turkey Lane, you can watch local women weave grass mats with designs as varied and complex as those you made as a child with your Spirograph. The large store also stocks Carib baskets, locally made soaps and toiletries, rums, jellies, condiments, woodcarvings, and masks made from the trunks of giant fougère ferns.

11 Grand Cayman

Flat, relatively unattractive, and full of scrubland and swamp, Grand Cayman and its sister islands (Cayman Brac and Little Cayman) nevertheless boast more than their share of upscale, expensive private homes and condos, owned by millionaire expatriates from all over who come because of the tiny nation's lenient tax and banking laws. (Enron, the poster child of shady business dealings, reportedly had more than 690 different subsidiaries here to help it avoid paying U.S. taxes.) Grand Cayman is also popular because of its laid-back civility—so civil that ships aren't allowed to visit on Sunday. George Town is the colony's capital and its commercial hub, and many hotels line the sands of the nation's most famous sunspot, Seven Mile Beach. Scuba divers and snorkelers come for the coral reefs and other formations that lie sometimes within swimming distance of the shoreline.

In 2004, Hurricane Ivan tore through Grand Cayman, causing substantial flooding, destroying many homes and businesses, and severely damaging power and sewage networks. Things were such a mess that the island was officially closed to tourists for 2 months. However, with tourism accounting for some 45% of the Caymans' GDP, cleanup was swift. Ships began returning in late November, and at press time, though you could still see roofs and walls torn off of buildings, rebuilding was underway and things were more or less back to normal.

COMING ASHORE   Cruise ships anchor off George Town and ferry their passengers to a pier on Harbour Drive, right in the midst of George Town's shopping district.

GETTING AROUND   Taxis line up at the pier to meet cruise ship passengers. Fares are fixed; typical one-way fares range from $12 to $20. **Motor scooters** and **bicycles** are another way to get around. Soto Scooters Ltd., Seven Mile Beach at Coconut Place (© **345/945-4465**), offers Honda Elite scooters and bicycles for about $30 and $15 daily.

LANGUAGE & CURRENCY   **English** is the official language of the islands. The legal tender is the **Cayman Islands dollar** (CI82¢ = US$1; CI$1 = US$1.22), but

U.S. dollars are commonly accepted. Be sure to note which currency price tags refer to before making a purchase.

BEST CRUISE LINE SHORE EXCURSIONS

Cruise lines typically offer about 30 shore excursions here, most of them of the swimming, snorkeling, sailing, submarine, and glass-bottom boat variety.

Stingray City ($49–$59, 2–3 hr.): The waters off Grand Cayman are home to Stingray City, one of the world's most unusual underwater attractions. Set in very shallow waters of North Sound, about 2 miles east of the island's northwestern tip, the site was discovered in the mid-1980s when local fishermen noticed that scores of stingrays were showing up to feed on the offal they dumped overboard. Today, anywhere from 30 to 100 relatively tame stingrays swarm around the hundreds of visiting snorkelers like so many aquatic basset hounds, eager for handouts. The guides bring buckets of squid and show you the correct way to feed the stingrays, which sort of suck the food right out of your hand. Stingrays are terribly gentle creatures, and love to have their bellies rubbed, but never try to grab one by the tail—their barbed stingers can inflict a lot of pain. Be sure to bring your waterproof camera for this one.

Atlantis Deep-Dive Submarine ($399, 1½ hr., including 55 min. dive): A real research sub takes two passengers at a time down to 800 feet to explore the Cayman Wall through a 3-foot viewing window. Powerful lights illuminate the sponge belt at 400 feet, and delicate coral and deep-sea creatures can be sighted even farther down. Those not quite so adventurous can sign up for the more prosaic **Atlantis Submarine Expedition** ($95, 1½ hr., including 45 min. dive), in which a 48-passenger sub takes you down to 100 feet through coral canyons, with an automatic fish feeder drawing swarms of colorful marine creatures.

Island Cycle Adventure ($59, 3 hr.): A great way to really get a feel for an island—and get some exercise—is via bicycle. You pick up your touring mountain bike at the Beach Club Colony Hotel, ride along the coastline for views of Seven Mile Beach, and then journey inland en route to the north side of the island to ride along the coast again.

ON YOUR OWN: WITHIN WALKING DISTANCE

In George Town, the small **Cayman Islands National Museum,** Harbour Drive (© **345/949-8368;** www.museum.ky), is housed in a veranda-fronted building that once served as the island's courthouse. Exhibits include Caymanian artifacts collected by Ira Thompson (beginning in the 1930s), and other items relating to the natural, social, and cultural history of the Caymans. There's a gift shop, theater, and cafe. Admission is $5 ($2.50 seniors); closed Sundays.

ON YOUR OWN: BEYOND THE PORT AREA

The only green-sea-turtle farm of its kind in the world, **Cayman Turtle Farm,** at Northwest Point, just beyond the town of Hell (© **345/949-3894;** www.turtle.ky), is the island's most popular land-based tourist attraction. Once a multitude of turtles lived in the waters surrounding the Cayman Islands, but today these creatures are an endangered species. The turtle farm's purpose is twofold: to replenish the waters with hatchlings and yearling turtles and, at the other end of the spectrum, to provide the local market with edible turtle meat. You can peer into 100 circular concrete tanks containing turtles ranging in size from 6 ounces to 600 pounds, or sample turtle dishes at a snack bar and restaurant. Admission is $6. Nearby **Hell** is mostly notable for its name (and the T-shirts bearing it), but there are also some unusual rock formations from which the town got its name. If you mail your postcards from here, guess what the postmark says.

BEACHES

Lined with condominiums and plush resorts, **Seven Mile Beach** begins north of George Town, an easy taxi ride from the cruise dock. It has sparkling white sands with a backdrop of Casuarina trees, and is known for its array of watersports and its translucent aquamarine waters. The average water temperature is a balmy 80°F (27°C).

SHOPPING

There's duty-free shopping here for silver, china, crystal, Irish linens, and British woolen goods, but we've found most prices to be similar to those in the United States. You'll also find cigar shops and international chains such as Coach, the leather-goods store. Please don't succumb and purchase turtle or black-coral products. You'll see them everywhere, but it's illegal to bring them back into the United States and most other Western nations.

12 Grenada

Once a British Crown Colony, the now-independent nation of Grenada ("Gre-*nay*-dah") produces more spices than anywhere else in the world, including clove, cinnamon, mace, cocoa, tonka beans, ginger, and a third of the world's nutmeg—and thus its nickname, the "Spice Island." **St. George's,** the country's capital, is one of the most colorful ports in the West Indies, nearly landlocked in the deep crater of a long-dead volcano, full of charming Georgian colonial buildings, and flanked by old forts. The island's coast is white and sandy, while its interior is a jungle of palms, oleander, bougainvillea, and other tropical foliage, crisscrossed by roads and trails.

Grenada was one of the hardest hit Caribbean islands during 2004's devastating hurricane season. Almost every building sustained some level of damage, but you can't keep a good island down. Known for its lushness and most extravagant fertility (results of a gentle climate and volcanic soil), Grenada started springing back almost immediately, its coastal greenery growing back rapidly and its rainforests filling out a little more slowly.

COMING ASHORE Ships either dock at the new multi-million-dollar pier in St. George's (which includes a spiffy new welcome center) or anchor in the much-photographed harbor and send their passengers to the pier by tender. **The Carenage** (St. George's main street) is only a short walk away from the pier.

GETTING AROUND Taxi fares are set by the government. A one-way taxi to Grand Anse (one of the Caribbean's best beaches) is about $15 for up to four passengers. You can also tap most taxi drivers as a guide for a day's sightseeing, for about $25 per hour. **Water taxis** also head from the cruise ship welcome center to Grand Anse. The round-trip fare is about $4.

LANGUAGE & CURRENCY **English** is commonly spoken on this island, and the official currency is the **Eastern Caribbean dollar** (EC$2.70 = US$1; EC$1 = US37¢), though dollars are accepted commonly. Always determine which dollars—EC or U.S.—you're talking about when discussing a price.

BEST CRUISE LINE SHORE EXCURSIONS

Because of Grenada's lush landscape, we recommend spending at least a few hours touring its interior, one of the most scenic in the West Indies.

Hike to Seven Sisters Waterfalls ($59 adult and child, 3½ hr.): After a 40-minute hike along a muddy path in the lush Grand Etang rainforest, passengers are free to take a swim in the natural pools or hop off the edge of the cascading waterfalls. It's gorgeous and lots of fun. Don't forget to wear your bathing suit and maybe a pair of Teva-type sandals.

Island Tour, Grand Etang Lake & Fort Frederick ($44, 4½ hr.): This is a great way to experience Grenada's lush, cool, dripping-wet tropical interior. Via bus, you travel past the red-tiled roofs of St. George's en route to the bright blue Grand Etang Lake, within an extinct volcanic crater some 570m (1,900 ft.) above sea level. On the way, you drive through rainforests and stop at a spice estate. Some tours include a visit to Annandale Falls and Fort Frederick.

ON YOUR OWN: WITHIN WALKING DISTANCE

In St. George's, you can visit the **Grenada National Museum,** at the corner of Young and Monckton streets (© 473/440-3725), set in the foundations of an old French army barracks and prison built in 1704. Small but interesting, it houses ancient petroglyphs and other archaeological finds, a rum still, Joséphine Bonaparte's bathtub from her girlhood in Martinique, and various Grenada memorabilia. Admission is $1. If you're up for a good hike, walk around the historical Carenage from the cruise terminal and head up to **Fort George,** built in 1705 by the French and originally called Fort Royal. While the fort ruins and the 200- to 300-year-old canons are worth taking a peek at, it's the 360-degree panoramic views of the entire harbor area that are most spectacular. You can pick up a rudimentary walking-tour map from the cruise terminal to help you find interesting sites along the way. **Church Street,** which leads right to the fort, has lots of quaint 18th- and 19th-century architecture as well as several 19th-century cathedrals and the island's Houses of Parliament.

ON YOUR OWN: BEYOND THE PORT AREA

You can take a taxi up Richmond Hill to **Fort Frederick,** which the French began in 1779. The British retook the island in 1783 and completed the fort in 1791. From its battlements you'll have a panoramic view of the harbor and the yacht marina.

Don't miss the mountains northeast of St. George's. If you don't have much time, 15m (50-ft.) **Annandale Falls** is just a 15-minute drive away, on the outskirts of the **Grand Etang Forest Reserve.** The overall beauty is almost Tahitian. You can swim and picnic surrounded by liana vines, elephant ears, and other tropical flora and spices. If you've got more time and want a less crowded spot, the even better **Seven Sisters Waterfalls** are farther into Grand Etang, an approximately 30-minute drive and then a mile hike along a muddy trail. It's well worth the trip and you'll really get a feel for the power and beauty of the tropical forest here. The falls themselves are lovely, and you can climb to the top and jump off into the pool below.

If you have time, head to **Levera National Park** in the north of the island for hikes through a mangrove swamp and a bird sanctuary. Just to the south of there, the 1912 **Morne Fendue Plantation House** at St. Patrick's (© 473/442-9330), offers a chance to enjoy old-time island recipes while you dine as an upper-class family would have in the 1920s. They serve a fixed-price ($16) lunch Monday to Saturday from 12:30 to 3pm. Call for reservations.

BEACHES

Grenada's **Grand Anse Beach,** with its 3.2km (2 miles) of wide sugar-white sands, is one of the best in the Caribbean, with calm waters and a great view of St. George's. There are several restaurants beachside, and you can also join a banana-boat ride or rent a Sunfish sailboat.

SHOPPING

Grenada is no grand Caribbean merchandise mart, so if you're cruising on to such islands as Aruba, St. Martin, or St. Thomas, you might want to postpone serious purchases. On the other hand, you can find some fine local handicrafts, gifts, and art here. The best buy is, of course, fresh **spices** and related items. Nutmeg products are especially popular. The Grenadians use every part of the nutmeg: They make the outer fruit into a tasty liqueur and a rich jam, and ground the orange membrane around the nut into a different spice called mace. You'll also see the outer shells used as gravel to cover trails and parking lots.

13 Jamaica

A favorite of North American honeymooners, Jamaica is the third largest of the Caribbean islands after Cuba and Hispaniola, with dense jungle in its interior, mountains rising as high as 2,220m (7,400 ft.), and many beautiful white-sand beaches along its northern coast, where the cruise ships dock. Most head for **Ocho Rios,** although more and more are opting to call at the city of **Montego Bay** ("Mo Bay"), 108km (67 miles) to the west. These ports offer comparable attractions, shore excursions, and shopping possibilities.

One of the most densely populated nations in the Caribbean, with a vivid sense of its own identity, Jamaica has a history rooted in the plantation economy and some of the most impassioned politics in the Western Hemisphere, all of which leads to a sometimes turbulent day-to-day reality. You've probably heard, for instance, that the island's vendors and hawkers can be pushy and the locals not always the most welcoming to tourists, and while there's some truth to this, we've had nothing but positive experiences, so keep an open mind.

LANGUAGE & CURRENCY The official language is **English,** but most Jamaicans speak a richly nuanced patois. The unit of currency is the **Jamaican dollar,** designated by the same symbol as the U.S. dollar (US$1 = J$61; J$1 = US2¢). Visitors can pay in U.S. dollars, but always find out if a price is being quoted in Jamaican or U.S. dollars—though it'll probably be obvious by the huge difference.

SHORE EXCURSIONS OFFERED FROM BOTH PORTS

Since there's little besides shopping near the docks at either Ocho Rios or Montego Bay, most passengers sign up for shore excursions. The following are usually offered from both ports.

Dunn's River Falls Tour ($45, 4–4½ hr. from Ocho Rios; $70, 7½ hr. from Mo Bay): These falls cascade 180m (600 ft.) to the beach and are the most visited attraction in Jamaica, which means they're hopelessly overcrowded when a lot of cruise ships are in port. Tourists are allowed to climb the falls, and it's a ball to slip and slide your way up with the hundreds of others, forming a human chain of sorts. Wear a bathing suit under your clothes, and don't forget your waterproof camera and your aqua-socks. (If you do forget, most cruise lines will rent you aqua-socks for an extra $5.)

The prettiest part of the falls, known as the Laughing Waters, was used in the James Bond classics *Dr. No* and *Live and Let Die*. This tour usually also visits other local attractions, with time allocated for shopping.

River Tubing Safari ($58 3½ hr.): This is one of the best excursions we've ever taken. After a scenic van ride deep into the pristine jungles, the group of 20 or so passengers and a couple of guides sit back into big black inner tubes (they have wooden boards covering the bottom so your butt doesn't get scraped on the rocks), and glide a few miles downriver, passing by gorgeous, towering bamboo trees and other lush foliage. It's sometimes peaceful and sometimes exhilarating—especially when you hit the rapids! If you're docking in Ocho Rios, this tour is usually on the White River. If in Montego Bay, it's on the Great River. *Note:* We find this trip much more interesting than the popular **Martha Brae River Rafting,** which takes you down the river on two-seat bamboo rafts. The cost is about the same.

Horseback-Riding Excursion ($89, 3–3½ hr.): Riders will love this trip, on which, after a 45-minute ride from the stables through fields, you'll gallop along the beach and take your horse bareback into the surf for a thrilling ride.

OCHO RIOS

Once a small banana and fishing port, Ocho Rios is now Jamaica's cruise ship capital, welcoming a couple of ships every day during high season. Though the area has some of the Caribbean's most fabled resorts, and Dunn's River Falls is just a 5-minute taxi ride away, the town itself is not much to see, despite there being a few outdoor local markets within walking distance. Don't expect to shop in the markets without a lot of hassle and a lot of very pushy hawking of merchandise—some of which is likely to be ganja (the wacky weed). In recent years an army of blue-uniformed "resort patrol" officers on bikes have been helping keep order.

COMING ASHORE   Most cruise ships dock at the **Port of Ocho Rios,** near Dunn's River Falls and adjacent to Island Village and several shopping options.

GETTING AROUND   You can walk to the shopping, but otherwise **taxis** are your best means of getting around on your own. They'll be waiting for you at the pier. Taxis licensed by the government display **JTB** decals, indicating they're official Jamaican Tourist Board taxis. Fixed rates are posted.

BEST CRUISE LINE SHORE EXCURSIONS

In addition to tours offered from both Jamaica ports, Ocho Rios also offers tours to several close-in attractions.

Prospect Plantation & Dunn's River Falls ($62, 4 hr.): About 4.8km (3 miles) east of town, Prospect Plantation offers a taste of Jamaica's colonial days (sans slavery), with a tractor-drawn jitney taking you among seasonal crops that include bananas, sugar cane, coffee, pineapple, and papaya. The trip includes a stop at Dunn's River Falls (see above).

Coyaba River Garden & Dunn's River Falls ($49, 3½ hr.): About a mile from town, Coyaba River Garden and Museum was built on the grounds of the former Shaw Park plantation, and displays artifacts from the Arawak, Spanish, and English settlements in the area. The gardens are filled with native flora, a cut-stone courtyard, and fountains. Like many of the other tours in Ocho Rios, it hits Dunn's Falls on the way back.

Mountain Biking to Chukka Cove ($69, 4 hr.): A minivan takes you into the mountains above St. Ann, where you hop on your bike for a ride down back roads, through meadows and woodlands to picturesque Chukka Cove, where you can take a swim.

Dolphin Cove ($34–$89, 2 hr.): Various excursions to this beachfront site allow you to gander at, touch, or swim with the resident dolphins. For about $10 more you can add on an hour and a half at (you guessed it) Dunn's River Falls.

ON YOUR OWN: WITHING WALKING DISTANCE

Adjacent to the cruise pier, **Island Village** (www.islandjamaica.com) is a 4-acre entertainment and shopping complex developed by Island Records' Chris Blackwell. Attractions include the ReggaeXplosion museum, a museum of Jamaican art, a casino, an outdoor concert venue and indoor theater, a beach with watersports, shopping (lots of it), and a branch of Jimmy Buffett's Margaritaville.

ON YOUR OWN: BEYOND THE PORT AREA

South of Ocho Rios, **Fern Gully** was originally a riverbed. Today, the main A3 road winds through a rainforest filled with wild ferns, hardwood trees, and lianas. For the botanist, there are hundreds of varieties of ferns; for the less plant-minded, roadside stands sell fruits and vegetables, carved-wood souvenirs, and basketwork. The road runs for about 6.4km (4 miles).

The 1817 **Brimmer Hall Estate,** Port Maria, St. Mary's (© **876/994-2309**), 34km (21 miles) east of Ocho Rios, is a working plantation where you're driven around in a tractor-drawn jitney to see the tropical fruit trees and coffee plants. Knowledgeable guides tell you about the processes necessary to produce the fine fruits of the island. Afterward, you can relax beside the pool and sample a wide variety of drinks, including an interesting one called "Wow!" The Plantation Tour Eating House offers typical Jamaican dishes for lunch. Tours run daily if there are enough people, so call ahead. Admission is $15. In the same general area, toward the coast, **Firefly,** Grants Pen, above Oracabessa (© **876/997-7201**), was the home of Sir Noël Coward and his longtime companion, Graham Payn, who, as executor of Coward's estate, donated it to the Jamaica National Heritage Trust. The recently restored house is as it was on the day Sir Noël died in 1973. It's open Monday to Thursday from 9am to 5pm. Admission is $10.

BEACHES

Island Village offers a beach immediately adjacent to the cruise port, with activities. **Mallards Beach,** at the Sunset Jamaica Grande (© **876/974-2201**) on Main Street, is shared by hotel guests and cruise ship passengers and tends to be overcrowded. Locals may steer you to the good and less-crowded **Turtle Beach,** southwest of Mallards. You might also want to check out the big **James Bond Beach** in Oracabessa, about 20 minutes from town. Bond author Ian Fleming's home, Goldeneye, is located nearby.

SHOPPING

Shopping in Ocho Rios is not as good as in Montego Bay and other ports, but if your money's burning a hole in your pocket, you can wander around the **Ocho Rios Craft Park,** opposite the Ocean Village Shopping Centre off Main Street. Some 150 stalls stock hats, handbags, place mats, woodcarvings, and paintings, plus the usual T-shirts and jewelry. The **Island Plaza** shopping complex, right in the heart of town, has paintings by local artists, local handmade crafts (be prepared to do some haggling), carvings, ceramics, and even kitchenware. At all of these places, prepare yourself for aggressive selling and fierce haggling. Every vendor asks too much for an item at first; it gives them the leeway to negotiate the price. (Note that some so-called duty-free prices are indeed lower than stateside, but then the Jamaican government hits you with a 15% "General Consumption Tax," so figure that in when shopping.)

MONTEGO BAY

Montego Bay has better beaches, shopping, and restaurants than Ocho Rios, as well as some of the best golf courses in the Caribbean. Like Ocho Rios, Mo Bay also has its crime, traffic, and annoyance, but there's much more to see and do here, at least nearby. (There's little of interest in the town itself except shopping.) Getting from place to place is one of the major difficulties here. Whatever you want to visit seems to be in yet another direction. Shore excursions and taxis are the way to go.

COMING ASHORE Montego Bay has a modern, recently expanded cruise dock, with the usual duty-free stores and tourist information.

GETTING AROUND If you don't book a shore excursion, a taxi is the way to get around. They'll be waiting for you at the pier. Taxis licensed by the government display **JTB** decals, indicating they're official Jamaican Tourist Board taxis. Fixed rates are posted.

BEST CRUISE LINE SHORE EXCURSIONS

In addition to tours offered from both Jamaica ports, Mo Bay also offers tours to several interesting plantations and great houses.

Rose Hall Great House ($43, 3 hr.): This is the most famous plantation home in Jamaica. Built about 2 centuries ago by John Palmer, it gained notoriety from the doings of "Infamous Annie" Palmer, wife of the builder's grandnephew, who supposedly dabbled in witchcraft and took slaves as lovers, killing them when they bored her. Annie was also said to have murdered several of her husbands while they slept, and eventually suffered the same fate herself. For what it's worth, many Jamaicans insist the house is haunted.

Greenwood Great House & Town Drive ($39, 3½ hr.): More interesting to some than Rose Hall, this Georgian-style building was the residence of Richard Barrett, a first cousin of Elizabeth Barrett Browning. On display are the family's library, portraits, antiques, and period musical instruments.

Croydon Plantation Tour ($59, 6 hr.): A guided tour of this mountain estate includes a quarter-mile walk over gently sloping terrain, with a lot of great views. Stops are made for refreshments and seasonal fresh fruits, and at the end you get a traditional Jamaican-style lunch.

ON YOUR OWN: BEYOND THE PORT AREA

There are no real attractions within walking distance. If you're not taking a shore excursion, consider a visit to **Rocklands Wildlife Station,** Anchovy, St. James (© **876/952-2009**). Lisa Salmon, known as the "Bird Lady of Anchovy," established this sanctuary, which is perfect for nature lovers and bird-watchers. You can feed small doves and finches from your hand, and with luck you can coax a Jamaican doctor bird to perch on your finger and drink syrup. Rocklands is about 1.2km (¾ mile) outside Anchovy on the road from Montego Bay. Admission is $8.

Montego Bay Golf Excursions

Montego Bay offers a number of excellent golf opportunities. Various cruise lines offer organized excursions, but you can also arrange play ahead of time on your own, and taxi it to the course.

- **Tryall Club** (© **876/956-5660**; www.tryallclub.com), 19km (12 miles) from Montego Bay, is an excellent, regal 18-hole, par-72 course that's often been the site of major golf tournaments, including the Jamaica Classic Annual and the Johnnie Walker Tournament. Greens fees are $145 plus $30 for a cart.
- **Wyndham Rose Hall Golf & Beach Resort,** Rose Hall (© **876/953-2650**), has a noted 18-hole, par-71 course with an unusual and challenging seaside and mountain layout. The 90m-high (300-ft.) 13th tee offers a rare panoramic view of the sea, and the 15th green is next to a 12m (40-ft.) waterfall, once featured in a James Bond movie. A fully stocked pro shop, a clubhouse, and a professional staff are among the amenities. Greens fees are $125.
- **Half Moon,** at Rose Hall (© **876/953-2560**; www.halfmoon-resort. com/golf), features an 18-hole, par-72 championship course designed by Robert Trent Jones Sr. Greens fees are $130, plus $20 for a mandatory caddy.
- **Ironshore Golf & Country Club,** Ironshore, St. James, Montego Bay (© **876/953-3681**), a well-known, 18-hole, par-72 course, is privately owned but open to the public. Greens fees are $30 to $50, depending on the season, plus $14 for a mandatory caddy.

BEACHES

Doctor's Cave Beach, on Gloucester Avenue across from the Doctor's Cave Beach Hotel (© **876/952-4355**; www.doctorscave.com), helped launch Mo Bay as a resort in the 1940s. Dressing rooms, chairs, umbrellas, and rafts are available. One of the premier beaches of Jamaica, **Aquasol Theme Park** (formerly Walter Fletcher Beach), is in the heart of Mo Bay. It's noted for tranquil waters, which makes it a particular favorite for families with children. Changing rooms are available, and lifeguards are on duty. Nearby, **The Pork Pit,** 27 Gloucester Ave. (© **876/952-1046**), is the best place to go for the famous Jamaican jerk pork and jerk chicken. Many beachgoers come over here for a big lunch. Picnic tables encircle the building, and everything is open-air and informal. Order half a pound of jerk meat with a baked yam or baked potato and a bottle of Red Stripe beer. Prices are very reasonable. Lunch costs $10.

On the main road 18km (11 miles) east of Montego Bay, the half-mile **Rose Hall Beach Club** (© **876/680-0969**) is a secure, secluded, white sandy beach, offering crystal-clear water, a full restaurant, two beach bars, a covered pavilion, an open-air dance area, showers, restrooms, and changing facilities, plus beach volleyball courts, various beach games, live music, and a full watersports activities program. *Note:* All of these beaches charge admission, which runs between about $4 and $6.

SHOPPING

The main shopping areas are at **Montego Freeport,** within easy walking distance of the pier; **City Centre,** where most of the duty-free shops are, aside from those at the large hotels; and **Holiday Village Shopping Centre,** across from the Holiday Inn on Rose Hall Road, heading toward Ocho Rios. The **Old Fort Craft Market,** a shopping complex with nearly 200 vendors licensed by the Jamaica Tourist Board, fronts Howard Cooke Boulevard up from Gloucester Avenue in the heart of Montego Bay, on the site of Fort Montego. With a varied assortment of handicrafts, this is browsing country. You'll see a selection of wall hangings, hand-woven straw items, and hand-carved wood sculptures, and you can also get your hair braided. Vendors can be extremely aggressive, so be prepared for some major hassles, as well as some serious negotiation. Persistent bargaining on your part will lead to substantial discounts. You can find the best selection of handmade Jamaican souvenirs at the **Crafts Market,** near Harbour Street in downtown Montego Bay. Straw hats and bags, wooden platters, straw baskets, musical instruments, beads, carved objects, and toys are all available here. That "jipijapa" hat will come in handy if you're going to be out in the island sun.

14 Key West

Located at the very end of the Florida Keys, Key West is America's southernmost city and has a vibe that mixes colorful Caribbean outpost with a dash of New Orleans high life. It's a fun-loving, heavy-drinking town with a lot of history, more than a little touristy goofiness, a thousand Hemingway look-alikes, and a large gay community. It's a regular melting pot. It's also, as many tour guides like to point out, the Pulitzer Prize winner capital of the U.S., with more winners per capita than anywhere else in the country. The proximity of most attractions to the cruise docks means there's little sense in taking an excursion here unless you have mobility problems. Wander around touristy Mallory Square and Duval Street, check out some of the theme bars, and then take a walk down some of the quieter side streets, maybe visiting Truman's Little White House or the Hemingway House museum. Or, you might want to spend your day playing golf, diving, or snorkeling. Several **"raw bars"** near the dock area offer seafood, including oysters and clams, although the king here is conch—served grilled, ground into burgers, made into chowder, fried in batter as fritters, or served raw in a conch salad (though beware, some of the quickie conch vendors near the docks are pretty skimpy with the conch ... can we say dough balls?). If you've got more of a sweet tooth than anything else, be sure to sample the decadent Frozen Chocolate Dipped Key Lime Pie on a Stick that you can pick up from several places in town.

COMING ASHORE Ships dock at **Mallory Square** (Old Town's tourist central), at the nearby Hilton Resort's **Pier B,** and at the U.S. Navy base's **"Outer Mole" pier.** All are on the Gulf side of the island. Passengers arriving at the Navy pier must take an official shuttle bus the short distance to and from Mallory Square, as individuals are not permitted to transit the base on their own.

LANGUAGE & CURRENCY English and the U.S. dollar.

GETTING AROUND The island is only 4 miles long and 2 miles wide, so getting around is easy. The most popular attractions are within walking distance of Mallory Square. The farthest is Hemingway House, about a mile down Duval. Many passengers opt for one of the island's tram tours, which are sold as shore excursions but are

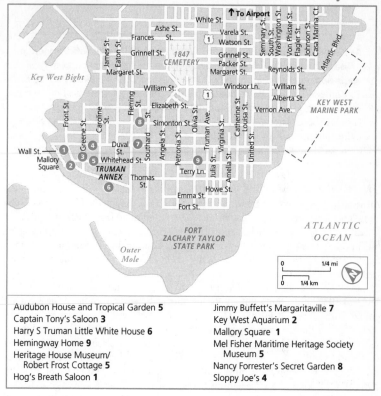

Audubon House and Tropical Garden **5**

Captain Tony's Saloon **3**

Harry S Truman Little White House **6**

Hemingway Home **9**

Heritage House Museum/
Robert Frost Cottage **5**

Hog's Breath Saloon **1**

Jimmy Buffett's Margaritaville **7**

Key West Aquarium **2**

Mallory Square **1**

Mel Fisher Maritime Heritage Society
Museum **5**

Nancy Forrester's Secret Garden **8**

Sloppy Joe's **4**

also available on a walk-up basis. The **Conch Tour Train** (© **305/296-4444;** www.conchtourtrain.com) is a narrated 90-minute tour that offers commentary on 100 local sites. The depot is located at Mallory Square, and trains depart every 30 minutes ($20 adults, $10 children 4–12, free 3 and under). The trip has only one stop where passengers can get on and off (at the Historic Seaport). If you want more flexibility, try the **Old Town Trolley** (© **305/296-6688;** www.trolleytours.com), which allows you to hop on and off its trains to explore on your own. Prices are the same as the Conch Train, and pickup stops are signposted around town. If you want wheels of your own, **bicycles** and **motor scooters** are a good bet here, and are widely available, with daily rates hovering around $12 and $45, respectively.

BEST CRUISE LINE SHORE EXCURSIONS

In addition to the Conch Train Tour described above, most lines offer walking tours and sometimes bike tours for those who like the services of a guide. But, this is really a port to explore on your own.

Key West Catamaran Sail & Snorkel Tour ($44, 3–3½ hr.): The popular Fury catamarans take passengers to a reef for some snorkeling and then finish the trip back to shore with music, booze, and a good time.

Deep-Sea Fishing in Key West

As Hemingway, an avid fisherman, would attest, the waters off the Florida Keys are some of the world's finest fishing grounds. You can follow in Papa's wake aboard the 40-foot *Linda D III* and *Linda D IV* (© **800/299-9798** or 305/296-9798; www.charterboatlindad.com), which offer the best deep-sea fishing here. Full-day charters for up to six people cost $675, half-day $475. Full-day shared charters are $175 per person, half-day $125. Make arrangements as far in advance as possible.

ON YOUR OWN: WITHIN WALKING DISTANCE

All attractions in Key West are within walking distance, though the Hemingway Home and Nancy Forrester's Secret Garden are at least 20 minutes from Mallory Square.

Bars—big, packed theme bars, usually with someone playing guitar and singing the hits in one corner—are a big draw in Key West. **Captain Tony's Saloon,** 428 Greene St. (© **305/294-1838**), is the oldest active bar in Florida, and is both heavily patronized by cruise ship passengers and tacky as hell. The 1851 building was the original Sloppy Joe's, a rough-and-tumble fisherman's saloon. Hemingway drank here from 1933 to 1937, and Jimmy Buffett got his start here before opening his own bar and going on to fame and fortune. The current **Sloppy Joe's,** 201 Duval St. (© **305/294-5717**), is the most touristy bar in Key West, visited by almost all cruise ship passengers, even those who don't normally go to bars. It aggressively plays up its association with Hemingway, with pictures of Hemingway look-alike contest winners plastered all over the walls. **Jimmy Buffett's Margaritaville,** 500 Duval St. (© **305/296-3070**), is kind of a refugee from Branson, Missouri, but if you've got a hankering for a cheeseburger from paradise or want to waste away again on margaritas, this is your place. Much less commercial is the open-air **Hog's Breath Saloon,** 400 Front St. (© **305/296-4222**), near the cruise docks. Raucous and loud, it's populated by visiting fishermen and bikers alike, all of them with drink in hand. Wherever you end up, try some of the favorite local beer, Hog's Breath, or some of the favorite local rum, Key West Gold (even though it's a cheat—it isn't actually made on the island). Most places recommended offer fast food to go with their drinks.

There's a bar at the **Harry S Truman Little White House,** 111 Front St. (© **305/294-9911;** www.trumanlittlewhitehouse.com), too, back in the back room where Truman and his friends played poker—though visitors can't drink there. The house, formerly the home of the Navy base commander, served as Truman's vacation home during his presidency and today remains just as he left it, decorated in late 1940s style. By the time the guides get through their well-organized hourlong tour you'll feel as if you've gone back in time. Admission is $10.

Hemingway Home, 907 Whitehead St. (© **305/294-1136;** www.hemingway home.com), provides a similar if less formal look back at the island's old days. "Papa" lived here with his second wife, Pauline, completing *For Whom the Bell Tolls* and *A Farewell to Arms* in the studio annex out back. Hemingway had some 60 polydactyl (many-toed) cats, whose descendants still live on the grounds. Admission costs $11.

Audubon House and Tropical Garden, 205 Whitehead St., at Greene Street (© 877/281-2473 or 305/294-2116; www.audubonhouse.com), is dedicated to the 1832 Key West sojourn of the famous naturalist John James Audubon. The ornithologist didn't live in this three-story building, but it's filled with his engravings. The main reason to visit is to see how wealthy sailors lived in Key West in the 19th century, and the lush tropical gardens surrounding the house. Admission is $10.

The Heritage House Museum and Robert Frost Cottage, 410 Caroline St. (© 305/296-3573; www.heritagehousemuseum.org), was the home of Jessie Porter Newton, the grande dame of Key West, and today her home is filled with mementos of the illustrious guests who partook of her hospitality, including Tennessee Williams, Gloria Swanson, and Robert Frost, who stayed in a cottage out back.

On the waterfront at Mallory Square, the **Key West Aquarium,** 1 Whitehead St. (© 305/296-2051; www.keywestaquarium.com), in operation since 1932, was the first tourist attraction built in the Florida Keys. The aquarium's special feature is a "touch tank" where you can feel a sea urchin, starfish, or a conch, the town's mascot and symbol. Admission is $9.

The **Mel Fisher Maritime Heritage Society Museum,** near the docks at 200 Greene St. (© 305/294-2633; www.melfisher.com), contains some of the more than $400 million in gold jewelry, doubloons, and other artifacts the late treasure hunter Mel Fisher plucked from the Spanish galleon *Nuestra Señora de Atocha,* which sunk off the Keys in 1622. Educational exhibits explain salvage operations and the history of the Spanish and piracy in the islands. Admission is $10

Nancy Forrester's Secret Garden, 1 Free School Lane, off Simonton between Southard and Fleming streets (© 305/294-0015), is the most lavish and verdant garden in town, with some 150 species of palms and thousands of orchids, climbing vines, and ground covers. Admission is $6.

BEACHES

Beaches are not too compelling here, but the best and closest to the cruise docks is **Fort Zachary Taylor State Beach** (© 305/292-6713), a 12-minute walk away. To get there, go through the gates leading into the Truman Annex (site of the Little White House).

SHOPPING

Within a 12-block radius of **Mallory Square** you'll find mostly tawdry, overpriced tourist merchandise, but if you're in the market for some Key West kitsch, you'll find flamingo snow globes, floppy straw hats, seashell ashtrays, and the like. At Mallory itself, shops sell seashells from the seashore—actually, from around the world, including some you'd hardly believe are real. They also sell wine bottle holders shaped like lobsters, but what the hell. As you move farther along **Duval Street** from Mallory you'll notice that the shops get more and more stylish. Could it be a coincidence that this part of town is the center of Key West's gay community? We don't think so.

15 Martinique

Fairy-tale romance and horrific disaster: Who could resist such an enticing combination? As if being the birthplace and childhood home of Empress Joséphine, sweetheart and wife of Napoleon, weren't enough, Martinique mesmerizes with the epic tragedy that befell St. Pierre one fair day in 1902: bustling cosmopolitan capital one minute, devastated volcanic graveyard of 30,000 souls the next. Love and death make quite a one-two punch, but they're just the hook. Look a bit deeper to appreciate Martinique's subtler attractions—quaint seaside villages, colonial ruins dating to when France and England vied for the island, and captivatingly beautiful rainforests and beaches. In 1946, Martinique became an overseas department of France, which it remains today.

COMING ASHORE   Most cruise ships dock in the heart of Fort-de-France, at the **Pointe Simon Cruise Dock,** which has quays for two large vessels. Because Martinique is a popular port of call, ships may also dock at the **Passenger Terminal** at the main harbor, a cargo port on the north side of the bay, a $10 (8.70€) cab ride from the center of town.

GETTING AROUND   Travel by **taxi** is convenient but expensive. Most cabs are metered, and you'll find them waiting at the cruise pier. To cross the bay to La Pagerie (Empress Joséphine's birthplace) and the resort area of Pointe du Bout, take one of the blue **ferries** that sail from east of the cruise dock in Fort-de-France at least once per hour. Round-trip tickets cost about $4.60 (6€). Avis, Budget, and Hertz all offer **rental cars,** too.

LANGUAGE   **French** is Martinique's official language, but you can get by with **English** at most restaurants and tourist sites. Martinique is an overseas region of France, so the **euro** (€) is the official currency (1€ = US$1.31; $1 = .77€). U.S. dollars are commonly accepted in tourist areas.

CALLING FROM THE U.S.   When calling Martinique from the U.S., dial the international access code **(011)** and **596** before the numbers listed here. The numbers listed here already begin with 596, but an effort by the French telephone authorities to standardize procedures requires that you dial those three digits twice.

BEST CRUISE LINE SHORE EXCURSIONS

Rainforest & Plantations 4WD Safari ($84, 4 hr.): Take your off-road vehicle through tropical forests and sugar-cane plantations (stopping to sample the crop) to a banana plantation and a distillery where you'll do short tours.

Martinique Snorkeling ($49, 3 hr.): Across the bay from Fort-de-France, the reef at Anse Dufour offers excellent snorkeling for experts and novices. The reef is filled with marine animals, including French grunts, blackbar soldierfish, and silversides. Snorkeling equipment is provided, as are professional instruction, supervision, and transportation.

ON YOUR OWN: WITHIN WALKING DISTANCE

Fort-de-France is a bustling town of 100,000 residents, full of ochre buildings, ornate wrought-iron balconies, cascading flowers, and tall palm trees. The town's narrow streets, cluttered with boutiques and cafes, climb from the bowl of the sea to the surrounding hills, forming a great urban amphitheater. There's plenty here to keep you busy.

At the eastern end of downtown, **La Savane** is a broad formal park with palms, mangoes, and manicured lawns, perfect for a promenade or rest in the shade. Its most famous feature is the **Statue of Empress Joséphine,** carved in 1858 by Vital Dubray. Expect her to be headless: Napoleon's Little Creole was unceremoniously decapitated in 1995 in commemoration of her role in reinstating slavery on the island in the early 1800s. Across the street, **Bibliothèque Schoelcher** (Schoelcher Library; © **596/70-26-67**) is one of Fort-de-France's great Belle Epoque buildings. Named in honor of Victor Schoelcher, one of France's most influential abolitionists, this elaborate structure, designed by French architect Henri Pick, was first displayed at the 1889 Paris Exposition. Four years later it was dismantled and shipped across the Atlantic. Today it houses Schoelcher's books as well as an impressive archive of colonization, slavery, and emancipation documents. Admission is free; closed Sunday.

Another Henri Pick masterpiece, **St. Louis Cathedral,** on rue Victor Schoelcher at rue Blénac, was built in 1895. A contemporary of Gustave Eiffel (of Eiffel Tower fame), Pick used massive iron beams to support the walls, ceiling, and spire. A grand example of Industrial Revolution architecture, it's been likened to a Catholic railway station. The organ, stained-glass windows, and ornamented interior walls are well worth a look and can be viewed every morning except Saturday.

Built in 1640, **Fort St. Louis,** Boulevard Alfassa, dominates the rocky promontory east of La Savane. A noteworthy example of 17th- and 18th-century military architecture, it first defended Fort-de-France in 1674 against Dutch invaders. Today, the bastion remains the French navy's headquarters in the Caribbean and as such is only open to visitors on special occasions.

The best of Fort-de-France's many museums, the **Musée Départemental d'Archéologie Précolombienne Préhistoire,** 9 rue de la Liberté (© **596/71-57-05**), traces 2,000 years of Martinique's pre-Columbian past with more than a thousand relics from the Arawak and Carib cultures. Admission is $4 (3.45€); closed Sunday.

You can expect to find great food all over town if you want to stop for lunch, and more than any other island in the French West Indies, Martinique gives French and Creole cuisine equal billing.

ON YOUR OWN: BEYOND THE PORT AREA

Martinique is much too large to tackle in a single day. You'll have to make some tough choices about which of its many museums, plantations, floral parks, and natural wonders to visit. Here are three suggested itineraries for the day.

NORTH OF FORT-DE-FRANCE   Martinique's Carib name, Madiana, means "island of flowers." To see what the Caribs were talking about, stroll through the **Jardin de Balata** (© **596/64-48-73**). Located about 8km (5 miles) north of town, this lush, Edenic garden showcases 200 species of plants, trees, and tropical flowers, as well as resident hummingbirds, frogs, and lizards. Admission is $8.45.

Yes, it's hot outside, but things could be worse. One of Martinique's must-see attractions, the village of **St. Pierre** on the northwest coast, was the cultural and economic capital of the island until 8am on May 8, 1902, when the **Mount Pelée** volcano exploded in fire and lava. Three minutes later, all but one of St. Pierre's 30,000 inhabitants had been incinerated, buried in ash and lava, or asphyxiated by poisonous gas. The town once hailed as the "Paris of the Antilles" became "the Pompeii of the Caribbean," and today it's no more than a sleepy fishing village, home to fewer than 5,000 souls. Ruins of a church, theater, and other buildings punctuate the town, memorials to St. Pierre's former glory. The one-room **Musée Volcanologique,** rue Victor Hugo (© **596/78-15-16**), traces the story of the cataclysm through pictures and relics excavated from the debris. Admission is $3.25. In lieu of walking from one ruin to another, you can hop on the Cyparis Express trolley from here for an hourlong tour (tickets $10.40). The trolley is named in honor of Cyparis, a prisoner locked behind thick cell walls, who was the sole human to survive the eruption. He later toured with P. T. Barnum's circus, showing off his burn scars.

Part sugar-plantation ruins, part tropical paradise, **Habitation Céron** (© 596/ 52-94-53) is the most evocative of Martinique's historical agricultural sites. This sprawling 17th-century estate, 15 minutes north of St. Pierre, is almost as wild and tranquil as the surrounding rainforest, but its verdigris cisterns, moss-covered stone buildings, and archaic, still functioning water mill are all haunted with the ghosts of a time when sugar was king, slaves toiled in the heat, and French colonists lived in languid comfort. Admission costs $7.80.

A few miles south of St. Pierre, **Le Carbet** is where Columbus landed in 1502, the first French settlers arrived in 1635, and the French painter Paul Gauguin lived for 5 months in 1887. The unassuming **Musée Paul Gauguin,** Anse Turin (© 596/ 78-22-66), sits not far from the hut the painter once occupied. They have no original paintings, but you will see biographical texts and whiny, self-pitying letters he wrote to his wife back in France. Admission is $5.20.

SOUTH OF FORT-DE-FRANCE   Marie Josèphe Rose Tascher de la Pagerie was born in 1763 in the quaint little village of **Trois Ilets,** across the bay from Fort-de-France. As Joséphine, she became the wife of Napoleon Bonaparte in 1796 and Empress of France in 1804. A small museum, the **Musée de la Pagerie** (© 596/68-33-06), sits in the former estate kitchen building, where Joséphine gossiped with her slaves. Displays include the bed that she slept in until she departed for France at age 16; portraits of her and of Napoleon; invitations to Parisian balls; and several letters, including a passionate missive from lovelorn Napoleon. Admission costs $4.

You'll have passed through a number of quaint coastal villages by this time but none sweeter than **Ste. Luce.** Absurdly picturesque with its blindingly white stucco walls, red-tile roofs, turquoise sea, and multicolored fishing boats, this town is pure sun-drenched maritime serenity. Swim or snorkel off the small, pleasant beach, meditate on horizon-dominating Diamond Rock (a former British citadel), or check out the village boutiques and cafes. For an unhurried taste of French island life, this is as good a place as any to spend the day.

BEACHES

Serious beach bunnies hop south of Fort-de-France to **Grand Anse des Salines,** widely regarded as Martinique's nicest strand. At the island's extreme southern tip, about an hour from the capital by car, it features coconut palm trees, views of Diamond Rock, and white sand that seems to go on for miles. Beachside stands offer refreshment. To get to the island's main **gay beach,** turn right at the entrance to Grand Anse des Salines and drive to the far end of the parking lot, near the sign for Petite Anse des Salines. Follow the path through the woods and then veer left till you find the quiet section with the good-looking guys.

Conveniently located across the bay from Fort-de-France, **Pointe du Bout** is Martinique's most lavish resort area. Aside from a marina and a variety of watersports, the area has some modest man-made, white-sand beaches. The sandy, natural beaches at nearby **Anse Mitan** and **Anses d'Arlet** are popular with both swimmers and snorkelers.

Beaches north of Fort-de-France have mostly gray (they like to call it silver) volcanic sand. The best of the bunch is **Anse Turin,** just to the side of the main Caribbean coastal road, between St. Pierre and Le Carbet. Extremely popular with locals and shaded by palms, it's where Gauguin swam when he called the island home.

Martinique Golf Excursions

When Robert Trent Jones Sr. designed **Golf de la Martinique** (© **596/68-32-81**) in 1976, he chose a picturesque, historic site: the seaside hills neighboring La Pagerie, the birthplace of Empress Joséphine. Thirty-two kilometers (20 miles) from Fort-de-France, this good, tough, 18-hole, 6,640-yard, par-71 course features emerald hills, swaying palms, constant vistas of the turquoise sea, and, thankfully, year-round trade winds that help keep things cool. The par-5 12th, with a dogleg to the right, is the most difficult hole. The fairway here is narrow, the green is long, and the wind, especially between December and April, is tricky. The 15th and 16th require shots over sea inlets. Facilities include a pro shop, a golf academy, a bar, a restaurant, and tennis courts. English-speaking pros are at your service. Greens fees and cart rental run about $120 for 18 holes, $81 for 9. A set of clubs is another $20. Some cruise lines offer an organized excursion to the club.

Martinique has no legal nudist beaches, but toplessness is as common here as anywhere in France. As a rule, public beaches lack changing cabins or showers, but hotel lockers and changing cabanas can be used by nonguests for a charge.

SHOPPING

Martinique offers a good selection of French luxury items—perfumes, fashionable clothing, luggage, crystal, and dinnerware—at prices that can be as much as 30% to 40% lower than those in the States. Unfortunately, because some luxury goods, including jewelry, are subject to a hefty value-added tax, the savings are ultimately less compelling. Paying in dollar-denominated traveler's checks or credit cards is sometimes good for a 20% discount. The main **shopping district** in Fort-de-France is bound by rue Ernest Deproge (on the waterfront), La Savane, rue Lamartine, and rue de la République, with **rue Victor Hugo** being the single most important stretch. Martinican goods, such as the excellent island rum, Creole jewelry, madras fabric, folk paintings, and hand-woven baskets, are good buys and more representative of the island. The **open-air market** in La Savane, at rue de la Liberté and rue Ernest Deproge, has the best selection of these items.

16 Nevis

Off the beaten tourist track, south of St. Martin and north of Guadeloupe, Nevis is the junior partner in the combined Federation of St. Kitts and Nevis, which gained self-government from Britain in 1967 and became a totally independent nation in 1983. Though smaller than St. Kitts and lacking a major historical site like that island's Brimstone Hill Fortress, Nevis is nevertheless the more appealing and upbeat of the two islands. Columbus first sighted the island in 1493, naming it Las Nieves, Spanish for "snows," because its 970m (3,232-ft.) mountain reminded him of the Pyrenees. Settled by the British in 1628, the island became a prosperous sugar-growing island as well as the most popular spa island of the 18th century, when people flocked in from other West Indian islands to visit its hot mineral springs. Nevis's two most famous historical residents were Admiral Horatio Nelson, who married a local woman here in 1787, and Alexander Hamilton, who was born here and went on to find fame as a drafter of the American Federalist Papers, as George Washington's treasury secretary, and as Aaron Burr's unfortunate dueling partner. Today, the island's capital city, **Charlestown,** has a lovely mixture of port-town exuberance and small-town charm, and the popular **Pinney's Beach** is just a knockout.

COMING ASHORE   Only small ships call on Nevis, docking right in the center of Charlestown and/or dropping anchor off the coast of Pinney's Beach.

GETTING AROUND   The entirety of Charlestown is accessible on foot, but if you want to visit Pinney's Beach or elsewhere on the island, you can get a **taxi** from Charlestown. Rates range from $5 up to about $17, which will get you to the island's farthest point. Taxis also offer island tours. Just negotiate a price with your driver.

LANGUAGE & CURRENCY   **English** is the language of both islands. The local currency is the **Eastern Caribbean dollar** (US$1 = EC$2.70; EC$1 = US37¢), though most shops and restaurants quote prices in U.S. dollars. Always determine which currency locals are talking about before making a purchase.

BEST CRUISE LINE SHORE EXCURSIONS
Some of the small-ship lines offer a day at Pinney's Beach as part of their regular visit, and might also offer hiking and snorkeling options, but the island is so small and easy to negotiate on your own that excursions are neither necessary nor advised.

ON YOUR OWN: WITHIN WALKING DISTANCE
If your ship docks in Charlestown, you're dead center of a perfect walking-tour opportunity. Charlestown is a lovely little place, laid back in somewhat the same manner as St. John, but with some of the really rural character of sister island St. Kitts.

If you head left from the docks and walk a little ways (maybe .4km/¼-mile) along Main Street, you'll come to the **Alexander Hamilton Birthplace** (© **869/469-5786;** www.nevis-nhcs.org/nevishistory.html), where the road curves just before the turnoff to Island Road. It's a rustic little two-level house set right on the coastline. On the first floor is the small **Museum of Nevis History** and gift shop (admission is $5; closes at noon Saturday; closed all day Sunday).

Backtracking along Main Street, you'll pass several serviceable if unremarkable shops. Keep walking through the center of town, saying "hi" to the occasional mama goat and kids you'll pass, and then turn left onto Government Road. One block up on the left, you'll find the **Jews' Burial Ground,** with graves from 1684 to 1768. When we were there, the dead were being entertained with reggae music drifting over from a shop across the street, while a breeze stirred the few trees on the property. All in all, not a bad resting spot.

Backtrack to Main Street, turn left, and continue on past the Grove Park Cricket Ground, bearing left when the road forks. Head up the hill (where you'll see several buildings standing alone on the hill to your right), and then turn at the first right, which will bring you back behind those buildings, the first of which is the inaccessible Government House and the second of which is the **Nelson Museum** (© **869/ 469-0408;** www.nevis-nhcs.org/nelsonmuseum.html). A very small, very homemade, and very appealing kind of place, it traces the history of Admiral Horatio Nelson's career enforcing England's Navigation Acts in the Caribbean, and also houses artifacts from Nevis's Carib, Arawak, and Aceramic peoples. The timeline of Nelson's Caribbean career includes ship models, ceramic and bronze Nelson figures, paintings of his battles and other scenes, a scrap from the Union Jack under which the admiral was standing when he was shot, and more memorabilia. Admission is $5; closes at noon Saturday; closed all day Sunday.

Once back outside, amble slowly off in the same direction you were going (right from the gate). Keep bearing right and you'll eventually be back on Main Street, in plenty of time to do a little shopping or stop into one of the local bars or restaurants.

ON YOUR OWN: BEYOND THE PORT AREA

The 3.2-hectare (8-acre) **Botanical Garden of Nevis** (© **869/469-3399**) is located 4.8km (3 miles) south of Charlestown on the Montpelier Estate. There are several gardens, including a tropical rainforest conservatory, a rose and vine garden, a cactus garden, a tropical fruit garden, and an orchid garden. Fountains, ponds, and re-creations of Mayan sculptures dot the grounds. Admission costs $9; closed Sunday.

BEACHES

The name to know on Nevis is **Pinney's Beach,** located north of Charlestown. A lovely spot for swimming, snorkeling, beachcombing, or just sitting back and watching the pelicans dive-bomb into the surf. It's home to the gorgeous Four Seasons resort and, as a counterpoint to conspicuous luxury, the rickety **Sunshine's Bar and Grill** (© **869/ 469-5817**), "Home of the Killer Bee," sitting right on the beach and offering beer and other refreshments along with the aforementioned Bee, a "killer" rum drink.

SHOPPING

Nevis is no shopping hub. A few uninteresting gift shops are dotted along Main Street, and the **Nevis Philatelic Bureau** at the Head Post Office, on Market Street next to the public market, 1 block south and 1 block east of the docks (© **869/469-5535**), has a range of Nevis stamps for collectors.

17 The Panama Canal

The Panama Canal is an awesome feat of engineering and human effort. Construction began in 1880 and wasn't completed until 1914, at the expense of thousands of lives, and the vast majority of the original structure and equipment is still in use. Transiting the canal, which links the Atlantic Ocean with the Pacific, is a thrill for anyone even vaguely interested in engineering or history.

Passing completely through the canal takes about 8 hours from start to finish, and is a fascinating procedure—the route is about 81km (50 miles) long and includes passage through three main locks, which, through gravity alone, raise ships over Central America and down again on the other side. Between the locks, ships pass through artificially created lakes such as the massive Gatun Lake, 26m (85 ft.) above sea level. It often costs ships about $100,000 to pass through, with fees based on each ship's weight. Your ship will line up in the morning, mostly with cargo ships, to await its turn through the canal. While transiting, there will be a running narration of history and facts about the canal by an expert who's brought on board for the day. The canal is so vital to the cruise industry that it's spawned its own word, *panamax,* meaning the maximum size a ship can be and still make it through. Panamax ships, it should be noted, make for a tight fit: Sometimes there's only a couple feet between their hull and the sides of the lock. Sitting in a lower-deck lounge and watching the walls go by less than an arm's length out the windows is a really, really disorienting experience.

Cruises that include a canal crossing are generally 10 to 14 nights long, with popular routes running between Florida and Acapulco, visiting a handful of Caribbean and Mexican ports and a few ports in Central America along the way, including Panama's San Blas Islands, Costa Rica's Puerto Caldera, and Guatemala's Puerto Quetzal. Many ships also do a **partial crossing** of the canal, sailing into Gatun Lake from the Caribbean side, docking to let passengers off for excursions, then sailing back out again.

COLÓN

In compliance with a treaty signed between the United States and Panama in 1977, canal operations passed from U.S. to Panamanian hands at the stroke of midnight on December 31, 1999. Not only did the transition go smoothly, but the canal changeover spurred government agencies and private developers in Panama to expand the canal zone's tourism infrastructure—not simply trying to attract as many ships as possible, but developing new attractions at the canal's Atlantic entrance to lure cruise passengers off their ships and into Panama's interior on shore excursions and for pre- and post-cruise stays. Even ships not transiting the canal are being wooed, with a long-term goal of making the city of Colón a home port for cruise ships sailing to the southern Caribbean.

The linchpin project in the new canal-area developments is **Colón 2000,** a $45-million private port development that opened in October 2000 in Colón, near the canal's Caribbean entrance, and that is capable of handling any size cruise vessel—even the 100,000-ton-plus ships that are too large to pass through the canal. Colón 2000's developer, Corporación de Costas Tropicales, has created a tour company, **Adventuras 2000** (www.colon2000.com), which offers a series of shore excursions highlighting Panama's history, culture, and diverse natural attractions (see "Best Cruise Line Shore Excursions," below). The project has opened many new jobs to locals, who are being trained as bilingual tour guides, drivers, and so on.

Colón 2000's glass-and-marble terminal building has a large lounge, an Internet cafe, a huge duty-free shopping mall (part of the Colón Free Zone, the second largest tax-free zone in the world), restaurants, and craft shops. Unfortunately, the town surrounding the splashy new development remains depressed. So there's no question passengers calling here should book an organized tour. Another new development in Colón, the Cristobal Cruise Terminal (Pier 6), offers piers for two ships of any size and has a duty-free shopping area, restaurants, and telephones.

BEST CRUISE LINE SHORE EXCURSIONS

The following excursions represent a sampling of those offered from Colón:

Emberá Indian Village Tour ($89, 3½ hr.): Today, Panama's Emberá Indians live much as they did in the early 16th century, when their first tourist—Vasco Nunez de Balboa, who "discovered" the Pacific Ocean—came through. You'll travel by dugout canoe up the Chagres River, visit the Emberá village, witness a performance of traditional dance, and (surprise, surprise) have an opportunity to purchase handicrafts.

of the Old Town, especially **Calle San Francisco** and **Calle del Cristo,** are a major shopping venue. Local handicrafts can be good buys, including *santos* (hand-carved wooden religious figures), needlework, straw work, hammocks, loose-fitting guayabera shirts, papier-mâché masks, and paintings and sculptures by local artists.

19 St. Barts

Chic, sophisticated St. Barts (or, technically, St. Barthélemy, a name no one ever uses) is internationally renowned as one of the ritziest refuges in the Caribbean, rivaled only by Mustique as the preferred island retreat of the rich and famous. Yet despite all the hoopla, St. Barts retains its charm, serenity, natural beauty, and incredibly French flavor—in contrast to most Caribbean islands, where descendants of African slaves form the majority, St. Barts's 7,000 year-round residents are primarily of French ancestry. Gustavia, the main port (whose name harks back to the 19th c., when Sweden controlled the island), is full of French restaurants and semi-chic, semi-boho nightspots. Many of the small luxe ships that call here stay into the evening so passengers can get a night out. Away from town, the island is full of dramatic hills and pristine white-sand beaches.

COMING ASHORE   Cruise ships anchor off **Gustavia,** the main town, and ferry passengers to the dollhouse-size harbor and town via tenders.

GETTING AROUND   Taxis congregate at Gustavia's harbor to take cruise passengers to the beaches. If you want some stylin' Euro-fun, rent a bright orange or red Smart Car, the hippest toys on the island, for a ride up and down St. Barts's picturesque, hilly roads. Budget and Avis, Hertz, and National have offices here.

LANGUAGE & CURRENCY   **French** is the official language, but virtually everyone speaks **English** as well. St. Barts is part of the French overseas region of Guadeloupe, so the **euro** (€) is the official currency (1€ = US$1.31; $1 = .77€). U.S. dollars are commonly accepted.

CALLING FROM THE U.S.   When calling St. Barts from the United States, dial the international access code **(011)** and **590** before the numbers listed here, which also begin with 590. That's right: If you want to make a connection, you have to dial 590 twice. It's just one of those oddities that makes the world go round.

BEST CRUISE LINE SHORE EXCURSIONS

Jet-Set Boat & Beach Excursion ($200–$400, 4 hr.): Circumnavigate St. Barts in a 40-foot cruiser, then tender ashore at St. Jean Beach for a swim, snorkel, and/or drinks from the open bar.

St. Barts on Horseback ($65, 2 hr.): Travel to northern St. Barts for a relaxed guided ride through the island's outback.

ON YOUR OWN: WITHIN WALKING DISTANCE

For a taste of the island's celeb vibe, make a beeline to **Le Select,** rue de la France at rue du Général de Gaulle (© **590/27-86-87**), the epicenter of Gustavia's social life for more than 50 years. This cafe's tables rest in a tree-shaded garden a block from the harbor. A full bar is available, as well as simple meals. The classic, funky ambience inspired Jimmy Buffet's "Cheeseburger in Paradise," and a mix of salty locals, celebrities, and chic tourists typically make up the clientele. Aside from hanging out, shopping, and eating, cruisers sticking close to port can also visit Gustavia's modest points of interest. **St. Bartholomew's Church,** rue Samuel Fahlberg, dates from the 1850s and features limestone and volcanic stone walls, as well as imported pitch pine pews. The **Municipal Museum,** on rue Duquesne, across from the dock (© **590/29-71-55**), is an unfocused but respectable introduction to the history, sociology, ethnology, economy, and ecology of the island. The most interesting items include Amerindian artifacts, rustic farm furnishings, and clothing used by early French settlers. Admission costs $2.60; closed Saturday afternoon and Monday morning.

ON YOUR OWN: BEYOND THE PORT AREA

Visiting the tiny fishing village of **Corossol** is a vibrant way to experience the St. Barts of the past. About 10 minutes by taxi from the dock, this quaint, totally un-chic hamlet is home to traditional folk who still live off the sea. It's your best bet for spotting women in traditional 17th-century bonnets and for watching roadside vendors weave items from palm fronds. On the town's waterfront, just to the left of the road from Gustavia, the **Inter Oceans Museum** (© **590/27-62-97**) catalogs thousands of shells, corals, sand dollars, sea horses, sea urchins, and fish from around the world, all displayed in endearingly homemade style (literally homemade: The museum is an extension of the owner's house). Don't miss the collection of sand from beaches around the world: A cocktail umbrella is planted in each specimen. Admission is $3.90; closed Mondays.

BEACHES

The 22 beaches of St. Barts are first-rate. Few are ever crowded, even during the peak season, and all are public, free, and easily accessible by taxi from the cruise pier (make arrangements with your driver to be picked up at a specific time). As St. Barts is a French island, toplessness is common at all beaches. If you're looking for an active beach strand, with restaurants and watersports, **Grand Cul de Sac** fits the bill, with waters that are shallow, warm, and protected. An even busier and equally social beach, **St. Jean** is actually two beaches divided by a rock promontory. Protected by a coral reef, the calm waters here attract families and watersports enthusiasts, including windsurfers, and there are numerous eating, drinking, shopping, and people-watching opportunities. **Gouverneur,** on the south central coast, is quiet and relatively remote. Its idyllic setting and unspoiled beauty make it No. 1 with locals. Farther east, in a wild and rustic area that was once the site of salt ponds, **Saline** is reached by a 3-minute hike over a sand dune. Most famous for its adult environment and nude bathers, it also boasts great bodysurfing waves.

SHOPPING

A duty-free port, St. Barts is a good place to buy liquor, perfume, and other French luxury items. Good buys on apparel, crystal, porcelain, and watches can also be found, especially during April, the biggest sale month. Moisturizer mavens can stock up on the island's own cosmetic line, Ligne St. Barth. Shops are concentrated in Gustavia and St. Jean, where the quality-to-schlock ratio is as high as anywhere in the Caribbean. Most shops and offices close for a long lunch, usually from noon to 2pm.

20 St. Kitts

Somewhat off the beaten tourist track, south of St. Martin and north of Guadeloupe, St. Kitts forms the larger half of the combined Federation of St. Kitts and Nevis, two islands separated by only about 3.2km (2 miles) of ocean. St. Kitts—or St. Christopher, a name hardly anyone uses—is by far the more populous of the two islands, with some 35,000 people. St. Kitts is almost ridiculously lush and fertile, dotted with rain-forests and waterfalls and boasting some lovely beaches along its southeast coastline, but it's also extremely poor, still dependent on the same sugar-cane crop that brought its English plantation owners riches (and its slaves hot misery) back in colonial days. Cane fields climb the slopes of its volcanic mountain range, and you'll see ruins of old mills and plantation houses as you drive around the island. Basseterre, the capital city, is full of old-time colonial architecture, but it's a small-scale place with little to offer visitors beyond a pleasant walk around. The island's most impressive landmark, **Brimstone Hill fortress,** is about 15km (9 miles) west of town.

COMING ASHORE   **Port Zante** stretches from the center of town into the deep waters offshore, with shopping, restaurants, and a welcome center on-site. New additions to the facility, including a second pier and expanded shopping, are due to be completed soon after this book hits the shelves.

GETTING AROUND   You can walk around Bassterre, but you need a **taxi** to get anywhere else. They greet cruise passengers (loudly) at the docks and also around the Circus, a public square near the docks at the intersection of Bank and Fort streets. Taxis aren't metered, so you must agree on the price before heading out. Always ask if the rates quoted are in U.S. dollars or Eastern Caribbean dollars.

LANGUAGE & CURRENCY   **English** is the language of both islands. The local currency is the **Eastern Caribbean dollar** (US$1 = EC$2.70; EC$1 = US37¢). Many shops and restaurants quote prices in U.S. dollars. Always determine which currency locals are talking about.

BEST CRUISE LINE SHORE EXCURSIONS

Brimstone Hill Fortress & Gardens ($46, 3 hr.): The price is right for this tour, making it a good way to visit the island's premier attraction. Among the largest and best-preserved forts in the Caribbean, **Brimstone Hill** (www.brimstonehillfortress.org) dates from 1690, when the British fortified the hill to help recapture Fort Charles, located below, from the French. In 1782, an invading force of 8,000 French troops bombarded the fortress for a month before its small British garrison, supplemented by local militia, surrendered. When the British took the island back the next year, they proceeded to enlarge the fort into "The Gibraltar of the West Indies." In all, the structure took 104 years to complete. Today it's the centerpiece of a national park criss-crossed by nature trails, with a population of green vervet monkeys to keep things lively. Perched on the upper slopes of a tall, steep hill, it's a photographer's paradise, with views of mountains, fields, and the Caribbean Sea—on a clear day you can see six neighboring islands. From below, the fort presents a dramatic picture, poised among diabolical-looking spires and outcroppings of lava rock. Its name comes from the odor of sulfur released by nearby undersea vents. Tours typically include a visit to the beautiful **Romney Gardens,** located amidst the ruins of a sugar estate between Basseterre and the fort. You can check out the lush hillside gardens (featuring giant ferns, orchids, poinsettias, and "The Tree," a 350-year-old Saman tree), say hi to the cows that graze just across the hill, or shop at **Caribelle Batik** (© 869/465-6253), one of the island's most popular boutiques, where artisans demonstrate their Indonesian-style hand-printing amid rack after rack of brightly colored clothes. (If you're coming here on your own, look for signs indicating a turnoff along the coast road, about 8km/5 miles north of Basseterre in the town of Old Road.)

Mount Liamuiga Volcano Hike ($102, 7 hr.): This dormant volcano, in the north-west area of the island, has long been known as "Mount Misery." It sputtered its last gasp around 1692, and today its summit is a major goal for hikers. On this excursion you'll hike about 1,140m (3,800 ft.) to the summit, traveling along narrow trails and through the island's cloud forest. It takes about 2½ hours to reach the top. Two lookout points offer views of the crater below. Refreshments are offered before the hike back down. This is a great trip if you're in shape.

Mountain Biking & Beach Tour ($71, 4 hr.): From the pier, you'll ride through Basseterre then out through sugar-cane fields and up 450m (1,500-ft.) Olivees Mountain for views and refreshments. After the ride down you'll stop at Friar's Bay for a swim and snack. It's a nice way to see this lush island.

Rainforest & Gardens Hiking Safari ($59, 4 hr.): Departing from Romney Gardens, you'll hike along a loop of trails through lush rainforest. With luck, you'll catch sight of some of the island's resident monkeys.

Sail & Snorkel Catamaran Trip ($68, 3½ hr.): A sailing catamaran takes you to secluded Smitten's Bay for snorkeling among diverse reef fish and coral formations. Complimentary rum punch is served aboard the boat on your return trip.

ON YOUR OWN: WITHIN WALKING DISTANCE

The capital city of Basseterre, where the docks are located, has typical British colonial architecture and some quaint buildings, a few shops, and a market where locals display fruits and flowers—but even this description might be giving you the wrong idea about this place. The truth is, it's a very poor town, with few attractions aimed at visitors. When we were last there, there were chickens walking around in front of the government buildings. **St. George's Anglican Church,** on Cayon Street (walk straight up Church St. or Fort St. from the dock), is the oldest church in town and is worth a look. **Independence Square,** a stone's throw from the docks along Bank Street, is pretty, with its central fountain and old church, but there's no good reason to linger unless it's to sit in the shade and toss back a bottle of Ting, the local grapefruit-based soda.

ON YOUR OWN: BEYOND THE PORT AREA

All the good out-of-town sites here are covered under "Best Cruise Line Shore Excursions," above.

BEACHES

The narrow peninsula in the southeast contains the island's salt ponds and also boasts the best white-sand beaches (approach via the windy, hilly road for a dramatic and gorgeous view). You'll find the best swimming at **Conaree Beach,** 4.8km (3 miles) from Basseterre; **Frigate Bay,** with its talcum-powder-fine sand; the twin beaches of **Banana Bay** and **Cockleshell Bay,** at the southeast corner of the island; and **Friar's Bay,** a peninsula beach opening onto both the Atlantic and the Caribbean. All beaches, even those that border hotels, are free and open to the public. You must, however, usually pay a fee to use a hotel's beach facilities.

SHOPPING

Basseterre is not a shopping town, despite handout maps that show a listing of shops that would put St. Thomas to shame. Look closer and you'll see entries such as "R. Gumbs Electrical," "TDC/Finco Finance Co.," and "Horsford Furniture Store." Turns out they just listed every business on every street in town, no matter whether it's of interest to visitors or not. Strength in numbers, we suppose. The port complex offers shopping. The most popular shop with visitors is probably **Caribelle Batik,** which is a stop on many shore excursions (see above).

21 St. Lucia

With a turbulent history shared by many of its Caribbean neighbors, St. Lucia (pronounced "*Loo*-sha") changed hands often during the colonial period, being British seven times and French seven times. Today, though, it's an independent state that's become one of the most popular destinations in the Caribbean, with some of the finest resorts. The heaviest development is concentrated in the northwest, between the capital of Castries and the northern end of the island, where there's a string of white-sand beaches. The interior boasts relatively unspoiled green-mantled mountains and gentle valleys, as well as the volcanic **Mount Soufrière.** Two dramatic peaks **(the Pitons)** rise along the southwest coast. **Castries,** the capital, has grown up around an extinct volcanic crater that's now a large harbor surrounded by hills. Because of fires that devastated many of its older structures, the town today has touches of modernity, with glass-and-concrete buildings, although there's still an old-fashioned Saturday-morning market on Jeremie Street. The country women dress in traditional cotton headdresses to sell their luscious fruits and vegetables, while weather-beaten men sit close by playing warrie (a fast game played with pebbles on a carved board) or fleet games of dominoes using tiles the color of cherries.

COMING ASHORE   Most cruise ships arrive at a fairly new pier at **Pointe Seraphine,** within walking distance of the center of Castries and boasting St. Lucia's best shopping right on-site. In the unlikely event that Pointe Seraphine is full up, your ship might dock instead at **Port Castries** on the other side of the colorful harbor. There's a shopping terminal here called La Place Carenage. Some smaller lines, such as Star Clippers, Seabourn, and Clipper, visit other sites around the island, anchoring off **Rodney Bay** to the north or **Soufrière** to the south and carrying passengers ashore by tender.

GETTING AROUND   There is an official **taxi** association servicing both Pointe Seraphine and La Place Carenage, with standard fares posted. You can hire a taxi to go to Soufrière, too. Many taxi drivers offer 2- to 3-hour tours, with a stop at the beach, for $60. Be sure you're talking U.S. or EC dollars before agreeing on a price.

LANGUAGE & CURRENCY   **English** is the official language. The official currency is the **Eastern Caribbean dollar** (US$1 = EC$2.70; EC$1 = US37¢), though shops and restaurants commonly take the U.S. dollar as well. Be sure you know which currency a price is being quoted in before paying.

BEST CRUISE LINE SHORE EXCURSIONS

Because of the difficult terrain, shore excursions are the best means of seeing this beautiful island in a day or less. In addition to the sampling below, most ships typically offer bus tours (many visiting the island's banana plantations), and snorkeling cruises.

Pigeon Island Sea Kayaking ($65–$70, 3 hr.): After transferring to Rodney Bay, you'll make the approximately 30-minute paddle out to the island, where you'll have time to swim, kayak some more, or make the steep climb up to Fort Rodney. From the summit, you'll have great views of the Pitons, and sometimes you'll even be able to see Martinique.

Rainforest Bicycle Tour ($69, 4½ hr.): After being dropped off by bus in the middle of the forest, you'll ride past banana plantations and the Errard Falls waterfall, and stop to sample various fruits that grow along the roadside. Some time for swimming is usually included at the falls. A different tour called **Jungle Mountain Biking** takes you by boat to the Jungle Biking facility, located on an 18th-century sugar plantation. There, you can explore 16km (10 miles) of trails at your own pace. Beach time is included at the end ($99, 4½ hr.).

Soody Nature Hike & Mineral Waterfall ($55, 7 hr.): Drive along the west coast through fishing villages, banana plantations, and the edge of the rainforest before arriving at Soufrière, location of the Pitons and the Diamond Botanical Gardens. A guided hourlong hike through the volcanic forest introduces you to the island's flora and fauna, and ends up at a therapeutic sulphuric waterfall where you can take a dip to cure what ails ya. Lunch at a Creole restaurant is included.

Beach Snorkel ($59, 3½ hr.): Snorkeling is spectacular around St. Lucia. This trip departs Castires harbor by boat, traveling an hour en route to the island's marine reserve, which has an area set aside especially for snorkeling. There's also a supersize 7-hour ($93) version of this trip that includes a buffet lunch.

ON YOUR OWN: WITHIN WALKING DISTANCE

The principal streets of Castries are **William Peter Boulevard** and **Bridge Street.** Don't miss a walk through town: People are very friendly, and Jeremie Street is chocka-block with variety stores of the most authentic local kind, selling everything from spices to housewares. A Roman Catholic cathedral stands on **Columbus Square,** which has a few restored buildings. Take a gander at the enormous 400-year-old "rain" tree, also called a "no-name" tree, which grows in the square. The nearby Government House is a late Victorian structure.

Beyond Government House lies **Morne Fortune,** which means "Hill of Good Luck." Actually, no one's had much luck here, certainly not the French and British soldiers who battled for **Fort Charlotte.** The fort switched between the two sides many times. You can visit the 18th-century barracks, complete with a military cemetery, a small museum, the Old Powder Magazine, and the "Four Apostles Battery"—four grim muzzle-loading cannons. The view of the harbor of Castries is panoramic from this point. You can also see north to Pigeon Island or south to the Pitons. To reach Morne Fortune, head east on Bridge Street.

Castries has a very colorful Central Market, right near the dock, which is also worth a visit. The airplane-hangar-size emporium sells local food, trinkets, and produce. Buy some banana ketchup or local cinnamon sticks to take home.

ON YOUR OWN: BEYOND THE PORT AREA

St. Lucia's first national park, the 44-acre **Pigeon Island National Landmark** (© **758/450-0603**), was originally an island but is now joined to the northwest shore of the mainland by a very environmentally unfriendly causeway. It's about 30 minutes by taxi from Castries. The park is ideal for picnics and nature walks, and is covered with lemongrass, which spread from original plantings made by British light opera singer Josset, who leased the island for 30 years and grew the grass to provide thatch for her cottage's roof. The island's **Interpretation Centre** contains artifacts and a multimedia display of local history, covering everything from the Amerindian settlers of A.D. 1000 to 1782's Battle of Saints, when Admiral Rodney's fleet set out from Pigeon

Island and defeated the French admiral De Grasse. Right below the interpretation center is the cozy **Captain's Cellar pub,** located in what was formerly a soldier's mess. From the tables outside you get wonderful views of the crashing surf on the Atlantic coast, just a few steps away. From here, you can walk up the winding and moderately steep path to a **lookout** from which you get a wonderful view that stretches all the way to Martinique. Two white-sand beaches lie on the island's west coast. Island admission is $5.

   La Soufrière, a fishing port and St. Lucia's second largest settlement, is dominated by Petit Piton and Gros Piton, collectively known as **the Pitons,** two of the dramatic pointed peaks that rise right from the sea to 738m and 786m (2,460 ft. and 2,619 ft.), respectively. Formed by lava and once actively volcanic, these mountains are now cloaked in green vegetation, with waves crashing around their bases. Their sheer rise from the water makes them such visible landmarks that they've become the very symbol of St. Lucia. Near the town lies the famous "drive-in" volcano, **La Soufrière,** a rocky lunar landscape of bubbling mud and craters seething with fuming sulfur. You can literally drive into an old crater and walk between the sulfur springs and pools of hissing steam. The fumes are said to have medicinal properties. A local guide is usually waiting nearby; if you do hire a guide, agree—then doubly agree—on what the fee will be. Nearby are the **Diamond Mineral Baths.** They were originally constructed in 1784 by order of Louis XVI, whose doctors told him that these waters were similar in mineral content to the waters at Aix-les-Bains. The baths were built to help French soldiers who had been fighting in the West Indies recuperate from wounds and disease.

BEACHES

If you don't take a shore excursion, you might want to spend your time on one of St. Lucia's famous beaches, all of which are open to the public, even those at hotel properties (though you must pay to use a hotel's beach equipment). Taxis can take you to any of the island's beaches, but we recommend that you stick to the calmer shores along the western coast, since the rough surf on the windward Atlantic side makes swimming potentially dangerous. Leading beaches include **Pigeon Island,** off the northern shore, with white sand and picnic facilities; **Vigie Beach,** north of Castries Harbour, with fine sand; **Marigot Beach,** south of Castries Harbour, framed on three sides by steep emerald hills and skirted by palm trees; and **Reduit Beach,** between Choc Bay and Pigeon Point, with fine brown sand. For sheer novelty, you might want to visit the black-volcanic-sand beach at **Soufrière.** Just north of Soufrière is a beach connoisseur's delight, **Anse Chastanet** (© **758/459-7000**), boasting an expanse of white sand at the foothills of lush, green mountains. This is a fantastic spot for snorkeling, with spectacular coral reefs starting only a little way offshore, providing shelter for thousands of fish and other sea creatures.

SHOPPING

You'll find some good but not remarkable buys on bone china, jewelry, perfume, watches, liquor, and crystal. Souvenir items include designer bags and mats, local pottery, and straw hats—again, nothing remarkable. *A tip:* If your cruise is also calling in St. Thomas, let the local vendors know; it may make them more amenable to bargaining. Built for cruise ship passengers, **Pointe Seraphine** has the best collection of shops on the island. You must present your cruise pass when making purchases here.

If you're in Soufrière, you might want to make a detour to the southwest, just past the small village of Choiseul, to the **Choiseul Craft Centre,** La Fargue (© 758/459-3226), a government-funded retail outlet and training school that perpetuates the tradition of handmade Amerindian pottery and basketware. Some of the best basket weaving on the island is done here, using techniques practiced only in St. Lucia, St. Vincent, and Dominica. Look for place mats, handbags, woodcarvings (including bas-reliefs crafted from screw pine), and pottery. It's open weekdays only.

22 St. Martin/Sint Maarten

Who can resist a two-for-one sale? That's what you get on St. Martin, a 96-sq.-km (37-sq.-mile) island that's been shared by France (with 52 sq. km/20 sq. miles of it) and the Netherlands (with 44 sq. km/17 sq. miles) for more than 350 years. Although the border between the two sides is virtually imperceptible—a monument along the road marks the change in administration—each side retains elements of its own heritage. The French side, with some of the best beaches and restaurants in the Caribbean, emphasizes quiet elegance. French fashions and luxury items fill the shops, and the fragrance of croissants mixes with the spicy aromas of West Indian cooking. The Dutch side, officially known as Sint Maarten, reflects Holland's anything-goes philosophy: Development is much more widespread, flashy casinos pepper the landscape, and strip malls make the larger towns look as much like Anaheim as Amsterdam. The 100% duty-free shopping has turned both sides of the island into a bargain-hunter's paradise.

COMING ASHORE   All cruise ships dock on the Dutch side, at **A. C. Wathey Pier,** about 1.6km (1 mile) southeast of Philipsburg. The majority of passengers are then tendered to the smaller Captain Hodge Pier at the center of town, but others choose to walk the distance on a newly developed boardwalk or take taxis. Smaller vessels sometimes dock on the French side of the island, at **Marina Port la Royale,** adjacent to the heart of Marigot.

GETTING AROUND   Taxis on both sides of the island are unmetered. Agree on a rate and currency before getting in. Dutch law requires that drivers list government-regulated fares based on two passengers. Privately owned and operated **minivans** have signs to indicate their destination, and can be hailed anywhere on the street. Fares are usually about $1.50. **Rental cars** are a great way to see both sides of the island. Avis, Budget, and Hertz all have offices here.

LANGUAGE & CURRENCY   Surprise, surprise: The official language on the Dutch side is **Dutch,** and the official language on the French side is **French.** Most people on both sides also speak **English.** The legal tender in Dutch Sint Maarten is the **Netherlands Antilles guilder,** or NAf (NAf1.79 = US$1; NAf1 = US56¢), and the official currency on the French side is the **euro** (1€ = US$1.31; $1 = .77€). U.S. dollars are widely accepted on both sides, and most prices are quoted in U.S. dollars, too.

CALLING FROM THE U.S.   When calling Dutch Sint Maarten from the United States, simply dial the international access number (011) before the numbers listed here. Calling French Saint Martin requires more of an effort: Dial 011, then **590** before the numbers listed. Yes, 590 appears in our listed numbers below, but those three digits must be dialed twice to make a connection.

BEST CRUISE LINE SHORE EXCURSIONS

"America's Cup" Sailing Regatta ($89, 2½ hr.): Get a taste of nautical exhilaration by competing in a race aboard an America's Cup–winning sailboat. This hands-on, extremely popular excursion lets you grind winches, trim sails, and duck under booms—after you've been trained by professionals, of course. Alternatively, sit back and watch others do all the work.

Pinel Island Shore Snorkel & Beach Tour ($39, 3½ hr.): After a scenic bus ride to the French town of Cul de Sac, along the northeast coast, hop on a tender to the small offshore island of Ilet Pinel for some of St. Martin's best snorkeling.

Amphibious Duck Adventure ($49, 1½ hr.): A little goofy, but how can you not enjoy a drive around Phillipsburg in a 12m (39-ft.) amphibious vehicle that's got calypso music playing and passengers armed with rum punch and their own duck quackers? From there the duck heads to the island's Great Salt Pond and up into the hills for a view, then drives right into Simpson Bay for a tour by water.

Hidden Forest Hike ($84, 5 hr.): A 45-minute drive to Loterie Farm, where you'll do a 2-hour hike through the tropical forest, eventually emerging at Pic Paradise, the island's highest point. Along the way, your guide will point out a secret freshwater spring and the island's famous guava berry trees. Return to the farm for a complimentary rum or fruit punch and a typical Caribbean farmhouse lunch.

Butterfly Farm & Marigot ($39, 3½ hr.): After a scenic drive through both the French and Dutch sides of the island, walk through a surrealistic enclosed garden that features pools, waterfalls, and hundreds of exquisitely beautiful and exotic butterflies from around the world. Amusing guides identify species, describe courtship and mating rituals, and give tips on attracting butterflies to your garden at home. Afterward, absorb the Creole charm and French atmosphere of Marigot.

ON YOUR OWN: WITHIN WALKING DISTANCE

Shopping, sunbathing, and gambling are the pastimes that interest most cruisers who hit this island, but folks with a taste for culture and history can make a day of it here as well.

ON THE DUTCH SIDE   Directly in front of the Philipsburg town pier, on Wathey Square, the **Courthouse** combines northern European sobriety with Caribbean brightness. Originally built in 1793 of freestone and wood, this venerable old building has suffered numerous hurricanes, but has been restored after each tempest and continues to house government offices. East of the Courthouse, at 7 Front St. (down a little shopping alley), the tiny **Sint Maarten Museum** (*©* **599/542-4917**) features modest, cluttered exhibits that focus on the island's history and geology. The second-floor gallery is open every day but Sunday. Admission is free; closes 2pm Saturday. Historically, **Fort Amsterdam** is the Dutch side's most important colonial site. Since 1631, the fort has looked out over Great Bay from the hill west of Philipsburg. The fort was the Netherlands' first military outpost in the Caribbean. The Spanish captured it 2 years later, making it their most significant bastion east of Puerto Rico. Peter Stuyvesant, who later became governor of New Amsterdam (now New York), lost his leg to a cannonball while trying to reclaim the fort for Holland. The site provides grand views of the bay, but ruins of the walls and a couple of rusty cannons are all that remain of the original fort.

Gambling is also big here, with several casinos clustered along Front Street in the heart of Philipsburg. All of them open early enough to snag cruisers.

ON THE FRENCH SIDE Fort St. Louis is Marigot's answer to Fort Amsterdam. Built in 1767 to protect the waterfront warehouses that stored the French colony's agricultural riches, the cannons of this bastion frequently fired on hostile British raiders from Anguilla. After restorations and modification in the 19th century, the fort was eventually abandoned. In addition to the fort's cannons, crumbling walls, and French tricouleur flag flapping in the breeze, the short climb up the hill flanking Marigot Bay's north end affords splendid vistas. As a respite from the sun, duck into Marigot's **Museum of Saint Martin** (✆ **590/29-22-84**), next to the Tourism Office and adjacent to the marina. Much more thorough and scholarly than its Philipsburg counterpart, this institution boasts a first-rate collection of Ciboney, Arawak, and Carib artifacts excavated from the island's Amerindian sites, plus a reproduction of a 1,500-year-old burial mound. Another display details the history of the plantation and slavery era, and early-20th-century photographs trace the island's modern development. Admission costs $6.50; closed Sunday.

BEACHES

St. Martin has more than 30 beautiful white-sand beaches, some social, some serene. The busier ones boast bars, restaurants, watersports, and hotels, where changing facilities are usually available for a small fee. Toplessness is ubiquitous, and nudism is common on the French side, and increasingly evident on the Dutch side as well.

ON THE DUTCH SIDE Great Bay Beach is your best bet if you want to stay in Philipsburg. This mile-long stretch is convenient and has calm water, but it lacks the tranquility and cleanliness of the more remote beaches.

Just west of the airport, on the west side of the island, **Maho Beach** boasts a casino, shade palms, and a popular beachside bar and grill. It's a good snorkeling spot, too. Farther west, **Mullet Beach** borders the island's golf course. Shaded by palm trees and crowded on weekends, it's popular with swimmers and snorkelers. On-site vendors rent an array of watersports equipment. **Dawn Beach,** on the east coast, is the best snorkeling site on the island. Rent equipment from Busby's Beach Bar, which is right on the sand.

ON THE FRENCH SIDE Far and away the island's most visited strand, **Orient Beach,** on the northeast coast, fancies itself "the Saint Tropez of the Caribbean." Hedonism is the name of the game here: plenty of food, drink, music, and flesh (a naturist resort occupies the beach's southern tip, but nudism isn't confined to any one area). Watersports abound. South of Orient Beach, the waveless waters of **Coconut Grove** or **Galion Beach** are shallow up to 30m (100 ft.) offshore. Protected by a coral reef, this area is No. 1 with kids and popular with windsurfers.

On the island's west coast, just north of the Dutch border, **Long Bay** is the island's longest beach and another refuge for adults seeking peace and quiet. There are no facilities here, but this wild beach bordering some of the island's grandest mansions is popular with the rich and (sometimes) famous. The water and sand here are silky.

SHOPPING

St. Martin is a true free port—no duties are paid on any item coming in or going out—and neither side of the island has a sales tax. Shops in the much busier Dutch side are concentrated in Philipsburg, along **Front Street** and the numerous alleys radiating from

St. Martin Golf Excursions

The **Mullet Bay Golf Course** (© 599/545-2801), on the Dutch side, has an 18-hole course designed by Joseph Lee that's considered one of the more challenging in the Caribbean, especially the back 9. Mullet Pond and Simpson Bay lagoon provide both beauty and hazards. Greens fee for 18 holes is $80, plus $18 per-person cart rental fee; for 9 holes it's $60 plus an $8 per-person fee; club rental is an additional $26 for 18 holes and $21 for 9. The course opens daily at 7am.

it. The district is largely nondescript, but you'll find all the usual jewelry/gift/luxury-item shops, as well as some quirky local boutiques. In general, prices in the major stores are non-negotiable, but at small, family-run shops, you can try your luck with a little polite bargaining. The T-shirt and souvenir epicenter is in the open-air market behind the Courthouse in front of the town pier. **Guavaberry Emporium,** 8–10 Front St., sells Guavaberry "island folk liqueur," an aged rum with a distinctive fruity, woody, almost bittersweet flavor; it's available only on St. Martin.

On the French side, Marigot features a much calmer, more charming, and sophisticated ambience, with waterfront cafes where you can rest your weary over-shopped feet. Many shops here close their doors for a 2-hour lunch break starting at noon. The wide selection of European merchandise is skewed toward an upscale audience, but French crystal, perfume, liqueur, jewelry, and fashion can be up to 50% less expensive than in the States.

23 U.S. Virgin Islands: St. Thomas & St. John

Ever since Columbus discovered the Virgin Islands during his second voyage to the New World in 1493, they have proven irresistible to foreign powers seeking territory, at one time or another being governed by Denmark, Spain, France, England, Holland, and, since 1917, by the United States. Vacationers discovered St. Thomas right after World War II and have been flocking here ever since. Tourism and U.S. government programs have raised the standard of living to one of the highest in the Caribbean, and today the island is one of the busiest and most developed cruise ports in the Caribbean, often hosting more than six ships a day during the peak winter season. **Charlotte Amalie** (pronounced "Ah-*mahl*-yah"), named in 1691 in honor of the wife of Denmark's King Christian V, is the island's capital and has become the Caribbean's major shopping center and one of its busiest cruise ports.

The most tranquil and unspoiled of the U.S. Virgins is St. John, the smallest of the lot, more than half of which is preserved as the gorgeous **Virgin Islands National Park.** A rocky coastline, forming crescent-shaped bays and white-sand beaches, rings the whole island, whose miles of serpentine hiking trails lead past the ruins of 18th-century Danish plantations and let onto panoramic ocean views. A few ships anchor directly off St. John, but those that dock in St. Thomas usually offer excursions here as well, via ferry.

St. Croix, the largest of the USVIs, was a popular cruise destination until 2002, when most lines pulled out citing lack of traveler interest and a rising crime rate. In late November 2004, though, Royal Caribbean began quietly dropping in on the island again, with several of its ships making overnight refueling stops following a day in St. Thomas. Passengers are able to go ashore between approximately 8pm and midnight, where they're greeted by a street fair put on expressly for their benefit, with Caribbean musicians, dancers, and food and crafts vendors. At press time, Royal Caribbean planned to continue these visits at least through October 2005. After that? We'll see.

LANGUAGE & CURRENCY **English** is spoken on all three islands, and the **U.S. dollar** is the currency. Americans get a break on shopping in the U.S. Virgins, since they can bring home $1,200 worth of merchandise without paying duty, as opposed to $400 from most other Caribbean ports. You can also bring back more liquor from here. See p. 75 for more **Customs** information.

ST. THOMAS

With a population of more than 50,000 and a large number of American expatriates and temporary sun-seekers in residence, tiny St. Thomas isn't exactly a tranquil tropical retreat. You won't have any beaches to yourself. Shops, bars, and restaurants (including a lot of fast-food joints) abound here, and most of the locals make their living off the tourist trade.

COMING ASHORE Most cruise ships anchor at **West Indian Dock/Havensight Mall.** Located at the eastern end of Charlotte Amalie Harbor, 2½ miles from the town center, it's got its own restaurants, bookstores, banks, postal van, and lots of duty-free shops. Many people make the long, hot walk to the center of Charlotte Amalie, but it's not a scenic route in any way, so you may want to opt for one of the $3 per-person open-air taxis. If Havensight is clogged with cruise ships, your ship will dock at the **Crown Bay Marina,** to the west of Charlotte Amalie. A taxi is your best bet—the 30-minute-plus walk into Charlotte Amalie feels longer on a hot day, and isn't terribly picturesque. A taxi ride into town from here costs about $4.

GETTING AROUND Taxis are the chief means of transport here. They're unmetered, but a guide of point-to-point fares around the island is included in most tourist magazines. Less formal, privately owned **taxi vans** make unscheduled stops along major traffic arteries, charging less than a dollar for most rides. If you look like you want to go somewhere, one will likely stop for you. They may or may not have their final destinations written on a cardboard sign displayed on the windshield.

BEST CRUISE LINE SHORE EXCURSIONS

In addition to the excursions below, a bajillion booze cruises, island tours, and beach/snorkeling tours are offered here. The waters off these islands are rated among the most beautiful in the world.

Coral World & Island Drive ($39–$42, 3 hr.): Coral World Underwater Observatory and Marine Park is St. Thomas's number-one attraction. The 3½-acre complex features a three-story underwater observation tower 100 feet offshore, plunging into the depths to provide views of tropical fish, coral formations, sharks, and other sea beasts. In the Marine Gardens Aquarium, saltwater tanks display everything from sea horses to sea urchins, and a Touch Pool lets you fondle some of them. Another tank is devoted to sea predators, including circling sharks. From here, the tour zips around the island for a brief tour, visiting Cassie Hill for great views of St. John and the British Virgin Islands.

The U.S. & British Virgin Islands

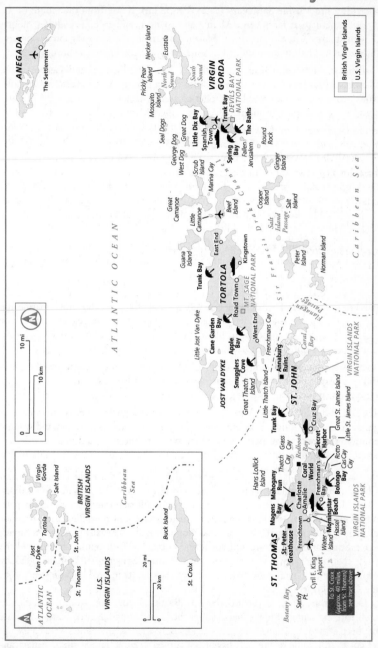

Kayaking the Marine Sanctuary ($72–$79, 3½ hr.): Kayak from the mouth of the marine sanctuary at Holmberg's Marina and spend nearly an hour paddling among the mangroves while a naturalist explains the mangrove and lagoon ecosystem. Includes a free half-hour to snorkel or walk along the coral beach at Bovoni Point.

Golfing at Mahogany Run ($170, 5 hr.): Designed by Tom and George Fazio, Mahogany Run is one of the most beautiful courses in the West Indies. This 18-hole, par-70 course rises and drops like a roller coaster on its journey to the sea. Cliffs and crashing sea waves are the ultimate hazards at the 13th and 14th holes. It's located on the north shore. You can also make arrangements for play on your own (© **800/ 253-7103,** ext. 1 or 340/777-6250, ext. 1). Greens fees are $130, including cart; the 20–30 minute taxi ride there will cost you about $10 each way.

St. John Eco-Hike ($64, 4 hr.): Take the ferry to St. John for a walkabout through the Virgin Islands National Park. The Lind Point Trail ascends about 250 feet to the Lind Point Overlook for views of St. John, St. Thomas, and the surrounding islands. An expert guide discusses the park's ecosystem and St. John's cultural history while you walk to Honeymoon Beach for a little swimming.

St. John Champagne Catamaran Sail ($79–$89, 4½ hr.): A sailing catamaran takes you to the pristine beaches of St. John. Snorkeling equipment, lunch, and champagne are provided. A 6-hour version of this tour is sometimes offered for $119.

Kon-Tiki Party Cruise ($39, 3 hr.): One of the liveliest party boats in the Caribbean sails over a coral reef where you can watch coral, sponges, and other marine life through glass panels—assuming you can see through those beer goggles you may be wearing by then. Steel band music plays throughout. At Palm Fringed Bay, you'll have time to swim before heading back to the pier.

Atlantis Submarine Expedition ($89, 2 hr.): Descend about 100 feet into the ocean in this air-conditioned submarine for views of exotic fish and sea life.

Water Island Bike Trip & Beach Adventure ($79, 3½ hr.): After a ferry ride to Water Island, a 5-minute bus ride brings you to the island's highest point, from which you get a nice downhill ride. Your guide will point out various historic sites and wildlife en route to Honeymoon Beach, where you can swim and enjoy a drink.

ON YOUR OWN: WITHIN WALKING DISTANCE

In days of yore, seafarers from all over the globe flocked to the old Danish town of Charlotte Amalie, including pirates and, during the Civil War, Confederate sailors. The old warehouses that once held pirates' loot still stand and, for the most part, house shops, shops, and more shops. The main streets (called "Gades" here in honor of their Danish heritage) are a veritable shopping mall, especially close to the waterfront. Stray farther landward and you'll find pockets of 19th-century houses and the truly charming, cozy, brick-and-stone **St. Thomas Synagogue,** built in 1833 by Sephardic Jews. There's a great view from here as well. It's located high on steep, sloping Crystal Gade.

Dating from 1672, **Fort Christian,** 32 Raadets Gade, rises from the harbor to dominate the center of town. Named after the Danish king Christian V, the structure has been everything from a governor's residence to a jail. Many pirates were hanged in its courtyard. Some of the cells have been turned into the rather minor **American-Caribbean Historical Museum,** displaying Indian artifacts of only the most passing interest. Admission is $3; closed weekends.

Seven Arches Museum, on Government Hill (© **340/774-9295**), is a 2-centuries-old Danish house completely restored to its original condition and furnished with antiques. You can walk through the yellow ballast arches and visit the great room with its view of the busy harbor. Admission is $5.

The **Paradise Point Tramway** (© **340/774-9809**) affords visitors a dramatic view of Charlotte Amalie Harbor at a peak height of 697 feet. The tramways transport customers from the Havensight area to Paradise Point, where riders disembark to visit shops and a popular restaurant and bar. The cost is $16 round trip.

ON YOUR OWN: BEYOND THE PORT AREA

The lush **St. Peter Greathouse Estate and Gardens,** at the corner of St. Peter Mountain Road (Rte. 40) and Barrett Hill Road (© **340/774-4999**), ornaments 11 acres on the volcanic peaks of the island's northern rim. It's the creation of Howard Lawson DeWolfe, a *Mayflower* descendant who, with his wife, Sylvie, bought the estate in 1987 and set about transforming it into a tropical paradise. It's filled with some 200 varieties of plants and trees, including an umbrella plant from Madagascar. There's also a rainforest, an orchid jungle, waterfalls, and reflecting ponds. From a panoramic deck you can see some 20 of the Virgin Islands. The house itself is worth a visit, its interior filled with local art. Admission is $10.

BEACHES

St. Thomas has some good beaches, all of which are easily reached by taxi. Arrange for your driver to return and pick you up at a designated time. All the beaches in the U.S. Virgin Islands are public, but some still charge a fee. Mind your belongings, as St. Thomas has pickpockets and thieves who target visitors. If you're going to St. John, you may want to do your beaching there instead (see "Beaches," under "St. John," below).

Located 3 miles north of Charlotte Amalie, across the mountains on the north side of the island, **Magens Bay Beach** was once hailed as one of the world's most beautiful, but it isn't as well maintained as it should be and is often overcrowded, especially when many cruise ships are in port. Admission is $3. Changing facilities, bathrooms, a snack bar, snorkel gear, and float rentals are available. In the northeast, near Coral World, **Coki Beach** is another good but often crowded spot. Snorkelers come here often. Also on the north side, **Sapphire Beach** is one of the finest on St. Thomas, set against the backdrop of the Doubletree Sapphire Beach Resort & Marina complex, where you can lunch or order drinks. Windsurfers like this beach a lot, and you can rent snorkeling gear and lounge chairs.

On the island's south side, **Morningstar** lies about 2 miles east of Charlotte Amalie at Marriott's Frenchman's Reef Beach Resort. You can wear your most daring swimwear here, and you can also rent sailboats, snorkeling equipment, and lounge chairs. To reach the beach take the cliff-front elevator at the Marriott. **Bluebeard's Beach Club,** just a little to the east, offers a secluded setting. Farther east still, the **Bolongo Bay Beach Club** lures those who love a serene spread of sand. You can feed hibiscus blossoms to iguanas and rent snorkeling gear and lounge chairs. They also offer a variety of watersports, including parasailing. At the far eastern end, little **Secret Harbor** sits near a collection of condos. With its white sand and coconut palms, it's a veritable cliché of Caribbean charm.

SHOPPING

Shopping is the number-one activity in Charlotte Amalie, and you'll sometimes find well-known brand names at savings of up to 40% off stateside prices—but you have to plow through a lot of junk to find the bargains. The main goodies are jewelry, watches, cameras, china, and leather, plus the local Cruzan Rum, which is so ridiculously cheap you'll think it's mismarked. Many cruise ship passengers shop at the **Havensight Mall,** where the ships dock, but the major shopping goes on along the harbor of Charlotte Amalie. **Main Street** (or Dronningens Gade, its old Danish name) is the main shopping area, with nearby **Back Street,** or Vimmelskaft, not too far behind. Many shops are also spread along the Waterfront Highway (also called Kyst Vejen) and along the side streets. All the usual Caribbean mega-tourist-shops sell all the usual jewelry, watches, perfume, gift items, and so on, but you'll also find some more singular boutiques and gift shops mixed in. At the **Vendors Plaza,** on the corner of Veterans Drive and Tolbod Gade, hundreds of street vendors ply their trades beneath oversize parasols. Food vendors set up on sidewalks outside.

ST. JOHN

A tiny gem, lush St. John lies about 3 miles east of St. Thomas across Pillsbury Sound. It's the smallest and least populated of the U.S. Virgins, only about 7 miles long and 3 miles wide, with a total land area of some 19 square miles. The island was slated for big development under Danish control, but a slave rebellion and the decline of the sugar-cane plantations ended that idea. Since 1956, more than half of St. John's land mass, as well as its shoreline waters, have been set aside as the Virgin Islands National Park, and today the island leads the Caribbean in eco- (or "sustainable") tourism. Miles of winding hiking trails lead to panoramic views and the ruins of 18th-century Danish plantations. Mysterious geometric petroglyphs incised into boulders and cliffs can be seen all over the island (ask a guide to point them out if you can't find them). These figures, of unknown age and origin, have never been deciphered. Since St. John is easy to reach from St. Thomas and the beaches are spectacular, many cruise ship passengers spend their entire day here.

COMING ASHORE   Cruise ships cannot dock at either of the piers in St. John. Instead, they moor off the coast at **Cruz Bay,** sending in tenders to the National Park Service Dock, the larger of the two piers. Most cruise ships docking at St. Thomas offer shore excursions to St. John's pristine interior and beaches.

GETTING AROUND   There are shopping, bars, and restaurants right by the docks. Otherwise, the most popular way to get around the island is by **surrey-style taxi.** Typical fares from Cruz Bay are $5.50 to Trunk Bay, $7 to Cinnamon Bay, and $11 to Maho Bay. Taxis wait at the pier. You can also rent open-sided **jeeps.** Avis and Hertz both have offices here. Just remember to drive on the left, even though steering wheels are on the left, too. Go figure.

BEST CRUISE LINE SHORE EXCURSIONS

St. John Island Tour ($45, 4½ hr.): Because most ships tie up in St. Thomas, tours of St. John first require a ferry or tender ride to Cruz Bay in St. John. Then you board open-air safari buses for a tour that includes a stop at the ruins of a working plantation (the Annaberg Ruins), as well as a pause at Trunk Bay or one of the other beaches. The island and sea views from the coastal road are spectacular.

ON YOUR OWN: WITHIN WALKING DISTANCE

Most cruise ship passengers dart through **Cruz Bay,** a cute little West Indian village with interesting bars, restaurants, boutiques, and pastel-painted houses. Wharfside Village, near the dock, is a complex of courtyards, alleys, and shady patios with a mishmash of boutiques, restaurants, fast-food joints, and bars. Located at the public library, the **Elaine Ione Sprauve Museum** (✆ **340/776-6359**) isn't big, but it does have some local artifacts, and will teach you about some of the history of the island. Admission is free; closed weekends.

ON YOUR OWN: BEYOND THE PORT AREA

In November 1954, the wealthy Rockefeller family began acquiring large tracts of land on St. John. They then donated more than 5,000 acres to the Department of the Interior for the creation of the **Virgin Islands National Park,** which Congress voted into existence on August 2, 1956. Over the years, the size of the park has grown steadily; it now totals 12,624 acres, including over two-thirds of St. John's landmass plus submerged land and water adjacent to the island. Stop off first at the **visitor center** (✆ **340/776-6201**) right on the dock at St. Cruz, where you'll find some exhibits and learn more about what you can see and do in the park. You can explore the park on the more than 20 miles of biking trails; rent your own car, Jeep, or Mini-Moke; or hike. If you decide to hike, stop at the visitor center first to watch an 18-minute video about the park and to pick up maps and instructions. The starting points of some trails are within walking distance while others can be reached by taxi for about $5 to $20. Within the park, try to see the **Annaberg Ruins,** Leinster Bay Road, where the Danes founded thriving plantations and a sugar mill in 1718. They're located off North Shore Road, east of Trunk Bay on the north shore.

BEACHES

For a true beach lover, missing the great white sweep of **Trunk Bay** would be like touring Europe and skipping Paris. That said, it's usually overcrowded. The beach has lifeguards and rents snorkeling gear to those wanting to explore the underwater trail near the shore. Snorkelers find good reefs at **Cinnamon Bay** and **Maho Bay,** and it's a great place to spot turtles and schools of parrotfish. Changing rooms and showers are available.

SHOPPING

Compared to St. Thomas, St. John is a minor shopping destination, but the boutiques and shops at Cruz Bay make up in interest and quality what they lack in number. Most of them are clustered at **Mongoose Junction** (www.usvi.net/shopping/mongoose) in a woodsy area beside the roadway, about a 5-minute walk from the ferry dock.

11

Alaska & British Columbia

A series of images: Two black bears eyeing us curiously, them padding along the shoreline of Dundas Bay, us drifting just yards away in a kayak. Walking along the Totem Trail at Sitka's National Historic Park, struck by the intense artistry of Southeast's Native cultures. Plucking a 1945 edition of John Steinbeck's *Cannery Row* off the shelf of a used bookstore in Juneau, then chatting with the 70-something proprietress about the ups and downs of the author's reputation. Watching Metlakatla's traditional Killer Whale Dancers perform at the town's clan house, and hearing one young member sound as enthusiastic as a hip-hop DJ as he talked about a new beat he'd created. Seeing a humpback whale breach for the first time, hurling his tanker trunk body gracefully into the air, then letting it fall back to water with the goofy joy of a beer-drinker in a belly-flop contest. Standing on deck at midnight, looking up at the Northern Lights for the first time and wondering if people ever get used to skies like that. Flying over Juneau's Mendenhall Glacier in a helicopter and realizing the immensity of the thing for the first time, then landing for an hour's visit and stooping to drink from the cold meltwater on its surface.

It's practically impossible not to be amazed by Alaska. Much of its coastline is wilderness, with snowcapped mountain peaks, enormous glaciers, dense rainforests, deep fjords, and the cycles of geologic time visible all around. Visit the towns, and you'll find people who retain the spirit of frontier independence that brought them here in the first place. Add Alaska's history and heritage, with its rich Native culture, its European influences, and its gold-rush and oil-pipeline chutzpah, and you have a destination that is utterly and endlessly fascinating.

The fact that some 750,000 cruise passengers arrive annually has had its impact, of course, turning some towns into veritable tourist malls populated by seasonal vendors and imported souvenirs. Even in the most touristy towns, though, it's easy to get out and experience the real thing. In Skagway, walk up one of the trails to the east of town and in 10 minutes you'd never know there are 6,000 other cruise passengers shopping behind you. In Ketchikan, walk southeast on Stedman Street and you're suddenly in Residential Alaska Land, where the real people live. Throughout the regions, you'll also find the influence of the region's great **Native peoples,** the Tlingit (pronounced "Klink-*get*"), Haida, and Tsimshian, who continue to make their presence felt in business, art, and politics.

Cruises in Alaska concentrate mostly on the **Inside Passage,** a series of connecting waterways threaded between the thousands of forested islands that make up the panhandle commonly known as Southeast Alaska or just **Southeast.** The passage actually begins in British Columbia, though ships tend to buzz through here without stopping en route to Alaskan waters, which begin just south of Ketchikan. From here, the region is home to scattered fishing towns, a number of larger towns and cities (including state capital Juneau), and many of the natural wonders visited by most ships, including Glacier Bay National Park, Tracy Arm fjord, and (mostly for small ships) Misty Fjords National Monument. The area teems with wildlife, including large populations of whale, bear, eagle, sea lion, sea otter, and mountain sheep. North of Southeast, ships sailing one-way itineraries also visit attractions like Hubbard Glacier and College Fjord along the **Gulf of Alaska,** which starts just above Glacier Bay.

HOME PORTS FOR THIS REGION
Vancouver, British Columbia, and **Seattle,** Washington, are the main southern termini for Alaska cruises, with ships either sailing round-trip or doing alternating north- and southbound departures between here and either Seward or Whittier, the two main port towns for **Anchorage.** Luxury lines Crystal and Silversea

also offer Alaska cruises that sail round-trip from **San Francisco.** Most of the small ships sail from one or another of the ports in Southeast (primarily **Juneau,** but also Ketchikan and Sitka), though some also operate out of Anchorage and Seattle.

LANGUAGE & CURRENCY English and dollars. You may want to get some Canadian dollars if you're sailing from Vancouver or visiting Victoria, but even that's not really necessary as most businesses will accept U.S. currency.

SHOPPING TIPS Shops throughout Alaska are chock-full of knock-off "Native Alaskan" art shipped in from Asia. So, when shopping for the real thing, ask the dealer for details about the artist, and also look for the **Silver Hand sticker,** a state certification that guarantees the item was, in fact, crafted in Alaska by a Native artist. The other thing that'll usually identify real pieces? Sky-high prices. You gets what you pays for.

1 Cruising Alaska's Natural Wonders

Every Alaska cruise will feature at least 3 days spent cruising the natural areas of Alaska's coast, including areas protected as national parks and national monuments. Regulations control access to some of them (most notably Glacier Bay, where only two large cruise ships and several smaller ones are permitted on any given day), while geography controls access to others: Misty Fjords, for instance, gets very narrow just where it gets most interesting, so only small ships can enter.

GLACIER BAY

There are about 5,000 glaciers in Alaska, but **Glacier Bay** (www.nps.gov/glba) definitely has The Big Mo, with the kind of name recognition the other glaciers can only dream about. Mostly, this is due to the fact that, in little more than 200 years, the area has gone from being a solid wall of ice up to 4,000 feet thick to being a 65-mile bay ecosystem full of wildlife, whales, and slowly returning vegetation, with glaciers extending up from its cold waters like fingers on a glove.

When first noted by Western man in 1794, Glacier Bay wasn't even a bay, but just an indentation in the shoreline of Icy Strait, plugged by a glacial cork. A mere 105 years later, the ice had receded some 35 miles, allowing naturalist **John Muir** to penetrate a landscape he described as "a solitude of ice and snow and newborn rocks," the latter not yet smoothed by the elements, and still retaining the heavy scratches left by the retreating glaciers. Today, that ice has retreated even farther, leaving behind a series of inlets headed by 11 tidewater glaciers, among them the **Johns Hopkins, Reid,**

Alaska

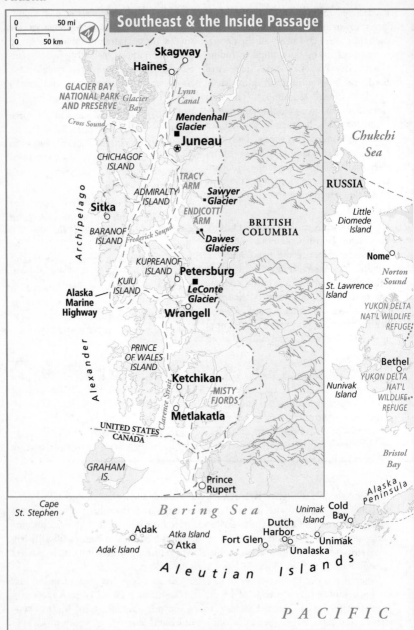

Southeast & the Inside Passage

0   50 mi
0   50 km

Skagway
Haines

GLACIER BAY
NATIONAL PARK
AND PRESERVE
Glacier
Bay
Lynn
Canal

Cross Sound

Mendenhall
Glacier
Juneau

CHICHAGOF
ISLAND

TRACY
ARM

ADMIRALTY
ISLAND

Sawyer
Glacier

ENDICOTT
ARM

Sitka

BARANOF
ISLAND
Frederick Sound

Dawes
Glaciers

BRITISH
COLUMBIA

KUPREANOF
ISLAND

Petersburg

KUIU
ISLAND

LeConte
Glacier

Alaska
Marine
Highway

Wrangell

PRINCE
OF WALES
ISLAND

Ketchikan

MISTY
FJORDS

Metlakatla

UNITED STATES
CANADA

GRAHAM
IS.

Prince
Rupert

Chukchi
Sea

RUSSIA

Little
Diomede
Island

Nome

Norton
Sound

St. Lawrence
Island

YUKON DELTA
NAT'L WILDLIFE
REFUGE

Bethel

YUKON DELTA
NAT'L
WILDLIFE
REFUGE

Nunivak
Island

Bristol
Bay

Alaska
Peninsula

Cape
St. Stephen

Bering Sea

Unimak
Island
Cold
Bay

Adak

Atka Island
Atka

Dutch
Harbor
Fort Glen

Unimak

Adak Island

Unalaska

Aleutian   Islands

PACIFIC

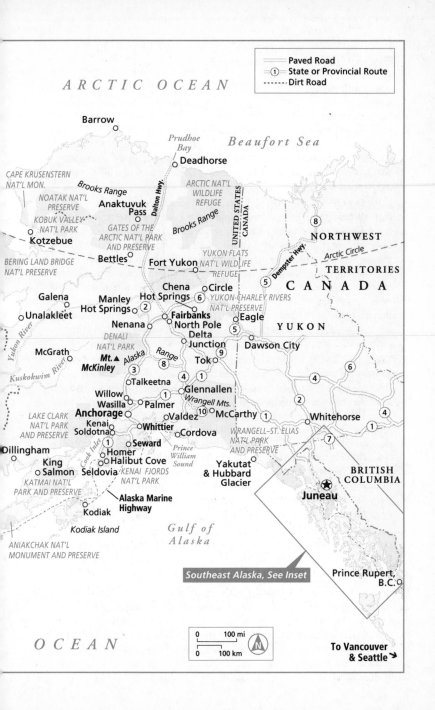

ARCTIC OCEAN

Barrow

Prudhoe Bay

Beaufort Sea

Deadhorse

CAPE KRUSENSTERN NAT'L MON.

Brooks Range

ARCTIC NAT'L WILDLIFE REFUGE

NOATAK NAT'L PRESERVE

Anaktuvuk Pass

KOBUK VALLEY NAT'L PARK

Kotzebue

GATES OF THE ARCTIC NAT'L PARK AND PRESERVE

Brooks Range

BERING LAND BRIDGE NAT'L PRESERVE

Bettles

Fort Yukon

YUKON FLATS NAT'L WILDLIFE REFUGE

(8)

NORTHWEST

Arctic Circle

TERRITORIES

CANADA

Galena

Manley Hot Springs

Chena Hot Springs

Circle

(5)

Dempster Hwy.

(6)

YUKON-CHARLEY RIVERS NAT'L PRESERVE

Unalakleet

(2)

Fairbanks

Eagle

YUKON

Nenana

North Pole

(5)

McGrath

DENALI NAT'L PARK

Delta Junction

Dawson City

Mt. ▲ McKinley

Alaska

Range

(8)

Tok

(9)

(6)

(3)

(4)

(1)

(4)

Talkeetna

Glennallen

(1)

Willow

Palmer

Wrangell Mts.

(2)

(4)

Wasilla

Valdez

McCarthy

(1)

Whitehorse

(1)

Anchorage

(10)

LAKE CLARK NAT'L PARK AND PRESERVE

Kenai

Soldotna

Whittier

Cordova

WRANGELL-ST. ELIAS NAT'L PARK AND PRESERVE

(7)

Dillingham

(1)

Seward

Homer

Prince William Sound

BRITISH COLUMBIA

King Salmon

Halibut Cove

KENAI FJORDS NAT'L PARK

Yakutat & Hubbard Glacier

Seldovia

KATMAI NAT'L PARK AND PRESERVE

Kodiak

Alaska Marine Highway

★ Juneau

Kodiak Island

Gulf of Alaska

ANIAKCHAK NAT'L MONUMENT AND PRESERVE

Southeast Alaska, See Inset

OCEAN

0   100 mi
0   100 km

Prince Rupert, B.C.

To Vancouver & Seattle ➚

Legend:
- Paved Road
- (1) State or Provincial Route
- Dirt Road

UNITED STATES / CANADA

Yukon River

Kuskokwim River

Cook Inlet

633

Glaciers: An Intro to the Ice

Along with whales, glaciers are the big drawing card on Alaska cruises, and with good reason: They're truly awesome. To see one spread between the bulk of massive mountains, flowing down into the sea, is to quite literally see how our world came to be. As the naturalist John Muir wrote while standing near an Alaskan glacier in the late 19th century, "Standing here with facts so fresh and telling and held up so vividly before us . . . one learns that the world, though made, is yet being made; that this is still the morning of creation."

HOW GLACIERS FORM   Glaciers form when snow accumulates over time at high altitudes. Successive snowfalls add more and more weight, compacting the snow underneath into extremely dense **glacial ice.** As the accumulation assumes mass, forming what is known as an **ice field,** gravity takes over and the ice field begins to flow very slowly downhill through the lowest, easiest passage. The glacier's enormous mass sculpts the landscape as it goes, grinding the shale and other rock and pushing rubble and silt ahead and to the sides. This sediment is known as **moraine.** *Terminal moraine* is the accumulation of rubble at the front of a glacier; *lateral moraine* lines the sides of glaciers. A dark area in a glacier's center—seen when two glaciers flow together, pushing their ice and crushed rubble together—is *median moraine.*

TYPES OF GLACIERS   Glaciers come in several different flavors. **Tidewater glaciers** are the kind most often seen on postcards; they spill down out of the mountains and run all the way to the sea. **Piedmont glaciers** are two glaciers that have run together into one. When seen from above, piedmonts resemble a highway interchange, edged by road slush, with the median moraine looking like lane dividers. There are also mountain or **alpine glaciers,** which are confined by surrounding mountain terrain and unable to flow. Other types—such as *hanging glaciers* that spill over rounded hillsides, *valley glaciers* that are confined by valley walls, and *cirque glaciers* that sit in basins and are usually circular (as opposed to river-shaped)—are essentially variants on these three main varieties.

GLACIAL BEHAVIOR   Glaciers are essentially rivers of ice that flow continually downhill. When they reach the sea, the effects of water and gravity cause **calving,** a phenomenon where large chunks of their ice face break off

Lamplugh, Margerie, and **Grand Pacific,** all of them in the bay's western arm and all regularly approached by cruise ships. Calving activity from these glaciers is the big draw (Johns Hopkins calves so much that ships can seldom approach closer than 2 miles, though it feels a lot closer), but don't forget to look at the land, which is a kind of living time-lapse photograph of earth's life cycles. Trees grow thick near the bay's head, but as you penetrate farther and farther you'll see less and less vegetation, and finally none at all. It just hasn't had time to grow back yet.

from the mass and crash into the sea, producing a sound like two 1,000-foot bowling balls colliding and cracking. The ice that's calved off floats away as an **iceberg.** Calvings are always a high point on a cruise.

Depending on temperature and the rate of precipitation, glaciers may either **advance** or **retreat.** Think of glaciers as human bodies and snowfall as calories—when the accumulation of snowfall (and resultant glacial ice) is greater than the amount of ice lost to melting and calving, the glacier grows, which is known as *advancing.* When the opposite occurs—when melting and calving outpace new buildup of ice—the glacier is said to be *retreating.* Glaciers can also be in a state of equilibrium, where the amount of snowfall roughly equals the amount of melt-off. Even where this is the case, the glacier is still a slow-moving river, always flowing downhill—it's just that its total length remains the same, with new ice replacing old at a more or less constant rate.

Some glaciers may **gallop,** surging forward as much as 10 to 150 feet a day, and some may recede or retreat at the same rate. Hubbard Glacier became a galloping glacier for a brief time in 1986, moving forward rapidly and blocking in Yakutat Bay for several months.

By the way, glacial ice isn't blue. It may look blue—and a startling, electric blue at that—but it's really a trick of the light. The ice absorbs all colors of the spectrum *except* blue, which is then reflected away, making the ice itself appear to be blue.

AN ICEBERG BY ANY OTHER NAME   When a glacier calves, the icebergs it forms are classified differently depending on their size, a system that allows one ship's captain to warn another of the relative ice hazard. Very large chunks are officially called **icebergs;** pieces of moderate size (usually 7 ft.–15 ft. across) are known as **bergy bits; growlers** are slightly smaller still, at less than 7 feet across, with less than 3 feet showing above water; and **brash ice** is any random smaller chunks. And remember the old adage: What you're seeing is only the tip—most of the berg is below the water.

If you want to explore glaciers further, the National Snow and Ice Data Center has a great glacier website, with many photos, a glossary, and other data, at **http://nsidc.org/glaciers**.

Glacier Bay was named a national park in 1925, and today each ship that enters this area takes aboard a park ranger to provide information about glaciers, wildlife (which includes mountain goats; brown bears; and minke, orca, and humpback whales), and history of Native peoples and white men in the bay. On large ships, the ranger will speak over the PA and may also give a presentation about conservation in the show lounge; on small ships, he or she will often be on deck throughout the day, speaking over the PA and/or just talking with the passengers and answering questions.

TRACY ARM & ENDICOTT ARM

Located about 50 miles due south of Juneau, these long, deep fjords reach back from the Stephens Passage stretch of the Inside Passage into the Coastal Mountain Range, their steep-sided waterways ending in active glaciers—the **North Sawyer** and **South Sawyer Glaciers** in Tracy Arm and **Dawes Glacier** in Endicott. All of them calve constantly, filling the waters with miles of brash ice and bergs that ping and thunk off your ship's hull as you approach the ice faces. The show can be pretty spectacular. Two years ago, we saw South Sawyer calve off a sheet of ice as big as our ship. Granted, we were on one of Cruise West's 100-passenger vessels, but still . . .

The passage through either fjord is incredibly dramatic, the sheer mountain walls rising literally a mile high straight from the water, cut by cascading waterfalls and tree-covered, snow-topped mountain valleys. Wildlife here might include Sitka black-tailed deer, bald eagles, mountain goats, and harbor seals (which often haul themselves out on ice floes to get some sun). You may also see the odd black bear. In 2003 we looked all day without luck, then, at dinner, our friend Cindy looked up from her salmon and spotted one on shore, eating a salmon of its own.

MISTY FJORDS NATIONAL MONUMENT

The 2.3-million-acre, Connecticut-size area of Misty Fjords starts at the Canadian border in the south and runs on the eastern side of the Behm Canal, which has Revillagigedo Island on the other side. (Ketchikan is on the western coast of Revillagigedo.) It is topography, not wildlife, that makes a visit here worthwhile, with volcanic cliffs rising up to 3,150 feet and plunging further hundreds of feet below the waterline, reminding you you're sailing in a flooded cleft between mountains. Peace and serenity are the stock-in-trade of the place, with its namesake mists imparting a storybook, *Lord of the Rings* kind of atmosphere, abetted by dense hemlock and spruce forests, high ridges covered in alpine grass, and the occasional flow of petrified lava rock down to the shoreline.

Only passengers on small ships will see Misty Fjords close up, as its waterway is too narrow in most places for big ships. The bigger ships pass the southern tip of the area and then veer away northwest to dock at Ketchikan, where shore excursions can take you back into the area by **floatplane.** Some fly in, do a water landing, and then fly out again. Others bring you to an excursion boat for exploration of the monument, then make the short cruise back to Ketchikan.

HUBBARD GLACIER

Hubbard lies at the northern end of **Yakutat Bay** and has two claims to fame: It's Alaska's widest ice face at about 6 miles across, and it's one of the fastest moving glaciers in Alaska. In the mid-'80s it moved so fast it created a wall across the mouth of **Russell Fjord,** one of the inlets lining Yakutat Bay. That effectively turned the fjord into a lake and trapped hundreds of migratory marine creatures inside. After causing such a hubbub, it receded to its original position again several months later. Still, it's an active mother, calving off a substantial amount of ice.

PRINCE WILLIAM SOUND & COLLEGE FJORD

Located directly south of Anchorage on the bottom side of the Kenai Peninsula, Prince William Sound suffered mightily following the *Exxon Valdez* oil spill in 1989, which killed innumerable marine creatures and birds. Today, following decades of cleanup, the area is on the rebound, with whales, harbor seals, eagles, sea lions, sea

Cruisetours—'Cause All Alaska Ain't on Water

Most folks who go to the trouble of getting to a place as far off the beaten path as Alaska try to stick around for a while once they're there rather than jet home as soon as they hop off the boat. Knowing this, the cruise lines have set themselves up in the land-tour business as well, offering a number of land-based extensions that can be tacked on to your cruise experience, either before you sail or after.

A typical **Anchorage/Denali/Fairbanks cruisetour** package might include a 7-night Vancouver-Anchorage cruise, followed by 2 nights in Anchorage and a scenic ride in a private railcar into **Denali National Park** for 2 more nights at one or another of the cruise line's lodges. A full day in the park allows guests to view the staggeringly beautiful wilderness expanse and its wildlife. If you're lucky, the cloud gods will part to give you a look at **Mount McKinley,** North America's highest peak at 20,320 feet. From there, you'll go by train to **Fairbanks,** spending 2 more days. Fairbanks itself isn't much to look at, but the activities available in outlying areas are fantastic, and include paddle-wheel day cruises on the Chena and Tanana rivers, jet boat rides, and excursions to gold mines and dredges. Passengers typically fly home from Fairbanks. A shorter variation of that itinerary might skip Fairbanks and return to Anchorage for departure.

Yukon Territory cruisetours typically combine a 3- or 4-day cruise between Vancouver and Juneau/Skagway with a land program into the Klondike. En route, passengers travel by rail, riverboat, motorcoach, and possibly air. Tours typically include overnight stops in **Whitehorse,** the territorial capital, and **Dawson City,** a remote, picture-perfect gold-rush town, then cross the Alaska border near Beaver Creek, travel to Fairbanks, and from there go through Denali to Anchorage. The tour can be taken in either direction.

A **Canadian Rockies cruisetour** offers some of the finest mountain scenery on earth. It's not just that the glacier-carved mountains are astonishingly dramatic and beautiful; it's also that there are hundreds and hundreds of miles of this wonderful wilderness high country. Between them, **Banff National Park** and **Jasper National Park** preserve much of this mountain beauty. Other national and provincial parks make accessible other vast and equally spectacular regions of the Rockies, as well as portions of the nearby Columbia and Selkirk mountain ranges. The beautiful **Lake Louise,** colored deep green from its mineral content, is located 35 miles north of Banff.

Other cruisetour options include an add-on to **Wrangell–St. Elias National Park,** east of Anchorage.

otters, puffins, and fish all returned to its waters. It's truly one of Alaska's most appealing wilderness areas, surrounded on three sides by the Chugach Mountains and only sparsely populated by humans, most of them congregated in a few isolated towns such as Valdez, Whittier, Cordova, and the Native villages of Tatitlek and Chenega.

College Fjord is in the northern sector of Prince William Sound, roughly midway between Whittier and Valdez. It's not one of the more spectacular Alaska glacier areas, being very much overshadowed by Glacier Bay, Yakutat Bay (for Hubbard Glacier), and others, but it's scenic enough to merit a place on a lot of cruise itineraries, mostly for **Harvard Glacier,** which sits at its head. The fjord was named by members of the 1899 Harriman Expedition, which saddled the glaciers lining College Fjord and neighboring Harriman Fjord with the names of prominent eastern schools—hence Harvard Glacier, Vassar, Williams, Yale, and so on. Perhaps the most spectacular of the sound's ice faces is **Columbia Glacier,** whose surface spreads over more than 400 square miles and whose tidewater frontage is nearly 6 miles across. Columbia is receding faster than most of its Alaska counterparts. Scientists reckon it will retreat more than 20 miles in the next 20 to 50 years, adding yet another deep fjord to Prince William Sound's already impressive collection.

2 Haines

Sitting near the northern end of the Lynn Canal, Haines (pop. 2,500) is a small, laid-back Alaska town, without the kind of self-referential tourist gloss that's so evident in neighboring Skagway, about 15 miles farther upwater. Despite a dramatic setting amid the peaks of the Fairweather Mountain Range, few ships dock here, partly because of a lack of large, deepwater docks, partly because of the lack of large, obvious attractions, so if you're sailing one that does, you'll be experiencing a town that maintains its local vibe well.

Haines was established in 1879 by Presbyterian missionary S. Hall Young and naturalist John Muir as a place to convert the Chilkoot and Chilkat Tlingit tribes to Christianity. They named it for Mrs. F. E. Haines, secretary of the Presbyterian National Committee, who had raised the funds for their exploration. The Tlingits called the place *Dei-Shu,* or "end of the trail," while traders knew the place as Chilkoot. The U.S. military arrived in the early part of the 20th century and constructed **Fort William H. Seward,** a very 19th-century-looking group of white clapboard structures arranged around a rectangular parade ground. The fort was decommissioned after World War II, and today its structures have been turned into private homes, B&Bs, and arts and performances spaces, some of them devoted to Native culture (see below). A recreation Tlingit tribal house sits at the center of the parade ground.

Ships that don't stop in Haines regularly offer excursions to the town from Skagway, traveling by boat. Some are simple tours of town attractions (cost: $85–$99); others combine a quick tour of town with a float or jet-boat ride through the **Chilkat Bald Eagle Preserve** (see below; the cost of these trips is typically $165–$175).

COMING ASHORE Small ships tie up to the Port Chilkoot Dock, directly opposite Fort Seward and ½ mile from downtown. Larger vessels must tender passengers in, dropping them either at Port Chilkoot or at the small-boat harbor in the downtown area. Visitor information is available at the dock.

GETTING AROUND It's easy to explore Fort Seward and the town on foot, or you can rent a bike at **Sockeye Cycle,** 24 Portage St. in Fort Seward, just uphill from the dock (© **907/766-2869**). Rentals cost $12 for 2 hours or $20 for 4 hours, helmet and lock included. They also offer bike tours of the area.

BEST CRUISE LINE SHORE EXCURSIONS

Chilkat Bald Eagle Preserve Float Trip ($99, 4 hr.): Head out to the Chilkat Preserve (see below) by bus, then suit up in boots and a life vest for a gentle float by rubber raft down the Chilkat River. An expert guide both rows and provides commentary on the area's natural environment, steering the raft close to shore to spot animal tracks and keeping an eye out for moose, bears, eagles, and wolves. A **jet-boat trip** is also available here ($99, 4 hr.), and though the trips generally report wildlife sightings, this seems to us a pretty noisy way to see a quiet place.

Chilkoot Lake Bicycle Adventure ($87, 3 hr.): After driving to your start point, you'll ride 8 miles along the shore of Lutak Inlet, where the river meets the sea. Highlights include some amazing views of the lake, glaciers, waterfalls, and mountains, and a chance at spotting eagles and bears.

Chilkat Rain Forest Nature Hike ($65, 4 hr.): This hike takes you through a rainforest and includes a narrative on forest flora and fauna by a naturalist. You might spot a bald eagle or two. Moderately difficult hiking is involved.

Taste of Haines Tour ($55, 2 hr.): Visit the Haines Brewing Company, the smallest brewery in Alaska, for a sample and a talk with the brewmaster, then head to a local smoked-salmon shop to sample and learn how the stuff is prepared.

Best of Haines by Classic Car ($54, 1 hr.): Explore Haines in style in a 1930s or 1940s vintage automobile. The entertaining guides share the history of the area, and you'll get an insight into how Hainesians live and make their livings.

Haines Walking Tour ($20, 1½ hr.): A leisurely walk from the dock, through Fort Seward, and into the town center.

ON YOUR OWN: WITHIN WALKING DISTANCE

The **Alaska Indian Arts Cultural Center,** located in the old fort hospital on the south side of the Fort Seward parade grounds (© **907/766-2160;** www.alaskaindian arts.com), has a small gallery selling traditional artwork and prints, plus a carvers' workshop where you may be able to see totem-carving in progress. Between the fort and the town center, the **American Bald Eagle Foundation and Natural History Museum,** Haines Hwy. at 2nd Avenue (© **907/766-3094;** http://baldeagles.org), is essentially a huge diorama featuring more than 180 stuffed eagles and other animals. Admission is $3. The place has a real folk-art quality that's entirely appropriate for Haines. Ditto for Dave and Carol Pahl's quirkily remarkable **Hammer Museum** on Main Street (© **907/766-2374;** www.hammermuseum.org), which displays more than 1,200—yes, 1,200—completely different hammers from all over the world, including whale-blubber hammers, bookbinders' hammers, little hammers used by 1920's nightclub patrons to applaud performers, and Tlingit ceremonial hammers. But, you ask, why hammers? Seems Dave came to Alaska 30 years ago with the dream of being a self-sufficient pioneer, and became intrigued when he realized he had more than a hundred just for his own use. Things grew from there. Admission costs $2. Also on Main Street, down near the small-boat harbor, the small **Sheldon Museum and Cultural Center** (© **907/766-2366;** www.sheldonmuseum.org) was established by local shopkeepers Steve and Bess Sheldon starting around 1925. It has a wonderful collection of Hainesiana: Tlingit artifacts, gold-rush-era weaponry, military memorabilia, and so on. Admission is $3.

ON YOUR OWN: BEYOND THE PORT AREA

Haines is probably the best place on earth to see bald eagles. About 20 miles outside town, the **Chilkat Bald Eagle Preserve** protects 48,000 acres of river bottom along the Chilkat River. Summer cruisers will miss the biggest eagle season (Oct to mid-Dec, when up to 3,000 eagles gather in the cottonwood trees, waiting to swoop down on late-spawning salmon), but a healthy 200 to 400 are in residence the rest of the year. You'll really need to take a float-trip shore excursion to see the place in the limited time you have here. The water is gentle, so much so that if your raft gets stuck, the guide will just hop out and push. Eagle sightings are practically guaranteed, and occasionally you might spot a moose along the shoreline too.

SHOPPING

More than a dozen galleries and shops are located around Fort Seward (mostly concentrating on Native arts) and the downtown area.

3 Juneau

Juneau's a great town. Fronted by the busy Gastineau Channel and backed by 3,819-foot Mount Juneau and 3,576-foot Mount Roberts, its location is beyond picture perfect. But it's the city's quirks we appreciate, like the fact that it's the capital of the state but is completely surrounded by water, forest, and the massive Juneau Icefield, and is therefore unreachable by land. Or the fact that the whole town lies at the base of a landslide zone, and has numerous treeless hillsides to prove it. Or that at one time a bull terrier named Patsy Ann was the official town greeter, trotting down to the docks whenever a ship came in. (Long dead now, there's a bronze statue of her in Marine Park.) We even appreciate the love-hate relationship the town has with the cruise industry, with many lamenting the fact that downtown and the Egan Expressway are completely overrun by visitors and tour buses from late May through September. Democracy thrives on debate, and we can't argue with the locals' concerns: On any given day, four or five cruise ships may be in port, ranging from the biggest in the fleets of Princess, Celebrity, Holland America, and the rest to the small ships of Cruise West, Glacier Bay, Clipper, and others. That means about 6,000 people are added daily to a population that numbers only 31,000 total—and those are spread out across the greater town's 3,255-square-mile area. It makes for a bit of chaos.

Tourism woes aside, modern Juneau is a product of Alaska's golden past. It was no more than a fishing outpost for local Tlingit Indians until 1880, when gold was discovered in a creek off the Gastineau Channel by Chief Kowee of the Auk Tlingit clan. Kowee passed the information on to German engineer George Pilz in return for 100 warm blankets and a promise of work for his tribe, and agreed to lead prospectors Joe Juneau and Richard Harris to the find. Mines quickly sprang up on both sides of the channel, including the **Alaska-Juneau Mine,** known locally simply as the A-J, which produced a whopping 3.5 million ounces of gold before it closed in 1944. You can still see its remains up on the slope of Mount Roberts.

Outside of town, the big attraction is **Mendenhall Glacier.** Twelve miles long and 1½ wide, it's the most visited glacier in the world.

COMING ASHORE Both large and small ships dock right in the downtown area, along Marine Way. Occasionally, overcrowding might mean a ship has to anchor in the channel and tender people to shore. A visitor information center is located in a green building right on the dock, near the base of the Mount Roberts Tram. The Patsy Ann statue is on the dock at Marine Park. Pat her head and consider yourself greeted.

GETTING AROUND   Most of the in-town sites are within walking distance of the pier, though some of it is tough going due to hills. The **Juneau Trolley Car Company** (© **907/789-4342**) also provides narrated tours of the downtown area. You can get off and on as you like at various marked sites. Fares are $14 adults, $10 kids. Visits to the Mendenhall Glacier and other sights out the Egan Expressway will require an excursion or taxi, which, as at every port town, you'll find waiting at the pier.

BEST CRUISE LINE SHORE EXCURSIONS

The number of excursions typically offered in Juneau is fairly stupefying, but mostly that's because a lot of mixing and matching is going on: a glacier visit paired with a salmon bake or a horseback trek, or a salmon bake paired with a flightseeing adventure, or a half-dozen different helicopter/glacier options. Here are some of the best.

Glacier Helicopter Tour ($215–$375, 2½–6½ hr.): This is one of the very best shore excursions we've ever taken. After transferring to the airport by bus, guests board helicopters for a flight that follows the flowing ice of Mendenhall Glacier high into the mountains. While glaciers are impressive enough from the water, it took this trip to really drive home to us how completely stupendous they really are, stretching away as far as the eye can see. It's literally like getting a glimpse back into the ice age. After about 20 minutes of flightseeing, your helicopter will touch down on the glacial ice, where (outfitted in special boots provided by the helicopter company) you'll have a chance to walk around on the surface. It's like being on Mars. Different packages give you more or less time on the glacier, with some options adding in additional activities, such as the **Glacier Dog-Sled Expedition** that combines a flight over the Juneau Icefield with a landing on the Norris Glacier, where you'll board dog sleds with an Iditarod veteran ($449, 3½ hr.). The **Extended Helicopter Glacier Trek** ($450, 6½ hr.) involves a flight onto the Juneau Icefield followed by 4 hours of hiking and climbing in rugged terrain, descending ice walls, and exploring glacial pools and ice caves along the way.

Mendenhall Glacier & Salmon Bake ($65, 4 hr.): Three for the price of one: a visit to the Macaulay Salmon Hatchery to learn about rearing or raising salmon; a visit to Mendenhall, where you can stick to the interpretive center or get closer to the ice on one of several different trails; and an all-you-can-eat salmon bake in a rustic setting, with folk-music entertainment, the ruins of an old mine to explore, and lush rainforest all around. A less expensive option ($40, 3 hr.) visits only the hatchery and glacier, while a more expensive one ($80, 4 hr.) replaces the salmon bake with a bus tour of the city.

Bike & Brew Tour ($80, 4½ hr.): This bicycle tour sets off outside town along Fritz Cove Road, offering views of picturesque Auke Bay and the Mendenhall Glacier. The 11-mile ride ends at the Alaska Brewing Company for a tour and sampling of the wares.

Mendenhall Glacier Float Trip ($105, 4 hr.): On the shore of Mendenhall Lake you'll board 10-person rafts. An experienced oarsman will guide you from there out past icebergs and into the Mendenhall River, where you'll encounter moderate rapids and stunning views. Expect a snack of smoked salmon and reindeer sausage somewhere along the way.

Mendenhall Lake Canoe Adventure ($130, 3½ hr.): Board 12-person Native canoes, paddling out onto the lake's water while a guide shares natural history and Native stories about the surrounding scenery and wildlife. You'll pull into shore near roaring Nugget Falls, just a few yards from the glacier face.

Mendenhall Glacier & Horseback Ride ($150, 3½ hr.): After driving to the Montana Creek trailhead, you'll saddle up for a 3-mile ride through Juneau's temperate rainforest, then transfer by van to Mendenhall Glacier.

ON YOUR OWN: WITHIN WALKING DISTANCE

Juneau town center is compact and fun to walk around, but if you want to escape the crowd or get an overview (literally), take the **Mount Roberts Tramway** (© 888/461-TRAM; www.goldbelttours.com) from the docks up to the clear air and overwhelming views at the 1,760-foot tree line. The ride only takes 6 minutes, but it's like entering another world. At the top there's a reception center with restaurant/bar, a gift shop (of course), and a theater showing a pretty good film about Tlingit culture, but try not to linger here too long. Instead, head outside to the network of paths that let on to really incredible views as you pass through a fascinating alpine ecosystem. If you're energetic, you can start a 6-mile round-trip to Mount Roberts's summit (at 3,819 ft.), though there are also several shorter loops. Watch your footing up here, especially if the trails are wet or covered in snow—a possibility in the shoulder seasons. (Tickets are $22 adults, $13 children 12 and under.) Most ships offer the tram as an excursion for the same price, but we suggest waiting till you get to town and buying a ticket on your own, as it's not worth the ride if you arrive on an overcast day. At the top of the mountain, you wouldn't be able to see a damn thing.

Heading in toward town, the legendarily notorious, realistically touristy **Red Dog Saloon** stands at right at the intersection where Egan Drive heads left toward Mendenhall Glacier and Franklin Street continues up into town. Through its swinging doors you'll find a slightly contrived but still infectious frontier atmosphere, with a sawdust-covered floor, live music, and walls covered with memorabilia and messages from previous visitors. You'll also find current visitors—lots of them. Locals hang across the street, at **The Alaskan Bar,** 167 S. Franklin, which occupies an authentic gold-rush hotel with a two-story Victorian barroom. Down Egan, **The Hangar** also serves a good brew, and there's also decent pizza.

Continue down Egan and make a right at Whittier to get to the **Alaska State Museum** (© 907/465-2901; www.museums.state.ak.us) and its large collection of art and artifacts. Opened as a territorial museum in 1900, it has a wildlife exhibit, reminders of the city's mining and fisheries heritage, and a first-class collection of artifacts reflecting the state's Russian history and Native cultures. A clan house in the Alaska Native Gallery contains authentic art you'd really find in its functional place. Admission is $5. Not far off, at the intersection of Main and Fourth streets, the fun little **Juneau-Douglas City Museum** (© 907/586-3572; www.juneau.lib.ak.us/parks rec/museum) displays artifacts and photographs from the city's pioneer and mining history and Tlingit culture, with special exhibits changing annually. The plaza in front is where the 49-star U.S. flag was first raised in 1959, when Alaska got its statehood before Hawaii did. Admission is $3. About 3 blocks away, at Fifth and Gold, the tiny, octagonal **St. Nicholas Russian Orthodox Church** was built in 1893 by local Tlingits who, under pressure to convert to Christianity, chose the only faith that allowed them to keep their language.

ON YOUR OWN: BEYOND THE PORT AREA

About 13 miles from downtown, at the head of Mendenhall Valley, the **Mendenhall Glacier** glows bluish white, looming above the suburbs like an Ice Age monster that missed the general extinction. Besides being a truly impressive sight, Mendenhall is the most easily accessible glacier in Alaska, with great views from the parking lot across the lake to the glacier's face, and a wheelchair-accessible trail that leads to the water's edge. The land near the parking lot shows the signs of the glacier's recent passage: little topsoil, stunted vegetation, and, in many places, bare rock that shows the scratch marks of the glacier's movement. Atop a bedrock hill, reached by stairs, a ramp, or an elevator, the Forest Service visitor center contains a glacier museum with excellent explanatory models, computerized displays, and ranger talks. Admission is $3. Trails of various lengths get you closer to the glacier, the easiest being a half-mile nature trail.

Along the Egan Expressway about 3 miles from downtown, the **Macaulay Salmon Hatchery,** 2697 Channel Dr. (© **877/463-2486;** www.dipac.net), has a visitor center where you can watch the whole process of harvesting and fertilizing salmon eggs. The resultant offspring are later released back into the wild. If that doesn't float your boat, the nearby **Alaskan Brewing Company** might (© **907/780-5866;** www. alaskanbeer.com). Located off Egan at Vanderbilt Hill Road (then right on Anka St. and right again on Shaune Dr.), they offer low-key tours with a sampling of beer at the end, and their logo-wear is even pretty hip. The brewery started small in 1986 when Geoff and Marcy Larson had the idea of bringing a local gold-rush-era brew back to life. It worked, and now Alaskan Amber and several other brews are found everywhere in Alaska, and mighty tasty too.

SHOPPING

The shops near the dock are mostly touristy, with cheap souvenir stores mixed in with jewelry shops, but there are some good picks among the litter, including **The Raven's Journey,** 439 S. Franklin, selling Tlingit and other Northwest Indian art; the **Decker Gallery,** 233 S. Franklin, selling the works of local artist Rie Muñoz; and **Galligaskins,** 219 S. Franklin St., selling clothing with Alaska-theme designs. If you're in need of reading material, this is probably the best port to buy a book, with several decent shops located downtown. If you're in need of smoked salmon (and who ain't?), **Taku Smokeries,** 550 S. Franklin (© **800/582-5122;** www.takusmokeries.com), will ship it anywhere in the U.S.

4 Ketchikan

Ketchikan sits just north of the Canadian border, and like many border towns it wears its mercantile heart on its sleeve. They call it "Alaska's first city" because it's the first port visited on most northbound cruises, but the way people throng the port area's gift shops, you'd think it was the last chance they had to use their credit cards before Judgment Day. Here's our advice: Walk down the gangway, take three deep breaths, and say to yourself, "I do not need to shop." Instead, walk right past the shops and head for one of the town's several **totem-pole** parks or take an excursion to **Misty Fjords.** When you get back you can spend a little time poking around the galleries and shops on Creek Street.

Shopping aside, the town's port area is interesting in that much of it is either landfill or sitting on stilts above the water. The town is also notable for being one of the soggiest in Alaska: The average annual rainfall is about 160 inches (more than 13 ft.!) and has topped 200 inches in its most intense years.

COMING ASHORE   Ships dock right at the pier in Ketchikan's downtown area.

GETTING AROUND   Ketchikan's downtown port area is completely flat and walkable. Taxis are available at the pier if you want to go out to Saxman Indian Village or Totem Bight Park on your own.

BEST CRUISE LINE SHORE EXCURSIONS

Misty Fjords Flightseeing ($220–$285, 2–4½ hr.): Everyone gets a window seat aboard the floatplanes that run these flightseeing jaunts over mysterious, primordial Misty Fjords National Monument (see "Cruising Alaska's Natural Wonders," on p. 631). The less expensive options tool around, make a water landing so you can step out onto the pontoon, then return to Ketchikan by air. The more expensive (and better) option transfers you to a tour boat after landing at the monument, allowing you to see more of it from sea level. The boat takes you back to Ketchikan at the end.

Neets Bay Bear Watch ($310, 3 hr.): A floatplane flies you to Neets Bay in Tongass National Forest, where you take a guided quarter-mile hike to Neets Creek, where a salmon hatchery draws an unusual number of black bears, which you can watch as they fish and feed. A similar trip is offered to Traitor's Cove, another salmon hatchery.

Saxman Native Village Tour ($49, 2½ hr.): This Native village, situated about 2½ miles outside Ketchikan, is home to hundreds of Tlingit, Tsimshian, and Haida and is a center for the revival of Native arts and culture. The tour includes a storytelling session and a performance by the Cape Fox Dancers at the Beaver Clan House, as well as a guided walk through the grounds to see the totem poles and learn their stories. Craftspeople are sometimes on hand in the working sheds to demonstrate totem-pole carving. A short bus tour of Ketchikan is usually appended to the end of the trip.

Rainforest Wildlife Sanctuary ($79; 2½ hr.): After an 8-mile coastal drive you'll do a half-mile hike with a naturalist guide, trying to spot eagles, bears, seals, and various birdlife. After, you'll have an opportunity to feed Alaskan reindeer, watch a totem pole carver at work, and take a tour of a historic sawmill.

Sport-Fishing ($169; 5 hr.): If catching salmon is your goal, Ketchikan is a good spot to do it. Chartered fishing boats come with tackle, bait, fishing gear, and crew to help you strike king and coho around the end of June, or pink, chum, and silver from July to mid-September. (*Note:* A $10 fishing license and $10 king-salmon tag are extra.)

Tatoosh Island Sea Kayaking ($125, 4½ hr.): There are typically two kayaking excursions offered in Ketchikan: this one (which requires you to take a van and motorized boat to the islands before starting your 90-min. paddle) and a trip that starts from right beside the cruise ship docks. Of the two, this one is far more enjoyable, getting you out into a wilder area rather than just sticking to the busy port waters. The scenery is incredible, and you have a good chance of spotting bald eagles, leaping salmon, and seals, who may be swimming around your boat or just basking on the rocks.

Totem Bight Historical Park & City Tour ($39, 2½ hr.): This tour takes you by bus around Ketchikan and through the Tongass National Forest to see a historic Native fish camp where a ceremonial clan house and totem poles sit amid the rainforest. A fair amount of walking is involved.

The Great Alaskan Lumberjack Show ($29, 1½ hr.): Touristy fun: Watch lumberjacks compete in logrolling, speed climbing, tree topping, chainsaw carving, and all of the other skills every lumberjack needs. The amphitheater, located behind Salmon Landing, just a few hundred yards from the pier, has covered grandstands to keep you from getting soggy. If you don't book this as an excursion, you can still buy tickets at the door for the same price.

ON YOUR OWN: WITHIN WALKING DISTANCE

Near the pier, the **Southeast Alaska Visitor Center** (© 907/228-6214) on Main Street is worth a stop for its museum, in which a number of exhibits and dioramas depict both the Native Alaskan cultures and the more modern business development of Ketchikan. Admission to the exhibits is $5.

The centerpiece of downtown Ketchikan is **Creek Street,** a row of quaint wooden houses built on pilings above a busy salmon stream. Today, the narrow, boardwalked street is filled mainly with boutiques and galleries specializing in offbeat pieces by local artists and funky restaurants, but back in the day it was Ketchikan's notorious and semi-condoned red-light district, with more than 30 brothels lining the waterway. That all came to an end in the mid-1950s, and today all that's left of it is the touristy **Dolly's House** museum, once the establishment of a madam who worked under the name Dolly Arthur. (Her real name was Thelma Copeland.) Like the house's old clientele, you have to pay to get inside. We don't know what the old patrons had to shell out, but today it'll cost you $4. At the end of Creek Street, a **funicular** takes you uphill to the Westmark Cape Fox Lodge, which offers nice views. Walk through the lobby and follow the signs to the **Married Men's Trail,** allegedly a route taken by local men to reach the "spawning grounds" below. It makes for a nice little hike back into town.

At the bottom, look for Park Avenue and follow it to the observation deck at the artificial **salmon ladder,** where you can watch the determined fish battle the current to their spawning grounds at the top of Ketchikan Creek. Farther on, at 601 Deermount St., the indoor **Totem Heritage Center** (© 907/225-5900) was built by the city in 1976 to house a fine collection of 33 original totem poles from the 19th century, retrieved from the Tlingit Indian villages of Tongass and Village Islands and the Haida village of Old Kasaan. The Tsimshian people are also represented in some exhibits. The poles have not been restored, and are displayed mostly unpainted, many with the grass and moss still attached from when they were rescued from the elements. Totem poles were never meant to be maintained or repainted—they generally disintegrate after about 70 years, and were constantly replaced—but these were preserved to help keep the culture alive. A high ceiling and muted lighting highlight the spirituality of the art. Well-trained guides are on hand to explain what you're looking at, and there are good interpretive signs, as well as authentic Native crafts for sale. Admission is $4.

Okay, now you can go shopping.

ON YOUR OWN: BEYOND THE PORT AREA

About 10 miles outside town on the Tongass Narrows, **Totem Bight State Historical Park** ((© 907/247-8574) presents poles and a clan house carved beginning in 1938. Working under the New Deal's Civilian Conservation Corps, Native craftsmen working with traditional tools copied fragments of historic poles that had mostly rotted away, thereby helping to preserve an aspect of Tlingit and Haida culture that had essentially been outlawed until that time. The setting, purportedly the site of a traditional fishing camp, is a peaceful spot at the end of a short walk through the woods. Admission is free. Closer to town (about 2½ miles south of the pier on the Tongass Hwy.), **Saxman Indian Village** (© **907/225-4846;** www.capefoxtours.com) has artifacts similar to those at Totem Bight Park, but with an added resource: You can see carvers work in the building to the right of the park. The place is really set up more for people on excursions (see above), but you can also visit the studio and the poles without joining a tour, using a pamphlet that costs $1.50 (note, however, that interpretive materials are scant compared to those at Totem Bight).

SHOPPING

You'll wonder whether the town should be renamed Kitschikan if you spend much time in the many souvenir stores that line Front Street and the rest of the port area, but there are a few decent shops in among them. Our favorites are all on **Creek Street,** which has galleries, kitchenware shops with moose-shaped cookie molds, bookshops, and other appealing stores.

5 Sitka

Geographically speaking, Sitka's not on the Inside Passage at all, but rather on the Pacific coast of Baranof Island, sheltered by a fringe of islands at the head of Sitka Sound. Its name, in fact, comes from the Tlingit *Shee Atika,* which means "people on the outside of Shee Island." Small ships can thread in through narrow Peril Strait, which separates Baranof and Chichagof islands, but the big cruise ships have to sail around Baranof into the open Pacific. This minor inconvenience—and the fact that Sitka lacks docking facilities for megaships, requiring that they send passengers ashore in tenders instead—means the town sees a lot fewer cruise ship visits than Juneau, Ketchikan, and Skagway. Because of this, it retains a more residential feel than similar-sized towns in Southeast, and a combination of location, multicultural heritage, an adaptive economy, and sheer local pride keep it just plain beautiful to look at, and remarkably little changed since the old days: Historic photographs bear a remarkable resemblance to today's city.

Sitka's history is Alaska's richest, bar none. The rich, powerful, and sophisticated Kiksadi Tlingit clan called this part of Baranof Island home for centuries. In 1799, however, they came face to face with European power when Alexander Baranof, manager of the fur-trading Russian-American Company, established a new fort here in order to expand their sea otter hunting operations and territorial claims. Faced with the prospect of subjugation, the Tlingit attacked the Russian's redoubt in 1802 and killed almost everyone inside, but were finally defeated 2 years later, allowing the Russians to establish their new North American capital here, which they named *Novoarkhangelsk* (New Archangel). Today, Sitka preserves the Russian buildings of Alaska's earliest white settlement and, more deeply, the story of the cultural conflict between Alaska Natives and the invaders, and their resistance and ultimate accommodation to the new ways.

COMING ASHORE Most passengers will arrive in Sitka by tender because the harbor is too small to accommodate large ships. Tenders drop you right in the downtown area, where small ships can also dock. Maps are available at the volunteer-staffed

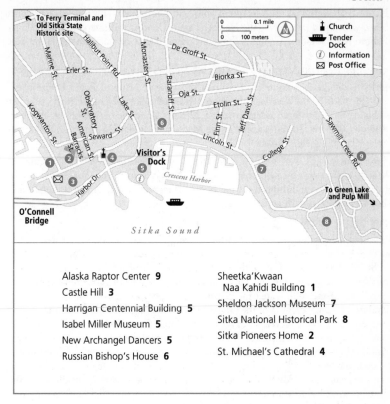

Alaska Raptor Center **9**
Castle Hill **3**
Harrigan Centennial Building **5**
Isabel Miller Museum **5**
New Archangel Dancers **5**
Russian Bishop's House **6**

Sheetka'Kwaan
 Naa Kahidi Building **1**
Sheldon Jackson Museum **7**
Sitka National Historical Park **8**
Sitka Pioneers Home **2**
St. Michael's Cathedral **4**

visitor information desk in the Crescent Harbor Dock's **Harrigan Centennial Hall,** which also houses the Isabel Miller Museum and the auditorium where the New Archangel Dancers perform (see below). The other docking facility is at the nearby O'Connell Bridge, where maps can be picked up from a volunteer at the information kiosk (mornings only). Map boards are located near both docking facilities.

GETTING AROUND   Unless you have mobility problems, we recommend walking in this town. You can hoof it to everything there is to see, and it's a beautiful place to explore. The Visitor Transit Shuttle bus also makes a circuit of the town's attractions throughout the day, meeting arrivals at the docks and stopping at the Sheldon Jackson Museum, the Historical Park, the Alaska Raptor Center, the Tribal Community House, and downtown. An all-day pass costs $7.

BEST CRUISE LINE SHORE EXCURSIONS

We advise against shore excursions here. The town is lovely enough by itself, and the various attractions have very good interpretive programs. If, however, you want something organized or want to get out in the wilds, here are a few options.

Sitka Historical Tour ($40–$45, 3 hr.): This bus excursion hits all the historic sights, including St. Michael's Cathedral, the Russian Cemetery, Castle Hill, and Sitka's

National Historic Park with its totem poles and forest trails. This tour is often combined with a performance by the New Archangel Dancers and/or a visit to the Alaska Raptor Rehabilitation Center. (Tours including either or both of the latter cost $45–$48.)

Sitka Bike & Hike ($70, 3 hr.): After transferring to Sawmill Creek, you'll ride 4 miles then hike approximately 1 mile in the Tongass National Forest before being brought back to the docking area. The **Advanced Bike Adventure** ($95, 4 hr.) is designed for experienced riders, covering 22 miles along the coast, with an elevation gain of 1,000 feet. Includes a visit to the Medvejie Fish Hatchery or a ½-mile hike to Beaver Lake. Lunch is included.

Sport-Fishing ($179, 4 hr.): An experienced captain will guide your fully equipped boat to a good spot for halibut and salmon; the rest is up to you. Your catch can be frozen or smoked and shipped to your home, if you wish. (*Note:* A $10 fishing license and a $10 king-salmon tag are extra.)

ON YOUR OWN: WITHIN WALKING DISTANCE

Essentially, everything in Sitka is within walking distance, though the farthest attraction, the Alaska Raptor Center (see below) might prove too far for some.

St. Michael's Cathedral, with its striking onion-shaped dome and its ornate gilt interior, is located on Lincoln Street, at the focal point of the downtown thoroughfare. One of the 49th state's most striking and photogenic structures, the current church is actually a replica of the original 1840s church, which burned to the ground one night in 1966. So revered was the cathedral that Sitkans, whether Russian Orthodox or not, formed a human chain and carried many of the cathedral's precious icons, paintings, vestments, and jeweled crowns from the flames. Later, with contributions of cash and labor from throughout the land, St. Michael's was lovingly re-created on the same site and rededicated in 1976. It still houses those religious symbols that the citizens worked so hard to rescue from the inferno, and is the official seat of the Russian Orthodox Church in Alaska. The vast majority of the church's congregation is made up of Alaska Native peoples, who were evangelized by the original cathedral's designer, Bishop Innocent Veniaminov, in the 19th century. Admission is $2.

Innocent's 1842 home, straightforwardly called **The Russian Bishop's House** (© **907/747-6281**), is a totally fascinating place a few blocks east at Lincoln and Monastery streets. It is now owned and operated by the National Park Service, which provides surprisingly enjoyable and informative tours of the bishop's furnished quarters and an impressive chapel. Born in 1797 in a remote Siberian village, Innocent first traveled to Alaska as a missionary in 1824, and was named the territory's first resident bishop in 1840. A giant for his time at 6 feet 3 inches, he was also something of a renaissance man, accomplished in architecture, carpentry (he built several of the pieces on display), ethnography, clockmaking, and linguistics. During his service, he became fluent in Tlingit and Aleut, and translated liturgical texts and his own spiritual treatises into these languages by adapting the Russian Cyrillic alphabet. Exhibits downstairs trace Sitka's history. Admission costs $4.

A little farther down Lincoln you'll see the campus of Sheldon Jackson College, founded by its namesake Presbyterian missionary in 1878 as a vocational school for young Tlingits. The **Sheldon Jackson Museum** (© **907/747-8981;** www. museums.state.ak.us), located on the grounds, contains a fine collection of Native artifacts, including Tlingit, Aleut, Athabascan, Haida, and Tsimshian peoples, as well as the Native peoples of the Arctic. The core of the collection was assembled by Jackson himself on his travels around the territory. Admission is $4.

Continue down Lincoln till you come to the **Sitka National Historical Park** (© 907/747-6281; www.nps.gov/sitk). This is where, in 1804, the Tlingit made their stand against Russia, holding off imperial gunboats and Aleut mercenaries for 6 days before finally melting away one night after taking heavy losses. The land was officially protected starting in 1890, and in 1910 the site was designated a National Historic Park, emphasizing the Native perspective. In the visitor center, exhibits explain the history and the art of totem carving, with 19th-century poles displayed in one hall and new ones created in the on-site Southeast Alaska Indian Cultural Center, which also has windowed workshops devoted to traditional crafts of metal, wood, beads, textiles, and woven grass. Outside, a rainforest trail winds along the coast of the 113-acre park past a collection of towering totems nestled among the spruce and hemlock. The battle site—just a grassy area now—is also along the trail, but among the trees and totems, with the sound of the lapping sea and raven's call, you can feel deep down what the Tlingits were fighting for. Admission costs $4

Beyond here, at 1101 Sawmill Creek Rd. (just across Indian River), the **Alaska Raptor Center** (© 907/747-8662; www.alaskaraptor.org) is just on the border between "within walking distance" and not. A nonprofit venture supported by tour companies, cruise lines, and public donations, the center was opened in 1980 to treat sick or injured birds of prey (primarily eagles), and to provide an educational experience for visitors. Birds that cannot be returned to the wild are sent to zoos or housed here permanently, providing guests the rare experience of standing just a few feet from a huge, unblinking eagle. The brand-new flight center offers an exciting view of the eagles training just prior to release. Admission costs $12 adults, $6 kids under 12.

Back in the center of town are several worthwhile sites. **Castle Hill,** up the stairs near the intersection of Lincoln and Katlian streets, was where the first U.S. flag was raised on Alaska soil, after the U.S. and Russia held a transfer ceremony here in 1867. You get a great panoramic view of town from the top. Across the street, FYI, the beautiful building behind the big bronze statue is the **Sitka Pioneers Home,** a state retirement home. Next to the Pioneers Home, the **Sheetka'Kwaan Naa Kahidi Building,** 200 Katlian St. (© 888/270-8687; www.sitkatribal.com), is a modern version of a traditional Tlingit tribal house. It hosts regular performances of traditional Tlingit dance, often coinciding with cruise ship visits. Show times are posted here and at the Centennial Hall. Behind the stage is the largest hand-carved wooden screen in Southeast Alaska, depicting Eagle and Raven, the two principle clans of the Tlingit people.

Next to the Crescent Harbor Dock, the **Isabel Miller Museum** at the Harrigan Centennial Hall (© 907/747-6455) outlines the city's history with art, artifacts, and a large diorama of Sitka as it was in 1867. Admission is free, though donations are welcome. Centennial Hall is also the home of the **New Archangel Dancers,** an all-woman company that gives 30-minute performances of Russian and Ukrainian traditional dance on most days that cruise ships are in port. Admission is $7, and tickets must be purchased at least a half-hour before the show. The schedule is posted at the hall, or you can call © 907/747-5516 for info.

SHOPPING

There are some good shops and galleries in Sitka, mostly on Lincoln and Harbor streets, with several shops selling Russian crafts clustered in the neighborhood of St.

Michael's Cathedral. The gift shop at the Sheldon Jackson Museum is an excellent place to buy Alaska Native arts and crafts and be assured of their authenticity.

6 Skagway

Located at the end of the picturesque Lynn Canal, Skagway served as the jumping-off point for the tidal wave of prospectors who arrived in 1897 for the short but intense Yukon Gold Rush. Greed is a great motivator, but not many of these fellas realized the hardships they'd have to endure before they could get close to the stuff, hiking some 3,000 vertical feet over 20 miles along either the **White Pass** or the **Chilkoot Pass** through the coastal mountain range to the Canadian border. By itself, that might not have been too bad, but by order of Canada's North West Mounted Police, they had to have at least a year's supply of provisions with them before they could enter the country. Numbed by wind and temperatures that fell at times to 50 below zero—Skagway's Tlingit name, *Skagua* means "home of the North Wind"—most inched their way up, carrying some of their supplies midway then returning for more. The process often required as many as 20 trips.

The town, such as it was then, was entirely a product of the rush, having been established as a dock and lumber mill by former steamboat captain William Moore and his son in the 1890s, after they realized the nearby pass would be a good entree to Canada if gold were ever discovered there. They were right, but rather than enriching the Moores as intended, the rush simply brought total anarchy to Skagway, with a swarm of opportunists arriving with the prospectors to either service or swindle them—usually both. The most notorious of the Skagway bad men was Jefferson Randolph "Soapy" Smith, a con man and thug who knew an open town when he saw it, and effectively took the town over before getting himself shot in a now mythic gunfight with city surveyor Frank Reid. Reid died in the fight too, and both were buried in the town's Gold Rush Cemetery—Reid inside, under a granite marker that reads "He gave his life for the honor of Skagway," Smith under a simple marker in unconsecrated ground. As is the way of things, it's Smith whose name is all over today's Skagway, part of the town's totally Disney-fied "wild and wonton frontier town" image.

Remember the actor Walter Brennan, who played the old coot in every other Hollywood Western from the '30s through the '50s? Well, every single person in Skagway seems to have gone to his acting school. Yes, people do live here (862 of them year-round, according to the latest census), but most of the folks you see in the summer are seasonal workers, brought in essentially as actors to man the set. And we gotta admit, it's some set, with the wide main drag, Broadway, lined end-to-end with gold-rush-era buildings and protected as a National Historic District. A few that look like real businesses turn out to be displays showing how it was back in frontier days, but most house gift shops—lots and lots of gift shops.

Pieces of history are preserved all around town, from cute touches like the huge watch painted on the mountainside, advertising long-gone Kirmse's watch-repair, to the monumental **White Pass and Yukon Route Railroad,** which opened in 1900 to carry late stampeders into Canada and bring gold out, and represents a remarkable engineering achievement. The round-trip to the summit of the pass, following a route carved out of the side of the mountain by an American/Canadian engineering team, takes 3 hours from the depot, located right at the foot of town. It's one of the first things you'll see when coming in from the cruise ship piers.

COMING ASHORE Ships dock at the cruise pier, at the foot of Broadway or off Congress or Terminal Way. Though the docks are in sight of downtown, it's about a 20-minute walk, so take one of the frequent shuttle buses if you don't feel like hoofing it.

GETTING AROUND Skagway is almost hermetically self-contained, like a theme park. The only street you really need to know about is Broadway, which runs through the center of town and off which everything branches. **Walking maps** describing the historic buildings and **trail maps** of the surrounding area are both available at the Arctic Brotherhood Hall on Broadway between 2nd and 3rd and at the National Historic Park visitors center, located in the railroad depot. Hikes range from 1 to 10 miles, and most involve some good hill-walking. The Skagway Streetcar Company also offers tours by van (see below).

BEST CRUISE LINE SHORE EXCURSIONS

White Pass & Yukon Route Railway ($97, 3½ hr.): The sturdy engines and vintage parlor cars of this famous narrow-gauge railway take you from the town past waterfalls and still-visible parts of the famous "Trail of '98" to the White Pass Summit, the boundary between Canada and the United States. On a clear day, you'll be able to see all the way down to the harbor, and you might see the occasional hoary marmot or other critter fleeing from the train's racket. A couple variations are offered, one an up-and-back trip to the summit, one a bus ride to the village of Carcross near Lake Bennett, Yukon Territory, where you have lunch at the Caribou Trading Post before boarding the train for the ride back to Skagway. Now the caveat to the whole experience: Don't bother going on an overcast day—you won't see anything. For that reason, you might want to eschew booking this as a tour, instead buying your tickets at the depot when you arrive. Schedule info is available at **www.wpyr.com**.

Dyea Ghost Town Bicycle Tour ($80, 3 hr.): Dyea, about 9 miles west, was established around the same time as Skagway but was abandoned completely after the gold rush. On this tour, you'll go partway by van before gearing up for a 6-mile ride through the remains of the town, past coastal tidal flats and wildflower fields.

Dyea on Horseback ($154, 3½ hr.): A van takes you to Dyea, where you tour the townsite aboard an even-tempered mount while your guide spins some history.

Sled Dog Musher's Camp ($109, 2¾ hr.): An introduction to the sled-dog life, with a tour of a musher's camp, a 20-minute ride through the forest aboard a wheeled sled, and a chance to cuddle husky pups.

Klondike Bicycle Tour ($80, 2½ hr.): After vanning it to the White Pass summit, you'll ride down the Klondike Highway, 15 miles from peak to sea, pausing along the way for photos.

Yukon Golf Odyssey ($170, 8 hr.): After a ride across the White Pass you'll head into the Yukon to the town of Carcross and its 9-hole, par-36 Meadow Lakes Golf & Country Club course, with four sets of tees on each hole and lengths ranging from 1,800 yards to 2,800 yards. Golfing in the Yukon! There's something to tell your regular partners.

Chilkoot Trail Hike & Float Trip ($99, 4½ hr.): From the pier, travel to the historic Dyea ghost town and hike the first 2 miles of the Chilkoot Trail through the rainforest. At the shore of the Taiya River you'll board 18-foot rafts for a float back to Dyea.

Skagway by Streetcar ($39, 2 hr.): As much performance art as historical tour, guides in period costume relate tales of the boomtown days as you tour the sights both in and outside of town. Though theatrical, it's all done in a homey style, as if you're getting a tour from your cousin Martha. The guide is as likely to point out funky oddities as major historical sights. After seeing the Historic District, the Lookout, the Gold Rush Cemetery, and other sights, guests see a little song-and-dance and film presentation about Skagway and become honorary members of the Arctic Brotherhood. This last part is very, very hokey.

ON YOUR OWN: WITHIN WALKING DISTANCE

Though Skagway's historic district includes some three dozen buildings from the 1890s and early 1900s, most are either privately owned or leased by the Park Service for use as businesses. Be sure to pick up the "Skagway Walking Tour" map mentioned above, in "Getting Around," and consult it as you wander around town. A little knowledge could transform that souvenir shop back into a dry-goods store. Everything here is within walking distance, though the Gold Rush Cemetery (see below) might be a bit far for some. If so, skip it; it's not that interesting by itself.

As you're coming into town from the docks, you'll be greeted by a few interesting sights. To the right, that fiendish looking machine near the tracks is a **rotary snowplow** that was used by the railroad whenever the White Pass tracks got snowed in. The two buildings just behind it, on the corner of 2nd and Broadway, house the offices of the **National Park Service,** with the **White Pass and Yukon Route** depot right next door. The NPS buildings are worth a stop for information and historical ambience (they once housed the original railroad depot and offices), while the latter merits a stop for its gift shop, which has some nifty railroad souvenirs.

Across the street, at the corner of Second Avenue, the **Red Onion Saloon** (© **907/ 983-2222**) was originally a dance hall and honky-tonk where the bartenders still serve drinks over the same mahogany bar as did their turn-of-the-century predecessors. Waitresses wear busty dance-hall outfits, as do the double-entendre-flinging docents who lure visitors to the former bordello upstairs for a $5 tour. If you have less time, you can even get a "quickie" tour for less. It sounds dumb, but it's actually very interesting, with rooms re-created to look as they would in the 1890s, and a decent presentation by the guides too.

On the same block, the **Arctic Brotherhood Hall** is mostly notable for its facade, covered in thousands of pieces of driftwood.

At the other end of town, at Seventh Avenue and Spring Street, the 1899 McCabe College building houses the **Skagway Museum** (© **907/983-2420**), a very professional display offering a look at Skagway's history through artifacts, photographs, and historical records. Items on display include a Tlingit canoe and Bering Sea kayaks, as well as a collection of gold-rush supplies and tools and Native American items including baskets and beadwork. Admission is $2. If you'd like to get out of town a while, continue walking about a mile and a half up State Street to the old **Gold Rush Cemetery,** where Frank Reid and Soapy Smith are buried.

Back on Broadway (so to speak), the ***Days of '98 Show*** has been playing at the Eagles Hall since 1927, which tells you how long Skagway has been relying on tourism. A melodrama of the Gay '90s featuring dancing girls, ragtime music, a recitation of Robert Service poetry, and (naturally) actors playing Smith and Reid in their historic shootout, the show is almost always offered as part of a shore excursion, but you can also buy tickets at the door for $14. Walk down Sixth from the theater and make a right to see the historic **Moore Cabin,** built in 1887 by Skagway founder William Moore.

SHOPPING

Skagway is all about shopping, but we'd avoid it. Most of the shops sell either cheap tourist gimcracks or jewelry. As we mentioned above, the most characteristic items from town are probably railroad items from the White Pass and Yukon Route, available at the depot.

7 Victoria, British Columbia

Cruises that start in Seattle or San Francisco typically visit Victoria on the way up to Alaska. Located on Vancouver Island, this lovely little city is the capital of British Columbia, and appropriately so as it's almost more British than Britain, with gorgeous Victorian architecture and lovely gardens among its main attractions. Take a tour around the island and you'll see gorgeous homes, stately government buildings, and views that include the snowcapped mountains of Washington State.

COMING ASHORE   Cruise ships dock at the Ogden Point cruise ship terminal on Juan De Fuca Strait, about a mile southwest of the **Inner Harbour** and the **Downtown/Old Town** area, where most attractions are located.

GETTING AROUND   Cruise lines offer a shuttle to the Inner Harbour, where flower baskets, milling crowds, and street performers liven the scene around the grand Fairmont Empress Hotel, famed setting for an English-style high tea.

BEST CRUISE LINE SHORE EXCURSIONS

City Tour & Butchart Gardens (US$60–US$65, 3½–4 hr.): Combines a bus tour of Victoria's highlights with a 2-hour visit to world-renowned Butchart Gardens (see below). Expanded trips include high tea at the gardens (US$75, 4 hr.).

City Tour with High Tea & Craigdarroch Castle (US$79, 4 hr.): After a bus tour of the major sights, this tour heads out to Craigdarroch Castle, an 1880s mansion built by a Scottish coal baron. The tour concludes with high tea at the Fairmont Empress Hotel.

Victoria Pub Crawl (US$59, 3½ hr.): Visit three of the city's finest pubs and sample its best local brews, all without having to choose a designated driver.

Orca & Wildlife Watching Adventure (US$99, 3½ hr.): A catamaran takes you out for 3 hours on the waters off southern Vancouver Island, home to killer whales, seals, porpoises, and myriad birds.

ON YOUR OWN: WITHIN WALKING DISTANCE

It's about a mile from the docks to the central attractions around the Inner Harbour, but let's call that walking distance, for argument's sake. Once there, the big attraction is the ivy-covered, grandly Edwardian **Fairmont Empress Hotel,** 721 Government St. (*©* **250/384-8111;** www.fairmont.com). Built in 1908, it has a grand lobby and is *the* place to go for British-style high tea. Many shore excursions include tea here, but if you plan to go on your own, call 2 weeks before your cruise for reservations and be sure to follow the dress code: no sleeveless shirts, tank tops, short-shorts, or cut-offs. To the side of the hotel you'll find the **Miniature World** museum

Victoria

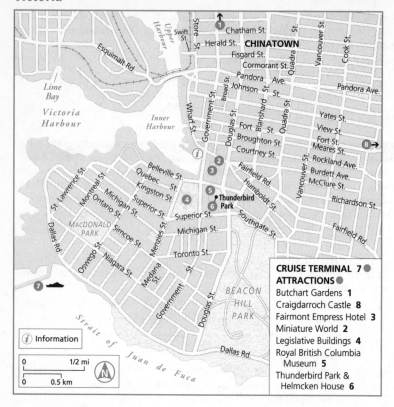

Information

Strait of Juan de Fuca

0   1/2 mi
0   0.5 km

CRUISE TERMINAL 7 ●
ATTRACTIONS ●
Butchart Gardens **1**
Craigdarroch Castle **8**
Fairmont Empress Hotel **3**
Miniature World **2**
Legislative Buildings **4**
Royal British Columbia
   Museum **5**
Thunderbird Park &
   Helmcken House **6**

(© 250/385-9731; www.miniatureworld.com), with quirky displays that include big dollhouses, the world's smallest working sawmill, and a model of London in 1670. Admission is US$6 (C$8) adults, US$4.50 (C$6) kids under 12. Nearby, British Columbia's **Legislative Buildings** exude typical British government gravitas, their stony bulk surrounded by vast lawns and headed by a statue of the city's namesake, Queen Victoria. You can take a tour of the interior, but you have to book in advance (© 250/387-3046).

Just to the east sits the **Royal British Columbia Museum,** 675 Belleville St. (© 888/447-7977; http://rbcm1.rbcm.gov.bc.ca), its entrance graced by towering totem poles and other large sculptural works by Northwest First Nations' artists. Inside, exhibits highlight the natural history of the province and Victoria's recent past, and another demonstrates how archaeologists study ancient cultures, using artifacts from numerous local tribes. Admission is US$8 (C$13) adults, US$6 (C$8.70) kids 6 to 18. The museum's **National Geographic IMAX Theatre** shows movies on various scientific themes and features exotic locations, such as the Amazon. Adjacent to the museum is **Thunderbird Park,** with Native totem poles and a ceremonial house. **Helmcken House,** 10 Elliot St., next to the park, is one of the oldest houses in British Columbia; it was the home of a pioneer doctor, and there are lots of torturous-looking medical tools to shudder over.

ON YOUR OWN: BEYOND THE PORT AREA

Some 13 miles north of downtown Victoria on the Saanich Peninsula, the 130-acre **Butchart Gardens,** 800 Benevenuto Ave., in Brentwood Bay (© **250/652-5256;** www.butchartgardens.com), started as a beautification project by the wife of a quarry owner, and today features English, Italian, and Japanese gardens, water gardens, and rose gardens. There are also restaurants and a gift shop on-site. You can catch a public bus from downtown Victoria for about US$1.75 (C$2.75) each way. A cab will cost you about US$50 (C$67) round-trip. Admission is US$16 (C$22) adults, US$8 (C$11) kids 13 to 17, US$1.50 (C$2.50) kids 5 to 12. The Highland-style **Craigdarroch Castle,** 1050 Joan Crescent (© **250/592-5323;** www.craigdarrochcastle.com), was built in the 1880s as the home of millionaire Scottish coal magnate Robert Dunsmuir. Four stories high and 39 rooms strong, it's topped with stone turrets and furnished in opulent Victoria splendor. City bus routes 11 and 14 will drop you off at the foot of Joan Crescent, a 2-minute walk to the castle's doorstep, or you can take an 8-minute taxi ride. Admission is US$7.50 (C$10) adults, US$2.60 (C$3.50) kids 6 to 12.

SHOPPING

Just north of the Inner Harbour area, Fort Street and Bastion Square are the center of Victoria's gallery and antiques scene, with shops selling English knick-knacks and regional Native art.

12

The Mexican Riviera & Baja

The so-called Mexican Riviera—the stretch of port cities and resorts extending from Mazatlán in the north to Acapulco in the south—is one of the classic cruise destinations, and not just because it's where *The Love Boat* used to sail every week. Blessed with miles of beaches backed by picturesque mountains, and with a climate that practically guarantees perfect beach weather any day of the year, this is the Caribbean for folks who live on the West Coast.

Spanish conquistadors and missionaries came to this coast in the 16th and 17th centuries to find riches, convert the heathen (frequently at sword-point), and establish ports for sailing to the Far East. But it wasn't until the mid–20th century that other travelers discovered that the region was almost tailor-made for relaxation. Hollywood arrived first, heading south for anonymity and great sport-fishing. Later the Spring Break crowd followed, seeking a place to get lewd and goofy on $1 beers. Today, the region still offers a bit of both, plus plenty of family-oriented relaxation, a dash of history, and a dash of culture, including lots of traditional and modern art.

In addition to the Riviera ports, many cruises on these itineraries also stop at **Cabo San Lucas,** at the tip of the Baja Peninsula, a town that's all about beaches and bars, but is also growing to accommodate some amazing golf courses and adventure-travel excursions.

HOME PORTS FOR THIS REGION Cruises to this region sail from San Diego, Los Angeles, and San Francisco.

LANGUAGE & CURRENCY Spanish is the tongue of the land, although **English** is spoken in most places that cater to tourists. The Mexican currency is the **nuevo peso** (new peso). Its symbol is the "$" sign, but it's hardly the equivalent of the U.S. dollar—the exchange rate is about $11 pesos to US$1 ($1 peso = about US9¢). Most tourist stores gladly accept U.S. dollars. *Note:* All prices in this chapter are given in U.S. dollars.

CALLING FROM THE U.S. & CANADA You need to dial the international access code **(011)** and **52** before the numbers listed here.

1 Acapulco

Why is it we think of Ricardo Montalban every time we think of Acapulco? Some kind of mixed 1970s TV series metaphor, we suppose, but it still works: The city is like Ricardo—you know he's not the bronzed TV star he once was, but he's still so charming that you go along with the act anyway. The town's temptations are hard to resist. Where else do men dive from cliffs into the sea at sunset, and where else does the sun shine 360 days a year? Though most beach resorts are made for relaxing, Acapulco has nonstop, 24-hours-a-day energy, and its perfectly sculpted bay is an adult playground filled with water-skiers and studs on WaveRunners. Back in the days when

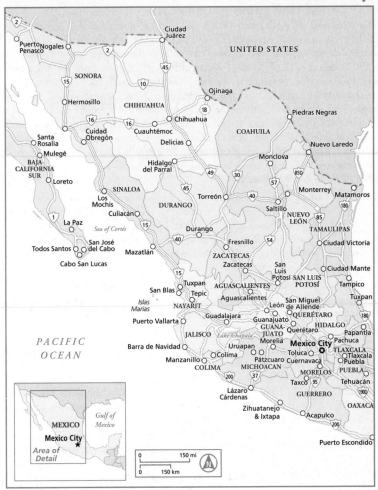

there was a jet set, this was their town, and it's not hard to understand why: The view of Acapulco Bay, framed by mountains and beaches, is just breathtaking.

COMING ASHORE   Cruise ships dock west of the Golden Zone hotel strip, a 5-minute walk from Old Acapulco's main plaza, the *zócalo,* right on the Costera (aka Avenida Costera Miguel Aleman), the main avenue through the tourist zone, lined with hotels, restaurants, shopping centers, and open-air beach bars. Fort San Diego is just above the docks.

GETTING AROUND   **Taxis** are more plentiful than tacos in Acapulco—and practically as inexpensive (only a few dollars) if you're traveling in the downtown area only. Just remember that you should always establish the price with the driver before starting out. The city **bus** system is also amazingly easy and inexpensive, with covered bus stops all along the Costera, posted with maps that show routes to major sights.

BEST CRUISE LINE SHORE EXCURSIONS

The Pyramids of Xochicalco ($149, 12 hr.): An air-conditioned bus takes you through the milelong Acapulco Tunnel then climbs into the Sierra Nevada and through the state of Guerrero, crossing one of the highest bridges in Latin America to reach **Xochicalco,** the "House of Beautiful Flowers." Dating from the 8th century B.C., this beautiful ceremonial center has artifacts and inscriptions indicating that its builders were in contact with the Mixtec, Aztec, Maya, and Zapotec. The most impressive building on the site is the *pirámide de la serpiente emplumada* (pyramid of the plumed serpent), with its magnificent reliefs. Underneath the pyramid is a series of tunnels and chambers with wall murals. The tour continues on to **San Jose de Vista Hermosa,** a former sugar-cane plantation built originally by conquistador Hernando Cortés, where you'll have lunch and time to look around. The drive to Xochicalco takes about 3½ hours each way.

The Silver City of Taxco ($149, 12 hr.): An air-conditioned bus takes you though the Acapulco Tunnel and into the Sierra, traveling to Taxco. Founded in 1528 by the silver- and gold-obsessed Spanish, the town is still an important producer of silver jewelry and other handicrafts. The tour also includes a visit to the baroque **Santa Prisca Church** and lunch at San Jose de Vista Hermosa (see above). The drive to Taxco is approximately 3½ hours each way.

Acapulco City Highlights & Cliff Divers ($42, 4 hr.): A bus tour that takes you from one end of Acapulco Bay to the other, taking in the beaches, resort hotels, and **La Quebrada,** where the world famous divers leap into the Pacific.

ON YOUR OWN: WITHIN WALKING DISTANCE

Acapulco's all about great beaches and watersports (and nightlife, which early-departing cruise passengers will have to put out of their minds), and as with most of the Mexican Riviera ports, the thing to do here is take in the surf and the seaside cafes. If you have an urge to explore the traditional downtown area, the shady *zócalo* (also called Plaza Alvarez) is worth a trip, allowing you a glimpse of local life and color. Inexpensive cafes and shops border the plaza, which is shaded by huge mango and rubber trees. At its far north end is the **Nuestra Señora de la Soledad** cathedral with its blue, onion-shaped domes and Byzantine towers. Though reminiscent of a Russian Orthodox church, it was actually built as a movie set, then later adapted into a house of worship. From the church, turn east along the side street going off at a right angle (Calle Carranza) to find an arcade with newsstands and more shops. The hill behind the cathedral provides a fantastic view of the town. Just follow the signs for **El Mirador** (lookout point), and take a taxi if it looks like too much of a walk for you.

Near the cruise docks, star-shaped **Fort San Diego,** was built in 1616 to defend the bay, and was later rebuilt after a 1776 earthquake leveled the original structure. After years of baking in the Acapulco sun, it was finally refurbished and turned into a museum directed by Mexico's department of archaeological and historic preservation. Today the fort houses the **Acapulco Historical Museum** (© 744/482-3828), whose displays illuminate Acapulco's past from pre-colonial times though the conquistador era to the silver trade between Acapulco and China, the Mexican war of independence, and beyond. A glass floor in several rooms allows visitors to see the remains of the original fort. Admission costs $3; closed Mondays.

All out-of-town activities are covered under "Shore Excursions," above.

BEACHES

In the old days, the downtown beaches—Manzanillo, Honda, Caleta, and Caletilla—were the focal point of Acapulco. The latter two remain popular with both visitors and locals, but today beaches and resort developments also stretch all along the 4-mile length of the bay's shore. Here's a rundown, going from west to east around the bay. **Playa la Angosta** is a small, sheltered, often-deserted cove just around the bend from **La Quebrada,** where the cliff divers perform. About 10 minutes south of downtown by taxi, on the Peninsula de las Playas, **Caleta** and **Caletilla** beaches have calm waters and thatched-roofed restaurants, with watersports equipment, beach chairs, and umbrellas for rent. From here, brightly painted boats ferry passengers to **Roqueta Island,** a good place to snorkel, sunbathe, hike to a lighthouse, visit a small zoo, or have lunch. The ride across costs about $5 round-trip.

East of the *zócalo,* the major beaches are **Hornos** (near Papagayo Park), **Hornitos, Paraíso, Condesa,** and **Icacos,** followed by the naval base (La Base) and **Punta del Guitarrón.** From here, the road climbs to the legendary Las Brisas hotel, then continues to the small, clean bay of **Puerto Marqués,** followed by **Punta Diamante,** about 12 miles from the *zócalo,* fronting the open Pacific and dominated by several resort hotels.

SHOPPING

Acapulco is not among the best places to buy Mexican crafts, but it does have a few interesting shops. The best are at the **Mercado Parazal** (often called the Mercado de Artesanías), on Calle Velázquez de León near Cinco de Mayo in the downtown *zócalo* area. When you see Sanborn's department store/drugstore, turn right and walk behind it for several blocks, asking directions if you need to. Here you'll find stalls of curios from around the country, including silver, embroidered cotton clothing, rugs, pottery, and papier-mâché, as well as on-site artists painting ceramics with village scenes. The shopkeepers aren't pushy, but they'll test your bargaining mettle. Before buying silver, examine it carefully and look for ".925" stamped on the back. This supposedly signifies that the silver is 92.5% pure, though the less expensive silver called "alpaca" may also bear this stamp.

Boutiques crowd the Costera, selling resort wear at prices lower than you generally pay in the United States.

2 Cabo San Lucas

Cabo San Lucas, the rowdier half of the conjoined towns commonly referred to as "Los Cabos," is one big bar-and-beach scene perched at the very tip of the Baja Peninsula, with the Pacific Ocean on one side and the mouth of the Sea of Cortez on the other. (Its quieter twin, San Jose del Cabo, is about 21 miles away, down a corridor lined with resorts.) Cabo made hardly a blip on the world's radar until after World War II, when Hollywood celebs and yachters started traveling here for sport-fishing. In 1973, the completion of the Transpeninsular Highway finally linked the town to the rest of North America, and, by the early 1980s, the Mexican government had realized the area's growth potential and began investing in new highways, a larger airport, golf courses, and modern marine facilities. Today, the town is a playground seemingly built entirely for vacationers' gratification, full of beaches, beach bars, bar-bars, craft shopping, restaurants, and did we mention bars? There's almost nothing of cultural or historic significance here (unless you're big on pop sociology), so your choices are to throw yourself into hedonism or sign up for a nature- or adventure-oriented excursion.

COMING ASHORE Cabo San Lucas lacks pier facilities for anything but small ships (in the 100-passenger range), so cruise ships must anchor just offshore and ferry passengers in by tender. You step ashore in the Cabo San Lucas Marina (in the Cabo San Lucas Bay harbor), which is chockablock with tour operators, information stands, shops, and transportation options.

GETTING AROUND The tender dock at the Marina is about a 10- to 15-minute walk from the town center, around the rim of the Y-shaped harbor. Essentially, everything in town is within a few blocks of the harbor rim. If you keep walking all the way around (at least a 30-min. walk, just because of the harbor's twists and turns), you'll reach the start of the beaches, but the fastest way to reach them is by **water taxi,** which costs about $3 per person. You can also catch a normal **taxi** for about $5 per carload, or a **bicycle taxi** for which you'll have to negotiate a rate. All are in vast supply right at the dock. Taxis can also take you to the golf courses on the corridor between Cabo San Lucas and San Jose del Cabo. Expect to pay between $15 and $25 each way.

BEST CRUISE LINE SHORE EXCURSIONS

In addition to the excursions listed here, the cruise lines typically offer almost two dozen other snorkeling, scuba, sailing, and bus tours.

Cabo San Lucas Sport-Fishing ($159, 5 hr.): Superb sport-fishing put Cabo San Lucas on the map. After boarding your sport-fishing vessel, you'll take a brief cruise to the fishing grounds, then spend a few hours trolling for marlin and sailfish. The good news: Beer is included. The bad news: Because the cruise ships can't store your catch, fishing for trophy fish is catch-and-release. Nontrophy fish are kept by the crew. A $10 fishing license is required.

Cabo Zodiac Whale-Watch ($65, 2½ hr.): Every year from January to March, Cabo San Lucas is visited by humpback, gray, and blue whales, and the best, most intimate, and action-packed way to see them is aboard one of these inflatable craft, which seat only 15 people.

ON YOUR OWN: WITHIN WALKING DISTANCE

Cabo is small and manageable, spreading out north and west of the harbor and edged by foothills, dramatically jagged rocks, and desert mountains. A wide **walkway** wraps most of the way around the harbor, lined with bars, restaurants, and shopping. On the other side of those bars and restaurants, about 650 feet from the water's edge, **Boulevard Marina** is the main artery that curves around the harbor—it essentially *is* the town, at least from a short-term visitor's standpoint. Bars and Mexican restaurants featuring fresh seafood crowd one another for space, so pick the one that seems to say "you." The most famous of the bunch is the **Cabo Wabo Cantina** (© 624/143-1188; www.cabowabo.com), partly owned by former Van Halen frontman Sammy Hagar. It's right in the center of town, with a big sign on Marina and the main entrance around back on Vicente Guerrero at Cárdenas. Expect a rock theme-bar atmosphere, with Van Halen videos and music playing on TV monitors. Unfortunately for cruise passengers, the place doesn't get happening till the evening, after your ship has sailed. Nearby, **El Squid Roe,** on Marina opposite Plaza Bonita (© 624/147-5127; www.elsquidroe.com), is another "Spring Break for Life" type bar of the Senor Frog and Carlos 'n Charlies variety. For an antidote to big bars, drop into **Slim's Elbow Room,**

Small-Ship Cruises in Baja's Sea of Cortez

The Baja Peninsula, stretching some 800 miles from the U.S. border to Cabo San Lucas, is almost like a sunbaked version of Southeast Alaska, a long, thin strip of mainland and islands, sparsely inhabited in places and often breathtakingly gorgeous. So, it's no wonder some of the same small-ship lines that sail Alaska in the summer move their ships south to offer cruises on the Sea of Cortez side of the peninsula, concentrating on nature, whale-watching, and visits to the region's historic ports. Usually sailing from **La Paz** (the capital city of Baja California Sur) or Cabo San Lucas, these small vessels spend time sailing among the sparsely inhabited **coastal islands,** where guests can hike the arid landscape and go tide-pooling along the rocky coast.

There are also visits to historic towns such as **Loreto,** site of the first permanent Spanish settlement on the peninsula, with its manicured fig trees, cobblestone streets, and lovely colonial architecture. Arts and crafts shops line the streets, and a museum at the historic mission—the first in the Californias, founded in 1697—offers a glimpse into Baja's past.

Most small-ship cruises also include an excursion by bus to **Bahía Magdelena** on the Pacific coast, where guides take you out in small *panga* boats to one of the world's best whale-watching grounds. Gray whales winter here, birthing their calves and getting ready for their trip back to the Arctic and Bering seas. On our last trip, a 40-foot mother gray and her calf swam right toward our small boat, ducking under on one side and coming up on the other. That's some close interaction, but not as close as some others get: Occasionally, a gray will pop her head up right next to the boats to see what's going on, and allow people to pat her on the head. Talk about up-close and personal. American Safari Cruises, Clipper Cruise Line, Cruise West, and Lindblad Expeditions all offer winter Baja sailings (see chapter 8 for more on these lines).

"The World's Smallest Bar," on Marina just in front of the building that houses Cabo Wabo. It's just a little bit bigger than a pool table.

ON YOUR OWN: BEYOND THE PORT AREA

Cruise ship passengers in town for just a few hours should stick to downtown Cabo and the beaches unless they're on a shore excursion and/or want to play **golf,** a sport with which Los Cabos is increasingly associated. Most of the courses are along the Corridor between the two towns.

- Designed by Jack Nicklaus, the 27-hole course at the **Palmilla Golf Club,** at the Palmilla resort (© **800/386-2465;** www.palmillaresort.com), sits on 900 acres of dramatic oceanfront desert and offers a choice of two back-9 options. Greens fees are $235, including cart.
- Just a few miles away is the 18-hole, 7,100-yard, Nicklaus-designed Ocean Course at the Corridor's **Cabo del Sol** resort (© **800/386-2465;** www.cabodelsol.com), known for its challenging three finishing holes. Tom Weiskopf designed the newer 18-hole Desert Course. Greens fees for both are $275, including cart.

- The 18-hole, 6,945-yard course at **Cabo Real,** by the Meliá Cabo Real Hotel in the Corridor (© **624/144-0232;** www.caboreal.com), was designed by Robert Trent Jones, Jr., and features holes that sit high on mesas overlooking the Sea of Cortez. Greens fees are $220, including cart.
- **El Dorado Golf Course** (© **624/144-5451;** www.caboreal.com) is a Jack Nicklaus Signature course next to the Westin Regina hotel at Cabo Real. Greens fees are $250, including cart.
- The **Raven Golf Club**'s 18-hole course, designed by Roy Dye (© **624/143-4653**), overlooks the juncture of the Pacific Ocean and Sea of Cortez, including the famous Land's End rocks. It includes the longest hole in Mexico, a 607-yard par-5. Greens fees are $159.

BEACHES

As your ship anchors offshore, you'll see the long, curving sweep of **Medano Beach** stretching into the distance to the right of town (on the east side of the bay). It looks to be about 5 minutes' walk from the docks, but looks can be deceiving: The Marina's two main arms stand between the tender dock and the sand, so you either have to walk all the way around (about a 30-min. trek) or hop a water taxi or regular taxi (see "Getting Around," above). At practically any point along the stretch you'll be able to rent WaveRunners, kayaks, windsurfing boards, and snorkeling gear. Restaurant/bars line the sand at intervals, with some quiet stretches in between.

As your ship comes into the bay, you may see a small beach off your port bow, nestled amid the rugged rocks that separate the bay from the Pacific. This is **Lovers Beach,** the most beautiful beach spot in town. It's only accessible by water taxi from the docks, and there are no facilities to speak of (just the occasional local selling drinks), but it's totally dreamy, with a real *From Here to Eternity* kind of vibe. At low tide you can cross through the famous arch that connects the two seas here. Swimming is generally safe only on the Sea of Cortez side, facing the bay. Farther north, along the Pacific Coast, Playa Solmar (at the Solmar and Playa Grande resorts) is a magnificent stretch of sand, but don't bother going unless you just want a view: There's a bad riptide, and swimming is prohibited.

SHOPPING

You'll find no shortage of shopping opportunities in Cabo, though you'll find few surprises either. Just beyond the tender dock at the harbor, a large, covered **handicrafts market** has scores of vendors selling pretty much the same merchandise you'll find in town: a mixture of T-shirts, handicrafts, blankets, trinkets, and tequila. In town, Cabo Wabo (see above) sells its own brand, **Tequila Cabo Wabo,** at its gift shop. Shops and handicraft marts alternate with jewelry stores and high-end (if not too inspiring) art galleries along Boulevard Marina.

3 Ixtapa/Zihuatanejo

Located side-by-side about 158 miles northwest of Acapulco, Ixtapa and Zihuatanejo are the odd couple of twin beach resorts. Ixtapa (eex-*tah*-pah) is a model of modern infrastructure, services, and luxury resorts, while Zihuatanejo (see-wah-tah-*neh*-hoh, or just "Zihua") is the quintessential Mexican beach village, a rustic retreat only 4 miles to the south—and, oddly, the place where cruise ships pull in. The area, with a backdrop of the Sierra Madre mountains and a foreground of Pacific Ocean waters, provides opportunities for beaching, scuba diving, deep-sea fishing, and golf. **Zihuatanejo** spreads out around a beautiful bay, with the downtown area to the north and a beautiful long beach and the Sierra foothills to the east. The heart of town is the Paseo del Pescador, a brick waterfront walkway bordering the Municipal Beach and boasting many shops and calm, casual restaurants. A good highway connects Zihua to **Ixtapa,** where tall hotels line the wide Playa Palmar beach, with lush palm groves and mountains as their backdrop. The main street, Boulevard Ixtapa, is full of small shopping plazas and restaurants, with the Marina Ixtapa at the north end of the beach from the hotel zone boasting excellent restaurants, private yacht slips, and an 18-hole golf course. Unless you want to play golf or explore Ixtapa's more resort-ish style, we recommend settling back for a quiet day in Zihua.

COMING ASHORE   Ships anchor in sheltered Zihuatanejo Bay and tender passengers to the town's municipal pier. The brick-paved Paseo del Pescador adjoins, with shops and restaurants within easy walking distance.

GETTING AROUND   You can walk around Zihuatanejo. **Taxi** fares between Ixtapa and Zihuatanejo run about $4.50, and fares within either town hover in the $2.50 to $5 range.

BEST CRUISE LINE SHORE EXCURSIONS

Zihuatanejo Sail & Snorkel ($64, 3 hr.): Climb aboard a trimaran and sail to Manzanillo Beach, one of the best snorkeling spots on the bay, where you'll drop anchor for direct access to the water.

Countryside Tour ($54, 3½ hr.): Leave Zihuatanejo by bus and head into the countryside, where you'll tour a fruit plantation that raises papaya, mango, grapefruit, and coconut, then visit an open-air factory to see bricks and floor tiles made using traditional methods. At Barra de Potosi lagoon, you can stroll the beach and watch local fishermen cast their nets in the lagoon.

ON YOUR OWN: WITHIN WALKING DISTANCE

In Zihuatanejo, here's what you do: Step off the tender, take a big breath, then let it out and order a beer or margarita. That's about it. **Paseo del Pescador** is full of nice little bars, shops, and seafood restaurants, and occasionally a musician will stroll by. For a little history, the **Museo de Arqueología de la Costa Grande** (no phone) traces the history of the Acapulco-to-Ixtapa/Zihuatanejo "Costa Grande" region starting in pre-Hispanic times (when it was known as Cihuatlán) through the colonial era. Most of the museum's pottery and stone artifacts give evidence of extensive trade with far-off cultures and regions, including the Toltec and Teotihuacán near Mexico City, the Olmec on the Pacific and Gulf coasts, and areas known today as the states of Nayarit, Michoacán, and San Luis Potosí. Local indigenous groups gave the Aztec tribute items, including cotton *tilmas* (capes) and *cacao* (chocolate), representations of which can be seen here. Located near Guerrero at the east end of Paseo del Pescador, it's worth the $1 admission and half-hour it'll take you to see the displays. Signs are in Spanish, but an accompanying brochure is available in English. Closed Mondays.

Beyond the port area there's only Ixtapa, and for cruise visitors, Ixtapa is mostly about . . .

BEACHES

IXTAPA   Ixtapa's main beach, **Playa Palmar,** is a lovely white-sand arc on the edge of the Hotel Zone, with dramatic rock formations silhouetted in the sea. The surf can be rough; use caution, and don't swim when a red flag is posted. Lovely **Playa Vista**

Hermosa, located just south of Ixtapa, fronting the Hotel Las Brisas Ixtapa, is framed by striking rock formations and is very attractive for sunbathing but has heavy surf and strong undertow. Use caution if you swim here. **Playa Linda,** about 8 miles north of Ixtapa, is the primary out-of-town beach, with watersports equipment and horse rentals available.

ZIHUATANEJO At Zihuatanejo's town beach, **Playa Municipal,** the local fishermen pull their colorful boats up onto the sand, making for a fine photo op. The small shops and restaurants lining the waterfront are great for people-watching and absorbing the flavor of daily village life. A cement-and-sand walkway runs from the *malecón* east along the water to **Playa Madera (Wood Beach),** which is good for bodysurfing. To the south is Zihuatanejo's largest and most beautiful beach, **Playa La Ropa,** a mile-long sweep of sand with calm waters and a great view of the sunset. Palm groves edge the shoreline, and some lovely small hotels and restaurants nestle in the hills. A taxi from town costs about $3. The beach's name stems from the sinking of a galleon that was carrying silk clothing *(ropa)* back from the Philippines. When the ship went down, its cargo washed ashore here, and hence the name "clothing beach." **Playa Las Gatas (Cats Beach),** across the bay from Playa La Ropa and Zihuatanejo, has exceptionally clear waters and a man-made reef that makes for calm swimming (good for kids) and good snorkeling. A little dive shop on the beach rents gear and there are a number of open-air seafood restaurants. Water taxis from the Zihuatanejo town pier can get you here for about $3 round-trip.

SHOPPING

IXTAPA Shopping in Ixtapa is not especially memorable, with T-shirts and Mexican crafts, plus brand-name sportswear. All of the shops are in the same area on Boulevard Ixtapa, across from the beachside hotels.

ZIHUATANEJO Zihuatanejo has its share of T-shirt and souvenir shops, but it's also a decent place to buy crafts, folk art, and jewelry. The **artisans' market** on Calle Cinco de Mayo is a good place to start shopping before moving on to specialty shops that spread inland from the waterfront. For a taste of local commerce, visit the **municipal market,** which sprawls over several blocks off Avenida Benito Juárez (about 5 blocks inland from the waterfront). Here, produce, fish, and nut vendors mix with stands selling huarache sandals, hammocks, and baskets.

4 Mazatlán

Almost straight across the Sea of Cortez from Cabo San Lucas, **Mazatlán**—"The Land of the Deer" in the old Nahuatl language—dates from the beginning of the 19th century, when German immigrants developed it as a shipping port. After a lull of about 160 years it gained new fame as a sport-fishing capital, then as a destination for American college kids on spring break. Today, families and mature vacationers are flocking here as well, taking advantage of the low prices and 10-plus miles of beaches. For cruise travelers, the town is like a barbell, with the historic **Downtown** area at the south end, the tourist-oriented **Zona Dorada** (Golden Zone) about 4 miles to the north, and the long, uninteresting curve of Avenida del Mar between.

COMING ASHORE Ships dock on the south side of town along a navigational channel, in the midst of substantial commercial shipping. Disembarking passengers must take a short tram from the ship to the welcome terminal, where they run a veritable gauntlet of gift and craft shops before popping out into air again on the far side.

GETTING AROUND   The port is about a 15- or 20-minute walk from the center of the old downtown, but you can also take a **taxi.** In fact, we challenge you *not* to—there are so many of them on hand at the pier that you might find yourself sitting in one without ever intending to. In addition to the green-and-white, fixed-rate Eco-Taxis, you'll also see hundreds of open-sided **Pulmonía** cars, which look like a cross between a jeep and a golf cart. Fares between the port (or Old Mazatlán) and the Zona Dorada average $4.50 to $6.50 for either option.

BEST CRUISE LINE SHORE EXCURSIONS

In addition to the tours listed here, cruise lines offer a lot of "mix-and-match" Mazatlán bus tours, taking in highlights of downtown and almost always heading through the Golden Zone for shopping.

Old Mazatlán Walking Tour ($33, 4 hr.): Start at the shoreside **Cerro de Neveria,** where divers plunge off a cliff into the sea, then amble through old Mazatlán's narrow, shady streets, visiting the **Teatro Angela Peralta** (see "On Your Own," below), stopping at a cafe for refreshment and **Nidart Gallery** (see "Shopping," below) for some shopping, then heading to the main plaza and the cathedral. It's not a bad way to get oriented, and you can continue walking on your own around the old market and then around the coast.

Sierra Madre Tour ($64, 7½ hr.): Travel by bus into the foothills of the Sierra Madre to the town of **Concordia,** founded in 1550 and famed for its furniture, handmade pottery, and Baroque church. Continue to **Copala,** a former gold-mining town founded in 1565, where you can wander the narrow, cobbled streets and see the old colonial houses and 16th-century stone church. The tour includes a traditional Mexican lunch and a shopping stop in the Zona Dorada.

Sport-Fishing Tournament ($139, 7 hr.): Everyone competes on this tour, in which passengers sail on 40-foot fishing boats and troll for marlin and sailfish. Beer is provided, and the winner gets a plaque. Now the bad news: Since the cruise ships can't store your catch, fishing for trophy fish is catch-and-release. Nontrophy fish are kept by the crew.

ON YOUR OWN: WITHIN WALKING DISTANCE

Though most people will probably take a taxi the short distance to downtown, we're going to consider it "walking distance" both for argument's sake and to distinguish it from the distant Golden Zone.

Downtown Mazatlán is centered around the palm-shaded **Plaza Principal,** also called Plaza Revolución and filled with vendors, pigeons, shoeshine men under blue Pacifico beer umbrellas, and old gentlemen resting in the shade. A Victorian-style wrought-iron bandstand sits at its center and the **Cathedral of the Immaculate Conception** hovers over one end. Built in the 1800s, the cathedral has twin, yellow-tiled steeples, while its interior has a vaulted ceiling and more than a dozen chandeliers. It's worth a quick peek. One block behind the cathedral is the covered **Mercado Municipal** (aka Mercado Pino Suarez, or just "the municipal market"). Taking up the whole city block between Juarez and Serdan, it's got its share of tourist shops but is more a place for locals, with stands selling fresh produce, meat, clothing, herbal remedies, and religious mementos. It's a vibrant slice of life, as are all the streets around it.

Backtrack along Juarez a few blocks to reach Mazatlán's **historic district,** a 20-square-block area centered around the pretty little **Plazuela Machado,** which boasts a few sidewalk restaurants and sometimes hosts local events. It's bordered by Frías, Constitución, Carnaval, and Sixto Osuna. On one corner of the square stands the Italian-style **Teatro Angela Peralta** (© **669/982-4447;** www.teatroangelaperalta.com), built between 1869 and 1881. A center of Mazatlán arts and culture for its first 40 years, the theater fell into decay following the Mexican revolution of 1910 and began a period of decay that lasted until the late 1980s, when a group of concerned citizens spearheaded its renewal. Today the 841-seat theater is a national historic monument and regularly hosts folkloric ballets, contemporary dance, symphony concerts, opera, and jazz. Its sumptuous, jewel-box-like interior, with three levels of dark, woody balconies, has been restored to its 19th-century glory. It costs $1 to tour the building. Half a block to the right of the building's entrance is the **Nidart Gallery** (see "Shopping," below). The blocks around the theater and Plazuela abound with beautiful old buildings and colorful town houses trimmed with wrought iron and carved stone. Many buildings were restored as part of a downtown beautification program, which seems well on its way to turning the neighborhood into a high-end cultural destination. Small galleries are beginning to move into the area as the neighborhood becomes the center of Mazatlán's artistic community. Check out the **town houses** on Libertad between Domínguez and Carnaval and the two lavish **mansions** on Ocampo at Domínguez and at Carnaval. For a rest stop, try the **Café Pacífico** (decorated with historic pictures of Mazatlán) or one of the other cafes on the Plazuela. Those with an interest in Mexican history can walk a couple blocks down Sixto Osuna to Venustiano Carranza, where you'll find the small **Museo Arqueológico de Mazatlán,** Sixto Osuna 76 (© **669/981-1455**), which displays both pre-Hispanic artifacts and contemporary art. Admission is free; closed Mondays.

If you're feeling like a good, tiring walk, head west down Constitución toward the ocean, then turn left and walk along the oceanside walkway on Paseo Clausen. Passing the beach at Olas Altas (the original Mazatlán beach strip) you'll see signs for **Cerro del Vigía (Lookout Hill).** Follow these up the steep hill at the edge of town, bending around the school and then hugging the coast. Below, accessible via several sets of stairs, is **Playa del Centenario,** a lovely stretch of pounding surf with views of the offshore Sea Lion rocks, the El Faro lighthouse (the second highest in the world, after Gibraltar), and Deer and Wolf islands, just off the Zona Dorada. Frigate birds and pelicans soar overhead, and down below there's sea-carved arches and patches of bright green vegetation. You'd be pounded to death if you tried to swim here, but it's a romantic picnic spot. At the point of the lookout, a stair-path leads out to a viewing platform that resembles the prow of a ship and lets onto some wonderful vistas. From here, continue following the coast road right around and back to the cruise docks.

ON YOUR OWN: BEYOND THE PORT AREA

Four miles from Downtown, the **Zona Dorada (Golden Zone)** begins where Avenida del Mar intersects Avenida Rafael Buelna and becomes Avenida Camarón Sábalo, which leads north through the tourist zone. While shops, restaurants, and bars are much more abundant here than downtown, it's very, very, very touristy, and only worth the drive if you're in a beach-party mood.

BEACHES

Much as we're not nuts about the Golden Zone, it is the better spot for beaches. At the beginning of the Zone you'll find **Playa Gaviotas** and several other beaches backed by resort hotels. Remember that all beaches in Mexico are public property, so

Mazatlán Golf Excursions

Mazatlán offers probably the best golf value in Mexico, with two notable courses open to the public.

- The 27-hole course at the **El Cid resort**, just east of the Zona Dorada (© **669/913-3333**; www.elcid.com), has 9 holes designed by Lee Trevino as well as 18 designed by Robert Trent Jones, Jr. It's open to the public, though preference is given to hotel guests and tee times book up quickly. Greens fees are $75 for 18 holes, plus $17 for the caddy.
- The **Estrella del Mar Golf Club**, across the channel from Downtown, on Isla de la Piedra (© **669/982-3300**; www.estrelladelmar.com), is an 18-hole, 7,004-yard course, also designed by Robert Trent Jones, Jr. Greens fees run $110, including cart.

all of these are accessible to you. Farther north, **Playa Sábalo** is perhaps the best beach in Mazatlán. The next point jutting into the water is Punta Sábalo, beyond which you'll find a bridge over a channel that flows in and out of a lagoon. Beyond the marina, more beaches stretch all the way to Los Cerritos.

At the western edge of downtown, **Playa Olas Altas** is a thin strip of curving beach backed by several low-key sidewalk bars. It's the closest beach to the docks, but lacks any amenities and any kind of "scene." Around a rocky promontory north of Olas Altas is **Playa Norte,** which offers several miles of good sand beach with numerous *palapa* bars, but busy Avenida del Mar is right there behind you, taking something away from the experience.

SHOPPING

La Zona Dorada is the biggest area for shopping, with hundreds of shops and stalls selling the usual for this part of Mexico: jewelry, shell-covered art, T-shirts, and lots of other touristy souvenirs, with a smattering of folk art mixed in, most of it of dubious quality. **Downtown** is more oriented toward locals, but is much more authentic. Small galleries and shops are beginning to appear in the historic district around the Teatro Angela Peralta, among them the wonderful **Nidart Galería,** Av. Libertad 45 at Carnaval (© **669/985-5991;** www.nidart.com), an exhibition space selling works created by local artists on-site, as well as works from around Mexico. This is quality stuff, and includes clay and leather sculptures and masks, paintings, woodwork, jewelry, and other items, priced much lower than you'd expect. Many city tours offered by the cruise lines include a stop here.

5 Puerto Vallarta

Looking at the vibrant, bustling Puerto Vallarta of today, it's hard to imagine that only 50 years ago the only tourists who stopped here landed on a dirt airstrip outside town. Established in the 1850s as a port for processing silver from the Sierra Madre mountains, the place only took off as a resort destination when Hollywood stars began arriving 110 years later. In 1963, John Huston brought stars Ava Gardner and Richard Burton here to film the Tennessee Williams play *Night of the Iguana,* and Burton's new love, Elizabeth Taylor, came along even though both were married to others at the time. Paparazzi arrived hot on their heels, and Puerto Vallarta was established as a tropical cauldron of sin and sun.

Downtown, a seaside promenade (or *malecón*) runs north-south beside Paseo Díaz Ordaz, adorned with public art and stretching the length of El Central—the center of town. From the waterfront, cobblestone streets reach a mere half-dozen blocks back into the hills. The areas bordering the **Río Cuale** river are the oldest parts of town, and a lovely island in midstream, **Isla Cuale,** is full of shops and lush foliage. Three bridges link the two sections of downtown, the most pleasant being a footbridge that hugs the shoreline. Isla Cuale can be accessed from any of them. The area north of the river is the main tourist zone, while the area immediately to the south is home to a growing number of sidewalk cafes and fine restaurants, plus the town's better beaches.

Many excursions here will take you outside town and up into the foothills of the Sierra Madre mountains. Farther up, the Huichol Indians still live in relative isolation, simultaneously protecting their culture from outside influences and making a living off their distinctive beaded artwork, which you'll see around town.

COMING ASHORE   Cruise ships dock at the Puerto Vallarta Marina, about 3 miles north of downtown along the busy Avenida Francisco Medina Ascencio. A plethora of craft and T-shirt shopping and several small bars and restaurants are clustered right in the port area, but it's not a destination in itself, so plan to take a taxi into town if you're not doing an excursion. Marina Vallarta, a resort and yacht harbor, is located just north of the terminal.

GETTING AROUND   Technically, you can walk into town. We did it, just to see if it's worth doing, and here's the scoop: It's not. Instead, take a shore excursion to get back into the hills, or take one of the taxis that greet ships at the dock, charging about $5. Once you're in the center of town, nearly everything is within walking distance both north and south of the river. And don't worry about getting back to the ship from here; the cabbies will find you.

BEST CRUISE LINE SHORE EXCURSIONS

Jungle Canopy Adventure ($94, 5 hr.): Ever wanted to be George of the Jungle? At a private reserve in the Sierra Madre, professional guides help you master the techniques of using horizontal traverse cables to travel through the jungle canopy, high up in the trees. Observation platforms give you a breather and a chance to observe the flora and fauna. At the end of your adventure, you rappel down a tree to the forest floor.

Deluxe Puerto Vallarta, Bullfight Demonstration & Show ($52, 4 hr.): A bus ride shows you some highlights of Vallarta (including Burton and Taylor's old homes) before arriving at the central plaza for a little shopping, then on to the Plaza Del Toros, where a Mexican-style rodeo precedes a non-lethal demonstration of the art of the *corrida*—no bulls are injured in the making of this motion picture.

Sierra Madre Hiking Expedition ($38, 4 hr.): Head by bus to Rancho Sierra Madre, where a local naturalist leads your 5-mile hike through the forest to a volcanic hot spring, where you can take a dip. Back at the ranch, you're free to wander around to check out the operation or just relax with a drink.

Hideaway at Las Caletas ($79, 7½ hr.): Las Caletas was Oscar-winning director John Huston's hideaway, so basically on this tour you get to live like a celeb, traveling to the cove by motor launch, relaxing on its palm-lined beaches and drinking in its bar, taking a nature hike, or going kayaking or snorkeling. Some of Huston's possessions are still on display.

San Sebastian/Sierra Madre Flightseeing ($169, 5 hr.): A 15-minute flight drops you off in the heart of the Sierra Madres, 4,200 feet above sea level, for a visit to the 17th-century silver-mining town of San Sebastian. Set in a mountain valley, it's full of colonial architecture and cobbled streets. The trip includes a walking tour of town, a visit to local homes to watch coffee being roasted, and lunch at a local restaurant.

Swimming with Dolphins ($154, 3 hr.): At the Dolphin Adventure Center, you get a half-hour in a saltwater pool with two Pacific bottlenose dolphins. Do we really have to say any more? A 7-hour, $270 **Dolphin Trainer for a Day** excursion lets you work with dolphin trainers in the water and out.

ON YOUR OWN: BEYOND THE PORT AREA

Assuming you don't want to make the hot, sometimes dusty 3-mile walk into town, let's call everything here beyond walking distance. Once in town, though, Puerto Vallarta's cobblestone streets are a pleasure to explore on foot, full of small shops, rows of windows edged with curling wrought iron, and vistas of red-tile roofs and the sea. Start with a walk up and down the *malecón,* taking in the fine collection of public art that stretches from end to end. Across from Carlos O'Brien's restaurant on the north end is Ramiz Barquett's *Nostalgia,* depicting a couple sharing a romantic moment while gazing out to the bay. Farther south is an array of fanciful, almost Dr. Seuss–like chairs by renowned Mexican artist Alejandro Colunga, one topped with a large octopus head, another with giant ears for backrests. Farther south is Sergio Bustamante's *Ladder to Heaven,* depicting children climbing a ladder to nowhere, and closer to the main square you'll find *Boy on the Seahorse,* which has become a Puerto Vallarta icon.

Near here, the main square is headed by the **Parish of Nuestra Señora de Guadalupe church,** topped with a curious crown held in place by angels. It's a replica of the one worn by Empress Carlota during her brief time in Mexico as Emperor Maximilian's wife. On its steps, women sell religious mementos; across the narrow street, stalls sell native herbs for curing common ailments. Stretching along the north end of the square, the municipal building has a large, folkloric **Manuel Lepe mural** inside in its stairwell.

Three blocks south of the church, head east on Libertad, lined with small shops and pretty upper windows, to the **Río Cuale municipal market** by the river (see "Shopping," below), then cross the bridge to Isla Cuale. Near the sea end of the island, the small **Museo Río Cuale** has a permanent exhibit of pre-Columbian ceramics, jewelry, and statuary. Admission is free.

Retrace your steps to the market and Libertad, and follow Calle Miramar to the set of rough stone steps. Follow these past the cute little blue-and-white **Graffity** café, then take the steep, narrow, pastel steps up to Calle Zaragoza, pausing on the stairs to catch your breath and also for a nice view of the sea. Once on Zaragoza, go right 1 block to the famous **arched pink bridge** that connected Richard Burton's and Elizabeth Taylor's houses.

BEACHES

For years, beaches were Puerto Vallarta's main attraction. Unfortunately, those near the cruise terminal are the worst in the area, with darker sand and seasonal inflows of stones. Stretching south to town, the **Hotel Zone** is known for broad, smooth beaches, open to the public and accessible primarily through hotel lobbies. Just south of town, the easiest beach to reach is **Playa Los Muertos** (aka Playa Olas Altas or Playa del Sol), just off Calle Olas Altas, south of the Río Cuale. The water can be rough, but the wide beach is home to several *palapa* restaurants that offer food, beverage, and beach-chair service. About 6 miles south of town along Highway 200, **Playa Mismaloya** is where *Night of the Iguana* was filmed, and also boasts clear water. Entrance to the public beach is just to the left of the Jolla de Mismaloya Resort. There's an *Iguana*-themed restaurant and bar on-site.

SHOPPING

Puerto Vallarta is one big shopping opportunity, with hundreds of small stores selling everything from fine folk art and modern art to tacky T-shirts, plus tremendous amounts of silver jewelry and sculpture depicting everything from Aztec calendars to Mickey Mouse. Puerto Vallarta's **municipal market** is just north of the Río Cuale, where Calle Libertad and Calle Rodríguez meet. The *mercado* sells clothes, jewelry, serapes, shawls, leather accessories and suitcases, papier-mâché parrots, stuffed frogs and armadillos, and, of course, T-shirts. Be sure to comparison-shop, and definitely bargain before buying. Upstairs, a sort of low-key food court serves inexpensive Mexican meals, giving adventurous diners a cheap, authentic dining experience. Exit the market by the corner of Encino and Maramoros and walk across the suspended plank-and-rope bridge to **Río Cuale Island,** where outdoor stalls sell crafts, gifts, folk art, and clothing.

Back in El Centro, head for the corner of Calle Galeana and Calle Morelos (right across from the *Boy on the Seahorse* statue) to find the **Huichol Collection Museum Gallery** (© 322/223-2141), the best place in town for authentic Huichol Indian art. Descendants of the Aztec, the Huichol live in the high Sierras north and east of Vallarta, and produce remarkable beadwork and "yarn painting" inspired by visions they experience during hallucinogenic peyote ceremonies. The colors explode from wall hangings, masks, bowls, and animal forms, the latter three made from carved wooden shapes to which incredibly intricate beadwork is added, eventually covering the entire surface. A Huichol artist is often at work in the back of the shop, and explanations in English tell you what you're looking at. Prices can be high for large pieces, but it's worth it for the quality.

Some of the more attractive shops are a block or two inland from the *malecón*, centered roughly around the intersection of Calle Corona and Calle Morelos. One block north, near the corner of Calle Aldama, **La Casa del Tequila** (© 322/222-2000) offers a tasting room where you can sample a selection of fine tequilas, plus a hacienda-style taco bar with swirling ceiling fans and cane seating.

13

Bermuda

This neat and tidy oasis in the middle of the Atlantic is edged in pink-sand beaches and rocky cliffs—and crawling with Brits in shorts. And not just any shorts, but shorts colored in perky tones of pink, green, or yellow, and paired with sports jackets, ties, and knee-highs. To the casual visitor, Bermuda is a pleasant paradox of sorts, mixing sane and proper, with a healthy dose of silly (back to those shorts again). But what really matters to the cruise passenger is that Bermuda is an orderly, beautiful, easy place to visit. Aside from the Caribbean, the island nation of Bermuda, sitting out in the Atlantic roughly parallel to South Carolina (or Casablanca, if you're measuring from the east), is the other major cruise destination from the U.S. eastern seaboard.

Although the Spanish discovered Bermuda in the early 16th century, it was the British who first settled here in 1609, when the ship *Sea Venture,* en route to Virginia's Jamestown colony, was wrecked on the island's reefs. No lives were lost, and the crew and passengers built two new ships and continued on to Virginia; but three crewmembers stayed behind and became the island's first permanent settlers. Bermuda became a crown colony in 1620 and remains one today, retaining a very **British character**—the island is divided up into parishes, driving is on the left, and horse-drawn carriages trot about, but the sun and the ubiquitous Bermuda shorts serve as proof you're in the islands.

That's not to say things aren't bustling when the ships are in town at Hamilton and St. George's, Bermuda's two main port towns, but a calm and controlled atmosphere reigns as visitors fan out across the island. There are many **powdery soft beaches** easily accessible by taxi or motor scooter, and Bermuda has more golf courses per square mile than any other place in the world. For shoppers, Front and Queen streets in Hamilton offer dozens of shops and department stores, most specializing in English items, while the interest of **history buffs** is piqued by the nearly 300-year-old St. Peter's Church, museums, and other sites within walking distance of the pier in St. George's. There are also impressive exhibits at the Maritime Museum, which is built into the ruins of Bermuda's oldest fort at the Royal Naval Dockyard, the island's third, and least used, port at the west end.

Cruise ships have been sailing to Bermuda for over a century, making it one of the earliest cruise destinations. The Quebec Steamship Company, which eventually evolved into the Furness Bermuda Line, began service from New York to Bermuda in 1874 with the small steamers *Canima* and *Bermuda* and then added the *Orinoco* in 1881, the *Trinidad* in 1893, and the liner *Pretoria,* acquired from the Union Line, in 1897.

Unlike most Caribbean itineraries, on which ships visit ports for a day at most, the majority of Bermuda-bound ships spend several whole days at the island. To protect its hotel trade and to maintain a semblance of order and keep the island from getting overrun by too many tourists, the government of Bermuda allows only six cruise ships—five on weekdays and the other on weekends—to visit the island on a regular basis during its season, late April through October, when the temperatures hover between 75°F and 85°F (24°C and 29°C) and extended rainfall is rare.

HOME PORTS FOR THIS REGION **New York** and **Boston,** are the main hubs for Bermuda cruises, with ships sailing round-trip on mostly 7-night itineraries. A few ships also sail to Bermuda round-trip from **Baltimore** and **Philadelphia.** Still a few more itineraries include Bermuda on **transatlantic crossings** in spring and fall.

LANGUAGE & CURRENCY English is the official language. The currency is the Bermuda dollar (BD$), which is pegged to the U.S. dollar on an equal basis—BD$1 equals US$1. There's no need to exchange any U.S. money for Bermudian.

SHOPPING TIPS While St. George's and the Royal Naval Dockyard both have their souvenir shops, Hamilton is the center of Bermuda's shopping universe. Here, it's all about English (and some Irish) goodies such as porcelain, crystal, wool clothing, cashmere sweaters, and linens, and it's all within walking distance, right outside of the terminal. Don't expect great deals, though—prices in Bermuda are generally on the high side.

1 Hamilton

Hamilton was once known as the "Show Window of the British Empire," and has been the capital of Bermuda since 1815, when it replaced St. George's. Today, it's the economic hub of the island.

COMING ASHORE Cruise ships tie up at docks smack dab in the middle of town. The terminal funnels passengers right into the main shopping drag on Front Street.

GETTING AROUND You can walk to all of the shops and department stores in town, or take a walking tour for a more historical perspective. Walking tour maps are available in the terminal. If you're beach bound or heading for a day of golf or some other attraction, there are taxis lined up outside the terminal (they're metered and expensive, starting at $3.75 when you get in the taxi, and $2 for each additional mile). Roads are well maintained, but narrow and winding. The islands bus and ferry system is also user-friendly. There are horse-drawn carriages at the terminal, and many folks go the scooter or moped route; there are rentals available near the terminal.

BEST CRUISE LINE SHORE EXCURSIONS

Though there's much you can do independently, from beach hopping to shopping and walking tours, if you crave a guide to narrate the highlights, or want to do something active such as snorkel or bike ride, the ships' organized tours are your best bet. The sampling below is generally offered from both Hamilton and St. George's.

Guided Walking Tour of St. George's ($23, 1 hr.): Learn about Bermuda's history, including its churches, art galleries, libraries, and private gardens.

Scenic South Shore Highlights ($43, 3 hr.): This minibus tour takes you from Hamilton to the Royal Naval Dockyard; en route, you'll stop by Gibbs Hill Lighthouse and one of the beaches, cross Somerset Bridge to Somerset Village, then head to the Royal Naval Dockyard and its attractions.

Railway Trail Cruise & Bike Tour ($59, 3 hr.): Bike where the original Bermuda Railway once ran on narrow gauge tracks. The tracks are gone, but a great trail remains

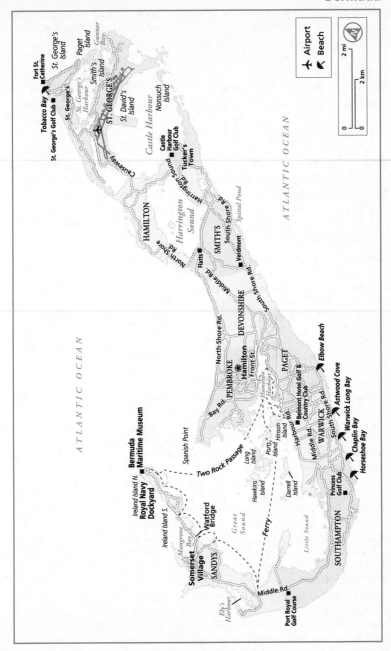

Bermuda

ATLANTIC OCEAN

Fort St.
Catherine

Tobacco Bay

St. George's Golf Club

St. George's

St. George's Island

Paget Island

Gunner Bay

Smith's Island

St. George's Harbour

ST. GEORGE'S

St. David's Island

Nonsuch Island

Castle Harbour

Castle Harbour Golf Club

Tucker's Town

Harrington Sound

Spittal Pond

South Shore Rd.

HAMILTON

North Shore Rd.

Flatts

SMITH'S

Verdmont

Middle Rd.

DEVONSHIRE

South Shore Rd.

North Shore Rd.

Bay Rd.

PEMBROKE

Hamilton

Front St.

Hamilton Harbour

PAGET

Elbow Beach

Belmont Hotel Golf & Country Club

Astwood Cove

Harbour Rd.

Ports' Island

Hinson Island

Middle Rd.

WARWICK

South Shore Rd.

Warwick Long Bay

Chaplin Bay

Horseshoe Bay

ATLANTIC OCEAN

Spanish Point

Bermuda Maritime Museum

Two Rock Passage

Long Island

Hawkins Island

Darrell Island

Little Sound

Princess Golf Club

SOUTHAMPTON

Ireland Island N.

Royal Navy Dockyard

Ireland Island S.

Mangrove Bay

Watford Bridge

Great Sound

Ferry

Somerset Village

SANDYS

Ely's Harbour

Middle Rd.

Port Royal Golf Course

✈ Airport
⚲ Beach

2 mi

2 km

0

0

2

2

behind, and this excursion is a great opportunity to get views of the ocean, and the island's lush gardens and bird life. The flat route covers 8km to 13km (5 miles–8 miles).

Snorkeling Trip ($60, 3 hr.): From Hamilton, board a boat and motor out to a snorkeling spot near the West End as the captain talks to passengers about Bermuda history and customs. Then, after an hour or so of snorkeling, the fun begins: The music is turned on, the dancing starts, and the bar opens as the boat heads back to port.

Coral Reef Glass-Bottomed Boat Cruise ($36, 1½ hr.): See the coral reefs and colorful fish living in Bermuda's waters, then view one of Bermuda's famous shipwrecks and enjoy a rum swizzle from a fully stocked bar.

Golf Excursion ($71–$160, half-day): Excursions include tee times for 18 holes at challenging courses such as Mid Ocean Golf Club, among the best in world; Riddells Bay Golf & Country Club, a veritable golfing institution built in 1922; Port Royal Golf Course; and St. George's Golf Club, designed by Robert Trent Jones. A taxi to and from the courses may be extra and club rental is about $30 extra, but carts are included. The golf excursions are often sold directly through an onboard golf pro who organizes lessons on the ship too.

ON YOUR OWN: WITHIN WALKING DISTANCE

A walking tour is a great option. Pick up a map in the cruise terminal and you're on your leisurely way to visiting sites from the 200-year-old post office to the exhibits in the Bermuda Historical Society Museum. If a nice relaxing lunch on the waterfront appeals to your sense of adventure, stroll on over to the **Wellington Room at the Waterloo House** (© 441/295-4480), an elegant Relais & Chateaux property on Pitts Bay Road, within walking distance of the ship docks. Lunch is served on the outdoor patio overlooking the colorful and idyllic harbor, and many snazzy-looking businesspeople lunch here. The fish chowder, laced with rum and sherry peppers, is a local favorite and a great choice. Lunch costs $30.

Consider a visit to the **Bermuda Underwater Exploration Institute** (© 441/292-7219); it's adjacent to the Hamilton docks near the roundabout on East Broadway. There are two floors of interactive exhibits about the ocean plus the highlight: a capsule that simulates a 3,600m (12,000-ft.) dive below the ocean's surface (it accommodates 21 people at a time). Open 9am to 5pm Monday to Friday and 10am to 5pm Saturday and Sunday; admission is $10.50 for adults and $5.50 for kids ages 7 to 16.

The **Bermuda Railway Trail** offers about 29km (18 miles) of trails divided into easy-to-explore sections. It was created along the course of the old Bermuda Railway, which stretched a total of 34km (21 miles) and served the island from 1931 to 1948, until the automobile was introduced. Armed with a copy of the *Bermuda Railway Trail Guide,* available at the various visitor centers located in and right outside the cruise terminals, you can set out on your own expedition via foot or bicycle (most of the moped/scooter rental agencies rent bicycles as well). Most of the trail winds along a car-free route, and there is a section of trail in St. George's and near Hamilton.

ON YOUR OWN: BEYOND THE PORT AREA The throngs head to the beaches, and for good reason. Many are powdery soft and some even pinkish (from crushed shells, corals, and other sealife), they're easily accessible by taxi or motor scooter from Hamilton and St. George's, and most (including Horseshoe Bay) are free. **Horseshoe Bay** in Southampton Parish is our top pick. Though you certainly won't have it to yourself since it's so popular with lots of other tourists, the horseshoe-shaped beach has scenic rocky cliffs at its edges and a vast soft plane of sand in the middle.

It's perfect for little kids too; Heidi took her 9-month-old twins here, and even when they flung sand into their eyes and mouths, it was so silky smooth it didn't matter! Horseshoe is free and there's a snack bar, bathrooms, and showers. Other beach options include **Elbow Beach** in Paget Parish, **Astwood Cove** (Warwick Parish), **Chaplin Bay** (Warwick and Southampton parishes), **Warwick Long Bay** (Warwick Parish), and **Tobacco Bay Beach** (St. George's Parish), where the water is very calm and the beach is tiny. The more adventurous can hop on a scooter and beach-hop among the many unnamed slivers of silky sand tucked into the jagged coastline. If you're itching to see more than Hamilton, and beaches aren't your bag, another great option is hopping on a local ferry (terminal is next to the cruise docks). For just a few bucks, either ride just for the view of Bermuda's colorful harbors and coastline, or head to the Royal Naval Dockyard on the island's far west end, where you can tour the historic fortress ruins and excellent museums.

2 St. George's

Quaint and historic, St. George's was the second English town established in the new world, after Jamestown in Virginia. King's Square, also called Market Square or the King's Parade, is the center of life here, and it's just steps from where the cruise ships dock.

COMING ASHORE   Cruise ships tie up at the docks smack dab in the middle of town.

GETTING AROUND   Same deal as Hamilton above. You can walk to a handful of historical attractions (see below), or if you're beach bound or heading off for a day of golf, there are taxis lined up steps from the ships in King's Square (they're metered and expensive, starting at $3.75 when you get in the taxi, and $2 for each additional mile). The island's bus and ferry system is also user-friendly (though you have to get to Hamilton or the Royal Naval Dockyard to catch a ferry), and many fearless folks go the scooter or moped route; there are rentals available near the terminal for between $35 and $45 per day.

SHORE EXCURSIONS   See "Best Cruise Line Shore Excursions" under Hamilton, above.

ON YOUR OWN: WITHIN WALKING DISTANCE

Like in Hamilton, a great option is grabbing a free walking-tour map from the tourism office in King's Square, just steps from your ship. Sites on the 17-stop tour include **Ordnance Island,** a tiny piece of land that juts into the harbor just in front of the dock, where a replica of *Deliverance* stands, the vessel that carried the shipwrecked *Sea Venture* passengers on to Virginia. Don't miss a quick stop at **St. Peter's Church,** on Duke of York Street, believed to be the oldest Anglican place of worship in the Western Hemisphere; some headstones in the cemetery date back some 300 years, and the present church was built in 1713. The **Carriage Museum,** at 22 Water St., is worth a look, harboring an interesting collection of the carriages used in Bermuda up until 1946, when the automobile arrived. The oldest stone building in Bermuda, the **Old State House,** built about 1620, sits at the top of King Street and was once the home of the Bermuda Parliament. At the intersection of Featherbed Ally and Duke of Kent Street is **St. George's Historical Society Museum,** which houses a collection of Bermudian historical artifacts and cedar furniture.

ON YOUR OWN: BEYOND THE PORT AREA

A mile or so from King's Square in St. George's (you could actually walk it without too much effort if you like a hardy trek), overlooking the beach where the shipwrecked crew of the *Sea Venture* came ashore in 1609, is **Fort St. Catherine,** which you'll want to see. Completed in 1614, and reconstructed several times after, it was named for the patron saint of wheelwrights and carpenters. The fortress houses a museum, with several worthwhile exhibits. Admission costs $5.

In **Flatts Village,** about halfway between Hamilton and St. George's, is the **Bermuda Aquarium, Museum & Zoo** (© 441/293-2727; www.bamz.org). There are interactive displays, huge aquariums, and seal feedings throughout the day. Open daily 9am to 5pm (last admission at 4pm); admission is $10 for adults and $5 for seniors and children ages 6 to 12. Children 5 and under are free.

You can also opt for the same beaches, golf courses, and other attractions mentioned in the Hamilton section. St. George's and Hamilton are about a 20- to 30-minute taxi ride apart (depending on traffic).

3 Royal Naval Dockyard

A few ships, usually the largest ones, dock at the **Royal Naval Dockyard,** sometimes called King's Wharf, on the west end; you can walk to the sprawling complex there. Constructed by convict labor, this 19th-century fortress was used by the British Navy until 1951 as a strategic dockyard. Today, it's a major tourist attraction whose centerpiece is the **Bermuda Maritime Museum** (© 441/234-1418; www.bmm.bm), the most important and extensive museum on the island. Exhibits are housed in six large halls within the complex, and the displays all relate to Bermuda's long connection with the sea, from Spanish exploration to 20th-century ocean liners. You can have a look at maps, ship models, and such artifacts as gold bars, pottery, jewelry, and silver coins recovered from 16th- and 17th-century shipwrecks, such as the *Sea Venture.* Admission is $10 adults, $5 kids. There are a handful of restaurants in the complex, as well as shops. Taxis are also readily available.

14

Hawaii

The words to a song we heard at a luau on Maui offer the best description of this magical land, "Welcome to my home, right next to paradise." Honeymooners flock here for a reason: The place is gorgeous. Even the Brady Bunch schlepped Alice and the six kids to Hawaii (you didn't see them going to Disney World, did you?). But it's not all about orchid leis and hula girls. The diverse landscape on this cluster of islands in the Pacific ranges from **fuming volcanoes,** to **crashing surf,** serene beaches, and **lush jungles.** In a place where the weather really is perfect all the time, it's no surprise that the locals are so mellow. Learn to surf, go to a luau, snooze on the sand, enjoy the local coffee, or check out the native Hawaiian culture, which the locals are fiercely proud of. The past survives alongside the modern world in a vibrant arts scene, which includes traditional Polynesian dance and music, as well as painting, sculpture, and crafts. You'll also likely get a glimpse of age-old customs such as outrigger canoe races, the most popular sport in all of Hawaii, and, of course, the ubiquitous ukulele playing.

Norwegian Cruise Line (NCL) rules the roost here, with two ships (and a third on the way) doing year-round cruises among the islands, round-trip from Honolulu. Intense lobbying in Congress gained NCL the right to have two of its three Hawaii vessels sail under the U.S. flag, which means the ships can concentrate solely on the islands and don't have to throw in a call to a foreign port (a requirement for foreign-flagged vessels). In isolated Hawaii, this is a real advantage that no competing line is currently able to offer (see NCL review on p. 201 for more details).

Aside from NCL's cruises, ships typically stop in the islands in April, May, September, and October. The four main ports here are **Oahu,** where you'll find the famous Waikiki beach; **Maui,** home of the historical town of Lahaina; **Kauai,** the most natural and undeveloped of the four; and the **Big Island,** where the state's famous volcanoes reside, including Mauna Kea and the still-active Kilauea.

HOME PORTS FOR THIS REGION **Honolulu,** on Oahu, is the main hub for inter-island cruises. Foreign-flagged vessels generally sail from the mainland—from ports such as Ensenada, Mexico; San Diego, California; Seattle, Washington; and/or Vancouver, Canada—hitting the Hawaiian Islands as they cruise between seasons in the Caribbean and Alaska.

LANGUAGE & CURRENCY While English is the official language, it is infused with a few native Hawaiian words, including the customary greeting, *aloha.* (Contrary to what you may believe, "Book 'em, Dano" is not actually a native phrase.) The U.S. dollar is the official currency.

1 Oahu

Oahu is a relatively small island, measuring 26 miles long and some 44 miles across at its widest, totaling 597 square miles of land, with 112 miles of coastline. Everyone ventures to Oahu seeking a different experience. Some talk about wanting to find the "real" Hawaii, some are looking for heart-pounding adventure, some yearn for the relaxing and healing powers of the islands, and others are drawn by Hawaii's aloha spirit, where kindness and friendliness prevail.

All kinds of memorable experiences can be yours. Imagine yourself sitting in a kayak watching the brilliant colors of dawn etch themselves across the sky, sipping a mai tai while you take in sweeping views of the south shore and the Waianae Mountains, battling a magnificent game fish on a high-tech sport-fishing boat, or listening to melodic voices chant the stories of a proud people and a proud culture that was overthrown little more than a century ago. By far the most social of the islands, Oahu has some of the best shopping and most fashionable promenade strips, as well as beautiful beaches with all the classic ingredients: tall palms, white sand, gentle surf, and plenty of sunshine. **Waikiki beach** offers the best of both worlds. Its trendy eateries, high-end hotels, and ritzy shops collide with a stunning beachfront. Its like Rodeo Drive meets South Beach, only better.

COMING ASHORE Ships dock alongside the festive, well-appointed **Aloha Tower** complex in Honolulu. Half shopping center, half cruise pier and promenade, this waterfront two-level mall centers around a five-story tower built in the 1920s. It's a landmark focal point that can easily be spotted around town.

GETTING AROUND Aloha Tower is a convenient jumping off point for either walking tours around the historic sites of downtown, or a short taxi ride to nearby beaches, shopping, and museums. Taxis queue up at the information booth near the adjacent parking area; a taxi to Ala Moana Beach costs about $6 for up to 5 people. If you miss out, call **City Taxi** (✆ 808/524-2121) or hop on the San Francisco–style open-air trolley called **Waikiki Trolley** (✆ 800/824-8804 or 808/593-2822; www.waikikitrolley.com) that runs to Ala Moana shopping center, Ala Moana Beach, and downtown. **TheBus** (✆ 808/848-5555; www.thebus.org) leaves every 30 minutes or so from in front of the Maritime Center and goes to several locations. You can also rent a car at the nearby airport, but with so many other transportation options, it's unnecessary (and the one-way road system can be confusing).

BEST CRUISE LINE SHORE EXCURSIONS

Pearl Harbor and USS *Missouri* ($75, 6½ hr.): For those old enough to remember World War II and those who can't forget 9/11, a tour of Pearl Harbor and the USS *Missouri,* is a deeply moving experience.

Historic and Cultural Honolulu ($39, 4½ hr.): A good sampler, this tour makes stops at Pearl Harbor, 'Iolani Palace, and Chinatown in downtown Honolulu, as well as Punchbowl National Cemetery. See "On Your Own: Within Walking Distance," below, for descriptions of these locations.

Grand Circle Island Tour ($69, 7 hr.): Given the island's immense natural beauty, a drive around the island is time well spent (make sure to bring your camera with you on the bus!). Views from inside Diamond Head Crater, an extinct volcano, rival those of the breathtaking carved shoreline at Hanauma Bay or the sweeping coastal vistas from Pali Lookout. Lunch is included.

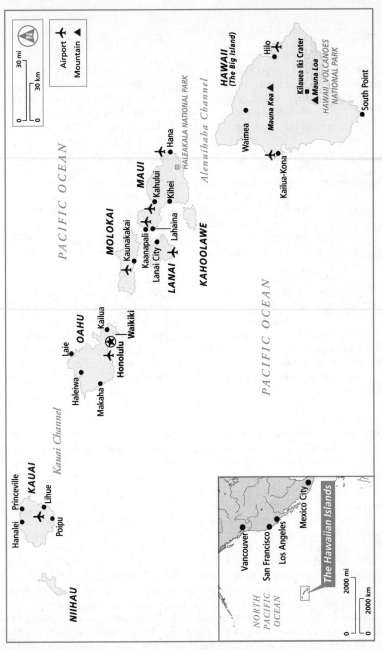

The Hawaiian Islands

Airport ✈ **Mountain** ▲

30 mi
30 km

PACIFIC OCEAN

Kauai Channel

KAUAI
Hanalei
Princeville
Lihue
Poipu

NIIHAU

OAHU
Laie
Haleiwa
Makaha
Kailua
Honolulu
Waikiki

MOLOKAI
Kaunakakai

LANAI
Lanai City
Kaanapali

MAUI
Lahaina
Kahului
Kihei
Hana

HALEAKALA NATIONAL PARK

KAHOOLAWE

Alenuihaha Channel

HAWAII
(The Big Island)
Hilo
Waimea
Kailua-Kona
Kilauea Iki Crater
Mauna Kea ▲
▲*Mauna Loa*
HAWAII VOLCANOES NATIONAL PARK
South Point

PACIFIC OCEAN

The Hawaiian Islands

Vancouver
San Francisco
Los Angeles
Mexico City

NORTH PACIFIC OCEAN

2000 mi
2000 km

If You're Embarking in Honolulu . . .

WHERE TO STAY

In the minds of many, Oahu and its most famous city, Honolulu, are synony-
mous. Honolulu's best-known neighborhood, Waikiki, is actually pretty
small, but its spectacular beach and array of resort hotels are the attractions
that originally put Hawaii on the tourist map. The choices for accommodations are nearly limitless, and range from budget to ultraluxury. For families
watching their wallet, there are nearly a dozen **Ohana Hotels** that offer
clean and affordable lodging in convenient downtown locations.

   Try the **Ohana Waikiki West,** 2330 Kuhio Ave. (© **808/922-5022**), located
2 blocks from Waikiki Beach. Downside? It's on a very busy part of Kuhio
Avenue. Rooms go for $159 per night, and can dip under $100 in low season. To escape the hustle and bustle, head over to the **Hawaiiana Hotel,**
260 Beachwalk, Honolulu (© **808/923-3811**), or next door to the **Breakers,**
250 Beachwalk (© **808/923-3181**). Both properties offer spacious motel
style rooms that surround a tranquil pool and garden starting at about $99
double.

   Trendy visitors should check into the **Aston Waikiki Beach Hotel,** 2570
Kalakaua Ave. (© **800/922-7866;** www.astonhotels.com), where New York
City chic meets Miami cool. Rates for a standard room start at $255 double,
but with surfboards adorning the walls of the lobby, who's counting? If it's
a Victorian setting you crave, don't miss the **Sheraton Moana Surfrider,** 2365
Kalakaua Ave. (© **808/922-3111;** www.sheraton-hawaii.com). Lovingly
referred to as the First Lady of Waikiki, this grand hotel debuted in 1901 as
the first true resort on the island and still retains the same elegance and

ON YOUR OWN: WITHIN WALKING DISTANCE

Right next to the pier is the **Hawaii Maritime Center** (© **808/536-6373**), where you
can learn about Hawaii's maritime history and view artifacts from the days of sailing,
whaling, yachting, and Matson Line cruising. Admission is $7.50 adults, $4.50 kids,
free for kids 5 and under. You can also visit the sailing ship, the *Falls of Clyde,* as well
as a replica of an ancient Polynesian canoe.

   A short walk up Richards Street, across Nimitz Highway, brings you into downtown Honolulu. If you go right on South King Street, you'll come to a statue of **King
Kamehameha I,** the famed Hawaiian ruler. Across the street, at the corner of South
King and Richards streets, stands **'Iolani Palace** (© **808/522-0832;** www.iolani
palace.org), America's only royal residence, where Hawaii's last monarch ruled until
1893. The building of this Italian Renaissance palace, which had electricity before
both the White House and Buckingham Palace, nearly bankrupted the kingdom.
Admission is $20 adults, $5 children (kids under 5 admitted only in the gallery). One
block farther up King Street, at 957 Punchbowl St., **Kawaiahao Church** (© **808/
522-1333**) is the first stone church built on Oahu and is home to a royal burial
ground. Admission is free. Next door, at 553 South King St., is the **Mission House
Museum** (© **808/531-0481**), a cute old mission house open for tours. Admission is

charm she started with 100 years ago. Rates for a standard cityview room start at $310.

WHERE TO DINE

On the second floor of the Aston Waikiki, **Tiki's Grill and Bar,** 2570 Kalakaua Ave. (© 808/923-TIKI), is a restaurant and open-air Tiki bar that overlooks the promenade and beach. The live music plays second fiddle to the sunset views and trendy crowd. The Kalua pig quesadilla is loaded with tender pork, plenty of cheese, and topped with fresh corn salsa. Main courses run $16.

Surprisingly popular is the **Cheesecake Factory** near the Royal Hawaiian Shopping Center (© 808/924-5001). Serving its standard plethora of trendy dishes in heaping portions, the alfresco dining and central location mean there's usually a wait for a table. Main courses cost $15.

With an equally long wait, but lower price tag, **Cheeseburger in Paradise,** 2500 Kalakaua Ave. (© 808/923-3731), delivers exactly that. Served in a basket, with a side of fries, the burgers come in nearly every incarnation, including chili, guacamole, bacon, and Island Style, with a slice of grilled Maui pineapple. There are also tasty salads and veggie or tofu burgers, with or without cheese. Main courses average $8.75.

For a serene outdoor dining experience, try dinner on the **Banyan Veranda** at the Sheraton Moana Surfrider Hotel (see "Where to Stay," above). Its prix-fixe dinner menu is served nightly from 5:30 to 9pm ($55 per person). Afternoon tea is served Monday to Saturday from 1 to 4:30pm and Sunday from 3 to 4:30pm.

$10 adults, $6 kids. Walking 5 blocks west from the museum along South King Street brings you to America's oldest **Chinatown.** Selling everything from flower leis to exotic fruit and vegetables, this crowded market area is a haggler's dream.

ON YOUR OWN: BEYOND THE PORT AREA

Just north of Lunalilo Freeway at the end of Puowaina Drive, is **Punchbowl Crater,** which houses the **National Memorial Cemetery of the Pacific** (© 808/532-3720). This natural landscape feature, called *hill of sacrifice* by early Hawaiians, now serves as a burial ground for 3,500 victims of war. Admission is free. To really learn about the history of Hawaii and its people, drop in at the **Bishop Museum,** 1525 Bernice St. (© 808/847-3511). Created in 1889, and now the State Museum of Natural and Cultural History, this Victorian building houses an extensive collection of artifacts from ancient Polynesians, Hawaiian royalty, turn-of-the-century immigrants, and more. Daily cultural shows and tours enrich the experience. Admission is $9.95 adults, $7.95 kids.

At **Pearl Harbor** (© 808/422-0561), you can't miss the *Arizona* **Memorial** (© 808/422-2771; www.nps.gov/usar), built right above the shallow water where the ship was sunk on December 7, 1941, or the battleship USS *Missouri* (© 808/423-2263; www.ussmissouri.com), on the decks of which peace was declared. Admission to *Arizona* is free. Tickets for *Missouri* are $16 for adults, $8 for children under 12, plus additional fees for guided tours. What you may not notice, and should, is the **USS *Bowfin* Submarine Museum and Park** (© 808/423-1341; www.bowfin.org). This National Historic Landmark offers a rare glimpse into the thrill and danger of life aboard a submarine. The self-guided audio tour is narrated by the vessel's last captain, who takes you through the cramped quarters where men slept nose-to-nose with torpedoes, bathed in miniscule showers, and took turns eating in the tiny galley. This tour is not recommended for people with claustrophobia or who may have difficulty going up or down ladders. Admission is $8 adults, $3 kids ages 4–12.

BEACHES

Nearby **Ala Moana Beach Park** on Ala Moana Park Drive has white sand and calm warm water, and is perfect for families. Like most beaches in Hawaii, it's free and uncrowded, especially on weekdays. There is a paved walkway and grassy areas where you can lounge or picnic under a tree. A taxi here costs less than $10 from the port, or you can catch a bus from the Maritime Center for $2.

A few miles farther south is the famous **Waikiki Beach.** One-way taxi fare will run about $13. This beach is popular with locals, who will often occupy the cement picnic tables under open-air shelters and play chess or just watch the action. While surprisingly small, it is favored for surfing, suntanning, or just people-watching. Restrooms, showers, and beach rentals are all to be had at the far end near Kapiolani Park.

Sandy Beach, on the eastern tip of the island, is a favorite spot for boogie boarding. While the white crashing surf may look appealing, take a moment to read the numerous warning signs, and take great care—lifeguards do more beach rescues here than anywhere else. If a red flag is flying, it means the surf is too dangerous to enter. A taxi will cost between $50 and $65 each way (keep in mind, many taxis can accommodate six or eight passengers, so the fare can be shared).

Another popular beach is **Hanauma Bay,** nestled in a volcanic crater just before Sandy Beach. You approach the beach from above, and pass through the Marine Education Center, which also provides a motorized tram that will take you down the steep road to the beach and back for $1 round-trip. There's a $5 entrance fee and the beach is closed every Tuesday. There is also a shuttle ($2 each way) from Waikiki to the bay that runs every half-hour between 9am and 1pm from city bus stops and several hotels. For more info, call **TheBus** at © 808/848-5555.

SHOPPING

The majority of stores in **Aloha Tower** cater to tourists, selling uniquely Hawaiian wares. Some fine carved wood and bark cloth can be found at a few shops on the second level. For those who like to indulge in serious window-shopping, head to **Kalakaua Avenue** at Waikiki Beach. Here you can find everything from Coach bags to board shorts, all on a bustling strip complete with statues, reflecting pools, street performers, and, at dusk, flaming Tiki torches and alfresco dining. To see some of the island's handmade artwork, drop into the **Nohea Gallery,** inside the lobby of the Sheraton Moana Surfrider Hotel, 2365 Kalakaua Ave. (© 808/922-3111; www. moana-surfrider.com).

2 Kauai

Kauai ranks right up there with Bora Bora, Huahine, and Rarotonga on any list of the world's most spectacular islands. All the elements are here: moody rainforests, majestic cliffs, jagged peaks, emerald valleys, palm trees swaying in the breeze, daily rainbows, and some of the most spectacular golden beaches you'll find anywhere. Soft tropical air, sunrise bird song, essences of ginger and plumeria, golden sunsets, sparkling waterfalls—you don't just go to Kauai, you absorb it with every sense. It may get more than its fair share of tropical downpours, but that's what makes it so lush and green—and creates an abundance of rainbows.

Kauai is essentially a single large shield volcano that rises 3 miles above the sea floor. The island lies 90 miles across the open ocean from Oahu, but it seems at least a half-century removed in time. It's often called "the separate kingdom" because it stood alone and resisted King Kamehameha's efforts to unite Hawaii. In the end, a royal kidnapping was required to take the Garden Isle: After King Kamehameha died, his son, Liholiho, ascended the throne. He gained control of Kauai by luring Kauai's king, Kaumualii, aboard the royal yacht and sailing to Oahu; once there, Kaumualii was forced to marry Kaahumanu, Kamehameha's widow, thereby uniting the islands.

A Kauai rule is that no building may exceed the height of a coconut tree—between three and four stories. As a result, the island itself, not its palatial beach hotels, is the attention-grabber. There are no opulent shopping malls here, but what Kauai lacks in glitz, it more than makes up for in sheer natural splendor, with verdant jungle, the endless succession of spectacular beaches, the grandeur of Waimea Canyon, and the drama of the Napali Coast. Many **Hollywood movies** were filmed here, including *Raiders of the Lost Ark, Six Days, Seven Nights,* and parts of all three *Jurassic Park* films.

COMING ASHORE   About the only fun thing to do at the dock at **Nawiliwili Harbor** is pronounce the name (*Nah*-willy-willy). Some of the small local malls offer free shuttle buses, but the real attraction is the phenomenal beach that is tucked quietly behind the Anchor Cove Shopping Mall, less than a mile from the pier.

GETTING AROUND   Taxis from the **Kauai Taxi Company** (© **808/246-9554**) and other companies typically meet cruise ships at the pier. Rates are $2 for the first ⅛ mile, and $2.40 each additional mile.

SHORE EXCURSIONS

Huleia River Kayak & Hiking Adventure ($62, 2¾ hr.): Right next to the pier is an entry point into a serene jungle river. As you paddle down in your two-person kayak, your expert guide explains the history of the nearby fishpond used by early Hawaiians and will point out where scenes from major adventure movies were filmed. Then your guide leads your group on a hike through the jungle, pointing out native, introduced, and culturally significant plants. A refreshing dip in a jungle stream or a Tarzan leap off a rope swing is definitely the high point.

Jungle Mountain Trek, Wagon & Zipline Adventure ($135, 7 hr.): Paddle a kayak through a mangrove forest, soar across a jungle stream on a highwire zipline, swing from a rope swing, leap off a waterfall, and more on this action-packed all-day adventure. This excursion takes you along jungle trails to some of the most beautiful waterfalls and ponds in the area. The beauty of the surrounding mountains is sublime, and it's impossible not to enjoy the guides' colorful retelling of ancient folklore while bouncing through a green valley in a tractor-pulled wagon surrounded by ridges and peaks that served as the inspiration of the folklore. Be sure to wear comfortable walking shoes, and bring a swimsuit and a towel. Lunch is served on a treehouse platform near a waterfall.

Waimea Canyon & Wailua River/Fern Grotto ($92, 7–8½ hr.): This excursion takes you to some of the most breathtaking and contrasting natural wonders of Kauai. First, visit the jagged red-earth cliffs and canyons of Waimea, the "Grand Canyon of the Pacific," whose depth measures 2,587 feet. Once you've had appropriate time to marvel at the view (don't forget a camera!), you're off via riverboat to explore the verdant green valley of Fern Grotto. Break in your shoes before you take this excursion. Lunch is included.

Tubing the Ditch ($87, 3 hr.): Travel to a former sugar-cane plantation in Kauai's interior and the headwaters of the Hanamaulu Ditch system, a series of open ditches, tunnels, and flumes that once provided irrigation for the farmlands. There you'll get an inner tube, be outfitted with helmet lamps, and begin your float trip through the tunnels. Not for the claustrophobic!

ON YOUR OWN: WITHIN WALKING DISTANCE

A few shopping malls are a short walk from the pier (see "Shopping," below) and a sunny beach even closer still (see "Beaches," below). Otherwise, you'll need wheels of some sort or another.

ON YOUR OWN: BEYOND THE PORT AREA

To understand life in a small town built around a sugar plantation, head to **Old Koloa town.** This tiny collection of small wooden buildings, now turned into shops and restaurants, was the new home for waves of immigrants who came to work on the sugar plantations. In the center of town is a small history center that houses a few artifacts from the turn of the century. Plaques on each building describe the original purpose and history. It's about an hour's drive from the harbor, so this is only a good bet for those who've rented wheels.

A visit to the **McBryde Garden** of the **National Tropical Botanical Garden,** Lawai Road, across the street from Spouting Horn, Poipu (© **808/742-2623;** www.ntbg.org), will leave you breathless as you wander amid the intoxicating array of tropical flowers and fragrances. Take a self-guided ethnobotanical tour ($15) to learn about the many useful and culturally significant plants growing in this green oasis. Trams run from 9:30am to 2:30pm, Monday through Saturday.

BEACHES

Nestled just behind the Anchor Cove Shopping Mall, less than a mile from the pier, is **Kalapaki beach.** Used by locals and tourists, this strip of natural beauty seems out of place next to the parking lot and strip mall. Protected by a jetty and patrolled by lifeguards, this beach is safe to swim and ideal for families with children. Restrooms are available at the nearby restaurants, where you can also change and grab a snack.

Beautiful **Poipu beach** can be reached by heading south from the port along Highway 50 for about 15 miles. This romantic spot has crystal blue water, pure white sand, palm trees, and even a patch of grass big enough for a game of Frisbee. At the eastern end is a small beach with lava rocks and moderate surf, while to the west, you'll see a string of small crescent beaches. Watch for rare and endangered Hawaiian monk seals that occasionally haul out and lounge on the beach. While seemingly tame, they are dangerous to approach and protected by law. In addition to lifeguards, there are showers, restrooms, and covered picnic areas. A taxi here costs about $32 each way.

Heading north on Highway 56, up the Coconut Coast, is **Kee Beach,** a favorite among locals. A deep, but calm swimming area in summer, is at the northern tip, though just off to the left when facing the sea are some dangerous and very sharp rocks just beyond the surf, so take care before you rush in. There are no lifeguards so stay in the area where everyone else is swimming. If no one is in the water, it is usually for good reason. A taxi runs about $65 each way, but many can carry up to six passengers, so you can share the cost with some of your shipmates.

SHOPPING

At the **Anchor Cove Shopping Mall** you can purchase some of the most breathtaking pearl jewelry this side of Asia. **South Pacific Gallery** stocks a wide variety of locally crafted jewelry and art. Don't miss **Seven Seas Trading Company,** with Asian and Hawaiian clothing, art, candles, statues, and more. For spectacular artwork made out of glass, go north on Kuhio Highway and stop in at **Kela's Glass Gallery,** 4-1354 Kuhio Hwy., Kapaa (© **888/255-3527** or 808/822-4527); or along the Coconut Coast, in the town of Hanalei, is the **Yellowfish Trading Company** (© **808/826-1227**), where kitschy Hawaiiana harkens back to the 1950s.

3 Maui

Maui, also called the Valley Isle, is just a small dot in the vast Pacific Ocean, but it has the potential to offer visitors unforgettable experiences: floating weightless through rainbows of tropical fish, standing atop a 10,000-foot volcano watching the sunrise color the sky, listening to the raindrops in a bamboo forest, and sunning on idyllic beaches. The island is also packed with interesting cultural sites and colorful history. Here, you set foot on the spot where ancient Hawaiian royalty and priests once walked, gathered, and worshipped. Later, at the turn of the century, it became a bustling home to native Hawaiians, immigrants, and missionaries. Cruise ships call on two ports, **Kahului** and **Lahaina.**

KAHULUI HARBOR

COMING ASHORE   Coming ashore at **Kahului Harbor,** an industrial port, may leave you less than inspired. Don't bother braving the maze of roads that weave around containers and warehouses, since all that lies beyond in the immediate vicinity are strip malls and roads. It's best to hop in a taxi to explore the island or sign up for one of the shore excursions.

GETTING AROUND   Taxis, as well as shuttle buses, line up in an orderly fashion under large well-marked signs at the pier. If for some reason you don't see one, try **Sunshine Cabs of Maui** (© **800/922-8294** or 808/879-2220) or **Islandwide Taxi and Tours** (© **808/874-TAXI**). Rates are $2.50 for the first ⅛ mile, 25¢ for each additional ⅛ mile.

SHORE EXCURSIONS

Haleakala Crater ($47, 5 hr.): Don't miss this chance to experience the dramatic landscape of a dormant volcano. Haleakala, whose vast crater measures 7½ by 2½ miles and is 3,000 feet deep, last erupted in 1790. As you ascend, the terrain changes from forest, to scrub, to a seemingly barren wasteland near the top. Surprisingly, it is here among the lava rocks and chilly slopes that some of Hawaii's most rare and endangered species of plants and animals can be found. Bring a sweater as temps at the top can sink as low as 40°F (5°C).

Maui Ocean Center and Iao Valley ($52, 4 hr.): This tour combines a visit to a modern interactive aquarium (see below for more information) that displays Hawaii's indigenous marine life, with a visit to Iao Valley, a lush state park and sacred site of religious and cultural significance for ancient Hawaiians.

Maui Whale-Watch ($49, 2 hr.): Some things have to be seen in person, and a breaching whale is one of them. The beauty and grace of these behemoths as they glide between our world and theirs is not to be missed. And, with such abundance here (about a third of all Pacific whales migrate here for the winter), your chances of seeing a whale are good (though not absolute). A guide from the Pacific Whale Foundation shares insights into the animal's behavior as you "listen in" to the mammals' conversation via underwater hydrophones.

ON YOUR OWN: WITHIN WALKING DISTANCE

The harbor functions as a working cargo port in addition to serving cruise ships, so there's not much to see in the immediate vicinity. Stick to shore excursions or take a taxi.

ON YOUR OWN: BEYOND THE PORT AREA

To see one of the most vibrant yet historic towns in Hawaii, go to **Lahaina** (for details, see "Lahaina," below).

For a unique eating experience, try some local fare at **Aloha Mixed Plate,** 1285 Front St. (© **808/661-3322**). Nowhere else short of a luau can you try the local favorites such as *kailua* roast pork (a full pig wrapped in palm leaves and cooked in a fire pit with lava rocks for 12 hr.), *lomi lomi* salmon (fresh salmon minced with raw tomatoes and spices), *lau lau* (pork cooked with taro leaves that taste like fresh spinach), and, of course, the Hawaiian staple, poi (a locally beloved, but flavorless, chocolate pudding). The cultural experience is well worth the short taxi ride from nearby Lahaina. Main courses average $8.

The **Maui Ocean Center,** 192 Ma'alaea Rd. (© **808/270-7000;** www.mauiocean center.com), invites you to explore Hawaii's native marine life in a safe and enjoyable setting. This modern family-friendly facility is the largest tropical reef aquarium in the Western Hemisphere and has both indoor and outdoor exhibits where you can go nose to nose with an octopus, watch a turtle swim, and even touch a squishy sea cucumber. Admission costs $20. To learn everything you ever wanted to know about whaling, head to the **Whaling Museum** in **Whaler's Village,** 2435 Kaanapali Pkwy. (© **808/661-5992;** www.whalersvillage.com). This compact museum houses a prized collection of scrimshaw and lets you step into the world of whaling through an innovative self-guided audio tour. Admission is free.

BEACHES

About 2 miles from the pier is the long and wide **Kanaha Beach Park.** Because there are no lifeguards here, swimming is at your own risk, though the white sand and sweeping vista make lounging on the sand and dabbling your toes in the water more than enough of a reward. Kanaha has restrooms, showers, a picnic area, picnic tables, a campsite, and parking. Head up to **Hookipa beach** to relax and watch windsurfers from around the world work the waves here. While not always safe for swimming, this is the best free windsurf stunt show in town. The beach has bathrooms, showers, picnic tables, barbecues, and parking.

SHOPPING

Your shopping options are to either head over to **Lahina** and **Whaler's Village,** 2435 Kaanapali Pkwy. (© **808/661-4567;** www.whalersvillage.com), or head south to the

Shops at Wailea, 3750 Wailea Alanui Dr. (© **808/891-6770;** www.shopsatwailea. com). Both shopping centers feature upscale classics (Louis Vuitton, Tiffany & Co.) as well as mainstream mall fixtures (The Gap, Banana Republic). They are also home to a number of restaurants.

LAHAINA

COMING ASHORE   Ships anchor offshore in Lahaina and tender passengers across the small harbor and alongside a pier right in the middle of town.

GETTING AROUND   Pretty much everything you could want to do from sight-seeing, to shopping, beaching, and diving, can be done within walking distance of the pier. If you do want to venture farther, taxis are usually waiting at the pier; if not, call **Alii Taxi** (© **808/661-3688**) or **Sunshine Cabs of Maui** (© **800/922-8294** or 808/879-2220).

SHORE EXCURSIONS

Atlantis Submarine Adventure ($99, 3½ hr.): If you don't scuba dive, this 65-foot air-conditioned submarine is the perfect way to view the spectacle of marine life nearly 150 feet below the surface.

Catch a Wave! ($80, 5 hr.): If you have ever wanted to surf the big kahuna, this is your chance. The gentle surf and excellent instructors nearly guarantee that anyone, young and old, can master the ancient Hawaiian art of surfing, even if it's only to stand up long enough for a souvenir snapshot ($10 for a CD of all photos taken of all participants). While not strenuous, this is not for the devout couch potato since you do have to paddle back to shore after you catch a wave.

Maui's Cultural Discovery ($39, 2 hr.): If history is your bag, don't miss this unique walking tour of Lahaina. Your guides are *kumu*, or teachers, and have in-depth knowledge of the ancient Hawaiian people as well as the more recent settlers. At the sacred sites, the *kumu* perform chants to show respect for the site and to keep the ancient tradition alive. The first sacred site is an ancient birthing stone near the dock. Others are now occupied by modern buildings, constructed over ancient temples or places of worship. The rest are off the beaten trail and not fully excavated, and really require a guide to bring them to life.

ON YOUR OWN: WITHIN WALKING DISTANCE

Lahaina (© **808/667-9193;** www.visitlahaina.com) is one of the most vibrant yet historic towns in Hawaii. It's rich in history, plus loaded with great shopping, watersports, and restaurants. Stop by the centrally located **Courthouse** to tour the small museum (headquarters for the Lahaina Art Society) there and check out the two art galleries, or grab a self-guided walking tour pamphlet. You can also check out the historical exhibits at the newly opened (and free) **Lahaina Heritage Museum** (© **808/661-1959**) on the second floor. Just outside the Courthouse, artists are camped under a great banyan tree, the largest you're ever likely to see.

As you meander among the shops and sites, clearly numbered plaques correspond to the walking tour. Head for the two-story **Pioneer Inn,** 658 Wharf St. (© **808/661-3636**), which was Maui's first hotel; the bar remains a favorite watering hole. Then check out the nearby **Baldwin House Museum,** 120 Dickenson St. (© **808/661-3262;** www.lahainarestoration.org), where a local missionary and medical doctor, Dwight Baldwin, single handedly vaccinated and thereby saved nearly the entire town from a deadly smallpox outbreak in the mid–19th century. Admission is $3. Stroll far-ther down Front Street, heading west, and drop in at the **Wo Hing Museum** (✆ **808/661-5553**), once an ancient Chinese fraternal society. Admission is $1. While the museum merits only a quick tour, don't miss the film loop playing in the adjacent cookhouse, where you can view footage of Hawaii shot by Thomas Edison nearly 100 years ago.

ON YOUR OWN: BEYOND THE PORT AREA
See "On Your Own: Beyond the Port Area," in the Kahului Harbor section above.

BEACHES
The beach at **Lahaina** is calm, clean, and a great place to watch surfers take their first lessons on the baby waves. Located between a stone break-wall and the shops at 505 Front St., this beach is known by locals as either 505 or the break-wall. There are rest-rooms, shops, and restaurants nearby. **Kaanapali beach,** directly behind **Whaler's Village** (see above), is a safe and popular beach stretching about a mile past several resorts. Beach chairs, umbrellas, kayaks, boogie boards, and other rentals are available at **Beach Activities of Maui** (✆ **808/661-5552;** www.mauiwatersports.com), located nearby next to the Westin Hotel. Restrooms and showers are both available.

SHOPPING
Front street in **Lahaina** is a shopper's mecca, with clothing boutiques full of aloha (also known as Hawaiian) shirts, jewelry stores selling pearls and tourmaline, and the usual assortment of art galleries. The best art can be found at the **Lahaina Arts Soci-ety** galleries inside the **Courthouse** at 648 Wharf St. (✆ **808/661-0111;** las@maui gateway.com). Also check out the **Village Gallery in Lahaina,** 120 Dickenson St. (✆ **808/661-4402**). Not far away on Honoapi'ilani Highway is the **Lahaina Cannery Mall** (✆ **808/661-5304;** www.lahainacannery.com), which used to be a huge pine-apple cannery, and now houses lots of shops carrying locally made handicrafts. For information on Whaler's Village, see "Shopping," in the Kahului Harbor section above.

4 The Big Island

The Big Island is the largest island in the Hawaiian chain (4,028 sq. miles—about the size of Connecticut), the youngest (800,000 years), and the least populated (with 30 people per square mile), and has an unmatched diversity of terrain and climate: fiery volcanoes and sparkling waterfalls, black-lava deserts and snowcapped mountain peaks, tropical rainforests and alpine meadows, a glacial lake, and miles of golden, black, and green (!) sand beaches. A 50-mile drive will take you from snowy winter to sultry summer, passing through spring or fall along the way. The island looks like the inside of a barbecue pit on one side, and a lush jungle on the other. It's a bizarre place, in a word, and takes some people aback because it doesn't fit the tropical stereotype.

Five volcanoes—one still erupting—have created this island, which is growing big-ger daily. At its heart is snowcapped Mauna Kea, the world's tallest mountain (meas-ured from the ocean floor), complete with its own glacial lake. Mauna Kea's nearest neighbor is Mauna Loa (or "Long Mountain"), creator of one-sixth of the island; it's the largest volcano on earth, rising 30,000 feet out of the ocean floor (of course, you can see only the 13,677 ft. that are above sea level). Erupting Kilauea makes the Big Island bigger every day—and, if you're lucky and your timing is good, you can stand just a few feet away and watch it do its work. In just a week, the Kilauea volcano can produce enough lava to fill the Astrodome.

HILO
COMING ASHORE   Ships pull alongside the docks at Hilo, which is not much more than an industrial port, so don't plan on walking into town. An organized shore excursion is your best bet here.

GETTING AROUND
In the unlikely event that there are no taxis waiting at the pier, you can call **Ace-1** (© **808/935-8303**). Note that because the island is so big, taxi rides can be quite expensive. Taxis are metered. The first ⅛ mile costs $2, as does each subsequent mile.

SHORE EXCURSIONS
Kilauea Volcano ($39–47, 4½ hr.): This park is by far Hawaii's premier tourism destination, and well worth a visit. On your tour, you'll get a look at the still-active Kilauea (5,000 ft. high), walk the extinct Thurston Lava Tube, and check out the exhibits at the National Volcano Observatory. There's no need to worry about dramatic eruptions; for the most part, Hawaii's volcanoes are quite tame.

Kilauea Lava Viewing Adventure ($99, 5 hr.): Drive 51 miles, climb 4,000 feet up Kilauea, and then descend to sea level to watch lava flowing into the sea. The land here is some of the newest on earth, formed by the cooling lava sometimes only hours before you arrive. It's often so hot it'll melt the soles of your sneakers if you don't keep moving. This is one that's only for the really fit, requiring a 2- to 6-mile hike on rough surfaces. Many folks who start out don't make it and have to head back to the van without seeing what they came to see.

Waipi'o Valley Horseback Ride ($119, 5–5½ hr.): There is no better way to appreciate the natural beauty of this sacred "Valley of the Kings" than from horseback. You'll ride along the rim of the valley until you reach Hiilawe falls—one of the most spectacular in Hawaii—where you can enjoy a vista of the Pacific. All riders must weigh no more than 230 pounds. Closed-toe shoes are required, and long pants are recommended.

Hawaii Tropical Botanical Garden ($34, 2½ hr.): Even if you are not a plant enthusiast, you will be awestruck by the sheer beauty of this garden set in one of the most spectacular locations in Hawaii. The orchids and other exotic plants (2,500 different species in all) are offset by the dramatic cliffs, vistas, and crashing surf below. The tour is self-directed along 1 mile or so of trails within the gardens. It's a shutterbug's paradise, so don't leave your camera on the ship.

ON YOUR OWN: BEYOND THE PORT AREA
To enjoy the beauty of a formal Japanese garden, head down Banyan Drive to **Liliuokalani Gardens,** right near **Coconut Island.** This picturesque 30-acre park has many bonsai trees as well as carp ponds, pagodas, and an arched bridge. For golfers, the small **Naniloa Country Club,** 120 Banyan Dr. (© **808/935-3000**), offers a small but challenging and rewarding course. Greens fees are $25 weekdays and $30 weekends, plus $15 cart fee. To truly understand the power and fury of the Pacific Ocean, visit the **Pacific Tsunami Museum** (130 Kamehameha Ave.). Be sure to speak with the volunteers on hand, many of whom have lived through the "walls of water" that hit Hilo in 1946 and 1960.

To learn more about Hawaii's marine ecosystems, visit the **Mokupapapa Discovery Center,** 308 Kamehameha Ave., Suite 109, in the South Hata Building (© **808/933-8195;** www.hawaiireef.noaa.gov). This education facility opened in May 2003, and is run by the National Marine Sanctuaries and the National Oceanic and Atmospheric Administration. Exhibits include a 2,500-gallon saltwater aquarium, a large number of photographs and murals, and several interactive research stations. Admission is free and it's open Tuesday through Saturday.

BEACHES

At the start of Banyan Drive (about 2 miles from the cruise dock) is **Reeds Bay Park,** a small beach popular with locals. While there are no lifeguards or facilities, the shallow water is well protected from waves and jagged rocks and is ideal for swimming.

Near the other end of Banyan Drive is Moku Ola, or **Coconut Island.** Accessible by a walking bridge, this serene destination is also popular with locals who want to stroll the shady perimeter, bathe in the rocky pools, or swim off the small grassy beaches. About 3 miles from the pier on Kalanianaole Avenue is **Leleiwi Beach Park.** Not a traditional white-sand beach, this one has black lava rocks that form small tide pools that are ideal for snorkeling. Keep an eye out for endangered sea turtles that are attracted to this spot. There are lifeguards, and facilities include showers, restrooms, and a small marine police station.

SHOPPING

The best shopping in Hilo can be found along Kamehameha Avenue in the heart of downtown. Stop by **Dreams of Paradise Gallery,** 308 Kamehameha Ave. (© **808/935-5670;** www.dreamsofparadisegallery.com), to see some impressive examples of local artwork, or to meet artist in residence and owner Suzan Starr. A wide selection of black pearl jewelry can be found at the adjacent **Black Pearl Gallery** (© **808/935-8556** or 800/343-2994; www.blackpearlgallery.com).

KAILUA-KONA

COMING ASHORE   Cruise ships anchor offshore here and tender passengers to the sleepy pier in Kailua-Kona. There's plenty to do within steps of this modest pier, including beach-hopping, shopping, and more. Taxis line up at the dock to whisk you away, but with so much to do at the pier, there is little reason to take one.

GETTING AROUND   Like the other ports in Hawaii, taxis await the arrival of cruise ship passengers, in this case lining up in front of the **King Kamehameha Hotel.** If you need to call for one, try **Speedy Shuttle** (© 808/329-5433); keep in mind, though, because the island is so big, long distance trips can be very pricey. **DJ's Rentals** (© 808/329-1700; www.harleys.com) is easily spotted right across from the Kailua Pier. They can hook you up with either a scooter or Harley Davidson, for full- ($45–$145) or half-day rentals ($45–$90). If two wheels are not enough, go all out with **Big Island Exotic Cars** (at the same kiosk) and rent a factory-built replica 1957 Porsche Speedster, or canary yellow Hummer. Single-day rates run from $249 to $449 depending on the vehicle and time of year.

To cruise the waterfront and around town, bicycles can be rented for $15 a day at **Dave's Bike and Triathalon Shop** (© 808/329-4522) across from the Kailua Pier behind Atlantis Submarine. Or try **Hawaiian Pedals** (© 808/329-2294) in the Kona Inn Shopping Village about half a mile down on Alii Drive.

SHORE EXCURSIONS

Catamaran Sail and Snorkel ($89, 3¾ hr.): Head out on a catamaran to Pawai Bay and enjoy a morning of cruising, music, snacking, and snorkeling. The bay is loaded with multicolored fish, rays, and lava-encrusted coral reefs. In winter there's a great chance you'll see whales or spinner dolphins breaching and cavorting.

Kona Cloud Forest Botanical Walk ($60; 3½ hr.): Knowledgeable naturalists guide you through a lush forest sanctuary on the slopes of the sleeping Hualalai Volcano. A good pick for someone who wants something more active than a bus tour, but less active than a fitness hike, covering about 1½ miles at a leisurely pace in cool mountainside weather. If you're into gardening, it's bliss; if you're into coffee, the end-of-tour stop at a Kona coffee farm will net you a free tasting and beans at a low price.

Big Island Helicopter Spectacular ($399, 4½ hr.): There is no better way to see the Big Island's beauty and volcanic fury than from a helicopter. On this journey you soar over the tropical valleys and waterfalls of the Kohala Mountains, the rainforest of the Hamakua Coast, and the spectacular lava flows of Hawaii Volcanoes National Park.

ON YOUR OWN: WITHIN WALKING DISTANCE

There is plenty to see and do right near the pier. Just head right down the seawall and enjoy the breathtaking view of the ocean on one side, and the endless stream of shops and galleries that line the opposite side of the street. Be sure and stop in at **Hulihee Palace,** 75-5718 Alii Dr. (© 808/329-1877), a two-story New England–style palace. Built in 1838 as a summer residence for Hawaii's royalty, it was at the time the largest and most elegant home on the island. Today it is a well-run and well-preserved museum. Admission is $6. Across the street is **Mokuaikaua Church** (© 808/329-1589), the oldest Christian church in Hawaii.

ON YOUR OWN: BEYOND THE PORT AREA

Saint Benedict's Catholic Church (© 808/328-2227), on Highway 19, is more commonly known as the "Painted Church," because of the colorful murals and frescoes that cover its walls and ceilings. It was painted by Father John Velge, the church's first priest, in an attempt to enlighten and educate his congregation, who were predominantly illiterate. Admission is free.

Ancient **Hawaiian petroglyphs** can be seen near the **King's Shops** at the **Waikoloa Beach Resort,** just off Waikoloa Beach Drive about 30 miles north on Highway 19 (© 808/886-8811). There are free tours that meet at the food court in the King's Shops Mall and depart weekday mornings at 10:30am and weekends at 8:30am, or the ancient markings can be toured on your own anytime. Follow the signs to the petroglyphs, and then take the small path that leads to a craggy trail through a lava field once used by Hawaiian travelers. Non-guests are welcome to visit **Hilton Waikoloa Village,** 425 Waikoloa Beach Dr. (© 808/886-1234; www.h-wv.com), and enjoy its spectacularly landscaped grounds and walkways that meander past enormous statues, dramatic waterfalls, sweeping coastal vistas, and $7 million worth of artwork. If you like Atlantis on Paradise Island in The Bahamas, you'll love this resort. Enjoy any of the nine restaurants, all of which can be reached either via air-conditioned tram, or open-air mahogany boats that run from one end of the property to the other. For a steep $75, families can also use the pools and man-made beach as well.

BEACHES

At the Kailua-Kona pier, you're practically standing on the beach at the **King Kamehameha Hotel.** Because all beaches are public in Hawaii, this small and sweet waterfront resort is yours to enjoy. For a modest fee, you can rent watersports gear, lounge chair, or umbrella. For those who prefer to swim without all the trappings, there is a miniscule scrap of beach just on the other side of the parking lot. Here the calm water makes for great paddling, swimming laps, or just floating your cares away. The best beach for snorkeling (especially for beginners) is **Kahaluu Beach Park,** located about 2 miles down Alii Drive from the pier. The salt-and-pepper-colored beach is convenient to restrooms, a snack truck, and sheltered picnic tables. While shallow, the water can become rough in the winter. Beautiful **Hapuna Beach State Park,** past the Hilton Waikoloa Village and Mauna Lani Resort, is about 35 miles up the Kohala Coast from the pier. Follow the highway signs and turn left toward the ocean off Highway 19. You'll be greeted by a large, white-sand beach; the area is serene, well maintained, and has a food pavilion, restrooms, and showers.

SHOPPING

There is ample shopping on Alii Drive, which starts at the Kailua Pier and extends southward along a nearly endless strip of small shopping galleries with similar names and equally similar wares. Artist Rapozo displays his prints in **Rapozo Images** (www.rapozo-studio.com) at the Seaside Mall. For something out of the ordinary, stop in at the **Eclectic Craftsman** (© 808/334-0562) in the Kona Marketplace to see the beautifully carved wood. Farther down, inside Waterfront Row, marvel at the marine life sculptures made from wood, stone, and metal at **Wyland Gallery** (© 808/334-0037; www.wyland.com).

15

New England &
Eastern Canada

Fishing boats piled with netting, Victorian mansions built by wealthy whalers, and lighthouses atop windswept bluffs are just a taste of what a journey along the coast of New England and Canada has in store. America and Canada were born in these parts, so you'll be in for lots of **historical sites** along the way, from Boston's Paul Revere House to the *Titanic* exhibit at the Maritime Museum in Halifax and Québec City's 17th-century Notre-Dame des Victoires Church. The legacies left by the French, English, Scottish, and other settlers that immigrated to these parts since the 17th century have lent ports along New England and eastern Canada their unique character, whether it's the Puritan ethic of stubborn independence and thriftiness that many New Englanders still cling to, or the French culture and language that thrive in the Providence of Québec.

The classic time to cruise here is in autumn, when a brilliant sea of **fall foliage** blankets the region. You can also cruise these waters in the spring and summer too, as the route becomes more popular. Big 2,000-passenger-plus ships go here as well as much smaller vessels carrying a tenth of that load. Depending on the size of the ship and the length of the cruise, itineraries may include passing through **Nantucket Sound,** around **Cape Cod,** or into the **Bay of Fundy** or **Gulf of St. Lawrence.** Some ships traverse the St. Lawrence Seaway or the smaller Saguenay

River. New England/Canada cruises range from 4 nights to 10 to 12, with most sailing to or from New York, Boston, Montréal, and Québec City.

HOME PORTS FOR THIS REGION **New York** and **Boston** are the main hubs for these cruises, while **Québec City** and **Montréal** also get there fair share of business.

LANGUAGE & CURRENCY English and dollars. You may want to get some Canadian dollars (US$1 = C$1.24) if you'll be spending a night or 2 in Québec or Montréal before hopping on a ship, but otherwise, when visiting ports such as Halifax and Saint John for the day, virtually all businesses accept the good ole U.S. dollar. Keep in mind, most goods in Canada are subject to a 7% tax plus an 11% provincial tax (the tax is already included in the price tag, however, unlike prices in the States).

SHOPPING TIPS You don't go on a New England/Canada cruise for the shopping, though there are a few choice spots. Of course, New York City, Boston, and Montréal, being major cities, offer lots of shopping ops, but other spots include Portland, Maine, where an L.L.Bean outlet is within striking distance at nearby Freeport. You can pick up nautical souvenirs and handicrafts in many ports, so if you're in the market for a whale paperweight, a woodcarving of a fisherman, or some oyster crackers, you'll be in luck.

1 Bar Harbor, Maine

In its heyday 100 or more years ago, Bar Harbor was one of the premier resort areas on the East Coast, attracting wealthy families looking for a rustic experience. Today it's a humbler place with no shortage of T-shirt shops and ice-cream parlors, but no less popular with tourists. Because of its beautiful natural setting, Bar Harbor is included on many cruise itineraries, getting more calls than Portland does, to the south. Overlooking Frenchman's Bay from its perch on Mt. Desert Island, which is connected to the mainland via a bridge, Bar Harbor's real pull is its accessibility to the lush **Acadia National Park,** which covers most of the 13 × 16-mile island. You'll see what we mean as you approach Frenchman's Bay with Cadillac Mountain looming just beyond the jagged coastline. Named "Isles des Monts-Deserts," meaning bare mountains, by French Explorer Samuel de Champlain in 1604, the region has been a favorite attraction for decades. Along with other tycoons of the 19th and early 20th centuries such as the Pulitzers, Astors, Vanderbilts, and Fords, John D. Rockefeller, Jr., fell in love with the area, which rivaled Newport, Rhode Island, as a ritzy summer get-away. As a testament to his love of the forested island, Rockefeller donated more than 10,000 acres to the national park.

COMING ASHORE While small ships less than 200 feet long can pull alongside the Town Pier, most ships must anchor offshore and send passengers to the Harbor Place pier via tenders. The ride to the pier only takes about 10 minutes. The two piers are next to each other smack dab in the downtown waterfront area.

GETTING AROUND Once in town, you can walk along the waterfront and to many shops, restaurants, and a few attractions (highlighted below in "Within Walking Distance"), but to see the Park, your best bet is signing up for one of your ship's shore excursions or renting a bicycle from a local dealer. Try **Harbor Bicycle Shop,** 141 Cottage St. (© 207/288-3886), or **Acadia Bike,** 48 Cottage St. (© 207/288-9605). You can also explore the park via horse and carriage. If you want a taxi and there aren't any waiting, try **At Your Service Taxi Cab Co.** (© 207/288-9222); they also offer guided tours of the Park.

BEST CRUISE LINE SHORE EXCURSIONS

Best of the Park and the Town ($59, 4 hr.): Traverse the 22-mile Park Loop Road of Acadia National Park via bus, with a stop to view Thunder Hole, where the right tidal conditions can send flumes of ocean spray high into the air. Visit the summit of Cadillac Mountain and pass the High Seas cottage, whose owner perished on the *Titanic* before she ever saw her dream home. See Sand Beach, Otter Cliffs, and Jordan Pond House, and make a stop to see how lobsters are caught. Afterwards, tour the elegant La Rochelle mansion, a fine example of turn-of-the-century grandeur, from its fireplaces, to moldings and seaside porches. You can also have a look at the Tiffany stained-glass windows at St. Saviour's Episcopal Church.

A Walk in the Park ($49, 2 hr.): A naturalist guide offers insight into the natural wonders of Acadia National Park on this walk, from the powerful glacial activity that gave the Maine coast its unique identity to the local wildlife, plant life, and fishing industry. Plus, learn the role that barons such as John D. Rockefeller, Jr., played in forming the park, and what Bar Harbor was like when Mt. Desert Island was the playground of America's rich and famous.

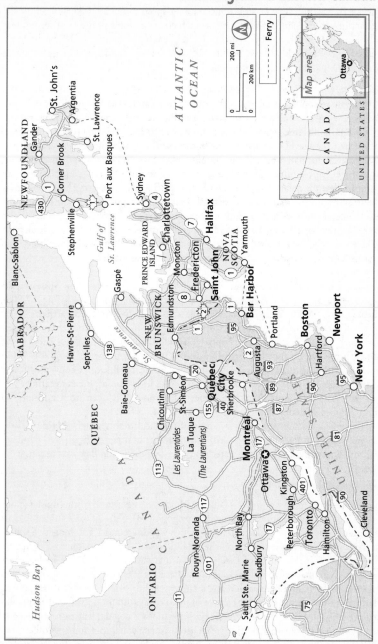

New England & Eastern Canada

Ferry

200 mi

200 km

ATLANTIC OCEAN

Map area

Ottawa

CANADA

UNITED STATES

St. John's

Argentia

Gander

St. Lawrence

NEWFOUNDLAND

Corner Brook

430

1

Port aux Basques

Stephenville

Sydney

4

Gulf of St. Lawrence

Charlottetown

7

Halifax

Blanc-Sablon

PRINCE EDWARD ISLAND

Moncton

Fredericton

Saint John

NOVA SCOTIA

Yarmouth

Gaspé

8

1

Bar Harbor

LABRADOR

Havre-St-Pierre

NEW BRUNSWICK

Edmundston

1

2

Portland

Boston

Newport

Sept-Îles

138

St. Lawrence

1

95

Augusta

Hartford

New York

QUÉBEC

Baie-Comeau

20

Québec City

2

93

89

90

95

Chicoutimi

St-Siméon

155

40

Sherbrooke

87

Les Laurentides

La Tuque

(The Laurentians)

Montréal

17

81

113

Ottawa

Kingston

401

90

Cleveland

117

Peterborough

Toronto

Hamilton

Rouyn-Noranda

North Bay

17

101

Sudbury

11

Sault Ste. Marie

75

ONTARIO

CANADA

UNITED STATES

Hudson Bay

695

Biking in Acadia ($49, 2½ hr.): Jump on a 24-speed mountain bike and follow the guide through the park's carriage trails, which crisscross some of the most scenic areas of the park. Constructed by John D. Rockefeller, Jr., beginning in 1913, the hard-packed gravel trails have been maintained well through the years. The guide makes stops to discuss the island's history and lore.

ON YOUR OWN: WITHIN WALKING DISTANCE

If for some reason you're allergic to beautiful forests and want to stay in town close to the ship, you can check out the great views of the area from the foot of Main Street at grassy **Agamont Park,** which overlooks the town pier and Frenchman Bay. From here, set off past the Bar Harbor Inn on the **Shore Path,** a wide, winding trail that follows the shoreline for half a mile along a public right of way. The pathway passes in front of many elegant summer homes (some converted to inns), offering a superb vantage point to view the area's architecture. From the path is a fine view of **The Porcupines,** a cluster of spruce-studded islands just off shore: A good spot to take note of the powerful force of glacial action, a south-moving glacier ground away at the islands, creating a gentle slope facing north. On the south shore, away from the glacial push (glaciers simply melted when retreating north), is a more abrupt, clifflike shore. The islands look like a small group of porcupines migrating southward—or so early visitors imagined.

For a glimpse of the area's past life, stroll on over to the new **Abbe Museum,** 26 Mt. Desert St. (© **207/288-3519;** www.abbemuseum.org), a sprawling 17,000-square-foot gallery housing a top-rate collection of Native American artifacts. (The original museum, next to Sieur de Monts Spring within the park itself, remains open and unchanged.) The museum is open year-round; admission is $4.50. Around the corner is the **Bar Harbor Historical Society,** 33 Ledgelawn Ave. (© **207/288-0000;** www.barharborhistorical.org), located in a handsome 1918 former convent. Browse artifacts from the resort town's glory days, as well as its low point, the devastating 1947 fire that destroyed more than 200 homes. The museum is open from mid-June to mid-October, Monday through Saturday; admission is free.

Somewhere during your stay, try some of the local freshly caught **Maine lobster** (served baked, stuffed, broiled, boiled, and a number of other creative ways) at one of the many restaurants along the waterfront area, including the Pier Restaurant at 55 West St.

ON YOUR OWN: BEYOND THE PORT AREA

You don't want to come to Bar Harbor without getting a taste of the most famous attraction: **Acadia National Park (www.nps.gov/acad).** Sign up for a guided hike or drive along the 27-mile Park Loop Road, which wends around 1,530-foot-high Cadillac Mountain, the highest point on the Atlantic coast. If you luck out and there's no fog, expect awesome views of spectacular natural sights like Thunder Hole, where ocean surf dramatically crashes against granite cliffs. Perhaps the best way to really experience the nature here is bicycling a stretch of the 55-mile car-free carriage trails that wind through the park (rent a bike in town or sign up for one of your ship's biking excursions). Horse-drawn carriage rides are another popular way to tour the park. No matter what your transport, there's a great chance you'll spot some wildlife, from the occasional moose, to beavers, foxes, eagles, hawks, and the peregrine falcon. You can also appreciate wildlife, such as seals and puffins, from the water via a kayaking excursion or a whale-watching trip. The best time to spot the great mammals in these parts is between April and October, when humpbacks, finbacks, minkes, and dolphins gather in the waters off the island to fill their bellies after a long winter.

SHOPPING You don't come here for the shopping, though if "I Love Maine" T-shirts and lobster potholders aren't your thing, there are few decent options. Head for the handful of interesting shops on **Main Street** selling locally made, and/or inspired, handicrafts and gifts. At **Island Artisans,** you can browse for local handicrafts such as tiles, sweet-grass baskets, pottery, jewelry, and soaps. Down the street is the **Bar Harbor Hemporium,** an interesting store dedicated to promoting products made from hemp, an environmentally friendly fibrous plant that can be used in making paper, clothing, and more. A few doors away is **In the Woods,** where you'll find a selection of, you guessed it, wood products from Maine, including bowls, cutting boards, children's games and puzzles, peg coat racks, spice racks, and more.

2 Halifax, Nova Scotia

It's safe to say that Halifax, Nova Scotia, is the top port of call for big ships on the New England and Eastern Canada circuit because of the city's large natural deep-water port and its especially pleasing harborside setting and tree-lined streets. Like New Brunswick, Nova Scotia was first inhabited by the Micmac Indians, who called the area Chebuctook, meaning Great Long Harbor. In 1605, the French staked their claim and started settling in the area calling it Acadia, or peaceful land. By 1621, the British had a foothold and named the land Nova Scotia (Latin for New Scotland), and in 1749, Edward Cornwallis founded Halifax. (The site was named after George Montagu Dunk, second earl of Halifax. Residents tend to agree that it was a great stroke of luck that the city avoided the name Dunk, Nova Scotia.) The city eventually became a thriving shipbuilding and trading center as well as a military hub for the Royal Army and Navy. Even into the 20th century, Halifax had strong military ties, serving as an important supply and convoy harbor in both World Wars. In recent years, it's evolved into a vital commercial and financial hub, as well as a home to a number of colleges and universities.

Typically, two ships are in port at one time, though occasionally as many as four or five ships are tied up. A band of marching, kilted bagpipers greets passengers, and the place is generally bustling. You'll notice that the locals are very fond of their Scottish ancestry (the reason the kilts and bagpipes keep turning up).

Though there's plenty of history to keep you occupied, you could skip the bookish stuff, and head right for one of the woody English-style pubs called the likes of the Split Crow or The Thirsty Duck. Inside, the ale is flowing and live music is usually part of the deal.

COMING ASHORE There couldn't be a more convenient port to call on; all ships call along the docks right in town and Halifax's attractions are just steps away.

GETTING AROUND Halifax is exceedingly walkable, though there are plenty of taxis at the docks if you're inclined to head for the hills. If you need to call a taxi, try **Leader's Limousine and Taxi Service** at (© **902/497-1117**). Taxi fares start at US$2.25 (C$2.90) no matter how short the ride is, and US$1.75 (C$2.20) is added per mile after that.

BEST CRUISE LINE SHORE EXCURSIONS

The *Titanic* Connection (US$39, 3 hr.): Burial site of 150 victims of the ill-fated *Titanic* nearly a century ago, Halifax was dubbed for a time as the "Funeral City," and

New England & Canada's Smaller Ports

Aside from the major ports listed in this chapter, there are a number of ports that small-ship lines such as American Canadian Caribbean Line (p. 329) and Clipper Cruise Lines (p. 342) include in their itineraries. Occasionally a big ship or two may also visit these ports.

Founded 350 years ago, **New London, Connecticut** (www.ci.new-london. ct.us), offers the visitor a taste of Colonial history in its vintage 17th-, 18th-, and 19th-century homes and buildings. If you're willing to travel a few miles, other nearby attractions include Mystic Seaport, Eugene O'Neill's summer home, and the Mohegan Sun and Foxwoods casinos.

Located in the northern reaches of Narragansett Bay, about 20 miles north of Newport, Rhode Island, visitors to **Fall River, Massachusetts** (www. fallriverma.org), can enjoy a trip on some historic boats, including the Battleship USS *Massachusetts*, submarine *Lionfish*, and other veterans of World War II. At the town's Marine Museum, you'll find artifacts from the *Titanic*, while at the Lizzie Borden Museum, you can get the down and dirty details on that famous unsolved murder mystery. The whaling capital of the world in the 19th century, **New Bedford, Massachusetts** (www.ci.new-bedford.ma. us), remains a major Atlantic deep-sea fishing port. Spend your time in port at the town's **Whaling Museum** (www.whalingmuseum.org) and enjoy ship replicas, whale skeletons and paintings, glasswork, and *scrimshaw*, which is carved whalebone or whale ivory. **Cuttyhunk,** a tiny island off the coast of New Bedford, is also included in a few small-ship itineraries. The sleepy stretch of land is all about beaches and serene strolls along rolling hills. **Nantucket Island, Massachusetts** (www.nantucketchamber.org), is classic New England, and was the world's top whaling hub before New Bedford stole the show. Today, the island is vastly popular, but still manages to maintain a low-key attitude. The island's great public beaches, including the Jetties or Surfside, are the great draw. **Martha's Vineyard** (www.mvy.com), also in **Massachusetts,** is New England's largest island. Besides its handsome old towns, the Vineyard is a haven for nature lovers. You'll find great beaches, though many are private, as well as dramatic cliffs and meadows that make for great long walks and bicycle rides.

Maine's largest city, **Portland** (www.visitportland.com), is set on a peninsula in scenic Casco Bay. The top attractions include the Portland Headlight,

its inhabitants were greatly commended on their response and compassion during the relief effort. Serving as a base for the *Titanic* recovery operation, Halifax received the bodies of more than 200 victims and implemented a system used to help identify the unknown by their belongings. This tour includes all aspects of Halifax's connection to this tragedy, including the historic pier from where the cable ships were dispatched to pick up victims; the church where memorial services were held; the temporary morgue sites which housed the bodies of such wealthy victims as John Jacob Astor; the cemeteries where rows upon rows of identical gravestones mark the final resting place of 150 victims; and the Maritime Museum of the Atlantic, which houses an excellent

America's oldest lighthouse in continuous use, and that bastion of practical outdoor ware, L.L.Bean, located in nearby Freeport.

Just southwest of Halifax is **Lunenburg** (www.town.lunenburg.ns.ca), Nova Scotia's main fishing port and a great area to spot whales. The 19th-century architecture that survives in this former British Colonial settlement landed Lunenburg on the prestigious UNESCO World Heritage list. Head for the hills when you debark in industrial **Sydney,** on **Cape Breton Island, Nova Scotia** (www.cbisland.com). It's the Cape Breton Highlands where you want to spend your time. The 175-mile-long Cabot Trail, all lakes, dramatic cliffs, and panoramic vistas, is the island's main attraction. You'll see Acadian fishing ports, pristine valleys, and some of the most picturesque coastline anywhere. If you're lucky, you'll spot moose, bald eagles, puffin, and humpback whales in the waters of the Gulf of St. Lawrence. In **Charlottetown** (www.visitcharlottetown.com) on **Prince Edward Island,** Canada's smallest province and the birthplace of Canada in 1867, you can visit historical sites, including the house of Lucy Maud Montgomery, who wrote the well-known novel *Anne of Green Gables* about the innocence and beauty of turn-of-the-20th-century life on the island. Or opt for a drive along one of the island's scenic highways, which wend past sandstone cliffs, rocky coves, lovely beaches, and fishing villages.

The string of humble towns along the beautiful Gaspe Peninsula on the southern shores of the St. Lawrence River, are set amidst the best of nature's bounty. Search for whales, go birding, or enjoy a walk along a seaside trail in **Gaspe, Perce,** or **Bonaventure Island** (www.infogaspesie.com). Francophiles will love **St. Pierre & Miquelon,** a group of small islands off the southern coast of Newfoundland that still cling to their French roots (many residents are descendants of Arcadians and Basques), speaking the language and offering classic French fare and wines in their restaurants. Not to be confused with Saint John, New Brunswick, a port that sees much more traffic than this small outpost, **St. John's** (www.stjohns.ca) is the capital of **Newfoundland** and the oldest city in all of Canada, dating back to 1582. The landscape in these parts can be exceedingly picturesque: The film *The Shipping News,* a montage of stunning seascapes, was filmed in Newfoundland.

permanent exhibit on the disaster, featuring the world's largest collection of wooden artifacts—including a post from the famous Grand Staircase, and one of the only intact *Titanic* deck chairs in the world.

Pub-Crawl (US$49, 2½ hr.): On this relaxing outing, you'll visit several of Halifax's favorite pubs and have a chance (of course!) to sample the local brew. Led by your kilted guide and a bagpiper, you'll walk through the streets of Halifax, taking in libations at some of the unique, Olde-English-style pubs. Throughout the tour, roving musicians along the way serenade visitors on the fiddle, guitar, mandolin, accordion, the washboard, and, of course, the bagpipes!

City Tour (US$32, 3 hr.): This tour includes the highlights of Halifax by both bus and on foot. Your guide will regale the group with stories of Halifax's rum running and privateering days as well as its *Titanic* connection, and the devastating Halifax Explosion, the tragic explosion between the ammunition ship *Mont Blanc* and the Norwegian supply ship *Imo* in 1917. The tour includes a visit to the Halifax Citadel, a hilltop fortress built between 1828 and 1856, which had been functioning as the British Imperial bastion of control in North America for many years. The group also strolls through the Victorian-style Public Gardens with your kilted guide and bagpiper.

Peggy's Cove (US$42, 3½ hr.): If it's the countryside you crave, escape to Peggy's Cove, a picturesque hamlet along the rugged Atlantic shoreline. The village sits on solid rock just above the crashing surf, and a kilted guide will lead a walking tour along the craggy coastline, with its bold glacier-formed outcroppings of granite rubbed smooth by eons of crashing waves, and past the town's impressive lighthouse. It's one of the most photographed spots in Canada. The scenic bus ride there and back affords passengers a nice view of Nova Scotia's quaint countryside.

ON YOUR OWN: WITHIN WALKING DISTANCE

There's plenty to do in this charming town on foot. While you can certainly sign up for the ship's guided walking tours, you can also just grab a free walking-tour map in the terminal. It's a good idea to start your tour at nearby **Pier 21** (which is likely right next to your ship), Halifax's version of Ellis Island, where more than a million immigrants have entered Canada. A few steps from here is the very worthwhile **Maritime Museum of the Atlantic,** 1675 Lower Water St. (© **902/424-7490;** http://museum. gov.ns.ca/mma), where exhibits include an impressive collection of *Titanic* artifacts and ship models. There's also a fascinating exhibit on the incredible **explosion** that leveled much of the city in 1917, when a French munitions ship collided with a Norwegian steamer. Admission is US$7 (C$8) adults. Other walkable attractions in town include the oldest continually operating saltwater ferry (since 1752) and North America's oldest operating naval clock, dating back to 1772.

The 17-acre Victorian-style **Public Gardens,** at Spring Garden and South Park streets, are also worthwhile, as is the 1750-built **St. Paul's church,** 1749 Argyle St. (© **902/429-2240**), the oldest Protestant church in Canada. Nearby is the **Chapel of Our Lady of Sorrows,** South and South Park streets (© **902/865-6663**), built in 1 day (Aug 1, 1843) by 2,000 men. At 1672 Barrington St., you can see one of the buildings put up in the late 1800s by George Wright, who was 1 of 33 millionaires on the maiden voyage of the doomed *Titanic.* A stroll through the **Halifax Citadel** (© **902/426-5080**), built between 1820 and 1856 in the shape of a star, is another must. Admission is US$7.25 (C$9). The fortress successfully defended Halifax Harbor, and the fortress was never attacked. You can still enjoy the panoramic views its strategic position affords, plus at noon daily a cannon dating back to the fort's early days is fired.

When we were in Halifax last year we saw a simple sign that said "Brewery Tour," with an arrow pointing left. When we followed it, we found ourselves at **Alexander Keith's Nova Scotia Brewery,** 1496 Lower Water St. (© **902/455-1474;** www.keiths. ca), the oldest brewery in North America, where we had the most amazing brewery tour we'd ever taken. Unlike the typical walk-through of a modern plant with a few historical exhibits, Keith's has restored significant portions of its plant to the way they looked when Keith established his business in 1820. Costumed actors take you through grain storehouses, historic brewing displays, and residential rooms en route to the 19th-century barroom for a sip (or two, or three) of Keith's brew. It's entertaining and fun. Tours run every half-hour May through early October from noon until 8 or 9pm (until 4pm Sun). Admission is US$7.50 (C$9.95).

ON YOUR OWN: BEYOND THE PORT AREA

For information on **Peggy's Cove,** see "Best Cruise Line Shore Excursions," above. Nearer to Halifax is the **Fairview Cemetery,** where 120 *Titanic* victims were buried in 1912. At least one of your ship's organized excursions will generally include a stop here, with the guide explaining Halifax's role in the ocean disaster.

SHOPPING

Locally made maritime handicrafts such as hooked rugs, pottery, wood items, quilt work and hand-knit woolens are big in Halifax. With its Scottish roots, you'll also find plenty of tartans and gifts made of pewter. There is no shortage of shops in and around the waterfront. Two indoor malls are located near the Grand Parade—**Scotia Square Mall** and **Barrington Place Shops,** flanking Barrington Street near the intersection of Duke Street. Another downtown mall, the 85-shop **Park Lane Shopping Centre,** is on Spring Garden Road about 1 block from the Public Gardens. For souvenir shopping, head to the **Historic Properties buildings** on the waterfront; for idle browsing, try the shops on and around Spring Garden Road between Brunswick Street and South Park Street.

3 Newport, Rhode Island

Where the rich retreated to before the Hamptons became hot, Newport was *the* place for America's wealthy aristocrats to summer at the turn-of-the-20th-century. From the Vanderbilts to the Astors, anyone who was anyone had a summer mansion here, a la 40-room palaces that the rich quaintly called cottages.

Sitting on the southern tip of Aquidneck Island in Narragansett Bay and connected to the mainland by three bridges, it's not difficult to understand how this picture-postcard seaside setting drew the elite who could have summered anywhere they darn well pleased. During the Colonial period Newport rivaled Boston and New York as a center of New World trade and prosperity. Wealthy industrialists, railroad tycoons, coal magnates, financiers, and robber barons were drawn to the area, especially between the Civil War and World War I. The Newport elite loved their extravagant pleasure yachts, and competition among them established Newport's reputation as a sailing center. In 1851, the schooner *America* defeated a British boat in a race around the Isle of Wight. The prize trophy became known as the America's Cup, which remained in the possession of the New York Yacht Club (with an outpost in Newport) until 1983. In that shocking summer, *Australia II* snatched the Cup away from *Liberty* in the last race of a four-out-of-seven series. An American team regained the cup in 1987, but in 1995 a New Zealand crew won it back. The strong U.S. yachting tradition has endured despite the loss of the Cup, and Newport continues as a bastion of world sailing and a destination for long-distance races. As you're shuttled through Newport's colorful harbor between your ship anchored offshore and the downtown pier, you may notice the handful of 12-meter America's Cup racing yachts moored in the harbor.

Today, Newport offers the beautiful sea and its scenic rocky coastline, as well as a bustling scene in town, all cobblestone streets, shady trees, cute cafes, and historical homes. Much of the hubbub is along the waterfront and its parallel streets: America's Cup Avenue and Thames Street. (The latter used to be pronounced "Tems," in the British manner, but was Americanized to "Thaymz" after the Revolution.) Though millions visit every year, Newport has managed to retain much of its small-town charm, unlike some ports, and hasn't been overtaken by T-shirt shops and fast-food outlets. Despite Newport's prevailing image as a collection of ridiculously ornate mansions and regattas of sailing ships inaccessible to all but the rich and famous, the city is, for the most part, middle class and moderately priced.

COMING ASHORE Ships large and small are calling on Newport these days, including the 2,600-passenger *Queen Mary 2* and *Golden Princess,* one of the largest cruise vessels in the world. No matter their size, all cruise ships anchor just a short distance offshore from downtown Newport, and shuttle passengers through the colorful harbor to the tender pier just a block from the information center (23 America's Cup Ave.); a kiosk is also often set up on the pier. You'll find all of Newport's most popular sights, including the famed mansions, within a short walk or drive of the downtown area.

GETTING AROUND After the pleasant trip through the harbor to shore (an excursion in and of itself), step off the tender pier and you're in the heart of Newport. Walk around the historic town by the sea to have a look at the 18th- and 19th-century architecture, or, if your goal is seeing the mansions and you don't want to sign up for your ship's guided tour, you can jump on the **RIPTA** (Rhode Island Public Transportation Authority) No. 67 vintage-style trackless trolley-bus that runs past many of the mansions as well as other significant important attractions. It'll cost you $6 for an all-day hop on/hop off pass, or $18 for a family of four. As the bus makes it way to the mansions, it stops at other historical attractions, including the 242-year-old Touro Synagogue (see below). If you want a taxi to drop you off at the mansions, try **Yellow Cab Service** (© **401/846-1500**). Another great way to get around town and out to the mansions is by bicycle. Among several rental shops is **Ten Speed Spokes,** 18 Elm St. (© **401/847-5609**).

BEST CRUISE LINE SHORE EXCURSIONS

Newport Walking Tour ($22, 1½ hr.): An expert Newport guide takes your group through a 10-block area of Colonial Newport, noted for nearly 200 restored 18th- and 19th-century Colonial and Victorian homes and landmarks. You will walk along the city's quaint and shady streets where no buses are allowed, and hear how tobacco heiress Doris Duke and many other residents led the fight to rescue this once neglected area. Stroll by the superb 1726 Trinity Church; architect Peter Harrison's Brick Market; the Touro Synagogue, the oldest Jewish house of worship in the country; the Quaker Meeting House; and the Old Colony House.

Guided Cliff Walk Tour ($29, 1½ hr.): If you'd like a guide who can regale you with tales of what used to go on during the bygone days of the Gilded Era, sign up for this tour. Stroll along a mile and a quarter of the path that wends between Newport's rocky coastline and the "backyards" of many of Bellevue Avenue's palatial cottages.

Mansion Tour ($59, 3½ hr.): This tour visits two of the city's fabled mansions— **Marble House,** featuring more than 500,000 square feet of white marble, and **The Breakers,** an over-the-top Italian Renaissance palace, which includes two rooms originally constructed in France and reassembled in Newport. Other mansion tours may include a different combination of estates.

ON YOUR OWN: WITHIN WALKING DISTANCE

This is a place for walking, if there ever was one. If you're reasonably fit, the famed mansions on Bellevue and Ocean avenues are within walking distance of the tender pier (1–4 miles), or you can take the trolley or a taxi (see "Getting Around," above). Mostly operated by the **Preservation Society of Newport County,** 11 European-palace-inspired summer cottages (as they were called by their humble owners) are open for touring, including the most famous, **The Breakers,** Ochre Point Avenue, east of Bellevue Avenue (© **401/847-1000**). Admission is $15. Commissioned in 1893 by Cornelius Vanderbilt, who made his millions in steamships and railroads, the marble 70-room Italian-Renaissance-style mansion perched above the sea was designed by Richard Morris Hunt, the Beaux Arts master who also designed the Metropolitan Museum of Art in New York City. Many of the other mansions are situated along Bellevue Avenue. **The Elms** and **Marble House** offer self-guided audio tours (admission $10), while the others have tour guides on-site who lead a new tour every 10 to 15 minutes. If you want something different from the plain vanilla tour, call ahead and reserve a spot on the Rooftop and Behind-the-Scenes tours at The Elms, to get a fascinating glimpse of how the staff lived and worked at this French-châteaux-style mansion built by Pennsylvania coal magnate Edward Berwind. For information on this tour, combination tours, and background info on most of Newport's mansions, call © **401/847-1000** or go to **www.newportmansions.org**.

Noteworthy private mansions open to the public include, **Astors Beechwood,** 580 Bellevue Ave. (© **401/846-3772**; www.astorsbeechwood.com), where daily tours are led by actors portraying the wealthy Astor family in the year 1891; the 60-room **Belcourt Castle,** 657 Bellevue Ave. (© **401/846-0669**; www.belcourtcastle.com), built from the inherited fortunes of August Belmont; and **Rough Point,** 680 Bellevue Ave. (© **401/849-7300**; www.newportrestoration.org), the former estate of heiress Doris Duke set along the Cliff Walk and featuring changing exhibits each year, such as one entitled "Jet Set to Jeans: The Wardrobe of Doris Duke." (Visitors wishing to go to Rough Point must purchase their tickets at **Newport Visitors Information Center,** 23 America's Cup Ave.—1 block from cruise ship arrivals pier—and then take a shuttle from the center to Rough Point. Shuttle departs every 20 min.)

A great way to visit the mansions and have a scenic walk to boot is to follow the 3.5-mile **Cliff Walk,** which meanders between Newport's rocky coastline and many of the town's Gilded Age mansion estates. It provides better views of many of them than can be seen from the street. Traversing its length, high above the crashing surf, is more than a stroll but less than an arduous hike. For the full 3.5-mile length, start at the access point near the intersection of Memorial Boulevard and Eustis Avenue; it's about a mile from the pier to the starting point. For a shorter walk, end at the Forty Steps (an access point between the path and the street), which is at the end of Narragansett Avenue, off Bellevue. If you want to do the entire Cliff Walk, but don't want to walk all the way back to the pier when you've reached the end, consider taking the trolley back (grab it on Bellevue Ave., just 1½ blocks from the walk). The round-trip trek could take 6 or 7 hours; keep in mind that there are some mildly rugged sections to negotiate, no facilities, and no phones. A number of mansions, such as the Breakers, Rosecliff, Astors Beechwood, Marble House, and Rough Point, are just on the other side of the walk; others are a few blocks inland from the path.

If you're up for a shorter stroll, just a few blocks from the pier is one of the most impressive concentrations of original 18th- and 19th-century Colonial, Federal, and Victorian houses in America, many of them designated National Historic Sites. Called **Historic Hill,** this section of town rises from America's Cup Avenue, along the waterfront, to Bellevue Avenue, the beginning of Victorian Newport. Spring Street serves as the Hill's main drag, and it's a treasure trove of Colonial, Georgian, and Federal structures. Chief among its visual delights is the 1725 **Trinity Church,** at the corner of Church Street. Said to have been influenced by the work of the legendary British architect Christopher Wren, it certainly reflects that inspiration in its belfry and distinctive spire, seen from all over downtown Newport and dominating Queen Anne Square, a greensward that runs down to the waterfront. You'll find that many of the historical buildings are owned by the **Doris Duke–founded Newport Restoration Foundation;** Duke spent her life giving away the fortune she inherited from her father's tobacco business (for more details, go to **www.newportrestoration.org**).

Whether you hop on the tourist trolley, sign up for your ship's bus tour, rent a bicycle, or walk, on route to the mansions you can also have a peak at several other worthy attractions, including the **Gothic Church of St. Mary's,** 70 Church St., where John F. Kennedy and Jacqueline Bouvier married; the 242-year-old **Touro Synagogue,** 85 Touro St. (© **401/847-4794;** www.tourosynagogue.org), said to be the country's oldest continually operating synagogue; and the **International Tennis Hall of Fame,** 194 Bellevue Ave. (© **401/849-3990;** www.tennisfame.org), one of the only places in North America where you can play on a grass court. Admission is $8. For tons of info on sightseeing in Newport, **www.gonewport.com** is a great resource.

SHOPPING

At the heart of the downtown waterfront, Bannister's Wharf, Bowen's Wharf, and Brick Marketplace have dozens of fairly generic stores. For a more interesting shopping experience, head to the shops along **Lower Thames Street.** For example, **J. T.'s Ship Chandlery** outfits recreational sailors with sea chests, ship lanterns, and foulweather gear. **Aardvark Antiques** specializes in salvaged architectural components. Books, nautical charts, and sailing videos are offered at **Armchair Sailor;** for vintage clothing, visit **Cabbage Rose. Spring Street** is noted for its antiques shops and purveyors of crafts, jewelry, and folk art. Spring intersects with **Franklin Street,** which harbors even more antiques shops in its short length.

4 Saint John, New Brunswick

Set along the Bay of Fundy at the mouth of the St. John River in New Brunswick, the city of Saint John (and it's always spelled out so as not to be confused with St. John's in Newfoundland) is a popular port of call on many big-ship itineraries. New Brunswick's largest city, Saint John sits along a sizeable commercial harbor and is the center of much of the province's industry. Like Halifax, the city was an important shipbuilding hub around the turn of the 20th century, and today its deep-water harbor can accommodate the world's largest liners

Don't expect a picture-postcard-perfect place overflowing with gardens and neat homes—Saint John is predominantly an industrial city. The large shipping terminals, oil storage facilities, and paper mills are the backdrop to the waterfront area. Still, if you make the effort, you'll see that the downtown boasts wonderfully elaborate Victorian flourishes on the rows of commercial buildings, like intricate brickwork along the cornices. A handful of impressive mansions lord over side streets, their interiors a forest of intricate woodcarving—appropriate for the timber barons who built them.

Like Halifax, the first Europeans to settle the area were the French, when Samuel de Champlain led an exploration party into the Bay of Fundy and founded the first French settlement in North America in 1604. A hundred years later, the British were on the scene, capturing Saint John, which, in 1785, became Canada's first incorporated city.

COMING ASHORE   Ships dock right at the **Pugsley Cruise Terminal,** which at press time was being rebuilt, in the industrial heart of the city, just steps from the city's downtown.

GETTING AROUND   If you haven't signed up for an organized tour, you can walk right into town (on top of the streets or via an underground passageway that connects many of Saint John's sites). Or opt for a 1-hour city highlights tour on the vintage bus-style trolleys or horse-drawn trolleys that meet the ship. If you'd rather travel by taxi, they queue up at the docks and work on set rates, depending on where you're going. Taxi tours are about US$30 (C$35) an hour for one to five passengers. If you need to call a taxi, try **Coastal Taxi Limited** (© **506/635-1144**) or **Diamond Taxi** (© **506/ 648-8888**). There's also a 2-hour **city bus tour** that departs twice a day from Barbour's General Store downtown for US$12 (C$17).

BEST CRUISE LINE SHORE EXCURSIONS

Historical Walking Tour (US$29, 2 hr.): See the restored historic district known as Trinity Royal and the bustling City Market that survives from the late 1800s. A bus takes groups to the farthest destination, the Loyalist Burial Ground, where the walk starts. Sights also include King's Square, Trinity Church, Barbour's General Store (a restored 19th-c. country store), Red Schoolhouse, and historic Prince William Street.

Reversing Falls Rapids & City Sights (US$99, 3 hr.): Reversing Falls is a much-photographed spot where the Bay of Fundy meets the St. John River, and strong tidal conditions cause harbor currents to reverse. This large tidal swing means some 2 billion gallons of water surge into the Bay twice a day—that's 2 *billion*. An amazing thing to witness. The tour begins with an orientation drive through Saint John, stopping at the Old City Market (open since 1876), before heading to Fallsview Park, donning life jackets and raingear, and boarding your high-speed jet boat for a ride over and around the rapids. You can take the jet boat ride without signing onto a tour by contacting **Reversing Falls Jet Boat Rides** (© **506/634-8987;** www.jetboatrides.com); the 20-minute rides cost US$25 (C$30) adults, US$20 (C$25) children.

Canadian Beer Tasting & Saint John Highlights Tour (US$46, 3 hr.): Heads up, beer-lovers: This is your chance to sample Canadian beers and enjoy a famous local Irish pub, O'Leary's. Also included is a drive around the Saint John area, time at the Old City Market, and a visit to the famous Reversing Falls.

ON YOUR OWN: WITHIN WALKING DISTANCE

A great way to get the lay of the land is by taking a 1-hour horse-drawn trolley or San Francisco–style bus trolley ride through the city (the later, which you must book through the cruise line); afterwards you can explore on your own. From the open-air carriage that seats just a handful of couples, the guide discusses the sights along the way, from the **Loyalist (or Old) Burial Grounds,** with gravestones dating back to

1784, to the flower- and tree-filled **King Square** park, which was designed in 1848 in the shape of the Union Jack to show loyalty to England. You'll see one of the city's top attractions, the **Old City Market,** a cavernous building dating back to 1876, as well as the 1825-built **St. John's Stone Church,** which was, like many buildings at the time, made from ships' ballast. Plus, you'll see Victorian homes and Georgian-style mansions, such as the 1881-built Loyalist House, on and around Germain Street. Sign up for the horse-drawn or bus-style trolley tours aboard ship (or you can just walk outside and hop on a horse-drawn trolley if you prefer winging it). You can see these same sights by walking around on your own or signing up for a guided walking tour, though only the bus-style trolley will take you to such sites as **Fort Howe,** a British fort built in 1777 overlooking the harbor and city, and the Reversing Falls Park.

Of the handful of museums in Saint John, the important one to visit is the **New Brunswick Museum,** on Market Square and open daily. Established in 1842, it's the oldest continuing museum in Canada. The original museum, known as the Gesner Institute, was begun by naturalist, Abraham Gesner. His natural history collection still exists today within the collections. Exhibits include a marine mammals gallery, whose focal point is "Delilah," the full skeletal remains of a 40-foot North Atlantic right whale that beached off Grand Manan in 1992. Other displays include local and Canadian art, plus you'll find the best collection of Loyalist artifacts on the North American continent, and the largest collection of ships' portraiture in Canada. Don't miss a peak at the cool tidal tube in the lobby that's connected to the harbor. Water in the tube rises and falls with the tide. Admission is US$4.50 (C$6).

ON YOUR OWN: BEYOND THE PORT AREA

If you don't sign on to one of the ship's shore excursions, you can walk to the Reversing Falls via the new **Harbour Passage trail** that winds along the waterfront. The trail starts at the Market Square boardwalk, about 5 minutes from Pugsley Terminal. Though not the most scenic walk you'll ever take (and not half as exciting as the jetboat ride), it's convenient and will take about 40 minutes; once at Reversing Falls you can opt to take a water taxi back to the ship (you can take the water taxi to the Falls as well), but keep in mind that the taxis operate on a fixed schedule. You can also catch it at the **Market Square Boardwalk** (**www.sjwaterfront.com** has more information on this trail system). To immerse yourself in an even more natural side of New Brunswick, book an excursion or take a taxi to **Irving Nature Park** (about a 15-min. drive), where a scenic and winding coastal road and walking trails bring you up-close to the Bay of Fundy's wildlife, including harbor seals and/or porpoises.

SHOPPING

Within a 10-minute walk of the cruise terminal, you'll find more than 100 shops, including those at the **Saint John Old City Market, Market Square, Brunswick Square,** and the stores on **King Street** and historic **Prince William Street.** You'll find the classic sweatshirts and baseball hat–type souvenirs as well as art galleries, antiques shops, and boutiques selling jewelry and handicrafts.

16

U.S. River Cruise Routes

In addition to sailing in the Caribbean, Central America, Alaska, Baja's Sea of Cortez, and New England/Canada, many of the small ships reviewed in chapter 8 also offer cruises on America's great rivers, visiting historic towns and sailing through gorgeous countryside. Experiences range from real Americana on the Mississippi and Erie Canal to a totally sybaritic experience sailing between vineyards in California's wine country. As these rivers cover a good chunk of the continental United States, and because each ship makes different stops along the way, we've limited ourselves to giving you a sort of virtual float along each river, with a sampling of the highlights seen on many regional cruises.

1 The California Wine Country

San Francisco's Bay Area easily qualifies as one of the world's greatest natural harbors, its shores fringed with national parklands and some of America's most prized residential communities. At the bay's eastern end, the Sacramento River Delta leads to the **Napa and Sonoma Valleys,** the United States' leading wine-growing region. While a driving holiday is a fine way to explore redwood and vineyard country, a cruise includes behind-the-scenes visits, expert presentations ashore and on board, and, of course, a designated driver. As an added benefit, many of the region's real scenic delights, including the graceful bridges and lovely islands of San Francisco Bay, are at their best when viewed from the water. Wine Country cruises draw mostly American passengers in the 30s to 70s age range.

Many of Napa and Sonoma's vineyards trace their ancestries back to immigrants who realized the soil and climate were perfect for growing European varietals from France, Italy, Germany, and Switzerland. New hybrid vines developed later, resulting in today's booming U.S. wine industry and the proliferation of prosperous wine estates, some of them designed in a modern California-ranch style, others Spanish Colonial or Spanish Mission, wooden Victorian, or European château. The sites you'll visit will vary depending on the date you sail, but most departures have a similar routing.

San Francisco (www.sfvisitor.org), the City by the Bay, is a must-see from the water. Its parallel streets run from the shore steeply up Knob, Russian, and Telegraph hills, with North Beach, Marina, and the Financial District sandwiched in between. The harbor entrance is flanked by dramatic natural headlands and spanned by the graceful **Golden Gate Bridge,** its towers often poking through a tongue of mist sweeping in from the colder Pacific.

The captain usually takes his ship under the span and sails until the ocean swells begin to rock, then makes a 180-degree turn to hug the **Sausalito** waterfront for several miles along the Marin County shore. A walk from the pier reveals Sausalito's varied lifestyles, from ramshackle houseboats to some of the most expensive waterfront property in America, and also lets you explore the city's popular boutique and art gallery district. An organized excursion visits the U.S. Army Corps of Engineers, caretakers of the inland waterways, where a 1.5-acre three-dimensional hydraulic Bay Model lays out the Bay's intricate water control system. From Sausalito, coaches drive north into the **Muir Woods National Monument** for a stroll amongst the California Redwoods, the world's tallest trees, set in a canyon beneath Mt. Tamalpais. A pedestrian tunnel has been carved through one trunk of amazing girth.

Sailing from Sausalito, the ship passes Tiburon, an upscale bedroom suburb ranging up the slopes of a peninsula jutting into the bay, then skirts **Alcatraz,** the once-notorious island prison that's now a national historic park. Nearby **Angel Island,** even more impressive in height and size, and once the Ellis Island of the West, now provides recreational facilities for picnic and hikes. From here, ships usually turn north, sailing past Berkeley and under the Richmond–San Rafael Bridge into a widening San Pablo Bay. Some cruises will sail through the narrow Carquinez Strait into the Sacramento Delta, an expansive area of marshlands and natural and man-made waterways. An early morning is likely to give rise to tule fog, a heavy misty that rises from the swampy bulrushes, and then burns off in the morning sun.

Your ship may dock at Vallejo at the mouth of the Napa River or continue sailing for several hours to land closer to the wine-growing region. From here, buses take passengers on full-day trips then return to the ship in the late afternoon.

The **Napa and Sonoma valleys** (**www.napavalley.org** or **www.sonomacounty. com**) run north by northwest between a ridge of low mountains rising not much more than 2,500 feet. The region is a major tourist area, more so in the fall during the harvest season and to a lesser extent in the green spring. While many of the vineyard names may be unfamiliar (Benziger, Markham, St. Supéry, and Schramsberg, for instance), you'll recognize the chardonnays, merlots, pinot noirs, and zinfandels they produce. And you'll get plenty of chances to sample them, either via **wine tastings** or by sipping the vintages chosen for dinner. These will include both table- and premium-quality varieties, including sparkling wines created using the champagne method.

A tour of **Benziger Vineyards** (**www.benziger.com**) includes a tractor-pulled tram tour into the Sonoma Hills for terrific views of the surrounding vineyard landscape, a blanket of color in the autumn. The **Markham Vineyards (www.markhamvineyards. com**) dates to 1874, when French immigrant Jean Laurent started his Laurent Winery on the site. Some visits include lunch in the 1879 stone cellar barrel room, which houses aging red wine.

St. Supéry (**www.stsupery.com**) is owned by third-generation French winemakers and is noted for its cabernet sauvignon and sauvignon blanc. Its 1880 Victorian house is on the National Register of Historic Places and includes an art gallery. **Schramsberg** (**www.schramsberg.com**) has a garden setting and produces well-regarded sparkling wine using the champagne method. Fermenting takes place along thousands of feet of tunnels dug by Chinese laborers brought in to work during the 19th century. Robert Louis Stevenson called Schramsberg's wine "bottled poetry."

The Chinese also helped to build the rail line that the **Napa Valley Wine Train** (**www.winetrain.com**) uses for its 30-mile town-and-country route. Some cruise departures include a ride in the wine-red lounge cars and full dinners while the train travels the Napa Valley.

If you're up early enough, your arrival back in San Francisco at the end of your cruise will probably coincide with dawn breaking over one of the world's most beautiful cities.

With luck, you've planned to stay on for a few days rather than rushing off to the airport. You can choose a location near Fisherman's Wharf, Ghiardelli Square, and Pier 39 or a more central one near Union Square. Both areas are close to those little cable cars that rise halfway to the stars. See chapter 9 for some great hotel picks in town.

LINES SAILING THESE ROUTES   **Clipper Cruise Line** (p. 342), **Cruise West** (p. 349), and **American Safari Cruises** (p. 337) all sail itineraries here in fall.

2 The Columbia & Snake Rivers, Pacific Northwest

The Columbia-Snake system is one of America's most important river systems, second only to the Mississippi-Missouri in the size of the area it drains. The Columbia River flows 1,200 miles from the Canadian Rockies in southeast British Columbia into Washington, and then forms the border with Oregon on its way to the Pacific. The 1,000-mile Snake River starts in Yellowstone National Park and flows through Idaho into eastern Washington, where it meets the Columbia.

The two rivers have historically served as the primary artery for east-west travel in the Pacific Northwest, used by the Nez Perce Indians as well as by later explorers, fur traders, settlers, military expeditions, and missionaries. Settlers came in increasing numbers in the few years prior to the 1846 Oregon Treaty, and in 1859, Oregon became the 33rd state. Washington, once part of Oregon, was organized as a separate territory in 1853, but did not become the 42nd state until 1889.

Today, the Columbia-Snake corridor provides a fascinating trip into more varied landscapes than one will find along any North American river. Beginning at the Pacific Ocean breakers, the river mouth near Astoria begins as a broad bay, narrows upriver to a more natural stream, and then squeezes dramatically through the deep **Columbia Gorge (www.fs.fed.us/r6/columbia/forest).** Thickly forested slopes rise to flanking high cliffs and snow melting into water cascades into pencil-thin waterfalls. The river's surface is turbulent and the winds strong, but a series of dams, construction on the first of which started during the Great Depression, tames the flow into a series of separate pools. **Navigation locks** lift boats and barges while parallel fish ladders provide a bypass for salmon heading upstream to spawn, and for the young heading in the other direction, toward the Pacific.

Beyond the gorge, the land becomes drier, and with the right soil and an ideal climate, **vineyards** have burgeoned in both Washington and Oregon to create the country's second-largest wine producing region in the U.S. after California. **Wildlife** is abundant here, as hundreds of thousands of birds come to roost and nest, especially in the **Umatilla Wildlife Refuge (http://midcolumbiariver.fws.gov/Umatillapage. htm).** By the time your ship reaches the Snake River, the land on either side shows few signs of habitation, instead rising from the waterline in layers of basalt laid down millions of years ago, forming multicolored buttes and mesas.

Portland, Oregon (www.pova.com), with a population of just over a half-million, is the embarkation city for nearly all Columbia-Snake cruises. The city has kept its human scale better than most, maintained a vibrant downtown and much of its traditional architecture, and prevented major expressways from slicing through its heart. Best known as the City of Roses, Portland boasts 250 parks, gardens, and greenways, and, since 1907, has celebrated the annual Portland Rose Festival for several weeks each June with an extravagant floral parade, music, car and boat races, and visits by U.S. Navy ships.

The city's core is **Pioneer Courthouse Square,** with a prosperous late-19th-century feel and street life generated by stores, offices, restaurants, and traditional-style hotels. On Saturdays and Sundays, the so-called **Saturday Market** is a huge draw for its open-air handicraft, clothing, and jewelry stalls.

High up and to the west of downtown, **Washington Park**'s terraced gardens display 400 varieties of roses, usually at their blooming peak during June and July and again in September and October.

Upon leaving Portland, cruises sail overnight downriver to where the widening Columbia meets the Pacific Ocean and call at **Astoria,** Oregon, tying up at a pier adjacent to the Columbia Bar lightship *Columbia* and Coast Guard cutter *Steadfast,* both of which are open for visitors. The **Columbia River Maritime Museum** is part of the pier complex, exhibiting the history of Columbia River trade in ship models, drawings, and photographs. Don't miss the 20-minute walk up Coxcomb Hill to 125-foot **Astoria Column,** which dominates the landscape from its 600-foot elevation. Erected in 1926 to mark the location of the first permanent American settlement west of the Rockies, it was designed by New York architect Electus D. Litchfield after the Trajan Column in Rome. Italian artist Attilio Pusterla created a bas-relief mural that scrolls around the column to depict the history of the town.

Organized excursions head downriver to **Fort Clatsop (www.nps.gov/focl),** a reconstructed stockade where Lewis and Clark spent 4 wet winter months in 1805–1806. Another stop, the seaside resort of **Cannon Beach,** is a big draw for its wooden weathered-cedar shopping district with typical craft-type boutiques.

Longview, Washington, gives access to **Mt. St. Helens (www.fs.fed.us/gpnf/msh nvm),** the site of the May 18, 1980, volcanic eruption that in minutes reduced the mountain's height by about 1,000 feet. The drive uphill winds through increasingly scarred hillsides covered in lava, ash, mud, and 150 square miles of destroyed forest to an interpretive center overlooking the cloud-enshrouded mountaintop and deep into a valley wasteland.

Bonneville Dam (www.nwp.usace.army.mil/op/b), dedicated by President Franklin Delano Roosevelt in 1937, signaled the first major WPA undertaking by the U.S. Army Corps of Engineers to create a safe passage through the Cascade Rapids. The dam created 48-mile-long Lake Bonneville, and its hydroelectric plants generate power sufficient to light 40,000 homes. The Visitors Center screens a slide film showing the dam under construction and describing how the salmon fish ladders work.

Farther upriver, the **Columbia Gorge Discovery Center (www.gorgediscovery. org)** exhibits the area's history and geology in a film that reveals how the Columbia Gorge was formed by violent volcanic upheavals and raging floods. Another film shows the building of the Columbia River Scenic Highway, which leads to Multnomah Falls. An exhibit illustrates how Lewis and Clark equipped their expedition.

Six thousand feet up the slopes of 11,245 foot **Mt. Hood (www.mthood.org)** stands Timberline Lodge, a timber-and-stone WPA hotel project built in 1932. The view is north to 12,307-foot, Mt. Adams, part of a line of volcano-formed mountains that include Mt. St. Helens and Mt. Rainier.

At The **Dalles Lock & Dam,** an excursion crosses the river to **Maryhill Museum (www.maryhillmuseum.org),** located high above the river in Washington. A Midwesterner named Sam Hill, son-in-law of James J. Hill of the Great Northern Railroad, established a museum exhibiting Queen Marie of Romania's royal regalia, Russian Orthodox icons, Rodin sculptures, a collection of 250 chess sets, miniature fashion costumes on stage sets, and Indian clothing, baskets, and weapons.

Pendleton, Oregon **(www.pendleton-oregon.org)** includes a stop at the roundup grounds for authentic Indian war dances, bareback riding, bucking broncos, calf roping, steer wrestling, or skits depicting respective male and female roles during pioneering days. In town, **Pendleton Underground** is an odd curiosity tour that shows how the Chinese laborers were relegated to living in a rabbit warren of rooms and passages under the streets and not permitted outside after dark. The Pendleton woolens factory tour ends in the Pendleton shops.

The **Tamastslikt Cultural Institute** presents a variety of Native American traditions, including dancing, drumming, and storytelling. Exhibits include horse regalia, war bonnets, bows, and demonstrations of saddle making. The **Whitman Mission,** established by Presbyterian missionaries, was the scene in 1847 of a massacre by the Cayuse, and the site thoughtfully tells the traumatic story of cultural clash. Nearby **Fort Walla Walla** exhibits a collection of carefully restored and re-created buildings that include a schoolhouse, doctor's office, railroad station, and houses arranged in a closed compound. Other buildings house farm equipment and a fire engine once drawn by a 33-mule team.

Finally, after passing through four **Snake River locks and dams,** your ship reaches the end of deep-water navigation at the border towns of Lewiston, Idaho, and Clarkston, Washington, 465 miles upriver from the Pacific Ocean. From here, an all-day **jet boat ride** heads into **Hells Canyon,** Idaho **(www.hellscanyonvisitor.com).** Set aside as a National Recreation Area, the Snake River, starting out as sluggish, increasingly becomes a fast-flowing stream of twisting rapids with 20mph currents. The high bluffs and mountains on either side increase in height, creating a canyon 7,900 feet deep—1,900 feet deeper than the Grand Canyon. Passengers are likely to see bighorn sheep standing still on rocky ledges, mule deer down by the water, eagles and osprey overhead, and Nez Perce Indian petroglyphs inscribed on the flat rock surfaces depicting more bighorn sheep.

LINES SAILING THESE ROUTES   **American West Steamboat Company** (p. 341) operates here almost year-round, taking off only January. **Cruise West** (p. 349), **Glacier Bay Cruiseline** (p. 367), and **Lindblad Expeditions** (p. 374) offer cruises here in the spring and fall. Additionally, **American Rivers Cruise Line** (© **800/901-9152;** www.americanriverscruiseline.com), the new operator of the riverboat *Columbia Queen,* cruises here from March through New Year's.

3 The Hudson River, Erie Canal & Great Lakes

Inland waters cruises in the U.S. Northeast sail waterways such as the Hudson River, the Erie Canal, the St. Lawrence Seaway, and the Great Lakes. No single cruise takes in all of these, but most mix and match—for instance, sailing portions of the Hudson, the Erie Canal, and the St. Lawrence.

UP THE HUDSON

The navigable portion of the **Hudson River (www.hudsonriver.com)** extends for about 150 miles from Manhattan to Albany and Troy, New York. The river is considered to be an estuary as tidal effects reach the base of the canal locks above Albany, and saltwater content extends about 60 miles northward from Manhattan, and even farther during long periods of dry weather. On a cruise, one gets superb water-level views of the Hudson Valley, the towering New Jersey Palisades, the rugged Hudson Highlands, sprawling country estates, and the mighty fortress at West Point.

Leaving **Manhattan**'s West Side, ships skirt the majestic skyline and cruise past the Upper West Side (wave to us as you go by!) to pass under the two-level George Washington Bridge. **Palisades Interstate Park (www.njpalisades.org)** rises on the New Jersey side, an especially beautiful scene during fall foliage season. Fishermen will be out in force on weekends, and it is once again safe to eat the catch, though everyday consumption is not recommended. After passing Yonkers, the Hudson widens into the Tappan Zee, passing under the **Tappan Zee Bridge** carrying the New York State Thruway north to Albany and west to Buffalo.

Looking carefully, one may glimpse **Washington Irving's house** in the Hudson Valley town of Sunnyside; Victorian gothic **Lyndhurst Castle,** owned by the National Trust for Historic Preservation; and **Philipsburg Manor,** a former 17th-century Dutch farming complex. From the decks you get a long-range view north to the Hudson Highlands, and at Ossining the stone walls of **Sing Sing Prison** parallel the river. For information on these attractions, check online at **www.hudsonvalley.org**.

As your ship approaches Bear Mountain State Park on the left and the Bear Mountain Bridge, a flag rises above the trees marking the **Bear Mountain Inn.** The river becomes noticeably narrower, and it is here that the Hudson Highlands cross, and the channel under the Bear Mountain suspension bridge dramatically deepens to over 300 feet as the surrounding land rises steeply.

On the cliff tops opposite, the grounds of the United States Military Academy at **West Point (www.usma.edu)** begin, marked first by officers' houses, the Hotel Thayer, and then the gray stone fortress-style buildings. At the base of the cliff, a launch docked near the West Shore Line station brings cadets and officers across the Hudson to Garrison station for trains to New York. The colorful cluster of wooden Victorian buildings across the street from the Garrison depot served as the setting for Dolly's return to Yonkers in the film *Hello Dolly.* Most cruises stop at West Point for tours of the academy and historic Hudson Valley homes.

Rising from the river you'll see the grassy grounds and yellow Federal-style buildings of the **Boscobel Restoration (www.boscobel.org),** a museum of early American furniture and decorative arts. Nearby, the 18th- and 19th-century river town of **Cold Spring** is full of restaurants (including the **Hudson House River Inn**), antiques shops, and collectibles stores. If you come back on your own, it also makes a good base for hiking the Hudson Highlands.

North of Cold Spring is **Bannerman's Island (www.hudsonvalleyruins.org),** on which you'll find the ruins of a mock 19th-century Scottish castle and estate. Built by a New York arms and surplus merchant as an arsenal and country retreat, the island's buildings were destroyed in an explosion and subsequent fires, leaving behind the stabilized ruins one sees today.

At **Poughkeepsie (www.cityofpoughkeepsie.com),** nearby sites include **Franklin Roosevelt's Hyde Park house;** wife Eleanor's cottage a short distance away; and the **Culinary Institute of America,** one of the leading U.S. cooking schools.

The Hudson passes numerous **lighthouses** and small river towns en route to Albany, the New York State capital, where Rockefeller's **Empire State Plaza** looms large ahead. Not all cruises come this far, and those that do (the ACCL ships) simply pass by to begin their trek through the Erie Canal.

INTO THE ERIE CANAL

The Erie's highlights are the **Waterford Flight** of five locks lifting the ship 150 feet, old factory towns such as Amsterdam and Little Falls, and the 22-mile Oneida Lake crossing. From Syracuse to Buffalo, ships pass through **Montezuma Wildlife Refuge** (**www.fws.gov/r5mnwr**) for possible sightings of bald eagles and Canada geese, past restored canal towns such as Fairport and Pittsford, and through the original canal's small locks and stone-arched aqueducts. These last structures were built by Frederick Law Olmsted, whose most famous work was New York's Central Park. Turning into the Oswego Canal, the vast expanse of **Lake Ontario** is ahead, and soon one is threading amongst the beautiful **Thousand Islands** (**www.thousandislands.com**). Stops are made at Clayton's Antique Boat Museum and Upper Canada Village, with houses, churches, and public and farm buildings spanning 100 years of Canadian architecture and small-town life. Small ships share the **St. Lawrence Seaway** (**www.grandslacs-voiemaritime.com**) with huge lake carriers and lock through to Montréal for a stop and a landing at Bay of Eternity in the dramatic **Saguenay fjord.** From here, your ship returns upriver to disembark at **Québec City** (**www.quebecregion.com**).

THE GREAT LAKES

Until the mid-1960s, the five **Great Lakes** (**www.great-lakes.net**) were popular summer cruising grounds for Canadian and U.S.-flag ships, some of which dated back to before World War I. When these ships went out of service, the industry died until American Canadian Caribbean Line and Clipper Cruise Lines started offering cruises here again in the late 1990s. A great idea, but keep in mind that the lakes are large bodies of water, and small, shallow-draft coastal cruisers like these can get bounced around during summer storms.

One exception in the last few years has been the appearance of the 14,903-ton, 410-passenger *C. Columbus,* a more stable oceangoing cruise ship operated by **Hapag Lloyd** (www.hl-cruises.com). While she caters mainly to German-speaking passengers, two or three bilingual cruises are offered annually in September and October, with announcements, menus, programs, and shore excursions in English.

Great Lakes itineraries are varied and may begin in any number of ports, such as Toronto, Windsor/Detroit, or Chicago. The following ports-of-call sampling will give you some idea of what there is to be seen. Cruises originating at Toronto will pass from Lake Ontario through the **Welland Canal** locks to Lake Erie, and an excursion will run to **Niagara Falls** (**www.tourismniagara.com**), including a wet boat trip in the *Maid of the Mist* to the base of the falls.

As you pass into Lake Huron, you'll see **Tobermory** (**www.tobermory.org**), a fishing port settled by Scots in the early 19th century and the center for a resort region in the beautiful island-studded Georgian Bay. **Mackinac Island** (**www.mackinacisland. org**) is entirely car-free and a popular summer resort. Its centerpiece, the venerable **Grand Hotel,** is one of the great hotels of North America, built in the 1890s and still maintaining its high standards. **Sault Ste. Marie,** strategically placed between lakes Huron and Superior, is the site for the **Soo Locks,** transited on some cruises that sail into the largest of the lakes. The Algoma Central rail excursion from the Soo into the North Country's **Agawa Canyon** (**www.agawacanyontourtrain.com**) is a highly scenic trip and includes a picnic lunch.

Large cities feature on all cruises in this region, including **Detroit** (**www.visit detroit.com**) for the Ford Museum and Deerfield Village, **Milwaukee** (**www. milwaukee.org**) for its German heritage and art museum, and **Chicago** (**www. chicago.il.org**) for its outstanding architecture, lakefront skyline, museums, neighborhoods, and the Chicago River. ACCL ships are the only ones to continue west across Illinois via an intricate series of waterways to the Upper Mississippi River and on south to New Orleans.

LINES SAILING THESE ROUTES **Clipper Cruise Line** (p. 342) offers cruises on the Hudson and the Great Lakes via the St. Lawrence Seaway. **American Canadian Caribbean Line** (p. 329) uses the Hudson to reach the Erie Canal for the passage across New York State to the Great Lakes and St. Lawrence Valley. **American Cruise Lines** (p. 336) cruises the Hudson River during the autumn. **Hapag-Lloyd** (see above; www.hl-cruises.com) does Great Lakes cruises.

4 The Mississippi River System

The **Mississippi River system (www.nps.gov/miss)** consists of some 50 rivers and tributaries, seven of which—the Atchafalaya, Arkansas, Ohio, Tennessee, Cumberland, Missouri, and Illinois—are navigable for considerable distances. Known as the Western Rivers because they formed part of the original American West, their drainage basin covers an area of 1,245,000 square miles or a full 41% of the contiguous 48 states, and includes all or parts of 31 states and 2 Canadian provinces. The Lower Mississippi is defined as the 954 miles between the mouth of the river just in from the Gulf of Mexico and the junction with the Ohio River. **New Orleans** is the principal embarkation port and terminus for most Lower Mississippi River cruises, its boat landing convenient to downtown via the Riverfront Trolley Line to Canal Street and thus into the French Quarter. See p. 483 for a more complete look at New Orleans.

THE LOWER MISSISSIPPI

Sailing from New Orleans, the heavily commercial waterway gives way to rural, mostly flat southern Louisiana. The river, however, remains a remarkable commercial artery used by the world's most impressive tow ships. As many as 30 to 40 barges may be strapped together to form a solid flotilla that can equal the carrying capacity of 1,800 to 2,400 tractor trailers with typical loads: grain, salt, lime, coal, rocks, and petroleum products.

The Lower Mississippi has been tampered with much more than the rest of the river system to improve navigation and flood control. While there are no locks, there are long stretches of levees, embankments built to straighten out the river and to prevent periods of high water from spilling off into the adjoining farmlands and flooding fields and towns, as so often happened in the past. Some levees are high enough to block the view inland except from the highest decks, through in other places the long-range vistas remain.

It's the Antebellum South (or the present-day interpretation of it) that lower river cruisers come to see. The rural plantation homes and the stately mansions clustered in towns and cities exhibit rich examples of American architecture, some rebuilt after the Civil War, others that have undergone considerable restoration after periods of neglect.

Laura Plantation, Louisiana (**www.lauraplantation.com**) was originally French owned, but during its most significant period it was under Creole influence. The main house, built around 1805, has a raised brick basement story with the upper floors executed in Federal style. Six slave quarters and a collection of outbuildings show the development of the sugar-cane industry that lasted into the 20th century.

Oak Alley, Louisiana (**www.oakalleyplantation.com**), built in 1837–1839, features a quintessential double line of live oaks that stretches from the river landing to the main Greek Revival–style house. **Houmas House,** Louisiana (**www.houmashouse.com**), an

1840 white-pillared Greek Revival mansion that lies at the end of a double line of equally old oak trees, was once the largest slave-holding plantation in the South.

Baton Rouge, Louisiana (**www.batonrougetour.com**), offers the nation's tallest state capitol building, a 34-story Art Deco masterpiece constructed on the orders of legendary governor Huey P. Long, the subject of endless stories. Nearby, the most enlightening experience takes place at the Louisiana State University's **Rural Life Museum,** arranged as if one stepped out the back door of the "Big House" to see how the rest of the working antebellum plantation was going about their daily lives.

St. Francisville, Louisiana (**www.stfrancisville.net**), boasts 140 structures listed on the National Register of Historic Places, including the Georgian Revival courthouse, Romanesque Revival Bank of Commerce & Trust, and French colonial, antebellum, neoclassical, gingerbread Victorian, and "dog trot" houses, the latter picking up their name from their design, with a long open corridor through which a dog could trot, if he had a mind to.

Natchez, Mississippi (**www.natchez.ms.us**), has 200 historic homes among more than 500 antebellum structures and up to about three dozen are open to the public. Take the steamboat's tour or buy your own tickets locally. In **Vicksburg,** Mississippi (**www.vicksburgcvb.org**), the National Military Park is the principal destination. An organized tour is the best way to appreciate the battle's significance and the incredible suffering that occurred during the 42-day siege that led to the city's final capture by Ulysses S. Grant on July 4, 1863.

Memphis, Tennessee (**www.memphistravel.com**), a city that bills itself as Home of the Blues and Birthplace of Rock 'n' Roll is usually an embarkation or disembarkation port for river cruises. Small ships dock at Mud Island River Park, a recreation and museum center, and a Main Street trolley gives access to the Beale Street Entertainment District and the National Civil Rights Museum, where Martin Luther King, Jr., was shot in April 1968. Outside town, **Graceland (www.elvis.com),** Elvis Presley's jazzed up Georgian-style home, draws the largest crowds north of New Orleans.

THE UPPER MISSISSIPPI

Some river aficionados consider cruises between St. Louis and St. Paul to be the most interesting because of the winsome combination of flanking high bluffs, pleasant farmlands, locking operations, and the intriguing small Victorian-era towns that the ships visit. In the fall, the foliage in Wisconsin rivals that of New England.

The upper Midwest's first inhabitants were the Native Sioux and Algonquin peoples, then came the French fur trappers and traders, prospectors to tap the rich lead deposits, entrepreneurs to invest in lumbering, and pioneering Anglo farmers to clear the land for agriculture. Ensuing manufacturing, trade, and transportation in the stretch between St. Paul and St. Louis created numerous river towns and cities of considerable if relatively short-lived importance, such as Cape Girardeau, Missouri; Burlington, Fort Madison, and Dubuque, Iowa; Galena, Illinois; LaCrosse, Wisconsin; and Winona, Wabasha, and Red Wing, Minnesota.

The Upper Mississippi officially begins at Mile 0, Cairo Point, Illinois (where the Ohio River converges), and ends 839 miles to the north at Minneapolis/St. Paul, Minnesota. Locking through is an interesting procedure, and on a 7-day Upper Mississippi cruise you'll be doing this an average of four times a day. Some locks are set up as tourist attractions, with observation towers and parks alongside. It's like a scene out of a history book, with passengers lining the ship's rails and visitors on land exchanging pleasantries while the boat sinks or rises in the chamber.

St. Louis, Missouri (**www.explorestlouis.com**), historically "The Gateway to the West," is a major embarking and disembarking port and worth a night or 2 before or after the cruise. Eero Saarinen's 630-foot **Gateway Arch,** completed in 1965, gives the city a much-needed icon as well as a monument of considerable beauty, especially when the stainless steel skin reflects the sun. The **Museum of Westward Expansion** offers an overview of the Lewis and Clark Expedition, and the St. Louis Union Station's Romanesque train shed is now a vast shopping and restaurant mall.

Hannibal, Missouri (**www.visithannibal.com**), opens the world of Mark Twain with a complex of museums and the cave that Tom Sawyer and Becky Thatcher explored.

St. Paul, Minnesota (**www.stpaulcvb.org**), is the beginning or end of an Upper Mississippi cruise. The city retains a compact center where most of the great civic architecture is located, such as the Beaux Arts–style Minnesota State Capitol Building (1905); the Minnesota Museum of American Art, housed in the Landmark Center downtown; and the top city attraction, the **James J. Hill House,** an elaborate Romanesque mansion built in 1891 for the Great Northern Railway baron.

THE OHIO RIVER

Some river aficionados consider the Ohio (**www.ohioriverfdn.org**) to be the most scenic and varied Midwestern waterway because of its twisting nature below Pittsburgh, its high bluffs, and its attractive agricultural landscapes. Add to that the small rivers towns, the rust belt cities with their active and abandoned industries, a wide variety of graceful bridges, the occasional cross-river ferries, and the impressive arrivals and departures at Pittsburgh and Cincinnati. Most cruises do not cover the entire Ohio River in one go, but include substantial portions such as between Cincinnati and Pittsburgh, or Cincinnati and Louisville to St. Louis or Memphis. Trips including the Cumberland and Tennessee rivers also include short stretches of the Lower Ohio en route to or from Memphis or St. Louis.

Most towns where the steamboats call put out a warm welcome, showing visitors how the river affected their respective roles in the development of Midwestern culture, manufacturing, and transportation.

The Ohio River, Mile 0, begins at the western Pennsylvanian junction of the Monongahela and Allegheny rivers at **Fort Point,** the very tip of the pie that forms downtown Pittsburgh. It is 982 twisting river miles to Cairo Point, where the Ohio joins the Mississippi (see above), and en route forms the borders of West Virginia, Ohio, Kentucky, Indiana, and Illinois.

The Ohio provides more water than the Upper Mississippi and itself is fed by the two Pittsburgh rivers, and by others such as the Kanawha, Big Sandy, Licking, Kentucky, Green, Wabash, Cumberland, and Tennessee. Eighteen locks and dams provide safe navigation, some replacing others that are now submerged in a constant effort to improve river commerce.

Architecturally rich downtown **Pittsburgh** (**www.visitpittsburgh.com**), known as the Golden Triangle, is clean and clear, with a compact center that's easy to navigate on foot. There's plenty to do if you're staying over before or after your cruise, including a visit to **Station Square,** the former Pittsburgh and Lake Erie Station and now a restaurant and shop complex; a ride on one of the two inclined railways for a terrific city view; a visit to the **Carnegie Museum of Art** and the **Carnegie Museum of Natural History;** or a stop at the **Andy Warhol Museum,** just across the 7th Street Bridge from downtown. The **Frick Art and Historical Center** is about 20 minutes east of downtown.

Leaving Pittsburgh, the 172 miles to Marietta, Ohio, are one of the loveliest rural stretches of river in the country. High banks define the stream, and where the woods part, farming fields spill right down to the water. **Marietta (www.mariettaohio.org)** is a quintessential Victorian riverfront community that still exudes its historical importance, and steamboats dock here adjacent to a lovely city park. The **Ohio River Museum,** minutes on foot from the landing, displays steamboat history in models, photographs, an excellent film, and the *W. P. Snyder, Jr.,* the last of the steam-powered stern-wheel towboats.

Maysville, Kentucky, derived its importance from firing bricks and manufacturing wrought-iron fences, gates, and ornamental street furnishings such as clocks, lampposts, benches, and signs. The town's prosperity is revealed in a 24-block, 160-building historic district that is on the National Register of Historic Places, featuring brick streets and Romanesque, Georgian, and Victorian styles, all walkable from the steamboat landing.

The graceful 1931 suspension bridge spanning the Ohio was the prototype for San Francisco's Golden Gate Bridge and leads to **Ripley,** Ohio **(www.ripleyohio.net),** once an important stop on the Underground Railroad. It served as the setting for Eliza's escape in Harriet Beecher Stowe's *Uncle Tom's Cabin.*

Arriving at **Cincinnati,** Ohio **(www.cincyusa.com),** the steamboats drop their stages at the Public Landing opposite the Great American Ballpark and just upriver from the **Roebling Suspension Bridge,** once the world's longest suspension bridge and the 1868 prototype for Roebling's masterpiece, New York's Brooklyn Bridge. Just up from the landing, downtown is anchored by Fountain Square and the 1931 Art Deco **Carew Tower,** which offers a great view from the 48th floor. Mt. Adams, a short taxi ride up one of Cincinnati's seven hills, combines a trendy residential neighborhood, restaurants, leafy Eden Park (where the **Cincinnati Art Museum** is located), and a wonderful Ohio River overlook.

You'll likely hit several towns and cities below Cincinnati. **Madison,** Indiana **(www.visitmadison.org),** is a repository of 19th-century residential architecture and bills itself as the most beautiful town in the Midwest. **Louisville,** Kentucky **(www.goto louisville.com),** is the home of the Louisville Slugger Museum and the 1914 steamboat *Belle of Louisville,* the city's icon and the oldest river steamer in the U.S. An excursion will take you out to Bluegrass Country and Churchill Downs, home of the annual Kentucky Derby. **Henderson,** Kentucky **(www.go-henderson.com),** boasts the WPA-constructed James J. Audubon Museum, dedicated to the wildlife of the area and housing the largest collection of Audubon memorabilia, including original drawings, paintings, and watercolors, and a complete collection of his publications. Finally, **Paducah,** Kentucky **(www.paducah-tourism.org),** located at the junction of the Tennessee and Ohio rivers, is a barge and tow repair center and home to the Museum of the American Quilters' Society, a nonprofit organization dedicated to the art, history, and heritage of hand-sewn and machine-made quilts.

Casting off from Paducah, your steamboat has just 47 miles to go to the meeting of the waters of the Ohio and Mississippi at Cairo Point. Depending on the itinerary, the boat will make a hard right for an upriver sail to St. Louis or go gently left downriver to Memphis.

LINES SAILING THESE ROUTES   Delta Queen Steamboat Company (p. 359) is the major player here, along with the **RiverBarge Excursions'** (p. 390) vessel *River Explorer.*

Index

CRUISE FREE!
Become a Group Leader

Do you have a family or school reunion group, a club or organization, a church group, or just some friends who want to cruise together? Then, you can cruise free by becoming a group leader!

- Family reunions
- Class reunions
- Clubs and organizations
- Meetings and Incentive groups
- Church groups
- Friends and family

Book eight cabins and one person cruises FREE!!!

Visit www.justcruisinplus.com for additional information on becoming a group leader.

Just Cruisin' plus

615-833-0922

or

800-888-0922

A Guide for Every Type of Traveler

FROMMER'S® COMPLETE GUIDES

For independent leisure or business travelers who value complete coverage, candid advice, and lots of choices in all price ranges.

These are the most complete, up-to-date guides you can buy. Count on Frommer's for exact prices, savvy trip planning, sight-seeing advice, dozens of detailed maps, and candid reviews of hotels and restaurants in every price range. All Complete Guides offer special icons to point you to great finds, excellent values, and more. Every hotel, restaurant, and attraction is rated from zero to three stars to help you make the best choices.

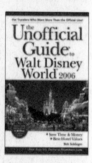

UNOFFICIAL GUIDES®

For honeymooners, families, business travelers, and anyone else who values no-nonsense, *Consumer Reports*–style advice.

Unofficial Guides are ideal for those who want to know the pros and cons of the places they are visiting and make informed decisions. The guides rank and rate every hotel, restaurant, and attraction, with evaluations based on reader surveys and critiques compiled by a team of unbiased inspectors.

FROMMER'S® IRREVERENT GUIDES

For experienced, sophisticated travelers looking for a fresh, candid perspective on a destination.

This unique series is perfect for anyone who wants a cutting-edge perspective on the hottest destinations. Covering all major cities around the globe, these guides are unabashedly honest and down-right hilarious. Decked out with a retro-savvy feel, each book features new photos, maps, and neighborhood references.

FROMMER'S® WITH KIDS GUIDES

For families traveling with children ages 2 to 14.

Here are the ultimate guides for a successful family vacation. Written by parents, they're packed with information on museums, outdoor activities, attractions, great drives and strolls, incredible parks, the liveliest places to stay and eat, and more.

Visit Frommers.com

Frommer's is a registered trademark of Arthur Frommer, used under exclusive license.

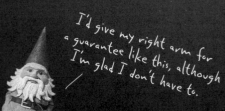